A TREATISE ON
COSMIC FIRE

BOOKS BY ALICE A. BAILEY

A TREATISE ON COSMIC FIRE

BY

ALICE A. BAILEY

LUCIS PUBLISHING COMPANY

LUCIS PRESS, LTD.

First Printing, 1925
Ninth Printing, 1973 (First Paperback Edition)
Sixteenth Printing, 2005

ISBN No. 0-85330-117-7
Library of Congress Catalog Card Number: 51006116

The publication of this book is financed by the Tibetan Book Fund which is established for the perpetuation of the teachings of the Tibetan and Alice A. Bailey.

This Fund is controlled by the Lucis Trust, a tax-exempt, religious, educational corporation.

The Lucis Publishing Company is a non-profit organisation owned by the Lucis Trust. No royalties are paid on this book.

This title is also available in a
clothbound edition.

It has been translated into Danish, Dutch, French, German, Greek, Italian, Russian and Spanish. Translation into other languages is proceeding.

LUCIS PUBLISHING COMPANY
120 Wall Street
New York, NY 10005

LUCIS PRESS, LTD.
Suite 54
3 Whitehall Court
London SW1A 2EF

MANUFACTURED IN THE UNITED STATES OF AMERICA
By FORT ORANGE PRESS, INC., Albany, NY

"To the God Who is in the FIRE and Who is in the
     waters;
To the God Who has suffused Himself through all
     the world;
To the God Who is in summer plants and in the
     lords of the forest;
To that God be adoration, adoration."

—Sh'vet Upanishad, **II.17.**

INTRODUCTION

The story of the many years of telepathic work by the Tibetan with Alice A. Bailey is revealed in her *Unfinished Autobiography,* published in 1951. This includes the circumstances of her first contact with him, on the physical plane, which took place in California in November 1919. Thirty years' work was planned. When this had been accomplished, and within thirty days after that period, Mrs. Bailey gained her release from the limitations of the physical vehicle.

The *Autobiography* also contains certain statements by the Tibetan in regard to his work and some information as to the reasons why it was undertaken. In the early stages the work involved careful attention to the physical plane conditions which might best help to make the telepathic process more successful. But during the latter years the technique was so perfected and the etheric mechanism of A.A.B. so skilfully attuned and adjusted that the whole process was practically effortless, and the reality and practical usefulness of telepathic interplay was demonstrated to an unique degree.

The spiritual truths dealt with involved in many cases the expression by the lower concrete mind (often with the insuperable restrictions of the English language) of abstract ideas and hitherto quite unknown concepts of spiritual realities. This unescapable limitation of truth has been frequently called to the attention of the readers of the books so produced but is all too often forgotten. Its constant remembrance will constitute in the years to come one of the chief factors in preventing the crystallisation of the teaching from producing yet one more dogmatic sectarian cult.

The present volume, *A Treatise on Cosmic Fire,* first published in 1925, was the third book jointly produced and carries inherent evidence that it will stand as the major and most far-reaching portion of the thirty-year teachings, notwithstanding the profundity and usefulness of the volumes published in the series

entitled *A Treatise on the Seven Rays* or of any other of the
books.

During the long course of the work the minds of the Tibetan
and A.A.B. became so closely attuned that they were in effect—
so far as much of the production of the teaching was concerned—a single joint projecting mechanism. Even to the end
A.A.B. often spoke of her amazement at the glimpses she obtained
through contact with the Tibetan's mind, of limitless vistas of
spiritual truths which she could not possibly have otherwise
contacted, and often of a quality she could not possibly express.
This experience was the basis of her often-proclaimed but frequently little-understood assertion that all the teachings she
was aiding in producing was in fact only the A B C of esoteric
knowledge, and that in the future she would gladly abandon any
pronouncement in the present teaching, when she found better
and more deeply esoteric teaching available. Clear and profound
as the teaching actually is in the books published in her name,
the truths imparted are so partial and subject to later revelation
and expansion that this fact, if constantly remembered, will give
us a second much-needed safeguard against that quality of the
concrete mind which constantly tends to produce sectarianism.

At the very beginning of the joint effort and after careful
consideration it was decided between the Tibetan (D.K.) and
A.A.B. that she as the working disciple on the outer plane should
shoulder as much as possible of karmic responsibility on that
plane, and that the teaching should go to the public over her
signature. This involved the burden of leadership in the esoteric
field and precipitated attack and condemnation from persons
and organisations whose positions and activities were more
Piscean and authoritarian.

The entire platform upon which esoteric teaching stands
before the public today has been liberated from the limitations
and follies of mystery, glamour, claim-making and impracti-
cality, by the position taken by the Tibetan and A.A.B. The
stand taken against dogmatic assertion has helped to establish
a new era of mental freedom for the students of the progressively
unfolding revelation of the Ageless Wisdom.

The age-old method of arriving at truth by the process of accepting new authorities and comparing them with previously established doctrines, while of undoubted value in the training of the mind, is gradually being transcended. In its place is emerging in both the religious and philosophical worlds a new capacity to take a more scientific position. Spiritual teaching will be increasingly accepted as an hypothesis to be proved less by scholasticism, historical foundation and authority, and more by the results of its effect upon the life lived and its practical usefulness in solving the problems of humanity.

Heretofore, advanced esoteric teaching has almost invariably been obtainable only by the student's acceptance of the authority of the teacher, varying degrees of personal obedience to that teacher and pledges of secrecy. As the new Aquarian dispensation progresses these limitations will disappear. The personal relation of the disciple to the Master remains, but already discipleship training has been attempted in Group formation. The record of one such experiment and attempt to use this new age method has been made available to the public in the book entitled *Discipleship in the New Age,* which gives the direct personal instructions by the Tibetan to a selected group.

In *A Treatise on Cosmic Fire* the Tibetan has given us what H. P. Blavatsky prophesied he would give, namely, the psychological key to the Cosmic Creation. H.P.B. stated that in the 20th century a disciple would come who would give the psychological key to her own monumental work *The Secret Doctrine* on which treatise the Tibetan worked with her; and Alice A. Bailey worked in complete recognition of her own task in this sequence.

FOSTER BAILEY

Tunbridge Wells
December 1950

EXTRACT FROM A STATEMENT BY THE TIBETAN

PUBLISHED AUGUST 1934

Suffice it to say, that I am a Tibetan disciple of a certain degree, and this tells you but little, for all are disciples from the humblest aspirant up to, and beyond, the Christ Himself. I live in a physical body like other men, on the borders of Tibet, and at times (from the exoteric standpoint) preside over a large group of Tibetan lamas, when my other duties permit. It is this fact that has caused it to be reported that I am an abbot of this particular lamasery. Those associated with me in the work of the Hierarchy (and all true disciples are associated in this work) know me by still another name and office. A.A.B. knows who I am and recognises me by two of my names.

I am a brother of yours, who has travelled a little longer upon the Path than has the average student, and has therefore incurred greater responsibilities. I am one who has wrestled and fought his way into a greater measure of light than has the aspirant who will read this article, and I must therefore act as a transmitter of the light, no matter what the cost. I am not an old man, as age counts among the teachers, yet I am not young or inexperienced. My work is to teach and spread the knowledge of the Ageless Wisdom wherever I can find a response, and I have been doing this for many years. I seek also to help the Master M. and the Master K.H. whenever opportunity offers, for I have been long connected with Them and with Their work. In all the above, I have told you much; yet at the same time I have told you nothing which would lead you to offer me that blind obedience and the foolish devotion which the emotional aspirant offers to the Guru and Master whom he is as yet unable to contact. Nor will he make that desired contact until he has transmuted emotional devotion into unselfish service to humanity,— not to the Master.

The books that I have written are sent out with no claim for their acceptance. They may, or may not, be correct, true and useful. It is for you to ascertain their truth by right practice and by the exercise of the intuition. Neither I nor A.A.B. are the least interested in having them acclaimed as inspired writings, or in having anyone speak of them (with bated breath) as being the work of one of the Masters. If they present truth in such a way that it follows sequentially upon that already offered in the world teachings, if the information given raises the aspiration and the will-to-serve from the plane of the emotions to that of the mind (the plane whereon the Masters *can* be found) then they will have served their purpose. If the teaching conveyed calls forth a response from the illumined mind of the worker in the world, and brings a flashing forth of his intuition, then let that teaching be accepted. But not otherwise. If the statements meet with eventual corroboration, or are deemed true under the test of the Law of Correspondences, then that is well and good. But should this not be so, let not the student accept what is said.

DEDICATED WITH GRATITUDE

TO

HELENA PETROVNA BLAVATSKY,

THAT GREAT DISCIPLE WHO LIGHTED HER
TORCH IN THE EAST AND BROUGHT THE
LIGHT TO EUROPE AND AMERICA IN 1875.

FOREWORD

This "Treatise on Cosmic Fire" has a fivefold purpose in view:

First, to provide a compact and skeleton outline of a scheme of cosmology, philosophy, and psychology which may perhaps be employed for a generation as a reference and a textbook, and may serve as a scaffolding upon which more detailed instruction may later be built, as the great tide of evolutionary teaching flows on.

Secondly, to express that which is subjective in comprehensible terms, and to point out the next step forward in the understanding of the true psychology. It is an elucidation of the relation existing between Spirit and Matter, which relation demonstrates as *consciousness*. It will be found that the Treatise deals primarily with the aspect of mind, with consciousness and with the higher psychology, and less with matter as we know of it on the physical plane. The danger involved in giving out information concerning the various energies of atomic matter is too great, and the race as yet too selfish to be entrusted with these potencies. Man is already, through the able work of the scientists, discovering the needed knowledge with adequate rapidity. The emphasis in this book will be found to be laid upon those forces which are responsible for the objective manifestation of a solar Logos and of man, and only in the first section will indication be given as to the nature of those energies which are strictly confined to the physical plane.

Thirdly, to show the coherent development of all that is found within a solar system; to demonstrate that everything which exists evolves (from the lowest form of life at the densest point of concretion up to the highest and most tenuous manifestation) and that all forms are but the expression of a stupendous and divine Existence. This expression is caused by the blending of two divine aspects through the influence of a third, and produces the manifestation which we call a form, starting it upon its evolutionary cycle in time and space. Thus is form brought to the point where it is an adequate medium for the demonstration of the nature of that which we call God.

Fourthly, to give practical information anent those focal points of energy which are found in the etheric bodies of the solar Logos, the *macrocosm*, and of man, the *microcosm*. As the etheric substratum which is the true substance underlying every tangible form is understood, certain great revolutions will be brought about in the domains of science, of medicine and of chemistry. The study of medicine, for instance, will eventually be taken up from a new angle, and its practice will be built upon a comprehension of the laws of radiation, of magnetic currents, and of the force centres found in men's bodies and their relationship to the force centres and currents of the solar system.

Fifthly, to give some information, hitherto not exoterically imparted as to the place and work of those myriads of sentient lives who form the essence of objectivity; to indicate the nature of those Hierarchies of Existences who form out of their own substance all that is seen and known, and who are themselves Fire and the cause of all the heat, warmth, life and motion in the universe. In this way the action of Fire on Water, of Heat in Matter, whether macrocosmically or microcosmically considered, will be touched upon and some light thrown upon the Law of Cause and Effect (the Law of Karma) and its significance in the solar system.

To sum up the matter, the teaching in this book should tend to an expansion of consciousness, and should bring about a recognition of the adequacy, as a working basis, for both science and religion, of that interpretation of the processes of nature which has been formulated for us by the Master Minds of all time. It should tend to bring about a reaction in favor of a system of philosophy which will link both Spirit and matter, and demonstrate the essential unity of the scientific and religious idea. The two are at present somewhat divorced, and we are only just beginning to grope our intellectual way out of the depths of a materialistic interpretation. It must not be forgotten, however, that under the Law of Action and Reaction, the long period of materialistic thought has been a necessary one for humanity, because the mysticism of the Middle Ages had led us too far in the opposite direction. We are now tending to a more balanced view, and it is hoped that this treatise may form part of the process through which equilibrium is attained.

In studying this treatise the student is asked to bear in mind certain things:

a. That in dealing with these subjects we are concerned with the essence of that which is objective, with the subjective side of manifestation, and with the consideration of force and of energy. It is well nigh impossible to reduce such concepts to concrete formulas and to express them in such a way that they can be easily apprehended by the average man.

b. That as we use words and phrases and speak in terms of modern language the whole subject necessarily becomes limited and dwarfed, and much of the truth is thereby lost.

c. That all that is in this treatise is offered in no dogmatic spirit but simply as a contribution to the mass of thought upon the subject of world origins and to the data already accumulated as to the nature of man. The best that man can offer as a solution of the world problem must perforce take a dual form and will demonstrate through a life of active service, tending to amelioration of environal conditions, and through a formulation of some cosmological scheme or plan which will seek to account as much as may be for conditions as they are seen to exist. Arguing as men do at present from the basis of the known and the demonstrated and leaving untouched and unaccounted for, those deep-seated causes which must be presumed to be producing the seen and known, all solutions as yet fail and will continue to fail in their objective.

d. That all attempts to formulate in words that which must be felt and *lived* in order to be truly comprehended must necessarily prove distressingly inadequate. All that can be said will be after all but the partial statements of the great veiled Truth, and must be offered to the reader and student as simply providing a working hypothesis, and a suggestive explanation. To the open-minded student and the man who keeps the recollection in his mind that the truth is progressively revealed, it will be apparent that the fullest expression of the truth possible at any one time will be seen later to be but a fragment of a whole, and later still be recognised to be only portions of a fact and thus in itself a distortion of the *real*.

This treatise is put out in the hope that it may prove useful to all broad-minded seekers after truth and of value to all investigators into the subjective Source of all that which is tangibly objective. It aims to provide a reasonably logical plan of systemic evolution and to indicate to man the part he must play as an atomic unit in a great and corporate Whole. This fragment of the Secret Doctrine, in the turning of the evolutionary wheel, goes out to the world making no claims as to its source, its infallibility or the correctness in detail of its statements.

No book gains anything from dogmatic claims or declarations as to the authoritative value of its source of inspiration. It should stand or fall solely on the basis of its own intrinsic worth, on the value of the suggestions made, and its power to foster the spiritual life and the intellectual apprehension of the reader. If this treatise has within it anything of truth and of reality, it will inevitably and unfailingly do its work, carry its message, and thus reach the hearts and minds of searchers everywhere. If it is of no value, and has no basis in fact, it will disappear and die, and most rightly so. All that is asked from the student of this treatise is a sympathetic approach, a willingness to consider the views put forth and that honesty and sincerity of thought which will tend to the development of the intuition, of spiritual diagnosis, and a discrimination which will lead to a rejection of the false and an appreciation of the true.

The words of the Buddha most appropriately have their place here, and make a fitting conclusion to these preliminary remarks:

THE LORD BUDDHA HAS SAID

that we must not believe in a thing said merely because it is said; nor traditions because they have been handed down from antiquity; nor rumours, as such; nor writings by sages, because sages wrote them; nor fancies that we may suspect to have been inspired in us by a Deva (that is, in presumed spiritual inspiration); nor from inferences drawn from some haphazard assumption we may have made; nor because of what seems an analogical necessity; nor on the mere authority of our teachers or masters. But we are to believe when the writing, doctrine, or saying is corroborated by our own reason and consciousness. "For this," says he in concluding, "I taught you not to believe merely because you have heard, but when you believed of your consciousness, then to act accordingly and abundantly."

—*Secret Doctrine* III. 401.

May this be the attitude of every reader of this "Treatise on Cosmic Fire."

ALICE A. BAILEY.

Note:—In the footnotes throughout this treatise "The Secret Doctrine" by H. P. Blavatsky is designated by the initials S. D. The page references are to the "Third Revised Edition."

FIRE

"What says the esoteric teaching with regard to *Fire?*"

Fire is the most perfect and unadulterated reflection, in Heaven as on earth, of the One Flame. It is life and death, the origin and the end of every material thing. It is divine Substance."

—Secret Doctrine I. 146.

Our earth and man (are) the products of the *Three Fires.*

—Secret Doctrine II. 258.

Fire and flame destroy the body of an Arhat; their essence makes him immortal.

—Secret Doctrine I. 35.

THE THREE FIRES

I. *The Internal Fire or Fire by Friction.*

"There is heat internal and heat external in every atom, the breath of the Father (Spirit) and the breath (or heat) of the Mother (matter)."

—Secret Doctrine I. 112.

II. *The Fire of Mind or Solar Fire.*

"The fire of knowledge burns up all action on the plane of illusion, therefore those who have acquired it and are emancipated are called 'Fires.' "

—Secret Doctrine I. 114.

III. *The Fire of Spirit or Electric Fire.*

"Lift up thy head, O Lanoo; dost thou see one, or countless lights above thee, burning in the dark midnight sky?"

"I sense one Flame, O Gurudeva; I see countless undetached sparks shining in it."

—Secret Doctrine I. 145.

CONTENTS

The above tabulation of the subjects dealt with in this treatise is of very real importance, for it forms the basis of that which we shall be considering. The total lack of a wider consciousness than the individual and the personal, acts as a bar to the true comprehension of things macrocosmic, but if the occult method is adhered to, if the Law of Correspondences is studied, and if we ever reason upward from the microcosm to the greater Whole, then glimpses will be caught of vast realms of realisation and vistas of spiritual unfoldment will open up before us, undreamt of hitherto.

CONTENTS OUTLINE IN DETAIL

SECTION TWO

CONTENTS

SECTION THREE

THE ELECTRIC FIRE OF SPIRIT

CHARTS

FULL PAGE TABULATIONS

INTRODUCTORY POSTULATES

INTRODUCTORY POSTULATES.

The teaching which is given in this Treatise on Cosmic Fire might be formulated in the following terms. These postulates are simply extensions of the three fundamentals to be found in the Proem in the first volume of the *Secret Doctrine* by H. P. Blavatsky.[1] Students are recommended to study them carefully; in this way their understanding of the Treatise will be greatly aided.

I. *There is one Boundless Immutable Principle; one Absolute Reality which antecedes all manifested conditioned Being. It is beyond the range and reach of any human thought or expression.*

The manifested Universe is contained within this Absolute Reality and is a conditioned symbol of it.

In the totality of this manifested Universe, three aspects are to be conceived.

1. The First Cosmic Logos, impersonal and unmanifested, the precursor of the Manifested.
2. The Second Cosmic Logos, Spirit-Matter, Life, the Spirit of the Universe.
3. The Third Cosmic Logos, Cosmic Ideation, the Universal World-Soul.

From these basic creative principles, in successive gradations there issue in ordered sequence the numberless Universes comprising countless Manifesting Stars and Solar Systems.

Each Solar System is the manifestation of the energy and life of a great Cosmic Existence, Whom we call, for lack of a better term, a Solar Logos.

[1] S. D., I, 42-44.

This Solar Logos incarnates, or comes into manifestation, through the medium of a solar system.

This solar system is the body, or form, of this cosmic Life, and is itself triple.

This triple solar system can be described in terms of three aspects, or (as the Christian theology puts it) in terms of three Persons.

ELECTRIC FIRE, or SPIRIT.

1st Person....Father.Life.Will.Purpose.Positive
energy.

SOLAR FIRE, or SOUL.

2nd Person....Son.Conscious-.Love-.Equilibrised
ness wisdom energy.

FIRE BY FRICTION, or Body, or Matter.

3rd Person....Holy.Form.Active Intelli-.Negative
Spirit. gence energy.

Each of these three is also triple in manifestation, making therefore

  a. The nine Potencies or Emanations.

  b. The nine Sephiroth.

  c. The nine Causes of Initiation.

These, with the totality of manifestation or the Whole, produce the ten (10) of perfect manifestation, or the perfect MAN.

These three aspects of the Whole are present in every form.

  a. The solar system is triple, manifesting through the three above mentioned.

  b. A human being is equally triple, manifesting as Spirit, Soul and Body, or Monad, Ego and Personality.

  c. The atom of the scientist is also triple, being composed of a positive nucleus, the negative electrons, and the totality of the outer manifestation, the result of the relation of the other two.

The three aspects of every form are inter-related and susceptible of intercourse, because

a. Energy is in motion and circulates.

b. All forms in the solar system form part of the Whole, and are not isolated units.

c. This is the basis of brotherhood, of the communion of saints, and of astrology.

These three aspects of God, the solar Logos, and the Central Energy or Force (for the terms are occultly synonymous) demonstrate through seven centres of force,—three major centres and four minor. These seven centres of logoic Force are themselves so constituted that they form corporate Entities. They are known as

a. The seven planetary Logoi.

b. The seven Spirits before the Throne.

c. The seven Rays.

d. The seven Heavenly Men.

The Seven Logoi embody seven types of differentiated force, and in this Treatise are known under the names of Lords of the Rays. The names of the Rays are

Ray I   ..Ray of Will or Power........1st Aspect
Ray II ..Ray of Love-Wisdom........2nd Aspect
Ray III ..Ray of Active Intelligence ...3rd Aspect
          These are the major Rays.
Ray IV ..Ray of Harmony, Beauty and Art.
Ray V   ..Ray of Concrete Knowledge or Science.
Ray VI ..Ray of Devotion or of Abstract Idealism.
Ray VII ..Ray of Ceremonial Magic or Order.

II. *There is a basic law called the Law of Periodicity.*

1. This law governs all manifestation, whether it is the manifestation of a solar Logos through the

medium of a solar system, or the manifestation of a human being through the medium of a form. This law controls likewise in all the kingdoms of nature.

2. There are certain other laws in the system which are linked with this one; some of them are as follows:

    a. The Law of Economy....the law governing matter, the third aspect.

    b. The Law of Attraction...the law governing soul, the second aspect.

    c. The Law of Synthesis....the law governing spirit, or the first aspect.

3. These three are cosmic laws. There are seven systemic laws, which govern the manifestation of our solar Logos:

    a. The Law of Vibration.
    b. The Law of Cohesion.
    c. The Law of Disintegration.
    d. The Law of Magnetic Control.
    e. The Law of Fixation.
    f. The Law of Love.
    g. The Law of Sacrifice and Death.

4. Each of these Laws manifests primarily on one or other of the seven planes of the solar system.

5. Each law sweeps periodically into power and each plane has its period of manifestation and its period of obscuration.

6. Every manifested life has its three great cycles:

Birth ....Life ....Death.
Appearance ....growth ....disappearance.

Involution .....evolution ......obscuration.
Inert motion ...activity ......,rhythmic motion.
Tamasic life ....rajasic life ....sattvic life.

7. Knowledge of the cycles involves knowledge of number, sound and colour.

8. Full knowledge of the mystery of the cycles is the possession only of the perfected adept.

III. *All souls are identical with the Oversoul.*

1. The Logos of the solar system is the Macrocosm. Man is the Microcosm.

2. Soul is an aspect of every form of life from a Logos to an atom.

3. This relationship between all souls and the Oversoul constitutes the basis for the scientific belief in Brotherhood. Brotherhood is a fact in nature, not an ideal.

4. The Law of Correspondences will explain the details of this relationship. This Law of Correspondences or of Analogy is the interpretive law of the system, and explains God to man.

5. Just as God is the Macrocosm for all the kingdoms in Nature, so man is the Macrocosm for all the sub-human kingdoms.

6. The goal for the evolution of the atom is self-consciousness as exemplified in the human kingdom.

   The goal for the evolution of man is group consciousness, as exemplified by a planetary Logos.[2]

   The goal for the planetary Logos is God consciousness, as exemplified by the solar Logos.

7. The solar Logos is the sum-total of all the states of consciousness within the solar system.[3]

[2] Ancient of Days. Daniel VII, pp. 13, 22.

[3] "We have all got into the habit of viewing the universe as a vast group of isolated bodies having very little connection with each other, while the fact is that the universe is one in its essence and many in its manifestations, descending from a homogeneity on the highest plane to more and more marked heterogeneity as it reaches the lowest planes."— *Some Thoughts on the Gita*, p. 54.

STANZAS OF DZYAN

STANZA I

The Secret of the Fire lieth hid in the second letter of the Sacred Word. The mystery of life is concealed within the heart. When the lower point vibrates, when the sacred triangle glows, when the point, the middle center, and the apex, connect and circulate the Fire, when the threefold apex likewise burns, then the two triangles—the greater and the lesser—merge into one flame, which burneth up the whole.

STANZA II

"Aum," said the Mighty One, and sounded forth the Word. The sevenfold waves of matter resolved themselves, and varied forms appeared. Each took its place, each in the sphere ordained. They waited for the sacred flood to enter and to fill.

The Builders responded to the sacred sound. In musical collaboration they attended to the work. They built in many spheres, beginning with the third. Upon this plane their work commenced. They built the sheath of atma and strung it to its Primary.

"Aum," said the Mighty One. "Let now the work proceed. Let the Builders of the air continue with the plan."

The Deva-Lord and Builders upon the plane of air worked with the forms within that sphere which is reckoned mainly theirs. They wrought for union, each in his group assigned. The moulds grew fast beneath their hands.

The sacred plane of juncture, the fourth great plane, became the sphere within the greater circle which marked the goal for man.

"Aum," said the Mighty One, He breathed forth to the fifth, the plane which is the burning-ground, the meeting place for fire. This time a cosmic note is heard beneath the sound systemic. The fire within, the fire without, meet with the fire ascending. The guardians of the cosmic fire, the devas of fohatic heat, watched o'er the forms that formless stood, waiting a point in time.

The builders of a lesser grade, devas who work with matter, wrought at the forms. They stood in fourfold order. Upon the threefold levels in empty silence stood the forms. They vibrated, they responded to the key, yet useless stood and uninhabited.

"Aum," said the Mighty One, "let the waters too bring forth." The builders of the watery sphere, the denizens of moisture, produced the forms that move within the kingdom of Varuna. They grew and multiplied. In constant flux they swayed. Each ebb of cosmic motion increased the endless flow. The ripple of the forms was seen.

"Aum," said the Mighty One, "let the Builders deal with matter." The molten solidified. The solid forms were built. The crust cooled. The rocks congealed. The builders wrought in tumult to produce the forms of maya. When the rocky strata were completed the work stood in completion. The builders of the lowest grade announced the work was finished.

Forth from the rocky strata emerged the covering next. The builders of the second agreed the work was done. The first and second on the upward way stood forth in fourfold form. The inner five was somewhat seen by those whose sight was keen.

"Aum," said the Mighty One, and gathered in His Breath. The spark within the peopling third impelled to further growth. The builders of the lowest forms, manipulating densest maya, merged their production with the forms built by the watery ones. Matter and water merged produced the third in time. Ascension thus progressed. The builders worked in union. They called the guardians of the fiery zone.

Matter and water mixed with fire, the inner spark
within the form were blended all together.

The Mighty One looked down. The forms met
His approval. Forth came the cry for further light.
Again He gathered in the sound. He drew to higher
levels the feeble spark of light. Another tone was
heard, the sound of cosmic fire, hid in the Sons of
Manas. They called to their Primaries. The lower
four, the higher three, and the cosmic fifth met at
the great inbreathing. Another sheath was formed.

STANZA III

The great Wheel turned upon itself. The seven lesser wheels rushed into being. They revolve like their Mother, around, within and forward. All that existeth was.

The wheels were diverse, and in unification, one. As evolved the great Wheel, the inner fire burst forth. It touched into life wheel the first. It circulated. A million fires rose up. The quality of matter densified, but form was not. The Sons of God arose, scanned the depth of Flame, took from its heart the sacred Stone of Fire, and proceeded to the next.

In turning next the Great Wheel launched the second. Again the flame burst forth, took to its heart the Stone and proceeded in revolution. The Sons of God again arose, and sought within the flame. "The form sufficeth not," they said, "remove from without the fire."

Faster revolved the greater Wheel, blue white emerged the flame. The Sons of God again came down and a lesser wheel revolved. Seven times the revolution, and seven times great the heat. More solid grew the formless mass, and deeper sank the Stone. To the heart of inmost fire the sacred Stone went down. This time the work was better done, and the product more perfected. At the seventh revolution, the third wheel rendered back the Stone. Triple the form, rosy the light, and sevenfold the eternal principle.

15

From out the greater Wheel, down from the vault of heaven, came into light the lesser wheel that counted as the fourth. The eternal Lhas looked down, and the Sons of God reached forth. Down to the inmost point of death They flung the sacred Stone. The plaudits of the Chohans rose. The work had turned a point. From the pit of outer darkness, They gathered forth the Stone, translucent now and unalloyed, of colour rose and blue.

The turning of the fifth wheel and its action on the Stone rendered it still more fit. Yellow the blending tint, orange the inner fire, till yellow, rose and blue mingled their subtle tones. The four wheels with the greater worked thus upon the Stone till all the Sons of God acclaimed, and said: "The work is done."

STANZA IV

In revolution fifth of the great Wheel the period set was reached. The lesser wheel, that responded to that fifth great turn, passed through the cycle and entered into peace.

The lesser wheels come forth and likewise do their work. The great Wheel gathers back the emanating sparks. The Five dealt with the work, the lesser two but wrought with detail. The Stone had gathered fire, lambent with flame it shone. The outer sheath met not the need till the sixth wheel and the seventh had passed it through their fires.

The Sons of God emerged from out their source, gazed on the sevenfold work, and stated it was good. The Stone was set alone. In dual revolution moved the greater Wheel. The fourth Lord of the greater Twelve handled the work of sevenfold fire. "It is not fit," He said, "merge thou this Stone within the wheel which started revolution."

The lords of the greater seven plunged the Stone within the moving wheel. The lords of the greater fifth and sixth likewise plunged their Stone.

Within the fire, deep at the inmost sphere, as whirled through space the greater Wheel, bearing the lesser seven, the two were fused. The fourth, the fifth, the sixth blended, merged and intermingled.

The aeon closed, the work was done. The stars stood still. The eternal Ones cried to inmost heaven: "Display the work. Draw forth the Stones." And lo, the Stones were one.

STANZA V

The moment manvantaric, for which had waited all the Triads, the hour that marked the solemn point of juncture, arrived within the scope of time, and lo, the work was done.

The hour for which the seven groups purushic, each vibrant to the sounding of the Word, seeking the adding of the power, had waited for millennia, passed in a flash of time, and lo, the work was done.

The First Degree in mighty acclamation deeming the hour propitious, sounded the triple note in three-fold reverberation. The echo reached the goal. They three times sent it forth. Restless the sphere of blue felt the vibration and answering, roused herself and hastened to the call.

The Second, with wise insistence, hearing the First sound forth, knowing the hour had likewise come, echoed the sound on note quadruple. This fourfold reverberation circled the gamut of the spheres. Again it was sent forth. Three times the note was sounded, pealing across the heavens. At the third intoning came the answer to the call. Vibrant as a key attuned, the eternal Primary replied. The blue to the dense one answered and responded to the need.

Quivering the sphere heard the third take up the note, pealing it forth, a full-toned chord smote on the ears of the Watchers of the Flame.

The Lords of Flame arose and prepared Themselves. It was decision's hour. The seven Lords of the seven spheres watched breathless the result. The great Lord of sphere the fourth awaited the on-coming.

The lower was prepared. The upper was resigned. The great Five waited for the point of equidistant merging. The foundation note ascended. Deep answered unto deep. The fivefold chord awaited the response from Those Whose hour had come.

Dark grew the space between the spheres. Radiant two balls became. The threefold thirty-five, finding the distance just, flashed like a sheet of intermittent flame, and lo, the work was done. The great Five met the Three and Four. The point intermediate was achieved. The hour of sacrifice, the sacrifice of Flame, arrived, and for aeons hath endured. The timeless Ones entered into time. The Watchers began Their task, and lo, the work proceeds.

STANZA VI

Within the cavern dark the fourfold one groped for expansion and for further light. No light above, and all around the gloom enveloped. Pitchy the darkness that surrounded it. To the innermost centre of the heart, throbbing without the Warming Light, crept in the icy cold of uttermost darkness.

Above the cavern dark shone all the light of day; yet the fourfold one saw it not, nor did the light pervade.

The rending of the cavern precedes the light of day. Great, then, must be the shattering. No help is found within the cave, nor any hidden light. Around the fourfold one lieth the vault of stone; beneath him menaceth the root of blackness, of utter denseness; beside him and above, naught but the same is seen.

The threefold Watchers know and see. The fourfold is now ready; the work of denseness is completed; the vehicle prepared.

Soundeth the trump of shattering. Blinding the power of the oncoming flame. The mystic earthquake rocks the cavern; the burning Flames disintegrate the maya, and lo, the work is done.

Gone is the gloom and the blackness; rent is the cavern's roof. The light of life shines in; the warmth inspires. The Lords on-looking see the work commence. The fourfold one becomes the seven. The chant of those who flame rises to all creation. The moment of achievement is attained.

Proceedeth the work anew. Creation moveth on its way, while waxeth the light within the cavern.

John 14:6: "Jesus said to him, 'I am the way, and the truth, and the life. No one comes to the Father except through me.

STANZA VII

Riseth the cave of beauty rare, of colour iridescent. Shineth the walls with azure tint, bathed in the
light of rose. The blending shade of blue irradiates
the whole and all is merged in gleaming.

Within the cave of iridescent colour, within its
arching circle, standeth the fivefold One demanding
further light. He struggleth for expansion, he
wrestleth towards the day. The Five demand the
greater Sixth and Seventh. The surrounding beauty
meeteth not the need. The inner warmth sufficeth
but to feed the urge for FIRE.

The Lords of Flame look on; they chant aloud:
"The time is come, that time for which We wait.
Let the Flame become the FIRE and let the light
shine forth."

The effort of the Flame within the crystal cave
becometh ever greater. The cry goes forth for other
aid from other Flaming Souls. The response comes.

The Lord of Flame, the Ancient One, the Mighty
Lord of Fire, the Point of Blue within the hidden
diamond, the Youth of Timeless Aeons, assisteth in
the work. The inner burning light and the outer
waiting fire,—together with the ROD,—meet on the
sphere of crystal, and lo, the work is done. The
crystal rends and quivers.

Seven times the work proceeds. Seven the efforts
made. Seven the applications of the Rod, held by a
Lord of Flame. Three are the lesser touches; four

the divine assistance. At the final fourth the work is done and the whole cave disrupts. The lighted flame within spreads through the rending walls. It mounteth to its Source. Another fire is merged; another point of blue findeth its place within the diadem logoic.

STANZA VIII

The greater Three, each with their seven lesser wheels, in spiral evolution, rotate within the timeless Now, and move as one. The cosmic Lords from Their high place, view the past, control the Now, and ponder on the Day be with us.

The Lhas of the eternal Sound, the product of the time that was, surmount the sevenfold display. Within the Ring-pass-not the Word of Love sounds forth.

The sevenfold Lords proceed with just vibration to carry out the work. They sound forth each a note of the deep logoic chord. Each to His greater Lord makes record due. In the solemn breathing forth the forms are built, the colour just apportioned, and the flame within reveals itself with ever growing light.

The Lord of Blue, Who gathereth all within the arc of Buddhi, soundeth His note. To Their source return the other six, blending Their colour diverse within Their Primary.

Blue to the green is added and completion quick is seen. The vibration of the third is added to the one. Blue to the orange blends, and in their wise admixture is seen the stable scheme. To the yellow and the red, to the purple and the ultimate is the vibration of the seventh adjusted as the Primary.

Each of the seven Lords, within Their seven schemes, adjusted to the second karmic circle, merge

Their migrating spheres and blend Their myriad atoms.

The forms through which They work, the lesser million spheres, the cause of separation and the curse of the Asuras, shatter when sounds the Sacred Word within a point in time.

The life logoic surges out. The streams of colour melt together. The forms are left behind, and Parabrahm stands complete. The Lord of the cosmic Third utters a Word unknown. The sevenfold lesser Word forms part of the vaster chord.

The Now becomes the time that was. The aeon mergeth into space. The Word of Motion hath been heard. The Word of Love succeedeth. The Past controlled the form. The Now evolves the life. The Day that is to be sounds forth the Word of Power.

The form perfected and the life evolved hold the third secret of the greater Wheel. It is the hidden mystery of living motion. The mystery, lost in the Now but known to the Lord of Cosmic Will.

STANZA IX

The thirty thousand million Watchers refused to heed the call. "We enter not the forms," they said, "until the seventh aeon." The twice thirty thousand million hearkened to the call and took the forms designed.

The rebellious ones laughed within themselves, and sought pralayic peace until the seventh aeon. But the seven great Lords called to the greater Chohans, and with the eternal Lhas of the third cosmic heaven entered into debate.

The dictum then went forth. The laggards in the highest sphere heard it echo through the scheme. "Not till the seventh aeon, but at the fourteenth seventh will the chance again come round. The first shall be the last and time be lost for aeons."

The obedient Sons of Mind connected with the Sons of Heart, and evolution spiralled on its way. The Sons of Power stayed in their appointed place, though cosmic karma forced a handful to join the Sons of Heart.

At the fourteenth seventh aeon, the Sons of Mind and Heart, absorbed by endless flame, will join the Sons of Will, in manvantaric manifestation. Three times the wheel will turn.

At the centre stand the buddhas of activity, helped by the lords of love, and following their twofold work will come the radiant lords of power.

The buddhas of creation from out the past have

26

come. The buddhas of love are gathering now. The buddhas of will at the final turn of the third major wheel will flash into being. The end will then be consummated.

STANZA X

The Fifth progresseth and from the remnants of the Fourth multiplied and reproduced. The waters arose. All sank and was submerged. The sacred remnant, in the place appointed, emerged at later date from out the zone of safety.

The waters dissipated. The solid ground emerged in certain destined places. The Fifth o'er-ran the Sacred Land, and in their fivefold groups developed the lower Fifth.

They passed from stage to stage. The watching Lords, recognising the rupas formed, gave a sign to the circulating Fourth and it speeded faster on its way. When the lesser Fifth had midway passed and all the lesser four were peopling the land, the Lords of Dark Intent arose. They said: "Not so shall go the force. The forms and rupas of the third and fourth, within the corresponding Fifth, approach too close the archetype. The work is far too good."

They constructed other forms. They called for cosmic fire. The seven deep pits of hell belched forth the animating shades. The incoming seventh reduced to order all the forms,—the white, the dark, the red, and shaded brown.

The period of destruction extended far on either hand. The work was sadly marred. The Chohans of the highest plane gazed in silence on the work. The Asuras and the Chaitans, the Sons of Cosmic Evil, and the Rishis of the darkest constellations, gathered their lesser hosts, the darkest spawn of hell. They darkened all the space.

*   *   *   *   *

From the coming of the heaven-sent One peace passed upon the earth. The planet staggered and belched forth fire. Part rose. Part fell. The form was changed. Millions took other forms or ascended to the appointed place of waiting. They tarried till the hour of progress should again sound forth for them.

*   *   *   *   *

The early Third produced the monsters, great beasts and evil forms. They prowled upon the surface of the sphere.

The watery Fourth produced within the watery sphere, reptiles and spawn of evil fame, the product of their karma. The waters came and swept away the progenitors of the fluidic spawn.

The separating Fifth built in the rupa sphere the concrete forms of thought. They cast them forth. They peopled the lower four, and like a black and evil cloud shut out the light of day. The higher three were hid.

*   *   *   *   *

The war upon the planet had been waged. Both sides descended into hell. Then came the Conqueror of form. He drew on the Sacred Fire, and purified the rupa levels. The fire destroyed the lands in the days of the lesser Sixth.

When the Sixth appeared the land was changed. The surface of the globe circled through another cycle. Men of the higher Fifth mastered the lower

three. The work was shifted to the plane whereon
the Pilgrim stood. The lesser triangle within the
lower auric egg became the centre of cosmic dissonance.

STANZA XI

The wheel of life turns within the wheel of outer form.

The matter of Fohat circulateth, and its fire hardeneth all the forms. The wheel that is not glimpsed moveth in rapid revolution within the slower outer case, till it weareth out the form.

The forty-nine fires burn at the inner centre. The thirty-five circulating fiery vortices extend along the circle of the periphery. Between the two passeth in ordered sequence the various coloured flames.

The great Triangles in their just arrangement hold hid the secret of the wheel of life. The cosmic fire radiates as directed from the second sphere, controlled by the Ruler of the merging ray. The cohorts of the third encircling sphere in varied ranks mark out the lesser threes.

The wheel of life still moves within the form. The devas of the fourth connect the thirty-five, and blend them with the central forty-nine. Above they work, seeking to merge the whole. Upward they strive, who in their myriad forms revolve within the wheels of lesser magnitude. The whole is one, yet on the lower spheres only the forms appear. They seem in their divisions more than can be grasped or met.

The many circulate. The forms are built, become too firm, are broken by the life, and circulate again. The few revolve, holding the many in the heat of motion. The one embraces all, and carries all from great activity into the heart of cosmic peace.

STANZA XII

The Blessed Ones hide Their threefold nature but
reveal Their triple essence by means of the three
great groups of atoms.   Three are the atoms and
threefold the radiation.

The inner core of Fire hides itself and is known
only through radiation and that which radiates.
Only after the blaze dies out and the heat is no
longer felt can the fire be known.

STANZA XIII

Through the band of violet that encircleth the Heavens passeth the globe of purple dark. It passeth and returneth not. It becometh enrapt in the blue. Three times the blue enfoldeth, and when the cycle is completed the purple fadeth and is merged into the rose, and the path again is traversed.

Three the great colours in the cycle that counteth as the fourth, violet, blue and rose, with the basic purple in revolution.

Four are the colours secondary in the cycle of discrimination in which the revolution taketh place. It is circled to the midmost point and somewhat passed. Yellow the band that cometh, orange the cloud that hideth, and green for vivification. Yet the time is not yet.

Many the circling fires; many the revolving rounds, but only when the complementary colours recognise their source, and the whole adjusteth itself to the seven will be seen completion. Then will be seen each colour in adjustment right, and the cessation of revolution.

SECTION ONE

FIRE BY FRICTION

THE FIRE OF MATTER

SECTION ONE

INTRODUCTORY REMARKS

I.   Fire in the Macrocosm
II. Fire in the Microcosm.
III. Fire in manifestation.

WE purpose in these few introductory remarks to lay
down the foundation for a 'Treatise on Cosmic Fire,'
and to consider the subject of fire both macrocosmically
and microcosmically, thus dealing with it from the standpoint of the solar system, and of a human being.   This
will necessitate some preliminary technicalities which
may seem at first perusal to be somewhat abstruse and
complicated but which, when meditated upon and studied,
may eventually prove illuminating and of an elucidating
nature, and which also, when the mind has familiarised
itself with some of the details, may come to be regarded
as providing a logical hypothesis concerning the nature
and origin of energy.   We have elsewhere, in an earlier
book, touched somewhat upon this matter, but we desire
to recapitulate and in so doing to enlarge, thus laying
down a broad foundation upon which the subject matter
can be built up, and providing a general outline which
will serve to show the limits of our discussion.

Let us, therefore, look at the subject macrocosmically
and then trace the correspondence in the microcosm, or
human being.

I. FIRE IN THE MACROCOSM

In its essential nature Fire is threefold, but when in
manifestation it can be seen as a fivefold demonstration,
and be defined as follows:

1. *Fire by friction,* or internal vitalising fire. These fires animate and vitalise the objective solar system. They are the sumtotal of logoic kundalini, when in full systemic activity.

2. *Solar Fire,* or cosmic mental fire. This is that portion of the cosmic mental plane which goes to the animation of the mental body of the Logos. This fire may be regarded as the sumtotal of the sparks of mind, the fires of the mental bodies and the animating principle of the evolving units of the human race in the three worlds.

3. *Electric Fire,* or the logoic Flame Divine. This flame is the distinguishing mark of our Logos, and it is that which differentiates Him from all other Logoi; it is His dominant characteristic, and the sign of His place in cosmic evolution.

This threefold fire may be expressed in ray terms as follows:

First, we have the animating fires of the solar system, which are the fires of the primordial ray of active intelligent matter; these constitute the energy of Brahma, the third aspect of the Logos. Next are to be found the fires of the divine Ray of Love-Wisdom, the ray of intelligent love, which constitutes the energy of the Vishnu aspect, the second aspect logoic.[4] Finally are to be found

[4] "That whereinto all enter, vishanti, is Vishnu; he who covers up, envelopes, surrounds, undertakes all, is Brahma; he who sleeps, shete, in everything, is Shiva. Shiva sleeps, lies hidden, in all and everything as the nexus, the bond, and this is the nature of desire. Vrinite signifies the envelopment, the covering with an envelope, the demarcation of the limiting bounds or the periphery, and so the formation or creation (of all forms); and this is action presided over by Brahma. Vishanti sarvani indicates that all things enter into It and It into all, and such is the Self, connected with cognition and Vishnu. The summation or totality of these is Maha-Vishnu.

"Maha-Vishnu, 'the overlord of all this world-system, is described as the Ishvara, white-coloured, four-armed, adorned with the conch, the discus, the mace, the lotus, the forest-wreath, and the kanstubha-gem, shining, vestured in blue and yellow, endless and imperishable in form, attributeless yet ensouling and underlying all attributes. Here, the epithet Ishvara indicates the rule; the four arms, the four activities of cognition, etc.; the white resplendence is the illumination of all things; the shankha, conch

the fires of the cosmic mental plane, which are the fires of the cosmic ray of will. They might be described as the rays of intelligent will and are the manifestation of the first aspect logoic, the Mahadeva aspect.[5] Therefore we have three cosmic rays manifesting:

The Ray of intelligent activity. This is a ray of a very demonstrable glory, and of a higher point of development than the other two, being the product of an earlier mahakalpa, or a previous solar system.[6] It embodies

or shell, indicates all sound, and the chakra, wheel or discus, all time, there being a connexion between the two; gada, the (whirling) mace, is the spiral method of the procession of the world and the lotus-flower is the whole of that procession; the vana-mala, the wreath of forest flowers, indicates the stringing together of all things into unity and necessity; the nila-pit-ambara, blue and yellow vestures, are darkness and light; the kaustubha jewel indicates inseparable connexion with all; Nirguna, attributeless, shows the presence of the nature of Negation; while saguna, attributeful, implies possession of name and form. The World-process (as embodied in our world-system) is the result of the ideation of Maha-Vishnu.''—*Pranava-Vada*, pp. 72-74, 94-95.

[5] Mahadeva is literally ''great Deva.'' The term is frequently applied to the first Person of the manifested Trinity, to Shiva, the Destroyer aspect, the Creator.

[6] ''One day out of this long life of Brahma is called Kalpa; and a Kalpa is that portion of time which intervenes between one conjunction of all the planets on the horizon of Lanka, at the first point of Aries, and a subsequent similar conjunction. A Kalpa embraces the reign of fourteen Manus, and their sandhies (intervals); each Manu lying between two sandhies. Every Manu's rule contains seventy-one Maha Yugas,—each Maha Yuga consists of four Yugas, viz., Krita, Treta, Dwapara, and Kali; and the length of each of these four Yugas is respectively as the numbers, 4, 3, 2 and 1.

The number of sidereal years embraced in the foregoing different periods are as follows:

	Mortal years
360 days of mortals make a year..................	1
Krita Yuga contains..............................	1,728,000
Treta Yuga contains..............................	1,296,000
Dwapara Yuga contains...........................	864,000
Kali Yuga contains...............................	432,000
The total of the said four Yugas constitute a Maha Yuga	4,320,000
Seventy-one of such Maha Yugas form the period of the reign of one Manu...........................	306,720,000
The reign of 14 Manus embraces the duration of 994 Maha Yugas, which is equal to..................	4,294,080,000
Add Sandhis, i.e., intervals between the reign of each Manu, which amount to 6 Maha Yugas, equal to....	25,920,000
The total of these reigns and interregnums of 14 Manus, is 1,000 Maha Yugas, which constitute a Kalpa, i.e., one day of Brahma, equal to..................	4,320,000,000

the basic vibration of this solar system, and is its great
internal fire, animating and vitalising the whole, and
penetrating from the centre to the periphery. It is the
cause of *rotary motion,* and therefore of the spheroidal
form of all that exists.

The Ray of intelligent love. This is the ray which
embodies the highest vibration of which our solar Logos
or Deity is capable in this present solar system. It is not
yet vibrating adequately nor has it yet attained the
peak of its activity. It is the basis of the cyclic spiral
movement of the body logoic, and just as the Law of
Economy is the law governing the internal fires of the
system so the cosmic Law of Attraction and Repulsion
is the basic law of this divine Ray.

The Ray of intelligent will. Little as yet can be said
about this ray. It is the ray of cosmic mind and in its
evolution parallels that of cosmic love, but as yet its
vibration is slower and its development more retarded.
This is definitely and deliberately so, and is due to the
underlying purpose and choice of the solar Logos, Who
seeks on His high level (just as do His reflections, the
sons of men) to achieve a more rounded out develop-

	Mortal Years
As Brahma's night is of equal duration, one day and night of Brahma will contain....................	8,640,000,000
360 of such days and nights make one year of Brahma, equal to	3,110,400,000,000
100 of such years constitute the whole period of Brahma's age, i.e., Maha Kalpa..................	311,040,000,000,000

That these figures are not fanciful, but are founded upon astronomical
facts, has been demonstrated by Mr. Davis, in an essay in the Asiatic
Researches; and this receives further corroboration from the geological
investigations and calculations made by Dr. Hunt, formerly President of
the Anthropological Society, and also in some respects from the researches
made by Professor Huxley.

Great as the period of the Maha Kalpa seems to be, we are assured
that *thousands and thousands of millions of such Maha Kalpas have passed,
and as many more are yet to come.* (Vide Brahma-Vaivarta and Bhavishyre
Puranas; and Linga Purana, ch. 171, verse 107, &c.) and this in plain
language means that the Time past is infinite and the Time to come is
equally infinite. The Universe is formed, dissolved, and reproduced, in an
indeterminate succession (*Bhagavata-gita,* VIII, 19)."—*The Theosophist,*
Vol. VII, p. 115.

ment, and He therefore concentrates on the development of cosmic love in this greater cycle.

This ray is governed by the Law of Synthesis, and is the basis of the systemic movement which may be best described as that of *driving forward through space,* or forward progression. Little can be predicated anent this ray and its expression. It controls the movements of the entire ring-pass-not in connection with its cosmic centre.[7]

The tabulation on page 42 may make the above ideas somewhat clearer.

These three expressions of the divine Life may be regarded as expressing the triple mode of manifestation. First, the objective or tangible universe; second, the subjective worlds or form; and thirdly, the spiritual aspect which is to be found at the heart of all.[8] The internal fires that animate and vitalise shew themselves in a twofold manner:

[7] The term ''ring-pass-not'' is used in occult literature to denote the periphery of the sphere of influence of any central life force, and is applied equally to all atoms, from the atom of matter as dealt with by the physicist or chemist through the human and planetary atoms up to the great atom of a solar system. The ring-pass-not of the average human being is the spheroidal form of his mental body which extends considerably beyond the physical and enables him to function on the lower levels of the mental plane.

[8] 1. The Primordial is the Ray and the direct emanation of the Sacred Four. S. D., I, 115, 116.
   The Sacred Four are:

	Unity			
a. Father	Mahadeva	1st Logos	Will	Spirit.
	Duality			
b. Son	Vishnu	2nd Logos	Love-Wisdom.	
	Trinity			
c. Mother	Brahma	3rd Logos	Intelligent	activity.
	Sacred Four			

   d. The united manifestation of the three—Macrocosm.
2. The manifested Quaternary and the seven Builders proceed from the Mother.—S. D., I, 402.
   a. The seven Builders are the Manasaputras, the Mind-born sons of Brahma, the third aspect. S. D., III, 540.
   b. They come into manifestation to develop the second aspect. S. D., I., 108.
   c. Their method is objectivity.
3. The re-awakened Energies sprang into space.
   a. They are the veiled synthesis...................S. D., I, 362
   b. They are the totality of manifestation...........S. D., I, 470
   c. They are pre-cosmic...........................S. D., I, 152, 470

TABULATION I.

Fire	Ray	Aspect	Expression	Law	Quality
1. Internal	Primordial	Intelligent Activity.	Rotary motion.	Economy	Fire by friction.
2. Of Mind	Love	Intelligent Love.	Spiral cyclic motion.	Attraction	Solar Fire.
3. Divine Flame	Will	Intelligent Will.	Forward Progression.	Synthesis	Electric Fire.

First as *latent heat*. This is the basis of rotary motion and the cause of the spheroidal coherent manifestation of all existence, from the logoic atom, the solar ring-pass-not, down to the minutest atom of the chemist or physicist.

Second, as *active heat*. This results in the activity and the driving forward of material evolution. On the highest plane the combination of these three factors (active heat, latent heat and the primordial substance which they animate) is known as the 'sea of fire,' of which akasha is the first differentiation of pregenetic matter. Akasha, in manifestation, expresses itself as Fohat, or divine Energy, and Fohat on the different planes is known as aether, air, fire, water, electricity, ether, prana and similar terms.[9, 10, 11] It is the sumtotal

[9] Akasha. Definition .... S. D., II, 538
It is the synthesis of ether.......................... S. D., I, 353, 354
It is the essence of ether............................ S. D., I, 366
It is primordial ether................................ S. D., I, 585
It is the third Logos in manifestation................ S. D., I, 377

[10] H. P. B., defines the Akasha in the following terms: S. D., II, 538.
"Akasha the astral Light can be defined in a few words: It is the Universal soul, the Matrix of the Universe, the Mysterium Magicum from which all that exists is born by separation or differentiation. In the various occult books it is called by different terms and it would be of value perhaps if we enumerate some of them here: There is one universal element with its differentiations.

Homogeneous.	*Differentiated.*
1. Undifferentiated cosmic substance.	1. Astral Light.
2. Primordial ether.	2. Sea of fire.
3. Primordial electric entity.	3. Electricity.
4. Akasha.	4. Prakriti.
5. Super-astral light.	5. Atomic matter.
6. Fiery serpent.	6. The serpent of evil.
7. Mulaprakriti.	7. Ether, with its four divisions, air,
8. Pregenetic matter.	fire, water, earth."

[11] Fohat is divine thought or energy (Shakti) as manifested on any plane of the cosmos. It is the interplay between Spirit and matter. The seven differentiations of Fohat are:
1. The Plane of divine life................. Adi .... Sea of fire.
2. The Plane of monadic life.............. Anupadaka.... Akasha.
3. The Plane of Spirit..................... Atma......... Aether.
4. The Plane of the intuition.............. Buddhi....... Air.
5. The Plane of mind..................... Mental ...... Fire.
6. The Plane of desire.................... Astral........ Astral Light.
7. The Plane of density................... Physical...... Ether.
—S. D., I, 105, 134, 135, 136.

of that which is active, animated, or vitalized, and of all that concerns itself with the adaptation of the form to the needs of the inner flame of life.

It might here be useful to point out that *magnetism* is the effect of the divine ray in manifestation in the same sense that electricity is the manifested effect of the primordial ray of active intelligence. It would be well to ponder on this for it holds hid a mystery.

The fires of the mental plane also demonstrate in a twofold manner:

First, as the *Fire of Mind,* the basis of all expression and in one peculiar occult sense the sumtotal of existence. It provides the relation between the life and the form, between spirit and matter, and is the basis of conscious-ness itself.

Second, as the *Elementals of Fire,* or the sumtotal of the active expression of thought, showing itself through the medium of those entities who, in their very essence, are fire itself.

These dualities of expression make the four necessary factors in the logoic quaternary,[12] or the lower nature of the Logos viewing His manifestation from one eso-teric angle; exoterically, they are the sumtotal of the logoic quaternary, plus the logoic fifth principle, cosmic mind.

The divine spark does not as yet manifest (as do the other two fires) as a duality, though what lies hidden in a later cycle, evolution alone will disclose. This third fire, along with the other two, makes the necessary five of logoic evolutionary development and by its perfected merging with the other two fires as the evolutionary process proceeds is seen the goal of logoic attainment for this greater cycle or period of this solar system.

---

[12] The quaternary is composed of the four lower principles and the sheaths through which they manifest as a coherent unit, being held together during manifestation by the life force of the indwelling entity.

When the primordial ray of intelligent activity, the divine ray of intelligent love, and the third cosmic ray of intelligent will meet, blend, merge, and blaze forth, the Logos will take His fifth initiation, thus completing one of His cycles. When the rotary, the forward, and the spiral cyclic movements are working in perfect synthesis then the desired vibration will have been reached. When the three Laws of Economy, of Attraction, and of Synthesis work with perfect adjustment to each other, then nature will perfectly display the needed functioning, and the correct adaptation of the material form to the indwelling spirit, of matter to life, and of consciousness to its vehicle.

II. FIRE IN THE MICROCOSM

Let us briefly consider therefore the correspondence between the greater whole and the unit man and then block out our subject in detail and consider the sections into which it will be wise to divide it.

Fire in the Microcosm is likewise threefold in essence and fivefold in manifestation.

1. There is *Internal Vitalising Fire,* which is the correspondence to fire by friction. This is the sumtotal of individual kundalini; it animates the corporeal frame and demonstrates also in the twofold manner:

First, as *latent heat* which is the basis of life of the spheroidal cell, or atom, and of its rotary adjustment to all other cells.

Second, as *active heat* or prana; this animates all, and is the driving force of the evolving form. It shows itself in the four ethers and in the gaseous state, and a correspondence is here found on the physical plane in connection with man to the Akasha and its fivefold manifestation on the plane of the solar system.

This fire is the basic vibration of the little system in which the monad or human spirit is the logos, and it

holds the personality or lower material man in objective
manifestation thus permitting the spiritual unit to contact the plane of densest matter. It has its correspondence in the ray of intelligent activity and is controlled
by the Law of Economy in one of its subdivisions, the
Law of Adaptation in Time.

2. There is next the *Fire or Spark of Mind* which is
the correspondence in man to solar fire. This constitutes
the thinking self-conscious unit or the soul. This fire of
mind is governed by the Law of Attraction as is its
greater correspondence. Later we can enlarge on this.
It is this spark of mind in man, manifesting as spiral
cyclic activity, which leads to expansion and to his
eventual return to the centre of his system, the Monad—
the origin and goal for the reincarnating Jiva or human
being. As in the macrocosm this fire also manifests in a
twofold manner.

It shows as that intelligent will which links the Monad
or spirit with its lowest point of contact, the personality,
functioning through a physical vehicle.

It likewise demonstrates, as yet imperfectly, as the
vitalising factor in the thought forms fabricated by the
thinker. As yet but few thought forms, comparatively,
can be said to be constructed by the center of consciousness, the thinker, the Ego. Few people as yet are in such
close touch with their higher self, or Ego, that they can
build the matter of the mental plane into a form which
can be truly said to be an expression of the thoughts,
purpose or desire of their Ego, functioning through the
physical brain. Most of the thought forms at present in
circulation may be said to be aggregations of matter,
built into form with the aid of kama-manas (or of desire
faintly tinged with mind producing thus an admixture of
astral and mental matter, mostly astral), and largely due
to reflex elemental action.

These dualities of expression are:

1. *Active fire* or prana.
   Latent fire or bodily heat.
2. *Mental energy* in the mental body.
   Purely mental thought forms, animated by self-engendered fire, or by the fifth principle, and therefore part of the sphere, or system of control, of the Monad.

These form an esoteric quaternary which with the fifth factor, the divine spark of intelligent will, make the five of monadic manifestation—manifestation in this case connotating a purely *subjective manifestation* which is neither altogether spiritual nor altogether material.

3. Finally there is the *Monadic Flame Divine*. This embodies the highest vibration of which the Monad is capable, is governed by the Law of Synthesis, and is the cause of the forward progressive movement of the evolving Jiva.

We now come, in due course, to the point of merging or to the end of manifestation, and to the consummation (viewing it monadically) of the great cycle or manvantara. What shall we therefore find? Just as in the macrocosm the blending of the three essential fires of the cosmos marked the point of logoic attainment, so, in the blending of the essential fires of the microcosm, do we arrive at the apotheosis of human attainment for this cycle.

When the latent fire of the personality or lower self blends with the fire of mind, that of the higher self, and finally merges with the Divine Flame, then the man takes the fifth Initiation in this solar system, and has completed one of his greater cycles.[13] When the three blaze forth as one fire, liberation from matter, or from material form is achieved. Matter has been correctly adjusted to spirit, and finally the indwelling life slips forth out of its sheath which forms now only a channel for liberation.

[13] These terms, Lower Self, Higher Self, Divine Self, are apt to be con-

III. FIRE IN MANIFESTATION.

To continue our consideration of the fires which sustain the economy of the visible solar system, and of the visible objective human being, which produce evolutionary development, and which are the bases of all objective efflorescence, it must be noted that they demonstrate as the sumtotal of the vital life of a solar system, of a planet, of the entire constitution of active functioning man upon the physical plane, and of the atom of substance.

Speaking broadly we would say that the *first fire* deals entirely with:

- a. Activity of matter.
- b. The rotary motion of matter.
- c. The development of matter by the means of friction, under the law of Economy. H.P.B. touches on this in the *Secret Doctrine*.[14]

The *second fire,* that from the cosmic mental plane, deals with:

- a. The expression of the evolution of mind or manas.
- b. The vitality of the soul.
- c. The evolutionary expression of the soul as it shows forth in the form of that elusive something which brings about the synthesis of matter. As the two merge by means of this active energising factor, that which is termed *consciousness* appears.[15] As

fusing until the student apprehends the various synonyms connected with them. The following table may be found helpful:

Father................	Son....................	Mother................
Spirit.................	Soul...................	Body..................
Life..................	Consciousness..........	Form..................
Monad.................	Ego....................	Personality...........
Divine Self...........	Higher Self...........	Lower Self...........
Spirit.................	Individuality..........	Personal Self.........
The Point.............	The Triad.............	The Quaternary.......
Monad.................	Solar Angel...........	Lunar Lords..........

[14] See S. D., I, 169, 562, 567, 569; II, 258, 390, 547, 551, 552.
[15] In the *Study of Consciousness* Mrs. Besant says (page 37): "Consciousness is the one reality, in the fullest sense of that much-used phrase;

the merging proceeds and the fires become more and more synthesised, that totality of manifestation which we regard as a conscious existence becomes ever more perfected.

d. The operation of this fire under the Law of Attraction.

e. The subsequent result in the spiral-cyclic movement which we call, within the system, solar evolution, but which (from the standpoint of a cosmos) is the approximation of our system to its central point. This must be considered from the standpoint of time.[16]

The *third fire* deals with:

a. The evolution of spirit.

Practically nothing can at this stage be communicated anent this evolution. The development of spirit can be only expressed as yet in terms of the evolution of matter, and only through the adequacy of the vehicle, and through the suitability of the sheath, the body or form, can the point of

it follows from this that any reality found anywhere is drawn from consciousness. Hence, everything which is thought, is. That consciousness in which everything is, everything literally, ''possible'' as well as ''actual'' —actual being that which is thought of as existent by a separated consciousness in time and space, and *possible* all that which is not so being thought of at any period in time and any point in space—we call Absolute Consciousness. It is the All, the Eternal, the Infinite, the Changeless. Consciousness, thinking time and space, and of all forms as existing in them in succession and in places, is the Universal Consciousness, the One, called by the Hindu the Saguna Brahman—the Eternal with attributes—the Pratyag-Atma—the Inner Self; by the Parsi, Hormuzd; by the Mussulman, Allah. Consciousness dealing with a definite time, however long or short, with a definite space, however vast or restricted, is individual, that of a concrete Being, a Lord of many universes, or a universe or of any so-called portion of a universe, his portion and to him therefore a universe—these terms varying as to extent with the power of the consciousness; so much of the universal thought as a separate consciousness can completely think, i.e., on which he can impose his own reality, can think of as existing like himself, is his universe.''

[16] Universal consciousness, manifesting as consciousness in time and space, as Mrs. Besant so ably expresses it, includes all forms of activity and spiral cyclic evolution from the standpoint of cosmic evolution, and in terms of absolute consciousness, may again be rotary.

spiritual development reached in any way be appraised. A word of warning should here be interpolated:—

Just as it is not possible upon the physical plane for the physical vehicle fully to express the total point of development of the Ego or higher self, so it is not possible even for the Ego fully to sense and express the quality of spirit. Hence the utter impossibility for human consciousness justly to appraise the life of the spirit or Monad.

b. The working of the flame divine under the Law of Synthesis—a generic term which will be seen eventually to include the other two laws as subdivisions.

c. The subsequent result of forward progressive motion—a motion which is rotary, cyclic and progressive.

The whole matter dealt with in this Treatise concerns the subjective essence of the solar system, not primarily either the objective or spiritual aspect. It concerns the Entities who indwell the form, who demonstrate as animating factors through the medium of matter, and primarily through etheric matter; who are evolving a second faculty, the fire of mind, and who are essentially themselves points of fire, cast off through cosmic friction, produced by the turning of the cosmic wheel, swept into temporary limited manifestation and due eventually to return to their central cosmic centre. They will return plus the results of evolutionary growth, and through assimilation they will have intensified their fundamental nature, and be spiritual fire plus the fire manasic.

The internal fire of matter is called in the *Secret Doctrine* "Fire by Friction." It is an *effect* and not a cause. It is produced by the two fires of spirit and of mind (electric and solar fire) contacting each other through the medium of matter. This energy demonstrates in matter itself as the internal fires of the sun, and of the planets and finds a reflection in the internal fires of man. Man is the Flame Divine and the fire of Mind brought into contact through the medium of substance or form. When evolution ends, the fire of matter is not cognisable. It persists only when the other two fires are associated, and it does not persist apart from substance itself.

Let us now briefly recognise certain facts regarding fire in matter and let us take them in order, leaving time to elucidate their significance. First we might say that the internal fire being both latent and active, shows itself as the synthesis of the acknowledged fires of the system, and demonstrates, for instance, as solar radiation and inner planetary combustion. This subject has been somewhat covered by science, and is hidden in the mystery of physical plane electricity, which is an expression of the *active* internal fires of the system and of the planet just as inner combustion is an expression of the *latent* internal fires. These latter fires are to be found in the interior of each globe, and are the basis of all objective physical life.

Secondly, we might note that the internal fires are the basis of life in the lower three kingdoms of nature, and in the fourth or human kingdom in connection with the two lower vehicles. The Fire of Mind, when blended with the internal fires, is the basis of life in the fourth kingdom, and united they control (partially now and later entirely) the lower threefold man or the personality; this control lasts up to the time of the first Initiation.

The fire of Spirit finally, when blended with the two other fires (which blending commences in man at the first initiation), forms a basis of spiritual life or existence. As evolution proceeds in the fifth or spiritual kingdom, these three fires blaze forth simultaneously, producing perfected consciousness. This blaze results in the final

purification of matter and its consequent adequacy; at
the close of manifestation it brings about eventually the
destruction of the form and its dissolution, and the termination of existence as understood on the lower planes.
In terms of Buddhistic theology it produces annihilation;
this involves, not loss of identity, but the cessation of
objectivity and the escape of Spirit, plus mind, to its
cosmic centre. It has its analogy in the initiation at
which the adept stands free from the limitations of
matter in the three worlds.

The internal fires of the system, of the planet, and of
man are threefold:

1. Interior fire at the centre of the sphere, those inner
   furnaces which produce warmth. This is latent
   fire.

2. Radiatory fire. This type of fire might be expressed in terms of physical plane electricity, of
   light rays, and of etheric energy. This is active
   fire.

3. Essential fire, or the fire elementals who are themselves the essence of fire. They are mainly divided
   into two groups:

    a. Fire devas or evolutionary entities.

    b. Fire elementals or involutionary entities.

    Later we will elaborate on this when we consider
    the Fire of Mind and deal with the nature of the
    thought elementals. All these elementals and
    devas are under the control of the fire Lord, Agni.
    When considering Him and His kingdom the sub-
    ject can be taken up at greater length.

We might here point out, however, that our first two
statements concerning the internal fires, express the
effect that the fire entities have upon their environment.
Heat and radiation are other terms which might be applied in this sense. Each of these effects produces a

different class of phenomena. Latent fire causes the active growth of that in which it is embedded and causes that upward pushing which brings into manifestation all that is found in the kingdoms of nature. Radiatory fire causes the continued growth of that which has progressed, under the influence of latent fire, to a point receptive of the radiatory. Let us tabulate it thus:

Systemic or Macrocosmic: The solar Logos or The Grand Man of the Heavens.

Latent or interior fire produces the internal heat which makes the solar system productive of all forms of life. It is the inherent warmth that causes all fertilisation, whether human, animal, or vegetable.

Active or radiatory fire retains in life and causes the evolution of all that has evolved into objectivity by means of latent fire.

Planetary, or the Heavenly Men:

What is laid down anent the system, as a whole, can be predicated of all planets which in their nature reflect the Sun, their elder brother.

Human, or the Microcosmic Man:

Human latent fire, the heat interior of the human frame causes production of other forms of life, such as—

1. The physical body cells.
2. Organisms nourished by the latent heat.
3. The reproduction of itself in other human forms, the basis of the sex function.

Human radiatory, or active fire, is a factor as yet but little comprehended; it relates to the health aura and to that radiation from the etheric which makes a man a healer, and able to transmit active heat.

It is necessary to differentiate between this radiation from the etheric, which is a radiation of prana, and magnetism, which is an emanation from a subtler body (usually the astral), and has to do with the manifestation of the Divine Flame within the material sheaths. The Divine Flame is formed on the second plane, the monadic, and magnetism (which is a method of demonstrating radiatory fire) is therefore felt paramountly on the fourth and sixth planes, or through the buddhic and astral vehicles. These are, as we know, closely allied to the second plane. This distinction is of importance and should be carefully recognised.

Having, therefore, made the above statements, we can proceed to take up somewhat in greater detail the interior fires of the systems, microcosmic and macrocosmic.

SECTION ONE

DIVISION A

THE INTERNAL FIRES OF THE SHEATHS.

I. The three channels.
II. Fire elementals and devas.

I. THE THREE CHANNELS FOR THE FIRE

FROM the very use of the term "sheath" it will be noted that we are considering those fires which manifest through the medium of those externalities, of those veils of substance which hide and conceal the inner Reality. We shall not here take up the subject of the sheaths on the higher planes, but simply deal with the fires that animate the three lower vehicles,—the physical body in its two divisions (etheric and dense), the emotional or astral body, and the mental sheath. It is frequently overlooked by the casual student that both the astral and the mental bodies are material, and just as material in their own way, as is the dense physical body, and also that the substance of which they are composed is animated by a triple fire, as is the physical.

In the physical body we have the fires of the lower nature (the animal plane) centralised at the base of the spine. They are situated at a spot which stands in relation to the physical body as the physical sun to the solar system. This central point of heat radiates in all directions, using the spinal column as its main artery, but working in close connection with certain central ganglia, wherever located, and having a special association with the spleen.

CHART I

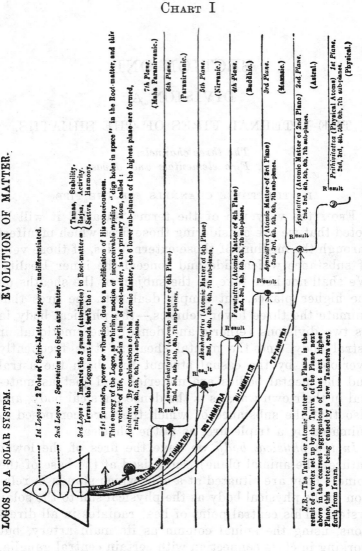

In the etheric body, which is an exact replica of its denser counterpart, we have the organ of active or radiatory fire, and, as is well known, the vehicle of prana. Its function is to store up the rays of radiatory light and heat which are secured from the sun, and to transmit them, via the spleen, to all parts of the physical body. Hence in the future it will come to be recognised that the spine and the spleen are of the utmost importance to the physical well-being of man, and that when the spinal column is duly adjusted and aligned, and when the spleen is freed from congestion and in a healthy condition, there will be little trouble in the dense physical body. When the physical furnace burns brightly and when the fuel of the body (pranic rays) is adequately assimilated, the human frame will function as desired.

The subject of the blending of these two fires, which is complete in a normal and healthy person, should engross the attention of the modern physician. He will then concern himself with the removal of nerve congestion or material congestion, so as to leave a free channel for the inner warmth. This blending, which is now a natural and usual growth in every human being, was one of the signs of attainment or of initiation in an earlier solar system. Just as initiation and liberation are marked in this solar system by the blending of the fires of the body, of the mind and of the Spirit, so in an earlier cycle attainment was marked by the blending of the latent fires of matter with the radiatory or active fires, and then their union with the fires of mind. In the earlier period the effects in manifestation of the divine Flame were so remote and deeply hidden as to be scarcely recognisable, though dimly there. Its correspondence can be seen in the animal kingdom, in which instinct holds the intuition in latency, and the Spirit dimly overshadows. Yet all is part of a divine whole.

The subject of the radiatory heat of the macrocosmic and microcosmic systems will be dealt with in detail in a later subdivision. Here we will only deal with the latent interior fire of the

      a. Sun.
      b. Planet.
      c. Man.
      d. Atom.

We must remember that in both the astral and the mental sheaths there exist the counterparts of the centres as found in the physical body. These centres concern matter and its evolution. One fundamental statement can be laid down anent the internal fires of all these four (sun, planet, man, and atom):

There exists in the Sun, in the planet, in man, and in the atom, a central point of heat, or (if I might use so limiting and inappropriate a term) a central cavern of fire, or nucleus of heat, and this central nucleus reaches the bounds of its sphere of influence, its ring-pass-not by means of a threefold channel.[17]

a. The Sun. Within the sun, right at its very heart, is a sea of fire or heat, but not a sea of flame. Herein may lie a distinction that perhaps will convey no meaning to some. It is the centre of the sphere, and the point of fiercest internal burning, but has little relation to the flames or burning gases (whatever terms you care

---

[17] "The divine essence that, pervading the entire universe of millions of solar systems, is caught up by our sun and passed out in a manifested form to the utmost boundaries of our solar system, so that this manifested essence may be the basic soil of the growth, preservation and destruction of our worlds, that divine essence is simple Nadam of our yogic philosophy and that Nadam or OM subsequently manifests itself as seven streams. The unmanifested is manifested by or borne by the subsequent ramifications. These streams are the seven vowels or seven notes. These seven vowels and notes must have special correlations with the seven vedic metres, since in the Vishnu Purana, Parasara describes the vedic metres as the coursers of the solar essence."—*Some Thoughts on the Gita,* p. 74.

to use) that are generally understood to exist whenever the sun is considered. It is the point of fiercest incandescence, and the objective sphere of fire is but the manifestation of that internal combustion. This central heat radiates its warmth to all parts of the system by means of a triple channel, or through its "Rays of Approach" which in their totality express to us the idea of "the heat of the sun."

1. *The akasha,* itself vitalised matter, or substance animated by latent heat.
2. *Electricity,* substance of one polarity, and energised by one of the three aspects logoic. To express it more occultly, substance showing forth the quality of the cosmic Lord Whose energy it is.
3. *Light Rays of pranic aspect,* some of which are being now recognised by the modern scientist. They are but aspects of the latent heat of the sun as it approaches the Earth by a particular line of least resistance.

When the term "channel or ray of approach" is used, it means approach from the centre of solar radiation to the periphery. What is encountered during that approach—such as planetary bodies, for instance—will be affected by the akashic current, the electrical current, or the pranic current in some way, but all of these currents are only the internal fires of the system when viewed from some other point in universal, though not solar, space. It is, therefore, obvious that this matter of fire is as complex as that of the rays. The internal fires of the solar system become external and radiatory when considered from the standpoint of a planet, while the internal fires of the planet will affect a human being as radiation in exactly the same way as the pranic emanations of his etheric body affect another physical body as radiatory. The point to be grasped in all these aspects is that one and all have to do with **matter or** substance, and not with mind or Spirit.

b. The Planet. Deep in the heart of the planet—such a planet as the Earth, for instance—are the internal fires that occupy the central sphere, or the caverns which —filled with incandescent burning—make life upon the globe possible at all. The internal fires of the moon are practically burnt out, and, therefore, she does not shine save through reflection, having no inner fire to blend and merge with light external. These inner fires of the earth can be seen functioning, as in the sun, through three main channels:

1. *Productive substance,* or the matter of the planet vitalised by heat. This heat and matter together act as the mother of all that germinates, and as the protector of all that dwells therein and thereon. This corresponds to the akasha, the active vitalised matter of the solar system, that nourishes all as does a mother.

2. *Electrical fluid,* a fluid which is latent in the planet though as yet but little recognized. It is perhaps better expressed by the term "animal magnetism." It is the distinctive quality of the atmosphere of a planet, or its electrical ring-pass-not. It is the opposite pole to the solar electrical fluid, and the contact of the two and their correct manipulation is the aim—perhaps unrealised—of all scientific endeavor at this time.

3. That emanation of the planet which we might term *Planetary Prana.* It is that which is referred to when one speaks of the health-giving qualities of Mother Nature, and which is back of the cry of the modern physician, when he wisely says "Back to the Earth." It is the fluidic emanation of this prana which acts upon the physical body, though in this case not via the etheric body. It is ab-

sorbed through the skin purely and the pores are its line of least resistance.

c. The Man. At the base of the spine lie hid the fires of the human system, or the internal fires of the Microcosm. The centre is located there, and from it the radiations go forth along the three channels, recognisable in the spine.

1. *Bodily warmth,* the channel along which the heat radiates ahd which finds the goal of its attention to be the heating of the corporeal frame. This vitalisation of the dense matter of the body finds its correspondence in the systemic akasha, and in planetary productive substance.

2. *Nervous response.* This is the vitalising tenuous fluid which applies itself to the stimulation of the nervous centres, and which creates electrical response to contact between the nerves and the brain. It should now be more closely studied. It corresponds to systemic electricity, and to planetary electricity.

3. *Pranic emanation.* The emanation, via the etheric body, which corresponds in man to solar prana and to planetary prana. This demonstrates principally in the health aura and has naught to do with magnetic qualities, as generally interpreted when considering a personality, or man as a unit. I make this repetition as it is very necessary that no mental confusion exists between that magnetism which is a spiritual emanation and that which is purely animal.

It might be wise here to point out that this triple manifestation of fire demonstrates in the astral and mental bodies likewise, having to do with the *substance* of those bodies. We might express this fire in its triple manifestation as the sumtotal of the essential fire, or life activity of the third Logos. It should be carefully borne in mind that the manifestation of the work of the three Logoi is the expression of the mind of some cosmic Entity. In the same way, the seven planetary Entities, the seven Heavenly Men, are seven Logoi (likewise cosmic Beings) Who in Their totality form the Body of the threefold Logos. We have, therefore:

1. The undifferentiated Logos—a cosmic Entity.
2. The Logos, threefold in manifestation:
    a. The cosmic Lord of Will Power.
    b. The cosmic Lord of Love and Wisdom.
    c. The cosmic Lord of Active Intelligence.
3. The triple Logos, sevenfold in manifestation., i.e. The seven planetary Logoi.[18, 19, 20]

[18] T. Subba Rao says on page 20, of *Esoteric Writings*: "As a general rule, whenever seven entities are mentioned in the ancient occult science of India in any connection whatsoever, you must suppose that those seven entities came into existence from *three primary entities* and that these three entities again are evolved out of a *single* entity or monad. To take a familiar example, the seven coloured rays in the solar ray are evolved out of three primary coloured rays; and the three primary colours co-exist with the four secondary colours in the solar ray. Similarly the three primary entities which brought man into existence co-exist in him with the *four secondary* entities which arose from different combinations of the three primary entities."

In Christian terminology these are the three Persons of the Trinity, and the seven Spirits which are before the Throne. Compare "Our God is a consuming fire." Heb: 12.29.

[19] "I have already said in speaking of this Logos, that it was quite possible that it was the Logos that appeared in the shape of the first Dhyan Chohan, or planetary Spirit, when the evolution of man was recommenced after the last period of inactivity on this planet, as stated in Mr. Sinnett's book, *Esoteric Buddhism*, and after having set the evolutionary current in motion, retired to the spiritual plane congenial to its own nature, and has been watching since over the interests of humanity, and now and then appearing in connection with a human individuality for the good of mankind. Or you may look upon the Logos represented by Krishna as one belonging to the same class as the Logos which so appeared. In speaking of himself Krishna says, (chap. x, verse 6):

"The seven great Rishis, the four preceding Manus, partaking of my nature were born from my mind: from them sprang, was (born) the human race and the world."

He speaks of the sapta Rishis and of the Manus as his manasaputras, or mind-born sons, which they would be if he was the so-called Prajapati, who appeared on this planet and commenced the work of evolution."—*The Theosophist*, Vol. VIII, p. 443.

[20] The following tabulation should be borne in mind:
Seven branch races make...........one subrace
Seven subraces make...............one rootrace
Seven rootraces make..............one world period

Each of these cosmic Entities is, in His essential essence, *Fire;* each manifests as fire in a threefold manner. In point of time the cosmic Lord of active Intelligence, considered from the standpoint of *cosmic* evolution, is more evolved than His two Brothers. He is the life of matter, its latent internal Fire. His is the fire essence that lies at the heart of the Sun, of the planet, and of man's material forms. He is the sumtotal of the Past.

The Lord of Cosmic Love now seeks union with His Brother, and, in point of time, embodies all the Present. He is the sumtotal of all that is embodied; He is conscious Existence. He is the Son divine and His life and nature evolve through every existent form. The Lord of Cosmic Will holds hid the future within His plans and consciousness. They are all three the Sons of one Father, all three the aspects of the One God, all three are Spirit, all three are Soul, and all three are Rays emanating from one cosmic centre. All three are substance, but in the past one Lord was the elder Son, in the present another Lord comes to the fore, and in the future still another. But this is so only in Time. From the standpoint of the Eternal Now, none is greater nor less than another, for the last shall be first, and the first last. Out of manifestation time is not, and freed from objectivity states of consciousness are not.

The fire of Spirit is the essential fire of the first Lord of Will plus the fire of the second Logos of Love. These two cosmic Entities blend, merge, and demonstrate as Soul, utilising for purposes of manifestation the aid of the third Logos. The three fires blend and merge. In this fourth round and on this fourth globe of our planetary scheme, the fires of the third Logos of intelligent matter are fusing somewhat with the fires of cosmic

Seven world periods make	....	one round
Seven rounds make	....	one chain period
Seven chain periods make	....	one planetary scheme
Ten planetary schemes make	....	one solar system

mind, showing as will or power, and animating the
Thinker on all planes. The object of Their co-operation
is the perfected manifestation of the cosmic Lord of
Love. This should be pondered upon for it reveals a
mystery.

The blending of the three fires, the merging of the
three Rays, and the co-operation of the three Logoi have
in view (at this time and within this solar system) the
development of the Essence of the cosmic Lord of Love,
the second Person in the logoic trinity. Earlier it was
not so, later it will not be, but now it is. When viewed
from the cosmic mental plane these Three constitute the
PERSONALITY OF THE LOGOS, and are seen *functioning as
one.* Hence the secret (well recognised as fact, though
not understood) of the excessive *heat,* occultly expressed, of the astral or central body of the triple personality. It animates and controls the physical body,
and its desires hold sway in the majority of cases; it
demonstrates in *time and space* the correspondence of
the temporary union of spirit and matter, the fires of
cosmic love and the fires of matter blended. A similar
analogy is found in the heat apparent in this second
solar system.

d. The Atom. The inner fires of the atom can likewise be seen functioning along similar lines, their demonstration being already somewhat recognised by science. This being so there exists no necessity for further
elaboration.[21]

---

[21] "It should be remembered that the mere scale does not matter, for
greatness and smallness are essentially relative. The destiny of each atom
is to create a brahmanda. Brahmandas like or smaller or larger than ours,
held together by a sun, are present in every atom. Vishvas, great world-
systems, exist in an atom, and atoms again exist in these vishvas. This is
the significance of 'many from one'; wherever we see the one we should
recognise the many also, and conversely. After securing the ability of,
and then actually, creating a brahmanda, the next step is the creation of a
jagat, then a vishva, then a maha-vishva and so on, till the status of maha-
vishnu is reached."—Bhagavan Das in the *Pranava Vada,* p. 94.

II. FIRE ELEMENTALS AND DEVAS

We might now briefly consider the subject of the fire
elementals and devas, and then deal with the relation
of the Personality Ray to this internal fire of the system
in its threefold manifestation.

Certain facts are known in connection with the fire
spirits (if so they may be termed). The fundamental
fact that should here be emphasised is that AGNI, the
Lord of Fire, rules over all the fire elementals and devas
on the three planes of human evolution, the physical,
the astral, and the mental, and rules over them not only
on this planet, called the Earth, but on the three planes
in all 'parts of the system. He is one of the seven
Brothers (to use an expression familiar to students of
the *Secret Doctrine*) Who each embody one of the seven
principles, or Who are in Themselves the seven centres
in the body of the cosmic Lord of Fire, called by H. P. B.
"Fohat." He is that active fiery Intelligence, Who is
the basis of the internal fires of the solar system. On
each plane one of these Brothers holds sway, and the
three elder Brothers (for always the three will be seen,
and later the seven, who eventually merge into the primary three) rule on the first, third and the fifth planes,
or on the plane of adi, of atma [22] and of manas. It is
urgent that we here remember that They are fire viewed

[22] *Atma* means as you all know the self or the ego or an individualised
centre of consciousness around which all worldly experiences in their dual
aspect of subjective and objective cluster and arrange themselves. It is
as it were one of the foci from which emerge rays of light to illumine the
cosmic waters and in which also converge the rays sent back by those waters.
In Theosophical writings, it is called the selfconscious individuality or the
Higher Manas. From this point of view, you will see that the Higher
Manas is the most important principle or the central pivot of the human
constitution or the true soul. It is the thread which ought to be caught
hold of by one who wants to know the truth and lift himself out of this
conditioned existence. To this it may be objected that Atma represents
the seventh principle of the theosophical septenary and that the Manas is
far lower in the scale. But the plain answer is that the seventh principle
is the ultimate state attainable by the self after crossing the ocean of
conditioned existence or samsara."—*Some Thoughts on the Gita*, p. 26.

in its third aspect, *the fire of matter*. In Their totality these seven Lords form the essence of the cosmic Lord, called in the occult books, Fohat.[23]

This is so in the same sense as the seven Chohans,[24] with Their affiliated groups of pupils, form the essence or centres in the body of one of the Heavenly Men, one of the planetary Logoi. These seven again in Their turn form the essence of the Logos.

Each of the seven Lords of Fire [25] are differentiated into numerous groups of fire entities, from the Deva-Lords of a plane down to the little salamanders of the internal furnaces. We are not dealing with the fiery essences of the higher planes at this stage in our discussion. We will only enumerate somewhat briefly some of the better known groups, as contacted in the three worlds.

1. *Physical Plane.*

Salamanders, those little fire elementals who can be seen dancing in every flame, tending the fires of the hearth and the home, and of the factory. They are of the same group as the fire spirits who can be contacted deep in the fiery bowels of the planet.

Fire spirits, latent in all focal points of heat, who are themselves the essence of warmth, and can be contacted

---

[23] Fohat, or electricity, is an Entity.
He is the primordial electric Entity .... S. D., I, 105.
He is ....Will ....S. D., I, 136.
He is ....Love-Wisdom ....S. D., I, 100, 144, 155.
He is ....Active Intelligence............S. D., I, 136.
Therefore He is God............................S. D., I, 167.
He is the sumtotal of the energy of the seven Spirits,
Who are the sumtotal of the Logos.—S. D., I, 169.
[24] *Chohan* (Tibetan). A Lord or Master. A high Adept. An initiate who has taken more Initiations than the five major Initiations which make man a "Master of the Wisdom."
[25] *The seven Brothers.* See S. D., I, 105. These seven are the seven differentiations of primordial electric energy.
Plane. As used in occultism, the term denotes the range or extent of some state of consciousness or of the perceptive power of a particular set of senses or the action of a particular force, or the state of matter corresponding to any of the above.

in the heat of the bodily frame, whether human or animal, and who are likewise the warmth terrestrial.

The Agnichaitans, a higher grade of fire spirit, who form a vortex of fire when viewed on a large scale, such as in volcanoes and large destructive burnings. They are closely allied to a still more important group of devas, who form the fiery envelope of the sun.

The pranic elementals, those minute fiery essences who have the ability to permeate the texture of the human body, of a tree, or of all that may be found in the human, vegetable and animal kingdoms, and who blend with the fires of the microcosmic systems.

Certain of the deva kingdom who may be described as ensouling certain of the great light rays, and Who are in Themselves the essence of those rays. Other forms of such elemental lives and of deva groups might be enumerated, but the above tabulation will suffice for our present purpose.

2. *The Astral Plane.*

The fiery essences of this plane are more difficult for us to comprehend, having not, as yet, the seeing eye upon that plane. They are in themselves the warmth and heat of the emotional body, and of the body of feeling. They are of a low order when upon the path of desire, and of a high order when upon the path of aspiration, for the elemental is then transmuted into the deva.

Their grades and ranks are many, but their names matter not save in one instance. It may be of interest to know the appellation applied to the devas of fire whose part it is to tend the fires that will later destroy the causal body. We need to remember that it is the up-springing of the latent fire of matter and its merging with two other fires that causes destruction. These elementals and devas are called the *Agnisuryans,* and in

their totality are the fiery essences of buddhi, hence
their lowest manifestation is on the sixth plane, the
astral.

Further information concerning these deva lives will
be found further on in the Treatise, where they are dealt
with at some length.

SECTION ONE

DIVISION B

THE PERSONALITY RAY AND FIRE BY FRICTION

I.   *The work of the three rays.*
    1. The personality ray.
    2. The egoic ray.
    3. The monadic ray.
II. *The personality ray and the permanent atom.*
III. *The personality ray and karma.*

I. THE WORK OF THE THREE RAYS

WE here touch upon a matter of wide general interest yet which is withal very little comprehended. I refer to the subject of the permanent atoms.[26] Each body or form wherein Spirit functions has, for its focal point on each plane, an atom composed of matter of the atomic subplane of each plane. This serves as a nucleus for the distribution of force, for the conservation of faculty, for the assimilation of experience, and for the preserva-

---

[26] *Permanent Atom.* An appropriated point of atomic matter. A tiny centre of force which forms the central factor and the attractive agency around which the sheaths of the incarnating Monad are built. These are strung like pearls upon the sutratma, or thread.
    Ray. A stream of force or an emanation. The solar Logos, or the Macrocosm, manifests through three major rays and four minor rays. The Monad or microcosm likewise manifests through three rays as mentioned in the text above. All rays express a peculiar and specialised type of force.
    Triad. This is literally Atma-buddhi-manas, the expression of the Monad, just as the personality is the expression of the Ego. The Monad expresses itself through the Triad, and in its lowest or third Aspect forms the Egoic or Causal body, the infant or germinal Ego. Similarly, the Ego expresses itself through the threefold lower man, mental, emotional, and etheric (these being the reflection of the higher Triad) and these three give rise to the dense physical manifestation.

tion of memory. These atoms are in direct connection with one or other of the three great rays in connection with the microcosm:—

  a. The *Monadic* Ray, the synthetic ray of the microcosm.
  b. The *Egoic* Ray.
  c. The *Personality* Ray.

Each of these rays has a connection with one or other of the permanent atoms in the lower threefold man, and has a direct action upon the spirillae [27] found within the atom. We have noted in *"Letters on Occult Meditation"* that the atoms of the lower threefold man underwent a twofold process:—

They were first vivified in rotation, and each held the light in ordered sequence until the lower triangle was entirely illumined.

Eventually transmutation took place, or (to word it otherwise) the polarisation eventually shifted into the three permanent atoms of the Triad, and out of the three permanent atoms of the lower triangle. The physical permanent atom is transcended and the polarisation becomes manasic or mental, the astral permanent atom is transcended and the polarisation becomes buddhic, while the mental unit is superseded by the permanent

---

[27] Spirilla: "In order to examine the construction of the atom, a space is artificially made, then, if an opening be made in the wall thus constructed, the surrounding force flows in, and three whorls immediately appear, surrounding the "hole" with their triple spiral of two and a half coils, and returning to their origin by a spiral within the atom; these are at once followed by seven finer whorls, which following the spiral of the first three on the outer surface and returning to their origin by a spiral within that, flowing in the opposite direction-form a caduceus with the first three. Each of the three coarser whorls, flattened out, makes a closed circle; each of the seven finer ones, similarly flattened out, makes a closed circle. The forces which flow in them, again, come from "outside," from a fourth-dimensional space. Each of the finer whorls is formed of seven yet finer ones, set successively at right angles to each other, each finer than its predecessor; these we call spirillæ.

"Each spirilla is animated by the life-force of a plane, and four are at present normally active, one for each round. Their activity in an individual may be prematurely forced by yoga practice."—*Occult Chemistry*, p. 28.

atom, of the fifth plane, the atmic. This is all brought about by the action of the three rays upon the atoms and upon the life within each atom. The relationship between these three rays and the permanent atoms might be summarised as follows:

The *Personality* Ray has direct action upon the physical permanent atom.

The *Egoic* Ray has a similar action upon the astral permanent atom.

The *Monadic* Ray has a close connection with the mental unit.

The effect which they have is threefold, but is not simultaneous; they work ever, as do all things in Nature, in ordered cycles. The stimulation, for instance, that is the result of the action of the monadic Ray upon the mental unit is only felt when the aspirant treads the Path, or after he has taken the first Initiation. The action of the egoic Ray upon the astral permanent atom is felt as soon as the Ego can make good connection with the physical brain; when this is so the egoic ray is beginning to affect the atom powerfully and continuously; this occurs when a man is highly evolved and is nearing the Path. This threefold force is felt in the following way:

First. It plays upon the wall of the atom as an external force and affects its rotary and vibratory action.

Second. It stimulates the inner fire of the atom and causes its light to shine with increasing brilliancy.

Third. It works upon the spirillae, and brings them all gradually into play.

II. THE PERSONALITY RAY AND THE PERMANENT ATOM

The *Personality Ray* deals with the first four spirillae, and is the source of their stimulation. Note here the correspondence to the lower quaternary and its stimulation by the ego. The *Egoic Ray* concerns itself with the fifth spirilla and with the sixth, and is the cause of their emerging from latency and potentiality into power and activity. The *Monadic Ray* is the source of the stimulation of the seventh spirilla.

There is great interest attached to this subject and wide reaches of thought and vast fields for investigation open up before the earnest student. This threefold action varies in point of time and sequence according to the ray itself upon which the Monad may be found; but the subject is too vast to be handled at this time.

In looking at the matter from the standpoint of fire the idea may be grasped a little through the realisation that the latent fire of matter in the atom is brought into brilliance and usefulness by the action of the personality Ray which merges with this fire and stands in the same position to the permanent atom in the microcosm as FOHAT does on the cosmic plane. The fire is there hidden within the sphere (whether the sphere systemic or the sphere atomic) and the personality Ray in the one case, and Fohat in the other, acts as the force which brings latency into activity and potentiality into demonstrated power. This correspondence should be thought out with care and judgment. Just as Fohat has to do with active manifestation or objectivity, so the personality Ray has to do with the third, or activity aspect in the microcosm. The work of the third aspect logoic was the arranging of the matter of the system so that eventually it could be built into form through the power of the second aspect. Thus the correspondence works out. By life upon the physical plane (that life wherein the physical permanent atom has its full demonstration) the matter is arranged and separated that must eventually be built into the Temple of Solomon, the egoic body, through the agency of the egoic life, the second aspect. In the quarry of the personal life are the stones prepared for the great Temple. In existence upon the physical plane and in the objective personal life is that experience gained which demonstrates as faculty in the Ego. What is here suggested would richly repay our closest attention, and open up before us reaches of ideas, which should eventuate in a wiser comprehension, a sounder judgment, and a greater encouragement to action.

III. THE PERSONALITY RAY AND KARMA

It might be wise here to recapitulate a little so that in the refreshing of the memory may come the basis of further knowledge. We dealt first with the three fires of the system, macrocosmic and microcosmic, and having laid down certain hypotheses we passed to the consideration of the first of the fires, that which is inherent in matter. Having studied it somewhat in its threefold manifestation in the various parts of the system, including man, we took up the matter of the personality Ray and its relationship to this third fire. We must recall here that all that has been dealt with has been in relation to matter, and for the whole of this first section this thought must be borne carefully in mind.

In our second section we will consider all from the standpoint of mind, and in the final from the standpoint of the Divine Ray. Here we are dealing with what H.P.B calls the primordial ray and its manifestations in matter.[28] All these Rays of Cosmic Mind, Primordial Activity, and Divine Love-Wisdom are but essential quality demonstrating through the agency of some one factor.

The *Primordial Ray* is the quality of motion, demonstrating through matter.

[28] See S. D., I, 108; II, 596.

The *Ray of Mind* is the quality of intelligent organisation, demonstrating through forms, which are the product of motion and matter.

The *Ray of Love-Wisdom* is the quality of basic motive that utilises the intelligent organisation of matter in motion to demonstrate in one synthetic whole the great Love aspect of the Logos.[29]

This line of thought can be worked out also correspondingly in the Microcosm, and will show how individual man is engaged in the same type of work on a lesser scale as the solar Logos.

At this point in the treatise we are confining our attention to the Ray of Active Matter, or to that latent heat in substance which underlies its activity and is the cause of its motion. If we think with sincerity and with clarity we will see how closely therefore the Lipika Lords or the Lords of Karma are associated with this work. Three of Them are closely connected with Karma as it concerns one or other of the three great Rays, or the three FIRES, while the fourth Lipika Lord synthesizes the work of his three Brothers and attends to the uniform blending and merging of the three fires. On our planet, the Earth, They find Their points of contact through the three "Buddhas of Activity," [30] (the correspondence should be noted here) and the fourth Kumara, the Lord of the World. Therefore, we arrive at the realisation that the personality Ray, in its relation to the fire of matter, is directly influenced and adjusted in its working by one of the Buddhas of Activity.

[29] S. D., I, 99, 108; II, 596.
[30] "Buddhas of Activity." The 'Pratyeka Buddhas.' This is a degree which belongs exclusively to the Yogacharya School, yet it is only one of high intellectual development with no true spirituality. . . . It is one of the three paths to Nirvana, and the lowest, in which a yogi—"without teacher and without saving others"—by the mere force of will and technical observances, attains to a kind of nominal Buddahood individually."— *Theosophical Glossary*

The karma [31, 32, 33] of matter itself is an abstruse subject and has as yet scarcely been hinted at. It is nevertheless indissolubly mixed up with the karma of the individual. It involves a control of the evolution of the monadic essence, the elemental essence and of the atomic matter of the plane; it is concerned with the development of the four spirillae, with their activity, with their attachment to forms when atomic, and with the development of the inner latent heat and its gradual fiery increase until we have within the atom a repetition of what is seen within the causal body: the destruction of the periphery of the atom by the means of burning. It deals with the subject of the building of matter into form by the interaction of the two rays, the Divine and the Primordial, producing thereby that fire by friction which tends to life and fusing.

The karma of form is likewise a vast subject, too

[31] "From the view taken of Karma as I have done it, you will see that no plane of the highest spirituality, be that the plane of the nirvanees, is outside the karmic wheel and when it is said in the Sanskrit writings and even in the Bhagavat Gita that men cross the karmic ocean, it must be understood with some allowance. The entities that have now succeeded in going outside the karmic wheel, have done so, only if that wheel be taken as the one that turns now. The cosmos is not going in one groove all the days of Brahma, but it is going on a higher and higher status as it fulfils its mission. Those who have attained unto a rest in a state of spirituality not reachable now, will therefore in a future day come within the action of the wheel, with perhaps a punishment for the great duties neglected for long ages."—*Some Thoughts on the Gita*, p. 40.

[32] *The Lipika* are the Spirits of the Universe. They are connected with the Law of Cause and Effect (Karma) and its recorders. Lipika comes from "Lipi" writing. For information concerning the Lipika Lords see S. D., I, pp. 152, 153.

The Buddhas of Activity, are the Triad Who stands closest to Sanat Kumara, The Lord of the World. They are the planetary correspondences to the three Aspects of the logoic third Aspect and are concerned with the force behind planetary manifestation.

Monadic Essence, the matter of the atomic (or highest) subplane of each plane. *Elemental Essence*, the matter of the six subplanes which are non atomic. It is molecular matter.

[33] "*Karma* may be defined to be the force generated by a human centre to act on the exterior world, and the reactionary influence that is in turn generated from the exterior world to act on him may be called karmic influence and the visible result that is produced by this influence under proper conditions may be called karmic fruit."—*Some thoughts on the Gita*, p. 53.

involved for average comprehension but a factor of real importance which should not be overlooked in connection with the evolution of a world, a synthesis of worlds, or of a system when viewed from higher levels. Everything is, in its totality, the result of action taken by cosmic Essences and Entities in earlier solar systems, which is working out through the individual atoms, and through those congeries of atoms which we call forms. The effect of the personality Ray upon the internal fires is therefore, in effect, the result of the influence of the planetary Logos of whatever ray is implicated, as He works out that portion of Karma which falls to His share in any one cycle, greater or lesser. He thus brings about and eventually transmutes, the effects of causes which He set in motion earlier in relation to His six Brothers, the other planetary Logoi. We get an illustrative parallel in the effect which one individual will have upon another in worldly contact, in moulding and influencing, in stimulating or retarding. We have to remember that all fundamental influence and effects are felt on the astral plane and work thence through the etheric to the dense physical thereby bringing matter under its sphere of influence, yet not itself originating on the physical plane.

SECTION ONE

DIVISION C

THE ETHERIC BODY AND PRANA [34]

I.   THE NATURE OF THE ETHERIC BODY

In our consideration of the internal fires of the system we shall find much of very real interest to the coming

[34] "Prana, or the vital principle, is the special relation of the Atma with a certain form of matter which by the relation of Atma organises and builds up as a means of having experience. This special relation constitutes the individual Prana in the individual body. The cosmic all-pervading Prana is not Prana in the gross sense, but is a name for the Brahman as the author of the individual Prana. . . . All beings, whether Devatas, men or animals, exist only so long as the Prana is within the body. It is the life duration of all. . . . Prana, or vitality, is the common function of the mind and all the senses."—*Serpent Power*, pp. 94, 95.

generation of thinkers for three main reasons, which might be enumerated as follows:

1. *Its Purpose and Description*

First. In the study of the etheric body lies hid (for scientists and those of the medical profession) a fuller comprehension of the laws of matter and the laws of health. The word *health* has become too localised in the past, and its meaning confined to the sanity of the body corporeal, to the co-operative action of the atoms of the physical body of man, and to the full expression of the powers of the physical elemental. In days to come it will be realised that the health of man is dependent upon the health of all allied evolutions, and upon the co-operative action and full expression of the matter of the planet and of the planetary elemental who is himself a composite manifestation of the physical elementals of all manifested nature.

Second. In the study of the etheric body and prana lies the revelation of the effects of those rays of the sun which (for lack of better expression), we will call "solar pranic emanations." These solar pranic emanations are the produced effect of the central heat of the sun approaching other bodies within the solar system by one of the three main channels of contact, and producing on the bodies then contacted certain effects differing somewhat from those produced by the other emanations. These effects might be considered as definitely stimulating and constructive, and (through their essential quality) as producing conditions that further the growth of cellular matter, and concern its adjustment to environing conditions; they concern likewise the internal health (demonstrating as the heat of the atom and its consequent activity) and the uniform evolution of the form of which that particular atom of matter forms a constituent part. Emanative prana does little in connection with form building; that is not its province, but it conserves the form through the preservation of the health of its component parts. Other rays of the sun act differently, upon the forms and upon their substance. Some perform the work of the Destroyer of forms, and others carry on the work of cohering and of attracting; the work of the Destroyer and of the Preserver is carried on under the Law of Attraction and Repulsion. Some rays definitely produce accelerated motion, others produce retardation. The ones we are dealing with here— pranic solar emanations—work within the four ethers, that matter which (though physical) is not as yet objectively visible to the eye of man. They are the basis of all physical plane life considered solely in connection with the life of the physical plane atoms of matter, their inherent heat and their rotary motion. These emanations are the basis of that "fire by friction" which demonstrates in the activity of matter.

Finally, in the study of the etheric body and prana comes comprehension of the method of logoic manifestation, and therefore much of interest to the metaphysician, and all abstract thinkers. The etheric body of man holds hid the secret of his objectivity. It has its correspondence on the archetypal plane,—the plane we call that of the divine manifestation, the first plane of our solar system, the plane Adi. The matter of that highest plane is called often the "sea of fire" and it is the root of the akasha, the term applied to the substance of the second plane of manifestation. Let us trace the analogy a little more in detail, for in its just apprehension will be found much of illumination and much that will serve to elucidate problems both macrocosmic and microcosmic. We will begin with man and his etheric body.

The etheric body has been described as a network, permeated with fire, or as a web, animated with golden light. It is spoken of in the Bible as the "golden bowl."

It is a composition of that matter of the physical plane which we call etheric, and its shape is brought about by the fine interlacing strands of this matter being built by the action of the lesser Builders into the form or mould upon which later the dense physical body can be moulded. Under the Law of Attraction, the denser matter of the physical plane is made to cohere to this vitalised form, and is gradually built up around it, and within it, until the interpenetration is so complete that the two forms make but one unit; the pranic emanations of the etheric body itself play upon the dense physical body in the same manner as the pranic emanations of the sun play upon the etheric body. It is all one vast system of transmission and of interdependence within the system. All receive in order to give, and to pass on to that which is lesser or not so evolved. Upon every plane this process can be seen.

Thus the etheric body forms the archetypal plane in relation to the dense physical body. The thinker on his own plane stands, in relation to the physical, as the Logos to His system. In the synthesis of thought it might be expressed thus: The thinker on the astral plane, the plane of desire and of necessity, stands to the physical body as the Logos on the cosmic astral plane stands to His system.

As we continue the study we will work out the correspondence in the cosmos, the system, and in the three worlds, for we need to remember that the analogy must be perfect.

1. Man, the Microcosm, the manifesting Monad, or One.
2. The Heavenly Man, the planetary Logos, or the manifesting group.
3. The Grand Man of the Heavens, the Macrocosm, the solar Logos, the manifestation of all groups and of all evolutions within His Body, the solar system.

All these bodies—the body of a man, a planetary Logos, and a solar Logos—are the product of desire originating on the planes of abstract mind, whether cosmic, systemic, or mind in the three worlds, whether cosmic desire-mind or human desire-mind, and all their bodies are "Sons of Necessity," as H.P.B. so aptly expressed it.[35, 36]

2. *Eight Statements.*

It is with the etheric bodies of all we are dealing, and with their vivification by prana (whether cosmic, solar, planetary or human), with the organs of reception and with the basis of emanations. Here, therefore, we can arrive at certain dicta anent the etheric body which for purposes of clarity might well be enumerated:

First. The etheric body is the mould of the physical body.

Second. The etheric body is the archetype upon which

[35] S. D., I, 74.

[36] "'This whole solar system being conceived of as one vast mechanism, with an exquisite adjustment of its parts in all major details, is only the physical expression of Vishnu, or the ethereal basic substance, as we may understand the word for the present. All the harmonies observable in the manifested cosmos are only the result of the harmoniously working energies that resolve ether into the expression that we recognise. All planets, worlds, human beings, etc., are only parts of the body, each functioning in subordination to the law which governs the whole. The evolution, preservation and destruction of the world is therefore one vast process called Yagna, which takes place in the body of Yagna Purusha, or the psychical body of nature. Humanity taken collectively is the heart and brain of this Purusha and therefore all the Karma generated by humanity, physical, mental, or spiritual, determines mainly the character of this Yagnic process. . . . Sri Krishna therefore calls the process the Yagnic life that he has been giving out to Arjuna as Yoga (1st Sloka 4th Chr). In fact, Yoga and Yagna are very closely allied and even inseparable, though at the present day people seem to disconnect the two. Yoga derived from the root Yuj to join means an act of joining. Now as the heart is the great centre in man, likewise the Yogee of the heart keeps his central position in the universe and hence his individuality. The individuality or the Higher Manas being the pivot of the human constitution or the centre on which two hemispheres of higher and lower existence turn as I have already said, the Yogee of the heart has a heavenly dome above and earthly abyss below and his yoga becomes twofold as a consequence. He joins himself on to the thing above in dhyana and the thing below in action. The word yagna derived from the root Yaj—to serve also means a twofold service, service done to the thing above through service done unto its expression the thing below.''—*Some Thoughts on the Gita,* pp. 18, 134.

the dense physical form is built, whether it is the form of a solar system, or of a human body in any one incarnation.

Third. The etheric body is a web or network of fine interlacing channels, formed of matter of the four ethers, and built into a specific form. It forms a focal point for certain radiatory emanations, which vivify, stimulate and produce the rotary action of matter.

Fourth. These pranic emanations when focalised and received, react upon the dense matter which is built upon the etheric scaffolding and framework.

Fifth. This etheric web, during incarnation, forms a barrier between the physical and astral planes, which can only be transcended when consciousness is sufficiently developed to permit of escape. This can be seen in both the microcosm and the macrocosm. When a man has, through meditation and concentration, expanded his consciousness to a certain point he is enabled to include the subtler planes, and to escape beyond the limits of the dividing web.

PHYSICAL SUB-PLANES	SOLAR SYSTEM PLANES
1. First ether. Atomic plane..	Adi. Divine. Sea of fire. First cosmic ether.
2. Second ether. Sub-atomic..	Anupadaka. Monadic plane. Akasha. Second cosmic ether.
3. Third ether. Super-etheric.	Atmic. Spiritual plane. Aether. Third cosmic ether.
4. Fourth ether. Super-gaseous	Buddhic. Intuitional Plane. Air. Fourth cosmic ether.

DENSE PHYSICAL	PLANES OF HUMANITY
5. Gaseous. Sub-etheric	Mental. Fire. Cosmic gaseous.
6. Liquid	Astral. Emotional plane. Water. Cosmic liquid.
7. Earthly. Dense	Physical plane. Earth. Cosmic dense.

When the Logos has expanded His Consciousness on cosmic levels He can then transcend the logoic etheric web, and escape beyond the ring-pass-not of His objective manifestation. In thinking out this analogy we must hold closely in mind the fact that the seven major planes of our solar system are the seven subplanes of the cosmic physical or the lowest cosmic plane.

We might note here the accurate working out of the correspondence in matter and the radiatory correspondence is equally accurate.

Sixth. In all the three bodies—human, planetary, and systemic or logoic—will be found a great organ within the organism which acts as the receiver of prana. This organ has its etheric manifestation and its dense physical correspondence.

In the system. In the system, the organ of cosmic prana, of the force vitalising matter, is the central sun, which is the direct receiver and dispenser of cosmic radiation. This is one of the threefold divisions of the Primordial Ray of active intelligence. Each of the cosmic Rays is in essence threefold, a fact which is oft overlooked, though logically obvious; each Ray is the vehicle for a cosmic Entity, and all existence is necessarily triple in manifestation. The central Sun has within its periphery a centre of reception with a surface radiation.

In the Planet. In the planet there will be found a similar organ or receiver within its etheric body, the locality of which is not for exoteric publication and cannot therefore be revealed. It is connected with the location of the two poles, north and south, and is the centre around which the globe rotates, and is the source of the legend of a sacred fertile land within the sphere of polar influences. The mythic land of exceeding fertility, of abundant luxuriance, and of phenomenal growth, vegetable, animal and human would naturally lie where prana is received. It is the esoteric Garden of Eden, the land of physical perfection. Surface radiation demonstrates, after distribution, as planetary prana.

In Man. The organ of reception is the spleen through its etheric counterpart. After distribution over the entire body via the etheric network it demonstrates in surface radiation as the health aura.

Seventh. Thus in all the three bodies will the resemblance clearly be seen, and the working out in perfect correspondence is easily demonstrable:

PRANA OF THE SOLAR SYSTEM

THE SOLAR SYSTEM

Entity manifesting .... The solar Logos.
Body of manifestation .... The solar system.
Receptive centre .... Pole of the central Sun.
Surface radiation or emanation. Solar prana.
Movement produced .... Systemic rotation.
Distributive effect .... Solar etheric radiation (felt cosmically).

THE PLANET

Entity manifesting .... A planetary Logos.
Body of manifestation .... A planet.
Receptive centre .... The planetary pole.
Surface radiation or emanation. Planetary prana.
Movement produced .... Planetary rotation.
Distributive effect .... Planetary etheric radiation (felt within the system).

A HUMAN BEING

Entity manifesting .... The thinker, a Dhyan Chohan
Body of manifestation .... Physical body.
Receptive centre .... The spleen.
Surface radiation or emanation. Health aura.
Movement produced .... Atomic rotation.
Distributive effect .... Human etheric radiation (felt by environment).

THE ATOM OF MATTER

Entity manifesting ....An elementary life.
Body of manifestation.........The atomic sphere.
Receptive centre ....Pole of the atom.
Surface radiation or emanation. Contribution of atom to the united health aura of body.
Movement produced ....Atomic rotation.
Distributive effect ....Atomic etheric radiation (felt within the physical form).

Eighth. When the "will to live" vanishes, then the "Sons of Necessity" cease from objective manifestation. This is logically inevitable, and its working out can be seen in every case of *entified objectivity.* When the Thinker on his own plane withdraws his attention from his little system within the three worlds and gathers within himself all his forces, then physical plane existence comes to an end and all returns within the causal consciousness; this is as much an abstraction in the three worlds of the Thinker as the Absolute is in the threefold solar system of the Logos. This demonstrates on the physical plane in the withdrawing from out of the top of the head of the radiant etheric body and the consequent disintegration of the physical. The framework goes and the dense physical form falls apart; the pranic life is abstracted bodily from out of the dense sheath, and the stimulation of the fires of matter ceases to be. The latent fire of the atom remains; it is inherent, but the form is made by the action of the two fires of matter—active and latent, radiatory and inherent—aided by the fire of the second Logos, and when they are separated the form falls apart. This is a picture in miniature of the essential duality of all things acted upon by Fohat.

There is a close connection between the spleen and
the top of the head in connection with the etheric body.
The organ of the spleen has an interesting correspondence to the umbilical cord which attaches an infant to
the mother for purposes of nourishment, and which is
separated at birth.   When a man starts to live his own
life of conscious desire, when a man is· born into a new
world of a subtler form of life, that interlaced cord of
etheric matter (which had united him to his physical
body) is broken; the "silver cord is loosed" and the man
severs his connection with the dense physical body and
passes out through the highest center of the body instead
of the lowest to life in a higher world and of another
dimension.   So it will be found in all the bodies and
sheaths of the microcosm, for the analogy will persist
on all planes during manifestation.   When more scientific knowledge has been gained it will be found that
the same procedure on a larger scale, takes place in
planetary manifestation.   A planet is but the body of
a planetary Logos, that body being etheric, and the
Logos expressing Himself through it and building upon
the etheric scaffolding a vehicle of manifestation.   The
MOON once was the body of expression for one of the
Logoi; the Earth now is, and the cycles change continuously.   The centre of escape for the etheric body is
found likewise in a physical planet, and the planetary
silver cord is loosed at the time appointed; but the times
and cycles, their commencement and termination are hid
in the mysteries of Initiation, and do not concern us.

Again in the solar system itself similar action will
eventuate at the close of a Mahamanvantara.   The Logos
will withdraw within Himself, abstracting His three
major principles.[37]   His body of manifestation—the Sun

---

[37] *Principles*, the basic differentiations, essential qualities or types of
energy upon which all things are built; they give the distinctive nature of
all forms.

and the seven sacred Planets, all existing in etheric matter—will withdraw from objectivity and become obscured. From the usual physical standpoint, the light of the system will go out. This will be succeeded by a gradual inbreathing until He shall have gathered all unto Himself; the etheric will cease to exist, and the web will be no more. Full consciousness will be achieved, and in the moment of achievement existence or entified manifestation will cease. All will be reabsorbed within the Absolute; pralaya,[38] or the cosmic heaven of rest will then ensue, and the Voice of the Silence will be heard no more. The reverberations of the WORD will die away, and the "Silence of the High Places" will reign supreme.

II. THE NATURE OF PRANA

In dealing with the subject of the etheric body and its functions as an assimilator and distributor of prana, we have dealt with it from the standpoint of its place in the scheme of things. We have considered this matter of etherics from the angle of correspondences, and have traced analogies in the system, the planet, and man. We have seen that it formed the foundation of the dense physical form, and in itself constituted a most important link between:

a. Physical man, and the emotional or astral plane.
b. Planetary Man, and essential emotional quality.
c. The Logos, the grand Heavenly Man, and the cosmic astral plane.

We might now narrow the subject down to the consideration of the etheric body of the human being and not touch upon correspondences to things systemic or cosmic at all, though it may be necessary to remind ourselves that for the wise student the line along which wisdom

[38] *Pralaya.* . . . A period of obscuration or repose—planetary, systemic or cosmic. An interlude between two periods of manifestation.

comes is the interpretative one; he who knows himself
(in objective manifestation, essential quality, and comprehensive development) knows likewise the Lord of his
Ray, and the Logos of his system. It is only then a
matter of application, conscious expansion, and intelligent interpretation, coupled to a wise abstention from
dogmatic assertion, and a recognition that the correspondence lies in quality and method more than in detailed adherence to a specified action at any given time
in evolution.

All that it is possible to give here is material which,
if rightly pondered on, may result in more intelligent
practical living in the occult sense of the term "living";
which, if studied scientifically, religiously and philosophically, may lead to the furthering of the aims of the
evolutionary process in the immediately coming lesser
cycle. Our aim, therefore, is to make the secondary body
of man more real, and to show some of its functions and
how it can eventually be brought *consciously* into the
range of mental comprehension.

Science, as we know, is fast reaching the point where
it will be forced to admit the fact of the etheric body,
because the difficulties of refusing to acknowledge it, will
be far more insuperable than an admission of its existence. Scientists admit already the fact of etheric matter; the success of photographic endeavor has demonstrated the reality of that which has hitherto been
considered unreal, because (from the standpoint of the
physical) intangible. Phenomena are occurring all the
time which remain in the domain of the supernatural
unless accounted for through the medium of etheric matter, and in their anxiety to prove the spiritualists wrong,
scientists have aided the cause of the true and higher
spiritism by falling back on reality, and on the fact of
the etheric body, even though they consider it a body of

emanative radiation—being concerned with the effect and not having yet ascertained the cause. Medical men are beginning to study (blindly as yet) the question of vitality, the effect of solar rays upon the physical organism, and the underlying laws of inherent and radiatory heat. They are beginning to ascribe to the spleen functions hitherto not recognised, to study the effect of the action of the glands, and their relation to the assimilation of the vital essences by the bodily frame. They are on the right road, and before long (perhaps within this century) the FACT of the etheric body and its basic function will be established past all controversy, and the whole aim of preventive and curative medicine will shift to a higher level. All we can do here is to give simply, and in a condensed form, a few facts which may hasten the day of recognition, and further the interest of the true investigator. Let me, therefore, briefly state what will be dealt with in our remaining three points:

The functions of the etheric body.

Its relation to the physical during life.

The ills or diseases of the etheric body (taking care to retain the original meaning of the word "disease.")

Its after death condition.

This will embody all that is as yet of practical use. More may later be forthcoming for our helping if that which is now given to the public is carefully followed up, and if investigators wisely, sanely and broadly study this important matter.

As the nature and functions of the etheric body of man assume their rightful place in the thought of the world and as it is realised that the etheric is the most important of the two physical bodies, man will be brought into closer conscious contact with the other evolutions that evolve in etheric matter just as he does in a dense physical body. There are certain large groups of devas, called "the devas of the shadows," or the violet devas, who are closely allied with the evolutionary development of man's etheric body, and who transmit to him solar and planetary radiation. The etheric body of man receives prana in different ways and of different kinds, and all these ways bring him into touch with varying entities.

1. *Solar prana.*

This is that vital and magnetic fluid which radiates from the sun, and which is transmitted to man's etheric body through the agency of certain deva entities of a very high order, and of a golden hue. It is passed through their bodies and emitted as powerful radiations, which are applied direct through certain plexi in the uppermost part of the etheric body, the head and shoulders, and passed down to the etheric correspondence of the physical organ, the spleen, and from thence forcibly transmitted into the spleen itself. These golden hued pranic entities are in the air above us, and are specially active in such parts of the world as California, in those tropical countries where the air is pure and dry, and the rays of the sun are recognised as being specially beneficial. Relations between man and this group of devas are very close, but fraught as yet with much danger to man. These devas are of a very powerful order, and, along their own line, are further evolved than man himself. Unprotected man lies at their mercy, and in this lack of protection, and man's failure to understand the laws of magnetic resistance, or of solar repulsion comes, for instance, the menace of sunstroke. When the etheric body and its assimilative processes are comprehended scientifically, man will then be immune from dangers due to solar radiation. He will protect himself by the application of the laws governing magnetic repulsion and attraction, and not so much by clothing and shelter. It is largely a question of polarisation. One hint might here be given: When men understand the deva evolution somewhat more correctly and recognise their work along certain lines in connection with the Sun and realise that they represent the feminine pole as they themselves represent the masculine (the fourth Creative Hierarchy being male)[39] they will comprehend the mutual relationship, and govern that relationship by law.

These solar devas take the radiatory rays of the sun which reach from its centre to the periphery along one of the three channels of approach, pass them through their organism and focalise them there. They act almost as a burning glass acts. These rays are then reflected or transmitted to man's etheric body, and caught up by him and again assimilated. When the etheric body is in good order and functioning correctly, enough of this prana is absorbed to keep *the form organised*. This is the whole object of the etheric body's functioning, and is a point which cannot be sufficiently emphasised. The remainder is cast off in the form of animal radiation, or physical magnetism—all terms expressing the same idea. Man therefore repeats on a lesser scale the work of the great solar devas, and in his turn adds his quota of repolarised or remagnetised emanation to the sumtotal of the planetary aura.

2. *Planetary prana.*

This is the vital fluid emanated from any planet, which constitutes its basic coloring or quality, and is produced by a repetition within the planet of the same process

[39] S. D., I, 232-238.
The whole cosmos is guided, controlled and animated by an almost endless series of Hierarchies of sentient Beings, each having a mission to perform.—S. D., I, 295.
Among these the Hierarchy of human Monads has a place.

which is undergone in connection with man and solar prana. The planet (the Earth, or any other planet) absorbs solar prana, assimilates what is required, and radiates off that which is not essential to its well-being in the form of planetary radiation. Planetary prana, therefore, is solar prana which has passed throughout the planet, has circulated through the planetary etheric body, has been transmitted to the dense physical planet, and has been cast off thence in the form of a radiation of the same essential character as solar prana, *plus the individual and distinctive quality of the particular planet concerned.* This again repeats the process undergone in the human body. The physical radiations of men differ according to *the quality* of their physical bodies. So it is with a planet.

Planetary emanative prana (as in the case of solar prana) is caught up and transmitted via a particular group of devas, called the "devas of the shadows," who are ethereal devas of a slightly violet hue. Their bodies are composed of the matter of one or other of the four ethers, and they focalise and concentrate the emanations of the planet, and of all forms upon the planet. They have a specially close connection with human beings owing to the fact of the essential resemblance of their bodily substance to man's etheric substance, and because they transmit to him the magnetism of "Mother Earth" as it is called. Therefore we see that there are two groups of devas working in connection with man:

a. Solar devas, who transmit the vital fluid which circulates in the etheric body.

b. Planetary devas of a violet color, who are allied to man's etheric body, and who transmit earth's prana, or the prana of whichever planet man may be functioning upon during a physical incarnation.

A very pertinent question might here be asked, and though we may not fully explain the mystery, a few sug-

gestive hints may be possible. We might ask: What
causes the apparent deadness of the Moon? Is there
deva life upon it? Does solar prana have no effect there?
What constitutes the difference between the apparently
dead Moon, and a live planet, such as the Earth? [40]

Here we touch upon a hidden mystery, of which the
solution lies revealed for those who seek, in the fact that
human.beings and certain groups of devas are no longer
found upon the Moon. *Man has not ceased to exist upon
the Moon because it is dead and cannot therefore support
his life, but the Moon is dead because man and these deva
groups have been removed from off its surface and from
its sphere of influence.*[41] Man and the devas act on every
planet as intermediaries, or as transmitting agencies.
Where they are not found, then certain great activities
become impossible, and disintegration sets in. The reason for this removal lies in the cosmic Law of Cause and
Effect, or cosmic karma, and in the composite, yet individual, history of that one of the Heavenly Men Whose
body, the Moon or any other dead planet at any time
happened to be.

3. *The prana of forms.*

It must first be pointed out that forms are necessarily
of two kinds, each having a different place in the scheme:

Forms that are the result of the work of the third and
the second Logos, and Their united life. Such forms
are the units in the vegetable, animal and mineral
kingdoms.

Forms that are the result of the united action of the
three Logoi, and comprise the strictly deva and
human forms.

There is also the still simpler form embodied in the substance of which all the other forms are made. This mat-

[40] S. D., I, 170-180.
[41] S. D., I, 179.

CHART II

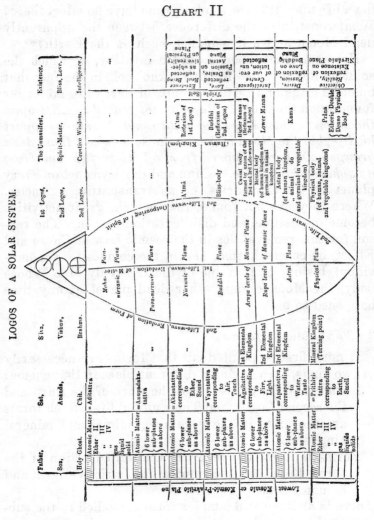

LOGOS OF A SOLAR SYSTEM.

FROM "THE THEOSOPHIST" FOR JANUARY, 1900.

ter is strictly speaking the:atomic and molecular matter, and is animated by the life or energy of the third Logos.

In dealing with the first group of forms, it must be noted that the pranic emanations given off by units of the animal and vegetable kingdom (after they have absorbed both solar and planetary prana) are naturally a combination of the two, and are transmitted by means of *surface radiation,* as in solar and planetary prana, to certain lesser groups of devas of a not very high order, who have a curious and intricate relationship to the group soul of the radiating animal or vegetable. This matter cannot be dealt with here. These devas are also of a violet hue, but of such a pale color as to be almost grey; they are in a transitional state, and merge with a puzzling confusion with groups of entities that are almost on the involutionary arc.[42, 43, 43a]

[42] *Involutionary Arc* is the term applied to the first part of the evolutionary process. It covers the ''path of descent,'' or the coming down of Spirit into ever denser matter until the lowest point is reached, the point of densest concretion. The latter half of the process is called *evolutionary* and marks the ascent or return of Spirit to its emanating source, plus the gains of the evolutionary process.

[43] *''The Three Outpourings.* In the diagram the ''symbols of the three Aspects (of the Logos) are placed outside of time and space, and only the streams of influence from them descend into our system of planes. . . . They represent in due order what are commonly called the three Persons of the Trinity. . . . It will be seen that from each of them an outpouring of life or force is projected into the planes below. The first of these in order is the straight line which descends from the third Aspect; the second is that part of the large oval which· lies on our left hand—the stream which descends from the second Aspect until it has touched the lowest point in matter, and then rises again up the side on our right hand until it reaches the lower mental level. It will be noted that in both of these outpourings the divine life becomes darker and more veiled as it descends into matter, until at the lowest point we might almost fail to recognise it as divine life at all; but as it rises again when it has passed its nadir it shows itself somewhat more clearly. The third outpouring which descends from the highest aspect of the Logos differs from the others in that it is in no way clouded by the matter through which it passes, but retains its virgin purity and splendour untarnished. It will be noted that this outpouring descends only to the level of the buddhic plane (the fourth plane) and that the link between the two is formed by a triangle in a circle, representing the individual soul of man—the reincarnating ego. Here the triangle is contributed by the third outpouring and the circle by the second. . . .''—*The Christian Creed,* by C. W. Leadbeater, pp. 39, 40.

[43a] See S. D., I, 98, 99, 100, 103.

1. *The root of life was in every drop of the ocean of immortality.* Every atom in matter was impregnated with the life of the Logos.

In dealing with the second group, the human form transmits the emanative radiations to a much higher grade of deva. These devas are of a more pronounced hue, and after due assimilation of the human radiation, they transmit it principally to the animal kingdom, thus demonstrating the close relationship between the two kingdoms. If the above explanation of the intricate inter-relation between the sun and the planets, between the planets and the evolving forms upon them, between the forms themselves in ever descending importance demonstrates nothing more than the exquisite interdependence of all existences, then much will have been achieved.

Another fact which must also be brought out is the close relationship between all these evolutions of nature, from the celestial sun down to the humblest violet *via the*

---

2. *The ocean was radiant light, which was Fire, Heat, Motion.* These three are the subjective life manifesting objectively. *Fire:* The essence of the first Logos. Electric fire. Spirit. *Heat:* Duality. The essence of the second Logos. Solar fire. The Son aspect. Consciousness. *Motion:* The essence of the third Logos. Fire by friction. Matter.

THE MACROCOSM.

First Logos......Fire............ The will to live or to be. Electric.
Second Logos....Heat............Duality, or love between two. Solar.
Third Logos.....Motion..........The fire of mind, the relation between Fire by friction.
This is the subjective expression.

The Sun........................ Will or power.
Venus-Mercury...................Love and Wisdom.
Saturn..........................Activity or intelligence.
This is the objective expression.

THE MICROCOSM.

The Monad...........Electric fire ....Will or power.
The Ego.............Solar fire............Love and wisdom.
The Personality...... Fire by friction ......Activity or intelligence.
This is the subjective expression.

The mental body................Will or power........Fire.
The astral body.................Love-wisdom........Heat.
The physical body............... Active intelligence...Motion.
This is the objective expression.

Physical body.

The brain............Monad...........Will or power. Electric fire.
The heart............Ego ....Love-wisdom. Solar fire.
Lower organs........Personality........Active intelligence.

deva evolution which acts as the transmitting transmuting force throughout the system.

Lastly, all work with fire. Fire internal, inherent and latent; fire radiatory and emanative; fire generated, assimilated and radiated; fire vivifying, stimulating and destroying; fire transmitted, reflected, and absorbed; fire, the basis of all life; fire, the essence of all existence; fire, the means of development, and the impulse behind all evolutionary process; fire, the builder, the preserver, and the constructor; fire, the originator, the process and the goal; fire the purifier and the consumer. The God of Fire and the fire of God interacting upon each other, till all fires blend and blaze and till all that exists, is passed through the fire—from a solar system to an ant—and emerges as a triple perfection. Fire then passes out from the ring-pass-not as perfected essence, whether essence emerging from the human ring-pass-not, the planetary ring-pass-not or the solar. The wheel of fire turns and all within that wheel is subjected to the threefold flame, and eventually stands perfected.

III. THE FUNCTION OF THE ETHERIC BODY

We will now continue with the discussion of the etheric body, and take up the consideration of its function and its relation to the physical body.

The two may wisely be considered together, for the inter-relation is so close that it is not possible to discuss them separately. Primarily the functions of the etheric body are three in number:

> 1. It is the receiver of prana.
> 2. It is the assimilator of prana.
> 3. It is the transmitter of prana.

1. *The receiver of prana.*

The etheric body may therefore be described as negative or receptive in respect to the rays of the sun, and as

positive and expulsive in respect to the dense physical
body. The second function—that of assimilation—is
strictly balanced or internal. As stated earlier, the
pranic emanations of the sun are absorbed by the etheric
body, via certain centres which are found principally in
the upper part of the body, from whence they are directed
downwards to the centre which is called the etheric
spleen, as it is the counterpart in etheric matter of that
organ. The main centre for the reception of prana at
present is a centre between the shoulder blades. Another
has been allowed to become partially dormant in man
through the abuses of so-called civilisation, and is situated slightly above the solar plexus. In the coming root-
race, and increasingly in this, the necessity for the expo-
sure of these two centres to the rays of the sun, will be
appreciated, with a corresponding improvement in physical vitality and adaptability. These three centres,

1. Between the shoulder blades,
2. Above the diaphragm,
3. And the spleen

make, if one could but see it, a radiant etheric triangle,
which triangle is the originating impulse for the later
pranic circulation throughout the entire system. The
etheric body is really a net-work of fine channels, which
are the component parts of one interlacing fine cord,—
one portion of this cord being the magnetic link which
unites the physical and the astral bodies and which is
snapped or broken after the withdrawal of the etheric
body from the dense physical body at the time of death.
The silver cord is loosed, as the Bible expresses it,[44]
and this is the basis of the legend of the fateful sister
who cuts the thread of life with the dreaded shears.

The etheric web is composed of the intricate weaving
of this vitalised cord, and apart from the seven centres

within the web (which correspond to the sacred centres, and of which the spleen is frequently counted as one) it has the two above mentioned, which make—with the spleen—a triangle of activity. The etheric web of the solar system is of an analogous nature, and likewise has its three receptive centres for cosmic prana. The mysterious band in the heavens, which we call the *Milky Way,* (S. D. II.250) is closely connected with cosmic prana, or that cosmic vitality or nourishment which vitalises the solar etheric system.

2. *The assimilator of prana.*

The process of assimilation is carried on in this triangle, and the prana which enters into either centre, circulates three times around the triangle before being transmitted to all parts of the etheric vehicle and from thence to the dense physical body. The main organ of assimilation is the spleen—the etheric centre and the dense physical organ. The vital essence from the sun is passed into the etheric spleen, and is there subjected to a process of intensification or devitalisation, according to the condition, healthy or not, of that organ. If the man is in a healthy state the emanation received will be augmented by his own individual vibration, and its rate of vibration will be keyed up before it is passed on into the physical spleen; or it will be slowed down and lowered if the man is in a poor condition of health.

These three centres are in the form that all centres take, of saucer-like depressions, resembling somewhat the appearance of small whirlpools, and which draw within their sphere of influence the currents that come their way.

The centres should be pictured as whirling vortices with a closely woven threefold channel passing from each centre to the other, and forming an almost separate circulatory system. This finds its point of departure for the entire system at the further side of the spleen to that at which the prana entered. The vital fluid circulates through and between these three centres three times, before it finally passes out from them to the periphery of its little system. This final circulation carries the prana, via the fine interlacing channels, to every part of the body, which becomes entirely impregnated by these emanations, if it might be so expressed. These emanations find their way finally out of the etheric system by means of surface radiation. The pranic essence escapes from the circumference of its temporary ring-pass-not as emanative human prana, which is the same prana as earlier received, plus the peculiar quality that any single individual may convey to it during its transitory circulation. The essence escapes, plus individual quality.

Here again can be seen the correspondence to the escape of all essences from within any ring-pass-not when the cycle has been completed.

This matter of the etheric body is of a very practical interest, and when its importance is better realised, men will attend to the distribution of prana within the body with closer attention, and will see that the vitalisation of the body, via the three centres, proceeds unhindered.

The subject has necessarily to be handled in a superficial manner, and only outlines and scattered hints can be given. Nevertheless, it will be found that if this teaching is studied with care, it will convey a knowledge of truths whose calibre and content will prove invaluable and of a kind hitherto not given out. The place of the etheric sheath as a separator or ring-pass-not, and its functions as a receiver and distributor of prana, are dealt with here in a larger sense than heretofore, and the subject may later be enlarged.

Two fundamental truths stand out from the aggregate of facts so slightly dealt with here:

First. The fourth etheric subplane of the physical plane is the immediate concern of

    a. Man, the Microcosm,

    b. The Heavenly Man, the planetary Logos,

    c. The Grand Man of the Heavens, the solar Logos.

Second. In this fourth chain and fourth round, the fourth ether is beginning to be studied, and—viewed as a separating web—it permits occasional exit to those of suitable vibration.

3. *The Transmitter of Prana.*

We have touched but little on the subject of the fire, the purpose of the etheric body being to convey it and distribute it to all parts of its system. We have dwelt on facts which might stimulate interest and emphasise the utility of this pranic vehicle. Certain facts need emphasis and consideration as we study this static ring and its circulating fires. Let me briefly recapitulate for the sake of clarity:

The System receives prana from cosmic sources via three centres, and redistributes it to all parts of its extended influence, or to the bounds of the solar etheric web. This cosmic prana becomes colored by solar quality and reaches the furthest confines of the system. Its mission might be described as the vitalisation of the vehicle which is the physical material expression of the solar Logos.

The Planet receives prana from the solar centre, and redistributes it via the three receiving centres to all parts of its sphere of influence. This solar prana becomes colored by the planetary quality and is absorbed by all evolutions found within the planetary ring-pass-not. Its mission might be described as the vitalisation of the vehicle which is the physical material expression of one or other of the seven Heavenly Men.

The Microcosm receives prana from the sun after it has permeated the planetary etheric vehicle, so that it is solar prana, plus planetary quality. Each planet is the embodiment of some one ray aspect, and its quality is marked predominantly on all its evolution.

Prana, therefore, which is active radiatory heat, varies in vibration and quality according to the receiving Entity. Man passes the prana through his etheric vehicle, colors it with his own peculiar quality, and so transmits it to the lesser lives that make up his little system. Thus, the great interaction goes on, and all parts blend, merge and are interdependent; and all parts receive, color, qualify and transmit. An endless circulation goes on that has neither a conceivable beginning nor possible end from the point of view of finite man, for its source and end are hid in the unknown cosmic fount. Were conditions everywhere perfected this circulation would proceed unimpeded and might result in a condition of almost endless duration, but limitation and termination result as the effects of imperfection giving place to a gradual perfection. Every cycle originates from another cycle of a relative completeness, and will give place ever to a higher spiral; thus eventuate periods of apparent relative perfection leading to those which are still greater.

The aim for this greater cycle is the blending, as we know, of the two fires of matter, latent and active, and their merging with the fires of mind and spirit till they are lost from sight in the general flame; the fires of mind and spirit burn up matter and thereby bring about liberation from the confining vehicles. The altar of earth is the birthplace of spirit, its liberator from the mother (matter), and its entrance into higher realms.

Hence, when the pranic vehicle is working perfectly in all three groups, human, planetary and solar, the union with latent fire will be accomplished. Here lies the reason for the emphasis laid on the necessity for building pure, refined physical vehicles. The more refined and rarefied the form, the better a receiver of prana will it be, and the less will be the resistance found to the uprising of kundalini at the appointed time. Coarse matter and crude immature physical bodies are a menace to the occultist, and no true seer will be found with a body of a gross quality. The dangers of disruption.are too great, and the menace of disintegration by fire too awful. Once in the history of the race (in Lemurian days) this was seen in the destruction of the race and the continents by means of fire.[45] The Guides of the race at that time availed Themselves of just this very thing to bring about the finish of an inadequate form. The latent fire of matter (as seen in volcanic display, for instance) and the radiatory fire of the system were combined. Planetary kundalini and solar emanation rushed into conjunction, and the work of destruction was accomplished. The same thing may again be seen, only in matter of the second ether, and the effects therefore will be less severe owing to the rarity of this ether and the comparatively greater refinement of the vehicles.

We might here note a fact of interest, though of a mystery insoluble as yet to most of us, and that is, that these destructions by fire are part of the tests by fire of an initiation of that one of the Heavenly Men Whose karma is bound up with our earth.

Each destruction of a portion of the web results in a greater facility of exit, and is in reality (when seen from the higher planes) a step forward and an expansion. A repetition of this takes place likewise in the system at the stated cycles.

[45] In the Secret Doctrine, Vol. I, p. 473, footnote, the destruction of Lemuria by fire is hinted at, and in the Secret Doctrine, II, 149, footnote, the words occur, ''Lemuria was not submerged but was destroyed by volcanic action, and afterward sank.''

4. *Disorders of the etheric body.*

We will now study the etheric body, and its ills and also its after death condition. This matter can be only briefly touched upon. All that may now be indicated is a general idea of the fundamental ailments to which the etheric may be subject, and the trend which applied medicine may later take when occult laws are better understood. One fact must here be brought out—a fact but little comprehended or even apprehended. This is the significant fact that the ills of the etheric vehicle, in the case of the microcosm, will be found likewise in the Macrocosm. Herein lies the knowledge that ofttimes explains the apparent miseries of nature. Some of the great world evils have their source in etheric ills, extending the idea of the etheric to planetary conditions and even to solar. As we touch upon the causes of etheric distress in man, their planetary and solar correspondences and reactions may perhaps be realised. We will need to bear carefully in mind when studying this matter, that all the diseases of the etheric body will appertain to its threefold purpose and be either:

a. *Functional,* and thereby affecting its apprehension of prana,

b. *Organic,* and thereby affecting its distribution of prana,

c. *Static,* and thereby affecting the web, when viewed solely from the angle of providing a physical ring-pass-not, and acting as a separator between the physical and the astral.

These three different groups of functions or purposes are each of paramount interest, lead to totally different results, and react in a different manner both outwardly and inwardly.

Viewed from the *planetary* standpoint the same conditions will be perceived, and the etheric planetary body (which is fundamentally *the* body in the case of the sacred planets, of which the Earth is not one) will have its functional disorders, which will affect its reception of prana, will suffer its organic troubles which may affect its distribution, and those disorders which permit of trouble in the etheric web, which forms the ring-pass-not for the involved planetary Spirit. Here I would point out that in the case of the planetary Spirits Who are on the divine evolutionary arc, the Heavenly Men Whose bodies are planets, the etheric web does not form a barrier, but (like the Karmic Lords on a higher plane) They have freedom of movement outside the bounds of the planetary web within the circumference of the solar ring-pass-not.[46].

Again from the *systemic* standpoint, these same effects may be observed, functionally, this time in connection with the cosmic centre; organically, in connection with the sum total of the planetary systems; and statically, in connection with the solar or logoic ring-pass-not.

We might now, for purposes of clarity, take up these three groups separately and briefly touch upon them and hint (for more will not be possible) at methods of cure and of adjustment.

a. Microcosmic functional disorders. These have to do with the reception by man, via the necessary centres, of the pranic fluids. We must always bear in mind, and thus keep the distinction clear, that these emanations of prana have to do with the heat latent in matter; when received and functioning through the etheric body correctly, they co-operate with the natural latent bodily

[46] The planetary Spirit is another term for the Logos of our planet, one of the "seven Spirits before the Throne," and therefore one of the seven Heavenly Men. He is on the evolutionary arc of the universe, and has passed many stages beyond the human.

The planetary Entity is on the involutionary arc and is a very low grade Entity. He is the sum total of all the elemental lives of the planet.

warmth, and (merging therewith) hold the body in a vitalised condition, imposing upon the matter of the body a certain rate of vibratory action that leads to the necessary activity of the physical vehicle, and the right functioning of its organs. It will, therefore, be apparent that the a. b. c. of bodily health is wrapped up in the right reception of prana, and that one of the basic changes that must be made in the life of the human animal (which is the aspect we are dealing with now) will be in the ordinary conditions of living.

The three fundamental centres whereby reception is brought about must be allowed to function with greater freedom, and with less restriction. Now, owing to centuries of wrong living, and to basic mistakes (originating in Lemurian days) man's three pranic centres are not in good working order. The centre between the shoulder blades is in the best receptive condition, though owing to the poor condition of the spinal column (which in so many is out of accurate alignment), its position in the back is apt to be misplaced. The splenic centre near the diaphragm is sub-normal in size and its vibration is not correct. In the case of the aboriginal dwellers in such localities as the South Seas, better etheric conditions will be found; the life they lead is more normal (from the animal standpoint) than in any other portion of the world.

The race suffers from certain incapacities, which may be described as follows:

First. Inability to tap pranic currents, owing to the unhealthy lives passed by so many. This involves the cutting off of the source of supply, and the consequent atrophying and shrinkage of the receptive centres. This is seen in an exaggerated form in the children of the congested quarters of any great city, and in the vitiated anemic dwellers of the slums. The cure is apparent— the bringing about of better living conditions, the employment of more appropriate clothing, and the adoption of a freer and more salubrious mode of living. When the pranic rays can find free access to the shoulders, and to the diaphragm, the subnormal state of the average spleen will adjust itself automatically.

Second. Over-ability to tap pranic currents. The first type of functional disorder is common and widespread. Its reverse can be found where conditions of life are such that the centres (through too direct and prolonged submittal to solar emanation) become over-developed, vibrate too rapidly, and receive prana in too great an amount. This is rarer, but is found in some tropical countries, and is responsible for much of the troublesome debility that attacks dwellers in these lands. The etheric body receives prana or solar rays too rapidly, passes it through and out of the system with too much force, and this leaves the victim a prey to inertia and devitalisation. Putting it otherwise, the etheric body becomes lazy, is like an unstrung web, or (to use a very homely illustration) it resembles a tennis racket which has become too soft, and has lost its resilience. The inner triangle transmits the pranic emanations with too great rapidity, giving no time for the subsidiary absorption, and the whole system is thereby the loser. Later it will be found that many of the ills that Europeans, living in India, fall heir to, originate in this way; and by attention, therefore, to the spleen, and by wise control of living conditions, some of the trouble may be obviated.

In touching upon similar conditions in the planet, both these types of trouble will be found. More cannot be said, but in the wise study of solar radiation upon the surface of the planet in connection with its rotary action, some of the group rules of health may be comprehended and followed. The spirit of the planet (or the planetary entity) likewise has his cycles, and in the absorption of

planetary prana, and in its correct distribution, lies the
secret of fertility and equable vegetation.   Much of
this is hidden in the fabled story of the war between
fire and water, which has its basis in the reaction of the
fire latent in matter, to the fire emanating outside of
matter, and playing upon it.   In the interval that has
to elapse while the two are in process of blending, come
those periods where, through karmic inheritance, reception is unstable and distribution inequable.   As the
point of race equilibrium is reached, so planetary equilibrium will likewise be attained, and in planetary attainment will come the equilibrium that must mutually
take place between the solar planets.   When they attain
a mutual balance and interaction then the system is stabilised and perfection reached.   The even distribution
of prana will parallel this balancing in the man, in the
race, in the planet and in the system.   This is but another way of saying that uniform vibration will be
achieved.

   b. *Microcosmic organic disorders.*   These are basically
two in number:

Troubles due to congestion.

Destruction of tissue due to over-absorption of prana,
or its too rapid blending with latent physical fire.

We have a curious illustration of both of these forms
of trouble in sun stroke and in heat stroke.   Though
supposedly understood by physicians, they are nevertheless altogether etheric disorders.   When the nature of
the etheric body is better understood, and its wise care
followed both these types of disease will be prevented.
They are due to solar pranic emanation; in one case the
effect of the emanation is to bring about death or serious
illness through the congestion of an etheric channel,
while in the other the same result is brought about by
destruction of etheric matter.

The above illustration has been used with definite intent, but it should be pointed out that etheric congestion may lead to many forms of disease and of mental incompetence. Etheric congestion leads to the thickening of the web to an abnormal extent, and this thickening may prevent, for instance, contact with the higher Self or principles and its resultants, idiocy and mental unbalance. It may lead to abnormal fleshy development, to the thickening of some internal organ, and consequent undue pressure; one portion of the etheric body being congested may lead to the entire physical condition being upset, resulting in diverse complaints.

Destruction of tissue may lead to insanity of many kinds, especially those kinds deemed incurable. The burning of the web may let in extraneous astral currents against which man is helpless; the brain tissue may be literally destroyed by this pressure, and serious trouble be caused through the etheric ring-pass-not having been destroyed in some one place.

In connection with the planet a similar state of affairs may be found. Later information may be forthcoming, which is at present withheld; this will show that whole races have been influenced, and certain kingdoms of nature troubled by planetary etheric congestion, or the destruction of planetary etheric tissue.

We have dealt with the functional and organic ills of the etheric, giving certain indications for the extension of the concept to other realms than the purely human. In the human kingdom lies the key, but the turning of that key opens up a door to a wider interpretation as it admits one into the mysteries of nature. Though that key has to be turned seven times, yet even one turn reveals untold avenues of eventual comprehension.[47, 48]

[47] *The keys to the Secret Doctrine*, by H. P. Blavatsky. See S. D., I, 343; II, note; II, 551.
  1. Every symbol and allegory has seven keys.—S. D., II, 567; III, 3.
  2. Only three keys available in the nineteenth century.—S. D., II, 543.
    Compare II, 617, 842.

We have considered the reception and distribution of pranic emanations in man, the planet, and the system, and have seen what produces temporary disorders, and the devitalisation or the over-vitalisation of the organic form. Now we can look at the subject from a third angle and therefore study:

c. Microcosmic static disorders, or a consideration of the etheric body in connection with its work of providing a ring-pass-not from the purely physical to the astral. As has been said, both here and in the books of H. P. B., the ring-pass-not [48a] is that confining barrier which acts as a separator or a division between a system and that which is external to that system. This, as may well be seen, has its interesting correlations when the subject is viewed (as we must consistently endeavour to view it) from the point of view of a human being, a planet and a system, remembering always that in dealing with the

3. There are seven keys to the Entrance door to the Mysteries.—S. D., III, 178. Compare I, 346; II, 330; II, 668; II, 731.
4. The keys, as hinted by H. P. B., are:
   a. Psychological.—S. D., II, 25, note; I, 389.
   b. Astronomical.—S. D., II, 25, note; I, 389; III, 198.
   c. Physical or physiological.—S. D., II, 25, note; III, 198.
   d. Metaphysical.—S. D., II, 25, note; II, 394.
   e. Anthropological.—S. D., I, 389; III, 198.
   f. Astrological.—S. D., II, 343.
   g. Geometrical.—S. D., II, 494; III, 176.
   h. Mystical.—S. D., I, 401.
   i. Symbolical.—S. D., II, 561.
   j. Numerical.—S. D., II, 198.
5. Each key must be turned seven times.—S. D., I, 22.
6. The Jews availed themselves of two keys out of the seven.
7. The Metaphysical key is available.—S. D., I, 338. Compare III, 198.
48 ‘‘The seven keys open the mysteries, past and future, of the seven great rootraces and of the seven kalpas.’’ Every occult book, symbol and allegory can be subjected to seven interpretations. There are three locks to be opened. Seven keys. Every book can be read exoterically, subjectively and spiritually. All the keys are not yet available. (See Secret Doctrine, I, 330, 343.) There is the physiological key, the psychological, the astrological and the metaphysical. The fifth key is the geometrical.
48a ‘‘Ring-pass-not. The circumference of the sphere of influence of any centre of positive life. This includes the fire sphere of magnetic work of the solar orb, viewing it as the body of manifestation of a solar Logos, and inclusive of an entire solar system. This term is also applied to the sphere of activity of a planetary Logos or to a planetary scheme and could equally well be applied to the sphere of activity of the human Ego.’’—S. D., I, 346.

etheric body we are dealing with *physical matter*. This must ever be borne carefully in mind. Therefore, one paramount factor will be found in all groups and formations, and this is the fact that the ring-pass-not acts only as a hindrance to that which is of small attainment in evolution, but forms no barrier to the more progressed. The whole question depends upon two things, which are the karma of the man, the planetary Logos, and the solar Logos, and the dominance of the spiritual indwelling entity over its vehicle.

IV.   MACROCOSMIC AND MICROCOSMIC ETHERS

1. *The Planetary Logos and the Ethers*

Man, the indwelling thinker, passes at night from out of his etheric ring-pass-not and functions elsewhere. Therefore, under the law, the planetary Logos likewise can pass His ring-pass-not at stated seasons which correspond in the planet to the hours of man's temporary repose, or pralaya.

The solar Logos likewise does the same during stated cycles, which are not the cycles succeeding those which we term solar pralaya, but lesser cycles succeeding the 'days of Brahma' or periods of lesser activity, periodically viewed.   All these are governed by karma, and just as the true Man himself applies the law of karma to his vehicles, and in his tiny system is the correspondence to that fourth group of karmic entities whom we call the Lipika Lords; He applies the law to his threefold lower nature.   The fourth group of extra-cosmic Entities Who have Their place subsidiary to the three cosmic Logoi Who are the threefold sumtotal of the logoic nature, can pass the bounds of the solar ring-pass-not in Their stated cycles.   This is a profound mystery and its complexity is increased by the recollection that the fourth Creative Hierarchy of human Monads, and the Lipika Lords in Their three groups (the first

group, the second, and the four Maharajahs, making the
totality of the threefold karmic rulers who stand between the solar Logos and the seven planetary Logoi),
are more closely allied than the other Hierarchies, and
their destinies are intimately interwoven.

A further link in this chain which is offered for
consideration lies in the fact that the four rays of mind
(which concern the karma of the four planetary Logoi)
in their totality hold in their keeping the present evolutionary process for Man, viewing him as the Thinker.
These four, with the karmic four, work in the closest co-
operation. Therefore, we have the following groups
interacting:

First. The four Maharajahs, the lesser Lipika
  Lords,[49] who apply past karma and work it out in
  the present.
Second. The four Lipikas of the second group, referred to by H. P. B. as occupied in applying future
  karma, and wielding the future destiny of the races.
  The work of the first group of four cosmic Lipika
  Lords is occult and is only revealed somewhat at the
  fourth Initiation (and even then but slightly) so it
  will not be touched upon here.
Third. The fourth Creative Hierarchy of human Monads, held by a fourfold karmic law under the
  guidance of the Lipikas.
Fourth. The four planetary Logoi[50] of Harmony,
  Knowledge, Abstract Thought and Ceremonial, who

[49] The four Lipika Lords stand between the first and second plane.—S. D.,
I, 155.
  a. They can pass the ring-pass-not.—S. D., I, 157.
  b. They are connected with karma.—S. D., I, 153.
  c. They are concerned with the Hereafter.—S. D., I, 151.
  d. They are in three groups.—S. D., I, 153.
  e. They are the spirits of the Universe.—S. D., I, 153.
[50] The four rays of mind are the four minor rays which form the logoic
Quaternary and which are synthesised eventually into a fifth ray, the third
major ray of active intelligence, or adaptability. The names of the rays
are as follows:

are in Their totality the Quaternary of Manas while in process of evolution, and who pass under Their influence all the sons of men.

Fifth. The Deva Lords of the four planes of Buddhi, or the plane of spiritual Intuition, Manas, or the mental plane, Desire, and the Physical, who are likewise allied to the human evolution in a closer sense than the higher three.

A further interesting correspondence is found in the following facts that are even now in process of development:

The fourth plane of Buddhi is the one on which the planetary Logoi begin to make Their escape from Their planetary ring-pass-not, or from the etheric web that has its counterpart on all the planes.

When man begins in a small sense to co-ordinate the buddhic vehicle or, to express it otherwise, when he has developed the power to contact ever so slightly the buddhic plane, then he begins simultaneously and consciously to achieve the ability to escape from the etheric web on the physical plane. Later he escapes from its correspondence on the astral plane, and finally from the correspondence on the fourth subplane of the mental plane, this time via the mental unit. This leads eventually to causal functioning, or to the ability to dwell, and to be active in, the vehicle of the Ego, who is the embodiment of the love and wisdom aspect of the Monad. Note here the correspondence to that proved fact, that many can even now escape from the etheric body, and function in their

The three major rays:
1. The Ray of Will or Power.
2. The Ray of Love or Wisdom.
3. The Ray of Active Intelligence.
The four minor Rays:
4. The Ray of Beauty, Harmony, Art or Rhythm.
5. The Ray of Concrete Knowledge or Science.
6. The Ray of Abstract Idealism.
7. The Ray of Ceremonial Order or Organisation.

astral sheath, which is the personality reflection of that same second aspect.

When a man takes the fourth Initiation, he functions in the fourth plane vehicle, the buddhic, and has escaped permanently from the personality ring-pass-not, on the fourth subplane of the mental. There is naught to hold him to the three worlds. At the first Initiation he escapes from the ring-pass-not in a more temporary sense, but he has yet to escape from the three higher mental levels, which are the mental correspondences to the higher ethers, and to develop full consciousness on these three higher subplanes. We have here a correspondence to the work to be done by the initiate after he has achieved the fourth solar plane, the buddhic. There yet remains the development of full consciousness on the three higher planes of spirit before he can escape from the solar ring-pass-not, which is achieved at the seventh Initiation, taken somewhere in the system, or in its cosmic correspondence reached by the cosmic sutratma, or cosmic thread of life.[51]

This fourth earth chain is in this connection one of the most important, for it is the appointed place for the domination of the etheric body by the human monad, with the aim in view of both human and planetary escape from limitations. This earth chain, though not one of the seven sacred planetary chains, is of vital importance at this time to the planetary Logos, who temporarily employs it as a medium of incarnation, and of expression. This fourth round finds the solution of its strenuous and chaotic life in the very simple fact of the shattering of

[51] Sutratma. The ''silver thread'' which incarnates from the beginning of a period of manifestation until the end, stringing upon itself the pearls of human existence. It is the line of energy which connects the lower personal man with his Father in Heaven via the ego, the mediating middle principle. Upon it are found those focal points of energy we call the permanent atoms.

the etheric web in order to effect liberation, and permit a later and more adequate form to be employed.

A further chain of ideas may be followed up in the remembrance that the fourth ether is even now being studied and developed by the average scientist, and is already somewhat harnessed to the service of man; that the fourth subplane of the astral plane is the normal functioning ground of the average man and that in this round escape from the etheric vehicle is being achieved; that the fourth subplane of the mental plane is the present goal of endeavor of one-fourth of the human family; that the fourth manvantara will see the solar ring-pass-not offering avenues of escape to those who have reached the necessary point; that the four planetary Logoi will perfect Their escape from Their planetary environment, and will function with greater ease on the cosmic astral plane, paralleling on cosmic levels the achievement of the human units who are the cells in Their bodies.

Our solar Logos, being a Logos of the fourth order, will begin to co-ordinate His cosmic buddhic body, and as He develops cosmic mind He will gradually achieve, by the aid of that mind, the ability to touch the cosmic buddhic plane.

These possibilities and correspondences have been somewhat dwelt upon, as it is necessary for us to realise the work to be done in connection with the etheric web before we take up the matter of the various causes which may hinder the desired progress, and prevent the appointed escape and destined liberation. Later we will take up the consideration of the etheric web, and its static condition. This will entail the recollection of two things:

First, that this static condition is only so when viewed from the standpoint of man at the present time, and is only termed so in order to make plainer the changes that must be effected and the dangers that must be offset. Evolution moves so slowly from man's point of view that it seems to be almost stationary, especially where etheric evolution is concerned.

Second, that we are only concerning ourselves with the physical etheric body and not with its correspondences on all planes. This is because our system is on the *cosmic etheric* levels, and hence is of prime importance to us.

2. *Cosmic and Systemic Ethers*

For the sake of those who read this treatise, and because the sequential repetition of fact makes for clarity, let us here briefly tabulate certain fundamental hypotheses that have a definite bearing upon the matter in hand, and which may serve to clear up the present existing confusion concerning the matter of the solar system. Some of the facts stated are already well known, others are inferential, while some are the expression of old and true correspondences couched in a more modern form.

a. The lowest cosmic plane is the cosmic physical, and it is the only one which the finite mind of man can in any way comprehend.

b. This cosmic physical plane exists in matter differentiated into seven qualities, groups, grades, or vibrations.

c. These seven differentiations are the seven major planes of our solar system.

For purposes of clarity, we might here tabulate under the headings physical, systemic, and cosmic, so that the relationship and the correspondences may be apparent, and the connection to that which is above, and to that which is below, or included, may be plainly seen.

CHART III

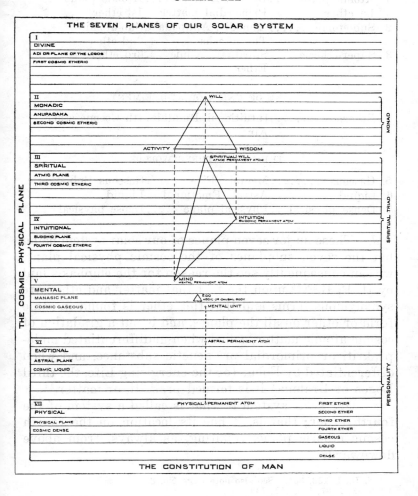

THE SEVEN PLANES OF OUR SOLAR SYSTEM

I	
DIVINE	
ADI OR PLANE OF THE LOGOS	
FIRST COSMIC ETHERIC	

WILL

II	
MONADIC	
ANUPADAKA	
SECOND COSMIC ETHERIC	

MONAD

ACTIVITY — WISDOM

III	SPIRITUAL WILL
	ATMIC PERMANENT ATOM
SPIRITUAL	
ATMIC PLANE	
THIRD COSMIC ETHERIC	

IV	INTUITION
	BUDDHIC PERMANENT ATOM
INTUITIONAL	
BUDDHIC PLANE	
FOURTH COSMIC ETHERIC	

SPIRITUAL TRIAD

V	MIND
	MENTAL PERMANENT ATOM
MENTAL	
MANASIC PLANE	EGO
	EGOIC OR CAUSAL BODY
COSMIC GASEOUS	MENTAL UNIT

VI	ASTRAL PERMANENT ATOM
EMOTIONAL	
ASTRAL PLANE	
COSMIC LIQUID	

PERSONALITY

VII	PHYSICAL PERMANENT ATOM	FIRST ETHER
PHYSICAL		SECOND ETHER
PHYSICAL PLANE		THIRD ETHER
COSMIC DENSE		FOURTH ETHER
		GASEOUS
		LIQUID
		DENSE

THE COSMIC PHYSICAL PLANE

THE CONSTITUTION OF MAN

THE PLANES

Physical Plane	Systemic Planes	Cosmic Planes
1. Atomic plane	Divine. Adi.	Atomic plane
1st ether	Primordial matter	1st ether
2. Sub-atomic	Monadic. Anupadaka	Sub-atomic
	The Akasha	2nd ether
3. Super-etheric	Spiritual. Atmic....	3rd ether
	Ether	

PLANE OF UNION OR AT-ONE-MENT

4. Etheric	Intuitional. Buddhic.	4th Cosmic ether
	Air	

THE LOWER THREE WORLDS

5. Gaseous	Mental. Fire	Gaseous Sub-etheric
6. Liquid	Astral. Emotional ..	Liquid
7. Dense physical ..	Physical plane	Dense physical

d. These major seven planes of our solar system being but the seven subplanes of the cosmic physical plane, we can consequently see the reason for the emphasis laid by H. P. B.[52, 53] upon the fact that matter and ether are synonymous terms and that this ether is found in some form or other on all the planes, and is but a gradation of cosmic atomic matter, called when undifferentiated mula-prakriti or primordial pre-genetic substance, and when differentiated by Fohat (or the energising Life, the third Logos or Brahma) it is termed prakriti, or matter.[54]

e. Our solar system is what is called a system of the fourth order; that is, it has its location on the fourth cosmic etheric plane, counting, as always, from above downwards.

[52] S. D., I, 136, 354. See also note page No. 8.
[53] S. D., I, 87, 136, 731, 732.
[54] *Mulaprakriti.* The Parabrahmic root, the abstract deific feminine principle—undifferentiated substance. Akasa. Literally, "the root of Nature" (Prakriti), or matter.

f. Hence this fourth cosmic etheric plane forms the meeting ground for the past and the future, and is the present.

g. Therefore, also, the buddhic or intuitional plane (the correspondence in the system of this fourth cosmic ether) is the meeting ground, or plane of union, for that which is man and for that which will be superman, and links the past with that which is to be.

h. The following correspondences *in time* would repay careful meditation. They are based on a realisation of the relationship between this fourth cosmic ether, the buddhic plane, and the fourth physical etheric subplane.

The fourth subplane of mind, the correspondence on the mental plane of the physical etheric, is likewise a point of transition from out of a lower into a higher, and is the transferring locality into a higher body.

The fourth subplane of the monadic plane is in a very real sense the place of transition from off the egoic ray (whichever that ray may be) on to the monadic ray; these three major rays are organised on the three higher subplanes of the monadic plane in the same way that the three abstract subplanes of the mental are the group of transference from off the personality ray on to the egoic.

The four lesser rays blend with the third major ray of active intelligence on the mental plane and on the atmic plane. The four Logoi or planetary Spirits work as one, on the atmic plane.

i. Another synthesis takes place on the synthetic second ray on the second subplane of the buddhic plane and the monadic plane, while the comparatively few Monads of will or power are synthesised on the atomic subplane of the atmic. All three groups of Monads work in triple form on the mental plane under the Mahachohan, the Manu, and the Bodhisattva, or the Christ; on the second or monadic plane they work as a unit, only demonstrating their dual work on the atmic plane, and their essential triplicity on the buddhic plane.[55]

The fourth etheric plane holds the key to the dominance of matter, and it might be noted that:

On the fourth physical ether man begins to co-ordinate his astral, or emotional body, and to escape at ever more frequent intervals into that vehicle. Continuity of consciousness is achieved when a man has mastered the four ethers.

On the fourth subplane of the mental plane, man begins to control his causal or egoic body, and to polarise his consciousness therein until the polarisation is complete. He functions then consciously on it when he has mastered the correspondences to the ethers on the mental plane.

On the buddhic plane (the fourth cosmic ether) the Heavenly Men (or the grouped consciousness of the human and deva Monads) begin to function, and to escape eventually from the cosmic etheric planes. When these three cosmic ethers are mastered, the functioning is perfected, polarisation is centred in the monadic vehicles, and the seven Heavenly Men have achieved Their goal.

j. On these etheric levels, therefore, the Logos of our

[55] The monads of the fourth Creative Hierarchy, the human Monads, exist in three main groups:
a. The Monads of Will.
b. The Monads of Love.
c. The Monads of Activity.
Mahachohan. The officer in our planetary Hierarchy who presides over the activities carried on in the four minor rays and their synthesising third ray. He has to do with civilisation, with the intellectual culture of the races, and with intelligent energy. He is the head of all the Adepts.
Bodhisattva. The exponent of second ray force, the Teacher of the Adepts of men and of Angels. This office was originally held by the Buddha, but His place was taken (after His Illumination) by the Christ. The work of the Bodhisattva is with the religions of the world, and with the spiritual Essence in Man.
The Manu. The One Who presides over the evolution of the races. He is the ideal man. He has to work with the forms through which Spirit is to manifest; he destroys, and builds up again. These three Individuals preside over the three Departments into which the Hierarchy is divided, and therefore represent in their particular sphere the three Aspects of divine manifestation.

system repeats, as a grand totality, the experiences of His tiny reflections on the physical planes; He co-ordinates His cosmic astral body, and attains continuity of consciousness when He has mastered the three cosmic ethers.

k. It is to be observed that just as in man the dense physical body in its three grades—dense, liquid and gaseous—is not recognised as a principle, so in the cosmic sense the physical (dense) astral (liquid) and mental (gaseous) levels are likewise regarded as non-existing, and the solar system has its location on the fourth ether. The seven sacred planets are composed of matter of this fourth ether, and the seven Heavenly Men, whose bodies they are, function normally on the fourth plane of the system, the buddhic or the fourth cosmic ether. When man has attained the consciousness of the buddhic plane, he has raised his consciousness to that of the Heavenly Man in whose body he is a cell. This is achieved at the fourth Initiation, the liberating initiation. At the fifth Initiation he ascends with the Heavenly Man on to the fifth plane (from the human standpoint), the atmic, and at the sixth he has dominated the second cosmic ether and has monadic consciousness and continuity of function. At the seventh Initiation he dominates the entire sphere of matter contained in the lowest cosmic plane, escapes from all etheric contact, and functions on the cosmic astral plane.

The *past* solar system saw the surmounting of the three lowest cosmic physical planes viewed from the matter standpoint and the co-ordination of the dense threefold physical form in which all life is found, dense matter, liquid matter, gaseous matter. A correspondence may be seen here in the work achieved in the first three rootraces.[56, 57]

[56] *Rootrace.* The Secret Doctrine teaches us that in this evolution or Round on this planet the Jivatma—the human soul—passes through seven main types or "rootraces." In the case of the two earliest of these, known

3. *The Protective Purpose of the Etheric Body.*

Now let us, after this somewhat lengthy digression, leave things cosmic and incomprehensible, and come down to practical evolution, and to the study of the matter of man's etheric body, and of the harm that may ensue to him should that body (through the breaking of the law) no longer perform its protective function. Let us see first of all what those protective functions are:

First. The etheric web acts as a separator or a dividing web between the astral and the dense physical body.

Second. It circulates the inflowing vitality or pranic fluid and carries on its work in three stages.

The first stage is that wherein the pranic fluid and

as the ''Adamic'' and the ''Hyperborean,'' the forms ensouled were astral and etheric respectively: ''huge and indefinite'' they were with a low state or outward-going consciousness exercised through the one sense (hearing) possessed by the first race, or through the two senses (hearing and touch) possessed by the second. But with the third race the Lemurian, a denser and more human type was evolved, this being perfected in the fourth or Atlantean race. The fifth race, the Aryan, is now running its course on this globe concurrently with a large part of the fourth race and a few remnants of the third. For it must be noted that, although each race gives birth to the succeeding race, the two will overlap in time, coexisting for many ages. Of existing peoples the Tartars, Chinese, and Mongolians belong to the fourth race, the Australian aborigines and Hottentots to the third.

[57] In the co-ordination of the Monadic, Atmic and Buddhic vehicles of the Heavenly Man, the vehicles of spiritual life, the higher esoteric correspondence to the prana flowing through the lower reflection, the etheric physical body, the point of synthesis is always on the atomic subplane, and the six merge and become the seventh. In this solar system the plane of synthesis is not included in the evolutionary scheme. It is the plane of gathering in and of pralaya. In the earlier system the fourth aetheric was in this position; it was to the evolving units of that period what the atomic plane is now, the highest point of achievement. The goal for all was the buddhic plane or the fourth cosmic aether. Three other planes are the goal now,—the buddhic, atmic and monadic, each time three planes and their eventual synthesis. In *the future* solar system the cosmic physical atomic aether (the plane of Adi in the system now) will be the starting point and the three planes to be dominated will be the three lowest cosmic astral planes. Man starts in where he leaves off, with cosmic physical matter perfected. His lowest body, therefore, will be the monadic or the body of the second cosmic aether. This will not be then counted as a principle any more than the threefold lower physical body of present day man is recognised as a principle.

The *present* solar system will see the surmounting of the three next cosmic physical planes, the fourth, third, and the second aethers, and the co-ordination of the cosmic etheric body.

solar radiations are received, and circulated three times around the triangle, thence being distributed to the periphery of the body, animating and vitalising all the physical organs and conducing to the automatic sub-conscious workings of the body of dense matter. When perfectly accomplishing its object it protects from disease, and the ills of the flesh are unknown to the man who absorbs and distributes prana with accuracy. This hint is recommended to all physicians, and when properly comprehended, will result in a basic change in medicine, from a curative to a preventive foundation.

The second stage is that in which the pranic fluids begin to blend with the fire at the base of the spine and to drive that fire slowly upwards, transferring its heat from the centres below the solar plexus to the three higher centres—that of the heart, the throat and the head. This is a long and slow process when left to the unaided force of nature, but it is just here that (in a few cases) a quickening of the process is permitted in order to equip workers in the field of human service. This is the object of all occult training. This angle of the matter we will take up in still greater detail when we handle our next point of "Kundalini and the Spine."

The third stage is that in which active radiatory matter or prana is blended ever more perfectly with the fire latent in matter; this results (as will be brought out later) in certain effects.

It produces a quickening of the normal vibration of the physical body so that it responds with more readiness to the higher note of the Ego, and causes a steady rising of the blending fires through the threefold channel in the spinal column. In the second stage this vitalising blended fire reaches a centre between the lower part of the shoulder blades, which is the point of conjunction, and of complete merging, of the fire from the base of the spine and the fire circulating along the pranic triangle. It will be remembered how one point of this triangle originates there. When the threefold basic fire and the threefold pranic fire meet and merge, then evolution proceeds with greatly increased velocity. This is effected definitely at the first Initiation when the polarisation becomes fixed in one or other of the three higher centres,—which centre being dependent upon a man's ray.

The result of this merging leads to a change in the action of the centres. They become "wheels turning upon themselves," and from a purely rotary movement become fourth dimensional in action, and manifest as radiant whirling centres of living fire.

The three major head centres (the sequence varying according to ray) become active and a similar process is effected between them as was effected in the pranic triangle. From being three centres that react faintly to each other's vibratory movement (feeling the warmth and rhythm of each other, yet separated), the fire leaps from centre to centre, and each whirling wheel becomes linked by a chain of fire till there is a triangle of fire through which the kundalini and pranic fires radiate back and forth. Circulation is also carried on. The fire of kundalini produces the heat of the centre, and its intense radiance and brilliance, while the pranic emanatory fire produces ever increasing activity and rotation.

As time elapses between the first and fourth Initiation, the threefold channel in the spine, and the entire etheric body is gradually cleansed and purified by the action of the fire till all "dross" (as the Christian expresses it) is burnt away, and naught remains to impede the progress of this flame.

As the fire of kundalini and prana proceed with their work, and the channel becomes more and more cleared, the centres more active, and the body purer, the flame of spirit, or the fire from the Ego, comes more actively *downwards* till a flame of real brilliance issues from the top of the head. This flame surges upwards through the bodies towards its source, the causal body.

Simultaneously with the activity of these fires of matter and of Spirit, the fires of mind, or manas, burn with greater intensity. These are the fires given at individualisation. They are fed continuously by the fire of matter, and their heat is augmented by solar emanatory fire, which originates on the cosmic levels of mind. It is this aspect of the manasic fire that develops under the forms of instinct, animal memory, and functional recollection which are so apparent in the little evolved man. As time progresses the fire of mind burns more brightly and thus reaches a point where it begins to burn through the etheric web—that portion of the web that can be found guarding the centre at the very top of the head, and admitting entrance to the downflow from the Spirit. By its means certain things are brought about:

The kundalini fire is consciously directed and controlled by the mind or will aspect from the mental plane. The two fires of matter by the power of the mind of man are blended first with each other, and, secondly, with the fire of mind.

The united result of this blending is the destruction (under rule and order), of the etheric web, and the consequent production of continuity of consciousness and the admission into the personal life of man of "Life more abundant," or the third fire of Spirit.

The downrush of Spirit, and the uprising of the inner fires of matter (controlled and directed by the conscious action of the fire of mind) produce corresponding results on the same levels on the astral and mental planes, so that a paralleling contact is brought about, and the great work of liberation proceeds in an ordered manner.

The three first initiations see these results perfected,

and lead to the fourth, where the intensity of the united
fires results in the complete burning away of all barriers,
and the liberation of the Spirit by conscious directed
effort from out its threefold lower sheath.   Man has consciously to bring about his own liberation.   These results
are self-induced by the man himself, as he is emancipated
from the three worlds, and has broken the wheel of rebirth himself instead of being broken upon it.

It will be apparent from this elucidation that the exceeding importance of the etheric vehicle as *the separator of the fires* has been brought forward, and consequently we have brought to our notice the dangers that
must ensue should man tamper injudiciously, ignorantly
or wilfully with these fires.

Should a man, by the power of will or through an
over-development of the mental side of his character,
acquire the power to blend these fires of matter and to
drive them forward, he stands in danger of obsession,
insanity, physical death, or of dire disease in some part
of his body, and he also runs the risk of an over-development of the sex impulse through the driving of the force
in an uneven manner upwards, or in forcing its radiation
to undesirable centres.   The reason of this is that the
matter of his body is not pure enough to stand the uniting of the flames, that the channel up the spine is still
clogged and blocked, and therefore acts as a barrier,
turning the flame backwards and downwards, and that
the flame (being united by the power of mind and not
being accompanied by a simultaneous downflow from the
plane of spirit), permits the entrance, through the burning etheric, of undesirable and extraneous forces, currents, and even entities.   These wreck and tear and ruin
what is left of the etheric vehicle, of the brain tissue and
even of the dense physical body itself.

The unwary man, being unaware of his Ray and therefore of the proper geometrical form of triangle that is

the correct method of circulation from centre to centre, will drive the fire in unlawful progression and thus burn up tissue; this will result then (if in nothing worse), in a setting back for several lives of the clock of his progress, for he will have to spend much time in rebuilding where he destroyed, and with recapitulating on right lines all the work to be done.

If a man persists from life to life in this line of action, if he neglects his spiritual development and concentrates on intellectual effort turned to the manipulation of matter for selfish ends, if he continues this in spite of the promptings of his inner self, and in spite of the warnings that may reach him from Those who watch, and if this is carried on for a long period he may bring upon himself a destruction that is final for this manvantara or cycle. He may, by the uniting of the two fires of matter and the dual expression of mental fire, succeed in the complete destruction of the physical permanent atom, and thereby sever his connection with the higher self for aeons of time. H. P. B. has somewhat touched on this when speaking of "lost souls"; [58, 59] we must here emphasise the reality of this dire disaster and sound a warning note to those who approach this subject of the fires of matter with all its latent dangers. The blending of these fires must be the result of spiritualised knowledge, and must be directed solely by the Light of the Spirit, who works through love and is love, and who seeks this unification and this utter merging *not* from the point of view of sense or of material gratification, but because liberation and purification is desired in order that the higher union with the Logos may be effected; this union must be desired, not for selfish ends, but because *group perfection* is the goal and scope for greater service to the race must be achieved.

[58] Lost Souls. See *Isis Unveiled*, Vol. II, p. 368; also S. D., I, 255, and S. D., III, 493, 513-516, 521, 525, 527.
[59] See S. D., III, 523-529.

V. DEATH AND THE ETHERIC BODY

It is not our purpose to give facts for verification by science, or even to point the way to the next step onward for scientific investigators; that we may do so is but incidental and purely secondary. What we seek mainly is to give indications of the development and correspondence of the threefold whole that makes the solar system what it is—the vehicle through which a great cosmic ENTITY, the solar Logos, manifests active intelligence with the purpose in view of demonstrating perfectly the love side of His nature. Back of this design lies a yet more esoteric and ulterior purpose, hid in the Will Consciousness of the Supreme Being, which perforce will be later demonstrated when the present objective is attained. The dual alternation of objective manifestation and of subjective obscuration, the periodic out-breathing, followed by the in-breathing of all that has been carried forward through evolution embodies in the system one of the basic cosmic vibrations, and the key-note of that cosmic ENTITY whose body we are. The heart beats of the Logos (if it might be so inadequately expressed) are the source of all cyclic evolution, and hence the importance attached to that aspect of development called the "heart" or "love aspect," and the interest that is awakened by the study of rhythm. This is true, not only cosmically and macrocosmically, but likewise in the study of the human unit. Underlying all the physical sense attached to rhythm, vibration, cycles and heart-beat, lie their subjective analogies—love, feeling, emotion, desire, harmony, synthesis and ordered sequence,—and back of these analogies lies the source of all, the identity of that Supreme Being Who thus expresses Himself.

Therefore, the study of pralaya, or the withdrawal of the life from out of the etheric vehicle will be the same whether one studies the withdrawal of the human etheric double, the withdrawal of the planetary etheric double, or the withdrawal of the etheric double of the solar system. The effect is the same and the consequences similar.

What is the result of this withdrawal, or rather what causes that something which we call death or pralaya? As we are strictly pursuing the text-book style in this treatise, we will continue our methods of tabulation. The withdrawal of the etheric double of a man, a planet, and a system is brought about by the following causes:

a. The cessation of desire. This should be the result of all evolutionary process. *True* death, under the law, is brought about by the attainment of the objective, and hence by the cessation of aspiration. This, as the perfected cycle draws to its close, will be true of the individual human being, of the Heavenly Man, and of the Logos Himself.

b. By the slowing down and gradual cessation of the cyclic rhythm, *the adequate vibration is achieved,* and the work accomplished. When the vibration or note is perfectly felt or sounded it causes (at the point of synthesis with other vibrations) the utter shattering of the forms.

Motion is characterised, as we know, by three qualities:

1. Inertia,
2. Mobility,
3. Rhythm.

These three are experienced in just the above sequence and presuppose a period of slow activity, succeeded by one of extreme movement. This middle period produces incidentally (as the true note and rate is sought) cycles of chaos, of experiment, of experience and of comprehension. Following on these two degrees of motion (which are characteristic of the atom, Man, of the Heavenly Man

or group, and of the Logos or the Totality) comes a
period of rhythm and of stabilisation wherein the point
of balance is achieved. By the force of balancing the
pairs of opposites, and thus producing equilibrium, pralaya is the inevitable sequence.

*c. By the severing of the physical from the subtler
body* on the inner planes, through the shattering of the
web. This has a threefold effect:

First. The life that had animated the physical form
(both dense and etheric) and which had its starting point
in the permanent atom and from thence ''pervaded the
moving and the unmoving'' (in God, the Heavenly Man,
and the human being, as well as in the atom of matter)
is withdrawn entirely within the atom upon the plane of
abstraction. This ''plane of abstraction'' is a different
one for the entities involved:

    a. For the physical permanent atom, it is the atomic
       level.
    b. For man, it is the causal vehicle.
    c. For the Heavenly Man, it is the second plane of
       monadic life, His habitat.
    d. For the Logos, it is the plane of Adi.

All these mark the points for the disappearance of the
unit into pralaya. We need here to .remember that it is
always pralaya when viewed from *below*. From the
higher vision, that sees the subtler continuously overshadowing the dense when not in objective manifestation,
pralaya is simply subjectivity, and is not that ''which is
not,'' but simply that which is esoteric.

Second. The etheric double of a man, a planetary
Logos, and a solar Logos, being shattered, becomes non-
polarised as regards its indweller, and permits therefore
of escape. It is (to word it otherwise) no longer a source
of attraction, nor a focal magnetic point. It becomes
non-magnetic, and the great Law of Attraction ceases to

control it; hence disintegration is the ensuing condition of the form. The Ego ceases to be attracted by its form on the physical plane, and, proceeding to inbreathe, withdraws its life from out of the sheath. The cycle draws to a close, the experiment has been made, the objective (a relative one from life to life and from incarnation to incarnation) has been achieved, and there remains nothing more to desire; the Ego, or the thinking entity, loses interest therefore in the form, and turns his attention inward. His polarisation changes, and the physical is eventually dropped.

The planetary Logos likewise in His greater cycle (the synthesis or the aggregate of the tiny cycles of the cells of His body) pursues the same course; He ceases to be attracted downward or outward, and turns His gaze within; He gathers inward the aggregate of the smaller lives within His body, the planet, and severs connection. Outer attraction ceases and all gravitates towards the centre instead of scattering to the periphery of His body.

In the system, the same process is followed by the solar Logos; from His high place of abstraction, He ceases to be attracted by His body of manifestation. He withdraws His interest and the two pairs of opposites, the spirit and the matter of the vehicle, dissociate. With this dissociation the solar system, that "Son of Necessity," or of desire, ceases to be, and passes out of objective existence.

Third. This leads finally, to the scattering of the atoms of the etheric body into their primordial condition. The subjective life, the synthesis of will and love taking active form, is withdrawn. The partnership is dissolved. The form then breaks up; the magnetism that has held it in coherent shape is no longer present, and dissipation is complete. Matter persists, but the *form* no longer persists.

The work of the second Logos ends, and the divine

incarnation of the Son is concluded. But the faculty or inherent quality of matter also persists, and at the end of each period of manifestation, matter (though distributed again into its primal form) is active intelligent matter plus the gain of objectivity, and the increased radiatory and latent activity which it has gained through experience. Let us illustrate: The matter of the solar system, when undifferentiated, was active intelligent matter, and that is all that can be predicated of it. This active intelligent matter was matter qualified by an earlier experience, and coloured by an earlier incarnation. *Now* this matter is *in form,* the solar system is not in pralaya but in objectivity,—this objectivity having in view the addition of another quality to the logoic content, that of love and wisdom. Therefore at the next solar pralaya, at the close of the one hundred years of Brahma, the matter of the solar system will be coloured by active intelligence, and by active love. This means literally that the aggregate of solar atomic matter will eventually vibrate to another key than it did at the first dawn of manifestation.

We can work this out in connection with the planetary Logos and the human unit, for the analogy holds good. We have a correspondence on a tiny scale in the fact that each human life period sees a man taking a more evolved physical body of a greater responsiveness, tuned to a higher key, of more adequate refinement, and vibrating to a different measure. In these three thoughts lies much information, if they are carefully studied and logically extended.

d. By the transmutation of the violet into the blue. This we cannot enlarge on. We simply make the statement, and leave its working out to those students whose karma permits and whose intuition suffices.

e. By the withdrawal of the life, the form should gradually dissipate. The reflex action here is interesting to note, for the greater Builders and Devas who are the active agents during manifestation, and who hold the form in coherent shape, transmuting, applying and circulating the pranic emanations, likewise lose their attraction to the matter of the form, and turn their attention elsewhere. On the path of out-breathing (whether human, planetary or logoic) these building devas (on the same Ray as the unit desiring manifestation, or on a complementary Ray) are attracted by his will and desire, and perform their office of construction. On the path of in-breathing (whether human, planetary or logoic) they are no longer attracted, and the form begins to dissipate. They withdraw their interest and the forces (likewise entities) who are the agents of destruction, carry on their necessary work of breaking up the form; they scatter it —as it is occultly expressed—to "The four winds of Heaven," or to the regions of the four breaths,—a fourfold separation and distribution. A hint is here given for careful consideration.

Though no pictures have been drawn of death bed scenes nor of the dramatic escape of the palpitating etheric body from the centre in the head, as might have been anticipated, yet some of the rules and purposes governing this withdrawal have been mentioned. We have seen how the aim of each life (whether human, planetary or solar) should be the effecting and the carrying out of a definite purpose. This purpose is the development of a more adequate form for the use of the spirit; and when this purpose is achieved then the Indweller turns his attention away, and the form disintegrates, having served his need. This is not always the case in every human life nor even in each planetary cycle. The mystery of the moon is the mystery of failure. This leads, when comprehended, to a life of dignity and offers an aim worthy of our best endeavour. When this angle of truth is universally recognised, as it will be when the intelligence of the race suffices, then evolution will proceed with certainty, and the failures be less numerous.

SECTION ONE

DIVISION D

KUNDALINI [60, 61] AND THE SPINE

> *I. Kundalini and the three triangles.*
>   1. In the head.
>   2. In the body.
>   3. At the base of the spine.
> *II. The arousing of Kundalini.*

VERY briefly, owing to the impossibility of revealing much on this necessarily dangerous subject, we will consider the subject of kundalini and the spine.

We must remember here that we are dealing with the etheric counterpart of the spine, and not with the bony structure which we call the spine or spinal column. This is a fact not sufficiently recognised by those who treat of the matter. Too much emphasis has been laid on the three spinal channels that compose the threefold spinal cord.

These channels are important in connection with the

---

[60] "*Kundalini*, the serpent power or mystic fire; it is called the serpentine or annular power on account of its spiral-like working or progress in the body of the ascetic developing the power in himself. It is an electric fiery occult, or fohatic power, the great pristine force which underlies all organic and inorganic matter."—H. P. Blavatsky.

[61] "Kundalini is the static form of the creative energy in bodies which are the source of all energies including Prana. . . .

"This word comes from the adjective Kundalin, or "coiled." She is spoken of as "coiled" because she is sleeping, lies coiled; and because the nature of her power is spiraline, . . .

"In other words, this Kundalini shakti is that which, when it moves to manifest itself, appears as the Universe. To say that it is "coiled" is to say that it is *at rest*—that is, in the form of static potential energy. . . . Kundalini shakti in individual bodies is power at rest, or the static centre round which every form of existence, as moving power, revolves." . .
—*The Serpent Power*, by Arthur Avalon.

nervous system of the man, but in relation to the matter in hand, they are not primarily so important as the etheric channel, which is the unit enclosing these three. Therefore, we must strictly remember that we are dealing with

a. The etheric channel,
b. The fire that passes up the channel,
c. The conjunction of this fire with the radiatory energising fire of the physical body at the point between the shoulder blades,
d. Their united ascension into the head,
e. Their blending eventually with the manasic fire which energises the three head centres.

I. KUNDALINI AND THE THREE TRIANGLES

The fire energising the triangle in the head is the higher correspondence to the triangle of prana, midway in the body, and its lower reflection at the base of the spine. We have, therefore, in the human unit three important triangles:

1. *In the head:* The triangle of the three major centres,
   a. The pineal gland,
   b. The pituitary body,
   c. The alta major centre.
2. *In the body:* The triangle of prana,
   a. Between the shoulders,
   b. Above the diaphragm,
   c. The spleen.
3. *At the base of the spine:* The three lower centres,
   a. A point at the bottom of the spinal column.
   b. and c. The two major sex organs in the male and female.[62]

[62] It is not my intention to lay any stress on the sex side of this subject, for these are organs with which the occultist has nothing to do. I will not therefore enumerate them in detail. I would only point out that in the transference of the fire at the base of the spine and the turning of its attention to the two higher triangles comes the redemption of man.

The merging of the fires of matter and the fires of mind results in the energising of the sumtotal of the atoms of the matter of the body. This is the secret of the immense staying power of the great thinkers and workers of the race. It results also in a tremendous stimulation of the three higher centres in the body, the head, the heart, the throat and in the electrification of this area of the body. These higher centres then form a field of attraction for the downflow of the third fire, that of Spirit. The many-petalled head centre at the top of the head becomes exceedingly active. It is the synthetic head centre, and the sumtotal of all the other centres. The stimulation of the centres throughout the body is paralleled or duplicated by the concurrent vivification of the many-petalled lotus. It is the meeting place of the three fires, those of the body, of the mind, and of the Spirit. The at-one-ment with the Ego is completed when it is fully stimulated, and combustion then ensues; this is duplicated in the subtler vehicles and causes the final consummation and the liberation of Spirit.

The merging of the fires of matter is the result of evolutionary growth, when left to the normal, slow development that time alone can bring. The junction of the two fires of matter is effected early in the history of man, and is the cause of the rude health that the clean-living, high-thinking man should normally enjoy. When the fires of matter have passed (united) still further along the etheric spinal channel they contact *the fire of manas as it radiates from the throat centre.* Clarity of thought is here essential, and it will be necessary to elucidate somewhat this rather abstruse subject.

1. The three major head centres (from the physical standpoint) are the:
    a. Alta centre,
    b. Pineal gland,
    c. Pituitary body.

2. They form a manasic triangle, after their juncture with the two fires of the two lower triangles, i.e., when they become synthetic.
3. But the purely manasic triangle prior to this merging is,
    a. The throat centre,
    b. The pineal gland,
    c. Pituitary body.

This is during the period when the human unit consciously aspires and throws his will on the side of evolution, thus making his life constructive.

The other fire of matter (the dual fire) is attracted upward, and merges with the fire of mind through a junction effected at the alta major centre. This centre is situated at the base of the skull, and there is a slight gap between this centre and the point at which the fires of matter issue from the spinal channel. Part of the work the man who is developing thought power has to do, is to build a temporary channel in etheric matter to bridge the gap. This channel is the reflection in physical matter of the antaskarana [63] that the Ego has to build in order to bridge the gap between the lower and higher mental, between the causal vehicle on the third subplane of the mental plane, and the manasic permanent atom on the first subplane. This is the work that all advanced thinkers are unconsciously doing now. When the gap is com-

* 1. "The Master-soul is Alaya, the universal soul or Atma, each man having a ray of it in him and being supposed to be able to identify himself with and to merge himself into it.
2. Antaskarana is the lower Manas, the path of communication or communion between the personality and the higher Manas or human soul.
    At death it is destroyed as a path or medium of communication, and its remains survive in a form as the Kama-rupa—the shell."
    —Voice of the Silence, page 71.
"The antaskarana is the imaginary path between the personal and the impersonal self, and is the highway of sensation; it is the battlefield for mastery over the personal self. It is the path of aspiration, and where one longing for goodness exists the antaskarana persists."—See Voice of the Silence, pp. 50, 55, 56, 88.

pletely bridged, man's body becomes co-ordinated with
the mental body and the fires of mind and of matter are
blended. It completes the perfecting of the personality
life, and as earlier said, this perfecting brings a man to
the portal of initiation—initiation being the seal set
upon accomplished work; it marks the end of one lesser
cycle of development, and the beginning of the transference of the whole work to a still higher spiral.

We must always bear in mind that the fires from the
base of the spine and the splenic triangle are *fires of
matter*. We must not lose this recollection nor get confused. They have no spiritual effect, and *concern themselves solely with the matter in which the centres of force
are located*. These centres of force are always directed
by manas or mind, or by the conscious effort of the indwelling entity; but that entity is held back in the effects
he seeks to achieve until the vehicles through which he is
seeking expression, and their directing, energising centres, make adequate response. Hence it is only in due
course of evolution, and when the matter of these vehicles
is energised sufficiently by its own latent fires that he can
accomplish his long-held purpose. Hence again the need
of the ascension of the fire of matter to its own place,
and its resurrection from its long burial and seeming
prostitution before it can be united with its Father in
Heaven, the third Logos, Who is the Intelligence of
matter itself. The correspondence, again, holds good.
Even the atom of the physical plane has its goal, its initiations and its ultimate triumph.

Other angles of this subject, such as the centres and
their relationship to manas, the fire of Spirit and manas,
and the eventual blending of the three fires, will be dealt
with in our next two main divisions. In this division we
are confining ourselves to the study of matter and fire,
and must not digress, or confusion will ensue.

II. THE AROUSING OF KUNDALINI

How this fire at the base of the spine can be aroused, the form its progression should take (dependent upon the Ray), the blending of the fire with pranic fire and their subsequent united progression, are things of the past with many, and fortunately for the race, the work was achieved without conscious effort. The second blending with the fire of manas has to be effected. Scarcely as yet have men succeeded in directing the fire up more than one channel of the threefold column; hence two-thirds of its effect in the majority is yet confined to the stimulation of the organs of race propagation. Only when the fire has circled unimpeded up another channel is the complete merging with the fire of manas effected, and only when it progresses geometrically up all the three—with simultaneous action and at uniform vibration—is the true kundalini fire fully aroused, and therefore able to perform its work of cleansing through the burning of the confining web and of the separating particles. When this is accomplished the threefold channel becomes one channel. Hence the danger.

No more can be imparted concerning this subject. He who directs his efforts to the control of the fires of matter, is (with a dangerous certainty) playing with a fire that may literally destroy him. He should not cast his eyes backwards, but should lift them to the plane where dwells his immortal Spirit, and then by self-discipline, mind-control and a definite refining of his material bodies, whether subtle or physical, fit himself to be a vehicle for the divine birth, and participate in the first Initiation. When the Christ-child (as the Christian so beautifully expresses it) has been born in the cave of the heart, then that divine guest can consciously control the lower material bodies by means of consecrated mind. Only when buddhi has assumed an ever-increasing control of the personality, via the mental plane (hence the need of building the antaskarana), will the personality respond to that which is above, and the lower fires mount and blend with the two higher. Only when Spirit, by the power of thought, controls the material vehicles, does the subjective life assume its rightful place, does the God within shine and blaze forth till the form is lost from sight, and "The path of the just shine ever more and more until the day be with us."

SECTION ONE

DIVISION E

MOTION ON THE PHYSICAL AND ASTRAL PLANES

I. PRELIMINARY REMARKS

I would point out primarily and emphasise the fact that the motion we are considering is that due to the fire latent in matter itself, a motion that is the prime characteristic and basic quality of the Primordial Ray of Active Intelligence. To express it otherwise: it is the outstanding faculty of the third Logos, of Brahma viewed as the Creator, and this faculty is the product or result of an earlier manifestation. Each of the three Logoi, when in manifestation and thus personified, is exemplifying some one quality which predominates over the others. Each, more or less, exemplifies all, but each demonstrates one of the three aspects so profoundly as to be recognised as that aspect itself. In much the same way, for instance, the different incarnating jivas carry a vibration which is their main measure, though they may also have lesser vibrations that are subsidiary to them. Let us get this clear, for the truth embodied is fundamental.

1. The threefold goal,
2. The threefold function,
3. The threefold mode of activity.

The Third Logos. The third Logos, or Brahma, is characterised by active intelligence; His mode of action is that which we call *rotary,* or that measured revolution of the matter of the system, first as a grand totality, setting in movement the material circumscribed by the entire ring-pass-not, and secondly differentiating it, according to seven vibratory rates or measures into the seven planes. On each of these planes the process is pursued, and the matter of any plane within the plane ring-pass-not shows first as a totality and then as a sevenfold differentiation. This differentiation of matter is brought about by rotary motion, and is controlled by the *Law of Economy* (one of the cosmic laws) with which we will deal later, only pausing here to say that this Law of Economy might be considered as the controlling factor in the life of the third Logos. Therefore:

a. His *goal* is the perfect blending of Spirit and matter.
b. His *function* is the manipulation of prakriti, or matter, so as to make it fit, or equal to, the demands and needs of the Spirit.

c. His *mode of action* is rotary, or, by the revolution of matter, to increase activity and thereby make the material more pliable.

All these three concepts are governed by the Law of Economy, which is the Law of Adaptation in time and space, or the line of least resistance. This line of least resistance is that which is sought for and followed on the matter side of existence. Incidentally, Brahma manifests Will, because He is purpose, and Love because in this solar system Love is the line of least resistance. While this is an occult statement worthy of consideration, yet it must be remembered that He is primarily activity and intelligence with the aim of adaptability, and that this is His main characteristic.

The Second Logos. The second Logos, Vishnu, the divine Wisdom Ray, the great principle of Buddhi seeking to blend with the principle of Intelligence, is characterised by Love. His motion is that which we might term *spiral cyclic.* Availing Himself of the rotary motion of all atoms, He adds to that His own form of motion or of spiralling periodical movement, and by circulation along an orbit or spheroidal path (which circles around a central focal point in an ever ascending spiral) two results are brought about:

a. He gathers the atoms into forms.
b. By means of these forms He gains the needed contact, and develops full consciousness on the five planes of human development, gradually rarefying and refining the forms as the Spirit of Love or the Flame Divine spirals ever onward towards its goal, that goal which is also the source from which it came.

These forms are the sumtotal of all spheres or atoms within the solar system, or within the solar ring-pass-not, and in their seven major differentiations they are the spheres of the seven Spirits, or the seven planetary Logoi.

All lesser spheres ranging downward from these major spheres, include all grades of manifestation down to the elemental essence on the arc of involution.[64] We need to remember that on the Path of Involution, the action of Brahma is primarily felt, seeking the line of least resistance. On the Path of Evolution the work of the second Logos is felt, beginning at a point in time and space which hides the mystery of the second chain, but finding its point of accelerated vibration or the unification of the two modes of manifestation—rotary-spiral-cyclic—in the middle part of what we call the third chain. This is after all the blending of the activity of Brahma with the onward progress of Vishnu. We have the correspondence to this in the sumtotal of the effects brought about in the second and third root races.

The activity of the second Logos is carried on under the cosmic Law of Attraction. The Law of Economy has for one of its branches a subsidiary Law of marked development called the Law of Repulsion. The cosmic Laws of Attraction and Economy are therefore the *raison d'être* (viewed from one angle) of the eternal repulsion that goes on as Spirit seeks ever to liberate itself from form. The matter aspect always follows the line of least resistance, and repulses all tendency to group formation, while Spirit, governed by the Law of Attraction, seeks ever to separate itself from matter by the method of attracting an ever more adequate type of matter in the process of distinguishing the real from the unreal, and passing from one illusion to another until the resources of matter are fully utilised.

---

[64] Elemental Essence is seen to consist of aggregations of matter, on one of the six non-atomic subplanes of the mental and the desire planes—aggregations which do not themselves serve as forms for any entity to inhabit, but as the material out of which such forms may be built.

Eventually the Indweller of the form feels the urge, or attractive pull, of its Own Self. The reincarnating jiva, for instance, lost in the maze of illusion, begins in course of time to recognise (under the Law of Attraction) the vibration of its own Ego, which stands to it as the Logos of its own system, its deity in the three worlds of experience. Later, when the body egoic itself is seen as illusion, the vibration of the Monad is felt, and the jiva, working under the same law, works its way back through the matter of the two planes of superhuman evolution, till it is merged in its own essence.

Therefore:

a. The *goal* of the second Logos is consciousness, to be achieved in co-operation with the third Logos.

b. His *function* is the building of forms to be His instruments of experience.

c. His *mode* of action is cyclic and spiral, the revolution of the wheel of existence in ordered cycles for a specific purpose, and the progression of these spheres of matter around a fixed centre, within the solar periphery.

These three concepts are governed by the Law of Attraction, or the law governing the interplay or the action and reaction.

a. Between the Sun and its six brothers.

b. Between the circling whirling seven planes of the solar system.

c. Between everything in the matter of all forms, the spheres of matter themselves and the aggregate of those spheres that are embodied in the forms of still others.

The First Logos. The first Logos is the Ray of Cosmic Will. His mode of action is a literal driving forward of the solar ring-pass-not through space, and until the end of this mahamanvantara or day of Brahma (the logoic

cycle) we shall not be able to conceive of the first aspect
of will or power as it really is. We know it now as the
will to exist, manifesting through *the matter* of *the forms*
(the Primordial Ray and the Divine Ray), and we know
it as that which in some occult manner links the system
up with its cosmic centre. In a manner inconceivable to
us the first Logos brings in the influence of other constellations. When this first aspect is better understood
(in the next mahamanvantara) the work of the seven
Rishis of the Great Bear,[65] and the supreme influence of
Sirius will be comprehended; in this present manifestation of the Son, or of the Vishnu aspect, we are concerned
more closely with the Pleiades and their influence via the
Sun, and, in relation to our planet, via Venus.

This subject of the first Logos, manifesting only in
connection with the other two in the system, is a profound mystery, which is not fully understood by even
those who have taken the sixth Initiation.

The first Logos embodies the ''will to live'' and it was
through His instrumentality that the Manasaputras came
into objective existence in relation to the human and deva
hierarchies. In this system, the blending of the Divine
Ray of Wisdom and the Primordial Ray of intelligent
matter forms the great dual evolution; back of both these
cosmic Entities stands another Entity Who is the embodiment of Will, and Who is the utiliser of forms—
though not the forms of any other than the Greater Building devas and the human hierarchies in time and space.
He is the animating principle; the *will-to-live* aspect of
the seven Hierarchies. Nevertheless these seven Hierarchies are (as says H. P. B.) the sevenfold ray of wisdom, the dragon in its seven forms.[66, 67, 68]. This is a

---

[65] ''The Hindus place their seven primitive Rishis in the Great Bear.
The prototypes or the animating source of the seven Heavenly Men, the
planetary Logoi, are considered the seven Existences who function through
the seven stars of the Bear.''—S. D., II, 668.

[66] S. D., I, 100-108.

[67] Subba Rao says in *Five Years of Theosophy*, page 102: ''As a gen-

deep mystery, and only a clue to it all can be found at this time by man in the contemplation of his own nature in the three worlds of his manifestation. Just as our Logos is seeking objectivity through His solar system in its threefold form of which the present is the second, so man seeks objectivity through his three bodies—physical, astral and mental. At this time he is polarised in his astral body, or in his second aspect in like manner as the undifferentiated Logos is polarised in His second aspect. In time and space as we now conceive it, the sum total of jivas are governed by feeling, emotion, and desire, and not by the will, yet at the same time the will aspect governs manifestation, for the Ego who is the source of personality shows in manifestation the will to love.

The difficulty lies in the inability of the finite mind to grasp the significance of this threefold manifestation, *but by thoughtful brooding over the Personality and its relation to the Ego, who is the love aspect and who nevertheless in relation to manifestation in the three worlds is the will aspect likewise,* will come some faint light upon the same problems raised to Deity, or expanded from microcosmic to macrocosmic spheres.

The Mahadeva aspect or the first Logos (who embodies cosmic will) is controlled by the Law of Synthesis, the cosmic law governing the tendency to unification; only in this case, it is not the unification of matter and Spirit, but the unification of the seven into the three, and into the one. These three figures primarily stand for Spirit,

eral rule, whenever seven entities are mentioned in the ancient occult science of India in any connection whatsoever, you must suppose that those seven entities came into existence from three primary entities; and that these three entities, again, are evolved out of a single entity or monad. To take a familiar example, the seven coloured rays in the solar ray are evolved out of three primary coloured rays; and the three primary colours coexist with the four secondary colours in the solar ray. Similarly the three primary entities which brought man into existence coexist in him with the four secondary entities which arose from different combinations of the three primary entities." Read also S. D., I, 190, 191.

⁶⁵ See S. D., I, 100, 108. Also Stanza III, 7A.

for quality, for principle, and not so primarily for matter, although matter, being inspired by spirit, conforms. The Law of Synthesis has a direct connection with One Who is still higher than our Logos, and is the law of control exercised by Him upon the Logos of our system. This is a spiritual relationship that tends to abstraction or to that synthesis of the spiritual elements that will result in their *conscious* return (the whole point lying in that word "conscious") to their cosmic point of synthesis, or of unification with their source. Their source is the ONE ABOUT WHOM NAUGHT MAY BE SAID, as we have earlier seen.

Therefore, in connection with the first Logos, we can sum up as we did with the other Logoi:

a. His *goal* is the synthesis of the Spirits who are gaining consciousness through manifestation, and who, by means of experience in matter, are gaining in quality.

b. His *function* is, by means of will, to hold them in manifestation for the desired period, and later to *abstract* them, and blend them again with their spiritual source. Hence the necessity of remembering that fundamentally, the first Logos controls the cosmic entities or extra-systemic beings; the second Logos controls the solar entities; the third Logos controls the lunar entities and their correspondences elsewhere in the system.

    This rule must not be carried too far in detail as long as man's mind is of its present calibre. The mystery lies in the realisation that all is carried on in a divine co-operation that has its base outside the system. Hence too the fact that the first Logos is called the Destroyer, because He is abstraction, if viewed from below upwards. His work is the synthesis of Spirit with Spirit, their eventual abstraction from matter, and their unification with their cosmic source. Hence also He is the one who brings about pralaya or the disintegration of form,—the form from which the Spirit has been abstracted.

If we carry the analogy down to the microcosm a glimpse can be gained of the same idea and hence ability to comprehend with greater facility. The Ego (being to the man on the physical plane what the Logos is to His system) is likewise the animating will, the destroyer of forms, the producer of pralaya and the One Who withdraws the inner spiritual man from out of his threefold body; he draws them to himself the centre of his little system. The Ego is extra-cosmic as far as the human being on the physical plane is concerned, and in the realisation of this fact may come elucidation of the true cosmic problem involving the Logos and "the spirits in prison," as the Christian puts it.

c. His *mode of action* is a driving forward; the will that lies back of evolutionary development is His, and He it is who drives Spirit onward through matter till it eventually emerges from matter, having achieved two things:

First, Added quality to quality, and therefore emerging plus the gained faculty that experience has engendered.

Second, Increased the vibration of matter itself by means of its own energy, so that matter at the moment of pralaya and obscuration will have two main characteristics,—activity, the result of the Law of Economy, and a dual magnetism which will be the result of the Law of Attraction.

All of these three concepts are governed by the Law of Synthesis, which is the law of a coherent will-to-be, persisting not only in time and space, but within a still vaster cycle.

These preliminary statements have been laid down in an endeavour to show the synthesis of the whole. In the use of words comes limitation, and a clouding of the idea; words literally veil or hide thoughts, detract from their clarity, and confuse them by expression. The work of the second and third Logoi (being the production of the objectivity of the essential Spirit) is more easy to grasp in broad outline than the more esoteric work of the first Logos, which is that of the animating will.

In terms of *fire* another angle of expression may perhaps elucidate.

The *third Logos* is fire in matter. He burns by friction, and gains speed and added vibration by the rotation of the spheres, their interplay thus producing friction with each other.

The *second Logos* is solar fire. He is the fire of matter and the electric fire of Spirit blended, producing, in time and space, that fire which we call solar. He is the quality of the flame, or the essential flame, produced by this merging. A correspondence to this may be seen in the radiatory fire of matter, and in the emanation, for instance, from the central sun, from a planet, or from a human being,—which latter emanation we call magnetism. A man's emanation, or characteristic vibration, is the result of the blending of Spirit and matter, and the relative adequacy of the matter, or the form, to the life within. The objective solar system, or the sun in manifestation, is the result of the blending of Spirit (electric fire) with matter (fire by friction), and the emanations of the Son, in time and space, are dependent upon the adequacy of the matter, and of the form to the life within.

The *first Logos* is electric fire, the fire of pure Spirit. Yet in manifestation He is the Son, for by union with matter (the mother) the Son is produced by Whom He is

known. "I and my Father are One" [69] is the most occult statement in the Christian Bible, for it not only
refers to the union of a man with his source, the monad,
via the ego, but to the union of all life with its source,
the will aspect, the first Logos.

We will now endeavor to confine ourselves strictly to
the subject of fire in matter, and its active effect upon the
sheaths of which it is the animating factor, and upon the
centers which come primarily under its control.

As we have been told, and as is generally recognised,
the effect of heat in matter is to produce that activity
which we call rotary, or the revolution of the spheres.
Some of the ancient books, and among them a few that
are not yet accessible in the occident, have taught that
the entire vault of heaven is a vast sphere, revolving
slowly like a stupendous wheel, and carrying with it, in
its revolution, the entire number of constellations and of
universes contained within it. This is a statement un-
verifiable by the finite mind of man at his present stage,
and with his present scientific accessories, but (like all
occult statements) it contains within .it the seed of
thought, the germ of truths, and the clue to the mystery
of the universe. Suffice it here to say, that the rotation
of the spheres within the solar periphery is a recognized
occult fact, and indications are available to prove that
science itself likewise formulates the hypothesis that the
solar ring-pass-not similarly rotates in its appointed place
among the constellations. But at this juncture we will
not deal with this angle of the subject, but will study the
rotary action of the spheres of the system, and of its
content—all the lesser spheres of every degree—remembering ever to keep the distinction clearly in mind that we
are dealing now simply with the inherent characteristic
of matter itself, and not with matter in co-operation with

[69] Bible.   John, 10: 30.

its opposite, Spirit, which co-operation brings about spiral-cyclic movement.

II. THE EFFECTS OF ROTARY MOTION

Every sphere in the body macrocosmic rotates. This rotation produces certain effects, which effects might be enumerated as follows:

1. *Separation* is produced by rotary movement. By means of this action, all the spheres became differentiated, and form, as we know, the following atomic units:

   a. The solar system, recognised as a cosmic atom, all the so-called atoms within its periphery being regarded as molecular.

   b. The seven planes, regarded as seven vast spheres, rotating *latitudinally* within the solar periphery.

   c. The seven rays, regarded as the seven veiling forms of the Spirits, themselves spheroidal bands of colour, rotating *longitudinally,* and forming (in connection with the seven planes) a vast interlacing network. These two sets of spheres (planes and rays) form the totality of the solar system, and produce its form spheroidal.

Let us withdraw our thought at this juncture from the informing Consciousnesses of these three types of spheres, and concentrate our attention upon the realisation that each plane is a vast sphere of matter, actuated by latent heat and progressing or rotating in one particular direction. Each ray of light, no matter of what colour, is likewise a sphere of matter of the utmost tenuity, rotating in a direction opposite to that of the planes. These rays produce by their mutual interaction a radiatory effect upon each other. Thus by the approximation of the latent heat in matter, and the interplay of that heat upon other spheres that totality is produced which we call "fire by friction."

In connection with these two types of spheres we might, by way of illustration and for the sake of clarity, say that:

    a. The planes rotate from east to west.

    b. The rays rotate from north to south.

Students should here bear carefully in mind that we are not referring here to points in space; we are simply making this distinction and employing words in order to make an abstruse idea more comprehensible. From the point of view of the totality of the rays and planes there is no north, south, east nor west. But at this point comes a correspondence and a point of real interest, though also of complexity. By means of this very interaction, the work of the four Maharajahs or Lords of Karma, is made possible; the quaternary and all sumtotals of four can be seen as one of the basic combinations of matter, produced by the dual revolutions of planes and rays.

> The seven planes, likewise atoms, rotate on their own axis, and conform to that which is required of all atomic lives.

> The seven spheres of any one plane, which we call subplanes, equally correspond to the system; each has its seven revolving wheels or planes that rotate through their own innate ability, due to latent heat —the heat of the matter of which they are formed.

> The spheres or atoms of any form whatsoever, from the form logoic, which we have somewhat dealt with, down to the ultimate physical atom and the molecular matter that goes to the construction of the physical body, show similar correspondences and analogies.

All these spheres conform to certain rules, fulfil certain conditions and are characterised by the same fundamental qualifications. Later we will consider these conditions, but must now continue with the effect of rotary action.

2. *Momentum,* resulting therefore in repulsion, was produced by the rotary movement. We have referred to the Law of Repulsion as one of the subsidiary branches of the great Law of Economy, which governs matter. Repulsion is brought about by rotary action, and is the basis of that separation which prevents the contact of any atom with any other atom, which keeps the planets at fixed points in space and separated stably from each other; which keeps them at a certain distance from their systemic centre, and which likewise keeps the planes and subplanes from losing their material identity. Here we can see the beginning of that age-long duel between Spirit and matter, which is characteristic of manifestation, one aspect working under the Law of Attraction, and the other governed by the Law of Repulsion. From aeon to aeon the conflict goes on, with matter becoming less potent. Gradually (so gradually as to seem negated when viewed from the physical plane) the attractive power of Spirit is weakening the resistance of matter till, at the close of the greater solar cycles, destruction (as it is called) will ensue, and the Law of Repulsion be overcome by the Law of Attraction. It is a destruction of form and not of matter itself, for matter is indestructible. This can be seen even now in the microcosmic life, and is the cause of the disintegration of form, which holds itself as a separated unit by the very method of repulsing all other forms. It can be seen working out gradually and inappreciably in connection with the *Moon,* which no longer is repulsive to the earth, and is giving of her very substance to this planet. H. P. B. hints at this in *the Secret Doctrine,* and I have here suggested the law under which this is so.[70, 71].

_____

[70] "The moon (our satellite) pouring forth into the lowest globe of our planetary chain (Globe D. "Earth"), all its energy and powers; and

3. *Frictional* effect on all other bodies atomic, producing:

   a. Vitality of the atom,

   b. Coherence of the atom,

   c. Ability to function.

   d. Heat supplied to the composite form of which it may form a fragmentary part, whether it is the heat supplied by the rotation of a planet within the form macrocosmic, or the rotation of a cell in the physical body within the form microcosmic.

   e. Final combustion or disintegration, when the fires latent and radiatory have achieved a specific stage. This is the secret of final obscuration and of pralaya, but cannot be dissociated from the two other factors of solar and electric fire.

4. *Absorption,* through that depression which is seen in all whirling spheres of atomic matter at whichever surface in the sphere corresponds to the point called in a planet the North Pole. Some idea of the intention that I seek to convey may be grasped by a study of the atom as portrayed in Babbitt's *"Principles of Light and Colour,"* and later in Mrs. Besant's *"Occult Chemistry."* This depression is produced by radiations which proceed counter to the rotations of the sphere and pass down from the north southwards to a midway point. From there they tend to increase the latent heat, to produce added momentum and to give specific quality according to the source from which the radiation comes. This absorption of extra-spheroidal emanation is the secret of the dependence of one sphere upon another, and has its correspondence in the cycling of a ray through any plane sphere. Every atom, though termed spheroidal, is more accurately a sphere slightly depressed at one location,

having transferred them to a new centre, becoming virtually a dead planet in which, since the birth of our globe, rotation has ceased.''—S. D., I, 179.
    [11] S. D., I, 179.

that location being the place through which flows the force which animates the matter of the sphere. This is true of all spheres, from the solar down to the atom of matter that we call the cell in the body physical. Through the depression in the physical atom flows the vitalising force from without. Every atom is both positive and negative; it is receptive or negative where the inflowing force is concerned, and positive or radiatory where its own emanations are concerned, and in connection with its effect upon its environment.

This can be predicated likewise of the entire ring-pass-not of the solar system in relation to its cosmic environment. Force flows into the solar system from three directions via three channels:

    a. The sun Sirius,
    b. The Pleiades,
    c. The Great Bear.

I would here point out the connection or correspondence in this statement to an earlier one made when speaking of solar radiation, and the channels through which it can be felt. These currents or radiations we call

    a. Akashic.
    b. Electrical.
    c. Pranic.

In considering the occult meaning of what is here suggested, one point in elucidation may be imparted, leaving the working out of the other two relationships to the student. The Pleiades are to the solar system, the source of electrical energy, and just as our sun is the embodiment of the heart, or love aspect, of the Logos (Who is Himself the heart of ONE ABOUT WHOM NAUGHT MAY BE SAID) so the Pleiades are the feminine opposite of Brahma. Think this out, for much is contained in this statement.

Certain broad statements have been laid down here concerning the rotation of matter, and the results produced in diverse spheres by that rotation. What is predicated of any one sphere or atom can be predicated of all, if it is in any way an occult statement of fact and we should be able to work out these four effects:

1. Separation, or the repulsive effect,
2. Momentum, or the interior effect,
3. Frictional, environal effect,
4. Absorption, the receptive or attractive effect,

in every grade and type of atom,—a solar system, a sun, a planet, a plane, a ray, the body of the Ego, or a cell in the physical body.

III. THE QUALITIES OF ROTARY MOTION

Every rotating sphere of matter is characterised by the three qualities, of inertia, mobility and rhythm.

1. *Inertia.* This characterises every atom at the dawn of manifestation, at the beginning of a solar cycle or mahamanvantara (or one hundred years of Brahma), at the commencement of a chain, of a globe, or of any spheroidal form whatsoever without exception. This statement, therefore, includes the totality of manifesting forms within the solar system.

Let us keep clearly in our minds that we are simply considering the three qualities of matter itself and are not considering consciousness. Inertia is the result of lack of activity and the relative quiescence of the fires of matter. These fires, during obscuration or Pralaya, though latent, are free from the stimulation that comes from the aggregation of atoms into form, and the consequent interplay of the forms upon each other. Where form exists and the Laws of Repulsion and Attraction are coming into force, making radiation therefore possible, then comes stimulation, emanative effect, and a gradual speeding up which eventually, from within the atom itself, by its own rotary movement produces the next quality.

2. *Mobility.* The inherent fires of matter produce rotary movement. Eventually this rotation results in radiation. The radiation of matter, the result of its dual heat, produces necessarily an effect upon other atoms in its environment (it matters not whether that environment is cosmic space, systemic space, or the periphery of the physical body of a man), and this interaction and interplay causes repulsion and attraction according to the polarity of the cosmic, systemic or physical atom. Eventually this produces coherence of form; bodies, or aggregates of atoms come into being or manifestation, and persist for the length of their greater or lesser cycles until the third quality is brought into definite recognition.

3. *Rhythm,* or the attainment of the point of perfect balance and of equilibrium. This point of perfect balance then produces certain specific effects which might be enumerated and pondered upon, even if to our finite minds they may seem paradoxical and contradictory.

The limitation lies with us and with the use of words, and not in any real inaccuracy. These effects are:

a. The disintegration of form,
b. The liberation of the essence which the form confines,
c. The separations of Spirit and matter.
d. The end of a cycle, whether planetary, human or solar,
e. The production of obscuration, and the end of objectivity or manifestation,
f. The reabsorption of the essence, and the merging again of differentiated matter with the root of matter,
g. The end of time and space as we understand it,
h. The unification of the three Fires and the bringing about of spontaneous combustion, if one might so express it,

i. The synthetic activity of matter in the three types of movement,—rotary, spiralling-cyclic and onward progression,—which unified movement will be produced by the interaction of the fires of matter, of mind and of Spirit upon each other.

When the point of rhythm or balance is reached in a solar system, in a plane, in a ray, in a causal body, and in the physical body, then the occupier of the form is loosed from prison; he can withdraw to his originating source, and is liberated from the sheath which has hitherto acted as a prison; and he can escape from an environment which he has utilised for the gaining of experience and as a battle ground between the pairs of opposites. The sheath or form of whatever kind then automatically disintegrates.

IV. ROTARY MOTION AND SYMBOLISM

Every rotating sphere of matter can be pictured by using the same general cosmic symbols as are used for the portrayal of evolution.

1. *The circle.* This stands for the ring-pass-not of undifferentiated matter. It stands for a solar system or the body logoic, viewed etherically; it stands for a planet or the body of a Heavenly Man viewed etherically; it stands for a human body, viewed likewise, etherically and it stands for them all at the prime or earliest epoch of manifestation. It stands finally for a single cell within the human vehicle, and for the atom of the chemist or physicist.

2. *The circle with the point in the centre.* This signifies the production of heat in the heart of matter; the point of fire, the moment of the first rotary activity, the first straining of the atom, motivated by latent heat, into the sphere of influence of another atom. This produced the first radiation, the first pull of attraction, and the

consequent setting up of a repulsion and therefore producing

3. *The circle divided into two.* This marks the active rotation and the beginning of the mobility of the atom of matter, and produces the subsequent extension of the influence of the positive point within the atom of matter till its sphere of influence extends from the centre to the periphery. At the point where it touches the periphery it contacts the influence of the atoms in its environment; radiation is set up and the point of depression makes its appearance, marking the inflow and outflow of force or heat.

We are here only showing the application of cosmic symbols to matter, and are not dealing with manifestation from any other angle than that of the purely material. For instance, we are applying the symbol of the point within the circle to the sphere of matter, and the point of latent heat. We are not handling at this point matter as informed by an entity who is to matter, when so informing, a point of conscious life.

We are dealing only with matter and latent heat, with the result produced by rotary movement of radiatory heat and the consequent interplay of bodies atomic. We are therefore dealing with the point we set out to consider while studying our fifth division, motion in the sheaths.

4. *The Circle divided into four.* This is the true circle of matter, the equal armed cross of the Holy Spirit, Who is the personification of active intelligent matter. This shows the fourth dimensional quality of matter and the penetration of the fire in four directions, its threefold radiation being symbolised by the triangles formed by the fourfold cross. This portrays the fourfold revolution of any atom. By this is not meant the ability of any atom to make four revolutions, but the fourth dimensional quality of the revolution which is the goal aimed at, and which is even now becoming known in matter during this

fourth round, and in this fourth chain. As the fifth
spirilla or fifth stream of force in an atom becomes developed, and man can conceive of a fourth-dimensional
rotary movement, the accuracy of this symbol will be
recognised. It will then be seen that all sheaths in their
progress from inertia to rhythm, via mobility, pass
through all stages, whether they are logoic sheaths, the
rays in which the Heavenly Men veil Themselves, the
planes which form the bodies of certain solar entities,
the causal body (or the sheath of the Ego on the mental
plane), the human physical body in its etheric constitution, or a cell in that body etheric. All these material
forms (existent in etheric matter which is the *true*
matter of all forms) are primarily undifferentiated
ovoids; they then become actively rotating or manifest
latent heat; next they manifest duality or latent and radiatory fire; the expression of these two results in fourth
dimensional action or the wheel or rotary form turning
upon itself.

5. *The swastika,* or the fire extending not only from
the periphery to the centre in four directions, but gradually circulating and radiating from and around the entire
periphery. This signifies completed activity in every
department of matter until finally we have a blazing,
fiery wheel, turning every way, with radiant channels of
fire from the centre to the ring-pass-not,—fire within,
without and around until the wheel is consumed and
there is naught remaining but perfected fire.

v. MOTION AND THE CENTRES

We can take up this matter of the centres along three
lines. Much has been written and discussed anent the
centres, and much mystery exists which has aroused the
curiosity of the ignorant, and has tempted many to
meddle with that which does not concern them. I seek to
elucidate somewhat and to give a new angle of vision to

the study of these abstruse matters. I do not in any way
intend to take up the subject from such an angle as to
convey rules and information that will enable a man to
vivify these centres and bring them into play. I sound
here a solemn word of warning. Let a man apply himself to a life of high altruism, to a discipline that will
refine and bring his lower vehicles into subjection, and to
a strenuous endeavor to purify and control his sheaths.
When he has done this and has both raised and stabilised
his vibration, he will find that the development and functioning of the centres has pursued a parallel course, and
that (apart from his active participation) the work has
proceeded along the desired lines. Much danger and dire
calamity attends the man who arouses these centres by
unlawful methods, and who experiments with the fires of
his body without the needed technical knowledge. He
may, by his efforts, succeed in arousing the fires and in
intensifying the action of the centres, but he will pay the
price of ignorance in the destruction of matter, in the
burning of bodily or brain tissue, in the development of
insanity, and in opening the door to currents and forces,
undesirable and destructive. It is not the part of a
coward, in these matters concerning the subjective life,
to move with caution and with care; it is the part of dis-
cretion. The aspirant, therefore, has three things to do:

1. Purify, discipline and transmute his threefold lower
   nature.
2. Develop knowledge of himself, and equip his mental body; build the causal body by good deeds and
   thoughts,
3. Serve his race in utter self-abnegation.

In doing this he fulfils the law, he puts himself in the
right condition for training, fits himself for the ultimate
application of the Rod of Initiation, and thus minimises
the danger that attends the awakening of the fire.

All that is intended to do in this treatise, is to cast some further light upon these centres, to show their interrelation, and to trace the effects produced by their rightful development. To do this, as before stated, the subject will be divided into the following divisions:

1. The nature of the centres.
2. The centres and the rays.
3. The centres and kundalini.
4. The centres and the senses.
5. The centres and initiation.

As can be seen from the above tabulation, the subject is not only vast but abstruse. This is principally owing to the fact that until the race is normally clairvoyant, it is not in a position to verify what is said, and has to accept the statements of those who profess to know. Later when man can see and prove for himself, it will be possible to check up these statements; the time is not yet, except for the few.

1. *The Nature of the Centres.*

Let us take the first point: I wish to enumerate the centres to be dealt with in this treatise, keeping the enumeration very closely to that laid down earlier, and dealing not with all the centres, but simply with those closely concerned with man's fivefold evolution.

As before stated, man, at the close of his long pilgrimage, will have passed through the five kingdoms of nature on his way back to his source:

1. The mineral kingdom,
2. The vegetable kingdom,
3. The animal kingdom,
4. The human kingdom,
5. The superhuman, or the spiritual kingdom,

and will have developed full consciousness on the five planes:

1. The physical plane,
2. The emotional or astral plane,
3. The mental plane,
4. The intuitional, or the buddhic plane,
5. The spiritual, atmic, or nirvanic plane,

by means of the five senses and their correspondences on all the five planes:

1. Hearing,
2. Touch,
3. Sight,
4. Taste,
5. Smell.

By the time the fifth round is reached, three-fifths of the human family will have attained this point and will have their five senses fully functioning on the three planes in the three worlds, leaving the two other planes to be subjugated during the remaining two rounds. I would here point out a fact that is little realised, that in this fivefold evolution of man and in this solar system, the two remaining rounds in any planetary cycle, and the sixth and seventh root-races in those cycles are always synthetic; their function is to gather up and synthesise that which has been achieved in the earlier five. For instance, in this root-race, the sixth and seventh sub-races will synthesise and blend that which the earlier five have wrought out. The analogy lies in the fact that in this solar system the two higher planes (the logoic· and the monadic) are synthetic. One is the synthesising plane for the Logos from whence He abstracts the essence in manifestation; the other for the Monad, from whence the Monad abstracts and garners the fruits of objectivity.

We will therefore only concern ourselves here with those centres which relate to the· evolution of the subtler bodies, the evolution of the psyche, and not with those connected with the evolution and propagation of the dense physical body. These centres are five in number:

1. That at the base of the spine, the only one dealt with that has a physical effect.
2. That situated at the solar plexus, the most important one in the body from the standpoint of the astral plane.
3. That found at the throat, the most important from the standpoint of the mental plane.
4. That in the region of the heart, which has an occult link with the buddhic plane.
5. That above the top of the head, which is the crown, and has relation with the atmic plane.

We do not deal with the lower centres of generation, nor with the spleen which has a direct connection with the etheric, and is the transmitter of prana; they have been dealt with earlier.

The centres in the human being deal fundamentally with the FIRE aspect in man, or with his divine spirit. They are definitely connected with the Monad, with the will aspect, with immortality, with existence, with the will to live, and with the inherent powers of Spirit. They are not connected with objectivity and manifestation, but with *force,* or the powers of the divine life. The correspondence in the Macrocosm can be found in the *force* which manipulates the cosmic nebulae and which by its whirling rotary motion eventually builds them into planets or spheroidal bodies. These planets are each of them an expression of the ''will to live'' of some cosmic entity, and the force that swirled, that rotated, that built, that solidified, and that continues to hold in form coherent, is the force of some cosmic Being.

This force originates on cosmic mental levels, from certain great foci there, descends to the cosmic astral, forming corresponding cosmic focal points, and on the fourth cosmic etheric level (the buddhic plane of our solar system) finds its outlet in certain great centres. These centres are again reflected or reproduced in the three worlds of human endeavor. The Heavenly Men, therefore, have centres on three solar planes, a fact to be remembered.

a. On the monadic plane, the plane of the seven Rays.
b. On the buddhic plane, where the Masters and their disciples form the forty-nine centres in the bodies of the seven Heavenly Men.
c. On the fourth etheric physical plane, where the sacred planets, the dense bodies in etheric matter of the Heavenly Men, are to be found.

Here again we can trace the microcosmic correspondence: In the human being the centres are found on the mental plane from which originates the impulse for physical plane existence, or the will to incarnate; from thence they can be traced to the astral level, and eventually to the etheric levels, to the fourth ether, where they practically go through the same evolution that the planetary centres went through, and are instrumental in bringing about objectivity,—being the force centres.

The centres are formed entirely of streams of force, pouring down from the Ego, who transmits it from the Monad. In this we have the secret of the gradual vibratory quickening of the centres as the Ego first comes into control, or activity, and later (after initiation) the Monad, thus bringing about changes and increased vitality within these spheres of fire or of pure life force.

The centres, therefore, when functioning properly, form the "body of fire" which eventually is all that is left, first to man in the three worlds, and later to the Monad. This body of fire is "the body incorruptible" [72] or indestructible, spoken of by St. Paul, and is the product of evolution, of the perfect blending of the three fires, which ultimately destroy the form. When the form is

[72] Bible. I Cor., XV, 53.

destroyed there is left this intangible spiritual body of fire, one pure flame, distinguished by seven brilliant centres of intenser burning. This electric fire is the result of the bringing together of the two poles and demonstrates at the moment of complete at-one-ment, the occult truth of the words "Our God is a consuming Fire." [73]

Three of these centres are called major centres, as they embody the three aspects of the threefold Monad—Will, Love and Intelligence:

1. The Head centre......The Monad. Will or Power.
2. The Heart centre.....The Ego. Love and Wisdom.
3. The Throat centre....The Personality. Activity or Intelligence.

The other two centres have to do primarily with the etheric body and with the astral plane. The throat centre synthesises the entire personality life, and is definitely connected with the mental plane,—the three planes, and the two higher planes, and the three centres with the two other centres, the heart and head. Yet, we must not forget that the centre at the base of the spine is also a synthesiser, as would normally be expected, if it is recognised that the lowest plane of all manifestation is the point of deepest reflection. This lowest centre, by synthesising the fire of kundalini and the pranic fires, eventually blends and merges with the fire of mind, and later with the fire of Spirit, producing thus consummation.

We must disabuse our minds of the idea that these centres are *physical things*. They are whirlpools of force that swirl etheric, astral and mental matter into activity of some kind. Because the action is rotary, the result produced in matter is a circular effect that can be seen by the clairvoyant as fiery wheels situated:

1. In the region of the spine, the lowest part.
2. Between the ribs, just below the diaphragm.

[73] Bible. Deut. IV, 24; Hebrews XII, 29.

3. In the region of the left breast.
4. In the centre of the throat.
5. Just above the top of the head.

I would like to describe these centres in greater detail, dealing with them as seen in etheric matter, and basing what I say upon a similar statement by Mr. C. W. Leadbeater in *"Inner Life," Vol. I, page 447-460.* We will note the colours and petals:

1. The base of the spine, four petals. These petals are in the shape of a cross, and radiate with orange fire.
2. The solar plexus, ten petals rosy color with admixture of green.
3. The heart centre, twelve petals glowing golden.
4. The throat centre, sixteen petals of a silvery blue, with blue predominating.
5. The head centre in its twofold divisions:
    a. Between the eyebrows, consisting of ninety-six petals, one-half of the lotus being rose and yellow, and the other half blue and purple.
    b. The very top of the head. A centre consisting of twelve major petals of white and gold, and nine hundred and sixty secondary petals arranged around the central twelve. This makes a total of ten hundred and sixty-eight petals in the two head centres (making the one centre) or three hundred and fifty-six triplicities. All these figures have an occult significance.

Just as the Monad is the sumtotal of all the three aspects, and of the seven principles of man, so is the head centre a replica of this, and has within its sphere of influence seven other centres with itself for synthesis. These seven centres are likewise divided into the three major and the four minor centres, with their union and consummation seen in the gorgeous centre surmounting and enveloping them all. There are also three physical centres, called *a.* The alta major centre,

b. The pineal gland,

c. The pituitary body,

with four lesser centres. These four lesser centres are blended in that centre which we call the alta major centre and need not concern us. I would here also point out that there is a close connection:

a. Between the alta major centre and the throat centre.

b. Between the heart centre and the pituitary body.

c. Between the head centre and the pineal gland.

It would repay the student to contemplate the interesting succession of triangles that are to be found and the way in which they must be linked by the progression of the fire before that fire can perfectly vivify them, and thence pass on to other transmutations. We might enumerate some of these triangles, bearing always in mind that according to the ray so will proceed the geometric rising of the fire, and according to the ray so will the points be touched in ordered sequence. Herein lies one of the secrets of initiation, and herein is found some of the dangers entailed in a too quick publication of information concerning the rays.

1. *The pranic triangle.*

    a. The·shoulder centre.

    b. The centre near the diaphragm.

    c. The spleen.

2. *Man controlled from the astral plane.*

    a. The base of the spine.

    b. The solar plexus.

    c. The heart.

3. *Man controlled from the mental plane.*

    a. The base of the spine.

    b. The heart.

    c. The throat.

4. *Man partially controlled by the Ego, advanced man.*

    a. The heart.
    b. The throat.
    c. The head, i.e., the four lesser centres and their synthesis, the alta centre.

5. *Spiritual man to the third Initiation.*

    a. The heart.
    b. The throat.
    c. The seven head centres.

6. *Spiritual man to the fifth Initiation*

    a. The heart.
    b. The seven head centres.
    c. The two many-petalled lotuses.

All these different periods show different triangular radiances. We must not infer from this that when the fire is centred in one triangle it is not demonstrating in others. Once the fire has free passage along any triangle it flames continuously, but always there is one triangle more radiant and luminous than the others, and it is from these glowing triangles of light, issuing from wheels and vortices of fire that the clairvoyant and the teachers of the race can appraise a man's position in the scheme of things, and judge of his attainment. At the culmination of life experience, and when man has reached his goal, each triangle is a radiant path of fire, and each centre a wheel of living fiery force rotating at terrific speed; the centre at this stage not only rotates in a specific direction, but literally turns upon itself, forming a living flaming iridescent globe of pure fire, and holding within it a certain geometrical shape, yet withal vibrating so rapidly that the eye can scarcely follow it. Above all, at the top of the head will be seen a fiery display that seems to put all the other centres into insignificance; from the heart of this many-petalled lotus issues a flame of fire with the basic hue of a man's ray. This flame mounts upward and seems to attract downward a sheet of electric light, which is the downflow from the spirit on the highest plane. This marks the blending of the fires and the deliverance of man from the trammels of matter.

We might now note that the evolution of these centres of force can be portrayed, not only in words, but under the same five symbols that have so often a cosmic interpretation.

1. *The circle.* At this stage the centre is seen simply as a saucer-like depression (as Mr. C. W. Leadbeater expresses it) of dimly glowing fire, a fire diffused throughout but of no real intensity. The wheel rotates slowly, but so slowly as to be almost inappreciable. This corresponds to the little developed stage, and to the early Lemurian root-race, and to that period wherein man was simply animal; all that was being formed was a field for the appearance of the spark of mind.

2. *The circle with the point in the centre.* The centre is here seen with a point of glowing fire in the middle of the saucer-like depression, and the rotation becomes more rapid. This corresponds to the stage wherein mind is beginning to be felt and thus to later Lemurian days.

3. *The divided circle.* At this stage the point of light in the centre of the vortex of fire is becoming more active; rotary motion causes it to burn more brightly, and to cast off rays of fire in two directions, which appear to split the vortex into two; the motion is much accelerated, and the dividing flame in the vortex shoots back and forth, stimulating the glow of the centre itself, till a much greater point of radiance is achieved. This corresponds to Atlantean days.

4. *The circle divided into four.* We come now to the point where the centre is exceedingly active, with the cross within its periphery rotating as well as the wheel itself, and causing an effect of great beauty and activity. The man has reached a stage of very high development

mentally, corresponding to the fifth root-race, or to the
fifth round in the larger cycle; he is conscious of two
activities within himself, symbolised by the rotating
wheel and the inner rotating cross. He is sensing the
spiritual, though actively functioning in the personal life,
and the development has reached a point wherein he is
nearing the Probationary Path.

5. *The swastika.* At this stage the centre becomes
fourth-dimensional; the inner rotating cross begins to
turn upon its axis, and to drive the flaming periphery to
all sides so that the centre is better described as a sphere
of fire than as a wheel. It marks the stage of the Path in
its two divisions, for the process of producing the effect
described covers the whole period of the Path. At the
close, the centres are seen as globes of radiant fire with
the spokes of the wheel (or the evolution of the cross
from the point in the centre) merging and blending into
a "fire that burneth up the whole."

A brief sentence has its place here owing to its relation
to this subject. Another sentence is also added here,
which, if meditated upon, will prove of real value and
will have a definite effect upon one of the centres, which
centre it is for the student himself to find out.

These two sentences are as follows:

> "The secret of the Fire lies hid in the second letter of the
> Sacred Word. The mystery of life is concealed within
> the heart. When the lower point vibrates, when the Sacred
> Triangle glows, when the point, the middle centre, and the
> apex likewise burn, then the two triangles—the greater
> and the lesser—merge with one flame which burneth up the
> whole."

> "The fire within the lesser fire findeth its progress much
> impelled when the circle of the moving and the unmoving,
> of the lesser wheel within the greater wheel that moveth
> not in Time, findeth a twofold outlet; it then shineth with
> the glory of the twofold One and of His sixfold brother.
> Fohat rusheth through space. He searcheth for his comple-

ment. The breath of the unmoving one, and the fire of the One Who seeth the whole from the beginning rush to meet each other, and the unmoving becomes the sphere of activity.''

We take up our second point in the consideration of the centres:

2. *The centres in connection with the Rays.*

This will give us a large range of subject to be dealt with, and much food for thought, surmise and wise conjecture. All that is here stated is given simply as basic or foundation facts, upon which may be erected a structure of conjecture, and of logical reasoning, employing the imagination, and thereby effecting two things:

These are an ability to expand our mental concept and to build the antaskarana, or that bridge which all who seek to function in the buddhic vehicle must build between higher and lower mind; hence the necessity for the use of the imagination (which is the astral equivalent to mental discrimination), and its ultimate transmutation into intuition.

All teachers, who have taken pupils in hand for training, and who seek to use them in world service, follow the method of imparting a fact (oft veiled in words and blinded by symbol) and then of leaving the pupil to follow his own deductions. Discrimination is thereby developed, and discrimination is the main method whereby the Spirit effects its liberation from the trammels of matter, and discerns between illusion and that which is veiled by it.

Not much can be here imparted, as the subject, if dealt with at all fully, would convey too much information to those liable to misuse it. As we know, the evolution of the centres is a slow and gradual thing, and proceeds in ordered cycles varying according to the ray of a man's Monad.

The life of the Pilgrim can be, for purposes of discussion, divided into three main periods:

1. That period wherein he is under the influence of the Personality Ray.
2. That wherein he comes under the Ray of the Ego.
3. That wherein the Monadic Ray holds sway.

The first period is by far the longest, and covers the vast progression of the centuries wherein the activity aspect of the threefold self is being developed. Life after life slips away during which the aspect of manas or mind is being slowly wrought out, and the human being comes more and more under the control of his intellect, operating through his physical brain. This might be looked upon as corresponding to the period of the first solar system, wherein the third aspect logoic, that of Brahma, Mind, or Intelligence, was being brought to the point of achievement.[74] Then the second aspect began in

[74] "When the last cycle of man-bearing has been completed by that last fecund earth; and humanity has reached in a mass the stage of Buddhahood and passed out of the objective existence into the mystery of Nirvana— then "strikes the hour"; the seen becomes the unseen, the concrete resumes its pre-cyclic state of atomic distribution.

But the dead worlds left behind the onsweeping impulse do not continue dead. Motion is the eternal order of things and affinity or attraction its handmaid of all works. The thrill· of life will again re-unite the atom, and it will stir again in the inert planet when the time comes. Though all its forces have remained statu quo and are now asleep, yet little by little it will—when the hour re-strikes—gather for a new cycle of man-bearing maternity, and give birth to something still higher as moral and physical types than during the preceding manvantara. And its "cosmic atoms already in a differentiated state" (differing—in the producing force in the mechanical sense of motions and effects) remain statu quo as well as globes and everything else in the process of formation." Such is the "hypothesis fully in accordance with (your) (my) note." For, as planetary development is as progressive as human or race evolution, the hour of the Pralaya's coming catches the series of worlds at successive stages of evolution; (i.e.) each has attained to some one of the periods of evolutionary progress—each stops there, until the outward impulse of the next manvantara sets it going from that very point—like a stopped time-piece re-wound. Therefore, I have used the word "differentiated."

At the coming of the Pralaya no human, animal, or even vegetable entity will be alive to see it, but there will be the earths or globes with their mineral kingdoms; and all these planets will be physically disintegrated in the pralaya, yet not destroyed; for they have their places in the sequence of evolution and their "privations" coming again out of the subjective, they will find the exact point from which they have to move on around

this present solar system to be blended with, and wrought out through it. Centuries go by and the man becomes ever more actively intelligent, and the field of his life more suitable for the coming in of this second aspect. The correspondence lies in similitude and not in detail as seen in time and space. It covers the period of the first three triangles dealt with earlier. We must not forget that, for the sake of clarity, we are here differentiating between the different aspects, and considering their separated development, a thing only permissible in time and space or during the evolutionary process, but not permissible from the standpoint of the Eternal Now, and from the Unity of the All-Self. The Vishnu or the Love-Wisdom aspect is latent in the Self, and is part of the monadic content, but the Brahma aspect, the Activity-Intelligence aspect precedes its manifestation in time. The Tabernacle in the Wilderness preceded the building of the Temple of Solomon; the kernel of wheat has to lie in the darkness of mother Earth before the golden perfected ear can be seen, and the Lotus has to cast its roots down into the mud before the beauty of the blossom can be produced.

The second period, wherein the egoic ray holds sway, is not so long comparatively; it covers the period wherein the fourth and fifth triangles are being vivified, and marks the lives wherein the man throws his forces on the side of evolution, disciplines his life, steps upon the Probationary Path, and continues up to the third Initiation. Under the régime of the Personality Ray, the man proceeds upon the five Rays to work consciously with Mind, the sixth sense, passing first upon the four minor Rays and eventually upon the third. He works

the chain of "manifested forms." This, as you know, is repeated endlessly throughout Eternity. Each man of us has gone this ceaseless round, and will repeat it forever and ever. The deviation of each one's course, and his rate of progress from Nirvana to Nirvana is governed by causes which he himself creates out of the exigencies in which he finds himself entangled."—From *The Mahatma Letters* to A. P. Sinnett, p. 67.

upon the third Ray, or that of active Intelligence, and from thence proceeds to one of the subrays of the two other major Rays, if the third is not his egoic Ray.

Enquiry might naturally arise as to whether the egoic ray is necessarily one of the three major rays, and if Initiates and Masters are not to be found upon some of the rays of mind, the minor four.

The answer lies here: The egoic ray can always be one of the seven, but we need to remember that, in this astral-buddhic solar system, wherein love and wisdom are being brought into objectivity, the bulk of the monads are on the love-wisdom ray. The fact, therefore, of its being the synthetic ray has a vast significance. This is the system of the son, whose name is Love. This is the divine incarnation of Vishnu. The Dragon of Wisdom is in manifestation, and He brings into incarnation those cosmic Entities who are in essence identical with Himself. After the third Initiation all human beings find themselves on their monadic ray, on one of the three major rays, and the fact that Masters and Initiates are found on all the rays is due to the following two factors:

First. Each major ray has its subrays, which correspond to all the seven.

Second. Many of the guides of the race transfer from one ray to another as They are needed, and as the work may require. When one of the Masters or Initiates is transferred it causes a complete re-adjustment.

When a Master likewise leaves the hierarchy of our Planet to take up work elsewhere, it frequently necessitates a complete re-organisation, and a fresh admission of members into the great White Lodge. These facts have been but little realised. We might here also take the opportunity to point out that we are not dealing with earth conditions when we consider the Rays, nor are we only concerned with the evolution of the Monads upon this planet, but are equally concerned with the solar system in which our earth holds a necessary but not supreme place. The earth is an organism within a greater one, and this fact needs wider recognition. The sons of men upon this planet so often view the whole system as if the earth were in the position of the sun, the centre of the solar organism.

Under the régime of the Ego, the ray upon which the ego can be found holds sway. This ray is simply a direct reflection of the monad, and is dependent upon that aspect of the spiritual triad which for the man is at any particular time the line of least resistance. By that we must understand that sometimes the ray will have for its centre of force the atmic aspect, sometimes the buddhic, and at other times the manasic aspect. Though the triad is threefold, yet its egoic outposts (if one may so express it) will be either definitely atmic, or predominantly buddhic or manasic. Here again I would draw attention to the fact that this triple demonstration can be seen under three forms, making in all a ninefold choice of rays for the Ego:

Atmic aspect.
   1. atmic—atmic
   2. atmic—buddhic
   3. atmic—manasic.

Buddhic aspect.
   1. buddhic—atmic
   2. buddhic—buddhic
   3. buddhic—manasic.

Manasic aspect.
   1. manasic—atmic
   2. manasic—buddhic
   3. manasic—manasic.

This literally means that the three major rays can each be subdivided (in connection with the Ego) into three divisions. This fact is also little appreciated.

The third period, wherein the monadic ray makes itself felt on the physical plane, is by far the shortest, and covers the period in which the sixth triangle holds sway. It marks the period of achievement, of liberation, and therefore, although it is the shortest period when viewed from below upward, it is the period of comparative permanence when viewed from the plane of the Monad. It covers the totality of time remaining in the one hundred years of Brahma, or the remainder of the process of manifestation.

When we study, therefore, the sets of triangles earlier referred to and the periods of ray dominance, we will find much room for thought. Let me here point out, however, that the six groups of triangles are in all but five if we eliminate the pranic triangle which has to do with matter itself and is not counted any more than the dense physical is counted a principle. Therefore we have:

a. Two triangles brought to vivification by the personality ray.
b. Two triangles brought to vivification by the egoic ray.
c. The synthesising triangle of the Monad.

We must, nevertheless, recollect that the complexity is increased by the fact that *the personality triangles will be brought to full activity according to the ray of the Monad or Spirit.* Therefore, no hard or fast rule can be laid down about development. The egoic triangles are dependent largely upon the reflection in the personality of the spiritual life force. They are the midway point, just as the causal or egoic body is the transmitting point (when sufficiently equipped and built) between the higher and the lower.

The permanent atoms are enclosed within the periphery of the causal body, yet that relatively permanent body is built and enlarged, expanded and wrought into a central receiving and transmitting station (using inadequate words to convey an occult idea) by the direct action of the centres, and *of the centres above all.* Just as it was spiritual force, or the will aspect, that built the solar system, so it is the same force in the man that builds the causal body. By the bringing together of spirit and matter (Father-Mother) in the macrocosm, and their union through the action of the will, the objective solar system, or the Son, was produced—that Son of desire, Whose characteristic is love, and Whose nature is buddhi or spiritual wisdom. By the bringing together (in microcosm) of Spirit and matter, and their coherence by means of force (or the spiritual will) that objective system, the causal body, is being produced; it is the product of transmuted desire, whose characteristic (when fully demonstrated) will be love, the expression eventually on the physical plane of buddhi. The causal body is but the sheath of the Ego. The solar system is but the sheath of the Son. In both the greater and the lesser systems, force centres exist which are productive of objectivity. The centres in the human being are reflections in the three worlds of those higher force centres.

Before taking up the subject of kundalini and the centres, it would be well to extend the information given above, from its prime significance for man, as that which concerns himself, to the solar system, the macrocosm, and to the cosmos. What can be predicated of the microcosm is naturally true of the macrocosm and of the cosmos. It will not be possible to give the systemic triangles, for the information would have to be so blinded that, except for those who have occult knowledge and the intuition developed, it would be practically useless intellectually, but certain things may be pointed out in this connection that may be of interest.

The Solar System. We might briefly look at this from

the standpoint of the centres of the Heavenly Men and of the Grand Man of the Heavens, the Logos.

a. The Heavenly Men. The Heavenly Men, in Themselves, embody centres just as does a human being, and on Their Own plane these centres of force can be found. Again we need to recollect that these centres of force on cosmic levels, and in manifestation in the objective system, demonstrate as the great force centres of which any particular group of adepts and Their pupils are the exponents. Every group of Masters and all the human beings incarnate or discarnate —who are held within the periphery of Their consciousness—are centres of force of some particular kind or quality. This is a fact generally recognised, but students should be urged to link up this fact with the information imparted on the centres of the human being, and see if much is not thereby learnt. These centres of force will demonstrate on etheric levels and on the subtler planes just as they do in a man, and they will be vivified as are the human centres by planetary kundalini, progressing in the desired triangles.

Two hints can here be given for thoughtful consideration. In connection with one of the Heavenly Men (which one cannot at this juncture be pointed out) we have one triangle of force to be seen in the following three centres:

   a. The force centre of which the Manu, and His group, are the expression.
   b. The centre of which the Bodhisattva or the Christ and His adherents are the focal point.
   c. The centre of which the Mahachohan and his followers are the exponents.

These three groups form the three centres in one great triangle—a triangle which is not yet in complete vivification at this stage of evolutionary development.

Another triangle in connection with our own planetary Logos is that formed by the seven Kumaras—the four exoteric Kumaras corresponding to the four minor head centres, and the three esoteric Kumaras corresponding to the three major head centres.[75, 76].

The second hint I seek to give, lies in the triangle formed by the Earth, Mars and Mercury. In connection with this triangle, the analogy lies in the fact that Mercury and the centre at the base of the spine in the human being are closely allied. Mercury demonstrates kundalini in intelligent activity, while Mars demonstrates kundalini latent. The truth lies hid in their two astrological symbols. In transmutation and planetary geometrising, the secret may be revealed.

b. *The Grand Man of the Heavens.* The seven Heavenly Men are the seven centres in the body of the Logos, bearing to Him a relationship identical with that borne by the Masters and Their affiliated groups, to some planetary Logos. Systemic kundalini goes forward to the vivification of these centres, and at this stage of development certain centres are more closely allied than others. Just as in connection with our planetary Logos, the three etheric planets of our chain—Earth, Mercury and Mars [77]—form a triangle of rare importance, so it may be here said that at the present point in evolution of the logoic centres, Venus, Earth and Saturn form one triangle of great interest. It is a triangle that is at this time undergoing vivification

[75] There are seven Kumaras connected with our planetary evolution, of Whom four are exoteric; the four exoteric have vehicles in etheric matter; three Kumaras are esoteric and have their vehicles in subtler matters still.

Sanat Kumara, The Lord of the world, is the representative on earth of the specialized force of the planetary Logos; the other six Kumaras transmit energy from the other six planetary schemes.

[76] S. D., I, 186-189.

[77] The chains of any planetary scheme are frequently called by the names of the seven sacred planets, making the study of the Law of Correspondences easier; similarly, the globes of any chain are called by planetary names, as is the case here. There are planetary schemes called Mars and Mercury.

through the action of kundalini; it is consequently increasing the vibratory capacity of the centres, which are becoming slowly fourth-dimensional. It is not yet permissible to point out others of the great triangles, but as regards the centres, we may here give two hints:

First. *Venus* corresponds to the heart centre in the body logoic, and has an inter-relationship therefore with all the other centres in the solar system wherein the heart aspect is the one of greater prominence.

Second. *Saturn* corresponds to the throat centre, or to the creative activity of the third aspect.

As evolution proceeds, the other centres attain a more pronounced vibration and the fire (circulating triangularly) will bring them into greater prominence; the two above mentioned, however, are of prime importance at this time. These two, with the lesser triangle of our chain, constitute the focal point of energy *viewed from our planetary standpoint.*

In addition to these some hints in connection with the microcosmic and macrocosmic centres, we might here give the cosmic correspondences at which it is possible to hint.

The Cosmos. Our solar system, with the Pleiades and one of the stars of the Great Bear, form a cosmic triangle, or an aggregation of three centres in the Body of HIM OF WHOM NAUGHT MAY BE SAID. The seven stars in the constellation of the Great Bear are the correspondences to the seven head centres in the body of that Being, greater than our Logos. Again, two other systems, when allied with the solar system and the Pleiades, make a lower quaternary which are eventually synthesised into the seven head centres in much the same way as in the human being after the fourth initiation.

1. The base of the spine.
2. The solar plexus.
3. The heart.
4. The throat.

The sevenfold head centre in its turn finds ultimate expression in the gorgeous twofold centre above the top of the head and surrounding it. Equally so, beyond the above named constellations is still another cosmic centre. The name of this centre is one of the secrets of the final initiation, the seventh. These are the only correspondences that may as yet be imparted. What lies beyond the solar ring-pass-not may be of intellectual interest,[78] but, for the purposes of microcosmic evolution it is a matter of no vast import.

3. *The Centres and Kundalini.*

As stated, it is not possible to impart much about kundalini, or the serpent fire. It might be of value, however, briefly to enumerate what has been said:

a. Kundalini lies at the base of the spine, and, in the normal average man, its main function is the vitalisation of the body.

b. Kundalini makes three at-one-ments during the period of evolution:
  1. With the radiatory fires of the body or prana at a point between the shoulder blades.
  2. With the fires of mind at a point at the very top of the spine, in the centre of the back part of the throat.
  3. With the fire of Spirit at the point where these two united fires of matter and of mind issue from the top of the head.

c. Each of the three channels within the spinal column have for specific purpose the blending of these threefold fires. We need to bear in mind that the

[78] S. D., I, 545, 726; II, 581, 582, 654.

fires *circulate,* and that, at the moment of achievement, every triangle in the body is vivified, every centre is fully functioning, and a threefold path of fire can be seen extending the entire length of the backbone.

d. When kundalini has blended with the pranic fire, the centres become three-dimensional. When it blends with mind or solar fire and the two fires are perfectly united, the centres become fourth-dimensional. When it blends with the electric fire of pure Spirit after the third Initiation, they take on two more dimensions.

e. Kundalini, as it is aroused, steadily increases the vibratory action, not only of the centres, but of every atom of matter in all the bodies—etheric, astral and mental. This quickening of activity has a dual effect of great interest:

1. It causes the elimination of all matter that is coarse and unsuitable, and casts it off in exactly the same way as a rapidly rotating wheel casts off or rejects from its surface.

2. It sweeps into its sphere of influence matter that is keyed to its own vibration, and builds it into its vibratory content. This is but a reflection of the action of the Logos in sweeping into differentiation the matter of the solar system. Kundalini is likewise the fire or force of matter, and therefore the life of the third Logos.

f. Kundalini has two effects upon the etheric web, as it is called.

1. By its gradually increasing action it purifies that etheric form and cleanses it from "dross," as the Christian expresses it.

2. Eventually, after the two fires of matter and the fire of mind have begun to blend (a slow and gradual process), the web itself is de-

stroyed, and by the time the third Initiation is reached, the man should have continuity of consciousness. This is so unless for certain work and for certain specific ends, the man consciously and willingly foregoes the burning of the web, a thing which can be brought about by the conscious action of the will.

4. *The Centres and the Senses, Normal and Supernormal.*

Before at all dealing with the centres and their relationship to the senses, it will be necessary first of all to point out certain facts of interest in connection with those senses,[79] and so clear the ground for further information.

[79] The seven senses or the avenues of perception.—S. D., I, 489, 490, The third or Indriya Creation.—S. D., III, 567.

Indriya—The control of the senses in yoga practice. These are the 10 external agents; the 5 senses which are used for perception are called 'Jnana-indriya' and the 5 used for action 'karma-indriya.'—Theosophical Glossary.

"Jnana-indriyas"—literally knowledge-senses . . . by which knowledge is obtained. . . . They are the avenues inward.

"Karma-indriyas"—literally action senses . . . those producing action. They are the avenues outwards.—*Study in Consciousness*, pp. 166-167.

1. Sensation is latent in every atom of substance.—S. D., II, 710.
2. The Sun is the heart of the system and sensation emanates from there. It is due to solar radiation.—S. D., I, 590, 662.
3. Knowledge is the end of sense.—S. D., I, 300.
4. There is a double set of senses, spiritual and material.—S. D., I, 582; S. D., II, 307, 308.
   This finds its reflection in the double set of physical senses noted in defining the indriyas.
5. The senses might be enumerated as follows: S. D., I, 583 and note 123; S. D., II, 600, 674, 675, 676.
6. The elements are the progenitors of the senses. . . .—S. D., II, 112, 113.

    a. Aether.....Hearing.....Sound ....Atmic plane
    b. Air........Touch.......Sound, touch ....Buddhic plane
    c. Fire........Sight........Sound, touch, sight ....Mental plane
    d. Water.....Taste.......Sound, touch, sight, taste..Astral plane
    e. Earth......Smell....... Sound, touch, sight, taste,
                                       smell ....Physical plane
7. Every sense pervades every other sense. . . .—S. D., III, 569.
   There is no universal order.
   All are on all planes.—S. D., III, 550.
8. The senses correspond with every other septenate in nature. See S. D., III, 448. Compare S. D., III, 497. Practical reading. . . .—S. D., I, 288

What are the senses? How many are there? And
what is their connection with the indwelling Man, the
Thinker, the Divine Manasaputra? These are questions
of vital moment, and in their due comprehension comes
the ability wisely to follow the path of knowledge.

The senses might be defined as those organs whereby
man becomes aware of his surroundings. We should
perhaps express them not so much as organs (for after
all, an organ is a material form, existent for a purpose)
but as media whereby the Thinker comes in contact
with his environment. They are the means whereby he
makes investigation on the plane of the gross physical,
for instance; the means whereby he buys his experience,
whereby he discovers that which he requires to know,
whereby he becomes aware, and whereby he expands
his consciousness. We are dealing here with the five
senses as used by the human being. In the animal these
five senses exist but, as the thinking correlating faculty
is lacking, as the "relation between" the self and the
not-self is but little developed, we will not concern ourselves with them at this juncture. The senses in the
animal kingdom are *group faculty* and demonstrate as
racial instinct. The senses in man are his individual as-
set, and demonstrate:

a. As the separate realisation of self-consciousness.
b. As ability to assert that individualism.
c. As a valuable means to self-conscious evolution.
d. As a source of knowledge.
e. As the transmuting faculty towards the close of life in the
   three worlds.

As we know, the senses are five in number and in order
of development are as follows:

a. Hearing.
b. Touch.
c. Sight.
d. Taste.
e. Smell.

Each of these five senses has a definite connection with one or other plane, and has also a correspondence on all planes.

Let us first take up each of these senses, point out some interesting facts in connection with them, and suggest their subplane correspondence.

PLANE	SENSE
1. Physical	Hearing.
2. Astral	Touch or feeling.
3. Mental	Sight.
4. Buddhic	Taste.
5. Atmic	Smell.

In the two lower planes in the three worlds—the astral and the physical—the five subplanes of human endeavor are the five highest. The two lowest subplanes, the sixth and seventh, are what we might express as "below the threshold," and concern forms of life beneath the human altogether. We have a corroborating analogy in the fact that the two earliest root-races in this round are not definitely human, and that it is the third root-race which is really human for the first time. Counting, therefore, from the bottom upwards it is only the third subplane on the physical and the astral planes which mark the commencement of human effort, leaving five subplanes to be subdued. On the mental plane the five lower subplanes have to be subjugated during purely human evolution. When the consciousness is centred on the fifth subplane (counting from below upwards) then the planes of abstraction—from the standpoint of man in the three worlds—supervene the two subplanes of synthesis, demonstrating through the synthesis of the five senses. In the evolution of the Heavenly Man we have exactly the same thing: the five planes of endeavour, the five lower planes of the solar system, and the two higher planes of abstraction, the spiritual or monadic and the divine, or logoic.

MICROCOSMIC SENSORY EVOLUTION

Plane

Physical ... 1. Hearing ....5th....gaseous
2. Touch, feeling ....4th....first etheric
3. Sight ....3rd....super-etheric
4. Taste ....2nd....sub-atomic
5. Smell ....1st....atomic

Astral ..... 1. Clairaudience 5th
2. Psychometry 4th
3. Clairvoyance 3rd
4. Imagination 2nd
5. Emotional idealism 1st

Mental ..... 1. Higher clairaudience ....7th ⎫
2. Planetary psychometry .....6th ⎬ FORM
3. Higher clairvoyance ....5th ⎪
4. Discrimination ....4th ⎭
5. Spiritual discernment ....3rd ⎫
Response to group vibration..2nd ⎬ FORMLESS
Spiritual telepathy ....1st ⎭

Buddhic .... 1. Comprehension 7th
2. Healing 6th
3. Divine vision 5th
4. Intuition 4th
5. Idealism 3rd

Atmic ...... 1. Beatitude 7th
2. Active service 6th
3. Realisation 5th
4. Perfection 4th
5. All knowledge 3rd

It can be noted that we have not summed up the two planes of abstraction on the atmic and the buddhic planes, the reason being that they mark a degree of realisation which is the property of initiates of higher degree than that of the adept, and which is beyond the concept of the evolving human unit, for whom this treatise is written.

We might here, for the sake of clarity, tabulate the five different aspects of the five senses on the five planes, so that their correspondences may be readily visualised, using the above table as the basis:

a. The First Sense......Hearing.

    1. Physical hearing.
    2. Clairaudience.
    3. Higher clairaudience.
    4. Comprehension (of four sounds)
    5. Beatitude.

b. The Second Sense....Touch or feeling.

    1. Physical touch.
    2. Psychometry.
    3. Planetary psychometry.
    4. Healing.
    5. Active service.

c. The Third Sense.....Sight.

    1. Physical sight.
    2. Clairvoyance.
    3. Higher clairvoyance.
    4. Divine vision.
    5. Realisation.

d. The Fourth Sense........Taste.

    1. Physical taste.
    2. Imagination.
    3. Discrimination.
    4. Intuition.
    5. Perfection.

e. The Fifth Sense.....Smell.

    1. Physical smell.
    2. Emotional idealism.
    3. Spiritual discernment.
    4. Idealism.
    5. All knowledge.

190 A TREATISE ON COSMIC FIRE

Let us now proceed to take up each of these senses in detail:

a. Hearing. This, very appropriately, is the first sense to be manifested; the first aspect of manifestation is that of sound, and necessarily therefore we would expect sound to be the first thing noticed by man on the physical plane, the plane of densest manifestation, and of the most marked effects of sound, regarding it as a creating factor. Pre-eminently the physical plane is the plane of hearing and hence the sense ascribed to the lowest plane of evolution, and of each of the five planes. On this seventh or lowest plane man has to come to full cognisance of the effect of the Sacred Word as it is in process of sounding forth. As it reverberates throughout the system, it drives matter into its appointed place, and on the physical plane finds its point of deepest materiality and of most concrete demonstration. The key for man to discover and turn, concerns itself with the revealing of the mystery of:

- *a.* His own sound.
- *b.* His brother's sound.
- *c.* His group sound.
- *d.* The sound of that one of the Heavenly Men with whom he is connected.
- *e.* The sound of the Logos, or the sound of nature; of the solar system, of the Grand Man of the Heavens.

Therefore, we note that on the physical plane a man has to find his own note, finding it in spite of the density of the form.

- *a.* On the physical plane he finds his own note.
- *b.* On the astral plane he finds his brother's note; through identity of emotion he comes to the recognition of his brother's identity.

c. On the mental plane he begins to find his group note.

d. On the buddhic plane, or the plane of wisdom, he begins to find the note of his planetary Logos.

e. On the atmic, or spiritual, plane the note logoic begins to sound *within* his consciousness.

I am differentiating thus for the sake of clarity. In evolution itself, due to the parallelism of nature, the distinctions are not so sharply made, and a man's ray, point of development, the work earlier accomplished, his temporary limitations, and other causes create a seeming confusion, but in the great scheme as seen from above downwards, the work proceeds as described.

Hearing on the astral plane is commonly called clair-audience, and means the ability to hear the sounds of the astral plane. It is a faculty that demonstrates throughout the entire astral body, and a man hears all over his vehicle and not only through the specialised organs, the ears, the product of physical plane action and reaction. This would necessarily be so, owing to the fluidic nature of the astral body. Man on the physical plane hears at the same time a certain range of sounds, and only a small and particular gamut of vibrations impinges upon his ears. There are many of the lesser sounds of nature which entirely escape him, while the major group sounds are not differentiated at all. As evolution proceeds and the inner sense of hearing becomes acute, these other physical plane sounds will likewise swing into his ken, and he will be acutely conscious of all sounds on the astral, and the physical plane—a thing, which if possible now, would result in the shattering of the body. If the note of nature, for instance, were to strike but once upon the ear of a man (a note made up of the totality of vibrations produced by all dense material forms) his physical body would be completely disrupted.

He is not ready yet for such a happening; the inner ear is not duly prepared. Only when the threefold hearing is consummated will completed hearing on the physical plane be likewise permitted.

Hearing on the mental plane is simply an extension of the faculty of differentiating sound. The hearing dealt with on all these planes is the hearing that has to do with the form, that concerns the vibration of matter, and that is occupied with the not-self. It has not to do with the psyche, or the telepathic communication that proceeds from mind to mind, but with the sound of the form or that power whereby one separated unit of consciousness is aware of another unit who is not himself. Bear this carefully in mind. When the extension of hearing becomes such that it concerns the psyche, then we call it telepathy or that wordless communication that is the synthesis of hearing on all the three lower planes and which is known by the Ego in the causal body on the formless levels of the mental plane.

On the buddhic plane, hearing (now of the synthetic quality called telepathy) demonstrates as complete comprehension, for it has involved two things:

1. A knowledge and recognition of individual sound,
2. A similar knowledge of group sound,

and their complete unification. This causes the most perfect comprehension, and is the secret of the Master's power.

On the atmic plane this perfected hearing is seen as beatitude. Sound, the basis of existence; sound, the method of being; sound, the final unifier; sound therefore realised as the *raison d'être,* as the method of evolution, and therefore as beatitude.[80]

[80] . . . "the chief agency by which Nature's wheel is moved in a phenomenal direction is *sound.* Sound is the first aspect of the manifested pentagon since it is a property of ether called Akas and as I already said Vedic recitation is the highest Yagnam containing in itself all minor

b. Touch. In taking up the subject of the second
sense, *that of touch,* we must note that this sense is pre-
eminently the sense of very great importance in this,
the second, solar system—a system of astral-buddhic consciousness.[81] Each of these senses, after having reached
a certain point, begins to synthesise with the others in
such a way that it is almost impossible to know where
one begins and the other ends. *Touch* is that innate recognition of contact through the exercise of manas or
mind in a threefold manner:

As recognition.
As memory.
As anticipation.

Each of the five senses, when coupled with manas, develops within the subject a concept embodying the past,
the present and the future. Therefore when a man is
very highly evolved, has transcended time (as known in
the three worlds), and can therefore look at the three
lower planes from the standpoint of the Eternal Now,
he has superseded the senses by full active consciousness. He *knows,* and needs not the senses to guide him
any longer to knowledge. But in time, and in the three
worlds, each sense on each plane is employed to convey
to the Thinker some aspect of the not-self, and by the aid

Yagnams and tending to preserve the manifested pentagon in the proper
order. In the opinion of our old philosophers sound or speech is next to
thought the highest karmic agent used by man.
Of the various karmic agencies wielded by man in the way of moulding
himself and surroundings, sound or speech is the most important, for, to
speak is to work in ether which of course rules the lower quaternary of
elements, air, fire, water and earth. Human sound or language contains
therefore all the elements required to move the different classes of Devas
and those elements are of course the vowels and the consonants. The
details of the philosophy of sound in its relation to the devas who preside
over the subtle world, belong to the domain of true Mantra Sastra which
of course is in the hands of the knowers.''—*Some Thoughts on the Gita,*
p. 72.
[81] Astral-buddhic consciousness is the term applied to the basic consciousness in our solar system. It is characterised by emotion, by feeling, sensation, which have eventually to be transmuted into intuition, spiritual perception and unity.

of mind, the Thinker can then adjust his relationship thereto.

> *Hearing* gives him an idea of relative direction, and enables a man to fix his place in the scheme, and to locate himself.
>
> *Touch* gives him an idea of relative quantity and enables him to fix his relative value as regards other bodies, extraneous to himself.
>
> *Sight* gives him an idea of proportion, and enables him to adjust his movements to the movements of others.
>
> *Taste* gives him an idea of value, and enables him to fix upon that which to him appears best.
>
> *Smell* gives him an idea of innate quality, and enables him to find that which appeals to him as of the same quality or essence as himself.

In all these definitions it is necessary to bear in mind *that the whole object of the senses is to reveal the notself, and to enable the Self therefore to differentiate between the real and the unreal.*[82]

[82] Sensations aroused by sense objects are experienced by means of the outer instruments of the Lord of the Body or senses (*Indriya*) which are the pathways through which the Jiva receives worldly experience. These are ten in number, and are of two classes:

a. The five organs of sensation..........*Jnanendriya*

      1. The Ear ....Hearing.
      2. Skin ....Feeling by touch.
      3. Eye ....Sight.
      4. Tongue ....Taste.
      5. Nose ....Smell.

b. The five organs of action............*Karmendriya*

      1. Mouth ....Speaking.
      2. Hands ....Grasping.
      3. Legs ....Walking.
      4. Anus ....Excretion.
      5. Genitals ....Procreation.

The organs of sensation are the reactive response which the Self makes to sensation. The organs of action are those through which effect is given to the Jiva's desires.

"The Indriya or sense is not the physical organ, but the faculty of mind operating through that organ as its instrument. The outward sense organs are the usual means whereby on the physical plane the functions of hearing

In the evolution of the senses, hearing is the first vague something which calls the attention of the apparently blind self

   a. To another vibration.
   b. To something originating outside of itself.
   c. To the concept of externality. When sound is first contacted the consciousness for the first time becomes aware of that which is without.

But all that is grasped by the dormant consciousness (by means of this one sense of hearing) is the fact of something extraneous to itself, and of the direction in which that something lies. This apprehension, in course of time, calls into being another sense, that of touch. The Law of Attraction works, the consciousness moves slowly outwards towards that which is heard; and when contact is made with the not-self it is called touch. This touch conveys other ideas to the groping consciousness, ideas of size, of external texture, and of surface differences; the concept of the Thinker is thus slowly enlarged. He can hear and feel, but as yet knows not enough to correlate nor name. When he succeeds in naming, he has made a big stride forward. We might note here, therefore, that the earliest cosmic symbols are applicable to the senses as well as elsewhere:

The point in the centre—consciousness and the not-self at a stage where sound alone is descriptive.
The divided circle—consciousness aware of the not-self, through a dual recognition.

and so forth are accomplished. But, as they are mere instruments and their power is derived from the mind, a Yogi may accomplish by the mind only all that may be done by means of these physical organs without the use of the latter. . . .
"The three functions of *attention, selection* and *synthesising* the discreet manifold of the senses, are those belonging to that aspect of the mental body, the internal agent, called *Manas.* Just as manas is necessary to the senses, the latter are necessary for manas. . . . Manas is thus the leading indriya, of which the senses are powers."—*Serpent Power,* by Arthur Avalon.

Sight follows on this, the third sense, and the one definitely marking the correlation of ideas, or the relation between; it parallels the coming of Mind, both in time and function. We have hearing, touch or feeling, and then sight. In connection with the correspondence it is to be noted that sight came in with the third root-race in this round, and that the third race saw also the coming in of Mind. The Self and the not-self were immediately correlated, and co-ordinated. Their close partnership became an accomplished fact, and evolution hastened forward with renewed impetus.

These three major senses (if I might so describe them) are very definitely allied, each with one of the three Logoi:

Hearing—The recognition of the fourfold word, the activity of matter, the third Logos.

Touch—The recognition of the sevenfold Form Builder, the gathering together of forms, their approximation and interrelation, the second Logos. The Law of Attraction between the Self and the not-self begins to work.

Sight—The recognition of totality, the synthesis of all, the realisation of the One in Many, the first Logos. The Law of Synthesis, operating between all forms which the self occupies, and the recognition of the essential unity of all manifestation by the means of sight.

As regards *taste* and *smell,* we might call them minor senses, for they are closely allied to the important sense of touch. They are practically subsidiary to that sense. This second sense, and its connection with this second solar system, should be carefully pondered over. It is predominantly the sense most closely connected with the second Logos. This conveys a hint of much value if duly considered. It is of value to study the extensions of physical plane touch on other planes and to see whither we are led. It is the faculty which enables us to arrive at the essence by due recognition of the veiling sheath. It enables the Thinker who fully utilises it to put himself *en rapport* with the essence of all selves at all stages, and thereby to aid in the due evolution of the sheath and actively to serve. A Lord of Compassion is one who (by means of touch) feels with, fully comprehends, and realises the manner in which to heal and correct the inadequacies of the not-self and thus actively to serve the plan of evolution. We should study likewise in this connection the value of touch as demonstrated by the healers of the race (those on the Bodhisattva line) [83] and the effect of the Law of Attraction and Repulsion as thus manipulated by them. Students of etymology will have noted that the origin of the word *touch* is somewhat obscure, but probably means to 'draw with quick motion.' Herein lies the whole secret of this objective solar system, and herein will be demonstrated the quickening of vibration by means of touch. Inertia, mobility, rhythm, are the qualities manifested by the not-self. Rhythm, balance, and stable vibration are achieved by means of this very faculty of touch or feeling. Let me illustrate briefly so as to make the problem somewhat clearer. What results in meditation? By dint of strenuous effort and due attention to rules laid down, the aspirant succeeds in touching matter of a quality rarer than is his usual custom. He contacts his causal body, in time he contacts the matter of the buddhic plane. By means of this touch his own vibration is temporarily and briefly quickened. Fundamentally we are brought back to the subject that we deal with in this treatise. The latent fire of matter attracts to itself that fire, latent in other forms. They touch, and recognition and awareness ensues. The fire of manas burns continuously and is fed by that which is attracted and repulsed. When the two

[83] The line of the Bodhisattva is that of Love-Wisdom, and of the detailed science of the soul; it is the teaching line and the path upon which all must eventually pass.

blend, the stimulation is greatly increased and the ability to touch intensified. The Law of Attraction persists in its work until another fire is attracted and touched, and the threefold merging is completed. Forget not in this connection the mystery of the Rod of Initiation.[84] Later when we consider the subject of the centres and Initiation it must be remembered that we are definitely studying one aspect of this mysterious faculty of touch, the faculty of the second Logos, wielding the law of Attraction.

Let us now finish what may be imparted on the remaining three senses—sight, taste, smell—and then briefly sum up their relationship to the centres, and their mutual action and interaction. That will then leave two more points to be dealt with in this first division of the Treatise on Cosmic Fire, and a summing up. We shall then be in a position to take up that portion of the treatise that deals with the fire of manas and with the development of the manasaputras,[85] both in their totality and likewise individually. This topic is of the most imperative importance as it deals entirely with man, the Ego, the thinker, and shows the cosmic blending of the fires of matter and of mind, and their utilisation by the indwelling Flame.

c. Sight. This sense, as said before, is the paramount correlating sense of the solar system.

Under the Law of Economy man hears. Sound permeates matter and is the basis of its subsequent heterogeneity.

Under the Law of Attraction, man touches and makes contact with that which is brought to his attention

---

[84] The Initiations spoken of in this Treatise are the major Initiations which bring about those expansions of consciousness which lead to liberation; these are taken in the causal body and from thence reflected into the physical; the Initiate never proclaims his initiation.

[85] *Manasaputras:* These are the Sons of Mind, the individual principle in man, the Ego, the solar Angel, in his own body on the abstract levels of the mental plane.

through sound waves of activity. This leads to a condition of mutual repulsion and attraction between the one who apprehends and that which is apprehended.

Having apprehended and then contacted his eyes are opened and he recognises his place in the whole order under the Law of Synthesis.

> Hearing............. Unity
> Touch............... Duality
> Sight............... Triplicity.

In these three senses the present is summed up for us. The work of evolution is to recognise, utilise, co-ordinate, and dominate the whole till the Self, by means of these three, becomes actively aware of every form, of every vibration, and of every pulsation of the not-self; then, through the arranging power of mind, the objective of the self will be to find the truth, or that centre in the circle of manifestation which is, for the Self, the centre of equilibrium, and the one point where the co-ordination is perfected; then the Self can dissociate itself from every veil, every contact, and every sense. This leads in every manifestation to three types of separation:

Involution. The separation of matter, or the one becoming the many. The senses are developed, and the apparatus is perfected by the Self for the utilisation of matter. This is under the Law of Economy.

Evolution up to the time of the Probationary Path. The merging of Spirit and matter, and the utilisation of the senses in a progressing identification of the Self with all forms from the lowest to those relatively refined. This is under the Law of Attraction.

Evolution on the Path. Again the separation of spirit from matter, its identification with the One, and the ultimate rejection of form. The senses then are synthesised into acquired faculty, and the Self has no further use for the not-self. It blends with the All-Self. This is under the Law of Synthesis.

If this is borne in mind it leads to a realisation that the separation of the Spirit from the material vehicle involves two aspects of the One great All; herein is seen the work of the Creator, the Preserver and the Destroyer.

In the final perfection of this third sense of sight, the term used is the wholly inadequate one of *realisation*. Let the student study carefully the lowest and highest demonstration of the senses as laid down in the tabulation earlier imparted, and note the occult significance of the expressions used in the summation.

Hearing	Beatitude.	This is realised through the not-self.
Touch	Service.	The summation of the work of the Self for the not-self.
Sight	Realisation.	Recognition of the triplicity needed in manifestation, or the reflex action of the Self and the not-self.
Taste	Perfection.	Evolution completed through the utilisation of the not-self and its realised adequacy.
Smell	Perfected Knowledge.	The principle of manas in its discriminating activity, perfecting the inter-relation between the Self and the not-self.

This all concerns the perfected, realised Personality.

In all these perfections is seen the *awareness* of the Self, and the graded process of identification, utilisation, manipulation and final rejection of the not-self by that Self who is now consciously aware. He hears the note of nature and that of his monad; he recognises their identity, utilises their vibration, and passes rapidly through the three stages of Creator, Preserver and Destroyer.

He *touches* or feels the vibration of the form or not-self in all its various grades, recognises his identity in time and space, and for purposes of existence or being and by means of the three Laws of Economy, Attraction and Synthesis utilises, blends and eventually dissociates himself. He *sees* the threefold evolutionary process and by means of the development of the inner vision, sees within the heart of the system macrocosmic and microcosmic, the one SELF in many forms, and finally identifies himself with that one Self by the conscious rejection of the not-self after its complete subjugation and utilisation.

d. Tasting. He *tastes* then finally and discriminates, for taste is the great sense that begins to hold sway during the discriminating process that takes place when the illusory nature of matter is in process of realisation. Discrimination is the educatory process to which the Self subjects itself in the process of developing intuition —that faculty whereby the Self recognises its own essence in and under all forms. Discrimination concerns the duality of nature, the Self and the not-self, and is the means of their differentiation in the process of abstraction; the intuition concerns unity and is the capacity of the Self to contact other selves, and is not a faculty whereby the not-self is contacted. Hence, its rarity these days owing to the intense individualisation of the Ego, and its identification with the form—a necessary identification at this particular time. As the sense of taste on the higher planes is developed, it leads one to ever finer distinctions till one is finally led through the form, right to the heart of one's nature.

e. Smelling is the faculty of keen perception that eventually brings a man back to the source from whence he came, the archetypal plane, the plane where his true home is to be found. A perception of difference has been cultivated that has caused a divine discontent within the

heart of the Pilgrim in the far country; the prodigal
son draws comparisons; he has developed the other four
senses, and he utilises them. Now comes in the faculty
of vibratory recognition of the *home vibration,* if it might
be so expressed. It is the spiritual counterpart of that
sense which in the animal, the pigeon and other birds,
leads them back unerringly to the familiar spot from
whence they originally came. It is the apprehension of
the vibration of the Self, and a swift return by means
of that instinct to the originating source.

The consideration of this subject awakens the realisation of the vastness of the region of thought concerned—
the region of the whole evolutionary development of the
human being. Yet all that is possible here, as elsewhere,
is to indicate lines of thought for careful pondering, and
to emphasise certain ideas which may serve as the foundation thoughts for the future mental activity of the immediate generation. The following facts must also be
borne in mind when considering the matter:

a. That the senses have been dealt with in this division of our Treatise on Cosmic Fire because they concern
the material form. Strictly speaking the five senses,
as we know them, are the means of contact built up by the
Thinker (polarised in his etheric body) and find their
expression in the physical form in those nerve centres,
brain cells, ganglia and plexus which exoteric science
recognises.

b. That these senses for all purposes of present manifestation, have their focal point on the astral plane and
are therefore largely under the stimulating action of the
solar plexus—that great focal point in the centre of the
body which is the stimulating agent for most of the human family at this time.

c. That as the higher triangle comes into play and the
polarisation steps up to the higher centres, the senses
begin to make themselves felt on the mental level and

man becomes *aware* on that plane. We have in the human body an interesting reflection of the transference of the polarisation from the Personality to the Ego, or into the causal body, in the division that exists between the higher and the lower mental planes, and the dividing line of the diaphragm between the higher and the lower portions of the body. Below the diaphragm we have the four lower centres:

1. The solar plexus.
2. The spleen.
3. Organs of generation.
4. Base of the spine.

Above are the three higher:

1. Heart.
2. Throat.
3. Head.

In the microcosm we have the lower quaternary separated from the Triad in a similar manner, and this analogy will bear pondering upon. By careful thought we can therefore work out the reflex action of the centres and the senses from the standpoint of the different planes, remembering that as the centres are awakened the process will be threefold:

First. The awakening on the physical plane, and the gradually increasing activity of the centres, until the Probationary Path is reached. This is paralleled by the increasing use of the senses, and their constant utilisation for the identification of the self and its sheaths.

Second. The awakening on the astral plane, and the gradually increasing activity of the centres, until the first Initiation is reached. This is paralleled by the tremendously keen use of the senses for the purposes of discriminating between the Self and the not-self.

Third. The awakening upon the mental plane, and the gradually increasing activity of the centres and the senses. The effect in both cases tends to identification of the Self with its own essence in all groups and the rejection of the sheaths and the forms.

This development is paralleled on the two higher planes simultaneously as in the lower, and as the astral senses come into perfected activity, the corresponding centres of force on the buddhic plane begin to function until the vibratory interplay between the two is consummated, and the force of the Triad can be felt definitely in the Personality via the astral.

Again the corresponding vortices on the atmic level come into active vibration as the mental centres become fourth dimensional, till we have a wonderful fiery activity demonstrating on all the three planes.

From the point of view of *fire*,[86] leaving the aura and

---

[86] The Fire of the manifested cosmos is Septenary.
The Threefold God manifests through the seven Fires:

1. Electric fire ....The seven Heavenly Men.
2. Solar fire ....Evolution of the seven Entities through their vehicles developing the seven principles.
3. Fire by friction ....The seven chains.
They are the seven centres of the Logos.
A Heavenly Man manifests through a chain.
1. He is electric fire ....The seven solar entities who inform each globe.
2. He is solar fire ....Evolution of the life through the forms, developing the seven principles.
3. He is fire by friction ....The seven globes.

Each Heavenly Man has seven principles.
A Man, the Microcosm, manifests through his vehicles:

1. He is electric fire ....The monad, a solar entity.
2. He is solar fire ....Evolution of the life through the vehicles in order to develop the seven principles.
3. He is fire by friction ......The seven sheaths:
    1. Atmic ....2. Buddhic.
    3. Causal ....4. Mental body.
    5. Astral body ....6. Etheric body.
        7. Physical body.

its colors out of temporary consideration, the evolutionary development marks an equally definite process.

  a. The vivification of the inner heat of the sheaths, or
  the tiny point of fire latent in every individual atom
  of matter. This process proceeds in all three bodies, at first slowly, then more rapidly, and finally
  simultaneously and synthetically.

  b. The bringing into activity from latency of the seven
  centres on all planes, beginning from the bottom
  upwards, until the centres (according to ray and
  type) are interrelated and co-ordinated. There are
  manifest thirty-five vortices of fire in the perfected adept,—all of radiant activity and all interacting.

  c. The vortices or wheels of lambent flame become in-
  terlinked by triangles of fire which pass and circulate from one to another, till we have a web of fiery
  lines, uniting centres of living fire, and giving truth
  to the statement that the Sons of Mind are
  FLAMES.

  d. These centres reach this condition of perfection as
  the Spirit or Will aspect takes ever fuller control.
  The unifying triangles are produced by the action of
  the fire of mind, while the fire of matter holds the
  form together in ordered sequence. So the interdependence of matter, mind and Spirit can be seen and
  demonstrates to the eye of the clairvoyant as the
  co-ordination of the three fires.

  e. In the Heavenly Man and His body, a chain of
  globes[87] likewise can be seen and we need here to re-

Physical Plane man manifests in the three worlds:
  1. Electric fire ....The higher self.
  2. Solar fire ....The seven centres.
  3. Fire by friction ....The sheaths.
[87] The Planetary Chains:
The seven Heavenly Men.........Form, the sun and the seven sacred
                              planets.—S. D., I, 100, 155.

member very carefully that the seven chains of a scheme are the expression of a planetary Logos. The Heavenly Men are expressing Themselves through a scheme of seven chains and the emphasis has been laid unduly, perhaps, upon the dense physical planet in any particular chain. This has caused the fact of the *chain* importance to be somewhat overlooked. Each of the seven chains might be looked upon as picturing the seven centres of one of the Heavenly Men. The idea of groups of Egos forming centres in the Heavenly Men is nevertheless correct, but in this connection the reference is to the centres of force on buddhic and monadic levels.[88]

Some of their names and qualities.

  a. The seven planetary Logoi, or the seven Spirits before the throne.
  b. The seven Kumaras ....S. D., III, 59, 327.
  c. Seven solar deities ....S. D., I, 114; I, 228; II, 92, 257.
  d. The primordial seven........S. D., I, 116.
  e. The seven Builders ....S. D., I, 152, 153.
  f. Seven intellectual Breaths....S. D., II, 332, note.
  g. The seven Manus ....S. D., I, 488.
  h. The Flames ....S. D., II, 258.
   They came from previous kalpasS. D., II, 99.
   Their nature is knowledge and love.
                           S. D., II, 275; S. D., II, 619.

The seven sacred planets are:

  1. Saturn ....2. Jupiter.
  3. Mars ....4. Sun (substitute for another).
  5. Venus ....6. Mercury.
              7. Moon (substitute for another).

Neptune and Uranus are not here enumerated, nor Vulcan.
The orbit of Neptune includes apparently the entire ring-pass-not.
Vulcan is within the orbit of Mercury.
Each one of the Heavenly Men manifests through a chain of seven globes. All the seven Logoi influence a chain, but one of Them is the incarnating Entity. They influence:

  a. Some globe in chain...b. Some plane ......c. Some round.
  d. Some world period ....e. Some rootrace ....f. Some subrace.
  g. Some branch race .....h. Some group ......i. Some human unit.

[88] In the *Secret Doctrine*, the Sons of Mind are spoken of as flames. In Stanza VII, 4, "These are the three-tongued flame of the four wicks. The wicks are the sparks, that draw from the three-tongued flame shot out by the seven flames. The spark hangs from the flame by the finest thread of Fohat."

In connection with this there is a fundamental point that must never be forgotten: these seven Heavenly Men might be considered as being in physical incarnation through the medium of a physical planet, and herein lies the mystery of planetary evolution. Herein lies the mystery of our planet, the most mysterious of all the planets. Just as the karma of individuals differs, so differs the karma of the various Logoi, and the karma of our planetary Logos has been a heavy one, and veiled in the mystery of personality at this time.

Again, according as the centres are active or inactive, so the manifestation differs likewise, and the study which opens up is of vast and abstruse interest in connection with the solar system.

5. *The Centres and Initiation*

We have dealt briefly with the evolution of the centres, with their function, their organisation and their gradually increasing activity from a point of comparative inertia until they are consummated motion. Then they become living wheels of flame, distinguished by a dual motion of the periphery and the inner revolving wheels, and by a fourth-dimensional effect, due primarily to the alignment of the inner subtler vortices with the comparatively exoteric etheric centres. This alignment is brought about eventually at initiation.

At the time that initiation is taken, the centres are all active and the lower four (which correspond to the Personality) are beginning the process of translating the fire into the three higher. The dual revolution in the lower centres is clearly to be seen and the three higher are commencing to be similarly active. By the application of the Rod of Initiation at the time of the initiation ceremony, certain results are achieved in connection with the centres which might be enumerated as follows:

a. The fire at the base of the spine is definitely di-

rected to whichever centre is the object of special attention. This varies according to the Ray, or the specialised work of the initiate.

b. The centre has its activity intensified, its rate of
evolution increased, and certain of the central spokes of
the wheel brought into more active radiance. These
spokes which are also called by some students lotus-
petals, have a close connection with the different spirillae in the permanent atoms. Through their stimulation
there comes into play one or more of the corresponding
spirillae in the permanent atoms on the three lower
planes. After the third Initiation, a corresponding
stimulation takes place in the permanent atoms of the
Triad, leading to the co-ordination of the buddhic vehicle, and the transference of the lower polarisation into
the higher.

c. By the application of the Rod of Initiation the
downflow of force from the Ego to the personality is
tripled, the direction of that force being dependent upon
whether the centres receiving attention are the etheric,
or the astral at the first and second Initiations, or whether
the initiate is standing before the LORD OF THE WORLD.
In the latter case, his mental centres or their corresponding force vortices on higher levels, will receive stimulation. When the World Teacher initiates at the first and
second Initiations, the direction of the Triadal force is
turned to the vivification of the heart, and throat centres,
and the ability to synthesise the force of the lower centres is greatly increased. When the One Initiator applies
the Rod of His Power, the downflow is from the Monad,
and though the throat and heart intensify vibration as
a response, the main direction of the force is to the seven
head centres, and finally (at liberation) to the radiant
head centre above, and synthesising the lesser seven
head centres.

d. The centres at initiation receive a fresh access of

vibratory capacity and of power, and this results, in
the exoteric life, as:

First. A sensitiveness and refinement cf the vehicles
which may result, at first, in much suffering to the
initiate, but which produces a capacity to respond
to contacts that far outweighs the incidental pain.

Second. A development of psychic faculty that again
may lead to temporary distress, but which eventually causes a recognition of the one Self in all selves,
which is the goal of endeavor.

Third. A burning away, through a gradual arousing
of kundalini, and its correct geometrical progression through the etheric web. This produces a resultant continuity of consciousness which enables
the initiate consciously to utilise *time* as a factor in
the plans of evolution.

Fourth. A gradual grasp of the Law of Vibration as
an aspect of the basic law of building; the initiate
learns consciously to build, to manipulate thought
matter for the perfecting of the plans of the Logos,
to work in mental essence, and to apply the law on
mental levels and thereby affect the physical plane.
Motion originates cosmically on cosmic mental levels, and in the microcosm the same order will be
seen. There is an occult hint here that will reveal
much if pondered upon. At initiation, at the moment of the application of the Rod, the initiate *consciously* realises the meaning of the Law of Attraction in form building, and in the synthesis of the
three fires. Upon his ability to retain that realisation and himself to apply the law, will depend his
power and progress.

e. By the application of the Rod, the fire of kundalini is aroused, and its upward progress directed. The
fire at the base of the spine, and the fire of mind are

directed along certain routes, or triangles, by the action of the Rod as it moves in a specified manner. There is a definite occult reason, under the Laws of Electricity, behind the known fact that every initiate, presented to the Initiator, is accompanied by two of the Masters, who stand one on either side of him. The three of them together form a triangle which makes the work possible.

The force of the Rod is twofold, and its power terrific. Apart and alone the initiate could not receive the voltage from the Rod without serious hurt, but in triangular formation transmission comes safely. The two Masters Who thus sponsor the initiate, represent two polarities of the electric All; part of Their work is therefore to stand with all applicants for initiation when they come before the Great Lord.

When the Rods of Initiation are held in the hands of the Initiator in His position of power, and at the stated seasons, they act as transmitters of electric force from very high levels,—so high indeed that the "Flaming Diamond" at certain of the final initiations (the sixth and seventh) transmits force, via the Logos, from outside the system altogether. We need to remember that this major Rod is the one used on this planet, but that within the system there are several such Rods of Power, and that they are to be found in three grades, if it may be so expressed.

First. The Rod of Initiation used for the first two initiations and wielded by the Great Lord, the Christ, the World Teacher. It is magnetised by application of the "Flaming Diamond"—the magnetisation being repeated when each new world Teacher takes office. There is a wonderful ceremony performed at the time that a new World Teacher takes up His work. During the ceremony He receives His Rod of Power—the same Rod as used since the foundation of our planetary Hierarchy—and holds it forth to the Lord of the World, Who touches it with His own mighty Rod, causing a fresh re-charging of its electric capacity. This ceremony takes place at Shamballa.[89, 90]

Second. The Rod of Initiation known as the "Flaming Diamond" and used by Sanat Kumara, the One Initiator, called in the Bible, the Ancient of Days. This Rod lies hidden "in the East" and holds the fire latent which irradiates the Wisdom Religion. This Rod was brought by the Lord of the World when He took form and came to our planet eighteen million years ago.

Once in every world period it is subjected to a similar process as that of the lesser Rod, only this time it is recharged by the direct action of the Logos Himself,— the Logos of the solar system. The location of this Rod is known only to the Lord of the World, and to the Chohans of the Rays, and (being the talisman of this evolution) the Chohan of the second Ray is—under the Lord of the World—its main guardian, aided by the deva Lord of the second plane. The Buddhas of activity are responsible for its custody, and under them the Chohan of the Ray. It is produced only at stated times when specific work has to be done. It is used not only at the initiating of men, but at certain planetary functions, of which nothing as yet has been given out. It has its place and function in certain ceremonies connected with the inner round [91] and the triangle formed by the Earth Mars

[89] *Shamballa*—The Sacred Island in the Gobi desert. The centre in central Asia where the Lord of the World, the Ancient of Days, has His Headquarters. H. P. B. says it is "a very mysterious locality on account of its future associations."—S. D., II, 413.

[90] *The World Teacher*—takes office cyclically. His cycles do not coincide with those of the Manu as the Manu holds office for the entire rootrace. The World Teacher gives out the keynote for the various religions and is the emanating source for periodical religious impulses. The duration of his cycles are not given out. The Buddha held office prior to the present World Teacher and upon his Illumination His place was taken by the Lord Maitreya whom the Occidentals call the Christ.

[91] *The inner round* is a mysterious cycle of which little can be told. It is not concerned with manifestation through the seven schemes or globes, but has to do with certain aspects of the subjective Life or the soul.

and Mercury. But more about this is not at this time permissible.

Third. The Rod of Initiation, wielded by the Logos of the solar system, is called among other things, the "Sevenfold Flaming Fire." It was confided to our Logos by the Lord of Sirius and sent to our system from that radiant sun. One of its purposes is for use in emergencies. This great talisman has never yet been employed in this particular manner, though twice it was nearly thus used,—once in Atlantean days, and once in the third year of the late war. This Rod of Power is used at the initiation of the seven Heavenly Men on cosmic levels. It is used also in the initiation of *groups,* a thing almost incomprehensible to us. It is applied to the centres of the seven Heavenly Men in the same general way as the lesser Rods are applied to the human centres, and the effects are the same, only on a vaster scale. This, needless to say, is a vast and abstruse subject, and concerns not the sons of men. It is but touched upon, as an enumeration of the Rods of Initiation would be incomplete without some reference to it, and it serves to show the wondrous synthesis of the whole, and the place of the system within an even greater scheme. In all things cosmic, perfect law and order are found, and the ramifications of the plan can be seen on all planes and all subplanes. This greatest Rod is in the care of the first great group of karmic Lords. It might be described as the Rod which carries a voltage of pure fohatic force from cosmic levels. The two lesser Rods carry differentiated fohatic force. This logoic Rod of Power is kept within the Sun, and is only re-charged at the beginning of every one hundred years of Brahma.

The reason why the Rods of Power are here discussed is that they have definitely to do with the centres which **are** *force vortices in matter* and which (though channels for spiritual force, or centres wherein the 'will to be' finds expression) demonstrate as activity in matter. They are the centres of existence, and just as one cannot, in manifestation, dissociate the two poles of Spirit and matter, so one cannot, in initiation apply the Rod without bringing about definite effects between the two. The Rods are charged with Fohat which is fire of matter plus electric fire, hence their effect. The mystery cannot be explained in greater detail as the secrets of initiation are not transmissible. More has been here imparted on this matter than hitherto, though there are those who have heard these things.

SECTION ONE

DIVISION F

THE LAW OF ECONOMY

I. Its effect in matter.

      ·1. Dissociation of atoms.
      2. Distribution of atoms.
      3. Vibratory rhythm.
      4. Heterogeneity.
      5. Inherent rotary activity.

II. Its subsidiary laws.

      1. The law of vibration.
      2. The law of adaptation.
      3. The law of repulsion.
      4. The law of friction.

I. ITS EFFECT IN MATTER

THIS law is the law governing the matter aspect of manifestation, and is the law characterising the work of the third Logos, and of the entities who are the embodiment of His will and the agents of His purposes. Each of the great cosmic Entities who take form as the three Logoi, is distinguished by different methods of activity, which might be described thus:

The third Aspect or Brahma aspect of the activities of those Entities who are His expression, is characterised by that method in the distribution of matter which we call the Law of Economy. It is the law governing the scattering of the atoms of matter and their dissociation from one another, wide distribution, vibratory rhythm,

214

heterogeneity and quality and their inherent rotary action. This Law of Economy causes matter always to follow the line of least resistance, and is the basis of the separative action of atomic matter. It governs matter, the opposite pole of spirit.

The second Aspect, the building, or Vishnu aspect, is governed by the Law of Attraction; the activities of the entities who embody this aspect are directed to the attracting of matter to Spirit, and the gradual approximation of the two poles. It results in cohesion, in the production of congeries of atoms in various formations, and this attraction is brought about by the attractive power of Spirit itself. It shows itself in:

1. Association,
2. Form building,
3. Adaptation of form to vibration,
4. Relative homogeneity of group unity,
5. Cyclic spiralling movement.

The line of least resistance is not the law for this aspect. The attractive power of Spirit in form-building, and in the adaptation of the form to the need, is the secret of the pain and resistance in the world; pain is only caused by resistance, and is a necessary phase in the process of evolution. This law of attraction is the law governing the Spirit, the opposite pole of matter.

The first Aspect, or the will to exist, is governed by the Law of Synthesis, and the activities of the cosmic entities who are its embodiments are governed by the law of enforced unity, and of essential homogeneity. It is the law that eventually comes into play after spirit and matter are blending, and adapting themselves each to each; it governs the eventual synthesis of Self with Self, and finally with the All-Self, and also of essence with essence in contra-distinction to the synthesis of matter and Spirit. It demonstrates as:

1. Abstraction,
2. Spiritual liberation,
3. Destruction of form through the withdrawal of Spirit (the Destroyer aspect)
4. Absolute homogeneity and absolute essential unity,
5. Progressive forward motion.

Thus can be seen the wonderful synthesis brought about by the evolutionary working of these three cosmic laws, —*each of them embodying the mode of work of certain cosmic Entities or Existences.* The final two will be taken up in their right place. Now we will touch but briefly upon the law of matter, that of Economy.

This is the law that lies back of what has been mistakenly called "The Fall" by religious writers, by which is defined in reality the involutionary process, cosmically considered. It led to a sevenfold differentiation in the matter of the system. Just as the Law of Attraction led to the sevenfold psychic differentiation of the Sons of Mind, and the Law of Synthesis results in the sevenfold perfection of the same Manasaputras, so we have an interesting connection between

The seven planes, or the seven grades of matter.
The seven Heavenly Men, the seven Divine Manasaputras, or the seven types of wisdom-love.
The seven qualities of wisdom, which are produced by the cosmic entities, the Kumaras by the aid of knowledge through the medium of matter.

This Law of Economy has several subsidiary laws which govern its effects on the different grades of matter. As said before, this is the Law swept into action by the sounds as uttered by the Logos. The Sacred Word, or the uttered Sound of the Creator, exists in different forms, and though in reality but one Word, has several syllables. The syllables all together form a solar phrase; separated they form certain words of power, producing different effects.[92]

The great WORD that peals through one hundred years of Brahma or persists in reverberation throughout a solar system, is the sacred sound of A U M. In differentiation and as heard in time and space, each of those three mystic letters stands for the first letter of a subsidiary phrase, consisting of various sounds. One letter, with a sequence of four sounds, makes up the vibration or note of Brahma, which is the intelligence aspect dominant in matter. Hence the mystery hidden in

[92] . . . "the Veda, the world song in human sound that was given to man for his use metaphysically from the standpoint of its meaning, and magically from the standpoint of its proper recitation. The world song obeying certain laws of proportions or the Pythagorean arithmetic and imparting its thrilling effect to the domain of cosmic substance, has induced the latter into a crystallisation process that the philosopher Plato called the geometry of the cosmos. The various forms that are observed from a molecule of salt crystal to the wonderfully complex organism of the human body are all the structures of the great cosmic geometriser known as Viswakarma, the deva carpenter in our Puranic writings. The revealed Veda whose function is to trace out the cosmos from one basic sound substance symbolised as Om, necessarily split itself into a primal three, a subsequent seven vowels and then into seven notes and then into seven combinations of the seven notes on a basic three and then into hymns. All these falling into the material field of the consonants, gradually produced the manifested crystallised forms which are collectively taken as the universe. The world to a thinker is the magic motion produced by the Orphean singer or the Hindu Saraswati. . . ."

"In the Vishnu Purana, second part, you will see that the power that resides in the sun is represented as the three-sided Vedic power, that the power as Rik creates, as Yajus preserves and as Sama destroys. Rik is therefore the creative song of the Devas in the Sun. Yajus the song of preservation and Sama the song of destruction of the Devas in the sun and construction of the Devas in the moon. Rik therefore is the song of the Devas and Sama the song of the Pitris and Yajua the intermediate song. The functions of the Vedas must of course vary according to the standpoint. If you take the Pitris, Sama is their constructive song, and Rik is their destructive note. The three Vedas correspond to every trinity in Nature and I request you will search for further information in the much abused Puranas. . . ."

"Of the various karmic agencies wielded by man in the way of moulding himself and surroundings, sound or speech is the most important, for, to speak is to work in ether which of course rules the lower quaternary or elements, air, fire, water and earth. Human sound or language contains therefore all the elements required to move the different classes of Devas and those elements are of course the vowels and the consonants. The details of the philosophy of sound in its relation to the devas who preside over the subtle world, belong to the domain of true Mantra Sastra which of course is in the hands of the knowers."—From *Some Thoughts on the Gita.*

the pentagon, in the fifth principle of mind, and in the five planes of human evolution. These five letters when sounded forth on the right note, give the key to the true inwardness of matter and also to its control,—this control being based on the right interpretation of the Law of Economy.

Another phrase, this time of seven letters, or a letter for each of the seven Heavenly Men, embodies the sound or note of the Vishnu aspect, the second aspect logoic, the form-building aspect. By its correct or partial sounding, by its complete or incomplete reverberation, are the forms built and adapted. The Law of Attraction finds expression in the manipulation of matter and its welding into form for the use of Spirit.

Then a third Word or phrase is added to the other two, completing the entire Word logoic and producing consummation. It is a Word of nine letters, making therefore the twenty-one sounds $(5 + 7 + 9)$ of this solar system. The final nine sounds produce spiritual synthesis, and the dissociation of the spirit from the form. We have a correspondence in the nine Initiations, each initiation marking a more perfect union of the Self with the All-Self, and a further liberation from the trammels of matter.

When the sense of hearing on all planes is perfected (which is brought about by the Law of Economy rightly understood) these three great Words or phrases will be *known*. The Knower will utter them in his own true key, thus blending his own sound with the entire volume of vibration, and thereby achieving sudden realisation of his essential identity with Those Who utter the words. As the sound of matter or of Brahma peals forth in his ears on all the planes, he will see all forms as illusion and will be freed, knowing himself as omnipresent. As the sound of Vishnu reverberates within himself, he knows himself as perfected wisdom, and distinguishes the note of his being (or that of the Heavenly Man in whose Body he finds place) from the group notes, and knows himself as omniscient. As the note of the first or Mahadeva aspect, follows upon the other two, he realises himself as pure Spirit and on the consummation of the chord is merged in the Self, or the source from which he came. Mind is not, matter is not, and nought is left but the Self merged in the ocean of the Self. At each stage of relative attainment, one of the laws comes into sway, --first the law of matter, then the law of groups, to be succeeded by the law of Spirit and of liberation.

II. THE SUBSIDIARY LAWS

The subsidiary laws under the Law of Economy are four in number, dealing with the lower quaternary:

1. *The Law of Vibration,* dealing with the key note or measure of the matter of each plane. By knowledge of this law the material of any plane in its seven divisions can be controlled.

2. *The Law of Adaptation,* is the law governing the rotary movement of any atom on every plane and subplane.

3. *The Law of Repulsion,* governs that relationship between atoms, which results in their non-attachment and in their complete freedom from each other; it also keeps them rotating at fixed points from the globe or sphere of opposite polarity.

4. *The Law of Friction,* governs the heat aspect of any atom, the radiation of an atom, and the effect of that radiation on any other atom.

Every atom of matter can be studied in four aspects, and is governed by one or other, or all of the four above mentioned laws.

a. An atom vibrates to a certain measure.

b. It rotates at a certain speed.

   c. It acts and reacts upon its environing atoms.
   d. It adds its quota to the general heat of the atomic
      system, whatever that may be.

These general rules relating to atomic bodies can be extended not only to the atoms of the physical plane, but to all spheroidal bodies within the system, and including the system also, regarding it as a cosmic atom.

The tiny atom of the physical plane, a plane itself, a planet, and a solar system all evolve under these rules, and all are governed by the Law of Economy in one of its four aspects.

It might be added in closing, that this law is one that initiates have to master before They can achieve liberation. They have to learn to manipulate matter, and to work with energy or force in matter under this law; they have to utilise matter and energy in order to achieve the liberation of Spirit, and to bring to fruition the purposes or the Logos in the evolutionary process.

SECTION TWO

SOLAR FIRE

(The Fire of Mind)

Introductory Questions.

SECTION TWO

INTRODUCTORY QUESTIONS

1. What is the relation of the Son to the Sun?
2. What is evolution, and how does it proceed?
3. Why is the solar system evolving along the lines of duality?
4. What is consciousness and what is its place in the scheme?
5. Is there a direct analogy between a system, a planet, man and an atom?
6. What is the mind aspect? Who are the Manasaputras?
7. Why is the progress of evolution cyclic?
8. Why is knowledge both exoteric and esoteric?
9. What is the relation between—

      a. The ten schemes,
      b. The seven sacred planets,
      c. The seven chains in a scheme,
      d. The seven globes in a chain,
      e. The seven rounds of a chain,
      f. The seven rootraces and subraces?

BEFORE taking up the subject of the fire of mind under the schedule already outlined, it might be of profit if certain facts are here pointed out, and one or two points clarified. The subject we are undertaking to elucidate is one of profound mystery, and is the basis of all that is now seen and known, both objectively and subjectively. We have somewhat studied that pole of manifestation called *matter*. The subject we are now entering upon concerns several things which might be considered in general terms as *Consciousness,* and in specified terms as including the following subjects,—hence its fundamental importance.

a. The science of objectivity.

b. The manifestation of the Son through the Sun and its attendant spheres, or the solar system in its entirety.

c. The evolutionary development of consciousness in time and space, therefore, the evolution of spirit and matter.

If the above three fundamentals are studied, it will be noted that they are very comprehensive, and, therefore, from the immensity of the theme, it will not be possible to do more than attempt to bring a general clarity of conception as to the broad outline of the process, and as to the gradual development of consciousness. For the sake of an intelligent following of this matter, it might be wise first to lay down a number of propositions which —(even if already known and appreciated)—will serve students as the scaffolding on which to erect the intended structure of knowledge. If a student of the Wisdom can grasp the nature of the general theme, he can then more easily and accurately fit the detailed information into its appropriate niche. Perhaps the best plan would be to formulate certain questions, and then proceed to answer them,—the answers to embody therefore the propositions that will be laid down. These questions arise naturally to the student of the *Secret Doctrine,* when he has reached the point where the big plan is becoming visible to him, but the pile of detailed material to be built in remains, as yet, inchoate. The questions we might ask and study are the following:

1. What is the relationship of the Son to the Sun?

2. What is evolution and how does it proceed?

3. Why is this solar system evolving along the lines of duality?

4. What is consciousness and what is its place in the present scheme of things?

5. Is there a direct analogy between the development of the following factors: a solar system, a planet, a man, and an atom?

6. What is the mind aspect and why is the manasic or mental principle of such importance? Who are the Manasaputras, or the Sons of Mind?

7. Why is the progress of evolution cyclic?

8. Why, as yet, do we consider certain knowledge as esoteric, and other aspects of knowledge as exoteric?

9. What is the relationship between
   a. The ten planetary schemes?
   b. The seven sacred planets?
   c. The seven globes in a chain?
   d. The seven rounds in a globe?
   e. The seven root races and the subraces?

When we have endeavored to answer in brief and concise fashion these nine questions, and have grasped, through their replies, something of the purpose lying behind the evolution of the consciousness of the Son (with all that is included in that expression) we shall be in a position to go more intelligently into a consideration of the plan, and to grasp more accurately the immediate stage ahead to be attained, working from our present standpoint as a basis.

We must ever remember that a curious interest and a far-seeing grasp of the plan of the Logos is of no importance to a man unless he correlates the present with that which he believes to lie in the future, unless he ascertains the point achieved, and realises wherein consists the work immediately to be undertaken in this gradual process of attaining full consciousness.

I. WHAT IS THE RELATIONSHIP OF THE SON TO THE SUN?

This question brings us primarily to a consideration as to Who is the Son, and what is His function. Two

CHART IV

CHART OF THE PLERÔMA ACCORDING TO VALENTINUS.

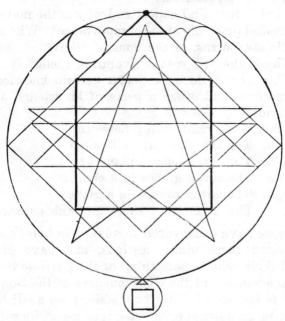

First the • (Point), the *Monad*, Bythus (the Deep), the unknown and unknowable Father. Then the △ (Triangle), Bythus and the first emanated pair or *Duad*, Nous (Mind) and its syzygy Aletheia (Truth). Then the ☐ (Square), the dual *Duad*, *Tetractys or Quaternary*, two males ||, the Logos (Word) and Anthrôpos (Man), two females, their syzygies, = Zoê (Life) and Ekklesia (the Church or Assembly), *Seven in all.* The Triangle the *Potentiality* of Spirit, the Square the *Potentiality* of Matter; the Vertical Straight Line the *Potency* of Spirit, and the Horizontal the *Potency* of Matter. Next comes the Pentagram ☆, the *Pentad*, the mysterious symbol of the Manasaputras or Sons of Wisdom, which together with their syzygies make 10, or the *Decad*; and last of all, the Hexalpha or interlaced Triangles ✡ the *Hexad*, which with their syzygies make 12, or the *Dodecad*. Such are the Contents of the Pleroma or Completion, the *Ideas* in the *Divine Mind*, 28 in all, for Bythus or the Father is not reckoned, as it is the *Root* of all. The two small circles *within* the Pleroma are the syzygy Christos-Pneuma (Christ and the Holy Spirit); these are *after*-emanations, and, as such, from one aspect, typify the descent of Spirit to inform and evolve Matter, which *essentially* proceeds from the same source; and from another, the descent or incarnation of the Kumâras or the Higher Egos of Humanity.

FROM "LUCIFER" FOR MAY, 1890.

factors are universally recognised in all systems that merit the name of philosophy; they are the two factors of spirit and matter, of purusha and prakriti. There is at times a tendency to confound such terms as "life and form," "consciousness and the vehicle of consciousness" with the terms "Spirit and matter." They are related, but clarity of view would be facilitated if it were realised that *prior to manifestation,* or to the birth of a solar system, it is more correct to utilise the words, Spirit and matter. When these two are inter-related *during manifestation,* and after the cessation of the pralayic interval or interlude between two systems, then the terms, life and form, consciousness and its vehicles, are more correct, for during the period of abstraction consciousness is not, form is not, and life, demonstrating as an actual principle, is not. There is Spirit-substance but in a state of quiescence, of utter neutrality, of negativity, and of passivity. In manifestation the two are approximated; they interact upon each other; activity supersedes quiescence; positivity replaces negativity; movement is seen in place of passivity, and the two primordial factors are no longer neutral to each other, but attract and repulse, interact and utilise. Then and only then, can we have form animated by life, and consciousness demonstrated through appropriate vehicles.

How can this be expressed? In terms of fire, when the two electric poles are brought into definite relationship we have demonstrated, along the line of occult sight and of occult feeling, both heat and light. This relationship is brought about and perfected during the evolutionary process. This heat and light are produced by the union of the two poles, or by the occult marriage of male and female, of Spirit (father) and matter (mother). In terms of the physical, this union produces the objective solar system, the Son of the Father and the Mother. In terms cf the subjective, it produces the Sun, as the sum total of the qualities of light and heat. In terms of fire, by the union or at-one-ment of electric fire (Spirit) and fire by friction (energised matter) solar fire is produced. This solar fire will be distinguished above all else by its evolutionary development, and by the gradual intensification of the heat to be felt, and of the light to be seen.

For a clearer comprehension of this abstract matter, we might consider the microcosm, or man evolving in the three worlds. Man is the product of the approximation (at present imperfect) of the two poles of Spirit (the Father in Heaven) and of matter (the Mother). The result of this union is an individualised Son of God, or unit of the divine Self, an exact replica in miniature on the lowest plane of the great Son of God, the All-Self, who is in Himself the totality of all the miniature sons, of all the individualised Selves, and of each and every unit. The microcosm, expressed in other terms or from the subjective point of view, is a miniature sun distinguished by the qualities of heat and light. At present that light is "under the bushel," or deeply hidden by a veil of matter, but in due process of evolution it will shine forth to such an extent that the veils will be lost from sight in a blaze of exceeding glory. At present the microcosmic heat is of small degree, or the magnetic radiation between the microcosmic units is but little *felt* (in the occult significance of the term), but as time proceeds, the emanations of heat,—due to intensification of the inner flame, coupled with the assimilated radiation of other units—will increase, and become of such proportions that the interaction between the individualised Selves will result in the merging to perfection of the flame within each one, and a blending of the heat; this will proceed until there is "one flame with countless sparks" within it, until the heat is general and balanced. When this is the case and each Son of God is a perfected Sun, characterised by perfectly expressed light and heat, then the entire solar system, the greater Son of God, will be the perfected Sun.

The system will then be characterised by a "blaze of refulgent glory," and by a radiation that will link it up with its cosmic centre, and thus effect the liberation of the Son, and His return to the far distant source from whence the primal impulse originated. Therefore, bear in mind:

First, that the Son is the radiant result of the union of Spirit and Matter, and may be considered as the totality of the solar system, the Sun and the seven sacred planets.

Second, that the Son manifests through his qualities of light and heat, as does the solar Sun.

Third, that the Son is the product of the electrical union of "fire by friction" and electric fire, and is Himself "solar fire" or the manifestation of the other two, hence *that which is seen and that which is felt.*

Finally, that the Son, therefore, is the middle manifestation, and is produced by that which is above, and that which is below, in the occult sense. Therefore, the Son on His own plane (the cosmic mental plane), is the egoic body of the Logos in the same sense as the egoic body of the microcosm is the product of the union of the Monad, or Spirit, and matter. Just as the body egoic of man (that which is called the causal body) is only in process of formation, and is not yet perfected, so we may predicate the same of the solar system, as it expresses the Life of God. It is in process of perfecting. The Son, manifesting through the Sun and its sphere of influence, is yet in a state of gradual development, and not until each cell within His body is fully alive and vibrating to a uniform measure, will He be "full grown" and perfected. Not until His radiation and His display of light is perfectly seen and felt, will His place among the heavenly constellations (the Son of God in a cosmic sense) be fully achieved.

Not until each cell in His body is a sphere of radiant glory—a blaze of fire and light, and a source of magnetic radiation or heat, occultly expressed, will the Son in the Heavens "shine forth." From the cosmic point of view, as we know, our sun is but of the fourth order, and on the lowest cosmic plane. When the Son has, through the Sun, attained full expression (that is, perfected His display of light and heat) then He will shine forth upon another plane, that of the cosmic mental. We have the analogy in the microcosm or man. When a man's light fully shines forth, when his magnetic radiation has reached the stage of vivid interaction or group activity, then he has attained full self-expression, and has included within his sphere of influence and control the mental plane. He is then considered a Master. He also is of the fourth order; he is the quaternary. The etheric plane is the centre of his life in the physical sense, just as we are told that the sun and the planets esoterically are considered as existing in etheric matter. As above, so below, is the occult law. Therefore, the relationship of the Son of the Father, and of the Mother, is to the Sun the same as man's relationship to the vehicle through which he functions. It is His mode of enterprise, His vehicle of expression; it is the form which His life animates for the specific purpose of

a. Gaining experience.
b. Making contact.
c. Developing full self-knowledge.
d. Achieving full mastery or control.
e. Attaining "manhood" cosmically. The cosmic Christ must measure up to the stature "of a full grown man," as it is expressed in the Christian Bible.[93]
f. Expanding His consciousness.

[93] Bible. Ep., 4:13.

All these stages have to be achieved on cosmic levels, in exactly the same sense as the microcosm, on systemic levels, likewise strives for similar ideals.

II. WHAT IS EVOLUTION AND HOW DOES IT PROCEED?

1. *Life Cycles.*

I do not propose to deal here with the evolutionary process in any other way than briefly to indicate that the whole method of evolution is simply that of adjusting the matter aspect to the Spirit aspect, so that the former proves entirely adequate as a body of expression for the latter. The life cycle of the Son is one hundred years of Brahma in the same sense as man has a life cycle consisting of a certain number of years, dependent upon his karma. During the life cycle of a man, he expresses what is in him at his particular stage, and gradually develops from the stage of the ante-natal period wherein the Self overshadows the matter aspect until the period wherein that Higher Self takes full possession of the prepared form. This stage varies with every individual. From that time on fuller self-consciousness is sought, and the man (if proceeding normally) expresses himself through the form ever more adequately. Each life of lesser cycle in the great cycle of the Ego or Self, sees that expression more complete, brings the form more under control and develops a conscious realisation of the Self until there comes a culminating cycle of lives in which the Self within rapidly dominates, and takes full authority. The form becomes wholly adequate; the fusion of the two poles of Spirit and matter is fully brought about; and the light (fire) and heat (radiation) is seen and felt systemically. Then the form is either consciously utilised for specific ends or is vacated, and the man is liberated. Electric fire and fire by friction are fused, and the consequent solar fire blazes forth in radiant glory.

Extend this idea from man, an individualised unit of

consciousness, to the great Heavenly Men, in one of
Whose bodies a man forms a cell. The body of expression
of each Heavenly Man is one of the sacred planets, and
They aim at the same goal as man—the attainment, on
Their own levels, of full expression, and the development
of Their vehicles of consciousness to a point where the
Spirit may blaze forth as light divine, and as heat. This
heat radiates consciously and with intense magnetic attraction between all the seven systemic groups, or planetary schemes. Their magnetic field of action will include
the planetary radius of one and all. Carry this thought
still further to include the Son, and the entire solar system which He animates; His attempt is to find full expression therein, so that eventually and consciously His light
may be seen and His heat, or magnetic radiation, may be
felt beyond His immediate sphere of influence, the logoic
ring-pass-not. Both the light of the Son and the heat of
the Son must be felt by the *opposite cosmic pole, that constellation which is our system's magnetic opposite.*

2. *The objective of the units of consciousness.*

Thus, the thought of union and of fusion underlies the
entire scheme of evolution; Man, the Heavenly Men, and
the cosmic Man (the Son of the Father and the Mother)
have to

- *a.* Radiate occult *heat* beyond their own individualised
  ring-pass-not.
- *b.* Occultly blaze forth and demonstrate light or fiery
  objectivity.
- *c.* Expand so as to include that which lies beyond their
  own immediate spheres.
- *d.* Fuse and blend the two fires so as to produce perfectly the central fire, solar fire.
- *e.* Blend Spirit and matter so that a body is produced
  that will adequately express Spirit.
- *f.* Merge the essence within the form, which is occultly

qualified during evolution, with the essence in all forms—humanly, in a planetary sense, and cosmically.

g. Attain human, systemic and cosmic *manhood*.

h. Achieve mastery on three planes of the solar system, humanly speaking.

i. Achieve mastery on five planes of the solar system, when speaking of a Heavenly Man.

j. Achieve mastery on three cosmic planes when speaking of the cosmic Christ, the Son, or the Logos manifesting objectively.

3. *The Manifesting Units of Consciousness.*[94]

If these stated aims are carefully considered, it will be seen how each has its place within the plan, and how

---

[94] "Matter, it must be remembered, is that totality of Existence in the Kosmos which falls within any of the planes of possible perception."— S. D., I, 560.

These Existences might be enumerated as follows:

1. The Seven Heavenly Men. In their totality they make up the Body of the Grand Man of the Heavens, the Logos.

    Other names for these Beings:

      a. The seven planetary Logoi or Spirits.
      b. The Prajapatis.
      c. The seven Lords of the Rays.
      d. The Dyhan Chohans.
      e. The seven Spirits before the Throne.
      f. The seven Archangels.
      g. The seven Logoi.
      h. The seven Builders.

               —S. D., I, 115, 130, 152, 535.

They are the informing Entities of the Divine Ray, the Ray of the second Logos, in much the same sense as Fohat and his seven Brothers are the totality of the Primordial Ray.—S. D., I, 100, 108, 155.

      a. *Matter* is fecundated by the Primordial Ray of Intelligence. This is the anima mundi, the soul of the world.
      b. The Primordial Ray is the vehicle for the Divine Ray of Love and Wisdom. The merging of these two is the aim of evolution.
      c. The Divine Ray is sevenfold. It brings in seven Entities.
      d. These seven are:

        1. The Logos of Will or Power.
        2. The Logos of Love and Wisdom.
        3. The Logos of Activity.
        4. The Logos of Harmony.
        5. The Logos of Concrete Science.
        6. The Logos of Devotion or Abstract Idealism.
        7. The Logos of Ceremonial Law or Order.

evolution is but a term used to express the gradual development in time and space of the inherent capacity of a human being, of a Heavenly Man, and of the Grand Man of the Heavens. The place and position of one and all to each other must be borne in mind, for no one can develop without the other. What, therefore, have we?

a. The Son, the Grand Man of the Heavens. He manifests through the Sun and the seven sacred planets, each of whom embodies one of His seven principles, just as He in His totality embodies one of the principles of a greater cosmic Entity.

b. A Heavenly Man. He manifests through a planet, and embodies one of the principles of the Son, the Logos. He Himself is likewise developing through seven principles, which are the source of His essential unity with all other Heavenly Men. Cosmically considered, the Son is developing the principle of a greater cosmic Being, that principle which we call love-wisdom. That is the fundamental characteristic He has to develop during His life cycle. Each Heavenly Man, therefore, embodies predominantly a subsidiary principle of the fundamental one. In like manner He Himself has six subsidiary principles, as has the Son.

c. A Human Being, Man. He manifests on the physi-

2. Men, The Monad, The Units of Consciousness. They, in their totality, make up the Bodies of the seven Heavenly Men. Each Monad is found upon one of the seven Rays.—S. D., I, 197, 285, 624; S. D., II, 85, 176, 196.

3. Devas.—S. D. I, 308; S. D., II, 107.
   Such devas are, for instance:
      a. The deva Lord of a plane. The sphere of his body is the entire plane.
      b. Groups of building devas.

4. Entities involved in the mineral, vegetable, and animal kingdoms.— S. D., I, 210, 298.
      a. The life of the third Logos—the atom of matter.
      b. The life of the second Logos—groups of atoms built into forms. plant, animal.
      c. The life of the first Logos—the forms indwelt by highest Spirit.

5. The spirit of a planet.—S. D., I, 178; S. D., II, 251, 500.
   He is the sum-total of the many involutionary lives upon a planet.

6. The atom.—S. D., I, 559, 620-622.

Summing Up: For the purpose and the goal see S. D., I, 70, 132.

cal plane through form, and has also seven principles; in each life cycle he works at their development. He likewise has His primary coloring, dependent upon the fundamental principle embodied by the Heavenly Man, Who is his originating source. Thus we have:

THE LOGOS

Father-Spirit............Mother-Matter.
producing

The Son or the Grand Man of the Heavens,
the conscious logoic Ego
evolving through

The Sun and the seven sacred planets
each embodying a

Cosmic principle, in six differentiations
by method of

a. Expansion, vibratory stimulation, magnetic interaction, or the law of attraction and repulsion.

b. Cyclic progress, rotary repetition, coupled to spiralling ascension,
and developing

    a. The quality of love-wisdom, through the utilization of form by the means of active intelligence.

    b. Full self-consciousness.

    c. A perfected solar system, or the form, adequate to the needs of the indwelling spirit.

Here a similar tabulation may be worked out to demonstrate the similarity of the process in the case of a Heavenly Man and a human being. If we ask why ten schemes, and in effect ten planets (seven sacred and three concealed) it is because the seven sacred planets are eventually merged into the three, and finally the three are blended into the one. This can be traced along the line of analogy as we consider the seven Rays. These seven Rays, which in manifestation are diverse, are eventually synthesised. The minor four are blended, we are told, into the third major ray, and the three major rays are finally merged into the one synthetic ray, the Love-Wisdom Ray (the Dragon of Wisdom, the occult serpent swallowing its tail).[95] This has been pointed out by H. P. B. We have, therefore, the three crowning rays, but seven seen during the evolutionary process. In connection with the Heavenly Men, functioning through the planets, there are, therefore, three planets which might be considered as synthesising planets, and four which are blended eventually, until the three have absorbed the essence of the four; finally the one absorbs the essence of the three, and the work is completed. This process lies many millennia ahead, during the inevitable period of the gradual obscuration of our system. Four of the Heavenly Men find Their magnetic opposites, and fuse and blend. First this takes place between Themselves, the negative and the positive rays merging and fusing, forming then the two from the four. Again the two merge, producing a united whole, and the one thus produced blends with the major third ray, the intelligence aspect,— the ray represented in our planetary Hierarchy by the Mahachohan. So the fusion will proceed until ultimately unity is reached in the system, and the Son has accomplished His purpose. He is perfected love-wisdom; his light shines forth cosmically; His magnetic radius touches the periphery of His cosmic opposite, and the marriage of the Son is effected. The two cosmic units merge.

If we here naturally ask which is the cosmic unit that is our solar opposite, we shall be told that that question

[95] Serpent swallowing its tail.—S. D., I, 704; II, 531.

lies hid for the present, though it is hinted at in the *Secret Doctrine,* and in other sacred books. A hint lies concealed in the relationship of the Pleiades to our earth, but not until a further precession of the equinoxes will it be more fully seen what is the exact relationship involved.[96]

III. WHY IS THIS SOLAR SYSTEM EVOLVING ALONG THE LINES OF DUALITY?

1. *The Problem of Existence.*

The third question involves one of the most difficult problems in metaphysics, and covers in its consideration the whole perplexing mystery of the reason why there is objectivity at all.

It is one that has been asked under different forms by men of every school of thought—by religious people who enquire:—"Why did God create at all? Why is existence forced upon one and all?"; by scientists in their search for the ultimate truth and in their endeavor to find out the motivation of all that is seen, and to account for sensuous life; by philosophers in their equally diligent search for that animating subjectivity that is expressing itself through all the moral and ethical sciences in every civilisation and among every people; by the biologist in his persistent application to search for the discovery of the source of life, and in his strenuous endeavour to account for the principle of life that is seen ever to evade his investigations; by the mathematician, who, dealing with the form side of manifestation in all the grades of mathematics, decides that God geometrises, that law and rule pervade universally, that the one exists by means of the many, and who yet is unable to solve the problem as to who that geometrising

[96] Students might compare the following references and then form their own conclusions.—S. D., I, 711 note, 545, 439; II, 811, 830, 581, 582, 426, 454, 654, 371.

identity may be. So the problems persist, and all the many lines of approach (in the endeavour to find the solution) end in the cul-de-sac of hypothesis, and in the recognition of an ultimate something of such an elusive nature, that men are forced seemingly to predicate a source of energy, of life, of intelligence, and to call it by diverse names according to the trend (religious, scientific or philosophical) of their minds. God, the Universal Mind, Energy, Force, the Absolute, the Unknown,—these terms and many others are forced from the lips of those who, by means of the form side, seek the Dweller within the form, and cannot find Him as yet. This failure to find Him is due to the limitations of the physical brain, and to the lack of development in the mechanism whereby the spiritual may be known, and whereby He may, and eventually will, be contacted.

The problem of duality is the problem of existence itself, and cannot be solved by the man who refuses to recognise the possibility of two occult facts:

1. That the entire solar system embodies the consciousness of an Entity, who originates on planes entirely without the solar ring-pass-not.
2. That manifestation is periodical and that the Law of Rebirth is the method that evolution takes in dealing with a man, a planetary Logos, and a solar Logos. Hence, the emphasis laid in the Proem of the *Secret Doctrine* on the three fundamentals,[97]
   a. *The Boundless Immutable Principle* and
   b. *The periodicity of the Universe.*
   c. *The identity of all souls with the Oversoul.*

When scientists recognise these two facts then their explanations will take a different line and the truth, *as it is,* will begin to illuminate their reason. Few men are yet ready for illumination, which is simply the light of the

[97] S. D., I, 42-44.

intuition breaking through the barriers that the rational faculty has erected. The duality of the solar system will eventually be recognised as dependent upon the following factors:

a. Existence itself.
b. Time and space.
c. The quality of desire or necessity.
d. The acquisitive faculty inherent in life itself. This faculty, by the means of motion, gathers to itself the material whereby it achieves its desire, whereby it fabricates the form through which expression is sought, and whereby it confines itself within the prison of the sheath in order to gain experience.

The supposition is correct that this theory takes for granted a mighty Intelligence who works thus through an ordered plan, and Who consciously takes shape and incarnates in order to carry out specific purposes of His own. But this hypothesis is but the rock bottom fact underlying the eastern teaching, and is one that is largely accepted, though diversely expressed and viewed by thinkers of all schools of thought throughout the globe. Even this conception is but a partial presentation of the real Idea, but owing to the limitations of man at this stage of evolution, it is sufficient as a working basis on which he may erect his temple of truth.

This Entity, Whom we call the solar Logos, is in no sense the same as the personal God of the Christian, who is no more nor less than man himself, expanded into a being of awful power, and subject to the virtues and vices of man himself. The solar Logos is more than man, for He is the sumtotal of all the evolutions within the entire solar system, including the human, which is an evolution standing at a middle point in relation to the other evolutions. On one side of him are ranged hosts of beings who are more than human, and who, in past kalpas, reached and passed the stage where man now is; on the other side are hosts of the subhuman evolutions who in future kalpas will achieve the stage of humanity. Man stands midway between the two, and is at the point of balance; herein lies his problem. He does not partake wholly of the material side of evolution, nor is he wholly the expression of the third Logos, the Brahma aspect of the Deity, Who is an expression of pure energy or intelligence, motivating that tenuous something which we call substance. He is not wholly Spirit, the expression of the first Logos, the Mahadeva aspect, which is an expression of pure will or necessitous desire, impelling to manifestation. It is the fundamental motive itself or the great will to be. Man is a product of the union of the two; he is the meeting place of matter or active intelligent substance, and of Spirit or the basic will. He is the child born of their marriage or at-one-ment. He assumes objectivity in order to express that which is in each of the two opposites, plus the result of their merging in himself.

2. *Its Nature and Duality.*

In terms of *quality* what have we?. Active intelligence at one with will or power produces that "Son of necessity" [98] (as H. P. B. expresses it) Who embodies intelligence, will or desire, and their united latent demonstration, love-wisdom.

In terms of *Fire* how might we express an analogous thought? The fire latent in matter—itself a product of an earlier manifestation of the same cosmic Identity, or the relatively perfected quality worked out by Him in a previous cosmic incarnation—is set in motion again by the desire of that same Identity to circle once more the wheel of rebirth. That "fire by friction" produces heat and radiation and calls forth a reaction from its

[98] S. D., I, 74.

opposite "electric fire" or spirit. Here we have the thought of the Ray striking through matter, for the action of electric fire is ever forward, as earlier suggested. The one Ray "electric fire" drops into matter. This is the systemic marriage of the Father and the Mother. The result is the blending of these two fires, and their united production of that expression of fire which we call "solar fire." Thus is produced the Son. Active Intelligence and Will are united and love-wisdom, when perfected through evolution, will be the outcome.

Electric fire or Spirit, united to fire by friction (heat) produces solar fire or light.

Hence, when the cosmic Entity takes form, there is added to the active intelligence which is the product of His earlier incarnation, a further quality, which is inherent and potential, that of love-wisdom. This is the ability to love that which is objective or the not-self, and ultimately to use with wisdom the *form*. Pure will is as yet an abstraction, and will only be brought into full development in another incarnation of the Logos. Mind or Intelligence is not an abstraction; it is something that is. Neither is love-wisdom an abstraction. It is in process of development or bringing into manifestation, and is the aspect of the Son.

What is above stated is in no way new, but these thoughts on essential duality are gathered together, in order to convey to our minds the necessity of viewing these things from the standpoint of their place in the cosmic scheme, and not from the point of view of our own planetary evolution and of man himself. *Humanity is that evolution through which the Son aspect is to express itself most perfectly in this cosmic incarnation.* Man blends the pairs of opposites, and the three fires meet in him. He is the best expression of the manasic principle and might be considered, from one very interesting

standpoint, the *chef-d'œuvre* of Brahma. He is the
sheath for the life of God; he is the individualised consciousness of the Logos, manifesting through the seven
divine Manasaputras, or Heavenly Men, in Whose bodies
each unit of the human family finds place. He is the
Vishnu aspect in process of development through the intelligence of Brahma, impelled by the will of Mahadeva.
Therefore, in a peculiar sense man is very important, as
he is the place of at-one-ment for all the three aspects;
nevertheless, he is very unimportant for he is not the
apex of the triangle, but simply the middle point, if we
view the triangle thus:

Spirit-Father.

The Son or man.

Matter-Mother.

The evolution of the Son, or the cosmic incarnation of
the Christ, is of immense importance in the plans of the
Being greater than the solar Logos, HE ABOUT WHOM
NAUGHT MAY BE SAID. The animating principles of allied
constellations and systems watch the progress of the
evolution of the Son with keenest attention.

Just as the planet called the earth is regarded as the
turning point or the battle-ground between Spirit and
matter, and is therefore, from that very consideration,
of great importance, so our solar system holds an analogous place in the cosmic scheme. The cosmic man, the
solar Arjuna, is wrestling for His individualised perfected self-consciousness, and for freedom and liberation
from the form, and from the not-self. So man on this
planet battles for similar ideals on his tiny scale; so battle in heaven Michael and His Angels, or the divine
Heavenly Men, Whose problem is the same on the higher
scale.

Duality, and the interplay between the two produces:

a. Objectivity, or the manifested Son or Sun.
b. Evolution itself.
c. The development of *quality.*
d. Time and space.

The questions we are now engaged in answering embody certain fundamental aspects of manifestation, viewed principally from the subjective or psychic angle.

IV. WHAT IS CONSCIOUSNESS? WHAT IS ITS PLACE IN THE SCHEME OF THINGS?

Consciousness might be defined as the faculty of apprehension, and concerns primarily the relation of the Self to the not-self, of the Knower to the Known, and of the Thinker to that which is thought about. All these definitions involve the acceptance of the idea of duality, of that which is objective and of that which lies back of objectivity.[99]

Consciousness expresses that which might be regarded as the middle point in manifestation. It does not involve entirely the pole of Spirit. It is produced by the union of the two poles, and the process of interplay and of adaptation that necessarily ensues. It might be tabulated as follows, in an effort to clarify by visualisation:

[99] ''Consciousness is the kosmic seed of superkosmic omniscience. It has the potentiality of budding into divine consciousness.''—S. D., III, 555.
The universe is an aggregate of states of consciousness.—S. D., II, 633.
Consciousness may be roughly divided into:
1. Absolute or God Consciousness....Unmanifested Logos.
     ''I am That I am.''
2. Universal or Group Consciousness..Manifested Logos.
     ''I am That.''   Consciousness of planetary Logos.
3. Individual or Self-Consciousness....Human consciousness.
     ''I am.''
4. Consciousness or Atomic Conscious-
     ness ....Sub-human consciousness.
The goal of consciousness for:
1. A planetary Logos............. Absolute consciousness.
2. Man ....Group consciousness.
3. Atom ....Self-consciousness.
     The Logos is the Macrocosm for Man.—S. D., I, 288, 295.
Man is the Macrocosm for the Atom. . . .
Summation: The Life and the Lives.—S. D., I, 281, 282.

First Pole	The Point of Union	Second Pole
First Logos	Second Logos	Third Logos.
Mahadeva	Vishnu	Brahma.
Will	Wisdom-Love	Active Intelligence.
Spirit	Consciousness	Matter.
Father	Son	Mother.
Monad	Ego	Personality.
The Self	The relation between	The Not-Self.
The Knower	Knowledge	The Known.
Life	Realisation	Form.

One could go on piling up terms, but the above suffices to demonstrate the relationship between the threefold Logos, *during manifestation*. Emphasis must be laid upon the above fact: The solar system embodies the above logoic relationship during evolutionary objectivity, and the whole aim of progressive development is to bring the Son of the Father and the Mother, to a point of full realisation, of complete self-consciousness, and to full and active knowledge. This Son is *objectively* the solar system, *inherently* will or power, and *subjectively* He is love-wisdom. This latter quality is in process of development through the utilisation of active intelligence.

The three manifested Persons of the logoic Triad seek full development by means of each other. The will to be, of the Mahadeva aspect, seeks, with the aid of the intelligence of Brahma, to develop love-wisdom, or the Son aspect, the Vishnu aspect. In the microcosmic system, the reflection of the threefold Logos, the man is endeavoring through the three vehicles to attain the same development on his own plane. On higher planes the Heavenly Men (through atma-buddhi-manas) aim at a similar progression. These two, the Heavenly Men plus the units in Their bodies, which are composed of deva and human monads form, in their totality, the Grand Heavenly Man. When man achieves, then the Heavenly Men likewise achieve; when They reach Their full growth and knowledge, and are self-conscious on all planes, then the Son achieves, and the solar system (His body of manifestation and experience) has served its purpose. The Son is liberated. Extend the idea of this threefold development of consciousness to the Logos in a still larger cycle (to that of the three solar systems of which this is the middle one) and we have repeated on cosmic levels in connection with the Logos, the process of the development of man in the three worlds.

THE MACROCOSM

The first solar system...embodied......the "I am" principle.

The second solar system. is embodying...the "I am that" principle.

The third solar system.. will embody....the "I am that I am" principle.

THE MICROCOSM

The first manifestation, the Personality, embodies the "I am" principle.

The second manifestation, the Ego, is embodying the "I am that" principle.

The third manifestation, the Monad, will embody the "I am that I am" principle.

Thus the different factors play their part in the general scheme of things, and all are interrelated, and all are interested parts and members one of the other.

V. IS THERE A DIRECT ANALOGY BETWEEN THE DEVELOPMENT OF A SYSTEM, A PLANET, A MAN AND AN ATOM?

If by this question the desire exists to demonstrate exact similarity, the answer must be: No, the analogy is never exact in detail but only in certain broad basic correspondences. In all the four factors, there will be found unchangeable points of resemblance, but in development the stages of growth may not appear the same in detailed evolution, viewed from the standpoint of a man in the three worlds, handicapped as he is by limited apprehension. The points of resemblance between the four might be summed up as follows, taking the atom on the physical plane as our starting point, and developing the concept from stage to stage:

An Atom.[1]

a. An atom consists of a spheroidal form containing within itself a nucleus of life.

b. An atom contains within itself differentiated molecules, which in their totality form the atom itself. For instance, we are told that the physical atom contains within its periphery fourteen thousand millions of the archetypal atoms, yet these myriads demonstrate as one.

c. An atom is distinguished by activity, and shows forth the qualities of:

   a. Rotary motion.
   b. Discriminative power.
   c. Ability to develop.

d. An atom, we are told, contains within itself three major spirals and seven lesser [2] which ten are in process

---

[1] In connection with *the Atom,* the *Secret Doctrine* says:
1. Absolute intelligence thrills through every atom.S. D., I, 298.
2. Wherever there is an atom of matter, there is
      life ....S. D., I, 245, 269, 279.
3. The atom is a concrete manifestation of the
      Universal Energy ....S. D., I., 201.
4. The same invisible lives compose the atoms, etc..S. D., I, 281.
5. Every atom in the universe has the potentiality
      of self-consciousness ....S. D., I, 132; II, 742.
6. Atoms and souls are synonymous in the lan-
      guage of Initiates........................S. D., I., 620, 622.
7. The atom belongs wholly to the domain of
      metaphysics ....S. D., I, 559.
8. Deity is within every atom ....S. D., I, 89, 183.
9. Every atom is doomed to incessant differentia-
      tion ....S. D., I, 167.
10. The object of the evolution of the atom is Man..S. D., I, 206.
11. A germ exists in the centre of every atom......S. D., I, 87; II, 622.
12. There is heat in every atom..................S. D., I, 112.
13. Every atom has 7 planes of being ....S. D., I, 174.
14. Atoms are vibrations........................S. D., I, 694.
[2] *Inner Life:* Vol. II, 177-179. *Occult Chemistry,* p. 22. *Occult Chemistry,* Appendix II and III. Babbitt's "*Light and Colour,*" pp. 97-101.

of vitalisation, but have not yet attained full activity. Only four are functioning at this stage, and the fifth is in process of development.

e. An atom is governed by the Law of Economy, is coming slowly under the Law of Attraction, and will eventually come under the Law of Synthesis.

f. An atom finds its place within all forms; it is the aggregation of atoms that produces form.

g. Its responsiveness to outer stimulation:

Electrical stimulation, affecting its objective form.
Magnetic stimulation, acting upon its subjective life.
The united effect of the two stimulations, producing consequent internal growth and development.

An atom therefore is distinguished by:

1. Its spheroidal shape. Its ring-pass-not is definite and seen.
2. Its internal arrangement, which comprises the sphere of influence of any particular atom.
3. Its life-activity, or the extent to which the life at the centre animates the atom, a relative thing at this stage.
4. Its sevenfold inner economy in process of evolution.
5. Its eventual synthesis internally from the seven into the three.
6. Its group relation.
7. Its development of consciousness, or responsiveness.

Having predicated the above facts of the atom, we can extend the idea now to man, following the same general outline:

A Man.

a. A man is spheroidal in form, he can be seen as a circular ring-pass-not, a sphere of matter with a nucleus

of life at the centre. In predicating this we are considering the true man in his fundamental position as the Ego,
with his sphere of manifestation, the causal body,—that
body which forms the middle point between Spirit and
matter.

b. A man contains within himself differentiated atoms,
which in their totality make up the objective form of the
man on the planes of his manifestation. All are animated
by his life, by his persistent will-to-be; all vibrate according to the point reached by the man in evolution. As seen
from the higher planes man demonstrates as a sphere
(or spheres) of differentiated matter, vibrating to a certain measure, tinctured by a certain color, and rotating
to a fixed key—the key of his life cycle.

c. A man is distinguished by activity on one or more
planes in the three worlds, and shows forth the qualities of:

1. Rotary motion, or his particular cycling on the
   wheel of life, around his egoic pole.
2. Discriminative capacity, or the power to choose and
   gain experience.
3. Ability to evolve, to increase vibration and to make
   contact.

d. A man contains within himself three major principles,—will, love-wisdom, active intelligence or adaptability—and their differentiation into the seven principles. These, making the eventual ten of perfected manifestation, are in process of vitalisation, but have not yet
attained full expression. Only four principles in man are
active, and he is in process of developing the fifth, or
manasic principle. Note how perfect is the analogy between man, viewed as the lower quaternary developing
the principle of mind, and the atom with its four spirillæ
active, and the fifth in process of stimulation.

e. A man is governed by the Law of Attraction, is

evolved through the Law of Economy, and is coming under the Law of Synthesis. Economy governs the material process with which he is not so much consciously concerned; attraction governs his connection with other units or groups, and synthesis is the law of his inner Self, of the life within the form.

f. Man finds his place within the group form. Egoic groups and the Heavenly Men are formed by the aggregate of human and of deva units.

g. His responsiveness to outer stimulation:

> *a.* Electrical stimulation, affecting the outer form, or pranic response.
>
> *b.* Magnetic stimulation, acting upon his subjective life. This emanates from his egoic group, and later from the Heavenly Man, in Whose body he is a cell.
>
> *c.* The united effect of these two stimulations, inducing steady growth and development.

A man is distinguished therefore by:

1. His spheroidal shape. His ring-pass-not is definite and seen.

2. His internal arrangement; his entire sphere of influence is in process of development. At present that sphere is limited and his range of activity is small. As the body egoic is developed, the nucleus of life at the centre increases its radius of control until the whole is brought under rule and government.

3. His life activity or the extent to which at any given time he demonstrates self-consciousness, or controls his threefold lower nature.

4. His sevenfold inner economy; the development of his seven principles.

5. His eventual internal synthesis under the working of the three laws from the seven into the three and later into the one.

6. His group relation.

7. His development of consciousness, of responsiveness to contact, involving therefore the growth of awareness.

A Heavenly Man.[3]

a. Each Heavenly Man is likewise to be seen as spheroidal in shape. He has His ring-pass-not as has the atom and the man. This ring-pass-not comprises the entire planetary scheme; the dense physical globe of any one chain being analogous in His case to the physical body of any man, and to the atom on the physical plane. Each scheme of seven chains is the expression of the life of an Entity, Who occupies it, as does a man his body, for purposes of manifestation and in order to gain experience.

[3] These Heavenly Men are:
1. The sum-total of consciousness................S. D., I, 626,
2. The Creators ....S. D., I, 477, 481-485.
   Compare S. D., II, 244.
   a. They are the seven primary creations, or the taking of the etheric body by a Heavenly Man.
   b. They are the seven secondary creations, or the taking of the dense physical body.
      Trace this in the Microcosm, and the work of the devas of the ethers in building the body.
   c. The aggregate of divine intelligence...........S. D., I, 488,
   d. The mindborn Sons of Brahma...............S. D., I, 493,
                                                     S. D., II, 610, 618.
   They are the logoic Quaternary, the Five, and the Seven.
   e. The seven Rays.................................S. D., I, 561,
                                                     S. D., II, 201.
      They are the seven paths back to God.......Spirit.
      They are the seven principles metaphysically.
      They are the seven races physically.
   f. The Lords of ceaseless and untiring devotion.....S. D., II, 92,
   g. The failures of the last system ....S. D., II, 243,
   h. The polar opposites to the Pleiades ....S. D., II, 579, 581.
   Our system is masculine occultly and the Pleiades is feminine.
   A Heavenly Man in His planetary scheme creates in a similar manner.
See S. D., II, 626.

b. A Heavenly Man contains within Himself that which corresponds to the cells within the vehicles of expression of a human being. The atoms or cells in His body are made up of the aggregate of the deva and human units who vibrate to His key note, and who respond to the measure of His life. All are held together and animated by His will to be, and all vibrate according to the point achieved by Him in evolution. From the cosmic standpoint a Heavenly Man can be seen as a sphere of wondrous life, which includes within its radius of influence the vibratory capacity of an entire planetary scheme. He vibrates to a certain measure, which can be estimated by the activity of the life pulsating at the centre of the sphere; the entire planetary scheme is tinctured by a certain color, is rotating to a fixed key which is the key of His life cycle within the still greater mahamanvantara or logoic cycle.

c. A Heavenly Man is distinguished by His activity on one or other of the planes which we call the Triadal, or Atma-Buddhi-Manas, in the same way as a man is distinguished by his activity on one of the planes in the three worlds, mental-astral-physical. Eventually a man is self-conscious on all three. Eventually a Heavenly Man is fully self-conscious on the higher three. Every forward movement or increased vitality in the aggregate of men in the three worlds, is paralleled by an analogous activity on the three higher planes. The action and the interaction between the life animating the groups or the Heavenly Men, and the life animating the atoms or men who form the units in groups is both mysterious and wonderful. A Heavenly Man on His own planes likewise shows forth the qualities of:

Rotary motion, or His particular cycling activity around His life wheel, a planetary scheme, and thus around His egoic pole.

Discriminating capacity, or the power to choose and
thereby gain experience. They are the embodiments of manas or the intelligent faculty (hence
Their title of Divine Manasaputras) which comprehends, chooses and discards, thus attaining
knowledge and self-consciousness. This manasic
faculty They developed in earlier kalpas or solar
systems. Their purpose is now to utilise that
which is developed to bring about certain specific
effects and to attain certain specific goals.

Ability to evolve, to increase vibration, to gain knowledge, and to make contact. This increased vibration is of a gradual and evolutionary order and
proceeds from centre to centre as it does in man,
and as it does in the case of the atomic spirillæ.
Their aim is to achieve uniformity of contact with
each other, and to merge eventually Their separated identities in the One Identity, retaining
simultaneously full self-consciousness or individualised self-apprehension.

d. A Heavenly Man contains within Himself three
major principles—will, love-wisdom, intelligence, and
their manifestation through the seven principles so often
discussed in our occult literature. These make the ten
of His ultimate perfection, for the seven are resolved into
the three, and the three into the one.

Each Heavenly Man has, of course, His primary coloring or principle as has man and the atom. Man has for
his primary coloring or principle that of the Heavenly
Man in Whose body he is a unit. He has also the other
two major principles (as has the Heavenly Man), and
their differentiation into the seven as earlier said. The
atom has for primary coloring or principle, that of the
egoic ray of the human being for instance in whose body
it finds place. This, of course, is in connection with the

physical atom in a man's body. This coloring manifests as the vibration setting the measure of the major three spirillæ and the minor seven.

Only four principles in the Heavenly Men are as yet manifesting to any extent, though One of Them is rather in advance of the others, and has the fifth principle vibrating adequately, while certain others are in process of perfecting the fourth. The Heavenly Man of our chain is vibrating somewhat to the fifth principle, or rather is in process of awakening it to life. His fourth vibration or principle in this fourth round or cycle, and on this fourth globe, is awakened, though not functioning as it will in the fifth round. Much of the trouble present in the planet at this time arises from the coming into activity of the higher or fifth vibration, which will be completed and transcended in the next or fifth cycle. The analogy, as in man and the atom, again holds good but not in exact detail.

e. A Heavenly Man is governed by the Law of Attraction, has transcended the Law of Economy, and is rapidly coming under the Law of Synthesis. Note therefore the gradual stepping-up of the control and the fact that:

First. The Law of Economy is the primary law of the atom. The Law of Attraction is coming into control of the atom. The Law of Synthesis is but slightly felt by the life of the atom. It is the law of life.

Second. The Law of Attraction is the primary law of man. The Law of Economy is a secondary law for man. It governs the matter of his vehicles. The Law of Synthesis is steadily beginning to be felt.

Third. The Law of Synthesis is the primary law of a Heavenly Man. The Law of Attraction has full sway. The Law of Economy is transcended.

The dense physical body is not a principle for a Heavenly Man, hence the Law of Economy is transcended.

The Law of Attraction governs the material process of form building. The Law of Synthesis is the law of His Being.

f. A Heavenly Man is finding His place within the logoic groups, and is seeking to realise His position among the seven and by realisation to approximate unity.

g. His responsiveness to outer stimulation. This viewed from the limited human standpoint touches on realms unattainable by man's intellect as yet. It deals with:

Electrical stimulation, and concerns the response to solar radiation, and to paralleling planetary radiation.

Magnetic stimulation, acting upon His subjective life. This radiation emanates from sources outside the system altogether. We might note the following facts:

Magnetic stimulation of the *physical atom* emanates from man on astral levels, and later from buddhic levels.

Magnetic stimulation of *man* emanates from the Heavenly Men on buddhic, and later on monadic levels.

Magnetic stimulation of a *Heavenly Man* emanates extra-systemically, from the cosmic astral, the united effect of these stimulations inducing steady internal development.

A Heavenly Man is distinguished therefore by:

1. His spheroidal shape. His ring-pass-not, during objectivity, is definite and seen.
2. His internal arrangement and His sphere of influence, or that activity animating the planetary chain.
3. His spiritual life control at any given period. It is the power whereby He animates His seven-

fold nature. Note the increase of influence as compared to man's threefold radius.

4. His eventual ultimate synthesis from the seven into
the three and from thence into one. This covers
the obscuration of the globes, and the blending into
unity of the seven principles which each globe is
evolving.

5. His evolution under Law and consequent development.

6. His group relation.

7. His development of consciousness and of awareness.

Finally, we must extend these ideas to a solar Logos,
and see how completely the analogy persists. The para-
graphs dealing with stimulation, magnetic and electric,
inevitably brings us back to the contemplation of fire, the
basis and source of all life.

A Solar Logos.

a. A solar Logos, the Grand Man of the Heavens, is
equally spheroidal in shape. His ring-pass-not comprises
the entire circumference of the solar system, and all that
is included within the sphere of influence of the Sun. The
Sun holds a position analogous to the nucleus of life at
the centre of the atom. This sphere comprises within its
periphery the seven planetary chains with the synthesising three, making the ten of logoic manifestation. The
Sun is the physical body of the solar Logos, His body of
manifestation, and His life sweeps cycling through the
seven schemes in the same sense as the life of a planetary
Logos sweeps seven times around His scheme of seven
chains. Each chain holds a position analogous to a globe
in a planetary chain. Note the beauty of the correspondence, yet withal the lack of detailed analogy.[4]

b. A solar Logos contains within Himself, as the atoms
in His body of manifestation, all groups of every kind,

[4] S. D., I. 136.

from the involutionary group-soul to the egoic groups on the mental plane. He has (for the animating centres of His body) the seven major groups or the seven Heavenly Men, who ray forth Their influence to all parts of the logoic sphere, and who embody within Themselves all lesser lives, the lesser groups, human and deva units, cells, atoms and molecules.

Seen from cosmic levels, the sphere of the Logos can be visualised as a vibrating ball of fire of supernal glory, containing within its circle of influence, the planetary spheres likewise vibrating balls of fire. The Grand Man of the Heavens vibrates to a steadily increasing measure; the entire system is tinctured by a certain color,—the color of the life of the Logos, the One Divine Ray; and the system rotates to a certain measure, which is the key of the great kalpa or solar cycle, and revolves around its central solar pole.

c. The solar Logos is distinguished by His activity on all the planes of the solar system; He is the sumtotal of all manifestation, from the lowest and densest physical atom up to the most radiant and cosmic ethereal Dhyan Chohan. This sevenfold vibratory measure is the key of the lowest cosmic plane, and its rate of rhythm can be felt on the cosmic astral, with a faint response on the cosmic mental. Thus the life of the logoic existence on cosmic levels, may be seen paralleling the life of a man in the three worlds, the lowest of the systemic planes.

On His own planes the Logos likewise shows forth:

First. Rotary motion. His life as it cycles through a day of Brahma, can be seen spiralling around His greater wheel, the ten schemes of a solar system.

Second. Discriminatory capacity. His first act, as we know, was to discriminate or choose the matter he needed for manifestation. That choice was controlled by:

Cosmic Karma.

Vibratory capacity.

Responsive coloring or quality.

Numerical factors involved in cosmic mathematics.

He is the embodiment of cosmic manas, and through the use of this faculty He seeks—by means of animated form—to build into His cosmic causal body, a paralleling quality of love-wisdom.

Third. Ability to progress, to increase vibration, and to gain full self-consciousness on cosmic levels.

d. The solar Logos contains within Himself the three major principles or aspects, and their differentiation into seven principles. These make the ten of His ultimate perfection and are eventually synthesised into the one perfected principle of love-wisdom. This ultimate principle is His primary coloring. Each principle is embodied in one of the schemes, and is being worked out through one of the Heavenly Men. Only four principles are as yet manifested to any extent, for the evolution of the Logos parallels that of the Heavenly Men.

e. The solar Logos is governed by the Law of Synthesis. He holds all in synthetic unity or homogeneity. His subjective life is governed by the Law of Attraction; His material form is governed by the Law of Economy. He is coming under another cosmic law as yet incomprehensible to men, which law is but revealed to the highest initiates.

f. The solar Logos is in process of ascertaining His place within the greater system in which He holds a place analogous to that of a Heavenly Man in a solar system. He seeks *first* to find the secret of His own existence, and to achieve full Self-Consciousness; *secondly* to ascertain the position and place of His polar opposite; *thirdly* to merge and blend with that polar opposite. This is the cosmic marriage of the Logos.

g. A solar Logos is distinguished by His responsiveness to outer stimulation. This concerns itself with:

Electrical stimulation or His response to electrical fohatic force emanating from other stellar centres, and controlling largely the action of our system and its movements in space in relation to other constellations.

Magnetic stimulation, acting upon His subjective Life, and emanating from certain cosmic centres hinted at in the *Secret Doctrine.* These find their source on cosmic buddhic levels.

It is their united effect which induces steady development.

The solar Logos is distinguished

1. By the spheroidicity of His manifesting existence. His solar ring-pass-not is definite and seen. This can only be demonstrated as yet by the endeavour to ascertain the extent of the subjective control, by the measure of the solar sphere of influence, or the magnetic attraction of the Sun to other lesser bodies which it holds in circular motion around itself.
2. By the activity of the life animating the ten schemes.
3. By the extent of the control exerted by the Logos at any given period.
4. By the ultimate synthesis of the seven schemes into three and thence into one. This covers the obscuration of the schemes and the unification of the seven principles which they embody.
5. By His subjection to the Law of His Being.
6. By His group relation.
7. By His unfoldment of Consciousness, the time fac-

tor being controlled by the measure of the unfoldment of all the conscious units in His body.

Here we have traced very briefly some of the analogies
between the four factors earlier mentioned, and have in a
cursory way answered the question. These points, if
dwelt upon, will be found of real assistance in developing
the mental appreciation of the student, and in increasing
his apprehension of the beauty of the entire solar scheme.

VI. WHAT IS THE MIND ASPECT? WHY IS THE MANASIC PRIN-
CIPLE OF SUCH IMPORTANCE? WHO ARE THE MANASAPUTRAS?

We are now to touch upon the profoundest mystery of
the whole manifested solar system—the mystery spoken
of by H. P. B. as the mystery of electricity.[5] It is intimately connected with the life of God as demonstrated
through His seven Centres, the seven Heavenly Men,
the Divine Manasaputras. This problem is not soluble as
yet exoterically and but little can be revealed to the general public. This is for three reasons:

First, the stage reached by man does not permit of his
correct apprehension of these abstractions.

Second, the greater part of the possible explanation is
only revealed to initiates who have passed the third Initiation, and even to them in a carefully guarded manner.

Third, the revelation of the close connection between
mind and fohat or energy, or between thought power and
electrical phenomena—the effect of fohatic impulse on
matter—is fraught with peril, and the missing link (if
so it might be termed) in the chain of reasoning from
phenomena to its initiatory impulse, can only be safely
imparted when the bridge between higher and lower mind,
is adequately constructed. When the lower is under the
control of the higher, or when the quaternary is merging into the triad, then man can be trusted with the re-

[5] S. D., I, 439, 221, 107.

maining four fundamentals. Three of these fundamentals are laid down for us in the Proem of the *Secret Doctrine*,[6] and with the evolving concept of psychology, make the revealed three and the dawning fourth. The other three are esoteric and must remain so until each man has for himself worked at his spiritual development, built the bridge between the higher and the lower mind, prepared the shrine in the temple of Solomon for the Light of God, and turned his activities into altruistic helping of the evolutionary plans of the Logos.

When these qualities are assuming a foremost place and when man has demonstrated the thoroughness of his will to serve, then the clue will be put into his hands and he will find the method whereby electrical impulse, demonstrating as heat, light and motion, is controlled and utilised; he will discover the source of the initial impulse from extra-systemic centres, and discover the basic rhythm. Then, and only then, will he be a truly intelligent co-operator, and (escaping from the control of the Law in the three worlds) wield the law himself within the lower spheres.

1. *The Nature of Manifestation.*

Here are three important questions to be dealt with as one, all bearing on the same subject, and all concerned with the fact of intelligent objectivity itself. Perhaps if we paraphrased the threefold query, and brought it down to microcosmic objectivity, the problem might not appear so complex. We might express it thus:

What is the thought aspect of a human being? Why is his mind and mental process of such importance? Who is the Thinker?

Man, in essential essence, is the higher triad demonstrating through a gradually evolving form, the egoic or causal body, and utilising the lower threefold personality

[6] S. D., I, 42-44.

as a means to contact the lower three planes. All this has for purpose the development of perfect self-consciousness. Above the triad stands the Monad or the Father in Heaven—a point of abstraction to man as he views the subject from the physical plane. The Monad stands to him in the position of the Absolute, in the same sense as the undifferentiated Logos stands to the threefold Trinity, to the three Persons of logoic manifestation. The parallel is exact.

1. The Monad.
2. The threefold Triad, Atma-Buddhi-Manas, or spiritual will, intuition, and higher mind.
3. The body egoic or the causal body, the shrine for the buddhic principle. This body is to be built by the power of the mind. It is the manifestation of the three.
4. The threefold lower nature, the points of densest objectivity.
5. This threefold lower nature is in essence a quaternary—the etheric vehicle, animating life or prana, kama-manas, and lower mind. Manas or the fifth principle, forms the link between the lower and the higher.[7]

We have, therefore, our lower four, our higher three, and the relation between them, the principle of mind. Here we have the seven formed by the union of the three and the four, and another factor, making eight. *The ultimate seven will be seen when buddhi and manas are merged.* Much has been hinted at in certain of our occult books about the eighth sphere. I would suggest that in this linking factor of intelligent mind, we have a clue to the mystery. When mind becomes unduly developed and ceases to unite the higher and the lower, it forms a sphere of its own. This is the greatest disaster that can overtake the human unit.

[7] S. D., I, 107.

Therefore we have:

Monad, the microcosmic absolute.
Pure Spirit.
The one and only.

The monadic trinity.

First aspect .... Atma or spiritual will.
Second aspect .... Buddhi, the Christ principle.
Third aspect .... Manas, or higher mind.

The Son aspect in objectivity.
The body egoic or causal body.

The lower quaternary.
1. The mental body.   3. Prana, or vital energy.
2. The astral or emotional body.[8]4. Etheric body.

The microcosm reproduces the solar system in miniature. The above deals with the objective forms, corresponding to the sun and the seven sacred planets. But the exoteric form is paralleled by a psychic development which we call the seven principles. Man develops seven principles, which might be enumerated as follows:

MICROCOSMIC PRINCIPLES [9]

Two higher principles:
        1. Active intelligence.
        2. Latent love-wisdom.

---

[8] Kamamanas—That blending of the mental and desire element that forms the personality or common brain-intelligence of the man.

"The energies that express themselves through the lower kinds of mental matter are so changed by it into slower vibrations that are responded to by astral matter that the two bodies are continually vibrating together, and become very closely interwoven."—*The Ancient Wisdom* by Mrs. Besant.

[9] 1. There are two main cosmic principles in nature:—
        a. Active and passive, male and female.—S. D., II, 556. I, 46.
        b. Buddhi and mahat. See also S. D., I, .357. II, 649. III, 273.
    2. These higher principles united produce the three and the seven.—
        S. D., I, 46.
        a. They are called the three Rays of Essence and the four Aspects.
           —S. D., I, 147.
        b. They can be called the three Vehicles with their three Aspects
           and Atma.—S. D., I, 182.

(The psychic nature of the Monad is twofold.)

1. The principle of atma. Spiritual nature. Will.
2. The principle of buddhi. Love nature. Wisdom.
3. The principle of manas. Intelligence nature, Activity.

Note here that the three principles in terms of the Triad with the two synthesising principles on the plane of the Monad, make five principles and give the key to H. P. B.'s numbering in certain places. We might express it thus:

I. The Absolute .... The Monad.
II. 1. Prakriti .... Active intelligence. The Divine
                             Manasaputra.
    2. Purusha .... Love-Wisdom. The Vishnu aspect.

On the plane of objectivity.

III. 3. Atma.
     4. Buddhi   } The Triad.
     5. Manas.

From the standpoint of evolution we regard the higher two and the highest one as the correspondence to the Absolute as He manifests in duality. This is prior to objectivity, which requires the presence of the three. In manifestation we might regard the principles as follows:

c. They are also called the three-tongued Flame of the Four Wicks.
        —S. D., I, 257.
        This is true cosmically and humanly.
The Principles of the Logos........   the seven Planetary Logoi.
                                —S. D., I, 358, 365.
The Principles of the planetary Logos... The vehicle called a chain.
                                —S. D., I, 194, 196. II, 626.
The Principles of man................. The different vehicles.
        Note also:—S. D., I, 176, 177. II, 630, 631. I, 189.
        Summation:—S. D., III, 475.
3. Cosmic Ideation, focussed in a principle results as the consciousness
    of the individual.—S. D., I, 351.
    a. Appropriation by the individual of a vehicle produces a display
        of energy of any particular plane. This energy will be of a
        peculiar colour and quality, according to the plane involved.
4. The seven principles are the manifestation of the one Flame.—S. D.,
    I, 45. III, 374.
Note also the function of the Gods in furnishing man with his principles.
S. D., I, 308.

First Principle . . . . . The sphere of manifestation, the monadic
                 egg.
Second Principle . . . Atma . . . . Will.
Third Principle . . . . Buddhi . . . . Pure reason, wisdom.
Fourth Principle . . . Manas . . . . Pure mind, higher mind.
Fifth Principle . . . . Manas . . . . Lower mind.
Sixth Principle . . . . . Kama-manas . .
Seventh Principle. . . Pure emotion, or feeling.

These are the principles for the microcosm viewed as
having transcended the physical bodies altogether, and
thus the tabulation deals entirely *with the subjective life,
or the development of the psyche or soul.*

This should be borne carefully in mind else confusion
will ensue. In our enumeration we are here dealing with
subjectivity and not with form. We have, therefore, considered:

    a. Sevenfold objectivity. . . . . the material forms.
    b. Sevenfold subjectivity. . . . the psychic evolution.
    c. Sevenfold spirituality. . . . .the life of the Entity.

We will note also that in the tabulation of the spiritual
life of the Monad we considered it as fivefold. This was
necessarily so in this fivefold evolution, but the remaining
two principles might be considered as:

    6. The life of the Heavenly Man in Whose body the
         human Monad finds a place.
    7. The life of the Logos in Whose body the Heavenly
         Man finds place.

It might be useful here to consider another enumeration of the principles of man [10] as he manifests in the

---

[10] Enumeration of the Principles.—S. D., II, 627, 631.
    1st Principle. . . . . .Dense physical body. Sthula Sharira.
    2nd Principle. . . . . .Etheric body. Linga Sharira.
    3rd Principle. . . . . .Prana. Vital energy.
    4th Principle. . . . . .Kama-rupa. The energy of desire.
                         —S. D., I, 136.
        (These are the lower four principles.)

three worlds, the planes whereon the subjective and the objective are united. What have we there? Let us begin where man begins, with the lowest:

7.	The etheric body	1.	The vital body.
6.	Prana	2.	Vital force.
5.	Kama-manas	3.	Desire Mind.
4.	Lower mind	4.	Concrete mind.
3.	Manas	5.	Higher or abstract mind.
2.	Buddhi	6.	Wisdom, Christ force, intuition.
1.	Atma	7.	Spiritual Will.

This is the lowest enumeration for little evolved man at the present time.

From the standpoint of the Ego what can be seen?

I. The Absolute.......Atma. Pure will-to-be.

II. *The Duad.*

      1. Buddhi............ Pure reason, wisdom.

      2. Manas............ Pure mind.

III. *The Triad.*

      3. The causal body.

      4. Lower mind.

5th Principle...............Manas. The energy of thought. The middle principle.—S. D., II, 83, 84. II, 332. S. D., II, 669.

6th Principle...............Buddhi. The energy of love.—S. D., II, 649, 676. S. D., III, 58.

7th Principle...............Atma. The synthetic principle.—S. D., I, 357, 201. S. D., III, 142.

See S. D., III, 201, note.

    a. Buddhi is the vehicle for atma.

    b. Manas is the vehicle for buddhi.

    c. Kamarupa is the vehicle for manas.—S. D., II, 171.

    d. The etheric body is the vehicle for prana.

Remember also:—

    a. That the physical body is not a principle.—S. D., II, 652. III, 445. III, 652.

    b. That atma is not a principle. See also S. D., III, 62, 63. III, 293.

(Other enumerations, differing in certain particulars will be found:—S. D., I, 177, 181, 685. II, 669. III, 476, 560. The latter is more esoteric.)

     5. Kama-manas.
     6. Prana.
     7. The etheric body.

In these various enumerations of the principles we are dealing with them (as H. P. B. has pointed out they must be dealt with)[11, 12] from differing standpoints, dependent upon the stage reached and the angle of vision. We have considered them thus in answering question six because we have sought to emphasise and to impress clearly upon our minds that the three lines of development must be remembered when considering the evolution of the Manasaputras.

2. *The Objective Development.*

This is sevenfold in evolution and in time, ninefold during obscuration, and tenfold at dissolution.

Macrocosmic

1. The seven sacred planets of the solar system.
2. The two which are hid, which are the synthesising planets.
3. The one final synthesising planet—the Sun. Seven added to two added to one make ten.

There are ten centres in the Grand Heavenly Man.

A Heavenly Man

1. The seven chains of a scheme.
2. The two synthesising chains.
3. One ultimate chain.

[11] H. P. Blavatsky says in the *Secret Doctrine* in connection with the Principles.
    a. That mistakes in the classification are very possible.—S. D., II, 677.
    b. That we must seek the occult meaning.—S. D., II, 652.
    That there are really six not seven principles.
    c. That there are several classifications.—S. D., III, 374, 446.
    d. That the esoteric enumeration cannot be made to correspond with the exoteric—S. D., III, 476.
    e. That the numbering of the principles is a question of spiritual progress.—S. D., III, 456, 460.
[12] S. D., III, 456.

There are ten centres in a planetary Logos.

Microcosm

1. The seven vehicles employed:
   - *a.* The atmic sheath.
   - *b.* The buddhic vehicle.
   - *c.* The causal or egoic body.
   - *d.* The mental body.
   - *e.* The astral body.
   - *f.* The etheric body.
   - *g.* The dense physical.
2. Two synthesising bodies:
   - *a.* The causal body.
   - *b.* The physical body.
3. One synthesising body:
   - *a.* The monadic sheath.

There are seven centres in the physical vehicle which correspond to these bodies, with the synthesising centres at the heart and throat; the head is then the ultimate synthesiser. This tabulation deals entirely with the form side, and with the vehicles indwelt by the Logos, the Manasaputras and by Man.

3. *The Subjective Development.*

This is also sevenfold:

1. Astral..........pure desire, emotion, feeling.
2. Kama-manas.....desire-mind.
3. Manas..........lower concrete mind.
4. Higher manas....abstract or pure mind.
5. Buddhi..........pure reason, intuition.
6. Atma............pure will, realisation.
7. Monadic........Will, love-wisdom, intelligence.

This deals with the sevenfold development of inherent love-wisdom by the aid of mind. This proceeds macrocosmically through the seven Heavenly Men, Who are actively intelligent, inherently love, and are objectively seen through Their forms, the planetary schemes. In Their totality They are the Logos, the Grand Man of the Heavens. In the case of a Heavenly Man the development proceeds through the seven groups of human entities who form Their psychic centres. These groups are on their own plane developing intelligence, are inherently love, and can be objectively contacted on the seven chains of a scheme. In the case of individual man, the development proceeds through his seven centres, which are the key to his psychic evolution. A man is also developing intelligence, is inherently love, and is objectively seen through one or other of his bodies.

What I seek to emphasise is the fact of the psychic development, and also that *subjective evolution is the main enterprise of the Logos,* of a planetary Logos and of a man. Active intelligent love (the bringing forth from latency of the inherent quality of love by the intelligent application of the mind faculty) will be the result of the evolutionary process. Just as objectivity is dual, life-form, so subjectivity is dual, mind-love, and the blending of the two produces consciousness. Spirit alone is unity, and is undivided; the development of Spirit (or its assumption of the fruits of evolution) is only to be realised and brought about when the dual evolution of the form and the psyche is consummated. Then Spirit garners the fruits of evolution and gathers to itself the qualities nurtured during manifestation,—perfect love and perfect intelligence showing forth then as active intelligent love-wisdom.

We might, therefore, answer the questions: "What is the Mind aspect and why is it so important?" by saying that the mind aspect is in reality the ability or capacity of the logoic Existence to think, to act, to build, and to evolve in order to develop the faculty of active love. When the Logos, Who is active intelligence, has run His life-cycle, He will be also love fully manifested throughout Nature. This can be likewise predicated of a Heavenly Man in His sphere and of a man in his tiny cycle. Thus the importance of manas can be fully seen. It is the means whereby evolution becomes possible, comprehension is achieved, and activity is generated and utilised.

Let us now consider how this question can be expressed in terms of Fire:

Objectively	*Subjectively*	
1. The sea of fire.	1. Our God is a consuming fire	Energising will.
2. The akasha ...	2. The Light of God	Form aspect.
3. The aether	3. The heat of matter	Activity aspect.
4. The air	4. The illumination of the intuition.	
5. Fire	5. The fire of mind.	
6. The astral light.	6. The heat of the emotions.	
7. Physical plane electricity ...	7. Kundalini and prana.	

Spiritually.

This is hid in a threefold mystery:

1. The mystery of electricity.
2. The mystery of the seven constellations.
3. The mystery of the ONE ABOVE THE LOGOS.

4. *The Heavenly Men and Man.*

The final part of question six is: Who are the Manasaputras?

This will be dealt with in greater detail in connection with our planet when taking up the subject of the coming of the Lords of Flame. It is desirable now to make certain facts clear which must form the basis of any thought upon this subject.

The Divine Manasaputras,[13, 14] Who are known in the *Secret Doctrine* by diverse names, are the Mind-born Sons of Brahma, the third aspect logoic.

They are the seven planetary Logoi, and are the Lords of the Rays, the seven Heavenly Men. They developed the mind aspect in the first solar system, that in which Brahma was paramount, and in Himself embodied objective existence. This He did in the same sense as that in which the second aspect (the Vishnu or Dragon of Wisdom aspect) is the sumtotal of existence in this the second system.

The cells in Their bodies are made up of the units of the human and deva evolutions in the same manner (only on a higher turn of the spiral) as the bodies of human beings are made up of living organisms, the various animated cells, or the lesser lives. This is a basic fact in occultism, and the relationship between the cells in the human vehicles, and the cells in the bodies of a Heavenly

[13] In the *Secret Doctrine* the Heavenly Men are spoken of as:
1. Agents of creation. They are the totality of manifestation.—S. D., I, 470.
2. They are pre-cosmic.—S. D., I, 470.
3. They are the sumtotal of solar and lunar entities.—S. D., I, 152, 470. Compare II, 374.
4. They are the seven Biblical Archangels.
    They are the seven Forces or creative Powers.
    They are the seven Spirits before the Throne.
    They are the seven Spirits of the Planets.—S. D., I, 472, 153.
5. In Their totality They are the Secret Unpronounceable Name.—S. D., I, 473.
6. They are the collective Dhyan Chohans.—S. D., I, 477.
7. They are the seven Kumaras. The seven Rishis.—S. D., I, 493. III, 196, 327.
8. They are the Sons of Light.—S. D., I, 521, 522.
9. They are the Hierarchy of creative Powers.—S. D., I, 233.
10. They are the veiled synthesis.—S. D., I, 362.
11. They are our own planetary deities.—S. D., I, 153.
12. They are all men, the product of other worlds.—S. D., I, 132.
13. They are closely connected with the seven stars of the Great Bear.—S. D., I, 488. S. D., II, 332. II, 579, 668. S. D., III, 195.
14. They are symbolised by circles.—S. D., II, 582.
15. They are collectively the fallen Angels.—S. D., II, 284, 541.

[14] *The Sons of Mind:* are known by various terms, such as:—"The Manasaputras, the Prajapatis, the Kumaras, the Primordial Seven, the Rudras, the Heavenly Men, the Rishis, the Spirits before the Throne.

Man, will be productive of illumination if carefully studied.

Just as a human being has an originating source, the Monad, and a semi-permanent vehicle, the causal body, but manifests through his lower principles (of which the dense physical is not one) so a Heavenly Man has an originating source, His Monad, a semi-permanent body on the monadic levels of the solar system, but manifests through three lower sheaths, our atmic, buddhic, and manasic levels. He is extraneous to the astral and physical planes just as a human being is to the physical. Man vitalises the physical vehicle with his force or heat but he does not occultly count it as a principle. So the Heavenly Man is extraneous to the two lower planes of manifestation though He vitalises them with His force. The human being realises his relationship (as a cell in the body) to a Heavenly Man only when he is developing the consciousness of the Ego on its own plane. If it might be so expressed, the groups of causal bodies are the lowest forms through which a Heavenly Man manifests, just as the physical body is the lowest through which a human being manifests, and this in its etheric connotation.

It should be borne in mind that the manifesting Existences embody certain planes, and have Their points of deepest involution on diverse levels:

a. A Man originates on the monadic level, has his main focal point on the fifth level, the mental, but is seeking full conscious development on the three lower planes, the mental, the astral and the physical.

b. A Heavenly Man has His source outside the solar system (as man outside the three worlds of his endeavor), has His main focal point on the second plane of the system, the monadic, and is seeking consciousness on the planes of the Triad,—this in relation to all the cells in His body. He developed consciousness on the three lower planes of the three worlds during the first solar system, again in relation to the cells in His body. Man is repeating His endeavor up to the fifth Initiation which will bring him to a stage of consciousness achieved by a Heavenly Man in a much earlier mahamanvantara. In connection with the initiations this should be carefully borne in mind.

c. *A solar Logos* has His origin on a still higher cosmic level, has His main focal point on the cosmic mental plane but is expressing Himself through the three lower cosmic planes just as man is seeking self-expression in the three worlds. Therefore, the seven major planes of the solar system are in the same relation to Him cosmically as the physical plane is to a human being. They form His etheric and dense bodies. It might be stated that:

1. He vitalises them by His life and heat.
2. He animates them.
3. He is fully conscious through them.
4. The etheric is *in time* His lowest principle, but the dense physical is not counted. The dense cosmic physical body is composed of matter of the three lower planes of the solar system, the mental, the astral and the physical. *The buddhic plane is consequently the fourth cosmic ether.*

d. The Heavenly Men form the seven centres in the body of the Logos. Therefore, They are the spheres of fire which animate His body, and each of Them expresses one form of His force manifestation, according to Their place within the body.

e. Human beings, when centred within their groups on causal levels, form one or other of the seven centres in the body of a Heavenly Man.

f. The solar Logos forms one centre in the body of a still greater cosmic ENTITY. Human beings therefore find their place within one of the forty-nine centres (not groups, for a centre may be made up of many groups, corresponding to the different parts) of the seven Heavenly Men.

A Heavenly Man, with His seven centres, forms one centre in the body of the solar Logos. I would here point out to you the close connection existing between *the seven Rishis of the Great Bear* and the seven Heavenly Men. The seven Rishis of the Great Bear are to Them what the Monad is to the evolving human unit.

VII. WHY IS THE PROGRESS OF EVOLUTION CYCLIC?

This question is one which necessarily appals us and makes us wonder.

Let us, therefore, deal with it as follows: Certain ideas are involved in the thought of cyclic progression, and these ideas it might pay us well to contemplate.

1. *The Idea of Repetition.*

This repetition involves the following factors:

a. Repetition in time: The thought of cyclic activity necessitates periods of time of differing length—greater or lesser cycles—but (according to their length) of uniform degree. A manvantara, or Day of Brahma, is always of a certain length, and so is a mahamanvantara. The cycles wherein an atom of any plane revolves upon its axis are uniform on its own plane.

b. Repetition in fact: This involves the idea of a key measure, or sound of any particular group of atoms that go to the composition of any particular form. This grouping of atoms will tend to the make-up of a particular series of circumstances and will repeat the measure or sound when an animating factor is brought to bear upon them. When the vitalising force is contacting at stated periods a certain set of atoms, it will call forth from them a specific sound which will demonstrate objectively as environing circumstances. In other words,

the interplay of the Self and the not-self is invariably
of a cyclic nature. The same quality in tone will be
called forth by the Self as it indwells the form, but the
key will ascend by gradual degrees. It is similar to the
effect produced in striking the same note in different
octaves, beginning at the base.

c. Repetition in space: This concept is involved
deep in the greater concept of karma, which is really the
law that governs the matter of the solar system, and
which commenced its work in earlier solar systems. We
have, therefore, *cycles in order,* and repetition in an
ever-ascending spiral, under definite law.

The thoughts thus conveyed might be expressed likewise as follows:

a. The solar system repeating
    its activity .... Repetition in Space.
b. A planetary chain repeating
    its activity .... Repetition in Time.
c. The constant consecutive re-
    verberation of a plane note,
    of a subplane note, and of
    all that is called into objec-
    tivity by that note .... Plane Repetition.
d. The tendency of atoms to
    perpetuate their activity,
    and thus produce similar-
    ity of circumstance, of en-
    vironment, and of vehicle.. Form Repetition.

When we carry these ideas on to every plane in the solar
system, and from thence to the cosmic planes, we have
opened up for ourselves infinitude.

2. *Repetition of Cyclic Action is Governed by Two
    Laws:*

Perhaps it is more accurate to say that it is governed
by one law, primarily, and a subsidiary law. This leads

to two general types of cycles, and is involved in the very nature of the Self and of the not-self. The interplay of the two by the aid of mind produces that which we call environment or circumstance.

The general law, which produces cyclic effect, is the Law of Attraction and Repulsion, of which the subsidiary law is the Law of Periodicity, and of Rebirth. Cyclic evolution is entirely the result of the activity of matter, and of the Will or Spirit. It is produced by the interaction of active matter and moulding Spirit. Every form holds hid a Life. Every life constantly reaches out after the similar life latent in other forms. When Spirit and matter sound the same note evolution will cease. When the note sounded by the form is stronger than that of Spirit, we have attraction between *forms*. When the note sounded by Spirit is stronger than that of matter and form, we have Spirit repelling form. Here we have the basis for the battlefield of life, and its myriads of intermediate stages, which might be expressed as follows:

a. The period of the domination of the form note is that of involution.
b. The period of the repulsion of form by Spirit is that of the battlefield of the three worlds.
c. The period of the attraction of Spirit and Spirit, and the consequent withdrawal from form is that of the Path.
d. The period of domination of the note of Spirit is that of the higher planes of evolution.

To the synchronisation of the notes, or to the lack of synchronisation, may be attributed all that occurs in the world cycles. Thus we have the production of harmony; first, the basic note of matter, then the note of Spirit gradually overcoming the lower note and usurping attention till gradually the note of Spirit overpowers all other notes. Yet it must be borne in mind that it is the note of the life that holds the form together. The note of the Sun, for instance, holds in just attraction the circling spheres, the planets. The notes synchronise and harmonise till the stage of adequacy is reached and the period of abstraction. Cyclic evolution proceeds. A human being, similarly, holds (by means of his note) the atoms of the three bodies together, being to them as the central sun to the planets. Primarily, nevertheless, it may be posited that the Law of Attraction is the demonstration of the powers of Spirit, whilst the Law of Repulsion governs the form. Spirit attracts Spirit throughout the greater cycle. In lesser cycles, Spirit temporarily attracts matter. The tendency of Spirit is to merge and blend with Spirit. Form repulses form, and thus brings about separation. But—during the great cycle of evolution—when the third factor of Mind comes in, and when the point of balance is the goal, the cyclic display of the interaction between Spirit and form is seen, and the result is the ordered cycles of the planets, of a human being, and of an atom. Thus, through repetition, is consciousness developed, and responsive faculty induced. When this faculty is of such a nature that it is an inherent part of the Entity's working capital, it has to be exercised on every plane, and again cyclic action is the law, and hence rebirth again and again is the method of exercise. When the innate conscious faculty of every unit of consciousness has become co-ordinated as part of the equipment of the Logos on every plane of the solar system, then, and only then, will cyclic evolution cease, will rotary movement on every plane of the cosmic physical plane be of such a uniform vibration as to set up action on the next cosmic plane, the astral.

3. *The Third Idea Involved Is That of the Two Types of Cycles*

1. *Rotation on the axis:* This is to be seen whether we are dealing with a minute atom of substance, with a planet revolving on its axis, with the rotation of the causal body, or with the rotation of a solar system.

- a. In relation to the human being, this might be considered as the rotation of the various sheaths around the central consciousness during any one incarnation.
- b. In relation to a Heavenly Man it might be considered as the rotation of a globe within a chain, or the period of one incarnation.
- c. In relation to a solar Logos it might be considered as one complete revolution of the Sun in space, with all that is included within the ring-pass-not.

2. *Rotation around an orbit.* This is the revolution of a sphere of life, not only on its axis, but along a spheroidal path or orbit around a central point.

- a. In connection with man this might be considered as the revolution of the wheel of life, or the passage of an entity through the three lower planes down into incarnation and back again.
- b. In connection with a Heavenly Man it might be considered as the cycle which we call a round in which the life of the Heavenly Man cycles through all the seven globes.
- c. In connection with the solar Logos it is the complete revolution of the solar system around its cosmic centre.

It is to be noted at this point that the ideas dealt with in connection with cyclic evolution cannot be posited apart from the concept of consciousness. The ideas of

time, of space, and of activity (from the point of view
of the occultist), can only be conceived as relative to
some conscious entity, to some Thinker.

Time to the occultist is that cycle, greater or lesser,
in which some life runs some specific course, in which
some particular period begins, continues, and ends, in
connection with the awareness of some Entity, and is
recognised only as time when the participating life has
reached a considerable stage of awareness. Time has
been defined as a succession of states of consciousness,[15]
and it therefore may be studied from the point of
view of

[15] The *Secret Doctrine* says:
1. The Universe is in reality but a huge aggregation of states of
   consciousness.—S. D., II, 633. I, 70, 626.
2. Spirit and consciousness are synonymous terms.—S. D., I, 43, 125,
   349, 350, 592, 593.
3. Every atom in the universe is endowed with consciousness.—S. D.,
   I, 105. II, 709, 742.
4. Six types of Consciousness as embodied in the Kingdom of Nature on the five planes of *Human* Evolution.—S. D., I, 123.
   II, 678.
   a. *The Mineral Kingdom* 1.
   Intelligent activity. All atoms show ability to select, to discriminate intelligently under the Law of Attraction and
   Repulsion.—S. D., I, 295.
   b. *Vegetable Kingdom* 2.
   Intelligent activity plus embryo sensation or feeling.
   c. *Animal Kingdom* 3.
   Intelligent activity, sensation plus instinct, or embryo mentality.—S. D., III, 573, 574.
   These three embody the sub-human consciousness.
   d. *Human consciousness* 4.
   Intelligent activity, love or perfected feeling or realisation and
   will, or intelligent purpose. The three aspects. S. D., I,
   215, 231.—S. D., II, 552. III, 579.
   This is Self-Consciousness—the middle point.—S. D., I, 297.
   e. *Spiritual Consciousness* 5.
   Buddhic realisation. The unit is aware of his group. The
   separated unit identifies himself with his ray or type.—
   S. D., III, 572. I, 183, 623.
   f. *Atmic Consciousness* 6.
   The consciousness of the unit of the Septenary solar system.
   —S. D., II, 673. II, 741.
   These two embody super-consciousness.
The seventh type embraces them all and is God Consciousness.—S. D.,
II, 740 note.
Study also S. D., I, 300, 301, 183, 221, 623. S. D., II, 32 note, 741, 552
note.—S. D., III, 573, 574, 558, 557, 584.

a. Logoic consciousness, or the successive states of divine realisation within the solar sphere.

b. Planetary consciousness, or the consciousness of a Heavenly Man as He cycles successively through the scheme.

c. Causal consciousness, or the successive expanding of the intelligent awareness of a human being from life to life.

d. Human consciousness, or the awareness of a man on the physical plane, and progressively on the emotional and the mental planes.

e. Animal, vegetable and mineral consciousness which differs from the human consciousness in many particulars, and primarily in that it does not co-ordinate, or deduce and recognise separate identity. It resembles human consciousness in that it covers the response to successive contacts of the units involved during their small cycles.

f. Atomic consciousness, demonstrating through successive states of repulsion and attraction. In this last definition lies the key to the other states of consciousness.

An atom revolves upon its axis. In its revolution it comes within the field of activity of other atoms. These it either attracts and swings into its own field of operation, or it repulses and drives them outside its range of activity, causing separation. One thing to be borne in mind in the concept of mutual attraction is the preservation of identity in cohesion.

A human being in objective manifestation likewise revolves upon his axis, or around his central point, his mainspring of animation; this brings him within the range of activity of other men, other human atoms. This similarly either tends to co-operation or cohesion, or to separation or repulsion. Again it must be borne in mind that even in cohesion identity is preserved.

A Heavenly Man, through the form of a planetary chain, similarly revolves upon His axis, and a like phenomenon may be observed. A planet repulses a planet similarly charged, for it is a known law that like particles repel each other, but occultly it is a known law that they will eventually attract each other as the vibration becomes sufficiently strong. A negative planet will be attracted by a positive, and so on through all forms. This is the manifestation of SEX in substance of every kind, from the tiny atom in the body to the vast planetary chains, and this is the basis of activity. Radiatory activity is simply the interplay between male and female, and this can be seen in the physical atom of the scientist, among men and women, and in the vaster atom of a solar system as it vibrates with its cosmic opposite.

We might, therefore, consider *time* as that process of activity, or that progression in development, wherein the indwelling Consciousness is seeking its opposite, and coming under the Law of Attraction, which leads to atomic, human, planetary, spiritual, solar and cosmic marriage. This idea is comparatively simple in relation to a human being, and can be seen in daily demonstration in his contacts with other men; these contacts are governed, for instance, very largely by his likes and dislikes. All these attractions and repulsions are under law, and their cause exists in *form* itself. The emotion of like or of dislike is nothing else but the realisation by the conscious entity of the swinging into his magnetic radius of an atomic form which he is led, by the very law of his own being, to either attract or repulse. Only when the form is transcended, and Spirit seeks out Spirit, will the phenomena of repulsion cease. This will be the inevitable finale at the cessation of solar evolution, and it will bring about pralaya. The duration of the interplay, the period of the search of Spirit for Spirit, and the vibratory process necessitated by the utilisation of the form, this we call Time, whether in connection with a man, a planetary Logos, or the Deity.

Space, again, is included in the idea of consciousness, and its utilisation of matter. Space, for the Logos, is literally the form wherein His conscious activities and purposes are worked out—the solar ring-pass-not. The space wherein a planetary Logos works out His plans is similarly as much of solar space as His consciousness is developed enough to use. Man again repeats the process and his ring-pass-not is included in the radius of his consciousness, and may be very circumscribed as in the case of the little evolved, or may be inclusive of a portion of planetary space of great extent, and even in the case of the very highly evolved may begin to touch the periphery of the sphere of influence of the planetary Logos in Whose body he is a cell.

Space for the atom (for instance, the atom in the physical body of man) will be the radius of the form in which is found the greater centre of consciousness of which it is a part and it will be both attracted and repulsed—attracted and built into the form of the greater Life, yet repulsed and thereby prevented from moving from a certain point within that form.

We have here dealt a little with time and space in their relation to a specific centre of consciousness; we have seen that they are simply *forms of ideas to express the cyclic activity of an entity.* The subject is exceedingly abstruse, due to the low stage of the human intelligence, which is as yet so occupied with the objective or material side of manifestation that the attraction existing between Spirit and Spirit is little more than a concept. When more of the human family have their centre of consciousness in the Ego and hence are busy with the work of repulsing matter, and with the withdrawal of

Spirit from form, then only will the transmutative process be comprehended, then only will time (as known in the three worlds) be transcended, and then only will space (as manifested to man through the three lower planes or the eighteen subplanes) be found to be a barrier. This same statement can be predicated of the seven Logoi and of the solar Logos, extending the idea to other planes, solar and cosmic. So also can it be narrowed down to the subhuman, and to the involutionary lives, remembering ever that as the consciousness is more confined and restricted so inertia, lack of response, and limitation of radiation will be seen.

By a close scrutiny of chart V, it will be apparent wherein lies the problem of the Logos, and wherein lies the accuracy of the correspondence between Him and His reflection Man.

First. Both are in objective manifestation on the physical plane.

Second. Both are at their point of deepest involution.

Third. Both are trammelled by matter, and are developing consciousness (egoic consciousness) on the physical plane—man on the solar physical, and the Logos on the cosmic physical plane.

Fourth. Man has to bring down into conscious full control, the God within. Through that control he must dominate circumstance, make his environment his instrument and manipulate matter. On cosmic levels the Logos does likewise. Both are far from achievement.

Fifth. Both work in, with, and by, electrical force.

Sixth. Both come under the laws governing forms and hence both are controlled in time and space by KARMA, which is the Law of forms. It has to do with quality, as force has to do with vibration.

Seventh. Both work through forms made up of:

a. Three main types of forms: A mental form, one aspect of manifestation; an astral form, a second aspect; and a physical form, the third aspect. The mental vibration sets the key measure and seeks to utilise and co-ordinate the physical body at *Will*. It deals with or links up the consciousness to the three forms in one direction; it repulses and causes separation in another. The astral vibration deals with the quality, with the attractive measure. It is the psychic element. The physical is the meeting ground of consciousness with the material form. This last is the result produced by the union of the key measure and the quality of tone.

b. Seven centres of force which hold the three forms in one coherent whole, and cause their vitalisation and their co-ordination. They put the triple unit into correlation with their main centre of consciousness on the higher planes, whether that centre is the causal body of man, of a planetary Logos, or of a solar Logos.

c. Millions of infinitesimal cells, each embodying a lesser life, each in a condition of constant activity, and each repulsing other cells so as to preserve individuality or identity, yet each held to each by a central attractive force. Thus we have produced the objective form of a crystal, a vegetable, an animal, a man, a planet, a system.

Finally, both work, therefore, in a dual manner and each demonstrates both attraction and repulsion.

Attraction of matter to Spirit and the building of a form for the use of Spirit is the result of electrical energy in the universe, which in each case brings the lesser lives or spheres into its range of influence. The magnetic force, the life of the Logos gathers together His body of manifestation. The magnetic force of the Heavenly Man, the planetary Logos, gathers out of the solar ring-pass-not that which He needs for each incarnation.

The magnetic force of the Ego gathers, at each rebirth, matter within the particular sphere or scheme within which the Ego has place. So on down the scale, we find the lesser pursuing its round ever within the greater.

Therefore we have (during a period of Attraction and Repulsion, or a life cycle) that which we call Time and Space, and this holds equally true in the life cycle of a Logos or an ant, or a crystal. There are cycles of activity in matter, due to some energising Will, and then Time and space are known. There are cycles of non-being when Time and Space are not, and the energising Will is withdrawn. But we must not forget that this is purely relative, and only to be considered from the standpoint of the particular life or entity involved, and the special stage of awareness reached. All must be interpreted in terms of consciousness.

The first type of cycle, or the period involved in one entire revolution of a sphere around its own centre of consciousness, is to the particular Entity involved (be he God or man) a lesser cycle. The second type of cycle or the period involved in the complete circling of an orbit, or the revolution of a sphere around the centre of which it is an integral part, we can consider as a greater cycle. The third type of cycle has not so much to do with the transition of the form through a certain location in space but as the cycle which includes both the greater and the lesser cycles. It has to do with the response of the ENTITY, to Whom our solar Logos is but a centre in His Body, to the contacts made on that centre and on its cosmic opposite. These two centres, for instance, our solar system and its cosmic opposite, in their interaction create a cycle period which has a relation to the "ONE WHO IS ABOVE OUR LOGOS." This is, of course, beyond human conception, but must be included in our enumeration of cycles if exactitude is to be achieved.

VIII. WHY IS KNOWLEDGE [16] BOTH EXOTERIC AND ESOTERIC?

We can now take up the question next in order, which was worded: *"Why do we consider certain aspects of knowledge esoteric and other aspects as exoteric?"*

The answer to this practically involves the realisation that some knowledge deals with the subjective side of life, and the other type of knowledge with the objective side; that one type of knowledge is concerned with energy and force (hence the danger of undue hasty revelation) and another with that which is energised. Therefore it will be apparent that until the faculty of ascertaining subjective information is achieved, whole ranges of facts will remain outside the scope of the consciousness of the majority.

As we have been told, the goal of evolution is the attainment of consciousness on all planes; owing to the small evolutionary attainment of the race only the physical plane is as yet in any way brought under *conscious* control. The knowledge which deals with that plane,

---

[16] In the *Secret Doctrine* we are told that *there are seven branches of knowledge mentioned in the Puranas.* S. D., I, 192.

Correspondences can here be worked out in connection with:—

    a. The seven Rays, the Lords of Sacrifice, Love and Knowledge.
    b. The seven states of consciousness.
    c. The seven states of matter or planes.
    d. The seven types of forces.
    e. The seven Initiations and many other septenates.

The Gnosis, the hidden Knowledge, is the seventh Principle, the six schools of Indian philosophy are the six principles.—S. D., I, 299.

These six schools are:—

    a. The school of Logic.......Proof of right perception.
    b. The atomic school.........System of particulars. Elements. Alchemy and chemistry.
    c. The Sankhya school.......System of numbers. The materialistic school. The theory of the seven states of matter or prakriti.
    d. The school of Yoga......Union. The rule of daily life. Mysticism.
    e. The school of Ceremonial Ritual. Worship of the devas or religion .... Gods.
    f. The Vedanta school.......Has to do with non-duality. Deals with the relation of Atma in man to the Logos.

The Gnosis or hidden knowledge is the same as Atma vidya, or Theosophy, and includes the other six.

the information which is concerned with densest objectivity, the sumtotal of facts connected with the five lower subplanes of the physical plane are (from the occult standpoint) considered exoteric. During the next two races the other two subplanes will be mastered, and the entire mass of knowledge concerned with physical and etheric matter, with energy, form and experience on the physical plane, will be easily available to man, and concern only his five physical senses.

Information and knowledge of the life evolving through the forms will for a considerably longer time be considered esoteric, as also will the apprehension and comprehension of the matter aspect, and the laws governing energy on the astral and the mental planes. This is stated in connection with average man, the rank and file of humanity. Objective or exoteric information is largely that obtained or ascertained by men in the Hall of Learning by means of the five senses, and by experiment. Experiment in due course of time and after many cycles of incarnation is transmuted into experience, and this produces eventually that which we call instinct, or the habitual reaction of some type of consciousness to a given set of circumstances, or of environment. These two factors of the senses and of experimental contact can be seen working out in the animal and human kingdoms; the difference between the two exists in the ability of the man consciously to remember, apprehend, anticipate, and utilise the fruits of past experience, and thus influence the present and prepare for the future. He employs the physical brain for this purpose. An animal likewise has an instinctual memory, apprehension, and an embryo anticipation, but (lacking mind) he is unable to adjust them to circumstances in the sense of prearrangement, and lacks the capacity consciously to utilise, and thus reap, the benefit of past events, and to learn from experience in the manner which a man does. The animal uses the solar plexus in the same way that a man uses the brain; it is the organ of instinct.

All that can be acquired by instinct and by the use of the concrete mind functioning through the physical brain can be considered as dealing with that which we call exoteric. It is thus evident how the range of fact will differ according to:

a. The age of the soul.
b. Experience developed and used.
c. Condition of the brain and the physical body.
d. Circumstances and environment.

As time progresses and man reaches a fair state of evolution, mind is more rapidly developed, and a new factor comes gradually into play. Little by little the intuition, or the transcendental mind, begins to function, and eventually supersedes the lower or concrete mind. It then utilises the physical brain as a receiving plate, but at the same time develops certain centres in the head, and thus transfers the zone of its activity from the physical brain to the higher head centres, existing in etheric matter. For the mass of humanity, this will be effected during the opening up of the etheric subplanes during the next two races. This is paralleled in the animal kingdom by the gradual transference of the zone of activity from the solar plexus to the rudimentary brain, and its gradual development by the aid of manas.

As we consider these points, it will become apparent that the esoteric aspects of knowledge are really those zones of consciousness which are not yet conquered, and brought within the radius of control of the indwelling Entity.

The point to be emphasised is that when this is realised the true significance of the esoteric and the occult will be appreciated, and *the endeavor of all* KNOWERS *will be to draw within the zone of their knowledge other*

*units who are ready for a similar expansion of conscious-
ness.* In this thought lies the key to the work of the
Brotherhood. They attract by Their force into certain
fields of realisation and endeavor and by that attraction
and the response of those human .atoms who are ready,
the group soul on the upward arc, or a particular centre
of a Heavenly Man, is co-ordinated.

In the same way the animal is brought at a certain
stage into the zone of influence of the lesser sons of
mind—human beings who are the elder brothers of the
animals, as the Masters of the Wisdom are the Elder
Brothers where humanity is concerned. So the interlocking proceeds and the division of responsibility.

IX.   WHAT IS THE RELATION BETWEEN:

  a. The ten planetary schemes?
  b. The seven sacred planets?
  c. The seven chains in a scheme?
  d. The seven globes in a chain?
  e. The seven rounds on a globe?
  f. The seven root-races and the seven subraces?

We have in this question a vast quantity of matter to
deal with and it will be impossible for us to do more
than to get a broad and general idea.

The subject is so vast and the comprehensiveness of
the interrelated points is so great that we shall only attain lucidity if we confine our attention to certain broad
general conceptions, leaving the subsidiary points for
more detailed elucidation at some later period.

1. *The Inter-related Parts*

Primarily I would suggest that we consider this subject only as it *concerns a Heavenly Man,* that we omit
from our immediate calculations the consideration of
the cellular composition of His body (those separated
units of consciousness which we call deva and human

beings), and that we view the matter from what is to the human being, the group concept, and not the individual.

The entire middle section of this treatise on the Fires has to do with the development of the consciousness of a Heavenly Man, and the application by Him of the knowledge gained (through the aid of manas or mind) in a previous solar system, to the acquisition of wisdom through objectivity, and to the transmutation of the earlier acquired faculty into applied Love. This is His work in the same sense that the work of the cells within His body is to develop the mind principle. When through experience in the three worlds the human units have accomplished this, they can then gain—through the final initiations—something of the group concept, or the conscious realisation of place, and of energised activity within the ring-pass-not of their particular planetary Logos. Therefore, we might consider the following points:

First: The work of the units who go to the make-up of a particular planetary Logos. This is of a threefold nature:

a. To attain the consciousness of the realised control of their own individual ring-pass-not, or of their own sphere of activity. This covers the period of evolution up to the first Initiation, or their entrance upon the Path, and thus into the spiritual kingdom. It concerns the awakening of consciousness on the three lower planes.

b. To attain the consciousness of the particular centre in the body of one of the planetary Logoi—which centre embodies their group activity. This carries them to the fifth Initiation, and covers the period wherein consciousness is awakened on the five planes of evolution.

c. To attain to the consciousness of the centre in the Body of the Logos of which any particular planetary

Logos is the sumtotal. This carries them to the seventh Initiation and covers the period of the awakening of consciousness on the seven planes of the solar system.

These expansions are attained by the aid of mind, transmuted in due course of time into love-wisdom, and entail the conscious control of the entire seven planes of the solar system, or of the lowest cosmic plane.

Second: The work of the Heavenly Men Who in their totality are the seven centres in the body of the Logos. This work is again threefold:

a. To attain to full self-consciousness, or to individual consciousness on the five planes; to vibrate with conscious activity within Their Own ring-pass-not, a planetary scheme. This covers a period in the scheme of involution, and of that period during the evolutionary stage which is comprised within the first three rounds up to the entrance upon the fourth round.

b. To attain to the consciousness of the solar Logos, within Whose body They form the centres. It entails the attainment by a Heavenly Man of a group consciousness of a sevenfold nature, or the achievement of accurate vibratory relationship with the other Heavenly Men Who form the other centres. It carries with it the capacity to have full conscious control on the seven planes of the solar system, and covers that period of development which is undergone in a planetary chain during the fourth, fifth, and sixth rounds. It should be borne in mind that a paralleling recognition should here be given to the fact that the solar Logos holds an analogous position in the body of a cosmic Entity to that held by a Heavenly Man in the body of a solar Logos.

c. To attain to the consciousness of a greater centre on cosmic levels. This covers the period of the seventh round, and gives to a Heavenly Man (when these rounds are viewed in the light of the Eternal Now, and not from the standpoint of time and of space) the consciousness of the cosmic astral, or the second lowest plane of the cosmic planes. A great deal of the problem to be seen slowly working out at this time to a solution is due to the fact that the control of the Heavenly Man, Whose body our scheme may be, is as yet but partial, and His cosmic experience is as yet but imperfect. This necessarily affects the cells in His body in the same way that lack of astral control in the case of a human being, affects his vehicle. It might here be pointed out that the evolution of the Heavenly Men is unequal, and that our planetary Logos has not the control, for instance, that the Heavenly Man of the Venus chain has achieved. In each round one subplane of the cosmic astral plane is brought under control, and the consciousness of the Heavenly Man expands to include one subplane more. The planetary Lord of Venus has dominated and controlled the five subplanes and is working on the sixth. Our planetary Logos is engaged in a similar work on the fourth and fifth. The work, as in all cycles, overlaps and it might be explained thus:

He is perfecting the control of the fourth subplane on the cosmic astral plane, and has nearly completed it. He is beginning to work at the control of the fifth subplane—a control which will be perfected in the fifth round.

He is sensing and responding to the vibration of the sixth subplane, but is not as yet fully conscious on that subplane.

We have a corresponding reflection to this in the fourth and fifth root-races on this planet, in which the astral consciousness of the Atlantean cycle is being perfected, the fifth principle is being developed, and the sixth is being gradually sensed. This deserves thoughtful consideration.

Third: The work of a solar Logos is again of a corresponding nature:

a. He has to attain to the full consciousness of His entire ring-pass-not, or of the seven planes of the solar system. This covers a period wherein five of the Heavenly Men, or five of His centres, and therefore, five schemes, reach a stage of accurate response to contact and stimulation.

b. He has to attain to the consciousness of the cosmic Logos within Whose body He is a centre. He must find by experience His place within the cosmic group of which He is a part, in much the same way as a planetary Logos pursues a similar course. This is achieved when all the Heavenly Men or each of the seven centres are awakened and functioning consciously and freely, with their systemic inter-relation adjusted and controlled by the Law of Action and Reaction. It brings within His control not only the seven subplanes of the cosmic physical plane (our seven major planes) but necessarily also the cosmic astral plane.

c. To attain to the consciousness of the centre in the body of the ONE ABOUT WHOM NOUGHT MAY BE SAID. This centre is formed by the sphere of influence of a cosmic Logos. In the body of a cosmic Logos, a solar Logos is a centre.

We must bear in mind that this enumeration is given from the standpoint of *the present,* and from the angle of vision (relatively limited) of the Heavenly Man of our particular scheme, and that it is therefore circumscribed by His peculiar conditions, which govern the intelligence of the cells in His body; it is given from the point of view of differentiation and not of synthesis. A synthetic absorption proceeds eventually in connection with all these Entities, and each undergoes a process, paralleling on His Own level that undergone by the Microcosm; in the case of the Microcosm the causal body or the body of the Ego acts as the synthesiser of the energy of the Quaternary or lower Self, and the spir-

TABULATION II

EVOLUTION IN THE UNIVERSE

Entity.	Vehicle	Centre	Space	Time
The Unknown	7 constellations	cosmic Logos	5 cosmic planes.	Period of three solar systems.
A cosmic Logos	7 solar systems	solar Logos	4 cosmic planes.	Period of one solar system.
A solar Logos	7 planetary schemes	Heavenly Man	3 cosmic planes.	Period of one planetary scheme.
A Heavenly Man	7 planetary chains	Chohans and groups	2 cosmic planes.	Period of one solar system.
A Man	7 etheric centres	a Principle	1 cosmic plane.	Period of one planetary scheme.

itual or monadic sheath as the synthesiser of the seven principles, making thus the three, the seven, and the ten.

In closing I would point out that the mind must carefully be kept from reducing all these ideas into a rankly materialistic concept. It must be rigidly borne in mind that we are dealing with the subjective life, and not with the objective form, and that we are considering, for instance, the synthesis of the principles or the qualitating energies and not the synthesis of form.

Through each etheric centre man is bringing to perfect vibration some one principle or quality through which the subjective life may express itself.

Through each chain in a scheme a Heavenly Man is endeavoring to do the same.

Through each scheme in a system, a solar Logos is working at the same thing; the goal is synthetic quality and not primarily the perfection of the form. The response of the energised form to the qualitative life is naturally—under the law—equal to the demand, but this is of secondary importance and is not the object in view.

We have seen that the work to be accomplished in all the above cases is necessarily threefold:

First. The development of individual consciousness.

Second. The development of group consciousness.

Third. The development of God consciousness, of that consciousness in each case which represents the highest spiritual Source, and which is recognised as the same in essence as the God within the individual, whether man or solar Logos.

This concept must be meditated upon by all thinkers and its synthesis emphasised. The relation of the cell to the group, of the group to the aggregate of groups, and of them all to the indwelling Entity Who holds them in synthetic correlation by means of the Law of Attraction and Repulsion is of vital moment. Two main ideas must always be borne in mind:

> That the terms "cell, group, or congery of groups"
> relate entirely to the form of vehicle, and thus
> to the *matter* aspect.

> That the idea of an Entity Who synthesises the groups
> and is the animating life of the cell has to do with
> the *Spirit* aspect.

These two concepts lead necessarily to a third, that
of the development of consciousness, which is the gradual expansion of the realisation of the Indweller in the
form, the apprehension by the Self of the relation of
the form to Itself, and of its slow utilisation and control.
This persists until that Realisation includes the cell, the
group, and the totality of groups. These ideas can be
applied to the three grades of consciousness referred to.
As follows:

Man, the lowest type of *coherent* consciousness (using
the word "consciousness" in its true connotation as the
"One who knows") is but a cell, a minute atom within
a group.

A Heavenly Man represents a coherent conscious
group.

A solar Logos on His Own plane holds an analogous
place to that of a Heavenly Man in a solar system, and
from a still higher standpoint to that of a man within
the solar system. When the place of the solar planes
within the cosmic scheme is duly apprehended it will be
recognised that on cosmic levels of a high order the
solar Logos is an Intelligence as relatively low in the
order of cosmic consciousness as man is in relation to
solar consciousness. He is but a cell in the body of
the ONE ABOUT WHOM NAUGHT MAY BE SAID. His work parallels on cosmic levels the work of man on the solar
planes. He has to undergo on the three lower cosmic
planes a process of developing an apprehension of His
environment of the same nature as man in the three
worlds. This fact should be remembered by all stu-

dents of this central division of our subject; above all the analogy between the cosmic physical planes and the solar physical planes must be pondered upon. It holds hid the fourfold mystery:

1. The mystery of the Akasha.
2. The secret of the fifth round.
3. The esoteric significance of Saturn, the third planet.
4. The occult nature of cosmic kundalini, or the electrical force of the system.

One hint on this fourth point may be given for wise consideration. When the electrical interplay between the planets is better ascertained (and by this I mean their negative or positive interplay), then it will be revealed which are related or connected, and which are nearing the point of balance. I would here point out very briefly certain facts, not pausing to elaborate or to elucidate, but simply making various statements which—as the knowledge of man progresses—will assume their rightful place in the ordered scheme. They will then be seen as enlightening and revealing the necessary sequence of development.

2. *The Work of the Atomic Units.*

a. The seven Heavenly Men, considered in relation to the Entity of Whom the solar Logos is a reflection, are as the seven centres in the physical body of a human being. This will be realised as the correspondence between the cosmic physical plane and the systemic physical plane is studied.

b. Three of these centres, therefore

Concern the lower centres of the cosmic Being.

Have their analogies on the dense, liquid and gaseous planes.

Are at present the object of the attention of cosmic kundalini.

c. One of these centres corresponds to the solar plexus and is the synthesiser of the lower three, thus making a quaternary.

d. The centre which is analogous to that at the base of the spine, or the reservoir of kundalini, has a permanence which is not seen in the other two lower centres. The Heavenly Man Who embodies this principle and is the source of generative heat to His Brothers, must be sought for by the aid of the intuition. Concrete Mind will not here avail.

e. The three higher centres, or the Heavenly Men Who correspond to the head, the heart and the throat of the solar Logos, have Their etheric analogies on the three higher etheric levels of the cosmic physical plane, just as the Heavenly Man Who embodies the logoic solar plexus finds His manifesting source on the fourth etheric.

f. This Heavenly Man, with His etheric vortex or wheel of force on the fourth cosmic ether, is in this fourth round, a vital factor in planetary evolution.

g. When the Heavenly Man, Who is at present demonstrating through the Earth scheme, has succeeded in vitalising His middle centre, or in directing the force of planetary kundalini away from the lower centres to the solar plexus centre, a new cycle will be reached, and much of the present distress will be ended. His work is as yet in an embryonic condition, and two and a half more cycles must transpire before He has accomplished the necessary work. When that is done, the result in connection with the human units in incarnation will be threefold:

Sex stimulation, as now understood, will be showing a tendency to manifest in creation, not so much on the physical plane, as on the astral and mental, demonstrating in the creations of art and beauty, and the objective work of the scientists.

Crime, as now seen, based largely on the sex emotion,

will be a thing of the past, and physical plane license, orgy and horror will be reduced seventy-five per cent.

The interplay between the three dense physical planets will be perfected and man will pass at will from one to another.

I would here point out the inadvisability of the method whereby the names of the globes in a chain, just as the names of a chain in a scheme, follow the planetary nomenclature. This has led to confusion.

A clue tending towards the correct understanding lies hid in the words: "Venus is the Earth's primary." [17]

It is not permissible to say much about this mystery, that *"Venus is the Earth's alter ego,"* nor is it advisable, but certain ideas may be suggested which—if brooded on—may result in a wider grasp of the beauty of nature's synthesis, and of the wonderful correlation of all that is in process of evolution.

Perhaps some idea may be gained if we remember that, in an occult sense, Venus is to the Earth what the higher Self is to man.

The coming of the Lords of Flame to the Earth was all under law and not just an accidental and fortunate happening; it was a planetary matter which finds its correspondence in the connection between the mental unit and the manasic permanent atom. Again, as the antaskarana is built by individual man between these two points, so—again in a planetary sense—is a channel being built by collective man on this planet to its primary, Venus.

In connection with these two planets, it must be remembered that Venus is a sacred planet and the Earth is not. This means that certain of the planets are to the Logos what the permanent atoms are to man. They embody principles. Certain planets afford only tem-

[17] S. D., II, 33. I, 323.

porary homes to these principles. Others persist throughout the mahamanvantara. Of these Venus is one.

Three of the sacred planets, it should be remembered, are the home of the three major Rays, of the embodied forms of the three logoic aspects or principles. Other planets are embodiments of the four minor rays. We might consider—*from the standpoint of the present*—that Venus, Jupiter and Saturn might be considered as the vehicles of the three super-principles at this time. Mercury, the Earth and Mars are closely allied to these three, but a hidden mystery lies here. The evolution of the inner round has a close connection with this problem. Perhaps some light may be thrown upon the obscurity of the matter by the realisation that just as the Logos has (in the non-sacred planets) the correspondence to the permanent atoms in the human being, so the middle evolution between these two (God and man) is the Heavenly Man, whose body is made up of human and deva monads, and Who has likewise His permanent atoms. Always the three higher principles can be distinguished in importance from the four lower.

The key is hidden in the fact that between the number of a globe in a chain and its corresponding chain lies a method of communication. The same is true likewise of the correspondence between a chain of globes and a scheme of analogous number. The connection between Venus and the Earth lies hid in number, and it took a moment of mysterious alignment between a globe, its corresponding chain and the scheme of allied number to effect the momentous occurrence known as the coming of the Lords of Flame. It occurred in the third root-race in the fourth round. Here we have an analogy between the quaternary and the Triad, carrying the interpretation up to a Heavenly Man. The chain was the fourth chain and the globe, the fourth. The fourth chain in the Venus scheme and the fourth globe in that chain were closely involved in the transaction.

h. The progress of development of the Heavenly Men is by no means uniform. One point has not been emphasised hitherto, and that is, that the problem before each of Them is dissimilar, and, therefore, it is not possible for man correctly to gauge the work done by Them and Their relative point of attainment. It has been said that as Venus is in the fifth round, the Venusian Lord is further progressed than His brothers. This is not altogether so. Just as in the development of humanity three main lines may be seen with four lesser lines merging into one of the three main lines, so in connection with the Heavenly Men, there are three main lines of which the Venusian is not one. The Lord of Venus holds place in the logoic quaternary, as does the Lord of Earth.

The main idea underlying the question we have been endeavoring to answer has to do with the relationship between the schemes, chains, rounds, and races, and it should be borne in mind that these manifestations bear the same relationship to a Heavenly Man as incarnations do to a human being. This gives the opportunity here to bring out perhaps a little more clearly the place of *cycles* in the evolution of all these Entities from a man up to a cosmic Logos, via a Heavenly Man and a solar Logos.[18] Just as it is pointed out in the *Secret Doctrine* that there are greater and lesser cycles in the evolution of a solar system, so it can be predicated equally of a Heavenly Man, of a human being, and of an atom. This brings us, therefore, to another statement:

i. The cycles in the evolutionary process of all these Entities may be divided mainly into three groups, though necessarily these groups can be extended into septennates and into an infinity of multiples of seven.

[18] S. D., I, 258.

In connection with a solar Logos the cycles might be called:

1. One hundred years of Brahma.
2. A year of Brahma.
3. A day of Brahma.

These periods have been computed by the Hindu students and are the sumtotal of *time* as we understand it or the duration of a solar system.

In connection with a Heavenly Man we have the corresponding cycles to those of the Logos:

1. The period of a planetary scheme.
2. The period of a planetary chain.
3. The period of a planetary round.

Within these three divisions, which are the differentiations of the three great cycles of incarnation of a planetary Logos, are numerous lesser cycles or incarnations but they all fall within one or other of the three main divisions. Such lesser cycles might be easily comprehended if it were pointed out that they mark such periods as:

a. The period of manifestation on a globe.
b. The period of a root-race.
c. The period of a sub-race.
d. The period of a branch race.

In order to apprehend even cursorily the identity of manifestation of a planetary Logos in a root-race, for instance, it must be remembered that the sumtotal of human and deva units upon a planet make the *body vital* of a planetary Logos, whilst the sumtotal of lesser lives upon a planet (from the material bodies of men or devas down to the other kingdoms of nature) form His *body corporeal,* and are divisible into two types of such lives:

a. Those on the evolutionary arc, such as in the animal kingdom.

b. Those on the involutionary arc, such as the totality of all elemental material forms within His sphere of influence. All the involutionary lives, as earlier pointed out, form the vehicles for the spirit of the planet, or the planetary entity, who is the sum-total of the elemental essences in process of involution. He holds a position (in relation to a Heavenly Man) analogous to that held by the different elementals that go to the make-up of man's three bodies, physical, astral and mental, and he is—like all manifesting beings—threefold in his nature, but involutionary. Therefore, man and devas (differentiating the devas from the lesser Builders) form the soul of a Heavenly Man. Other lives form his body, and it is with body and soul that we are concerned in these two divisions of our thesis on fire. One group manifests the fire of matter, the other group the fire of mind, for the devas are the personification of the active universal mind, even though man is considered manasic in a different sense. Man bridges in essence; the devas bridge in matter.

In connection with Man the cycles are equally threefold:

1. The Monadic cycle, which corresponds in man to the 100 years of Brahma, and to a planetary scheme.
2. The Egoic cycle.
3. The Personality cycle.

In these thoughts on cycles we have opened up a vast range of thought, especially if we link the idea of egoic and personality cycles to the vaster periods in connection with a planetary Logos. The idea is capable of vast expansion, and is governed by certain fundamental ideas that must be carefully considered and contemplated.

The cycles in a man's *personality* manifestation demonstrate in groups of fours and sevens, and follow the usual evolutionary sequence, as:

a. *Differentiation,* the involutionary process, or the one becoming the many, the homogeneous becoming the heterogeneous.

b. *Balance,* or the process of karmic adjustment.

c. *Synthesis,* or spiritualisation, the many again becoming the One.

d. *Obscuration,* or liberation, the end of the evolutionary process, or the freeing of Spirit from the limitations of matter.

By this we must understand that all incarnations on the physical plane are not of equal importance, but some are of more moment than others; some, from the point of view of the Ego, are practically negligible, others count; some are to the evolving human Spirit of importance analogous to the incarnation of a planetary Logos in a globe, or through a root-race, whilst others are as relatively unimportant to him as the manifestation of a branch-race is to a Heavenly Man.

As yet, owing to the small point of development of the average man, the astral incarnations or cycles count for little, but they are by no means to be discounted, and are oft relatively of more importance than the physical. In due course of time the astral cycles will be better comprehended and their relation to the physical. When it is realised that the physical body is not a principle but that the kama-manasic principle (or desire-mind principle) is one of the most vital to man then the period or cycle in which a man functions on the fifth subplane of the astral (the fundamentally kama-manasic plane) will assume its rightful place. It is so again with the mental cycles and so with the causal. The causal cycles or the egoic cycles, which include all the groups of lesser cycles in the three worlds correspond to a complete round in the cycles of a Heavenly Man. There are seven such cycles, but the number of lesser cycles (included within the seven) is one of the secrets of Initiation.

The egoic cycles proceed in groups of sevens and of threes, and not in groups of fours and sevens as do the personality cycles, and the same ratio must be predicated of the central cycles of a Heavenly Man and of a solar Logos.

The monadic cycles proceed in groups of ones and of threes as do the basic cycles of those great Entities of which man is the microcosmic reflection. If the general concept here laid down is studied in relation to the schemes, and other forms of manifestation to each other and, if the microcosm himself is studied as the clue to the whole, some idea will begin to permeate the mind as to the purpose underlying all these manifestations. It should be borne also in mind that just as the average man in each incarnation achieves three objects:

1. The development of consciousness or the awakening of the faculty of *awareness,*
2. The achievement of a certain proportion of permanent faculty, or the definite increase of the content of the causal body,
3. The making of karma, or the setting in motion (by action) of causes which necessitate certain unavoidable effects,

so a Heavenly Man at one stage of His evolution does the same. As man progresses and as he enters upon the Probationary Path and the subsequent Path of Initiation, he succeeds in bringing about some further noticeable developments.

1. As before, his consciousness expands, but he begins to work intelligently from above and does not work blindly on the lower planes.

2. The building of the causal body is carried to full completion, and he begins next to shatter what he earlier wrought, and to destroy the Temple so carefully constructed, finding it too to be a limitation.

3. He ceases to make karma in the three worlds, but begins to work it off, or, literally, to "wind up his affairs."

So do the Heavenly Men, for They likewise have a cosmic *path* to tread, analogous to that trodden by man, as he nears the goal of his endeavor.

Again we can with exactitude carry the concept further still, and predicate action of a similar nature by the solar Logos.

The consideration of this question is nearly concluded and it must be apparent that the relation between the aforementioned manifestations is of a *psychic* nature (using the word *psychic* in its true sense, as having reference to the psyche, or soul, or consciousness) and deals with the gradual expansion of Soul-Knowledge in a Heavenly Man. A word of warning should here be sounded. Though all these cosmic Beings find in man a reflection of Their Own Nature, yet the analogy of resemblance must not be pushed to extremity. Man reflects, but he reflects not perfectly; man is evolving, but he is not occupied with the same problems in exact detail as are the perfected Manasaputras.

Man aims at becoming a Divine Manasaputra, or perfected Son of Mind showing forth all the powers inherent in mind, and thus becoming like unto his monadic source, a Heavenly Man. *A Heavenly Man* has developed Manas, and is occupied with the problem of becoming a Son of Wisdom, not inherently but in full manifestation. *A solar Logos* is both a Divine Manasaputra and likewise a Dragon of Wisdom, and His problem concerns itself with the development of the principle of cosmic Will which will make Him what has been called a "Lion of Cosmic Will."

Throughout all these graded manifestations the law holds good, and the lesser is included in the greater. Hence the need for the student to preserve with care a due sense of proportion, a discrimination as to time in evolution, and a just appreciation of the place of each unit within its greater sphere. Having sounded this note of warning we can now proceed with the concluding remarks anent this final question.

It has been stated that a mystery lies hid in the 777 incarnations. This figure provides room for much speculation.[19] It should be pointed out that it does not hold the number of a stated cycle of incarnations through which a man must pass, but holds the key to the three major cycles previously mentioned. Primarily this number applies to the planetary Logos of our scheme and not so much to other schemes. Each Heavenly Man has His number and the number of our Heavenly Man lies hid in the above three figures, just as 666 and 888 holds the mystery hid of two other Heavenly Men. This number *777 is also the number of transmutation,* which is the fundamental work of all the Heavenly Men. The basic work of man is accumulation and acquisition, or the acquiring of that which must later be transmuted. The work of transmutation, or the true cycle of 777 commences on the Probationary Path, and is definitely the activity of a Heavenly Man being realised and responded to by the cells in His Body. Only when His Body has reached a certain vibratory movement can He truly influence the individual cells. This work of transmuting *cell activity* was begun on this planet during the last root-race, and the divine alchemy proceeds. The progress made is as yet but small, but each transmuted

*S. D., I, 191.

conscious cell increases the speed and the accuracy of the work. Time alone is needed for the completion of the work. In connection with this matter of transmutation comes the legend of the Philosopher's Stone, which is literally the application of the Rod of Initiation, in one sense.

SECTION TWO

DIVISION A

MANAS OR MIND AND ITS NATURE

I. Three manifestations of manas.
II. Some definitions of manas:
1. Manas is the fifth principle.
2. Manas is electricity.
3. Manas is that which produces cohesion.
4. Manas is the key opening the door into the fifth kingdom.
5. Manas is the synthetic vibration of five rays.
6. Manas is the intelligent will or ordered purpose of an existence.

WE enter now upon a very important division of our subject, and take up for consideration the Fire of Mind, cosmically, systemically, and humanly considered. We have dealt with the fire of matter, and studied for a while its purpose, origin and work. We considered somewhat the factor of Consciousness, and saw that the great work of a solar Logos, with all included manifesting lives, was the development of a conscious control, and a psychic awareness within certain set limits. Having laid down these preliminary foundation thoughts, we need now to block out, for the sake of clarity, the mass of material that is available on the subject of the manasic fire, which is the animating principle of consciousness itself. Let us first of all get one broad general outline and then proceed to fill in the details.

I. THREE MANIFESTATIONS OF MANAS [20]

1. The fire of mind, cosmically considered.

[20] ''Manas is the individuality or the spiritual Ego on the side of the higher Triad, and the personality or the kamic ego on the side of the lower

2. The fire of mind viewed systemically.

3. The fire of mind in connection with a human being.

In other words, what we are endeavoring to do is to study Mind in a solar Logos, a planetary Logos and in the Microcosm. Each of these three main divisions may be dealt with under four lesser heads which may be expressed as follows:

a. The origin of cosmic, systemic and microcosmic mind.

b. The place of mind in evolution in all three cases.

c. The present stage of development of mind in each of the three groups.

d. The future of mind, or of manasic unfoldment.

When we have taken up these points, we should have a clearer idea as to the purpose and place of the fire of the intelligence, and should be able accurately to comprehend its correlating synthetic work.

Before, however, following up these ideas it might prove of value to us if we sought to define this principle of manas and see what is already understood by it.

II. DEFINITIONS OF MANAS OR MIND

1. *Manas, as we already know, is the fifth principle.*

Here enter in certain factors and analogies that it would be of profit to us to mention at this juncture.

This fifth principle embodies the basic vibration of the fifth plane, either cosmically or systemically considered. A certain sound of the logoic Word, when it

quaternary. Manas is the pivot of the human structure, or the centre on which the spiritual and material parts of man are made to turn.''

"Lower manas is only a ray of the higher manas let into the fleshly tabernacle for illuminating its being and giving it thought, desire and memory.''

"It is because manas is the turning point in the cycle that H. P. B. has considered it under the two aspects—higher and lower—the higher the attainer and experiencer of spiritual heights and the lower, the soul of the lower three, the triangle that completes embodiment. Manas is therefore the battle-ground of forces contained in the microcosm. . . . The stage of evolution which we have reached is the very starting point of the great struggle.''—*Some Thoughts on the Gita.*

reaches the mental plane, causes a vibration in the matter of that plane, arrests its tendency to dissipate, causes it to take spheroidal form, and builds it literally into a body which is held in coherent shape by a mighty deva. Entity, the Raja Lord of the mental plane. Exactly the same procedure ensued on cosmic levels, when a still mightier sound was uttered by the ONE ABOUT WHOM NAUGHT MAY BE SAID, and the utterance of this caused a vibration on the fifth cosmic plane. Certain great Entities became active, including such relatively unimportant Beings as our solar Logos and His group.

This fifth principle is the distinctive coloring of a particular group of solar Logoi on the causal level of the cosmic mental, and is the animating factor of Their Existence, the reason of Their manifesting through various solar systems, and the great Will-to-be that brings Them forth into objectivity.

Manas has been defined as mind, or that faculty of logical deduction and reasoning, and of rational activity that distinguishes man from the animals. Yet it is something much more than that for it underlies all manifestation, and the very shape of an amoeba, and the discriminative faculty of the lowest atom or cell, is actuated by mind of some kind or another. It is only as the place of that discriminating cell or atom within its greater sphere is apprehended, and recognised, that any clear conception will be gained of what that coherent rational inclusive mentality may be.

2. *Manas is electricity.*[21]

The fire of Mind is fundamentally *electricity*, shown in its higher workings, and not considered so much as

---

[21] Electricity:
. . . "We know of no phenomenon in nature—entirely unconnected with either magnetism or electricity—since, where there are motion, heat, friction, light, there magnetism and its Alter Ego (according to our humble opinion)—electricity will always appear, as either cause or effect—or rather both if we but fathom the manifestation to its origin. All the

force in matter. Electricity in the solar system shows itself in seven major forms, which might be expressed as follows:

Electricity on the first plane, the logoic or divine, demonstrates as the Will-to-be, the primary aspect of that force which eventually results in objectivity. Cosmically considered, it is that initial impulse or vibration, which emanates from the logoic causal body on the cosmic mental plane, and makes contact with the first cosmic etheric, or the solar plane of adi.

Electricity on the monadic plane demonstrates as the first manifestation of form, as that which causes forms to cohere. Matter (electrified by "fire by friction") and the electric fire of spirit meet and blend, and form appears. Form is the result of the desire for existence, hence the dynamic fire of Will is transmuted into the burning fire of Desire. I would call attention to the choice of those two phrases, which might also be expressed under the terms:

Dynamic electrical manifestation.
Burning electrical manifestation.

Here on the second plane, the sea of electrical fire, which distinguished the first plane, is transformed into the akasha, or burning etheric matter. It is the plane of the flaming Sun, just as the first plane is that of the fire mist

phenomena of earth currents, terrestrial magnetism and atmospheric electricity, are due to the fact that the earth is an electrified conductor, whose potential is ever changing owing to its rotation and its annual orbital motion, the successive cooling and heating of the air, the formation of clouds and rain, storms and winds, etc. This you may perhaps find in some text book. But then Science would be unwilling to admit that all these changes are due to Akasic magnetism incessantly generating electric currents which tend to restore the disturbed equilibrium."

. . . "The sun is neither a Solid nor a Liquid, nor yet a gaseous glow; but a gigantic ball of electro-magnetic Forces, the store-house of universal Life and Motion, from which the latter pulsate in all directions, feeding the smallest atom as the greatest genius with the same material unto the end of the Maha Yug."—*Mahatma Letters to A. P. Sinnett,* pp. 160, 165.

or the nebulæ. This idea will be easier to comprehend if it is borne in mind that we are dealing with the *cosmic physical plane.*

Certain things take place on the second plane which need realisation, even if already theoretically conceded:

Heat or flaming radiation is first seen.

Form is taken, and the spheroidal shape of all existence originates.

The first interplay between the polar opposites is felt.

Differentiation is first seen, not only in the recognised duality of all things, but in differentiation in motion; two vibrations are recognised.

Certain vibratory factors begin to work such as attraction, repulsion, discriminative rejection, coherent assimilation, and the allied manifestation of revolving forms, orbital paths and the beginning of that curious downward pull into matter that results in evolution itself.

The primary seven manifestations of logoic existence find expression and the three, with the four, commence Their work.

The seven wheels, or etheric centres in the body etheric of that great cosmic Entity, of Whom our solar Logos is a reflection, begin to vibrate and His life activity can be seen.

We are at this juncture considering the manifestations of electricity on the different planes of the cosmic physical plane, or on our solar systemic planes. Hence, all that can be seen in manifestation is fundamentally *physical electricity.* We have seen that the primary manifestation is that which vitalised, tinctured, and pervaded the matter of space, thus embodying—in connection with logoic manifestation—that which is analogous to the vital heat, activity and radiation of a human being, manifesting on the solar physical plane. Certain electrical phenomena distinguish a human being, only (as they have not been expressed or considered in terms of electricity) the analogy has been lost sight of. These demonstrations might be considered as:

First, that coherent VITALITY which holds the entire body revolving around the central unit of force. It must here be remembered that the entire manifestation of a solar system consists of the etheric body, and the dense body of a Logos.

Second, that radiatory MAGNETISM which distinguishes man, and makes him active in two ways:

In relation to the matter of which his vehicles are composed.

In relation to the units which form his group.

Third, that ACTIVITY on the physical plane which results in due performance of the will and desire of the indwelling entity, and which in man is the correspondence of the Brahma aspect.

These three electrical manifestations—vitality, magnetism, and fohatic impulse—are to be seen at work in a solar Logos, a Heavenly Man and a human being. They are the objective manifestations of the psychic nature, which (in a solar Logos, for instance) we speak of in terms of quality, and call will, wisdom, activity. Therefore, it should be noted here that the first three planes of the cosmic physical plane—the logoic, monadic, and atmic planes—are of prime importance and are the basic planes from whence emanate the secondary four; in other words, the first three cosmic ethers embody in a literal sense those three Entities whom we know as Mahadeva, Vishnu, and Brahma. In a similar sense these Three find Their densest objectivity in the three physical ethers. The lower four manifest during evolution, but are eventually synthesised into the higher three. It should be also remembered that on all the seven subplanes of a solar plane a process, in connection with electrical phenomena in etheric matter, will parallel all the processes on the major planes. This is easily to be seen on the mental plane, for instance, in connection with Man. Theoretically, the absorption of all faculty by the causal body, and the discontinuance of all enforced objectivity in the three worlds at the close of the synthesising period is conceded. On the other planes it is not so obvious. On the buddhic plane, the Builders on the evolutionary arc, or a large part of the deva evolution, undergo a paralleling synthesis. On the physical plane a mysterious synthesis in connection with the "spirit of the Earth" is undergone, and the first three ethers are related to him in a way as yet little understood.

We might sum it up thus:

First, the balancing of electrical phenomena, or the achievement of synthesis in connection with Man, transpires on the three higher levels of the mental plane.

Second, a similar process in connection with a *Heavenly Man* transpires on the three higher subplanes of the monadic plane. Viewed in a larger sense it takes place on the three major planes—the atmic, buddhic, and manasic—just as in the three worlds of human evolution —the physical, astral, and mental—the synthesising process proceeds on the higher of the three involved.

Third, in connection with a solar Logos (within the system and not considering His cosmic synthesis) the three higher subplanes of the logoic plane see His final absorption or abstraction, and the three planes of the three Logoi are similarly concerned.

It should here be carefully borne in mind that we are dealing with electrical matter, and are therefore concerned with cosmic etheric substance; all matter in the system is necessarily etheric. We are consequently dealing literally with physical phenomena on all planes of

the system. In time and space we are concerned with
units of different polarity which—during the evolutionary process—seek union, balance, equilibrium or synthesis, and eventually find it. This electrical interplay
between two units causes that which we call light, and
thereby objectivity. During evolution this demonstrates
as heat and magnetic interaction and is the source of all
vital growth; at the achievement of the desired goal,
at union, or at-one-ment, two things occur:

> *First,* the approximation of the two poles, or their
> blending, causes a blazing forth, or radiant light.
> *Second,* obscuration, or the final disintegration of mat-
> ter owing to intense heat.

This can be seen in connection with man, a Heavenly
Man and a solar Logos, and their bodies of objectivity.
In man this polarity is achieved, the three different types
of electrical phenomena are demonstrated, and the light
blazes forth, irradiating the causal body, and lighting
up the entire sutratma, or thread (literally the Path)
which connects the causal vehicle with the physical brain.
Then disintegration or destruction ensues; the causal
body vanishes in a blaze of electrical fire, and the real
"man" or self is abstracted from the three world-bodies.
So will it be seen in the body of a Heavenly Man, a
planetary scheme, and so likewise in the body of the
Logos, a solar system.

The difficulty in apprehending these thoughts is great,
for we are necessarily handicapped by lack of adequate
terms, but the main ideas only are those I seek to deal
with, and the one we are primarily concerned with in
this division is *the electrical manifestation of magnetism,*
just as earlier we dealt cursorily with the same electrical
phenomena, manifesting as the activity of matter.

Therefore you have:

1. Activity......electrical manifestation of matter.
2. Magnetism....electrical manifestation of form.
3. Vitality.........electrical manifestation of existence.

This is literally (as pointed out by H. P. B.)[22] fire by friction, solar fire, and electric fire.

Fire by friction is electricity animating the atoms of matter, or the substance of the solar system, and resulting in:

The spheroidal form of all manifestation.
The innate heat of all spheres.
Differentiation of all atoms one from another.

Solar fire is electricity animating forms or congeries of atoms, and resulting in:

Coherent groups.
The radiation from all groups, or the magnetic interaction of these groups.
The synthesis of form.

Electric fire is electricity demonstrating as vitality or the will-to-be of some Entity, and manifests as:

Abstract Being.
Darkness.
Unity.

We have seen that electrical manifestation on the first plane caused initial vibration, and on the second its activity resulted in the archetypal form of all manifestation from a God to man, and an atom.

On the third plane, which is primarily the plane of Brahma, this electrical force showed itself in intelligent purpose. The will-to-be, and the form desired, are correlated by intelligent purpose underlying all. This intelligent purpose, or active will, utilising an instrument, brings us to that most difficult of metaphysical problems, the distinction between will and desire. It is not possible here to handle this delicate subject, save simply to point out that in both will and desire, intelligence or manas is a fundamental factor, and must be recognised. This permeating principle of manas—colouring as it does both the will aspect and the desire aspect—is the cause of much confusion to students, and clarity of thought will eventuate only as it is realised:

First, that all manifestation emanates, or is electrified, from the cosmic mental plane.

Second, that the Universal Mind, or the divine thinker, is the intelligent Principle which makes Itself known as the Will-to-be, Desire or Love-of-Being, and that active intelligent purpose which animates the solar system.

Third, that Maha-deva, or the Divine Will, Vishnu, the Wisdom aspect, or the manifested "Son of Necessity," and Brahma or active purpose are the sum-total of intelligent consciousness, and are (to the manifesting cosmic Entity) what the mental body, the desire body, and the physical body are to man, the thinker in the three worlds, functioning in the causal body. We must not forget that the causal body contains the three permanent atoms or the three spheres which embody the principle of intelligence, of desire, and of physical objectivity. Always must the analogy be held between the threefold Logos and threefold man, and definiteness of thought and of concept results when the one likeness between these is pondered on. Man is a unit, functioning as a unit in the causal body. He is a triplicity functioning under the will aspect, or mental body; under the desire or wisdom aspect, the astral body; and under the activity aspect, the physical body. He electrifies or vitalises all three bodies or aspects, unifying them into one, and bringing about—by means of the Intelligence He is—coherency of action, simultaneity of purpose, and synthetic endeavour.

Finally, therefore, it is apparent that, no matter from what angle we study, the threefold Logos (or His reflection, the microcosm) through *the Manasic principle,* intelligently reduces matter to form, and utilises that form for the fulfilment of the will, desire and purpose of the indwelling Existence; this principle *can be seen underlying all three aspects.*

There is no need here to point out the different triplicities which can be built up on the basic idea of Spirit and Matter, linked by Intelligence. This has often been done. I but seek to emphasize that INTELLIGENCE is the main quality of the Logos; that it shows as will, as desire or wisdom, and as activity; and that the reason for this is due to the work earlier accomplished by the cosmic Entity, involving cycles which have passed into the dim mist of retrospect, even from the angle of vision of a solar Logos.

This developed manasic principle is the intelligent purpose that is bringing about at-one-ment on each plane of the solar system in connection with the subplanes. It will eventually bring about the synthesis of all the planes, and thus bring the cosmic physical plane, as a unified whole, under the complete control of that cosmic Entity Who is seeking expression through that threefold manifestation we call a solar system, or the body logoic.

On this third plane that intelligent principle demonstrates as coherent activity, either systemic, planetary, or monadic, and also as the triple vibration of spirit-matter-intelligence, sounding as the threefold Sacred Word, or electricity manifesting as sound.

We have here an interesting sequence or inversion, according to the angle of vision, involving the planes as we know them:

Electricity as vibratory impulse. This causes the aggregation of matter, and its activity within certain bounds, or its awakening to activity within the solar ring-pass-not. This is the first syllable of the Sacred Word.

Electricity as Light, causing spheroidal objectivity. This is the birth of the Son. It covers the enunciation of the second syllable of the Sacred Word.[23]

Electricity as Sound. Here we have the completed threefold Sacred Word.

On the fourth plane this electrical force shows itself as colour. In these four we have the fundamental concepts of all manifestation; all four have an electrical dynamic origin; all are basically a differentiation or effect of impulse, emanating from the cosmic mental plane and taking form (with intelligent purpose in view) on the cosmic physical. Man repeats the process on his tiny scale, dealing only with three planes, and flashing into objectivity on the solar physical. It will be demonstrated later as science attains more and more of the truth that

1. All physical phenomena as we understand the term have an electrical origin, and an initial vibration on the first sub-plane of the physical plane.

[23] "Through perfectly concentrated meditation on the light in the head comes the vision of the Masters who have attained."

"The tradition is that there is a certain centre of force in the head, perhaps the 'pineal gland,' which some of our Western philosophers have supposed to be the dwelling of the soul,—a centre which is, as it were, the doorway between the natural and the spiritual man. It is the seat of that better and wiser consciousness behind the outward looking consciousness in the forward part of the head; that better and wiser consciousness of "the back of the mind," which views spiritual things, and seeks to impress the spiritual view on the outward looking consciousness in the forward part of the head. It is the spiritual man seeking to guide the natural man, seeking to bring the natural man to concern himself with the things of his immortality. This is suggested in the words of the Upanishad already quoted. "There, where the dividing of the hair turns, extending upward to the crown of the head'; all of which may sound very fantastical, until one comes to understand it."

"It is said that when this power is fully awakened, it brings a vision of the great Companions of the spiritual man, those who have already attained, crossing over to the further shore of the sea of death and rebirth. Perhaps it is to this divine sight that the Master alluded, who is reported to have said: 'I counsel you to buy of me eye salve, that you may see.' "— *Yoga Sutras of Patanjali,* Book III, 32. (C. Johnston's Edition.)

2. That Light, physical plane light, has a close connection with, and uses, as a medium, the second ether.
3. That sound functions through the third ether.
4. That colour in a peculiar sense is allied to the fourth ether.

We must note here that in the development of the senses, hearing preceded sight, as sound precedes colour.

An interesting analogy may here be noted between the fourth cosmic ether, and the fourth ether on the physical plane of the solar system. Both are in process of becoming exoteric—one from the standpoint of man in the three worlds, and the other from the standpoint of a Heavenly Man. The fourth ether is even now being investigated by scientists, and much that they predicate concerning ether, the atom, radium, and the ultimate "protyle" has to do with this fourth ether. It will eventually be brought under scientific formula, and some of its properties, knowledge concerning its range of influence, and its utilisation will become known unto men. Paralleling this, the buddhic plane, the plane of the Christ principle, is gradually becoming known to those advanced beings who are individually able to cognise their place in the body of a Logos of a planetary scheme. The influence of the buddhic plane, and the electrical force that is its peculiar characteristic, are beginning to be felt, and its energy is also beginning to have a definite effect on the egoic bodies of men; the fourth ether of the physical systemic plane is likewise assuming its rightful place in the minds of men, and the electrical force of that subplane is already being adapted and utilised by man in the assistance of the mechanical arts, for methods of transportation, for widespread illumination, and in healing. These four adaptations of electricity:

1. For mechanical uses,
2. For transportation,
3. For illumination.
4. In healing,

are but the working out on the physical plane of parallel-ing utilisation of buddhic electrical force.

It might here be asked why colour primarily is spoken of as the buddhic manifestation of electricity. We are employing the word "colour" here in its original and basic sense as "that which veils." Colour veils the sevenfold differentiation of logoic manifestation and, from the angle of vision of man in the three worlds, can be seen only in its full significance on the buddhic plane. All fire and electrical display will be seen to embody the seven colours.

Again another correspondence between the fourth cosmic ether and the fourth physical ether lies in the fact that they are both primarily concerned with the work of the great builders, bearing in mind that they build the *real* body of the Logos in *etheric* matter; the dense physical vehicle is not so much the result of their work as it is the result of the meeting of the seven streams of force or electricity, which causes that appar-ent congestion in matter that we call the dense physical planes (the three lower subplanes). This apparent con-gestion is, after all, but the exceeding electronic activity or energy of the mass of negative atoms awaiting the stimulation that will result from the presence of a cer-tain number of positive atoms. This needs to be borne in mind. The work of evolution is based on two methods and demonstrates as:

Involution, wherein the negative electrons of matter preponderate. The percentage of these feminine elec-trons is one of the secrets of initiation and is so vast during the involutionary stage that the rarity of the posi-

tive atoms is very noticeable; they are so rare as only
to serve to keep the mass coherent.

Evolution, wherein, due to the action of manas, these
negative atoms become stimulated and either dissipate
back into the central electrical reservoir, or merge in
their opposite pole, and are consequently again lost.
This results in:

> Synthesis.
> Homogeneity.
> The rarity instead of the density of matter. The
> fourth cosmic ether, the buddhic, is the plane of
> air, and is also the plane of absorption for the
> three worlds. This rarefication of dense matter
> (as we know it) simply means that at the close
> of the evolutionary process it will have been trans-
> muted and be practically, from our point of view,
> non-existent; all that will be left will be the posi-
> tive atoms, or certain vortices of force which—
> having absorbed the negative—will demonstrate
> as electrical phenomena of a form inconceivable
> to man at his present stage of knowledge. These
> vortices will be distinguished by:
>
> 1. Intense vibratory activity.
> 2. The predominance of one certain colour ac-
>   cording to the quality of the etheric display,
>   and its source.
> 3. Repulsion to all bodies of similar vibratory
>   rate and polarity. Their attractive quality
>   at the end of evolution will cease owing to
>   the fact that naught remains to be attracted.

The vortices in each planetary scheme will be, during
evolution, seven. Later, during the period of obscuration, three of the vortices will approximate their masculine pole and eventually but one will be left. In man
a similar procedure can be seen in connection with his

seven centres during the process of initiation. First there are seven, then three absorb the lower four through electrical interaction. We are here viewing the subject wholly from the point of view of our present discussion. Finally, only the head centre is left, for it is the positive pole to all the others.

This question of the electrical polarity of the centres is one of real difficulty, and little can be communicated on the matter. It may be safely pointed out, however, that the generative organs are the negative pole to the throat centre as is the solar plexus to the heart. The order of the development of the centres, the ray-type and colour, coupled to the fact that during certain stages of the evolutionary process different centres (such as the base of the spine) are positive to all the others, not even excluding the head centre, leads to the vast complexity of the subject. Likewise certain of the planetary schemes are positive and others negative; three of the schemes are dual, both negative and positive. The same can be predicated anent a solar system, and, curiously enough, anent the planes themselves. For instance, in connection with the earth scheme we have a positive polarity of a temporary nature based on the type of incarnation our particular Heavenly Man is undergoing on our planet. By this is meant that there are masculine and feminine incarnations undergone by Heavenly Men as by men, considering the entire subject from the angle of electrical polarity and not from sex as understood in connection with the physical body.

Venus is negatively polarised, and hence it became possible for a mysterious absorption by the Earth of Venusian force. Again in this connection the question of sex may serve to elucidate. The karmic tie between the two Heavenly Men—one in a positive incarnation and the other in a negative—caused the working out of an old debt and a planetary alliance. *Light* flashed forth

in Lemurian days in a number of great groups of the
human family when these two opposite poles made electrical connection. It needed the joint work of the two
Heavenly Men, working on buddhic levels (the fourth
cosmic ether) to bring about the blazing forth of the
light of manas in the causal groups on the fifth cosmic
gaseous plane, the mental plane of the solar system.
It will be remembered that it was earlier pointed out
that the majority of men function consciously on the
fifth subplane of the three planes in the three worlds.
In them the fifth principle is beginning to function, but
not in sufficient force as yet to do more than keep them
in line with the electrical force flowing from the fourth
cosmic ether down to the next subplane of the cosmic
physical.

It must ever be borne in mind that each plane and
each subplane which is numerically allied, is embodying
the same type of force, and is consequently of the same
polarity.

Again, the astral plane and the buddhic plane are
related, as we already know; the astral is negative in
relation to the buddhic plane. When the polarity of the
different planes is known, when the polarity of the subplanes is comprehended, and when the interaction between them and the corresponding cosmic planes is
grasped, then will man be free, but not before. When
the polarity of the ethers to each other and their relationship to the whole is comprehended, human evolution
will have run its course. A Master has solved the problem of electrical phenomena in the three worlds, hence
His freedom. Further, when the relationship of the
negative form to the positive Spirit is grasped, and their
joint connection with the cosmic Entities Who indwell
the whole system is somewhat apprehended, group liberation will be achieved.

Perhaps in considering this abstruse matter it may

help to clarify the point of view if it is recollected that man is essentially positive in his own nature but his vehicles are negative; hence he is the central unit of positive electricity that draws and holds to him atoms of an opposite polarity. When he has merged and blended the two poles, and produced light of a definite magnitude during any particular incarnation (which magnitude is settled by the Ego prior to incarnation) then obscuration takes place. The electrical manifestation burns up and destroys the medium, and the light goes out; what we call physical death ensues, for the electrical current burns up that which had caused objectivity, and that which *shone*. Let us carry this idea further and realise that these units called men (who are positive as regards their own vehicles) are but the negative cells in the body of a Heavenly Man, and are held within His sphere of influence by the force of His electrical life. Bear in mind again that the Heavenly Men are thus positive as regards the lesser lives, but in Their turn are negative as regards the greater Life that contains Them.

Here again is demonstrated the truth of the teaching given by H. P. B.

Electric Fire ..... Positive .... Spirit.
Fire by Friction.. Negative ... Matter.
Solar Fire .... Light ...... The two blended and thus producing the objective blaze.

We have thus considered the question of the electrical origin of all manifestation in connection with the four higher subplanes of the solar system—*those four planes which are the four cosmic ethers, and therefore form the body of objectivity of a Heavenly Man in exactly the same sense as the four physical ethers of the solar system form the etheric body of a man.* I have here repeated the fact, as its importance has not yet been grasped by the average occult student; this fact—when conceded and realised—serves in a wonderful way to clarify the whole subject of planetary evolution. We have now reached the three planes wherein man functions, or the gaseous, liquid, and dense subplanes of the cosmic physical.

The whole subject of the akasha will be greatly clarified as exoteric science delves into the question of the ethers. As knowledge of the four types of ethers is available, as the vibratory action of these ethers is realised, and as the details concerning their composition, utilisation, light-bearing capacity, and the various angles from which they may be studied become known then paralleling knowledge anent the corresponding four cosmic ethers will be forthcoming. Much concerning them may be deduced from the already apprehended facts which relate to the four solar physical ethers.

For instance, the fourth ether (which is even now being what we might call "discovered"), is at this stage characterised by certain things. I might enumerate a few of these facts with exceeding brevity, as follows:

a. It is the ether which the violet ray uses as a medium.

b. The fourth ether is that whereof the majority of the etheric bodies of men are made.

c. The fourth ether is largely the principal sphere of influence of the "devas of the shadows," or those violet devas which are closely concerned with the physical evolution of man.

d. It is the etheric sphere within which, at a little later date, the human and the deva evolutions will touch.

e. From this fourth etheric sphere the dense physical bodies are created.

f. It is the sphere of physical individualisation. Only when the animal to be individualised was fully conscious on that subplane of the physical plane was it possible to co-ordinate the corresponding spheres on the astral and mental planes and by means of this triple co-ordination to effect the necessary steps which enabled the quaternary to succeed in its effort to approximate the Triad.

g. This fourth ether in this fourth round and on this fourth chain has to be completely mastered and controlled by the Human Hierarchy, the fourth creative. Every unit of the human family has to attain this mastery before the end of this round.

h. It is the sphere wherein the initiations of the threshold are undergone, and the fivefold initiations of the physical plane are entered upon.

Much more might be further added to this list, but I have sought only to point out those which can be easily realised as having a correspondence on the buddhic plane, the fourth cosmic ether. It should be borne in mind that our physical plane in its subplanes has its analogy likewise to the entire cosmic physical plane.

COSMIC PHYSICAL PLANE

1. Adi ......First c o s m i c ether.	1. Atomic subplane ......First ether.
2. Monadic ..Second cosmic ether.	2. Sub-atomic ..Second ether.
3. Atmic ....Third c o s m i c ether.	3. Super-etheric. Third ether.
4. *Buddhic ..Fourth cosmic ether.*	4. *Etheric ......Fourth ether.*
5. Mental ...Cosmic gaseous.	5. Gaseous.
6. Astral ....Cosmic liquid.	6. Liquid.
7. Physical ..Cosmic dense.	7. Dense physical.

The solar physical plane might also be expressed accurately as follows, working out the analogy to the major planes:

SOLAR PHYSICAL PLANE

First subplane ...atomic........first ether.....physical adi.
Second subplane..sub-atomic....second ether..physical anupadaka.
Third subplane...super-etheric..third ether....physical atmic.
Fourth subplane..etheric ......fourth ether...physical buddhic.
Fifth subplane ...gaseous .... physical mental.
Sixth subplane... liquid .... physical astral.
Seventh subplane.dense .... physical dense.

In both the cosmic and solar physical planes, the plane of buddhi is ever the plane of at-one-ment, or the meeting ground of diversities, and of their blending—not into a fundamental unity—but into group unity. This is owing to the fact that the buddhic plane is pre-eminently the plane most concerned with the evolution of the Heavenly Men. What I have therefore predicated anent the fourth physical ether can likewise be extended to the fourth cosmic ether, and find its analogy on the buddhic plane. The place, for instance, of *violet* in the spectrum is of prime importance in connection with the greater cycles, and marks the end of a cycle and the beginning of a new one. The buddhic plane is peculiarly the plane of violet, even though all the colours find their place there; the Lord of the Ray of Ceremonial Magic, Who embodies the violet ray or hierarchy, has a special relationship to the buddhic plane. It must be borne in mind that each planetary Logos works primarily on one of the seven planes; from this we can infer that His influence finds its line of least resistance on some one plane, even though it be exerted on all planes.

Again, extend the second statement anent the etheric composition of the bodies of men to Those of the Heavenly Men, and it will be found that just as the majority of human etheric bodies are built of matter of the fourth ether, so it may also be said that four of the Heavenly Men have Their etheric vehicles composed of this fourth cosmic ether (buddhic matter).

Further, the two great evolutions (human and deva) find their group unity on the buddhic plane, and portions of both hierarchies blend and merge so as to form the body of the divine Hermaphrodite.[24, 25] Earlier, at certain fixed points, they may temporarily approximate each

---

[24] The Pairs of Opposites:—
—From *The Science of Social Organisation,* by Bhagavan Das.
[25] The Divine Hermaphrodite—this is the great Being, planetary or solar, who manifests in Himself the pair of opposites.

other. On the buddhic plane definite and permanent alliance may be seen. On this plane also the ''devas of the shadows'' who are concerned in the building of the planetary scheme, pursue their work, and thus parallel the work done in the three worlds by the lesser builders who work with the etheric body of man. So can the analogies be worked out, for ever this Law of Resemblance holds good; yet ever must it be remembered that the analogy is of a psychic nature, and demonstrates in work, activity, and quality, and not in literal identity of form.

As time elapses the work of the Heavenly Men in the cosmic etheric spheres will be better comprehended, and assisted intelligently by those lesser intelligences who— by the study of the physical ethers—will eventually hold the key of the greater manifestation. Science is the handmaiden of wisdom, and opens the door to those infinite reaches and to those cosmic expanses, where stand Those vaster Intelligences, Who manipulate the matter of the higher planes, and bend it to the desired form, causing the vibrations thus set up to be felt at the furthest bounds of the solar ring-pass-not. Automatically then all lesser lives and all the denser materials are swept and carried into the needed channels and forms. *Vibration* or initial activity, *light,* or activity taking form and animating form, *sound* the basis of differentiation and the source of the evolutionary process, and *colour* the sevenfold differentiation — thus is the work carried on. We have been dealing with these four in connection with a solar Logos, and equally with the work of a Heavenly Man and of Man, of the human monad.

Students should also bear in mind another point that is often forgotten, which is that every plane can be studied and divided in two ways:

First. The seven subplanes can be divided into the

higher three planes or the abstract planes, and the lower four or the concrete planes. This division is the best and most purely metaphysical, for it embodies the entire idea of the Self, the Not-Self, and the Intelligence, with their synthesis, which produces the objective universe, whether solar system, planetary scheme, or human incarnation. In connection with the Logos it is fully discussed and illuminatingly considered in the first volume of the *Secret Doctrine,* where the work of the Father and the Mother in producing the Son through conscious intelligent co-operation is handled by H. P. B. in a masterly manner.

In connection with man the point can be grasped more easily if the causal body on the abstract levels of the mental plane is considered in connection with the lower four or concrete levels from whence manifestation emanates.

Second. Dividing the seven subplanes into the same higher three but making the fourth plane the plane of meeting or of at-one-ment, and regarding the lower three as the planes of endeavour. This division primarily concerns man.

Both these divisions will be seen later as existing on every plane in the system and as having their origin in electrical force which shows itself differently on each plane but acts on all under three laws: Attraction or Repulsion, Economy, and Synthesis. The lower three planes or subplanes act under the Law of Economy primarily; the plane of meeting or of union acts under a phase of the Law of Attraction. Paralleling them, of course, during evolution are their opposites, showing as Dispersion, Repulsion, and Differentiation.

The question of the electrical manifestation of the akasha on the seven planes has therefore to be studied in its three main divisions, then plane by plane or the sevenfold consideration, and finally as the forty-nine fires. Throughout it must be recollected that the subject is still further complicated by the factor of time which brings these forty-nine fires at different stages under different spheres of influence and under the three laws of the cosmos. Thus the same fire at different periods will show itself forth as constructive light, or again bring about combustion and eventual obscuration as the result of burning out.

In connection with the manifestation of electricity on the mental, astral and physical planes. We will not enlarge upon the subject, as it will later be discussed as fully as may be possible. Suffice it to say that the law holds good and that what is laid down as fact anent a Heavenly Man on His Own planes is equally true of man on the four lower planes. Thus:

A SOLAR LOGOS

1. Electrical vibration ....the plane logoic or adi.
2. Electrical light ....the plane monadic or anupadaka.
3. Electrical sound ....the plane of atma.
4. Electrical colour ....the plane of buddhi.

A HEAVENLY MAN

1. Electrical vibration ....the plane monadic.
2. Electrical light ....the plane of atma.
3. Electrical sound ....the plane of buddhi.
4. Electrical colour ....the mental plane.

MAN

1. Electrical vibration ....buddhic plane.
2. Electrical light ....the mental plane.
3. Electrical sound ....the astral plane.
4. Electrical colour ....the physical plane.

We need to remember here that we were earlier dealing with the Logos, and with the Heavenly Men as incorporate parts of His body of manifestation. In the tabulation above given we are dealing with each separately, and it should be observed that the manifestation of the groups of causal bodies on the mental plane is the colour manifestation of a Heavenly Man and His lowest point of objectivity. In man his lowest point of objectivity is the fifth subplane of the physical plane, as the liquid and the dense subplanes are not counted as principles any more than the cosmic liquid and dense (the astral and the systemic physical planes) count with a Heavenly Man.

We have seen that manas or mind is the fifth principle, or the basic vibration of the cosmic mental plane, the fifth plane; it was therefore impulse originating from the causal levels of the cosmic mental plane, which drove our solar Logos into manifestation, in the same way that the force which brings man into incarnation emanates from his causal body on the mental plane of the solar system. We have seen also that manas is that discriminative faculty which animates all substance, and which is also the electrical fire of the system showing forth as attraction and repulsion, with all that is involved in those two words. In the widest sense of the idea the Laws of Economy and of Synthesis are only divisions of that same cosmic law of which Attraction and Repulsion are also manifestations. This cosmic law, demonstrating thus in a threefold manner, might (for lack of a better term) be called *the Law of Being,* and is of a nature so incomprehensible to the finite mind of man that he can only sense it partially through the aforesaid three branches.

3. MANAS IS THAT WHICH PRODUCES COHESION

We come now to our third definition: The manasic principle is above all else that cohesive something which enables an Entity (whether Logos, Heavenly Man, or man) to work:

a. Through form, and thus exist.

b. By means of progressive development or cyclic
   evolution.

c. On certain planes, that are, for the entity concerned, the battleground of life, and the field of
   experience.

d. By the method of manifestation, which is a gradual
   growth from a dim and distant dawn through an
   ever increasing splendour of light to a blaze of
   effulgent glory; then through a steadily dimming
   twilight to final obscuration. Dawn, day, midday,
   twilight, night—thus is the order for the Logos,
   for a planetary Logos, and for man.

If the above four points are carefully studied, it will
be found that they are fairly comprehensive, and embody the four points that are as yet the only ones available for man in this fourth round.

Man regards himself as a synthesised aggregate of
physical body, emotional nature, and mentality, yet
knows himself as more than these three, and recognises
himself as the utiliser of form, of emotion, and of mentality, holding them all together coherently so that he is
a unit. A planetary Logos similarly does the same, with
the difference that manas is not the medium whereby
he is a coherent whole. Owing to his more advanced
stage of development, *wisdom* is for Him the dominant
factor. *A solar Logos achieves through Will what a
planetary Logos does through wisdom or buddhi, and
man (on his tiny scale) through manas.* Yet, as both
planetary Logos and man are but parts of their greater
whole, the electric fire of will permeates them also, merging with the solar fire of buddhi, and fanning the fires
of matter. In all these distinctions and differentiations
it must be remembered that they do not exist from the
logoic standpoint, but are only to be predicated in rela-

tion to the lesser bodies which are included in the solar ring-pass-not.

A man is a coherent unit in objective manifestation for very brief periods on the physical plane simply because as yet he works only through manas and not through wisdom. His cycles are consequently soon run, and gone like a flash in the night. A planetary Logos, Who is perfected manas and works through wisdom, has longer cycles, and from the angle of vision of man endures for æons; His life is the basis of the comparative permanence of the egoic cycles of man. The cycle of objectivity of a solar Logos persists for the greater mahamanvantara or solar cycle because it is based on will as well as on wisdom and manas. Therefore, it will be apparent that:

a. *Manas or intelligence* is the basis of the separative manifestation of man.

b. *Wisdom or buddhi* is the basis of the group manifestation of a Heavenly Man.

c. *Will* is the basis of the One Life which synthesises all groups.

Therefore again, in studying this Fire of Mind, we must remember that it is that which man is developing and with which he is learning to work, but that it is also that which a Heavenly Man has developed in an earlier system; it is to Him as automatic in its action as is the subconscious activity of a man's physical organs.

4. MANAS IS THE KEY TO THE FIFTH KINGDOM IN NATURE

We might also define manas as the key to the door through which entrance is made into the fifth kingdom of nature, the spiritual kingdom. Each of the five kingdoms is entered by some one key, and in connection with the first two kingdoms—the mineral and vegetable—the key or method whereby the life escapes into the higher kingdom is so inexplicable to man at his present stage

of intelligent apprehension that we will not pause to
consider it.   In relation to the animal kingdom it might
be said that the key whereby entrance is effected into the
human kingdom is that of *instinct*.   This instinct, towards the final stages of the animal's evolution, and as it
becomes more and more detached from the group soul,[26]
becomes transmuted into mentality, or into that embryo
mind which is latent in animal-man, and which simply
needed the stimulating vibration which emanated from
the Earth's Primary to be fanned into something definitely human.   We must always bear in mind that the
method of individualisation on this globe was not the one
followed on others, and that many of the present advanced units of humanity individualised normally, and
through the driving force of evolution itself.   They found
(to express it as far as possible in terms of fire), their
opposite electrical pole through the activity of animal
instinct, and by the blending of the two a human being
was produced,—the union of the three fires in the causal
vehicle.

Man passes into the fifth kingdom through the transmutation of the discriminative faculty of mind, which—
as in the animal's individualisation—brings about at a
certain stage a spiritual individualisation which is the
correspondence on higher levels to what transpired in
Lemurian days.   Therefore, we have:

Instinct..The key from the animal into the human
kingdom or from the third into the fourth
kingdom.

Manas...The key from the human into the spiritual
kingdom, or from the fourth kingdom into
the fifth kingdom.

[26] "*A Group-soul* is a collection of permanent Triads in a triple envelope
of monadic essence.   The permanent Triads are a reflection upon the lower
planes of the spiritual Triads on the higher.   This description is true of
all group-souls functioning on the physical plane, but gives no idea of the
extreme complexity of the subject."—From *A Study in Consciousness*, by
Annie Besant.

Higher we need not go, for the transmutation of manas proceeds, and much as yet remains to be done.

5. MANAS IS THE SYNTHESIS OF FIVE RAYS

One other definition might be given even though its abstruseness may prove but a bewilderment to the student.

Manas is the united faculty of four of the Heavenly Men, synthesised through a fifth Heavenly Man on the third plane of the system. These five Heavenly Men were the logoic embodiment in an earlier system and achieved the fullness of manasic life. Their synthetic life is that which is primarily understood when we speak of Brahma, that cosmic Entity Who is the sum-total of logoic active intelligence. For lack of better terms we call Them the Lords of the four minor Rays, Who find Their synthesis through the third Ray of Activity. They have been called in an endeavour to express the principles which They embody:

1. The Lord of Ceremonial Magic.
2. The Lord of Abstract Idealism, or Devotion.
3. The Lord of Concrete Science.
4. The Lord of Harmony and Art.

These four function through the fourth cosmic ether, and have vehicles of buddhic matter. They merge into the greater life of the Lord of the third Ray of Aspect on atmic levels, and these four (with the one synthetic Ray), are the totality of manasic energy. They are the life of the five lower planes. They are the five Kumaras, and two remain, making the seven Kumaras or Builders of the universe; these five have been called the five Mind-born Sons of Brahma.[27]   Manas, therefore, is the psychic effect of Their united group work, and shows forth in different ways according to the units involved, the forms

[27] S. D., I, 119, 493; II, 111, 112.

animated, and the planes concerned. They demonstrate predominantly on the five lower subplanes of each plane, and this factor should be remembered in connection with the major initiations of manas. Nevertheless—as They are the sumtotal of the third or Brahma aspect—Their main sphere of influence is on the lowest or third division of the manifested universe or on the mental, astral, and physical planes.

I would here suggest a third division of the major planes of the system which will hold much of interest for the real student of occultism.

First Logos ...Mahadeva ..Will Aspect ....First plane.
Second Logos..Vishnu .....Wisdom Aspect..Second, T h i r d, Fourth.
Third Logos ...Brahma ....Intelligence ....Fifth,   S i x t h, Seventh.

In these five definitions of manas we have suggested scope for thought and much has been hinted at for those who have ears to hear. Many more explanatory words might be spoken but we aim to start students thinking for themselves, and seek to see them defining these ideas in their own words.

6. MANAS IS THE INTELLIGENT WILL OR PURPOSE OF AN EXISTENCE

Manas might finally be defined as the intelligent will and ordered purpose of every self-conscious entity. I would urge the student to bear in mind certain basic facts which will serve to keep his mind clear, and which will enable him to comprehend something of the place which this fire of mind holds in the cosmos and the solar system, and (needless to say), in his life also,—the reflection of the other two.

He should ever remember that manas is a *principle of the Logos,* and necessarily therefore is felt in all those evolutions which are a part of His nature but is allied especially to the throat and head centres; it is the active intelligent factor which enables a solar Logos, a planetary Logos or Heavenly Man, and a human being to:

a. Use intelligently a form or vehicle.
b. Build faculty into the causal body.
c. Reap the benefit of experience.
d. Expand the consciousness.
e. Make progress towards a specified goal.
f. Discriminate between the two poles.
g. Choose the direction in which his activity shall trend.
h. Perfect the form as well as use it.
i. Obtain control of active substance, and turn its forces into desired channels.
j. Co-ordinate the different grades of matter, and synthesise the utilised forms till each and all show a unanimous line of action and express *simultaneously* the will of the Indweller.

All these ends are the result of the manasic development and perhaps the student might apprehend the underlying idea more clearly if it is realised that

a. The Spirit employs *manas* in all that concerns matter, the electrical substance, or the active akasha.
b. The Spirit employs *buddhi* in all that relates to the psyche, that relates to the soul of the world, to the soul of an individual, or to the soul of every form.
c. The Spirit employs will or *atma* in all that relates to the essence of all, to itself, considering the essence and the Self as pure Spirit as distinguished from spirit-matter.

In the first case, the distinctive quality of manas is discrimination which enables the Spirit to differentiate between:

1. The Self and the Not-Self.
2. Spirit and Matter.
3. The planes and the subplanes.
4. The different grades of atomic matter in the system.
5. Vibrations, engendered by will, working through love-wisdom, and energising substance.
6. All that concerns forms of every kind and in every type of essential existence.

In the second case, the buddhic principle has for its distinctive quality love, and demonstrates as wisdom working through love and producing:

1. Unity between all Selves.
2. Group coherence.
3. Qualities that are distinctively along the line of what we call love.
4. Effective work in connection with evolution, or the fundamentals of hierarchical work.

In the third case the Spirit employs the will aspect or atma (in man), which has, for its distinctive feature, that coherent force which keeps the purpose of the entity ever in view, working it out through love in substantial form.

I have pointed out these distinctions as it serves to bring the scope, and equally the limitations, of the active mental principle somewhat more clearly before the student. In the *Hall of Ignorance* the accumulative side of manas and its ability to store and acquire knowledge and information is being developed. A man, for instance, acquires facts, and application, and sets up vibrations which have to be worked out intelligently. The acquisitive side of this principle is showing forth. In the *Hall of Learning* the discriminative side is being developed, and the man learns not only to choose but to discard, and he begins to merge the two poles intelligently. In the

Hall of Wisdom he discards also, and perfectly blends the two poles, thereby producing that objective something we call light. The illuminating side of manas is shown. He becomes an intelligent creator, and by the time he has taken the four major initiations he has:

1. Developed perfectly the Brahma aspect, which— as pointed out—functions primarily in the three worlds. It is the active intelligent aspect.
2. Achieved the point of development at which a Heavenly Man, the Divine Manasaputra, commenced this circle of manifestation we call a solar system.
3. Transmuted manas into wisdom or love.
4. Synthesised the Rays of Activity or Intelligence and is beginning to merge this synthesis into the higher one of love-wisdom.

To sum it all up in words of fire: *The fire of matter has blazed out perfectly, and the vibratory activity of the man has been keyed up to synchronise with that of a Heavenly Man, thus enabling a man to function consciously, or be vitally active on the buddhic plane.*

The fire of mind has blended with the fire of matter and has stimulated it to such an extent that it has brought about the liberation of the entity, man, from the three worlds, and has occultly "obscured" his manifestation on the three planes in exactly the same way as the manifestation of a Logos "goes out" (occultly) when the fires are sufficiently fierce. As regards the fire of Spirit, or pure electric fire, this is finally synthesised with the other two and brings about the escape of the life on to another plane cosmically considered.

A MAN

a. The blending of the fire of matter and of the fire of mind liberates from the three worlds.

b. The blending of electric fire with the two other fires brings about liberation from the five lower planes, and enables a man to function consciously on the cosmic physical plane.

A HEAVENLY MAN

a. The blending of the fire of matter and of mind liberates from the three planes of His manifestation.

b. The blending of the electric fire in His case brings about escape from the planetary ring-pass-not and enables Him to function consciously on the cosmic astral plane.

A SOLAR LOGOS

a. The blending of the fire of matter and of mind liberates Him from the solar ring-pass-not, and gives Him the freedom of the cosmic physical, astral and the lower subplanes of the cosmic mental planes.

b. The blending of electric fire with the other two enables Him to function consciously in His causal body thus paralleling the work of Man in the three worlds.

SECTION TWO

DIVISION B

MANAS AS A COSMIC, SYSTEMIC AND HUMAN FACTOR

I.   The Origin of Manas, or Mind

1. *Cosmic Manas.*
    a. The process of individualisation.
    b. The method of initiation.

2. *Planetary Manas.*
    a. Consciousness and existence.
    b. Will and ordered purpose.

3. *Human Manas.*
    a. Man and the planetary Logos.
    b. The Logos of our scheme.
    c. Venus and the Earth chain.

4. *Manas and the Earth Chain.*
    a. The Earth chain and the incarnating monads.
    b. The fourth kingdom and the Hierarchy.
    c. A Prophecy.
    d. A Summation.

II.   The Position of Manas

1. *Manas and Karma.*
2. *Manas and karmic purpose.*

III.   The Present Stage of Manasic Development

1. *In the planets.*
2. *In the system.*
3. *On the Earth.*

IV. THE FUTURE OF MANAS

1. *The characteristics of Manas.*

   a. Discrimination.
   b. Ordered activity.
   c. Adaptability.

2. *Developments of the Human Mind.*

   a. Ray effects.
   b. Animals, men and the rays.
   c. Types of Karma.

3. *Manas in the Final Rounds.*

   a. The transmutative process.
   b. Synthesis.

I. THE ORIGIN OF MANAS OR MIND

WHAT we are dealing with here (taking these three factors in their order), is the fire of mind in connection with a solar Logos. It has been earlier pointed out that mind has already been developed in a Heavenly Man, and therefore we must equally predicate anent a solar Logos that cosmic mind, or the fifth Principle, is His prime characteristic, and was perfected by Him in an earlier system. We might now consider our first subdivision:

1. *Cosmic Manas.*

Whence comes this fire? Where originates this vital heat, or vibratory activity, which is predominantly a feature of all conceivable Beings? How far back is it possible for us to go? Can we conceive of its origin? What is this downpouring fire that animates the darkness of matter?

   a. The Process of Individualisation. Perhaps it may help somewhat if we here consider the question of INDI-VIDUALISATION, or the process of intelligent self-realisa-

CHART V

EVOLUTION OF A SOLAR LOGOS

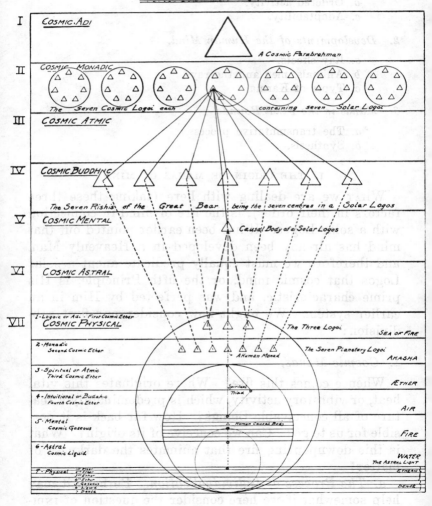

I	COSMIC ADI	A Cosmic Parabrahman
II	COSMIC MONADIC	

The Seven Cosmic Logoi each   containing   seven   Solar Logoi

III COSMIC ATMIC

IV COSMIC BUDDHIC

The Seven Rishis of the   Great   Bear   being the seven centres in a   Solar Logos

V COSMIC MENTAL   Causal Body of a Solar Logos

VI COSMIC ASTRAL

VII
1 - Logoic or Adi - First Cosmic Ether
COSMIC PHYSICAL   The Three Logoi   SEA OF FIRE

2 - Monadic
Second Cosmic Ether   A Human Monad   The Seven Planetary Logoi   AKASHA

3 - Spiritual or Atmic
Third Cosmic Ether   ÆTHER

4 - Intuitional or Buddhic
Fourth Cosmic Ether   Spiritual Triad   AIR

5 - Mental
Cosmic Gaseous   Human Causal Body   FIRE

6 - Astral
Cosmic Liquid   WATER   THE ASTRAL LIGHT

7 - Physical
1st Ether
2nd Ether
3rd Ether
4th Ether
5 Gaseous
6 Liquid
7 Dense
ETHERIC
DENSE

tion which so strikingly differentiates men from the animals. At individualisation the two poles are approximated, and at their meeting light streams forth, irradiating the cave of matter, and lighting the pathway that must be trodden by the Pilgrim on his way back to his source.

This irradiation brings about, in connection with man,

Self-realisation.

Purpose.

Separation from all other individualised selves, or spheres.

Consciousness, above all.

Ability to evolve.

Capacity to "shine ever more and more unto the perfect day."

This is equally true of a solar Logos, and of a Heavenly Man.

Individualisation is literally the coming together (out of the darkness of abstraction), of the two factors of Spirit and matter by means of a third factor, the intelligent will, purpose and action of an Entity. By the approximation of these two poles light is produced, a flame shines forth, a sphere of radiant glory is seen which gradually increases the intensity of its light, its heat and its radiance until capacity is reached, or that which we call perfection. We should note and distinguish the words *light, heat* and *radiance,* which are the distinctive features of all individualised entities from Gods to men.

Man is beginning to arrive partially at the secret of this phenomenon through his ability to produce through scientific knowledge, that which is called electric light and which is used by man for illumination, heat and healing. As more anent this matter is discovered by physical plane students, the whole question of existence and of creative activity will become clearer.

As regards the origin of the fire of mind something

more may be learned through studying *the various meth-ods of individualisation.* In connection with man these methods are three in number as far as we can tell, though the probability of there being several other methods which are inconceivable to man's finite comprehension, is quite possible.   These methods are:

First, the method pursued on the moon-chain (the plan-etary manifestation previous to ours), when, through innate force and energy, the conjunction of the three fires was brought about and the fire of matter contacted the fire of Spirit through the latent presence of the fiery spark of mind.   This spark of mind, working through the instinct, drove the material form or substance, into such activity that it was enabled to reach up to heights where its opposite pole could be contacted.   Animal-man aspired; Spirit answered; the vibration of the germ of mentality had permeated the substance like yeast.   Thus was consciousness awakened.   In the previous solar sys-tem, in connection with the Heavenly Men, this was the method pursued by Them, and These advanced cosmic Beings entered into consciousness and mastered the three lower planes of the cosmic physical,—the planes which man is endeavouring to master now.   They individualised as the result of work accomplished during incomprehen-sible æons of endeavour.[28]   The earlier solar system was much longer in duration than this one will be, and force in matter was generated by the progression of the ages. *It was the period of the vitalisation of the spirillæ in the physical permanent atom of the Logos.*

In this method of individualisation, the emphasis is laid on the fact that the principle of manas is a part of the logoic character, and is part of His very nature. It, therefore, has its origin in His Being or Self; it is

---

[28] The period of the individualisation of a solar Logos goes back further still and need not concern us here, save to remember that the Law of Analogy holds good.

part of the content of the logoic Causal Body, and therefore permeates all manifestation which originates with Him. Hence the accuracy of the statement that cosmic manas originates on the cosmic mental plane, and is a portion of the fire that animates that plane.

Second, in the second solar system, and in connection with the method employed therein, another point merits attention. This fire of mind has its source in a constellation until recently unrecognized by exoteric science as having any relation of an intimate nature to our solar system, owing to its tremendous distance away. *The sun "Sirius" is the source of logoic manas* in the same sense as the Pleiades are connected with the evolution of manas in the seven Heavenly Men, and Venus was responsible for the coming in of mind in the Earth chain. Each was primary to the other, or was the agent which produced the first flicker of consciousness in the particular groups involved. In every case the method was that of a slow evolutionary growth till the consciousness suddenly blazed forth owing to the interposition of force, apparently from an extraneous source,

1. The Logos .... Solar System .... Sirius
2. Seven Heavenly Men ...... Planetary scheme. Pleiades
3. Heavenly Man .... Earth chain ..... Venus

This second method therefore is that which is brought about by the hastening of the evolutionary process through influences from outside; these tend to awaken consciousness, and to bring about the merging of the poles. The first method touched upon was that of the earlier solar system. The method we are now considering is the distinctive one of this solar system and will persist till the end of the mahamanvantara.

That the earlier method was seen in the moon-chain is only evidence of the steadfastness of the Law of Repetition by which every large cycle includes, in its earlier stages, all the lesser, and repeats the earlier procedure. This is a recognised fact, for instance, in the building of man's physical body, for the fœtus reproduces all earlier stages and forms till the human is achieved; again, as we know, the fourth round reproduces briefly the earlier three but has its own distinctive quality.

b. The Method of Initiation. In this second method the "Rods of Initiation" are used to effect certain re-sults. These rods are of four kinds:

1. *Cosmic,* used by a cosmic Logos in the initiations of a solar Logos, and of the three major planetary Logoi.

2. *Systemic,* used by a solar Logos in the initiations of a planetary Logos.

3. *Planetary,* used by a planetary Logos for initiatory purposes, and for the third, the fourth, and fifth major initiations, with the two higher.

4. *Hierarchical,* used by an occult Hierarchy for minor Initiations, and for the first two initiations of manas by the Bodhisattva.[29]

When man individualised in Lemurian days (about eighteen million years ago), it was the application of the Rod of Initiation to the Logos of our Earth chain which brought about the event and touched into activity certain centres in His body with their corresponding groups. This application, bringing about consciousness on some plane, may be regarded as literally the awakening of the lives concerned to participate in intelligent work on the mental plane. Animal man was conscious on the physical, and on the astral planes. By the stimulation effected by the electric rod this animal man awoke to consciousness on the mental. Thus the three bodies were co-ordinated, and the Thinker enabled to function in them.

[29] The above information about the "Rods" is taken out of *Initiation Human and Solar,* page 126.

All Rods of Initiation cause certain effects:

a. Stimulation of the latent fires till they blaze.

b. Synthesis of the fires through an occult activity that brings them within the radius of each other.

c. Increase of the vibratory activity of some centre, whether in man, a Heavenly Man, or a solar Logos.

d. Expansion of all the bodies, but primarily of the causal,—this also in speaking of all the three types of Entities.

All these results were seen when the Heavenly Man of our scheme took initiation eighteen million years ago. This initiation was brought about—as earlier pointed out—by a peculiar juxtaposition of chains, globes and schemes, and caused such a stimulation of all the latent manasic units within His body that a downflow of pure manas from the planetary manasic permanent atom was possible along the path of the planetary antaskarana—a channel which *exists* in the case of the planetary Logos, and which has not to be built as in the case of man. Along with this juxtaposition came a similar alignment with one of the Pleiades, permitting of manasic influence from that source.[30, 31]

Third, the third method of individualisation is the one to be followed in the next solar system, though it will have its faint beginnings in this one. It is not based on latent activity as in the first case, nor in electrical polarity as in the second, but in a peculiar process of *"occult abstraction"* (using the word "abstraction" in its basic sense as "the drawing out" of essence). This occult abstraction is brought about by an effort of the will at present incomprehensible. The first method of individualisation

[30] "The Secret of the Pleiades and of their relation to the Seven Rishis of the Great Bear, and therefore to our Seven Heavenly Men, is not yet to be revealed. It is known only in detail to the Chohans of the Seventh Initiation, though the fact that there is such a relation is now exoteric." H. P. B. speaks of it in the *Secret Doctrine.*

[31] See S. D., II, 711, 725, 726.

is that of the third aspect, or latent activity, and follows
the line of least resistance under the Law of Economy;
the second method is the purely electrical one, and works
under the Law of Attraction; whilst the third method
lies hidden in dynamic will and is as yet to us impossible
and incomprehensible.

2. *Planetary Manas.*

We sought in the foregoing, to understand somewhat
the origin of manas—whether cosmic, or otherwise—
through the consideration of human individualisation
and the method thereof. We saw that individualisation is
the conscious apprehension of the Self of its relation to
all that constitutes the Not-Self, and that it is evoked in
three ways, of which only two as yet are even dimly comprehensible. In each case this awakening of consciousness is preceded by a period of gradual development, is
instantaneous at the moment of Self-Realisation for the
first time, and is succeeded by another period of gradual
evolution. This period of gradual evolution leads up to
another crisis which we call *initiation*. In one we have
initiation into conscious existence, in the other initiation
into spiritual existence or group identification.

For a *solar Logos* individualisation dates back to
stages far anterior to the triplicity of solar systems
which constitutes for Him the Eternal Now, but which
from man's point of view embody the past, the present,
and the future. A *planetary Logos* individualised in a
previous system; *a man* individualises in this; the *planetary entities,* now involutionary, will individualise in the
next.

a. Consciousness and Existence. From the wider
point of view the terms initiation and individualisation
are synonymous; they both express the idea of an expansion of consciousness, or of entrance into a new kingdom of nature. The faculty of acquiring knowledge

must be realised as paralleling the development of the
sense of sight, or vision, as earlier pointed out. The fire
of mind shone forth and illuminated animal man in
Lemurian days, during that vast cycle wherein sight
opened up for him the physical plane. The relationship
between sight and mind is a very close one, and must not
be lost from sight. In the first round, and in the first
root-race of this round, *hearing* was the sense developed. In the second round and the second root-race
touch was evolved. In the third round and corresponding root-race *sight* was added to the other two, and the
Self which hears, and the Not-self which is touched, or apprehended as tangible, are related and connected by sight,
—the correspondence to the intelligence that links. Thus
is brought about the blending of the three fires, and
illumination is present. But through all this evolutionary development the ONE Who hears, touches, and sees,
persists and interprets according to the stage of the
development of the manasic principle within Him. This
basic Interpreter is the Entity Who is independent of
an existence which ever necessitates a form. His is the
life that causes matter to vibrate and He is therefore
"fire by friction"; His is the life of pure Spirit which
wills to be, and which utilises form, and is therefore electrical impulse on the cosmic physical plane or "electric
fire"; His is the life that not only animates the atoms and
electrifies them by His Own nature, but likewise knows
itself to be one with all yet apart from all,—the thinking,
discriminating, Self-realising something that we call
MIND or Solar Fire. Universal mind or manas permeates all, and is equally that Self-knowing, individualised Entity Whose body contains our solar Logos as
well as certain other solar Logoi; Whose fire, heat and
radiation embrace certain other solar systems and unify
them with our own system so that one complete vital
body forms the manifestation of this mighty cosmic Be-

ing. Vortices of force on the cosmic etheric plane form
the etheric framework of seven solar systems in the same
way that the bodies of the seven Heavenly Men are the
etheric centres for a solar Logos, and as the seven centres in man (existing in etheric matter), are the animating electrical impulse of his life.

To express the origin of manas apart from manifestation through a congery of systems, a solar system, or a
man is for us impossible. Only as one grasps the fact
that each planetary scheme, for instance, serves as the
body of a Heavenly Man Who is the directing Mind in
that scheme, and the animating principle of manas or the
active discriminating faculty which every atom in that
scheme evinces; only when it is realised that a solar
Logos is similarly the manasic principle of those large
atoms we call schemes in their totality; only when it is
apprehended that a cosmic Logos is again the instigating
mind of the still vaster atoms we call systems; only when
it is admitted that man is the animating discriminative
faculty of the tiny spheres which form his body of manifestation; and finally, only when all this is meditated
upon, and its truth accepted, will this question of the origin of manas assume a less abstruse character, and the
difficulty of its comprehension be less appalling.

Man, the Thinker, the Knower, the manasic princirle
in the centre of the many spheres which form his bodies,
manipulates electrical force in three departments (the
physical, astral and mental bodies) through seven centres which are the focal points of force, and of its intelligent dispersal throughout his little system to the myriads
of lesser atoms, which are the cells in these spheres.

A Heavenly Man equally, and in a wider sense, the
Thinker and Knower, the manasic or mind principle plus
the buddhic or Christ principle, manipulates electrical
force through three principal vehicles or globes in atmic,
buddhic, and manasic matter, dispersing it from thence

to the myriads of cells which correspond to the deva and human units.

A *solar Logos* in a still wider sense is the permeating universal Mind, the manasic principle, plus the buddhic and the will principle, working in three major schemes, by means of seven centres of force, and through the myriads of groups which are the cells in His body, in the same way as human beings are the cells in the body of a Heavenly Man.

The *cosmic Logos* of our system works similarly through three major systems (of which ours is not one), utilising seven solar systems (of which ours is one), for the distribution of His force and having myriads of sevenfold groups as the cells of His body.

b. *Will and ordered purpose.* Thus all that we can really predicate anent the origin of manas is that it is the unified will-activity, or the purposeful expression of the realised Identity of some great Self which colours the life and swings into intelligent co-operation all the lesser units included in its sphere of influence. Each of us, in illustration, is the thinking purposeful Entity who acts as the manasic principle, and the spring of action, to all the units included in our three bodies. Each of us sways them to our will; we act, and by acting, force co-operation as we see fit. The Logos does the same on a larger scale. In this thought lies light on the question of karma, of free-will and of responsibility. *Manas is, really* WILL *working itself out on the physical plane,* and the truth of this will be seen when it is realised that all our planes form the cosmic physical plane, whereon an Entity, inconceivably greater than our Logos, is working out a set purpose through the Logos, through us, through all Spirit-substance that is included within His sphere of radiatory activity.

Certain problems of real interest are prone to enter our minds, but they serve only to develop abstract thought and to expand the consciousness, for they are as yet insoluble and will remain so. Some of them might be enumerated as follows:

1. Who is the cosmic Entity in Whose scheme our Logos plays his little part?
2. What is the nature of the great purpose He is working out?
3. Which centre in His body is represented by our solar system?
4. What is the nature of the incarnation He is now undergoing?
5. What are the ten systems—the three and the seven —of which our solar system is one? Must we look for the major three within the seven, or extraneously?
6. What is the coloring or basic quality of this cosmic Entity?
7. Is the colouring of the fourth cosmic ether (the buddhic plane), blue, or is it violet to correspond with our fourth physical ether? Why is buddhi exoterically regarded as yellow in color?
8. Which are the primary three centres in the body of our solar Logos and which the minor four?
9. What is the karma of the different schemes?
10. What is the over-balancing karma of the Logos Himself as it affects the ten schemes within His system?

All these questions, and numbers of others, will arise in the mind of the interested student, but beyond the formulation of them he may not as yet go, though the fifth round will see the realisation, by men, of the nature of the karma of the Logos of our chain. Words, as oft we have been told, blind and stultify.

In summing up, this quality of manas may be somewhat apprehended if the student regards it as the intelligent will, the active purpose, and the fixed idea of some Entity which brings about existence, utilises form, and works out effects from causes through discrimination in matter, separation into form, and the driving of all units within His sphere of influence to the fulfilment of that set purpose. Man is the originating source of mind as regards the matter of his vehicles, and their latent manasic impulse. So again with a Heavenly Man and His larger sphere of influence, and so with the solar Logos. Each discriminated, and thus formed His ring-pass-not; each has a purpose in view for every incarnation; each is actively following and intelligently working to effect certain ends, and thus each is the originator of manas to His scheme; each is the animating fire of intelligence to his system; each, through this very manasic principle individualises, expands gradually this self-realisation till it includes the ring-pass-not of the Entity through Whom the fifth principle comes to him; and each attains initiation, and eventually escapes from form.

3. *Human Manas.*

We are now to consider primarily man and the manasic principle, its development in the fourth Creative Hierarchy, the human Monads, with special reference to our Earth chain.

We have seen that, to all intents and purposes, manas is the active will of an Entity working itself out through all the lesser lives who go to the content of the ring-pass-not or sphere of influence of the indwelling Existence. Therefore—as concerning man on this chain—he is but expressing the purpose and the will in action of the planetary Logos in Whose body he is a cell or lesser life.

Certain mysteries arise consequently for our consideration which are connected with the life cycles of the Heavenly Man of our scheme, and particularly in relation to that special incarnation of His which we call the cycle

of manifestation on the dense physical globe, the earth.
He wears the planetary body as man wears the robe of
the physical body, and by means of this objective form
He works His purposes out on the physical plane,
through the factor of mind achieving certain goals. Incidentally, the cells in His body conform to that Mind
which plays upon them, just as man, the intelligent
principle of incarnation on the physical plane, brings
into conformity with *his* purpose the atoms of his body,
and stimulates ever more and more the spirillæ of those
atoms by the force of his mind playing upon them.

Here comes the opportunity to make clear something
that is oft lost sight of in the general fog surrounding
this subject. *The human and deva units* on the upward
arc, who are the cells in His body, *go to the formation
of the centres, and not to the remainder of the cellular
vital substance of His vehicles.* Man has a body made up
of matter which is applied to different uses, yet which
forms a unit. In this unit there are certain areas of
more vital importance than other areas *from the standpoint of energising force.* Such an area as the heart
may, in this connection, be considered and compared (as
regards force value) with such an area as the calf of the
leg. The entity, man, utilises both, but the heart centre
is of paramount importance. Thus is it also with a
Heavenly Man. The two great Hierarchies—deva and
human—are force centres in the body of a planetary
Logos; the other evolutions of an involutionary nature
extant within the scheme, and the remainder of the active
substance of the globes, and all contained therein, go
to the content of the remainder of His body.

a. *Man and the planetary Logos.* With the deva
evolution at this point we have nought to do. I seek to
concentrate attention on man, as he functions on earth.
In order to clarify the idea of manas and its relation to
a human being it is necessary to point out certain things

in connection with a Heavenly Man which must be borne in mind.

First, that each Heavenly Man holds the position of a centre in the body of a solar Logos; therefore, the Logos of a scheme will embody some outstanding characteristic. The ten schemes are the seven, and the synthesising three—not the seven and a lower three. The lower centres were vital in the last solar system (from the esoteric standpoint), and are not counted in this; they were synthesised and absorbed during the obscuration process of System I.

Secondly, each Heavenly Man is consequently the embodiment of a particular kind of electrical force which flows through His scheme as man's force flows through some one of the etheric centres in his body. Each scheme, as each human centre, will

a. Vibrate to some one key.
b. Have its own colouring.
c. Resemble, when seen from the higher planes, a vast lotus.
d. Possess, according to its vibratory capacity, a definite number of petals.
e. Be connected in geometrical formation with certain other centres of Heavenly Men, making systemic triangles.[32]
f. Be characterised by different stages of activity according to the initiation towards which the Logos may be working. Thus, at one period one centre or Heavenly Man may be the subject of logoic attention, and of specialised stimulation, and at another period a totally different scheme may be the object of vitalisation. For some time the Logos has turned His attention to the *Earth Scheme* and to *Saturn,* whilst *Uranus* is receiving

[32] A hint of this triangle of force was conveyed in *Letters on Occult Meditation,* page 79-84, when speaking of man and his centres.

stimulation.   Much is therefore accentuated, and
increased evolutionary development is the consequence of this divine attention.

When these facts are borne in mind it will be seen that
the interaction, and the complexity, is of vast proportions, and man can do no more than accept the fact, and
leave the explanation until his consciousness is of greater
scope.

Third, one of the mysteries revealed at initiation is that
of the logoic centre which our scheme represents, and
the type of electrical fire which is flowing through it.
The "Seven Brothers," or the seven types of fohatic
force, express Themselves through the seven centres, and
the One Who is animating our scheme stands revealed
at the third Initiation.   It is by knowledge of the nature
and quality of the electrical force of our centre, and by
realisation of the place our centre holds in the body
logoic, that the Hierarchy achieves the aims of evolution.
It will be obvious that the Heavenly Man Who stands
for the kundalini centre, for instance, will work differently, and have a different purpose and method, from
His Brother Who stands for the heart centre in the
body logoic, or to the Heavenly Man Who embodies the
logoic solar plexus.   From this it is apparent that:

a. The type of electrical force
b. The vibratory action
c. The purpose
d. The evolutionary development
e. The dual and triangular interaction

of all the Heavenly Men will differ, and so will the evolutions that form the cells in Their Bodies differ likewise.
Little has as yet been revealed anent the types of evolutions which are to be found in the other schemes of our
system. Suffice it to say that in all the schemes, on some

globe in the scheme, human beings or self-conscious units, are to be found. Conditions of life, environment and form may differ, but the human Hierarchy works in all schemes.

It must also be borne in mind that just as all seven Heavenly Men are found in the body logoic, and are Themselves under the influence of seven solar Logoi (using the word "influence" in its astrological sense), so in a planetary scheme with its seven globes each is astrologically under the influence of all the seven Heavenly Men. A scheme is but a replica of a system. Each of the Heavenly Men pours forth His radiation or influence, and stimulates in some way some other centre or globe. To word it otherwise, His magnetism is felt by His Brothers in a greater or less degree according to the work being undertaken at any one time. At present the Heavenly Men, representing centres at different stages of stimulation, being not all equally developed and being not as yet psychically unified, this magnetic interplay is little realised, and the psychic flow from one scheme to another is little utilised or comprehended. As time elapses this interplay of force will become more evident and the force will be consciously employed. When men, for instance, know

The quality of the force flowing through their particular scheme;

The purpose and name of the centre they stand within;

The centre or Heavenly Man with Whom the Logos of their scheme is allied;

Which two schemes form, with their own, a triangle for logoic force at a certain stage of evolutionary development;

The secret of the cycles, or the periods of stimulation or obscuration;

then will the body logoic begin to achieve its purpose;

then will the Logos of our system begin to blend and merge and co-ordinate all His vehicles; then will the force flow through all the centres unimpeded; and then will the glory shine out, and each cell in every body—logoic, planetary, deva and ·human, blaze forth with perfected glory, vibrate with adjusted accuracy, and a major cosmic initiation be taken.

b. The Logos of our Scheme. The Heavenly Man or planetary Logos of the Earth scheme can be considered in various ways, and as is our custom we will simply tabulate the statements anent Him which, when considered at length by the individual student, should serve to make the FACT of the essential Personality of this great Entity, the work that He is endeavouring to accomplish, and the relationship of the human Hierarchy to Him, a greater reality. We must bear in mind in studying this matter that it will not be possible to reveal for general publication details as to His specific Identity, His number and His scope of conscious development. Such mysteries, as earlier pointed out, are reserved for those who are pledged to keep silent. But some general idea may be conveyed before we take up specifically this chain and round.

It might be asked wherein all this information is of use, and what purpose it serves in this hour of the world's need. Apart from the fact that the cyclic giving out of the truth works under the law, and may not be gainsaid, it is suggested for consideration that much advantage will be felt when men in large numbers conceive of the purpose of specific manifestations, when they realise that all forms are but the modes of expression of certain Entities or Beings, Who occupy them for cycles of definite duration in order to attain a purpose, and that each life—great or small—serves its own ends, yet subserves the greater ends of the Being in Whose body it is a corporate part. The details of the plan may not be given.

The general outline—solar, planetary, and hierarchical —may be suggested, and by the very suggestion, bring order into the thoughts of men as they view the apparent chaos of the moment. Let us not forget, that when order is brought about, and united thought produced on the mental plane, then order transpires eventually on the physical plane.

The planetary Logos of this scheme is one of the four minor Logoi, or Lords of the Rays, and is specially concerned therefore with the development of one attribute of manas. Each of the four minor Rays is, as we know, eventually synthesised, or absorbed into that Ray which is represented on our earth by the Mahachohan. He is the Lord of the third major Ray or Aspect, and synthesises the four. *These four Rays with their synthesising Ray make the five rays of Manas or Mind.* We can consider them as:

a. The fivefold Brahma Aspect.

b. They were the five Rays of prime importance in the first solar system, and were the five individualised Heavenly Men, called the Mind-born Sons of Brahma. Through the individualisation of the four in that system the individualisation of the great cosmic Entity we call Brahma was brought about. He individualised and the four go to the content of His body.

c. They are represented on our earth by the five Kumaras Who obeyed the Law, and took human form, as H. P. B.[33] hints in several passages in the *Secret Doctrine.*

This scheme is considered as the fourth and the one of the most importance in the system during this particular cycle for the following reasons:

Our *solar system,* being considered as of the fourth
[33] S. D., I, 493.

order, and *our scheme* being the fourth in order, there is consequently a moment of special opportunity afforded our planetary Logos through the alignment brought about. It eventuates in the turning of the attention of the logoic kundalini fire towards this centre, our scheme, and the subsequent results are in process of working out.

Within the scheme *the chain* that concerns us the most, and which is temporarily of the most vital importance to the planetary Logos, is the Earth chain, the fourth in order again, thus bringing about another alignment of very grave moment. This carries with it special opportunity, and permits of the entry of force from the cosmos itself, or of extra-systemic electrical vitality. This super-stimulation results in what looks to us like cataclysms, and a stupendous shattering of forms, but it is simply the necessary sequence to the vitalisation of the life within the form, and the breaking of the limiting form unable to bear the cosmic action.

Again within the chain, *the globe* at present receiving planetary polarisation, or at present embodying in a special sense the life of the planetary Logos is the Earth, the fourth in order. This brings about a still further alignment.

Add to the above facts the accepted knowledge that this is the *fourth round* and we have a fivefold alignment which is of paramount significance to us all, though it had even greater significance and force in the fourth root-race, and brought about that stupendous psychic event—the opening of the door of Initiation to the human Hierarchy.

These very important facts merit close attention, and the consideration of all occult students. They hold the key whereby some comprehension of manas and of planetary evolution may come about. What have we, therefore, in this special cyclic alignment?

1. A solar system of the fourth order.
2. The fourth scheme in the system.
3. The fourth chain in the scheme.
4. The fourth globe in the chain.
5. The fourth round.[34]

All these are found active within the same cycle, and all therefore bring about a simultaneous alignment which results in the clearing of a channel direct from the heart of our scheme through every ring-pass-not to the cosmic correspondence, found outside the solar sphere.

To the above realisation, we must add yet the further fact that the fourth Creative Hierarchy is the one whose evolution we are considering, and it will be apparent to the most superficial student that in these thoughts lies hidden the clue, not only to man but to the entire cyclic evolution in which he is taking part.

The fourth Creative Hierarchy is essentially the Hierarchy of manas. This is no play on words, but a statement of deep occult significance. The statement has been made with entire accuracy that five Hierarchies out of the twelve have passed out and that seven remain. Of these seven, our human Hierarchy is the fourth, making it literally the ninth when counting the entire twelve. In this connection it would be well to link up the statements that have been made to the effect that the five Kumaras or Heavenly Men Who definitely embody the manasic principle (or the five Rays over which the systemic correspondence to the Mahachohan presides) de-

[34] Compare also the following correspondences:

The sacred Tetraktys	The manifested Logos.
The Fourth Creative Hierarchy	The Human.
The Fourth Principle	Lower Mind.
The Fourth Race	Kamamanas.
The Fourth Element	Water, S. D., I, 95. I, 640.
The Four Truths	S. D., I, 70.
The Four Propositions	S. D., I, 107.
The Four Initiations	S. D., I, 227.
The Fourth Plane	Buddhi, fourth cosmic ether.
The Fourth physical sub-plane	The Fourth Ether.
The Fourth Round	The Present.

veloped manas in an earlier system; They passed out of the wave of manasic influence *as far as Their own Nature* is concerned.

We must remember also that nine is the number of Initiation, or of the major Initiations of Manas, wherein man becomes a perfect Nine, or literally *is* the number of his Hierarchy. This is from the standpoint of the three systems, though his present systemic number may be four.

In occupying ourselves with these various statements anent our scheme and its Ruler we have seen that this particular cycle, or incarnation of His, is one of great importance, not only to Himself but to the entire system. The planetary Logos of this scheme is primarily occupied with a particular group of units, or with those Monads who vibrate to His key, are colored by the same colour as Himself, answer to the same number, and are esoterically known by the same Name. One point here needs emphasis: all Monads pass at different times under the influence of the different planetary Logoi, and all are found at some time in each scheme. This does not mean that every human unit passes a period of incarnation in each scheme. It means that on some one globe in every scheme, human units will be found either prior to physical incarnation, between different egoic cycles (a totally different thing to periods between physical lives), between different rounds or manvantaras, or between the various root-races and subraces. As stated in various occult books, many of the present advanced humanity individualised on the moon chain, and only took physical bodies in the earth chain during the fourth root-race, thus escaping incarnation during the first three rounds, and the first two races of the fourth round. In the interim, they came under the planetary influence of another Logos of a scheme, and were occupied during that immense period of time in fanning the manasic flame, and developing the attributes of manas, so that the Atlantean root-race found them adequately equipped to cope with life conditions.

This participation in the life and influence of the different schemes is effected in four different ways:

First, through passing the interim between egoic cycles of physical incarnation on the particular globe of their scheme, which numerically coincides with the particular other scheme whose influence is desired, either from deliberate choice or karmically necessitated. Each globe in a chain is occultly linked with the chain of its own number, and with the scheme of a similar number. For instance: Globe 2, Chain 2, and scheme 2 during round 2 are specially linked and vitalised, and are the focal point of peculiar attention on the part of the Logos of that scheme. Similarly (again in illustration) globe 2, chain 2 during round 2 in *any scheme* such as the fifth, for instance, are aligned or connected esoterically with the second scheme. This gives opportunity for the units in the body of any Logos to come under the influence of another Logos, and within his vibratory radiation.

Second, through a direct transference of the units in incarnation in any scheme (during an interlude) to some globe in another scheme where they are subjected to the stimulation and vibration peculiar to that scheme. These two methods are the most usual. This transference will seem mysteriously impossible unless the student is careful to realise that it is the transference of the individualised *lives and not the transference of the forms which they occupy.* The whole matter is psychic, and based on the unity of the anima mundi. It is only possible at those periods when two Heavenly Men are mutually finding each other—under the Law of Attraction—and thus swinging into the magnetic radius of each other.

Third, through a conscious passage of the initiate,

through initiation, from one scheme to another. This is frequently done, and hints of it have been given by different writers and thinkers, though several have confused the globes of their own chain with the scheme of the same number, or have mistaken another chain within the scheme for another scheme.

Fourth, the fourth method of transference of consciousness, and the bringing of the life units under the focal power of a Lord of a Ray, can be brought about through knowledge of certain mantrams and formulæ. On this we may not enlarge as these mantrams are esoteric and the use of them is fraught with much danger to the uninitiated.

The planetary Logos of this scheme is called "the First Kumara," the One Initiator, and the statement is made that He came to this planet from Venus, Venus being "the Earth's primary." This needs elucidation somewhat, though it may not be permitted to do more than convey a few hints as to the truth. The fact is one of the most mysterious in the development of our scheme, and in it lies hidden the secret of this world cycle. It is not easy to convey the truth and words but seem to veil and cloak.

Perhaps a hint may be given in pointing out that there is an analogy between the coming in of the Ego in full sway and its taking hold at certain periods in the life of a human being. At seven years we are told the Ego "takes hold," and again at adolescence; at twenty-one that hold may be made still firmer. Again, as lives are passed, the Ego (in connection with a human being) grips its vehicles and so sways them to his purpose with more effect and fullness. The same procedure can be seen in relation to a Heavenly Man and His body of manifestation, a scheme. It must be remembered that every scheme has seven chains; that each chain has seven globes, making a totality of forty-nine globes;

that each globe is again in turn occupied by the life of the Logos during what we call seven rounds, making literally three hundred and forty-three incarnations, or fresh impulses to manifest. We must add to these major manifestations such lesser ones as those named by us root-races, and subraces, also branch races, and thus we are faced with a complexity that is enough to stagger the average student. The planetary wheel of life turns on its lesser scale the wheel of life of the little pilgrim we call man; as it turns, it sweeps the life of the evolving planetary Logos into ever new forms and experiences until the fire of Spirit burns up all lesser fires.

As earlier pointed out, each Heavenly Man is linked with one of His Brothers under the Law of Mutual Attraction, which manifests so degradingly as yet upon the physical plane, through the life of the human unit, imprisoned in physical form. *Psychically* the link is of a different nature, and such a link is found between the planetary Logos of the scheme we call Venus, and the Logos of our scheme. This psychic interaction has its cyclic ebb and flow, as ebbs and flows all life force. In Lemurian days came a period of close interaction which brought about an incarnation on the physical planet of the Logos of our scheme, the Head of the Hierarchy, and the One Initiator. This could not have been effected had not the planetary Logos of the Venus scheme been in a position to link up closely with ours.

c. Venus and the Earth Chain. This question of the coming of the Lords of Flame to the planet Earth is deeply involved (as stated above) in the relationship existing between the Heavenly Man of the Earth scheme and the Lord of the Venus scheme. Until more detailed information is permitted publication anent these two great Entities, little more can be done beyond indicating some probabilities, and pointing out certain factors which students should carefully bear in mind. The statement has been made that (owing to the Venusian scheme being in its fifth round) its humanity is consequently further advanced than ours, and can help us, and that this help came in Lemurian days. This is an instance of a partial truth and its misinterpretation. The Venusian scheme is—as stated in the *Secret Doctrine* [35]—in its fifth and last round; its humanity is very far ahead of ours in certain particulars, but the momentous occurrence in the third root-race was due to the following causes, and not to the factor of the greater advancement of a certain group of human beings:

First, the Venus Scheme, viewed as a logoic centre, is more active than ours, and therefore its radiatory magnetism is far more widely spread. Its radiation is such that on the buddhic plane it swept within its magnetic radius that chain in our scheme which is composed predominantly of buddhic matter. Then, via that chain, it magnetised the corresponding globe in our chain, and this resulted in a specific vitalisation in the dense planet itself.

Second, just as in the case of man, certain triangles of force are found at different stages of evolution, or (to word it otherwise) different centres become geometrically linked, such as the

   a. Base of the spine,
   b. Solar plexus,
   c. Heart;

or again,

   a. Solar Plexus,
   b. Heart,
   c. Throat,

so, in the case of a Heavenly Man, or of a solar Logos, a similar event occurs. Such an event transpired in this round in relation to the centre which our planetary Logos

[35] S. D.. I, 187. II, 33-36, 626.

embodies. It became geometrically linked with two other centres, of which Venus was one, and logoic Kundalini—circulating with tremendous force through this adjusted Triangle—brought about that intensification of vibration in the human family which resulted in individualisation. We might here enumerate the schemes as a basis for our further work:

The seven planets, centres, or schemes:
1. Vulcan (the sun, exoterically considered).
2. Venus.
3. Mars.
4. *Earth.*
5. Mercury.
6. Jupiter.
7. Saturn.

The three synthesising planets:
1. Uranus.
2. Neptune.
3. Saturn.

The One Resolver.

The SUN.

I would caution you here against attaching any importance to the sequence followed in numbering these seven schemes, either in connection with their order of development or importance, or their position in relation to the central planet, the sun, or to each other. Only two are to be considered numerically accurate *at this stage and in this round,* i.e., our Earth, the fourth scheme, and Venus, the second. Venus is either the second or the sixth scheme, according to whether the schemes are counted mystically or occultly. Inversely, Jupiter will be either the second or the sixth, and it must be remembered that:

a. The planets Venus and Jupiter are exceedingly closely connected with the Earth, and form eventually an esoteric triangle.

b. Saturn is the synthesising scheme for the four planets which embody manas purely and simply, or is the major resolution of the minor four, and eventually for all the seven.

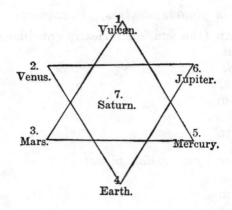

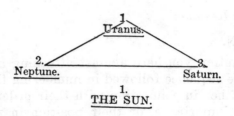

c. Mercury, the star of the intuition, or of transmuted manas, is, at this stage, considered as the fifth scheme.

Therefore, the Heavenly Men of Venus and Jupiter are magnetically linked with the Heavenly Man of our scheme. The relationship of the Logos of Jupiter and His influence will not be realised nor felt until the sixth

round is in full force, though during the sixth root-race
His vibration will be acknowledged and sensed; in the
middle of the fifth round the Logos of Mercury will,
with the Logos of the Venus scheme, and of our Earth,
form a temporary triangle of force. We have here information given that has only been hinted at hitherto
but for which, in this fifth subrace and in this fourth
round, the world is now ready; it holds the solution of
the mystery of this round.

Third, the statement that the great Kumara or the
One Initiator came to this planet from Venus is true
in so far as it embodies the fact that He came to this
dense planet (the fourth) in the fourth chain *from that
chain in our scheme which is called the "Venus" chain,
and which is the second chain.* He came via the second
globe in our chain; His scarcely felt vibration was sensed
(occultly) in the second round, but only in the third
root-race of the fourth round did conditions permit of
His physical incarnation and of His coming as the
Avatar. Very reverently might it be said that the first
three rounds and the two succeeding root-races in this
chain correspond to the period prior to birth; and that
His coming in the fourth round with the subsequent
awakening of manas in the human units find their analogy in the awakening of the life principle in the unborn
infant at the fourth month.

The analogy holds good, for a Heavenly Man at the
end of the seventh round reaches full maturity, but
requires the final process of rounding out and perfecting which He attains during the two final periods

a. Of synthesis into the major three schemes.
b. Of resolution into the final one;
making again—with reverence may it be said—the nine
cycles which cover the gestation of a Heavenly Man,
and which precede His birth into yet higher worlds.
In this lies much food for thought, and much of moment

for the profound student. We might couple with these suggestions the recollection that we are speaking here only of the Logos of our own scheme, and must carefully differentiate other cycles for the other Logoi—a thing as yet impossible for us. As this is meditated upon and studied, the wonder and beauty of the plan will become apparent.

A clue to the idea of the final Avatar is likewise to be seen here. Many temporary incarnations precede this consummating one, which will be the incarnation wherein the Heavenly Man, in the full beauty of His completed seven cycles, and prior to His merging into His synthesising goal, will demonstrate as the embodiment of that perfected quality, or logoic aspect, for which He primarily stands. As a centre in the body logoic, He will be fully vitalised, and the logoic kundalini will have stimulated, and aroused to perfection His systemic Lotus. For a brief period He will shine forth radiant as the Sun in His glory; then the kundalinic fire will pass in higher progressive spirals, and He will gradually become centred in the corresponding logoic head centre, the higher triangle or the major three schemes. To illustrate by means of a human being, the microcosm: Man attains a period of high development wherein his heart and throat centre are perfected and vitalised; they become radiant whorls of fire, fourth dimensional in action, and allied with each other and with some other centre; they become likewise the object of the attention of human kundalini. This is a period of great activity and magnetic usefulness. It is succeeded by still another, wherein the three head centres are synthesising their seven minor correspondences, and the force of kundalini passes there. As above, so below.

I have especially mentioned these two centres in the microcosm as they are closely concerned (on a larger scale) with the particular cycles through which our

Chart VI

The Divine Septenary hanging from the Triad thus forming the Decad and its permutations 7, 5, 4, 3. (S.D. Vol. I, pp. 259)

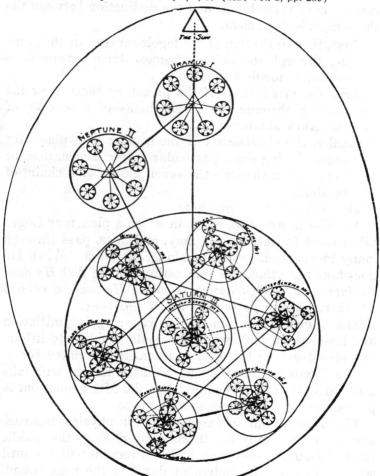

Solar Septenary Chart—From the middle of the Third Root Race, at the Fourth Round to "The Judgment Day" in the middle of the Fifth Round

THE DENSE PHYSICAL PLANETS

Earth	4th Chain 4th Globe	Mars	4th Chain 4th Globe
Jupiter	3rd Chain 4th Globe	Vulcan	3rd Chain 4th Globe
Saturn	3rd Chain 4th Globe	Venus	5th Chain 5th Globe
	Mercury	4th Chain 5th Globe	

planetary Logos passes, and because they represent the third and second aspects.

We need to bear in mind that the stimulation of the centres is of three kinds, and the distinction between the three must be kept clear.

First, the vitalisation of the logoic centres, or the pour ing through the seven schemes, during stupendous cycles, of logoic kundalini.

Next, the vitalisation of the planetary centres, or the pouring through the seven chains of a scheme, of planetary kundalini.

Finally, the vitalisation of the centres of a planetary Logos during some particular major incarnation, or the pouring through the seven globes of a chain, of kundalini.

It should be stated here that:

A major incarnation is one in which a planetary Logos takes some initiation. He may, and does, pass through many incarnations without taking initiation. When He does take initiation, it is interesting to note that *He does so during some incarnation in which He takes a vehicle of etheric matter as is the case at this time.*

The Logos of our scheme is preparing for initiation and hence the terrific tests and trials, incident to life on our planet during this cycle, are easily accounted for.

The Logos of our scheme, Sanat Kumara, will take a major initiation in the middle of the fifth round, but is preparing for a minor one at this time.

The Logos of our scheme has been in physical incarnation (having a body of etheric matter) since the middle of the Lemurian root-race, and will remain with us until what is called "the judgment day" in the next round. At that point in His career He will have achieved the necessary vitalisation of the particular centre which is occupying His attention, will have "seen of the travail of His Soul" in connection with the units of the human

Hierarchy who go to the composition of this centre, and will drop His present form, will turn His attention to another and higher centre, and give of His force to the units of a different calibre, from another branch of the human Hierarchy, who respond to the vibration of that centre.

It would be well to enlarge here a little on the connection between Venus and the Earth, which is hinted at in some of the occult books, and is somewhat touched upon in this. I have stated that the interaction between the two schemes is due largely to their positive and negative polarity, and I pointed out that a similar relation underlies the relation of the Pleiades and the seven schemes of our solar system, and also the relation of Sirius and the system itself. This, therefore, sweeps into close interaction three great systems:

1. The system of Sirius,
2. The system of the Pleiades,
3. The system of which our sun is the focal point,

making, as we will have noted, a cosmic triangle. Within our system there are several such triangles, varying at different stages; according to their relation to each other, the differentiated force of the different schemes can pass from scheme to scheme, and thus the units of life on the different rays or streams of force become temporarily intermingled. In all these triangles (cosmic, systemic, planetary, and human) two points of the triangle represent each a different polarity, and one point represents the point of equilibrium, of synthesis or merging. This should be borne in mind in studying both the macrocosmic and the microcosmic centres, for it accounts for diversity in manifestation, in forms and in quality.

A correspondence might here also be pointed out which

may serve to convey light to those who have eyes to see:

The Venus scheme, being in the fifth round, had the fifth principle of manas co-ordinated and developed, the minor four manasic aspects had been synthesised, and the buddhic aspect was being provided with a means of expression through the medium of the perfected fifth. Our Heavenly Man, in the fifth round, will have attained a paralleling point in evolution, and the fifth principle will, as stated, be no longer the object of His attention as regards the human units.

Five stages of activity mark the development and utilisation of the mind principle; there are three stages of acquisition, and two wherein that which has been acquired is used. This is too intricate a calculation for us to enter into it here, and it cannot be undertaken except by an initiate, for it involves ability to study the cycles of the earlier solar system, but it might be noted that (judging from the microcosm on the earth planet) this is just what might be expected. Man developed manas in this round during the third, fourth and fifth root-races, and utilises it for the development of the intuition and of the higher consciousness during the sixth and seventh. During an incarnation by a planetary Logos in a chain, during one round He demonstrates through His seven centres or globes manas on three globes, and utilises it for specific purposes on the final two. This is a lesser cycle to that in which we view the seven chains as His seven centres. These words are chosen with care; I say not "acquires manas"; He but produces that which is inherent. It must be remembered that just as the planes of a solar system stand for a different purpose, vibrate to a different key, and serve their own specific ends, so do the globes serve an analogous function.

   a. Globe 1, is that of ultimate abstraction, and of origination. It is the initial globe of manifestation.

b. Globe 2, is the first sheath in which a Heavenly Man embodies Himself.

c. Globes 3, 4, 5, are those through which He demonstrates the possession of the manasic principle.

d. Globes 6 and 7, are the ones through which He manifests buddhi, through forms built by means of the manasic principle.

This can be equally predicated on a larger scale of a chain.

An interesting correspondence of a very occult nature can be worked out by the advanced student in connection also with the seven schemes. There are two which may be considered primarily archetypal, causal, or involving abstraction; three in which manas is manifested, and two in which already buddhi is manasically demonstrating. Of these two, Venus is one and thus we have the three and the two which make the five schemes of the five Kumaras, Who are Brahma.[36]

Just as Venus is negatively polarised to our Earth scheme, so the seven stars of the Pleiades are negatively polarised to our seven schemes.

A very pertinent question might here be asked. We might justly enquire (in connection with the point that Venus is negatively polarised, and also that the Pleiades are equally so) why they should be termed negative if they are the donors and not the receivers, for to be negative is surely to be receptive. This is indeed so, but the question arises in our minds, owing to lack of information, and consequent misapprehension. Venus may have had much to do with the impartation of the stimulation which resulted in great events on Earth via the Venus chain of our scheme, but *our scheme gave, in a mysterious manner, more than was received,* though the

---

[36] Students must carefully differentiate between the five Mind born Sons of Brahma, the five true Kumaras and their representatives on our earth planet, Those Who stand around Sanat Kumara Who may be stated (esoterically understood) to represent Himself.

gift was not of the same nature. The coming in of the Venusian influence to our chain, and to our planet, with the subsequent stimulation of certain groups in the fourth Creative Hierarchy, the human, caused a paralleling event of even greater magnitude in the Venus scheme. This affected the sixth Hierarchy, one of the deva Hierarchies, dwelling in the Venus scheme. This stimulation emanated via our sixth chain (or the second according to the angle of vision) and affected a corresponding chain in the Venus scheme. The magnitude of the difference may be seen in the fact that in our case *one globe alone* was affected, whereas the influence of our scheme on the Venusian was such that *an entire chain* was stimulated. This was brought about through the positive polarity of the Heavenly Man of the Earth scheme.

Therefore, enlarging the concept, we can note the fact that our Heavenly Men are the transmitters, via their seven schemes, to the seven stars of the Pleiades. Our solar system is negatively polarised as regards the sun Sirius, which influences our entire system psychically via the three synthesising schemes—Uranus, Neptune, Saturn—the latter, Saturn, being the focal point for the transmission of cosmic manas to the entire seven schemes.

4. *Manas and the Earth Chain*

We have brought our consideration of our first point, the origin of cosmic and systemic manas, down to certain facts concerning our chain, and have (with the utmost brevity) passed in review the larger aspect of the question. We touched first of all upon the subject of cosmic manas, as it concerned our Logos and the Heavenly Men. Then we considered it more specifically in its relation to the individual Heavenly Men, and finally brought it down to that which more nearly concerns ourselves—

manas and the Heavenly Man of our scheme. Having
proceeded thus far, we considered the stimulation of
manas in our own chain, and saw that, in connection
with our Earth, it came:

Via the Venus chain of our scheme.
As the result of a stimulation, originating in the Venus
scheme.
Because logoic kundalini had vitalised one of the systemic triangles of force, of which (temporarily)
Venus and the Earth formed two points of the triangle.
This produced the individualisation of those, particularly in the human Hierarchy, who form a particular centre in the body of the planetary Logos.

a. *The Earth Chain and the Incarnating Monads.*

We have reached, therefore, a point wherein (having
cursorily dealt above with the origin of cosmic, systemic,
and planetary manas), it is now possible for us to come
definitely down to the consideration of our Earth chain
within the Earth scheme, and see something of the origin
of the manasic principle *in the present group of incarnating egos,* units of the fourth Creative Hierarchy. It
is necessary here for students to remember that only one
group in the fourth Hierarchy was affected by the coming in of manas in the third root-race, and that therefore
in incarnation on the planet at this time are component
parts of the two groups: one group, which received the
manasic stimulation during this world period, and another group which received the stimulation during the
previous chain. The last named group can be seen incarnating in all those who tread the Probationary Path,
who are counted as the advanced units of the race, and
considered as the notables among men. Owing to the
difference between the two groups may be traced much
of the world unrest. This difference lies in the following

factors, which, for purposes of clarity, it might be well to enumerate:

The fact that each group forms a different centre in the body of a Heavenly Man.

The difference in the method of individualisation.

The different rate of vibration of the two centres.

The fact, therefore, that in each chain the planetary Logos takes a different initiation, affecting different centres; and so bringing into manifestation different lesser entities.

Students, when considering these things, need to view the matter from the following angles—some quite possible lines of approach for us, others which we are only capable as yet of dimly anticipating. The occult fact, as stated by the English poet Pope, ''The proper study of mankind, is man,'' is embodied in the investigation of all these vast cycles.

The cosmic angle. This involves the study of the place of the solar Logos within His greater sphere, the study of extra-systemic psychology and astronomy, and the consideration of the relation existing between our system and other constellations, and of our path in the vast arc of the heavens. It bears on the relation of the various suns with their circulating attendants, and of the planets with each other; it concerns the study of their individual polarisation, and their interaction with their polar opposites. It will lead the student into regions of logical speculation, into the study of cosmic electricity, and the universal Law of attraction, and is as yet much beyond the comprehension of even the most advanced students at this time, and will only become a science (reduced to form and text-book if I might so express it) during the final part of the next round.

The systemic angle. This deals with the place of the Heavenly Men within the body logoic, Their mutual interplay, and Their rational interdependence, and with the cycles wherein each in turn, or in dual formation, is the recipient of logoic force. It necessitates the study of the solar system as a unit, of the astronomical and orbital relation of the Sun to the planets. The systemic triangles will eventually become a subject of popular speculation, then of investigation, of scientific demonstration, and finally be known to be proved and authenticated fact,—but the time is not yet. The different polarities of the schemes will be studied, and information, that is now imparted only to initiates of the third Initiation, will eventually become exoteric. In due course of time systemic information along the lines of:

    a. The vitalisation of the schemes
    b. Interaction between two schemes
    c. The periods of incarnation of a planetary Logos on
        the physical plane
    d. The initiation of the planetary Logos,

will be reduced to law and order. As yet but dim speculations and hints that appeal only to the spiritual and the intuitive are in any way possible. The early part of the next round will see more widespread knowledge and interest in this matter.

The planetary angle. This point of view concerns itself with the history of the individual scheme, and with the consciousness, and evolution of some particular Heavenly Man. The student in studying along these lines must endeavour to get some grasp of the scheme as a unit, as a body corporate with its seven centres and forty-nine globes, and with the triangle formed between them. Separate chains are either

    The object of planetary stimulation,
    The sphere of the incarnation of a planetary Logos,
    Emerging into objectivity,

Manifesting,
Gradually entering into obscurity.

This point of view is as yet impossible for the average thinker, for it involves an expansion of consciousness unattainable by man. Nevertheless the endeavour to comprehend serves a useful purpose, for it sets a goal for man and enables him to enlarge his present concept.

The chain angle. This brings the whole idea more within the range of possibility, and has already been indicated to students in *Volume II,* of the *Secret Doctrine.* The student is narrowed down to the contemplation of the seven globes of the chain of which he is a component, though microscopic, part. He has for investigation the globes as seen in *time,* with their mutual interplay; he has for study the part each one may be playing in the great cycle of a Heavenly Man. For instance, in the present Earth chain which concerns us the most nearly, the fourth globe is of paramount interest, inasmuch as it is the physical plane vehicle for a Heavenly Man in dense objective incarnation. Yet it must not be forgotten that, though manifesting thus objectively, He embodies in totality the chain and the scheme. The idea may be clarified for the student if it is stated that:

A scheme, in its totality, corresponds to the Monad, or to the monadic auric egg, in connection with a human being and his forty-nine cycles.

A chain,[37] in its totality corresponds to the body egoic of a human being, to the causal body with its seven great

---

[37] Chain—a series of seven globes or worlds which form the field of evolution during the planetary cycle or manvantara. The first three of these globes—generally known as A., B. and C. form a descending arc, the densest physical matter of the descent being reached in the fourth globe, D, of which our earth is an instance. The fifth globe, E, on the ascending arc (correspondence to C on the descending arc) usually belongs to the astral plane, and the sixth and seventh F and G (correspondence to B and A on the descending arc) to the Rupa and Arupa levels of the mental plane; these therefore are invisible to ordinary sight.

cycles mentioned elsewhere in these pages, and hinted at in certain occult books.

A *globe*, with its seven races corresponds to a particular series of incarnations in connection with a man, incarnate or discarnate, for all globes are not on physical levels.

A *physical globe*, in a chain corresponds to a particular physical incarnation of a man. The planetary Logos takes physical form in His planet and is its life and works out His purposes.

A *root-race*, simply is analogous to the "seven parts" (as Shakespeare phrases it) as played by the midget, man. In a root-race a Heavenly Man is simply living out His life, working through some experience in the great work of developing buddhi or corporate action, (for buddhi is the unifying principle of groups) and, in the process of experiencing and developing, He sweeps into His vibratory capacity all the cells in His body. In the case of a human being the cells in his body (the material cells) are involutionary lives, animated by the third Logos, co-operating with the second Logos. In the case of a planetary Logos, the cells in His body are evolutionary lives (deva and human units) animated by the life of the second Logos, co-operating with the first Logos, and utilising the activities of the third Logos for purposes of manifesting.

Having pointed out these things, the place the Earth chain and globe play in the evolution of the planetary Logos of the Earth scheme should be clearer to the student.

The wheel turns, and in its turning sweeps into objectivity one of its seven globes, or brings into manifestation on the physical plane that great Entity Whose life animates the whole scheme. It must be borne in mind that just as man is handicapped by his physical body, and finds himself unable to express through it the entire content of his egoic consciousness, so a Heavenly Man, when taking to Himself a dense physical vehicle in any particular chain, is also handicapped, and is unable to express in perfection on the globe the full beauty of His Life or the splendour of His manifesting Consciousness.

It might here be stated in connection with the planetary Logos of our scheme that:

a. He is in physical incarnation.
b. He is midway through His career upon the cosmic Path of Initiation, and consequently is to take the fourth Initiation in this chain. Well may this globe, therefore, be considered the globe of sorrow and of pain, for through it our planetary Logos is undergoing that which the mystic calls "the Crucifixion."
c. The cells in His body—those cells through which He feels, and senses, and experiences,—are, in this world period, rent by pain and suffering, for His is the consciousness at the centre of the Body, and theirs is the capacity to suffer, so that by means of them He may learn the meaning of systemic dispassion, be dissociated from all forms and material substance, and upon the cross of matter eventually find liberation and the freedom of the Spirit.

The same equally can be predicated of a solar Logos with the following interesting sequence carefully borne in mind:

The solar Logos has for objective nine initiations, the third cosmic Initiation being His goal.
Our planetary Logos has for objective seven initiations, the second cosmic Initiation being His goal.
Man has for objective five initiations, the first cosmic Initiation being his goal.

CHART VII

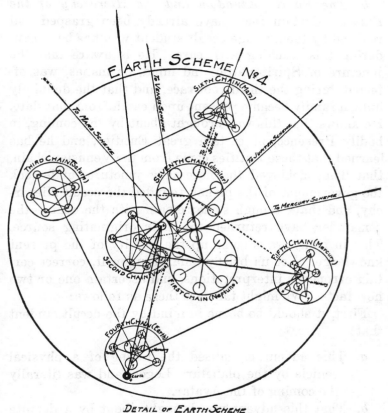

EARTH SCHEME No 4

SIXTH CHAIN (Mars)

To Venus Scheme

THIRD CHAIN (Saturn)

To Venus Scheme

To Mars Scheme

SEVENTH CHAIN (Jupiter)

To Jupiter Scheme

To Mercury Scheme

SECOND CHAIN (Venus)

FIFTH CHAIN (Mercury)

FIRST CHAIN (Neptune)

FOURTH CHAIN (Earth)

Earth

DETAIL OF EARTH SCHEME
AS SHOWN ON
SOLAR SEPTENARY CHART

If we link this up with that earlier imparted concerning
initiation and the sun Sirius, we will have a clue to the
triple cosmic Path.

*b. The Fourth Kingdom and the Hierarchy of the
Planet.* Certain facts have already been grasped and
realised by the average occult student who has been pondering this teaching with care. He is aware that the
juncture of Spirit-matter and mind, or manas, was effected during the third root-race, and that the definitely
human family became present upon earth from that date.
He knows that this was brought about by the coming, in
bodily Presence, of certain great Entities, and he has
learned that these Entities came from the Venusian chain,
that They achieved the necessary juncture, undertook
the government of the planet, founded the occult Hierarchy, and that—though some remain with the chain—the
remainder have returned to Their originating source.
This in many ways sums up the totality of the present
knowledge. Let us briefly enlarge upon it, correct certain erroneous interpretations, and ascertain one or two
new facts. We might tabulate these as follows:

First, it should be borne in mind by the occult student
that:

a. This advent signalised the taking of a physical
   vehicle by the planetary Logos, and was literally
   the coming of the Avatar.
b. That this advent was brought about by a definite
   systemic alignment which involved:
   The Venus scheme of the system.
   The Venus chain of the Earth scheme.
   The Venus globe of the Earth chain.
c. That the planetary Logos did not come from the
   Venus scheme but from the Venus chain of His own
   scheme, the Earth scheme. Owing to systemic

alignment logoic kundalini could flow through a
certain triangle of which two points were Venus
and the Earth.   This caused an acceleration of
vibration, and enabled the Heavenly Man of our
scheme to take a minor initiation, and to set about
His preparations for a major initiation.

Next, it should also be remembered that in considering
this matter we must be careful to view it not only as it
affects our own globe and its present humanity, but from
the systemic and cosmic point of view, or from the angle
of its importance to a planetary Logos and a solar Logos.   Hence it is a fact that this event was not only the
result of the taking of a minor initiation by our Earth
Logos, but in the Venus scheme it was signalised by the
taking of a major initiation by the Venusian planetary
Logos on His fifth chain.   In connection with a solar
Logos it followed upon the stimulation of one of His
centres and from the geometrical progression of the fire
through the earlier mentioned Triangle.

It has been stated that one hundred and four Kumaras
came from Venus to the Earth; literally the figure is one
hundred and five, when the synthesising Unit, the Lord
of the World Himself, is counted as one.   There remain
still with Him the three Buddhas of Activity.   I would
call attention to the dual significance of that name,
"Buddha of Activity," bearing out, as it does, the reality
of the fact that Entities at Their stage of evolution are
active love-wisdom and embody in Themselves the two
aspects.   The three Buddhas of activity have a correspondence to the three persons of the Trinity.

These Entities are divided into three groups of thirty-
five each, and in Themselves embody the three major centres of the planetary Logos, those three groups which we
know as the "three departments," for it should be emphasised that each department forms a centre:

a. The Head centre.... The Ruling Department
b. The Heart centre.... The Teaching Department
c. The Throat centre... The Mahachohan's Department. This centre synthesises the lesser four, just as the third Ray synthesises the minor four.

These Kumaras (or Their present substitutes) can also be divided into the seven groups which correspond to the seven Rays, and are in Themselves the life of the centre for which They stand. Fifteen, therefore, of these Entities (again the ten and the five) form a centre in the body of the planetary Logos, and the three Kumaras about Whom we are told (Who in Themselves are fivefold, making the fifteen) are the entifying Lives of the particular centre which is involved in the coming Initiation of the Heavenly Man, and to which the human units at this time, and during this greater cycle, belong.

Another fact that should be noted about these great Beings is, that when viewed in Their seven groups, They form:

a. Focal points for the force or influence emanating from the other solar centres or schemes.
b. The seven divisions of the occult Hierarchy.

They exist, as does the Heavenly Man Himself, in etheric matter, and are literally great Wheels, or centres of living Fire, manasic and electric fire; They vitalise the body of the Heavenly Man and hold all together as an objective whole. They make a planetary triangle within the chain, and each of Them vitalises one globe.

It is not permitted at this stage to state, for exoteric publication:

Which Ray, or logoic emanation is embodied by our planetary Logos.

Which centre in the solar system is called the Earth
scheme.

Which scheme is our polar opposite, or which Heavenly
Man is most closely allied to ours.

Which particular centre in the body of the planetary
Logos He is at present endeavouring to vitalise.

These points are, as may be inferred, too dangerous to
impart, and those students whose intuition suffices to attain the information will see for themselves the necessity
for silence.

c. A Prophecy. We might now, prior to continuing
with our subject, name the different chains of the Earth
scheme. We must bear carefully in mind the fact that
these are simply names, affixed to the chains and globes
for the sake of clarity. As this subject is more widely
studied it will inevitably be found advisable to call the
chains by their numbers, and to drop the names as at
present used:

1. Neptune.
2. Venus.
3. Saturn.
4. Earth.
5. Mercury.
6. Mars.
7. Jupiter.

It is necessary here to take the opportunity to sound a
note of warning to students in connection with the charts
which have been inserted in the Treatise.

They depict only one cycle in logoic evolution, and
cover only the present greater period in the working out
of which we are engaged. They might be roughly described as embracing that period in the system which
began for us in the middle of the third root-race of this
round and continues until the period called "the Judg-

ment'' in the coming fifth round. When that time comes
our planetary Logos will have attained the initiation
which is His present goal; the fifth round of the Venusian
scheme will be closing, and the Venus scheme will begin
to pass into obscuration, preparatory to transferring her
life to the synthesising planet with which she is connected; Mercury will be reaching the apotheosis of
achievement, and with Mars and the Earth, will form a
systemic triangle. We are speaking here of *schemes,*
and not of chains.

We must recognise another triangle within the Earth
scheme, of the chains called ''the Earth chain,'' the
Venus chain, and the Mercurian chain, but this triangle
entirely concerns the centres of the planetary Logos of
our scheme. A systemic formation of great importance
in the next round should be pointed out which will bring
three schemes:

> The Earth scheme,
> Mars,
> Mercury,

into such a position in relation to each other that the
following results will eventuate:

1. A systemic triangle will be formed.

2. Logoic kundalini will circulate freely between these
three points.

3. A certain great logoic centre will be vitalised and
the attention of logoic kundalini will pass from the present triangle in process of forming (the Earth, Venus, and
a scheme whose name it is advisable to withhold) to the
other.

4. An entirely new group of human beings will sweep
into incarnation in our Earth scheme. Three fifths of
the present humanity, being on the Probationary Path,
or the Path of Initiation, at that time, will have their
centre of consciousness definitely on the mental plane,

whilst two fifths will remain focussed on the astral. These two fifths will pass into temporary pralaya, preparatory to their transference to another scheme, as the Earth scheme will no longer provide for them an adequate place of nurture.

5. Entities will come in from Mars to the Earth scheme, and will there find their necessary field of endeavour.

6. Mercurian life will begin to synthesise, and to be transferred to its synthesising planet. In the case of Mercury this synthesising planet is not Saturn, but one of the other two higher major centres.

7. The "Judgment Day" in the fifth round, or the point of attainment of our Heavenly Man, will see a period of planetary strife on mental levels which will cause the present world unrest to seem as nothing. As pointed out earlier, this present struggle has been to test the ability of the entities within the present human forms to appreciate their mental forces, and through the power of MIND to transcend feeling, or pain. The struggle in the fifth round will be between higher and lower mind, and the battle ground will be the causal body.[38] The

[38] *The Causal Body.*

"This influence or force, or result, or whatever it may be called, of the antecedent actions of man, forms as it were a seed, from which germinates the plant, yielding good or bad fruit, to be eaten by him during his subsequent existence. (Vishnu Purana I, XIX, 5). This seed is technically called the Karana Sarira, the causal body (Paingala Upanishad II), as it is the cause of man's enjoyment or suffering. This Karana Sarira is composed of the fifth Kosa (Anandamaya) of man and adheres to the soul so long as the soul remains enveloped in the gross or subtle body (Sthula or Sukshma Sarira); and vanishes entirely when the soul extricates itself from the trammels of the said two bodies; for then, the soul attains its primeval purity, and burns up as it were every trace of its combination with the body, including this causal body (Karana Sarira). This happens when the soul is prepared for final emancipation, Moksha. Till then, of course, the Karana Sarira, the seed, the result of prior actions, remains effective, and asserts a strong controlling influence over man's actions."— *The Theosophist,* Vol. VII, III, p. 59.

"An ordinary person will by Vasana (Aroma or smell) repeat (In Jagra, the waking state) the old story dreamt in a dream that has passed way. So also will he, who, investigating the true nature of the self has attained to real knowledge, express himself and still will never become Chidabhasa (chidabhasa is the reflection of atma in the Karana Sarira, which is the

struggle now being waged on the planet is between a few Egos (or the leaders of the many races who are necessarily in place and position owing to their egoic polarisation) and many personalities, who are swept into the vortex through group association; it is necessarily terrific, and forces the destruction of the form. The struggle in the fifth round, being on mental levels, will be between Egos and egoic groups, each working consciously, and with intellectual application, to bring about certain group results. It will result in the triumph (the ultimate triumph) of Spirit over matter, in the driving out of certain groups as yet unable to shake themselves free from the trammels of matter, and who prefer captivity to the life of the Spirit; it will mark the beginning of the obscuration of our scheme, and the gradual passing into pralaya, during the remaining two and a half rounds of our entire seven chains. It is an interesting occult fact that our Earth should now be in her fifth round, and paralleling the Venusian scheme, but the moon chain of our scheme saw a period of temporary retardation of the evolutionary process of our Heavenly Man; it resulted in a temporary slowing down of His activities, and caused "lost time," if such an expression might reverently be permitted. The Lords of the Dark Face, or the inherent forces of matter for a time achieved success, and only the fifth round of our chain will see their ultimate defeat. The Venusian scheme also had its battleground, but the planetary Logos of that scheme overcame the antagonistic forces, triumphed over material forms, and was consequently in a position—when the right time came—to apply the needed stimulation or an

vehicle of ignorance). *He who has become a celestial being will nevertheless be called 'man' till the causal body that has already died (by the birth of Pragna, or wisdom) is completely consumed by the predominant fire of wisdom.*"—*Kaivalyanavanita*, Part II, 31.

"By the rarest fire of True Wisdom the body of avidya (i.e. the causal body) will be reduced to ashes."—*Kaivalyanavanita*, Part I, 98.
Copied from *The Theosophist*, Vol. VIII.

increased fiery vibration to our Earth scheme. The fact that outside aid was called in during the third root-race of this chain, and that the evolution of manas brought about the individualisation, in physical form, of the Avatar, needs to be pondered on. The Divine Manasaputra, the Lord of the World, took form Himself through the driving impulse of manas, inherent in His nature, and in some mysterious way this was aided by another Heavenly Man of another scheme. His co-operation was required.

d. *Summation.* We have been studying the origin of manas, and we saw first, that it is the active will, intelligently applied, of an Entity, and then that this active intelligent will affects all lesser lives in cyclic evolution within the Body of that particular actively willing Existence. This is true of all Beings from the Logos downwards. Perhaps in summing up it might be expressed thus:

The originating source of manasic activity *in a solar system* is that great cosmic Entity Who embodies our solar Logos as a centre in His Body along with six other solar Logoi Who are, in Their totality, His seven centres.

The originating source of manasic activity *in the planetary schemes* is that cosmic Entity we call the solar Logos. He is the active, directing Intelligence Who is working with definite purpose through His seven centres.

The originating source of the manasic principle in a *planetary scheme* is that lesser cosmic Entity Whom we call a planetary Logos. He works through His seven chains as does the Logos through His seven planetary centres. It is interesting here to note that when the solar Logos is being manasically impelled to work out some purpose of His greater Source (THE ONE ABOUT WHOM NAUGHT MAY BE SAID) He may cause a vivification in one or other of His centres according to the purpose in view. This occurred in the forming of the triangle of which Earth and Venus are two points, and (affecting the Heavenly Men of these two schemes) stimulated Them to take initiation, and led the planetary Logos of our scheme to form a lesser triangle within His sphere of activity, which triangle eventuated in His taking a lesser initiation, and in the manasic impregnation of animal man. Thus were swept into objective activity that group of monads who go to the composition of a particular centre.

Similarly, and microcosmically, a human being is the manasic incentive and the origin of active, intelligent will to all the cells within his threefold body,—astral, mental and physical. His is the directing intelligence, and his the source of all action and endeavour within his periphery, and, like his greater corresponding spheres, a solar Logos and a planetary Logos, he works through seven centres.

Thus we have traced the origin of manas as far as it is possible to do at this time. The mystery of manas is hidden in existence itself, and holds the secret of life and conceals and veils those Entities Whose outstanding quality and characteristic it is. To the life of that little entity we call an atom in the physical body of a man, the Thinker in the causal body, his greater directing intelligence, is as obscure and unknown as the Logos is to the Thinker, Man, himself. The analogy is nevertheless accurate.[39] Man's physical body, for instance, considering it

---

[39] *Forms.*

The *Atharva Veda,* as the summation, instructs us in the principles which equally underlie the methods of the World-process, and of the atom-process—a world in miniature. Whether 'World-process' or 'atom-process' —depends on the speaker and his point of view. As every mantra of this Veda reflects the operations of the World-process, so does it reveal to us cognition within cognition, memory within memory, power within power, world within world, fact within fact, action within action, duty within duty, sin within sin, individuality within individuality, ascending and descending from every point in space, endlessly, ceaselessly. Atoms make up molecules, molecules compounds, compounds cells, cells tissues, tissues organs, organs bodies, bodies communities; communities classes and races; classes and races kingdoms; kingdoms of many grades and varied linkings make up a planet, planets make up a solar system, solar systems a vaster system, and so on, unending; nowhere is found simplicity indivisible;

as a corporate whole composed of many lesser lives, suffers or prospers as its directing Intelligence acts with wisdom-love or otherwise. The manasic principle actuates all that occurs within the man's aura, and he suffers, or he makes progress, according to the application of that principle.

So, reverently may the same be said of the body of the solar Logos, a system, and so may it be said of the planetary Logos and His scheme.

II. THE POSITION OF MANAS

1. *Manas and Karma.*

Having seen that *manas is the intelligent purpose of some Being, working out in active objectivity,* and having touched upon the inter-relation existing between certain of these Entities, it may now be possible to vision—even if somewhat cursorily and dimly—the true position of the manasic principle in all three cases. The whole mystery of this principle is hidden in two fundamentals:

The mystery of the resolution of the six-pointed star, into the five-pointed star.[40, 41]

The mystery of the Lords of Karma, Who are, in themselves, the sole recipients of the Mind purposes

nowhere complexity final. All is relative.—From *Pranava-Vada*, pp. 334-335.

[40] It might be of interest to note the correspondences between these six forces and the "shaktis" of the Hindu philosophy. The *Secret Doctrine* says that:—

The Six are the six forces of Nature.
What are these six forces? See S. D., I, 312.
    a. They are types of energy.
    b. They are the dynamic quality or characteristic of a planetary Logos.
    c. They are the life force of a Heavenly Man directed in a certain direction.
These "shaktis" are as follows:—
    1. Parashakti—Literally, the supreme force, energy and radiation in and from substance.
    2. Jnanashakti—The force of intellect or mind.
    3. Ichchhashakti—The power of will, or force in producing manifestation.
    4. Kriyashakti—The force which materialises the ideal.

of that cosmic ENTITY Who enfolds our solar Logos
within His consciousness.

When, therefore, the esoteric side of astrology, and of
mystical geometry, has been studied, and alliance has
been made between these two sciences, a flood of light will
be thrown upon this matter of the intelligent principle;
when the inner workings of the Law of Cause and Effect
(the law whereby the Lipika Lords govern all Their
action) is better comprehended, then—and then only—
will the sons of men be able to study with profit the place
of manas in the evolutionary scheme.   At the present
time it is not possible to do more than point out the
direction of the path which must be trodden before this

5. Kundalini shakti—The force which adjusts internal relations to
   the external.
6. Mantrikashakti—The force latent in sound, speech and music.
These six are synthesised by their Primary, the Seventh.
[41] The *Secret Doctrine* says that:—
*It is on the Hierarchies and the correct number of these Entities that
the mystery of the universe is built.*

    Ten—The line and the circle.   The symbol of the Heavenly Men.
       —S. D., I, 117.

        The ten are the arupa universe................S. D., I, 125.
        The ten are manifested existence.............S. D., I, 467.
        The ten are sumtotal........................S. D., I, 428.
    Six— The six-pointed star.   The subjective life and the objective
       form, overshadowed by Spirit.

        The six are the six forces of nature...........S. D., I, 236.
        The six Heavenly Men.......................S. D., I, 402.
        The six planes..............................S. D., I, 236.
       Force or energy, matter or substance, and Spirit.
        The six are the double triangle................S. D., I, 143.
        The six are the symbol of objectivity.........S. D., II, 625.
        They are the deva aspect of manifestation.....S. D., I, 241.
  Five—This is the pentagon, the Makara, the five pointed Star.   Com-
      pare S. D., I, 218, 219.

        Five is the symbol of a planetary Logos.......S. D., II, 618.
        Five is the symbol of the microcosm ....S. D., II, 608.
        Five is the symbol of creation.................S. D., II, 613.
        It is the second and the third Logos united in evolution.
In the merging of the five and the six you have the totality of manifestation, the male and female blended in the Divine Hermaphrodite.   Summing up, S. D., I, 235-239.   II, 610, 638.

      The first order..............The essential Lives.   Spirit.
                          The Self.
      The sixth order..............The objective form.   Matter.
                          The Not-Self.
      The fifth order..............Intelligence.   Manas.
                          The relation between.

abstruse matter can be made clear, and to indicate certain lines of investigation which might (if strenuously and scientifically followed) yield to the student a rich reward of knowledge. Until the intuition is better developed in the average man, the very principle of manas itself forms a barrier to its due understanding.

2. *Manas and karmic purpose.*

If it is realised by the student that manas and intelligent purpose are practically synonymous terms, it will be immediately apparent that karma, and the activities of the Lipika Lords, will be involved in the matter. It will also be apparent that only as the lower mind is transmuted into the abstract or higher mind and from thence into the intuition, will man be able to understand the significance of manas. We may perhaps ask why this must be so. Surely it is because the abstract mind is the agent on cosmic levels whereby the Entity concerned formulates His plans and purposes. These plans and purposes (conceived of in the abstract mind) in due course of evolution crystallise into concrete form by means of the concrete mind. What we call the archetypal plane in connection with the Logos (the plane whereon He forms His ideals, His aspirations and His abstract conceptions) is the logoic correspondence to the atomic abstract levels of the mental plane, from whence are initiated the impulses and purposes of the Spirit in man,—those purposes which eventually force him into an objective form, thus paralleling logoic manifestation. First the abstract concept, then the medium provided for manifestation in form, and, finally, that form itself. Such is the process for Gods and for men, and in it is hidden the mystery of mind and of its place in evolution.

For the sake of clarity, let us take the microcosm for momentary study. It should be realised by all students that man is Spirit or the Self, working through matter or the Not-Self, by means of the intelligence or manas, and it should also be realised that the statement of this fact (which is equally true of a solar Logos, a Heavenly Man, and a human being) involves the admission of certain deductions based on manifestation itself. One of these deductions is that by means of this principle of manas *form* is built. Therefore, the whole subject of the Builders has to be studied—those entities who are the embodiment of Universal Mind, who are the animating lives within the form, and who are the Divine Manasaputras in their comprehensive totality. In the occult realisation of this lies hid the secret of the close relationship between man and the deva evolution, man being the repository (through the Heavenly Man of Whose body he forms a part) of the purpose of the Logos, and the devas in all their higher grades being the cohesive attractive factor which manipulates matter, and which moulds it into shape. The two are partners, indispensable to each other, and without the two working in close co-operation this objective solar system would immediately disintegrate, just as man's dense and etheric bodies disintegrate when the Spirit withdraws, and the Builders cease their work.

Three hierarchies in particular are concerned with objective manifestation in etheric matter, the fourth, or strictly human hierarchy, and the fifth and sixth or the deva hierarchies. The other hierarchies fulfill other purposes connected with the life of the Spirit in the higher forms in the cosmic ethers, but in connection with our present subject these three hierarchies work on the lower levels of the cosmic physical plane the subplanes of which we call the mental, astral, and physical planes. When the five and the four are perfectly blended, we shall have achieved the nine of a major initiation, and when the six is added we shall have the resolution into one of the groups embodied by a Kumara, as has been hinted earlier. This marks the resolution of the six-pointed star finally into the five-pointed star; this is a great mystery, and concerns primarily the Heavenly Man of our scheme, and only incidentally the groups within His body of etheric manifestation.

It will, therefore, be apparent that if all manifestation is the embodiment in *form* of a cosmic conception, and the working out of it in concrete shape, manas or intelligence is a basic factor of the process and the means whereby the link is made between the abstract and the concrete. This is already realised to be true in connection with man, and it is equally true of cosmic entities. As man progresses towards the heart of the mystery he awakens to a realisation that the aim of evolution for him is to build *consciously* the channel between the levels which are to him the planes of the abstract or of the ideal, and the concrete ones whereon he normally functions. This connecting channel has been inadequately called, and is literally "THE PATH" itself. He builds it:

By means of the manasic principle consciously applied.

By the process of transcending the karmic limitations of the three lower planes.

Through the method of dominating matter, or the Personality, considering it as the Not-Self.

Through the expansion of his consciousness through graded steps until it includes the planes he seeks to reach, and thereby demonstrating the truth of the statement that in order to tread the Path he must become that Path itself, and the accuracy of the occult truth that the antaskarana is itself but illusion. Ponder on this, for it carries illumination for those who have eyes to see.

In the process of treading that Path and of achieving the goal, man is resolved into the five-pointed star, finally into the triangle of Spirit. Between these two stages is a mysterious esoteric stage wherein he is resolved into the four,—not this time the four of the lower quaternary, but a higher four. He becomes part of the consciousness of that occult group hinted at in various places which stands next to the three Logoi, the four great Maharajahs, the dispensers of karma, the repositories of cosmic purpose, who are reflected (but only reflected) in the logoic Quaternary, or in those four Heavenly Men Who embody (with their synthesising third) logoic manas. These four with the synthesising one are in Themselves the sumtotal of manas, the Brahma aspect, or Intelligence in activity. Karma works through manas, and only as the six-pointed star (or the sumtotal of concrete mind in its various divisions) becomes the five-pointed star, or the synthesis of the lower into the abstract or higher, is the transmutation into the three, or the Spiritual Triad, made possible via the four, or the formless repositories of karmic purpose; thus is liberation achieved, thus is man set free, and the microcosm attains BEING without the necessity of form-taking. A hint here in connection with the microcosm may help: When the microcosm has transcended the three worlds of matter and has become the five pointed star, he passes into the consciousness of the Monad, or pure Spirit, via the fourth plane of buddhi. For him the buddhic plane is the plane of karmic correspondence. On it he enters into the sphere of conscious co-operation in the working out of karma for a Heavenly Man, having completely worked out his personal karma in the lower three spheres. The student whose intuition suffices can work out the planes which correspond to the buddhic plane, for a Heavenly Man and for a solar Logos. This will only be possible if the concept is extended to cosmic levels and beyond the systemic.

Through the ideas here imparted it may be possible for the student to think out, for himself, some aspects of the place of manas in cosmic evolution. It necessitates a somewhat synthetic viewpoint, and the steady holding of the thought of PURPOSE in all activity, whether cosmic, systemic, planetary, or microcosmic. It is the fire of divine impulse permeating all forms and driving those forms to certain action and achievement.

The fire of matter earlier dealt with is the dynamic fire of motion, which keeps in activity each atom of matter. The fire of mind is the coherent impulse and purpose, driving the forms (built up of active matter) in a specific direction, and along certain destined paths. It is consequently karmic impulse, originating cause, and operating will. It is likewise the result or the effect of this action in time, and only as the Triad comes into play, via the esoteric four, are the fires of both mind and matter burnt out and the fire of Spirit set free.

III. THE PRESENT STAGE OF MANASIC DEVELOPMENT
IN THE THREE GROUPS

Literally, should we paraphrase this sentence, we might express it in the form of an enquiry as to the point attained in the active working out of the purposes of the great Entities involved in cosmic and systemic manifestation; we might also enquire if the intelligent will of the cosmic Logos and of the solar Logos and equally (within the system) of the different planetary Logoi, proceeded satisfactorily to a stage where it can be both appreciated and somewhat comprehended. These thoughts are involved in the consideration of this point, and open up for us much of very real interest. It should here be pointed out that the manasic principle (whether cosmic, systemic, or human) manifests in five ways, is transmuted into wisdom after its fivefold manifestation, and eventually is resolved into pure will or power. Herein lies the clue; all the objective display we see around us in connection with the Heavenly Men, and with the cells of Their bodies, lies hidden in this. Herein may be found the mystery of the five Kumaras, Who are awaiting the final resolution, and herein is secreted the knowledge of divine alchemy, which is based on the five elements, and is concerned with their transformation into a primal element through the medium of an intermediate stage.

1. *In the Planets.*

Occult students need, in considering these points, to remember very clearly the distinction between transmutation and the final resolution; between the process of transforming the five elements, esoterically understood, and the final resolution of the transmuted essences into their synthesis. This has a vital bearing upon our subject, for resolution is as yet by no means possible, and the process of transmutation is only just beginning in the majority of cases. In studying these subjects we have necessarily to confine ourselves to the Heavenly Men, for the human units—as cells in Their body—are of course included in all that is posited about Them, and until it is known which cosmic Logos recognises our solar Logos as a centre in His body, and which six other systems are affiliated with ours, it will not be possible to touch upon the systemic stage of manasic development. But in connection with the Heavenly Men certain facts are possible of theoretical comprehension, even though not as yet demonstrable to the scientific mind. We will, as usual, tabulate our premises, and thus keep clearly in mind, and visualised, the points under investigation:

First. It might first be said that the third aspect, combined with the second, or Brahma and Vishnu allied, go to the totality of the Divine Manasaputras. They are Will utilising matter, or active intelligent substance, in order to demonstrate Love-Wisdom; all this is based on purpose, and has causation as a fundamental. This

Brahma aspect is fivefold and, with the Vishnu aspect, makes the six, or the pentagon, having Mahadeva or Will in the centre of all manifestation.

Second. This fivefold Brahma aspect or the five Kumaras, are in full manifestation, and, with the reflection of the other two aspects, make the seven of our manifested system.

Third. Mercury and Venus are in process of transmutation, and the manasic principle in both these schemes, having reached a high stage of development, is being transmuted into Love-Wisdom. When three fifths of the units (deva and human) that go to the composition of the vehicles of any planetary Logos are entering upon the Path, then the process of transmutation is entered upon. The faculty of MIND is then an instrument for creative use, and not the "slayer of the real," and a barrier to the free life of the Spirit.

Again, it must be noted that Earth, Mars, Jupiter, Saturn, and Vulcan are as yet developing manas, and the stage achieved in each varies, and is not for exoteric publication. The Heavenly Men of these schemes have not yet succeeded in bringing Their bodies to the stage where transmutation on a large scale is possible. They are approaching it, and when the necessary three fifths is reached, then They will begin to transmute on a larger scale. The Earth scheme has about one fifth in process of transmutation in one or other of the globes at this time and Vulcan has very nearly two fifths.

We might here point out that though we are concerned primarily with manas in the *human* cells in the body of a planetary Logos, yet we must remember that the deva units in some schemes preponderate. Although from the standpoint of a human being the devas are in no way considered as coming under the influence of manas, as we understand it, yet from another angle they *are* manas itself, the active creative force, the fifth and the sixth

Hierarchies in full display. We should ponder upon the
relationship (a necessarily close relationship) between
the fifth deva Hierarchy and the fifth logoic principle,
and we should also bear in mind that—viewing the whole
matter from the angle of vision of a Heavenly Man—
the devas are a corporate part of His nature, and He is a
Manasaputra, a creative Builder, and the fivefold aspect
of Brahma. The sumtotal of manas is pure deva essence,
and it is only as union is made between this fivefold third
aspect and the other two aspects that what we understand
as MAN—whether Heavenly Man or human—comes into
being. The devas are united with these other two factors
and the result is:

> *a.* A solar Logos.
> *b.* A Heavenly Man.
> *c.* A human being.

This is a great mystery and is allied to the mystery of
electricity (or of fohatic life) which H. P. B.[42] refers to.
The Messengers, the Builders, the devas, are flaming fire,
radiant electric matter, and only in time and space, only
during manifestation and only through the cycles of objectivity, is such an entity as man possible, or can a
Heavenly Man come into existence. Outside a solar ring-
pass-not, for instance, and as far as our evolution is
concerned, we have radiant electric substance, active, intelligent ether, ensouled by the deva evolution.[43] These

---

[42] S. D., I, 107.

[43] *Pitris.*

"What I called spirituo-ideal constitution is what is known as swarga
in our Sanscrit works and the entities that are functioning there are called
the Pitris, which of course means fathers. These Pitris are often heard of
in a sort of antithetical way to the Devas in our puranas and this has led
some of our Hindoos, many theosophists included, to think that the Pitris
and Devas are in two distinct spheres of life. Now Pitris and Devas always
exist together, the Devas giving the consciousness and the Pitris forming
the body. The two are relative terms. If the Pitris be water the Devas
are the fire in the water. If the Pitris be fire, the Devas are the flame in
that fire. If the Pitris be the flame, the Devas are the conscious principle
that actuates the flame and gives to the flame the power of illumining the
world and making it exist as a factor of our consciousness. From the

work blindly and under the laws of cosmic electricity. (We must differentiate with care between cosmic electricity, and the electrical akasha of the system, which is electrical substance confined and brought under another set of laws through the instrumentality of another factor, that of pure Spirit.) Outside the ring-pass-not, we have that abstraction which we call pure Spirit. This "pure Spirit," or abstract, conscious Being, through conscious karma periodically seeks to manifest, and wills to work out a purpose under the laws of Its Own being, and is thus impelled by the attractive quality of its opposite pole, intelligent substance, to blend with it. The meeting of these two polarities, and their point of merging, causes that flash in the cosmic universe which we call a sun, and results in light or objectivity. Within the ring-pass-not, therefore, the electric fire of pure Spirit can only manifest through merging or union with electrical substance, and is, therefore, during evolution and for the major portion of the process, limited by it. In fact, little as it is realised, the deva evolution controls for the greater portion of manifestation up to the beginning of the transmutative process. They build incessantly the confining form.

When the process of transmutation is effected by the five Heavenly Men, then the whole system is reaching a very high stage of evolution, and with the two schemes which will be entering into the stage of obscuration, the resolving process will commence. The plan, viewed largely, will be as follows:

The four schemes which form the logoic Quaternary

highest to the lowest plane of life, the Pitris furnish the objective aspect and the Devas the subjective aspect and life itself is a stream that forms the middle line. . . . When instead of three lokas the cosmos is divided more accurately into seven lokas, you may assort the three higher lokas to the Devas, the three lower to the Pitris and the middle to the life stream which may be conceived as the point in which the Deva essence is changed into Pitric essence or the no loka is made fit to appear as a loka down below or the unmanifested becomes the manifested."—*Some Thoughts on the Gita*, p. 56.

will merge into their synthesising scheme, that of Saturn, while Venus and Mercury will merge into Uranus and Neptune. No importance need be attached to the sequence of these names. The dual fact is all that is necessary to grasp.

Neptune, Uranus, and Saturn will, therefore, have absorbed the essence of manifestation and (in connection with the solar Logos) they correspond to the three permanent atoms in the causal body of a man. We say "correspond" for the analogy is not in detail. Uranus and Neptune are reflections of the logoic astral and mental permanent atoms. Saturn is *in fact* the correspondence to the logoic physical permanent atom. This is an occult mystery and must not be separated from its allied truth in the cosmic scheme.

Viewing manas as the vibratory activity of all atoms and narrowing our concept down to our own scheme it is interesting to note that some correspondences can be traced as we study this fifth principle during the present round, the fourth. The manasic principle is the basis of the coming into activity and the mental recognition of the following facts in nature.

The fifth spirilla within the atom of matter will become active. This fifth spirilla is beginning faintly to vibrate, while the fourth spirilla in this fourth round is assuming a vibration that will cause the intense vitalisation of the vehicles, and eventually bring about the shattering of the form, and the subsequent escape of the Spirit into a form composed of matter which responds to the vibration of the fifth spirilla.

The fourth ether is coming into recognition, and along with it will come the knowledge of the lives which it embodies. Hence the success of spiritualistic endeavour, for the larger number of the average discarnate entities at this stage who are willing to make contact with the physical plane are clothed in matter of this ether. The devas of this ether will also come to be known before the end of this round, and alliance will be made between the fourth Creative Hierarchy of men, and the devas of the fourth ether.

The fourth plane, the buddhic, by the aid of manas, will gradually be realised. This will be done as manas is transmuted into wisdom. By a few in this round the fifth principle will be superseded by the principle of buddhi. Right on from now till the middle of the next round there will be an overlapping of the four and the five—manas and the buddhic principle—thus making the nine, or perfected man, the initiate.

It might also be remarked that more and more will the control of the fourth Kumara be evidenced and felt. On this I cannot enlarge, being only permitted to make the statement.

The consciousness of the mass of the human family will gradually pass on to the fourth subplane of the mental plane, and be more and more controlled by purely concrete mind. Unless this is paralleled by a steady influx of egos on to the buddhic plane in conscious activity, and thus out of the control of manas pure and simple, a very serious condition will have to be handled by the Hierarchy.

The work of the four Maharajahs who apportion karma *within* the ring-pass-not will reach its culminating point during the fourth round. In the next round, the work of the Lipikas who handle affairs in connection with our system *outside* the ring-pass-not will become more prominent. This is necessarily so, as the Lipika Lords dispense the law to those who have merged themselves with their divine principle, and are no longer held by the material forms of the three worlds. The Lords of Karma, or the Maharajahs, work with the sons of men in the three worlds, and through manasic principle.

2. *In the System.*

We have now for consideration some further points on the subject of manasic development within the system and then we can proceed to discuss the future of manas, our final subheading.

It will be apparent to all of us that the vastness of the subject and the enormous cycles of time involved tend to obscurity and lack of definiteness. Only the highlights stand out, and only broad general concepts, and the impartation of fundamental facts (to the exclusion of detail) are in any way possible in this treatise. Certain ideas stand out clearly against the background of intricate plans, against the apparent confusion caused by the overlapping of cycles, both great and lesser, and against accumulation of chaotic detail. This apparent chaos, and even seeming contradiction, is the result of our imperfect evolution, the result of our entire lack of perspective incident upon our place in the planetary scheme, and the result of the shortness of our vision. Broad outstanding generalisations are all that we can appreciate at our present stage, and they might be summed up as three in number:

Position or the place of the system within its greater whole, and the corporate nature of all manifestation. This involves the concept of:

A cosmic system, involving lesser systems and holding them together by the power of a unified life.[44]

A solar system, a portion of that greater system of mani-

---

[44] *Diversity from Unity.*

"Now, according to the Adepts of ancient Aryavarta, *seven principles* are evolved out of these three primary entities. Algebra teaches us that the number of *combinations* of things, taken *one* at a time, *two* at a time, *three* at a time, and so forth $= 2^n - 1$. Applying this formula to the present case, the number of entities evolved from different combinations of these three primary causes amount to $2^3 - 1 = 8 - 1 = 7$. As a general rule whenever seven entities are mentioned in the ancient occult sciences of India in any connection whatsoever, you must suppose that these seven entities come into existence from three primary entities; and that these three entities, again, are evolved out of a single entity or Monad."—*The Theosophist*, Vol. VIII, p. 449.

festation, equally involving lesser forms of objectivity, and holding them likewise unified by the power of its own life.

A planetary scheme, or subdivision of that solar system. This likewise persists as a unit by itself, yet has no existence apart from other units.

Groups or unified bodies within the scheme. These are again individualised, yet at the same time are a part of the greater whole.

Congeries or aggregations of cells, the subdivisions of groups. These must be similarly interpreted.

The cells, or the individualised units, within the groups. Each of these is a conscious entity, yet each has no existence apart from its groups.

Each of these divisions is characterised by:

An ensouling life, which—as far as we are concerned, emanates from the ONE ABOUT WHOM NAUGHT MAY BE SAID, Who ensouls the seven solar systems, down through the Lord of a solar system, through the cosmic Entities we call the Heavenly Men, and the solar Entities ensouling groups and through that peculiar central manifestation we call a human being to the little cell within the body of that human being, and the atom which is the basic material whereof all forms in all the kingdoms of nature are made.

Intelligent activity, or the display of purpose or manas, the fifth principle in every type of manifestation. This, as earlier pointed out, is the intelligent plan of the Entity concerned working out in time and space.

Power to evolve or progress. This is literally the distinctive ability of the ensouling life within the form to progress intelligently from lower to higher forms of manifestation. This is above all the peculiar and perfected attribute of the fifth principle.

Capacity to cohere. This is the ability of all intelligent, active Lives during evolution to conform to the Law of Attraction and Repulsion, and thus form a conscious, intelligent part of a greater life. It is literally

the transmutation of manas into wisdom.   Though all
that IS exists in form yet little is as yet brought under
the intelligent control of the entity within the form.
Only the Heavenly Men and Their superior embracing
lives are consciously and intelligently working through
and dominating the form, for only They, as yet, are perfected manas.   Beneath them come many grades of consciousness.   Man is gradually achieving that conscious
control over matter in the three worlds which his divine
Prototypes, the Heavenly Men, have already achieved.
They are attaining a similar control on higher levels.
Below man come many lives who are blind and unconscious of the congery or subdivision of which they form
part.   Thus can be seen, in general outline, the place of
manas at the present stage.

Relation.   Another outstanding feature that is the result of our studies is that of relation.   The realisation
of this in future years will lead to the study of the different polarities of the different spheres (from a planetary scheme to an atom) within the solar ring-pass-not,
and of the relation existing between:

> *a.*   A scheme and the totality of schemes.
> *b.*   Scheme and scheme.
> *c.*   Chain and chain.
> *d.*   Globe and globe.
> *e.*   Group and group.
> *f.*   Subdivision and subdivision.
> *g.*   Unit and unit.[45]
> *h.*   Cell and cell.

The interrelation of all these factors and their profound interdependence is one of the most important
points for us to grasp; though this whole relation is
governed by the law of Attraction and Repulsion, and

---

[45] I use the word ''unit'' in connection with all that is in any degree self-
conscious, or individualised.   It must, therefore, be remembered that this
phrase refers to nothing below the human kingdom.

therefore comes more under what we call the second aspect, yet self consciousness itself is the result of the manasic principle, and the close co-operation between these two factors of mind and love-wisdom, or the two laws of Attraction and Synthesis, must ever be carefully remembered.

Limitation. This is a prime factor to be borne in mind in considering a cosmos, a system, a scheme, a chain, or any form of limiting sphere down through them all to the physical atom of the scientist. It presupposes:

    a. Capacity beyond that manifested.

    b. Duality, or that which is limited and the limiting substance.

    c. Purpose, for in an ordered scheme of existence, the limitation persists just as long as it is required in order to attain certain ends. It is succeeded by "abstraction" occultly understood, and in its literal sense.

When these three factors:

    Position,
    Relation,
    Limitation,

are studied within the system, the close connection of all the groups within the whole will be evidenced, and the need of each part for all other parts will be brought out.

As regards cosmic position, relation and limitation, little can be said, as e'en to the Heavenly Men Themselves the matter is obscure. That this is necessarily so must be apparent when Their place in the scheme of things is realised and Their relative unimportance is considered. Therefore, we can do no more than accept the fact of the inconceivable magnitude of that EXIST-ENCE which is manifesting through seven solar systems, and the extension of this concept of Being to embrace the entire vault of the Heavens. It is interesting to bear in mind in this connection that all that is seen, being objective forms or Beings in manifestation through certain spheres of light, may not be all that is, but that there may lie back of everything visible a vast realm or realms of Existences. The very brain of man reels in contemplation of such a concept. Yet just as there are tens of millions of human beings out of objective manifestation, or discarnate, on the subtler planes of the solar system, so there may be cosmic entities, in rank equal to the ONE ABOUT WHOM NAUGHT MAY BE SAID, Who are in a similar sense discarnate, and found in realms subtler than that of the manifestation of light.

3. On the Earth.

a. The five Kumaras. We might now consider briefly the subject of the five Kumaras, Who are the sum total of manas on the Earth. I have stated that the Lord of the World, the first Kumara, is the planetary Logos of our scheme in physical incarnation, but nowhere has the impression been conveyed that the three Kumaras, associated with Him, are three other planetary Logoi. This is in no way the case. These three, called the "Buddhas of Activity," are but the viceregents upon our planet of those three planetary Logoi, Who, with our planetary Logos, make the sum total of the logoic Quaternary. Associated with them are the three esoteric Kumaras, mentioned in the *Secret Doctrine*,[46] Who represent the three other Logoi, and so make focal points for all the logoic forces within our chain. In each chain such representatives are found, six focal points embraced by the seventh, the planetary Logos of the scheme, Who holds them all within His aura.

[46] S. D., I, 493.

Their work is threefold:

First. They are the centres in the body of the planetary Logos. Each chain corresponds to one centre, and the globes are but the lesser wheels within any particular centre. The life of the Logos in this incarnation on the Earth is flowing through three centres and beginning to stimulate a fourth, hence four globes are involved and the three Kumaras (so called for lack of a better term) are vitally intelligently active; three are in abeyance and one is beginning to function. The globes correspond to the chains. This fourth Kumara is as yet practically unrealised, but as hinted at earlier His day is about to dawn.

Second. They act as transmitters of a particular type of force to those units who go to the content of any particular centre. They are, in fact, the agents for the Lords of the Rays to the Monads of any ray in incarnation in any particular chain and on any particular globe.

Third. They are the agents for:

a. The Lord of a Ray as stated above.
b. The four Maharajahs.
c. The planetary Logos of Their own scheme.
d. The great Deva of the Earth planet.

They work with the law; They are the cognizers of the intelligent purpose of the planetary Logos, and know His plans; They are the vital activity of the planet, and in a subtle sense they are not only the Ray representatives but likewise the link between the chain and the scheme.

It might here be stated that the relative failure that was the fate of the *Moon chain* in our scheme has greatly handicapped Their work, and made it imperative for Them to employ drastic measures in order to offset that failure. Herein lies another clue to the world turmoil.

b. The Moon chain. It might be of interest here, if, before passing on to other matters, we took up the very difficult subject of the moon chain and answer certain pertinent questions that may have arisen in the minds of students.

The enumeration of the chains and of the schemes as given in the two charts is entirely *for the present,* and covers a period comparatively recent, carrying forward the history of evolution to the middle of the next round in our chain. Had we been given the charts embracing pre-Lemurian days, and extending back a distance into the (humanly speaking) unfathomable past, we would have seen the moon chain portrayed with the Neptune chain omitted. In the chart as given two chains are apparently lacking, the moon chain and the Uranus chain. The reasons are abstruse, but something may be hinted at as follows:

The Moon chain with the Earth chain formed two units, or two polarities, negative and positive. The point of merging was reached, and the Earth chain absorbed or synthesised the moon chain in the same sense as certain of the schemes will merge until only three will apparently be left. Therefore the Earth chain is essentially dual in its nature, being the sumtotal of a male and a female chain. This is a mystery impossible to elucidate further, but it is dealt with in certain occult books, and hinted at by H. P. B.[47]

In due course of time another merging in the scheme will eventuate and then Uranus (the chain of that name in our scheme) will flash into objectivity. Forget not that the schemes manifest as seven, as ten, as three from the angle of the Eternal Now, or—from the point of view of a Heavenly Man—the manifestation may be written as ③⑦ . In time and space the order might be stated to be 7-3-10, and at certain stages 10-7-3. As

[47] S. D., I. Section IX, Vol. I, 176-200.

the opposites merge the ten become the seven and the three, and it is during this process that entire chains and globes, and eventually schemes, will apparently vanish from objectivity, and drop out of sight. They will be simply absorbed. During the twofold process of evolution, it might be numerically expressed as:

During involution the sequence is seen as three, then seven and finally ten.

During evolution the sequence is ten, then seven and finally three.

The involutionary process is over practically and the evolutionary is approximately midway through. This will be marked by the disappearance or absorption of certain chains as they find their polar opposites, and a simultaneous appearance of the more subtle chains or globes as the manasic principle enables man to see them. The moon chain is in process of disappearance, and only a decaying body is left; the life of the second and the first Logos has been withdrawn from it, and only the latent life of matter itself remains. Simultaneously Neptune arose over the horizon, and took its place as one of the seven manifesting chains of the planetary Logos. We are here dealing with the Neptune chain of the earth scheme.

The Moon chain has in itself a curious occult history, not yet to be disclosed. This differentiates it from the other chains in the scheme and even from any other chain in any scheme. An analogous situation or correspondence will be found in another planetary scheme within the solar system. All this is hidden in the history of one of the solar systems which is united to ours within a cosmic ring-pass-not. Hence the impossibility of yet enlarging upon it. Each Heavenly Man of a scheme is a focal point for the force and power and vibratory life of seven stupendous ENTITIES in exactly the same sense as the seven centres in a human being are the focal points for the influence of a corresponding heavenly Prototype. Our Heavenly Man, therefore, is esoterically allied to one of the seven solar systems, and in this mysterious alliance is hidden the mystery of the moon chain.

Certain brief hints may be given for the due consideration of students:

The Moon chain was a chain wherein a systemic failure was to be seen.

It is connected with the lower principles, which H.P.B. has stated are now superseded.

The sexual misery of this planet finds its origin in the moon failure.

The progress of evolution on the moon was abruptly disturbed and arrested by the timely interference of the solar Logos. The secret of the suffering in the Earth chain, which makes it merit the name of the Sphere of Suffering, and the mystery of the long and painful watch kept by the SILENT WATCHER,[48] has its origin in the events which brought the moon chain to a terrific culmination. Conditions of agony and of distress such as are found on our planet are found in no such degree in any other scheme.

[48] "... it is He, again, who holds spiritual sway over the initiated Adepts throughout the whole world. He is, as said, the "Nameless One" who has so many names, and yet whose names and whose very nature are unknown. He is the 'Initiator,' called the 'Great Sacrifice.' For, sitting at the Threshold of Light, he looks into it from within the Circle of Darkness, which he will not cross; nor will he quit his post till the last Day of this Life-Cycle. Why does the Solitary Watcher remain at his self-chosen post? Why does he sit by the Fountain of Primeval Wisdom, of which he drinks no longer, for he has naught to learn which he does not know—aye, neither on this Earth, nor in its Heaven? Because the lonely, sore-footed Pilgrims, on their journey back to their Home, are never sure, to the last moment, of not losing their way, in this limitless desert of Illusion and Matter called Earth-Life. Because he would fain show the way to that region of freedom and light,.from which he is a voluntary exile himself, to every prisoner who has succeeded in liberating himself from the bonds of flesh and illusion. Because, in short, he has sacrificed himself for the sake of Mankind, though but a few elect may profit by the Great Sacrifice."—S. D., I, 229.

The misuse of the vibratory power of a certain centre, and the perversion, or distortion of force to
certain erroneous ends, not along the line of evolution, account for much of the moon mystery.

Certain results, such as the finding of its polar opposite, were hastened unduly on the moon chain, and
the consequence was an uneven development and
a retardation of the evolution of a certain number
of deva and human groups.

The origin of the feud between the Lords of the Dark
Face and the Brotherhood of Light, which found
scope for activity in Atlantean days, and during the
present root race, can be traced back to the moon
chain.

We have here all that it is possible to give out at this
time, and much that has hitherto not been permitted
publication. It is necessary again to emphasise the need
of attaching no importance to the names of the chains
and globes, and the necessity of a numerical enumeration; at the same time should the student decide to number the chains, and globes, he must carefully bear in
mind that the sequence of numbers has no reference
or relation to place or time, nor to sequence of appearance, or order of manifestation.

IV.   THE FUTURE OF MANAS

It is only intended to handle this immense subject
primarily in its relation to MAN, leaving the student
to work out for himself much of what might be said,
and to expand the concept from the unit to the group,
and from the group to the totality of groups within the
solar system. We will only touch upon the development
of the mind in man and hint at some probable developments; we shall endeavour to show that manas, as it
evolves, leads to certain distinct characteristics, which

distinguish it from other developments which may be seen. The subject therefore will be discussed under the following subheadings:

1. The characteristics of manas.
2. Probable developments of the human mind.
3. Manas in the final rounds.

In studying all these points the emphasis is, of course, to be laid upon the future, and I enlarge not upon that which is already developed.

1. *Characteristics of manas.*

The main characteristics of manas might be summed up under three heads:

a. Discrimination.
b. Ordered activity.
c. Adaptability.

Let us study these a little and note wherein in days and cycles to come they will be seen working out.

a. Discrimination. This is necessarily almost the statement of a platitude. All students recognise the discriminative quality of manas and its selective capacity; all recognise the faculty in man which enables him to distinguish intelligently between the Self and the Not-Self. What we are apt to forget is that this faculty persists on all planes, and is threefold in manifestation:

First. Discrimination between the I-consciousness, and that which is cognised in the external world. This is the ability to distinguish between oneself and all other forms extant. It is universally developed and has reached a fairly high stage of evolution.

Second. Discrimination between the Ego and the Personality. This narrows the concept down to the sphere of a man's own consciousness, and enables him to differentiate between his subjective self or soul, and the bodies which hold that soul enshrined. This is not

by any means so universally developed. Most men do
not as yet distinguish with accuracy between themselves
as the THINKER, persistent in time and space, and the
vehicle through which they think, which is ephemeral
and transient. The real recognition of this essential
duality, and the scientific appreciation of it is to be
seen in the mystics, the advanced thinkers of the race,
the conscious aspirants, and those nearing the Portal
of Initiation.

Third. Discrimination between soul and Spirit, or
the realisation by the man that not only can he say,
"I am"; not only can he realise that *"I am That"*; but
that he can advance to a still further realisation, and
say, *"I am That I am."*

In all these expansions and appreciations the discriminative faculty of manas is utilised.

Therefore, we can see for ourselves the future development, and whereto it will lead mankind. Man now
knows himself as a separated unit of consciousness; he
now distinguishes between himself and all other materialised selves; he now realises himself as distinct from
every other functioning sphere of matter from the materialised Logos to the cell in his own physical body, and
the cell in all bodies on the physical plane. This separative instinct, this distinguishing self-centredness has
been the nursery wherein the infant, man, has segre-
gated himself until he is of full strength, and able to
take his share in the work of his group. Only the voluntary merging of interest and of aim is of value, and
only that is seen in man as he nears the final part of
the path of evolution. It is incident upon an earlier
stage of intense self-assertion and intense self-realisation. This stage is with us now; it marks all manifestation, and is the basis of the preservation of identity.
It distinguishes:

The Logos and all forms within His body.

The planetary Logoi and all forms within Their bodies.

Man and all forms within his body.

That which must be emphasised is the little realised concept that this assertion of "I am" distinguishes not only man, but is *the mantric word which preserves the integrity of all groups* likewise. When man can say "I am That" he is beginning to sense his oneness with his group. When groups make a similar assertion they are beginning to realise their identity with all other groups. When a planetary Logos echoes the words "I am That" He is approaching the hour of synthesis, or of absorption. When a solar Logos utters the words, a year of Brahma will be drawing to a close, and the hour of conscious merging with His greater group will be approaching. Broadly (in relation to man) it might be stated that:

"*I am*" refers to the *personality* consciousness on three lower planes, or to all that is considered as inferior to the causal body. It concerns a man's realisation of his place upon the *globe* within a chain.

"*I am That*" refers to his *egoic* consciousness, and to the planes of the Triad. It concerns a man's realisation of his place within the *chain* and his relationship to the group of which he forms a part.

"*I am That I am*" refers to a man's *monadic* consciousness, and his relationship to the planes of abstraction. It concerns his realisation of his position in the *scheme.*

When the initiate can say "I am That I am," then he has merged himself with his divine essence, and is freed from form. The first occult assertion marks his emancipation from the three lower kingdoms, and his conscious functioning in the three worlds. This occurred at individualisation through the instrumentality of manas. The second occult assertion marks the gradual emancipation of man from the lower three kingdoms, and his complete freeing from lower form domination at the fifth initiation. At the final assertion, the initiate not only distinguishes between the Self, and all other forms of manifestation; he not only distinguishes between his own identity and the soul, as well as matter in form, but he can discriminate between the three— Spirit, Soul, and Matter—and with this realisation he is entirely liberated from manifestation for this greater cycle. This inherent discriminative faculty of manas, displayed on ever higher spirals leads a man

Into matter and form,
Through all forms of matter on all planes and
Finally brings about his eventual abstraction *from* all forms and matter, plus the aggregate of transmuted knowledge which the evolutionary process has procured for him.

b. Ordered activity. Here comes in the concept of intelligent purpose, pursuing a fixed and settled plan, and working out a preconceived ideal in time and space. The Microcosm comes into incarnation through impulse based on intelligent purpose originating in his case on the mental plane—the plane of the manasic principle. An interesting point might here be indicated. The fifth plane, the mental, may be considered on a large scale as holding, in the case of a Heavenly Man, a position symbolically analogous to that held by the causal bodies of the units on His Ray. Some causal bodies are on the third and some on the second subplanes, and the intricacy is excessive and various, producing geometrical forms allied somewhat to those portrayed upon the charts. All is ordered activity of the units (each pursuing his own self-centred purpose and following the inclination of the lower self, whose slogan is "I am"). This will gradually give place to the ordered activity of the groups in which the units recognise the oneness of their self-interest, and therefore intelligently, actively, and with conscious purpose work for the good of the body corporate. The vibration which occultly accompanies the sounding of the words "I am That" by the units on the physical plane is only very faintly beginning to make itself felt. Units here and there are sounding it forth by their lives, and are thus passing on the vibration, and setting it in motion against the cruder, coarser one of "I am."

The time for the sounding of the final mantric phrase by ordered active groups lies ahead in the sixth and seventh rounds, and will not reach its full vibration in this solar system at all. "I am That" will peal forth fully consummated in this system of duality, for the third initiation sees the initiate comprehending its mantric force. Nevertheless, initiates of the sixth and seventh Initiations will not preponderate in this system. After the fifth round and the passing into temporary obscuration of two fifths of the human family, the remaining units will achieve an approximate standing as follows:

One fifth will mantrically sound the words "I am That I am."

Two fifths will achieve the fifth Initiation and will know themselves as "I am That." They will also be cultivating response to the higher note.

One fifth and a half will attain the third Initiation, and will know themselves as "I am That" in full consciousness.

The remaining units will be those who are treading the Path, and beginning to know themselves as the group.

In reference to what has been said anent the second characteristic of manas, a very interesting development may be looked for during the coming century. This is the intensification of business organisation, and the bringing (under law and order), of the entire life of:

Families and groups of families,
Cities and groups of cities,
Nations and groups of nations,

until the human race in every department of its exoteric life will conform to rule,—this voluntarily, and with manasic realisation of group need. The whole trend of mental effort during the next subraces will be towards the synthesis of endeavour, thus ensuring the good of the corporate body involved. Many interesting events will occur and many experiments will necessarily be made (some to prove successful and some failures), before manas, or purposeful, ordered, intelligent activity, will control in the life of the peoples of this world. It is not possible to enter into this in greater detail, as the subject is too vast.

Let us now take the third attribute of manas and its future demonstration.

c. *Adaptability.* This is, as we know, the prime attribute ascribed to the third Ray, or the Brahma aspect. Therefore, fundamentally it may be considered as the attribute of intelligence which adapts the matter aspect to the Spirit aspect, and is a characteristic inherent in matter itself. It works under the two laws of Economy, and of Attraction and Repulsion; the work of the Mahachohan being primarily along this line. Consequently the four lesser Rays of Attribute which are synthesised into the third Ray of Aspect, Adaptability, or Active Intelligence, are fundamentally concerned, and the future of manas is therefore involved in the growing influence of these four Rays:

1. Harmony, Beauty, Art or Unity.
2. Concrete Science or Knowledge.
3. Abstract Idealism.
4. Ceremonial Magic.

2. *Development of the Human Mind.*

When the future results brought about by the four types of force mentioned above are somewhat realised, and their relationship to the adaptation of matter to Spirit (through the building into form), is studied, much of profound significance will be sensed by the student. In the foretelling of mental developments along these four lines and the prophesying of definite achievement, indications may be given of the path which concrete science may follow. Let us, therefore, take these four types of force, or these four planetary influences, and study them separately, bearing ever in mind that:

a. Each of them has swung into power during earlier world cycles.

b. One of them, being the influence of our own planetary Logos, is ever present with us, and is the major influence or vibration on the planet.

c. Certain of them are passing out of power at this present time, and others are coming in.

d. During the remainder of this round and the entire fifth round these four rays of attribute will circulate into and out of power ceaselessly; towards the end of the fifth round the third Ray of Aspect will predominate, having begun its work of synthesising and its influence will be paralleled in the sixth round by the gradually growing power of the second Ray of Aspect,—the two types of influence overlapping. In the seventh round, the power of the second Ray will predominate and the influence of the third will weaken. The first Ray will make itself felt. The first Ray, that of

Mahadeva [49] or the Destroyer, will set its second great impulse upon our planetary evolution by the obscuration of two fifths of the human family. The impress to be set by the first Ray upon our human family on this globe might be considered as threefold:

First. At human individualisation in the middle of the third rootrace. This was produced by a vast destruction of the forms we call animal-man. This point has seldom been brought out in teaching. The advent of the Lords of the Flame, the electrical storm which ushered in the period of man, was distinguished by disaster, chaos, and the destruction of many in the third kingdom of nature. The spark of mind was implanted and the strength of its vibration, and the immediate effect of its presence caused the death of the animal form, thus producing the immediate possibility of the newly vitalised causal bodies vibrating to such purpose that new physical vehicles were taken. That was the Will aspect manifesting in the fourth round in connection with the human family.

Second. In the fifth round, *at the so-called Judgment.* This will bring about the apparent destruction of two-fifths of the human family, and the translation of the indwelling units of consciousness to other spheres, more

---

[49] The Trinity. ''Maha-Vishnu presides over the summation and totality of all this. In every Brahmanda the activity is fourfold, and the chief functionaries are Brahma, Vishnu, and Shiva. Subdivisions of their functions give rise to the names and offices of Narayana, etc.

''Among these functions, that of making or creating goes with action and belongs to Brahma. Again, ''that which has been made is maintained by knowledge;'' this maintenance or preservation is the work of Vishnu. Further, because it is necessary that what has appeared should disappear, therefore is there a destroyer, and he is Shiva, connected with desire, which first affirms and next denies, acts and reacts, now attracts and then repels, begins with craving for, and, after satiety, revolts from its object and casts it off. It precedes action, or Brahma, as longing for manifestation; and it succeeds knowledge or Vishnu, after maintenance or enjoyment of that manifestation, as a sense of fatigue, a growth of inertness, a need for rest by winding up the manifestation.''—From *Pranava-Vada,* pp. 82-84, 311.

suited to their stage of evolution. This event will be regarded at the time as a catastrophe, but the Knowers will
see and know, and three fifths of the human family will
understand the reason.

Third. At the final reabsorption of the perfected
monads into their emanating source in the seventh round.
This will be marked by obscuration and the destruction
of the form. Suffering will be practically nil, as the
human units involved will have reached a stage where
they can consciously co-operate in the process of abstraction. It is evident therefore that as regards the human
family (the manasaputras in incarnation), the fourth,
fifth, and seventh rounds hold hid the key to the first
aspect. For the devas it is the first, second and sixth.
For the involutionary entity, whom we call the "spirit
of the planet" it is simply the third.

The third Ray holds sway all the time, for the second
Ray only came into power in the second round. It holds
sway simultaneously with the second Ray until the end
of the age, when it begins gradually to obscure as the first
Ray swings into influence again. Remember, nevertheless, that all three are at all times present. It is simply a
question of degree and of cyclic evolution.

We might now take the four minor Rays, which, with
the third, make the sumtotal of manas, and see wherein
their influence may be expected. The subject is so stupendous that we cannot possibly do more than touch upon
certain points, nor can we enlarge along the line of the
mechanistic development of forms to utilise the force.
This is all hidden in the science of electricity, and as
exoteric science discovers how:

To utilise the power in the air, or to reduce electrical
phenomena to the uses of man;

To build forms, and create machines to contain and distribute the electrical forces of the atmosphere;

To harness the activity of matter, and to drive it to-
    wards certain ends;

To employ the electrical force in the air to vitalise, re-
    build, and heal the physical body;

then the phenomena of the Rays, working in cycles, will
be comprehended, and vast opportunities will be seized
by man to bring about specific ends during specific cycles.

    a. Ray effects. The Ray of Harmony, Beauty and Art,
or the second manasic aspect (adaptability being the
third) will work out in the following ways:

In the development of the intuition by the means of the
knowledge of sound vibration, and the higher mathematics. This is being already touched upon exoterically.

Music, as a means to be employed in building and destroying, will be recognised, and the laws of levitation
and of rhythmic movement in all forms, from an atom to
a solar system, will be studied. The manipulation of
matter of all kinds by the means of sound will be practised on the two lower planes, and when the synthesis of
the four rays into the third is in process of accomplishment, then a similar knowledge will be displayed on the
mental plane.

The laws of fire will be gradually permitted exoteric
publication; there are twenty-seven occult laws which are
only revealed after initiation at this stage of evolution.
In them are summed up the basic laws of color and of
music and rhythm. When music produces warmth or
stimulation, and when pictures, for instance, glow or reveal the subjective within the objective, then will this
fourth Ray of Harmony be coming to fruition.

    Let us keep the numbering of the Rays clearly in mind.

The numbers preceding the names have to do with the
sevenfold manifestation, and the numbers succeeding the
names concern the fivefold manifestation of Brahma.

	1. Will or Power.
Rays of Aspect:	2. Love or Wisdom.
	3. Adaptability or active intelligence.... 1.
	4. Harmony, Beauty or Art .... 2.
Rays of Attribute:	5. Concrete Knowledge or Science ..... 3.
	6. Abstract Idealism .... 4.
	7. Ceremonial Magic .... 5.

We must now continue with our consideration of the four types of force, emanating from certain great Entities, and the future results that may be expected from their effect upon man, remembering ever that these four influences (with their synthesis, the third Ray of Aspect) sum up, in themselves, the fifth logoic principle of manas. They are, literally, the radiatory effects of the Divine Manasaputras. We are concerned primarily with the results to be brought about in the units in Their bodies.

The coming into power of this fourth Ray at any time (and such an advent may be looked for towards the close of this lesser cycle, which ended in 1924) will produce a corresponding activity in connection with the fourth subplane in each plane, beginning with the fourth physical ether; this will result in the following effects:

First, physical plane scientists will be able to speak with authority anent the fourth ether, even though they may not recognise it as the lowest of the four etheric grades of substance: its sphere of influence and its utilisation will be comprehended, and "force" as a factor in matter, or the electrical manifestation of energy within definite limits, will be as well understood as is hydrogen at this time. Indications of this can already be seen in the discovery of radium, and the study of radioactive substances and of electronic demonstration. This knowledge will revolutionise the life of man; it will put into his hands that which occultists call "power of the fourth order" (on the physical plane). It will enable him to

utilise electrical energy for the regulation of his everyday life in a way as yet incomprehensible; it will produce
new methods of illuminating, and of heating the world
at a small cost and with practically no initial outlay. The
fact of the existence of the etheric body will be established, and the healing of the dense physical body, via
the etheric body, by *force* utilisation and solar radiation,
will take the place of the present methods. Healing will
then fall practically into two departments:

1. Vitalisation, by means of:
    a. Electricity.
    b. Solar and planetary radiation.
2. Definite curative processes, through the occult
    knowledge of:
    a. The force centres.
    b. The work of the devas of the fourth ether.

Transportation on sea and land will be largely superseded by the utilisation of air routes and the transit of
large bodies through the air, by means of the instantaneous use of the force or energy inherent in the ether
itself, will take the place of the present methods.

Religious students will study the side of manifestation
we call the "life side" just as the scientist studies that
called "matter," and both will come to a realisation of
the close relation existing between the two, and thus the
old gap and the ancient warfare between science and religion will be in temporary abeyance. Definite methods
of demonstrating the fact that life persists after the death
of the physical body will be followed, and the etheric web
will be recognised as a factor in the case. The connection
between the different planes will be sought, and the analogy between the fourth etheric subplane and the fourth
or buddhic plane (the fourth cosmic ether) will be studied,
for it will be realised that the life of those Entities,
Whom we recognise as the planetary Logoi, pours

through our scheme from the fourth cosmic plane, the cosmic buddhic, and thus in a very special sense through all lesser correspondences. The alignment will be as follows:

   a. The fourth cosmic plane, the cosmic buddhic.
   b. The fourth cosmic ether, the fourth plane of the system, the buddhic.
   c. The fourth etheric subplane of our physical plane.

There is thus a line of least resistance from the planes of the cosmos, producing a special activity in connection with the Heavenly Men, demonstrating on Their Own plane, and sequentially in connection with the units in Their bodies on lower levels. Lines of force, extending from our scheme extra-systemically, will be a recognised fact, and will be interpreted by scientists in terms of electrical phenomena, and by the religious man in terms of life,—the life force of certain Entities.

Philosophic students will endeavour simultaneously to link these two schools of thought, and to demonstrate the factor of the intelligent adaptation of the electrical phenomena which we call matter,—of that energised active material we call substance,—to the life purpose of a cosmic Being. In these three lines of thought, therefore, —scientific, religious, and philosophic,—we have the beginning of the *conscious* building, or construction of the antaskarana of that group which we call the fifth root-race.

On the fourth subplane of the astral plane, a similar activity will be noted as in process. The inflowing force will cause an astral stimulation in the bodies of many of the human family who are still on that subplane, and will bring about an awakening of the desire for harmony in a new manner. This will work out relatively well in the sixth subrace. It should be remembered that numbers of the old Atlanteans (fourth rootrace men) will respond to the stimulation and will find their way into incarnation at that time, for the four and the six are always closely allied. We have another suggestive analogy in the fact that the devas of the fourth ether will be soon swinging into recognised utility and that in the sixth subrace the deva evolution will be exceedingly prominent. The fourth plane is the plane of at-one-ment for certain deva and human units, and certain groups (the fourth Creative Hierarchy and the sixth Deva Hierarchy) have a pronounced karma to work out together. One can now see the supreme importance of the human Hierarchy, the fourth in this sequence of planes and ideas.

Second Cosmic Plane	Seven Cosmic Logoi.
Fourth Cosmic Plane	Seven Rishis of the Great Bear.
Second Solar Plane	Seven Heavenly Men.
Fourth Solar Plane	Seven centres of the seven Heavenly Men in the fourth cosmic ether.
Fourth subplane of the solar physical	Seven centres of the human unit in ether of the fourth order.

The beauty of the interlocking system will be apparent, even though it may not be so immediately understandable wherein lies the relation between these complexities of entities. We must ever remember that we are considering the force or life-energy of these entities as it pours into, and works through definite, material, substantial forms.

On the fourth subplane of the mental plane there will be, in the immediate future, a period of intensified evolution for the units of the fifth rootrace, prior to their passing out of and into another race, globe, chain, or scheme. We have on the fourth subplane of the fifth plane the centre of interest for the present race and the day of its opportunity. Here can be seen the awakening of the higher consciousness, and the first ripple of perception of, and vibratory response to, the causal body. In this connection, we must ever remember that the periphery of the causal body encloses the permanent atoms. It is the plane of testing, of the major initiations of the Threshold; it is the battleground in man, and from this plane he must secure the right to enter the Path, and procure that control over his lower bodies which will make him a master, and not a slave.

Thus one could progress the idea and fill many books with suggestions as to that which may be expected during the next few centuries but it does not serve any useful purpose to enlarge further. I might, in summing up these ideas, point out that the immediate future achievement consists in the utilisation of force and of electrical energy for the more harmonious adjustment of the life of man.

One or two more suggestions might be made anent the influence of this fourth Ray of mind, and primarily it might be pointed out that more time has been given to the consideration of this Ray than will be possible with most of the others on account of its holding a place of such importance in this fourth chain of the earth scheme, and on the fourth globe, our earthly planet. Each planetary Logos pours forth His influence in different rounds, planes, chains, globes, races, and subraces according to their numerical relationship to the scheme of which He is the vitalising Life. Temporarily, and as the cycle progresses, these forms become receptive and negative, and are thus responsive to the positive influence of the planetary Logos.

One further point I would make, and as it is of an esoteric and occult nature, it can be but hinted at. At the fourth Initiation, the force of the Logos of the fourth Ray is a vital factor in the initiation. It is through the application of the Rod of Initiation that His Life energy is applied to the initiate, or the electrical force that emanates from Him is geometrically circulated through certain centres, producing the necessitated stimulation. At the fifth Initiation similarly the force of the third Logos may be felt, and at the sixth that of the second Logos, while at the seventh the dynamic fire of the first Logos circulates through the body of the Chohan.

It might be tabulated thus:

1. The magical force of the seventh Logos is felt at the first Initiation.
2. The aggressive fire of the sixth Logos is felt at the second Initiation.
3. The illuminating light of the fifth Logos is felt at the third Initiation.
4. The harmonising life of the fourth Logos is felt at the fourth Initiation.
5. The blending power of the third Logos is felt at the fifth Initiation.
6. The unifying heat of the second Logos is felt at the sixth Initiation.
7. The dynamic electricity of the first Logos is felt at the seventh Initiation.

Let us now pass on to the brief consideration of the future influence of the third manasic ray of "Concrete Knowledge or Science." As I have elsewhere pointed out this ray concerns itself with the building of form, with the utilisation of matter, with the embodying of ideas, or of entities, whether cosmic, systemic, lunar, or subhuman. The planetary Logos of this fifth systemic Ray holds a peculiar position in the scheme of things. He is the embodiment of the fifth logoic principle of manas. His is the synthesising scheme for the five schemes of the five Kumaras Who are Brahma, when viewed as the sum total of the third logoic aspect, though He is not the synthesising factor for the seven schemes which are the sum total of logoic manifestation considered as the union of the second and third aspects. This is a point of prime importance to bear in mind. His is the influence that leads to the scientific adaptation of matter to form,

and His is the life that unifies ever the three and the five.
Let us see if, by illustration, we can make this idea more
simple. He is, as we know, the embodiment of the fifth
principle. His influence, therefore, may ever be felt in
His numerical correspondences, for He is the Lord of the
fifth Ray in the system, and Ruler of the third Manasic
Ray when considering only the third aspect. At individualisation, or at the coming into incarnation of the
self-conscious units, the fifth principle linked the higher
three and the lower four. This took place in the third
rootrace and produced a form wherein dwelt Spirit on
the third subplane of the fifth plane. All these analogies
will bear pondering upon and the numerical relationship
is not by chance. His was the power that acted via certain schemes, chains, and globes, and produced results in
the cells and groups of cells in the body of our particular
planetary Logos. This is given by way of elucidation,
and by way of indicating the relative importance of the
influence of a planetary Logos upon another planetary
Logos during different stages of evolution.

This influence has waxed and waned since that time,
dying down during the fourth rootrace, and waxing
steadily greater during this fifth or Aryan. The planetary Logos Whose influence it is has not yet reached the
zenith of His power, in this race. For a period immediately ahead His electrical energising force will pour on
to our planet, and will bring about fresh discoveries anent
matter and form, and fresh revelations concerning energy
in matter.

During the coming subraces His cycle will begin to pass
out, and the influence of His Brother, the fourth Logos
of Harmony, will reach its zenith for this round. During
the fifth round the power or electrical radiation of the
fifth Logos will again be strongly felt, for it is His round,
and just as He was largely responsible for the manasic
stimulation of animal man in the third rootrace, so in

the fifth round will he be instrumental in causing that great separation which we call the "Judgment." Remember in this connection that these Logoi—when pouring Their influence through a scheme or other septenary—work through Their numerical correspondence in the chains and globes. In the fifth round, for instance, the fifth chain (a centre in the body of the Heavenly Man) will be the recipient of this fifth type of force and will transmit and circulate it to the other chains via their fifth globe. Until the race has further evolved the mystery lies securely hid, and the inability of man to find out the enumeration of the schemes, chains, and globes, or to discover whether they are counted from within outwards, or vice versa, conceals that which must be hid.

The influence of this fifth Logos will be felt very considerably now on the fifth subplane of all the planes, specially in the three worlds of human endeavour, and as we are here dealing with man we can count from what is erroneously termed "the bottom up." Therefore, the mental unit of men in this fifth subrace will receive increased stimulation, enabling man to vibrate on the fifth subplane which literally is the third subplane on the abstract level of the mental plane, on which the causal body is found. The fifth spirilla will, consequently, become active and the electrical force, or the fohatic current, will pour through it, and enable those men who are at the right stage to utilise this force in order to take the first initiation.

As this fifth influence becomes more and more felt, its effects will be seen on the astral plane in an intelligent conscious control which will be based not so much on the desire for harmony as on a desire for a scientific, intelligent manipulation of astral matter. When this is the case, the higher psychism will begin to make itself felt. On the physical plane a great deal of interesting electrical phenomena will be seen, and the opportunity of the

Manu to separate races, to segregate types, and to submerge and detach continents will be great. This is the
ray of separative force, and its place, as a factor in the
erection and destruction of forms, is very interesting.

It may be asked wherein this can all be interpreted in
terms of fire, and thus the integrity of the thought-form
of this book be preserved. Whenever the words influence,
radiation, or the power of a ray, are used, we are dealing
inferentially with electrical phenomena, or with energy
of some kind. This energy, or electrical manifestation,
this "mystery of electricity" to which H. P. B. refers,[50]
is the foundation of all manifestations, and lies back of all
evolution. It produces light in ever-growing brilliancy;
it builds and moulds the form to the need of the indwelling Entity; it brings about coherence and group activity;
it is the warmth that causes all growth, and that fosters
not only the manifestations of the vegetable and animal
kingdoms but induces interaction between the human
units, and lies behind all human relationships. It is magnetism, radiation, attraction and repulsion, life, death,
and all things; it is conscious purpose and essential will
in objective manifestation, and he who has solved what
lies back of electrical phenomena has solved not only the
secret of his own Being, but knows his place within his
greater sphere, a planetary Logos, is conscious of the
Identity of that cosmic Existence we call a solar Logos,
and realises somewhat the place of our system and its
electrical relationship with the seven constellations.

We have now to deal with the influence of a force that
is waning and passing out of dominance, that of the sixth
Ray of Devotion or Idealism. It will not be possible to
predicate much anent it, beyond pointing out certain
general ideas which may be of value in the contemplation
of Ray cycles in general.

[50] S. D., I, 107.

These Ray influences work through their focal points in all cases (macrocosmic and microcosmic) and these are the etheric centres. The centres, in the case of all Beings, are ever seven in number, and are composed of deva and human units in group activity, or of force vortices which contain in latency, and hold in ordered activity, cells with the potentiality of human manifestation. Forget not the occult truism that all forms of existence pass at one stage of their career through the human kingdom.

Cosmic, or extra-systemic rays, impinge upon or circulate via centres found on the second cosmic ether, but which, at the present stage of objectivity, become systemically visible in the fourth cosmic ether, the buddhic.

One permanent cosmic Ray is the ray of our Logos Himself, and the subrays of this ray permeate His entire system. Six other cosmic Rays, animating other systems, influence ours, finding their reflections in the subrays of our logoic Ray. To these six cosmic influences our Heavenly Men respond. They absorb the influence, being centres in the body logoic, pass it through Their schemes, circulate it through Their own centres (chains), and transmit it on to other schemes, coloring it with Their Own peculiar shade and qualifying it by Their own peculiar tone or note. The whole system of ray influence, or radiatory warmth, considered both physically and psychically, is one of an intricate circulation and interaction. The radiation or vibration passes in ordered cycles from its originating source, the One Ray, or systemic Logos, to the different centres in His body. Viewed from the physical standpoint this ray force is the energising factor in matter. Viewed from the psychical point of view it is the qualitative faculty. From scheme to scheme, from chain to chain, and from globe to globe, this force or quality passes and circulates, both adding, and at the same time abstracting, and returns to its focal point with two noticeable differences:

a. The radiatory heat is intensified.

b. The qualitative character or colour is increased.

The effect on the form side is equally noticeable, and the warmth or quality of a Ray not only affects the psyche of a man, a planetary Logos, and a solar Logos, but has a definite effect on material substance itself.

Ray influences work equally on the deva and human Hierarchies, as they function in a planetary or logoic body. Clarity of thought might eventuate if we ever bear in mind that all forms are dual, both in evolution and in essential nature. They are the product of the work of the Builders (deva forces) and of active intelligence (the human units) and the two are indivisible in the Divine Hermaphrodite, or Heavenly Man. They are stimulated in both aspects of their Being by the ray influence.

Let us now tabulate these ideas somewhat:

Entity	Force Centres	Psychical Manifestation	Physical Manifestation
1. Solar Logos.	Heavenly Men.	Deva Builders.	A solar system.
	They energise and are active life.	They work in matter and hold the life.	
2. Planetary Logos	Human group units	Deva Builders.	A scheme.
3. A Man	Seven etheric centres	Elemental builders	Bodies.

Each of these divisions can be studied separately and in due course of time (when it may be safe to transmit information more freely anent the devas) it will be seen that a deva Lord of a plane, for instance, works through force centres, manifests objectively through the colour which is His psychical display, and ensouls the matter of a plane just as a Heavenly Man ensouls His scheme. The idea can be extended likewise to chains, globes, races, and rounds. Duality always will be seen,—human and deva manifestation forming the sumtotal, and always will energy and quality progress in parallel lines.

As the ray influence passes away from a race or a planet, a scheme or a solar system, it must not be supposed that it is completely abrogated; it has simply passed beyond the periphery of whatever ring-pass-not it was energising, and the force of its influence is being focussed elsewhere. The original recipient becomes a channel, or transmitting agent, and not so much an absorber or container. Words again are handicapping us, and proving their inadequacy to express an idea. What the student should recognise is that during a cycle of ray influence, the object of its immediate attention receives and absorbs it, and transmutes it according to its need, and not so much therefore is available for transmission. When the cycle is drawing to a close more and more of the ray influence or magnetism will be felt elsewhere, until practically all of it will be passed on unabsorbed.

This is what is beginning to happen in relation to this sixth Ray of Devotion. Egos who are on that particular Ray will take form elsewhere on other globes, and in other chains, and not so much on our planet. The vibrations of that Ray will quiet down as far as we are concerned, and find increased activity elsewhere. To phrase it otherwise, our planet and all thereon will become positive and non-receptive, and will temporarily repulse this particular type of force. A psychical manifestation of this can be seen in the dying down of what is called *Christian* enthusiasm. This Ray, on which the Chohan Jesus may be found, will no longer pour its force to the same extent into the form He built, and it will necessarily slowly but surely disintegrate, having served its purpose for close on two thousand years. Later again the same force will be felt returning, and a new form will be found slowly coming into being, but along more adequate lines.

It will consequently be apparent how the knowledge of these cycles, and of the force manifestation or obscuration of a Ray will eventually lead to a working with the Law, and to an intelligent co-operation with the plan of evolution. It might here be stated that the seven Kumaras (the four exoteric and the three esoteric) co-operate with this Law, and work exoterically, or esoterically according to the Ray in power, with the exception of the first Kumara, the Logos of our scheme, Who —being the synthesizing point for all—remains ever in objective activity.

It is this Ray activity which governs the obscuration or manifestation of a system, and a scheme with all that is included in these manifestations. Hence the emphasis laid in all occult books on the study of cycles, and on the differentiation of the one hundred years of Brahma into its component parts. In this knowledge lies hid the mystery of Being itself, of electrical force, and of fohatic synthesis.

I will make no more comments on the future effects of the Ray which is passing into temporary obscuration as far as we are concerned. We shall later take up at greater length than has been possible with the other Rays, the subject of the seventh type of force now coming into power, and which is therefore a vital factor in the immediate evolution of man.

The fifth principle of manas is at this time beginning to demonstrate mainly through the seventh type of force (or the fifth when considering only the Brahma aspect of manifestation). It will be immediately apparent, therefore, that this incoming Ray is peculiarly situated at this time, and that its influence will be manifested under very favourable conditions. It is pouring its force out upon the seventh plane, the physical, during the fifth rootrace and the fifth subrace, and consequently the opportunity is great. In all that has been said anent the Rays it will be apparent that from the present standpoint two are paramountly concerned with the evolution of man: the *fourth Ray of Harmony,* which is the dominant ray of the greater cycle which includes the fourth round and globe, and the *seventh Ray of Ceremonial Magic,* which is one of the foremost influences concerned in all objective manifestations. These two Rays, or the force of these two planetary Logoi, are largely instrumental in bringing about coherency in our chain, the fourth of the fourth scheme, and on our physical globe, the Earth. The fourth and the seventh interact, one acting temporarily as a negative force and the other as a positive.

The fifth Kumara, the Lord of the seventh Ray (for it is necessary to keep in mind His dual position as one of the points of the five-pointed Star of Brahma, and as one of the Triangles in the sevenfold logoic body) has a unique position as the "Ruler of the Building Devas" of the physical plane, the devas of the ethers, in cooperation with their Deva Lord. He guides and directs the production of the form by means of certain occult words. He works, therefore, through the etheric body of all forms and it is through His inflowing force that we may look for that increased stimulation of the matter of the etheric brain which will make the physical brain receptive to the higher revealing truth, and will put into the hands of scientists the secrets of the fourth and third ethers. The development of the matter of the brain parallels the stage of development of its atomic correspondence, and in the vitalisation of the fifth spirilla and the consequent reflex action of the seventh, we may look to see the mind of man assume proportions, and attain achievement, as yet unthought and undreamt.

We might consider the effect of this incoming force along three lines:

First. The type of force, or the logoic quality, with its
function and aim.

Second. Its work in relation to:

    a. The animal kingdom.

    b. The human kingdom.

    c. The deva kingdom.

Third. The results to be looked for during the coming
centuries.

The type of force, or the nature of the Heavenly Man
of the seventh Ray, is fundamentally constructive. It
will be necessary here to touch somewhat upon His character and His place in the logoic scheme, calling attention to the need of refraining from personalisation and
externalisation. The Heavenly Man of the scheme in
which the Ray of Ceremonial Magic is embodied is one
of the main transmitters of radiation from the Sun to
the system and has a close connection with logoic kundalini. Herein lies a hint. The Raja-Lord of the etheric
levels of the physical plane works in close alliance with
Him and this will be apparent if we bear in mind that
the Lord of a plane is its embodied activity. He is the
energising force that expresses itself as a unified Identity in the matter of a plane, and we might therefore get
some idea of the coherency of Their mutual work if we
bear in mind that

The Raja-Lord of a plane is the sum total of the substance of that plane.

The planetary Logos Who is most closely connected
with any particular plane is its quality and colouring.

By the united action and work of these two Entities
all is accomplished,—the Lord of the Builders construct-

ing the forms which the Lord of Life utilises to develop consciousness within.

The force or vibration of any Ray might be summed up as:

a. The intelligent purpose of an Entity, a planetary Logos.

b. His life energy working in, through, and upon His body of manifestation.

c. His magnetic radiation as it affects (though in lesser degree) His Brothers in manifestation.

d. His peculiar colouring or quality, His main psychological aspect, demonstrating through His own activities within His own scheme.

e. The effect of the same as it influences His Brothers within the body corporate of the solar Logos.

f. His life force as it radiates beyond His own periphery as active energy and stimulating activity— being literally one of the aspects of Fohat. The activity aspect of a Heavenly Man is as much an aspect of Fohat as Brahma is the sumtotal of Fohat. The Heavenly Men are, by virtue of physical manifestation, Fohat and His Brothers.

When this is borne in mind it will be seen that each of the planetary Logoi, equally with a solar Logos, and with Their reflections, human beings, demonstrate through the aspects.

In their totality all these are the expression of the incarnating Logos; in the one case His fohatic energy builds the kingdoms of nature, giving them Body; in the other He gives them their psychical value, and finally through them all He demonstrates as Existence or Being.

Similar tables can be worked out for a Heavenly Man and a human being, laying the emphasis always upon the development of the middle or psychic aspect.

With these thoughts in mind it should be possible to

TABULATION III

THE ASPECTS AND EVOLUTION

Aspect	Manifestation	Objectively	Subjectively	Evolutionary Aspect
Activity	The Seven Brothers	Seven etheric centres	Seven types of force	Involution and evolution of the kingdoms of nature.
Sumtotal.	Fire by friction. The Brahma or matter aspect. The Mother.			
Love-Wisdom Dragon of Wisdom.	Seven Heavenly Men	Seven schemes	Seven Rays	Seven types of deva and human Monads.
Sumtotal.	Solar fire. Vishnu aspect. Subjectivity or the psyche. The Son in manifestation.			
Will	Seven Cosmic Entities	Seven Heavenly Men	Seven qualities	Seven Hierarchies.
Sumtotal.	Electric Fire, the One Life. Mahadeva. Spirit.			

see more clearly what the coming in of a Ray, such as the present one, or its passing out, may involve. In the particular case under discussion, we have the coming in of a Ray that is intimately connected with the plane of manifestation, the physical plane, which is (within the greater cycle) responsible for man's very existence, and the source of his future hope.

This seventh Ray (fifth) ever manifests in a period of transition from one kingdom to another, and this holds hid the mystery of the particular form of service of its planetary Logos. He governs the processes of:

Transmutation
Incarnation
Transference.

In these three words His life-work is summed up; in these three words is embodied the nature of this great Entity, Who presides over the processes of blending and merging and adaptation; Who, through His knowledge of cosmic Sound, guides the life forces of certain solar and lunar entities from form to form, and is the link between the soul awaiting incarnation, and its body of manifestation. This is equally true whether we are considering the incarnation of a man, of a group, of an idea, or of all entities of lesser grade to the solar Being Who manifests through a globe, or the regent of the globe under the planetary Logos. All entities of higher rank than this great evolutionary Being come into incarnation through the linking work of an extra-systemic Being. In all periods of the transference of the life from

System to system,
Scheme to scheme,
Chain to chain,

this cosmic Deity pours forth His power and influence. In all periods of lesser transition of the life from

Globe to globe,
Plane to plane,
Kingdom of nature to another kingdom,

the Lord of the seventh Ray plays a similar part.

Herein lies the reason for His inflowing force at this time, for a profound movement is in order of accomplishment, and a transference is in progress which calls for His particular type of energy. A transference is being effected of certain groups of human and deva Monads out of the human kingdom into the fifth or spiritual kingdom. During His cycle of close on two thousand five hundred years, a specific number of men will pass on to the Path of Initiation, and take at least the first Initiation, thus transferring their centres of consciousness out of the purely human into the early stages of the spiritual.

During this same cycle, a transference of units from out of the animal kingdom into the human will proceed in the fifth chain and from thence on to another chain, thus producing a period of even greater activity than on our own globe. Similarly I may point out (even though it is not possible to give more than a hint) that the force of the cosmic Transferrer is being called into activity by the transference during this cycle of a special group of highly advanced units of the human and deva kingdoms (members of the occult Hierarchy) to another scheme altogether. Certain units also—from among the Lipika Lords—are taking advantage of this cosmic influence to transfer their activity to another system, giving place to others Who will work out the karma of the new age. The power of these agencies permeates the entire globe and extends throughout the chains and schemes which lie in the line of its path. It will fundamentally affect the vegetable kingdom, obscuring old types and bringing in new; it will work in the mineral kingdom and give a new impetus to the chemical processes, causing incidentally a setting loose of radioactive units, and a consequent accretion of knowledge by the scientist. In the elemental kingdoms and the group souls found therein, it produces facility in the transference of atoms.

So far-reaching are the effects of this Ray, both on the deva and human units in their different kingdoms that entirely new environments will evolve for the utilisation of the new types and entirely new characteristics will be found emerging in the race of men.

We have somewhat considered the type of force which expresses itself by means of the seventh Ray and have seen that it is the great transmuting, and transferring agent of the Logos. We have seen that it has a powerful effect both on deva and human units; we have found that the prime function of the Logos of the seventh Ray is beyond all else, that of adaptation, or the moulding of the form and the rendering of it suitable to the needs of any particular Entity. In all the constructive work of form-building, certain factors enter in which must here be enumerated as they concern vitally this particular Heavenly Man, and the particular plane, the physical, on which we undergo experience. These are:

First. *The will* or the one-pointed purpose of some entity.

Second. *The material* through which the life proposes to manifest. This material, as we know, is found within the ring-pass-not in seven grades, and in forty-nine sub-grades.

Third. *The Builders* who are the vehicle for the divine purpose, and who mould matter upon a particular plan. These Builders evolve the forms out of their own nature and substance.

Fourth. *A plan* by which the work is carried out and which is imparted to the Builders, being latent in their consciousness. They evolve the form of the Grand Heavenly Man, of the Heavenly Men, of the human units, and of all forms from within outwards, and produce the self-identified Existences as a mother builds and produces a conscious Son out of the matter of her own body, carrying certain racial earmarks yet independent, self-conscious, self-willed and threefold in manifestation. The fact of the identity of the deva evolution with the essence they manipulate must ever be borne in mind.

Finally. Certain Words or *Mantric Sounds,*[51] which—

---

[51] They have in India an ancient system of psychical teaching called Yoga, in which the recitation of certain mantrams, or verses of Sanskrit, is prescribed. Especially important is said to be the way in which the mystical syllable Om, or Aum, is pronounced. Learned Brahmans tell me that the illimitable psychic potentiality of the Sanskrit charms, or mantrams is only drawn out by the adoption of a certain very accurate rule of pronunciation (swara). They say that by formulating the words correctly a vibration is set up in the akaz, or that part of the ether of space which enwraps our 'globe, which makes man the master over all the spirit denize. s of the various kingdoms of nature. It first re-acts upon the astral double or ethereal body of the man himself, purifying its grossness, stimulating its psychic powers out of the normal state of latency, and gradually fortifying them up to the point of mastery over nature's finer forces.—*The Theosophist*, Vol. XIII, pp. 229, 613.

"The primal single sound (Aum or Om) is the highest uttered word of power and knowledge. It is verily as Brahman itself. The regulation of the breath is the chiefest tapas-discipline. Higher than the Savitri is no mantra. Higher than silence is truth.

The Creator stored the veritable essences of the Three Vedas in the three letters that make up the Sacred Word, in the three utterances that name and form the three worlds, and in the three parts of the veda-verse that invokes the sun. Each part He milked from one Veda. Whoso ponders on these, morning and evening, after having learnt the Vedas previously, he verily studies the whole of the Vedas every day. These are the gateway unto Brahman.

By repeated dwelling on their significance, and tuning his desire and modelling his thought to that significance, the seeker after Brahman shall, without fail, attain all perfection, whether he discharge any other duty or not; for the very name of the Brahmana is 'the friend of All creatures' (and the Gayatri is the prayer for the blessing of all creatures by our radiant Father in Heaven, the Sun)."—*Unknown.*

There are specific formulæ known to all initiates of a certain grade (and even to many who have not attained that grade, a number have become known and are used—sometimes in ways that result in no good to the insufficiently instructed user), some one or other of which is specially adapted to produce nearly every possible effect that can be imagined. . . .

Well may *Isis Unveiled* (p. 514) tell us that 'sounds and colors' are all spiritual numerals; nor is that all, for odors, metals and planets are equally spiritual numerals. Each planet (or spiritual plane) has relation to a metal and a color. These again are in co-relation with a corresponding odor and sound.

The sphere of aura that surrounds every human being has one very important 'fold' or 'layer,' which invariably bears the color of the

uttered by a greater Life—can ever drive the lesser lives
to the fulfillment of constructive purpose. These Words
are uttered by

A solar Logos. The threefold Word gives rise to a
    sevenfold vibration.
A Heavenly Man, Who—through utterance—sweeps
    into evolutionary objectivity His scheme and all
    that is therein.
The Monad, whose threefold word gives rise to a seven-
    fold vibration.
The Ego, who—through sonorous utterance—produces
    a human being in the three worlds.

The analogy existing between these four should be carefully noted.

Certain Words belong to the different aspects, and the
Words of the first aspect set in vibration the matter that
evolves through the seven cycles of solar systems. Their
relation to the Words of the present solar system is
analogous to the primordial substance which lies back of
our present creation. The Words of the second aspect
concern us closely, but the Words of Brahma are at the
present stage more closely connected with our work upon
the physical plane. These Words, where the three worlds
are concerned, very largely fall into a group of mantrams,
hidden in the consciousness of the Lords of the fifth and
seventh Rays; by their intelligent utterance the third
aspect (the Brahma or manasic aspect) is brought into
contact with the first aspect and produces that which we
call the "Conscious Son" or Sun. Upon the mental plane
they are sounded by the Lord of the fifth Ray, causing
a vibration not only in what we might call "the lower
levels" but producing response on the first or archetypal

metal and planet to which that particular individual has most affinity;
and it is on this layer that the magnetic part of odors and all sound
vibrations impinges.—*The Theosophist*, Vol. VII, p. 218.

plane and on the cosmic mental plane likewise. On the physical plane the words, uttered by the seventh Logos, produce the following results:

First. The anchoring of the permanent atoms within their group soul, or the union of matter and consciousness.

Second. The guidance of the stream of life into any particular kingdom, or the blending of form and consciousness.

Third. The transference of the conscious, sentient life from form to form, from group to group, from kingdom to kingdom within the hierarchies.

In connection with the human kingdom, the fifth Ray had to function or pour forth its influence in order to produce self-consciousness within the conscious form.

It will consequently be seen that the utterance of sound along the line of force by the trained adept can both utilize deva activity to effect certain results in connection with the form side of manifestation, and can drive the life within to definite action. Hence the extreme danger —as has been frequently pointed out—of the knowledge of these mantrams and the need to safeguard them from interference and misuse. Power over form and over force lies always ready in the hand of those who have done three things:

First. Developed the consciousness of the group in which they themselves find place.

Second. Learned the secret of the notes and tones to which that group responds.

Third. Apprehended certain set words and phrases and the due method of chanting and intonation.

They cannot bring about results outside the periphery of the group whose consciousness is theirs. For instance, an adept can work with forms and force within

THE FACTOR OF MANAS 451

the ring-pass-not of his own planetary Logos within the three worlds, within the ring-pass-not of the polar opposite of his Logos, or within the ring-pass-not of three planetary Logoi who form a systemic triangle. He cannot exhibit this power in the higher planes nor within the spheres of the synthesising and neutral schemes. After the sixth Initiation his power extends to the two planes beyond the three worlds, the buddhic and the atmic, and within the spheres of the entire Brahma aspect as we visualise it as the totality of the schemes of the five Kumaras who are Brahma. At the seventh Initiation he has power on all the seven planes and within the entire number of schemes; all the Sacred Words are then his and he can work in matter of all grades, sound all notes, and control all types of force. He stands ready then to guide the life to regions outside the solar sphere of influence. But on the physical plane he works primarily with the Words of the seventh Logos, which fall naturally into five groups:

1. Mantrams which deal with etheric matter, and control the devas of the ethers.

2. Mantrams which deal with dense physical matter and control the sub-human evolution through certain groups of devas.

3. Words specifically connected with the human Hierarchy, and which are very carefully guarded from the knowledge of man himself.

4. Words concerning the deva evolution which control, and bring different groups of devas into the line of the will of the utterer. These are in many ways the most dangerous and all knowledge of them is withheld from men below the rank of initiates of the third order.

5. Words which affect the life side of manifestation and which drive it into, or out of, form.

There is a sixth group intimately connected with electrical manifestation, which is beginning to work out in the formula of scientists, and students of radio-activity and electrical phenomena, but fortunately for themselves they remain formulas on paper and are not as yet embodied in sound.

In dealing very briefly with the question of mantrams, it is to be recognised that "The time is not yet" for their general publication. No purpose would be immediately served by the impartation of mantric forms. Inevitably the time will come when they will be known, but at this time no one would be benefited by the knowledge of them for the following reasons:

Knowledge of things occult does not suffice for their wise utilisation.

The development of the intuition by means of aspiration, endeavour, failure, and renewed effort ending in success is of far more profit to the Ego than the quick results brought about by the use of sound.

The "Words" are used for the manipulation of matter and its bending into form along the line of evolution. Until the inner faculty of clairvoyance is somewhat developed, this knowledge of mantrams remains practically useless and may be even a menace. When a man can see a need for correction and for adjustment in a brother's vehicle, and can awaken in his brother a desire to adjust that which is amiss, wise assistance can be given by the one who sees and sounds. Think this out, for it holds the key to the reason for the safeguarding of the words.

Selflessness, sight, and sincerity of purpose must all three exist before the sounds can be imparted. Selflessness and sincerity are sometimes found but the occult use of the inner vision is still rare.

We must keep closely in mind (as we take up this matter of the incoming Ray and the effects to be looked for from its influence) that we are only considering the mind aspect in the three evolutions. I do not purpose to say much anent human development as much has been already hinted at in the preceding pages, and a hint suffices for the true student, but it may be possible to state in broad outline the coming developments and to tabulate the results to be expected. Suggestions only are possible.

Development of etheric vision universally. This will be due to two causes:

First, the scientific recognition of the existence of the etheric levels, thereby freeing people from the onus of adverse public opinion, and enabling them to reveal what they have individually long realised. Etheric vision is comparatively common even now. But comment concerning it is rare, owing to the fear of criticism.

Secondly, the increased activity of the devas of the ethers, which throws the matter of the etheric levels into more active vibration, with consequent reflex action on the eye of man.

Increased mental activity and the spread of education (of the concrete mental kind) everywhere. This will result in:

Increased competition between units and between groups.

The organization of business on lines hitherto undreamt of.

The foundation of groups and aggregations of groups whose sole purpose will be to synthesise all the lines of human endeavour, and thus bring about unification of effort, and economy of force in the scientific, business, philosophic, educational, and religious worlds.

The foundation of schools of medicine along new lines, whose purpose will be to study the etheric body, its relation to the dense physical body, and its function as the receiver, storer, and transmitter of the vital fluids of the system.

The foundation of the new Church, which will be no longer along devotional and idealistic lines but which will be an outgrowth of the old idealism, demonstrating through mental forms. It will have for its basis the scientific recognition of the unseen world and its due appreciation and apprehension by means of accurate scientific ceremonial. This ceremonial of the universal church—being founded on the mental unity of all peoples—will not be ceremonial as it is now understood, as it will be the guarded, guided, scientific utilisation of sound and color to bring about certain desired ends, such as

The aligning of the Ego,

The influencing of groups,

The making of contact with the Occult Hierarchy,

The co-operation with the devas in order to further the constructive ends of evolution,

and many other objects which will grow out of the scientific comprehension of the constitution of man, the nature of vibration or radioactivity, and the demonstrated reality of the hitherto metaphysical hypothesis and religious dogma of the unseen world of thought and of spiritual existence.

Increased facility in approaching the Path. This will be based on the fact that so many of the then existent humanity will have personal knowledge of the ruling powers and forces, will perhaps be on the Probationary Path, or will be initiates of the first degree. Thus the present scepticism will become non-existent. The dangers then will be along other lines—those incident to the very influence of this ray itself: the dangers of crystallisation into form so that the true spiritual devotee may become rare, and the scientific aspirant will take his place.

The true occultist is a scientist and a devotee, and where these two are not merged, we have the mystic and the man in danger of black magic, being governed by the intellect and not by selflessness; there are dangers incident also upon contact with the deva evolution and the knowledge of the powers and forces made available through their agency.

The coming into incarnation of numbers of old magicians and occultists, and the rapid growth therefore of recognised psychic powers among the people. This psychism, being tinged with mentality and not being of a purely astral quality, will be even more dangerous than in Atlantean days, for back of it will be some degree of will, conscious purpose, and intellectual apprehension, and unless this is paralleled by the growth of spiritual realisation, and by the steady grip of the Ego upon the lower personality, a period of real danger may ensue. Hence the need of pointing out and of realising the menace, so that the truth of the inner life and the need of serving the race as an essential to advancement may be proclaimed far and wide.

Paralleling the incoming of this large band of seventh Ray magicians (some linked to the Brotherhood and some to the purely manasic groups) is the proposed advent of certain members of the Hierarchy (initiates below the fourth Initiation) and of certain disciples and probationers, all on this Ray and all true psychics, who hope through their endeavours to offset the vibrations, and ward off the menace incident to the advent of the other group. The arranging of this and the preparing of the way for them in the different countries, specially in Europe and North America, is occupying the attention at this time of the Master R— and the Master H—.[52]

A group of scientists will come into incarnation on the

[52] The Master R. or Rakoczi, is the Hungarian Master, living at this time in Hungary, and is the Regent of Europe and America, under the "great

physical plane during the next seventy-five years who will be the medium for the revelation of the next three truths concerning electrical phenomena. A formula of truth concerning this aspect of manifestation was prepared by initiates on the fifth Ray at the close of the last century, being part of the usual attempt of the Hierarchy to promote evolutionary development at the close of every cycle of one hundred years. Certain parts (two fifths) of that formula have worked out through the achievements of such men as Edison and those who participate in his type of endeavour, and through the work of those who have dealt with the subject of radium and radioactivity. Three more parts of the same formula have still to come, and will embody all that it is possible or safe for man to know anent the physical plane manifestation of electricity during the fifth subrace.

All that we have here considered covers the time till the coming in of the new subrace. This race will summarise and carry to a temporary conclusion the manasic effort of the fifth rootrace of mental growth, and will cause results of stupendous import. During the sixth subrace, the emphasis will not be so much on the *development* of mind, as it will be on the *utilisation* of the concrete mind, and its acquired faculty, for the development of the powers of abstract thought. Perhaps too much importance has been attached to the statement of some occult writers that the sixth subrace will be intuitive. The intuition will be awakening, and will be more prominent than now, but the outstanding characteristic will be the ability of the units of the sixth subrace to think in abstract terms, and to use the abstract mind. Their function will be to perfect (as far as may be in this round)

Brotherhood.'' He works through various organisations and movements including Masonry. He is one of the Masters who take pupils.
The Master H. or Hilarion, is a Cretan Master, is interested in the Spiritualistic Movement and is responsible for *Light on the Path.*

the group antaskarana,[53] or the link between the mental and the buddhic. This bridge will be of a usable nature during the sixth rootrace in which the intuition will show real and general signs of existing. In this rootrace, units only show signs here and there of real intuition, having built the necessary bridge in their individual selves. In the sixth rootrace small groups will be intuitive.

It is needless to say more here anent the influence of the seventh Ray upon the sons of men. More later may be available but enough has been suggested to form the basis of useful speculation.

b. Animals and human beings and the Rays. We will now take up two points and study the effect of the incoming force on the human and animal kingdoms.

These points are of profound interest to the occult student for two reasons. The topic we have now to consider is the effect of the incoming seventh Ray during the coming centuries upon the animal kingdom and the deva evolution. The profundity of the interest lies in the fact that in the one case we are dealing with the evolution immediately behind the human and from which man is not as yet wholly emancipated, and in the other we are concerning ourselves with a paralleling evolution, and one that is of vast importance in the scheme of things. Let us take up first this *seventh Ray and its effect upon the animal kingdom.*

Practically little is known to man concerning this kingdom of nature, save what science has vouchsafed anent the physical organisms, and a few occult statements which have been given out at various times; the development of the animal consciousness and its immediate future is as yet but little understood.

The most important of the occult facts concerning this

Antahkarana is the lower manas, the path of communication between the personality and the higher manas, or human soul.—*H. P. Blavatsky.*

third kingdom as they relate to our present subject, may be enumerated as follows:

1. The animal kingdom holds the same relation to the human kingdom as the dense physical body does to the seven principles and still finds its connecting link with man through the close correspondence between their bodies of objectivity.

2. The animal kingdom is the third of the kingdoms and is (from the esoteric point of view and as regards its relation to mankind) the mother aspect, prior to the overshadowing by the Holy Spirit, the manas aspect. Think out this resemblance, and trace the analogy between the cosmic mother, the systemic mother, and the same mother aspect as seen in the animal kingdom as a basis for the evolution of man.

Each of the kingdoms of nature acts as the mother to the succeeding one in the evolutionary process. Any group, which may be under consideration, should in due course of evolution give birth to offspring, who will—in themselves—embody some ideal, and who receive their objective *forms on some plane* from the earlier group. From the third kingdom springs the fourth, and from this fourth will emerge the fifth, each receiving

a. Germ protection,
b. Form,
c. Gradual development,
d. Nourishment,

until in each case the human child, or the Christ child, is brought to the birth. This is a very occult truth, and though the facts have been recognised and taught anent the fourth and fifth kingdoms, the work and place·of the animal has not received its due recognition.

3. During the third rootrace, animal individualisation took place, and the self-conscious unit, called Man, came into being. I have somewhat dealt with the question of

individualisation elsewhere and seek not here to enlarge upon it. I would only point out a correspondence that holds hid the key to the mystery of individualisation.

In this chain, individualisation took place during the third rootrace and in the fourth round, speaking in this connection of a round through a chain of globes, and not the life force of a planetary Logos circulating through the seven chains in a scheme. It is of peculiar interest at this time that we are in the fourth round in a chain as well as in the fourth round as regards the scheme of seven chains. It has led to evolutionary possibilities of great import. On the moon chain individualisation took place during the fifth race of the third round, and in the next chain to ours on the evolutionary arc individualisation will take place during the sixth race of the second round,—in each case this refers to a planetary round through a chain of globes.

4. In the fourth rootrace the "door" (as it is called) between the two kingdoms became closed, and no more of the animal kingdom passed into the human. Their cycle temporarily ended and—to express it in terms of fire or of electrical phenomena—the animal kingdom and the human became positive to each other, and repulsion instead of attraction supervened. All this was brought about by the swinging into power of a profoundly long cycle of the fifth Ray. This was necessitated by the need of man to develop along the manasic line, and resulted in a period of·repulsion of the animal units, leaving their consciousness to be stimulated on astral lines.

Owing to this repulsion, we have one reason (and one of the least fundamental) for the destructive war and the long cycle of cruelty that has been waged between man and the animals. It can be evidenced in the terror of man in connection with wild animals of the jungles and the deserts, and in the terrible toll of life that such animals have exacted during the centuries. This must not be forgotten. For thousands of years, wild animals have —specially before the coming in of firearms—destroyed the defenseless, and during those years, had statistics been taken, the numbers of human beings killed would reach a stupendous figure. Now, in this age, the balancing is taking place and in the slaughter of animals equilibrium is being reached. I do not refer to the wanton cruelties practised under the name of science, nor to certain practices which take place under religious guise in different lands. The source of these enormities must be sought for elsewhere. It is hidden in the karma of that Being, Who for a period—during the moon chain— held office as the Entity Who is the informing evolutionary Life of the animal kingdom. This is a point of view needing careful pondering. Each of the kingdoms of nature is the expression of a Life or Being; man, for instance, being the expression of one or other of the Heavenly Men; the sumtotal of humanity (the fourth Hierarchy) being found, with the deva evolution, as the centres of the solar Logos. The animal kingdom likewise is the expression of the life of a Being Who is a part of the body of the Logos or of the planetary Logos, but not a centre of conscious energy. (A correspondence is found in the human body, which has its seven centres of force or energy, but also other organs upon which objective manifestation depends in lesser degree.) Such an Entity finds expression through the animal kingdom, of which He is the informing Soul, and He has definite place in the planetary or logoic body. This is a hint which has hitherto not been exoteric and is to be commended to the consideration of students. I would add that some of the tragedies underlying existence at this time are karmically incident upon temporarily faulty relations between an entity who dominated at one period of the third or moon-chain, and the one holding analogous position in this the fourth or earth chain. This latter is the sumtotal of the lowest human principle, if we count the dense physical or animal body of man as a principle. In their lack of agreement lies the clue to the cruelties practised on animals by man.

We have enumerated six occult statements anent the animal kingdom, the third kingdom of nature. They related to the past, and we will now add one further statement to them and then proceed to consider the present and to foretell certain eventualities that may be looked for in the future.

As we have seen, during the third rootrace, opportunity for the animal kingdom occurred and many individualised. In the fourth rootrace this cycle of opportunity ceased temporarily, and something happened which is analogous to what will occur in the fifth rootrace in connection with man, at the so-called "Judgment Day." In Atlantean days the lives which composed the third kingdom of nature were divided into two groups:

A number of these lives were "passed," and the tide of life sweeps through them, permitting of their incarnating in animal form on earth, and their gradual evolution.

The remainder were rejected, and as a group they became temporarily quiescent, and will not manifest in physical form until the next round.

In the fifth round, a corresponding division will take place in the fourth kingdom, and the lives in that kingdom will be subjected to an analogous test; some will be passed and will continue their evolution on this planet, while others will be rejected, and will go into temporary pralaya.

After the rejection in the fourth rootrace of three-fourths of the animal units, the remaining triads (or one-fourth) proceeded on their way holding the promise of opportunity for all in time, and the guarantee of their own attainment in the next round. Just as the human Monads, who are passed in the fifth round, will enter into the fifth kingdom, or respond to its vibration before the climax of the seventh, so the animal monads (if I may employ such a term) who were passed in this round will achieve individualisation during the fifth and enter the fourth kingdom. This will be brought about by the strong manasic impulse which will characterise the whole cycle of the fifth round, and will thus be effected normally and as the result of due evolutionary growth. An electrical stimulation of the nature of the occurrence in Lemurian days will not be required.

Since the great division in the fourth rootrace, the animal kingdom has been primarily occupied with the stimulation and development of kama. This is the basis of the endeavour being made by the Brotherhood *by the aid of man* to fan the emotional instinct (or the embryo love aspect) through the segregating of the domestic animals, and the consequent play made upon the third spirilla in the animal atoms by human magnetism or radiatory energy. The sumtotal of the domestic animals— the animal units brought into closest connection with man —form the heart centre in the body of that great Entity Who is the life of the animal kingdom. From the heart flow all the influences which will eventually permeate the entire body. These units are those which will be finally separated from the group soul at the reopening of the door into the human kingdom in the next round.

Let us now consider the immediate present, and the advent of this seventh ray of ceremonial magic. The effect upon the animal kingdom of the force of this ray will be far less than upon the human, for it is not yet ready to respond to the vibration of this planetary Logos, and will not be until the sixth round when His influence will bring about great events. Nevertheless, certain effects might here be noticed.

Owing to the increased activity of the deva evolution, and specially of the devas of the ethers, the lesser builders will be stimulated to build, with greater facility, bodies of a more responsive nature, and the etheric bodies of both men and animals and also their responsiveness to force or prana will be more adequate. During the sixth subrace, disease as we know it in both kingdoms will be materially lessened owing to the pranic response of the etheric bodies. This will likewise bring about changes in the dense physical body and the bodies of both men and animals will be smaller, more refined, more finely attuned to vibration, and consequently more fitted to express essential purpose.

Owing to the recognition by man of the value of mantrams, and his gradual comprehension of the true cere monial of evolution, coupled with the use of sound and colour, the animal kingdom will be better understood, and better trained, considered and utilised. Indications of this already can be seen; for instance, in all our current magazines at this time, stories which deal with the psychology of animals, and with their mental attitude to man, are constantly appearing, and by the means of these and through the force of the incoming Ray, man may (if he cares to do so) come to a much wider sympathy with his brothers of less degree. Thus by the turning by man of his thought force upon the animals, stimulation of their latent mentality will ensue, leading in due course of time to the crisis in the next round. More attention should be paid by occult students to the effect of the consciousness of one group upon another group, and the advancement of the lesser, by the means of the stimulating power of the greater, should be studied. The following facts should be realised:

a. The powerful vibration of the Lords of the three Rays, and of Their radiation, stimulates the four Heavenly Men and develops Their apprehension, enabling Them to expand Their consciousness.

b. The consciousness of the Heavenly Men stimulates all the units in Their bodies, but causes specialised response from those who are actively and intelligently working at the development of group consciousness. The vibration, for instance, of a planetary Logos has a peculiar effect upon all those who are initiates, adepts and chohans, and brings their three major spirillæ to the necessitated vibration. This work is begun when the sixth spirilla (in the minor group of seven) is active.

c. The consciousness of man is stimulated and developed when—at a certain stage—he can respond to the vibration of members of the Occult Hierarchy, and is thus nearing the portal into the fifth kingdom. This coincides with the vibratory activity of the fifth spirilla.

d. In like manner, the less evolved units of the race, who are scarcely more than animals, are brought to the necessary stage of vibration by the play upon their mental bodies of the combined vibrations of men, whose fourth spirilla is functioning adequately. In these last two cases we are dealing with the spirillæ of the mental permanent atom. In the other two we are dealing with occult mysteries, bound up in the vivification of solar and not human permanent atoms.

e. The fourth Creative Hierarchy, viewed as a unit functioning on this planet (and leaving out of consideration its manifestation in other schemes) works in a magnetic manner, and in a stimulative capacity upon the animal kingdom, the force of its vibration pouring on to *the astral bodies* of the animals, and producing response. This awakens to a more effective apprehension all the units of the animal kingdom. Hence it can be seen how close is the interplay, and the interdependence, and how closely united all these greater and lesser lives are with each other. Growth and development in one part of the body logoic produces a corresponding advance in the whole. No man, for instance, can make definite and specialised progress without his brother benefiting,—this benefiting taking the form of:

The increase of the total consciousness of the group.

The stimulation of units in the group.

The group magnetism producing increased healing or blending effects upon allied groups.

In this thought lies, for the servant of the Master, incentive to effort; no man who strives for mastery, who struggles to attain, and who aims at expansion of consciousness but is having some effect—in ever widening spirals—upon all whom he contacts, devas, men, and animals. That he knows it not, and that he may be totally unaware of the subtle stimulating emanation which proceeds from him may be true, but nevertheless the law works.

The third effect of the coming in of this ray is one that may at first repel—it will cause a great destruction in the animal kingdom. During the next few hundred years many of the old animal forms will die out and become extinct. To supply the wants of man, through disease, and through causes latent in the animal kingdom itself, much destruction will be brought about. It must ever be borne in mind that a building force is likewise a destroying one, and new forms for the animal evolution are, at this time, one of the recognized needs. The immense slaughter in America is part of the working out of the plan. The inner life or fire which animates the animal groups, and which is the life expression of an Entity, will, under this seventh influence, blaze up and burn out the old, and permit the escape of the life, to newer and better forms.

Our subject for immediate consideration concerns the

deva evolution, and the effect of the incoming ray upon them.

The first point to be noted is that this influence at this time affects primarily the devas of the physical plane, the devas of the ethers, or of the shadows, as they are sometimes called, and not, to the same extent, the devas of the astral or mental planes. Every Ray affects in more or less degree the plane or subplane which is its numerical correspondence; the student should bear this in mind, and should therefore recollect that for all purposes of investigation at this time the seventh Ray of Ceremonial Magic will have a powerful influence:

On the seventh or physical plane, regarding it as a unit.

On the seventh subplane or the lowest subplane on the physical, the astral and the mental planes.

On the seventh or lowest human principle: prana in the etheric body.

On all Monads in incarnation who are seventh Ray Monads.

On a peculiar group of devas who are the agents, or "mediates" between magicians (either white or black) and the elemental forces. This group is occultly known as "The Mediatory Seventh," and is divided into two divisions:

    a. Those working with evolutionary forces.

    b. Those working with involutionary forces.

One group is the agent of constructive purpose, and the other of destructive. More need not be submitted anent this group as they are not easily contacted, fortunately for man, and can as yet only be reached by a particular group ritual *accurately* performed,—a thing as yet practically unknown. The Masons eventually will be one of the chief agents of contact, and as men are as yet not ready for such power as this will put into their hands,

true masonry will develop but slowly. Nevertheless, under the magnetic force of this seventh Ray,
the growth of masonry is inevitably sure.

This Ray of Ceremonial Magic will consequently have
a very profound effect upon the physical plane, for not
only is this plane coming under its cyclic force but at
all times its planetary Logos has a special effect upon
it; the Raja-Lord of this plane is what is occultly termed
the "Reflection in the Water of Chaos" of the planetary
Logos. Hence in the matter of this plane (which is the
body of the Raja-Lord) certain very definite events are
occurring which—though invisible to the ordinary man
—are apparent to the eye of the spiritual man or adept.

The matter of the plane becomes receptive to positive
force for the feminine or deva aspect, being negative, becomes responsive to the positive energy of the Heavenly
Man. This energy, finding the line of least resistance,
pours into the substance of the plane, or the substantial
body of the Deva Lords. Owing to the receptive condition of this body it follows certain lines and produces
definitely *constructive* results.

Constructive results transpire in the negative etheric
matter of the plane and on the four higher subplanes.
On the lower three a contrary effect is produced, and
the energy of the Heavenly Man will lead to the destruction of form, preparatory to the building work. The
building ever originates on, and proceeds from, etheric
levels. Cataclysms of a world wide nature will occur
during the next one thousand years; continents will be
shaken; lands will be raised and submerged, culminating
in the profound material disaster which will overtake the
world towards the close of the fourth branch race of the
sixth subrace. This will usher in the infant sixth root-
race.

The devas of the ethers, with which we are most concerned, will be affected in several ways, and the results upon the other evolutions will be far-reaching. We must remember always that the devas are the qualities and attributes of matter, the active builders, who work consciously or unconsciously upon the plane. Here I would point out that all the devas of the higher levels of the mental plane, for instance, and of the systemic planes from there on to the centre (the divine plane, the plane of the Logos, sometimes called Adi) co-operate consciously, and are of high rank in the system, and of position equal to all the ranks and grades of the Hierarchy from a first degree initiate up to, but not including, the Lord of the World Himself. Below these higher levels, where the concrete is touched, we have lesser grades of devas who work unconsciously, with the following exceptions, who are conscious forces and entities and of high position:

a. The Raja-lord of a plane.
b. Seven devas who work under Him, and are the entities who inform the matter of the seven sub-planes.
c. Fourteen representatives of the Rays, Who cycle into and out of power, according to the Ray, waxing or waning.
d. Four devas who are the *plane* representatives of the four Maharajahs (the Lords of Karma) and are the focal points for karmic influence in connection with man. The four Maharajahs are the dispensers of karma to the Heavenly Men, and thus to the cells, centres, and organs of His body necessarily; but the whole system works through graded representatives; the same laws govern these agents of plane karma as govern the systemic and cosmic, and during plane manifestation they are, for instance, the only unit *in form*

permitted to pass beyond the plane ring-pass-not. All other units in manifestation on a plane have to discard the vehicle through which they function before they can pass on to subtler levels.

c. Types of Karma. We might here enumerate the different types of KARMA, even though we have not the time to enlarge upon the subject. A book by itself of vast proportions could not contain all that might be said. We should bear in mind that KARMA is imposed upon the ensouling entity through the medium of matter or of substance itself (which is coloured by it) and that this matter or substance is *intelligent material composed of deva essence.*

Cosmic Karma—Imposed upon the solar Logos from outside of the system.

Systemic Karma—The working out by the Logos of effects set in motion in previous Kalpas, and which influence His present type of Body.

Planetary Karma—The individual karma of a Heavenly Man, which is just as different from that of another Heavenly Man, as is the karma of the different members of the human family.

The Karma of a chain, which is bound up in the life experience of that entity who ensouls a chain, and is a centre in the body of a Heavenly Man, in the same sense as a Heavenly Man within His scheme is a centre in the body of the solar Logos.

Globe Karma—The individual destiny of the entity who is a centre in the body of the ensouling Life of a chain.

These five existences above enumerated, who are worked upon by karma, are all cosmic and solar Lords of Light, Who achieved intelligence, and passed through the human kingdom many kalpas ago.

Plane Karma—This is inextricably mixed up with the

karma of the planetary Logos and of the Raja-Lord, and is dependent upon the interplay between these two opposite poles,—the masculine and feminine aspect of the Divine Hermaphrodite.

The Karma of a subplane, or the destiny of certain lesser entities who manifest through these planes.

In these two types of karma, we have what one might term the "Karma of the Hierarchies" as it has been brought about since the manifesting of the solar system. It is the result of the past of this system, and not so much the working out of effects originating in previous solar systems.

The Karma of the kingdoms of nature as we know them on our planet:

   a. The mineral kingdom.
   b. The vegetable kingdom.
   c. The animal kingdom.

This is necessarily the karma of the different lunar Lords who ensoul these kingdoms, and who are working out their purposes through them. We must note that we have touched therefore upon cosmic, solar, and lunar karma. In the latter is hid the great mystery of the Moon, and her place in the planetary scheme.

The Karma of the Human Hierarchy [54, 55, 56] in its seven groups, and of the individual Monads. This in itself is a vast and intricate subject and—during the particular cycle of the Earth globe—can be divided into:

[54] Karma and Reincarnation, the fourth and fifth doctrines of the Wisdom-religion. These two are, in reality, the A, B, C, of the Wisdom-religion. Karma is the sum total of our acts, both in the present life and in the preceding births. It is of three kinds:—

        1. *Sanchita* karma
        2. *Prarabdha* karma
        3. *Agami* karma

"*Sanchita karma* includes human merits and demerits accumulated in the preceding and in all other previous births. That portion of the *Sanchita karma* destined to influence human life in one or the present incarnation is called *Prarabdha.* The third kind of karma is the result of the merits and demerits of the present acts. *Agami* extends over all your words,

a. World karma. (The seven root-races.)

b. Racial karma, or the destiny and purpose of each root-race.

c. Subrace karma, for each subrace has its own destiny to work out.

d. National karma.

e. Family karma.

f. Individual karma.

All these different types of karma are intermingled and bound up in a manner inconceivable and inextricable

thoughts, and acts. What you think, what you speak, what you do, as well as whatever results your thoughts, words, and acts produce on yourself, and on those affected by them, fall under the category of the present karma, which will be sure to sway the balance of your life for good or for evil in your future development.''—*The Theosophist*, Vol. X, p. 235.

⁶⁵ ''Karma (action) is of three kinds:—

1. Agami:—The bodily actions good and bad—done after the acquisition of the discriminative knowledge. (Vide *Sri Sankaracharya's Tatwa Bodh,* question 34).

2. Sanchita:—The actions formerly done, serving as seeds to grow the countless births; the store of former actions preserved. *Ibid,* question 35).

And 3. Prarabdha:—The actions of this body (i.e. birth) which give pleasure or pain in this life alone. (*Ibid.*, question 36.).''—*The Theosophist*, Vol. VIII, p. 170.

⁶⁶ Karma. ''It must be remembered that in every action of man the influence of his prior karma constitutes an important element. For the accomplishment of every action, says, Sri Krishna, we need five essentials:—

1. The actor.
2. The determined will.
3. Implements for committing the act, such as hands, tongue, etc.
4. The exercise of these implements.
5. The influence of antecedent conduct.

The work which a man does with his body, speech or mind, whether it be just or unjust, has these five essentials or factors engaged in the performance. (*Gita*, XVIII, 13, 14, 15.)

These five essentials of karma are divided into 2 groups in the Mahabharata:—1, man's present action (including the first four essentials) and, 2, the result of his past action (which forms the fifth essential).

''At the same time it must be remarked that the result of human existence is not the work of a day or even a cycle. It is the aggregate sum of actions committed during innumerable previous existences. Each action may in itself be as slight as can be conceived, like the minutest filaments of cotton,—such that hundreds of them may be blown away by a single breath; and yet, as similar filaments when closely packed and twisted together form a rope, so heavy and strong that it can be used to pull elephants and even huge ships with, so the articles of man's karma, however trivial each of them may be in itself, would yet by the natural process of accretion, combine themselves closely and form a formidable Pasa (rope) to pull the man with, i.e. to influence his conduct for good or evil.''—*The Theosophist*, Vol. VII, p. 60.

to man; even the adepts cannot untangle the mystery beyond that of the groups affiliated with them, while the Chohans of the higher degrees work with the karma of the larger groups (which are the aggregates of the lesser groups).

All the lesser grades of devas, "The Army of the Voice," on each plane, the lesser builders and elementals in their myriads, work unconsciously, being guided and directed by words and sound. In this way vibrations are set up in the essence of the planes by the conscious Builders.

There is not much to be added at this point anent the deva evolution; much that might be imparted is perforce withheld owing to the danger arising from superficial knowledge, unaccompanied by wisdom and the inner vision. There are three more points to add to the four already given, concerning primarily the relationship of the devas to man in the future, and their closer approximation to him through the incoming type of force. This approximation, though inevitable, will not have for the human hierarchy results entirely beneficent, and before the true method of contact is comprehended, and the consequent association wisely utilised, much suffering will eventuate and much bitter experience will be undergone. When it is remembered that the devas are, in their totality, the mother aspect, the great builders of form, and the nourishers of that which is as yet unable to guard itself, any return of man to a closer dependence upon the devas is as if a full grown man returned to the care of his mother, offering up his self-reliance in exchange for material benefit. The devas are the mother of the form, but the self-conscious unit, MAN, should realize his independence of the form, and should follow the path of Self-expression. This should be pondered on, for in days to come (when units here and there contact the devas, and inevitably pay the penalty) it may be helpful if the reason is understood, and man realises his necessary separation from these Essences *in the three worlds.* Approach between the two lines of evolution becomes possible on the plane of buddhi, but then it is an approach of two essences, and not an approach of the concrete to the essence. Man, while functioning in material, substantial forms in the three worlds, may not trespass across the separating line between the two evolutions. Only on the planes of solar fire or on the cosmic etheric levels may contact be permitted; on the planes of the cosmic dense physical plane (our mental, astral and physical planes) disaster only results from contact. I have dwelt on this point, for the danger is real, and near at hand.

The deva evolution will, through this seventh Ray force have much to do with the transmission of prana to units of the three higher kingdoms of nature, and this easier transmission (from the etheric levels of the physical plane) will parallel a correspondingly easier transmission of spiritual or psychical force from the fourth cosmic ether, the buddhic plane. The results of this pranic transmission will be more healthy physical bodies among the sons of men. This need not be looked for at this time, and will only begin to be noticeable about three hundred years hence, when the incoming seventh Ray Egos will be numerically strong enough to be recognised as the prevailing type for a certain period. Their physical bodies, owing to their being built for seventh Ray force will respond more readily than the others, though first Ray egos and fifth Ray Egos will benefit enormously from this influence. The etheric devas will build during a peculiarly favourable period, and the physical bodies then constructed will be distinguished by:

a. Resilience,
b. Enormous physical magnetism,

c. Ability to reject false magnetism,
d. Capacity to absorb solar rays,
e. Great strength and resistance,
f. A delicacy and refinement in appearance as yet unknown.

The etheric levels of the plane will be full of an increased activity, and slowly but surely, as the decades slip away, man will become conscious of these levels, and aware of their inhabitants. The immediate effect of this greater etheric energy will be that a numerically larger number of people will possess etheric vision, and will be able normally and naturally to live consciously on etheric levels. The majority of men only function consciously on the three lower levels of the physical—the gaseous, the liquid, and the dense—and the etheric levels are as sealed to them as are the astral. In the coming centuries, man's normal habitat will be the entire physical plane up to, though not including, the second subplane. The fourth and third etheric levels will be as familiar to him as the usual physical landscape to which he is now accustomed.

The centre of attention of medical and scientific students will be focussed on the etheric body, and the dependence of the physical body upon the etheric body will be recognised. This will change the attitude of the medical profession, and magnetic healing and vibratory stimulation will supersede the present methods of surgery and drug assimilation. Man's vision being then normally etheric, will have the effect of forcing him to recognise that which is now called the "unseen world," or the superphysical. Men in their etheric bodies will be noted, and communicated with, and the devas and elementals of the ethers will be studied and recognised. When this is so, then the true use of ceremonial ritual as a protection and safeguard to man will assume its right place.

The work of the devas in connection with the animal and the vegetable kingdoms will be likewise recognised, and much that is now possible through ignorance will become impossible and obsolete. The time will come, when the attitude of man to the animal kingdom will be revolutionised, and the slaughter, ill-treatment, and that form of cruelty called "sport," will be done away with.

A mysterious change in the attitude of men and women to the sex question, marriage and the work of procreation will result from the development of etheric vision, and the consequent recognition of the devas. This change will be based on the realisation of the true nature of matter, or of the mother aspect, and of the effect of the Sun upon substance. The unity of life will be a known and scientific fact, and *life in matter* will no longer be a theory but a fundamental of science. This cannot be enlarged upon here.

3. *Manas in the Final Rounds.*

a. The transmutative process. Transmutation is a subject that from the earliest ages has occupied the attention of students, scientists and alchemists. The power to change, through the application of heat, is of course universally recognised, but the key to the mystery, or the secret of the systemic formula is advisedly guarded from all searchers, and is only gradually revealed after the second Initiation. The subject is so tremendous that it is only possible to indicate in broad general outlines how it may be approached. The mind of the public turns naturally to the transmutation of metals into gold with the aim in view of the alleviation of poverty. The mind of the scientist seeks the universal solvent which will reduce matter to its primordial substance, release energy, and thus reveal the processes of evolution, and enable the seeker to build for himself (from the primordial base) the desired forms. The mind of the alchemist searches for the Philosopher's Stone, that effective transmuting agent which will bring about revelation, and the power to impose the will of the chemist upon the elemental forces, which work in, by, and through matter. The religious man, especially the Christian, recognises the psychic quality of this transmutative power, and frequently speaks in the sacred books, of the soul being tried or tested seven times in the fire. All these students and investigators are recognising one great truth from their own constricted angle, and the whole lies not with one or another, but in the aggregate.

In defining transmutation as it is occultly understood, we might express it thus: *Transmutation is the passage across from one state of being to another through the agency of fire.* The due comprehension of this is based on certain postulates, mainly four in number. These postulates must be expressed in terms of the Old Commentary, which is so worded that it reveals to those who have eyes to see, but remains enigmatic to those who are not ready, or who would misuse the knowledge gained for selfish ends. The phrases are as follows:

I. He who transfers the Father's life to the lower three seeketh the agency of fire, hid in the heart of Mother. He worketh with the Agnichaitans, that hide, that burn, and thus produce the needed moisture.

II. He who transfers the life from out the lower three into the ready fourth seeketh the agency of fire hid in the heart of Brahma. He worketh with the forces of the Agnishvattas, that emanate, that blend, and thus produce the needed warmth.

III. He who transfers the life into the gathering fifth seeketh the agency of fire hid in the heart of Vishnu. He worketh with the forces of the Agnisuryans, that blaze, that liberate the essence, and thus produce the needed radiance.

IV. First moisture, slow and all enveloping; then heat with ever-growing warmth and fierce intensity; then force that presses, drives and concentrates. Thus is radiance produced; thus the exudation; thus mutation; thus change of form. Finally liberation, escape of the volatile essence, and the gathering of the residue back to primordial stuff.

He who ponders these formulas and who meditates upon the method and suggested process will receive a general idea of the evolutionary process of transmutation which will be of more value to him than the formulas whereby the devas transmute the various minerals.

Transmutation concerns the life of the atom, and is hidden in a knowledge of the laws governing radioactivity. It is interesting to note how in the scientific expression 'radioactivity,' we have the eastern conception of Vishnu-Brahma, or the Rays of Light vibrating through matter. Hence the usually accepted interpretation of the term 'atom' must be extended from that of the atom of chemistry to include:

a. All atoms or spheres upon the physical plane.
b. All atoms or spheres upon the astral and mental planes.
c. The human being in physical incarnation.
d. The causal body of man on its own plane.
e. All planes as entified spheres.
f All planets, chains and globes within the solar system.
g. All monads on their own plane, whether human monads or Heavenly Men.
h. The solar Ring-Pass-Not, the aggregate of all lesser atoms.

In all these atoms, stupendous or minute, microcosmic or macrocosmic, the central life corresponds to the positive charge of electrical force predicated by science, whether it is the life of a cosmic Entity such as a solar Logos, or the tiny elemental life within a physical atom. The lesser atoms which revolve round their positive centre, and which are at present termed electrons by science, are the negative aspect, and this is true not only of the atom on the physical plane, but of the human atoms, held to their central attractive point, a Heavenly Man, or the atomic forms which in their aggregate form the recognised solar system. All forms are built up in an analogous manner and the only difference consists—as the text-books teach—in the arrangement and the number of the electrons.[57] The electron itself will eventually be found to be an elemental, tiny life.

The second point I seek to make now is: *Radiation is transmutation in process of accomplishment.* Transmutation being the liberation of the essence in order that it may seek a new centre, the process may be recognised as radioactivity technically understood and applied to all atomic bodies without exception.

That science has but recently become aware of radium (an example of the process of transmutation) is but the fault of science. As this is more comprehended it will be found that all radiations, such as magnetism or psychic exhalation, are but the transmuting process proceeding on a large scale. The point to be grasped here is that the transmuting process, when effective, is superficially the result of outside factors. Basically it is the result of the inner positive nucleus of force or life reaching such a terrific rate of vibration, that it eventually scatters the electrons or negative points which compose its sphere of influence, and scatters them to such a distance that the Law of Repulsion dominates. They are then no more attracted to their original centre but seek another. The atomic sphere, if I might so express it, dissipates, the electrons come under the Law of Repulsion, and the central essence escapes and seeks a new sphere, occultly understood.

We must remember always that all within the solar system is dual, and is in itself both negative and positive: positive as regards its own form, but negative as regards its greater sphere. Every atom therefore is

[57] Atom and Electron: See *Consciousness of the Atom,* page 17-22.

both positive and negative,—it is an electron as well as an atom.

Therefore, the process of transmutation is dual and necessitates a preliminary stage of application of external factors, a fanning and care and development of the inner positive nucleus, a period of incubation or of the systematic feeding of the inner flame, and an increase of voltage. There is next a secondary stage wherein the external factors do not count so much, and wherein the inner centre of energy in the atom may be left to do its own work. These factors may be applied equally to all atoms; to the mineral atoms which have occupied the attention of alchemists so much, to the atom, called man who pursues the same general procedure being governed by the same laws; and to all greater atoms, such as a Heavenly Man or a solar Logos.

The process might be tabulated as follows:

1. The life takes primitive form.
2. The form is subjected to outer heat.
3. Heat, playing on the form, produces exudation and the factor of moisture supervenes.
4. Moisture and heat perform their function in unison.
5. Elemental lives tend all lesser lives.
6. The devas co-operate under rule, order and sound.
7. The internal heat of the atom increases.
8. The heat of the atom mounts rapidly and surpasses the external heat of its environing.
9. The atom radiates.
10. The spheroidal wall of the atom is eventually broken down.
11. The electrons or negative units seek a new centre.
12. The central life escapes to merge with its polar opposite becoming itself negative and seeking the positive.
13. This is occultly obscuration, the going-out of the light temporarily, until it again emerges and blazes forth.

More detailed elucidation will not be possible here nor advisable:

It will be apparent, therefore, that it should be possible, from the standpoint of each kingdom of nature, to aid the transmuting process of all lesser atoms. This is so, even though it is not recognised; it is only when the human kingdom is reached that it is possible for an entity consciously and intelligently to do two things:

First: aid in the transmutation of his own positive atomic centre from the human into the spiritual.

Second: assist at the transmutation

  a. From the lower mineral forms into the higher forms.
  b. From the mineral forms into the vegetable.
  c. From vegetable forms into the animal forms.
  d. From animal forms into the human or consciously and definitely to bring about individualisation.

That it is not done as yet is due to the danger of imparting the necessary knowledge. The adepts understand the transmuting process in the three worlds, and in the four kingdoms of nature, which make them a temporary esoteric three and exoteric four.

Man will eventually work with the three kingdoms but, only when brotherhood is a practice and not a concept.

Three points must now be considered in this connection:

Conscious manipulation of the fires.
Devas and transmutation.
Sound and colour in transmutation.

It is necessary here to point out, as I have done in other matters under consideration, that only certain facts can be imparted, whilst the detailed work concerning *process* may not be dealt with owing to the inability of the race as yet to act altruistically. Much misapprehension crept in, owing to this very thing, in the early days of hierarchical effort to give out some of the Wisdom fundamentals in book form, and this is bravely dealt with by H. P. B.[58, 59] The danger still persists, and greatly handicaps the efforts of Those, Who—working on the inner side—feel that the thoughts of men should be lifted from the study of the ways of physical existence to broader concepts, wider vision, and synthetic comprehension. Indication only is possible; it is not permissible here to give out the transmutative formulas, or the mantrams that manipulate the matter of space. Only the way can be pointed to those who are ready, or who are re-

[58] The difficulty of giving one the Wisdom Religion is dealt with by H. P. B. in the *Secret Doctrine* as follows:—

1. Opinion must be reserved because:—
   a. Complete explanation for initiates only.
   b. Only a fragmentary portion of the esoteric meaning given.
   c. Only adepts can speak with authority.—S. D., I, 188, 190. II, 55, 90.
   d. The teachings are offered as a hypothesis.—II, 469.
2. We must lose sight entirely of:—
   a. Personalities.
   b. Dogmatic beliefs.
   c. Special religions.—S. D., I, 3, 4.
3. We must be free from prejudice.—S. D., III, 1.
   We must also:
   a. Be free from conceit.
   b. Free from selfishness.
   c. Ready to accept demonstrated truth.
4. We must find the highest meaning possible. S. D., III, 487.
5. We must be also non-sectarian.—S. D., III, 110.
6. We must remember the handicap of language.—S. D., I, 197, 290, 293.
7. We must aim to become a disciple.—S. D., 188. II, 246. III, 129.
8. We must eventually develop powers.—S. D., I, 518. II, 85.
9. We must lead the life of Brotherhood. S. D., I, 190.
10. We must remember that H. P. B. makes no claim to infallibility.—S. D., II, 25 note, 273. I, 293.

H. P. B. says:—

"I speak with 'absolute certainty' only so far as my own personal belief is concerned. Those who have not the same warrant for their belief as I have would be very credulous and foolish to accept it on blind faith. . . . What I do believe in is:—

1. The unbroken oral tradition revealed by living divine men during the infancy of mankind to the elect among men.
2. That it has reached us unaltered.
3. That the Masters are thoroughly versed in the science based on such uninterrupted teaching."—*Lucifer*, Vol. V, p. 157.

"The Secret Doctrine is no 'authority' *per se;* but being full of quotations and texts from the Sacred Scriptures and philosophies of almost every great religion and school, those who belong to any of these are sure to find support for their arguments on some page or another. There are, however, Theosophists, and of the best and most devoted, who do suffer from such weakness for authority."—*Lucifer*, Vol. III, p. 157.

[59] See Preface and Introduction, *Secret Doctrine*, Vol. I.

covering old knowledge (gained through approach to the Path, or latent through experience undergone in Atlantean days) and the landmarks indicated hold sufficient guidance to enable them to penetrate deeper into the arcana of knowledge. The danger consists in the very fact that the whole matter of transmutation concerns the material form, and deva substance. Man, being not yet master even of the substance of his own sheaths, nor in vibratory control of his third aspect, incurs risk when he concentrates his attention on the Not-Self. It can only be safely done when the magician knows five things:

1. The nature of the atom.
2. The keynote of the planes.
3. The method of working from the egoic level through conscious control, knowledge of the protective sounds and formulas, and pure altruistic endeavour.
4. The interaction of the three fires, the lunar words, the solar words, and later a cosmic word.
5. The secret of electrical vibration, which is only realised in an elementary way when a man knows the keynote of his own planetary Logos.

All this knowledge as it concerns the three worlds is in the hands of the Masters of the Wisdom, and enables Them to work along the lines of energy or force, and not with what is usually understood when the word 'substance' is used. They work with electrical energy, concerning Themselves with positive electricity, or with the energy of the positive nucleus of force within the atom, whether it is the atom of chemistry, for instance, or the human atom. They *deal with the soul of things.* The black magician works with the negative aspect, with the electrons, if I might so term it, with the sheath, and not with the soul. This distinction must be clearly borne in mind. It holds the clue to the non-interference of the

whole Brotherhood in material matters and affairs, and
Their concentration upon the *force* aspect, upon the centres of energy. *They reach the whole through the agency
of the few centres in a form.* With this preamble we will
now take up the consideration of the

Conscious Manipulation of the Fires

It will now be apparent that the whole process of
transmutation, as we can˙deal with it at present, concerns itself with the two fires which reached a high stage
of perfection in a past solar system:

    a. The fire of an atom in its twofold aspect—internal
        and radiatory.

    b. The fires of mind.

It is with these that transmutation concerns itself from
the human standpoint, and the third fire of Spirit is not
at this stage to be considered.

This *conscious* manipulation of the fires is the prerogative of man when he has reached a certain point in his
evolution; the unconscious realisation of this has led
naturally to the attempts of the alchemist to transmute
in the mineral kingdom. A few of the older students
right through the ages have comprehended the vastness
of the endeavour of which the transmutation of the baser
metals into gold was but preliminary and a symbol, a
pictorial, allegorical, concrete step. The˙whole subject
of transmutation is covered by the work of the Hierarchy
in all its three departments on this planet, and we might
get some idea of the matters involved if we studied this
vast hierarchical standpoint, getting thereby a concept
of the work done in aiding the evolutionary process. It
is the work of transferring the life from one stage of
atomic existence to another, and it involves three distinct steps, which can be seen and traced by means of the
higher clairvoyance, and from the higher planes. These
steps or stages are:

The fiery stage—the blending, fusing, burning period, through which all atoms pass during the disintegration of form.

The solvent stage, in which the form is dissipated and substance is held in solution, the atom being resolved into its essential duality.

The volatile stage, which concerns primarily the essential quality of the atom, and the escape of this essence, later to take a new form.

Radioactivity, pralayic solution, and essential volatility might express the thought. In every transmuting process without exception these three steps are followed. Occultly expressed in the old Commentary they are thus stated:

"The fiery lives burn within the bosom of Mother.

"The fiery centre extends to the periphery of the circle and dissipation supervenes and pralayic peace.

"The Son returns to the bosom of Father, and Mother rests quiescent."

The Masters, in concert with the great Devas, concern Themselves with this transmutative process, and each department might be considered as dealing with one of the three stages:

The Mahachohan's department in its five divisions deals with the burning of the fiery lives.

The Manu's department concerns itself with the form or the ring-pass-not which encloses the burning lives.

The Bodhisattva's department deals with the return of the Son to the bosom of the Father.

Within the department of the Mahachohan, a secondary division along these lines might be outlined:

The seventh and fifth Rays are occupied with the return of the Son to the Father and are largely centred in pouring forth energising power when it becomes necessary to transfer the life of the Son from an old form into a new, from one kingdom of nature to another on the Path of Return.

The third and sixth Rays deal with the burning of the
fiery lives.

The fourth blends the two fires within the atomic form.

It will be seen from a close study of these subdivisions,
how close is the co-operation between the different
groups, and how inter-related are their activities. The
work of the Hierarchy can be interpreted always in terms
of alchemy, and Their activities deal with a threefold
transmutation. This work is carried on by Them *consciously,* and supervenes upon Their own emancipation.

A Master transmutes in the three worlds and principally concerns Himself with the process upon the eighteen subplanes, the great field of human evolution, and
with the passage of the life throughout the dense physical body of the Logos. *The Chohans* of the sixth Initiation work in the fourth and fifth ethers of the logoic
etheric body (the buddhic and atmic planes), and deal
with the passage of the life of Spirit from form to form
in those worlds, having in view the transmutation of
units in the spiritual kingdom into the monadic. Those
on still higher levels—*the Buddhas and their Confrères
of the first and third Rays*—deal with the passage of the
life into the sub-atomic, and atomic planes of the cosmic
physical. What has been said applies to all hierarchical
efforts in all schemes and on all globes, for the unity of
effort is universal. In every case, conscious self-induced
control, or authority, precedes ability to transmute. *Initiates* learn to transmute and superintend the passage
of the life out of the animal kingdom into the human
after the third Initiation, and during the earlier stages
of initiation, formulas that control the lesser devas, and
which produce results in the merging of the second and
third kingdoms are communicated; they work under safe-
guards and supervision.

Advanced intellectual man should be able to co-operate in the synthesis of the work, and deal with the trans-

mutation of the metals, as the ratio of their intellectual development to that of the mineral elements, and builders whom they would control, is the same as in the above mentioned cases and grades of consciousness, but owing to the disastrous developments in Atlantean days, and the consequent stultification of spiritual evolution for a time until karma has been adjusted, the art has been lost; or rather, the knowledge has been safeguarded until a period is reached in the racial progress wherein the physical body is pure enough to withstand the forces contacted, and to emerge from the process of chemical transmutation enriched, not only in knowledge and experience, but strengthened in its own inner fibre.

As time proceeds, man will gradually do four things:

1. Recover past knowledge and powers developed in Atlantean days.
2. Produce bodies resistant to the fire elementals of the lower kind which work in the mineral kingdom.
3. Comprehend the inner meaning of radioactivity, or the setting loose of the power inherent in all elements and all atoms of chemistry, and in all true minerals.
4. Reduce the formulas of the coming chemists and scientists to SOUND, and not simply formulate through experiment on paper. In this last statement lies (for those who can perceive) the most illuminating hint that it has been possible as yet to impart on this matter.

It may seem that I have not communicated much information anent this conscious manipulation of the fires. That lies in the inability of the student to read the esoteric background of the above communicated statements. Conscious transmutation is possible only when a man has transmuted the elements in his own vehicles; then only can he be trusted with the secrets of divine alchemy.

When through the latent internal fires of the matter of his own sheaths he has transmuted the chemical and mineral atoms of those sheaths, then can he safely—through affinity of substance—aid the work of mineral transmutation of the first order. Only when (through the radiatory fires of the sheaths) he has transmuted the correspondence to the vegetable kingdom within his own organism can he alchemically do work of the second order. Only when the fires of mind in himself dominate, can he work with the transmutative processes of the third order, or with the transference of life into the animal forms. Only when the Self within, or the Ego in the causal body, is in control of his threefold personality can he occultly be permitted to be an alchemist of the fourth order, and work in connection with the transmutation of the animal monad into the human kingdom, with all the vast knowledge that is included in that idea. Much lies ahead to be accomplished, but in the appreciation of the magnitude of the task need be no place for discouragement, for in the wise outlining of the future, in the cautious promulgation of knowledge concerning the necessitated stages, will come strenuous effort and aim on the part of many aspirants, and the evolutionary bringing in of those who can achieve.

The problem of speaking clearly on this subject of transmutation is a very real one, owing to the vastness of the subject and the fact that in the transmutation process the magician or alchemist *works with deva essence through the control of the lesser Builders in co-operation with the greater Devas.* In order, therefore, to bring about clarity of thought and definiteness of conjecture in this respect, I desire primarily to lay down certain postulates which must be carefully borne in mind when considering this question of transmutation. They are five in number and concern specifically the field wherein the transmuting process is carried on. The student must recollect at this juncture the distinction that is made between the work of the black and the white magician. It might be helpful here before proceeding further to look at these distinctions as far as they concern the matter in hand:

First.   The white Brother deals with positive electrical energy. The dark Brother deals with the negative electrical energy.

Second.   The white Brother occupies himself with the soul of things. The black Magician centres his attention upon the form.

Third.   The white Magician develops the inherent energy of the sphere concerned (whether human, animal, vegetable or mineral) and produces results through the self-induced activities of the central life, subhuman, human or super-human. The black Magician attains results through the agency of force external to the sphere involved, and produces transmutation through the agency of resolvents (if so I might term it) or through the method of the reduction of the form, rather than through radiation, as does the white Magician.

These differences of method need to be carefully considered and their reaction visualised in connection with different elements, atoms, and forms. To return to our statement of our five postulates anent the transmutation of substance, the resolution of the life, or the transference of energy into different forms.

THE FIVE POSTULATES

Postulate I. All matter is living matter, or is the vital substance of deva entities. For instance, a plane, and forms built of that particular plane substance, is the material form or sheath of a great deva, who is the essence back of manifestation and the soul of the plane.

Postulate II. All forms, vibrating to any keynote, are fabricated by the building devas out of the matter of their own bodies. Hence they are called the great Mother aspect, for they produce the form out of their own substance.

Postulate III. The devas are the life which produces form-cohesion. They are the third and second aspects blended, and might be considered as the life of all forms that are subhuman. A magician, therefore, who transmutes in the mineral kingdom works practically with deva essence in its earliest form on the upward arc of evolution, and has to remember three things:

a. The effect of the backward pull of the involutionary lives which lie back of the mineral, or, in effect, its heredity.

b. The sevenfold nature of the peculiar group of devas which constitute its *being* in an occult sense.

c. The next transition stage ahead into the vegetable kingdom, or the occult effect of the second kingdom on the first.

Postulate IV. All deva essences and builders on the physical plane are peculiarly dangerous to man, for they work on the etheric levels and are—as I have earlier pointed out—the transmitters of prana, or the vital, animating substance, and hence they set loose upon the ignorant and the unwary, fiery essence which burns and destroys.

Postulate V. The devas do not work as individualised conscious units through self-initiating purposes as does a man, a Heavenly Man or a solar Logos (viewed as Egos) but they work in groups subject to:

a. Inherent impulse, or latent active intelligence.

b. Orders issued by the greater Builders.

c. Ritual, or compulsion induced through colour and sound.

When these facts are remembered and considered, some comprehension of the place the devas play in transmutation may be achieved. The position that fire occupies in the process is of peculiar interest here, for it brings out clearly the difference of method between the two schools.

In the transmutative process as carried on by the Brotherhood, the inner fire which animates the atom, form or man is stimulated, fanned and strengthened till it (through its own internal potency) burns up its sheaths, and escapes by radiation from within its ring-pass-not. This is seen in an interesting way as occurring during the process of the final initiations when the causal body is destroyed by fire. The fire within burns up all else and the electric fire escapes. The true alchemist therefore in days to come will in every case seek to stimulate the radioactivity of the element or atom with which he is working and will centre his attention upon the *positive* nucleus. By increasing its vibration, its activity, or its positivity, he will bring about the desired end. The Masters do this in connection with the human spirit and do not concern Themselves at all with his 'deva' aspect. The same basic rule will be found to apply in the case of a mineral as well as of a man.

The process as carried on by the Dark Brotherhood is the reverse of this. They centre the attention upon the form, and seek to shatter and break that form, or the combination of atoms, in order to permit the central electric life to escape. They bring about this result through external agencies and by availing themselves of the destructive nature of the substance (deva essence) itself. They burn and destroy the material sheath, seeking to imprison the escaping volatile essence as the form disintegrates. This hinders the evolutionary plan in the case of the life involved, delays the consummation, interferes with the ordered progress of development, and puts all the factors involved in a bad position. The life (or entity) concerned receives a setback, the devas work destructively, and without participation in the purpose of the plan, and the magician is in danger, under the Law of Karma, and through the materialising of his own substance by affinity with the third aspect. Black magic of this nature creeps into all religions along this very line of the destruction of the form through outer agency, and not through the liberation of the life through inner development and preparedness. It produces the evils of Hatha Yoga in India and similar methods as practised in certain religious and occult orders in the Occident also. Both work with matter on some plane in the three worlds, and do evil that good may come; both control the devas, and attempt to produce specific ends by manipulation of the matter of the form. The Hierarchy works with the soul within the form and produces results that are intelligent, self-induced and permanent. Wherever attention is centred on the form and not on the Spirit, the tendency is to deva worship, deva contact and black magic, for the *form* is made of deva substance on all planes.

This must be considered well in connection with every form for it holds the key to many mysteries.

We have seen how in this question of the transference of the life from form to form, the work proceeds under rule and order, and is effected through the co-operation of the devas in the first instance, and the application of external agents to the atom or form involved, and in the second place (involving the most important and lengthy stage of the procedure) through the subsequent reaction within the atom itself, which produces an intensification of the positive burning centre, and the consequent escape (through radioactivity) of the volatile essence.

At all the different stages, the fire elementals perform their part, aided by the fire devas who are the controlling agents. This is so on all the planes which primarily concern us in the three worlds—different groups of devas coming into action according to the nature of the form concerned, and the plane on which the transmutation is to take place. Electric fire passes from atom to atom according to law, and "fire by friction" responds, being the latent fire of the atom, or its negative aspect; the process is carried on through the medium of solar fire, and herein lies the secret of transmutation and its most mysterious angle. Fire by friction, the negative electricity of substance, has been for some time the subject of the attention of exoteric science, and investigation of the nature of positive electricity has become possible through the discovery of radium.

Keely, as H. P. B. hinted,[60] had gone far along this path, and knew even more than he gave out, and others have approached, or are approaching, the same objective. The next step ahead for science lies in this direction, and should concern the potential force of the atom itself, and its harnessing for the use of man. This will let loose upon earth a stupendous amount of energy. Nevertheless, it is only when the third factor is comprehended, and science admits the agency of mental fire as embodied in certain groups of devas, that the force of energy that is triple, and yet one in the three worlds, will become available for the helping of man. This lies as yet far ahead, and will only become possible towards the end of this round; and these potent forces will not be fully utilised, nor fully known till the middle of the next round. At that time, much energy will become available through the removal of all that obstructs. This is effected, in relation to man, at the Judgment separation, but it will produce results in the other kingdoms of nature also. A portion of the animal kingdom will enter into a temporary obscuration, thus releasing energy for

[60] S. D., I, 172, 607-611.

the use of the remaining percentage, and producing results such as are hinted at by the prophet of Israel [62]
when he speaks of "the wolf lying down with the lamb";
his comment "a little child shall lead them" is largely the
esoteric enunciation of the fact that three fifths of the human family will stand upon the Path, 'a little child' being
the name applied to probationers and disciples. In the
vegetable and mineral kingdoms a corresponding demonstration will ensue, but of such a nature as to be too
obscure for our comprehension.

The central factor of solar fire in the work of transmutation will come to be understood through the study
of the fire devas and elementals, who are fire, and who
are, in themselves (essentially and through active magnetic radiation), the external heat or vibration which
produces:

The force which plays upon the spheroidal wall of the
atom.

The response within the atom which produces radiation or the escape of volatile essence.

Speaking cosmically, and regarding the solar system as
itself a cosmic atom, we would consider that:

The abstractions or entities who indwell the form are
"electric fire."

The material substance which is enclosed within the
ring-pass-not viewing it as a homogeneous whole,
is "fire by friction."

The fire devas from the cosmic mental plane (of whom
Agni and Indra are the embodiers along with one
whose name is not to be given) are the external agencies who carry on cosmic transmutation.

This triple statement can be applied to a scheme, a
chain, or a globe also, remembering ever that in connec-

[62] Bible, Isaiah 11:6.

tion with man the fire which is his third aspect emanates from the systemic mental.

We have dealt in broad and general manner with this question of electricity and have seen that fire essence or substance is resolved through internal activity and external heat in such a manner that the electric fire at the centre of the atom is liberated and seeks a new form. This is the aim of the transmutative process and the fact that hitherto alchemists working in the mineral kingdom have failed to achieve their objective has been due to three things:

First. Inability to contact the central electric spark. This is due to ignorance of certain of the laws of electricity, and above all, ignorance of the set formula which covers the range of the electrical influence of that spark.

Second. Inability to create the necessary channel or "path" along which the escaping life may travel into its new form. Many have succeeded in breaking the form so that the life has escaped but they have not known how to harness or guide it and all their labour has consequently been lost.

Third. Inability to control the fire elementals who are the external fire which affects that central spark through the medium of its environment. This inability is especially distinctive of the alchemists of the fifth root race who have been practically incapable of this control, having lost the Words, the formulas, and the sounds. This is the consequence of undue success in Atlantean days, when the alchemists of the time, through colour and sound so entirely controlled the elementals that they utilised them for their own selfish ends and along lines of endeavours outside their legitimate province. This knowledge of formulas and sounds can be comparatively easily acquired when man has developed the inner spiritual ear. When this is the case, the transmutative processes of the grosser kind (such as are involved in the manufacture of pure gold) will interest him not at all and only those subtler forms of activity which are connected with the transference of life from graded form to form will occupy his attention.

The following facts might also be pointed out:

First. That every kingdom of nature has its note or tone, and the mantric sounds, which concern any transmutative process within that kingdom, will have that note as the key or base note.

Second. That the note of the mineral kingdom is the basic note of substance itself, and it is largely the sounding of the note combinations, based on this key, which produces the great world cataclysms, wrought through volcanic action. Every volcano is sounding forth this note, and, for those who can see, the sound and colour (occultly understood) of a volcano are a truly marvellous thing. Every gradation of that note is to be found in the mineral kingdom which is itself divided into three main kingdoms:

   a. The baser metals, such as lead and iron, with all allied minerals.

   b. The standard metals, such as gold and silver, which play such a vital part in the life of the race, and are the mineral manifestation of the second aspect.

   c. The crystals and precious stones, the first aspect as it works out in the mineral kingdom—the consummation of the work of the mineral devas, and the product of their untiring efforts.

When scientists fully appreciate what it is which causes the difference between the sapphire and the ruby, they will have found out what constitutes one of the stages of the transmutative process, and this they cannot do until the fourth ether is controlled, and its secret discovered. As time progresses, the transmutation, for instance, of coal into diamonds, of lead into silver, or of certain metals into gold, will hold no appeal for man, for it will be recognised that the outcome of such action would cause deterioration of the standard, and result in poverty instead of the acquirement of riches; man will eventually come to the realisation that in atomic energy, harnessed to his need, or in the inducing of increased radioactivity, lies for him the path to prosperity and riches. He will, therefore concentrate his attention on this higher form of life transference and

    a. Through knowledge of the devas,
    b. Through external pressure and vibration,
    c. Through internal stimulation,
    d. Through colour applied in stimulation and vitalisation,
    e. Through mantric sounds

he will find the secret of atomic energy, latent in the mineral kingdom, and will bend that inconceivable power and force to the solution of the problems of existence. Only when atomic energy is better understood and the nature of the fourth ether somewhat comprehended, shall we see that control of the air which lies inevitably ahead.

Third. By the discovery of the note of the vegetable kingdom, by its conjunction with other of nature's notes, and by its due sounding forth in different keys and combinations will come the possibility to produce marvellous results within that kingdom, and to stimulate the activities of those devas who work with flowers, fruits, trees and herbs.

Every root race has its own particular style of vegetation, or certain basic forms and designs which can be traced in all countries where the race locates. These results are brought about by the interaction between the basic note of the vegetable kingdom itself, and the note of the race of men who are evolving simultaneously. The union of these two notes is that which produces distinctive vegetation, though it should be remembered that when the human note dominates too strongly it is apt to drive out the life of the forms of this second kingdom. The devas who work in this kingdom are a special group, and have a closer and more peculiar relation to it than have the builders or devas in any other kingdom. The transmutative process is effected more easily in the vegetable kingdom than in any other owing to this very factor, and also to the incentive given to this second kingdom and its evolutionary process by the coming of the Lords of the Flame from the second or Venus globe—preeminently the globe with which this kingdom has a mysterious connection. If I might express it in other words: the cosmic Entity, Who is the life of the second globe and its informing principle, has a close connection with the solar Entity Who is the informing life of the entire vegetable kingdom. This analogy can be worked out in connection with the other kingdoms, globes and other forms and accounts somewhat for the fact that this fourth [63, 64] globe is above everything else the globe of human evolution in this scheme; it gives also the clue to the mystery of the Presence of the great Kumara Himself upon earth. These thoughts merit close attention.

[63] The Fourth Round. The present (our) Round being the middle Round (between the 1st, 2nd, and 3rd, and the 5th, 6th and 7th) is one of adjustment and final equipoise between Spirit and matter. It is that point, in short, wherein the reign of *true* matter, its grossest state (which is as unknown to Science as its opposite pole—homogeneous matter or substance) stops and comes to an end. From that point physical man begins to throw off ''coat after coat,'' of his material molecules for the benefit and subsequent formation or clothing of the animal kingdom, which in its turn is passing it on to the vegetable, and the latter to the mineral kingdoms. Man having evoluted in the *first* Round from the animal via the two other kingdoms, it stands to reason that in the present Round he should appear before the animal world of this manvantaric period. But see the *Secret Doctrine* for particulars.—*Lucifer*, Vol. III, p. 253.

[64] S. D., I, 107.

The note of the human kingdom, sounded in quadruple intensity on this globe, has produced portentous happenings, and I would suggest to all occult investigators the close study and scrutiny of the following manifestations in time and space:

1. The fourth Creative Hierarchy .... The human.
2. The fourth scheme .... Our earth scheme.
3. The fourth chain .... The earth chain.
4. The fourth globe .... Our planet.
5. The fourth kingdom .... The human.
6. The fourth round .... The first strictly human round.
7. The four Kumaras .... Embodiers of humanity.
8. The fourth plane .... The buddhic, the human goal.
9. The fourth ether .... The physical correspondence of the buddhic plane.

One fundamental sound is responded to by all these varied factors; it is the note that is the cause of their existence and the basis of their being. This note, if sought for and found, will bring into close alliance all of these factors till they are blended into a great occult unity; it will bring likewise into co-operation the band of devas who are the essences of the fourth human principle.

  b. Synthesis. We have seen that during the coming races and subraces certain very definite development may be looked for in connection with manasic unfoldment; and it is worth while to note particularly that as far as the evolution of manas in this round is concerned its highest efflorescence may be looked for during the next five hundred years. The coming in of the two final root races marks the point of synthesis, and the gradual utilisation of that which has been manasically achieved; this will be brought about by a development of abstract thought, and of intuitive recognition. In other words, manas has (during the past three root races) been principally applied to the understanding of objective existence, to the adaptation of the Dweller in the form to his environment on the physical plane. From now on the trend of activity will be towards the understanding of the subjective side of manifestation, and towards the comprehension of the psyche of the individual life, divine, planetary, or human. In the next round, all the previous stages will be recapitulated, and manas will demonstrate in ways inconceivable as yet to the half awakened consciousness of man. In that round three-fifths of the human family will be fully aware, functioning with uninterrupted continuity of recollection on the physical, astral, and lower mental planes. The emphasis of manasic evolution will be laid upon the achievement of causal consciousness, and upon the scientific construction of the bridge which should unite the causal vehicle and the permanent manasic atom on the abstract levels.

During the sixth and seventh rounds we shall again have the synthesising process at work in a manner analogous to that which lies ahead in the sixth and seventh root races of this round.

To express the whole matter in larger terms: The Heavenly Man will be achieving the consciousness of his causal body on cosmic levels, with a consequent reaction, repolarisation and alignment of His body of manifestation. Under the law this will work out as demonstrated quality, and ordered intelligent purpose in every kingdom of nature, and will produce unifying results within those kingdoms of a kind inexplicable to man at his present stage of manasic development. We need not, therefore, give further time to the consideration of them, for the mental concept of man could not measure up to the magnitude of the theme.

In summing up what I have written anent this matter of the discriminative faculty, the intelligent activity, the adaptability nature, and the transmutative power of manas, I would like to point out that so far-reaching are these developments that every department of nature, macrocosmic and microcosmic, will show forth these aspects, and show them forth in a ninefold manner before the consummation is achieved, and man has found his course.

Let us, therefore, look for a brief moment at the microcosmic manifestation, leaving the student as far as he is able to work out analogous ideas in relation to the Heavenly Man and the solar Logos:

Manasic characteristics and the planes

I. *On the Physical Plane:* Here this quality demonstrates as:

   a. The selective power of the atoms of the body.

   b. The adaptability of the physical form to its environment and to its circumstances.

   c. The ordered purpose of the informing Life, as it affects the physical form and atoms.

   d. The transmutative power, inherent in man though as yet unrecognised by him, which has brought him to his present stage of physical existence from that of animal man. It concerns also the transference of the life on to manasic levels.

II. *On the Astral Plane:*

   a. The discriminative power of man to choose between the pairs of opposites.

   b. His adaptability to emotional conditions, and his power to attain eventual equilibrium.

   c. The power of man, through conscious purpose, to *clear* his astral body of foreign matter, and to ensure its translucence.

   d. The transmutative inherent power which transmutes, or transfers the life into buddhic forms eventually.

III. *On the Mental Plane:*

   a. In the selective power of man to choose the form through which to manifest.

b. His adaptability to mental currents and vibration, and his utilisation of them to control the lower forms.

c. The working out of purpose through the medium of the two lower vehicles. Impulse emanates from the mental plane.

d. The transmutative power which transforms the entire lower threefold man into a new form, the causal body. This process of transmutation is carried on through the entire series of incarnations.

IV. *On the Abstract Levels of the Mental Plane.*

a. The ability of the Ego to discriminate as to time and space in the three worlds.

b. Egoic adaptation of matter and circumstance of time and environment to the specific need under the Law of Karma.

c. The 'Intelligent Purpose' which lies back of all physical objectivity, and which is seen working out in every life.

d. The transmutation or transference into the Triad of the life of the Ego as it functions in the causal body. This results in dissociation from manifestation in the three worlds. To effect this transmutation (which is a point at times overlooked) the Thinker in the causal vehicle has to do three things:

    1. Build and equip the causal body.

    2. Bring about conscious connection or control of the threefold lower nature through the agency of the permanent atoms.

    3. Bridge the interlude between the causal body on its own level, and the manasic permanent atom.

V. *On Buddhic Levels:*

  a. Discriminative power here demonstrates as ability to distinguish between the abstract and the concrete, and to arrive at conclusions apart from the ordinary apparatus—the mental body and the physical brain.

  b. Adaptability to Hierarchical enterprise shown by the Initiate or Master, and His receptivity to life impulses and spiritual currents emanating from the planetary Logos of His Ray—a thing at this stage impossible of conscious realisation.

  c. In the ordered purpose which guides the choice by a Master of one of the seven Paths of endeavour. Thus choice is based on KNOWLEDGE, and not on desire.

  d. In the conscious transmutation He undertakes in the work of evolution, and in the gradual transference of His own life, and the life of His group, into the monadic aspect which is reflected in the buddhic.

VI. *On Atmic Levels:*

  a. In the selective work of the adept as it relates to planetary manifestation, and the discriminative power which guides all action relating to His own planet, and the two others associated with the Earth, as a systemic triangle.

  b. The adaptation of groups (deva and human) to certain types of influence, and vibration, which emanate extra-systemically, and which from high cosmic levels play upon groups, fostering certain attributes for which we have, as yet, no terminology.

  c. The synthesising work of the Brahma aspect as it works out in the blending of the four minor rays into the third major.

d. The transmutation which results in planetary obscuration in connection with five of the Heavenly
Men and which—as in the previous work of synthesis—concerns microcosmic evolution and is par-
ticipated in by man. I would call attention to an
interesting point: as more and more of the Monads
are resolved back into their source it produces a
gradual obscuration of the particular Heavenly
Man in Whose body they are the cells. Though
this may look to human vision as extending over a
profoundly long period, from the point of view of
universal or group consciousness it is occurring
now. For instance, such an event as the obscuration of the manifestation of the Logos of our
Earth scheme is already in process and began in
Lemurian days.

VII. As regards monadic discrimination, adaptability,
purpose and transmutative power it is needless to
enlarge.

All these ideas and concepts are of value only in so
far as they produce within the Thinker a more intelligent
appreciation of the grandeur of the divine plan, an appropriation of the energy and force which is his by right of
participation in the processes of manifestation, and a
wise co-operation in the furtherance of the evolutionary
plan as it affects him individually and his groups.

SECTION TWO

DIVISION C

THE EGOIC RAY AND SOLAR FIRE

I. The Nature of the Causal Body

1. It is formed by the contact of the two fires of Spirit and matter.
2. It is produced at individualisation.

II. The Nature of the Permanent Atoms

1. Their purpose.

   a. They are force distributors.
   b. Conservers of faculty.
   c. Assimilators and transmuters.
   d. Vehicles of memory.

2. Their place in the Egoic Body.

   a. The astral permanent atom.
   b. The atomic triangle.

3. The Spirillae and the Egoic Ray.

   a. The composition of the permanent atoms.
   b. The planes and fiery energy.
   c. The three fires.

4. Summary.

III. The Egoic Lotus

1. Wheels or centres of energy.
   a. Centres of force.
   b. The causal body, the monadic heart centre.

2. *The twelve-petalled Lotus.*

    a. The knowledge petals.
    b. The love petals.
    c. The sacrifice petals.

3. *Summary.*

I. THE NATURE OF THE EGOIC OR CAUSAL BODY

The subject of the egoic Ray and its relation to the second fire is one of vital import to three types of people: Those who are interested in the true psychology, or in the evolution of the psyche; those who are on or nearing the Path, and hence are coming more and more into touch with their own Ego; those who work with the souls of men, the servers of the race.

The reason for this is because in the due comprehension of this subject, that of the Ego functioning in the causal body, comes the ability to work scientifically with the problem of one's own evolution, and to do good work in aiding the evolution of one's brother.

1. *Egoic manifestation is produced through the medium of two fires.*

Let us therefore consider somewhat the subject of the egoic Ray and the causal body, viewing it from the standpoint of the microcosm, and leaving the student to work out for himself the analogies where the Logos is concerned, conjuring him to bear in mind that the analogy must ever be drawn with due emphasis upon the fact that all that the human unit can comprehend is the manifestation of the solar Logos in a physical body.

In all manifestation, as we well know, we have duality producing triplicity. Spirit meets and contacts matter; the result of that contact is the birth of the Son, or the Ego, the consciousness aspect. The egoic manifestation is therefore the middle aspect, the place of at-one-ment,

and (after due evolutionary cycles) the place of balance,
or of equilibrium. It should be noted that the analogy
between the Logos and man is not accurate, for man has
to undergo the whole process *within* the solar periphery,
whilst the Logos (within that periphery) goes through
the stage analogous to that which the man undergoes
when his astral sheath clothes itself with etheric matter and he takes physical incarnation, which was
touched upon when considering the subject of "Fire by
friction." It will consequently be apparent that, in considering the manifestation of the Ego, we are dealing with
the point of central emphasis in man's threefold manifestation. We are concerning ourselves with that division
of his nature which concerns the process of making him
the perfect six-pointed star during the preliminary stage
(the threefold personality and the threefold Triad
merged and blended and perfectly produced through the
intermediate point the causal body) and which, when the
physical body is eliminated, makes him the five-pointed
star or perfected manasaputra.

To state the whole in terms of fire: The causal body
is produced by means of the positive life, or fire, of the
Spirit (electric fire) meeting the negative fire of matter,
or "fire by friction"; this causes the blazing forth of
solar fire. This central blaze inevitably in due course
burns up the third fire, or absorbs its essence, and is
itself eventually blended with the fire of Spirit and passes
out of objective display.

I seek here to deal with the subject of the causal body
in two different ways—one along the old lines and the
other strictly along the lines of occult electrical phenomena.

2. *Egoic manifestation is produced at individualisation.*

The causal body is that sheath of mental substance
which is formed at the moment of individualisation by

the contact of the two fires. The force or energy that pours through from the higher planes (the breath of the Monad, if you care so to term it) produces a vacuum, or something analogous to a bubble in koilon, and the sheath of the causal body—the ring-pass-not of the central Life is formed. Within this sheath are to be found three atoms, which have been termed the mental unit, the astral permanent atom and the physical permanent atom; they correspond individually to the seventh principle of each of the three persons of the microcosmic triad, a reflection (in the three worlds of the microcosm) of the three Persons of the logoic Trinity. H. P. B. hints at this in connection with the Logos when she speaks of the visible sun being the seventh principle of the Brahma aspect, the physical permanent atom of the Logos.[65, 66]

II. THE NATURE OF THE PERMANENT ATOMS

1. *The purpose of the permanent atoms.*

The three permanent atoms are in themselves centres of force, or those aspects of the personality which hold hid the fires of substance, or of objectivity; it cannot be too strongly pointed out at this juncture that, in considering the threefold man in the three worlds, we are dealing with substance which (in connection with logoic manifestation) is considered the dense physical. Surrounding these three atoms is the causal sheath, answering the following purposes:

It separates one unit of egoic consciousness from another unit of consciousness, yet is itself part of the gaseous body (the fifth cosmic physical subplane) in the physical body of the planetary Logos, Who is the central life of any particular group of Monads. This fact has been little appreciated, and merits careful consideration.

[65] S. D., III, 143.
[66] S. D., I, 574.

It holds hid spiritual potentialities in its inherent ability to respond to the higher vibration; from the moment of individualisation till it is discarded at initiation, the life within steadily develops these potentialities, and produces certain definite results by the utilisation of the three permanent atoms. It gradually vivifies and awakens them until, on the three planes, the central life has an adequate point of contact which can originate the necessitated vibration in the matter of the plane.

The permanent atoms on each plane serve a fourfold purpose as regards the central or egoic life:

They are the distributors of a certain type of force.

They are the conservers of faculty or ability to respond to a particular vibration.

They are the assimilators of experience and the transmuters of that experience into quality. This is the direct result of the work of the egoic Ray as it plays upon the atom.

They hold hid the memory of the unit of consciousness. When fully vibrant they are the *raison d'être* for the continuity of the consciousness of the man functioning in the causal body. This distinction must be carefully made.

We must always remember in studying these difficult matters that we are dealing with the logoic dense physical body and that:

The mental unit is found in logoic gaseous matter.

The astral permanent atom in logoic liquid matter.

The physical permanent atom in dense physical substance.

And they therefore have their place in matter of the three lowest subplanes of the physical body of the Logos. Consequently when in the process of evolution, and through initiation, man achieves the consciousness of the Spiritual Triad, and transfers his polarisation into the three triadal permanent atoms, he is simply able to function *consciously* in the etheric body of his particular planetary Logos. Work out the analogy in the microcosmic development and note how in order to function consciously in his individual etheric body a man has to burn through what has been called the etheric web, and study how the fires of initiation produce something analogous in the planetary etheric body, and eventually in the cosmic etheric. As each unit of consciousness, through self-induced effort, achieves the goal and crosses the 'burning-ground,' a microscopic portion of the etheric web of the planetary etheric body is consumed by fire; this results in a definite gain for that great Entity, the planetary Logos, through the relatively unimportant liberation of the force of one cell in His body. When all the units or cells in His body have achieved, He too is set free from dense manifestation and *physically dies*. This stage is succeeded by the comparatively brief one of etheric existence (covering the period of planetary obscuration), and then He is liberated from incarnation altogether.

Viewing this process from the standpoint of the Logos, the Brahma aspect passes out, or the life withdraws from the physical permanent atom, leaving later stages on cosmic levels, with which we need not concern ourselves. These cover the withdrawal of the logoic life from out of the other two aspects. In a solar system, which is a physical incarnation of the Logos, the Brahma aspect is apparently the most important, it being the medium of expression, yet it is the subjective aspect, or the life-desire of the Logos which is fundamentally of moment; this concerns His endeavour on high levels, and on cosmic planes beyond the ken of the highest Chohan.

It might be of value here if I pointed out that the Egoic Ray of the human unit [67] with which we are con-

---

[67] The human Ray. ''Each human centre is a crystallised ray of the Absolute One that has worked through processes of evolution into what is known as a human being.''—*Some Thoughts on the Gita.*

cerning ourselves, manifests *as regards each ray* just as does the logoic manifestation. *Each* of the seven Rays, viewed in connection with the causal bodies of men, demonstrates as a unity on the first subplane, as a triplicity on the second and as seven on the third, forming there the forty-nine groups which most concern evolving man. According to the angle of vision, this numbering of groups may be increased or lessened, but for purposes of studying the aspects of mind, the above enumeration suffices. In the course of his many septenary lives, and as the cyclic sevens pass over him, man passes under the influence of the seven sub-rays of his own Ray. Then he begins to synthesise and merge the seven into the major three sub-rays, returning thus to unity on his own egoic Ray.

> *First.* The septenary status governs the time from individualisation till he enters upon the Path.
>
> *Second.* The threefold status governs the time up till the third Initiation.
>
> *Third.* He achieves the unity of his Ray by the fifth Initiation, and is then *consciously* a part of the body of the Heavenly Man.

The same idea can be worked out in connection with the awakening of the life forces within the permanent atoms, viewing each atom as the seventh principle in each of the three aspects of the personality.

2. *Their Place in the Egoic Body.*

   a. The importance of the astral permanent atom. There is one fact to be grasped in connection with the place of the permanent atom within the causal periphery and its evolution, that needs to be emphasised with care, and that is that the *astral permanent atom* in this solar system is the recipient of a great flow of force or energy, and receives more stimulation and energising than any of the others, and this for the following reasons:

First. The centre of polarisation for the fourth, or human kingdom, is in the astral consciousness viewing this kingdom as a unity in expression. From the astral, and through the desire nature, the majority of men inevitably direct and control the physical vehicle. The astral body is in the direct line of force via the buddhic from monadic levels, 2-4-6.

Second. The goal set before humanity is that of becoming Masters of the Wisdom, or conscious units in the Body of the Dragon of Wisdom or of Love. This a man achieves when he can function consciously in the buddhic vehicle, or when the astral permanent atom is superseded by the buddhic permanent atom.

Third. The next reason is that the second aspect of the Logos (that of love or the manifestation of the love nature of the Logos through the medium of the·Son) is the one demonstrated in this system. This system is:

a. A Son of Necessity, or of desire

b. Vibrant to the key of the cosmic Ray of Love

c. The form through which this ray of cosmic Love (shown in the inter-relation between the Self and the Not-Self, or through duality) is expressing itself

d. Governed by the cosmic Law of Attraction. The monads of love are the dominating quality. (I choose this word 'quality' specifically.)

Fourth. The centre in the cosmic body of the ONE ABOUT WHOM NOUGHT MAY BE SAID of which our solar Logos is the embodied force is the *heart centre.* Here we have one of the clues to the mystery of electricity. The sacred planets, with certain allied etheric spheres within the ring-pass-not, are parts of that heart centre, and are 'petals in the Lotus,' or in the heart centre of that great unknown Existence Who stands to the solar Logos as He in His turn stands to the Heavenly

Men Who are His centres, and specially as He stands to the particular Heavenly Man Who is the embodied force of the logoic Heart centre. Therefore, it will be apparent to the careful student that the entire force and energy of the system and its life quality will be that which we call (having perforce to use handicapping, misleading words) LOVE. This will account for the fact that the force that plays through that cosmic heart centre will be the paramount force found in the manifestation of a solar Logos, and of a Heavenly Man; it will likewise produce its microcosmic analogy, and reflective reactions; hence the relative importance of the astral permanent atom within the causal periphery. It is in the direct line of active force emanating from the cosmic existence, and passing to it in ever lessening degree, via the solar Logos in His system of love, and the planetary Logos within a scheme, the Dragon of Wisdom-Love.

This force when rightly directed and properly controlled is the great transmuting agency, which eventually will make of the human unit a Master of the Wisdom, a Lord of Love, a Dragon of Wisdom in lesser degree.

Finally: this solar system, the objective physical manifestation of the Logos, is interpenetrated by His astral body, as is the case with the human manifestation. As the Logos is polarised in His cosmic astral sheath and has not yet attained cosmic mental polarisation His force or desire nature is the main incentive for the subjective Life and lives that underlie the form.

If the student will ponder with care these five facts, he will get a clue to the problems of existence as realised around us, to the causes of the heat of the solar system, to the method of the cosmic Law of Attraction and Repulsion, which governs all atomic forms, and to the question of SEX which is apparent in every kingdom of nature. They give the clue also to the constitution of the Divine Hermaphrodite.

Therefore, it is necessary to bear in mind the relative importance of the permanent atom of the second aspect of the personality within the causal periphery, and to remember that the force which flows through that atom and which is the animating force of the astral body is following the lines of least resistance and really might be considered as bearing upon his physical manifestation in a manner twice as strong as that reaching him through the other two.   The Logos expresses Himself now through the Divine Ray, His second aspect, and this Ray is the sumtotal of the radiation of the Lords of Wisdom, the Heavenly Men, the Dragons Who are Unity and Who are Love.   Through Them this force flows, and They in turn clothe Themselves with form, or as H. P. B. expresses it 'The primordial Ray becomes the vahan for the Divine Ray.' [68]   Their life animates every atom of substance when built into form, and Their life is the sumtotal of Logoic magnetism, or the great desire nature of the Logos going out after the Not-Self, producing the cosmic Marriage; it is the logoic demonstration of the sex appeal, His search for His polar opposite, and their mystic union.

This process is repeated by the microcosm following the line of his being, and this brings him likewise into incarnation, or into mystic union with form.

b. The atomic triangle.   The causal sheath is to the clairvoyant therefore a sphere of vibrant living substance; within it can be seen three fiery points.   At the heart of the sphere is a central blaze of light, emitting

---

[68] *The Divine Ray contains within itself seven other rays.*
It is the swan with the seven young ones.
It is the Logos of love-wisdom with the seven planetary Logoi.
It is the Grand Man of the Heavens, with the seven Heavenly Men.
It is the One Boundless Principle, with the seven principles.
                    This is subjectively.
It is the seven planets with their informing entities.
It is the seven planes with their animating principles.
    Love-Wisdom is the manifestation of the astral (or desire) nature of the Solar Logos.—S. D., I, 103.

rays; these rays are given as seven in number, and play upon these points or circles (analogous to the electrons in the atoms of science) and *at this stage* produce most effect upon the astral permanent atom. The physical permanent atom has a position relatively close to the positive centre, and the force plays through it, and passes on to the astral permanent atom in the form of five rays of parti-coloured light which blend with the intensely vivid hue of the astral permanent atom, and increase its intensity until the blaze is so excessive that it appears to the onlooker as if the two points blended, or the two electrons merged, and (in merging) produce such an intensity of light that they are seen as dissolving. The mental unit, having a position within the causal body analogous to the planet furthermost from the sun, becomes vibrant likewise, and the two other points (considered now as one) begin to interact with the mental unit, and a similar process is set up and is pursued until these two points—circulating around their positive centre— also approach each other, blend, merge, and dissolve. The centre of positive life gathers or synthesises the three points, and thus the *three fires of the personality* repeat on their tiny scale the microcosmic procedure as seen in the synthesis of electric fire, solar fire, and fire by friction, and only a blazing unit is left. This blazing unit, through the combined heat of its being, burns up the causal body, and escapes back on to the planes of abstraction. Thus man is the Path itself, and also the pilgrim upon the Path; thus does he burn, but is also the burning-ground.

The analogy holds true in the case of the microcosm viewed from monadic levels in his manifestation as Monad, Ego and Personality, and thus the process is carried on as it concerns a Heavenly Man, and likewise a solar Logos. Should the brain suffice to hold the concept, thus

is the process also on cosmic levels for such high existences as the seven Rishis of the Great Bear, and that still
greater Being, the ONE ABOUT WHOM NOUGHT MAY BE
SAID.

3. *The Spirillae and the Egoic Ray.*

We will take up now the subject of the spirillae within
the permanent atom, and see in what manner they are
affected by the egoic ray, remembering always that we
are considering them as:

First. The interior economy of the life germ on the
three planes which concern man in the three worlds;
second, as the seventh principle in each of the three
sheaths; and third, as the positive nucleus of force which
holds together the matter of the three sheaths.

Let us therefore study two things:

> The composition of the permanent atom.
> The difference between the mental unit and the astral
> and physical permanent atoms.

To do this with clarity, and so bring some kind of definite
concept into being from the dark regions of abstraction,
let us tabulate:

a. The composition of the permanent atom: The permanent atom of the astral and physical planes is a sphere
of physical or astral substance, composed of atomic matter, and characterised by the following qualities:

Responsiveness. This is its inherent power to respond
to the vibration of some one of the Heavenly Men, as it
is transmitted via the deva, or Brahma aspect, of His
threefold nature. The permanent atom finds its place
within the sphere of influence of one or other of the great
devas who are the Raja-Lords of a plane.

Form Building Power. These devas sound forth two
syllables of the threefold microcosmic word and are each
(on their own plane) the coherent agency which gathers

substance into form, and attracts matter for purposes of objectivity. The *astral* sound produces the microcosmic 'Son of Necessity,' and when it reverberates on the *physical* plane produces physical incarnation, and the sudden appearance on etheric levels of the seven centres. The building of the dense physical is the result of consequent automatic action in deva essence, for it must ever be borne in mind that man is essentially (as regards the physical plane) an etheric being, and his dense physical body is esoterically regarded as 'below the threshold' and is not considered a principle.

Relative Permanency. In the seventh principle of all manifesting entities is stored up and developed capacity, acquired ability, and the atomic memory, or in other words the *heredity* of the Thinker, viewing him from the physical standpoint or from the emotional. There is no permanence whatever in the sheaths; they are built into temporary forms, and dissolved when the Thinker has exhausted their possibilities, but the seventh principle of each sheath gathers to itself the achieved qualities and stores them up—under the Law of Karma—to work out again and to demonstrate as the *plane impulse* at each fresh cycle of manifestation. This permanency is itself likewise only a relative one, and as the inner fire within the atom burns more brightly, as the external fires of the ego or solar fire beat upon it with ever increasing intensity, the atom in due time is consumed, and the inner blaze becomes so great that it destroys its encompassing wall.

Heat. Herein lies the distinction between the permanent atoms on all planes, and the atomic matter of which they form a part. It is not easy to make this distinction clear, nor is it desirable at this time; the true facts of the case are one of the guarded secrets of initiation, but the distinction between the permanent atom, and atomic matter, may be somewhat comprehended if we state:

The permanent atom is one that has been appropriated by one of the lives that form the *centres* in the body of a solar Lord, whilst atomic matter *per se* goes to the formation of other parts of His great body of light.

A permanent atom is one which has come under the attractive power of the second aspect, whilst atomic matter itself is vitalised by the life of the third aspect.

A permanent atom follows the line of the least resistance of force, and is passing out of the control of the Deva Lord and coming under the control of positive life. This concerns the evolution of consciousness in substance.

A permanent atom comes under the direct control of the lower of the three groups of Lipika Lords, and is the agency through which They work in the imposition of karma upon the particular entity who may be utilising it. They work directly with the permanent atoms of men, and produce results through the agency of form until they have exhausted the vibratory capacity of any particular atom; when this is the case the atom passes into the stage of obscuration, as does the seventh principle of any sheath. It comes under the influence of the first aspect, manifesting as the Destroyer.

Remember that in these affirmations we are concerning ourselves with the microcosm, and with the permanent atoms which are related to him; as regards the solar Logos manifesting in the system, we are concerned with but one permanent atom, and this is His physical permanent atom. It is thus true that within the permanent physical atom of the solar Logos lies hid the ability to respond consciously to the vibration of all the planes, lies hid the secret of the karmic purpose of His incarnation, and lies concealed the mystery of His functional activity; but we cannot penetrate the secret as yet of His three lower permanent atoms as they function as a unity within His causal vehicle. Until we can do this it is useless for us to conjecture as to His fundamental Being.

The difference between them: The mental unit is in a unique and peculiar position as regards man, the Thinker in the causal body. This point will be discussed shortly, suffice it to say here that its mystery lies hid in the nature of the Heavenly Men Themselves. The following correspondence holds the key to this mystery, but it can only be indicated, leaving it to the student to work out the truth for himself. On the three planes of logoic manifestation—the highest three—we have the three aspects manifesting; on the buddhic plane, the fourth cosmic ether, we have the logoic etheric centres demonstrating, or those force vortices which animate the three lower planes of the dense physical manifestation. In connection with the Heavenly Men we have a secondary manifestation, and on the buddhic plane we have Their third aspect found, leaving for Their paramount manifestation of force, the cosmic gaseous plane, or the manasic plane; They are essentially the divine Thinkers, the Manasaputras. In connection, therefore, with the Microcosm, viewing him as part of a centre in the body of a Heavenly Man, we have a lesser descent within the gaseous or fire manifestation of a solar Lord. This concerns the three higher subplanes of what might be considered as the manifestation of Man's three higher aspects in mental matter, whilst on the fourth subplane we have the mental centres of man within the periphery of his mental body, of which the mental unit is the unifying factor. This is—as has been earlier said—a deep mystery, and one that can be no further amplified.

b. The Planes and Fiery Energy. It seems desirable

that we should here discuss the analogies on each plane,[69] with the seven sub-planes, reminding the student that we are speaking of the planes as the field of evolution of a solar Logos, and not only as a field for the development of man. In the solar system we have:

First, the three higher planes, which have been rightly called the planes of the three aspects; second, the seventh logoic principle is on the first plane, and we can consider it as the impulse in physical matter which produced His body of objectivity.

On the second plane are found the seven Heavenly Men, Who are His principal centres of force. There are others, but we are not here concerned with Them. These latter have achieved a certain specific goal, and are the

---

* 1. The seven systemic planes are:

    1. Divine plane...Logos......1st cosmic ether.
    2. Monadic plane..Monad..... 2nd cosmic ether.
    3. Spiritual plane ....3rd cosmic ether.
    4. Intuitional plane ....4th cosmic ether.
    5. Mental plane..Ego........gaseous plane.
    6. Astral plane ....liquid plane.
    7. Physical ....gross.

2. The seven differentiations in terms of fiery energy are:

    a. Plane of divine life........Father..............Sea of fire.
    b. Plane of monadic life.......Son................Akasha.
    c. Plane of atma.............Holy Ghost.........Aether.
    d. Plane of buddhi, intuition.. Central............Air.
    e. Plane of mind.......................................Fire.
    f. Plane of desire.....................................Astral Light.
    g. Plane of physical...................................Ether.

        Thought........Thoughtforms........Materialisation.
            Microcosm............Macrocosm.

3. Planes of logoic evolution.....the seven planes.
   Planes of Son's evolution.....the six planes.
   Planes of monadic evolution...the five planes.
   Planes of human evolution.....the three worlds.

    Seven is the number of the totality of manifestation.
    Three is the number of consciousness.
    One is the number of Life or Spirit.

4. Electric fire .....Solar fire ....Fire by friction.
   Father ....Son ....Holy Ghost.
   Spirit ....Consciousness ....Matter.

embodiment of centres which are now quiescent or out of manifestation, the logoic kundalini having turned its attention elsewhere. Under another enumeration they make the ten of the esoteric life, and can also be enumerated as twelve, thus forming the twelve-petalled Lotus, or the heart centre in the Body of the ONE ABOUT WHOM NOUGHT MAY BE SAID.

On the fourth cosmic ether the buddhic plane, are found the etheric centres of the Logos. There are to be found the esoteric planets and the Sun, viewed as the centre of the buddhic principles, and from thence the Logos animates His dense physical manifestation.

Finally, on the three lower planes we have His gaseous, liquid, and dense bodies or sheaths, forming in themselves a unity in one peculiar sense; they are as much a coherent whole as the three higher planes form a unified triple expression of the three persons of the Trinity.

We have a similar analogy in the subplanes of each plane in the system, and this will become ever more apparent as man achieves a greater clarity of vision, and can consciously ascertain for himself the truth about the subjective life. Let us briefly take these planes and study the life or force manifestation on each, laying the emphasis upon the lower four, and not so much upon the planes which do not concern man so closely.

The Logoic Plane. The first, the second, and the third subplanes of the first cosmic ether respond specifically to the vibration of one of the three aspects, or to those cosmic Entities Whose influence reaches the matter of the planes from without the system altogether. On the fourth subplane comes a primary blending of the three fiery Lives, producing archetypally that force manifestation of electricity which eventually causes the blazing forth of the Sons of Light on the next plane. In this electrical connotation we have the three higher planes ever embodying the threefold Spirit aspect, the lower three embodying the threefold substance aspect, and then a plane of at-one-ment whereon an approximation is made which, on the path of return, marks the moment of achievement, and the point of triumph. This is succeeded by obscuration. Hence on every plane in the solar system we have a fourth plane whereon the struggle for perfect illumination, and subsequent liberation takes place, the battle ground, the Kurukshetra. Though for man the fourth plane, the buddhic, is the place of triumph, and the goal of his endeavour, for the Heavenly Man it is the battle-ground, while for the solar Logos it is the burning-ground.

This differentiation of the subplanes of the systemic planes *into a higher three, a lower three, and a central plane of harmony is only so from the standpoint of electrical phenomena, and not from the standpoint of either pure Spirit, or pure substance, viewed apart from each other. It concerns the mystery of electricity, and the production of light.* The three higher planes concern the central Forces or Lives, the three lower concern the lesser Forces or Lives. We must bear this carefully in mind, remembering that to the occultist there is no such thing as substance, but only Force in varying degrees, only Energy of differentiated quality, only Lives emanating from different sources, each distinctive and apart, and only Consciousness producing intelligent effect through the medium of space.

I would point out that the Lord Agni shows forth His fiery life on the atomic subplane of each plane; He shows forth as solar fire on the second, third and fourth, and as 'fire by friction' on the fifth, sixth and seventh. From the point of view of the microcosm, the Spark in the Flame, man demonstrates as electric fire on the second plane, or the second cosmic ether; as solar fire on the third, fourth and the three higher subplanes of the fifth plane, and as fire by friction on the lower subplanes of the fifth, on the sixth, and seventh planes.

c. *The Planes and the Three Fires.* On every plane we have, relatively speaking:

a. Electric fire demonstrating as the prime condition on the higher three.

b. Fire by friction as the most significant factor on the lower three.

c. Solar fire, showing forth as the blaze produced by union on the central plane.

In the solar system this is to be seen in connection with a Heavenly Man on the buddhic plane, where They blaze forth through Their etheric centres. In connection with man on the mental plane, we have a similar condition: the three higher subplanes concern the Spirit aspect in the causal body, the three lower subplanes concern primarily the mental sheath, or fire by friction; the fourth subplane is that on which the force centres of the mental body are to be found. So it is on the physical plane for man—his etheric centres being located in matter of the fourth ether.

Each of the three Persons of the Trinity manifests equally as does a man, as Spirit, Soul or Ego, and Substance. In connection with Brahma, we have the Spirit aspect animating the three higher subplanes of every plane, or the first fire aspect. His soul aspect is found on the fourth subplane of each plane whereon are situated the etheric centres of all manifested entities. His substance aspect is primarily contacted on the three lower subplanes. Hence we have the forty-nine fires of matter, or the seven fires of each plane, the union of the higher three and the lower three producing that blaze which we call the wheels of fire or the centres on the fourth subplane of each plane.

In connection with the second aspect there is a similar

condition. Solar fire blazes forth in its electrical aspect on the second plane, and demonstrates thus also on the third and fourth planes, but finds its central demonstration on manasic levels, shining through the causal vehicles of the egoic groups. Only two and a half planes then remain through which the fire by friction aspect may manifest, eighteen subplanes in all which concern the third aspect of the second Person of the logoic Trinity.

For man, the microcosm, a similar differentiation is possible; His Monad can be studied in its threefold essence on its own plane, his egoic aspect likewise, and the Brahma aspect of the Ego is found within the permanent atoms. Students should therefore study with care:

1. *The Planes.* The manifestation of Brahma, the third or substance aspect, and should apply to this Entity the same triple constitution as is apparent in the other two. The planes of electric fire, the planes of his lower nature, and the point of blazing forth or conflagration for him (the etheric centres) must be carefully studied. Brahma is the positive life of matter; He is the revelation of substance and the blaze that can be seen.

2. *Vibration.* The manifestation of the second aspect. These vibrations of consciousness are the major three words which are the sumtotal of egoic life, the minor three which govern the third aspect of the Ego, and the chord of at-one-ment which is that which is sounding forth now.

The three aspects of Spirit as they are seen can only be expressed in terms of the other two in this solar system, and of their nature extra-systemically nought can profitably be said at this stage of cognition.

The above thoughts upon the planes, and the ninefold nature of all that is, take one into regions as yet almost beyond the grasp of man; yet *only when the substance* aspect is studied by the scientist in its triple nature will truth be approximated, and the true nature of electrical phenomena be comprehended; then and only then will electricity be harnessed and utilised by man as a unity, and not just in one of its aspects as at present; the negative electricity of the planet is all that is as yet contacted for commercial purposes. It must be remembered that this term is used in the sense of negative in relation to solar electricity. When man has found out how to contact and utilise positive solar electricity in combination with negative planetary electricity, we shall have a very dangerous condition brought about, and one of the factors which will eventually manifest in the destruction of the fifth root race by fire. At that great cataclysm—as the Bible says "the Heavens will melt with fervent heat." [70] This will be seen in a still greater degree in the next round, and will cause that destruction by fire of the forms of the men who have failed, which will liberate the lives on a stupendous scale, and thus temporarily 'purify' the Earth from elements which would tend to hinder the evolutionary process. As the cycles pass away, the balancing of these fiery currents will be gradually brought about, and will result in a planetary condition of harmony, and of esoteric equality, which will provide ideal environment for harmonious man.

Only when the soul aspect is studied by the psychologist in its threefold essential nature will the mystery of consciousness become apparent, and the nature of the three magnetic groups, in their various subdivisions with their consequent effectual radiation become a factor in the public life. This concerns itself with the definite development of the psyche under law, with the scientific expansion of the consciousness, and will eventually bring about conditions wherein the work, preliminary to the first initiation, will be purely exoteric, and no longer

[70] Bible. II Peter, 3:10.

part of an esoteric process. In due course of time, it will
be found that the self-induced efforts whereby a man consciously prepares his centres for the application of the
Rod of Initiation at the first Initiation, will be the subject
of books, and of lectures, and form part of the ordinary
thought of the masses. This again will eventuate in a
cleavage between the two groups in the middle of the
fifth round. It must be remembered that this cleavage
will be part of a natural process, and not a drastic ruling,
imposed upon an unwilling people. The KNOWERS and
the students of the Knowledge—actuated by group consciousness, and working consciously—will separate
themselves *in group formation* from those who know not,
and from those who care not. This cleavage will be self-
induced, and a natural outgrowth of the group life; it
will in itself be of a temporary nature for the fundamental aim in view will be the bringing about of an eventual closer merging; it will mark primarily the line of
demarcation between the lower four Rays of consciousness, and the higher three. It is also a mystery hid in the
relationship between the four exoteric Kumaras,[71] and
the esoteric three, and from the point of view of man
separates those who are developing the consciousness of
the Triad from those who as yet are living the life of the
Quaternary. It concerns those who respond to the solar
Lords, distinguishing them from those who recognise as
yet only the control of the lunar Lords. In terms of
Fire: those who warm themselves by means of fire by
friction and respond not to the heat of solar fire remain
within the cavern, thus living in the dark; whilst those
whose being is irradiated by the Sun of Wisdom, and
who bask in the rays of solar heat dwell in the light, and
enjoy an ever increasing freedom, and vital existence.

The true significance of the three aspects of Spirit is
only becoming apparent to the initiate of high degree,

[71] S. D., i, 116, 493; II, 112, 149.

and cannot be expressed in words, nor comprehended by man before he has passed out of the human kingdom into the spiritual. Therefore, it is needless for us to pause here to consider it at greater length.

We might sum up the matter in terms of the Old Commentary from which source H. P. B. quoted so often:

"The Blessed Ones hide Their threefold nature, but reveal Their triple essence by means of the three great groups of atoms. Three are the atoms, and threefold the radiation. The inner core of fire hides itself and is known only through radiation and that which radiates. Only after the blaze dies out and the heat is no longer felt can the fire be known."

We can now resume our consideration of the mystery of the mental unit, and note wherein it differs from the other permanent atoms; we might then briefly summarise a mass of esoteric information anent the permanent atoms, which will suffice for many years to come as the basis of investigation for occult students. The permanent atoms, and their internal economy, will remain a mystery for a long time, and only a few general indications can here be given.

The fundamental difference between the mental unit and the other two atoms consists in the fact that it contains only four spirillae instead of seven. This is brought about by the very facts of evolution itself, for the mental unit is the first aspect of the personality triad, or of man functioning in the human kingdom on the three lower planes. At his transference into the spiritual kingdom, these three aspects—the mental body, the astral body, and the physical body—are synthesised into the higher by a dual process:

1. His polarisation shifts from out of the lower three atoms into the Triadal atoms.
2. The force which these atoms generate and embody is merged and blended into the higher force points.

A permanent atom is the positive nucleus or germ substance to the sheath wherein it is found. It is that which is the basis of form-building, and it is literally a vibrant point of force, emanating from the second aspect of the Monad, which aggregates to itself, and subsequently builds into form, the negative or third aspect. But it must here be remembered that this second aspect is itself dual, and that in considering the permanent atoms we are dealing with the feminine aspect of the second Person. The spirillae therefore are but streams of force, or second aspect vitality which circulates geometrically within the circumscribing wall of substance, composed of third aspect force or substance. What has been said of objectivity, or of the cosmic atom can be equally well predicated of the permanent atom of man the microcosm:

"The primordial ray is the vehicle of the divine Ray." [72] *Negative force forms a receptacle for positive force. Atoms are but force centres, and the centres as we know of them are but aggregates of force points which have reached a specific point in evolution, and are responding to the first great aspect in some degree, or to electric fire.*

This sentence, is one to be seriously pondered, for it holds hid much information for the student, and when duly comprehended will result in the light of knowledge being shed upon the problems of manifestation. It concerns the secret of the position of the different kingdoms of nature within the logoic body, and their place and part, for all depends upon the type of force which animates, upon the interplay of that force in substance, upon the dual, triple, or united aspect of force, and upon its septenary demonstration in form-building.

Every atom is a focal point of force, the force of substance itself, the life or vitality of the third aspect, the

[72] S. D., I, 108.

life of that cosmic Entity Who is *to the Logos* the negative aspect of electricity.

Every form [73] and aggregate of atoms, is simply a force
centre produced by the action of positive force and its
interaction with negative energy. It is the vitality of the
second aspect working in conjunction with the third, and
producing—in time and space—that illusion or maya
which temporarily blazes forth, and attracts attention,
creating the impression that matter is a concrete something. There is no such thing as concretion in reality;

[73] *Forms.*
1. *Divine ideation passes from the abstract to the concrete or visible form.*
    a. The objective is an emanation of the subjective.—S. D., I, 407.
    b. Impulse is spirit energy causing objectivity.—S. D., I, 349;
       S. D., I, 683.
    c. The Logos renders objective a concealed thought.—S. D., II, 28.
2. *Three things required before any form of energy can become objective.*—S. D., I, 89.
    1. Privation.....Separation. Initial impulse. Energy. Will.
    2. Form........Quality or shape. Nature. Love.
    3. Matter.......Objective sphere. Intelligent activity.
              See S. D., III, 561.
3. *Life precedes form.*—S. D., I, 242.
    a. The Thinker ever remains.—S. D., II, 28.
    b. Force of life is the transformation into energy of the thought
       of the Logos.—See S. D., III, 179.
4. *Spirit evolves through form and out of form.*—S. D., I, 680.
    a. Spirit has to acquire full self-consciousness.—S. D., I, 215.
    b. Form imprisons spirit.—S. D., II, 775.
    c. The principle of limitation is form.—S. D., III, 561.
    d. Spirit informs all sheaths.—S. D., I, 669 note.
    e. Spirit passes through the cycle of Being.—S. D., I, 160.
5. *The devas are the origin of form.*—S. D., I, 488.
    They exist in two great groups:
    a. The Ahhi are the vehicle of divine thought.—S. D., I, 70.
    b. The Army of the Voice.—S. D., I, 124.
    They are the sum-total of the substance of the four higher planes
  and of the three lower.
6. *There is a form which combines all forms.*—S. D., I, 118.
              See S. D., I, 77.
    This Form is the sum-total of all that is manifested, or the entire
solar sphere or system. This contains:
    a. The ten planetary schemes and all that is therein.
    b. All the lesser interplanetary bodies.
    c. The deva and human evolutions.
    d. The kingdoms of nature everywhere.
    e. The involutionary and evolutionary Gods.
    f. Every atom of substance on every plane.
7. *All forms are destroyed periodically.*
    Read carefully S. D., I, 397-401.

there is only force of different kinds, and the *effect* produced on consciousness by their interplay.

Back of all forms and of all substances (as yet but little contacted and realised) lies a third type of force, which utilises these two other factors to produce eventual harmony, and which is itself on its own plane the sumtotal of the second. It can be called:

- *a.* The one synthesising Life.
- *b.* Electric fire.
- *c.* The point of equilibrium.
- *d.* Unity or harmony.
- *e.* Pure Spirit.
- *f.* Dynamic Will.
- *g.* Existence.

It is a Force, working through a dual manifestation of differentiated force, through the energy of matter, the coherency of forms, through force centres, and force points. It is FOHAT in triple demonstration, of which the final or third is as yet unknown and inconceivable.

This brings me to the consideration of the fact earlier stated that the mental unit possesses but four of the streams of force. Each of the streams of force in the permanent atoms vibrates to the note of a particular subplane, and serves as the medium for the vitalisation of the matter of the subplane, which is built into any particular body around a permanent atom. It is the force of the Heavenly Man as it animates the cells of His form, and holds them as a coherent unity. Here it must be remembered that, from the point of view of the microcosm, the aspect of pure Spirit or of Electric Fire remains in this solar system as an abstraction. A man can attain group consciousness; he can vibrate to the note of the Heavenly Man in Whose body he is a cell; he can demonstrate in relative perfection fire by friction and solar fire, but it remains for a later mahamanvantara to reveal the true nature of Spirit. Therefore in man, functioning in the human family, this fact is apparent and the correspondence to be seen. Until he passes out of the three worlds, and until he becomes a Master of the Wisdom, he has this truth concealed in these three aspects. The mental is not a septenary permanent atom, but only responds to four types of force, and not to the entire range of vibrations. Herein lies a reason for tolerance. Until a man is coming consciously under the control of the Ego and is beginning to sense the vibration of the manasic permanent atom, it is useless to expect him to respond to certain ideals, or to grasp certain aspects of truth. The mental unit suffices for his need, and no bridge exists between it and the manasic permanent atom.

Two and a half planes are concerned with the evolution of man, per se, in the fourth kingdom, and he only begins to transcend them as he nears the Path and treads it. From the standpoint of average man in physical incarnation, the egoic consciousness, within the causal periphery, is as abstract as is the Logos viewed as the Dweller within the system. These two and a half planes are of peculiar interest to the Logos, as they embody:

That which, for Him, lies *below* the threshold of consciousness.
Those centres from which logoic kundalini is turning.
That which is not considered a principle.
That which is gradually passing into obscuration.

It is impossible to enlarge further upon this mystery.

4. *Summary.*

Before proceeding further, however, it might be well to sum up some of the facts anent the spirillae and the atom, and then we can take up the subject of the causal body and man, the individual.

1. The four lower spirillae are definitely under the influence of the personality Ray.

2. The fifth and sixth spirillae are more specifically under the egoic Ray, whatever that Ray may be.

3. The fifth spirilla has a peculiar value inasmuch as it synthesises the lower four. It is the third when counting the streams of spiral force from the standpoint of the atomic pole. It vibrates to five types of force.

4. The spirillae are literally ten in number, three major and seven minor. But from the unity point of view, they are the four and the major three, the remaining lesser three being counted as one with their major, inasmuch as they are direct reflections.

5. The permanent atoms are not heart-shaped as portrayed in certain books. A certain number of atoms are of that type but they are not the permanent atoms which are more definitely spheroidal and are slightly flattened at the top, where the correspondence to the polar depression may be found, and equally flattened at the under surface.

6. The arrangement of the spirillae within the permanent atoms varies on each plane and the ones most frequently described are those of the physical plane. The arrangement of these tiny force vortices and their internal economy on each plane is one of the secrets of initiation and may not be revealed. One hint only may be given to guide the student: The astral permanent atom has its internal streams of force arranged so that the spirals do approach quite closely the conformation of a heart, though the pointed end is eliminated. The buddhic permanent atom has its spirillae arranged so as to form approximately a figure eight with a central stream bisecting the double spiral.

7. The closer the approach to reality the simpler will be found the arrangement of the spirilla. These streams of force show a septenary arrangement in the

lower three permanent atoms of man, while the higher three contain but three spirillae—the major three.

8. It should be noted that there are but six permanent atoms connected with human evolution, while a Heavenly Man has but five, and even then only one in the solar system. (The mystery of a planet and its central life has not yet been revealed. It is connected with another manifestation of which as yet nought is known.)

9. It should be remembered that we are dealing with a physical incarnation of these great Entities and that Their permanent atoms, with the exception of the physical, are extra-systemic.

10. The causal body of the Heavenly Men is upon the third subplane of the cosmic mental plane, while that of the solar Logos and those of the three Persons of the logoic Trinity are upon the first subplane.

11. The permanent atoms of men are upon the atomic subplane of each plane, with the one exception of the mental unit. Those of the animal groups are upon the second subplane; those of the vegetable groups are upon the third subplane; those of the mineral groups are upon the fourth subplane. There is, therefore, a close analogy between these focal points of force of the group—human or otherwise—and a chain, a globe, and a round, and in their due application comes enlightenment. The sumtotal of the permanent atoms of any particular kingdom form the streams of force or spirillae in the greater atoms of solar entities or of lunar entities, while the sumtotal of the permanent atoms of man *in the spiritual kingdom* (the three triadal atoms, atma-buddhi-manas) form the spiral streams of force within certain centres.

12. As the permanent atoms become radioactive in due course of evolution, the result within the centre is a marked increase of vibration.

13. The permanent atoms concern solar entities when they are found on or above the higher mental. They

concern lunar entities on the lower mental, the astral and the physical planes.

14. It should be noted that in this solar system the following entities manifest through:

I.   *One permanent atom . . . the physical.*
     1. A solar Logos.
     2. The three major Rays, or Lords of Aspect.
     3. The seven Heavenly Men.
     4. The forty-nine Regents of the planetary chains.
II. *Two permanent atoms . . . the physical and the astral.*
     1. The seven Lords of the globes in every chain.
     2. The forty-nine Root Manus.
     3. The seventy-seven Embodiers of form—a group of solar Lords Who are concerned with form building, working primarily on the first ray.
     4. Certain of the Avatars, Who are selected by the Logos to carry a certain type of force at stated intervals and thus further the evolution of the psyche.
III. *Three permanent atoms . . . physical, astral, and mental.*
     1. The Lords of the third Kingdom, the animal. They are seven Entities whose bodies are made up of animal souls just as the Heavenly Men embody for man the Buddhic principle, so these lords embody for the animal kingdom the manasic principle, which is the goal of the evolutionary process for them.
     2. Certain great entities who embody a whole range of existences upon five of the planets, of which the earth is not one, but who in due course of time will come to be recognised as having a powerful effect upon man on the earth, via the three Buddhas of Activity. A hint as to this esoteric influence comes to man in the close connection existing between the Earth and Mercury. As yet it is not possible to enlarge further.
     3. The entities who are the sumtotal of those group souls who contain definite permanent triads. Nine triads constitute the body of one of these entities.
IV. *Through four permanent atoms . . . physical, astral, mental and buddhic.*
     1. Eight groups of solar Entities Who form the subjective life of the seven centres in the body of Brahma, viewing Him as a separate cosmic Entity,

dissociated from His two brothers. They are the
seven Sons of Fohat, with the eighth Son included,
and They are the final differentiation of the forty-
nine fires, prior to Their union with the fire of Eros.
Thus is it expressed by H. P. B.[74]

2. That Entity Who works through the FORM of a
planetary occult Hierarchy, using it as His body
of manifestation, and regarding it as the centre
through which His force can flow. It should be
remembered that all such groups on every planet
form a vehicle for the life of a great Individual Who
gives to that Hierarchy its distinctive colouring and
its unique keynote.

3. A number of solar Deities Who are the radiators of
solar magnetism, and the life of *form*.

4. A peculiar group of Beings connected with a certain
constellation and the lesser Dragon, who have their
habitat on Neptune and work with the sixth principle in the solar system. They take physical form,
animated by purified desire, controlled by mind, and
are the dispensers of love-wisdom by means of certain of the "Halls of Wisdom" on the various
planets. The words "Halls of Wisdom" in their
esoteric significance describe a stage of consciousness
not a location.

V. *Through five permanent atoms . . . physical, astral, mental, buddhic and atmic.*

1. The Lords of certain subplanes who work under the
Raja-Lord of a plane and who are themselves vibration and activity.

2. The lesser Heavenly Men on the buddhic level, Who
reflect Their higher prototypes on the second plane
of the system.

3. The entities who are the sum-total of group consciousness on egoic levels, remembering that these
groups are differentiated and are formed of aggregates of seven, until there are formed forty-nine
groups of seven egoic vehicles forming one group
which is the body of this lesser solar Deity. There
is a multiplicity of these groups of forty-nine. This
has been somewhat stated before when it has been

[74] S. D., I, 139, 144.

announced that a Master with His particular band of disciples and initiates form a group or force centre. These groups have their permanent atoms as do all lives seeking objective expression.

4. The entities who are the sumtotal of the vegetable kingdom in its diversity of manifestation in different globes, chains and schemes.

VI.   *Through six permanent atoms . . . physical, astral, two mental, buddhic and atmic.*
MAN.

All that is here stated is an enlargement of the data given about the "Army of the Voice," [75] and an endeavour to show that many diverse lives (all embodying lesser lives, or embodied in greater ones themselves) are to be found within the various schemes. We have dealt only with those likewise which are superhuman or human, with those who have been or are MEN. We have not dealt with the subhuman, or with the lunar lords or lesser pitris, for their day is not yet, and they progress as the tide of evolution progresses, unconsciously and not self-consciously. We have dealt with these entities and their permanent atoms in connection with their manifestation in a solar system, and have not carried it beyond the solar ring-pass-not. *All the permanent atoms concern physical matter and manifestation.* The highest permanent atom of man, the atmic, is, after all, an atom of the third cosmic ether, and this should be pondered upon and studied. We have considered these various personalities (and the word 'personality' is chosen deliberately, for what are They but personalities, or Beings, in physical incarnation?) from the standpoint of Their lowest force point first. We have discussed the permanent atom as a point of contact with the force of a plane, of a planet, of a chain, of a scheme, or of a system. This should ever be borne in mind.

It is to be recognised that much that is written above
[75] S. D., I, 121.

may seem incomprehensible, but when scientists come to understand and regulate *force,* that which is written here will become plainer; it will be seen that we have dealt with the positive force in all negative forms above, and including the human kingdom.

III. THE EGOIC LOTUS [76]

We must now deal with the subject of the causal body on its own plane from the point of view of FIRE. We have studied it briefly from the more ordinary angle, and in materialistic terms, considering it as a vehicle of rarefied substance, containing within itself the seventh principle of each of the two lower sheaths of the microcosm, and the mental unit. This latter is that which embodies the first aspect in manifestation, and which is analogous to the first logoic aspect—one that in this solar system does not come to full demonstration.

I would like to point out here that in studying the solar system as the physical manifestation of a solar Logos, we are investigating:

   a. The physical permanent atom of a solar Logos as contained within the logoic causal body on its own plane.
   b. The seven types of force, or the seven logoic spirillae within that permanent atom. This, if real-

---

[76] *The Egoic Lotus* ". . . the laws of karma are adjusted, the clue being found in the mastery of the sixteen rays of the Ego, for which sixteen rays sixteen mantras or words are given, the real pronunciation being however reserved for initiates only."—*Kali Upanishad.*

"The mystery of the sixteen rays of the Ego will be revealed when the force of the Sacred Tetraktys is merged with that of the Holy Twelve."
—*The Old Commentary.*

The Primordial is the Ray and the direct emanation of the first Sacred Four.—S. D., I, 115, 116.

The Sacred Four are:—

Father .... Spirit. Existence. Unity.
The Son .... Soul. Love-Wisdom. Duality.
Mother .... Matter. The trinity.

and their united manifestation making
The active evolving solar system, the logoic ring-pass-not.
This is the Macrocosm.

ised, gives a new outlook upon the subject of plane vibration.

c. The close correspondence between the planes and the seven spirillae in the permanent atom of a solar Logos.

We have touched upon these spirillae and their function very briefly, and can now approach the question of the egoic Ray and the fire of mind from the subjective point of view, or in terms of fire.

1. *Centres or Wheels of Energy.*

a. *Centres of force.* We shall again reach the clarity of vision desirable if we study the subject of monadic development from the angle of vision of the human unit. It has been taught in many occult text books that man has seven centres of force (or ten, according to some calculations); that three of these centres are paramount, and eventually synthesise the other four, or absorb their force or energy. This produces their eventual obscuration, or their passing out of manifestation; they occultly 'die.' This is paralleled in the logoic centres, the planetary schemes, which also in due course of time pass into obscuration, and transmit their energy to the major three schemes. The three main centres in the Microcosm are the Head, the Heart and the Throat.

1. The Head centre...The Monad .....Will .... Spirit.
2. The Heart centre..The Ego ....Love .... Consciousness.
3. The Throat centre.The Personality. Activity..Matter.

It will, therefore, be apparent that just as in man these centres are related to the threefold spiritual man in his total development, so the three types of centres—microcosmic or macrocosmic—come gradually more and more under the vitalising power of one of the three aspects of the Logos. These centres are recognised also as focal points of active force, manifesting to the vision of the clairvoyant as fiery wheels or the flaming petals of a lotus.

b. *The causal body . . . monadic heart centre.* In studying the egoic body it should be remembered that the causal body is the correspondence in the monadic manifestation to the *heart centre.* It is a flaming wheel of fire within the monadic auric egg, which embraces the five planes of monadic manifestation; it is also seen as the twelve-petalled Lotus. Of these twelve petals, the innermost three are unrevealed, or are embryonic, and hence the causal body is frequently considered as a nine-petalled Lotus, or as a wheel of fire with only nine spokes or whorls. This is essentially true as regards the evolutionary process, but when a man has succeeded in awakening or unfolding the nine petals, or in arousing the fire of the nine spokes or whorls (which is practically consummated at the three major Initiations) the inner three are revealed. They respond to the monadic vibration, to the aspect of pure Spirit; it is the stimulation or revelation of these inner petals, by the One Initiator at the third and fourth Initiations which brings about the final conflagration and the blazing up of the causal body with the subsequent liberation of the central positive Life or Fire.

2. *The Twelve-Petalled Egoic Lotus*

Solar Fire is dual. It is the fire of matter or substance and the fire of mind blended. This makes man the six-pointed Star of Light, for each of these fires is triple. The fire of mind is also in essence dual, bringing in another triplicity, thus making the nine. When a man has awakened the nine fires, and has unfolded the nine petals, and when he has received the stimulus which is imparted at initiation, through being brought into *conscious* contact with the electric spark of his own particular Heavenly Man, they all blend and merge. The inner three which complete the twelve, and which are concerned with the final, and essentially spiritual stages, of his evolution, are really related more intimately to the evolution of the Heavenly Man, and are connected with the stimulus which He receives Himself in contacting the logoic electric spark, or the pure Spirit aspect of the Logos.

It should here be noted that this ninefold development is hinted at in the *Secret Doctrine* in the various places where H. P. B. deals with the Kumaras [77] or the Heavenly Men, of Whom the microcosm is a reflection. She calls Them the Lords of Knowledge, the Lords of Love and the Lords of Sacrifice. Each of Them is a nine-petalled Lotus in the logoic body. They are the flaming Wheels, and in Their various names, as found in the *Secret Doctrine,* may be discovered the clue to the mystery. Let us realise this clearly, nevertheless, as regards the microcosm, and later extend the idea to the Heavenly Men. Let us picture the nine-petalled egoic lotus, the heart centre in the monadic consciousness, unfolding each of its petals in groups of three upon the three subplanes of the higher mental. Their unfoldment is worked out through the evolutionary process, undergone on the three planes in the three worlds, or within the three Halls of Ignorance, of Learning, and of Wisdom.

a. *First Group of Petals—Knowledge Petals:*

1. The *Petal of Knowledge* for the physical plane. Through the breaking of the Law and the ensuing suffering the price of ignorance is paid and knowledge is achieved. This unfoldment is brought about through physical plane experience.

2. The *Petal of Love* for the physical plane. Unfolds through physical relationships, and the gradual growth of love from love of self to love of others.

[77] S. D., II, 257.

3. The *Petal of Sacrifice* for the physical plane. This
    unfoldment is brought about through the driving
    force of circumstances, and not of free will. It
    is the offering up of the physical body upon the
    altar of desire—low desire to begin with, but as-
    piration towards the end, though still desire. As
    man in the early stages of his evolution is polar-
    ised on the physical, much of this is undergone
    unconsciously and without any realisation of what
    is being consummated, but the result in the causal
    body is seen in a twofold increase of heat or of
    activity:

> The physical permanent atom becomes radio-
> active or a radiant point of fire.

> The lower three petals become vibrant and be-
> gin to unfold until fully developed.

b. *Second Group of Petals—Love Petals:*

1. *The Petal of Knowledge,* for the astral plane; un-
    foldment is brought about by the conscious bal-
    ancing of the pairs of opposites, and the gradual
    utilisation of the Law of Attraction and Repul-
    sion. The man passes out of the Hall of Ignorance
    where, from the egoic point of view, he works
    blindly and begins to appreciate the effects of his
    physical plane life; by a realisation of his es-
    sential duality he begins to comprehend causes.
2. *The Petal of Love* for the astral plane; unfoldment
    is brought about through the process of gradually
    transmuting the love of the subjective nature or of
    the Self within. This has a dual effect and works
    through on to the physical plane in many lives of
    turmoil, of endeavour and of failure as a man
    strives to turn his attention to the love of the Real.
3. *The Petal of Sacrifice* for the astral plane; unfold-
    ment is brought about by the attitude of man as he

consciously endeavours to give up his own desires
for the sake of his group. His motive is still
somewhat a blind one, and still coloured by the
desire for a return of that which he gives and
for love from those he seeks to serve, but it is
of a much higher order than the blind sacrifice to
which a man is driven by circumstances as is the
case in the earlier unfoldment. As this threefold
enlightenment or unfoldment proceeds, again a
dual result is seen:

> The astral permanent atom comes into full
> activity and radiance, as regards five of its
> spirillae, and the two atoms of the physical
> and the astral planes are equally vibrant.

> The three petals of the central ring of the egoic
> lotus come also into full unfoldment, and the
> heart centre of the Monad is seen as a wheel
> of fire with six of its spokes in full display
> of energy and rapidly rotating.

c. *Third Group of Petals—Sacrifice Petals:*

1. *The Petal of Knowledge* for the mental plane; its
   unfoldment marks the period wherein the man
   consciously utilizes all that he has gained or is
   gaining under the law for the definite benefit of
   humanity.

   Each of the groups of petals is distinguished by a
   predominant colouring; *Knowledge,* on the physical plane, with the colouring of the other two
   subsidiary; *Love,* on the astral plane, with the
   light of sacrifice weaker in tone than the other
   two, which practically show forth in equal brilliancy. On the mental plane, the light of sacrifice
   comes to its full display, and all that is seen is
   coloured by that light.

2. *The Petal of Love* on the mental plane is unfolded

through the conscious steady application of all
the powers of the soul to the service of humanity
with no thought of return nor any desire for reward for the immense sacrifice involved.

3. *The Petal of Sacrifice* for the mental plane: demonstrates as the predominant bias of the soul as
seen in a series of many lives spent by the initiate prior to his final emancipation. He becomes
in his sphere the "Great Sacrifice."

This stage can be seen objectively to the eye of the
clairvoyant as dual in effect:

a.   The mental unit becomes a radiant point of
light; its four spirillae transmit force with
intense rapidity.

b.   The three higher petals unfold, and the
nine-petalled lotus is seen perfected.

The causal body is then (expressed in terms of
fire) a blazing centre of heat, radiating to its group
warmth and vitality. Within the periphery of the
egoic wheel can be seen the nine spokes rotating
with intense rapidity and—after the third Initiation—becoming fourth dimensional, or the wheels
"turn upon" themselves.[78] In the midst forming a
certain geometrical triangle (differing according
to the ray of the Monad) can be seen three points
of fire, or the permanent atoms and the mental
unit, in all their glory; at the centre can be seen
a central blaze of glory growing in intensity as
the three inner petals respond to the stimulation.
*When the fire of matter, or "fire by friction," be-
comes sufficiently intense; when the fire of mind, or
solar fire (which vitalises the nine petals) becomes
equally fierce, and when the electric spark at the
innermost centre blazes out and can be seen, the*

[78] Bible. Ezekiel, 1:15:21.

entire causal body becomes radioactive. Then
the fires of substance (the vitality of the permanent atoms) escape from the atomic spheres, and
add their quota to the great sphere in which they
are contained; the fire of mind blends with its
emanating source, and the central life escapes.
This is the great liberation. The man, in terms
of human endeavour, has achieved his goal. He
has passed through the three Halls and in each
has transferred that which he gained therein to
the content of his consciousness; he has in ordered sequence developed and opened the petals
of the lotus—first opening the lower three, which
involves a process covering a vast period of time.
Then the second series of petals are opened, during a period of time covering his participation intelligently in world affairs until he enters the
spiritual kingdom at the first Initiation; and a
final and briefer period wherein the three higher
or inner ring of petals are developed and opened.

In closing what may be said on this subject of the
egoic Ray and fire of mind, I would request the student
to bear the following points in mind:

First. That the order of the development of the petals
and the stimulation of the fires depends upon the Ray
of the Monad, and the subray upon which the causal body
finds itself. This thought would bear expansion, and
would prove a fruitful source of study to the occult investigator.

Second. That this unfoldment proceeds slowly in the
early stages, and only proceeds with rapidity as the
man himself works at it with conscious effort.

The Ego takes no active interest in the development
until the second petal in the second series is beginning
to open. Before that time, the work proceeds under the

law of its being and through the inherent life of the second Logos which is the life of the petals of the lotus. The life of the first Logos, working through the SELF (who dwells in a form built by the life or energy of the second Logos out of force-substance animated by the life of the third Logos) only responds to opportunity when the above mentioned stage is reached.

Finally: The ceremony of initiation is only undergone when the causal body is in a condition to respond to the Will aspect of the Heavenly Man (the first aspect) and to do this through the glad co-operation of the fully conscious self.

More on this is not now possible, but enough has here been indicated to open up various lines of study. These, if followed, will lead the student to much of practical value and application.

3. *Summary.*

Our next subject concerns itself with the elementals of the mental plane, with the thought forms they animate, and with the consideration of them as force centres, capable of producing results—constructive, if rightly directed; destructive, if left blindly to follow their own course. Before taking up this matter, however, I want to gather together some threads of thought in connection with the matter just dealt with. If we have carefully followed the data given about the egoic manifestation on its own plane, and the fires of the causal body, we shall have noted the close resemblance between that egoic body, viewed as a force centre, and certain aspects of logoic manifestation.

The causal body has been seen as a wheel of fire, containing within its periphery three focal points of energy, the permanent atoms. They are analogous, as earlier pointed out, to the seventh principle of each of the three aspects—will or power, love-wisdom, and active intelligence. Each of these focal points has its own internal economy, as seen in the spirillae, which are essentially streams of force, responding to stimulation and vibration, aroused within and without their limiting ring-pass-not. The internal life of the permanent atom, and that which animates and produces its activity, is the life of the third aspect; the force playing upon it and through it is the life of the second aspect. As evolution proceeds the intensity of the life forces from within and those which affect it from without, grows gradually stronger and stronger, and the light of the permanent atoms increases, the petals of the lotus unfold, and the spokes of the radiatory fire come into action. Bear in mind here, that *the permanent atoms are concerned with the substance aspect of Existence or Becoming, while the petals of the lotus, or the fiery spokes of the wheel, deal specifically with the psychical aspect, or the development of consciousness; the central nucleus, or the three inner petals, embodies the aspect of pure Spirit.*

All three lines of evolution are proceeding simultaneously, and have a reflex action the one upon the other; it is this which produces the consequent perfection of unfoldment. It is neither possible nor desirable to follow each line of this threefold evolution separately, nor to consider them as dissociated from each other. The interplay is too accurate, and the mutual stimulation too important to be neglected by the student of egoic evolution.

It is, as stated elsewhere, through the permanent atoms that the Ego comes en rapport with his objective world; he works upon and through his environment successfully or blindly just in so far as he can energise his permanent atoms, and bring the spirillae out of latency into potency. This only becomes possible as he unfolds the petals of the lotus. It must be remembered that the three lower petals when fully unfolded affect, through their vitality, the three major spirillae in the physical permanent atom. As the second ring of petals gradually opens, the astral permanent atom undergoes a similar process, leading up to the full arousing of the spirillae within the mental unit.

Here I would point out that there is a slight difference in the case of the mental unit, for the four spirillae of the mental unit are aroused to full activity when *the knowledge petal* of the final three opens. The opening of the remaining two reveal the glowing threefold flower which lies at the centre of egoic manifestation.

It would be wise to sound a note of warning here in connection with this question of egoic unfoldment. What has been said here has been but the formulation of the general plan of egoic unfoldment as interpreted in terms of consciousness or of fire. In studying the subject with due personal application, the student should bear in mind the following facts:

First, that according to the Ray of the Monad, so will the petals unfold. For instance, if the Ray of the Monad is the second Ray, the knowledge petal will be the first to open, but the second petal of love will almost parallel its development, being for that particular type of Ego the line of easiest unfoldment; the knowledge petal will be for it the most difficult to open.

Second, that the effects of one circle of petals opening will be felt within the next circle at an early stage and will cause a vibratory response, hence the greater rapidity of the later stages of unfoldment as compared with the first.

Third, that there exist many cases of uneven or unequal unfoldment. Quite frequently people are found with perhaps two petals unfolded in the first circle and one still in latency, while a petal within the central or second ring may be in full development. This is the explanation frequently of the power in service along certain lines displayed by some, coupled with a comparatively low stage of development or of consciousness (egoically speaking). This is due to varying causes, such as the karma of the Monad itself on its high plane and the strength of the monadic grip upon the ego; many lives given to a particular line of action, resulting in the setting up of a strong vibration—one so strong that it renders the development of response to subsidiary vibrations difficult of attainment; certain peculiar conditions hidden in the evolution of any particular Lord of a Ray, and the effect of that condition upon a particular group of cells; the group karma of a collection or congery of causal bodies, and their mutual interplay. Every egoic unit or monadic force centre has a definite effect upon the group or community of Egos in which it may have a place, and as the interaction proceeds results are sometimes produced of a temporarily unexpected nature.

These points should be carefully borne in mind by the student of egoic evolution. This whole subject is of interest in that it is the next step ahead for the students of occult psychology. Much will be eventually ascertained which will throw new light upon the possibility of work upon the physical plane for man. The whole secret of success in any endeavour or enterprise is primarily based on two things:

First, the ability of the Ego to work through the personality, using it simply as the medium of expression.

Second, the karma of the egoic group as it becomes more apparent on the physical plane. Hitherto, much has been said and taught about individual karma. Group karma in the future will slowly assume its rightful place in the thought of students, and this will lead to more intelligent co-operation, to a more sympathetic understanding of group responsibilities, and to a more adequate solution of group problems.

The study of occult psychology involves a true conception of the nature of the Ego, or the arousing of the Ego to full activity in manifestation; it will necessitate the sound formulation of the laws of egoic unfoldment, of the methods whereby, petal by petal, the lotus may be brought to perfection, and of the triple nature of its evolution; it will bring about an eventual apprehension of the true meaning of force, and of energy in its dual aspect—internal vibration and external radiation; it will produce the centering of the attention of all advanced students upon the centres—in this case *not* the physical centres on etheric levels but upon the psychical centres, such as the Ego in the causal body and egoic groups. This will produce later a better comprehension of the effect of one consciousness upon another consciousness on the physical plane, and this knowledge will be scientifically utilised to produce specific results in group evolution, and thus some of the world problems will find solution. Finally, the laws of fire will be studied, the nature of heat, of radiation and of flame will be occultly investigated, and the action of one fire upon another fire, the result of radiation from one conscious sphere to another will be realised; the method of arousing consciousness on the different planes by action upon the fires of the causal body and their stimulation will be gradually revealed.

The whole question is slowly, very slowly, coming to the fore in human thought (even though this is little realised) through the study of vocational education, business efficiency, and the place of the human unit in any trade or enterprise. Men are being spoken of and considered in terms of potential force factors, and this is a step in the right direction.

Approaching the same question from the personality standpoint and not the egoic, the time is fast approaching when the emphasis will be laid in education upon

how best the young can be taught to contact their own
ego or higher energy; how best they can be led to appropriate the knowledge and ability of their higher self
for use on the physical plane; how best they can ascertain their group formation, and thus work along with
their group, and in unison with the total energy of that
group; how best their threefold lower self—physical,
astral, and mental—can be brought into direct alignment with their higher centre of force, and thus draw
down a continuous supply of energy for the strengthen-
ing of their three vehicles, and their wise manipulation;
how best the various spirillae can be awakened and the
energy within their own cells released for action. All
this will be a thing of gradual evolution, but I have here
outlined the trend of the future study, as in the formulation of possibility lies its eventual realisation. Such a
process must necessarily be slow. The powers of the
ego are stupendous and if released now through the
agency of an unready personality would lead to dire
disaster. But the time will come, and in the meantime
a due apprehension of inherent capacity will profit all
who have the intuition to recognise the goal.

SECTION TWO

DIVISION D

THOUGHT ELEMENTALS AND FIRE ELEMENTALS

I. Thought Forms

1. *Their function.*
    - a. To respond to vibration.
    - b. To provide the vehicle for an idea.
    - c. To carry out specific purpose.
2. *The Laws of Thought.*
    - a. Three cosmic laws.
    - b. Seven systemic laws.

II. Thought Elementals and Devas

1. *The Ruler of Fire . . . Agni.*
    - a. Agni and the solar Logos.
    - b. Agni and the mental plane.
    - c. Agni and the three Fires.
2. *The Fire Devas . . . the Greater Builders.*
    - a. Introductory statements.
    - b. The functions of the devas.
    - c. The devas and the planes.
3. *The Solar Angels . . . the Agnishvattas.*
    - Introductory remarks.
    - a. On the fifth Principle.
    - b. On Individualisation.
    - c. On Incarnation.
    - d. On the Building of the Causal Body.
4. *The Fire Elementals . . . the Lesser Builders.*
    - a. Introductory.
    - b. Physical plane elementals.
    - c. Elementals of the ethers.
    - d. Elementals and the Microcosm.

550

III. Man, as a Creator in Mental Matter

1. *The creation of thought forms.*
2. *The process of thought form building.*

IV. Man and the Fire Spirits

1. *The Will aspect and creation.*
    a. The condition of the magician.
    b. Construction of thought forms.
    c. The occult significance of speech.
2. *The nature of Magic.*
    a. Black magicians and white.
    b. The source of black magic.
    c. Conditions for white magic.
3. *Fifteen rules for Magic.*
    a. Six rules for the mental plane.
    b. Five rules for the astral plane.
    c. Four rules for the physical plane.

Under this division we shall briefly give an outline of the study which we will undertake upon this vast and stupendous subject, for, as it definitely concerns the evolution of man and his power eventually to create, it will be wise for us to take up the matter in some detail.

This section is not intended to give interesting bits of information anent the devas; I only seek to deal with the matter in its practical application to man, and to give as much of the necessary knowledge as will enable a man to control and build his own system, to understand the method of creation and to comprehend somewhat the lesser lives and the paralleling deva evolution with which he may be concerned.

I. THOUGHT FORMS

1. *Their Function.*

It will be noted that in studying this matter we have not started with that which is most apparent, the exoteric form in mental matter, but with the inner life or Idea within the form and with the Laws that govern the crea-

tive aspect. This function of every thought form is
threefold:

To respond to vibration
To provide a body for an idea
To carry out specific purpose.

Let us first study the logoic thought form and then
turn our attention to the thought forms fabricated by
the Thinker from the systemic mental planes and in
mental matter. We have to note that, in the case of the
Logos, all upon which we have to base our conclusions
are His physical manifestation, and His quality, psychic
nature, aroma, emanation or magnetism, as we see it
working out through the form. Hence we are very much
handicapped.

a. *Response to Vibration.* It is always recognised
in occult circles that the whole object of human evolution is to enable the Thinker to respond to every contact
fully and consciously, and thus to utilise his material
sheath, or sheaths, as adequate transmitter of such contact. The most easily studied human thought-form is
the one the Ego creates through which to function. He
builds his sheaths by the power of thought, and the
dense physical body is the best sheath that—at any particular stage of evolution—he can at the time manufacture. The same can be predicated of the solar Logos.
He builds by the power of thought a body which can respond to that group of vibrations which are concerned
with the cosmic physical plane (the only one we can
study). It is not yet adequate, and does not fully express
the logoic Thinker.

The vibrations to which the systemic thought-form
must respond are many in number, but for our purposes
might be enumerated as mainly seven:

1. The vibrations of the cosmic physical plane, viewing it as all the matter of that plane which exists

outside the logoic ring-pass-not. It concerns the pranic and akashic fluids and currents.

2. The vibrations of the cosmic astral plane as they affect the physical form of divine manifestation. This involves cosmically the action upon our solar Logos of the emotional quality of other cosmic entities, and concerns the magnetic effect upon Him of their psychic emanation. This, in view of the fact that His dense physical body is not a principle, is of a more potent nature than the first set of vibrations, as is the case also in man's evolution.

3. Vibrations from that which, within the logoic consciousness, is recognised as the logoic Higher Self, or His emanating source. This brings the solar system within the vibratory radius of certain constellations which have a position of profound importance in the general evolution of the system.

4. Vibrations from Sirius via the cosmic mental plane.

5. Vibrations from the seven Rishis of the Great Bear, and primarily from those two Who are the Prototypes of the Lords of the seventh and fifth Rays. This is a most important point, and finds its microcosmic correspondence in the place which the seventh Ray has in the building of a thought-form, and the use of the fifth Ray in the work of concretion. All magicians who work with matter and who are occupied with form-building (either consciously or unconsciously) call in these two types of force or energy.

6. Certain very remote vibrations, as yet no more appreciable in the logoic Body than is monadic influence in that of average man, from the ONE ABOUT WHOM NAUGHT MAY BE SAID, that cosmic

Existence Who is expressing Himself through seven centres of force, of which our solar system is one.

7. A series of vibrations which will become more potent as our Logos nears that period which is occultly called "Divine Maturity," which emanate from that constellation in the Heavens which embodies His polar opposite. This is a deep mystery and concerns the cosmic marriage of the Logos.

It will be apparent, therefore, how little can as yet be predicated anent the future of the solar system until the vibrations of the sixth and seventh order become more powerful, and their effects can consequently be studied more easily. It is not possible here to do more than indicate the seven types of vibrations to which our solar Logos (functioning in a material body) will in due course of time consciously, and fully, respond. He responds to vibrations of the first, second, third and fourth order quite fully at this time, but as yet (though responding) cannot fully, and consciously, utilise these types of energy. The vibration of the fifth order is recognised by Him, particularly in three of His centres, but is not as yet fully under His control. The other two are sensed, and felt, but so remotely as to be almost outside the range of His consciousness.

In carrying out these ideas in connection with man and the thought forms which he fabricates (such as his material sheaths), the correspondence can be worked out within the system, and from the point of view of the planetary schemes in which man has his place. The work of man as he builds in mental thought matter and constructs forms extraneous to himself, we shall deal with later.

The methods whereby vibratory response is brought about might be enumerated as follows:

Through the factor of time in evolution.

Through extra-systemic stimulation and intensive training, whether for a Logos or a man.

Through the process of Initiation, and the application of the Rods of Initiation.

The factor of evolution is recognised and studied by many schools of thought, esoteric or exoteric. The extra-systemic stimulation involves a large number of factors, but the main two to be remembered are that this stimulation will be applied:

Through the group to the unit.

Through a more evolved "Kingdom of Nature" to a less evolved.

As regards the third factor of Initiation, it must be borne in mind that we are here considering only the great initiations, and not the numerous expansions of consciousness which can be traced through all kingdoms and all manifestations.

In connection with what we have considered above, anent the primary function of a thought-form (the power to respond to vibration) I would emphasise the necessity of remembering that that response must be made by the inner embodied Idea, and that it will then through a complex reflex action, bring about response from the material sheath which veils it. Vibration is the result of subjective impulse, and makes its appeal to the subjective consciousness through impact upon whatever may be understood as substance; this impact is transmitted direct to the inner life, and in due turn is retransmitted to substance in the form of recognition or realisation. An analogous process may be studied in the nerve reactions of the physical frame, and their alliance with the brain consciousness.

As will be seen in the three worlds of man's emprise, man will work as a Creator and will follow a similar procedure. His thought forms will be constructed of mental matter, chosen specifically because it vibrates to the same type of vibration as the Idea seeking embodiment, and these forms will persist—as does the logoic thought form, the solar system—for just as long as the factor of Will, or dynamic vitality, continues to hold it together.

This brings us to our next point:

b. *To Provide a Body for an Idea.* In this statement we have latent the basic principle of incarnation, and of activity, even of existence itself. It involves the expansion of our idea to include the cosmic mental plane as we consider the Logos, and as the creative faculty of man is studied we are taken to the mental plane of the solar system. One fundamental thought must here be given and pondered upon: *This creative impulse, this tendency towards the concretion of the abstract, this inherent ability to "take form" has its fullest expression as yet in physical matter. The "raison d'être" is that—for man—all substances with which he creates, all forms which he builds, and all processes of concretion which he carries on, are created, built and carried on within the physical body of the Logos.* Herein can be found the reason for the emphasis laid in nature on the sex aspect, and on that of physical reproduction; it can be seen in all the kingdoms of nature, with the exception of the first and fifth. This is a most significant point and the exceptions should be studied in their widest connotation, for they contain the basic mystery of sex on the involutionary path, and on the evolutionary. In them we have the two extremes. It will have been noted that as the idea that the solar system is the physical vehicle of the Logos and His body of manifestation is grasped, many problems become elucidated, and two points especially will gradually be apprehended by the student, if he meditates and studies:

First. That in due course of time, as the Logos

achieves liberation from the trammels of physical matter, the whole objective system will come to be regarded
as an idea or concept, clothed in a veil or sheath of subtler matter than the physical, and the logoic body
will be viewed as the product of will and desire, and
physical matter in any of its grades will not enter into
its composition; it will simply be a desire body. This
will bring about a condition of affairs inconceivable to
us and only to be somewhat apprehended by the man
who can function upon the systemic buddhic plane, the
fourth cosmic ether. Bear in mind here that our astral
plane is but the sixth subplane of the cosmic physical
plane and that this provides us with no real grounds
from which to reason concerning the cosmic astral plane.
Only when the astral plane is a calm receiver of buddhic
impulse, or a liquid reflector of that plane (which will
not be till the close of the mahamanvantara) shall we
be able to formulate any ideas anent the cosmic astral
plane.

Second. That the entire sex aspect of manifestation,
as we understand it in the different kingdoms of nature,
is an expression of the energy of the Logos, as it flows
through and stimulates that centre in His body which
corresponds to the generative organs. All the creative
functions of the vegetable, animal, and human family,
viewing them as a whole, are as yet purely physical,
and based on lower desire. The desire of the Logos for
physical incarnation is as yet the dominant note. Later
His desire for that will be less and will become transmuted into desire for creation on mental levels only.
This is what brings the Destroyer aspect into activity,
leading to eventual obscuration, and the physical
"death" of the solar system. Indication that this aspect is coming into power will be seen when two great
events transpire:

a. The ability of man consciously to create on mental levels, and the consequent transmutation of his lower sex impulses into higher.

b. The mental vitalisation of another large section of the animal kingdom.

When these two things can be seen working out in any round, it will be indicative of a decided mental polarisation of the Logos; we can only become cognisant of this by studying His body of manifestation in its component parts.

What is here predicated anent the logoic thought form can be equally well stated about that of a Heavenly Man, and a planetary scheme. As His cosmic polarisation becomes more mental, and as His cosmic desire nature becomes transmuted, the force that plays through His centres will correspondingly be seen to vary in direction; He will withdraw force from certain of His lower centres and globes; He will cease to be interested in *physical* incarnation, and He will eventually withdraw within Himself. His thought-form will show a gradual diminution of vitality; the dense physical globe will die and pass out of objectivity, and other globes will temporarily hold His life, though not for long. In due course of time the entire scheme will be obscured, and He will function only in His cosmic astral body.

Such is the case too with a chain and its informing Life, viewing a chain as simply a centre in the body of the planetary Logos, yet having its own central factor. This can be seen in the Moon in a most interesting way. The desire of its Occupant was no longer for physical manifestation; He therefore withdrew His life. All that is left is the devitalised shell; the two other aspects have gone and only the third aspect, the inherent life of matter itself, remains gradually to dissipate also as the centuries elapse. In connection with man, a similar condition is seen in the gradual disintegration of the physical body after death; the two other aspects are removed, and the form decays.

As these fundamental facts are grasped, and man begins to appreciate his position as Creator, the entire aspect of the sex question will also change; and emphasis will be laid upon the laws of *mental* creation, on the formulation of thought-forms in a scientific manner, and the dense physical aspect of creation will be in abeyance. When this is so, then will man be coming into his divine right, and the human kingdom be fulfilling its legitimate function. The sex aspect—as at present expressing itself—and the whole process of reproduction is one which man shares with the animal kingdom, and is based upon his animal instincts, and his dense physical nature, which is not a principle. When he is totally emancipated from the animal kingdom, and the third and fourth kingdoms stand distinct from each other, then the sex nature, and the organs of reproduction will be viewed by the average man in a very different manner than at present. Creation will eventually be *the result of thought impulses and not desire impulses;* the process will be then (once the initial impulse on the mental plane has been given), as normal, as safe, and as unconscious as the act of breathing is now. When this is so (and the time is a long way ahead), physical reproduction will still continue, but the physical form will be spoken of in terms of concretion and of energy, and the emphasis will be laid upon that which is to be embodied. This stage will be entered upon when the functions of the etheric body are scientifically grasped and understood and the laws of creative thought are a matter of public knowledge and discussion; it will coincide with a period wherein the animal kingdom will again be under manasic impression, and individualisation will again be permitted.

It will be generally recognised at that time that Spirit-matter are two aspects of the one Unity, and the present terminology of Spirit, and material substance, will have given place to the broader concept of negative and positive energy as the two aspects of the One Energy. All phenomena will then be expressed in force terms, and the sex question—or the union of the male and female, the negative and the positive, on the physical plane—will be redeemed and purified.

An embodied idea, therefore, is literally a positive impulse, emanating from mental levels, and clothing itself in a veil of negative substance. These two factors in turn will be regarded as emanations from a still greater force centre, which is expressing purpose through them both.

A thought form, as constructed by man, is the union of a positive emanation and a negative. These two are the emanations of a Unity, the coherent Thinker.

c. *To Carry Out Specific Purpose.* We touch here upon the most vital element in the building of thought-forms. In our first point we touched upon the aspect of consciousness, or "response to sensation, or feeling," and thus brought into our study of the building process the second aspect logoic, that of the Ego, or the realisation of essential duality. In our second point the more objective aspect was somewhat elaborated, and the tangible form dealt with, thus bringing in the third logoic aspect, that of intelligent substance, or that through which consciousness seeks expression. Now the will or purpose aspect is to be considered, bringing therefore the first aspect logoic, or the "will-to-be" to the fore. When this third point is meditated upon with care, it will be noted (as might be expected) that it includes the other two, and synthesises them.

Certain factors must be borne in mind as we consider these words "specific purpose." By their tabulation we shall endeavour to make as clear as may be, this very complex matter. The ideas involved are:

The Factor of Identity. Specific purpose is the practical application of the will, or intent, of a conscious intelligent Existence as it shows itself in:

- *a.* Its source
- *b.* Its mission
- *c.* Its method
- *d.* Its objective.

All these will vary according to the nature of the emanating Identity. All thought forms—logoic, planetary, and human—(for no other entities of lesser grade work as mental creators), emanate from a mind, are built for the purpose of carrying out some active work, demonstrate under set rules and laws, and have a definite goal, or expected consummation.

The Factor of Time. Specific purpose in the solar system is the gradual evolution of a definite plan originating in the Mind of the Logos, and slowly, and cyclically, achieving consummation. Three vast periods of time are consumed in the process:

The period of construction, wherein the form is built.
The period of utilisation, wherein the form is occupied, vitalised by a central Life, and employed.
The period of dissolution, wherein the form is devitalised, destroyed and dissipated.

In the first stage, that which concerns the tangible, that which deals with objectivity, is the more emphasised, and of supreme importance. In the second stage, the life within the form, or the subjective consciousness, comes gradually to the fore, and the *quality,* or the psyche of the thought-form, becomes apparent. In the final stage, the thought form (having performed its mission), separates into its basic duality, and will or energy (which lies, as a unity, back of duality), ceases in intent.

The objective life (*spiritual* life where cosmic thought-forms are concerned; *manasic* life when solar thought forms are constructed; and *elemental* life where human thought-forms are built) withdraws and the form dissipates.

In all these cases it will be apparent that only in the study of the development of the *quality* of the thought-form will its inherent purpose be revealed; only as its emanative processes are comprehended will the nature of its mission become recognisable. This is true fundamentally of all forms. Where the relatively unimportant forms—such as those constructed by man at this time—are concerned, this can easily be discovered, and to the trained clairvoyant each form reveals:

By its colour,
By its vibration,
By its direction,
By its keynote,

the nature of the inner life, the quality of its vibration and the nature of its goal. In the summation of all these points will the purpose reveal itself.

The Factor of Karma. Every thought-form comes under the law of Karma through the effect it produces. At this stage in the history of the system—that vast transitional stage between dense physical life and existence in the logoic etheric body—it is not easy for us to differentiate between those thought forms which are effects and those which are causes. It should be remembered here that *only cosmic and solar lords formulate thoughts.* The lunar Lords and all lesser intelligences do not do so. Therefore, the two above mentioned groups come under karmic law. They only are self-conscious, and therefore responsible. Where self-consciousness is not, there is no responsibility. Hence animals are not held to be responsible, and though they suffer on the physical plane and in their physical vehicles, on the subtler planes they are freed from karma, for they have neither memory nor anticipation; they lack the correlating faculty and as the spark of mind is missing, they are held free from the law of retribution, except where the physical body is concerned. The reason for the suffering in the animal kingdom is hidden in the mystery of the sin of the mindless,[80] and in that terrible period spoken of in the *Secret Doctrine,* which resulted in abortions and distortions of all kinds. Had this period not occurred, and this particular type of "miscarriage of purpose" not taken place, we should not have had the fearful karmic relationship which now exists between the third and the fourth kingdom.

The effect of the life and persistence of a thought-form, if maleficent and destructive, works out as "evil karma" if beneficent it works as "good karma" in the group in which the emanator has a place. This is what is meant by there being no karma attached to the working out of a good and altruistic deed.

The Factor of the Lesser Builders. Here a most interesting factor comes in upon which we shall enlarge later, when considering the elementals. The specific purpose of a thought-form is connected very closely with the type of deva essence of which it is constructed, and (in connection with man on the mental plane), with the type of elemental which he can control, and send forth as the occupier, or vitalising agency of the thought-form. Roughly speaking, a *solar Logos* works only through the greater Builders, the Manasaputras in Their

[80] *The sin of the Mindless.* See S. D., II, 195, 201. This sin has to do with the period of the Separation of the Sexes in the early third rootrace, the Lemurian. The same historical fact is hinted at also in the Bible in Genesis VI, 2:4.

"They (the sexes) had already separated before the ray of divine reason had enlightened the dark region of their hitherto slumbering minds, and had *sinned.* That is to say, they had committed evil unconsciously by producing an effect which was unnatural."

See also S. D., II, 721, 728.

various grades on the two higher planes of the solar system. He works through Them, and sends Them forth upon the mission of constructing, and vitalising the systemic thought-form, with a specific purpose in view. The *planetary Logoi* work primarily through the Builders of the next three planes (atma-buddhi-manas), who construct and control the work of the planetary schemes. *Men* work through the builders of the lower mental planes, and the astral plane, for the human thought-forms are kama-manasic; the physical plane builders are swept automatically into action by the force of the currents, and energies set up in subtler matter, by the great Builders.

The inserted tabulation opposite may make this clear. If the table is carefully studied, it will be seen that the fivefold earlier enumeration concerns the most important kingdoms in nature, whilst the final two are peculiarly interesting in that the mineral kingdom can in no sense be considered a principle, but simply the densest point of concretion of the abstract, and that the vegetable kingdom has a peculiar place in the economy of the system as the transmitter of the vital pranic fluid; the vegetable kingdom is definitely a bridge between the conscious and the unconscious. Here I am using these words in their broadest and most general sense. Though it is known that the mineral kingdom has a consciousness of its own, yet *sensation* is more distinctly recognisable in the second kingdom, and the distinction between the consciousness of the mineral and that of the animal is so vast that their respective consciousnesses are basically unlike. Between these stands the vegetable kingdom, approximating more generally the animal consciousness than the mineral, and having a most esoteric relationship to the deva evolution.

All these kingdoms of nature are "forms of thought"; all have body, vitality, quality and purpose, and all are

TABULATION IV

THE BUILDING ENTITIES

	Quality	Entity	Centre	Personality	Kingdom	
1.	Atma	Logos	Head (Brain)	Grand Heavenly Man	Seventh	Unity
2–3	Buddhi manas	Planetary Logos	Heart and Throat	Heavenly Men	Sixth and Fifth	Duality
4.	Mental	Man	Solar Plexus Base of spine	Man	Fourth	Triplicity
5.	Astral	Animal	Generative Organs		Third	Duality
6.	Etheric	Vegetable	Spleen		Second	Transitional
7.	Dense	Mineral	None		First	Unity

sent out by a greater life than their own upon a specific mission; they are sent forth by those who are self-conscious and are a blend of mind, spirit and objective form. Only the self-conscious can create, and only they are capable of purpose, of co-ordination, of direction and control.

Even though it may seem that much has been left unsaid, yet in due consideration of the above four points in connection with ''purpose'' in a thought-form, much can be worked out by the student himself.

In extending these ideas to a solar Logos, many questions of interest arise which are profitable only in so far as they expand the concept, and widen the horizon of the Thinker. The logoic purpose is not yet. comprehensible to man; it does not profit him to meditate thereon, yet in the formulation of ideas, and their apprehension by thinkers may come the gradual dawning of a day of recognition, and a subsequent co-operation with that divine purpose. Let us, therefore, formulate some of these questions, leaving the future to reveal the answer:

1. What may be the purpose of the present incarnation of the solar Logos?
2. What is the purpose which may perhaps be working out in our own planetary scheme and what is the basic plan of our planetary Logos?
3. Wherein does it differ from other planetary schemes?
4. What is the purpose lying back of the relation existing between our Earth and Venus?
5. Is the purpose of the animal kingdom, as a whole, in any way to be ascertained?
6. What is the purpose back of the present root-race evolution? Can we realise it?
7. What is the purpose behind the differing national forms?

Let us next bring the whole idea down to a more practical basis, and formulate questions along the following lines:

1. In what type of matter do I usually formulate thoughts?
2. What is the psychic quality of my thought-forms?
3. With what specific purpose do I use mental matter?
4. Do I work in mental matter consciously or unconsciously?
5. Do I vitalise my thought-forms with a high or a low order of entity?
6. Do I study the laws of construction?
7. Do I realise the power of the will to vitalise?
8. Do I destroy thought-forms when they have accomplished their purpose by a conscious act of the will?
9. Do I make forms which bring karmic effects, or do I build those which go to the good of the group?

Many such thoughts will arise, and in the study of thought man learns the laws of being.

2. *The Laws of Thought.*

There are three great laws, that we might term the fundamental laws of the cosmos, of that greater system (recognised by all astronomers), of which we form a part, and seven laws inherent in the solar system. These seven we might consider secondary laws, though, from the standpoint of humanity, they appear as major ones.

a. *Three Cosmic Laws.* The first of the cosmic laws is the *Law of Synthesis*. It is almost impossible for those of us who have not the buddhic faculty in any way developed, to comprehend the scope of this law. It is the law that demonstrates the fact that all things—abstract and concrete—exist as one; it is the law governing the thought form of that One of the cosmic Logoi in Whose consciousness both our system, and our greater centre, have a part. It is a unit of His thought, a thought form in its entirety, a concrete whole, and not the differentiated process that we feel our evolving system to be. It is the sumtotal, the centre and the periphery, and the circle of manifestation regarded as a unit.

The second law is the *Law of Attraction and Repulsion.* Fundamentally, the law describes the compelling force of attraction that holds our solar system to the Sirian; that holds our planets revolving around our central unit, the sun; that holds the lesser systems of atomic and molecular matter circulating around a centre in the planet; and that holds the matter of all physical plane bodies, and that of the subtle bodies co-ordinated around their microcosmic centre.

The third law is the *Law of Economy,* and is the law which adjusts all that concerns the material and spiritual evolution of the cosmos to the best possible advantage and with the least expenditure of force. It makes perfect each atom of time, and each eternal period, and carries all onward, and upward, and *through,* with the least possible effort, with the proper adjustment of equilibrium, and with the necessary rate of rhythm. Unevenness of rhythm is really an illusion of time, and does not exist in the cosmic centre. We need to ponder on this, for it holds the secret of peace, and we need to grasp the significance of that word *through,* for it describes the next racial expansion of consciousness, and has an occult meaning.

In the nomenclature of these laws much is lost, for it is well nigh impossible to resolve abstractions into the terms of speech, and not lose the inner sense in the process. In these laws we again have the threefold idea demonstrated, and the correspondence, as might be expected, holds good.

The Law of Synthesis. . The Will Aspect. . . . 1st Aspect.
The Law of Attraction. The Love Aspect. . . . 2nd Aspect.
The Law of Economy. . The Activity Aspect. 3rd Aspect.

b. *Seven Systemic Laws.*—Subsidiary to the three major laws, we find the seven laws of our solar system. Again we find the law of analogy elucidating, and the three becoming the seven as elsewhere in the logoic scheme. In each of these seven laws we find an interesting correlation with the seven planes. They are:

1. *The Law of Vibration,* the basis of manifestation, starting on the first plane. This is the atomic law of the system, in the same sense that on each of our planes the first subplane is the atomic plane.
2. *The Law of Cohesion.* On the second plane cohesion is first apparent. It is the first molecular plane of the system, and is the home of the Monad. Divine coherency is demonstrated.
3. *The Law of Disintegration.* On the third plane comes the final casting-off, the ultimate shedding of the sheaths, of the fivefold superman. A Chohan of the sixth Initiation discards all the sheaths beneath the monadic vehicle, from the atmic to the physical.
4. *The Law of Magnetic Control* holds sway paramountly on the buddhic plane, and in the development of the control of this law lies hid the control of the personality by the Monad via the egoic body.
5. *The Law of Fixation* demonstrates principally on the mental plane and has a close connection with manas, the fifth principle. The mind controls and stabilises, and coherency is the result.
6. *The Law of Love* is the law of the astral plane. It aims at the transmutation of the desire nature, and links it up with the greater magnetism of the love aspect on the buddhic plane.
7. *The Law of Sacrifice and Death* is the controlling factor on the physical plane. The destruction of the form, in order that the evolving life may progress, is one of the fundamental methods in evolution.

The Intermediate Law of Karma.—There is also an intermediate law, which is the synthetic law of the system of Sirius. This law is called by the generic term, the Law of Karma, and really predicates the effect the Sirian system has on our solar system. Each of the two systems, as regards its internal economy, is independent in time and space, or (in other words), in manifestation. We have practically no effect on our parent system, the reflex action is so slight as to be negligible, but very definite effects are felt in our system through causes arising in Sirius. These causes, when experienced as effects, are called by us the Law of Karma, and at the beginning they started systemic Karma which, once in effect, constitutes that which is called *Karma* in our occult and oriental literature.

The Lipika Lords of our system, the systemic Lords of Karma, are under the rule of a greater corresponding Lord on Sirius.

We have therefore:

1. The three cosmic laws of Synthesis, Attraction and Economy.
2. The Sirian law of Karma.
3. The seven laws of the solar system.

As we have been told, our seven major vibrations are the vibrations of the lowest cosmic plane; there is our habitat. Our Logos Himself, the heart of His system, is on the cosmic astral plane; he is polarised there. Just as the units of the fourth Creative Hierarchy, the human, are evolving through the use of physical bodies, but are polarised at this time in their astral vehicles, so we have seen that the objective solar system forms the physical body of the Logos, though His polarity is in His astral body. It is significant that in this greater manvantara, the Logos is to take the fourth cosmic Initiation. A hint which may enlighten lies in the correspondence which exists between this statement and the fourth root-race development, and this, the fourth or astral round.[81]

The system of the Sirian Logos is on the cosmic mental plane, and in a subtle way, incomprehensible to us, our Logos, with His system, forms a part of a still greater Logos. This does not involve loss of identity, though the matter is too abstruse to express more adequately. It is in this analogy that the basic idea can be found of all teaching given out about the Grand Heavenly Man. The whole conception of these laws is bound up in this idea. We have the three laws of the cosmic higher planes, holding in a synthesis of beauty the greater and the lesser system. Next we have the great law of Sirius, the Law of Karma, on the third subplane of the cosmic mental plane, which law really controls our Logos, and His actions, in the same way as the ego—in due course of evolution—controls the human personality.

We need to remember that, under the Law of Correspondences, we shall have a relationship in the Cosmos, similar to that existing in the microcosm between the ego and the personality. The suggestion holds much that we might consider with benefit. We must not, however, carry the analogy too far; as we have not yet evolved to where we have planetary consciousness, still less systemic, how can we really expect even to conceive of the A B C of cosmic truth? Just broad hints, wide conceptions, and generalities, are as yet possible. Of one thing we can be sure, and that is that *identity ever remains.*

Let me explain by illustration:

Each one of us, in due process of evolution, forms part of one of the Heavenly Men, Who Themselves form the

---

[81] *The present Round*, which is the fourth, is the one in which desire, or response to contact and sensation is being brought to its fullest expression. In the next round, the fifth, the fifth principle of mind, or manas, will reach fruition.

seven centres in that greater Heavenly Man, the Logos. Yet, though we are merged with the whole, we do not lose our identity, but forever remain separated units of consciousness, though one with all that lives or is. In like manner our Logos loses not His identity, even though He forms part of the Consciousness of the Logos of Sirius. In His turn, the Sirian Logos forms one of the seven Grand Heavenly Men, who are the centres in the body of ONE OF WHOM NOUGHT MAY BE SAID.

The Laws and the Planes.—We might, while studying the seven laws of the solar system, take them plane by plane, showing certain things—three in all:

1. We might study their effect as they demonstrate on the path of involution.
2. As they manifest on the path of evolution, or return.
3. We might also touch on the laws as they affect the human and deva organisms that evolve by means of them.

As we do this, we shall gradually get a broad general idea of how this system of ours (the thought-form of the Logos), was gradually built up, how it is controlled and held together, and how numerous and intricate are the interrelations. Certain fundamental hypotheses are assumed, which must form the background for all we would say. We must assume first that a Builder, or some Creative Mind, is working to bring about an ordered production, and is seeking to manifest through a demonstrable objective. The objective universe is but the product of some subjective mind. Next we must posit that the material for the building of this universe lay ready to the hand of the Builder, and that this material itself is the fruit of some previous system, all that is left of some past consummated product. Given, therefore, the Builder and the material, we must next accede to the proposition that this Builder proceeds with His building under some definite laws that guide His choice of material, that control the form that He erects, and that indicate to Him the process to be followed in the consummating of His idea. We must not forget that three great symbols stand, in the mind of the Logos, for each of His three systems, that the whole exists for Him as a concrete thought-form, for He is learning to manipulate the matter of the cosmic mental plane on concrete levels, in the same way that man is working on the laws of thought, and on the building of thought-forms.

It is impossible to do more than sense the symbols of the systems past and present. Perhaps if we could visualise a swastika of ten arms revolving at right angles, of a radiant green colour, all the ten arms emanating from a central blazing sun, we might have some idea of the thought-form that formed the basis of *System I, the activity system.* The basic thought-form for *the second system* embodies the green swastika of the first manifestation, and adds to it concentric and interlaced circles in blue, in groups of three, linked by one large circle. Both symbols are, of course, in the higher dimensions. The symbol for the next system is unknown. After grasping and conceding these three basic ideas, we can now proceed to the working out of the laws of the system on the seven planes, remembering always that these seven laws hold good on the numerically corresponding subplane on each plane. Let me briefly illustrate:

The fourth law, Magnetic Control, for instance, holds sway on the fourth subplane of each plane, in the fourth round, and in the fourth root-race specially. We shall then have the correspondence as follows:

4th Law ....Magnetic Control.
4th Ray ....Harmony or beauty.
4th Plane ....The buddhic.

4th Subplane ....Buddhic Magnetic Control.
4th Round ......Dense Physical Magnetism, controlling sex
                manifestation on the physical plane, and
                inspired by astral desire, the reflection of
                the buddhic.
4th Root-Race ...The Atlantean, in which the above qualities
                specially demonstrated.

1. *The Law of Vibration.*—This is the law of the first plane, and it governs all the atomic subplanes of each plane. It marks the beginning of the work of the Logos, the first setting in motion of mulaprakriti. On each plane the vibration of the atomic subplane sets in motion the matter of that plane. It is the key measure. We might sum up the significance of this law in the words, "light" or "fire." It is the law of fire; it governs the transmutation of differentiated colours back to their synthesis. It controls the breaking up of the One into the seven, and then the reabsorption back into the One. It is really the basic law of evolution, which necessitates involution. It is analogous to the first movement the Logos made to express Himself through this solar system. He uttered the Sound, a threefold Sound, one sound for each of His three systems, and started a ripple on the ocean of space. The Sound grows in volume as time progresses, and when it has reached its full volume, when it is fully completed, it forms one of the notes in the major cosmic chord. Each note has six subtones, which, with the first, make the seven; the Law of Vibration, therefore, comprises eighteen lesser vibrations and three major, making the twenty-one of our three systems. Two multiplied by nine (2x9), makes the necessary eighteen, which is the key number of our love system. Twenty-seven holds hid the mystery of the third system.

On the path of involution, the seven great Breaths or Sounds drove to the atomic subplane of each plane, and there the basic vibration repeated in its own little world the method of logoic vibration, giving rise itself to six subsidiary breaths. We get the same correspondence here as we did in the matter of the Rays, for we shall find that the lines of vibration are 1-2-4-6. Logically this would be so, for involution is negative, receptive, and corresponds to the feminine pole, just as the abstract rays were 2-4-6. This truth requires meditation, and an attempt to think abstractly; it is linked to the fact that the whole second system is receptive and feminine; it concerns the evolution of consciousness of the psyche.

On the path of evolution this law controls the positive aspect of the process. All is rhythm and movement, and when all that evolves on each plane attains the vibration of the atomic subplane, then the goal is reached. When, therefore, we have achieved the first main vibrations, and have perfected vehicles for all evolutions (not merely the human), of fivefold atomic subplane matter, then we have completed the round of evolution for this system. In the coming system we shall add the next two vibrations that complete the scale, and our Logos will then have completed His building.

The fourth Creative Hierarchy, that of the human Monads, has to learn to vibrate positively, but the devas proceed along the line of least resistance; they remain negative, taking the line of acquiescence, of falling in with the law. Only the human Monads, and only in the three worlds, follow the positive line, and by resistance, struggle, battle and strife learn the lesson of *divine* acquiescence. Yet, owing to the increase of friction through that very struggle, they progress with a relatively greater rapidity than the devas. They have need to do this, for they have lost ground to make up.

The Law of Vibration is the law of progress, of movement and of rotation. On the seventh or lowest plane, the vibration is slow, clogged and lethargic from the

standpoint of the first, and it is in learning to vibrate or
to rotate more rapidly, that we mount the path of return.
It involves, therefore necessarily, the building in of finer
matter into the vehicles, both deva and human. In this
second system, on the five planes of human evolution, we
have the five vehicles—physical, astral, mental, buddhic
and atmic—which have all to be purified, rarefied, intensified and refined. In the two lowest, the physical and
the astral, only matter of the five higher subplanes, of
their respective planes, is to be found, for the two lowest
subplanes are too low for deva or human bodies; they
were dominated in the first system. The mental body
is the first in which we find matter of all the subplanes.
The aim of evolution for us is love dominated by intelligence—or intelligence dominated by love, for the interaction will be complete. The human race came into the
chain at a point where it naturally took bodies of the
fifth astral and physical subplanes, and we can see here
an analogy to the coming into the fourth root-race of the
more advanced Egos.

2. *The Law of Cohesion.*—This is one of the branch
laws of the cosmic Law of Attraction. It is interesting
to notice how this law demonstrates in this Love-System
in a threefold manner:

On the plane of the Monad, as the law of cohesion, the
law of birth, if we might use that term, resulting in
the appearance of the Monads in their seven groups.
Love the source, and the Monad of love, the result.

On the plane of buddhi, as the law of magnetic control. It shows itself as the love-wisdom aspect, irradiating the ego, and eventually gathering to itself the essence
of all experience, garnered, via the Ego, through the
personality lives, and controlled throughout from the
plane of buddhi. Magnetism, and the capacity to show
love, are occultly synonymous.

On the astral plane, as love demonstrating through the

personality. All branches of the law of attraction, demonstrating in this system, show themselves as a force that ingathers, that tends to coherence, that results in adhesion, and leads to absorption. All these terms are needed to give a general idea of the basic quality of this law.

This law is one of the most important of the systemic laws, if it is permissible to differentiate at all; we might term it the law of coalescence.

On the path of involution it controls the primal gathering together of molecular matter, beneath the atomic subplane. It is the basis of the attractive quality that sets in motion the molecules and draws them into the needed aggregations. It is the measure of the subplanes. The atomic subplane sets the rate of vibration; the Law of Cohesion might be said to fix the colouring of each plane. It is the same thing in other words. We need always to remember in discussing these abstract fundamentals that words but dim the meaning, and serve but as suggestions and not as elucidations.

In manifestation the cosmic Law of Attraction controls all these subsidiary laws, just as the Law of Synthesis governs pralaya and obscuration, and the law of Economy deals with the general working out, along the line of least resistance, of the logoic scheme. During manifestation we have most to do with the Law of Attraction, and it will be found, on study, that each subsidiary law is but a differentiation of that law.

This second law of the system governs specially the second plane, and the second subplane on each plane. It might be interesting to work this out and trace the underlying correspondence, bearing in mind always that all that can be done is to point out certain things, and indicate lines of thought that may lead, if pursued, to illumination.

Ray Two and Law Two are closely allied, and it is

interesting to realise that it is on the second subplane
of the monadic plane that the majority of the Monads
have their habitat; there are a few Monads of power or
will on the atomic subplane, but their numbers are not
many, and they simply form a nucleus in evolutionary
preparation for System III, the power system. The
majority of the Monads are on the second subplane and
they are the Monads of love; on the third subplane can be
found quite a number of the Monads of activity, but
numerically not as many as the Monads of love. They
are the failures of System I.

There is a direct channel, as we know, between the
atomic subplane on each plane. This is more or less
true of each subplane and its corresponding higher subplane numerically, and there is, therefore, a direct and
quite expansive channel between the second subplane
on all planes, enabling the Monads of love to link up
with peculiar facility with all their vehicles when composed of second subplane matter. After initiation, the
causal body is found on the second subplane of the
mental plane, and monadic control then commences.

The Monads of love return (after life in the three
worlds and the attainment of the goal) to their originating second subplane, that being also the goal for the
monads of activity who have to develop the love aspect.
In the five worlds of human evolution both groups of
Monads have to control atomic and molecular matter as
well and this is done by the utilisation to the full (as full
as may be possible in this second system), of the will or
power aspect.

The "Kingdom of God suffereth violence and the violent take it by force," or by Will or power. It is not
Will, as we shall know it in the final system but it is Will
as known in this system, and it has to be utilised to the
uttermost by the evolving Monad in his struggle to control each *atomic* subplane. The Monads of power have

a much greater struggle, and hence the fact so often apparent that people on what we term the power Ray, have so often a hard time, and are so frequently unlovable. They have to build in on all the six planes the love aspect, which is not prominent in their development.

A hint has been given us as to the approximate figures governing the Monads:

35 Thousand million Monads of love
20 Thousand million Monads of activity
5 Thousand million Monads of power

making a total of sixty thousand million human Monads. The Monads of power, though in manifestation, are as yet very rare in incarnation. They came in, in large numbers, at the close of the moon chain, and will come in again in full numerical strength in the last two rounds of the present chain.

We might now briefly trace the correspondence in the second round and the second root-race, showing how the Law of Cohesion was specially active at these periods. A condition of nebulosity of a pronouncedly volatile condition, marked the first round and race. Movement, and the accompaniment of heat, is their distinguishing quality, much as in System I, but in the second round, and also in the second race, a definite cohesion is noticeable, and form is more clearly recognisable in outline. Cohesion is also plainly to be seen as the distinguishing feature of our present system, the second. It is the aim of all things to unite; approximation, unification, a simultaneous attraction between two or more is ever to be seen as a governing principle, whether we look at the sex problem, or whether it demonstrates in business organisation, in scientific development, in manufacture, or in politics. Well might we say that the *At-one-ment* of the many separated is the keynote of our system.

One more suggestion may be given: On the path of

involution this law governs the gathering together and the segregation of matter; on the evolutionary path it controls the building of forms. It has been stated that the matter of the lowest subplane forms the basis of a new plane; therefore we have on the atomic subplane a point where merging takes place, which makes it a plane of synthesis, just as in the same way the first or logoic plane is the plane of synthesis for this system. There takes place the merging of evolution into an inconceivably higher state.

3. *The Law of Disintegration.*—This is the law that governs the destruction of the form in order that the indwelling life may shine forth in fullness. It is another aspect of the Law of Cohesion—the reverse side (if one might so express it), and is just as much a part of the divine plan as that of attraction. It is one of the laws that ends with the solar system, for the great laws of attraction, cohesion and love last on into that which is to come. The Law of Disintegration has its correspondence in cosmic law, but it is almost incomprehensible to us. The Law of Economy holds the key to this law. When the Monad has circled through all disintegrating forms, and has achieved the sixth Initiation, it is resolved into its primal monadic source, and the five lesser sheaths are destroyed. Later on the Monads themselves are synthesised, not disintegrated. This law controls only from the third plane, and ceases action in this particular fashion when the third plane is transcended.

This law is one of the most difficult for the race to understand. Some of its workings (those on the path of evolution), can be seen and somewhat comprehended, but on the path of involution, or of construction, the working out of the law is not so apparent to the superficial observer.

On the path of involution it controls the process of the

breaking up of group souls; it governs the periods when
the permanent triads are transferred from one form to
another; it works through the great world cataclysms,
and we need to remember that it governs, not only the
physical plane catastrophes (as we erroneously term
them), but the corresponding cataclysms on the astral
plane, and the lower levels of the mental plane. It
governs physical plane disruptions, especially those affecting the mineral world; it controls the disintegration,
on the astral plane, of thought-forms; it dissolves the
astral vehicle when left behind, and the mental likewise.
The dissipation of the etheric double is the result of its
working.

Again we can correlate this law with that of Attraction, for the two interact upon each other. This law
breaks up the forms, and the Law of Attraction draws
back to primal sources the material of those forms, prior
to rebuilding them anew.

On the path of evolution the effects of this law are
well known, not only in the destruction of the discarded
vehicles touched upon above, but in the breaking up of
the forms in which great ideals are embodied,—the forms
of political control, the forms in which nature itself
evolves, apart from those in which individual consciousness manifests, the great religious thought-forms, the
philanthropic concepts and all the forms which science,
art, and religion take at any one particular time. All
eventually break under the working of this law.

Its workings are more apparent to the average human mind in its manifestations at this time on the physical plane. We can trace the connection between the
atmic and the physical plane (demonstrating on the
lower plane as the law of sacrifice and death), but its
effect can be seen on all the five planes as well. It is
the law that destroys the final sheath that separates the
perfected Jiva. It has not yet been fully brought out

(for the law of correspondences has been little studied, nor is it readily apparent) that on the third subplane of each plane this law works in a special manner, causing a very definite breaking-up of something that is tending to separation. Like all that works in the system, the process is slow; the work of disintegration begins on the third subplane, and is finished on the second, when the Law of Disintegration comes under the influence of the Law of Cohesion, the disintegration having effected that which makes cohesion possible. We can see an illustration of this on the mental plane. The causal body of the average man is on the third subplane, and as a man becomes fit for the merging into the Triad, that causal body has to be discarded and done away with. Under the Law of Sacrifice and Death, the disintegration is begun on the third level and is consummated on the second, when the man merges with the Triad, preparatory to the final merging with the Monad.

Another illustration of the same thing can be found on the physical plane. When a man has reached the point where he can sense and see the fourth ether, he is ready for the burning away of the etheric web, which has its location midway between the third and second subplane matter which composes his physical body. When this disintegration is effected, the man merges with his astral vehicle, establishing a consequent continuity of consciousness. This correspondence, and this disintegration, can be traced on each plane, till finally on the atmic level on its third subplane comes the final disintegration, which results in a merging with the monadic consciousness.

The third Ray, that of adaptability or activity, has a close connection with this law. It is through activity (or the adaptation of matter to need), that the form comes into being; through activity it is employed, and through that very adaptation it becomes a perfect form, and at the moment of perfection loses its usefulness; it crystallises, breaks, and the evolving life escapes to find for itself new forms of greater capacity and adequacy. It is so in the life of the reincarnating Ego; it is so in the rounds and races of humanity; it is so in the solar system; it is so in all cosmic processes.

In the third chain, the moon chain, we have an interesting related fact. On the moon chain the point of attainment for the individual was the arhat or fourth Initiation,—the initiation which marks the final breaking with the three worlds, and the disintegration of the egoic body.

At the end of the third root-race came the first of the great cataclysms that broke the race form, and inaugurated a new one, for it was the first definitely human race as we now know it. The analogy will be found to hold good no matter from what angle the subject may be studied. In the third subrace a correspondence can be traced, though it is not yet apparent to the circumscribed vision which characterises most of us. Close proximity to an effect often veils a cause.

4. *The Law of Magnetic Control.*[82]—This law is the basic law controlling the Spiritual Triad. Through this law, the force of evolution drives the Ego to progress through the cycle of reincarnation back to union with his kind. Through separation he finds himself, and then—driven by the indwelling buddhic or Christ principle—transcends himself, and finds himself again in all selves. This law holds the evolving lower self in a coherent form. It controls the Ego in the causal body, in the same way that the Logos controls the Monad on the second plane. It is the law of the buddhic plane; the

---

[82] Note the correspondence that can be traced here. On the second plane we have the Law of Cohesion—love. On the second plane of the manifesting Triad, the Law of Magnetic Control—love. Again lower down on the second plane of the Personality, the Law of Love. The accuracy of the analogy is quite interesting, and provides room for speculation.

Master is one Who can function on the buddhic levels, and Who has magnetic control in the three worlds. The lower is always controlled from above, and the effect the buddhic levels have on the three lower is paramount, though that is scarcely yet conceded by our thinkers. It is the Law of Love, in the three worlds, that holds all together, and that draws all upward. It is the demonstration, in the Triad, of the Law of Attraction.

On the path of involution this law works with the permanent atoms in the causal body. It is the buddhic principle, and its relation with the lower permanent atom of the Triad is the mainspring of the life of the Ego. On the path of descent it has much to do with the placing of the permanent atoms, but this matter is very abstruse, and the time has not yet come for further elucidation. At the third outpouring, (in which the fourth kingdom, the human, was formed), it was this Law of Magnetic Control that effected the juncture of astro-animal man, and the descending Monad, using the spark of mind as the method of at-one-ment. Again we can see how it works. The monadic plane, the buddhic plane, and the astral plane are all three closely allied, and we find there the line of least resistance. Hence the facility with which the mystic contacts the buddhic and even higher planes. The lines of least resistance in the three systems are:

System   I. Physical, mental, and atmic.
                 The atmic was the highest point of
                 achievement in that system.
           II. Astral, buddhic and monadic.
           III. Mental, atmic and logoic.

Note the correspondence therefore to be seen between the fourth kingdom and the working of this, the fourth law. It is of vital moment in this fourth chain.

As regards human evolution, this fourth law is of prime importance at this time. The aim of human en-

deavour is both to be controlled by this law, and likewise to wield it in service. It is the law whereby sex
expression, as we know it, is transmuted and elevated;
sex is only the physical plane demonstration of the Law
of Attraction; it is the working out of that law in the
human kingdom, and in all the lower kingdoms, too. The
love of all that breathes, and the attraction that works
out in service, is the same thing as demonstrated in the
Triad. Sex expression, the coming together of two, becomes transmuted into the coming together of many for
acts of service, which will give birth to new ideals, and
to a new race—the spiritual.

Here I might point out a numerical fact that may be
of interest in connection with the fourth hierarchy.
This human hierarchy is the fourth, as we know, yet if
we count the five hierarchies that have passed on, it is
in reality the ninth. Nine is the number of initiation,
the number of the adept, and of the man who functions
in his buddhic vehicle.

The fourth Ray also operates in close connection with
the fourth Law. It is the Ray of Harmony or Beauty—
Harmony through control, that control entailing the
knowledge of wisdom. It is the harmony of similarity;
it is the equilibrising of all through the realisation of the
laws of magnetism that produce the co-ordination of the
many diverse into the one homogeneous; magnetism governs the synthesis of the many aspects into a form of
unity. This harmony is reached through the fifth plane,
and the fifth Ray of Concrete Knowledge acts as a step
to the fourth, for many who work on the fifth Ray pass
eventually to the fourth. In this system the fifth Ray
is of paramount importance in the development of all
egos. Each must pass some time on it before definitely
remaining on his monadic Ray. In many incarnations
much time is spent on the fifth subplane of each plane,
which is governed principally by the fifth Ray. All pass

then on the fourth subplane governed by the fourth
Ray, and in this particular period of the fourth round in
the fourth chain, more time is spent on the fourth subplane by evolving Egos than on any other. Many come
into incarnation directly on to this plane, and it is here
that they begin to think harmoniously.

The Laws in the Three Worlds.—We will now take up
and briefly study the three most important laws affecting the evolving human being, as he lives his life in the
three worlds. These laws are:

> 1. The Law of Fixation.
> 2. The Law of Love.
> 3. The Law of Sacrifice and Death.

These laws are all dominated and controlled eventually by the three higher laws in the system—the Laws
of Magnetic Control, of Disintegration, and of Cohesion. There is a direct connection between these seven
laws and the seven Rays or Vibrations, and if we study
the correspondence we shall recognise the fact that the
first law, that of Vibration, is the controlling law of the
six, demonstrating through the second law, that of Cohesion, just as the solar Logos is at this time manifesting Himself through His second aspect in this the second
solar system.

The first Ray of Will or Power is the first aspect
of the All-self, and in the third outpouring,[83] came

[83] *The Three Outpourings.* ''In the diagram the symbols of the three
Aspects (of the Logos) are placed outside of time and space, and only
the streams of influence from them descend into our system of planes. . . .
They represent in due order what are commonly called the three Persons
of the Trinity. . . . It will be seen that from each of them an outpouring
of life or force is projected into the planes below. The first of these in
order is the straight line which descends from the third Aspect; the second
is that part of the large oval which lies on our left hand—the stream
which descends from the second Aspect until it has touched the lowest
point in matter, and then rises again up the side on our right hand until
it reaches the lower mental level. It will be noted that in both of these
outpourings the divine life becomes darker and more veiled as it descends

down to the fifth plane, along with the other monads. A subtle correspondence exists between the monads of Will on the fifth plane, the fifth law, and the fifth Ray.

The second Ray or the Love-Wisdom aspect wields a control on the fourth and sixth planes, and dominates the Laws of Cohesion and Magnetic Control, and the astral Law of Love. There is a direct interlinking between the abstract Rays and the laws of the planes where they specially control.

The third Ray which is the Activity aspect, controls the Laws of Disintegration and of Death, on the third and seventh planes.

Therefore, it will be apparent to the careful student of the wisdom that:

1. *The Power Aspect*—Ray 1, Planes 1 and 5, and the Laws of Fixation and Vibration, form one interlocking whole.
2. *The Love Aspect*—Ray 2, Planes 2, 4, 6, and the Laws of Cohesion, Magnetic Control, and of Love, form another unit.
3. *The Activity Aspect*—Ray 3, Planes 3 and 7, and the Laws of Disintegration, Sacrifice and Death, make still another group.

It is logical for the first Ray only to have control, as yet, on two planes, for the Power Aspect waits for another system in order to demonstrate in full development. Ray two, the synthetic Ray for our system, con-

into matter, until at the lowest point we might almost fail to recognise it as divine life at all; but as it rises again when it has passed its nadir it shows itself somewhat more clearly. The third outpouring which descends from the highest aspect of the Logos differs from the others in that it is in no way clouded by the matter through which it passes, but retains its virgin purity and splendour untarnished. It will be noted that this outpouring descends only to the level of the buddhic plane (the fourth plane) and that the link between the two is formed by a triangle in a circle, representing the individual soul of man—the reincarnating ego. Here the triangle is contributed by the third outpouring and the circle by the second. . . .''—*The Christian Creed*, by C. W. Leadbeater, pp. 39, 40.

trols on three planes; it has the preponderance, for
paramountly we are the Monads of Love, and Love is
our synthesis. Ray three, the dominant Ray of the system which is past, its synthetic Ray, controls on two
planes, and on one that is little understood, for, just as
the physical body is not considered a principle, so there
is a sphere of activity that is not included in our
enumeration, it is past and gone. Some explanation of
this lies hid in the occult words, "The Eighth Sphere."

In regard to the four minor Rays of Harmony, Concrete
Science, Devotion and Ceremonial Order, their control
exists in degrees on all the planes, but they have their
particular emphasis in the evolution of the reincarnating
ego in the three worlds at this time. These four Rays
control, in a subtle and peculiar manner, the four kingdoms of nature—mineral, vegetable, animal and human
—and at their merging into the three Rays of Aspect
(the Activity Ray of the Mahachohan being the synthesiser of the lower four in our planetary scheme) have
a correspondence with the merging of man (the product of the three kingdoms and the fourth) into the superman kingdom, the spiritual. The fourth Ray and the
fourth Kingdom form a point of harmony for the lower
three, and all four then pass into the major or upper
three. This is worthy of our serious thought, and the
analogy of the fourth plane will also be apparent. For
this system, the buddhic plane, the human kingdom, and
the fourth Ray of Harmony or Beauty or Synthesis,
have a point of correspondence, just as the fourth root-
race is the one in which the synthesis is first observed—
the door into the fifth kingdom of Spirit being then
opened; the fourth rootrace also developed the astral
capacity that made contact with the fourth or buddhic
level possible.

In a subtle way too (I use the word subtle for lack of
a better, meaning a statement of actuality that seems an

illusion), the three minor Rays, Concrete Science, Devotion and Ceremonial Law, have each a connection with the three kingdoms of nature below the human, and with the three laws of the three lower worlds.

The Ray of Ceremonial Order has special significance at this time; it controls life in the mineral world, and in the final stages of involutionary life at the point where the upward turn of evolution is made. Through Ceremonial Order comes the control of the lesser builders, the elemental forces, the point of synthesis in the lowest plane of all, the period of transition. In all such periods the seventh Ray comes in (as now) the Ray of Law and Order, of accurate arrangement and formation. It is the reflection on the physical plane of the Power and Activity Aspects working in synthesis. Rays 1, 3, 7, have an interplay, as we know. Ray seven is the appearance in combination of the forces of evolution. It is the manifestation of Power and Activity on the lowest plane of all. It is allied to the laws of the third and seventh planes, Disintegration and Death, for all periods of transition are periods of the destruction and building of forms, and the shattering of the old in order that newer and better chalices of life may be constructed.

The Ray of Devotion has a definite though little known connection with the vegetable kingdom. We must remember that it is linked to a subsidiary law of the cosmic Law of Attraction. It is in the vegetable kingdom that we find one of the first and temporary approximations between the evolving human Monad, and the evolving deva Monad. The two parallel evolutions touch in that kingdom, and then again follow their own paths, finding their next point of contact on the fourth or buddhic level, and a final merging on the second.

The concrete Rays have an especial effect on the *negative* evolution of the devas, who form the feminine aspect of the divine hermaphroditic Man, working along the lines of more positive development. The abstract Rays do a similar work on the *positive* human hierarchy, tending towards a more receptive attitude. This hierarchy forms the masculine aspect of the divine Hermaphrodite. But at three points on the path of evolution the Monads of Love, working on the abstract qualities, touch the devas of activity working on concrete faculty. The perfection of the two evolutions marks the point of attainment of the divine Heavenly Man; it is the perfecting of the two major centres, creative activity and love, of the Logos. In their lower aspect these centres are known as the centres of generation and the solar plexus, but are transmuted, as evolution proceeds, into the throat and heart centres. Then, in a dual synthesis, they will pass on into the third system, that in which the Power aspect is developed, and the head centres will be complete. This achieved, our Logos has triumphed, and measured up to the sixth cosmic Initiation, just as He should measure up in this system to the fourth.

The Ray of Concrete Science has a peculiar relationship to the animal kingdom, in that it is the Ray that governs the merging of that kingdom into the human. The planet, Venus, in her fifth round, gave the impetus which produced the spark of mind in animal man—a fact well known. It is also the fifth Ray, and has an interesting connection with the fifth Law of Fixation. We might study, too, with profit, the analogy that can be seen between these factors and the fifth root-race, the race of peculiarly strong development of the concrete mind. The Law of Analogy always holds good.

With this as a basis, the three laws of the personality become replete with life, and can be summed up in the well-known term, "The Law of Rebirth and Death in the three worlds." The fifth law governs a fixed point in the personality, that of the fifth principle.

The Law of Love in the astral body also has its points for consideration. There is a direct link between the astral body (love in the personality), the buddhic vehicle (love in the Triad), and the Monads of Love. Later on, this will be understood more fully, but it is the main channel for the basic law of the system, Love. These three points mark periods of completion, and likewise starting-points for fresh endeavour in the life of the evolving Monad—from the personality to the Triad, from the Triad to the Monad, from the Monad back again to its source.

5. *The Law of Fixation.*—This is the governing law of the mental plane, finding its greater correspondence in the Law of Karma on cosmic mental levels. "As a man thinks, so is he;" according to his thoughts are his desires and acts, and so results the future. He fixes for himself the resultant karma. The word "Fixation" is chosen for two purposes: First, because the word implies the capacity of the thinker to shape his own destiny, and secondly because the word implies a stabilising idea, for as evolution progresses, the Ego evolves the faculty of forming definite concrete thought-forms, and, through these stable products, of subduing the fluctuations of the astral body.

This law of the fifth, or mental plane is one of the most important laws with which we have to do at any time, and it will find its most complete demonstration in the next, or fifth round. In relation to this fourth round the following facts may be gathered about its working:

It is the law under which the evolving personality builds up, during the course of many lives, the causal body; it fixes the matter inhering in that body, placed there by the man as the ages slip away, and crystallises it. Before the fourth Initiation the crystallisation is complete, and the inevitable shattering that is the result of crystallisation in all forms, takes place, setting the indwelling life free for further progress. All forms are but hindrances and limitations, and ultimately must go, but they have their needed place in the development of the race. Eventually the causal body of the entire race itself disintegrates.

This law governs the crystallisation of all forms prior to their shattering in the process of evolution.

It governs the *time* of rebirth, being one of the subsidiary branches of the Law of Karma. Each of the seven subsidiary laws is linked to one of the cosmic laws, or with the Sirian Law of Karma. We need always to remember that the consciousness of the cosmic mental plane is the logoic goal of attainment, and that the Sirian Logos is to our solar Logos what the human Ego is to the personality. The Law of Karma, or cosmic Fixation, is the law of the cosmic mental plane, and controls the corresponding law in our system.

In the fifth round this law will act as the divider, temporarily crystallising and fixing into two great classes the human Monads, as they evolve. One group then (containing those who will reach the goal), will pass gradually out from under the domination of this law, and will come under the Law of Magnetic Control. The other will remain under the law in a static condition, until in a later period a fresh opportunity will come; old forms will break, and in another mahāmanvantara, and in its fifth period, will come the chance for which they will have waited, when they can again swing into the current of evolution and the imprisoned spirits may mount again towards their source.

In an occult sense this law is for us the one with which we are the most intimately concerned. It plays an important part in the hands of the Lords of Flame, and is one of Their main factors in controlling the three worlds. Note here an interesting fact, that Venus is the sixth planet (esoterically the second), and is in her fifth round, and hence is ahead of us along every line.

This law demonstrates the static quality of love, static temporarily, but necessarily so when viewed from the standpoint of time, the great deluder. On the path of involution this law again works with the permanent atoms in the three worlds, with the building in of material around those atoms, in connection with the building devas and the reincarnating Egos. The devas are the mother aspect, the builders of the body, and the reincarnating Jivas are the son aspect; yet the two are but one, and the result is the divine hermaphroditic man.[84]

6. *The Law of Love.*—It is not easy, in this brief digest, to approach the tremendous problem of the place love plays in the evolving scheme of things as understood by three-dimensional man. A treatise could be written on the subject, and yet leave it unexhausted. Much light comes if we can ponder deeply on the three expressions of Love: Love in the Personality, Love in the Ego, and Love in the Monad. Love in the Personality gradually develops through the stages of love of self, pure and simple and entirely selfish, to love of family and friends, to love of men and women, until it arrives at the stage of love of humanity or group love consciousness which is the predominant characteristic of the Ego. A Master of Compassion loves, suffers with, and remains with His kind and with His kin. Love in the Ego gradually develops from love of humanity into love universal—a love that expresses not only love of humanity, but also love of the deva evolutions in their totality, and of all forms of divine manifestation. Love in the Personality is love in the three worlds; love in the Ego is love in the solar system, and all that it contains; whilst love in the Monad demonstrates a measure of cosmic love, and embraces much that is outside the solar system altogether.

[84] See page 512.

This term "The Law of Love," is after all too generic a term to apply to one law governing one plane, but will have to suffice for the present, as it conveys the type of idea that is needed, to our minds. The Law of Love is in reality but the law of the system in demonstration on all the planes. Love was the impelling motive for manifestation, and love it is that keeps all in ordered sequence; love bears all on the path of return to the Father's bosom, and love eventually perfects all that is. It is love that builds the forms that cradle temporarily the inner hidden life, and love is the cause of the disruption of those forms, and their utter shattering, so that the life may further progress. Love manifests on each plane as the urge that drives the evolving Monad onwards to its goal, and love is the key to the deva kingdom, and the reason of the blending of the two kingdoms eventually into the divine Hermaphrodite. Love works through the concrete rays in the building of the system, and in the rearing of the structure that shelters the Spirit, and love works through the abstract rays for the full and potent development of that inherent divinity. Love demonstrates, through the concrete rays, the aspects of divinity, forming the *persona* that hides the one Self; love demonstrates through the abstract rays in developing the attributes of divinity, in evolving to fullest measure the kingdom of God within. Love in the concrete rays leads to the path of occultism; love in the abstract rays leads to that of the mystic. Love forms the sheath and inspires the life; love causes the logoic vibration to surge forward, carrying all on its way, and bringing all to perfected manifestation.

In System I, Activity, Desire for Expression, and the *Impulse to Move* was the basic note. That activity produced certain results, certain permanent effects, and thus formed the nucleus for the present system. Ordered Activity is the foundation of this system of ordered

Love, and leads to system three, wherein ordered Activity, with ordered Love for its impulse, results in ordered loving Power.

The sixth Ray of devotion and the sixth law of love have a close alliance, and on the sixth plane comes the powerful working out in the lower Triad, the Personality, of the Law of Love. On the astral plane, the home of the desires, originate those feelings which we call personal love; in the lowest type of human being this shows itself as animal passion; as evolution proceeds it shows itself as a gradual expansion of the love faculty, passing through the stages of love of mate, love of family, love of surrounding associates, to love of one's entire environment; patriotism gives place later to love of humanity, often humanity as exemplified in one of the Great Ones. The astral plane is, at the present time, the most important for us, for in desire—not corrected or transmuted—lies the difference between the personal consciousness and that of the Ego.[85]

In the sixth Scheme, that of Venus, this can be seen clearly; it is the scheme of love. Viewed from one angle, the Venusian Scheme is the second, and from another it is the sixth. It depends upon whether we reason from the circumference to the centre or the reverse.

It is the home of the planetary Logos of the sixth Ray. This may sound like a contradiction, but it is not so really; we must remember the interlocking, the gradual shifting and changing, that takes place in time on all

---

[85] Why do we consider this matter of the devas of the middle system (as we might call those connected with this system and with buddhi and kama-manas) in our consideration of thought forms? For two reasons: One is that all that is in the solar system is but substance energised from the cosmic mental and astral planes, and built into form through the power of electrical law; all that can be known is but forms ensouled by ideas. Secondly, that in the knowledge of the creative processes of the system, man learns for himself how in time to become a creator. We might illustrate this by remarking that one of the main functions of the Theosophical movement in all its many branches is to build a form which can be ensouled, in due time, by the idea of Brotherhood.

the Rays. In the same way the Earth chain is the third if viewed from one aspect and the fifth viewed from another.

In the sixth chain of each scheme, this sixth law and the sixth Ray have a very important significance, whilst the seventh chain of each scheme is always synthetic— Love and Activity in a perfect balance. The same effect can be demonstrated in the sixth Round. In the sixth Round of the present chain of the Earth scheme, the sixth law will demonstrate with great clarity and force, as love shown in brotherhood, love translated or transmuted from the astral to the buddhic. So in the sixth rootrace and the sixth subrace a similar analogy will be seen. Out of the shattered form of the fifth subrace of the fifth root race, built up under the fifth Ray of Concrete Knowledge, with the aid of the fifth Law of Fixation, will emerge the sixth subrace of brotherly love —love shown in the realisation of the one life latent in each Son of God.

7. *The Law of Sacrifice and Death.* This law links itself to the third law, that of Disintegration following the connection that always exists between the atmic and the physical plane. The Law of Disintegration controls the fivefold destruction of forms in the five lower worlds, and the Law of Death controls similarly in the three worlds. It is subsidiary to the third law. The Law of Sacrifice is the Law of Death in the subtle bodies, whilst what we call death is the analogous thing in the physical body. This law governs the gradual disintegration of concrete forms and their sacrifice to the evolving life, and is closely linked in its manifestation with the seventh Ray. This Ray is the one that largely controls, that manipulates, that geometrises and that holds sway over the form side, governing the elemental forces of nature. The physical plane is the most concrete exemplification of the *form side;* it holds the divine life imprisoned or

enmeshed at its densest point, and it works at this time in line with the seventh law. In a mysterious way this law is the reverse side of the first, or the Law of Vibration. It is Vulcan and Neptune in opposition, which is as yet an almost incomprehensible thing for us. The densest form of expression on the physical plane is after all but a form of synthesis; just as the rarest form of expression on the highest plane is but unity or synthesis of a finer kind. One is the synthesis of matter, and the other the synthesis of life.

This law governs the seventh chain in each scheme; each chain having achieved the fullest expression possible in the scheme, comes under the Law of Death, and obscuration and disintegration supervenes. In a cosmic sense and analogy, it is the law that governs the coming in of pralaya at the end of a system. It is the law that shatters the cross of the cosmic Christ, and places the form of the Christ within the tomb for a period of time.

The Principle of Mutation. In concluding the above information about the laws, it is needful that we all recognise the extreme danger of dogmatising about these matters, and the risk of laying down hard and fast rules. Much must remain unexplained and untouched, and much also will serve to raise only questions in our minds. Comprehension is as yet impossible. Until fourth-dimensional sight is ours, it will scarcely be possible for us to do more than hint at, and get a passing vision of, the complexity and the interweaving in the system. It is not easy for us to do more than grip as a mental concept the fact that the rays, schemes, planets, chains, rounds, races and laws form a unit; seen from the angle of human vision the confusion seems unimaginable, and the key of its solution to be so hidden as to be useless; yet, seen from the angle of logoic sight, the whole moves in unison, and is geometrically accurate. In order to give some idea of the complexity of the arrangement, I would like here to point out that the Rays themselves circulate, the Law of Karma controlling the interweaving. For instance, Ray I may pass around a scheme (if it is the paramount Ray of the scheme) with its first subray manifesting in a chain, its second in a round, its third in a world period, its fourth in a root race, its fifth in a subrace, and its sixth in a branch race. I give this in illustration, and not as the statement of a fact in present manifestation. This gives us some idea of the vastness of the process, and of its wonderful beauty. It is impossible for us, sweeping through on some one Ray, to visualise or in any way to apprehend this beauty; yet, to those on higher levels and with a wider range of vision, the gorgeousness of the design is apparent.

This complexity is for us very much increased because we do not yet understand the principle governing this mutation. Nor is it possible for even the highest human mind in the three worlds to do more than sense and approximate that principle. By mutation I mean the fact that there is a constant changing and shifting, an endless interweaving and interlocking, and a ceaseless ebb and flow, in the dramatic interplay of the forces that stand for the dual synthesis of Spirit and matter. There is constant rotation in the Rays and planes, in their relative importance from the standpoint of time, which is the standpoint most closely associated with us. But we can rest assured that there is some fundamental principle directing all the activities of the Logos in His system, and by wrestling to discover the basic principle on which our microcosmic lives rest, we may discover aspects of this inherent logoic principle. This opens to our consideration a wide range of vision, and though it emphasises the complexity of the subject, it also demonstrates the divine magnitude of the scheme, with its magnificent intricacies. The reason the fourth is a major round is because in this round two things happened—the spark of mind was implanted and the door was opened from the animal kingdom into the human; and later, another door opened, on to the Path leading from the human kingdom into the spiritual— again a dual reason. The fifth round is a major round because it marks a point in evolution where those who will achieve the goal, and those who will not, are sharply differentiated into two groups; the seventh is a major round because it will mark the merging of the two evolutions, the human and the deva.

The major root races are chosen under the Law of Correspondence. In the third root race came the third Outpouring, the merging and the point of contact between the Spiritual Triad and the Lower Quaternary. The fifth root race marks a point where higher and lower manas approximate, and where the concrete mind, meeting its highest development of this round, gives place to the intuition from above. Here again we have a twofold reason. The seventh root race again demonstrates dual attainment, love in activity, the basis of the third system of Will or Power.

The three major Rays, being dual, are their own sufficient explanation. They are at present the mode of expression of the three aspects, and demonstrate under their appropriate Logoi, Who manipulate world affairs through the three departments, of which the rulers on our planet are the Lord Maitreya, the Manu, and the Mahachohan. The three major planes demonstrate easily their unique position—on plane two we have the home of the Monads of Love, on plane five we find the habitat of their reflections, the reincarnating Egos, and

on the physical plane we find the working out at its
densest point of the life of the Spirit.

This principle of mutation governs every department
in the Law of Correspondences, and certain things can
be stated as regards the system, and its component parts
which will be found illuminating if we remember that
they are facts *for the present*. Let me again illustrate:
we have been told that the three major Rays *at this time*
are the first, the second, and the seventh. But later, the
Rays now major may become subsidiary, and others take
their place, though for this solar system the second Ray,
being the synthetic Ray, will always be a major Ray.
Perhaps we can here get a hint on this great principle,
though we must be careful not to draw it out to too fine
a conclusion. For this system the major Rays will
always be the dual Rays—the negative-positive Rays,
the masculine-feminine Rays—this being the dual system.
The major Rays for system three will be those in triple
manifestation.

The following table may be found of interest, if regarded as relative, and as holding information for the
present time, but also as being subject to change and
circulation:

7 Rays ....Major 1-2-7 ...Four subsidiary converging on
the fifth.

7 Principles ..3 Major ......Monad, Ego and Personality,
synthesising at various stages
the four subsidiary.

7 Chains .....Major 1-4-7 ...

7 Planes ......Major 2-5-7 ...

7 Manvantaras.Major 3-4-7 ...

7 Rounds .....Major 4-5-7 ...

7 Root races ..Major 3-5-7 ...

7 Sub races ...Major 1-5-6 ...

7 Initiations ..Major 1-4-5 ...if viewed from the angle of
human attainment, and 1-5-7
if viewed from a higher.

II. Thought Elementals and Devas.

1. The Ruler of Fire—Agni.

a. *Agni and the Solar Logos.*

Thus far in this treatise we have considered the first section of the book which has dealt somewhat with the internal fires of the system, both macrocosmic and microcosmic. In this the second section we are dealing with the fire of mind. This section, together with the nine introductory questions, constitutes the main part of the treatise. In it we have dealt with the nature and function of mind and with the egoic ray. We have dealt also, somewhat, with the form side of thought, with its material manifestation and with its substance.

We proceed now to take up the consideration of *the Ruler of Fire, AGNI,* and are brought to the study of the vitality that energises and the Life that animates; to the contemplation of the Fire that drives, propels, and produces the activity and organisation of all forms. The realisation of this will reveal the fact that what we are dealing with is the "Life and the lives,"[86] as it is called [87]

---

[86] *The Life and the Lives.* H. P. B. says in the *Secret Doctrine.*
"Occultism does not accept anything inorganic in the Kosmos. The expression employed by Science 'inorganic substance' means simply that the latent life, slumbering in the molecules of so-called 'inert matter' is incognisable. All is Life, and every atom of even mineral dust is a Life, though beyond our comprehension and perception. . . . Life therefore is everywhere in the Universe . . . wherever there is an atom of matter, a particle or a molecule, even in its most gaseous condition, there is life in it however latent and unconscious."—S. D., I, 269, 281, 282.

[87] The Life and the Lives.
1. Everything lives and is conscious, but all life and consciousness is not similar to the human.—S. D., I, 79.
    a. Life is the one form of existence manifesting in matter.
    b. Matter is the vehicle for the manifesting of soul.
    c. Soul is the vehicle for the manifesting of Spirit.
Therefore: 1st Logos, 2nd Logos, 3rd Logos co-operate.
Illustration:
    Life of the 3rd Logos—animating atoms of matter.
    Life of the 2nd Logos—animating the forms, or aggregate of atoms.
    Life of the 1st Logos—animating the composite forms.
2. The one Life synthesises this triplicity.
Let us work this out in the Macrocosm and Microcosm.

in the *Secret Doctrine;* with Agni, the Lord of Fire, the Creator, the Preserver, and the Destroyer; and with the forty-nine fires through which He manifests. We are dealing with solar fire per se, with the essence of thought, with the coherent life of all forms, with the consciousness in its evolving aspect, or with Agni, the sumtotal of the Gods. He is Vishnu and the Sun in His glory; He is the fire of matter and the fire of mind blended and fused; He is the intelligence which throbs in every atom; He is the Mind that actuates the system; He is the fire of substance and the substance of the fire; He is the Flame and that which the Flame destroys.

Students of the *Secret Doctrine* when they read carelessly are apt to consider Him only as the fire of matter and omit to note that He is Himself the sumtotal—and this is especially the case when they find that Agni is the Lord of the mental plane.[88] He is the animating life of the solar system, and that life is the life of

Fohat, Prana, Electricity, Magnetic Fluid, are all terms used for this one vitalising life.

The Microcosm is animated and vitalised by prana, and its actions controlled by the indwelling Thinker.

The Macrocosm is animated and vitalised by Fohat; its actions are controlled by the informing Intelligence we call the Logos.

[88] ". . . Agni, who is the source of all that gives light and heat. So that there are different species of Agni (fire); but "whatever other fires there may be, they are but the ramifications of Agni, the immortal'' (Rig Veda, L, 59 I). The primary division of Agni is threefold. "Agni," says the Vishnu Parana, "has three sons, Suchi, Pavamana, and Pavaka" (I, x). Suchi means the Saura, or Solar fire; Pavamana means Nirmathana, fire produced by friction, as the friction of two pieces of wood; and Pavaka means the vaidyuta or fire of the firmament, i.e. the fire of the lightning, or electric fire.

The sources of these three fires, I may observe in passing, constitute the three principal deities spoken of in the Veda, namely, Surya, the sun, representing the solar fire; Indra (and sometimes, Vayu) the rain-producing deity, representing the fire of the firmament; and Agni, representing the terrestrial fire, the fire produced by friction (Nirukta, VII, 4); and all these three, be it remembered, are merely the ramifications of one Agni; which in its turn is an emanation from the Supreme One, as the reader will find from the allegorical description given of Agni as being the mouth-born son of Brahma, in the Vishnu purana.

Now, each of the triple forms of Agni has numerous subdivisions. The solar fire is distinguished by several divisions according to the nature of the rays emitted by the great luminary.''—*The Theosophist,* Vol VII, p. 196.

God, the energy of the Logos, and the manifestation
of the radiance which veils the Central Sun. Only as
He is recognised as Fohat, the energy of matter, as
Wisdom, the nature of the Ego and its motivation, and
as essential unity, can any due conception be arrived
at as to His nature or being. He is not the solar Logos
on the cosmic mental plane, for the egoic consciousness
of the Logos is more than His physical manifestation,
but *Agni is the sumtotal of that portion of the logoic
Ego which is reflected down into His physical vehicle;
He is the life of the logoic Personality, with all that is
included in that expression.* He is to the solar Logos
on His own plane what the coherent personality of a
human being is to his Ego in the causal body. This is a
very important point to be grasped, and if meditated
upon will bring to the student much enlightenment. His
is the life that fuses and blends the threefold nature of
the Logos when in physical incarnation; His is the coherent force that makes a unity of the triple logoic Personality, but man can only arrive at His essential nature
by the study of the logoic physical vehicle—hence the
difficulty; he can only understand by a consideration of
His psychic emanation as it can be sensed and viewed by
passing the history of the races in retrospect. Man's
personality reveals his nature as his life progresses; his
psychic quality unfolds as the years slip away, and when
he passes out of incarnation he is spoken of in terms of
quality, good or bad, selfish or unselfish; the effect of his
"emanation" during life is that which remains in men's
minds. Thus only can the logoic personality express
itself, and our knowledge of His nature is consequently
limited by our close perspective, and handicapped by
the fact that we are participants in His life, and integral
parts of His manifestation.

It is only as we begin to function upon the buddhic
plane that we can in any way "live in the subjective"

side of nature, and it is only as our knowledge of the
spiritual life increases, and as we pass definitely through
the portal of initiation into the fifth kingdom that we
can appreciate the distinction between the dense physical, and the vital body. Only as we become polarised
in the cosmic etheric body and are no longer held prisoner by a dense material sheath (for the three lower
planes are but the dense body of the Logos) do we come
to a fuller understanding of the psychic nature of the
Logos, for we stand then in the body which bridges the
gulf between the dense physical, and the astral body of
the Logos. Only when this is the case do we understand the function of the Lord Agni as the vital life
of the cosmic etheric, as the vitality of the Heavenly
Men and the activity of Their sheaths.

b. *Agni and the Mental Plane.*

I seek to deal with a very important point here, emphasising the close connection between Agni, the sumtotal of the life force of the logoic threefold personality, as He is seen at work on the mental plane (which
closely concerns man), and that manifesting driving
force or intelligent will which emanates from the cosmic
mental plane. There is a very interesting series of correspondences to be worked out here and we might briefly
indicate the lines to be followed in this connection by
the ensuing tabulation:

The 5th cosmic plane .... The cosmic mental.
The 5th systemic plane .... The mental plane.
The 5th subplane of the phys-
    ical .... The gaseous.
The 5th principle .... Manas.
The 5th Law .... Fixation, the Law of Concretion.
The 5th Ray .... Concrete knowledge.
The 5th round .... The round of manasic attain-
                             ment.

The 5th root-race .... The Aryan. Mental development.

The 5th sub-race .... The Teutonic and Anglo-Saxon. Concrete mind.

The 5th group of Devas .... Fire Devas of the mental plane.

The 5th Manvantara .... Three-fifths of the manasaputras achieve.

The 5th scheme .... The Lord of concrete science.

The 5th Mahamanvantara (or solar system) .... The solar Logos achieves His fifth major Initiation.

The 5th chain .... Principal evolution—fire devas.

The 5th Hierarchy .... The greater Builders.

Vibrations of fifth order ...... Manasic.

It will, therefore, be apparent that when the system is viewed in reverse order and the physical plane is counted as the first (as it often is when considering it as the field of strictly human evolution), that the third plane—the mental plane—comes under the same group of correspondences and Agni, as the energising factor of the dense physical body of the Logos, or as the fire of His most concrete manifestation, vitalising, warming and holding all together, has to be considered.

Three hierarchies are, in this mahamanvantara, of profound significance, the fourth or human Creative Hierarchy, and the two deva hierarchies, the fifth and sixth.

The fourth Hierarchy in the larger scheme is literally the ninth, for five hierarchies have earlier passed on and are considered as pure abstractions. In this system concretion concerns us, and the blending of form and of energy into one coherent whole. In the ninth, tenth and eleventh Hierarchies lies the clue to the nature of Agni, the Lord of fire, the sumtotal of systemic vitality. He who understands the significance of these figures, and their relation to each other as *the triple division of a Unity in time and space* will have dis-

covered one of the keys which will unlock a door hitherto
fast closed. They are the numbers of achievement, of
potentiality brought into full activity and of innate
capacity demonstrating in perfect fruition. All potentiality lies in the vitalising, energising power of Agni,
and in His ability to stimulate. He is life itself, and the
driving force of evolution, of psychic development and of
consciousness. This fact is hidden in these figures, and
not the evolution of substance, which is but a result,
emanating from psychic causes. These three numbers
are the basis of the cyclic calculations which concern
the egoic cycles, and the cycles of Vishnu, as distinguished from the cycles dealing with the third aspect.
Occult students have not sufficiently grasped the fact
that objectivity is an inevitable result of an inner conscious subjective life. When this is better apprehended,
bodies on the physical plane, for instance, will be purified, developed and beautified through a scientific attention paid to the development of the psyche, to the
unfoldment of the Ego, and to the stimulation of the egoic
vibration. The cause will be dealt with and not the
effect, and hence the growing appreciation by the human
family of the study of psychology, even though as yet
they are but studying the kama-manasic body, and have
not reached back to the egoic consciousness. The lunar
Lords have had their day; now Agni, as the solar Lord
of life and energy, will assume due importance in human
life.

c. *Agni and the Three Fires.*

In studying the manifestation of Agni in the solar
system it should be remembered that we are considering
here His essential nature as *actuating fire.* We have
seen that He is the threefold logoic personality, but
He is the threefold Logos in a subjective sense, and the

TABULATION V

AGNI—LORD OF FIRE

Aspect	Fire	Result	Subjective Manifestation	Origin of Energy	Objective Manifestation
First, Will	Electric Fire	Activity of Spirit	The One Life. Unity. Spiritual. Dynamic. Coherence. Synthesis.	Central Spiritual Sun	The solar system (etheric and dense)
Second, Love-Wisdom	Solar Fire	Activity of Consciousness. Egoism. Vitality. Magnetism.	The seven Heavenly Men. The seven Rays. The seven types of Mind	The Heart of the Sun	The seven Rays manifesting through the seven planetary schemes
Third, Activity	Fire by Friction	Activity in matter. Atomic vitality. Energy.	The seven fires. The akasha.	The physical Sun	The seven planes

form aspect is only subsidiary. Perhaps a tabulation may make this point clearer.

Each of these three aspects of the One Fire, showing as the Creative Fire, Preserving Fire, and Destroying Fire, must be studied as electrical phenomena, and this under the aspects of light, flame, and heat, of electricity, radiance and motion, of will, desire and action. Only thus will the true nature of Agni be apprehended. As the logoic personality He is demonstrating through a triplicity of sheaths forming a unity, and only thus will it become apparent why at this stage in evolution the material aspect is the most considered.

The entire system is the physical sheath of the Logos and consequently the most easily cognised, for the Logos is as yet centred in His cosmic sheaths and can only reveal Himself through their medium.

Man's just apprehension of this mystery of electricity will only come about as he studies himself, and knows himself to be a triple fire, manifesting in many aspects.

MAN, A FIRE

Monadic fire	Electric fire	Spirit Will	The Central Spiritual Sun.
Egoic fire	Solar fire	Consciousness Love-Wisdom	The Heart of the Sun.
Personality fire	Fire by friction	Physical man	Physical Sun.

Each of these fires can also be studied in a threefold manner and under three aspects.

THE MONAD

Will aspect	Electric fire	Flame	Spiritual Will.
Love-wisdom	Solar fire	Light	Spiritual Love.
Active Intelligence	Fire by friction	Heat	Spiritual Intelligence.

THE EGO

Will	Atma	Electric fire	The spark The Jewel in the Lotus	Conscious Will.
Love- Wisdom	Buddhi	Solar fire	The rays The twelve- petalled lotus.	Conscious Love.
Active Intelli- gence	Manas	Fire by friction	Substance The perma- nent atoms.	Conscious Activity.

THE PERSONALITY

Will	Mental body	Electric fire	Lower mind	Thought
Love	Astral body	Solar fire	Kama	Desire
Activity	Physical body	Fire by friction	Prana	Activity

I seek to emphasise here the fact that in this three-fold manifestation there is a ninefold unfoldment. It should ever be borne in mind that seven is the number which governs the evolution of substance and of form building in the solar system, but that nine is the number governing the development of the consciousness within that form of the psyche. This is seen in the sevenfold display of logoic life through the planetary scheme, and the ninefold nature of egoic unfoldment.

If the student here substitutes for the words, Monad, Ego and personality, the three aspects of the Logos, and will bear in mind that as yet all that he can ascertain or cognise is the lowest of the logoic manifestations—the personality—it will be apparent why so much must remain mysterious to even the higher grades of initiates, and why even the perfected Dhyan Chohan cannot pene-trate the secrets of the Logos outside His system.[89] They

[89]H. P. B. in the *Secret Doctrine* refers to ". . . the solution of the riddle . . . before which even the highest Dhyan Chohan must bow in

can cognise much concerning Agni, the Lord of Fire, but until They can contact that of which He is an emanation, a reflection or a ray, there is a limit to what may be known.

Agni is Fohat, the threefold Energy (emanating from the logoic Ego) which produces the solar system, the physical vehicle of the Logos, and animates the atoms of substance. He is the basis of the evolutionary process, or the cause of the psychic unfoldment of the Logos, and He is that vitality which ultimately brings about a divine synthesis in which the form approximates subjective demand, and after being consciously directed, and manipulated, is finally discarded. This is the goal for the Logos as it is for man; this marks the final liberation of a human being, of a Heavenly Man and of a solar Logos.

We could divide the process into three periods:

First. The period wherein the fire of matter (the heat of mother) hides, nourishes and brings to birth the infant Ego. This is the period of purely personality life, when the third aspect dominates, and man is in the veil of illusion.

Second. The period wherein the Ego, or subjective life within the form, passes through certain stages of unfoldment, and comes to an ever fuller consciousness. This is the period of egoic development, and is produced by the gradual merging and blending of the two fires. It is the life of service and of the Path.

Third. The period wherein the egoic consciousness itself is superseded by spiritual realisation, and the fire of Spirit blends with the other two.

At first the personality acts the part of mother, or of material aspect, to the germ of the inner life. Then

silence and ignorance—the Unspeakable Mystery of that which is called by the Vedantins, Parabrahman.''—S. D., I, 352.

the Ego manifests its life within the personal life, and produces a shining forth which "groweth ever more and more until the perfect day." [90]   At that perfect day of revelation it is seen what man in essence is, and the Spirit within is revealed. This can be studied from the Christian angle, and Paul was but voicing an occult truth when he enunciated the facts concerning the birth of the Christ within the heart, and the growth of the higher life at the expense of the lower. Thus also can it be taught along occult, and not mystic, lines in the recognition (by science) of the vitalisation of the permanent atoms (the force centres of the sheaths or substance), of the unfoldment of the egoic lotus, and the awakening of its petals, and in the final revelation of the jewel in the lotus.

All that can be said of man can be predicated of the Logos on an inconceivably greater scale. As man discovers the laws of his own material sheaths—the laws of substance—he is ascertaining the nature of the fires of the outer man or Fohat, as he vitalises the logoic vehicle; the fires of his own sheaths are aspects of Agni as the fire of matter. As he ascertains the nature of consciousness, and the laws of psychical unfoldment he is studying the nature of the vitality of the subjective man, and the laws of conscious being, thus studying Agni as He manifests as Light and Cool Radiance, shining through the vehicle. Later (for the time is not yet) as he comes to comprehend the nature of his Monad, the spiritual or essential life which is developing consciousness by means of the sheaths, he will discover the nature of Agni as He shews forth as pure electricity. Even though this is not yet possible, nevertheless the statement as to the lines of investigation which can be pursued, and the realisation of that which may eventually

[90] Bible.   Proverbs IV, 18.

be achieved, may cause men's minds to turn to the study
of the real and of the true.

2. The Fire Devas the Greater Builders.

I have divided the groups of devas and elementals
into evolutionary and involutionary Builders—those who
are in themselves positive force, and those which are
negative force, the conscious and the blind workers. It
is absolutely essential that students bear in mind here
that we are studying the mystery of electricity and therefore must remember the following facts:—

a. Introductory Remarks.

The Mystery of Electricity. The greater Builders are
the positive aspect of substance or of electrical phenomena whilst the lesser Builders are the negative
aspect.

Two types of force are represented in the activities of
these two groups and it is their interaction and interplay
which produces Light, or the manifested solar system.

Their sumtotal is substance in its totality, the intelligent active form, built for the purpose of providing a
habitation for a central subjective life.

They are also the sumtotal of the Pitris,[91] or Fathers
of mankind, viewing mankind as the race itself, the
fourth kingdom in nature, the Heavenly Men *in physical
manifestation.* This is a most important point to emphasise. These deva activities in relation to Self-Consciousness (which is the distinctive characteristic of
humanity) can best be studied in the large, or through

[91] *The Lunar Pitris.*
"The great Chohans called the Lords of the Moon, of the airy bodies:
"Bring forth Men," they were told, "men of your nature. Give them
their forms within. She (Mother Earth) will build coverings without (for
external bodies). Males—females will they be. Lords of the Flame also.
. . . They went each on his allotted lands: Seven of them each on his lot.
The Lords of the Flame remained behind. They would not go. They
would not create."—*Stanza* III, 12, 13, S. D., II, 79, 81.

the consideration of groups, of races, and of the life of the scheme, the manifestation of one of the Heavenly Men. When the student brings his study of deva work down to the terms of his own individual life he is apt to become confused through too close a juxtaposition.

The greater Builders are the solar Pitris, whilst the lesser Builders are the lunar ancestors. I would here explain the occult meaning of the word "ancestor," as used in esotericism. It means literally initiatory life impulse. It is that subjective activity which produces objectivity, and concerns those emanatory impulses which come from any positive centre of force, and which sweep the negative aspect into the line of that force, and thus produce a form of some kind. The word "ancestor" is used in connection with both aspects.

The solar Logos is the initiatory impulse or Father of the Son in His physical incarnation, a solar system. He is the sumtotal of the Pitris, in the process of providing *form*. The union of Father (positive force) and Mother (negative force) produces that central blaze which we call the form, the body of manifestation of the Son. *A Heavenly Man* holds an analogous position in relation to a planetary scheme. He is the central germ of positive life or force, which, in due course of time, demonstrates as a planetary scheme, or an incarnation of the planetary Logos. *A man* similarly is the positive life or energy which, through action on negative force, creates bodies of manifestation through which he can shine or radiate.[92, 93, 94]

The lesser Builders [95] are the negative aspect and are swept into action in group formation through the play

---

[92] The Lunar Pitris created the physical man.—S. D., I, 114, 197.
They exist in three great classes.
1. The most developed. They form, in Round one, the sumtotal of the three kingdoms, and achieve a human form.—S. D., I, 203.
In Rounds two and three they are the sumtotal of that which will eventually be human.

of positive force upon them, or through the action of the conscious Minds of the system. At the present stage of evolution—during the period of Light—it is difficult for the human being (until he has attained the consciousness of the Ego) to differentiate between the types of force, and to work *consciously* with these dual aspects. An Adept of the Light works with force in substance, viewing substance as that which is negative, and therefore occultly to be moved, and He can do this because He has (in the three worlds of His endeavour) achieved unity, or the point of balance and equilibrium, and can therefore balance forces and deal with positive and negative energies as appears best in the interests of the plan of evolution. The Brother of Darkness, knowing himself to be positive force in essence, works with negative substance, or with the lesser Builders to bring about ends

In Round four at the beginning they form the etheric bodies of our Earth humanity.
2. Those whose bodies are taken by the Solar Angels.—S. D., I, 203.
3. The sum total of the three kingdoms at present known.
⁹⁰ The Earth gives man his body; the Gods give him his five inner principles . . . Spirit is one.—S. D., I, 248.
1. The Earth gives the dense physical.
2. The Lunar Gods give him three lower principles—
    a. Etheric body
    b. Prana
    c. Kama—manas
3. The Solar Gods give him two principles—
    d. Lower mind
    e. Higher mind
4. The Monad is the unified two highest principles—
    f. Buddhi
    g. Atma

—S. D., I, 248.

⁹¹ The totality of form. God is "One, notwithstanding the innumerable forms which are in Him," so is man, on earth the microcosm of the macrocosm.—S. D., II, 197; II, 303; III, 584.
Everything is comprised in man.
He unites in himself all forms.
The mystery of the earthly man is the mystery of the Heavenly Man.
The potentiality of every organ useful to animal life is locked up in man, the Microcosm of the Macrocosm.—S. D., I₁, 723.
⁹⁵ *Pitris*—The ancestors or creators of mankind. They are of seven classes, three of which are incorporeal and four corporeal. These are usually called the Lunar Pitris or Ancestors and must not be confounded with the Solar Pitris or Angels, who give *mind* to man, and create the relatively permanent body of the ego, or Higher Self.

of his own, incited thereto by selfish motive. The Brothers of Light co-operate with the positive aspect in, and of, all forms—the building devas of evolutionary intent—in order to bring about the purposes of the Heavenly Man Who is the sumtotal of planetary physical manifestation.

It can be seen, therefore, how necessary it is that the functions of the devas of all grades be comprehended. It is however equally important that man should refrain from the manipulation of these forces of nature until such time as he "knows" himself, and his own powers, and until he has fully unfolded the consciousness of the ego; then, and only then, can he safely, wisely, and intelligently co-operate in the plan. As yet, for the average man or even the advanced man this is dangerous to attempt and impossible to accomplish.

Now, let us add a few more statements upon which the student can ponder before we pass on to study specifically the three main groups of building devas on the three planes in the three worlds which most intimately concern man.

The building devas [96] are the Ah-hi, or Universal Mind. They contain within their consciousness the plan logoic,

---

[96] Devas. ". . . he would have (1) divided the Devas into two classes—and called them the "Rupa-devas" and the "Arupa-devas" (the "form" or objective, and the "formless" or subjective Dhyan Chohans; and (2) would have done the same for his class of "men" since there are Shells and "Mara-rupas"—i.e. bodies doomed to annihilation. All these are:

  (1) "Rupa-devas"—Dhyan Chohans, having forms. ⎫
  (2) "Arupa-devas"—Dhyan Chohans, having no forms. ⎬ Ex-men.
  (3) "Pisachas"—(two-principled) ghosts. ⎭
  (4) "Mara-rupa"—Doomed to death (three principled).

  (5) Asuras—Elementals—having human form. ⎫
  (6) Beasts—Elementals second class—animal elementals. ⎬ Future men.

  (7) Rakshasas—(Demons) Souls or Astral Forms of sorcerers; men who have reached the apex of knowledge in the forbidden art. Dead or alive they have, so to say, cheated nature; but it is only temporary—until our planet goes into obscuration, after which they have nolens volens to be annihilated.

It is these seven groups that form the principal divisions of the Dwellers of the subjective world around us."—*Mahatma Letters to A. P. Sinnett,* 107.

and inherently possess the power to work it out in time and space, being the conscious forces of evolution.

They not only embody the Divine Thought but are that through which it manifests, and its actuating activity. They are essentially motion. The lesser builders are more particularly the material form which is actuated, and in their cohorts are the substance of matter (considering substance as that which lies back of matter).

They are that which produces concretion and which gives form to the abstract. The terms "rupa" and "arupa" devas are relative,[97] for the formless levels and the formless lives are only so from the standpoint of man in the three worlds; the formless lives are those which are functioning in and through the etheric body of the Logos, formed of the matter of the four higher planes of the system. From this point of view the mental plane provides an interesting consideration:—its three higher subplanes are positive, and centralise the positive force of the plane. This focussing of the positive affects the negative substance of the four lower planes and brings about likewise:

a. The formation of force centres on the causal levels, those force centres being egoic groups in their various divisions.
b. The concretion of substance, or the building of the dense physical body of the Logos.

On the physical plane of the solar system an analogous process can be seen taking place as regards the physical

---

[97] Rupa..........with form or body.
Arupa.........formless or bodiless.
Generally speaking, the term *rupa* is applied to all forms in the three worlds whilst the term *arupa* is applied to all forms through which existences manifest on the four higher levels of the solar system and the abstract levels of the mental plane.

body of man, or his concrete manifestation. In his case, the fourth subplane is the focal point of positive force. On that plane are located *the etheric centres of man, which have, in the evolutionary process and in the work of force direction, a relationship to his physical body similar to the relationship which groups of Egos on the mental plane have to the dense physical body of the Logos. This is a profound occult hint.*

In the words "prana and the etheric body" (or life force and form) we have the key to the mystery of the solar and lunar pitris, and a hint as to the place of the physical body in the scheme of things.

The solar Pitris and devas find their force expression most adequately through man, with all that is included in that term. They are the source of his self-consciousness, and it is their action upon the negative aspect which produces the human Ego (on a large scale, viewing them in their totality as cosmic force); it is their action upon the negative or mother aspect which, on cosmic levels, produces that Self-conscious Unity, a solar Logos, functioning through His physical vehicle. From the Christian standpoint, the greater Builders are the Holy Spirit, or force overshadowing and fecundating matter, whilst the negative or lesser Builders correspond to the Virgin Mary.

The lunar Pitris, and lesser builders from the systemic point of view find their fullest expression in the animal kingdom. When they, as the initiatory impulse, had produced animal man they had performed their prime function, and just as (on a smaller scale and in connection with only one of the Heavenly Men) the moon is a dying and decadent world, so on a systemic scale and therefore covering a vast period of time, the work of the lunar Pitris is slowly coming to a conclusion as the power of the third kingdom, the animal, over the human is being superseded by spiritual power; the systemic correspondence to lunar pitric activity will occultly die out.

The lunar Pitris,[98, 99] the builders of man's lunar body and their correspondence in the other kingdoms of nature, are the sumtotal of the dense physical body of the Logos, or the substance of the mental, astral and physical planes (the gaseous, liquid and dense bodies which form a unity, His physical vehicle, viewing it apart from the etheric). They are the product of an earlier solar system; their activities date from there. That system stands to the present one as the lunar chain to ours. That is why the physical body is considered no principle (either for man or the solar Logos); that is why the lower nature is considered evil, and why man must "slay his lunar body."[1] Evil is that which can be controlled and subdued but which is permitted to govern. The positive can always manipulate the negative. When the negative line is followed and the line of least resistance to that which is no principle, is pursued, then we have evil.

In the first solar system the negative substance aspect, the Mother aspect or matter, was perfected. The lower Pitris dominated. In this system force activity lies in the hands of the solar Pitris or greater devas. At the close of the mahamanvantara they will have built accord-

[98] The Lunar, or Barhishad Pitris have the following function:—S. D., II, 99.
1. They are the Ancestors of Man.—S. D., II, 107.
2. They are the Fashioners of his form.
3. They possessed the physical creative fire.
4. They could only clothe the human monads.
5. They could not make man in their likeness.
6. They could not give him mind.—S. D., II, 82.
7. They build his external form.
8. They give the lower principle.—S. D., II, 92.
[99] Temporarily they are the Conquerors of Spirit.—S. D., II, 66.
a. Spirit becomes immersed in material forms.
b. Forms are the battle ground.
c. Eventually Spirit will slay the forms.—S. D., II, 67.
d. Note the esoteric order.—S. D., II, 88, 92, 100; II, 116.
[1] In the *Voice of the Silence* the words occur:
"Before that Path is entered, thou must destroy thy lunar body, cleanse thy mind body, and make clean thy heart."

ing to the plan a perfect sheath or vehicle of expression for the Divine Thought, and this through the manipulation of negative substance; they utilise the heat of the Mother to nourish the germ of the Divine Thought, and to bring it to fruition. When the germ has developed to maturity the Mother aspect no longer has a place, and the Man occultly is freed or liberated. This idea runs through all manifestations, and the kingdoms of nature or the form (no matter what form it may be) nourish the germ of that which is the next step on in the evolutionary process, and are considered the Mother aspect. This aspect is eventually discarded and superseded. For example, the third kingdom, the animal, in the early stages nourishes and preserves the germ of that which will some day be a man; the personality is the preserver of that which will some day unfold into spiritual man.

It will thus become apparent to students how the Heavenly Man, viewing Him as a solar Deity, a self-conscious Entity, works with His negative aspect through positive force, from logoic etheric levels upon the three aspects of the logoic dense physical, thus bringing to maturity the atoms and cells of His Body, fostering the germ of self-consciousness, fanning the flame until each unit becomes fully group conscious and aware of his place within the body corporate. Each human being likewise, functioning in the three worlds, works in a corresponding way upon the conscious cells of his bodies, until each atom eventually achieves its goal. The Heavenly Man works necessarily through egoic groups, pouring positive force upon them until they emerge from passivity and negativity into potency and activity. Man works correspondingly through his centres upon his sheaths, and has a responsibility to the lesser lives which under the karmic law must be worked out. This is the basis of the evolutionary process.

b. The Functions of the Devas.

Having predicated certain basic facts about the devas, viewing them as the sum total of the energy of substance and of substance itself, we come down to more technical details and to the more detailed consideration of these building forces as they construct the thought-form of the Logos, the solar System. From this consideration of them certain practical knowledge will eventuate:

First. Knowledge of how to build in mental matter in the three worlds, and how to employ the devas of the gaseous plane of the cosmic physical.

Second. Realisation of how to combine the pairs of opposites, and thus give body and form to concept.

Third. Materialisation upon the physical plane of the embodied idea.

1. *Manifestation of the Logoic Aspects.* This is achieved through the close consideration of the laws of being, and of the method pursued by the Logos in giving His conception form, thus working out His purpose, or will, through that form. In the three planes of man's endeavour we have reflected the three aspects of the Logos as they produce manifestation:

The Mental Plane . . . reflection of the first aspect. The plane of concept, of the union of Father-Spirit-Will and Mother-Matter-Energy. This is the work of the Logos, and this union produces the Son, for Divine Thought takes form. The body of the Ego is there found.

Astral Plane . . . reflection of the second aspect, the Son. Materialisation proceeds through desire, and the form grows and evolves, becoming more adequate.

Physical Plane . . . Manifestation. The thought-form (of man or the Logos) appears in activity. The Son is born on the physical plane, the thought of the Thinker (divine or human) becomes an entity, separated from its originating source, yet energised by the vitality emanating from him.

All this becomes possible—speaking now from the human standpoint—through the action of the devas who are that which embodies thought, and that which give it its separated energy, as distinct from the purpose which will work out to fruition as the form becomes adequate as a medium of expression.

2. *Deva force substance.* As we consider the devas of the seven planes of the solar system, and especially as we consider those who work in the three worlds, we must bear in mind the following statements:

The First Statement. They are the devas who are the dual force-substance of the lowest cosmic plane, the cosmic physical. As regards the three worlds, they are the deva force and substance [2] which compose the dense physical body of the Logos, hence man is limited, as he works on these planes, to those devas who are primarily regarded (from the higher levels) as having no part in the seven principles of the Logos; to those devas who form the gaseous, liquid, and concrete form of the Logos, the devas of concrete fire, of water and of earth in its densest aspect; to those devas who are the automatic, subconscious builders, carrying on the work of the dense physical vehicle of the Logos in the same sense as the builders in man's body work automatically and unconsciously, producing the cells and energising the bodily functions. This is the basis of the danger to man in tampering with these forces. He is too close to them in many ways; he identifies himself with them and until

[2] The Solar Angels are dual in Nature.
"Manas is dual—Lunar in the lower, Solar in its upper portion."— S. D., II, 520, 675.
   a. The solar aspect is attracted towards Buddhi.
   b. The other descends into, or is attracted by the lower animal.
   c. The Solar Angels form the "Soul" or Second Aspect.
   d. The chief "Soul" is Manas, or mind."—S. D., II, 521.

he has attained the consciousness of the Ego, and has with full knowledge established his identity with the Spirit aspect and not with substance, he is liable to be swept into the line of blind force, and become a lost soul should he trespass ignorantly, and curiously, into their domain.

He is concerned also with those devas who are as yet animated by the life and purpose which distinguished the evolution of the first solar system. That life is the life of God, and that purpose is the working out of His will, but it is evil from our present standpoint, for it is superseded as far as man is concerned by a different purpose and goal. Therefore, identification with that which is past, retrogression and the methods of old are for a man a return along the path of self-conscious evolution, and lead eventually to a loss of the egoic principle, or of ego-ism, which distinguishes a man (human or heavenly) from the rest of evolution.

The Second Statement. The hope for the devas and for the form aspect lies in the fact that each of the subplanes of the cosmic physical plane comes under the direct influence of cosmic forces, originating on the six other cosmic planes. Of these forces everything is unknown and inconceivable, except the vague and general indications of these currents and forces as they may be felt as emanating from the cosmic planes.

The cosmic mental plane. This manifests for us in the three types of force to be seen on the systemic mental plane. These three types have not been sufficiently studied, and are:

a. The force which plays through all the manasic permanent atoms, and which produces basically that manifestation which we call the three worlds.
b. The force which animates those groups of "lotuses"

which we call egoic groups or centres—aggregations of causal bodies.

c. The force which vitalises all the mental units and which is distributed thence to all the other permanent atoms.

These three types of force deal with the substance aspect —permanent atoms, causal vehicle, and mental units, and are therefore directly impressing themselves upon the devas who build these forms out of their own substance, and thus develop the divine plan. These three types of force affect substance, but with a psychic intent, being themselves swayed and actuated according to divine purpose, and from high levels. They emanate from the concrete levels of the cosmic mental plane (being therefore the force flowing through the mental unit of the Logos), and are concerned with the force centre which focalises the logoic mental body. They are the force of Agni in His first aspect. He is that fire which is distinctive of the cosmic mental plane, reflected in the cosmic gaseous subplane of the cosmic physical plane— our systemic mental plane.

The Cosmic Astral Plane. The force from this plane plays through our systemic astral plane, the cosmic liquid physical sub-plane, and it is practically subject only to two differentiations, each of them occultly embodied in two great groups of devas:

First. The devas who are the substance or force of the astral plane, viewing it as the sumtotal of desire, of feeling and of sensation. They are, therefore, the nerve centers, or nerve plexi, of the logoic physical body, for the systemic astral plane provides the nervous system of the logoic physical body. It is the body of intensest vibration from the physical standpoint, and the vehicle through which all is transmitted to that portion of the logoic physical body which corresponds to the brain in man. I can elucidate this no further, but the few words here imparted open up a tremendous range of thought, and give the key to much which transpires and which is distressing in solar evolution as well as human.

Second. Those devas who are the sumtotal of the astral light. They are the agents of the karmic lords, who are in themselves deva entities of an inconceivably advanced evolution and who, in their own substance,

1. Record.
2. Produce effects from cause.
3. Direct force.

This particular group of devas emanate from a great force centre which we generalise by calling it by the name of the sun Sirius. Sirius-kama-manas—the cosmic astral plane and the systemic astral plane—make a close interlocking chain, and form the line of least resistance for a particular type of negative force to pour through.

The Cosmic Physical Plane. This is the force (external and internal) of the solar system itself, and of its environing space. It might be regarded as the pranic forces, pouring through the logoic etheric body (our four higher subplanes) which are positive to the lower three, impregnating these lower three planes (a reflection in substance, or in the Brahma aspect, of the union of Father-Mother) and producing the purely concrete manifestation. This is why the physical vehicle has such control during long stages of man's evolution, for the *force* of this type of energy is necessarily felt more strongly than any other. It is deva force, and substance, which is so close to us as powerfully to delude us. Here lies the mystery of maya, and here is to be found the secret of illusion. Here exists for man the first great stage of the battle for full Self-consciousness, and for identification with the God-aspect, and not with the matter-aspect. Here lies the occult reason why man is called by his father's name and not his mother's. When man has dominated the deva essences of the physical plane, he controls next those of the astral and dominates the mental essences. Having achieved this *in his own* nature he can then safely become a magician and contact, control and work with, the devas in connection with the plans of the Heavenly Man. In the realisation of the three types of force, will be found for man the key to the mystery of his centres.

The secret of the note of the head, the heart, and the throat centre is found here and their blending with the lower centres so that the note of the higher *sounds* out, and the lower produces only harmony. Upon the note of nature the Logos has to superimpose a higher note. To the natural note of the centre (which is found through the development of the lower centre, which is its reflection or correspondence) must be added the dominant note of the higher centre, and, in the dual harmony the centre vibrates as desired. The note is the result of correct activity. That is why the lower centres of man are (in the early stages of his career) the controlling factor. He has to learn their note, and from it to attain the key of the higher. Then the higher takes the prominent place, and the lower only serves the purpose of providing that which is understood as occult "depth." Why is this? Because in these notes those groups of devas who are the force and energy of the centres (which are centres in substance) are contacted and controlled. Through their activity, directed through the centres, the material sheaths—physical, astral and mental—are built.

These ideas of force and the sheaths are the basis of the astrological teaching that is one of the keys to the *Secret Doctrine*.[3] We should therefore bear in mind that

---

[3] *The Astrological Key* is referred to in the S. D., Vol. II, 26.

the Deva Lords, Agni, Varuna, Kshiti,[4] represent in the exoteric teaching the substance aspect of the dense body of the Logos, whilst the force aspect as flowing through the etheric body of the Logos is considered under various names, such as Shiva, Surya, Brahma. Yet the two aspects are but one.

The Third Statement. The final point I seek to make here is that *in connection with these three lower planes and their many groups of devas it must be remembered that their polar opposites are to be found in the great devas of the highest three planes.*

Divine .....1st Cosmic.. Primordial
               ether .....Fire ..... Mental Plane..Fire.
Monadic ....2nd Cosmic..Akasha .....Astral Plane...Astral
               ether   light.
Spiritual
  or Atmic..3rd Cosmic..Æther......Physical Plane. Ether
               ether

The particular type of differentiated force which they embody, when brought into union with each other is that which causes concretion, or the appearance, in space and time, of the dense physical body. This should be carefully considered, along with the very interesting fact that on the fourth plane of our system (the fourth cosmic ether, or buddhic plane) we have the sphere of certain occult happenings which cannot be more than hinted at, because their true significance is one of the secrets of initiation. They are an aspect of the plan of the Logos which can be contacted *direct* by those who have expanded their consciousness adequately.

---

[4] Agni, the God of Fire in the Veda; the oldest and the most revered of the Gods in India. He is the triple aspect of Fire and therefore the sum total of manifestation. He is regarded also as the Lord of the mental plane (the 5th plane) whose symbol is Fire.

Varuna, the God of Water, in the sense of the waters of space, or the waters of matter. He is regarded also as the Ruler of the astral plane (the 6th plane) whose symbol is water.

Kshiti, the God of the Earth in the sense of dense substance, and not a planetary body; he is the God of the physical plane, the seventh plane.

The buddhic plane, or fourth cosmic ether, is the plane whereon:

a. The sacred planets function.

b. Man will eventually function freed from the triple lower man.

c. The true meaning of the words "Divine Hermaphrodite" is there to be comprehended.

d. It is predominantly the plane of life-force, and one of the planes of generation.

e. Here man will for the first time understand and utilize his relationship with the devas.

f. It will see the fruition of the combined evolutionary process of the two solar systems.

g. It is the plane from whence all planetary avatars emanate.

h. The Heavenly Men take the first Initiation on this plane.

i. On this plane the true inner significance of the "Sun" is apprehended.

More I cannot say, but careful study of that which is here given may open up much that is of significance in the study of the macrocosm and the microcosm.

c. The Devas and the Planes.

Preliminary Remarks. We have considered in broad and general terms the various types of force which animate deva substance, and its origin. Now we can study more specifically the deva entities in their various groups, having laid down the fundamentals in connection with them.

In this particular section students must remember that we are not considering those builders of involutionary development which are spoken of in theosophical and occult literature as the elemental essences. We are discussing those who are on the evolutionary arc, and who are the agents of cosmic force, whilst the lesser builders are the agents specifically of solar and of lunar force. Solar force implies the various differentiations of the threefold cosmic force as it manifests within the solar system. Solar force can also (as far as the creative or building faculty of man is concerned) be termed planetary force, for every human being (be he Adept or ordinary man) builds and creates his thought forms —consciously or unconsciously—within the planetary spheres in the three worlds.

We shall now come to a considerable amount of tabulation, for all that it is wise and possible to give at this time are certain facts, names and outlines which can only be demonstrated through the law of correspondence. The key to comprehension is always this law. The basic differentiation in the solar system is as follows:

Agni.....Electric fire . Spirit...Central Spiritual Sun..Energy

Surya....Solar fire ...Vishnu..Heart of the Sun ....Light

Brahma..Fire by friction.......Physical visible Sun ..Fohat

As *electric fire* the Logos manifests as the seven aspects of Will, spiritual impulse or purpose.

As *solar fire* He manifests as the seven Rays, or as the Light of Wisdom, the Consciousness, radiating through the form.

As *fire by friction* He manifests as the seven Sons of Fohat, the seven great fires, or the active heat of intelligent substance.

These three aspects of the God of Fire, and of the fire of God, are the three Entities of the logoic Trinity, and each in turn manifests through seven other Entities Who form their total manifestation.

Sevenfold electric fire. The seven types of spiritual existences, or the seven Spirits before the Throne in Their essential essence; the dynamic force or will lying back of all manifestation. They form on their own plane in a peculiar sense the logoic "Jewel in the Lotus," and hence are inconceivable to our intelligence in this solar system, as They are not revealed until the "Son be made perfect," or the logoic consciousness is fully awakened. They are esoterically the "Spirits of Darkness."

Sevenfold solar fire. The seven Heavenly Men, the sumtotal of Light, the seven Rays of manifestation of the Spiritual Sun. In time and space these seven Rays of Light become the nine (the major three, with the third demonstrating as seven) and are thus esoterically the nine petals of the logoic Ego as He manifests in His physical vehicle. They are esoterically the "Sons of Light."

Sevenfold fire by friction. The seven brothers of Fohat. The seven manifestations of electricity, or of electrical phenomena. These are the seven Raja-Lords or Devas of the seven planes; they are the seven Fires, or those seven states of activity through which consciousness is expressing itself. They are the vehicles of consciousness and the seven vibrations. They are esoterically the "Brothers of energy."

Therefore it will be apparent that the sumtotal of logoic manifestation as it can be seen in existence in time and space is:

Seven Spirits .... sevenfold will.
Seven Rays .... sevenfold quality or psyche.
Seven Deva Lords .... sevenfold form.

The latter are literally the seven spirillae, or force vibrations within the logoic physical permanent atom. This needs to be carefully borne in mind and pondered upon. The seven Rays are the sumtotal of the psychic nature of the Logos, as it radiates through His physical form— His seven qualities, the aggregate of the expression of His desire, or love nature. The seven Spirits are the sumtotal of His Will-to-be aspect, the synthetic Life of His total manifestation, that which causes the persistence of the form, and its evolution for as long as the logoic Ego seeks physical existence.

To carry the simile, or analogy, even further back and thus bear in mind the resemblance between microcosmic and macrocosmic development we have:

1. The seven Spirits who find Their originating incentive on:

    a. The cosmic lower mental levels.

    b. The logoic "Jewel in the Lotus."

    c. The cosmic atmic plane.

2. The seven Heavenly Men are in the line of force from:

    a. The cosmic astral plane.

    b. The logoic nine-petalled lotus.

    c. The cosmic buddhic plane (the seven Rishis of the Great Bear).

3. The seven Sons of Fohat find their vital force emanating from:

    a. The cosmic physical plane.

    b. The logoic permanent atoms (within the causal body).

    c. The cosmic higher mental levels.

Yet these three are but the expressions of One Existence, for behind the Logos in physical incarnation is to be found the logoic Monad, expressing Itself through the logoic Ego, and its reflection, the logoic Personality.

All these spiritual Essences are individualised self-conscious Identities, and the "Fiery Lives" are real, and conscious, vital Existences. Thus we see the Logos manifesting as One Unity yet Three in One; we see the three-fold Unity differentiating into the seven great Lives, containing within Themselves all lesser lives.

Another broad differentiation must next be touched upon:

   a. The seven Fires form the forty-nine Fires.

   b. The seven Heavenly Men manifest through forty-nine lesser Rays.

   c. The seven Spirits shew forth as forty-nine Existences.

In connection with the Spirit aspect it will prove unprofitable to carry the thought any further. Of Spirit *per se* we can know nothing, and beyond predicating the forty-nine [5] solar Manus (each of the Heavenly Men is expressing Himself on the physical plane through seven Manus) it is impossible to go. Therefore, in discussing these abstract questions, we will concern ourselves only with the seven Rays of Light, or Heavenly Men, and the seven Fires.

Each of the seven Rays of Light differentiates into seven making the forty-nine aspects of the logoic psychic nature, as it shews itself on the cosmic physical plane, and each of the seven Fires manifests as seven lesser Fires, making the forty-nine Fires referred to by H. P. B. in the *Secret Doctrine.*[6] The seven Heavenly Men manifest each through seven lesser Entities, Who form the psychic centres in Their body in the same manner as They—in Their turn—form the psychic centres in the logoic vahan or vehicle. Each of the seven Fires, or Deva Lords, of a plane manifest through seven lesser devas, who form the central fire, and consciousness of the substance of a subplane. It is with their mutual interplay and work that we are now concerned, or with the study of matter as it is affected and built into form through the medium of Divine Thought or Will.

Of the higher Fires (the Lords of the four higher planes) I do not seek to deal, for it only profits us to

---

[5] The fortynine Manus. They are the patrons or guardians of the race cycles in a manvantara, or Day of Brahma. There are seven races in a world period, and there are seven world periods.

[6] See S. D., I, 567.

study the construction of thought-forms in the three worlds through the medium of deva essences; these are vitalised and manipulated by the Builders, the Dhyan Chohans, the Heavenly Men through the force of Their Life, through Their knowledge of the logoic Will or purpose, and through the power of Their psychic nature. Thus They are occupied in building the logoic physical body, and in carrying out His plans in that body, in this way fulfilling the purpose for which He incarnated. Their work is infinitely greater than this, for it lies primarily on cosmic levels, but this is what concerns us, and all that we can, in any way grasp. Man in the three worlds of human endeavour works at two things:

First. The building of his body of manifestation, a threefold body.

Second. The construction of thought-forms, which he builds of mental matter and vitalises by desire, and which he holds within his aura, thus constructing a tiny system of his own.

Both man, and the Heavenly Men, work in deva substance; both co-operate with the devas; both manifest will, psychic quality and intelligent activity as they pursue their work but a difference lies, not only in degree, but in consciousness. Man works usually unconsciously. The Heavenly Men, on cosmic levels, work for the most part consciously. Herein lies a hint as to the stage of evolution of our Logos.

This matter is of real difficulty, for the subject is abstruse and profound. We will now leave these basic ideas, and deal more specifically with the devas with whom we are immediately concerned, or with the three groups I have outlined—the Agnichaitans, the Agnisuryans, and the Agnishvattas. They are concerned primarily with the evolution of the dense body of the Logos, the liquid, gaseous and dense subplanes of the cosmic physical, or the three worlds of human endeavour; with the magnetic radiation of the Logos through His physical vehicle, and with the radiatory emanations of the particular Heavenly Man Who is expressing Himself through our planet. Finally they are concerned with the evolution of consciousness [7] in the three worlds, and particularly with the individualisation of the human unit of consciousness, and with the vitalisation of the centres in the body of the Heavenly Man with Whom we are peculiarly connected.

The subject of our consideration now is the fire devas of the physical plane, those great building devas who are working out the purposes of the Logos in his dense, physical body. Let us get our ideas as clear as possible on this matter; in the following tabulation, the status of these devas will be apparent at a glance:

Name	Cosmic Plane	Systemic Plane	Nature	Ruler
Agnichaitan ...	7th subplane... cosmic physical	Physical..	Densest concretion	Kshiti
Agnisuryan ...	6th subplane... cosmic physical	Astral ...	Liquid ...	Varuna
Agnishvatta ...	5th subplane... cosmic physical	Mental ...	Gaseous ..	Agni

The Agnichaitans. These are the devas who construct, and build in matter of the densest kind in connection with logoic manifestation. They function on the seventh subplane of the cosmic physical plane, and are the producers of the greatest concretion. In the planetary body of our planetary Logos they are the builders of the Earth, His densest form, and throughout the entire solar system they are the sum-total of that activity and vibra-

[7] The Lunar Angels have to reach the plane of the Solar Angels.—S. D., I, 203.
They have to win immortality.—S. D., III, 518, 519.
Self-consciousness is their goal.—S. D., I, 205; II, 622.

tion which demonstrates through what we call "solid substance."

Therefore, it will be apparent that under the law they will have a peculiarly powerful effect on the lowest sub-plane of the systemic physical plane; hence their esoteric appellation of the "Agnichaitans of the inner or central heat." They are the totality of the lowest vibration in the cosmic physical vehicle.

The Agnisuryans are the builders on the sixth sub-plane of the cosmic physical plane, our systemic astral plane. They represent, as I have before hinted, the sympathetic nervous system in the logoic physical body, just as their brothers of the seventh vibration represent the sumtotal of the circulatory or blood system. A hint to the student who is interested in the physiological key lies in the relationship between the two great groups of devas who build and construct the most objective portion of logoic manifestation, and the two groups of corpuscles which in their mutual interaction hold the body in health; there is an analogy also in the relationship between the devas of the astral plane, and the motor and sensory nerves of the physical body. I will not enlarge upon this angle of vision.

These devas have to do, in a very esoteric sense, with the nerve plexus in the:

a. Solar system. (Physical Sun)
b. Planetary scheme. (Dense Planet)
c. Human physical body. (Dense Body)

and are therefore a powerful factor in the eventual vitalisation of the centres in man. The etheric centres, or the focal points of force of a Heavenly Man are on the fourth cosmic ether, the buddhic plane. The astral plane is closely allied to the buddhic, and as the etheric centres of our Heavenly Man, for instance, come into full activity, the force is transmitted through the astral correspond-

ence to the fourth physical ether, in which the centres
of man exist.

The Agnishvattas are the builders on the fifth or gaseous subplane of the cosmic physical, and—from the
human standpoint—are the most profoundly important,
for they are the builders of the body of consciousness
per se. From the psychic standpoint of occult physiology,
they have a close connection with the physical brain, the
seat or empire of the Thinker, and as at this stage all
that we can know must be viewed kama-manasically, it
will be apparent that between the sympathetic nervous
system and the brain is such a close interaction as to
make one organised whole. This microcosmic correspondence is of interest, but in studying these groups
of devas at present we will view them principally in
their work as systemic and planetary builders, leaving
the student to trace out for himself the human analogy.
He will learn thereby. Having indicated certain lines of
thought, we will now take up these groups one at a time
and consider them.

The Agnichaitans—Physical Plane Devas.

These devas are the sumtotal of physical plane substance. This plane is, as we know, divided into two
parts:

The four ethers, four subplanes.

The demonstrably concrete or dense three subplanes.
We have here a subdivision of the seventh subplane of
the cosmic physical plane making the lowest manifestation one that is divided into forty-nine subplanes or
states of activity. For purposes of active work, the
devas of the system are divided into forty-nine groups
—the forty-nine fires. The Agnichaitans in turn are
also divided into forty-nine groups, thus reflecting the
whole.

1. The Raja-Lord. Kshiti. The life of the physical plane.

2. Three groups of Agnichaitans concerned with:

A. The force or energy of physical substance. That electrical aspect which produces activity.

B. The construction of forms. They produce the union of negative and positive substance, and thus bring into being all that can be seen, and touched in the exoteric and ordinary connotation.

C. The internal heat of substance which nourishes and causes reproduction. They form the purely mother aspect.

These three groups are subdivided again into seven groups which form the matter of each subplane, viewing that matter as the body of manifestation of one of the seven devas through whom the Raja-Lord of the plane is manifesting.

These seven groups are again divided into seven, making forty-nine.

The three groups function as follows:

Group A. on the first subplane. They are the sumtotal of the atomic matter of the physical plane.

Group B. on the second, third and fourth etheric subplanes. They are the substance of those planes, the transmitters of prana, through which prana flows to the most concrete aspects of the logoic dense vahan, or vehicle.

Group C. the lowest three subplanes; they are the devas who are the essences of all that is tangible, visible and objective.

A very real distinction must be made by students between the centres and the remainder of the body, as they investigate the construction of the body of the solar Logos or of a planetary Logos.

The centres are allied or connected with consciousness, and are composed of self-conscious units—the human Monads. The remainder of the body is composed of deva substance, yet the two together form a unity. The deva units therefore far outnumber the human, and deva substance is also feminine and negative, the human Hierarchy being masculine. Through the positive activity of the centres, the negative deva substance is influenced, built and energized. This is true of a solar Logos, a planetary Logos and a human being.

Three types of force, therefore, play upon or through these devas:

a. That energizing the devas of the first subplane, the atomic. This emanates directly from the first aspect of Brahma, or Agni, considering Him as a selfconscious Identity, the third Person of the logoic Trinity, and therefore Spirit, Soul and Body Himself in His separated essential nature.

b. That energizing the devas of construction, or the form building groups; this comes from the second aspect of Brahma, and is prana, issuing from the physical Sun, and working under the Law of Attraction.

c. That energizing the devas of the lowest three orders, emanating from Brahma in His third aspect. Thus in the dual force, or the aspects of matter itself, interacting the one upon the other, densest forms of all are produced. Yet these three function as one.

Group C. Agnichaitans. In considering these groups of Agnichaitans, we must remember that we are dealing with that manifestation of the Logos with which exoteric science is dealing, and that as regards Group C, science is already making fair progress in the accumulation of knowledge; it remains yet for science to acknowledge the "entified" nature of substance,[8, 9] and thus account for the life that energizes the substance of the three lower subplanes. This recognition by science that all forms are built of intelligent lives will come about when the science of magic begins again to come to the fore, and when the laws of being are better understood. Magic concerns itself with the manipulation of the lesser lives by a greater life; when the scientist begins to work with the consciousness that animates substance (atomic or electronic), and when he brings under his conscious control the forms built of this substance, he will gradually become cognizant of the fact that all entities of all grades and of varying constitutions go to the construction of that which is seen. This will not be until science has definitely admitted the existence of etheric matter as *understood by the occultist,* and until it has developed the hypothesis that this ether is in differing vibrations. When the etheric counterpart of all that exists is allocated to its rightful place, and known to be of more importance in the scale of being than the dense vehicle, being essentially the body of the

[8] The "entified" nature of all substance is technically known as Hylozoism. H. P. B. says:

"Hylozoism, when philosophically understood, is the highest aspect of Pantheism. It is the only possible escape from idiotic Atheism based on lethal materiality, and the still more idiotic anthropomorphic conceptions of the Monotheists; between which it stands on its own entirely neutral ground. Hylozoism demands absolute Divine Thought, which would pervade the numberless active creating Forces, or "Creators," which Entities are moved by, and have their being in, from and through that Divine Thought. . . . Such active "Creators" are known to exist and are believed in because perceived and sensed by the Inner Man in the Occultist."—S. D., II, 167, 168.

[9] An atom is an entified abstraction.—S. D., I, 559-560.
  a. The informing entity of the system is the Logos.
  b. The informing entity of a plane is its raja-Lord.
     Such as Indra, Agni, Varuna, Kshiti.
  c. The informing entity of a planet is its planetary Logos.
  d. The informing entity in the Microcosm is a Dhyan Chohan.
  e. The informing entity in the causal body is the Divine Thinker.
  f. The informing entity in a physical atom is an elemental life.
  Fire is in all things.—S. D., I, 146; II, 258.
  a. The informing entity is Fire.—S. D., I, 145, 146.
  b. The matter of the form is permeated with fire.—S. D., I, 112.
  c. The developing mind is cosmic fire.—S. D., I, 114.

life, or vitality, then the rôle of the scientist and the occultist will merge.

H. P. B. has said [10] that the dense physical is not a principle, and this point is frequently overlooked in connection with man and the Logos. Its importance cannot be too strongly realised for it has the effect of transferring the point of centralisation, or of polarisation in the case of man into his etheric body, composed of matter of the four higher subplanes of the systemic physical plane, and in the case of the Logos, of the four higher subplanes of the cosmic physical plane. The point is one of a very real complexity, for it involves the realisation that, from the standpoint of the occultist, the lowest vibration with which he may concern himself is that of the systemic etheric in its four lesser allied vibrations; similarly macrocosmically the lowest logoic vibration with which the greater Adepts are concerned is the cosmic etheric. The three lowest systemic and cosmic vibrations are the result of :

Reflex action on the part of negative substance for the lower three are negative to the higher four.

Synchronous vibration, inherent in negative substance, the residue of an earlier system, and embodying therefore *past karma* for the Logos and for man.

Vibrations that are gradually being superseded by the imposition of a higher note; therefore for both man and the Logos, they occultly form the ''body of death.''

This brings us to the point which we are seeking to make anent this third group of the lowest devas. They are very destructive where man is concerned, for they embody the final and therefore powerful vibration of the past system, the conscious activity of dense matter. Hence there is consequently a profound truth in the

[10] See S. D., II, 621.

statement that man is at the "mercy of the elements."
Man can physically be burned and destroyed by fire;
he is helpless before volcanic action, and cannot protect himself from the ravages of fire, unless in the initial
stages of such deva endeavour. The occult importance
of the war man wages on the fire devas for instance is
very real in connection with the fire department in any
city. The time lies far ahead as yet, but it will surely
come, when the personnel of these departments will be
chosen for their ability to control the agnichaitans when
manifesting destructively, and their methods will no
longer be that of water (or the calling in of the water
devas to neutralise the fire devas), but that of incanta-
tion, and a knowledge of the sounds that will swing into
action forces which will control the fiery destructive
elements.

The third group of these devas is very definitely connected with the control of the Manu's department, and
of the great devas associated with that department on
this planet. Through their activity during certain cycles
the entire surface of the Earth is changed through the
medium of volcanic action; continents are raised and
submerged; volcanoes are active or quiescent, and thus
the world is purified by fire. In their own department
these Agnichaitans are kept busy building the mineral
forms through the agency of fire; they are the alchemists
of the lower regions, and through contact with them,
and through the knowledge of "the words" by which
they are controlled, the future scientific alchemists (I
use this expression in contradistinction to the idealistic
alchemists of the past) will work with minerals and
with the lives embodied in all mineral forms.

The secret of the transmutation of the baser metals
into gold will be revealed when world conditions are
such that gold is no longer the standard and hence the
free manufacture of gold will not lead to disaster, and

when scientists work with the life aspect, or with positive electrical life, and not with the substance or form aspect.

We have seen that the work of the lowest group of Agnichaitans is to build continents by fire, to purify by fire during alternate cycles, and to construct the metals and the minerals. It is also concerned with the tending of the fires of the hearth, or those fires which warm, cheer and produce livable conditions in a planet, and incidentally in a home. This is of very vital import, for it means that they are connected with the central basic fires in the bowels of the Earth, with the central basic fire that nourishes and warms the physical forms of all the kingdoms of nature, and consequently with the kundalini fire at the base of the spine in individual man.

It is not advisable for us further to enlarge upon their functions. It should be noted that in connection with the matter aspect there is less to be said than on consciousness, and on the hylozoistic aspect of manifestation. The reason lies in the fact that exoteric science is slowly, yet steadily, finding out the nature of phenomena, and discovering for itself the character of electrical manifestation. In their slowness of discovery lies safety. It is not wise nor right yet for the true nature of these different forces and powers to be fully known; therefore, it is not possible for us to do more than indicate certain broad general lines. In due course of time, as the human family becomes centred in the higher, and not in the lower nature, and as the force from the higher planes can more easily impose itself on the lower, the facts concerning these Lives and Builders, their methods of work, and the laws of their being will be known. Knowledge at this time would be productive of two results. It would first of all bring the human family into the power (as yet blind and destructive) of

certain elementals, who are of a nature analogous to that
of the physical body. Hence destruction of the form
would ensue, or paralysis and insanity on a large scale
would eventuate. Secondly, it would put power into
the hands of certain of the Brothers of the Left Hand
Path [11] and of a number of unconscious magicians (of
whom there are quite a number) who would use it only
for selfish, evil and material ends. Hence no more can
be said anent dense physical substance and its embodiers. The Agnichaitans of the third group are as
yet a menace to man, and are only handled in group
formation, and on a large scale by the head of the Manu's
department through their own rulers—certain devas of
a development equal to that of the sixth Initiation.

The occult Hierarchy of our planet is primarily concerned with the development of self-consciousness in
man, and with the intelligent interpretation of the happenings of Nature; it is concerned with a wise co-operation with the building Forces of nature; and the object
of its main endeavour is the vitalisation and activity
of the centres in the Heavenly Man of our planet, and
in the individual units of the human family.

The occult Hierarchy is a great force centre, the
heart, head, and throat of the Heavenly Man as these
three centres function in a triple co-ordination. Paralleling their activities along the line of consciousness (and
primarily consciousness or intelligence as it demonstrates through the third and fourth kingdoms) is to be
found a great hierarchy of devas who concern themselves with the development of that portion of the body
of a Heavenly Man which is not included in the active
centres. Perhaps some idea of what I seek to convey

[11] *The Left-hand Path* is that followed by the Black Magician, and by the
Brothers of the Shadows. It originates in the use of the forces of nature
for selfish ends; it is characterised by intense selfishness and separative-
ness, and ends in Avitchi, the 8th sphere, the home of lost souls, or those
shells of the lower man which have become separated from their egoic or
individual life principle.

may be gathered from an illustration. The occult Hierarchy is concerned with the unfoldment of the nine-petalled Lotus in the Heavenly Man, and in man (the former through reflex action between the cosmic physical and the cosmic mental), while the great deva Hierarchy is concerned with the permanent atoms, with the egoic body, and with the development of the spirillae. Thus the function of the Agnichaitans of the lowest furnaces—macrocosmically and microcosmically—will be seen and comprehended by the wise student.

Group B. Agnichaitans. In taking up the matter of the second group of Agnichaitans—Group B—we are dealing with that important group of devas who are designated in some works as the ''devas of the shadows.'' Their function is primarily a fourfold one, and they are the basis of motion or of activity on all planes, which activity is produced by the interplay of the negative and positive aspects of Brahma, the manifested God.

First, they are the builders of the etheric bodies of all sentient existences, and primarily of all the etheric bodies of men.

Second, they are the transmitters of prana.

Third, they perform a very definite function in the evolutionary process of linking up the four kingdoms of nature, being essentially the transmuters and transmitters of the lower into the higher. They build between each kingdom—mineral, vegetable, animal and human—that which in each case corresponds to the antaskarana, or the bridge linking higher and lower manas, and which therefore is the channel for the transmission of the life from out of the lower human kingdom into the higher spiritual one. It will be found that between each of the different stages of consciousness (from the subconscious through the self-conscious to the superconscious) there is a period of linking, of building, and of bridging, and this is carried out by the agency of certain groups of devas on all the planes. These three groups on the physical plane find their counterparts and their work paralleled on higher levels. The point to be remembered is that this work of bridging from one stage or from one kingdom to another has to be performed under the following conditions:

a. As the result of an impulse emanating from the lower, or originating in the active desire of the lower to embrace or contact the higher. This is of paramount importance, for all progress must be self-induced, self-initiated, and be the result of an inner activity.

b. As the result of reflex action from the higher stage or kingdom; it is brought about by the activity of the lower which calls forth a response from the higher. All vibration, it must be remembered, travels along waves of living substance.

c. As the result of extraneous stimulation produced by the activity of certain conscious powers, interested in the process of evolutionary development.

All these conditions can be seen in the process of the initiation of man, and of his transference from the fourth kingdom into the spiritual. His efforts must be self-induced, or the effect of his own self-conscious endeavour; they will meet with a response from his superconsciousness, the atmic aspect or Spirit and this dual interplay will be further aided by the Guardians of the Rites of Initiation. Yet all three effects are felt in spirit-matter; all proceed under the law of vibration, and this law is literally the response of deva substance to force emanating from some conscious or unconscious source.

Fourth, these "devas of the shadows," perform certain activities of an interesting and varied kind, but of such diversity as to make enumeration wellnigh impossible. We might attempt with brevity to state a few of these functions, remembering ever that what can be predicated of them on the physical plane can also be predicated of their correspondences on all the planes. This we can leave to the student to work out for himself, begging him again to bear in mind that we are dealing with the devas on the evolutionary arc, which may be divided into the following classes, amongst many others.

Class 1. The special agents of magic. They are peculiarly susceptible to the building vibrations of the seven rays.

Class 2. A group of Agnichaitans who manifest as physical plane electricity. They are a group who are coming somewhat under the control of man, and will be more and more dominated by him.

Class 3. A group who form the health auras of all the three middle kingdoms of nature (vegetable, animal and human) either collectively or individually. Man is coming into contact with them along medical lines and beginning somewhat to recognise them. One of the great errors into which the human family has fallen has been the endeavour to administer mineral drugs to man for medicinal purposes. It has resulted in a combination of deva substances which was never intended. The relation of man to the lower kingdoms, and particularly to the animal and mineral, has brought about a peculiar condition in the deva world and has tended to complicate deva evolution. The use of animal food (and the use of minerals as medicine in a lesser degree) has produced a commingling of deva substance, and of vibrations which are not attuned to each other. The vegetable kingdom is in a totally different situation, and part of its karma has lain in the providing of food for man; this has resulted in a needed transmutation of the life of that kingdom into the higher stage (the animal) which is its goal. The transmutation of vegetable life takes place necessarily on the physical plane. Hence its availability as food. The transmutation of the life of the animal into the human kingdom takes place on kama-manasic levels. Hence the non-availability, esoterically understood, of the animal as food for man. This is an argument for vegetarian living which needs due consideration.

Class 4. A very important class of etheric devas (as far as man is concerned) who are definitely the constituent substance of his centres. They occupy this position for karmic reasons, and are, from many angles, some of the most highly evolved of the devas of the shadows. They are distinguished by their ability to respond to a particular set of planetary vibrations in a peculiar manner, and in their essential essence, and in their own peculiar sphere enable man to react to Ray stimulation. Each centre is under the influence of one or other of the planets. In this fact lies the ability of man eventually—through the agency of his centres—to put himself en rapport with the sevenfold soul of the world.

Class 5. We have here a very important group of devas, who are peculiarly active and esoterically dominant during this round; they are the Agnichaitans who form the centre which vibrates to the measure of kundalini in its many forms and demonstrations; this is the centre at the base of the spine. In this centre we have a very effective display of the two polarities, for the petals of the centre which is the seat of kundalini, and the fire or vitality which animates them are negative and positive to each other. This centre is to be found in some form or other in all sentient beings and upon it largely depends:

a. Consciousness at one of its seven stages.
b. Continuity of existence.
c. Perpetuation of species or reproduction on some or other of the planes.

It might be of interest here to note that this centre is literally a fourfold radiation, and the "Cross of the Holy Spirit," the equal armed Cross, is its symbol. This four-petalled lotus is the result of evolution. In the first kingdom of nature, the mineral, through which a specific Entity is manifesting, this centre is a unity on etheric levels, for only one petal is to be seen. In the vegetable kingdom, viewing it as the expression of a great Existence, two petals are becoming active. In the third kingdom, the animal, the centre at the base of the spine will be found to have three petals, whereas in man, the lotus is vibrating in a fourfold manner. At each initiation of the great Being Who is manifesting through our planet, one of these petals becomes unfolded on etheric levels, so that at individualisation, the four became active, and His selfconscious activity was brought right down on to the physical plane. The analogy can be seen typified at His great Initiation which took place in the fourth round and the third rootrace; the correspondence between the third kingdom and the fourth, and their production of the esoteric seven is one of the lines of study for the occultist.

As each of the petals of the etheric centres becomes vibrant, or an at-one-ment is brought about in deva substance, a quickening takes place on allied levels in the cosmic etheric body of the planetary Logos, and of the solar Logos. Certain correspondences in the petals of the egoic lotus of the different units of the human family, and (on cosmic levels) in the solar and planetary egoic bodies become apparent. It should also be borne in mind that these basic centres, wherein the kundalini fire lies hidden, are found in the following Existences, as They function in physical bodies:

1. A solar Logos.
2. A planetary Logos.
3. Those Entities Who are the sumtotal of consciousness as it expresses itself through the different kingdoms of nature—manifesting through them as a man manifests through his body.
4. The Lord of a chain.
5. The Lord of a globe.
6. Certain Beings Who form the life of specific groups. They are esoteric, and Their function is one of the secrets of initiation.
7. Man.
8. Animals.

It should be here also remarked that in the logoic manifestation one of the planetary schemes forms the centre in the logoic body which harbours kundalini. This scheme, whose name must not as yet be revealed, is largely given over to deva control—the two groups of devas meeting there, and performing their function of animating the dense physical body of the Logos in the same way as the kundalini in man at this stage animates his dense physical vehicle. Later, as the third major scheme assimilates the life-activity of the lower four, this kundalini fire will be withdrawn, and will be transmuted into the activity of the logoic Throat centre.

In planetary manifestation, one of the chains performs a similar work in the evolutionary process of the planetary Logos. Again the same can be predicated of one of the globes in a chain. In this fourth round, therefore, it can be seen why the fire at the base of the spine (viewing it in its esoteric significance, and in connection with the Logos, and the Logoi, and not only in connection with man) plays so dominant a part in the stimulation of the logoic Quaternary, or of His Lower Self. Herein is found the mystery of present evil, the source of present distress, and the basis of planetary experience. The kundalini fire in the logoic body is at the height of its activity in stimulating His physical body—our lower three systemic planes—and the four petals of that particular centre are coming into full activity in this fourth round. It must be remembered that He is the sum-total of all the centres in manifestation, and the aggregate of all the fires of kundalini in every department of nature. The trouble in our planet, and likewise the hope for our planet, lies in this very fact. The etheric centre of our planetary Logos being in matter of the fourth cosmic ether (the buddhic plane) stimulates at present His lower quaternary, our three worlds of human endeavour. The direction of the force lies here, and not until the next round (when three-fifths of the human kingdom will be developing the buddhic vehicle), will the point of equilibrium for Him be reached, and the direction of the serpent fire be directed higher.

This holds the clue to much. A further clue to the sad condition to be seen in the world (especially along sex lines) lies in the fact that those units of the human family who contribute to the constitution of this particular centre out of the seven, are frequently at this stage over-vitalised, the physical vehicle vitality indicating to them the line of least resistance. To word it otherwise: The deva forces who form the centre, and are likewise the activity of the centre, are as yet over-dominant, and the power they acquired in the earlier solar system has not yet been transmuted into spiritual power.

We have above considered a few of the devas of the ethers but have of necessity left many untouched. The vastness of our subject will be apparent when it is remembered that in dealing with the devas we are dealing with that which is the basic substance of manifestation, or Spirit-matter; with the negative or the mother aspect, in the divine duality, and with the sum total of all that is. We are concerned with the tangible form, using the word "tangible" as that which can be apprehended by consciousness in one or other of its many states. The utter impossibility of cataloguing the forms and aspects of deva substance, or of tabulating the myriad groups and classes will be borne in on our comprehension. On all the planes these three groups will be found, and all are recipients of force. An analogy likewise exists between these three groups of devas on the systemic physical plane, and their correspondences on the cosmic physical plane. Briefly it might be pointed out that we have:

Group A.......	The plane Adi ....Divine	
	Systemic atomic.	evolution.
Group B.......	The three worlds of the Triad.......Spiritual	
	Logoic etheric.	evolution.
Group C.......	The three worlds...................Human	
	Logoic dense physical.	evolution.

In this lies much of interest for the student as it makes clear the correspondence between the evolution of substance and the evolution of spirit.

As regards the devas of Group B, little more can be said. Only a few more generalities are advisable.

These devas, especially those of the fourth ether, are so closely connected with man that one of the immediate developments ahead will be his awakening to a realisation of their existence, and his consequent gradual domination of them. This domination will be the result of several things but will only be complete when he can function on the fourth cosmic ether, the buddhic plane. One of the things the Hierarchy at this stage is seeking to do, is *to retard* this awakening of the mass of mankind to this realisation, for that event will necessitate many adjustments, and, at the beginning, may produce many apparently evil effects. The development of the physical eye is a thing which is proceeding under the Law, and inevitably the whole race of men will at length attain that dual focus which will enable man to see both the dense and the etheric forms. At this stage his inability to do so is largely due to a lack of pranic vitality. This is mainly the result of wrong conditions of living, and the misuse of food. The present general trend towards juster and purer conditions of life, the return of man to simpler and saner ways, the widespread feeling for bathing, fresh air, and sunlight, and the greater desire for vegetable, and nut foods, will result inevitably in a more ready assimilation of the pranic fluids. This will produce certain changes, and improvements, in the physical organs, and in the vitality of the etheric body.

Therefore, those of us who see somewhat of the Plan are urged to spread the knowledge of the Wisdom Religion, and above all to break loose from the preconceived dogmas of pre-war days. It should be pointed out here that the war was a great occult event, and caused a vital change in many of the plans and arrangements of the Hierarchy. Modifications have been necessitated, and some events will have to be delayed whilst others will be hastened. One of the profoundest effects of the war was felt among the devas of the shadows, and primarily among those of the fourth order. The etheric web which protected certain groups in the human and animal kingdoms was rent in various places, and the results of that disaster have to be offset. Another effect upon the devas resulting from the war, as it worked, can be seen among the devas of Group A, or those devas who *are* (in an occult sense) the physical permanent atoms of all self-conscious beings. The fourth spirilla was tremendously stimulated, and its evolution hastened

to an extraordinary degree, so that some of the lesser
evolved men, through the stress of danger and experience, had this fourth spirilla brought up to, and beyond,
that of normal humanity. Through this stimulation of
the fourth spirilla of the units of the fourth Creative
Hierarchy in this fourth round on the fourth globe in
this fourth scheme, a tremendous push onward along the
evolutionary path has been effected, and hence one of
the great objects of the war has been achieved. A still
more terrific stimulation was given in the fourth root-
race during the war of that period, and the result was
the passing on to the Path of Initiation of many who
normally would not even now be treading it. A similar
effect can be looked for at this time, and the Hierarchy
is preparing itself for the taking over of much of an
extra-planetary nature owing to the almost immediate
availability of comparatively large numbers of the sons
of man. We must not forget that this stimulation of
the spirillae affects the matter aspect, or deva substance.
Man is literally deva substance, and a God, thus being
a true reflection of the solar Logos.[12, 13]

[12] "Thus God dwells in all,
    From life's minute beginnings, up at last
    To man—the consummation of this scheme
    Of being, the completion of this sphere
    Of life: whose attributes had here and there
    Been scattered o'er the visible world before,
    Asking to be combined, dim fragments meant
    To be united in some wondrous whole,
    Imperfect qualities throughout creation,
    Suggesting some one creature yet to make,
    Some point where all those scattered rays should meet
    Convergent in the faculties of man. . . .

    When all the race is perfected alike
    As man, that is; all tended to mankind,
    And, man produced, all has its end thus far:
    But in completed man begins anew
    A tendency to God. Prognostics told
    Man's near approach; so in man's self arise
    August anticipations, symbols, types
    Of a dim splendour ever on before
    In that eternal circle life pursues.
    For men begin to pass their nature's bound,
    And find new hopes and cares which fast supplant

Group A.   Agnichaitans.   We have seen that on all planes the groups of devas can be divided into three

> Their proper joys and griefs; they grow too great
> For narrow creeds of right and wrong, which fade
> Before the unmeasured thirst for good; while peace
> Rises within them ever more and more.
> Such men are even now upon the earth,
> Serene amid the half formed creatures round.''
>
> —*Paracelsus* by Robert Browning.

[a] 1. Man is an animal, plus a living God, within his physical Shell.—
S. D., II, 85.   S. D., II, 284.
   a. Man is the Macrocosm for the animal, therefore he contains all
      that is meant by the term animal.—S. D., II, 179, 187.
   b. Divine consciousness is received from the living God.—S. D., II,
      103.
   c. The animal forms the basis and the contrast for the divine.—
      S. D., II, 100.
   d. The light of the Logos is awakened in animal man.—S. D., II, 45.
2. Man is the Tabernacle, the vehicle only, of his God.—S. D., I, 233,
   281; II, 316; III, 66.
Compare S. D., II, 174.   Read Proverbs VIII.
Study Biblical description of Tabernacle:—
   a. Outer court, the place of animal sacrifice and purification.
   b. The Holy place, the place of consecration and service.
   c. The Holy of Holies.
The first corresponds to the life of the personality.
The second to that of the Ego, or Higher Self.
The last to that of the Monad, or Divine Self.
3. Man contains in himself every element found in the universe.—
   S. D., I, 619; III, 584.
   a. All in nature tends to become Man.—S. D., II, 179.
   b. All the impulses of the dual, centripetal and centrifugal force
      are directed towards one point—Man.—S. D., II, 179.
   c. Man is the storehouse . . . he unites in himself all forms.—S. D.,
      II, 303.
   d. The potentiality of every organ useful to animal life is locked
      up in Man.—S. D., II, 723.
4. Man tends to become a God and then God, like every other atom in
   the universe.—S. D., I, 183.
Compare the atom and the Microcosm, man. Illustration:—S. D., I, 174.
Every atom has seven planes of being.—S. D., I, 205.   Read S. D., I, 201.
   a. Every atom contains the germ from which he may raise the tree
      of knowledge.   (Of good and evil, therefore conscious dis-
      crimination).—S. D., II, 622.
   b. It is the spiritual evolution of the inner immortal man that forms
      the fundamental tenet of the occult sciences.—S. D., I, 694.
   c. Atoms and souls are synonymous terms in the language of the
      initiates.—S. D., I, 620-621.
5. Human beings . . . those Intelligences who have reached the appropriate equilibrium between Spirit and Matter.—S. D., I, 132.
Read also carefully:—S. D., I, 267, 449; S. D., II, 190.
   a. On the descending arc Spirit becomes material.—S. D., I, 693.
   b. On the middle turn of the base both meet in man.—S. D., I, 214,
      271.

main groups, even though usually studied in their dual capacity of involutionary and evolutionary force units. Broadly speaking, these groups can be viewed as:

a. Those which embody the positive aspect, or positive electrical phenomena.
b. Those which embody the negative aspect.
c. That group which—in time and space—is the union of the two aspects and which—during evolution—demonstrates the third type of electrical phenomena.

Another grouping of this triplicity can be made which brings them into line with the order of manifestation as laid down in the ancient cosmogony, and this we followed when we enumerated the groups of Agnichaitans.

Group A—Corresponds to the manifestations of existence as seen on the highest plane, or that aspect which is understood by the term Agni.
Group B—Corresponds to the Vishnu-Surya aspect.
Group C—Corresponds to the Brahma or the creative Logos aspect.

We have recapitulated thus, as it is desirable to have the thought clearly defined.

We have touched upon the two lower groups of devas. Now, we might take up the consideration of Group A, the most important group on the physical plane from the standpoint of creation, and of objectivity, for they are the life of matter itself and the intelligence animating the forms of all that exists on the systemic physical

c. On the ascending arc Spirit asserts itself at the expense of the material.
d. This is true of Gods and of men. See S. D., II, 88.
e. Man is therefore a compound of Spirit and matter.—S. D., II, 45.
f. In man the intelligence links the two.—S. D., II, 102, 103.
See note to S. D., II, 130. Compare S. D., II, 394.

plane; they are not self-conscious intelligence, but consciousness as understood by the occultist.

Each of the atomic subplanes in the solar system is
closely interrelated with the others, and the seven atomic
subplanes of all the planes form a unity, and are essentially the cosmic physical plane as the term is occultly
understood. The subplanes of which they are the originating source bear the same relationship to them as the
six principles do to the seventh. Therefore, the devas of
Group A are the concentrated creative force of the subplanes, the origin of the objective side of physical manifestation, and the source of the seven Breaths of the
creative Logos on the physical plane. But it must be
remembered that in each scheme the creative impulse
or will is the planetary Logos of the scheme, Who as
truly creates His body of Manifestation under the Law
(His dense physical planet) as man—under the same
Law—creates his physical body, or as the solar Logos
(at the other end of the scale) creates His body, a solar
system.

This has a definite and esoteric bearing upon the subject under discussion, and the essential differences between the Heavenly Men seeking manifestation will be
seen in Their schemes, and therefore in the types of
devas through whom They function, and out of whose
essence Their form is made.

It might be expressed thus: Just as each man has a
body which, in its main characteristics and form, resembles other bodies, yet in its quality and personal
distinctive features is unique, so each of the Heavenly
Men builds for Himself a body out of deva substance or
spirit-matter which is of the same nature as that of His
brothers, and yet which is distinctive, coloured by His
own peculiar colouring, vibrant to His own particular
key, and able to demonstrate His own unique quality.
This is produced through the peculiar type of deva

essence He chooses, or (to word it perhaps more
occultly) it has involved the response of certain peculiar
groups of devas to His note. They embody in themselves just those constituents which He requires to build
His body or scheme. It will, therefore, be recognised
that the devas of Group A, being what we might call the
key-devas, are of prime importance, and, from our present standpoint, must remain abstract and esoteric. If
we consider this under the Law of Analogy, and study
the essentially esoteric nature of the plane of the Logos
(the first plane, called Adi) the reason for this will be
apparent. If the devas of Group A could be recognised,
or even contacted by advanced men, the study of their
nature, colouring and tone would reveal to unprepared
humanity the colouring and tone of our particular
planetary Logos. For this knowledge the race is not
ready. It would reveal also, through the study of the
Law of Action and Reaction, which of the incarnating
Egos were on the ray of this Logos; the deductions from
this would lead men into dangerous realms, and put
power into hands as yet unprepared to wield it wisely.

Therefore, Group A of Agnichaitans must remain profoundly esoteric, and their true nature can only be revealed to the Adept of the great Law.

Thus only a few hints are permissible, and these deal
simply with the relationship of man to these entities.
He is related to them primarily because his physical
permanent atom is directly energised by them, being a
part of their essential nature, and having a place in
their form. It will be apparent to any student that if
the permanent atoms of the lower man are within the
causal periphery the devas of the three worlds on the
atomic subplanes must work in the closest co-operation;
there must be unity of purpose and of plan.

The devas of the atomic levels of all the planes in our
scheme work in close affiliation:

a. With each other, thus making seven groups who are the sumtotal of the Brahma aspect of our planetary Logos.

b. With the seven groups who constitute the atomic matter of that scheme which is the polar opposite of ours.

c. With that particular group in that scheme which is one of the points in a systemic triangle of which our scheme and our opposite scheme are the other two.

d. With corresponding groups in lesser degree in all the systemic schemes.

e. With the scheme which corresponds to the first aspect, or the plane of Adi.

f. With those devas who form the spirit-substance of the manifestation of that particular Rishi of the Great Bear Who is the prototype of our particular planetary Logos.

g. With those devas who form the substance of that one of those esoteric existences who are spoken of in the *Secret Doctrine* [14] as "The wives of the seven Rishis," or the seven sisters, the Pleiades. One of these seven sisters has a close connection with our Heavenly Man, and therefore we have an interesting cosmic interplay as follows:

    1. One of the seven Rishis of the Great Bear.
    2. One of the seven Sisters, or a Pleiad.
    3. The Heavenly Man of our scheme.

This interplay will be threefold and as far as we are concerned just now will involve a transmission of life force through the atomic matter of our planes, circulating in deva substance. This will materially affect certain types of humanity more than others, according to their ray and nature, and this effect will demonstrate in

[14] See S. D., II, 579-582.

a vivification of the spirillae of the permanent atoms
and of the centres.

Agnisuryans—Astral Plane Devas.

We start here upon a consideration of those groups
of devas who are the substance of the astral plane, the
Agnisuryans. They may be considered in the following
manner, and by the employment of synonymous terms,
some general idea of their function may be arrived at
before we begin to differentiate them into groups and
study their relation to:

1. The various entities who are the soul of the differ-
    ing kingdoms, or groups, such as the animal king-
    dom, the human kingdom, and higher in the scale
    of consciousness than men—the planetary Logos.
2. Man himself.
3. The plane as a totality.

We might consider these devas:

First, as the substance of the astral plane in its seven
grades.

Second, as that aspect of logoic manifestation which
corresponds to the liquid subplane in the systemic physical plane.

Third, as the vehicle of the deva lord Varuna.

Fourth, as the animating lives of that involutionary
matter of the astral plane which we call the elemental
essence, and as the vitality energising the desire elementals of all that is sentient. Viewed in this aspect in
connection especially with man, they are the correspondence on the astral plane to the "devas of the shadows,"
for the desire bodies of all human beings are composed
of matter of the second, third and fourth subplanes of
the astral plane. This is a point which should be closely
considered, and the analogy between the etheric body,
the vehicle of prana vitalising the dense physical, and

man's astral body, and the method of its vitalisation will be found illuminating.

Fifth, from the standpoint of the physical plane, as the sumtotal of material activity (even though subjective) which produces that which is tangible and objective. Just as the solar system is a "Son of Necessity," or of desire, so the physical bodies of all that exist are the product of the desire of some greater or lesser entity within the system.

It might be apposite here to point out the lines along which energy—whether manasic, pranic, or astral—enters the system and reaches a particular plane, thus finding its way to all units of consciousness, from an atom to a solar Logos.

The dense physical plane itself is energised via:

a. The planetary etheric body.
b. The mental plane, or the cosmic gaseous subplane.
c. The atmic plane, or the third cosmic ether.
d. The plane of adi, or the first cosmic ether.

and inferentially (by means of the logoic permanent atom) a similar flow of force enters from cosmic levels.

The astral plane is energised via:

a. The buddhic plane, the fourth cosmic ether.
b. The monadic plane, the second cosmic ether.
c. The cosmic astral plane, and thus to the Heart of all Being.

The mental plane is energised via:

a. The atmic plane, the third cosmic ether.
b. The plane adi, the first cosmic ether.
c. The cosmic mental plane, beyond which it is unnecessary for us to go.

It will be noted by the careful student that these planes might be looked at in connection with the three worlds as demonstrating two types of force,—first, a force which tends to differentiation such as on the mental plane (the plane of inherent separation) and on the physical plane (the plane of actual separation); secondly, a force which tends to unity, such as on the astral plane, and on the plane of essential harmony, the buddhic plane. It must be remembered that we are considering force as it flows through, or permeates, deva substance. A hint as to the truth lies in the fact that at present the astral body of man is positive to the physical plane, negative to the mental, and positive to the buddhic plane. As evolution proceeds, the astral body should become positive to the mental, and thus prove incapable of being swayed by thought currents, and the separative processes of that plane, and negative to the buddhic plane, or receptive to the forces from that plane. When it has attained equilibrium, and the forces are evenly balanced, the astral body should become the transmitter from the buddhic plane, the fourth cosmic ether, via the gaseous, to the dense physical plane. This thought should be studied in connection with the burning of the etheric web of the planet, thus illumination may come. Literally, there is no such division on the astral plane as we find on the mental or on the physical planes. On both those planes, we have a division into two: the mental plane being divided into higher and lower, rupa and arupa, concrete and abstract, and the physical plane into the etheric levels and the dense subplanes.

There is, therefore, a correspondence between these two. The reason for this apparent division (considering the question apart from the states of consciousness of a human being) is due to the stage of development of the great devas who embody the plane, who ensoul it, and who manifest through it as a man manifests through his body. Varuna, the Lord of the astral plane, has achieved a more unified conscious control than His brothers of the mental and physical planes. He comes into manifestation in connection with one of the Heavenly Men, Who is the Lord of a major Ray. The other two are linked up with the Lords of a minor Ray. There is a suggestive hint for students in this information. We may justly ask why, if this is so, it should apparently manifest so disastrously in connection with man? There are several reasons for this, one being that the force flowing through the vehicle of the great deva, the plane, is consequently stronger than in the other two cases, and this is owing to His more advanced stage of development and also to the fact that the Logos Himself is polarised in His astral body. Another reason is that he has a peculiar link with the Ruler of the animal kingdom, and as the human being has not yet dissociated himself from, nor learnt to control, his animal nature, he too comes under the influence of this tremendous force. There are other reasons hidden in the karma of our Heavenly Man, but the above reasons suffice.

1. *The Function of the Agnisuryans.* The devas of the astral plane are those with whom man is very specially connected at this time owing to his astral polarisation, and to the place desire and feeling play in his development. Consciousness expands through contact, through intelligent appreciation of that which is contacted, and through realisation of that which is to be gained through a specific contact. That which is contacted depends upon reciprocal vibration, and the place therefore of desire (which is the going out after sensation) and of feeling (which is the reflex of that desire) is of real importance; they put man constantly in touch —even though he realises it not—with deva substance of some kind or another. Even when man has reached a relatively high stage of evolution, the demonstration of that point of attainment is seen in the type of not-self which he contacts; it is only when he is an initiate that

he begins to approximate, and to know the meaning of the essential unity which lies at the heart of Being, and to comprehend the oneness of the Universal Soul, and the Unity of that subjective Life which secretes itself behind form of every kind. It should never be forgotten that the matter aspect is found on all planes; also that forms are ever to be found, until the solar ring-pass-not is transcended and the Logos escapes from His present limitation. Owing to this the devas of the astral plane assume a very important place in the three worlds.

Previously, we considered them in a fivefold aspect, dividing them into five groups. At this point we will limit our consideration to the relationship of self-conscious units such as Man and the planetary Logos to this deva substance. A great distinction exists between man and his prototype, a Heavenly Man.

The astral plane plays a very real part in the evolution of man, having a close connection with one of his principles. Astral matter and vibration is one of the controlling factors in the lives of the great majority of people. To the Heavenly Man, astral matter corresponds to the liquid portion in the physical body of man, and is for Him therefore no principle.

The astral plane is man's principal battle-ground and the area of his most intense field of sensation,—mental sensation (esoterically understood) is for him as yet only a possibility. The astral body is the seat of man's most violent vibration, and these vibrations are a potent cause of his physical plane activities. If man only realised it, the devas of the astral plane at present very largely control what he does and says, and his goal of evolution (his immediate goal) is to liberate himself from their control in order that he, the real Ego or thinker, may be the dominating influence. To be explicit, and thus to illustrate this point: the little elemental lives which form the body of the emotions, and the positive life of any evolutionary deva who (through similarity of vibration) is linked to any particular man and who gives to him an astral body of a coherent and positive power, are as yet practically in control of the majority. Man usually does as his desires and instincts prompt him. If this evolutionary deva is of a high order (as will be the case in a highly developed man) the vibration will be high, and the desires and instincts will be good and exoterically right. Nevertheless, if the man is controlled by them, he is as yet under deva influence, and must free himself. If the deva life is of a low order, the man will demonstrate low and vicious instincts, and desires of a vile calibre.

If these remarks are rightly apprehended, some understanding will come of what is meant when the deva evolution is spoken of as being a "parallel evolution" to that of man. In the three worlds the two lines of evolution parallel each other, and must not be consciously one. In the planes of the Triad they are known as a unity, producing the Divine Hermaphrodite, or the Heavenly Man,—the self-conscious human units embodying the three aspects of divinity, while the conscious deva units embody the divine attributes. The two, blended together, form the body of manifestation, the centres and substance of the Heavenly Man. Great is the mystery, and until man knows his place within the conscious whole, he should reserve his opinion as to the meaning thereof. It will be apparent, therefore, in view of the connection between the astral plane with its unified work, and the buddhic plane with the conscious harmony there experienced, that the astral body of man calls for the closest study and understanding. A link will be found through its medium with the buddhic plane and harmonious activity on the physical plane will be produced. The student of occultism should study carefully in this connection:

a. The physical sun, and its relation to prana and the etheric body.

b. The subjective sun, and its connection with the astral plane, with the kama-manasic principle, and the astral body.

c. The central spiritual sun, and its relation to the Spirit or atma in man.[15]

d. The heart of the sun, and its relation to the lower and higher mental bodies, producing that peculiar manifestation we call the causal body. In this connection it must be remembered that the force which flows from the heart of the sun, works through a triangle formed by the Venusian scheme, the Earth and the sun.

That another triangle was also formed involving two planets was to be expected under the law, and the triangles vary according to the scheme involved.

Cosmically there is a very interesting series of triangles which will be found by the student of esoteric astronomy and of occult cycles. They originate in the central sun of our particular group of solar systems. This series involves the Pleiades. The fact that this is so will not be known until the last decade of the present century, and will not be recognised by science till that time when certain lines of knowledge and discovery will bring scientists to a realisation that there is a third type of electricity, which ever balances and forms the apex of the triangle. But the time is not yet.

All that is here said is expressed in terms of deva groups and deva forces, which form (in their aggregate) substance responsive to analogous vibration. This is occultly expressed under certain definite names. It is possible, therefore, to transmit safely information of a character incomprehensible to the profane in such a phrase, for instance, as: "The triangle of . . . of . . . and of Group . . . of the Agnisuryans formed itself, and in the turning of the Wheel produced the third." This conveys to the mind of the occultist the knowledge

[15] S. D., II, 250, 251.

that in the flow of force from a particular constellation, outside our system altogether, through a particular planetary scheme, and thus through the astral body of a planetary Logos, a condition was brought about which produced the appearance of the third kingdom in nature, the sentient conscious animal kingdom. Some such similar phrase embodies also the deva connection with man's individualisation, but it profits not to pass it on; the above is only quoted in order to do three things:

1. Demonstrate somewhat the nature and extent of the forces flowing through our system.
2. Show the close connection we have with the deva evolution.
3. Emphasise the triangular nature and interrelation of all that eventuates.

It might be advisable here to bring out a point in connection with the devas of the lower planes (those with whom man is peculiarly connected). They can be divided into certain groups, indicating their place in the scale of consciousness. Perhaps the question may here be asked why we are dealing only with those deva groups which are to be found in the three worlds. Occultly understood, these devas (of the type we are considering) are only found in the dense physical body of the Logos,— being the substance of the lower three subplanes of the cosmic physical. The old Commentary says as follows:

> "The spheres of fire seek location upon the lower three. They originate by medium of the fifth, yet merge upon the planes of yoga. When the fiery essences permeate all, then there is no more the fifth nor sixth, nor seventh, but only the three shining by medium of the fourth."

Therefore, for the purposes of our present study, the devas are only to be found in the three worlds. Beyond those three planes we have the three aspects of the major three manifesting through the fourth; we have consequently the spheres of the planetary Logoi upon the plane of buddhi. They synthesise all that has been developing through the denser manifestation. From the standpoint of the esoteric philosophy, the cosmic physical plane on which our entire solar system has its place must be studied in a dual manner:

1. From the point of view of the Heavenly Men, covering the evolutions of the four higher planes, or the etheric levels. Of these we can know practically nothing until after initiation, at which time the consciousness of the human being is transferred gradually on to the cosmic etheric planes.
2. From the standpoint of the human being in the three worlds. Man is the consummating evolution in the three worlds, just as the Heavenly Men are in the higher four.

In the three worlds, we have the parallel evolutions— deva and human in their many varying grades—the human naturally concerning us the most intimately, though the two evolve through interaction with each other. In the higher four worlds, we have this duality viewed as a unity, and the aspect of the synthetic evolution of the Heavenly Men is the one considered. It would interest us much could we but understand a little of the point of view of those great devas Who co-operate intelligently in the plan of evolution. They have Their own method of expressing these ideas, the medium being colour which can be heard, and sound which can be seen. Man reverses the process and sees colors and hears sounds. A hint lies here as to the necessity for symbols, for they are signs which convey cosmic truths, and instruction, and can be *comprehended alike by the evolved of both evolutions*. It should be borne in mind, as earlier pointed out, that:

a. Man is demonstrating the aspects of divinity. The devas are demonstrating the attributes of divinity.

b. Man is evolving the inner vision and must learn to see.

   The devas are evolving the inner hearing and must learn to hear.

c. Both are as yet imperfect, and an imperfect world is the result.

d. Man is evolving by means of contact and experience. He expands.

   The devas evolve by means of the lessening of contact. Limitation is the law for them.

e. Man aims at self-control.

   Devas must develop by being controlled.

f. Man is innately Love,—the Force which produces coherency. The devas are innately intelligence,—the force which produces activity.

g. The third type of force, that of Will, the balancing equilibrium of electrical phenomena, has to play equally upon and through both evolutions, but in the one it demonstrates as self-consciousness, and in the other as constructive vibration.

In the Heavenly Man these two great aspects of divinity are equally blended, and in the course of the mahamanvantara the imperfect Gods become perfect. These broad and general distinctions are pointed out as they throw light upon the relationship of Man to the devas.

The devas of the physical plane, though divided into the three groups A, B, C, are under another grouping spoken of as *"the Devas of the Seventh Order."* The seventh order is peculiarly linked to the devas of the first order on the first plane. They are the reflectors of the mind of God of which the first order is the expression, and manifest it as it has worked through from the

archetypal plane. This seventh order of devas is directly
under the influence of the seventh Ray, and the planetary
Logos of that Ray works in close co-operation with the
Raja-Lord of the seventh plane. As the goal of evolution for the devas is the inner hearing, it will be apparent
why mantric sounds and balanced modulations are the
method of contacting them, and of producing varying
phenomena. This seventh order of devas is the one with
which the workers on the left hand path are concerned,
working through vampirism and the devitalisation of
their victims. They deal with the etheric bodies of their
enemies, and by means of sounds affect deva substance,
thus producing the desired results. The white Magician
does not work on the physical plane with physical substance. He transfers His activities to a higher level,
and hence deals with desires and motives. He works
through the devas of the sixth order.

The devas of the sixth order are those of the astral
plane, and are the devas who have the most to do with
the forces which produce the phenomena we call love,
sex impulse, instinct, or the driving urge and motive
which demonstrates later on the physical plane in activity of some kind. The positive vibration set up on the
astral plane produces results on the physical and that is
why the White Brother, if He works with the devas at
all, works only on the astral plane and with the positive
aspect.

These devas of the sixth order, as might be expected,
are closely linked with those of the second order on the
monadic plane, and with the heart centre of the particular Heavenly Man on Whose Ray they may be
found. They are allied too to the deva forces on the
buddhic plane and in these three great orders of devas
we have a powerful triangle of electrical force,—the
three types of electricity which are met with in occult
books. It should be borne in mind that the equilibrising

type of force (at present an unknown type) flows in
from the buddhic plane at this time, and the apex of the
triangle is there.

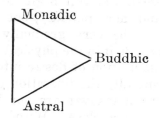

These three orders are (in this solar system) the most
potent, especially in this fourth round. They influence
particularly the fourth kingdom of nature, and are the
basis of that search for balance, of that aspiration towards harmony, union and yoga which distinguishes man
in all grades; it shows in its lower manifestation as the
sex instinct as we know it, and in its higher as longing
for union with God.

These devas of the sixth order come under the special
influence of the Lord of the sixth Ray of Abstract Idealism, and it is their connection with Him which facilitates
the working through of the archetypal idea on to the
physical plane. The sixth Creative Hierarchy likewise
is specially connected with this particular order of devas,
and through this dual influence is produced that physical
manifestation which is definitely objective,—one type of
force working through the etheric manifestation, and
the other through the dense physical.

This will as yet prove an insoluble mystery to the
student, but in the significance of numbers much can be
discovered. This angle of the matter should be studied
in order to bring out the true meaning of this sixth
order of devas, whose symbol is the six-pointed Star set
at a particular angle and in full manifestation. The
six-pointed star is the sign that a "Son of Necessity"

(no matter whether God or man) has sought physical incarnation. The devas of the sixth order, the Agnisuryans, are a prime factor in bringing this about. In the sixth round these devas will begin to make their presence felt more and more potently, but the strength of their vibration will be very gradually turned upwards, and not downwards into the physical plane. This will involve the transmutation of desire into aspiration, and will produce eventually the liberation of the planetary Logos, and bring a manvantara (or His cycle of physical incarnation) to a close. Withdrawal of the force of desire results likewise in the cessation of man's physical existence. The old Commentary expresses this truth in the following words:

"The Sixth retire within themselves; they turn towards the Fifth, leaving the Seventh alone."

In continuing our consideration of these deva orders, it should be pointed out that these three lower deva orders—the lower fifth, the sixth and the seventh—have a close connection with the moon. They are the building agents which (working on the involutionary matter of the three worlds) construct the lower three bodies of incarnating man. They are a branch of the lunar Pitris, but the fact should be remembered that this particular branch of pitris are those functioning in our particular scheme, and are closely allied to our planetary Logos. Groups of these Pitris are found wherever man is in incarnation in all the schemes, but in other schemes they differ somewhat from ours, as the "Mystery of the Moon" is connected with a peculiar esoteric condition which concerns our own planetary Logos.

Wherever man is in incarnation, the Builders of his bodies are to be found but they will differ in:

a. Their rate of vibration.
b. Their stage of development.

    c. Consciousness.

    d. Fohatic, magnetic and dynamic force.

It should be remembered also that each round sees the deva substance or the deva evolution changing; they also evolve and, therefore, the subject of the devas in their dual aspect as the negative and positive substance which produces objectivity must be studied in a three-fold manner if a true idea is to be approximated. Therefore, the devas—who are the sum-total of substance—must be considered from:

    The standpoint of round development.

    The standpoint of any particular planetary Logos as they form His body of manifestation, a scheme.

    The standpoint of the human kingdom.

When this is not done, a wrong and narrow idea is the result. In future time, as may be seen from a study of the *Secret Doctrine*,[16] the Logos in His septenary Nature will be seen as the Macrocosm for Man, whilst the Microcosm, Man himself, will be seen also as the Macrocosm for the three lower kingdoms. This is simply one way of studying the evolution of the conscious Entity—God, Man, or lesser life—by means of deva substance; it involves the study of the positive and negative inter-action. As says the old Commentary again:

"When Father approaches Mother, that which will be taketh form. The union of the two concealeth the true mystery of Being.

When the two great devas seek each other, when they meet and merge, the promise of life is fulfilled.

When the one who sees and knows stands midway between his parents, then can be seen the fruition of knowledge, and all is known upon the planes of consciousness.

When Anu, the infinitesimal, is seen to contain Ishvara in His potency, when the lesser spheres and cycles expand into the circle of the Heavens, then shall the essential Unity be cognised and manifested fully.

When the One that holds the life becomes the three behind which that life is hidden; when the three by revolution become the seven and the ten; when the thirty million crores of deva lives repeat the revolution; when the central point is reached and reveals the three, the nine, and the inner blazing JEWEL, then is the circle of manifestation consummated, and the One again becomes the ten, the seven, the three and the point.''

Herein lies the key to the mystic marriage, and to the student of occultism much may be revealed through the study of these pairs of opposites; it will cause the revelation of the process (in time and space) whereby this union and its fruit is consummated, and the resultant creation of the divine Hermaphrodite is seen upon His Own high plane.

We must ever keep clearly in mind that we are dealing in this section with the evolutionary devas who are the positive Life animating involutionary matter or deva substance. Consequently, the correspondence of the mystic marriage of Spirit and matter can be seen working out also in deva substance itself, through the interaction of negative and positive deva lives. Substance itself represents essential duality; forms repeat the same duality, and when we arrive at man himself again, we have duality plus a third factor. These three orders of deva substance—the lower fifth, the sixth and seventh—are a very mysterious group as far as man is concerned.[17]

---

[17] Sankaracharya and Buddha. The great sage Sankaracharya who is known to us all as the leading head of the adwaitic movement that was set on foot subsequent to the time of the equally great Sage known as Gautama Buddha, the head of the doctrine of Buddhi or Buddhism. Both are great Masters of compassion and may be conceived as the two hemispheres of the burning globe of light that is placed on the central mental mount to impart light to the East and the West. The two great Masters are mystically connected, if you will listen to H. P. B., and to understand the natures of these two beings is to understand the nature of the entire cosmos divisible as two hemispheres, the one being the land of the sun-rise of thought eternal and the other being ''the Pillar to the West upon whose face the rising sun of thought eternal poureth forth its most glorious waves.'' They are representatives for us (the poor children of the dust of the ground) of the two

They have scarcely been hinted at as yet in occult literature, but they contain within themselves the secret of
our planetary individualisation. They were the group
which had much to do with the "sin of the mindless,"
and are very closely associated with animal man. To
the power and control which these pitris assumed must
be ascribed much of the disastrous early happenings
referred to in the *Secret Doctrine,* such as the above
mentioned "sin," and also the early "failures" in building suitable vehicles for Spirits seeking incarnation.
Here also may be found the beginnings of that mysterious divergence which we call the "left and right hand
paths," which conditions (existing within the body logoic
and consequently being part of the divine consciousness) originated in the remote "space of time," when
the sons of God were seeking form. It has to do with a
special condition in the astral body of our planetary
Logos, and with His history as it lies hidden in the astral
light.

It concerns that which He has to surmount and many
of the problems which face the occultist, including the
"sin of the mindless," the failure in Atlantean days, and
even that mysterious "failure" of the Buddha (which
has a planetary significance only hinted at in the *Secret
Doctrine*)[18] can be traced back to the condition of the deva
substance of which the astral body of our planet, and the
astral bodies of all forms are formed. Our planetary Logos is one of the Lords spoken of as being a
lesser lord, and more "full of passion" than the higher
three. Not even yet is His work completed, and deva

great powers known in the Puranas as Siva and Vishnu, the universal sower
and reaper, who by their interaction are said to support the universe of
progress.—*Some Thoughts on the Gita,* pp. 92-3.
    [18] The Stanzas at the beginning of Volume II of the *Secret Doctrine*
make these failures apparent.—S. D., II, 195, 201, 721, 728.
    The Failure of the Buddha. See S. D., III, 376-588.
    The Imperfect Gods are referred to in S. D., I, 214, 449; II. 223; III,
209.

substance in its various living orders is not yet brought fully under His control. The deva evolution has far to travel.

If this idea be extended to the solar system, it will be apparent that the astral vehicles of the different planetary Logoi differ. This difference is necessarily dependent upon *Their cosmic astral life which directly affects the systemic astral, or the physical liquid subplane of the cosmic physical*. This is a point but little realised. The dense physical body of the planetary Logos exists, as we know, in a threefold condition—dense, liquid, and gaseous—and each is acted upon directly from the corresponding cosmic plane. The condition of the various physical planets will some day be found to be dependent upon this fact.

When the psychic nature of the planetary Logos is understood (which knowledge is entered upon after initiation, being a part of the Wisdom) the *nature* of the different schemes, as regards their watery aspect, for instance, will be found to be connected with a particular astral state. As the initiate progresses in wisdom, he intuitively comprehends the essential nature of the seven groups, or of the logoic Septenate, which is that concerning their colour or quality. This colour or quality is dependent upon the psychic nature of any particular planetary Logos, and His emotional or desire nature can thereby be somewhat studied by the initiate. This will lead eventually to a scientific consideration of the effect of this nature upon His dense physical body, and particularly that portion of it which we call the astral plane, the liquid sub-plane of the cosmic physical plane. A reflection of this (or a further working out, if that term is preferred) is found in the liquid portions of the physical planet.

The seventh subplane of the cosmic physical plane can be subdivided into seven, which are our seven physical subplanes. It is this knowledge which enables a magician to work. Given a certain physical phenomenon—such as the weight of water, for instance, upon a planet—and an initiate of the higher orders can form deductions from it as to the quality of the exalted Life manifesting through a plane. He arrives at this knowledge through a process of reasoning from the liquid (sixth) subplane of the systemic physical plane to:

    a. The liquid subplane of the cosmic physical, our systemic astral plane.

    b. The fourth cosmic ether, the buddhic plane.

    c. The second cosmic ether, the monadic plane, or the plane of the seven Heavenly Men.

    d. The cosmic astral plane, thus getting in touch with the desire nature of the God.

This method naturally involves a vast knowledge of the deva substance and predicates an intuitive realisation of their orders and groups, the keynotes of those orders and of the planes, and also of the triple nature of substance and a knowledge of how to work with the third type of electrical force, which is the type of energy which puts a man in touch with extra-systemic phenomena. Hence that force still remains unknown, and is only contacted as yet by high initiates.

It will again be apparent why the Agnisuryans are of such supreme importance; they embody force which is a direct emanation from the cosmic astral plane and which reveals—when triply blended—the desire nature of our Heavenly Man, and of any particular planetary Logos. In the two opposites, which are called by the theologians "Heaven and Hell," we have two of these types of force hinted at, and in this thought we have indicated one of the keys to the astral plane.

    2. *Summary.* Before passing to the consideration of

those devas who are concerned with the construction of man's causal body, and who are the linking group between the Triad and the Quaternary, both in man and the Logos, we will briefly enumerate the principal groups of Agnisuryans on the systemic astral plane, as they, in their totality, form the body of manifestation of the great deva or Raja-Lord of the plane.

First. The Raja-Lord of the Plane, the great deva Varuna, Who is the central Life of the substance of the astral plane of our planetary scheme. He is Himself an outpost of the consciousness of that greater Deva Who embodies the substance of the solar astral plane, or the sixth subplane of the cosmic physical plane. He again in His turn reflects His prototype, that great cosmic Entity Who ensouls the cosmic astral plane.

Second. Seven great Devas, who are the positive force of each of the seven subplanes of the systemic astral plane.

Third. Various groups of devas, performing different functions carrying out varying activities, and producing constructive results. They might be enumerated as follows, bearing in mind the fact that we are but touching upon a few of the many groups, and that there are numbers whose name is utterly unknown to man and would be unintelligible if mentioned:

1. Those devas who form the permanent atomic substance of all the Monads, both in and out of physical incarnation. They are divided into seven groups according to the Ray of the Monad.

2. Those devas who form the "liquid" aspect in the physical body of the planetary Logos and of the solar Logos. They are myriads in number, and include deva existences ranging all the way from those who ensoul the astral plane, and the astral currents of the highest religious and aspirational nature, to the little water

spirits which are reflections of such astral entities precipitated in watery physical matter.

3. A group of devas, who form the desire body of that great entity who ensouls the animal kingdom. They are the total kamic manifestation (divorced from mentality) of animal desire in its incentive impulsive aspect.

4. Certain devas who—being of the third order—form the Heaven of the average orthodox Christian or believer of any faith. Another group—being the seventh order—form the Hell for the same class of thinker.

5. Those devas who form the astral life of any thought-form. These we will deal with later when studying thought-form construction.

6. A mysterious group of devas intimately connected at this time with the sex expression in the human family on the physical plane. They are a group who are, at this juncture, swept into being, and they embody the fire of sex expression as we understand it. They are the impulse, or instinct, back of physical sex desire. They were peculiarly dominant in the fourth root-race, at which time sex conditions reached a stage of unbelievable horror from our point of view. They are gradually being controlled, and when the last of the Lemurian Egos has passed into the fifth root-race they will be slowly passed out of the solar system altogether. They are connected with the passional "fire" of the solar Logos and with one of His centres in particular; this centre is being gradually obscured and its fire transferred into a higher centre.

7. There is also a group of devas connected with the Lodge of Masters, whose work it is to build the aspirational forms towards which average man may aspire. They are divided into certain groups—three in number —connected with science, religion and philosophy, and through these groups of deva substance the Heads of the three departments reach men. It is one of Their

channels for work. The Master Jesus is particularly active at this time along this line, working in collaboration with certain adepts on the scientific line, who—through the desired union of science and religion—seek to shatter the materialism of the west on the one hand and on the other the sentimental devotion of the many devotees of all faiths. This is made possible now through the passing out of the sixth Ray and the coming in of the seventh. It should be borne in mind by all students when considering the planes, plane substance and energy that they are in a condition of flux and change all the time. The matter of all planes circulates, and cyclically certain portions become more energised than others; the matter of the planes is thus under a threefold influence, or—to word it otherwise—deva substance is subjected to a threefold cyclic stimulation:

1. *Ray stimulation,* dependent upon any Ray being in or out of power. It is inter-systemic and planetary.
2. *Zodiacal stimulation,* which is an extra-systemic stimulation, and is also cosmic and cyclic.
3. *Solar stimulation,* or the impact of direct solar force or energy upon the substance of a plane; this emanates from the "Heart of the Sun" and is peculiarly potent.

All the planes are subjected to this threefold influence but in the case of the buddhic and the astral planes, the force of this third stimulation is very great. The adepts —working in conjunction with the great devas—utilise cyclic opportunity to effect definitely constructive results.

8. A group of devas closely connected with the mysteries of initiation. They form what is esoterically called the "path of the Heart," and are the bridge between the astral and the buddhic planes. They are in no way

connected with the permanent atoms in the causal body, but are very definitely associated with the central tier of petals in the egoic lotus, or with the "petals of love." Force interacts between these three petals on the one hand, and the devas who form the "Path of the Heart" upon the other, those who are the bridge of astral-buddhic matter whereby initiates of a certain mystic type make the "great approach."

9. Devas of all degrees and vibratory capacity who make up the bulk of the desire forms of every kind.

10. The devas of transmutative force. They are a peculiar group of devas who embody the "fires of transmutation" and are called by various names, such as:

The furnaces of purifications.
The melting elements.
The gods of incense.

It is impossible to enumerate more now, and likewise profitless and it has only been deemed advisable to bring these many types of deva substance to the notice of students on account of the pre-eminent importance of the astral body in the three worlds. It is by the domination of these deva lives, and the "transmutation of desire" into aspiration, and by the purificatory fires of the astral plane that man eventually succeeds in attaining buddhic consciousness.

It has been the recognition of the cleansing power of the occult fluids—water and blood—that has led to the emphasis laid by Christians (even though erroneously interpreted) upon these two.

3. THE SOLAR ANGELS, THE AGNISHVATTAS.

Introductory Remarks.

We start here upon the consideration of the Agnishvattas, or the Fire devas of the mental plane, and are

thus launched upon the most stupendous subject in connection with our planetary evolution; it is the one having
the most occult significance for man, for these solar
Angels [19] concern his own essential nature, and are also
the creative power by which he works. For all practical purposes, and for the elucidation of the spiritual
evolution of man, this immediate section is of the greatest interest and importance; it should be one of the most
widely studied sections of this treatise. Man is ever
profoundly interested in himself, and before he can duly
develop must comprehend *scientifically* the laws of his
own nature, and the constitution of his own "mode of
expression." He must realise likewise somewhat of the
inter-relation of the three fires in order that he may himself at some future date "blaze forth."

The question of these Fire Dhyanis and their relation
to man is a most profound mystery, and the entire matter is so clothed in intricate legends that students are
apt to despair of ever arriving at the desired, and necessary clarity of thought. Not yet will it be possible
entirely to dispel the clouds which veil the central mystery, but perhaps, by due tabulation and synthesis, and
by a cautious amplification of the data already imparted,
the thoughts of the wise student may become somewhat
less confused.

There are two statements in the *Secret Doctrine* which
are often overlooked by the casual reader but which, if

[19] Solar angels are therefore entities of a high spiritual order—with a
refined consciousness that corresponds to the material substance in which
they are clothed. In order to connect this with what I have said already,
you may consider the solar angels as collectively forming the Lord Brahma
of the lotus isle. The angels are called by various names as planetary
spirits, Asuras, etc., but in order to get a proper idea of their nature, you
may consider them as standing in the same relation to the spiritually
regenerated and released world Brahmins or the Nirmanakayas as these
stand to the ordinary humanity. The angels were such Brahmins in previous Mahamanvantaras, who spent those enormous periods in suffering
and toil for the sake of rearing wisdom in the world and hence they
emerged as angels from the infinite womb of Aditi under their karmic
impulse after a period of Mahapralaya.—*Some Thoughts on the Gita*,
page 137.

duly pondered upon, convey much information. Let us
make note of these two statements:

1. Two connecting principles are needed. This requires a living spiritual Fire of the middle principle from the Fifth and third states of Pleroma.
   This fire is the possession of the Triangles.
2. These Beings are Nirvanis from a preceding Mahamanvantara.

We have been considering somewhat the devas of evolutionary tendency who are grouped roughly together
as the lunar Pitris.[20] These lunar Pitris are divided into
four groups and are concerned with the building of man's
dual physical body, with his astral body and with his
lower mental body; these sheaths are energised by their
force through the medium of the permanent atoms. But
for the purposes of the subjective nature of man, they
are to be considered in their three groups—etheric,
astral and lower mental. The work of the Agnishvattas
(the self-conscious principles, the Builders or construc-
tors of the egoic body on the higher mental levels) is to
unite the higher three principles—atma, buddhi, manas
—and the lower three, and thus become in very truth the
middle principle in man. They themselves originate
from the logoic middle principle.[21] Thus the esoteric
seven is completed. The physical body in its denser
manifestation is, as we know, not esoterically considered
a principle.

The devas of the lower mental levels in relation to

[20] The Lunar Pitris are all Nature Spirits.—S. D., II, 107.
  1. They possess, or are the containers of the fire of the third aspect.
     —S. D., II, 81.
  2. Their work precedes that of the Solar Angels.—S. D., I, 268.
  3. They exist in seven classes as do the Solar Angels.—S. D., II, 96.
     a. Three incorporeal, which are the three elemental kingdoms of
        nature, providing man with his etheric, astral and mental
        bodies.
     b. Four corporeal which are the forms of the four kingdoms of
        nature.—S. D., II, 93.
     c. See S. D., II, 233.
[21] S. D., II, 83.

man work through the mental unit, and are, roughly
speaking, divided into four groups, being in fact the
first condensation of the threefold lower body of man.
They form part of his lunar body. They are directly
linked with the highest spiritual essences, and represent
the lowest manifestation of force emanating from the
cosmic mental plane, and finding its link with the human
Hierarchy through the mental units. They are the gaseous devas of the logoic physical body. We will not deal
with them in greater detail at this moment for as we
study the subject of the fifth principle certain points will
become clearer; their work in connection with man can
be enlarged upon as we proceed. More detail at this
moment would but serve to complicate.

Let us be quite clear in our minds just what we are in
process of considering. We are dealing with:

1. That fifth state of consciousness called the mental
   plane,
2. The substance of that plane as it exists in its dual
   aspect, rupa and arupa,[22]
3. The lives who ensoul that matter, especially in
   their relation to man,
4. The Egos or the self-conscious units who form the
   middle point in manifestation,
5. The building of the causal body, the opening of the
   egoic Lotus, and the construction of those groups
   we call egoic groups,
6. The individuality of those Existences whom we call:
   a. Agnishvattas.
   b. Manasa devas.
   c. Fire dhyanis.
   d. Solar angels, or solar Pitris.
   e. The Asuras.

and many other names mentioned in the occult books.

[22] For rupa and arupa definitions see pages 615, 616.

Much confusion exists in the minds of students as to the distinction between the Agnishvattas who incarnated in man, and those who simply were responsible for the implanting of the manasic or mental spark in animal man. This opens up for us the entire question of individualisation itself, and the incarnation of certain spiritual existences who—when in bodily form—are spoken of as Avatars, as Buddhas of Activity, or as direct manifestations of the Logos. The entire mystery is hidden in the relationship of the individual Monads who form the various centres in the body of a planetary Logos and the self-conscious Identity of that planetary Logos Himself. The student must here bear in mind the fact that the mental plane is the first aspect of the *dense* physical body of the planetary Logos, the buddhic plane being a cosmic etheric plane, and the one whereon are to be found the etheric centres of a Heavenly Man.

From the buddhic plane (in a planetary or solar sense) comes the vitality and impulse which galvanises the dense physical vehicle into purposeful and coherent action; it is on the mental plane, therefore, that this impulse is first felt and the contact between the two realised. Herein lies a hint which will serve a purpose if pondered upon. The student should study the place and purpose of the mental plane, and its relation to the planetary Logos and a solar Logos. As he investigates more closely the nature of his own etheric body, he must extend that knowledge to higher levels, and must endeavour to comprehend the constitution of the greater sphere of which he is but a part. As the nature of his own centres, and their effective action upon his own dense physical body, is better understood, he will pass to a fuller comprehension of the corresponding effect in the body of the Logos.

It is on the mental plane (the reflection in the three worlds of the third and fifth states of Pleroma), that the full force of etheric vitality is felt. A hint as to the

significance of this may be found in the fact that the
etheric body of man receives, and transmits prana directly to the physical body, and that the vitality of the
physical frame is to be gauged largely by the condition
and action of the heart. The heart circulates vitality
to the myriads of cells that constitute the dense physical
sheath; something analogous is seen in the fact that
these fire devas are "the Heart of the Dhyan chohanic
body,"[23] for their energy comes from the spiritual sun,
in the same sense that the energy of the pranic devas of
the etheric body comes from the physical sun. This
energy of the Agnishvattas manifests on the mental
plane, the gaseous subplane of the cosmic physical just
as the energy of the etheric centres on the fourth etheric
subplane manifests first and potently on the gaseous matter of the physical body. This is why the Sons of
Wisdom, embodying the buddhic principle, the life force,
or love aspect, are nevertheless known on the fifth plane
as the self-conscious principles; buddhi uses manas as
a vehicle, and occult writers often speak in terms of the
vehicle. The Ego, or the self-conscious Identity is in
essence and in truth Love-Wisdom, but manifests primarily as intelligent consciousness.

We should endeavor to study carefully the following
statement which is concerned with kama-manas, and
which deals with the conditions which produce individualisation, or which call forth into self-conscious Being
the Monads seeking full self-expression. It is as follows:

*Only as the heart centre of a Heavenly Man (each in
His cycle and each differing cyclically) becomes vitalised
and attains a certain vibratory capacity does the individualisation of the Monads become possible under the Law.*

Again, it is only as the threefold dense physical body
of a planetary Logos (as expressed by our three worlds,
the mental, astral and dense physical planes) has reached

---

[23] This name is given to them in the *Secret Doctrine*, Volume II, page 96.

a corresponding vibration and retraced the cyclic development of the previous mahamanvantara, that there is produced that vibratory contact which causes the shining out upon the mental plane of the egoic groups. It brings forth a manifestation of the heart impulses of the Heavenly Man, and thus swings into objectivity those Monads (energised by the life of the Heart) who form various centres. The old Commentary says:

"When the Heart of the Body throbs with spiritual energy, when its sevenfold content thrills under the spiritual impulse, then the currents spread and circulate and divine manifestation becomes a Reality; the divine Man incarnates."

The physical plane analogy is seen at the life stimulation which is felt between the third and fourth month during the prenatal period, when the heart of the child thrills with life and individual existence becomes a possibility.

This life vibration emanates from the soul of the mother (the correspondence to the Pleroma or universal soul) and is coincident with the awakening of the third spirilla in the permanent physical atom of the infant. It must be borne in mind that just as in each round all the preceding stages are rapidly recapitulated, and just as in the prenatal period the fœtus recapitulates during the formative process the history of the preceding kingdoms, so in the solar system a similar procedure can be seen. When a certain point is reached and the lower three planes are vibrating, or energised, then cosmic incarnation becomes a possibility; the "Heart" occultly awakens, and the "Son of God," the expression of the desire and love of the Logos, is born.[24, 25] The cosmic incarnation of certain exalted Beings is consummated, and one of the indications of this is the appearance of the egoic groups

[24] Compare S. D., I, 203; II, 108, 122, 279.

[25] These three planes are the correspondences to the three lower spirillae in the physical permanent atom of the solar Logos and the planetary Logos.

on mental levels, and the resultant individualisation.
Method and time may vary according to the nature of
any particular planetary Logos, but for each and all the
"Heart of the Body" has to thrill with awakening life
before the response comes from the lower. The lunar
Pitris have to carry on their work in our scheme and
system before the solar angels, thrilling with expectancy,
take possession of the forms prepared through their
endeavour, and stimulate them into self-conscious life and
separated existence. Thus the four great schemes in the
solar system, which are the vehicles for four of the planetary Logoi (Who constitute the logoic Quaternary),
have to reach a certain stage of vibratory capacity, and
of consciousness before a similar happening occurs in its
fullness in the solar system, and the lower four and
higher three are synthesised. The logoic heart is thrilling, and response comes already from all the schemes,
as three spirillae are vibrating in all of them, but the Son
of God is not yet fully and cosmically self-conscious. As
response comes the centres awaken. One logoic centre
is responding fully to the heart stimulation, and that is
Venus, who is passing through the final round.

If the student endeavours to dissociate our solar system
from that which preceded it, and if he considers the
pralaya at the close of this mahamanvantara to be a
final one, and the utter consummation of all things, he
errs. In the preceding system the cosmic physical plane
attained a certain vibratory capacity, and the devas of
the internal furnaces became (relatively speaking) highly
evolved, the "fires of matter" then blazing forth. Certain Existences attained self-consciousness in that earlier
system, and are the "nirvanis" spoken of by H. P. B.[26]
As might be expected, they are characterised by active
intelligence, achieved and developed by means of material evolution during a previous mahamanvantara. They

[26] See S. D., II, 83, 84, 243.

are the Manasa devas and in their totality are the vehicles of the Divine mind, the dhyan-chohanic forces, the aggregate of the Ah-hi. In this solar system the vibration of the cosmic astral plane is becoming dominant, and through that vibration, travelling via the fourth cosmic ether (whereon as earlier stated are the etheric centres of the planetary Logoi) and our systemic astral plane, certain eventualities become possible. The "Sons of desire," logoic or human, can learn certain lessons, undergo certain experiences, and add the faculty of love-wisdom to the intelligence earlier gained.

Our solar Logos, and the Heavenly Men, are polarised on the cosmic astral plane, and the effect of Their life energy as it flows through the systemic "Heart" can be seen in the activity of the astral plane, and in the part sex and passion play in the development of man. At the close of this mahamanvantara there will be ready for manifestation in the coming third system nirvanis who will be, in very essence, "active intelligent love"; they will have to wait until the five lower planes of the system have reached a stage of vibratory development which will permit them to enter, as the nirvanis in this system waited until the three lower planes became adequate in vibratory response. We are here speaking in terms of the Heavenly Men. In the Earth scheme, the analogy is hidden in the advent of the Egos in the third round, in the third root race and in the third chain. Individualisation, as we understand it, was not possible until the "third state of pleroma" was reached, either universally where a Heavenly Man is concerned, or relatively in connection with a human unit.

Considering the same subject from below upwards it is the animal in the third kingdom which individualises. Viewing it from above downwards it is the fifth kingdom, the spiritual, which ensouls the third and produces the fourth, or self-conscious human kingdom. These figures

should be studied for they hold the mystery ᴗid, and
though the true occult meaning will not be revealed untii
the third major Initiation, nor fully comprehended until
the fifth, yet light may stream in on a difficult point.
Equally so in the next solar system, individualisation
(if such an inadequate term may be applied to a state of
consciousness inconceivable even to an initiate of the
third Initiation) will not be possible until the second or
sixth stage of Pleroma. Consciousness will blaze forth
then on the Monadic plane, and it will be the plane of
individualisation. All states of consciousness below that
high level will be to the Logos what the consciousness of
the three worlds is to Him now. Just as the physicai
body of man is not a principle, so all planes at this time
below the fourth cosmic ether are not considered by the
Logos to be a principle.

Our present solar Angels or fire devas will then have a
position analogous to that of the lunar Pitris now, for
all will form a part of the divine consciousness, and yet,
will be esoterically considered as "below the threshold"
of consciousness. Man has to learn to control, guide
and use the deva substances of which his lower sheaths
are made; this goal involves the development of full
self-consciousness, which is brought about through the
agency of the solar Angels or builders and vitalisers of
the egoic body; they are those through whom self-consciousness becomes a fact. In the next solar system
they too will no longer embody the type of consciousness
towards which man aspires; he will have to rise to still
greater realisations, and again by occultly "putting his
foot upon" them these higher realisations will become
possible. In this solar system he has to mount by the
putting his foot upon the serpent of matter. He rises by
domination of matter and becomes himself a serpent of
wisdom. In the next solar system he will mount upward
by means of the "serpent of wisdom," and by the domi-

nation and control of the Agnishvattas, achieve something of which even the illuminated mind of the highest Dhyan-chohan can not yet conceive.

a.   The Fifth Principle.

The solar Angels are the Pitris, the builders of the body of the Ego, and the producers of individualisation or the realised consciousness, the Agnishvattas, the great devas of Mind.

Certain broad and general affirmations have been laid down with the purpose in view of opening up this stupendous and practical subject, and in an endeavour to link up this solar system in its fundamental manasic aspect with the past and the future.

The section we are now approaching concerns the development of the divine Manasaputras, viewing them as a collective whole, containing the Divine Mind, and considering the individual Monad, who responds to Their life as a part of the body of these Dhyani Buddhas.

(a.) *Cosmically considered.* An occult sentence has its place here. It holds the key to the mystery of the fivefold Dhyanis:

"The higher Three in cyclic unison sought to know and to be known. The lower Three (for we count not here the eighth) knew not nor saw; they only heard and touched. The fourth had not a place. The Fifth (which also is the fourth) formed at the middle point a cosmic TAU, which was reflected on the cosmic Seventh."

H. P. B. states [27, 28] that the individualised Monad has more spiritual consciousness than the monad itself on its own plane, the second. It must be remembered here that the planetary Logoi are only in physical incarnation in our system, their bodies of individualisation being on the cosmic mental plane, therefore full expression for them

[27] S. D., I, 200, 201.
[28] See S. D., I, 201; II, 251, 252.

is impossible during manifestation. Relatively therefore, *during manifestation,* man is able to express
himself fully when he attains the "consciousness of the
high places." It should, therefore, be pointed out at
the very beginning of our study of this fifth principle
that the divine Manasaputras on their own plane must
be considered from the standpoint of physical incarnation, whereas man can be considered from what is, for
him, a spiritual aspect.[29]

Human individualisation, or the emergence of the self-
conscious units on the mental plane, is involved in a
larger development, for it synchronizes with the appropriation of a dense physical body by the Planetary
Logos; this body is composed of matter of our three
lower planes. As the etheric centres of the Manasaputras on the fourth cosmic etheric plane become vitalised,
they produce increased activity on the systemic mental
plane, the cosmic gaseous, and the *consciousness* of the
Heavenly Man and His life energy begins to make itself
felt. Simultaneously, under the Law, mind force or
manasic energy pours in from the fifth cosmic plane,
the cosmic mental. This dual energy, contacting that
which is inherent in the dense physical body of the Logos
itself, produces correspondences to the centres upon that
plane and the egoic groups appear. They blend in latency the three types of electricity, and are themselves
electrical phenomena. They are composed of those
atoms, or types of lives, which are a part of the fourth

```
                        1.
                        2.
                        3.
                        4.
    ➤ Kingdom————————————Principle.
                        5.
                        6.
                        7.
                        8.
```

This has a cosmic and systemic significance and to throw light upon that
occurrence which concerns our own scheme, the Stanzas on the coming of
the Lords of Flame should here be studied.

Creative Hierarchy, the aggregate of purely human Monads. Similarly, this triple force, produced by this conscious appropriation by the Heavenly Man, animates deva substance and the dense physical body of the planetary Logos is manifested objectively. This is what is meant by the statements that devas are found only in the three worlds. It is a statement analogous to the one that humanity is only found in the three worlds; nevertheless, the human Monads in their seven types are found on the plane of spirit—as it is the plane of duality—the deva monads are likewise found there.

Students should ever bear in mind that these occult subjects can be expressed in a twofold manner:

In terms of the three worlds, or from the standpoint of the logoic dense physical body.

In terms of force or energy, or from the standpoint of the logoic body of prana or vitality, the four cosmic ethers.

What we understand by the fifth principle is but the expression on the causal plane of that force or energy which emanates from the logoic causal body on the fifth cosmic plane, via the logoic correspondence to the mental unit. (These correspondences involve a concept far in advance of what is possible even to an initiate at this time). In the fifth round, the inner significance may become more apparent to the disciple. As the logoic will is gradually transmuted into desire and thus the physical incarnation is produced, a tremendous downflow of vitalising force from the fifth cosmic plane takes place, until it arrives at our fifth plane, the mental. This force it is which—at the correct cyclic moment—causes certain eventualities in time and space and in the three worlds, His dense physical body. The first of these events is the appropriation *by the Logos* of that dense physical vehicle, and the flashing into manifestation of the physical Sun and the physical planets. Though this, from our standpoint, covers an inconceivably vast period of time, to the Logos it is but the brief period of gestation which all bodies undergo. A second momentous occurrence is the appropriation *by the various Prajapatis,*[30] or Heavenly Men of their physical bodies—again at varying times and according to their evolutionary stage. This is of later date for the seven than for the three. An idea of the meaning of this distinction can be gleaned by the student, as he studies the process of the incarnating ego.

What do we consequently find? First of all, impulse, or the will-to-be, emanating from the mental plane; then desire, emanating from the astral plane, producing manifestation on the dense physical.

This idea must be extended to the three Logoi or logoic Aspects and we then have the key to the mystery of the nine Sephiroth, the triple Trimurti.

The other event might be noted,—the appropriation at a still later period in time and space by the individual Monads of their bodies of manifestation.

The pouring in of this force of energy, emanating from the fifth logoic Principle, brings about two things:

The appropriation by the sevenfold Logos of His dense physical body.

The appearance on the fifth systemic plane of the causal bodies of the human Monads.

or

For the greater Life it was incarnation.

For the lesser lives it was individualisation.

This needs pondering upon.

---

[30] *Prajapatis.* The Progenitors; the givers of life to all on this earth. They are seven and then ten corresponding to the seven and ten Sephiroth. Cosmically, they are the seven Rishis of the Great Bear; systemically they are the seven planetary Logoi, and from the standpoint of our planet they are the seven Kumaras.

See S. D., I, 109, 122, 459, 661; II, 33, 36; footnote 80.

It will, therefore, be apparent to all thinkers why this fifth principle stirred the third aspect into self-conscious activity.

(b.) *Hylozoistically considered.*[31] In continuing our consideration of the fifth logoic Principle, we will now view it in its hylozoistic aspect. We have seen that it can be regarded as the force, the energy or the quality which emanates from the logoic mental unit on the cosmic mental plane; this necessarily has a definite effect on the fifth systemic plane, and on the fifth subplane of the physical plane, the gaseous. Before taking up the subject of the Agnishvattas in detail, there are three points which should be borne in mind.

First, it should be remembered that all the planes of our system, viewing them as deva substance, form the spirillae in the physical permanent atom of the solar Logos. This has earlier been pointed out, but needs re-emphasising here. All consciousness, all memory, all faculty is stored up in the permanent atoms, and we are consequently dealing here with that consciousness; the student should nevertheless bear in mind that it is on the atomic subplanes that the logoic consciousness (remote as even that may be from the Reality) centres itself. This permanent atom of the solar system, which holds the same relation to the logoic physical body as the human permanent atom does to that of a man, is a recipient of force, and is, therefore, receptive to force emanations from another extra-systemic source. Some idea of the illusory character of manifestation, both human and logoic, may be gathered from the relation of the permanent atoms to the rest of the structure. Apart

---

[31] *Hylozoism:*—From Greek "ule," matter; "zoon," animal; and "ism." Ism is a suffix embodying the doctrine or abstract idea of the noun to which it is attached. Hylozoism is the doctrine that all matter is endowed with life.

"When we have attained to this conception of hylozoism of a living material universe, the mystery of nature will be solved."—*Standard Dictionary.*

from the permanent atom, the human physical body does not exist.

Again, forms differ as do kingdoms according to the nature of the force flowing through them. In the animal kingdom that which corresponds to the permanent atom responds to force of an involutionary character, emanating from a particular group. The human permanent atom responds to force emanating from a group on the evolutionary arc and the Ray of a particular planetary Logos in Whose body a human Monad has a definite place.

Secondly, it must be noted that in view of the above it will be apparent that we are, at this period of manasic inflow and development, concerned with the coming into full vitality and activity of the fifth logoic spirilla; this vitalisation shows itself in the intense activity of the mental plane, and the threefold nature of the electrical phenomena to be witnessed upon it.

a. The atomic subplane.manasic perma-
            nent atoms....Positive
b. The fourth subplane. mental units......Negative
c. The egoic groups.....causal bodies....Equilibrium
                                or neutral

This is in process of demonstration during the course of evolution. We are dealing here with the substance aspect and considering energy in its various manifestations. The response of deva substance to the inflow of force on the mental plane has a threefold effect in connection with the Logos or the Septenate:

1. It produces a greatly increased vitality in the logoic centres on the fourth cosmic ether, due to reflex action, which is felt both above and below the plane of activity.

2. It stimulates the efforts of the highest specimens of the third kingdom, and a dual effect is produced

through this, for the fourth kingdom in nature makes its appearance on the physical plane and the Triads are reflected on the mental plane in the causal bodies to be found thereon.

3. As earlier said, the dense physical is linked and co-ordinated with the etheric bodies of the solar Logos and of the planetary Logos. Therefore, the lower three planes are synthesised with the higher four, and the devas of an earlier maha-manvantara or solar cycle are brought into conjunction with those of a newer order who were awaiting just conditions. The physical incarnation of the Logos is completed. The lower three kingdoms, being negative to the higher force, the mutual attraction of these two and their interaction bring into being the fourth or human kingdom. The three fires of mind, Spirit and matter are brought together and the work of full self-consciousness begun.

Finally, the student should very carefully study here the significance of the numbers three, four and five in the evolution of consciousness. Numerology has hitherto been studied primarily, and rightly, from the substance aspect, but not so much from the standpoint of conscious energy. The Triad, for instance, is usually looked upon by our students as the triangle formed by the manasic, buddhic and atmic permanent atoms; the cube stands for the lower material man, and the five-pointed star has frequently a very material interpretation. All these angles of vision are necessary, and must precede the study of the subjective aspect, but they lay the emphasis upon the material rather than upon the subjective; the subject nevertheless should be studied psychologically. In this solar system, the above numbers are the most important from the angle of the evolution of consciousness. In the earlier system, the numbers six and seven held the mystery hid. In the next system, it will be two and one. This refers only to the psychical development. Let me illustrate: The five-pointed star on the mental plane signifies (among other things) the evolution, by means of the five senses in the three worlds (which are also capable of a fivefold differentiation) of the fifth principle, the attainment of self-consciousness, and the development of the fifth spirilla.

On the buddhic plane, when flashing forth at initiation, this number signifies the full development of the fifth principle or quality, the completed cycle of the Ego upon the five Rays under the Mahachohan, and the assimilation of all that is to be learned upon them, and the attainment —not only of full self-consciousness, but also of the consciousness of the group wherein a man is found. It infers the full unfoldment of five of the egoic petals, leaving four to open before the final initiation.

The five-pointed star at the initiations on the mental plane flashes out above the head of the initiate. This concerns the first three initiations which are undergone in the causal vehicle. It has been said that the first two initiations take place upon the astral plane and this is correct, but has given rise to a misunderstanding. They are felt profoundly in connection with the astral and physical bodies and with the lower mental, and effect their control. The chief effect being felt in those bodies, the initiate may interpret them as having taken place on the planes concerned, for the vividness of the effect, and the stimulation works out largely in the astral body. But it must ever be remembered that the major initiations are taken in the causal body or—dissociated from that body—on the buddhic plane. At the final two initiations, which set a man free from the three worlds and enable him to function in the logoic body of vitality and to wield the force which animates that logoic vehicle, the initiate becomes the five-pointed star, and it descends upon him, merges in him, and he is *seen at its very centre*. This descent is brought about through the action of the Initiator, wielding the Rod of Power, and puts a man in touch with the centre in the Body of the planetary Logos of which he is a part; this is consciously effected. The two initiations, called the sixth and seventh, take place on the atmic plane; the five-pointed star "blazes forth from within itself" as the esoteric phrase has it, and becomes the seven-pointed star; it descends upon the man and he enters into the Flame.

Initiation and the mystery of numbers primarily concern consciousness, and not fundamentally "ability to function on a plane," nor the energy of matter, as might be gathered from so many occult books. They deal with the subjective life, life as part of the consciousness and self-realization of a planetary Logos, or Lord of a Ray, and not *life in matter* as we understand it. A Heavenly Man functions in His pranic vehicle, and there His consciousness is to be found as far as we are concerned in this system; He works *consciously* through His centres.

To sum up: There is a stage in the evolution of consciousness where the three, the four and the five blend and merge perfectly. Confusion on this point arises from two causes which are the point of individual achievement of the student. We interpret and colour statements according to the state of our own inner consciousness. H. P. B. hints at this [32] when dealing with the principles; also the interpretation of these figures varies according to the key employed. The fifth or spiritual kingdom is entered when the units of the fourth kingdom have succeeded in vitalizing the fifth spirilla in all the atoms of the threefold lower man; when they

[32] See S. D., III, 456.

have unfolded three of the egoic petals and are in process of unfolding the fourth and fifth and when they are becoming conscious of the pranic force of the Heavenly Man.

(c.) *The Solar Angels and the Fifth Principle.* We can now study the Entities concerned with this fifth principle and their effect upon the evolution of consciousness.

Where man is concerned these solar Angels, the Agnishvattas, produce the union of the spiritual Triad, or divine Self, and the Quaternary, or lower self. Where the Logos is concerned, whether solar or planetary, they produce conditions whereby the etheric, and the dense physical become a unit.

They represent a peculiar type of electrical force; their work is to blend and fuse, and above all else they are the "transmuting fires" of the system, and are those agents who pass the life of God through their bodies of flame as it descends from the higher into the lower, and again as it ascends from the lower into the higher. They are connected in their highest groups with that portion of the logoic head centre which corresponds to the heart, and here is the clue to the mystery of kamamanas. The kamic angels are vitalised from the "heart" centre and the manasic angels from the logoic head centre, *via the point within that centre connected with the heart*. These two dominating groups are the sum-total of kama-manas in all its manifestations. The solar angels exist in three groups, all of which are concerned with the self-consciousness aspect, all of which are energised and connected with the fifth spirilla of the logoic permanent atom, and all of which work as a unit.

One group, the highest, is connected with the logoic head centre, whether solar or planetary. They work with the manasic permanent atoms and embody the will-to-be in dense physical incarnation. Their power is felt on the atomic subplane and on the second; they are the substance and the life of those planes. Another group is connected definitely with the causal bodies of all Egos and are of prime importance in this solar system. They come from the heart centre, and express that force. The third group, corresponding to the throat centre, show forth their power on the fourth subplane through the mental units. They are the sumtotal of the power of the Ego to see, to hear and to speak (or sound) in the strictly occult sense.

A hint may here be given to those who have power to see. Three constellations are connected with the fifth logoic principle in its threefold manifestation: Sirius, two of the Pleiades, and a small constellation whose name must be ascertained by the intuition of the student. These three govern the appropriation by the Logos of His dense body. When the last pralaya ended, and the etheric body had been co-ordinated, a triangle in the Heavens was formed under law which permitted a flow of force, producing vibration on the fifth systemic plane. That triangle still persists, and is the cause of the continued inflow of manasic force; it is connected with the spirillae in the logoic mental unit and as long as His will-to-be persists, the energy will continue to flow through. In the fifth round, it will be felt at its height.

In considering the Entities [33] who gave the manasic principle to man, we must remember that they are the beings who, in earlier manvantaras have achieved, and who—in this round—waited for a specific moment at

[33] A very natural question might here be asked:—Why do we consider this matter of the devas of the middle system (as we might call those connected with this system and with buddhi and kama-manas) in our consideration of thought forms? For two reasons:—One is that all that is in the solar system is but substance energised from the cosmic mental and astral planes, and built into form through the power of electrical Law; all that can be known is but forms ensouled by ideas. Secondly, that in the knowledge of the creative processes of the system, man learns for himself how in time to become a creator. We might illustrate this by remarking that one of the main functions of the Theosophical movement in all its many branches is to build a form which can be ensouled, in due time, by the idea of Brotherhood.

which to enter, and so continue their work. A parallel case can be seen at the entry—in Atlantean days—of Egos from the moon-chain. The parallel is not exact, as a peculiar condition prevailed on the moon, and a peculiar karmic purpose brought them all in at that time.

It should here be remembered that in the moon the fifth principle of manas incubated normally, and instinct gradually developed until it imperceptibly merged into manas, being of a similar nature; in this round a peculiar condition necessitated extra-planetary stimulation, and this special group of Pitris effected a transition of the lower into the higher through a downflow of energy via the Earth's Primary from an extra-systemic centre.

The central three rounds, as in the planes and principles, are the most important for the evolution of the self-conscious units in this system, and this working towards perfection of the three, the four, and the five, mark, for the planetary Logos, as for man, the cycle of maturity. The earlier and later cycles mark that of growth towards maturity, and the garnering of the fruits of earlier experience. The three Halls again can be here considered from this aspect, and the central period allocated to the Hall of Learning.

On all the planets these manasadevas are found working, ever in their three groups but varying the methods employed according to the stage of the evolution of the planet concerned, and the karma of its planetary Lord. Their method of work on the Earth can be studied in the *Secret Doctrine* and has a most significant interest for men at this time.[34] The three groups should be carefully considered from the standpoint of their occult work, which is hinted at under the terms of:

    a. Those who refused to incarnate.

    b. Those who implanted the spark of manas.

    c. Those who took bodies and moulded the type.

[34] See all the earlier part of the *Secret Doctrine,* Volume II.

The second group, the intermediate, can be subdivided into two lesser groups:

  a. Those who implant the spark of manas,
  b. Those who fan and feed the latent flame in the best types of animal man,

thus again making five.   These statements have been accepted at their face value, but little attention is paid to the real meaning.   Much profit would come if the student would study the subject from the standpoint of energy, and of magnetic interaction.   Those who refused to incarnate or to energise with their life the prepared forms, were acting under Law, and their opposition to incarnation in these forms was *based on magnetic repulsion*.   They could not energise the forms provided, for it involved the opposition of that which is *occultly the same*.   The lesser was not negative to the greater Life.   Where the Spark was implanted we have the receptivity of the negative aspect to the positive force and therefore the progress of the work.   In every case we have deva substance of one polarity energised by another polarity with the goal in view of producing— through their mutual interaction—a balancing of forces, and the attainment of a third type of electrical phenomena.

The question of the coming of the Lords of Flame is discussed hereafter under the heading ''Individualisation.''   At this point we are only dealing with the work of these chohanic forces in a systemic and cosmic sense. These solar entities, being liberated intelligent Essences were in pralaya of a secondary nature when the time came for their reappearance in manifestation.   When the WORD sounded forth which produced desire in the Triad for self-expression, and when the sound of the lower manifestation had blended with it, and had risen up into the Heavens, as the occult books express it, an effect was produced which caused a response in certain allied constellations; this set loose energy which swept into the solar system, carrying with it those solar angels who "rested in the Heart of God until the hour was come." Their appearance upon the mental plane brought about the union of Spirit and matter, and from this union was born a self-conscious Identity, the Ego. On cosmic levels, an analogous process occurs in connection with such stupendous Identities as a solar Logos, and the septenary Lives.

As the energy of a human being, seeking incarnation, passes down from the plane of intensive purpose, the mental plane, into the physical vehicle on the gaseous or fifth subplane, so a somewhat analogous stimulation takes place in the body logoic. A somewhat similar process can also be seen in connection with this energy in a human body as it stimulates the life of the individual cell, and brings about relatively its intelligent co-operation in group work, and its ability to take its place in the body corporate. It is so with the human Monads, the cells in the body logoic. When science recognizes this fact (which will scarcely be yet awhile) attention will be turned to the volatile essences of the body, to the heart centre particularly, and its relation to these gaseous elements. The heart will be found to be not only the engine which circulates the life fluids, but also the generator of a certain type of intelligent essence which is the positive factor in the life of the cell.

Some idea can be gathered from this as to the microcosmic process, for the individualization of the units is brought about through a macrocosmic happening which produces effects in the microcosm.

A final point here needs emphasising. Occultly understood, the five Kumaras or the five Mind-born Sons of Brahma are the embodiers of this manasic force on our planet; but They only reflect (in the Hierarchy of our planet) the function of the five Kumaras or Rishis who are the Lords of the five Rays manifesting through the four lesser planets and the synthesising planet.

These five Kumaras are the channels for this force and one of Them, the Lord of the planet Venus, embodies in Himself the function of the fifth Hierarchy. This accounts for the activity of Venus at the moment of individualisation in this round. In the next round, this fifth Hierarchy will be utilising our Earth scheme in this way, and we shall then see manas in full fruition working out in the human family. This fifth Hierarchy of Agnishvattas in their many grades embody the "I principle" and are the producers of self-consciousness, and the builders of man's body of realisation. In time and space, and on the mental plane, they are Man himself in essential essence; they enable him to build his own body of causes, to unfold his own egoic lotus, and gradually to free himself from the limitations of the form which he has constructed, and thus to put himself— in due course of time—into the line of another type of energy, that of buddhi. To word it otherwise, through Their work man can become conscious without the manasic vehicle, for manas is but the form through which a higher principle is making itself known. The life of God comes cyclically under the influence of the different Hierarchies or forces, all of which temporarily build for it a vehicle, pass it through their substance, give to it in this way a certain quality or colouring, and increase thereby its vibratory capacity until eventually the life is set free from hierarchical limitation. It then returns to its eternal Source plus the gain of its experiences and with the increased energy which is the result of its various transitions.

Let us bear carefully in mind, that the Rays are the positive aspect in manifestation and pass down into negative matter, deva or hierarchical substance, thus causing certain evidences of activity. The Hierarchies are the negative aspect as far as the Rays are concerned and are responsive to Ray impulse. But within each Ray and each Hierarchy in this system a dual force again will be found. The Sons of God are bisexual. The deva substance is also dual, for the evolutionary devas are the positive energy of the atom, cell or subhuman form, for instance, while the electrons or lesser lives within the form are negative.

The mystery of the Manasaputras is hidden in this, and in the function of the fifth Hierarchy, and it is not possible to reveal more of it. The secret of Buddhi, the sixth or Christ principle, which concerns these Sons of God, and the secret of the fifth Hierarchy which is the vehicle or recipient of buddhi, cannot be mentioned outside initiated circles. It holds hid the possibility of egoic unfoldment, and keeps secret the karma of the Heavenly Men, the five Kumaras.

The fifth principle of manas is embodied in the five Kumaras, and if the student studies the significance of the first five petals which are unfolded in the egoic lotus, he may touch upon the fringe of the mystery. The fifth Ray, which is the Ray of the fifth Kumara, is potently responsive to the energy flowing through the fifth Hierarchy. As the student of occultism knows, the Lord of the fifth Ray holds that place in the Septenary enumeration, but under the fivefold classification, he holds the third or middle place.

1. The cosmic Lord of Will or Power.
2. The cosmic Lord of Love-Wisdom.
3. The cosmic Lord of Active Intelligence.........1.
4. The cosmic Lord of Harmony...................2.
5. The cosmic Lord of Concrete Knowledge.......3.
6. The cosmic Lord of Abstract Idealism..........4.
7. The cosmic Lord of Ceremonial Magic..........5.

This should be pondered on, and His close connection therefore, as a transmitter of force within the Moon chain, the third chain, in connection with the third kingdom, the animal, and with the third round, must be borne in mind. One symbol that may be found in the archaic records in lieu of His Name or description is an inverted five-pointed star, with the luminous Triangle at the centre. It will be noted that the points involved in this symbol number eight—a picture of that peculiar state of consciousness brought about when the mind is seen to be the slayer of the Real. The secret of planetary avitchi [35] is hidden here, just as the third major scheme can be viewed as systemic avitchi, and the moon at one time held an analogous position in connection with our scheme. This must be interpreted in terms of consciousness, and not of locality.

In the fifth round, at its middle point, certain things will eventuate.

The fifth Hierarchy will rise to its full power. This will precede the Judgment Day, and will mark a point of tremendous struggle, for the manasic vehicle "manas" (which they embody) will rebel against the translation of the life within (the buddhi). There will, therefore, be seen on a racial scale and involving millions simultaneously, a repetition of the self-same struggle which embroils the man who seeks to transcend mind and to live the life of Spirit. This will be the final Armageddon, the planetary kurukshetra, and will be succeeded by the Judgment Day when the Sons of Manas will be cast out and the Dragons of Wisdom rule. This only means that those in whom the manasic principle is over-potent or under-developed will be considered as failures and will

---

[35] *Avitchi.* A state of consciousness, not necessarily after death or between births for it can take place on earth as well. Literally it means "uninterrupted hell." The last of the eight hells we are told where "the culprits die and are reborn without interruption—yet not without hope of final redemption."
See S. D., III, 510, 521, 528, 529.

have to wait for a more suitable period for development, while those who are living the buddhic life, and in whom it is waxing stronger—spiritual men, aspirants, disciples of various degrees, initiates and adepts—will be left to pursue the natural course of evolution on this scheme.

The mystery of Capricorn is hidden in these five and in the Biblical words "the sheep and the goats." [36] The Christian hints at this when he speaks of the Christ reigning on earth a thousand years during which the serpent is imprisoned. The Christ principle will triumph for the remainder of the manvantara, and the lower material nature and mind will be held in abeyance until the next round, when fresh opportunity will arise for certain groups of the discarded, though the majority will be held over until another system. Something similar again will take place on the fifth chain but as it concerns a centre in the planetary Logos of which we know but little, we need not here enlarge upon it.

The planetary chains embody centres, and as they are awakened and come under stimulation, they swing into physical incarnation certain types of manasaputras. The type dominated by the fifth chain energy is little known as it is yet in process of evolution within another scheme, the fifth, so it is waste of our time to consider it. It is connected with the unfoldment of the fifth egoic petal of a planetary Logos on His Own plane and consequently with the activity of the fifth spirilla. When the hour strikes, these units of energy will "come in" from another scheme on a stream of cosmic energy which will swing through a particular systemic triangle, just as when the egos came in this round.

It might here be pointed out that the solar Angels concerned with the fifth Hierarchy are naturally a potent factor in the evolution of the fifth or spiritual kingdom; they are that which make it possible, for they not only

---

[36] Bible. Rev., 20:6-7. Matt., 25:32.

bridge the gap between the fourth and third kingdoms, but bridge that found between the fourth and fifth.

We need not consider any further this question of the fifth principle, for two reasons:

First, that the subject has been sufficiently covered for our purpose in an earlier section, and secondly, that the full revelation in connection with cosmic manas and the entities who come in on that influence may not further be revealed at this moment. That which is given in the *Secret Doctrine,* and supplemented here by further details, will suffice for the investigations of students for another generation. Each generation should produce those able to ascertain subjective fact for themselves; they will utilize that which is exoteric and known as stepping stones on the path to perfect knowledge. They will know, and they will give out, and only the next cycle of fifty years after their work is accomplished will see the recognition by the many of the truth revealed by the few. In the case of H. P. B. this is apparent. On the tide of the present endeavour, the *Secret Doctrine* will be vindicated and her work justified.

b. On Individualisation.

(*a.*) *The Work of the Solar Angels.* Let us briefly consider the general construction of the body of the Ego enumerating its component parts and bearing in mind that the form is ever prepared prior to occupancy. From the study of this body, we can get some idea of, and some light upon macrocosmic Individualisation.

The causal body, called sometimes (though inaccurately) the "karana sarira," has its place on the third subplane of the mental plane, the lowest abstract plane, and the one whereon the Ray of the third Logos provides the necessary "light for construction." (This is because each subplane comes specially under the influence of its Number, Name, or Lord.) When the hour strikes and the vehicles for buddhi are to be co-ordinated certain great Beings, Lords of the Flame, or Manasa-devas, through driving external force, come in conjunction with the material of that subplane, and vitalise it with Their Own energy. They form a new and positive impulse which co-ordinates the material of the plane and produces a temporary balancing of forces. Hence the meaning of the "white," or transparent condition of the new causal body. It remains with the new-born ego first to upset the equilibrium, and then to regain it, at the close of the process, producing a radiant form, full of primal colours.

At the coming in of the Manasadevas to produce self-consciousness and to bring about the incarnation of the divine Egos, four things occur on that plane. If the student adds to these four those which have been already imparted in various occult books anent the effect of indi-vidualisation on animal man and his appearance as a self-conscious identity on the physical plane, a working hypothesis is provided whereby man can scientifically undertake his own unfoldment. These four are given in the order of their appearance in time and space:

First. There appear upon the third subplane of the mental plane certain vibratory impulses—nine in number—corresponding to the fivefold vibration of these Manasadevas in conjunction with the fourfold vibration set up from below and inherent in the matter of this subplane, the fifth from the lower standpoint. This produces "the ninefold egoic lotus," which is at this stage tightly closed, the nine petals folded one upon the other. They are vibrant, and scintillating "light" but not of excessive brightness. These "lotus buds" are in groups, according to the influence of the particular ones of the fivefold Dhyanis Who are acting upon it and Who form it out of Their own substance, colouring it faintly with the "fire of manas."

Second. There appears a triangle on the mental plane, produced by manasic activity, and this triangle of fire begins slowly to circulate between the manasic permanent atom, and a point at the centre of the egoic lotus, and thence to the mental unit, which has appeared upon the fourth subplane through innate instinct approximating mentality. This triangle of fire, which is formed of pure electrical manasic force, waxes ever brighter until it produces an answering vibration from both the lower and the higher. This triangle is the nucleus of the antaskarana. The work of the highly evolved man is to reduce this triangle to a unity, and by means of high aspiration (which is simply transmuted desire affecting mental matter) turn it into the Path and thus reproduce in a higher synthetic form the earlier "path" along which the descending Spirit came to take possession of its vehicle, the causal body, and from thence again work through the lower personal self.

Third. At a certain stage of vibratory activity, the work of the Lords of the Flame having produced a body or form and a vibration calling for response, there occurs a practically simultaneous happening.

A downflow of buddhi takes place along the line of the manasic triangle until it reaches a point at the very centre of the lotus. There, by the power of its own vibration, it causes a change in the appearance of the lotus. At the very heart of the lotus, three more petals appear which close in on the central flame, covering it closely, and remaining closed until the time comes for the revelation of the "jewel in the Lotus." The egoic lotus is now composed of twelve petals, nine of these appear at this stage in bud form and three are completely hidden and mysterious.

At the same time, the three permanent atoms are enclosed within the lotus, and are seen by the clairvoyant as three points of light in the lower part of the bud, be-

neath the central portion. They form at this stage a
dimly burning triangle. The causal body, though only
in an embryonic condition, is now ready for full activity
as the æons slip away, and is complete in all its threefold
nature. *The matter aspect,* which concerns the material
form of the man in the three worlds, or his active intelligent personal self can be developed and controlled
through the medium of the mental unit, the astral permanent atom and the physical permanent atom. *The
Spirit aspect* lies concealed at the heart of the lotus,
in due course of time to stand revealed when the manasadevas have done their work. The will that persists forever is there. *The consciousness aspect* embodying the
love-wisdom of the divine Ego as it reveals itself by
the means of mind is predominantly there, and in the
nine petals and their vibratory capacity lies hid all opportunity, all innate capacity to progress, and all the
ability to function as a self-conscious unit, that entity
we call Man.[37] Mahadeva sits at the heart, Surya or
Vishnu reveals Him in His essence as the Wisdom of
Love and the Love of Wisdom, and Brahma, the Creative
Logos makes that revelation possible. The Father in

[37] *The Solar Lord, the Divine Ego.* Of the two courses of soul development referred to by H. P. B. in her ''Voice of the Silence'' as the path of
''Dhyana'' and ''Dharma'' or the ''Paramitas,'' Ramayana is based upon
the latter. The ''Seven Portals,'' referred to in the book of the same
name, correspond very probably to the seven cantos of this sacred poem.
But I have read only the first canto, and I shall give you the analysis of it,
so far as I know. Excluding the preface to the poem, the first thing, in
the first canto, is a description of the peculiar circumstances that attended
Rama's birth in Dasaratha's family. Dasaratha is, as you all know, a
descendant of solar kings, who began to rule over this earth from the
time of Manu the Vyvaswatha. As his name implies, he is a king whose
car can travel in ten directions, or taking the occult microcosmic sense,
he is king of the human body, which has ten senses of action and perception
that connect it with the ten directions. You are thoroughly familiar with
the idea that our ancient philosophers used to describe the body as a town
with nine gates. The nine gates are, as you know, the nine orifices of the
human body. If you add to the nine one more for the orifice known as
the Brahma-rundra or the door of Brahma, you get ten gates corresponding to the ten directions. The word ''Dasaratha'' indicates the consciousness connected with our senses, which consciousness is inferior to
the consciousness which we call mind.—*The Theosophist,* Vol. XIII, p. 340.

Heaven is to be revealed through the Christ, the Son, by the method of incarnation made possible through the work of the Holy Spirit. All this has been brought about by the sacrifice and instrumentality of certain cosmic entities who "offer Themselves" up in order that Man may be. From their very essence, they give out that which is needed to produce the individualising principle, and that which we call "self-consciousness," and thus enable the divine Spirit to enter into fuller life by means of limitation by form, by means of the lessons garnered through a long pilgrimage, and through the "assimilation of manifold existences."

The *fourth* point to be noted is that when these three events have occurred, the light or fire that circulates along the manasic triangle is withdrawn to the centre of the lotus, and this "prototype" of the future antaskarana, if so it may be expressed, disappears. The threefold energy of the petals, the atoms and the "jewel" is now centralised, because impulse must now be generated which will produce a downflow of energy from the newly made causal vehicle into the three worlds of human endeavour.

We have dealt with the method of individualisation through the coming in of the Lords of the Flame because it is the prime method in this solar system; whatever methods may be pursued in the varying schemes and chains, this—at the middle stage—is the universal rule. Karmic conditions having to do with a planetary Logos may effect modifications, and bring into action manasadevas whose activity may not be the same in working detail, but the results are ever similar, and the divine Egos in their causal bodies have analogous instruments to work through. . . .

A *final* point which is of profound significance is that *the Agnishvattas construct the petals out of Their Own substance, which is substance energised by the principle of "I-ness," or ahamkara. They proceed to energise the permanent atoms with Their own positive force, so as to bring the fifth spirilla in due course of time into full activity and usefulness.* All possibility, all hopefulness and optimism, and all future success lies hid in these two points.

As we have seen, the work of the Agnishvattas on the mental plane resulted in a downflow of force or energy from the Monad (or Spirit) and this, in conjunction with the energy of the lower quaternary produced the appearance of the body of the Ego on the mental plane. In ordinary electric light, we have a faint illustration of the thought I seek to convey. By the approximation of the two polarities, light is created. By an analogous type of electrical phenomena, the light of the Monad shines forth, but we have to extend the idea to the subtler planes, and deal with seven types of force or energy in connection with the one polarity and with four in connection with the other. A scientific formula for the process of individualisation conveys this dual approximation with its differing types of energy in one symbol and a number, but it cannot here be revealed.

The Manasadevas are themselves energised by force from the cosmic mental plane—a force which has been in operation ever since the individualisation of the solar Logos in kalpas far distant. They, in Their corporate nature, embody the will or purpose of the Logos, and are the cosmic "prototypes" of our solar Angels. The solar Angels on the mental plane of the system embody as much of that will and purpose as the Logos can work through in one single incarnation and as They, in Their groups, can develop. They work, therefore, through egoic groups and primarily, after individualisation, upon the mental units of the separated identities who go to the constituency of the groups. This is Their secondary work. Their work in part might be described as follows:

Primarily, they bring about the union of the divine Ego and the lower personal self. This has been dealt with.

Secondly, they work through the mental units, impressing upon the atom that portion, microscopic as it may be, of the logoic purpose which the individual can work out on the physical plane. At first their influence is unconsciously assimilated, and the man responds to the plan blindly and ignorantly. Later, as evolution proceeds, their work is recognised by the man in a conscious co-operation with the plan of evolution.[38] After the third initiation, the will or purpose aspect predominates.

It might here be noted that it is the positive force of the Manasadevas that produces initiation. Their function is embodied by the Hierophant. He, seeing before Him the vehicle for buddhi, passes the voltage from the higher planes through His body, and by means of the Rod (charged with positive manasic force) transmits this higher manasic energy to the initiate so that he is enabled to know consciously and to recognise the plan for his group-centre through the immensely increased stimulation. This force descends from the manasic permanent atom via the antaskarana and is directed to whichever centre the Hierophant—under the Law—sees should be stimulated. He stabilises the force, and regulates its flow as it circulates throughout the egoic Lotus, so that when the work of unfoldment is accomplished the sixth principle at the Heart of the Lotus can stand revealed. After each initiation the Lotus is more un-

[38] *The Sacrificer or Yajamana.* The yajamana is the person who has sacrificed himself for the good of the world and who has undertaken to mould the affairs of it, in obedience to the law. If the human body be taken as the sacrificial ground, the manas in him is the yajamana. All the doings of man in all his life from birth to death, form one grand yagnic process that is conducted by the true human entity called the Manas. He, who is willing to sacrifice his body, speech, and thought to the good of all the world, is a real yagnika and all the higher lokas are reserved for him. The central keynote of yagnika's life is to do good unto all, irrespective of caste and creed even as the sun shines for all.—*Some Thoughts on the Gita,* page 90.

folded and light from the centre begins to blaze forth—
a light or fire which ultimately burns through the three
enshrining petals, and permits the full inner glory to
be seen, and the electric fire of spirit to be manifested.
As this is brought about on the second subplane of the
mental plane (whereon the egoic lotus is now situated)
a corresponding stimulation takes place in the dense
substance which forms the petals or wheels of the centres
on the astral and etheric levels.

(b.) *Individualisation and the races.* If this treatise
serves no other purpose than to direct the attention of
the scientific and philosophic students to the study of
force or energy in man and in groups, and to interpret
man and the human family in terms of electrical phenomena, much good will have been accomplished. The
polarity of a man, of a group, and of a congery of groups,
the polarity of the planets and their relationship to
each other and to the Sun, the polarity of the solar system
and its relationship to other systems, the polarity of one
plane to another, and of one principle to another, the
polarity of the subtler vehicles, and the scientific application of the laws of electricity to the totality of existence
on the physical plane will bring about a revolution upon
the planet second only to that effected at the time of
individualisation. I would point out here a certain
significant fact which students will do well carefully to
consider.

In the third rootrace [39] individualisation took place.
It was an event which became possible through certain
conditions and polar relationships, and because the
scientific laws were understood and the Knowers took

---

[39] Root races. *The Secret Doctrine teaches that these seven groups of
human units inhabit seven continents during evolution.*—S. D., II, 6, 7, 8.

    a. First race......................The Imperishable Sacred Land.
    b. The 2nd race...................The Hyperborean Land.
    c. The 3rd race...................Lemurian.
    d. The 4th race...................Atlantean.
    e. The 5th race...................Aryan.
    f. Two more races will succeed the present one.

advantage of a peculiar electrical condition to hasten the evolution of the race. It was electrical phenomena of a stupendous kind, and produced the "lights which ever burn." It was the result of the knowledge of natural law and its adaptation to opportunity.

In the fourth rootrace another adaptation of force occurred. Again time and opportunity were taken advantage of to open the door into the fifth kingdom by the method of forced initiation. A third type of electricity played its part in bringing about this event, and it is the effect of this electrical phenomenon upon the units (who are themselves centres of energy) which—scientifically viewed—indicates a man's suitability for the ceremony of initiation, and his availability as a transmitter of spiritual energy to the world. Every initiate is technically a transmitter of force and his work is consequently threefold:

1. To provide a threefold vehicle capable of the necessary resistance to the force and able to receive and hold it.
2. To transmit it as energy to the world which he serves.
3. To store up a certain amount of it for a twofold purpose:
a. To provide a reservoir of force for emergencies and for special work as required by the Great Ones.
b. To act as a dynamo for the immediate group which all advanced souls, disciples and initiates gather around them on some one or other of the planes in the three worlds.

In the fifth rootrace, another tremendous happening may be looked for, and the time lies immediately ahead. It had its beginning in the energy which eventually culminated in the world war. The first effect of the appearance of fresh electrical stimulation from extra-systemic

A TREATISE ON COSMIC FIRE

centres, is ever to bring about a primary destruction leading on to revelation. That which is imprisoned must be loosed. So it will be in this rootrace, the fifth. Certain cosmic forces are at work and the full effect of their energy is not yet apparent. This incoming force, the Hierarchy will avail itself of in order to push forward the planetary plans. In every case the effect of the phenomenon is felt in some one or other of the kingdoms beside the human. In the individualisation period, it is apparent that a tremendous stimulation took place in *the animal kingdom*—a stimulation which has persisted, and which has led to the phenomenon of "domestic animals" as we call them, and their relatively high stage of intelligence as compared to the wild animals. In Atlantean days the opening of the door into the fifth ¹ingdom, or into the stage of buddhic consciousness, had a profound effect upon *the vegetable kingdom*. This effect can be seen working out in such results as are achieved by Burbank, and which are of a nature corresponding to the initiatory process in man, involving a rapid achievement of relative perfection.

In the tremendous event which is impending, in the great revelation which is near at hand, the Hierarchy will again take advantage of the time and the energy to bring about certain events which will work out primarily in the human kingdom but which will also be seen as force regeneration in *the mineral kingdom*. The energy, when first felt in the human kingdom, brought about the conditions which caused the tremendous activity which resulted in war, and which is causing the present world stress; in the mineral kingdom it affected certain of the minerals and elements, and the radioactive substances made their appearance. This characteristic (or radioactivity) of pitchblende and the other involved units is comparatively a new development under the evolutionary law, and one which, though latent, only needed the drawing forth of the type of energy now beginning to pour in on the earth. This force began to flow in at the end of the eighteenth century, and its full effect is by no means yet felt, for it will be several hundred years before it passes away. By means of it, certain discoveries are possible, and the new order comes in upon it. The Great Ones, Who know the time and the hour, will bring about, in our rootrace, that which corresponds to the occurrences in the earlier third and fourth races.

(c.) *Methods of Individualisation.* We have seen how the characteristic method of individualisation in this solar system is the result of force emanating from the cosmic mental plane, which sweeps into activity those entities whose function it is to form the body of the ego out of their own living substance on the mental plane and thus, through their own quality and nature, endow human units on the physical plane with the faculty of self-consciousness, thus producing Man. It is their work also to energise the mental units of all men, and to co-ordinate, by means of the force which they embody, and to energise the sheaths of the threefold lower man, so that they may in due course of time intelligently express the will and purpose of the indwelling Thinker. Through the carrying out of this function in the case of the human family, certain planetary and systemic conditions are brought about.

The dense and etheric bodies of the Logos and of the planetary Logoi are merged, and one coherent vehicle of expression is provided for these cosmic Entities.

In the producing of self-consciousness in the human family, the full conscious occupation by the Logos involved is consummated. It is the moment of fruition, and (from a certain esoteric standpoint) marks the attainment of one perfected Septenary. The three involutionary or elemental kingdoms and the three sub-human

kingdoms find their seventh principle in the fourth kingdom in nature, $3 + 4 = 7$. When the life of God has
circled through these seven kingdoms, then full self-
consciousness is achieved from a certain relative standpoint, and the Son is on the way to attainment. This
relative perfection has then to be carried on to other
stages, but they are stages in which the separated self-
consciousness of the Identities concerned (whether human or planetary) must eventually merge itself in universal consciousness.

Certain centres in the bodies logoic and planetary are
also stimulated and the Rays (if it might be so expressed)
become radioactive. It is this radiation which will
eventually bring about *conscious* group activity, which
will lead to interaction between the planets, and which,
under the Law of Attraction and Repulsion, will bring
about eventual synthesis.

On extra-systemic or cosmic levels, the individualisation process produces a corresponding activity in the
egoic body of the Logos, and hence increased vibration
in that centre in the body of the ONE ABOUT WHOM
NOUGHT MAY BE SAID, which our Logos represents. It
also produces a reaction or "occult recognition" in the
prototype of the Septenate, or in the seven Rishis of
the Great Bear, and this reaction in cosmic circles will
persist until the end of the mahamanvantara, when the
Logos is set free (even though temporarily), from physical plane existence.

It also brings about a setting loose of force from
the cosmic mental plane which is cyclic in character.
In this round, the fourth, the maximum force of this
cycle was felt in the third root race. In the next round,
during the fourth root race, and for a very brief period,
a fresh cycle will reach its zenith, and will again open
the door of individualisation in order to permit the
entry of certain very advanced Egos who are seeking

incarnation in order to carry out a special piece of work. This round will provide no bodies adequate to their need. The next round may do so if the plans proceed as anticipated. In this case the Manasadevas concerned will not individualise animal men as in the previous round, but will stimulate the mental germ in those members of the present human family who—as H. P. B. says—though apparently men, are without the spark of mind.[40] During the next seven hundred years, these low aboriginal races will practically die out and will not—in this round —reincarnate. They will be *rejected*. In the next round opportunity will again occur, and the Manasadevas will again renew their work of forming individualistic nuclei for the development of self-consciousness. The Egos awaiting opportunity will not, of course, enter in until the human type of that era is sufficiently refined for their purpose. They are concerned with the unfoldment of the sixth petal of the logoic egoic Lotus, and are of such a nature that we can scarcely conceive of them. They are on the line of the Buddhas of Activity, but the above named are free for this mahamanvantara, whereas these particular Egos have yet somewhat to work out. They could only ''come in'' in the middle of the fifth round, and were a group of initiates who arrested their own evolution (technically speaking) in order to take up a special piece of work on the planet Vulcan; therefore, they must return to continue and complete that which has been left undone. Owing to the results of their experience on Vulcan, the physical vehicle necessitated is of such an order that they could not at this time, and in this round, incarnate without disaster.

Individualisation in the next round will begin to show indications of the third method,—that of the next system.

---

[40] Such are the Veddhas of Ceylon, the Bushman of Australia, and certain of the lowest of the African races.
See S. D., II, 206, 300, 439.

This method has been described as that of "occult abstraction." It will concern itself with the withdrawal from out of the lowest type of the then existing men (through knowledge of the etheric constitution of the body) of the vitality latent in it, and a temporary turning of that latent fire to the increase of the activity of the germ or spark of mind; this will be effected by a dynamic action of the will. This seems impossible, and well nigh senseless phraseology when considered in terms of consciousness and of spirituality, but let the student study the phenomenon in terms of the cosmic physical plane, and from the standpoint of the gaseous and etheric subplanes, and he will see that in all these septenary fires it is ever the fire of matter in reality, and these sevenfold diversifications of electrical phenomena can ever affect each other.

Thus, in the mahamanvantara, the three methods of individualisation in connection with our planetary scheme are to be seen

a. *In the Moon chain,* the gradual evolution of self-consciousness under natural law.

b. *In the Earth chain* that of achieved self-consciousness through the aid of extraneous agencies. It is the distinctive method of this system.

c. *In the next round and chain* the method will be abstraction through will power, but this in an embryonic manner.

I have dealt with these three from the standpoint of our own scheme. In all the schemes whereon man is found at some period or another, these three methods will be contacted. They mark the gradual control by the Logos on cosmic levels of His threefold lower nature. In the first, the correspondence lies in the latent consciousness of matter, and works under the Law of Economy. It concerns primarily the Self-consciousness of the Logos in His dense physical body, and His polarisation therein. It is likewise the same for a Heavenly Man, and a part of the mystery of evil is to be found in the readiness of certain of these cosmic entities (particularly our planetary Logos in the moon chain) to remain polarised in the physical etheric body after having supposedly dominated the material aspect, or gained the control of the third Fire in an earlier system. A hint lies here for the wise student anent present evil on this planet.

The second correspondence concerns the latent "consciousness of desire," and works under the Law of Attraction; it is the law for this system, and deals with the ability of the Logos to "love wisely," in the occult sense of the term. It has relation to the polarisation of the Logos in His astral body, and produces the phenomenon called "sex activity" on all planes in the system. In the earlier system, emancipation was effected through the faculty of *discrimination,* though that word as used to-day is but a faint indication of the systemic process in those days. Through the force engendered during the process that vibration was set up which persists to-day in matter. It is evidenced by the active intelligence and the discriminative selective capacity of the atom of substance. In this system emancipation will be brought about through the line of occult *dispassion;* this likewise will leave its mark upon matter, tinging it in such a way that in the third system, primordial substance will demonstrate a second quality. In the next system "non-attachment through abstraction" is as near as we can get to the method of the liberating process but it is useless for man to speculate upon this as his mind cannot conceive of the condition.

(*d.*) *Avatars, Their nature and Their Work.* We have, in our discussion above, connected the phenomenon of individualisation with the appropriation by the Logos, or by a planetary Logos, of Their dense physical vehicles, and Their self-conscious existence through the medium of the physical body. A very difficult and mysterious subject might be touched upon here,—that of AVATARS, and though it will not be possible for us to expound it fully, as it is one of the most occult and secret of the mysteries, perhaps a little light may be thrown upon this profound subject.

For purposes of clarity and in order to elucidate a matter of extreme difficulty to the occidental mind above all (on account of the fact that it has not yet grasped the rationale of the process of reincarnation), it would be wise to divide the differing types of avatars into five groups, bearing in mind that every avatar is a Ray, emanated from a pure spiritual source, and that a self-conscious entity only earns the right to this peculiar form of work through a previous series of lives of achievement.

1. Cosmic Avatars.
2. Solar Avatars.
3. Inter-planetary Avatars.
4. Planetary Avatars.
5. Human Avatars.

As just said, an avatar is a Ray of effulgent and perfected glory, clothing itself in matter for the purpose of service. All avatars in the strict sense of the word are liberated souls, but the cosmic and solar avatars are liberated from the two lower planes of the cosmic planes. While the planetary and the interplanetary avatars are liberated from the cosmic physical plane, our systemic planes, the human avatar has achieved freedom from the five planes of human endeavour. In a strictly technical and lower sense, a Master in physical plane incarnation is a type of avatar, for He is a "freed soul" and therefore only chooses to incarnate for specific purpose, but we will not deal with Them. Let us again subdivide these groups so as still further to clarify our ideas:

1. *Cosmic Avatars:* They represent embodied force from the following cosmic centres among others:

   a. Sirius.
   b. That one of the seven stars of the Great Bear which is ensouled by the prototype of the Lord of our third major Ray.
   c. Our cosmic centre.

They represent entities as far removed from the consciousness of Man, as man is from the consciousness of the atom of substance. Thousands of those great cycles which we call "a hundred years of Brahma" have passed since They approximated the human stage, and They embody force and consciousness which is concerned with the intelligent co-ordination of the starry Heavens.

They have achieved all that man can conceive of as the transcendence of will, of love and of intelligence, and in the synthesis of those three have added qualities and vibrations for which we have no terms, and which cannot be visioned by even our highest adepts. Their appearance in a solar system is very unusual, and is only recognised on the highest two planes. Yet, owing to the material nature of our solar system, Their advent is literally the appearance in a physical form of a spiritual Being Who is fully conscious.

Such entities from Sirius appear at the occasion of the initiation of the solar Logos, and They have a peculiar connection with the five Kumaras and through Them (using Them as focal points for force) with the Mahachohan's department in all the occult Hierarchies of the system. Only once has such a Being visited our system, in connection with the appearance in time and space of the five mind-born Sons of Brahma. The effect of such a visit as that of the Avatar from Sirius is seen as the sumtotal of civilisation and culture, viewing these from the standpoint of the entire system and in one flash of time.

An avatar from the cosmic centre will appear as pralaya is nearing and will produce in the body of the Logos that which we call "Death." He is the cosmic *Reaper,* and (to reduce the above to words of an understandable nature) He belongs to a group which represents the abstracting energy of the cosmos, of which we find faint correspondences in the work of the "destroyer" aspect of the Logos, and in the forces which produce physical death, and the disintegration of the physical body of man. It is not possible to say more on these fundamentally esoteric matters, and the value of what is said lies largely in the bringing to the mind of the student the reality of our cosmic interrelation.

2. *Solar Avatars:* These avatars are of three types though there are really many more. They are also extra-systemic visitors, and are mainly concerned with certain processes in the system, among others the administration of the law of cause and effect, or of karma. They embody the karma of the past kalpas as far as our Logos is concerned, and give the initiatory impulse to the processes of adjustment, of expiation and of recognition as it concerns the present system as a whole. One such Entity, the "Karmic Avatar" appeared upon the second logoic vibration, being swept in on the second Breath; He has stayed until now: He will remain with us until all the schemes have entered upon their fifth round, and are nearing their "Judgment Day." At that time, He can withdraw, leaving the planetary Logoi concerned to fulfil the karmic purpose unwatched. The vibratory impulse will then be so strong and the realisation of the buddhic principle so consciously vivid that nothing can then arrest the onward march of affairs. Under Him work a number of cosmic entities who, as stated in the *Secret*

Doctrine,[41] have the privilege of "passing the ring-pass-not"; these are, nevertheless, not avatars for They are Themselves evolving through the administration of karma. It is Their work, and opportunity to progress. An avatar can learn nothing from the place of His appearance. His work is to apply the force of some type of electrical energy to substance in one of its many grades, and thus bring about anticipated results.

Another type of solar avatar, Who can be seen appearing in the schemes, has relation to the heart centre of a planetary Logos, and appears on the higher planes (never on the lower) when the heart activity is making itself felt, and when the energising process is seen to bring about three things:

  a. An expansion of consciousness.
  b. An increase of spiritual light and brilliancy.
  c. Planetary radioactivity.

It is this planetary phenomenon which produces (in connection with the fourth kingdom in nature) the throwing open of the door of initiation to man. Such avatars do not come in connection with any particular Hierarchy but only in relation to the total system. They produce the blending of the colours, and the synthesis of the units in their groups.

At the initiation of a planetary Logos, an avatar may appear in His scheme on the seventh globe from that cosmic centre or star which is ensouled by the particular Rishi Who (in the constellation of the Great Bear) is His cosmic prototype. This is, for the Entity concerned, the taking of a physical form, for our higher planes are but matter from Their standpoint. This has been emphasised frequently, as its significance is not yet sufficiently grasped. By means of the appearance of this Avatar on the seventh globe, the planetary Logos is

[41] These are the Lipika Lords. See S. D., I, 157.

enabled to preserve continuity of cosmic consciousness even when in physical incarnation; this solar avatar performs the same function for the planetary Logos as the Guru does for His disciple. He makes certain events possible by means of the stimulation and protection of His aura, and He acts as a transmitter of electrical energy from the cosmic centre. We must be careful to hold this analogy very lightly, for the real work accomplished cannot be grasped by man. This avatar has naturally a direct effect upon the centres of the Heavenly Man and therefore upon the units or human Monads, but only indirectly and upon the Monad on its own plane. This influence meets with little response from the Monad until after the third Initiation when its conscious life becomes so strong that it grips afresh its egoic expression in one direction, and awakens to planetary realisation in another. This type of avatar appears only at the time of the initiation of a planetary Logos. The number of initiations taken by a planetary Logos in this system vary from two to four.

3. *Interplanetary Avatars.* A very interesting group of avatars is here to be found. They are mainly concerned with three things: first with the superintendence of the transfer of force units or *egoic* groups from one scheme to another (not with individual units from chain to chain). They appear usually twice in the history of a scheme, and though unable to take physical bodies of grosser material than those formed of atmic and the buddhic substance, they work with impulse in mental matter and thus effect these group transfers. They Themselves are subdivided into three groups:

a. Those effecting the transfer from the minor schemes or Ray manifestations on to the third Ray; They concern Themselves with the result of the merging of the polar opposites in the four lesser schemes until but one is left; and then with the transference of the life and quality of this remaining one on to the third Ray.

b. Those dealing with the transference and inter-action of the life forces between the three major Rays.

c. Those producing the final systemic transfer at the end of the age.

Secondly, certain avatars from the fourth Creative Hierarchy, for esoteric and for us inexplicable reasons, leave Their Own Hierarchy, and appear in one or other of the deva Hierarchies. This happens only once in the history of each scheme and occurs at the time of its densest physical appearance, and has relation to the transference of deva impulse from one scheme to another. They are connected in this way with the ap-pearance of the self-conscious units, being the primal embodiment of the latent self-consciousness of the atom of deva substance. They set the type for the devas of any particular scheme.

Once in the history of each scheme, an avatar from the constellation Capricorn appears on mental levels. This level is the lowest one on which these interplanetary deities appear. No more can be communicated on this matter. "The mystery of the goat" lies hidden here. This avatar makes His appearance in the third round of the third chain, and disappears in the fifth round of the fourth chain.

These interplanetary avatars come in, as the products of much earlier kalpas when systemic conditions are re-fined enough to permit of Their appearance. They are the nirmanakayas of an earlier solar cycle Who now again take the opportunity to effect (in an active sense and through physical manifestation) certain uncom-pleted work.

4. *Planetary Avatars.* These emanate from the cen-

tral planetary Logos of a scheme and embody His will and purpose. They are of two different kinds. The first type is a manifestation on etheric physical levels of the planetary Logos Himself for a specific length of time. It involves the definite taking of a physical body by one of the Kumaras. Such an avatar is to be seen in Sanat Kumara, Who, with the three other Kumaras, embodies the four planetary quaternic principles. In a very real sense, Sanat Kumara is the incarnation of the Lord of the Ray Himself; He is the Silent Watcher, the great Sacrifice for humanity.[42]

As noted in the above paragraph, there are secondly three Entities Who embody planetary principles. They are (speaking from the present standpoint) the dynamic energy which holds together the three lower kingdoms, viewing these kingdoms as units and not as differentiations. They are closely connected with the energy aspect of the three earlier chains, and it only needed the work of an interplanetary avatar (at the formation of the triangle which resulted in the individualisation period in Lemurian days) to enable Them to take etheric bodies and incarnate among men. They act as focal points for the energy of the planetary Logos on His own plane. The first Kumara is in a mysterious sense the energy which produces self-consciousness in the human family. The three other kumaras, or the three Buddhas of Activity, act as similar focal points for the energy which animates the three lower kingdoms, and which produces their differing grades of consciousness. It is not possible to express this great mystery more clearly but if the student couples these few hints with those earlier given in the *Secret Doctrine,* the mystery of the "Holy Four" may be somewhat clarified from the standpoint of energy and evolution.

The times and seasons of their appearing vary ac-

[42] S. D., I, 494; II, 112, 149, 333.

cording to the particular karma of the Lord of the Ray, and nothing in connection with these great cycles, and incarnation periods, can be revealed to the unpledged and the profane.

5. *Human Avatars.* These are fully dealt with by H. P. B. and there is nothing further to add to her information, for the time is not ripe.[43] All the above has its place here, as it concerns the mystery of force and consciousness, and the fullest manifestation of a planetary Logos and of a solar Logos in a dense physical body is hidden in the appearance of these various avatars and in their effect.

(*e.*) *Individualisation, a form of Initiation.* There is but little more that can be said at this time anent individualisation. What has been said here and in the *Secret Doctrine* is but a manner of endeavouring to express profound and significant facts, concerning existence and manifestation, in terms of human thought, and through the limiting medium of language. From the most esoteric standpoint "Man is a deva;" he is Spirit and deva substance, united through the work of conscious deva energy. He unites within himself the three aspects of the Deity. He is, while in objectivity:

1. The Self, the Not-Self, and the intelligent link in a very vital sense.
2. He is Shiva, Vishnu, and Brahma, in synthetic manifestation.
3. He is the medium whereby the Will of God, the Love of God, and the Mind of God become intelligible and apparent.
4. He is positive electrical force, plus negative electrical force, plus the equilibrising medium.
5. He is the Flame, the Fire, and the Spark in essential manifestation.
6. He is electric fire, solar fire and fire by friction.

[43] S. D., III, Section 41; III, 345.

But the point which it is necessary here to emphasise, is that man does not, in space and time and in the three worlds, demonstrate all these aspects simultaneously, but only simultaneously towards the close of the process of evolution. As in the Macrocosm, Brahma manifests activity first, then the second or middle aspect and finally the first or purposeful will makes itself seen, so with the microcosm.

The Brahma aspect, that in which the Not-Self or material aspect is apparent and predominant. This covers the sub-human stages, and the first three cycles of the Personality Life:

 a. First cycle............savage state.
 b. Second cycle ....average man.
 c. Third cycle............intellectual successful man.

The Vishnu aspect, that in which the love-wisdom aspect gradually predominates and emerges through the medium of the Brahma aspect. It covers the final two stages of the human personality life, and that period of egoic growth which embraces the final two Initiations:

 a. First cycle ....The Path of Probation.
 b. Second cycle ....The Path of Initiation.
         (till the third Initiation)
 c. Third cycle ....That covering the fourth and
         fifth Initiations.

This is the temporary consummation, but just as in the animal kingdom, the human mind was latent and instinctive, and just as in the human kingdom the buddhic aspect is latent and instinctive, so during the final cycle of human endeavour, the Atma, or highest aspect of the Monad, is also latent and instinctive. This must produce later stages of development. There are no gaps in evolution, and no periods wherein there is total absence of any one aspect; all are ever present but they

"show forth" in alternation. Only when the fires of
matter are blazing brightly, and become radiatory, does
it become possible for the fire of mind to show forth,
even though ever inherently present. Only when these
two fires of matter and of mind have reached a stage of
energetic heat and light, can the electric fire of Spirit
show forth in its glory. Only again when these three are
unitedly burning does the fire of matter die down for
lack of that which it may consume, and only when that
occurs is it possible for the fires of mind (on mental
levels) to burn up that which it has hitherto animated.
When this is accomplished, the fire of pure Spirit (increased and intensified by the gaseous essence of the fire
of matter, or "fire by friction," and coloured, and rendered radiatory by the fire of mind) blazes forth in perfected glory, so that naught is seen save one vibrant
flame. This idea can be extended away from Man to a
Heavenly Man, and again to the Logos in His cosmic
relationship.

Individualisation marks one stage of the process in
the intensification of "fire by friction." It has relation
to the achievement of Brahma, and marks a point in the
energising of substance. Certain forms are ready for
self-consciousness. Two cosmic Rays of differing polarities are mutually attracted.

Initiation marks a stage in the intensification of "solar
Fire." It has relation to the achievement of Vishnu,
and marks a point in the evolution of consciousness,
through self-consciousness to group consciousness, or
universal consciousness.

Identification with the aggregate of all groups might
be the term used to express the final stages of the evolutionary process; it marks a period towards the close of
the mahamanvantara when all groups begin *consciously*
to work out the eternal Will. It involves a type of
realisation, incredible to man now but which is conceiv-

able (though not yet practicable) to the Chohans of the
Hierarchy now on Earth. They work consciously carrying out the Will of the planetary Logos in the planet,
but even They are as yet far from appreciating fully the
Will and purpose of the Logos as He works through the
system.   Glimpses They may get, and an idea of the
general plan, but the details are as yet unrecognisable.

c.   On Incarnation.

(a.) Cosmic, Planetary and Human. We leave now
the consideration of self-consciousness, as it is produced
through the medium of the particular type of deva substance which the Agnishvattas provided for the body of
the Ego, and pass on to the study of incarnation, cosmic,
planetary and human. A hint as to the constitution of
these solar Pitris and Manasadevas may come to the
student who ponders upon the place of the egoic unit in
the body of the planetary Logos, and in the particular
centre of which it forms a component part.   These
Manasadevas and Dhyan Chohans who produce self-
consciousness in man are indeed the energy and substance of the cosmic Heavenly Man.

The word "incarnation" in its root meaning conveys
the fundamental truth involved in the taking of a dense
physical body, and should technically be applied only
to that period of manifestation which concerns the three
lower subplanes of the:

  a. Cosmic physical plane, in relation to a solar Logos
     and to a planetary Logos.
  b. Systemic physical plane, in relation to man.

This connotation has been preserved where the cosmic
entities are concerned, but when man is under consideration the term has been applied to the unification of the
etheric double with the dense physical body, or to the
appropriation by man of the vehicle composed of the

substance of the lowest subplane of the cosmic physical plane in its lowest aspects. This distinction has a certain significance and should be remembered. This appropriation is governed by the same laws which governed the appropriation by the Logos of His physical vehicle. In order to get an idea of what the procedure is, it might be of value if we considered the different kinds of pralaya, and pondered upon those periods which ensue between incarnations. From the point of view of any unit involved, a pralaya is a period of quiescence, of cessation from a particular type of activity, involving objectivity, yet from the point of view of the great whole with which the unit may be involved, a pralaya may be considered merely as a transference of force from one direction into another. Though the unit may be temporarily devitalised as regards its form, yet the greater Entity persists, and is still active.

Let us take up the matter first from the human standpoint, and study pralaya as it affects the Monad in incarnation.[44] There are five types of pralaya with which we may legitimately concern ourselves. We should notice first the fact that this condition is primarily one that concerns the relationship between Spirit and matter, in which a condition in substance is brought about through the action of the energising factor, the Spirit. It has, therefore, to do with the relation of the greater devas as They carry out Their work of form-building

[44] There are fundamentally three kinds of Pralaya. See S. D., I, 397-398.

1. *Solar pralaya.*	This comes at the end of one hundred years of Brahma. It marks reabsorption into unity. It marks end of manifestation of solar system. Concerns the solar Logos.
2. *Incidental pralaya.*	This succeeds the days of Brahma. It marks periods between manvantaras. Temporary form ceases but duality remains. Concerns a planetary Logos.
3. *Individual pralaya.*	Achieved by a man at the fifth initiation. Marks attainment of perfection. Concerns the monad.

There is also the pralaya in connection with human evolution which we call devachanic. It concerns the personality.

under the Law of Will cf God to the lesser devas who
represent living substance. It will be apparent to the
student that it concerns the relation of the Holy Spirit
to the Mother in the production of the Son, and then the
relation of the Son to the Mother. If the ideas formulated
in this treatise have been carefully followed, it will be
obvious that in studying the question of pralaya, we
are studying the relation (in time and space) of the
positive energy of the solar Logos, the planetary Logos,
and of Man to the substance through which alone manifestation is possible. Through this relation, existence
on the objective planes can be brought about.

(b.) *The Nature of Pralaya.* We can view pralaya
as the work of "abstraction," and as the method which
brings the form under the Destroyer aspect of Spirit,
working ever under the Law of Attraction, of which the
Law of Synthesis is but a branch. The basic law of the
system is that which governs the relation of all atoms
to the aggregate of atoms, and of the Self to the Not-self.
It is (from the occult standpoint) the most powerful
force-demonstration in the system, and should the law
inconceivably cease to work, instantaneously the system
and all forms therein, planetary, human and other would
cease to be. By an act of will the planetary schemes
persist, by an act of will the system is; by an act of
the egoic will man appears. When the Will of the Logos,
of the Heavenly Man, and of the human divine Ego is
turned to other ends, the substance of Their vehicles
is affected, and disintegration sets in. The five types of
pralaya which concern the human unit are as follows:

(1) *The period of pralaya between two incarnations.*
This is of a triple nature and affects the substance of
the three vehicles, physical, astral and mental, reducing
the form to its primitive substance, and dissipating its
atomic structure. The energy of the second aspect (that
of the form-builder) is withdrawn by the will of the Ego,

and the atoms composing the form become dissociated from each other, and are resolved into the reservoir of essence to be re-collected again when the hour strikes. This condition is brought about gradually by stages of which we are aware:

The first stage is the withdrawal of the life force in the etheric vehicle from the threefold (dense, liquid and gaseous) dense physical body and the consequent "falling into corruption," and becoming "scattered to the elements." Objective man fades out, and is no more seen by the physical eye, though still in his etheric body. When etheric vision is developed, the thought of death will assume very different proportions. When a man can be seen functioning in his etheric physical body by the majority of the race, the dropping of the dense body will be considered just a "release."

The next stage is the withdrawal of the life force from the etheric body or coil, and its devitalisation. The etheric coil is but an extension of one aspect of the sutratma or thread, and this thread is spun by the Ego from within the causal body much as a spider spins a thread. It can be shortened or extended at will, and when the period of pralaya has been decided upon, this thread of light, or of solar fire (note the word "solar") is withdrawn, and gathered back to the atomic subplane where it will still vitalise the permanent atom and hold it connected within the causal body. The life impulses are then—as far as the physical plane is concerned—centralised within the atomic sphere.

The third stage is the withdrawal of the life force from the astral form so that it disintegrates in a similar manner and the life is centralised within the astral permanent atom. It has gained an increase of vitality through physical plane existence, and added colour through astral experience.

The final stage for the human atom is its withdrawal

from the mental vehicle. The life forces after this four-fold abstraction are centralised entirely within the egoic sphere; contact with the three lower planes is still inherently possible by means of the permanent atoms, the force centres of the three personality aspects.

In each incarnation the life forces have gained through the utilisation of the vehicles,

a. An increased activity, which is stored in the physical permanent atom.

b. An added colouring, which is stored in the astral permanent atom.

c. A developed quality of strength, or purpose in action, which is stored in the mental unit.

These are wrought into faculty in devachan.

Devachan [45, 46] is a state of consciousness, reflecting, in

[45] Deva-Chan. "(3) 'Who goes to Deva Chan?' The personal Ego, of course, but beatified, purified, holy. Every Ego—the combination of the sixth and seventh principles—which, after the period of unconscious gestation is reborn into the Deva-Chan, is of necessity as innocent and pure as a new-born babe. The fact of his being reborn at all shows the preponderance of good over evil in his old personality. And while the Karma (of evil) steps aside for the time being to follow him in his future earth-reincarnation, he brings along with him but the Karma of his good deeds, words, and thoughts into this Deva-Chan. 'Bad' is a relative term for us—as you were told more than once before,—and *the Law of Retribution is the only law that never errs.* Hence all those who have not slipped down into the mire of unredeemable sin and bestiality—go to the Deva-Chan. They will have to pay for their sins, voluntary and involuntary, later on. Meanwhile they are rewarded; receive the *effects* of the *causes* produced by them.

"Of course it is a *state*, one, so to say, of *intense selfishness* during which an *Ego* reaps the reward of his *unselfishness* on earth. He is completely engrossed in the bliss of all his personal earthly affections, preferences, thoughts, and gathers in the fruit of his meritorious actions. No pain, no grief nor even the shadow of a sorrow comes to darken the bright horizon of his unalloyed happiness; for, *it is a state of perpetual 'Maya.'* . . . Since the conscious perception of one's *personality* on earth is but an evanescent dream that sense will be equally that of a dream in the Deva-Chan—only a hundredfold intensified."

. . . .

"'Bardo' is the period between death and rebirth—and may last from a few years to a kalpa. It is divided into three sub-periods (1) when the *Ego* delivered of its mortal coil enters into *Kama-Loka* (the abode of Elementaries); (2) when it enters into 'Gestation State'; (3) when it is reborn in the *Rupa-Loka* of Deva-Chan. Sub-period (1) may last from a few minutes to a *number* of years—the phrase 'a few years' becoming puzzling and utterly worthless without a more complete explanation; Sub-the life of the Personality, that higher state which we call nirvanic consciousness, and which is brought about by egoic action. It is but a dim reflection in the separated units (and therefore tinged with selfishness and separative pleasure) of the group condition called nirvanic. In this high state of consciousness each separate identity, though self-realising, shares in the group realisation, and therein lies bliss for the unit. Separation is no longer felt, only unity and essential oneness is known. Therefore, as might be naturally deduced, there is no devachan for the savage or little evolved man, as they merit it not, and have not the mentality to realise it; hence, therefore, the rapidity of their incarnations, and the brevity of the pralayic period. There is little in their case for the Ego, on its own plane, to assimilate in the residue of incarnations, and hence the life principle withdraws rapidly from out of the mental form, with the resulting impulse of the Ego to reincarnate almost immediately.

When the life of the personality has been full and rich, yet has not reached the stage wherein the personal self can *consciously* co-operate with the ego, periods of personality nirvana are undergone, their length depending upon the interest of the life, and the ability of the man to meditate upon experience. Later, when the Ego dominates the personality life, the interest of the man is raised to higher levels, and the nirvana of the soul be-

period 2nd is 'very long'; as you say, longer sometimes than you may even imagine, yet proportionate to the *Ego's* spiritual stamina; Sub-period 3rd lasts in proportion to the good *Karma*, after which the *monad* is again reincarnated.''

.   .   .   .   .   .

. . . ''Every effect must be proportionate to the cause. And, as man's terms of incarnate existence bear but a small proportion to his periods of inter-natal existence in the manvantaric cycle, so the good thoughts, words, and deeds of any one of these 'lives' on a globe are causative of effects, the working out of which requires far more time than the evolution of the causes occupied.''—From *Mahatma Letters to A. P. Sinnett*, pp. 100-105-106.

[46] *Devachan.* A state intermediate between two earth lives into which the Ego enters after its separation from its lower aspects or sheaths.

comes his goal. He has no interest in devachan. Therefore, those upon the Path (either the probationary Path,
or the Path of Initiation) do not, as a rule, go to devachan, but immediate incarnation becomes the rule in
the turning of the wheel of life; this time it is brought
about by the conscious co-operation of the personal
Self with the divine Self or Ego.

(2) *The period between egoic Cycles.* Herein is hid
the mystery of the 777 incarnations and concerns the
relation of the unit to his group on the egoic plane, prior
to the unfoldment of the fifth petal. It concerns man
in the period between the savage stage and that of the
disciple, when he is an average man but still in the two
Halls. The mystery of all root races lies here, and the
egoic cycles coincide with the building of racial forms,
and civilisations. A man will reincarnate again and
again in the various subraces of a root race until a certain
cycle has been covered; then he may undergo a pralayic
condition until in a later (and sometimes much later)
root race he will respond to its vibratory call, and the
egoic impulse to incarnate will again be felt. In illustration of this, we should bear in mind that the more advanced humanity of today did not incarnate until the
fourth root race. These cycles are one of the mysteries
of initiation, though one of the earlier mysteries, and
are revealed at the second initiation as they enable the
initiate to comprehend his position, to see somewhat
the nature of the karmic impulse, and to read his own
record in the astral light.

These might be considered the two lesser pralayic
periods and concern primarily life in the three worlds.

(3) *Next comes the period wherein the man has attained freedom.* A man has at this stage succeeded,
under law, in "abstracting" himself, the freed soul, from
out of the matter of the three worlds. He has used and
worked with deva substance and has gained all the vibra-

tory contact possible, and has secured all the intended "realisations" and "revelations"; he can no longer be held imprisoned by the devas. He is free until, consciously and willingly, and in another round, he can return as a member of a Hierarchy to continue His work of service for the little evolved humanity of that distant time. As this concerns the seven paths of opportunity for a Master we will not deal with it here.[47] This is the great human pralaya.

(4) *Planetary Pralaya.* Man, after these cyclic happenings, is now a conscious part of his group, and a vibrant point in a centre in the body of a Heavenly Man, consciously alive and consciously aware of his place in the great whole. This involves a realisation as to the centre of which he is a point of energy, a knowledge of the type of force he is to transmit, and to manipulate from cosmic levels, and a conscious relation with the six other centres in the planetary Life with which he is associated.

This period of conscious activity in etheric substance (of which the planetary body is formed) persists according to the karma of the planetary Lord, for the unit is now consciously associated with planetary karma, and is a participant in the working out of the will and purpose of the Lord of His Ray. On the higher planes of the system, this stage persists for the length of the life of a scheme; to which a period of pralaya succeeds that has its beginning towards the end of the seventh round in any scheme or of the fifth if the Law of Persistence of a scheme is working out through cycles of five. I am

[47] The seven Paths upon one of which all must pass:—

    Path 1.   The Path of Earth Service.
    Path 2.   The Path of Magnetic Work.
    Path 3.   The Path of the Planetary Logoi.
    Path 4.   The Path to Sirius.
    Path 5.   The Ray Path.
    Path 6.   The Path of the Solar Logos.
    Path 7.   The Path of Absolute Sonship.

here generalising and speaking in broad terms; the karma
of the units differ and a man—according to the path he
chooses after the fifth initiation—stays and works within
his own scheme, but changes may occur through the following factors:

  a. Planetary karma.
  b. The will of the Lord of his Ray.
  c. Orders emanating from the solar Logos which are
      conveyed to him after liberation via the planetary
      Logos and through the medium of the chohan of
      his Ray.

He is then "abstracted" under a mysterious planetary
law which only works on cosmic etheric levels, and is
transferred to his destination. If we interpret all the
above in terms of energy and of radioactivity and thus
avoid the dangers of materialistic interpretation, the
meaning will become clearer.

(5) *The Great Pralaya.* This interval comes at the
close of every one hundred years of Brahma, and sweeps
into dissolution forms of every kind—subtle and dense—
throughout the entire system. It is a period analogous
to that dealt with when we considered the abstraction
of man from his etheric vehicle, and his ability then to
function on the astral plane, dissociated from his dual
physical form. Within the system a process similar to
that undergone when man withdraws the etheric body
out of the dense physical vehicle, will be seen towards
the close of the mahamanvantara. It will cover the
period wherein the lesser four Rays merge and blend,
seeking duality, and their polar opposites. Eventually
the four become two, the two become one, and all are
then synthesised into the third major Ray. The time is
not yet, but lies countless aeons ahead. It is the first
appearance of the destroyer aspect in connection with
the planetary schemes, and marks the beginning of the

time when the "Heavens will melt with fervent heat," and the Sun becomes seven suns.[48]

The microcosmic correspondence can be seen in the following process. The physical permanent atom absorbs the entire life force of the physical body, and its inherent heat and light is thereby increased until at the fourth initiation the seven spirillae are fully vitalised, and vibrant. The internal heat of the atom, plus the external heat of the egoic body wherein it has its place, produces then that which destroys the permanent atom. Temporarily, and just prior to destruction, it becomes a tiny sevenfold sun owing to the radiation and activity of the spirillae. So with the physical sun of the system; it will in a similar manner become seven suns, when it has absorbed the life essence of the fully evolved planes, and of the planetary schemes thereon. The ensuing conflagration is the final work of the Destroyer aspect. It marks the moment of the highest development of deva substance in the system, the consummation of the work of Agni and his fire angels, and the initiation of Brahma. Atomic substance will then *individualise* (which, as we know, is the goal for the atom) and after the great pralaya the next solar system will start with the threefold Spirit manifesting through substance which is essentially distinguished by active intelligent love. This is necessarily incomprehensible to our fourth round minds.

We have thus considered the various types of pralaya, in so far as they affect the human unit; each unit finds its ways eventually into one of the cosmic astral centres of the particular cosmic Entity Who is the Lord of his Ray, and therefore at the great pralaya those human units who have achieved, and who have not passed to other distant cosmic centres, will find their place there.

Before we take up planetary and cosmic pralaya, we might here consider the relationship of the Agnishvattas

[48] See S. D., II, 746, 747.

(who caused the individualisation of animal man on this planet), to other and previous cycles of evolution, and why we have only dealt with them from the point of view of a mahamanvantara, and of a kalpa. The reason we have not considered specifically the group of Agnishvattas, Kumaras and Rudras connected with the Earth has been because we have handled the entire subject from the planetary standpoint, and not from that of the human family. The student who seeks detailed information as to the Agnishvattas of the Earth chain has but to study the *Secret Doctrine*. We have attempted to carry the thought of the student beyond his own tiny sphere to the consideration of the work of the Manasadevas in the solar system. In every scheme They have Their place, but in some—as in the Jupiter scheme —They are just beginning Their work, and in others— as in the Vulcan and Venus schemes—Their work is nearly completed. Venus is in her last round, and has nearly developed her fourth kingdom to perfection, or as much as it is possible in the system. In the Earth scheme, They are in full tide of work, and only in the next round will They demonstrate the height of Their activity. They pass cyclically through the schemes and under Law—the Law of Karma for the planetary Logos, for They are essentially concerned with His Life as it actuates His centres. They come into a scheme on a wave of manasic energy from the head centre of the Logos, and in the process of passing through his Heart centre three things occur:

1. They become differentiated into seven groups.
2. They direct Themselves as streams of energy to some particular scheme.
3. Their contact with a scheme is that which produces the manifestation of the fourth Creative Hierarchy, and leads to the Monads taking form in the three worlds.

These entities who sacrifice Themselves for the human Hierarchy (and we must note here the accuracy of the fact that They emanate from the logoic head centre, or from the will aspect), are the true Saviours who give Their lives for the good of the race. *They stand in relation to the totality of the schemes as the Occult Hierarchy of any particular planet stands to men upon that planet.* During pralaya They are withdrawn (as all else), from manifestation, and return to a cosmic centre of which the logoic head centre is but a dim reflection; they return the richer for experience.

The old Commentary says:

"The deva shineth with added light when the virtue of the will hath entered. He garnereth colour as the reaper garners wheat, and storeth it up for the feeding of the multitude. Over all this deva host the mystic Goat presideth. Makara is, and is not, yet the link persisteth."

Rounds come and go but (except from the standpoint of a particular planet), the Manasadevas are forever present, but their influence is not forever felt.

In considering planetary pralaya we might briefly enumerate the following periods of quiescence:

Between Two Globes in a Chain.   This covers the period of abstraction of the seeds of all life, and its transference from one sphere to another.   The seed manu of a globe gathers all the life forces into Himself, as does the Logos at the close of a system, and as also transpires at the close of a chain, and holds them quiescent in His aura.   This covers a period of a manvantara, or of one day of Brahma.

Between Two Chains.   This covers the period of a mahamanvantara, or of one year of Brahma.

There are many ways of arriving at the greater cycles, but there is no need to confuse with the intricacies of figures.   The ten Prajapatis or Rishis, or the ten planetary Logoi, manifest through Their ten schemes in time and space, the hour of Their appearing differing. Each likewise manifests as does the Logos through a septenate and a triad, making again a ten of perfection.

Between Two Solar Systems. This covers the period of one hundred years of Brahma, and through the study of the planetary cycles comprehension of these greater cycles may come. Complication comes to the student nevertheless in the fact that two of the schemes cover their cyclic periods in five rounds, while others have seven; one scheme has but three rounds, but a mystery is hidden here: on the inner round one planet has nine cycles to run before the purpose of its Lord is completed.

Certain lesser periods of pralaya do not concern man at all, but concern *the atom of matter as it is released from form of any kind in the subhuman kingdoms. Pralaya is the result of radioactivity carried to a conclusion.*

(c.) Types of Human Rebirth. In our study of the building of thought-forms and the agencies for their construction, we have considered:

1. The deva substance out of which they are constructed.
2. The energy which animates them and its source.
3. Their appearance in time and space, or their incarnation.
4. Their disappearance or pralaya.
5. The constructing entities who in a threefold manner produce these forms, utilising the process of:

    a. Meditation, which is ever the preliminary to construction.
    b. Dynamic force, or the positive energy which seizes upon its polar opposite (negative substance), and utilises it.

    c. The impartation of colour or quality, which moulds that which has been prepared.

    d. A secondary vitalisation, which sets in separate motion the thought-form thus created.

We will now consider the mystery of rebirth, or the incarnation of those lives which exist in subtler matter, and yet which seek form according to law, and touch upon their specific intent on dense physical levels. We can consider this in connection with the cosmic entities who seek existence on the physical plane of the cosmos, our solar systemic planes, or the reincarnating jivas who are driven by the Law towards earthly manifestation in order to become fully conscious, and acquire (by means of sentient existence), added faculty and power.

H. P. B. has said that rebirths may be divided into three classes:[49]

    a. Those of Avatars.

    b. Those of Adepts.

    c. Those of jivas seeking development.

To those who are endeavouring to grasp somewhat the mystery of rebirth and its laws and purpose, and who are confused when considering the mystery of the Buddha, and the secret purpose of that mysterious Entity, the Silent Watcher; to those who find the problem of understanding the position of the Kumaras and Their relation to the planetary Logos almost an insuperable one, it might be wise to say: Study and meditate upon the difference existing between the lower principles and the higher three; study and meditate upon the place and position of these lower principles in the body of the planetary Logos and ponder upon the correspondence between:

    a. The devachan of the reincarnating jiva.

    b. The nirvana of the Adept.

[*] See S. D.. III, 364, 365, 367.

    c. The pralaya of a cosmic Entity, such as the Lord of
      a chain, the Lord of a scheme, and the Lord of a
      Ray.

I say *correspondence* in its esoteric significance, and do
not seek to infer analogy in detail, but only in purpose
and in experience. It may be said of all three states
that they are periods of development, long cycles of
meditation, and interludes between stages of activity.
Hence the emphasis laid in the East and in all occult
schools of development upon meditation, for it is the
means of bringing to the unit under development the
capacity which will produce:

    a. Abstraction, or liberation from form.
    b. Creative power.
    c. Direction of energy, through an act of the will.
    d. Future constructive activity.

By means of meditation, a man finds freedom from the
delusion of the senses, and their vibratory lure; he finds
his own positive centre of energy and becomes consciously able to use it; he becomes, therefore, aware of
his real Self, functioning freely and consciously beyond
the planes of sense; he enters into the plans of the
greater Entity within Whose radiatory capacity he has
a place; he can then consciously proceed to carry out
those plans as he can grasp them at varying stages of
realisation; and he becomes aware of essential unity.
But when a man has thus freed himself from the objects
of sense in the three worlds he again becomes aware of
the need of further meditation, and it is this (to man in
the three worlds), inconceivable form of meditation that
engrosses the attention of the Adept, and which is undertaken by Him in two great stages, each preceding the
two final Initiations, the sixth and the seventh. I refer
not here only to Adepts who "make the sacrifice," and
choose rebirth for service on the planet, but to all adepts.
Freedom to work on any Path must be gained by occult

meditation; freedom to escape beyond the ring-pass-not is also thus attained, and likewise the curious state of quiescence which is achieved by Those Who have offered for service as the occult Hierarchy in the next round. In Them have to be stored the psychic seeds of knowledge which will be available in the fifth round; this necessitates for Them an attitude of receptivity to occurrences at the close of each root-race, when there is, on subtler levels, a gathering in of psychic force, and its storing with Those prepared for its reception.   Their work is analogous to that of the Seed-Manu, Who Himself works through a septenate as do these storers of the psychic life-forces.

Again for such cosmic Entities as the planetary Logoi periods of meditation transpire, but these concern Them on the cosmic planes, and only the effects are felt on this. They meditate in Their physical brains, and therefore in substance as does man, but the process is carried on in the etheric brain.   This should be pondered on, for it holds the mystery hid.   Also, the fact that some of these Lords of the Rays are more proficient in meditation than others, and thus achieve differing results which work out in Their schemes, should be carefully borne in mind.

(d.) *The Future Coming of the Avatar.*

THE COMING AVATAR

"From the zenith to the nadir, from dawn to fall of night, from the emergence into being of all that is or may be to the passing into peace of all that hath achieved, gleameth the orb of blue and the inner radiant fire.

From the gates of gold down to the pit of earth, out from the flaming fire down to the circle of gloom, rideth the secret Avatar, bearing the sword that pierceth.

Naught can arrest His approach, and none may say Him nay. To the darkness of our sphere He rideth alone, and on His approach is seen the uttermost disaster, and the chaos of that which seeketh to withstand.

The Asuras veil their faces, and the pit of maya reeleth to the foundation. The stars of the eternal Lhas vibrate to that sound,—the WORD uttered with sevenfold intensity.

Greater the chaos becometh; the major centre with all the seven circulating spheres rock with the echoes of disintegration. The fumes of utter blackness mount upwards in dissipation. The noise discordant of the warring elements greets the oncoming One, and deters Him not. The strife and cries of the fourth great Hierarchy, blending with the softer note of the Builders of the fifth and sixth, meet His approach. Yet He passeth on His way, sweeping the circle of the spheres, and sounding forth the WORD.

*   *   *   *   *   *   *

From the nadir to the zenith, from eve unto the Day be with us, from the circle of manifestation to the centre of pralayic peace, is seen the enveloping blue, lost in the flame of achievement.

Up from the pit of maya back to the portals of gold, forth from the gloom and darkness back to the splendour of day, rideth the Manifested One, the Avatar, bearing the shattered Cross.

Naught can arrest His return, none can impede His Path, for He passeth along the upper way, bearing His people with Him. Cometh the dissolution of pain, cometh the end of strife, cometh the merging of the spheres and the blending of the hierarchies. All then is re-absorbed within the orb, the circle of manifestation. The forms that exist in maya, and the flame that devoureth all, are garnered by the One Who rideth the Heavens and entereth into the timeless Æon.''

(*From the Archives of the Lodge.*)

We have touched upon the subject of *Avatars* and the various classes into which they might be divided. We might now enlarge somewhat more upon the methods. The methods whereby certain cosmic Existences and certain highly evolved Entities appear among men to do a specific work might be very inadequately, and cursorily summarised, as follows:

The method of overshadowing.

The method of embodying some principle.

The method seen in the mystery of the Bodhisattva, or
the Christ.

The method of direct incarnation.

The handicap of words is great, and the above phrases
but convey a hint as to the true meaning.   Therein lies
safety for the student, for the real significance would be
incomprehensible to him, and would but mislead him and
guide him along the path of misunderstanding.   Until a
man is a pledged initiate, he cannot comprehend the
matter.   Of these, the most ordinary method is the first.
All these methods of manifestation will perhaps be better
understood by the student if he *interprets them always in
terms of force and energy,* and if he notes that dim reflections of the same processes, and faint analogies can be
traced among the reincarnating jivas.   When a man has
reached a certain development and can be of service to
the world, cases occur when he is *overshadowed* by a great
adept, or—as in the case of H. P. B.—by One greater
than an adept.   A chela can be a centre through which his
master can pour His energy and force for the helping of
the world, and in certain important crises men have been
overshadowed by more than one of the Great Ones.[50]

[50] *Discipleship   or   Chelaship.*   . . . The   ancient   mysteries   were   but
a school of spiritual training and perfection in true wisdom; that the preliminary qualification was the purification of the heart from all sensual
passions and false preconceptions; that, while the hand of the Master
might lead the neophyte through the dangers of the stage where, like the
infant, he could not walk alone, he was obliged, in the higher paths, to
learn to guide and guard himself, as the adult man has to do in ordinary
life; that the ultimate goal was the expansion of the self˙into infinite
existence and potentialities; and, lastly, that, however the initial forms and
ceremonies may have differed in appearance, an identical aim was in view.—
The Theosophist, Vol. IX, p. 246.

The pure heart and clean mind alone permit one to attain salvation.
This was his doctrine. So, likewise, is it taught in the Aryan Mahabharata
(Sec. CXCIX. Vana Parva) which says:

"Those high souled persons that do not commit sins in word, deed,
heart and soul, are said to undergo ascetic austerities, and not that they
suffer their bodies to be wasted by fasts and penances. He that hath no
feeling of kindness for relatives cannot be free from sin, even if his body
be pure.   That hard-heartedness of his is the enemy of his asceticism.
Asceticism, again, is not mere abstinence from the pleasures of the world.
He that is always pure and decked with virtues, he that practices kindness

What occurs on lower planes is but a reflection of higher processes, and in this thought may lie illumination. A man is a force centre, either for his Ego, when sufficiently evolved, or, via his Ego, of his group force; when very highly developed he can consciously be overshadowed by an exponent of a different type of force, which blends with his group, or Ray, force, and produces significant results in his life on earth.

Again when an Ego is highly evolved he may choose during any particular incarnation to work paramountly through any one principle among the lower four; when this is the case the man's life on earth is significantly that of an *embodied principle*. He seems to strike one note and to sound out one tone. His work is clearly to be seen along one line. He is a fanatic of high degree, but accomplishes big things for his subrace, even though the physical brain may not be consciously aware of the egoic impulse. This process has a curious relation to the obscuration, or fading out, of the personality, for the particular principle embodied works through a corresponding permanent atom, and its spirillae become over-rapidly developed, and hence their term of service wears to a close. This is a fact which is nevertheless taken advantage of when a superman, or great adept, becomes the embodiment (during a rootrace) of a principle; the vestures or sheaths of which the permanent atom is the nucleus (through the innate strength of the developed spirillae) are preserved by the aid of mantric formulas. The vibration is perpetuated for a specific length of time, and for as long as the vesture or sheath may be required. A hint is here conveyed which may be of service.

Again, when a man has become a disciple he may, if he so wish, remain upon the astral plane and work there, and —at his pleasure, and under the adjustment of karma by

his Guru—he may take immediate physical birth. A hint
as to the *mystery of the Bodhisattva* may be found in
these two thoughts, provided the student transfers the
whole concept to the etheric levels of the cosmic physical
plane, and remembers that on these levels the adept
works altogether as a part of a group, and not as a separated Identity, as does the ego in the three worlds.
Therefore, the energy pouring through Him may be:

  a. That of a particular centre in the body of the
     planetary Logos in its total force.
  b. That of a particular set of vibrations within that
     centre, or a part of its vibratory force.
  c. That of the energy of a particular principle, either
     one of His own higher principles which He is seek-
     ing to bring to bear upon the earth, by taking in-
     carnation for that specific purpose, or the energy
     of one of the planetary logoic principles, as it
     pours through Him via a particular spirilla or life
     current in the permanent atom of the planetary
     Logos.

When these types of force are centralised in any particular adept, and He is expressing simply that extraneous force and nothing else, the effect is shown on the
physical plane in the appearance of an avatar. *An avatar is, but an adept is made,* but frequently the force,
energy, purpose or will of a cosmic Entity will utilise the
vehicles of an adept in order to contact the physical
planes. This method whereby cosmic Existences make
Their power felt can be seen working out on all the planes
of the cosmic physical plane. A striking instance of this
can be seen in the case of the Kumaras, Who, under certain planetary forces, and through the formation of a
systemic triangle, gave the impulse to the third kingdom
which produced the fourth by bringing it into conjunction with the fifth. These Kumaras, Sanat Kumara and

His three pupils, having achieved the highest initiation possible in the last great cycle, but having as yet (from Their standpoint) another step to take, offered Themselves to the planetary Logos of Their Ray as "focal points" for His force, so that thereby He might hasten and perfect His plans on Earth within the cycle of manifestation. They have demonstrated three out of the four methods. They are *overshadowed* by the planetary Logos, and He works directly as the Initiator (in relation to man) through Sanat Kumara, and with the three kingdoms in nature through the three Buddhas of Activity,—Sanat Kumara, being thus concerned directly with the ego on the mental plane, and His three Pupils being concerned with the other three types of consciousness, of which man is the summation. At the moment of initiation (after the second Initiation) Sanat Kumara becomes the direct mouthpiece and agent of the Planetary Logos. That great Entity speaks through Him and for one brief second (if one can use such a term in connection with a plane whereon time, as we understand it, is not) the planetary Logos of a man's Ray consciously—via His etheric brain—turns His thought upon the Initiate, and "calls him by His Name."

Again the Kumaras are *embodied principles,* but in this connection we must remember that this means that the force and energy of one of the principles of the Logos are pouring through Them via that which—to Them— corresponds to the Monad. Through Them, during Their period of incarnation and voluntary sacrifice, the great Prototype of the planetary Logos begins to make His Presence felt, and force from the constellation of the Great Bear faintly vibrates on earth. At initiation, man becomes aware consciously of the Presence of the planetary Logos through self-induced contact with his own divine Spirit. At the fifth Initiation he becomes aware of the full extent of this planetary group influence, and of his part in the great whole. At the sixth and seventh Initiations the influence of the planetary Prototype is sensed, reaching him via the planetary Logos working through the Initiator.

The method of *direct incarnation* was earlier seen when the Kumaras were in physical form. This only applied to some of Them; Sanat Kumara and His Pupils are in physical form, but have not taken dense physical bodies. They work on the vital etheric levels, and dwell in etheric bodies. Shamballa, where They dwell, exists in physical matter as do the Kumaras, but it is matter of the higher ethers of the physical plane, and only when man has developed etheric vision will the mystery lying beyond the Himalayas be revealed. Therefore, *Sanat Kumara is the planetary Logos yet He is not.* A reflection of this method of direct incarnation can be seen when a disciple steps out of his body and permits his Guru, or a more advanced chela, to use it.

The mystery of the Bodhisattvas [51] has been touched upon by H. P. B. and until students have assimilated and studied what she has said, there is no more to add. Apprehension of truth is ever the factor that calls for fresh revelation.

A very interesting period will come about the year 1966 and persist to the end of the century. It is one for which the Great Ones are already making due preparation. It concerns a centennial effort of the Lodge and of the Personages taking part therein. Each century sees a centennial effort of the Lodge along a particular line of force made to forward the ends of evolution, and the effort for the twentieth century will be upon a larger scale than has been the case for a very long time, and will involve a number of Great Ones. In a similar effort during the nineteenth century, H. P. B. was concerned, and a fairly large number of chelas. In the effort immediately ahead,

[51] S. D., I, 82, 83.

several of the Great Ones are concerned and the Master
of the Masters Himself; in Their "forthcoming" for
work three out of the various methods of appearing mentioned earlier will be seen in full activity, and it is on
these three that we might now touch.

In the appearing of the Bodhisattva Himself, the *mystery of the Bodhisattva* will be seen in its fullest sense,
and it is not for us here to enlarge upon it. Suffice it to
say that the vestures of the GREAT ONE will be used,
but time will show whether the coming Lord will clothe
upon those vestures a physical vehicle at this particular
juncture, or whether the astral plane may not be the
field of His activity. If the student ponders upon the
consequences entailed in the appropriation of this vesture, much light upon probable happenings will be
thrown. The vestures act in a dual capacity:

a. They are very highly magnetised, and therefore
   have a profound and far-reaching effect when
   utilised.
b. They act as a focal point for the force of the Lord
   Buddha and link up the coming Lord with Him,
   enabling Him to increase His Own stupendous resources by drawing upon still higher force centres,
   via the Lord Buddha.

This force will find its expression upon the astral plane,
producing vast results of a quieting nature and bringing,
by reflex action, peace on earth. The transmutation of
desire into aspiration, and the transformation of low
desire into high desire, will be some of the effects, while
the result of the force flowing through will produce profound reactions of the deva denizens of that plane.
Through the vibration thus set up will come the possibility of many (who would otherwise not do so) taking
the first initiation. Later, towards the end of the greater
cycle, the coming Avatar will again employ the vestures

with all that is entailed thereby, and will take a physical body, thus demonstrating on the physical plane the force of the Logos in the administration of the Law. When He comes at the close of this century and makes His power felt, He will come as the Teacher of Love and Unity, and the keynote He will strike will be regeneration through love poured forth on all. As He will work primarily on the astral plane, this will demonstrate on the physical plane in the formation of active groups in every city of any size, and in every country, which will work aggressively for unity, co-operation and brotherhood in every department of life—economic, religious, social and scientific.

These groups will achieve results now impossible, owing to the retention of buddhic force, but later this force will be set loose on earth via the medium of the Great Lord, operating as an aspect of the Logos, and as a focal point for the consciousness and energy of the Buddha.

It is this impending probability which is held in mind during the century at the annual recurrence of the Wesak festival. Students would do well to further the ends of the occult Hierarchy by a similar concentration at the time of the festival, thus setting up currents of thought which will have a great appeal in the occult sense of that term.

Indication of the nearing of this event will be seen in the reaction which will be set up during the next twenty-five years against crime, sovietism, and the extreme radicalism which is now being made use of by certain powers to achieve ends contrary to the plans of the Lord. The era of peace will be ushered in by a gathering together on earth of the forces which stand for construction, and development, and by a conscious deliberate banding together of groups in every land who embody the principle (as far as they can vision it) of Brotherhood. Watch the signs of the times, and be not discouraged over the immediate future. The appearance of the Great Lord on the astral plane (whether followed by His physical incarnation or not) will date from a certain Wesak festival at which a mantram (known only to those attaining the seventh Initiation) will be pronounced by the Buddha, thus setting loose force, and enabling His great Brother to fulfil his mission. Hence the gradual recognition of the Wesak festival, and its true significance in the occident is desirable, and opportunity will be offered to all who are willing to place themselves in the line of this force, and thus become vitalised by it, and consequently available for service. The reaction mentioned above, will also become possible through the pressure brought to bear by the present children, many of whom are chelas and some initiates. They have come in to prepare the way for the coming of His Feet.

When the hour strikes (five years prior to the date of His descent) they will be in the full flower of their service and will have recognised their work, even though they may not be conscious of that which the future holds hid.

When the hour has come (and already a few cases are to be found), many cases of *overshadowing* will be seen and will demonstrate in a threefold manner. In all countries, in the orient and the occident, prepared disciples and highly evolved men and women, will be found who will be doing the work along the lines intended, and who will be occupying places of prominence which will make them available for the reaching of the many; their bodies also will be sufficiently pure to permit of the overshadowing. It will only be possible in the case of those who have been consecrated since childhood, who have been servers of the race all their lives, or who, in previous lives, have acquired the right by karma. This threefold overshadowing will manifest as:

First. An impression upon the physical brain of the

man or woman, of thoughts, plans for work, ideals and intentions which (emanating from the Avatar) will yet be unrecognised by him as being other than his own; he will proceed to put them into action, unconsciously helped by the force flowing in. This is literally a form of higher mental telepathy working out on physical levels.

Second. The overshadowing of the chela during his work (such as lecturing, writing, or teaching), and his illumination for service. He will be conscious of this, though perhaps unable to explain it, and will seek more and more to be available for use, rendering himself up in utter selflessness to the inspiration of His Lord. This is effected via the chela's Ego, the force flowing through his astral permanent atom; and it is only possible when the fifth petal is unfolded.

Third. The conscious co-operation of the chela is necessitated in the third method of overshadowing. In this case he will (with full knowledge of the laws of his being and nature) surrender himself and step out of his physical body, handing it over for the use of the Great Lord or one of His Masters. This is only possible in the case of a chela who has brought all the three lower bodies into alignment, and necessitates the unfolding of the sixth petal. By an act of conscious will he renders up his body, and stands aside for a specific length of time.

These methods of overshadowing will be largely the ones used by the Great Lord and His Masters at the end of the century, and for this reason They are sending into incarnation, in every country, disciples who have the opportunity offered them to respond to the need of humanity. Hence the need of training men and women to recognise the higher psychism, and the true inspiration and mediumship, and to do this scientifically. In fifty years time, the need for true psychics and conscious mediums (such as H. P. B., for instance) will be very great if the Master's plans are to be carried to fruition, and the movement must be set on foot in preparation for the coming of Him for Whom all nations wait. In this work many have their share, provided they demonstrate the necessary endurance.

Naturally, the first group will be the largest, for it does not necessitate so much knowledge, but more risk is entailed with them than with the others—the risk of a perversion of the plans, and of disaster to the unit involved. The second group will be less numerous, and the last group will involve only a handful, or two or three in certain countries. In this case, it will be verily true that, through sacrifice, the Son of Man will again tread the highways of men, and His physical incarnation be a fact. Very few will be thus available for His use, as the force He carries requires a peculiarly resilient instrument, but due preparation is being made.

Again the method of *direct incarnation* will be employed by certain of the Masters and initiates through the process of:

a. Physical birth.

b. Appropriation of a suitable vehicle, or body.

c. Direct creation by an act of will. This will be rare.

The second, or middle, method will be the one most frequently employed. Six of the Masters, as yet quite unknown to the average occult student by name, have already sought physical incarnation—one in India, another in England, two in northern America, and one in central Europe, whilst another has made a great sacrifice, and taken a Russian body in the desire to act as a peace centre in that distracted land. Certain initiates of the third Initiation have taken feminine bodies,—one in India will in due time do much toward the emancipation of the women of India, whilst another has a peculiar work to do in connection with the animal kingdom which likewise is awaiting the day of His appearing.

The Master Jesus will take a physical vehicle, and with certain of His chelas effect a re-spiritualisation of the Catholic churches, breaking down the barrier separating the Episcopal and Greek churches from the Roman. This may be looked for, should plans progress as hoped, about the year 1980. The Master Hilarion will also come forth, and become a focal point of buddhic energy in the vast spiritualistic movement, whilst another Master is working with the Christian Science endeavour in an effort to swing it on to sounder lines. It is interesting to note that those movements which have laid the emphasis so strongly on the heart or love aspect, may respond more rapidly to the inflow of force at the Coming than other movements which consider themselves very advanced. The "mind may slay" the recognition of the Real, and hatred between brothers swing the tide of love-force away. The three Masters so closely allied with the theosophical movement are already making Their preparations, and will also move among men, recognised by Their Own and by those who have eyes to see. To those of Their chelas on earth who undergo the necessary discipline, opportunity will be offered to work on the astral plane and, should they so choose, an immediate incarnation, provided they have achieved continuity of consciousness. He Who is known as D. K. is planning to restore—via His students—some of the old and occult methods of healing and to demonstrate:

a. The place of the etheric body.
b. The effect of pranic force.
c. The opening up of etheric vision.

It is not permissible to say more in connection with the plans of the Great Ones. Their appearing will not be simultaneous in time, for the people could not stand the tremendously increased inflow of force, and recognition of Them and of Their methods will depend upon the intui-

tion, and the training of the inner senses. They come
with no herald, and only Their works will proclaim Them.

(*e.*) *Impulse and Incarnation.* Perhaps light upon
this very difficult question of the incarnating jivas, of
adepts and of avatars may come if the student remembers that:

1. *An ordinary man* demonstrates the third aspect of
intelligent activity in his personality life, and is evolving
consciously the second aspect, or the egoic manifestation
on the physical plane.

2. *An adept* in incarnation is demonstrating fully the
second aspect as well as the third, and in his own internal life is in process of evolving the first aspect, or is
endeavouring to bring through the monadic life into conscious activity on the buddhic plane.

3. *An avatar* demonstrates one of two things, according to his peculiar karma:

a. *The pure light of the Monad,* brought through by
     means of the perfected Ego and personality on to
     the physical plane. The line of force extends
     straight through from monadic levels to the
     physical.
b. *The light of the Logos* Himself in one or other
     aspect, this being transmitted consciously via the
     Monad straight through to the physical plane from
     the planetary Logos, or even from the solar Logos
     Himself.

In the first two cases, desire for sentient existence, or
desire for service to humanity, are the factors which produce physical manifestation (one through the force of
evolution itself, the other through a conscious act of the
will). Desire for sentient existence is but the latent second aspect seeking expression by means of the Not-Self,
and in the other case the manifested second aspect consciously utilises form as a means to an end. In the case

of all avatars it is the will aspect which is brought into play, and which produces appearance—either the will of the perfected adept, such as the Buddha Himself, or (as in the case of the true Avatar, Who is, and Who has not achieved) the will of the planetary Logos or of the solar Logos, taking form for a specific purpose. It involves a higher display of the creative faculty than that displayed by the Adept in the creation of His body of manifestation, the Mayavirupa.[52] The terms "appropriation of a physical body" and "creation of a physical body" must be extended to include all the planes of the solar system, and not just our physical plane, the seventh subplane of the cosmic physical.

The causes which combine to produce incarnation, are seen to be three:

1. Egoic impulse.
2. The activity of the solar and lunar Angels.
3. Karma, or the place which antecedent action plays in producing manifestation.

We can hardly dissociate them in the consideration of our subject owing to the innate constitution of the egoic body itself and the factor the indwelling consciousness plays in producing appearance through an act of will. Let us briefly, therefore, reconsider what we have learned anent the egoic body and its constitution, and then take up the steps followed by the Ego in producing results in the three worlds.

We have seen that on the third level of the mental plane, the egoic lotus is found and the student should picture it to himself as follows:

Concealed at the very centre or heart of the lotus is a brilliant point of electric fire of a blue-white hue (the

---

[52] *The Mayavirupa* is literally the illusory form; it is the body of temporary manifestation which the Adept creates on occasion through the power of the will and in which He functions in order to make certain contacts on the physical plane and to engage in certain work for the race.

jewel in the lotus) surrounded, and completely hidden, by three closely folded petals. Around this central nucleus, or inner flame, are arranged the nine petals in circles of three petals each, making three circles in all. These petals are formed out of the substance of the solar Angels, as are the central three,—substance which is not only sentient as is the substance of the forms in the three worlds and the lunar bodies, but which has an added quality of "I-ness" or of self-consciousness, enabling the spiritual unity at the centre (by means of it) to acquire knowledge, awareness, and self-realisation. These nine petals are of a predominant orange hue, though the six other colours are found as secondary colours in a varying degree. The inner three petals are of a lovely lemon-yellow hue. At the base of the lotus petals are the three points of light which mark the position of the permanent atoms, and which are the medium of communication between the solar Angels and the lunar Pitris. By means of these permanent atoms the Ego, according to its state of evolution can construct his lunar bodies, acquire knowledge on the lower three planes, and thus buy his experience, and becomes *aware*. On a higher turn of the spiral, the Monad through the egoic petals, and thus with the aid of the solar Angels, acquires knowledge and equally on more exalted levels becomes aware.

The light within these permanent atoms has a dull red glow and we have, therefore, all the three fires demonstrating in the causal body—*electric fire* at the centre, *solar fire* enclosing it as the flame encloses the central nucleus or essence in a candle flame, and *fire by friction*, this latter fire resembling the glowing red wick which lies at the base of the higher flame.

These three types of fire on the mental plane—meeting and unified in the egoic body—produce in time a radiation or warmth which streams out from all sides of the lotus, and forms that spheroidal shape noted by investigators. The more fully developed the Ego may be, and the more the petals are unfolded, the greater the beauty of the surrounding sphere, and the more refined its colouring.

At the early stages after individualisation, the egoic body has the appearance of a bud. The electric fire at the centre is not apparent, and all the nine petals are closed down upon the inner three; the orange colour has a dead aspect and the three points of light at the base are just points and nothing more; the triangle which is later seen connecting the points is not demonstrated. The surrounding sphere is colourless and is only to be appreciated as undulatory vibrations (like waves in the air or ether) reaching barely beyond the petal outline.

By the time the third Initiation is reached, a wondrous transformation has transpired. The outer sphere is palpitating with every colour in the rainbow, and is of wide radius; the streams of electrical energy circulating in it are so powerful that they are escaping beyond the periphery of the circle, resembling the rays of the sun. The nine petals are fully unfolded, forming a gracious setting for the central jewel, and their orange hue is now of a gorgeous translucence, shot with many colours, that of the egoic ray predominating. The triangle at the base is now quickened and scintillating, and the three points are small blazing fires, showing to the eye of the clairvoyant as sevenfold whorls of light, circulating their light from point to point of a rapidly moving triangle.

By the time the fourth Initiation is reached, the activity of this triangle is so great that it looks more like a wheel in rapid revolution. It has a fourth dimensional aspect. The three petals at the centre are opening up, revealing the "blazing jewel." At this initiation, through the action of the Hierophant wielding the electric Rod of Power, the three fires are suddenly stimulated by a downflow of electric, or positive force, from the

Monad, and their blazing out in response produces that
merging which destroys the entire sphere, dissipates all
appearance of form, and produces a moment of equilibrium, or of suspension, in which the "elements are consumed with fervent heat." The moment of highest radiation is known. Then—through the pronouncement of a
certain Word of Power—the great solar Angels gather
back into themselves the solar fire, thus producing the
final dissipation of the form, and hence the separation
of the life from the form; the fire of matter returns to
the general reservoir, and the permanent atoms and the
causal body are no more. The central electric fire becomes centralised in atma-buddhi. The Thinker or
spiritual entity stands free of the three worlds, and functions consciously on the buddhic plane. Between these
two stages of quiescent (though self-conscious) inertia
and of that radiant activity which produces a balancing
of forces, is a long series of lives.

In our consideration of the subject of the reincarnating jivas, we have touched upon three subjects:

a. Avatars, with the intent of disposing of the confusion in the minds of students as to certain types of
appearances. In our present study we shall deal only
with the process followed by ordinary men.

b. Pralayas, with the intent of arousing in the mind
of the student the idea of interludes of quiescence dependent upon the intervening periods of activity.

c. The appearance of the body egoic and its general
conformation, with the intent of awakening the realisation of the student to the fact that evolution affects that
body also, and not only man's forms in the three worlds.
The effects of the process are interdependent, and as
the lower self develops, or the personality becomes more
active and intelligent, results are produced in the higher
body. As these effects are cumulative, and not ephemeral

as are the lower results, the egoic body becomes equally more active and its manifestation of energy is increased. Towards the close of the evolutionary period in the three worlds a constant interchange of energy is seen to be taking place; the lower forms become irradiated with light, and reflect the higher radiance; the egoic body is the Sun of the lower system, and its bodies reflect its rays, as the moon reflects the light of the solar sun. Similarly the egoic Sun,—through the interaction— shines with ever greater intensity and glory. On the higher levels a similar interaction takes place for a brief period between the Monad and its reflection the Ego, but only in the coming solar system will this inter- action be carried to its logical conclusion.

Having, therefore, very briefly dealt with these three topics, we can now proceed to consider the process fol- lowed by the Ego when seeking manifestation in the three worlds. Let us endeavour in our thoughts to interpret all these processes in terms of energy and of force.

The old Commentary says:

"When the Spark is touched to the four wicks, and when spiritual Fire in its threefold essence meets with that which is combustible, the Flame bursts forth. Faint the flicker at the first appearing, and near to death it seems, but the wicks smoulder and glow, and the heat is retained. This is cycle the first, and is called that of the *glowing* wheel.

The flicker grows into a tiny flame and the four wicks burn, but are not consumed, for the heat does not suffice. The light of these three fires is yet so small that the cave is not illumined. Nevertheless, the flame and the essential heat can be felt by the One Who approaches and watches. This is the second cycle, and is called that of the *warming* wheel.

The tiny flame becomes a lighted lamp. The fire flares up, but much smoke is there, for the wicks are burning fast, and the heat suffices for their quick destruction. The lamp, set in the midst of darkness, makes the thick blackness manifest itself; the light and warmth are felt. This, the third cycle, is called that of the *lighted* wheel.

The four wicks and the flame appear as one, and nearly all
the smoke is gone, for flame is mostly seen. The cave itself is
lighted up, though the lamp is yet apparent. Cycle the fourth
is called the hour of the *flaming* wheel.

The final cycle comes when even the lamp itself is burned,
destroyed through the intensity of heat. The One Who watches,
seeing the work accomplished, fans the central point of fire and
produces a sudden flaming. The wicks are naught—the flame is
all. This, so the Sacred Science says, is called the cycle of the
wheel *consumed.*"

Here in the arcane symbology is hid (in terms of
energy and of radiant activity) the whole secret of egoic
energy, and of impulse making its presence felt in the
substance of the lower planes; the student should interpret the above sentences both macrocosmically and microcosmically. In all manifestation, the originating impulse
comes from the first aspect which is hidden at the heart
of the egoic lotus, but this hidden Identity works under
law, and in the earlier stages (the first three cycles) the
process goes on under the Law of Economy, which is the
law of substance itself; in the final two cycles· this law
becomes merged (though not superseded, being still potent) with the Law of Attraction, which is·the fundamental law of the divine Self. It is the failure to realise this
which has resulted in the confusion existing in the minds
of many metaphysicians as to which demonstrated first,
desire or will, and as to the distinction between them,
between impulse and purpose, and between instinct and
intention. In the earlier stages man reincarnates under
the Law of Economy, and though the will aspect lies
back of the process, yet for a long time it is the pull of
sensation and its reflex in consciousness, desire, which
produces rebirth. Sensation, being a quality in matter
or substance, the Self in the beginning identifies Itself
with sensation. Later, when the Self is beginning to
identify Itself with Itself, and to recognise the nature of
the Not-Self, the Law of Attraction and Repulsion be-

comes more active, and conscious will and purpose are displayed. Here it should be remembered that a profound difference in time and space exists between the Logos, or Macrocosm, and Man, the Microcosm. Average man comes into incarnation through egoic impulse, based on desire and on the relation of the second aspect to the third aspect or of the Self to the Not-Self. He will eventually bring about (through evolution) the revelation of the first aspect, and then egoic impulse (based on conscious mental apprehension of the purpose in view) will be the dominant factor, and will demonstrate through a definite will to act. In connection with the Logos, the first stage has been left far behind, and logoic manifestation is based on will and purpose and on conscious intelligent activity. The reason for this is that the Logos, and the planetary Logoi likewise, are on the path of cosmic initiation.

Therefore, though the originating impulse comes from the central point, it is not at first apparent. At the moment of individualisation, the dim outline of a form such as earlier described has made its appearance on mental levels, and (which is a point not as yet recognised by students) it becomes apparent that a period on mental levels has transpired given over to a preparation for the imminent event. Through the activity of the solar Angels the twelve petals have gradually taken form, as the point of electric fire at the heart has begun to make itself felt even though not as yet localised. Then the first three petals take shape, and close down upon the vibrant point, or "jewel" under the potency of the Law of Attraction. One by one the nine other petals take shape as the vibrations begin to affect solar substance, the three types of petals being each under the influence of one or other of the major Rays; these, in their turn, come under the influence of force from cosmic centres.

As earlier said, these petals form a bud, each being closely folded. Only faint vibrations are to be seen pulsating in the bud, just enough to testify to its being a living organism. Shadowy and dim can the ring-pass-not be seen, the encircling limit of the activity of the coming Consciousness. It is an ovoid or sphere, and very small as yet. This process of forming the egoic lotus has gone on silently from the moment that the lower animal man, or the lower four principles, had reached a point where the energy (generated by him) could begin to make itself felt on mental levels. When the fire of the lower prepared sheaths (the threefold fire of substance itself) becomes radioactive, this nebulous appearance on the third subplane of the mental plane begins to be organised, as the result of the downward pull of the higher by the lower, and as the response of the Spirit aspect to the radiations, or attraction, of matter. But individualisation as we understand it is not yet effected. This process of radioactivity on the part of the lower, and of a downflow of energy from the higher, covers a long period wherein the solar Angels are working on Their Own plane and the lower Pitris are also working on theirs; one group is producing the nucleus of the egoic body, and the other the receptacle for the life of God, or the Monad in the three worlds.

Then comes a set time in the life of the planetary Logos wherein His centres become active in a particular manner; this is coincident with the incarnation of the Monads, and their descent into the three worlds. A systemic triangle is formed (for ever the three produce the seven), and through this setting loose of threefold energy, the work of the solar and lunar Pitris is co-ordinated, and the three permanent atoms are appropriated by the jiva concerned, and appear at the base of the egoic lotus. Individualisation has taken place and the work of at-one-ment is completed; the fourth kingdom

in nature is a "fait accompli;" the Monad has clothed
itself in material sheaths, and the self conscious unit
appears on the physical plane. If all that H. P. B. has
to say anent the first three rounds of our Earth scheme
is read as dealing with the period of condensation of
the causal body upon the mental level, and as covering
the time leading up to the appearance in the fourth round
of man as we now have him, some light may be thrown
upon this difficult matter.

The egoic lotuses can be seen grouped together, and
each of them forms part of a group. These groups in
their turn form part of a vaster lotus which embodies
the consciousness of a still greater Entity whose "jewel"
may be found on the second subplane. All these in their
turn may be divided into seven fundamental groups.
These seven groups or aggregates of egoic lotuses form
the seven types of consciousness of those Entities Who
are the seven centres of force for our own planetary
Logos. These seven in their turn will be synthesised on
higher levels into the three higher centres, till the entire
energy and force which they represent is gathered up,
and absorbed by the centre corresponding to the highest
head centre of the planetary Logos. Each Logos embodies one type of cosmic energy. Each of His centres
embodies this type of energy in one of its seven differentiations. Each of these seven in turn manifests
through egoic groups, and these again are composed of
those points of energy we call Egos.

These multitudes of egoic groups form a radiant interlocking whole, though all are diverse and differing,
both as to their point of development, and their secondary colouring. Just as the petals in the egoic lotus of
the incarnating jivas unfold in differing order and at
different periods, so the egoic groups also unfold diversely as to time and sequence. This produces a wonderful appearance. Again just as the Master can (by

studying the group or larger lotus of which He is a part),
ascertain the condition of the human units who go to
its constitution, so the planetary Logos can ascertain
through *conscious identification* (note the term) the condition of the various groups through whom His work
must be accomplished.

It will now be apparent to the student that the appearance of the incarnating jivas on the physical plane will
be governed by three things:

> First of all, on impulse based on the will-purpose
> of the Life animating the aggregate of groups on
> any subray, or one of the seven larger groups.
>
> Second, on impulse based on the will, tinged by
> desire, of the Life animating a man's egoic group.
>
> Third, on impulse, based on the desire of the Ego
> for physical plane manifestation.

As identification of a man with his group becomes
matured the desire impulse becomes modified until it is
eventually superseded by group will. If these facts are
pondered upon it will be apparent that Egos come into
incarnation therefore not singly but according to group
urge, and thus collectively. This is the basis of collective karma, and of family karma. The individual urge,
which is, of course, a reaction to group urge, is the result
of personal karma. Hence, though we may by these reflections, have thrown some light upon this question of
reincarnation, we have nevertheless said much to increase
the magnitude of the question, and its complexity. Average man is confined to the use of the physical brain, and
is, therefore, unable to think in group terms.

This egoic impulse in any group or any group unit
makes itself felt as a pulsation, or access of energy, emanating from the central point. This central activity is
produced by the action of the planetary Logos working
through the groups in His centres, and according to the

centre under stimulation so will the groups concerned be
affected. Beyond mentioning this fact, we cannot enlarge, for the subject is stupendous, and beyond a man's
comprehension; it is only necessary for him to appreciate
his dependence in this matter upon the planetary Logos.

From the group centre, therefore, emanates an urge
to renewed activity, and this spreads throughout the
group lotus until the units who respond to that particular
ray vibration occultly "awaken." All this time (as far
as the jivas are concerned) this aspect of force has been
that of the first aspect, and has passed from the central
points to other central points. The positive nuclei in
each case are affected by this flashing forth of electric
fire, or energy. Each point concerned responds by a primary contraction followed by an outgoing or expansive
display of energy. Each Identity concerned proceeds to
sound a WORD. This sound expands into a mantram and
the solar angels vibrate in response. There is a point
of interest to be noted here.

a. The first aspect works through a Word of Power.
b. The second aspect works through mantric combinations.
c. The third aspect works through mathematical formulas.

Having sounded the Word the first aspect, represented
by the electric fire at the centre of the lotus, sinks back
into quiescence, and becomes an abstraction as far as the
self-conscious unit is·concerned. The work has been begun, the necessary vibration has been set up, and the
whole process then proceeds under law. The solar angels
have begun their activity, and until their work has
reached a very high stage, the Spirit aspect must become,
in the causal body, an analogy to the Silent Watcher.
As the solar Angels continue sounding out the mantram
which is the basis of their work, the lunar Pitris respond

to certain sounds in that mantram (not to all by any means at first) and gather out of those sounds the formula under which their work must proceed. So the Word is the basis of the mantram, and the mantram is the basis of the formula.

At each incarnation, finer forms are required, and the formulas therefore grow more complicated, and the sounds on which they are based become more numerous. In time, the formulas are completed, and the lunar Pitris respond no more to the sounds or mantrams chanted on the mental plane. This is indicative of the stage of perfection, and shows that the three worlds have no more a downward pull for the jiva concerned. Desire for lower manifestation and experience has no more sway, and only conscious purpose is left. Then, and only then, can the true Mayavirupa be constructed; the Master then sounds the mantram for Himself, and builds *without formulas* in the three worlds. At the time too that man begins to tread the Probationary Path, the mantrams of the solar Angels begin to die down, and slowly (as the petals of the inner circle open up) the true Word emerges until the three enshrining petals burst open, and the central spark is revealed. Then the Word is fully known, and mantrams and formulas have no further use. Thus is the beauty of the scheme revealed. When the planetary Logos is concerned, the Word sounded on cosmic levels is being resolved into mantrams on the cosmic etheric planes, for He is in a position to create consciously on those levels; He works nevertheless through formulas on the dense physical planes of His scheme, our three worlds of endeavour.

To return to the reincarnating jivas: When the initiatory impulse has been given, the vibration thrills through the petals, and activity starts in those of them which respond to the note of that Word. The solar Angels direct the vibration, and the mantram for that particular

type of Ego is begun. Finally the vibration reaches the
mental unit at the base of the lotus bud, and the lunar
Pitris are called into activity. They begin to work out
their formulas for the particular type of vehicle which is
required.

(f.) Activity of the Pitris. The joint activity of the
solar and the lunar Pitris [53] in the process pursued by the
reincarnating Ego is our next subject of consideration
The Ego, driven by desire for physical experience, has
made the initial move and a vibration, emanating from
the centre of the lotus bud, has reached the lotus petals,
and has consequently vibrated in deva substance, or in

---

[53] The joint activity of solar and lunar Pitris.—S. D., II, 258.
 1. ''The spark hangs from the flame by the finest thread of Fohat.
   a. The three-tongued flame that never dies........**Triad.**
   b. The four wicks.............................Quaternary.
   c. The thread of Fohat........................Thread of Life.
 2. It journeys through the seven worlds of maya.
   Macrocosmically...................the seven planetary schemes.
   Planetary ....the seven chains of a scheme.
   Microcosmically..................the seven globes of a chain.
Note and meditate upon:—
''. . . the divine Septenary hanging from the triad, thus forming the
Dead and its permutations. Seven, five and three.''
 3. It stops in the first, and is a metal and a stone; it passes into the
second and behold—a plant; the plant whirls through seven forms and
becomes a sacred animal.''
Compare S. D., I, 266.
Note the kabalistic aphorism:—''A stone becomes a plant; a plant, a
beast; a beast, a man; a man, a spirit; and the spirit, God.—S. D., I, 267.
 4. From the combined attributes of these, Manu, the Thinker, is formed.
   —See S. D., II, 179, 187.
 5. Who forms him? The seven lives and the One Life.—See S. D., II,
   268.
   The seven groups of lives who form the three lower bodies. The
   lunar Pitris or fathers of the material forms.
 6. Who completes him? The fivefold Lha.
   Who unites the higher Spiritual Triad and the lower self?
   a. The fivefold Gods of the intelligence.
   b. The fifth principle of mind.
 7. Who perfects the last body? Fish, sin, and soma.
   a. Fish, sin and soma collectively compose the three symbols of the
     immortal being.
   b. Fish—symbol of the buddhic principle, the manifested life on
     earth. Note the avatara of Vishnu. The sign of Pisces, the
     fish. Jesus the fisher of men.
   c. Sin—The fall of man, involution of Spirit.
   d. Soma—Moon. The work of lunar Pitris, providing bodies.
Read stanza VII, 6, S. D., I, 285.

matter vitalised by the Agnishvattas. As they are galvanised into activity (according to the group affected) the vibration is increased, and a dual sound is emitted. This dual sound is the basis of the mantram upon which the Ego's cycle of incarnation is founded. The vibration, pulsating through the outer circle of petals (for the two inner circles and the three central petals are not as yet responsive) arrives at the triangle formed by the three permanent atoms, and vivifies the three lower spirillae, causing a slight response in the fourth, and leaving the higher three yet dormant. In each round one of the spirillae has been 'created,' and in this fourth round (through the creation of the fourth spirilla) the fourth or human kingdom can come into being. The word 'creation' must be occultly understood, and means the appearance in active manifestation of some form of energy. Only in the next round will the fifth spirilla be an active functioning unit in a sense incomprehensible now.

Students should bear in mind that this applies primarily to the humanity individualised on this globe, and was also equally true in the earlier chain; units, however, which come into this fourth or Earth Chain from the earlier one, are much ahead of earth's humanity, and their fifth spirilla is awakening into organised activity in this round. All in Nature overlaps.

When therefore this vibration from the central Will has arrived at the atomic triangle it is an indication that the entire lotus is turning its force *downwards,* and for the period of manifestation the flow of egoic energy is towards the lower, and consequently away from the higher. There is at this stage very little turning of egoic energy in the direction of the Monad, for it has not yet generated enough force, and is not as yet radioactive towards the Spirit aspect. Its activities are primarily internal and self-centred for the greater part of the time, or are directed towards arousing the permanent atoms, and not towards the unfolding of the petals. This should be carefully borne in mind.

The work of the solar Angels is of a triple nature:

(1.) *Directing the vibration towards the atomic triangle.* Here a very interesting fact must be borne in mind. The three permanent atoms, or the three points of the triangle, do not always hold the same relative position as regards the centre of the lotus, but according to the stage of development so will be the position of the atoms, and so will be the apprehension of the inflowing force. In the earlier stages, the physical permanent atom is the first to receive the inflow, passing it through its system to the astral permanent atom and the mental unit. This force is circulated four times around the triangle (this being the fourth round) until the mental unit is again contacted and the energy becomes centralised in the fourth spirilla of the mental unit. Then and only then do the lunar Pitris begin their work, and commence the co-ordination of the substance which will form the mental sheath, next working with the astral body and finally with the etheric body.

At a later stage in the evolution of man (the stage wherein the average man is now) the astral permanent atom is the first contacted, and the energy circulates through it to the other two. At the stage of advanced intellectual man, the mental unit takes the primary place. In this case there is now the possibility of the alignment of the three bodies which will later be an accomplished fact. The fifth spirilla in the lower two atoms increases its vibration. As we know, there are only four spirillae in the mental unit and the moment that that is in full activity, the co-ordination of the antaskarana becomes a possibility. Changes are now taking place in the egoic lotus, and the petals are unfolding, that unfoldment being partially dependent upon the vibration in the spirillae and their awakening.

The student should bear in mind the fact that as soon as the mental unit has become the apex of the atomic triangle a condition is brought about wherein force in the future will enter the three atoms simultaneously through the three unfolded petals of the outer circle, and the man has therefore reached a very definite stage in evolution. The direction of force, and its application to the atoms is the work of the solar Pitris. As evolution proceeds, their work in this connection becomes more complex, for the petals are unfolding, and the triangle is revolving more rapidly.

(2.) *Pronouncing the mantram which will make possible the 777 incarnations.*

Each of the figures in this triplicity stands for:

    a. A cycle of egoic manifestation.
    b. A particular sound which will enable the Ego to express some subray of this egoic ray.
    c. The three circles of petals which will unfold as the result of incarnation.
    d. The particular group of manasadevas who form the causal body of the Ego concerned.

The mantric sounds are therefore based on these figures, and through the mantram (which grows in volume, depth and number of sounds involved as time elapses) the force is directed, the petals concerned are stimulated into activity, and the lunar Pitris become aware of the work to be done in preparation for any incarnation.

(3.) *Building into the causal body that which is required for its completion.*

In the early stages this work is comparatively small but as the third stage of development is reached, and the man is demonstrating character and ability, their work is rapidly increased, and they are kept fully occupied in the work of perfecting the egoic body, in expanding the egoic consciousness, if metaphysical terms are preferred. All this is accomplished by means of the material furnished by the lower self. When that lower Personality becomes gradually radioactive, these radiations are attracted to the positive ego, and are absorbed into its nature through the activity of the solar Angels.

These three activities are the main work of the solar Pitris where man is concerned. Where the group, and not the individual, is concerned, their work lies along the line of adjusting the egoic units in their groups, and of making them group conscious, but this is only possible towards the final stages of evolution when the work of the highest group of Agnishvattas is in order. The middle group who form the nine petals are always the most active. They work in connection with the lower group who are the direct transmitters of energy to the atomic triangle, receiving it from the middle group. More of their work it is not possible to detail, for the work of the Agnishvattas is vast and intricate, and differs also in the various schemes in certain particulars. Those who are working in the Uranus, the Neptune, and the Saturn scheme work somewhat differently to those functioning in the Venus, the Vulcan, the Mars, the Mercury, the Jupiter, the Earth and the exoteric Saturn scheme, and so do the Manasadevas of the inner round. We should note here that we again have a triplicity of groups, representing a triplicity of force, and herein lies a hint. In the central list of schemes the middle and lower group of Agnishvattas are active. In the others the higher group and middle group hold sway as these planets are the most occult and sacred in manifestation, and are concerned only with egos who are on the Path, and who are therefore group-active. In connection with Uranus, Neptune and Saturn, this might be expected as they are the synthesising planetary schemes, and provide conditions suitable only for the very advanced stages. They are the "reaping" planets.

Much confusion in connection with Egos exists in the minds of our students on account of their failure to realise that (as H. P. B. has pointed out)[54] the *Secret Doctrine* is primarily concerned with the planetary scheme of our Earth, and has little to impart anent the other schemes, and their methods of evolving self-consciousness. The general procedure on the mental levels is the same, but as each scheme embodies one particular type of force, the peculiarity of that force will colour all its evolution, and the work of the Agnishvattas will correspond. It is not possible to state what is the peculiar colouring of the Ray which is embodied in our scheme, as it is one of the most secret of the mysteries revealed at initiation, but students must bear in mind that in the fundamentals laid down here we are not dealing specifically with our scheme.

A great deal has been said in modern occult literature anent the process followed in the perfecting of those Egos who choose to remain with the Hierarchy of our planet, and their methods of development (through chelaship to adeptship). But nothing practically has been imparted anent the many egos who reach a certain high stage of evolution in our scheme and who are then transferred to one of the three synthesising schemes, passing first to the scheme which is the polar opposite to ours, and from thence to the synthesising scheme. *They are numerically more than those who remain within the Earth scheme.* Whichever may be the synthesising scheme to which they are attracted, it marks and indicates their start upon one of the three cosmic paths. The work of the Manasadevas is carried on throughout the entire system, and a constant circulation transpires, and a constant transmission of energy, and of force units embodying that energy, goes on throughout the entire system. This transmission becomes possible in any scheme when the

[54] S. D., I, 41, 83.

fourth or human kingdom becomes radioactive; it really marks the setting in of the period of obscuration. Venus is a case in point. Metaphysically stated, it marks the point when the Logoi begin to dissociate Themselves from Their dense physical bodies, or from the three worlds of human endeavour.

The three groups of Agnishvattas concerned with the evolution of man on the mental level have each a specific function, as we have already seen, and the lowest of the three deal primarily with the transmission of force or energy to the three permanent atoms. In the dual sounding of the egoic mantram by the lowest of the three groups changes are brought about and the lunar Pitris (who concern themselves with the lower three vehicles) enter upon their work, the key being given to them by the solar Angels.

These lunar Pitris embody the substance of man's lower bodies, just as the solar Pitris sacrifice themselves to give him his egoic body, and his consciousness.[55, 56] They are substance in its dual aspect, and the Lunar Pitris in their higher grades are the positive energy of atomic substance, and in their lower are the negative

[55] The Ego is described thus in the *Secret Doctrine*: Each is a pillar of Light. Having chosen its vehicle, it expanded, surrounding with an akashic aura the human animal, with the Divine Principle settled within the human form.''—S. D., III, 494.

They are the Fire Dhyanis, and emanate from the Heart of the Sun.''—S. D., II, 96.

Read the words of the Commentary on S. D., II, 96.

They are the Sons of Fire and fashion inner man.—S. D., II, 114.

[56] The solar Angels (Sons of Wisdom) are entities seeking fuller consciousness.—S. D., II, 176, 177; II, 643.

    a. They had intellect through previous contact with matter.

    b. They were incarnated under the law of Karma.—S. D., III, 517.

    c. They had to become all wise.

    Read carefully S. D., II, 243 note.

    d. These solar Angels are high intelligences.—S. D., II, 259.

    e. They are Nirmanakayas.[57]—S. D., II, 266.

    f. They are the celestial yogis.—S. D., II, 257.

[57] ''Nirmanakaya'' is a name made up of two words which signify ''having no body,'' and has no reference whatever to moral qualities. It is a state of consciousness. The great Teachers of Nirvanic spheres are called by this name.

aspect of the same substance. They might be considered, *in connection with man,* as triple in their ranks:

a. The highest group of all receives the energy from the higher levels, and ensouls the spirillae of the three permanent atoms.

b. The second group, being the positive energy that attracts, builds and forms the body of man on the three planes.

c. The lowest group are the negative aspect of energised substance and the matter of the three sheaths.

In connection with the solar system they embody the Brahma aspect, being the product of earlier cycles wherein conscious activity was achieved, but self-consciousness was only arrived at by certain cosmic entities who passed through conscious substance, and gave to it that potentiality which will enable atomic substance—after many kalpas—to develop self-consciousness. In connection with a planet, they are called by a mysterious name which may not be revealed, as it conceals the mystery of the scheme which preceded ours, and of which ours is a reproduction. There are Pitris who work in connection with a planet, and with a solar system as well as those working in connection with the human kingdom. They embody the energy of substance as demonstrated in a system, a scheme and a human cycle.

There are also in connection with our peculiar Earth scheme, those lunar Pitris who reached their present stage of activity in the moon chain. They are deva groups but (unlike the Agnishvattas) they have not passed through the human stage; for them it has yet to be achieved, and their present experience in connection with the human Hierarchy has that end in view. It should be remembered that it is a fundamental law in occult development that any life can only give out that which it has possessed, and possession of the varying attributes of consciousness from that of the atom up to the consciousness of a solar Logos, is the result of long cycles of acquirement. The solar Pitris, therefore, could give to man his consciousness; the lunar Pitris could give to him the instinctual consciousness of his vehicles. In their aggregate in all the kingdoms of nature, on this planet and elsewhere, they give to the planetary Logos and to the solar Logos the sumtotal of the *form consciousness* of Their respective bodies. This is the case in every scheme in the system, but in the Earth chain a peculiar condition of affairs was brought about through the planetary failure coincident with the moon chain; this is the cause of the present balancing of forces on this chain. The fourth chain in every scheme sees the work of the solar Pitris in connection with man begun. It sees also the Pitris of his sheaths in activity through the impulse given by the solar Angels. The matter of those sheaths has passed through three chains and three rounds and is vibrant to a note which is tuned to the. . . . To word it otherwise, the third can be clearly sounded, and is followed naturally by the fifth, or the dominant. The simultaneous sounding of the third and the fifth, basing it upon the planetary keynote, produces the effect of a threefold chord, or a fourth tone, a complex sound. I am here dealing with the chord of the human hierarchy as a whole. Within the hierarchy there is again diversity, based upon the hierarchical chord, and this produces the many egoic chords and notes; these produce in their turn objective manifestation.

We can now trace the progress of egoic energy as it passes down from the abstract levels to the permanent atoms. On each plane the work is threefold, and might be tabulated as follows:

1. The response within the permanent atom to the vibration set up by the solar Pitris; to word it other-

wise: the response of the highest group of lunar Pitris
to the chord of the Ego. This definitely affects the spirillae of the atom, according to the stage of evolution of the
Ego concerned.

2. The response of the substance to the atomic vibration upon the particular plane involved. This concerns
the second group of Pitris, whose function it is to gather
together the substance attuned to any particular key, and
to aggregate it around the permanent atom. They work
under the Law of Magnetic Attraction, and are the attractive energy of the permanent atom. On a tiny scale each
permanent atom has (to the substance of a man's
sheaths) a position relative to that which the physical
sun holds to the substance of the system. It is the
nucleus of attractive force.

3. The response of the negative substance concerned
and its moulding into the desired form through the dual
energy of the two higher groups of Pitris. Some thought
of the unity of this threefold work has been given in the
differentiation of the substance of any plane into:

a. Atomic substance.
b. Molecular substance.
c. Elemental essence.

This differentiation is not entirely accurate, and a
truer idea of the underlying concept might be conveyed
if the word "energy" took the place of "substance and
essence." This third group of Pitris is really not correctly termed Pitris at all. The true lunar Pitris are
those of the first and highest group, for they embody one
aspect of the intelligent will of Brahma, or of God-in-
substance. The third group are literally the lesser Builders, and are blind incoherent forces, subject to the energy
emanating from the two higher groups. Occultly these
three groups are divided into the following:

a. The Pitris who see, but touch nor handle not.

b. The Pitris who touch but see not.

c. The Pitris who hear but neither see nor touch.

As they all have the gift of occult hearing, they are char-acterised as the "Pitris with the open ear"; they work entirely under the influence of the egoic mantram.   If these differentiations are studied a great deal may be-come apparent anent a very important group of deva workers.   They are a group who only come into mani-festation as a *co-ordinated triplicity* in the fourth round in order to provide vehicles for man; the reason for this lies hid in the karma of the seven Logoi, as They ener-gise the fourth, fifth and sixth Hierarchies.   In the earlier round in each scheme these three groups attain a certain stage of necessitated growth, and embody the highest evolution of the substance aspect.   Only the high-est and most perfected of the atoms of substance find their way into the vehicles of man,—those which have been the integral parts of the higher evolutionary forms.

(g.) The Work of Form-building. This work of form-building proceeds under definite laws, which are the laws of substance itself; the effect is the same for human, planetary and solar vehicles.   The different stages might be enumerated as follows:

1. *The Nebulous.* The stage wherein the matter of the coming sheath begins to separate itself gradually from the aggregate of plane substance, and to assume a nebulous or milky aspect. This corresponds to the "fire-mist" stage in the formation of a solar system and of a planet. The *Pitris of the Mist* are then active as one of the many subsidiary groups of the three major groups.

2. *The Inchoate.* Condensation has set in but all is as yet inchoate, and the condition is chaotic; there is no definite form. *"The Pitris of the Chaos"* hold sway, and are characterised by excessive energy, and violent activ-ity, for the greater the condensation prior to co-ordina-

tion the more terrific are the effects of activity. This is true of Gods, of men, and of atoms.

3. *The Fiery.* The internal energy of the rapidly congregating atoms and their effect upon each other produces an increase of heat, and a consequent demonstration of the spheroidal form, so that the vehicle of all entities is seen to be fundamentally a sphere, rolling upon itself and attracting and repulsing other spheres. *"Pitris of the Fiery Spheres"* add their labours to those of the earlier two and a very definite stage is reached. The lunar Pitris on every scheme, and throughout the system, are literally the active agents in the building of the dense physical body of the Logos; they energise the substance of the three planes in the three worlds, the mental, the astral and the dense physical planes of the system. This needs much pondering upon.

4. *The Watery.* The ball or sphere of gaseous fiery essence becomes still more condensed and liquefied; it begins to solidify on its outer surface and the ring-pass-not of each sheath is more clearly defined. The heat of the sphere becomes increased and is centralised at the core or heart of the sphere where it produces that pulsation at the centre which characterises the sun, the planet, and the various vehicles of all incarnating entities. It is an analogous stage to that of the awakening of life in the foetus during the prenatal stage, and this analogy can be seen working out in the form-building which proceeds on every plane. This stage marks the co-ordination of the work of the two higher groups of lunar Pitris, and the *"Pitris of the Dual Heat"* are now intelligently co-operating. The heart and brain of the substance of the slowly evolving form are linked. The student will find it interesting to trace the analogy of this, the watery stage, to the place the astral plane holds in the planetary and systemic body, and the alliance between mind and heart which is hidden in the term "kama-manas." One

of the profoundest occult mysteries will be revealed to the consciousness of man when he has solved the secret of the building of his astral vehicle, and the forming of the link which exists between that sheath and the astral light in its totality on the astral plane.

5. *The Etheric.* The stage is not to be confined to the building of the physical body in its etheric division, for its counterpart is found on all the planes with which man is concerned in the three worlds. The condensation and the solidification of the material has proceeded till now the three groups of Pitris form a unity in work. The rhythm set up has been established and the work synchronised. The lesser builders work systematically and the law of Karma is demonstrating actively, for it should be remembered that it is the inherent karma, colouring, or vibratory response of the substance itself which is the selective reaction to the egoic note. Only that substance which has (through past utilisation) been keyed to a certain note and vibration will respond to the mantram and to the subsequent vibrations issuing from the permanent atom. This stage is one of great importance, for it marks the vital circulation throughout the entire vehicle of a particular type of force. This can be clearly seen in relation to the etheric body which circulates the vital force or prana of the sun. A similar linking up with the force concerned is to be seen on the astral and the mental planes. *"The Pitris of the Triple Heat"* are now working synthetically, and the brain, the heart and the lower centres are co-ordinated. The lower and the higher are linked, and the channels are unimpeded so that the circulation of the triple energy is possible. This is true of the form building of all entities, macrocosmic and microcosmic. It is marked by the active co-operation of another group of Pitris, termed *"The Pitris of Vitality"* in connection with the others. Group after group co-

operate, for the three main bodies are distributed among many lesser.

6. *The Solid.* This marks the final stage in actual form building, and signifies the moment wherein the work is done as regards the aggregating and shaping of substance. The greater part of the work of the lunar Pitris stands now accomplished. The word "solid" refers not solely to the lowest objective manifestation, for a solid form may be ethereal, and only the stage of evolution of the entity involved will reveal its relative significance.

All that has been here laid down as to the progressive stages of form construction on every plane is true of all forms in all systems and schemes, and is true of all thought-form building. Man is constructing thought-forms all the time, and is following unconsciously the same method as his Ego pursues in building his bodies, as the Logos follows in building His system, and as a planetary Logos uses in constructing His scheme.

A man speaks, and a very diversified mantram is the result. The energy thus generated swings into activity a multitude of little lives which proceed to build a form for his thought; they pursue analogous stages to those just outlined. At this time, man sets up these mantric vibrations unconsciously, and in ignorance of the laws of sound and of their effect. The occult work that he is carrying on is thus unknown to him. Later he will speak less, know more, and construct more accurate forms, which will produce powerful effects on physical levels. Thus eventually in distant cycles will the world be "saved," and not just a unit here and there.

In connection with this building of man's sheaths certain interesting points of manifestation occur which might be dealt with now, leaving the student to work out the correspondences in relation to the system and the planet, and giving only general indications which may be of use to him in his conclusions.

In all the work of form-building, certain very vital occasions occur which concern the Ego even more than the sheaths themselves, though the reflex action between the lower personal self and the higher is so close as to be well nigh inseparable.

The moment wherein the Ego appropriates the sheath. This takes place only after the fourth spirilla is beginning to vibrate, and the period differs according to the power of the ego over the lower self. In connection with the dense physical vehicle, an analogy can be seen when the Ego ceases from his work of overshadowing, and at some period between the fourth and seventh year makes his contact with the physical brain of the child. A similar occurrence takes place in connection with the etheric vehicle, the astral, and the mental.

The moment wherein the energy of the Ego is transmitted from one sheath to a lower one. It is often overlooked that the path of incarnation is not a quick one, but that the Ego descends very slowly and takes possession gradually of his vehicles; the less evolved the man, the slower is the process. We are dealing here with the period of time which transpires after the Ego has made the first move towards descent, and not with the time which elapses between two incarnations. This work of passing on to a plane for purposes of incarnation marks a definite crisis, and is characterised by the exertion of the will in sacrifice, the appropriation of the substance in love, and its energising into activity.

The moment wherein the particular type of force with which any particular sheath is energised is appropriated. This brings the sheath concerned:

- *a.* Under the influence of the egoic ray,
- *b.* Under the influence of a particular subray of the egoic ray,
- *c.* And through that influence,—

Under certain astrological influences,
Under certain planetary radiations,
Under the influences of certain force currents,
emanating from certain constellations.

These three events have a very interesting analogy in
connection with the work of the Logos in the construction
of His physical body, the solar system, and also in certain correspondences which can be seen embodied in facts
dealt with at the first three Initiations.

From the standpoint of the lower self, the two most
vital moments in the work of the reincarnating Ego, are
those in which the mental unit is re-energised into cyclic
activity, and in which the etheric body is vitalised. It
concerns that which links the centre at the base of the
spine with a certain point within the physical brain via
the spleen. This is dealing purely with the physiological
key.

We might now touch upon a very interesting point
concerning the dense physical body, dealing therefore
with that which is not considered a principle either in the
macrocosm or the microcosm. As we know, man is essentially mental man, and astral man; then the two take to
themselves an etheric sheath for purposes of objective
work. That is *the true lower man, these two in the
etheric body.* But later—in order to know even on the
lowest plane of all—man takes to himself a coat of skin,
as the Bible expresses it, and puts on (over his etheric
body) that outer illusory form we know so well. It is
his lowest point of objectivity and his direct "imprison-
ing." This appropriation of a dense sheath by the Ego
is subject to a very peculiar piece of karma connected
with the four Kumaras, or Heavenly Men, Who form the
logoic Quaternary. In the schemes which concern the
logoic Triad (or those of the three major Rays or Heavenly Men) dense physical incarnation is not the appointed

lot, and man functions in his lowest manifestation in etheric matter.

This appropriation of the lowest body is distinguished in several ways from the approach to the other sheaths. For one thing, there is no permanent atom to be vitalised. The physical plane is a complete reflection of the mental; the lowest three subplanes reflect the abstract subplanes and the four etheric subplanes reflect the four mental concrete planes. The manifestation of the Ego on the mental plane (or the causal body) is not the result of energy emanating from the permanent atoms as a nucleus of force but is the result of different forces, and primarily of group force. It is predominantly marked by an act of an exterior force, and is lost in the mysteries of planetary karma. This is equally true of man's lowest manifestations. It is the result of reflex action, and is based on the force of the group of etheric centres through which man (as an aggregate of lives) is functioning. The activity of these centres sets up an answering vibration in the three lowest subplanes of the physical plane, and the interaction between the two causes an adherence to, or aggregation around, the etheric body of particles of what we erroneously term "dense substance." This type of energised substance is swept up in the vortex of force currents issuing from the centres and cannot escape. These units of force, therefore, pile up according to the energy direction around and within the etheric sheath till it is hidden and concealed, yet interpenetrating. An inexorable law, the law of matter itself, brings this about, and only those can escape the effect of the vitality of their own centres who are definitely "Lords of Yoga" and can—through the conscious will of their own being—escape the compelling force of the Law of Attraction working on the lowest cosmic physical subplane.

An interesting analogy (accurate on general lines

though in detail not so apparent) exists between the building of the antaskarana on mental levels between the mental unit and the manasic permanent atom (whereby the Path of Liberation is travelled, and man set free) and the opening up of the channel between the centre at the base of the spine and the brain and thence to the head centre. Through this latter channel man escapes out of the dense physical body, and continuity of consciousness (between the astral and the physical planes) is reached. In the one case, through right direction of force, the etheric web no longer forms a barrier; it is destroyed and the man is fully conscious *in the physical brain* of what transpires on the astral plane. In the other case, the causal body also is eventually destroyed through the right direction of force. We will not here take up the specific work of building upon the scaffolding of the etheric body the dense physical form. It has been sufficiently dealt with in other books. We will only want to touch upon two more points which are of interest in this consideration of the work of the lunar Pitris in building man's body.

In connection with the building of the dense body, it should be stated that it appears as a human form, much in the nature of a cross within the ovoid of the other spheres. It is notably of a fivefold nature:

> Head.
> Two Arms.
> Two Legs.

According to the position assumed by the man, he is seen as a symbol of the cross and is then fourfold (the two legs being considered as one lower limb) or, if separated, as fivefold, and has been then considered as the symbol of the five-pointed star. This fivefold nature of the dense physical body is brought about through the fact that only five centres primarily are really active in average man

up to the third Initiation; all are there, and all are vitalised, but only five in this fivefold normal evolution are
dominant. The force emanating from these five, therefore, sweeps the dense substance into a close aggregation. As two of the centres are not functioning as
actively as the other five, an ovoid is not formed as in the
case of the etheric, astral and mental sheaths. The fivefold shape of physical man is the result of the fivefold
direction of force currents from five centres.

It might be interesting also to point out that the interaction of the energy of the solar Pitris and of the lunar
Pitris produces a very definite effect upon the lower
group of lunar Pitris, and is one of the means whereby
they will eventually reach the stage at which the solar
Pitris are. This (if fully realised by man) will bring
him to a very careful control of his sheaths, and to a
close attention to the direction in which his force or
energy is turned. He is responsible for the work of aiding in the evolution of substance, being himself a manasaputra.

(h.) Incarnation and Karma. In resuming our consideration of the process pursued by the reincarnating
Ego, it is necessary to point out that the entire subject
radically concerns *energy,* and that according to the place
in evolution of the unit of force involved, so will the
length of time required for the process be brief, or the
reverse. In the early stages, the initiatory impulse is
heavy and slow, and the matter required for the sheaths
is of a correspondingly ''low'' grade, that is, it is of low
vibratory capacity, and the time elapsing between the
first vibration outwards on the mental plane, and the co-
ordination of the dense physical body is a long one.
Later on, the vibration becomes more powerful and the
effects therefore are more rapidly felt. At the close of
evolution, when the human unit is upon the Path and
consciously controlling his destiny, and working off

karma, the intervals intervening between two incarnations are brief or not as the man may choose in the interests of the work to be done, and according to his intention to achieve liberation from form. It must also be remembered that as the evolutionary process proceeds, the egoic activity calls out response not only from substance in the three worlds, but also from the formless levels of the system. The response will be felt finally on monadic levels. Then, after a moment of equilibrium, the effect of the rhythm is felt entirely on the higher planes, and leaves the lower.

The word "moment" is used here in its occult significance to specify a period of time, and must be considered as a period relative to a day or year of Brahma. One of the secrets of initiation is concerned with the apprehension of cycles, and with their duration, and the following terms have to be appreciated, their duration recognised, and their antithesis (an intervening pralaya) duly considered before a man is considered a true occultist.

a. 100 years of Brahma . . . . An occult century. The period of a solar system.

b. One year of Brahma . . . . The period of seven chains, where the seven planetary schemes are concerned.

c. One week of Brahma . . . . The period of seven rounds in one scheme. It has a chain significance.

d. One day of Brahma . . . . The occult period of a round.

e. One hour of Brahma . . . . Concerns interchain affairs.

f. One Brahmic minute . . . . Concerns the planetary centres, and therefore egoic groups.

g. One Brahmic moment . . . . . . Concerns an egoic group, and its relation to the whole.

These are the greater periods of time, and when their significance is comprehended, much that is now obscure will be revealed. As yet, it is only to initiates that the true figures are given, the figures in the *Secret Doctrine,* such as the 100 years of Brahma, strike *the general average* but it must be ever remembered that in considering the figures where a scheme, for instance, is concerned, much latitude has to be allowed for individual planetary karma, and idiosyncrasy.

The following points are worthy of consideration when upon this subject, and deal with some interesting factors.

All the planetary Rishis are not equally "long-lived," in the occult sense of the term, and the seven planetary Logoi of the seven sacred planets are at different stages of evolution; Their vibratory response, therefore, differs, producing varying effects in time.

The three major planetary schemes (Uranus, Neptune, and Saturn) have not, as yet, received their fullest stimulation, and will not do so until the "energy of the sacred seven" has been transferred to Them. Figures, therefore, as regards their duration and persistence are not in order.

The figures for the planets concerned with the "inner round" differ as to *length of time* but not as to space location from those of other planets.

The true figures in connection with any planetary scheme and its occult activity are not ascertainable by the man who cannot be trusted with the significance of the other planetary bodies (of great number) within the solar ring-pass-not. The entire solar sphere is full of such bodies, characterised by the same features as are the seven and the ten, and each of them in some degree has an effect upon the whole. Figures, therefore, cannot be considered as final until the effect of the lesser planetary bodies upon their immediate neighbours is known, and the extent of their planetary radiation has been gauged. There are more than 115 of such bodies to be reckoned with, and all are at varying stages of vibratory impulse. They have definite orbits, they turn upon their axis, they draw their "life" and substance from the sun, but owing to their relative insignificance, they have not yet been considered factors of moment. This attitude of mind will change when etheric vision is a fact, and the reality of the existence of an etheric double of all that is in manifestation will be recognised by scientists. This fact will be demonstrated towards the close of the century, and, during the early part of the next century a revolution in astronomical circles will occur which will result in the study of the "etheric planets." As these bodies are organs of energy, permeating the dense form, the study of the interaction of solar energy, and the occult "give and take" of planetary bodies will assume a new significance. Certain planetary bodies (both greater and lesser) are "absorbers," others are "radiators," while some are in the stage of demonstrating a dual activity, and are being "transmuted." All these circumstances require to be considered by the initiate who is dealing with cycles.

Figures also must be computed when the effect upon the planets of what are called "asteroids" is known. This is much greater than exoteric science has so far admitted, but the significance of this must eventually be interpreted in terms of energy and on etheric levels.

Another factor in computation which must also be considered is the effect of the various moons upon any planetary scheme, and the true meaning of the eighth sphere in connection with dense substance. Every moon is occultly a "point of corruption," or that which is passing off in noxious gases. The transmutation of the form has been proceeded with in their case to a point where all that represents *vital* energy has left, all solar life has passed off, no remnants of pranic energy remain, and that which is to be seen is simply the decay of the physical body,— a decay which is proceeding on etheric levels as well as on physical. The decay of a moon has as great an evil effect upon all that contacts it as a decaying body on earth has upon its surroundings. It is occultly "offensive." This will be more truly apprehended when the etheric double of our moon is studied. As the moon becomes small through the process of disintegration, its effect upon the Earth will be correspondingly lessened, and this stage will be paralleled by a consequent greater freedom from evil impulse of the sons of men. Better conditions among the animals will be another result above all else, and the dying out of that which is noxious in the animal kingdom. By the time the seventh round is reached, the evil effect of the then moon (which will have to all intents and purposes practically disappeared) will be finished. During the fifth round, men will discover how to neutralise any remaining effects through scientific achievement and knowledge of the necessary sounds and mantrams, and thus much evil will be offset. The etheric moon is included in these remarks. The greatest effect of moon conditions is to be seen working out predominantly in the terror, and present distress in the animal kingdom.[58]

A further factor in cyclic computation lies in the effect of the following stars and constellations upon our system and upon any particular scheme within the system:

- *a.* The Great Bear.
- *b.* The Little Bear.
- *c.* The Pole Star, especially where our planet is concerned.
- *d.* The Pleiades.
- *e.* The constellation of Capricorn.
- *f.* Draco.
- *g.* Sirius.
- *h.* The various constellations and stars of the Zodiac.

[58] Bible. Romans, 8:22.

The mystery is hidden in esoteric astrology, and until the subject of energy working through the etheric body, of radioactivity, and of the transmutation of all bodies from a lower state into a higher is better comprehended, the true mystery of the "influence" of these various bodies upon each other will remain at its present stage—an unrevealed secret. If the radiatory effect of a human being or of a group of human beings upon each other is as yet practically an unknown thing from the standpoint of practical science, so the occult effect of these greater forms upon each other remains unknown. Science recognises certain effects, leading and tending to the general coherence of the universe, just as the general laws of the social order among men are theoretically apprehended, but the true scientific realisation of energy-radiations emanating from the etheric bodies of all these suns and groups of suns, and from all these planets and groups of planets is little understood. Their atomic activity is recognised, but that department of their being, which finds its correspondence in "animal magnetism" in man, is little realised, while the even more potent factor of the magnetic radiation of their astral bodies is totally uncalculated, nor is it admitted. All these factors have to be allowed for in any consideration of the factor of time and cycles, and the true esoteric knowledge is not to be gained by the study of figures by the lower mind. It comes as the result of the intuition and is stimulated at initiation.

All that has here been pointed out, can be applied equally (though in a very finite sense) to the ego and its cycles, and also equally, considerations other than the purely "personal" will enter into its time periods. The influence of other groups and of other units, the effects of radiation from other rays, and of certain types of force as yet unrevealed, and thus outside our consideration, are concerned with its appearing, with the duration of its manifestation, its subsequent obscuration, and final pralayic interval. As the Ego has time periods corresponding to those of Brahma, and its "100 years" and its "777 incarnations" have a solar analogy, so equally groups of Egos differ as to time, just as the planetary schemes are analogous in evolution but differ where their periods are concerned. The Law of Periodicity is one, but as it is based upon initial impulse, and upon the rhythmic beat of the "central heart" or the "central sun" of any organism (solar system, planetary scheme, planetary chain, egoic group or individual egoic life) the true nature or "family" of any such organism must be ascertained before cyclic pronouncements can be made with any hope of approximate accuracy. This was why H. P. B. sought to emphasise the need of studying the "astral family" and occult heredity of any person, for in the astral is to be found the clue to the "egoic family or group." With this clue the student can then ascertain the characteristics of his group on egoic levels, its place among other egoic groups, and eventually his ray or group centre. As time elapses, the true study of heredity and esoteric transmission will open up, and the whole fabric of thought built up around such modern expressions as:

a. Consanguinity or blood ties
b. Physical heredity
c. Atavism
d. Intermarriage
e. Family relationships
f. The family unit
g. Soul mates
h. Divorce and many other terms

will be shifted to higher planes, and will be recognised and used in connection with soul relationships. They are, as yet, but a faint realisation on the physical plane of certain inner relations, which are seeking outer response. When all aggregates of ideas are interpreted in terms of force and energy, in terms of attraction and repulsion, or the vibratory response of units to each other, and of aggregates of units to other groups, we shall have the clearing up of many problems and a simplification of life. Men will be true to their group affiliations, and the present misgrouping and mismating will gradually, through knowledge, die out.

We can now take up the consideration of karma in its relation to the act of reincarnation. As we are well aware, the law of karma is the most stupendous law of the system and one which it is impossible for the average man in any way to comprehend, for, if traced back along its central root and its many ramifications, one eventually reaches the position where causes antedating the solar system have to be dealt with, and this point of view can only be usefully grasped by a high initiate.

This great law really concerns, or is based on causes which are inherent in the constitution of matter itself and on the interaction between atomic units whether we use this expression in connection with an atom of substance, a human being, a planetary atom or a solar atom.

We might express it also in saying that the will aspect or initiatory impulse is primarily that which produces cause, which is cause itself. It should be remembered ever that *cause* involves the idea of duality, i.e., that which initiates, and that which is produced simultaneously by the initiation. The two ideas are inseparable, yet nevertheless the second idea in its most abstract connota tion must not be considered literally as an *effect;* true effect involves a third idea. Some appreciation of the problem may be gleaned by a consideration of phenomena which ever involves this dual initiatory cause and its objective effect:

a. Spirit-matter in dual activity produces the objective universe.

b. Electric fire and fire by friction when brought into contact produce solar fire; it flashes forth from darkness, yet a darkness which is potent with energy.

c. Will-desire is the cause of incarnation; the will-to-be reacting on substance (whose main quality is desire or responsiveness to sensation) produces the forms through which the central Life or Existence seeks expression.

d. Ideas and thought-matter together produce thought-forms.

If the student considers these points, it will become apparent that it is not possible for him to do more than study the *effects* produced by the juxtaposition of the pairs of opposites; he cannot dissociate them in his mind and deal with Spirit *per se,* or with matter *per se* any more than the atom of substance in man's physical body can dissociate itself from that body, and consider itself independently of form influences. All atoms are always controlled by the following factors, just as a man in the body of a planetary Logos, and a planetary Logos within His greater Whole will be equally controlled by the same basic principles:

The influence and quality of the organ or unit in which it finds a place. In the human atom this means his group force or influence.

The life influence of the entire physical body of which any atom is a corporate part. In the human atom this means the influence of the particular centre in which his egoic group has a place, and the type of energy which it embodies.

The life influence of the desire or astral body, the strongest karmic agency which has to be considered.

In the human atom, this involves the influence of the three centres in the body of the Heavenly Man which form any specific "force triangle," and which have much to do with the liberation of *groups of Egos* from manifestation.

The life influences of the mental body, or of that principle which imposes upon the atom the quality of activity in form, which governs the reaction of the atom to its group life, and which enables the quality of its life to be demonstrated. In the human atom this concerns those causes which are incident to a man's Ray, or literally the influence of the life of the planetary Logos as He functions as a self-conscious Life on His Own plane, as He works out His Own plans, and consequently sweeps into activity the cells of His body as mere incidents where He (the basic central life) is concerned.

The life impulse of the Thinker functioning in the causal body who—though a great abstraction or the Absolute where the cellular life is concerned—is nevertheless a potent and active factor in the imposition of rhythm upon the atom in every body. In the human atom, this brings in the influence of the life of the solar Logos, for that Life imposes rhythm upon every human atom in the system, and does so through the agency of substance and its inherent quality, sensation.

In these thoughts, we have but approached the study of karma from a fresh angle, and endeavoured to show the sources of the "influences" which play upon all atomic lives.

The atom likewise is controlled by its own "esse," or by its own inherent nature or vibration, which was the quality of matter itself before it was aggregated into a solar system, and which was the vibratory activity produced through the rhythmic life of an earlier solar system. This is equally true of all atoms of all grades, but only in connection with the atom of substance, and to some degree with the human atom, is it in any way possible to ascertain the predisposing causes. Until the mystery of the Great Bear is revealed and is known as it is, and until the influence of the Pleiades is comprehended, and the true significance of the cosmic triangle formed by

a. The seven Rishis of the Great Bear,
b. The seven planetary Logoi of our solar system,
c. The seven Pleiades or Sisters,

is revealed, the karma of the seven sacred planets will remain unknown. All that we can see is its working out in the solar system. The intricacy of the whole subject will be apparent when it is borne in mind that not only do these three groups form a cosmic triangle, but that within that triangle many lesser triangles have to be studied. Any one of the seven Rishis with one of our planetary Logoi and one of the seven Sisters may form a subsidiary triangle, and all must thus be studied.

In connection with the karma of the solar Logos, the subject is even more abstract and incomprehensible. It lies hidden—not in the seven constellations—but in the three constellations which concern the three bodies of His Personality and which in themselves are but manifestations of a central LIFE past our concept and our recognition. It concerns the manifestation in time and space of the ONE ABOUT WHOM NAUGHT MAY BE SAID, and Whose relationship to the solar Logos finds a faint analogy in that of the planetary Logos to man, the human unit. It profits not to extend the thought any further.

We are but seeking to emphasise the fact of the interdependence of all atoms and forms, to lay stress upon the reality of the variety of influences which play upon all that is manifesting, and to call attention to the fact of the karma of the past aeons, kalpas and that unknowable period in which the initiatory impulses were set up which are still persisting, and which God, man and atoms are still working out and off. Influences or vibrations, calling forth response, play upon every form and atom in the solar system and all that can be predicated of them is that they tend to develop consciousness of some kind, impose certain rhythms according to that conscious response, and produce aggregations or group activity.

The liberation from karma about which would-be occult students so glibly talk is after all but the freeing of the atom from its own personal problem (the problem of response to unitary sensation), and its conscious acquiescence in group response and work. It marks the dissociation of the human atom from the rhythm imposed upon him by the lower "influences" which find their channel of approach through his vehicles, or lunar bodies, and his consequent willing recognition of the will-impulse of his greater whole, or the life of the egoic group—a centre in the planetary body. It involves atomic control, but involves also conscious subjection to the karma of the Heavenly Man. Man is no longer the slave of the rhythm of matter *per se,* but controls it in the three worlds of his endeavour; he is still nevertheless controlled by the group karma of the planetary centre, by its influence, life and vibratory impulse. The same can be predicated of a Heavenly Man, and of a solar Logos.

We might, in closing, express the same thought in terms of fire, remembering that words only limit and confine the thought, and that the main reason for this mode of approach is to bring pictorially before man some aspects of the central idea.

"Electric fire, or will-impulse" in conjunction with "fire by friction" produces light or "solar fire." Electric fire is force or energy of some kind, and hence in itself is fundamentally an emanation. "Fire by friction" is substance with the quality of heat as its predominant characteristic; it is latent heat or sensation. Both these ideas, therefore, convey the idea of duality. An emanation must have its originating source, and heat is but the result of friction, and is necessarily dual. Both these concepts involve facts long antedating the solar system, and hidden in the Universal Mind. All that we can scientifically ascertain is the nature of that which is produced by their approximation, and this is solar fire or light. These thoughts may make clear somewhat the significance of the number five, esoterically considered. Electric fire, being an emanation is essentially dual in concept, and so is fire by friction; they together produce solar fire, and thus the esoteric fifth.

It will be apparent that when a man speaks of karma, he is dealing with something much wider than the interplay of effect and cause within the sphere of his own individual routine. He is, in all things, governed by causes originating in the aggregate of lives which form his egoic group, by the aggregate of groups which form one petal in a centre of a Heavenly Man, by force or purpose circulating through a triangle of centres, and by the life energy or purposeful will of the planetary Logos Himself. Finally he is governed by the will of the solar Logos as it demonstrates itself in initiatory activity. Beyond this we need hardly go, but enough has been said to show that every human atom is under the dominance of forces outside his own consciousness, which sweep him and others into situations from which there is no escape, and which are to him incomprehensible.

This has been at no time better illustrated than in the event of the late war and in present world conditions; these are effects of causes having their origin in the renewed activity of a certain planetary triangle, and in the vibration set up by our planetary Logos on the moon-chain, and which had a faint beginning in an earlier solar system. This vibration impinged primarily upon certain atoms and groups of atoms in His body, principally those composing the human and animal kingdoms, and produced the apparently dire results which we have been witnessing. So great was the effect of His energy, that the vegetable kingdom was somewhat (though not so much) affected, and the mineral kingdom felt the effect in a startling manner, far more than the vegetable kingdom and almost as much as the animal. Here we have a setting of circumstances outside human and even group control, which illustrates the helplessness of man in certain conditions, and which serves to bring in factors apparently apart from the individual vibration of the fourth kingdom.

Nevertheless, within limits, man definitely does "control his destiny," and can initiate action which produces effects recognisable by him as being dependent upon his activity along a particular line. He does, on a miniature scale, repeat the procedure of the Logos on a vaster scale, and thus is the arbiter of his own destiny, the producer of his own drama, the architect of his own home, and the initiator of his own affairs. Though he may be the meeting place of forces outside his control, yet he can utilize force, circumstance and environment and can turn them, if he so will, to his own ends.

The working out of karmic law in a man's own life might be broadly divided into three divisions, in each of which a different type of energy is demonstrating, producing effects upon the lower and higher bodies of a definite nature.

In the very early stages, when man is scarcely more than an animal, the vibratory activity of the atoms of his three sheaths (and of the lowest primarily) governs all actions on his part. He is the victim of the vibratory activity of physical substance, and much that occurs is the consequence of the interaction between the Ego and its lowest manifestation, the physical sheath. The centre of attention is the physical body and only faintly are the two subtler bodies responding. The egoic impulse is slow and heavy, and the vibration is directed to producing response between the egoic consciousness and the atoms of the physical body. The physical permanent atom is more active than the other two. It is the aspect of "fire by friction" which is fanned by the egoic breath, with a triple object in view:

  a. Co-ordinating the physical body.
  b. Increasing the resistance of the etheric web, a work which was only carried to the desired point by the middle of the Atlantean root-race.
  c. Bringing certain of the lower centres to the necessary stage of expression.

The heat of the atoms in the bodies is increased during this stage, and their atomic life co-ordinated, while the triangle between the three permanent atoms becomes a demonstrable fact and not a faint indication.

During the second stage, the law of karma or karmic influence (through the inevitable reflex action produced by the increased activity of the sheaths) turns its attention to the working out of desire, and its transmutation into the higher aspiration. Through experience, the pairs of opposites are recognised by the Thinker, and he becomes no longer the victim of the vibratory impulses of his physical body; the factor of intelligent choice becomes apparent. The man begins to discriminate between the pairs of opposites, choosing ever in the early stages that which appeals most to his lower nature and that which he believes will bring him pleasure. The centre of the attention of the Ego is the astral body, and it becomes so closely co-ordinated with the physical body that the two form one united expression of desire. The mental body

remains comparatively inactive at this stage. The love
nature of the Ego is in process of being developed, and
this stage is the longest of the three. It deals with the
evolution of the petals of the egoic lotus, and with the
blending of solar fire and of fire by friction. Reflex action between the lower and the higher during this middle
period produces three effects, which will be seen, if carefully studied to convey much information anent the working out of the law of Karma. These three effects are:

1. The development of the astral permanent atom with
   a concurrent stimulation of the physical permanent
   atom, and thus the growth and evolution of the two
   sheaths concerned.
2. The co-ordination of the threefold man through the
   innate vitality of the astral body and its effect upon
   the mental and the physical. This is the kama-
   manasic period, and as this body is the only complete sphere in the threefold lower man, it is the
   most powerful body inherently for it embodies (as
   does the solar system) the heart aspect, or embryonic love nature, which it is the object of macrocosmic and microcosmic evolution to develop.
3. Finally the unfoldment of the nine egoic petals in
   three stages.

In the working out of the law we must therefore note
that man is first of all the victim of the impulses of dense
substance or of the brahma aspect, and thus repeats rapidly the evolutionary process of the preceding solar system; in the second stage he is the victim of desire, or of
his own love nature.

In the third stage, the law of karma works through a
man's mental nature, and awakens in him recognition of
the law, and an intellectual apprehension of cause and
of effect. This is the shortest stage but is also the most
powerful; it concerns the evolution of the three inner

petals shielding the "jewel," and their ability to disclose at the right moment that which lies hidden. It covers the period of the evolution of advanced man, and of the man upon the Path. In connection with the human family it covers the first half of the next round, prior to the great separation. Electric fire is beginning to make its radiations felt, and the will or purpose of the Ego is now consciously realised upon the physical plane. The three permanent atoms form a triangle of light, and the petals of the lotus are rapidly unfolding. When the will and purpose of the Ego are realised by man in his waking consciousness in the physical brain, then the law of karma in the three worlds is becoming neutralised, and man is on the verge of liberation. He has exhausted the initial vibration, and there is no response within his sheaths to the threefold vibration of the three worlds; he stands freed from the three kingdoms and the fourth.

d.   On the building of the Causal Body.

We enter now upon one of the most vitally practical parts of our Treatise on Fire, that which deals with the building of the causal body, or body of manifestation of the Ego. It concerns the work of the solar Angels, or the true self-conscious Identity, man. If the student has in any way apprehended the general trend of the earlier pages, he will now be in a condition of mind which will enable him to interpret all that is said in terms of energy, or of that vibratory activity which is produced by the three major phases of electrical phenomena, the union which produces that divine manifestation called Man, or, when the aggregated units are considered, the human kingdom.

(a) *Introductory remarks.*   We have studied somewhat the constitution of the Triangles, or Pitris, Who, through self-sacrifice, endow man with self-consciousness, building his egoic vehicle out of Their own essence. We

have touched briefly upon the lunar Pitris, who endow
man with his lower sheaths and principles through which
the energy of the solar Lords may make itself felt, and
we shall now proceed to study three things:

First, the effect of the higher energy upon the lower
bodies, as it gradually makes itself felt during the evolutionary process, and thus simultaneously "redeems"
man in an occult sense, and also "elevates" the lunar
Pitris.

Second, the effect of this energy on the mental plane
in the development and unfoldment of the egoic lotus.

Third, the awakening to activity of the central Life
within the lotus. This activity demonstrates in a twofold
manner:

a. As the realisation by the man on the physical plane
within the physical brain of his divine nature, resulting in a consequent demonstration of divinity
upon earth, prior to liberation.

b. As the conscious activity of the individual Ego on
the mental plane in co-operation with its group or
groups.

In the first case, we have the effect of the egoic life upon
its sheaths, and their subsequent control, and in the second case we have the self-awakening of the egoic unit on
its own plane; in the third case, we have a group realisation, or the entrance by the unit into the consciousness of
the Heavenly Man.

It will not be possible to do more than indicate broad
general lines of development. The subject of egoic evolution cannot be fully comprehended until after initiation,
but it is felt now by the Teachers on the inner side that
the main principles had better be given out at once in
view of the unexpected development (since the opening
of this century) of two great sciences:

The Science of Electricity. The investigations of scientists have been greatly stimulated by the discovery of radium, which is an electrical phenomenon of a certain kind, and by the knowledge this discovery brought of the radioactive substances; the development of the many methods of utilising electricity has also greatly aided. This science has brought man to the threshold of a discovery which will revolutionise world thought on these matters, and which will eventually solve a great part of the economic problem, thus leaving many more persons free for mental growth and work.   This expansion of knowledge can be looked for before one hundred and fifty years have transpired.

The Science of Psychology.   The psycho-analytic theories which (though indicative of progress) are yet tending in a wrong direction, may prove disastrous to the higher development of the race unless the true nature of the "psyche" is elucidated.   When the public mind has apprehended, even cursorily, the following briefly stated facts, the trend of popular education, the object of political science, and the goal of economic and social endeavour will take a new and better direction. These facts might be summed up in the following postulates:

I.   Man is *in essence* divine.[59] This has ever been enunciated throughout the ages, but remains as yet a beautiful theory or belief, and not a proven scientific fact, nor is it universally held.

[59] Each human being is an incarnation of God.—S. D., III, 449.   Compare:—S. D., II, 541; S. D., III, 475; and the Biblical words: "I have said, Ye are Gods." "Know ye not that ye are the Temple of the Holy Spirit?"

No Being can become a God without passing through the human cycles.—S. D., II, 336.

Man therefore is like God in that he represents the pairs of opposites, good and evil, light and darkness, male and female, etc.   He is a duality. He represents also God in that He is a triplicity, being three in one, and one in three.—See S. D., II, 553.

By man the divine Monad is meant.—S. D., II, 196.

II. Man is in fact a fragment of the Universal Mind,
     or world soul,[60] and as a fragment is thus par-
     taker of the instincts and quality of that soul, as
     it manifests through the human family. There-
     fore, unity is only possible upon the plane of
     mind. This, if true, must lead to the tendency to
     develop within the physical brain a conscious
     realisation of group affiliations on the mental
     plane, a conscious recognition of group relation-
     ships, ideals and goal, and a conscious manifes-
     tation of that continuity of consciousness which
     is the object of evolution at this time. It will
     further produce the transference of the race con-
     sciousness from the physical plane to the mental,
     and a consequent solving through ''knowledge,
     love, and sacrifice'' of all present problems.
     This will bring about emancipation from the
     present physical plane disorder. It must lead to
     the education of the public as to the nature of
     man, and the development of the powers latent
     within him—powers which will set him free from
     his present limitations, and which will produce
     in the human family a collective repudiation of
     the present conditions. When men everywhere
     recognise themselves and each other, as divine
     self-conscious units, functioning primarily in the
     causal body but utilising the three lower vehicles
     only as a means of contact with the three lower
     planes, we will have government, politics, eco-
     nomics and the social order readjusted upon
     sound, sane and divine lines.

III. Man in his lower nature, and in his three vehicles,
     is an aggregate of lesser lives, dependent upon
     him for their group nature, for their type of
     activity, and collective response, and who—

● S. D., I, Proem., pp. 42-44.

through the energy or activity of the solar Lord
—will themselves later be raised, and developed
to the human stage.

When these three facts are understood, then and only
then will we have a right and just comprehension of the
nature of man.

Again, this realisation will bring about three changes
in the thought of the age:

(1) *A readjustment of the medical knowledge of man*,
resulting in a truer understanding of the physical body,
of its treatment, and of its protection, and thus producing a juster apprehension of the laws of health. The
aim of the physician will then be to find out what it is in
a man's life which is preventing egoic energy from flood-
ing every part of his being; to find out what lines of
thought are being indulged in which are causing that
inertia of the will aspect which is so conducive to wrong-
doing; to ascertain what it is in the emotional body which
is affecting the nervous system, and thus obstructing the
flow of energy from the love petals of the egoic lotus
(via the astral permanent atom) to the astral body, and
from thence to the nervous system; to discover what is
the hindrance in the etheric body which is preventing the
right flow of prana, or of solar vitality to every part of
the body.

It is essential that in days to come medical men should
realise that disease in the physical body is incidental to
wrong internal conditions. This is already being somewhat considered but the whole question will remain but a
beautiful theory (even though an incontrovertible one in
view of the achievements of mental scientists and of the
various faith healers) until the true nature of the ego, its
constitution, its powers, and its field of influence are duly
apprehended.

This revelation will come when medical men accept this

teaching as a working hypothesis, and then begin to note, for instance, the powers of endurance shown by the great souls of the earth, and their capacity to work at high pressure, and to remain practically immune from disease until (at the close of a long life of usefulness) the Ego deliberately chooses to "die-out" of physical existence. It will come when the medical profession concentrates upon preventative action, substituting sunshine, a vegetarian diet, and the application of the laws of magnetic vibration and vitality for the present regimen of drugs and surgical operations. Then will come the time when finer and better human beings will manifest on earth. When also physicians learn the nature of the etheric body, and the work of the spleen as a focal point for pranic emanations, then sound principles and methods will be introduced which will do away with such diseases as tuberculosis, debility, malnutrition and the diseases of the blood and of the kidneys. When doctors comprehend the effect of the emotions upon the nervous system, they will turn their attention to the amelioration of environal conditions, and will study the effects of the emotional currents upon the fluids of the body, and primarily upon the great nerve centres, and the spinal column. When the connection between the dense physical and the subtler bodies is a fact established in medical circles, then will the right treatment of lunacy, of obsessions, and of wrong mental conditions be better comprehended, and the results more successful; finally, when the nature of egoic force, or of energy is studied, and the function of the physical brain as the transmitter of egoic intent is better comprehended, then the coördination of man's entire being will be studied, and illness, debility and disease, will be traced to their just cause, and will be treated through the cause and not just through the effect.

(2) *The entire social world of thought* will apply itself to the understanding of the emotional nature of

humanity, to the group relationships involved, and to the interaction between individuals and other individuals, between groups and other groups. These relationships will be interpreted wisely and broadly and a man will be taught his responsibility to the lesser lives which he ensouls. This will produce a just direction of individual force, and its utilisation for the stabilisation, the development, and the refining of the substance of the different vehicles. Men will also be taught their definite responsibility under law to their own individual families. This will bring about the protection of the family unit, and its scientific development; it will cause the elimination of marital troubles, and the abolition of abuses of different kinds, so prevalent now in many family circles.

Responsibility to the community in which a man is placed will likewise be emphasised. Men will be taught the true esoteric meaning of citizenship—a citizenship based upon egoic group relations, the law of rebirth, and the real meaning of the law of karma. They will be taught national responsibility, and the place of the community within the nation, and of the nation within the comity of nations. Men will finally be taught their responsibility to the animal kingdom. This will be brought about in three ways:

1. Man's truer understanding of his own animal nature.
2. A comprehension of the laws of individualisation, and the effect of the influence of the fourth, or human, kingdom upon the third, or animal, kingdom.
3. The work of an Avatar of a lesser order Who will come in the beginning of the next century to reveal to man his relationship to the third kingdom. His way is being prepared by the many who in these days are developing public interest through the

various societies for the benefit and protection of
animals, and through the many stories to be found
in books and current periodicals.

We are told by H. P. B.[61] that the sense of responsibility
is one of the first indications of egoic control, and as
more and more of the human family come under egoic
influence, conditions will be bettered slowly and steadily
in every department of life.

(3) *In the educational world,* an apprehension of
man's true nature will bring about a fundamental change
in the methods of teaching. The emphasis will be laid
upon teaching people the *fact* of the Ego on its own plane,
the nature of the lunar bodies, and the methods of aligning the lower bodies so that the Ego can communicate
direct with the physical brain, and thus control the lower
nature and work out its purposes. Men will be taught
how, through concentration and meditation, they can ascertain knowledge for themselves, can develop the intuition, and thus draw upon the resources of the Ego. Then
will men be taught to *think,* to assume control of the
mental body, and thus develop their latent powers.

In the above few remarks are indicated very briefly
and inadequately the results which may be looked for
from a true understanding of the essential nature of
man. It has been written in view of the necessity these
days of a statement as to the real or inner man, and as
to the laws of the kingdom of God. That inner man has
ever been known to be there, and the "kingdom within"
has ever been proclaimed until H. P. B. came and gave
out the same old truths from a new angle, giving an
occult turn to mystic thought. Now comes the opportunity for man to realise the laws of his own being, and
in that realisation those who stand on the verge of intuitional apprehension of knowledge and those of scientific
bent who are willing to accept these truths as a working

hypothesis to be utilised as a basis for experiment until proven false, will have the chance to solve the world problems from within. Thus will the Christ principle be manifested upon earth, and thus will the Christ nature be demonstrated to be a fact in nature itself.

The value to the public thought of a true explanation of the evolution of the Ego, and its gradually developing power on earth is very great. There are two ways in which man may view this matter, both of which provide food for meditation, and well merit serious consideration. Both of them have been somewhat dealt with by thinkers of many schools of thought, and hence do not require any lengthy elucidation. The problem may be regarded as one calling for the elevation of the inner consciousness of the human unit (functioning in the physical body) to the higher levels of the mental plane, and therefore involves a raising or expansion of his waking consciousness till it becomes aware of this higher life. This is the way of mystical approach, and many instances of its successful accomplishment can be studied in the lives of the mystics of all ages. By sheer devotion and strenuous application, and by a severe disciplining of the physical body, the mystic effects his entrance into the heart centre of his little system, and his life becomes irradiated by the beams of his own central sun—the egoic light divine. The problem may again be regarded as one in which the effort of the man is concentrated in an attempt to bring down into the physical brain consciousness, and thus on to the physical plane, the life and power and energy of the inner centre, the Ego. This involves necessarily a scientific apprehension of the laws of being, and a recognition of the dual nature of the Self. It involves a devotion to the work of bringing about a domination of the lunar lords through the radiant control of the solar Lord. This is the occult method. It is the method of studying the constitution of those entities who form the fourfold lower nature, the personality, and a close investigation of those divine Essences Who build the body of the Ego or higher self. To this must be added a severe application of the laws of nature to the individual problem.

What is proposed in this Treatise is to follow the latter method, as the aim is to make clear the rationale of the process.

(b) *The evolution of the petals.* The building of the causal body is the result of dual energy, that of the lower self with its reflex action upon the higher unit, and that of the natural energy of the self as it makes its direct impress upon the substance of the egoic lotus. It should here be remembered that, subtle though the material may be, the egoic lotus is as truly substance of a particular vibration as is the physical body, only (owing to its rarity) physical plane man regards it practically as non-substantial. It is in fact, as earlier pointed out, the result of the dual vibration of the fivefold Dhyanis or Gods in conjunction with the fourfold Quaternary, or the Pitris of the lower vehicles. Through a conscious effort of the planetary Logoi, these Dhyanis and lower Pitris are brought into a close relationship. This produces (upon the third subplane of the mental plane) a ninefold vibration or whorl in the gaseous matter of the plane—for this is the cosmic gaseous subplane—which, after a certain period of persistence, assumes the form of a nine-petalled lotus. This lotus is folded over in bud shape upon the central point, or heart of the lotus—that spark of electric fire which by its action or innate vitality working upon the substance of the lotus, attracts to itself sufficient of that substance to form three inner petals, which closely shield the central spark; these are nevertheless of the same substance or essence as the nine other petals. The student must be careful not to materialise his concept too much and it might therefore be wise for him to view

Chart VIII

THE EGOIC LOTUS AND THE CENTERS

COSMIC PHYSICAL PLANE

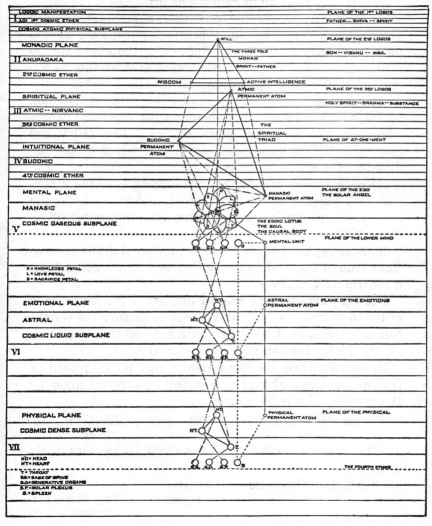

this manifestation from other angles and employ other terms to express the same idea. For instance, the body of the Ego may be viewed in the following four ways:

As nine vibrations, emanating from a central point, which, in its pulsation or radiations produces three major vibrations of great force pursuing a circular activity around the centre; the nine vibrations pursue a diagonal path until they reach the periphery of the egoic sphere of influence. At this point they swing around, thus forming the well-known spheroidal form of the causal body.

As nine petals of a lotus, radiating from a common centre, and hiding within themselves three central petals, which conceal a central point of fire. The radiations from the tip of each petal are those which cause the illusion of a spheroidal shape.

As nine spokes of a wheel, converging towards a central hub, which is in itself threefold, and which hides the central energy or dynamo of force—the generator of all the activity.

As nine types of energy which produce definite emanations from a threefold unit, again itself an outgoing from a central unit of force.

For all purposes, the second definition will be the one of the most use to us in our attempt to picture the constitution, nature, method of development and true evolution of the Ego, functioning in the causal body.

In terms of fire, the same truths may be expressed as follows, and this should be carefully pondered upon by the student of this Treatise:

1. Electric fire. Spirit .... Will aspect ...Jewel in the lotus.

2. Solar fire...Consciousness .Love aspect ...The nine petals.

3. Fire by friction ...Substance ....Activity aspect ......The three permanent atoms.

In *electric fire,* the Monad is represented in its three-fold nature, and stands for that type of manifestation which will be brought to its highest stage of development in the next solar system.

In *solar fire,* these solar Pitris in their ninefold formation represent and make possible the unfolding of the consciousness of the Monad through the medium of the Ego in the three worlds of human evolution.

In *fire by friction,* the lunar Pitris are represented and constitute the lower self, the personality, or those vehicles by means of which the Ego in turn is to acquire experience on the lower planes.

Yet these three are one in manifestation within the egoic auric egg, and the interchange of energy and vitality proceeds steadily. Spirit uses the Soul, or the Ego, as a vehicle of enlightenment, and the Ego uses the lower Quaternary as its medium of expression. The evolution of Spirit can really therefore be divided into three stages:

First. The stage in which the lunar Pitris function primarily, and prepare the lower sheaths for occupancy. The lower vibrations control, and "fire by friction" is that which warms and nourishes to the practical exclusion of all else.

Second. The stage in which the solar Pitris gradually become predominant, in which the egoic consciousness is developed. The sheaths are occupied by the Thinker, are gradually controlled by him, are bent to his will and purpose, and are eventually discarded. The middle vibrations control and solar fire irradiates; it lights up in due course of evolution the lower sheaths; it gradually increases its heat, and eventually aids in the destruction of the forms.

Third. The stage in which electric fire is revealed, and through the intensity of its blaze puts out the other fires. The lunar Pitris have fulfilled their work, the solar Pitris have developed the self-conscious unit, man, and the monad (having utilised both) discards both, and withdraws into itself, this time plus the gain of material existence, and plus developed love-wisdom.

In terms of the old Commentary, the truth is thus stated:

"The Lord of Life Himself sits at the heart and watches. The Lords of solar fire pursue their task and sacrifice themselves to the lunar Lords of all the lower planes. They die, but resurrect. They pass without, and come again. Yet the Lord of Life sits still.

The lunar Lords begin to die; their power begins to wane with each successive cycle. The solar Lords shine forth in triumph and consign the fourfold ones to fire,—the fire which burns and dissipates the form.

Many times the work repeats itself; the cycles wax and wane, until the day triumphant when the solar Lord acclaims himself and knows himself the ruler.

The Lord of Life then turns Himself, and arises in His might. He consumes the solar Lords, and they perish as did the lunar Lords. He speaks a Word; the fire descends. The blaze bursts forth. Gone is the lower fire through the flame of solar burning, gone is the middle fire through the intensity of fire from Heaven.

Naught remaineth save a threefold flame of violet, indigo and yellow. THAT disappears. Then darkness reigns. Yet the Lord of Life persists, though invisible."

As we know, the egoic lotus consists of three circles,— each circle being composed of three petals, and all shielding the inner bud where hides the jewel. It is with the evolution of these petals that we are concerned, with their formation, their vitalisation, their nurturing, and eventual unfoldment. It will be useful for the student at this stage to remember that we are primarily dealing with the development of the second aspect in man, the love-wisdom aspect, and are only secondarily considering the third aspect, that of activity which finds its energising centres in the three permanent atoms.

These three circles of petals are called in the esoteric terminology:

1. The "outer knowledge" triad, or the lords of active wisdom.
2. The middle "love" triad, or the lords of active love.
3. The inner "sacrificial" triad, or the lords of active will.

The first is the summation of experience and developed consciousness; the second is the application of that knowledge in love and service, or the expression of the Self and the Not-Self in reciprocal vibration; and the third is the full expression of knowledge and love turned toward the conscious sacrifice of all to the furthering of the plans of the planetary Logos, and to the carrying out of His purposes in group work. Each of these three groups of petals come under the definite guidance of three groups of Agnishvattas, who form them out of their own substance and who in essence *are* the threefold Ego during its manifestation. Through them flows the force and coherent energy of those mysterious Entities whom (when considering the human family as a whole) we call—

a. The Buddhas or Lords of Activity.
b. The Buddhas or Lords of Compassionate Love.
c. The Buddhas of Sacrifice, of Whom the Lord of the World is, to man, the best known exponent.

Through these three groups flows that threefold energy which, on the mental plane, finds its medium of expression in connection with the human kingdom, in the three groups of Agnishvattas or solar Pitris above referred to. These groups form the substance of the three circles of petals, and each group has also a special influence upon the particular petal belonging to their especial scale of vibrations. For the sake of clarity, we might tabulate the various petals so that the student may get a clearer comprehension of the conformation of his own causal vehicle, and some idea of the various triangular relationships:

I. *The outer "knowledge" triad:*

a. Petal 1 ....Knowledge on the physical plane.
Colours: Orange, green and violet.
b. Petal 2 ....Love on the physical plane.
Colours: Orange, rose and blue.
c. Petal 3 ....Sacrifice on the physical plane.
Colours: Orange, yellow and indigo.

These three petals are organised and vitalised in the *Hall of Ignorance,* but remain unopened and only begin to unfold as the second circle is organised.

II. *The middle "love" triad:*

a. Petal 1 ....Higher Knowledge applied through love on the physical and astral planes.
Colours: Rose, and the original three.
b. Petal 2 ....Higher intelligent love on the physical and astral planes.
Colours: Rose and the corresponding three.
c. Petal 3 ....Loving intelligent sacrifice on the physical and astral planes.
Colours: Rose and the same three.

These three petals preserve the fundamental orange but add the colour rose in every petal, so that four colours are now seen. These petals are organised and vitalised in the *Hall of Learning,* but remain unopened. The outer tier of petals simultaneously unfolds till it is open entirely, revealing the second circle; the third remains shielded.

III. *The inner "sacrificial" triad:*

a. Petal 1 ....The Will to sacrifice through knowledge on the mental plane, and thus intelligently to dominate the entire threefold lower man.
Colours: Yellow and the four colours, orange, green, violet and rose.

CHART IX

THE EGOIC LOTUS

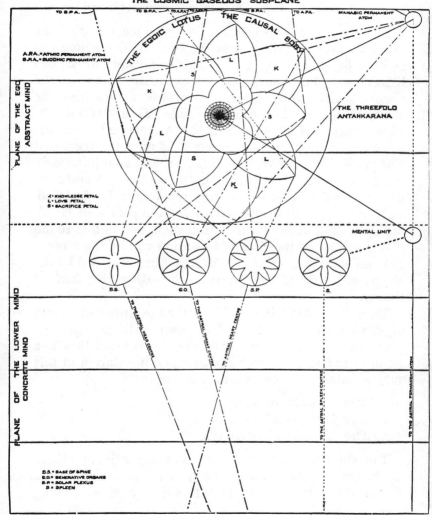

THE COSMIC GASEOUS SUBPLANE

THE EGOIC LOTUS

THE CAUSAL BODY

A.P.A. = ATMIC PERMANENT ATOM
B.P.A. = BUDDHIC PERMANENT ATOM

MANASIC PERMANENT ATOM

THE THREEFOLD ANTAHKARANA

K = KNOWLEDGE PETAL
L = LOVE PETAL
S = SACRIFICE PETAL

MENTAL UNIT

B.S. = BASE OF SPINE
G.O. = GENERATIVE ORGANS
S.P. = SOLAR PLEXUS
S = SPLEEN

b. Petal 2 . . . . The will to sacrifice through love on the mental plane, and thus to serve.
Colours: Yellow and the four colours, orange, violet, rose and blue.
c. Petal 3 . . . . The utter sacrifice of all forever.
Colours: Yellow, orange, rose, blue and indigo.

In the mystery of these subsidiary colours and of the gradual shining forth within the lotus of five colours in any one petal at one time, is veiled the mystery of the five Kumaras.[62] The student who seeks the significance of the preponderance of orange and of rose is approaching the secret of the two Kumaras Who fell. More it is not possible to say, but the colours hold the esoteric key to this great occurrence. This inner circle of petals is organised and vitalised in the *Hall of Wisdom,* and simultaneously the middle circle unfolds, so that two rows of petals are duly opened, and only the third remains to be unclosed. This final opening is effected during the period of treading the stages of the Path of Initiation, and in this round it is hastened by the rites of initiation and by the strenuous and abnormal efforts of the man himself, aided by the electrical work of the Initiator, wielding the Rod of Power.

Though we have thus divided off the different stages of development, we have but dealt with the general average, gathering our facts from the records to which we have access and which are grouped in relation to this subject into the three groups, related to:

a. The Monads of power.
b. The Monads of love.
c. The Monads of activity.

The student must remember that according to these groupings, so will be the tendency of the petals to unfold. For instance, in the case of the majority of men, being

---

[62] S. D., I, 483.

Monads of Love, the love petals are more easily awakened, for love is the nature of the present manifestation
and the line of love in some direction (low, high, or spiritual) is the line of least resistance for the many. Yet
the Monads of activity are numerous and influential and
the first petal in each ring is for them the easiest to
unfold. For both groups the "knowledge" petal is the
first opened, owing to the inherent nature of the Manasadevas themselves, and their basic vibration. For all,
sacrifice is the hardest, for it involves ever the two factors of intelligence and love,—intelligent knowledge and
a love that goes out to that which must be saved through
sacrifice.

In these three circles of petals lies concealed another
clue to the mystery of the 777 incarnations. The figures
do not convey an exact number of years, but are figurative and symbolical; they are intended to convey the
thought of three cycles of varying duration, based upon
the septenary nature of the manifesting monad.

First. The 700 incarnations. These concern the unfoldment of the outer circle. This is the longest period.
The initial vibration is slow and heavy, and millenia of
lives have to elapse before the interchange of energy
between the Ego and its reflection, the personal self (the
lower threefold man) is such that the consciousness of
the man occultly "awakens" in the Hall of Learning.
For advanced man at this time these incarnations took
place upon the moon chain and in some cases upon certain planets connected with the inner round. This is the
circumstance which necessitated his "coming-in" during
the Atlantean root-race. Men of this type refused to
incarnate earlier, as the bodies were too coarse; this was
the cyclic reflection (on the lowest plane) of the refusal
of the Monads to incarnate at the dawn of manvantaric
opportunity. No real "sin" was committed; it was
their privilege to discriminate, and this refusal has its

bearing upon conditions upon Earth, being the basis of
the great class distinctions which—in every land—have
been so fruitful of trouble and the esoteric foundation of
the "caste" system, so abused now in India. The problem of labor and capital has its roots in the subjective
distinction between "equipped and unequipped" Egos,
between those units of the human family on earth who
have passed out of the Hall of Ignorance, and those who
are yet groping in its dark and gloomy corridors; between those Egos who are only "bud" Egos, and those
who have organised the outer circle of petals, and whose
petals are ready to open up.

The idea of a septenate of centuries must be carefully
pondered upon, and as ever in all occult matters, the idea
of triplicity must be also borne in mind with a synthesising period, which is a summation of the triple co-
ordination:

3 periods of 3 tens................	90 years.
1 synthesising period	10 years.
	100 years.
This seven times repeated.......	7
	700 years.

Each cycle (again figurative cycles) leaves one of the
petals more vitalised, and has a definite effect on each.

Second. The 70 incarnations. These concern the unfoldment of the middle circle. Much may be learned from
a consideration of the occult significance involved in the
sending out of their followers by any initiate (such as
the Christ) in groups of seventy, going two and two.
These seventy incarnations primarily effect the development of love in the personal life, the evolution of the
astral nature, based on the recognition of the pairs of
opposites, and their equilibrising in love and service.

This cycle covers the period passed by the man in the

Hall of Learning and has its correspondence in the Atlantean root-race and its conflict between the Lords of the Dark Face and the Brotherhood of Light. Within the life of each individual, a similar conflict wages during this period, ending with the final kurukshetra or battle-ground which earns for the man the right to tread the Probationary Path, and eventually the privilege to stand before the Portal of Initiation. Again the numerical significance of the numbers must be studied; this time they are hid in the number ten, or three cycles of three lesser periods, each making nine, and one synthesising period, leading up to the consummation of one period within the greater cycle; this is signified by the ten of relative perfection.[63, 64] The interplay between kamic impulse and manasic energy has produced a realisation within the consciousness of the Ego of that

[63] *The Number 10.*—See S. D., I, 125, 126.
  1. *The three, enclosed within the circle are the sacred Four.*
     a. *Adi-Sanat,* the Number, Unity. The Logos, or the One in physical incarnation. God and man function as unities on their respective physical planes.
     b. *The Voice of the Word,* the Numbers, for He is one and nine. The second aspect. The embodied Idea. Consciousness.
     c. *The formless Square,* the matter aspect, substance and form. Limitation.
        Trace these out in connection with:—
          a. A solar Logos informing a solar system.
          b. A planetary Logos, informing a planetary scheme.
          c. Man, informing his bodies of manifestation.
  2. *The ten are the arupa universe.*
  The emphasis here is laid upon the subjective Lives, or the Intelligent Consciousness within the forms.
  These ten might be called:—
     I. The first Logos . . . Shiva . . . Father . . . Will.
     II. The second Logos . . . Vishnu . . . Son . . . Love-wisdom.
     III. The third Logos . . . Brahma . . . Holy Ghost . . . Intelligence overshadowing Matter, Mother.
        1. The Lord of Cosmic Will.........................First   Ray.
        2. The Lord of Cosmic Love........................Second   Ray.
        3. The Lord of Cosmic Intelligence.................Third   Ray.

        4. The Lord of Cosmic Harmony....................Fourth   Ray.
        5. The Lord of Cosmic Knowledge..................Fifth   Ray.
        6. The Lord of Cosmic Devotion...................Sixth   Ray.
        7. The Lord of Cosmic Ceremonial.................Seventh Ray.
  They are the subjective consciousness, the cause of manifestation.
[64] S. D., I, 214; II, 393, 445, 446.

which he has learned within the two Halls; the outer circle of petals is unfolded, and the central ring is ready to open.

Third. The 7 incarnations. These are those passed upon the Probationary Path. This is an interesting period in which certain things are effected which might be described in the following terms:

The two outer rings of petals are stimulated in a new and special sense through the conscious act of the probationary disciple. Much of the work hitherto has been pursued under the ordinary laws of evolution and has been unconscious. Now all that changes as the mental body becomes active, and two of the will petals are co-ordinated, and one "awakes" vitality and unfolds.

The fire or energy from these two rings begins to circulate along the atomic triangle and when this is the case it marks a very momentous epoch; a dual work has been consummated in the personal lower life and in the egoic:

a. The permanent atoms have the four lower spirillae fully active (two groups of two each) and the fifth is in process of arousement into equal activity. The triangle is in circulatory action but has not yet achieved its full brightness nor its rotary or fourth dimensional revolution.

b. The two circles of petals are "awake," one being wide open and the other on the verge of opening.

Thus in the life of the probationer two aspects of the divine life are making themselves apparent, and though as yet much remains to be done, nevertheless when the inner circle of petals is awakened—through the instrumentality of the curious and abnormal process of initiation—the remaining aspect will be brought into similar prominence, and produce the perfected man in the three worlds. Thus is the work of the Solar Pitris consummated.

The fact of the abnormality of the process of initiation must here be emphasised.

Initiation is in the nature of a great experiment which our planetary Logos is making during this round. In earlier and perhaps in later rounds the whole process will follow natural law. In this round and on this chain, our planetary Logos on His high level is what is esoterically called "sitting for yoga," and is definitely undergoing certain processes of training in order to stimulate His centres. This fact is being taken advantage of by the Hierarchy on Earth to produce certain results in the races under Their guidance. The whole process is optional, and a man may—if he so choose—follow the normal process, and take aeons of time to effect what some are choosing to do in a briefer period, through a self-chosen forcing process.

At the termination of the 777 incarnations, a man passes through the door of initiation and enters upon a brief synthesising process, or a final period in which he garners the fruits of the experience in the two first halls, and transmutes knowledge into wisdom, transforms the shadow of things seen into the energy of that which is, and achieves the final liberation from all the lower forms which seek to hold him prisoner. This period of initiation itself is divided into seven stages, but only five of these concern the evolution of the Ego, just as the five Kumaras concern primarily the evolution of Humanity in the system and on this planet. Thus again we have the four exoteric Kumaras, of Whom two fell, and the three esoteric, of whom One gathers the life forces of the four exoteric, making with Them the five above mentioned. The student must study this question from the point of view of energy or life force, considering it from the aspect of polarity and of the mystic marriage, from

the comprehension of the real meaning of the sex relation, of the meeting and merging of the pairs of oppo
sites, and the work of the one who synthesises where
every type of energy is concerned. For instance:

a. The Ego synthesises or gathers in the life forces of
   the fourfold lower man.
b. The Mahachohan's Ray on Earth synthesises the
   life forces of the lower four. This Ray is the third
   subray of our planetary Ray.
c. The third major Ray of the solar system blends
   the minor four.
d. The fifth Kumara blends and unites in Himself the
   work of the lower four.

The reflection of all this in the Microcosm can be
studied by the man who understands how the physical
body is the vehicle of all the principles.

By the time the third Initiation is taken, the inner
circle of petals is opened and the full-blown lotus in all
its beauty can be seen. At the fourth Initiation the inner
bud bursts open through the effect of the electrical force
of the Rod, which brings in the power of the synthetic
ray of the solar system itself; the inner jewel is thus
revealed. The work has been accomplished; the energy
resident in the permanent atoms, has vitalised all the
spirillae whilst the perfected force of the lotus, and the
dynamic will of the central spark are brought into full
and united activity. This brings about a threefold display of vital force which causes the disintegration of the
form and the following results:

a. *The permanent atoms become radioactive,* and their
   ring-pass-not is therefore no longer a barrier to
   the lesser units within; the electronic lives in their
   various groups escape, and return to the eternal
   reservoir. They form substance of a very high

order, and will produce the forms of those existences who, in another cycle, will seek vehicles.

b. *The petals are destroyed* by the action of fire, and
the multiplicity of deva lives which form them
and give to them their coherence and quality are
gathered back by the solar Pitris of the highest
order into the Heart of the Sun; they will be
directed outward again in another solar system.
The atomic substance will be used for another man-
vantara, but the solar Pitris will not again be
called upon to sacrifice themselves until the next
solar system when they will come in as planetary
Rays, thus repeating upon monadic levels in the
next system what they have done in this.   They
will then be the planetary Logoi.

c. *The central Life electric returns to its source,* escaping out of prison and functioning as a centre of
energy on planes of cosmic etheric energy.

We have endeavoured above to convey a general idea
of the evolutionary process in connection with the Ego.
and its progression under karmic and cyclic law. If the
student ponders upon these two laws it will become apparent to him that both might be summed up under the
generic term of the *Law of Rhythm.* All manifestation
is the result of active energy producing certain results,
and expenditure of energy in any one direction will necessitate an equal expenditure in an opposite.   This in
terms of the Ego and its life experience brings about
three stages:

First. The stage wherein the energy manifested acts
outwardly. The Self becomes identified with its sheaths.
This is the strictly personal stage.

Second. The stage wherein adjustment under law is
being sought, and the Self is neither entirely identified
with its sheaths, nor identified entirely with Itself.   It is

learning to choose between the pairs of opposites. This
is the period of the fiercest strife and turmoil, and the
battlefield wherein the adjustment has to be made; it is
the laboratory period wherein enough transmutative
force is generated by the disciple to carry him to the
opposite extreme of the earlier stage,—that stage
wherein the energy will manifest *within* and not without.

Third. The stage wherein the energy of the Ego is
centred at the heart of the circle, and not in the periphery, being applied from thence through the conscious
effort of the Ego in group service. The pull of the lower
nature is superseded, and the attraction of that which is
higher even than the Ego is felt. The earlier process has
then to be repeated on a higher turn of the spiral, and
monadic energy begins to work upon the Ego as the egoic
worked upon the personality. The Monad, which has
been identifying Itself with the Ego (its outer manifestation) begins again to seek its own true centre "within
the Heart," and on the higher levels results affecting distribution and conservation of energy may again be seen.

It is necessary to emphasise this procedure because it
is important that all occultists should learn to interpret
and to think in terms of energy and of force, in contra-
distinction to the sheaths or instruments employed. The
mystic has recognised this "force" factor, but has only
worked with the *positive* force aspect. The occultist
must recognise and work with three types of force, or
energy, and therein lies the distinction between his work
and that of the mystic. He recognises:

1. Positive force . . . . . Or that which energises.
2. Negative force . . . . Or that which is the recipient
                           of energy; that which acts
                           or assumes form under the
                           impact of positive force.

3. Light, or harmonic
   force ....That which is produced by the
                     union of these two. The re-
                     sult is *radiant energy,* and is
                     the result of the equilibris-
                     ing of the two others.

These three aspects of energy have been called, as has
been often said:

   a.   Electric fire .....positive energy ....Father.
   b.   Fire by friction...negative energy ...Mother.
   c.   Solar fire ....radiant energy ....Sun or Son.

Each of these two last aspects demonstrates within
itself in a dual manner, but the effect is a unified whole
as regards the great Unity in which they are demonstrating.

The problem of the devas may be somewhat better
understood if it is remembered that they in themselves
embody the two types of energy. For instance, the solar
Pitris are the substance of the egoic bodies and groups,
and the medium of expression for the Spirit aspect, for
Spirit manifests by means of soul. The lunar Pitris, who
form the personal lower self, being the aggregate of the
lower sheaths, are energised and used by the solar
Lords. These solar Angels again are in many groups
and express within their own ranks a dual energy, both
positive and negative. There is the positive life of the
egoic lotus which co-ordinates, preserves, and actuates the
petals, and there is also the energy of the petal substance
itself, or the negative aspect which is swept by the positive force of the greater solar Lords into living whorls
or wheels which we symbolically call "petals." There is
a close analogy in connection with the planetary Logos,
and the solar Logos between *prana,* the life force which
animates the etheric body of man, and by means of that

force coheres the dense physical body, and that synthesising life force of the Logos which animates every atom on every plane of the system. If this is meditated upon, and the fact of all our planes being the etheric and dense manifestation of the solar Logos is realised, then the place played by the solar Angels may become somewhat elucidated, and their relation to the planetary Logos and to the solar Logos may become also clearer.

We must not only study them in connection with ourselves and with our effort to identify ourselves with the solar Lords of the lunar Pitris, but must recognise also:

   a. The solar Angels of a planetary scheme.
   b. The solar Angels of the solar system.
   c. The lunar lords of the scheme and system.

The word "lunar" is here an anachronism and is technically inaccurate. The moon or moons in any scheme are systemic effects, and are not causes. In certain planetary relationships, they are considered causes, but in connection with our solar system they are not. Yet also, in connection with a system, there exist cosmically certain bodies in space which have as definite an effect upon the system as the moon has upon the earth. This is something as yet unknown and incomprehensible to metaphysicians, scientists and astronomers. War wages cosmically as yet between the systemic "lunar" lords, and those Entities who are analogous to the solar Lords on cosmic levels. Until our students extend their concept to include in their calculations the logoic astral and mental bodies as the Logos seeks to express emotion and mind on the physical plane (through His physical body, a solar system) they will not progress far towards the heart of the solar mystery. Until the force of the cosmic lunar Lords is sought for, the fact of there being entire constellations beyond our solar system in process of disintegration in time and space in a manner similar to

the disintegration of the moon will not be known nor the
effects of this traced. Eventually our solar system will
pass into a similar state. The true mystery of evil [65] lies
here, and the true reality of the "War in Heaven" must
here be sought. Similarly it must be remembered that
planetary schemes pass into obscuration and "die out,"
through the withdrawal in all cases of the positive life
and energy and of the electric fire which is the animating
principle of every system, scheme, globe, kingdom in
nature, and human unit. This produces again in every
case the dying out of the "solar radiance," or of the
light produced by the commingling of the negative and
positive energy. All that is left in every case again is
the habitual energy of the substance upon which, and
through which, the positive energy has had such a re-

[65] *Problem of Evil.*
The following quotation is from a trance writing, given through Dr.
Anna Kingsford; it runs thus:
"You have demanded also the origin of evil. This is a great subject,
and we should have withheld it from you longer, but that it seems to
us now that you are in need of it. Understand then that Evil is the
result of Creation. For Creation is the result of the projection of Spirit
into matter; and with this projection came the first germ of evil. We
would have you know that there is no such thing as a purely spiritual
evil, but evil is the result of the materialisation of Spirit. If you examine
carefully all we have said to you concerning the various forms of evil,
you will see that every one is the result of the limitation of the power to
perceive that the whole Universe is but the Larger Self. . . . It is, then,
true that God created evil; but yet it is true that God is Spirit, and being
Spirit is incapable of evil. Evil is then purely and solely the result of
the materialisation of God. This is a great mystery. We can but indicate it tonight. . . . God is perception itself. God is universal percipience.
God is that which sees and that which is seen. If we could see all, hear
all, touch all, and so forth, there would be no evil, for evil comes of the
limitation of perception. Such limitation was necessary if God was to
produce aught other than God. Aught other than God must be less than
God. Without evil, therefore, God would have remained alone. All things
are God according to the measure of the Spirit in them."
That is to say, a perfected humanity will be a perfect vehicle of the
divine Spirit (see the Mercaba of Ezekiel, 1st Chapter). Great is our
indebtedness to the Seers who throw out for us flashes of light on the
darkness and mystery of human life, where the struggling Spirit within
is so often buried in the depths of this mysterious Chaos, thereby making
visible the darkness, so that we are enabled to see a few steps of the Way
ahead, thus encouraging us to press forward with renewed assurance that
the mists and clouds will be dispelled, and we shall in due time enter the
fulness of the divine Presence.—*The Theosophist*, Vol. XXIX, p. 50.

markable effect. This negative type of force gradually
dissipates, or disperses itself, and seeks the central reservoir of energy. The spheroidal form is thus disintegrated. This can be seen working out now in the case of
the moon, and the same rule holds good for all bodies.
We might word it otherwise:—The solar Devas (or radiant energy) return to the central Heart or to the source
which breathed them out. This leaves the lesser deva
substance dependent upon its own internal heat, as it
involves the withdrawal of that which built substance into
form. This deva substance is of many kinds and perhaps
the consequent procedure can be more clearly understood
if we say that as the form breaks up the lesser builders
and devas return to their *group soul*. Certain of them,
those who form the bodies of the fourth kingdom in nature, and who are therefore the highest kind of substance
through which consciousness can manifest in the three
worlds, are on the road *towards individualisation,*—they
are nearer the human stage than the substance of the
three other kingdoms. They occupy a place in the deva
evolution analogous to that which a man holds in the
human kingdom (note that I say kingdom, not evolution)
who is nearing the Path. The goal for the devas (below
the rank of solar Pitris) is individualisation, and their
objective is to become men in some future cycle. The
goal for a man is initiation, or to become a conscious
Dhyan Chohan, and in some distant cycle to do for the
humanity of that age what the solar Pitris have done for
him, and make their self-conscious expression a possibility. The goal for a solar Pitri is, as said earlier, to
become a logoic Ray.[66]

[66] The Goal for the Pitris:
The lunar Pitris are on a level with the lower Principles.—S. D., II, 82.
  a. They create our lower principles ....S. D., II, 92.
  b. They possess creative fire but not divine fire...S. D., II, 81, 82.
  c. They evolve the human form ....S. D., I, 203.
  d. They will eventually become men.............S. D., I, 203.
            Compare S. D., II, 99.

To return to the matter which we were considering:—
Just as the moon is a deterrent or malefic force where
the Earth is concerned, and productive of evil "influences," so all such disintegrating bodies are equally destructive. Such bodies exist within the solar ring-pass-
not,[67] unrecognised as yet, and disintegrating constellations (of which there are many in the universe, unknown
and unrecognised by scientists) have an equally malefic
effect upon our system, and upon all that passes into
their sphere of influence.

There is one such constellation, situated between the
lesser Dipper and our system, and another, interrelated
with the Pleiades and our system which still have a profound effect upon the physical body of the solar Logos.

The above paragraph is specifically worded thus because the effects are felt in the *lowest* sheath of all, and
are responsible for much that is ignorantly termed
"black magic." These two constellations have run their
cycles and are "dissolving." Some of their life force
and energy has been transferred to our solar system,

The higher Principles are latent in the animals.—S. D., II, 266, 279.
    a. The solar Pitris embody the fifth principle.... S. D., I, 241.
    b. They give consciousness to man..............S. D., I, 204.
    c. They furnish the vehicle for the incarnating
        Monad, forming the egoic body ....S. D., I, 237.
    d. They develop the human type ....S. D., II, 243.
                    Compare S. D., II, 96.
[67] Unseen Planets: "Not all of the Intra-Mercurial planets, nor yet
those in the orbit of Neptune, are yet discovered, although they are strongly
suspected. We know that such exist and where they exist; and that there
are innumerable planets "burnt out" they say,—in Obscuration we say;—
planets in formation and not yet luminous, etc." . . .
    "When so attached the 'tasimeter' will afford the possibility not only
to measure the heat of the remotest of visible stars, but to detect by their
invisible radiations stars that are unseen and otherwise undetectable, hence
planets also. The discoverer, an F. T. S., a good deal protected by M.,
thinks that if, at any point in a blank space of heavens—a space that
appears blank even through a telescope of the highest power—the tasimeter
indicates an accession of temperature and does so invariably; this will
be a regular proof that the instrument is in range with the stellar body
either non-luminous or so distant as to be beyond the reach of telescopic
vision. His tasimeter, he says, 'is affected by a wider range of etheric
undulations than the Eye can take cognisance of.' Science will Hear
sounds from certain planets before she Sees them. This is a Prophecy."—
Mahatma Letters to A. P. Sinnett, p. 169.

just as the lunar life force was transferred to our earth, and this it is that is the cause of much cyclic evil. The process of decay and the evil emanations induced still have power to influence forms which are responsive to what was for them an earlier vibration. The substance of these forms is magnetically linked with the decaying body, much as the etheric double is connected with its dense sheath, and effects are therefore manifested. Purificatory fire is the only cure for this magnetic corruption, and this is being utilised freely by the planetary Logoi in Their schemes, and by the solar Logos in the system.

PURIFICATORY FIRE

"The fire burned low. A dull red glow slumbered within the Heart of Mother. Its warmth was scarcely felt. The first and second of the inner lines throbbed with the burning, but the rest were cold.

The Sons of God looked down from the innermost centre. They looked, then turned away Their gaze and thoughts to other spheres. Their hour had not yet come. The elemental fires had not prepared the altar for the Lords. The sacrificial fire waited in its high place and the steady glow beneath increased.

The fire burned clearer, and the first and second slowly lighted up. Their glow became a line of brilliant fire yet the five remained untouched. The Sons of God again looked down. For one brief second They thought upon the Mother, and as They thought the third caught fire. Swiftly They looked away for the form as yet relayed to Them no call. The heat was latent and no outer warmth ascended to Their place.

The æons passed. The glow increased. The Spheres took form, but dissipated rapidly, lacking coherent force. They passed. They came again. Action incessant, noise and fire and smouldering heat characterised Their cycles. But the Lhas in Their high heaven spurned this elemental work and gazed within Themselves. They meditated.

* * * * * * *

The glow became a steady burning and tiny flames were seen. The first, the second, and the third became three lines of fire and one triangle was consummated. Yet the four are seen quiescent

and respond not to the heat. Thus do the cycles and the elemental lives pass and repass, and their work continues.

The forms are set, yet brief their span. They move not, yet
they pass. The hour has come for the great awakening. They
pass no longer down but mount.

This is the interlude for which the Lhas in Their high place
have waited. They may not enter yet the forms prepared, but
feel Their hour approaching. They meditate anew, and for a
minute gaze upon the myriad threefold fires until the fourth
responds.

The sixty seconds passed in dynamic concentration produce
forms of triple kind, three sets of forms, and myriads in the
three. The Heart of Mother contracts, and expands with these
sixty fiery breaths. The lines become allied, and cubes are
formed, shielding the inner fire. The altar is prepared, and
four square stands. The altar glows, red at the centre and warm
without.

* * * * * * *

The altar flames. Its heat mounts up, yet it burns not, nor is
consumed. Its heat, which has no flame, reaches a higher
sphere; the Sons of God for a brief period warm Themselves,
yet approach not nearer to it until the passing of another cycle.
They await the hour, the hour of sacrifice.

The solar Lords, taking the Word as sounded by the Sons
of God, arise in the fierceness of their solar life and approach
the altar. The four lines glow and burn. The sun applies a
ray; the solar Lords pass it through Their substance and again
approach the altar. The fifth line awakens and becomes a glowing point, and then a dull red line, measuring the distance 'twixt
the altar and the One Who watches.

The fivefold fire dynamic begins to flicker and to burn. It
lights not yet without; it simply glows. The æons pass away,
the cycles come and go.

Steadily the solar Lords sacrifice Themselves; They are the
fire upon the altar. The fourth provides the fuel.

* * * * * * *

The Sons of God still watch. The work nears its final consummation. The Eternal Lhas in Their high place call each to
each, and four take up the cry: ''The fire is burning. Does the
heat suffice?''

Two answer to each other: " 'The fire is burning; the altar is well-nigh destroyed. What happens next?'" "Add to the fire with fuel from Heaven. Breathe on the blazing fire and fan its flame to utter fierceness."

Thus the command goes out from One Who watches, silent hitherto, through countless æons. They send forth breath. Something prevents the passage of the breath. They call for aid. One makes His appearance Who has not yet been seen.

He lifts His hand. The one, the two, the three, the four and five merge into one and mingle with the sixth. The flame mounts up, responding to the breath. The final disappearance of the cube is needed and then the work stands forth."

From the archives of The Lodge.

(c) *The Names of the Egoic Lotuses.* We might consider briefly the work of forming the egoic lotus on its own plane; this is as the result of the work of the Agnishvattas, after its segregation in space, and the formation of its ring-pass-not. We have touched upon the remotest and earliest stages. One point we have not yet emphasised but which is of interest to the thoughtful student. This is the fact of the difference existing between the egoic bodies owing to their varying stages of development. For instance, up till the middle of the Atlantean rootrace [68] (when the door of individualisation was closed), Egos were to be seen at many differing stages from the newly organised "buds," representing freshly individualised men, to the highly developed causal bodies of the different disciples and initiates, who were superintending the evolution of the race. Now the egoic bodies might be grouped from the evolutionary standpoint as follows:

On the third subplane of the mental plane:

Bud egos. Our planetary scheme, being at the midway point in its evolution, there are therefore no unopened "buds" strictly speaking. All the egoic lotuses have at least one petal open. All the lotuses are organised, but there are vast differences among those of small develop-

[68] S. D., I, 196.

ment, showing forth in the brilliancy of the permanent atoms, and in the stage of petal unfoldment.

Brahmic lotuses in which the first or knowledge petal is fully unfolded. They are so called as they represent on the physical plane the fully active intelligent unity, the man of small mental development, the lowest type of workers, agriculturists, and peasants on every continent. They are also called "third class creators," as they express themselves only through the act of physical creation on the physical plane, and their function is largely to provide vehicles for those of their own group.

The lotuses of Brahman, in which the second petal is showing signs of opening and the second aspect in its lowest manifestation is showing signs of demonstration. They stand as representing certain groups of Egos from certain planetary schemes, notably Jupiter and Venus, who are a grade higher than the class above, but which have as yet a long way to go. They are called "second class creators," for though they demonstrate on the physical plane in the act of physical creation, yet they are more swayed by love than by animal instinct as in the first case. They are to be found incarnating at this time in the Orient, particularly in India and in the Latin countries, and just lately in America.

Primary lotuses. These are a group of special interest brought in under the influence of the Lord of the fifth Ray, and therefore fundamentally allied to the energy which is the special manifestation in this system and the basis of all achievement, that is, manas. They were quiescent during the Atlantean root-race but have come in during the fourth and fifth subraces of this root-race. They are a group a good deal more advanced than the earlier classes but need much to develop the second petal. With them the first and the third petals in the first circle are opening, but the middle petal is yet shut. The middle tier also shows no signs of vitality. Owing

to conditions in their emanating planet, their development has been one-sided, and hence their entering on a
wave of energy into this scheme in order to "round"
themselves out, as it is called. They may be seen in the
purely intellectual selfish scientific type. They are responsible for much of the advanced application of
mechanical science to the needs of men, and for the introduction of certain types of machinery; they work largely
in connection with the energy of the mineral kingdom.
By this it must be inferred that the solar Lords who
embody this type are linked with a group of lunar Lords
who respond magnetically to the devas of the mineral
kingdom. Their work for the race has at present a dele-
terious effect, but when the second petal is opened, the
wonders then to be achieved by them in loving service
along their own particular line will be one of the factors
which will regenerate the fourth kingdom. They will
achieve emancipation in the fifth round, four fifths of
them passing on to the Path and one fifth set back for
another cycle.

Lotuses of passion or desire. They are so called because their fundamental nature is embodied love in some
one or other form. The bulk of the Monads of Love are
among this large group and they are to be seen incarnating in the bulk of the well-to-do, kindly people of the
world. They are divided into five groups, of whom three
individualised upon this planet, and two were the very
latest to individualise upon the moon chain. They have
two petals unfolded and the third is for them at this time
the object of their attention. Many may succeed in unfolding it before the seventh rootrace of this round but
the bulk of them will unfold it in the second rootrace of
the next round, and will stand ready before the close of
the round to pass on to the probationary path, having
unfolded one tier of petals, and organised the second.
All these lotuses of the first circle are divided into groups
but interplay goes on between them; energy in any centre

produces reflex energy in another. It must be remembered that in closing the door in Atlantean times to the animal kingdom, and the consequent temporary cessation of the forming of any more "bud lotuses" the effect was dual, in directions other than the human or the animal. It was the result of the internal decision on the part of the planetary Logos to turn His attention away from the act of creation on the systemic mental plane to the work of progressive evolution. This caused a cessation of certain types of activity, producing a quiescence in certain of His centres, and an increased activity in others. It also had an effect upon the solar Angels, and consequently upon the Heart of the solar system from whence they are drawn. Floods of energy or streams of force from the heart of the sun (the subjective Sun) were arrested and directed elsewhere, while the Pitris already active began to centre their attention upon the work begun, and temporarily new beginnings were out of order. It must not be forgotten here that the work of the solar Pitris *from their point of view,* is not primarily the evolution of man, but is the process of their own development within the plan of the solar Logos. The evolution of the human race is, for them, but a method.

Perfected men are in the councils of the planetary Logos of their particular ray; the solar Pitris are in the council of the solar Logos.[69]

It might be of value here if we temporarily stopped our consideration of the egoic groups and briefly tabulated the evolutions, remembering that in this tabulation, the planes of differentiation alone are concerned; on the plane of the unmanifest or of the subjective, only unity is known. It must again be remembered that the term "unmanifest" is one of relative importance only, and concerns *man's apprehension* of all that is. To the solar Logos the planes of the unmanifest are objective. Man has not as yet achieved etheric vision, and the etheric

[69] All these will become solar Logoi of varying grades.

TABULATION VI

Lives	Goal
1. Planetary Logoi .... The major Three.	Cosmic liberation; the final cosmic Initiations.
2. The minor four planetary Logoi.	Cosmic Initiation, or the first four Initiations.
3. The informing Lives of a planetary globe....	Manus of a cosmic chain. Not a seed manu, but a periodical manu of lesser degree. This involves an unrevealable mystery, connected with certain Hierarchies of color.
4. The informing life of a kingdom in nature...	Transference in one of three directions; a. To the line of the solar Pitris. b. To Sirius, as a karmic adjuster. c. To the solar system of the next order to work in connection with the planetary Logoi of his own line as ruler of a kingdom or life wave in the system, and not just in a scheme.
5. The solar Pitris....................	The highest three groups will become major planetary Logoi; the lower four groups will become minor planetary Logoi.
6. The human evolution.................	To become the solar Pitris of another cycle. To follow any of the paths earlier enumerated. Those who become solar Pitris, being the bulk of humanity, return to Sirius to be breathed out again into activity.
7. The lunar Pitris....................	To become men. They will in their higher grades pass directly into the animal evolution of the next cycle and so eventually individualise. Their three higher grades will become animal-men, and the lower four will contribute to the quaternie forms of the men of the next creation.
8. The animal evolution	Human kingdom.
9. The vegetable evolution	The animal kingdom.
10. The mineral evolution	The vegetable kingdom.
11. The four higher grades of lesser Builders.	They will form the manifested double or form of that mysterious third evolution of the next system; that is, the etheric body of the planetary entity. This mysterious life is as yet an unfathomable mystery and one which will not be revealed till the final one of the triplicity of solar systems of our solar Logos.
12. The three lower grades of the lesser Builders.	The physical body in its densest form of the planetary entity.

subplanes are to him as yet unmanifest. The solar Logos has cosmic etheric vision fully developed, and because He is on the cosmic Path all is known and fully revealed to Him within the solar System.

It might here be noted that the planetary Entity is the sumtotal of all the elemental lives of the lesser Builders functioning as, or forming, the substance of any particular globe in physical objectivity. The mystery of the whole subject lies hidden in three things:

First, the fact that our three planes, physical, astral, and mental, form the dense body of the solar Logos, and are therefore not considered as forming principles.

The second fact is that the lesser "lives" or the elemental essence are the "refuse" of an earlier system, and react to inherent impulses so powerfully that it was only possible to control them through the dynamic will of the Logos, consciously applied. The word "refuse" must be interpreted analogically, and as is understood when it is said that man gathers to himself in each fresh incarnation matter to form his dense physical body which is tinged with the earlier vibrations of preceding incarnations. These "lives" have been gradually drawn in during the entire mahamanvantara as it became safe and possible to control and bend them to the will of the greater Builders. Much of the earlier energy-substance in systemic construction has been passed on into that force-matter which we call that of the lunar Pitris, and its place has gradually been taken by this type of energy, gathered in from the greater sphere in which our Logos has place. The twelve evolutions are after all but the twelve types of energy, manifesting ever in three groups of forces, and again as one group when synthesised during the process of manifestation. They are fourfold in interaction, and have a systemic ebb and flow about which little is known.

Third, the fact of the coming into incarnation of the

informing "life" of this low grade substance, who is an
entity from a point in the Heavens which may not be
mentioned: He embodies influences of a manasic nature,
but manas at its very lowest vibration. Perhaps some
idea of this may be gathered if it is stated that there is a
resemblance between this vibration, or this energising
life, and the basic vibration of the solar system preceding
this one. We must remember that our basic vibration
was the result of the evolutionary process of the entire
earlier system. This entity has the same analogous relation to the deva evolution as the mysterious "bridges"
which baffle scientists, and which are found between the
vegetable and the animal kingdom, and the mineral and
the vegetable; they are neither the one nor the other. On
a large scale, this "life" or the informing entity of the
lower life of the physical plane of the solar system is
neither a full exponent of the subconscious life of the
earlier system, nor of the elemental life of this; only in
the next system will be seen the manifestation of a form
of consciousness of a type at present inconceivable to
man. Esoterically he is stated to have "neither sight
nor hearing"; he is neither deva nor human in essence.
He is occultly "blind," utterly unaware; he is capable
only of movement, and resembles the foetus in the womb;
that which is coming to the birth only the next greater
cycle will reveal. The mystery of the moon [70] or of the
"divine lunatic" is connected somewhat with the revelation (through the premature compassion of our planetary Logos) of the life of this nature, informing the dense
globe of the moon chain. On His high level, pity awoke
in the heart of the planetary Logos for certain involutionary existences within the moon chain, and (like the
Buddha on a lesser scale and at a much later date) compassionate zeal brought the karmic results with which we
are still concerned. The "beast" must be driven back

[70] S. D., I, 172, footnote.

for his own good to run his cycle, hidden in his den and confined within safe limits until the dawning of a new system brings him conscious opportunity.

More we may not say. It must be remembered that the mysteries of existence are as yet but little cognised by man. In cases where profound mysteries lie, man is often totally unaware of it; and frequently man remains blind and deaf where no mystery is but only revelation for those who have eyes to see and ears to hear. When man has penetrated to those secrets which lie behind the lower kingdoms in nature, when he has solved the problem of the constitution of the interior of the Earth, and has from there worked his way back to knowledge of the working of the involutionary path and the lives which tread that path, then and then only will he begin to realise the strangeness of that which lies beyond his ken.

One further hint may be given, which will serve to throw a beam of light upon the problem for those who are ready, and will add to the confusion of the non-intuitive: —From the standpoint of the ONE ABOUT WHOM NAUGHT MAY BE SAID, to Whom our solar system is but a centre (*which* centre being one of the three truths revealed at the seventh Initiation)

a. System   I ......was characterised by the organisation of a centre, and the mysterious life we have been speaking about was produced by the "lowest vibration of the centre."

b. System II ......is characterised by the activity in three dimensions of this centre, and the evolution of three types of consciousness, deva, human and subhuman, in all their many grades and hierarchies. It is the period of the balancing of the forces in the centre.

c. System III ......will be characterised by the fourth dimensional activity of the centre, and the twelve types of evolution will become four types of force.

This is next to impossible for man to understand and will seem inexplicable, but this hint is imparted in order that man may realise the interdependence of the various systems, and the place they hold in a greater scheme; the intent is not to give the student uncorrelated facts of no apparent use to him. Without the premise of our position within a vaster scheme, man's deductions will remain inaccurate.

We will now proceed with our enumeration of the groups of Egos according to their characteristics, but it might be wise to deal first with a problem which may be in some minds and see if it is not capable of solution. Two problems come before the mind of the thoughtful student; one concerns the position (in connection with any particular planetary scheme) of those vast groups of Egos, which are embodied by Lives, emanating from any one of the seven Rays, and associated with any of the various schemes. The other deals with the effect produced by the "coming-in" of Egos on the mental plane which are not "bud" Egos, but are possibly very fully developed, such as disciples and initiates.

These thoughts may be clarified if certain statements are made relating to the mental plane, and which will serve as indications as to the direction in which the solution of these problems may be sought.

The mental plane is, as H. P. B. has pointed out, the vastest of all the planes with which we are concerned. It is the key plane of the solar system. It is the pivotal plane upon which the great Wheel turns. It is the meeting place of the three lines of evolution and has been for this reason esoterically termed *"the council chamber of the Three Divinities."* On this plane, the three Persons of the logoic Trinity meet in united work. Below two Persons may be seen associated; above another duality functions, but only on this plane do the Three make an at-one-ment.

All the Logoi of the differing schemes are expressing Themselves upon this plane. There are certain schemes in the system which find their lowest manifestation on this plane, and have no physical body such as the Earth, and the other dense planets. They *exist* through the medium of gaseous matter, and their spheres of manifestation are simply composed of the four cosmic ethers and the cosmic gaseous. But all the great Lives of the solar system do possess bodies of our systemic mental matter, and therefore on that plane communication between all these Entities becomes a possibility. *This fact is the basis of occult realisation,* and *the true ground for the at-one-ment.* Matter of the abstract levels of the mental plane enters into the composition of the vehicles for all these greater Existences and through the medium of this energised substance each can get *en rapport* with each, no matter what Their individual goal of attainment may be. The units, therefore, in Their bodies can equally get in touch with all other Egos and groups once they have achieved the consciousness of the mental plane (causal consciousness) and know the varying group "keys," the group tones and colors.

It will consequently be apparent to the careful student that in this fact lies the true relationship between the various groups of Egos, no matter what degree of evolution, or what ray and in which scheme they may be. The basic truth here involved may be better grasped if the following occult phrases are studied:

"*Within the Hall of Ignorance* kama-manas rules. The man, weighed down by much misplaced desire, seeks for the object of his heart's attention within the murky halls of densest maya. He finds it there but dies ere garnering all the longed-for fruit. The serpent stings him, and the joy desired recedes from out his grasp. All seeking thus the selfish fruits of karma must each despise each other; hence strife and greed, ill-will and hatred, death and retribution, karmic invocation and the thunderbolt of vengeance characterise this Hall.

Within the Hall of Learning intellect rules and seeks to guide. Desire of a higher kind, the fruit of manas and its use, supplants the lower kamic urge. Man weighs and balances, and in the twilight Halls of Intellection seeks for the fruit of knowledge. He finds it but to realise that knowledge is not all; he dies upon the open field of knowledge, hearing a cry beat on his dying ears: "Know that the knower greater is than knowledge; the One who seeks is greater than the sought.

Within the Hall of Wisdom the Spirit rules; the One within the lesser ones assumes supreme control. Death is not known within these halls, for its two great gates are passed. Discord and strife both disappear and only harmony is seen. The knowers see themselves as One; they recognise the field wherein knowledge grows as Brahmic dissonance and differentiation. Knowledge they know as method, an instrument of purpose utilised by all and just a germ of eventual recognition. Within this hall union of each with each, blending of one and all, and unity of action, goal and skill marks every high endeavor."

If these words are pondered on, it will be realised that true union exists in the realisation that the greater life ever includes the lesser, and that each expansion of consciousness brings man closer to this realised Oneness.

Therefore, if one might venture to express an abstraction and a state of consciousness in terms of time and space, and through the limitation of language, it might be stated that on egoic levels, or on the three higher subplanes of the mental plane, there exists a channel of communication, based on similarity of vibration and oneness of endeavour, between every one of the planetary schemes, within the solar ring-pass-not. Here, and here alone (as regards the three worlds and the human kingdom), becomes possible the establishing of egoic relationships and the transmission of thought substance between

a. Units and egoic groups.
b. Groups and other groups.

   c. Greater groups with still greater or with lesser
     ones.

   d. Egos in one planetary scheme with those in an-
     other.

The Ah-hi, the greater Builders,[71] Who are the Lords
working out the will of the solar Logos, mainly use two
planes for communication with each other and with Their
cohorts:

   First, *the second plane,* where They communicate by
     means of a spiritual medium incomprehensible to
     man at present.

   Second, *the mental plane,* where They communicate
     with all lesser lives by means of a type of mental
     telepathy.

The "coming-in" of advanced Egos from the inner
round, or from other planetary schemes, or from subtler
spheres where they have been in pralaya awaiting opportunity is produced in a triple manner and is the result of a triple activity. It is caused by an understanding
between the planetary Logos of a scheme, and a brother
planetary Logos whereby an exchange is effected. The
student must here think in terms of force and energy, of
magnetic interaction and the *conscious* transmission of
energy out of the body of the planetary Logos, via the
centres or a centre, into the body of another planetary
Logos. *The cause here is the will or purpose, the object
is sensation, and the method is force transference.* Exactly the same understanding lies back of the coming in
of egos from the inner round, only this time the energy is
sent forth by certain existences (working in connection
with any planetary Logos) who are the "custodians of
the inner circle." This touches upon a mystery and deals
with the coming-in of high Egos, of Avatars, of Buddhas,

---

[71] From a Sensa word meaning "serpents." These are the Dragons of
Wisdom. See S. D., I, 55, 69, 70.

of masters, of initiates, and of disciples, and ot all who have to wait for group, and not individual, urge for the fulfillment of cyclic karma on a large scale, and whose "wheels" are controlled by cosmic forces and not by purely systemic forces.

Another factor might be termed the karmic results of seeds sown in days long past, and hidden in the mysteries of the earlier system, scheme, or chain as the case may be. All these three groups of manifestation follow karmic impulse, and this impulse it is which controls the time period, and method of the appearance in any group of planetary egos, of newly born lotus buds, or of lotuses which are termed "mystically transplanted." These latter are probably of a high degree of unfoldment. This is possible in individual cases and in the case of entire groups.

A third factor has to do with the transference of Egos or lotuses from one sphere of activity to another and this necessarily produces conditions calling for the appearance of similar centres to take their place. Energy transmitted must be supplied from elsewhere, and this is another predisposing factor for the appearance of egoic lotuses in any scheme. The law of the conservation of force holds good on any plane.

This whole question of the transference of egoic lotuses from any one scheme to another, or from chain to chain, on the mental plane is one of very real intricacy, and cannot be elucidated to the unpledged disciple. Only these general indications are in any way possible.

It must also be remembered in connection with our planet that Egos appear in those groups whose lotuses are not produced as the result of the Law of Attraction working between the animal kingdom of the globe and the higher Triads, but which are Egos who have individualised elsewhere, and who therefore come in with their petals already organised, and perhaps with several petals unfolded. This has necessarily a profound effect both upon the groups in which they appear, and upon the type of man who will make his appearance subsequently in physical plane incarnation. This is touched upon in the *Secret Doctrine* when the question of the early teachers and divine kings who occupied the ill-favoured bodies of the early humanity, is broached.[72, 73]

To continue with our consideration of egoic groups: It might be briefly stated that the egoic groups in connection with our planet may be roughly grouped according to the stage of lotus organisation, as follows:

a. Egos who were produced through the individualisation process in Lemurian days. They are the true Earth humanity, along with the second group.

b. Egos who have individualised during the Atlantean root-race until the door was shut.

c. Egos who have "come-in" from the moon chain and who are much more evolved than the earth humanity.

d. Egos who have been swept in since Atlantean days to take the place of those Egos who have achieved liberation, and whose causal bodies have disappeared, or whose lotuses have "died out" leaving a vacuum in force substance which must be supplied and filled. They usually come in from one of two schemes:

1. From the scheme embodied by the polar opposite of our planetary Logos.

2. From that scheme which is allied with these two in forming a systemic triangle.

[72] See the early part of the *Secret Doctrine*, Volume II.
[73] C. W. Leadbeater had a dim apprehension of this idea when he referred to those boat loads of Egos from the moon chain. He has of course materialised the idea far too much; if the same fundamental idea is expressed in terms of force and of the appearance of force centres within the earth chain, which force centres are the result of energy emanating from an earlier chain and producing whorls in the ether or substance of the mental plane, then the true significance may be more easily grasped.

These cases are necessarily rare at present but will become more frequent as more and more of the human race take the fourth Initiation.

e. Certain rare Egos or lotuses from schemes not enumerated in the above triplicity. They are usually only brought in so that they may perfect certain developments in their own nature, to carry out experimental work in connection with the deva kingdom, or to produce certain group results desired by the planetary Logos. They frequently do not descend into dense physical incarnation but work primarily on mental and astral levels, returning to their own spheres eventually for the final stages of liberation.

All these lotuses in their myriad differentiations have specific effects upon each other on mental levels, and these effects are as yet utterly unrealised by man. Nevertheless, they are the basis of the true psychology, and the grounds of all true activity. The student would do well to ponder upon the effect any advanced Ego would be likely to have upon:

a. Other Egos in his group.
b. The solar Pitris who are the substance of the group.
c. The lunar Pitris, who are linked with the solar Pitris through the permanent atoms.

We have enumerated above certain classifications of groups of Egos to be found on the causal levels of the mental plane, so as to give students some idea of the vastness of the subject, and the complexity of the problem. It must be remembered that on the third subplane of the mental plane there is no individual separation such as we find when in physical manifestation, but nevertheless group separation is to be seen. These groups are far too many to enumerate in detail. We have outlined and named five of the larger groups as catalogued under one scheme of tabulation in the Hall of Records. Other methods of enumeration exist, and even under the one here used, these five groups are each subdivided into ten groups, and these again are broken up into lesser units, all of them being known and portrayed under certain symbols.

When we come to the second subplane of the mental plane (the plane whereon the egoic bodies of advanced humanity, of disciples, and of initiates are found) the method of grouping will be according to:

a. Ray.
b. Subray.
c. Department (whether under the Manu, the Maha-chohan or the Bodhisattva on our earth scheme or their analogies on other schemes).
d. The Master's group.

These egoic lotuses are all organised, and have a number of petals unfolded whilst some are in the final stages of development.

They have also been grouped under the following three heads:

Lotuses of revelation. Those in which the "jewel" is just about to be revealed.

Lotuses with perfume. Those whose occult "smell" or aroma is permeating their environment. They are those Egos who have not yet completely unfolded the final tier of petals, but whose lives are of magnetic force in the three worlds, and whose careers are distinguished by altruistic service.

Radiant lotuses, or those whose light is beginning to shine forth as lights in a dark place.

They are grouped also according to primary colour, to subsidiary colouring, according to key or tone, and one tabulation is entirely numerical. It might be of interest to the student if we here pointed out that in the Hall of Records in connection with the human Egos certain of the records under symbological terminology keep a minute account of the following facts concerning each unit:

The *lunar* record. This deals with all the lower vehicles and forms, employed by the human Monads and concerns itself with:

a. Their rate of vibration,
b. Their type,
c. Their key number,
d. The particular group of lunar Lords who are concerned with those bodies,
e. The detailed history of the elemental lives who construct the bodies.

This information is employed by the karmic official responsible for the production of a new set of vehicles at each incarnation, in order to assist the working out of karma. The history of the lunar bodies is stored up in the permanent atoms.

The *solar* record. This deals with the more permanent egoic vehicle, and concerns itself with:

a. The rate of vibration.
b. The history of the petal unfoldment.
c. The history of any particular group of solar Angels concerned with the formation of the lotus.
d. The activity of the deva substance out of which the lotus is constructed.
e. Group relationships.

This information is used by the Master Who has made Himself responsible for the stimulation and the growth of any particular series of Egos, and also by advanced Egos who are consciously working with their group.

The *consciousness* record. This concerns the response of the indwelling Entity to its surroundings. It deals with the utilisation of knowledge by the knower, and is in many ways the most intricate and the most lengthy of the records.

These records are mostly used by the Lord of the World and His pupils to ascertain information in connection with the planetary centres. They are arranged in such a way that the entire record of any group, however vast and extensive, is embodied in seven sheets of symbols, each containing forty-nine symbols. These sheets are changed and corrected once every seven years, and are precipitated on astral matter by an effort of will by the Chohan responsible for the particular group involved.

(*d.*) *The Petals and the Etheric Centres.* It remains now to point out the close connection between the unfoldment of the petals in the egoic lotuses and the etheric centres in man. *It is through the centres that psychic energy flows.* Students should carefully bear in mind the two following facts:

First, the etheric body is vitalised, as we know, by prana. Pranic energy is the stimulator of animal activity, and of physical plane development. Its effect is primarily upon the atoms of the physical body and it has a triple effect upon the substance of the physical body:

a. It preserves the animal health of the body.
b. It constructs and builds in the body, through its energy and force currents, what is needed to replace the daily wear and tear.
c. It is the medium whereby man comes into physical touch with his brother man. Physical magnetism is largely, even if not wholly, dependent upon prana.

The etheric centres are the force vortices formed in etheric matter by astral impulse, transmitted via the astral centres. These astral centres in their turn are the transmitters of still higher energy, and thus the statement is technically true that the etheric centres are the source of man's psychic energy, and are therefore affected by the unfoldment of the petals. Every petal is in its turn a type of force centre, and the energy emanating from it affects the etheric centres, and produces every type of psychic energy of the true kind.

The energy flowing from the Ego is but little felt in the early stages of development. Man follows his allotted path through animal and racial instinct, and can be safely left to the stimulation emanating from his group centres, and to the ordinary driving force inherent in form, and to the earlier life waves. It is only when he has reached a comparatively advanced stage (in comparison with that of animal man) that egoic or psychic force pours through his centres in such a way as to produce results in consciousness—of these he will eventually become profoundly aware within his physical brain. I do not here refer to the ordinary animal psychism displayed by the higher animals, and found among certain of the post Lemurian races. This is a type of consciousness inherent in the atoms, and is a constituent part of the "soul of the world." It is unconscious and uncontrolled and has no part in this teaching. I refer to the conscious psychism which is displayed by advanced humanity, by disciples and initiates of all grades. This kind is the result of the pouring in of egoic energy through the etheric centres (mainly through five of them) in such a way that the consciousness of the physical brain becomes aware of it, and also aware of:

a. Its purpose,

b. Its technique,

c. The effects produced within the lower self of the man himself and also upon others, *d.* His ability to employ it or not as he may desire. It is under his control.

The centres with which the student is concerned are, as we know, four in number:

a. The head,
b. The heart,
c. The throat,
d. The base of the spine.

These are the only ones which should receive consideration. His work is to transfer the force or energy out of the two lower—the spinal and the solar plexus—into the three higher. It is presumed that he has already transferred, or is in process of transferring, the energy of the generative organs into the centre of desire, the solar plexus, with the aim in view of guiding it still higher to the throat centre. The splenic centre, being the vehicle of prana, is specially developed under evolutionary law, and its energy is not transferred to another centre, but is consciously diffused. When its correspondence in the head centre is awakened, this becomes the organ of occult healing; through it the healer (by an act of will), absorbs prana and vitality from the ethers, and then breathes it out again upon the object to be healed by an act of compassionate healing.

In connection with the etheric centres, we should note the fact that the major head centre is twofold in structure, and consists of a lotus of ninety-six petals between the eyebrows, and of a twelve-petalled lotus at the top of the head, with ninety-six petals in a subsidiary whorl. The significance of these figures is profound. In every case the figure twelve is met with, showing a definite relation to the basic psychic lotuses on egoic levels. Twelve multiplied by eight stands for the twelve petals in each case, while in the figure eight lies hidden the idea of duality:

a. The four of the quaternary,
b. The four of the egoic auric egg (the three aspects, and the ring-pass-not.)

We must note also, that the idea of twelve in connection with the centres is found in three of them:

a. The higher head centre,
b. The secondary head centre,
c. The heart centre.

If the student studies this condition, and links up the idea of the three tiers of petals in the twelve-petalled lotus, he may find illumination. More it is not possible to give at this stage.

It is only when the etheric centres—the two head centres and the heart centre—are fully active with their twelve petals completely unfolded that the central circle of petals in the egoic lotus (the fourth or inner circle) unfolds. The significance of the four circles in the egoic lotus, and the eight circles of twelve petals each in the etheric lotuses on the mental plane is of great importance.

The centres with which man has to deal are necessarily five at this stage owing to the following facts, which must be studied if a man desires to awaken his centres according to plan, and if he wishes safely to follow along the line of the true psychic unfoldment:

The fact that the energy starts from the fifth plane, the mental, where man is concerned,

The fact that it is through the agency of the fifth principle that man can consciously work at his own unfoldment,

The fact that the path of evolution is for man a fivefold one, covering the five planes of human unfoldment; and is divided into five stages as regards the Ego,

The fact that although this is the second solar system from the standpoint of the egoic cycles of the Logos,

or His second major egoic cycle, yet it is the fifth
when viewed from another angle, that of the lesser
cycles. It corresponds to the fifth period in human
evolution, that in which man treads the Path. The
Logos is now treading the cosmic Path.

The fact that the fifth spirilla is in process of awakening. This has to be effected before the interplay of
energy between the egoic lotus and the etheric centres becomes so powerful as to awaken man's physical brain, and cause him to become aware of the
inner currents. This takes place usually when the
fifth petal is organised.

This whole question can also be viewed in a larger
manner from the standpoint of the five Kumaras. It
must be remembered that the aggregate of the etheric
centres of any particular group of men form the force
centres or minute "energy units" in the larger petals of
their group centre. These again form petals in some particular planetary centre, and the aggregate of these petals
form those larger centres of energy which we call "planetary centres." These in their turn form centres of force
for the Logos.

Yet the mystery in connection with this is so profound
that unless the student carefully guards himself from too
mathematical and material a concept, he will go astray.
The etheric centres of man are not on the same plane as
the etheric centres of a planetary Logos. His centres
are on the plane of the fourth cosmic ether, the systemic
buddhic plane, and it is only when man has taken the final
initiation that his energy becomes incorporated into that
of the planetary centre on its own plane. The etheric
centres of the planetary Logos are transmitters and
transmuters of force, and bear the same relation to Him
as do the *physical* centres to a human being. All the
dense physical centres, such as the mouth, for instance,

are transmitters of some type of energy arising in the
human brain or will.

The understanding of force, of force transmission, and
of the effects of liberated force upon the higher planes is
the secret of occult knowledge. Force or energy flows in
from the Ego. It works through the etheric centres and
produces results on the three planes, varying according
to the age of the soul. As yet, through lack of alignment,
this egoic force does not reach the physical brain as
fully as it later will, but it does reach the astral centres,
and is frequently the cause of much of that lack of emotional control everywhere to be seen. The astral substance is as yet insufficiently organised, and when aroused
by egoic energy moves violently. Astral substance is
played upon by two counter streams of force: first, the
egoic, and secondly, that vibration set up through countless ages on the physical plane, which is latent in substance itself, and is the result of an earlier solar system.
This it is which produces the violent action and reaction
to be seen in every life.

It is not possible to give more data concerning the unfoldment of the petals and their connection with the
etheric centres. Three hints of practical import anent
this stupendous subject may however be given which, if
duly pondered upon, may carry illumination to those who
are ready.

The first is that the etheric centres become active in a
fourth dimensional sense (or become wheels turning upon
themselves) when the aspirant has complied with certain
details.

He must work upon the unfoldment of the fifth and
sixth petals, or the final two in the second circle and must
endeavour to bring about two things in connection with
his threefold lower nature:

a. He must align his three bodies so that there is a direct channel of contact formed between the Ego and the physical brain.

b. He must strive to bring about a stabilisation of both the astral body and the mind, and must aim at that emotional equilibrium which is produced by the conscious "balancing of forces."

He must study the laws of transmutation and be a student of that divine alchemy which will result in a knowledge of how to transmute the lower force into the higher, of how to transfer his consciousness into the higher vehicles, and of how to manipulate energy currents so that his own nature is transformed. He will then become a channel for the light of the Ego, and for the illumination of buddhi to pour through for the saving of the race, and the lighting of those who stumble in dark places. He must demonstrate the laws of radioactivity in his own life on the physical plane. His life must begin to radiate, and to have a magnetic effect upon others. By this I mean he will begin to influence that which is imprisoned in others, for he will reach—through his own powerful vibrations—the hidden centre in each one. I do not mean by this the physical or magnetic effect that many quite unevolved souls have upon others. I refer to that spiritual radiation that is only responded to and realised by those who themselves are becoming aware of the spiritual centre within the heart. At this stage the man is recognised as one who can speak occultly "heart to heart." He becomes a stimulator of the heart centre in his brother, and one who arouses men into activity for others.

The second hint is that as the aspirant becomes progressively radioactive, and as the energy of the inner God demonstrates more and more through the lower personality, the "heat radiations" become so powerful that very definite results are produced of a personal, and also of an environal, nature. A few of these results might be enumerated as follows:

The etheric web, separating the lower physical consciousness of the brain from the astral plane begins to undergo a lengthy process of destruction, and the first "rents" in the web occur. It is through these that the student becomes aware of the inner planes, becomes conscious in the physical brain of the inner happenings, and can (if a disciple) make his contacts with his Ego and (via that ego) with his Guru.[74] This marks a very important development.

The higher head centre increases its activity and becomes capable of receiving flashes of illumination from the higher planes. This happens only occasionally at first but with increasing frequency as the years progress, and the "rents" become more numerous.

The various triangles become vivified and proceed to increased activity in due geometrical progression, whilst the centre between the shoulder blades, the converging point for certain fires, becomes active. This marks a definite stage in the process of transferring the fires into the higher centres. Roughly speaking, this period of the transference of the heat or energy of the lower centres into the higher may be divided into two parts: first, that in which the centres in the lower part of the body (those below the diaphragm) are transferred into the centres in the higher part of the torso. These centres in the torso are three in number, the heart, the throat, and the centre between the shoulder blades. We must here note that the throat centre is situated in the lower part of the throat, and properly belongs to the torso and not to the head. It should also be stated here that the centre between the shoulder blades is not a "sacred" centre, but is of a temporary nature, and is created by the aspirant himself during the process of transference.

[74] A Guru is a spiritual teacher.

The second stage is that in which the energy of the lower six centres:

a. The throat,
b. The heart,
c. The solar plexus,
d. The spleen,
e. The organs of generation,
f. The base of the spine,

are—in due order according to a man's ray and subray—transferred into the correspondences within the head centre. These seven head centres are the reflection in the microcosm of those ''mansions prepared in the Heavens'' which receive the sevenfold energy of the monad. These are the chambers prepared by the lower energy which are to be the recipients of ''soul or the higher psychic energy.''

The final hint which can be given, may be summed up in the words that as the aspirant progresses,[75] he not only balances the pairs of opposites, but the secret of his brother's heart becomes revealed to him. He becomes an acknowledged force in the world, and is recognised as one who can be depended upon to serve. Men turn to him for assistance and help along his recognised line, and he begins to sound forth his note so as to be heard not only in human but in deva ranks as well. This he does, at

[75] Aspirant.

''The practices which make for union with the Soul are: fervent aspiration, spiritual reading, and complete obedience to the Master.

The word which I have rendered ''fervent aspiration'' means primarily ''fire''; and, in the Eastern teaching, it means the fire which gives life and light, and at the same time the fire which purifies. We have, therefore, as our first practice, as the first of the means of spiritual growth, that fiery quality of the will which enkindles and illumines, and, at the same time, the steady practice of purification, the burning away of all known impurities.''

''Their aim is, to bring soul-vision, and to wear away hindrances.''

''The Rules are these: purity, serenity, fervent aspiration, spiritual reading, and perfect obedience to the Master.''

''The perfection of the powers of the bodily vesture comes through the wearing away of impurities, and through fervent aspiration.''—*Yoga Sutras of Patanjali*, Book II, 1, 2, 32. 43 (C. Johnston's Edition).

this stage, through the pen in literature, through the spoken word in lecturing and teaching, through music, painting and art. He reaches the hearts of men in some way or another, and becomes a helper and server of his race.

Two more characteristics of this stage might here be enumerated.

The aspirant has an appreciation of the occult value of money in service. He seeks nothing for himself, save that which may equip him for the work to be done, and he looks upon money, and that which money can purchase, as something which is to be used for others and a means to bring about the fruition of the Master's plans as he senses those plans. The occult significance of money is little appreciated, yet one of the greatest tests as to the position of a man upon the probationary path is that which concerns his attitude to and his handling of that which all men seek in order to gratify desire. Only he who desires naught for himself can be a recipient of financial bounty, and a dispenser of the riches of the universe. In other cases where riches increase, they bring with them naught but sorrow and distress, discontent and misuse.

At this stage also the aspirant's life becomes an "instrument of destruction" in the occult sense of the term. Wherever he goes the force which flows through him from the higher planes, and from his own inner God, produces at times peculiar results upon his environment. It acts as a stimulator of both the good and the evil. The lunar Pitris who form the bodies of his brothers and his own body are likewise stimulated, their activity is increased, and their power greatly aggravated. This fact is used by Those Who work on the inner side to bring about certain desired ends. This it is also which oft times temporarily causes the downfall of advanced souls. They cannot stand the force pouring into them, or upon them, and through the temporary over-stimulation of their centres and vehicles they go astray. This can be seen working out in groups as well as in individuals. But, inversely, if the lunar Lords of the lower self have been earlier subjugated and brought under control, then the effect of the force and energy contacted is to stimulate the response of the physical brain consciousness and the head centres to egoic contact. Then the otherwise destructive force becomes a factor for good and helpful stimulation, and can be used by Those Who know how, to lead men on to further illumination.

All these stages have to work out on all the three lower planes and in the three bodies; this they do according to the particular Ray and subray. In this fashion the work of the disciple is carried forward, and his testing and training carried out until the two circles of petals are unfolded, and the third is organised. Thus he is brought, through right direction of energy and wise manipulation of force currents, to the Portal of Initiation, and graduates out of the Hall of Learning [76] into the great Hall of Wisdom—that Hall wherein he gradually becomes "aware" of forces, and powers, latent in his own Ego and egoic group. It is the Hall wherein he gains the right to use the force of the egoic group, for he can now be trusted to wield it only for the helping of humanity. After the fourth Initiation, he becomes a sharer in, and can be trusted with some part of the energy of the planetary Logos and thus be enabled to carry forward the plans of that Logos for evolution.

---

[76] The three Halls through which the soul of man must progress are spoken of in *The Voice of the Silence*, pp. 19, 20.

1st Hall... Hall of Ignorance... infant humanity..... Physical plane.
2nd Hall... Hall of Learning....average man........astral plane.
3rd Hall...Hall of Wisdom.....spiritual man.......mental plane.

The longest time is spent in the Hall of Ignorance. The later period in the Hall of Learning is called the Probationary Path. In the Hall of Wisdom the Initiate approaches the central mystery of Being.

(*e.*) *Initiation and the Petals.* In considering the connection of the petals and their unfoldment through initiation, there is little which it is permissible to give out at this time for the information of the general public. All that is possible is to give certain statements, containing:

a. Hints as to the right direction of the energy,
b. Suggestions as to the basic mysteries which man has to solve,
c. Indications as to certain correspondences,
d. Practical points for constructive thinking.

Students must remember that the aim of all truly occult teachers is not to give information but to train their pupils in the use of thought energy. It will therefore be apparent why this method of instruction is the one invariably used. It is the method which involves the dropping of a hint on the part of the Teacher, and the correlation perhaps of certain correspondences, coupled with a suggestion as to the sources of light. It involves, on the part of the pupil, the following recognitions:

a. That the hint may be worth following.
b. That meditation is the pathway to the source of light, and that *the hint dropped is the "seed" for meditation.*
c. That facts, ill-assorted and uncorrelated, are menaces to knowledge and no help.
d. That every aspect of truth, progressively grasped, has to be assimilated, and welded into the experience of the student.
e. That unless the correspondences agree in an atomic, personal, planetary and cosmic fashion, they are not to be trusted.
f. That much information is withheld until the student is a disciple, and still more until he is a pledged initiate. The reason for this is to be found in the

fact that all knowledge concerns energy, its application, and its use or misuse.

Let us now continue with our consideration of the petals and Initiation.

Each of the three circles of lotus petals is closely connected with one of the three Halls. This has been earlier referred to. Much of the work connected with the *first tier of petals* is part of the experience in the Hall of Ignorance. The act of organising and preparing for unfoldment is the most important stage, and that with which man is the most concerned. The act of petal opening is of briefer duration, and is produced by the pouring in of solar heat or fire, and thus bringing about a fresh access of energy. This is produced in our earth scheme through the co-operation of the Mahachohan, of the Chohan of a man's egoic group, and the particular Ego concerned.

The following tabulation may be found helpful:

I. *Knowledge Petals. First circle.*

a. Organised in the Hall of Ignorance.
b. Guided by the force and energy of the Mahachohan.
c. The third group of solar Pitris affected.

II. *Love Petals. Second circle.*

a. Organised in the Hall of Learning.
b. Guided by the force of the Bodhisattva.
c. The second group of solar Lords affected.

III. *Will or Sacrifice Petals. Third circle.*

a. Organised in the Hall of Wisdom.
b. Guided by the force and energy of the Manu.
c. The first group of solar Angels affected.

At the stage which we are considering (that of the organisation and unfoldment of the first tier of petals), the egoic influence felt at the beginning is but small, but when the three petals become sufficiently active and alive through the energy accumulated and stored up in the

ego during the activities of the personal life, a form of
initiation then takes place which is a reflection (on a
lower plane) of the great manasic initiations. The energy
in the outer circle of petals causes it to spring apart
from the next circle, and to unfold. This threefold energy
becomes interactive and a very definite stage is thus
reached. This series of initiations is seldom recognised
within the physical brain consciousness owing to the
relatively inchoate stage of the bodies, and the unre-
sponsiveness of the brain matter. Yet they are nevertheless initiations of a definite though less important
character, and they involve primarily the display (within
the personal life of the man) of an intelligent recognition
of his group relationships on earth. This recognition is
frequently selfish in character, as, for instance, that which
the union worker displays, but it is indicative of group
interplay.

A similar process takes place when the second circle
of petals is organised and ready for unfoldment. This
time the World Teacher, the Master and the Ego concerned are co-operating, for these smaller initiations deal
with the love nature, with astral or emotional organisation, and with the recognition (by the man in his personal
life) of some form of unselfish love, and of a love for
some object, person or ideal which leads to altruistic endeavor, and to the negation of the lower self.

This brings us to the third group of petals or to the
unfolding of the will or sacrifice petals, based on intelligent purpose and pure love. The force in this group calls
in a different factor, that of the Manu, as well as the force
of the Bodhisattva, and the desired effect is produced
through the full co-operation of the fully awakened Ego,
aided by his own Master (if he is evolving in a cycle
wherein hierarchical effort for humanity takes the form
it does in this present one), and the Manu. Eventually
(after the second Initiation) the Lord of the World comes

in as a factor,—the Lord of world power, fully expressing itself in love.

Speaking generally, therefore, it might be stated that egoic groups in whom the knowledge petals are being organised and unfolded come under the primary influence of the Mahachohan; those in whom the love aspect, or the second circle of petals, is opening come under the primary influence of the Bodhisattva, with the knowledge unfoldment paralleling the work; whilst those in whom the third tier is being opened come under the energy direction of the Manu, with the two other types of force co-ordinated. It will be apparent to the careful reader that in this fact lies hid the secret of why the Mahachohan holds office longer than either of His two Brothers, holding it as He does for an entire world period. The key to these cycles lies hid in the following thoughts: the Bodhisattva and the Manu change more frequently and pass on to other work owing to the fact that They each embody one type of triple force, whereas the Mahachohan is the focal point for five types of energy, each in its turn triple in nature.

In each case of petal unfoldment, certain types of force are generated, dealt with, assimilated, and used, at first unconsciously and finally with full intelligence.

In the *Hall of Ignorance* the force of the energy of Brahma (the activity and intelligence of substance) is that mostly dealt with, and the man has to learn the meaning of activity based on:

a. Inherent energy,
b. Absorbed energy,
c. Group energy,
d. Material energy or that which is hidden in physical plane matter.

In the *Hall of Learning* the disciple becomes aware of, and uses the energy of, the second aspect in form-building, in social relations, in family and other group affiliations. He comes to the true recognition of sex and its relations but as yet views this force as something to be controlled and not something to be consciously and constructively utilised.

In the *Hall of Wisdom* the initiate comes to the knowledge of the first great aspect of energy, the dynamic use of will in sacrifice, and to him is then committed the key to the three fold mystery of energy. Of this energy in its threefold aspect he became aware in the other two halls. At the third, fourth and fifth Initiations the three keys to the three mysteries are given to him.

The key to the mystery sensed in the first Hall, the mystery of Brahma, is handed to him and he can then unlock the hidden energies of atomic substance. The key to the mystery of sex, or of the pairs of opposites, is thrust into his hand, and he can then unlock the hidden forces within all forms. The key to the mystery of sacrifice and to the secret of the Silent Watchers in the cosmos is revealed to him, and he learns to unlock the hidden energies of the will aspect. The dynamo of the solar system is shown to him, if it might so be expressed, and the intricacies of its mechanism revealed.

The following are the three basic mysteries of the solar system:

1. *The mystery of Electricity.* The mystery of Brahma. The secret of the third aspect. It is latent in the physical sun.
2. *The mystery of Polarity,* or of the universal sex impulse. The secret of the second aspect. It is latent in the Heart of the Sun, i.e., in the subjective Sun.
3. *The mystery of Fire* itself, or the dynamic central systemic force. The secret of the first aspect. It is latent in the central spiritual sun.

These three mysteries which we have touched upon above, come in a peculiar sense under the jurisdiction of

certain great Lords or Existences, and They have much
to do with the revealing of the mystery to those prepared
initiates Who come under Their influence during the final
stages of the Path.

The mystery of electricity has three keys, each of which
is held in the hands of one of the Buddhas of Activity.
Theirs is the prerogative to control the electrical forces
of the physical plane, and Theirs the right to direct the
three major streams of this type of force in connection
with *our present globe*. These three streams are concerned with atomic substance, out of which all forms are
constructed. In connection with *our chain* there are three
mysterious Entities (of whom our three Pratyeka Buddhas are but the Earth reflections) Who perform a similar
function in connection with the electrical forces of the
chain. *In the scheme,* the planetary Logos has also three
co-operating Existences Who are the summation of His
third Aspect, and who perform therefore work similar to
that performed by the three aspects of Brahma in the
solar system. The mystery of this threefold type of
electricity is largely connected with the lesser Builders,
with the elemental essence in one particular aspect,—its
lowest and most profound for men to apprehend as it concerns the secret of that which "substands" or "stands
back" of all that is objective. In a secondary sense it concerns the forces in the ethers which are those which
energise and produce the activities of all atoms. Another
type deals with the electrical phenomenon which finds
its expression in the light which man has somewhat harnessed, in the phenomena such as thunder storms and the
manifestation of lightning, with the aurora borealis, and
in the production of earthquakes and all volcanic action.
All these manifestations are based on electrical activity
of some kind, and have to do with the "soul of things,"
or with the essence of matter. The old Commentary
says:

"The garment of God is driven aside by the energy of His movements, and the real Man stands revealed, yet remains hidden, for who knows the secret of a man as it exists in his own self-recognition."

The mystery of electricity deals with the "garment" of God, just as the mystery of polarity deals with His "form."

In the mystery of Polarity, we have three different types of force manifesting and thus it is apparent that the two mysteries deal with the six forces. These three types of force are manipulated by the Buddhas of Love. They, through Their sacrifice, concern Themselves with the problem of sex, or of "magnetic approach" on all the planes. The Buddha of Whom we speak and Who contacts His people at the full moon of Wesak, is one of the three connected with *our globe,* having taken the place of One Who passed on to higher work in connection with *the Chain,* for the same hierarchical grading is seen as in connection with the Buddhas of Action. One group might be considered the divine Carpenters of the planetary system, the other the divine Assemblers of its parts and the Ones Who, through the magnetic influence They wield, unite the diversities and build them into form.

The present ideas anent Sex must be transmuted and raised from the existing lower connotation to its true significance. Sex—in the three worlds—has to do with the work of the lunar Pitris and the solar Lords. It signifies essentially the form-building work in substance, and its energising by the spiritual aspect. It signifies the elevation of the material aspect through the influence of Spirit as the two together perform their legitimate function in co-operation and thus—by their mutual union and blending—produce the Son in all His glory. This method of interpreting it is equally true of all the Existences manifesting on any plane, systemic and cosmic. Certain factors enter into the thought of sex which might be enumerated as follows:

a. Mutual attraction,
b. Complementary suitability,
c. Instinctual appeal,
d. Approach, and recognised co-operation,
e. Union,
f. The next stage is the temporary importance of the material aspect, that of the Mother, the feminine aspect,
g. The withdrawal into a temporary retirement of the Father,
h. The work of creating the Son,
i. The evolution and growth of the Son, both materially and in consciousness,
j. Emancipation of the Son from his Mother, or the liberation of the soul at maturity from matter,
k. Recognition by the Son of the Father and his return to that Father,

The final result of all these successive stages being that all the three aspects have performed their functions (their dharma) on the physical plane and all three have demonstrated certain types of energy.

The Father aspect manifests in giving the initial impulse or the positive electrical demonstration which is the germ of the created Son, and Whose Life is embodied in the Son. The occult significance of the words of the Christ in answer to the cry "Lord, show us the Father" is little appreciated. "He that has seen Me has seen the Father, for I and my Father are One," He said.[77]

The Mother, or the negative aspect, builds and nourishes, guards and cherishes the Son through the antenatal, and the infant stages, and stands around Him during later stages, giving of the energy of her own body and activity in ministry to His need.

[77] Bible. John XIV, 8.

The Son, the combined energy of Father and of Mother, embodies both types and all the dual sets of qualities, but has a character all His Own, an essence which is His peculiar nature, and an energy which leads Him to fulfil His Own ends and projects, and which will eventually cause Him to repeat the process of producing,—

1. Conception,
2. Creation,
3. Conscious growth,

as did His Father.

When we reach *the mystery of Fire,* we are concerned with that mysterious extra-systemic energy which is the basis of both the activity of Mother and the Life of the Son. The Son in very deed "becomes His Mother's husband," as say the ancient Scriptures. This is but an enigmatical phrase unless interpreted in terms of the combination of energy. Only when the Son has reached maturity and knows Himself as essentially the same as the Father can He consciously perform His Father's function, and produce and perpetuate that which is needed for the sustaining of cosmic generation.

The electricity of substance, the electricity of form, and the electricity of Life itself must blend and meet before the true Man (whether Logos, or human being) realises himself as creator. Man at this stage knows somewhat of the electricity of substance, and is coming to the belief as to the electricity of form (even though as yet he calls it magnetism) but as yet he knows nought of the electrical reality of life itself. Only when the "jewel in the Lotus" is about to be revealed, or the third circle of petals is about to open up, does the initiate begin to have a realisation of the true meaning of the word "life" or spirit. The consciousness has to be fully awakened before he can ever understand that great energising something of which the other types of energy are but expressions.

There are only two more points to be considered in connection with the petals and initiation.

First, it should be noted that the words "knowledge, love and sacrifice" mean much more occultly than the apparent significance of the terms. Each circle of petals stands for one of these three ideas, and each circle again embodies these three aspects of existence in a greater or lesser degree. These three concepts are the modes of expression of the three great qualities which (from the standpoint of the Past, the Present and the Future) characterise the natures of all the manifesting entities—Gods, men and devas. From the standpoint of the central factor in manifestation, man, it should be realised that *knowledge* was inherent in the previous solar system, and is the faculty of which he has to avail himself. It is there available for his use. It is the hidden energy of the planetary Logos which he has to learn to focus through his physical brain, and thus apply.

Love is the faculty inherent in the present. It is the hidden energy of the planetary Logos of which he must avail himself and focus in his heart centre and thus apply.

Sacrifice is the faculty which will be his in the future, which he will intelligently focus through the highest head centre and thus apply. It is dependent upon his development of consciousness, and therefore upon his recognition of the esoteric purpose of his group, and of the planetary existences. As it involves what is termed "a solar and lunar act of abnegation" it involves, therefore, a due comprehension of solar and of lunar energy, and a bringing of both these two groups to a stage of co-operative activity. It concerns, therefore, the nature of the Jewel in the lotus, and it is only when the three sacrifice petals in the three tiers are unfolded that this particular type of energy is released. The lunar Lords of the three bodies have been controlled, and their vibration synchronised, so that the great act of sacrifice finds them ready for the final process of renunciation. The solar Lords, in their three major groups, are equally ready for the final sacrifice, which involves the "rupture between the sun and the moon" as it is called. This results in the breaking of the magnetic link between the true man, and the vibratory sensitive substance of which his three world bodies are made. The need for incarnation is no longer felt, the chains of karma are broken, and the man is liberated. The "lunar Lords return to their own place" or —as the Christian expresses it—"Satan is bound for a thousand years," [78] this meaning only that pralayic peace is the lot of these entities until the return of manvantaric opportunity.

The final sacrifice involves also the disappearance of the lower triangle, or the severing of the connection between the three permanent atoms in the lower part of the causal body or egoic lotus, and the central unit of energy. The energy of these atoms is set loose through the intense heat produced by the union of the three fires and is reabsorbed into the general reservoir in interplanetary space. The fiery triangle is lost sight of in the general blaze, and the deva essences who temporarily formed it cease their activity.

Again, the solar Angels complete their initial sacrifice by a final one, and offer themselves upon the fiery altar. The causal body is completely destroyed. The four lower groups of solar Pitris return to the heart of the subjective sun, or to that inmost centre of the system from whence they came, whilst the three higher groups are carried (by the force and energy generated in the fiery furnace and blaze, and through the stimulation produced by the blazing forth of the central jewel) straight to the central spiritual sun, there to abide until another kalpa calls them forth to sacrifice Themselves, this time as planetary Logoi. The student must bear in mind that

[78] Bible. Rev. XX, 2.

in thinking of the Pitris, he must ever think in group terms. The Pitris who formed the egoic body of a human being do not—alone and isolated—form planetary Logoi. The forty-nine groups of solar fires concerned in the great work are those spoken of, and they become the forty-nine planetary Logoi in connexion with seven solar systems. In them is hid the mystery of the three who become the sixteen—united or synthesised by the seventeenth—a correspondence upon cosmic levels of the seven with the eighth sphere. This must remain practically an insoluble mystery to man at present.

The four groups who found their way to the Heart of the system will reappear as the four planetary Logoi who are the twenty-eight and who thus produce the possibility of the ten of perfection in another series of manifesting systems.

The seven types of solar energy find the "path of return" to their central emanating source; by the disruption of the tie between them and the lunar lords (who are esoterically spoken of as "dead or dying on the field of battle") the great sacrifice is consummated, and they are free to return in triumph.

The occult significance of these words in connection with the energy standing behind and working through all appearance might be expressed as follows:

Knowledge [79] is the right apprehension of the laws of energy, of the conservation of force, of the sources of

[79] 1. *There are seven branches of knowledge mentioned in the Puranas:*—S. D., I, 192.

2. *The Gnosis, the hidden Knowledge, is the seventh Principle, the six schools of Indian philosophy are the six principles.*—S. D., I, 299.
These six schools are:

    a. The school of Logic.........Proof of right perception.
    b. The atomic school...........System of particulars. Elements. Alchemy and chemistry.
    c. The Sankhya school.........System of numbers. The materialistic school. The theory of the seven states of matter or prakriti.

energy, of its qualities, its types and its vibrations. It involves an apprehension of:

   a. The different key vibrations.
   b. The centres whereby force enters.
   c. The channels along which it circulates.

d. The school of Yoga........Union. The rule of daily life. Mysticism.
e. The school of Ceremonial Religion ....Ritual. Worship of the devas or Gods.
f. The Vedanta school..........Has to do with non-duality. Deals with the relation of Atman in man to the Logos.

3. *There are four branches of knowledge to which H. P. B. specially refers:*—S. D., I, 192.

These four are probably those with which man has dealt the most, in this fourth round and fourth chain.

Compare S. D., I, 70, 95, 107, 227.

The four Noble Truths. The four Vedas. The four Gospels. The four basic admissions. The four ready Elements. The four grades of Initiation.

a. Yajna Vidya ....The performance of religious rites in order to produce certain results. Ceremonial magic. It is concerned with *Sound*, therefore with the Akasha or the ether of space. The "yajna" is the invisible Deity who pervades space.
   Perhaps this concerns the physical plane?

b. Mahavidya ....The great magic knowledge. It has degenerated into Tantrika worship. Deals with the feminine aspect, or the matter (mother) aspect. The basis of black magic. True mahayoga has to do with the form (second aspect) and its adaptation to Spirit and its needs.
   Perhaps this concerns the astral plane?

c. Guhya vidya ....The science of mantrams. The secret knowledge of mystic mantrams. The occult potency of sound, of the Word.
   Perhaps this concerns the mental plane?

d. Atma vidya................True spiritual wisdom.

4. *Knowledge of truth is a common inheritance.*—S. D., II, 47, 3.

5. *Knowledge is a relative subject, and varies according to the grade achieved.*

   a. Ranges of further knowledge open up before a planetary Logos.—S. D., II, 740.

   b. The four truths can be arrived at by unaided man.—S. D., III, 420.

6. *Finally, Knowledge is a dangerous weapon:*

This is due to: Personal Selfishness.

It is only safe when:

   a. One gives oneself up to it, body, soul and spirit.—S. D., III, 62, 63.

d. The triangles and other geometrical figures which it produces during evolution.

e. The cycles and the ebb and flow of energy in connection with the different types of planetary manifestation, including all the kingdoms of nature.

f. The true significance of those force aspects which we call "periods of pralaya" and those we call "periods of manifestation." It also involves a right realisation of the laws of obscuration.

All this the man has been learning in the various Halls through practical experience, involving pleasure and pain; these, in the final initiations, bring him to a realisation not only of the existence of these forces but of how to wield and manipulate them. This is knowledge: to rightly direct force currents, first in the three worlds of human endeavour, and then in the solar system.

Love is the right apprehension of the uses and purposes of form, and of the energies involved in form-building, the utilisation of form, and the eventual dissipation of the superseded form. It involves a realisation of the Laws of Attraction and Repulsion, of the magnetic interplay between all forms, great and small, of group relationships, of the galvanizing power of the unifying life, and the attractive power of one unit upon another, be it atom, man, or solar system. It involves an understanding of all forms, form purposes, and form relationships; it concerns the building processes in man himself, and in the solar system; and it necessitates the development of those powers within man which will make him a conscious Builder, a solar Pitri of a coming cycle. This

b. One has an unshakeable belief in one's own divinity.—S. D., III, 62, 63.
c. One recognises one's own immortal Principle.
d. One knows oneself.—S. D., III, 435, 436.
e. All the virtues are practised.—S. D., III, 262.
f. One has experience.—S. D., III, 481.
g. One realises knowledge is the fruit of Spirit alone.—S. D., III, 453.
h. Knowledge is acquired through the region of the higher mind.—S. D., III, 453.

is one of the great revelations at initiation: the unveiling
to the initiate of the particular cosmic centre whence
emanates the type of force or energy which he, the initiate, will be concerned with when he becomes in due
course of time a solar Pitri, or divine manasaputra to a
coming humanity. Hence he must have, not only knowledge, but the energy of love likewise to enable him to perform the function of linking the higher three and the
lower four of a future race of men at some distant period,
thus permitting of their individualising through *the sacrifice of his own fully conscious middle principle.*

Sacrifice involves even more than what has been already pointed out. It involves the following factors:

   a. Knowledge of the purposes and intentions of the
       planetary Logos,
   b. Realisation of the particular and peculiar type of
       energy, and of the quality of his own Ray Lord,
   c. Comprehension of the different groups of existences
       who are participating in planetary evolution and
       in solar manifestation,
   d. A revelation as to certain cosmic enterprises in
       which our planetary Logos is acting as an intelli-
       gent co-operator. Thus is brought in the factor of
       extra-systemic force.

When all these and other factors are considered, it is
evident that the energy set loose in sacrifice to these
plans and intentions involves such a vast field of comprehending wisdom that it is not possible for the average
man ever to sense it. It deals with the purposes and
plans of the Silent Watchers over the three planes—the
five, and the seven; it deals with the dynamic force of the
great Destroying Angels on all the planes, who will eventually—through the manipulation of the three forms of
energy—bring to an end all that is. These angels are a
mysterious group of fohatic Lives Who sound forth the

trumpets of destruction, and by means of the notes sounded produce that shattering which will set loose the energy of forms.

The second point is very briefly given. It concerns the innermost circle of petals, or that set of three petals, or those three streams of whirling energy, which immediately surround the "jewel in the lotus." Each of these three petals is related to one of the three circles, and is organised as each of the three circles is unfolded. They form, therefore, a synthesis of knowledge, love or sacrifice, and are closely connected through the type of force flowing through them with one of the three higher centres of the planetary Logos of a man's particular ray. This central unit of threefold force is dealt with in a specific manner at initiation.

At the first, the second, and the third Initiations, one of the three petals opens up, permitting an ever freer display of the central electric point. At the fourth Initiation, the jewel (being completely revealed) through its blazing light, its intense radiatory heat, and its terrific outflow of force, produces the disintegration of the surrounding form, the shattering of the causal body, the destruction of the Temple of Solomon, and the dissolution of the lotus flower. The work of the Initiator in this connection is very interesting. Through the medium of the Rod of Initiation and of certain Words of Power, He brings about results of a co-ordinating, transmuting and liberating nature.

Through the action of the Rod as wielded at the first two Initiations, the two outer circles unfold, the energy of the two is set free and the two sets of force as embodied in the six petals are co-ordinated and become interactive. This stage of petal adjustment succeeds upon that called earlier "unfoldment" and has to do with the simultaneous action of the two tiers of petals. The interplay between the two circles is completed, and the circulation of the force currents perfected. According to a man's ray and subray, so is the Rod applied to what might be termed the "key" petal. This of course differs according to the unit of force involved. It is of interest to note here that, as the petal substance is deva substance and as the energy of the petals is the energy of certain manasadevas (one of the three higher orders of Agnish-vattas) the initiate is overshadowed (the word is not entirely satisfactory in explaining the type of deva service here necessitated, but it must suffice) by a great deva who represents the equilibrium of substantial vibration which is brought about by the efforts of the initiate, aided by the adepts who present him, and who each represent one of the two polarities of force. This is temporarily stabilised by the Initiator. These three factors,

1. The representing deva,
2. The two adepts,
3. The initiator,

form, for a brief second, a triangle of force with the initiate at the centre. Through them circulates the terrific power, the "fire from Heaven," which is brought down from the higher triad through the agency of the electrical rod.

This application of extra-egoic force is in itself of a threefold nature, as symbolised by the three protective agencies and the threefold nature of the Rod itself. It emanates in a primary sense from the planetary Logos of a man's ray, and proceeds from that one of the planetary centres which corresponds to either the head, heart, or throat centre in a human unit. This energy is applied to the corresponding tier of petals and to the corresponding petal in a tier according to the initiation taken, and according to the primary and secondary ray. A close connection can be traced here between the petals and the centres on the etheric level of the physical plane, and thus it can be seen how (when the necessary work is done) it is possible to have a direct transmission of force from the higher planes to the lower in the following order:

a. From the logoic centre, or the planetary Logos, to the Monad on its own plane.

b. From that Monad to one of the three tiers of petals, according to the aspect or ray concerned.

c. From the tier of petals, viewed as a unit, to one of the petals in the circle, according to the quality and type of force, using the petal as a transmitting agency.

d. From the particular petal in which the force is momentarily centred to one of the permanent atoms, again according to ray and type of force.

e. From the permanent atom via the atomic triangle, and the mental, and astral centres, to that one of the three higher centres in the etheric body particularly concerned.

f. From the etheric centre to the physical brain.

We have here put very briefly the process of force transmission from the Monad to man on the physical plane, and hence it will be apparent why the emphasis is so consistently laid upon the necessity for bodily purity (in all the three bodies), and upon the alignment of those bodies so that the flow of force may be unimpeded. The effects of this downflow of force may be viewed in a twofold manner, that is, in a material and in a psychic sense.

The *material effect,* or the result of this stimulation upon the forms and upon the atoms in the forms, is to render them radioactive, or to set loose the energy of substance. This is the liberating of the energy imprisoned within the form, and concerns the Brahma aspect, and the evolution of matter itself. It affects the lunar bodies, and therefore relates to the lunar Lords or Pitris, causing a weakening of their hold upon the lesser builders, bringing them more under the force streams from the solar Angels, and leading to a situation which will eventually result in a return of the lunar Pitris of all degrees to the central point for force substance. In a *psychic sense* the result of the downflow is a stimulation of consciousness, and the acquisition (through that stimulation) of the psychic powers latent in man. His three higher physical centres, the pineal gland, the pituitary body, and the alta major centre are affected, and man becomes psychically aware in the physical brain of the higher influences, happenings and powers. According to the ray concerned, so is the centre affected. The force of the lunar Lords, which has succeeded in keeping these three organs quiescent, is superseded and the solar Angels pour in their energy.

All this again is closely connected with the threefold energy of the physical body, and produces effects within the spinal column which arouses the kundalini fire at the base of the spine, causing it to mount along the triple spinal channel, again according to ray and aspect involved. More anent this may not here be said, as the dangers of a premature knowledge along this line are far greater than the dangers of ignorance. Suffice it to point out that the fires at the lower centres,—those below the diaphragm—have, by the time the second initiation is reached, usually mounted to the centre between the shoulder blades; at the second initiation they rise as far as the head, and all the fires of the torso are then active. All that remains then to do is to centralise them, to produce the necessary geometrical interplay between the seven head centres, and then to focus them all prior to the final liberation in the highest centre of all.

4 The Fire Elementals, the Lesser Builders.

a. Introductory.

It will be apparent now that in our consideration of the deva Builders, great and small, of the solar system, we have hitherto practically confined ourselves to those who are the functioning agents in the three worlds of human endeavour. We have dealt briefly with the Builders on the evolutionary arc, the greater entities who either have passed through the human kingdom, and therefore have left that stage of evolution behind them in earlier cycles, or are at this time the "solar agents" of human manifestation. All these forms of divine existence represent—in their own place—aspects of *positive force.* We come now to the consideration of the lesser builders in the three worlds, those who represent the *negative* aspect of force, being on the involutionary arc, and who are, therefore, the recipients of energy and influences. They are worked upon by energy, and through the activity of the greater Builders are forced into different directions in space, being built into the differing forms. The energy that works upon them, as is well known, emanates from the second aspect, and in their totality they form the great Mother.

I would call to the attention of all students the fact that these lesser builders are literally a "sea of fire" upon which the great breath, or the Aum, takes effect. Each fiery spark, or atom, becomes (through the action of the Word), vitalised with new life, and impregnated with a different type of energy. In the union of the life of atomic substance itself with that which causes the atoms to cohere, and to form vehicles of some kind or another, can be seen demonstrating the "Son of God." Herein lies the essential duality of all manifestation; this duality is later supplemented by the life of the One Who sounds the Word. Thus is the cosmic incarnation brought about with the three factors entering in.   This has been sufficiently dealt with in earlier pages.

Much that will have to be said will be of a tabulatory nature, and the only way in which students can check up the approximate accuracy of that which is imparted will be through a careful meditation upon:

a. The Law of Correspondences.
b. The realisable probabilities.
c. The indications in occult literature of a corroborative nature.

Students should remember that we are dealing with involutionary substance, or atomic matter.   This atomic matter is *living* substance, each atom being a tiny life palpitating with the vitality of the third Logos.   These lives, being negative energy, are responsive to their polar opposite, and can (under the Law of Attraction and Repulsion) be built into forms which are the expression of the second aspect.   Eventually the forms themselves become in their turn negative, and responsive to still another type of force, becoming recipients of the life of the first Logos when the fourth or human kingdom is reached.

This Treatise seeks to prove, that in the fourth kingdom the three fires meet:

a. Fire by friction, or the negative Brahma Aspect, the third Aspect.
b. Solar Fire, or the positive negative Vishnu Aspect, the second Aspect.
c. Electric Fire, or the positive Shiva Aspect, the first Aspect.

Man in the three worlds, consciously or unconsciously, recapitulates the logoic process, and becomes a creator, working in substance through the factor of his positive energy.   He wills, he thinks, he speaks, and thought-forms eventuate.   Atomic substance is attracted to the enunciator. The tiny lives which compose that substance are forced (through the energy of the thinker), into forms, which are themselves active, vitalised and powerful. What man builds is either a beneficent or a maleficent creation according to the underlying desire, motive, or purpose.

It is essential that we endeavour to make practical what is here to be imparted, as it is useless for man to study the groups of lesser builders, their functions and their names, unless he realises that with many of them he has an intimate connection, being himself one of the great builders, and a creator within the planetary scheme. Men should remember that through the power of their thoughts and their spoken words they definitely produce effects upon other human beings functioning on the three planes of human evolution and upon the entire animal kingdom. The separative and maleficent thoughts of man are largely responsible for the savage nature of wild beasts, and the destructive quality of some of nature's processes, including certain phenomena, such as plague and famine.

It is of no value to man to know the names of some of the "army of the voice" unless he comprehends his relationship to that army, unless he apprehends the responsibility which is his to be a beneficent creator, working under the law of love, and not impelled to the creative act through selfish desire, or uncontrolled activity.

b. *Physical Plane Elementals.*

It should be remembered that the devas we have been considering are the originators of impulse, and the manipulators of energy in their own degree, and on their own plane. In connection with them are to be found, therefore, the recipients of force, or the multitude of lives of an elemental nature which form the sumtotal of the matter of a plane. These are swept on waves of energy, through the impulse of the Breath, and as the result of vibratory action, into all forms as we know them on the physical plane. Therefore, in connection with manifestation *on the physical plane* the devas may be divided into three groups:

1. *The transmitters of the will of God,* the originators of activity in deva substance. These are the greater builders in their various groups.
2. *The manipulators of the initiated energy.* These are the myriads of workers with force who transmit the impulse in their turn to the elemental essence. They are the builders of lesser degree, but are on the evolutionary arc as are the first group.
3. *The recipients of force,* the sumtotal of the living substance of a plane. These lives are passive in the hands of the builders of greater degree.

The three groups to be considered are:

1. The elementals of densest matter.
2. The elementals of liquid matter.
3. The elementals of gaseous matter.

We must bear in mind as we study these three groups that we are not concerned with the transmitters, but with the manipulators and with the recipients of energy.

The Elementals of Densest Matter. These are the workers and builders which are concerned with the tangible and objective part of all manifestation. In their totality they literally form that which can be touched, seen, and contacted physically by man. In considering these matters we must never dissociate the various groups in our minds in a too literal sense, for they all interpenetrate and blend, in the same manner as man's physical body is compounded of dense, liquid, gaseous, and etheric matter. Diversity, producing a unity, is everywhere to be seen; this fact must constantly be borne in mind by the occult student when studying the sub-human forms of existence. There is a distinct danger in all tabulations, for they tend to the forming of hard and fast divisions, whereas unity pervades all.

Among the manipulating devas of the lowest level of the dense physical plane are to be found certain subterranean forms of existence, of which hints are to be found in the ancient and occult books. There is to be found in the very bowels of the earth, an evolution of a peculiar nature, with a close resemblance to the human. They have bodies of a peculiarly gross kind, which might be regarded as distinctly physical as we understand the term. They dwell in settlements, or groups, under a form of government suited to their needs in the central caves several miles below the crust of the earth. Their work is closely connected with the mineral kingdom, and the "agnichaitans" of the central fires are under their control. Their bodies are constituted so as to stand much pressure, and they are not dependent upon as free a circulation of air as man is, nor do they resent the great heat to be found in the earth's interior. Little can here be communicated anent these existences, for they are connected with the lesser vital portions of the physical body of the planetary Logos, finding their microcosmic correspondence in the feet and legs of a man. They are one of the factors which make possible the revolutionary progressive activity of a planet.

Allied with them are several other groups of low class entities, whose place in the scheme of things can only be described as having relation to the grosser planetary functions. Little is gained by enlarging upon these lives and their work; it is not possible for man in any way to contact them, nor would it be desirable. When they have pursued their evolutionary cycle, they will take their place in a later cycle in the ranks of certain deva bodies that are related to the animal kingdom.

It is commonly supposed that all the fairies, gnomes, elves, and like nature spirits are to be found solely in etheric matter, but this is not so. They are to be found in bodies of gaseous and liquid substance likewise, but the mistake has arisen for the reason that the basis of all that which can be objectively seen is the etheric structure, and these little busy lives frequently protect their dense physical activities through the agency of glamour, and cast a veil over their objective manifestation. When etheric vision is present then they can be seen, for the glamour, as we understand it, is only a veil over that which is tangible.

Students must at this juncture remember that all dense physical forms, whether of a tree, an animal, a mineral, a drop of water, or a precious stone, are in themselves elemental lives constructed of living substance by the aid of living manipulators, acting under the direction of intelligent architects. It will immediately become apparent why it is not possible in any way to tabulate in connection with this particular lowest group. A beautiful diamond, a stately tree, or a fish in the water are but devas after all. It is the recognition of this essential livingness which constitutes the basic fact in all occult investigation, and is the secret of all beneficent magic. It is not my purpose, therefore, to deal more specifically with these lowest forms of divine life, except to impart two facts, and thus give indication of the solution of two problems which have oft disturbed the average student; these are, first, the problem as to the purpose of all reptilian life, and, secondly, the specific connection of the bird evolution with the deva kingdom.

The secret of the *reptile kingdom* is one of the mysteries of the second round, and there is a profound significance connected with the expression "the serpents of wisdom" which is applied to all adepts of the good law.

The reptile kingdom has an interesting place in all mythologies, and all ancient forms of truth impartation, and this for no arbitrary reason. It is not possible to enlarge upon the underlying truth which is hidden in the karmic history of our planetary Logos, and is revealed as part of the teaching given to initiates of the second degree.

The second great life impulse, or life wave, initiated by our planetary Logos, when brought in conjunction with the first, was the basis of that activity which we call evolutionary energy; it resulted in a gradual unrolling, or revelation, of the divine form. The heavenly serpent manifested, being produced out of the egg, and began its convolutions, gaining in strength and majesty, and producing through its immense fecundity millions of lesser "serpents." The reptile kingdom is the most important part of the animal kingdom in certain aspects, if such an apparently contradictory statement can be made. For all animal life can be seen passing through it during the prenatal stage, or returning to it when the form is in advanced decomposition. The connection is not purely a physical one, but it is also psychic. When the real nature and method of the kundalini, or serpent fire, is known, this relation will be better understood, and the history of the second round assume a new importance.

The secret of life lies hidden in the serpent stage,— not the life of the Spirit, but the life of the soul, and this will be revealed as the "serpent of the astral light" is truly approached, and duly studied. One of the four Lipika Lords, Who stand nearest to our planetary Logos, is called "The Living Serpent," and His emblem is a serpent of blue with one eye, in the form of a ruby, in its head. Students who care to carry the symbology a little further can connect this idea with the "eye of Shiva" which sees and knows all, and records all, as does the human eye in lesser degree; all is photographed upon the astral light, as the human eye receives impressions upon the retina. The same thought is frequently conveyed in the Christian Bible, in the Hebrew and Christian recognition of the all-seeing eye of God. The application and value of the hints here given may be apparent if the subject of the third eye is studied, and its relation to the spine, and the spinal currents investigated. This third eye is one of the objects of kundalinic vivification, and in the spinal territory there is first the centre at the base of the spine, the home of the sleeping fire. Next we have the triple channel along which that fire will travel in due course of evolution, and finally we find at the summit of the column, and surmounting all, that small organ called the pineal gland, which when vivified causes the third eye to open, and the beauties of the higher, subtler planes to stand revealed. All this physico-psychical occurrence is possible to man owing to certain events which happened to the Heavenly Serpent in the second, or serpent, round. These happenings necessitated the formation and evolution of that peculiar and mysterious family we call the reptilian. These forms of divine life are very intimately connected with the second planetary scheme, being responsive to energy emanating from that scheme, and reaching the earth via the second globe in the second chain. A group of special devas (connected with a particular *open* sound in the planetary Word), work with the reptile evolution.

It should be noted here that this evolution on the etheric planes has a closer effect upon man than on the physical. If students will apply themselves to the consideration of these facts, to the investigation of the serpent lore in all lands, mythologies and scriptures, and if they will link up all this knowledge with that concerning those heavenly constellations which have a serpent appellation (such as, for instance, the Dragon), much illumination may come. If the intuition suffices, knowledge may then be imparted which will make clearer the connection between the physical bodies with their centres, and the psychic nature.

The *bird kingdom* is specifically allied to the deva evolution. It is the bridging kingdom between the purely deva evolution and two other manifestations of life.

First. Certain groups of devas who desire to pass into the human kingdom, having developed certain faculties, can do so via the bird kingdom, and certain devas who wish to get in communication with human beings can do so via the bird kingdom. This truth is hinted at in the Christian Bible and Christian religious representations by angels or devas being frequently represented as having wings. These cases are not many, as the usual method is for the devas gradually to work themselves towards individualisation through expansive feeling, but in the cases which do occur these devas pass several cycles in the bird kingdom, building in a response to a vibration which will ultimately swing them into the human family. In this way they become accustomed to the use of a gross form without the limitations, and impurities, which the animal kingdom engenders.

Second. Many devas pass out of the group of passive lives in the effort to become manipulating lives via the bird kingdom, and before becoming fairies, elves, gnomes, or other sprites, pass a certain number of cycles in the bird realm.

Why the two above events occur will not be apparent to the casual reader, nor will the true connection between the birds and the devas be accurately realised by the occult student unless he applies himself to the consideration of the "bird or swan out of time and space," and the place that birds play in the mysteries. Herein lies for him the clue. He must remember likewise the fact that every life of every degree, from a god to the most insignificant of the lesser devas, or builders, must at some time or another pass through the human family.

As H. P. B. has pointed out,[80] birds and serpents are closely connected with wisdom, and therefore with the psychic nature of God, of men, and of devas. The study of mythology should reveal certain stages and relationships which will make this matter clearer.

The Elementals and Lesser Devas of Liquid Matter. A very interesting illustration of the interpenetration of all the living matter of creation can be seen in connection with the atmosphere surrounding our planet. In it is to be found:

    a. Moisture, or those living essences which are the liquid elementals.

    b. Gaseous substance, or those lives which are linked to all fiery essences, being volatile and the result of heat.

    c. Etheric matter, or the lowest orders of the devas of the ethers.

This major triplicity, when in conjunction, produces that which we breathe, and that in which we live and move and have our being. To the thoughtful student the air is full of symbology, for it is a synthesis, and that which bridges the higher and the lower strata of manifestation.

We must centre our attention first upon those lives which constitute the sumtotal of all that is watery, and liquid throughout manifestation, and in dealing with this we must remember that we are concerned with the most occult of investigations, and with matters which are very closely connected with man's evolution.

The many groups of the water devas of the manipulatory class have been roughly grouped by mythological writers, under the terms undines, mermaids, and other

[80] S. D., Section X, Vol. I, 384, 435; II, 306.

expressions, but their diversity is great, and this will be necessarily apparent when it is remembered that the sumtotal of water upon the earth (oceans, seas, rivers, lakes and streams), far exceeds the dry portion, or land, and every drop of moisture is in itself a tiny life, fulfilling its function and running its cycle. The mythic forms above referred to are but those myriad lives built into a form through which an evolutionary deva is seeking expression.

The extreme interest of this subject might be expressed under certain statements which will give the student some idea of the close attention which should, and eventually will be paid to this subject of the deva lives of watery manifestation. As said above, the aggregate of these lives is greater than the aggregate of those lives which form the sum total of solid earth as we understand the term, even though they do not exceed the number of lives which form the gaseous portion of manifestation; this gaseous portion is found in the atmosphere, interpenetrating dense matter, and filling in a large degree the interior caverns of the planet. The microcosmic resemblance to the great Life of the planet is seen in the fact that both forms are but outer sheaths or frameworks, sheltering an inner "vault"; both forms are hollow, both have their negative and positive extremities, their poles, so to speak, and internally much proceeds affecting the outer evolutions.

One of the most occult of the planets, Neptune, presides over the "devas of the waters"; their presiding deva Lord, Varuna, the Raja of the astral plane, being an emanation from that planet. Students will find it of profound interest to study the close interaction therefore between:

1. The sixth plane, the astral plane, and the sixth subplane of the physical plane, the liquid subplane.

2. The sixth subplane of each plane in the solar system, and their relation to each other.

Herein will be found one reason why men of a relatively
low type of physical body, and having an astral body
with some sixth subplane matter in it are responsive to
higher things and have a spiritual aspiration.   The influence emanating from the sixth subplane of the buddhic
plane calls out a reciprocal response from the sixth subplane matter in other bodies, and the sixth principle of
buddhi under the Law of Correspondences intensifies
that vibration.

The name Neptune is one under which the planetary
Logos of one of the major three schemes is known upon
our planet.   Certain of His influences and energies affect paramountly the deva essence of this sixth subplane
matter, reaching them via the Raja Lord Varuna.   This
knowledge is of practical value astrologically, for it will
enable men to understand the nature of their own physical bodies, and above all of their astral bodies.   It is an
occult fact that the type of astral matter in a man's
body decides the quality of the watery substance of his
physical body.   There is, in occultism, no dissociating
the physico-psychic natures, for the latter determines
the former.   The planet Neptune therefore has a profound effect and a close connection under the Law of
Correspondences with the sixth, or astral plane, which
is the plane of the liquid portion of the logoic physical
body, with the sixth subplane of the physical plane, or
with the liquid portion of the human physical body and
of the planetary physical body, also with the sixth type
of energy or force, or the sixth ray.

The major scheme over which Neptune presides forms
a systemic triangle of great interest for esoteric astrologers with the sixth scheme and one other.   This is symbolised in the three pronged trident which the god Nep-

tune is always portrayed as holding, the prongs being literally the symbolic triangles connected with each other by three lines of force.

This planet has also a vital relation to the sixth logoic principle, or Buddhi, and therefore the sixth principle of man. No man begins to co-ordinate the buddhic vehicles until he comes under Neptunian influence in some life or another. When this is the case, his personality horoscope will show Neptunian influence dominating somewhere.

The Neptunian scheme governs one of the three paths of return, and gathers to itself eventually all those Egos who attain primarily through the manipulation of the sixth type of energy usually called devotion. It is Neptunian influence likewise which presides over and makes possible the second Initiation, wherein the initiate produces results in the astral body, and wherein his astral centres are the object of the Hierophant's attention. This particular type of energy flows through three centres:

a. That particular head centre which is linked to the heart centre.
b. The heart centre.
c. The solar plexus.

The planet Neptune, along with the planetary Logos of the sixth ray controls the astral centres in man. This statement involves much esoteric macrocosmic significance. When it is remembered that all centres—human and divine—are composed of deva essence, the connection between this influence and the devas, and their reflex effect upon man, will immediately become apparent.

In the mystery of the sea and the secret of its occult "drying up" or absorption, will be revealed eventually the significance underlying:

a. The sex impulse, macrocosmically and microcosmically interpreted.
b. The cessation of desire.
c. The direction of fire to the throat centre instead of
   to the generative organs.
d. Pralaya and obscuration.
e. The meaning of the words "There shall be no more
   sea" found in the Christian Bible.

When meditating upon these thoughts, students will
find it well to bear in mind the fact that Neptune is one
of the major or synthesising planets, that it is an
"absorbing" or "abstracting" planet, and that it is connected with the process whereby eventual perfection is
demonstrated. The Son is made perfect, and the cosmic
incarnation is brought to a close.

There is again a very close esoteric connection between the fact lying behind the Biblical words "the Spirit
of God moved upon the face of the waters,"[81] and the
ordered lawful activity of the Great Mother as she performs her work of body-building under the impulse of
desire. The true relation between the astral plane and
the physical plane will only become apparent as students
carefully bear in mind that the astral plane of the solar
system is the sixth subplane of the cosmic physical
plane, and constitutes the sumtotal of the liquid substance of the logoic physical body. When this is realised, the work of the deva essence takes due place; the
factor of desire, or of astral motion, and its reflex action
upon the physical body via the sixth subplane will become apparent, and the Great Mother will be seen actively engaged, under the influence of desire, in the work
of building, nourishing, and producing that warmth and
moisture which make manifestation possible. The
Mother is the greatest of the devas, and closely linked

[81] Bible. Gen., 1:2.

with the devas of the waters, for moisture of some kind or another is an essential to all life.

The sixth principle, therefore, or the love aspect (the Christ principle), and the sixth plane, are connected; there is an interplay of energy between the fourth cosmic ether, or buddhic energy, and the sixth plane, or astral energy. The devas on both these planes belong essentially to groups over which Neptunian influence presides, hence the astral plane can, and eventually will, directly reflect the buddhic.

The *greater building devas* on the second plane of the solar system, the monadic plane or the second cosmic ether, direct the energies of the manipulating devas of the fourth cosmic ether, the buddhic plane.

The *manipulating devas* of the fourth cosmic ether will, in due course of evolution, work out the plan in objective perfection through the medium of the living substance of the lesser devas of the liquid or astral plane. When they have done this two results will be seen: first, the astral plane will perfectly reflect the buddhic plane and, secondly, the result of that will be that the physical plane will produce the exact vehicle needed for microcosmic or macrocosmic expression through the force of water, or desire.

All this is revealed to esotericists in the symbology of the circulatory system in man. As the blood system, with its two types of channels (arteries and veins) and its two types of builders (the red and the white corpuscles), is studied from the occult standpoint, much will be ascertained of a revolutionary nature. The laws of the path of outgoing, and of the path of return, with the two groups of deva lives therein concerned, will be apprehended by man. A further hint may here be given. In the physical body of man in connection with the circulatory system, we find, in the three factors—the heart, the arteries, and the veins—the clue to the three types of devas, and also to the systemic triangle which they represent, and further, to the three modes of divine expression. There is a planetary as well as a systemic circulation, and it is carried on through the medium of deva substance everywhere, macrocosmically as well as microcosmically.

The devas of the sixth physical subplane can be divided into three groups, and these again into seven and into forty-nine, thus corresponding with all groups in the solar system. These groups (in their essential nature) respond to that "which lies above more than that which lies below," which is only an occult way of expressing a relationship of an intimate nature between the devas of fire and the devas of water, and a negation of a close connection between the water devas and the earth. Occultly expressed, through the action of the fire devas, the water devas find liberation.

The devas of water find for themselves the path of service in their great work of nourishing all the vegetable and animal life upon the planet; the goal for them is to enter into that higher group of devas which we call the gaseous or fire devas. These, through the action of their fire upon the waters, produce that sequence of evaporation, condensation, and eventual precipitation which—through its constant activity—nourishes all life upon the earth. Thus again can the psychic laws of love be seen at work in the deva kingdom as in the human; first, the withdrawal or segregation of the unit from the group (called individualisation in man, and evaporation in the water realm). Next, condensation, or the amalgamation of the unit with a newer or higher group, this we call condensation for the devas of the waters, and initiation in man; finally, the sacrifice of the group of human or deva atoms to the good of the whole. So does the law of service and sacrifice govern all the second aspect divine in all its departments great or small. Such is the law. But in the human kingdom, though love is the fulfilling of the law, it is arrived at along the path of pain and sorrow, and every true lover and server of humanity is stretched upon the cross until for them the sixth principle dominates, and the sixth type of matter in their bodies is completely subjected to the higher energy.[82] In the case of the devas, love is the fulfilling of the law without pain or sorrow. It is for them the line of least resistance, for they are the mother aspect, the feminine side of manifestation, and the easy path for them is to give, to nourish, and to tend. Therefore, the devas of the waters pour themselves out in service to the vegetable and animal kingdoms, and in the transmutative fires all that holds them on the sixth subplane will eventually be overcome, and through occult "distillation and evaporation" these devas will eventually form part of the gaseous fiery group and become those fires which are the basis of the divine alchemy.

Speaking generally, it must be remembered that the earth devas of densest matter become, in the course of evolution, the devas of the waters, and find their way eventually on to the astral plane, the cosmic liquid; the devas of the waters of the physical plane find their way, through service, on to the gaseous subplane, and then to the cosmic gaseous, becoming the devas of the mental plane. This literally and occultly constitutes the transmutation of desire into thought.

The gaseous devas become eventually the devas of the fourth ether, and from thence in long aeons, find their way to the cosmic fourth ether, the buddhic plane. These three groups are therefore *cosmically* connected with:

[82] "Measure thy life by loss instead of gain,
　Not by the wine drunk but by the wine poured forth;
　For Love's strength standeth in Love's sacrifice;
　And he who suffers most has most to give."
　　　　　　　　　—*The Disciples*, by Mrs. Hamilton King.

1. The cosmic astral plane and the constellation whence emotional and desire energy originates.
2. The cosmic mental plane, and therefore with the constellation Sirius.
3. The cosmic buddhic plane, and the constellation of the Pleiades.

Thus can the whole process be worked out, if man carefully studies his own nature, and the law of analogy.

The Devas of the Gaseous Subplane. In dealing with the elementals, or lesser devas, under the manipulatory devas of this extensive group, we are dealing with the devas of fire, and with the fiery essences of substantial nature which can be seen manifesting in myriads of forms. Certain of the subdivisions of this group are known to students, such as:

The Salamanders, or the fiery lives which can be seen by clairvoyants leaping in the flames of a furnace or of a volcano; this group can be subdivided into four groups according to color—red, orange, yellow, and violet—the last of which approximate very closely to the devas of the fourth ether.

The Agnichaitans; this is a term applied to the fiery lives, which are the sumtotal of the plane substance, as seen in the first part of our treatise, and also to the tiny essences which compose the fires of manifestation. As the nature of physical plane electricity is understood and studied, and its true condition realised, the reality of the existence of these agnichaitans will stand revealed.

As the race becomes clairvoyant, as it surely will in a great degree before the close of this rootrace, these gaseous devas will stand revealed, and men will realise that they are working with fiery lives, and that they are themselves closely allied to these lives through the fires of their own bodies. The clairvoyance which is in process of developing in this rootrace is entirely physical, and, under the law, its development is to be anticipated, for the Aryan rootrace is that one wherein man—in this fourth round—comes to full self-consciousness. This involves complete physical vision, and the use in perfection of the three physical plane senses of hearing, touch, and sight. In the next rootrace, astral clairvoyance will be prevalent, though not universal, and thus contact with the buddhic plane will be more easily achieved. In the earlier rootraces of the next round, the fifth, there will be a recapitulation of the activities of this round, until, in the fifth rootrace, the sumtotal of that achieved in this round will be seen. Men will then begin to demonstrate mental clairvoyance. Thus the cycles mingle and overlap, in order that no unit of life, however small and unimportant, may fail in opportunity.

These agnichaitans of the third subplane come particularly under the influence of Saturnian energy. They are the great fusers of substance, and it is in connection with them that the transmutation of metals becomes possible. They have a relationship to the mineral kingdom analogous to that which the watery devas have to the vegetable and animal. They are, as will be apparent, connected with the throat centre of a planetary Logos and of a solar Logos, and it is through their activity that the transmission of sound through the air becomes possible. It might surprise students and inventors could they but realise that the present rapid growth of wireless communication everywhere is due to the swinging into contact with the human vibration of a group of fiery deva lives hitherto uncontacted.

Just as each plane has its seven subplanes, so likewise each subplane can be subdivided, thus making forty-nine fires on every plane, or the three hundred and forty-three fires of the solar system. Herein can be found the clue to the mystery of the ''fourth between the three' which has at times bewildered students of the occult records. There are several ways of reading these figures, 3 4 3, but the only occult method which can be hinted at here, lies in the recognition of the three higher planes, the three lower planes, the fourth plane of meeting between them. This fourth plane has occultly been called "the meeting place." When it is remembered that the goal for these gaseous devas is the fourth cosmic ether, or the buddhic plane and that they (in their major and minor groups) are the internal macrocosmic and microcosmic fires, some idea may be gained as to the true significance of the eventual at-one-ment between the two lines of evolution for the goal for man likewise is the buddhic plane.

On the third subplane, therefore, in its fifth division of deva essences, certain groups are now being contacted in this, the fifth rootrace; the result of this contact can be seen in the stimulation of responsive vibration, which is demonstrated already in the discovery of wireless intercourse and of radium.

There will also be seen a paralleling increased vibration of the human spirillæ which will result, before the end of the round, in the awakening to full activity of the fifth spirilla of the human physical permanent atom.

Hence the work of the Mahachohan at this time in connection with seventh ray (which is temporarily acting as the synthesis of the five types of energy over which He presides), might be summed up as follows:

First, He is utilising the seventh type of energy in order to further the recognition by the human unit of the subtler substance of the physical plane. This seventh ray is a primary factor in the production of objectivity. The energy of the planetary Logos of the seventh scheme dominates the seventh plane; it is the ray whereon deva substance and Spirit can meet and adapt themselves to each other with greater facility than on any other ray except the third.

Man, at present, is fully conscious, through some one or other of his senses, on the three lower subplanes; it is intended that he shall be equally conscious on the four higher. This has to be brought about by the stimulation of the deva substance which composes his bodies. This will be accomplished through the dynamic will of the transmitting devas as they energise the manipulatory devas, and thus affect the myriads of lesser lives which compose man's body, and also by an increased responsiveness of the indwelling man or thinker to the contact made upon his body. This increased awareness will be brought about by the arousing of the fifth spirilla, by the unfolding of the fifth petal in the egoic lotus, and by the gradual opening of the third eye through the arousing and uniform activity of five factors: the centre at the base of the spine, the three channels in the spinal column, and the pineal gland.

All these factors involve the activity of deva essence, plus the resultant awareness of the thinker. This will be followed by the conscious use of the newly-awakened powers. In this manner the close interrelation and interdependence of the two lines of evolution becomes magnificently apparent.

Second, the Mahachohan is working specifically at this time (in co-operation with the Manu), with the devas of the gaseous subplane; this is in connection with the destroying work they are to effect by the end of this rootrace, in order to liberate Spirit from constricting forms. Volcanic action therefore may be looked for, demonstrating in unexpected localities, as well as within the sphere of the present earthquake and volcanic zones. Serious disturbance may be looked for in California before the end of the century, and in Alaska likewise.

The work of the Mahachohan can also be seen in the

effect that the devas of the kundalini fire are producing upon man. These are a peculiar group of Agnichaitans who have reached a stage of evolution which permits of their being separated off from their group into a group connected with a certain fire in man's bodies. This fire owing to its present activity, and the direction of that activity, is responsible for the reaction against physical marriage, and for the desire evinced by highly evolved men everywhere to evade the marriage relation, and confine themselves to creation upon the mental or astral planes. This is due to the present inclination of the manipulatory devas of the lower generative organs to seek the throat centre, and to function there, utilising the strength of the kundalini fire to bring this about. All this is under the law of evolution, but in the interim between cause and justified effect much harm, evasion of the law, and consequent suffering can be seen. Owing, therefore, to the violent reaction at this time against the safeguarding laws of civilisation, it has been decided that the nature and functions of the devas must be somewhat revealed to man, and that their place in the scheme of things, and man's close connection and dependence upon them, must be given out.[83] At the same time, the means whereby they can be contacted, and the words whereby they can be controlled, will be withheld.

Laxness in the marriage relation, due to this particular cause, is only seen amongst the highly evolved and amongst the independent thinkers of the race. Similar laxness amongst the masses, and the low types of humanity, is based upon a different reason, and their promiscuity is due to certain developments of the animal nature in its lowest manifestation. These two causes

---

[83] If man can be brought to a realisation of the nature of his own being and of his constitution, and can be led to comprehend the rationale of that which can be seen occurring, and if the thinkers of the race can be shown the risks incident upon present happenings in the deva evolution, much danger may be averted. Hence the decision to extend the scope of this book to include more detailed information anent the deva evolution.

will bear consideration by those who have the present needs of civilisation at heart.   They can then co-operate with the Mahachohan in the work of effecting the very necessary transfer of force from a lower to a higher centre, and prevent (through knowledge), the incidental license.   This will bring about a refusal to besmirch the great love or sex impulse of nature.

The ceremonial ray has been often called "the marriage ritual of the Son," because upon this ray Spirit and matter can meet and have union.   This fact also should be borne in mind during the next one hundred years, for they will see great changes in the marriage laws.   The present laxity will inevitably bring a reaction, and the laws will become more stringent, in order to safeguard the race during a transition period.   These laws will not be along the line of making escape from the marriage relation more difficult, but will take effect at the other end, so to speak; the rising generation will be properly taught and guarded, and indiscriminate, hasty marriage will not be permitted, nor will juveniles be allowed rashly to enter into the marriage obligation.   There is no need to enlarge further upon this, for in working out their own problems men learn, and all that those upon the inner side are permitted to do is to give a hint or an indication.

Another angle of the Mahachohan's work at this time is connected with *sound,* and therefore with the particular devas whom we are considering.   Through the mismanagement of men, and their unbalanced development, the sounds of earth, such as those of the great cities, of the manufactories, and of the implements of war, have brought about a very serious condition among the gaseous devas.   This has to be offset in some way and the future efforts of civilisation will be directed towards the spreading of a revolt against the evils of congested living and to the dissemination of an impulse of a widespread nature to seek the country and wide spaces. One of the main interests in the future will be a tendency towards the elimination of noise, owing to the increased sensitiveness of the race. When the energy of water and of the atom is harnessed for the use of man, our present types of factories, our methods of navigation and of transportation, such as steamers and railway apparatus, will be entirely revolutionised. This will have a potent effect not only on man but on the devas.

c. The Elementals of the Ethers.

We will consider now the etheric levels of the physical plane or the four highest subplanes of the physical plane. These etheric levels are but gradations of physical plane matter of a rarer and more refined kind, but physical nevertheless. They are termed in most textbooks:

1. The first ether, or atomic matter.
2. The second ether, or sub-atomic matter.
3. The third ether, or super-etheric matter.
4. The fourth ether, or simply etheric matter.

The fourth ether is the only one as yet recognised by scientists, and is the subject of their present investigations, little though they may realise it.

On the atomic subplane are the permanent physical atoms of all humanity and the *appropriated atoms* of the deva kingdom. The devas do not develop as do the human race. They reincarnate in groups, and not as individuals, though each group is composed of units, and has nothing of the nature of the involutionary group soul. The group soul on the involutionary path and that upon the evolutionary are unlike; one is passing on to differentiation and is composed of entities animated by one general life; the other has differentiated, and each entity is a separate unit of the one life, complete in itself, yet one with the whole.

There are many types of life to be contacted on the four etheric levels, but we can only concern ourselves at present with the deva life, remembering that the deva evolution is of equal importance to that of the human. These devas are many in number, are of involutionary and evolutionary nature, and of all grades and types. Ruling over them on the physical plane is the great deva Kshiti. He is a deva of rank and power equal to a Chohan of a Ray; He presides over everything outside the human kingdom upon the physical plane, and He has for His council the four subordinate deva lords of the four etheric levels. He, with these subordinate devas, presides over a subsidiary council of seven devas who handle all that concerns the deva evolution, and the work of the greater and the lesser builders.

The deva Ruler of the fourth, or lowest ether, has delegated a member of His council to meet with certain of the Masters at this time for two specific purposes, first, to see whether the approximation of the two lines of evolution, human and deva, might be now tentatively permitted, and, secondly, to reveal some of the methods of healing and the causes of physical disability which are inherent in the etheric double.

Devas of all kinds and colours are found on the physical etheric levels, but the prevailing hue is violet, hence the term so often employed, the "devas of the shadows." With the coming in of the ceremonial ray of violet, we have the amplification therefore of the violet vibration, always inherent on these levels, and the great opportunity therefore for contact between the two kingdoms. It is in the development of etheric vision (which is a capacity of the physical human eye) and not in clairvoyance that this mutual apprehension will become possible. With the coming in likewise of this ray will arrive those who belong thereon, with a natural gift of seeing etherically. Children will frequently be born who will see etherically as easily as the average human being sees physically; as conditions of harmony gradually evolve out of the present world chaos, devas and human beings will meet as friends.

As the two planes, astral and physical, merge and blend, and continuity of consciousness is experienced upon the two, it will be difficult for human beings to differentiate at first between devas of the astral plane, and those of the physical. At the beginning of this period of recognition, men will principally contact the violet devas, for those of the higher ranks amongst them are definitely making the attempt to contact the human. These devas of the shadows are of a dark purple on the fourth etheric level, of a lighter purple, much the same colour as violet, on the third etheric level, a light violet on the second, whilst on the atomic subplane they are of a glorious translucent lavender.

Some of the groups of devas to be contacted on the physical plane are as follows:

Four groups of violet devas, associated with the etheric doubles of all that exists on the physical plane. These four are in two divisions, those associated with the building of the etheric doubles, and those out of whose substance these doubles are built.

The green devas of the vegetable kingdom. These exist in two divisions also. They are of high development, and will be contacted principally along the lines of magnetisation. The greater devas of this order preside over the magnetic spots of the earth, guard the solitude of the forests, reserve intact spaces on the planet which are required to be kept inviolate; they defend them from molestation, and with the violet devas are at this time working definitely, though temporarily, under the Lord Maitreya. The Raja Lord of the astral plane, Varuna and his brother Kshiti, have been called to the council chamber of the Hierarchy for specific consultation, and just as the Masters are endeavouring to prepare humanity for service when the World Teacher comes, so these Raja Lords are working along similar lines in connection with the devas. They are arduous in Their work, intense in Their zeal, but much obstructed by man.

The white devas of the air and water who preside over the atmosphere work with certain aspects of electrical phenomena, and control the seas, rivers, and streams. From among them, at a certain stage in their evolution, are gathered the guardian angels of the race when in physical plane incarnation. Each unit of the human family has his guardian deva.

Each group of devas has some specific method of development and some means whereby they evolve and attain a particular goal.

For the *violet* devas the path of attainment lies through feeling, and through educating the race in the perfecting of the physical body in its two departments.

For the *green* devas the path of service is seen in magnetisation, of which the human race knows nothing as yet. Through this power they act as the protectors of the vegetable plant life, and of the sacred spots of the earth; in their work lies the safety of man's body, for from the vegetable kingdom for the remainder of this round comes the nourishment of that body.

For the *white* devas the path of service lies in the guarding of the individuals of the human family, in the care and segregation of types, in the control of the water and air elementals, and much that concerns the fish kingdom.

Thus in the service of humanity in some form or another lies attainment for these physical plane devas. They have much to give and do for humanity, and in time it will be apparent to the human unit what he has to give towards the perfecting of the deva kingdom. A great hastening of their evolution goes forward now coincident with that of the human family.

There is another group of devas about which much may not as yet be communicated. They have come in from another planetary scheme, and are specialists in their particular line. They have attained, or passed through, the human kingdom, and are of equal rank with certain members of the Hierarchy, having chosen to stay and work in connection with the physical plane evolution. They are not many in number, being only twelve. Four work in the violet group, five in the green group, and two in the white, with a presiding officer of rank equal to a Chohan. The number of the deva evolution is six, as that of man is now five, and as ten stands for perfected man, so twelve stands for perfection in the deva kingdom. This group presides over the three earlier enumerated. Certain subsidiary groups are found.

Under group 1 are found all the elementals working with the etheric doubles of men, all the elementals forming the etheric bodies wherein is life, and all the elementals working with the etheric counterparts of so-called inanimate objects. These are named in the order and the importance of their development. The violet devas are on the evolutionary path; the elementals are on the involutionary path, the goal for them being to pass into the deva kingdom of violet hue.

Under group 2 work the fairies of plant life, the elves who build and paint the flowers, the radiant little beings who inhabit the woods and the fields, the elementals who work with the fruits, vegetables, and with all that leads to the covering of the earth's surface with verdure. Associated with them are the lesser devas of magnetisation, those attached to sacred spots, to talismans and to stones, and also a special group to be found around the habitations of the Masters wherever situated.

Under group 3 work the elementals of the air and the sea, the sylphs, the water fairies, and the devas who guard each human being.

Here only general hints are given. This list is not complete and does not include the grosser elementals, the brownies, and those that inhabit the dark spaces of the earth, the cities and the subterranean spots of the earth's crust.

The devas of the ethers carry on their foreheads a translucent symbol in the form of a crescent moon, and by this they may be distinguished from the astral devas by those able to see clairvoyantly.

As we consider the devas of the ethers, we find that they fall naturally—as far as manifestation is concerned—into two main groups. Each group is represented on each of the four subplanes, and this grouping must be considered as but one method of differentiation out of the many possible. These groups are, first, those devas who are the transmitters of prana to all forms of life; they are a group of intermediary devas, and may be regarded as the energy providers in their various differentiations; secondly, those devas who form the etheric bodies of every form in manifestation. These constitute the bulk of the lesser devas.

There are naturally many other organised intelligences in the great Army of the Voice in connection with this primary division of the physical plane, but if the student will consider these two groups, and will investigate their relationship to man and to the Heavenly Man within Whose body they are to be found, he will learn much which will enable him to comprehend problems hitherto considered insoluble, and will find many things revealed which will tend to revolutionise the findings of modern science, and bring about changes in the care of the physical body.

The Devas and Energy. Before we take up the consideration of these two groups it might be wise here to emphasise the necessity of remembering that when we consider the etheric levels of the physical plane we are dealing with those planes upon which the *true form* is to be found, and are approaching the solution of the mystery of the Holy Spirit and the Mother. In this realisation, and its extension to include an entire solar system, will come a clarifying of the connection between the four higher planes of the system and the three worlds of human endeavour. We have, in the *macrocosm,* the four planes of super-conscious life, or those four central vibrations which are the basis of the life and energy of the etheric body of a planetary Logos and of a solar Logos, and the three planes of conscious and of self-conscious life which form the dense physical vehicle of a Heavenly Man, and of the Grand Man of the Heavens.

By a close scrutiny of these conditions in the macrocosm and in the microcosm will come a comprehension of the reason why the physical vehicle is never considered a principle at all by occultists. The Holy Spirit, the One Who overshadows and Who implants the germ of life in the waiting acquiescent Virgin Mother or matter (causing her to awaken and to commence her great work of producing the divine incarnation) is a primary factor from the standpoint of the second solar system. In a way incomprehensible to modern thinkers, the Mother, or the divine Aspirant to the mysteries of the cosmic marriage, was (in a previous system) the dominant factor. In this system in connection with substance it is the Holy Spirit. The work, therefore, on etheric levels, and the energy and activity originating therefrom, are the factors that primarily are responsible on the physical plane for all that is tangible, objective, and manifested. The accretion of matter around the vital body, and the densification of substance around the vital etheric nucleus are in themselves the result of interaction, and the final interchange of vibration between that which might be called the residue from an earlier manifestation, and the vibration of this present one.

It is here—in the relation between positive electrical energy in its fourfold differentiation, and the triple negative receptive lower substance—that scientists will eventually arrive at certain definite deductions and discover:

- a. The secret of matter itself, that is, matter as we know and see it.
- b. The key to the process of creation upon the physical plane, and the method whereby density and concretion on the three lower levels are brought about.
- c. The formulas for organic transmutation, or the key to the processes whereby the elements as we know them can be disintegrated and recombined.

Only when scientists are prepared to admit the fact that there is a body of vitality which acts as a focal point in every organised form, and only when they are willing to consider each element and form of every degree as constituting part of a still greater vital body, will the true methods of the great goddess Nature become their methods.   To do this they must be prepared to accept the sevenfold differentiation of the physical plane as stated by Eastern occultism, to recognise the triple nature of the septenary manifestation.

- a. The atomic or Shiva energy, the energy of the first subplane or the first etheric plane.
- b. The vital form building energy of the three ensuing etheric levels.
- c. The negative receptive energy of the three planes

of the dense physical, the gaseous, the liquid and the truly dense.

They will also eventually consider the interplay between the lower three and the higher four in that great atom called the physical plane. This can be seen duplicated in the atom of the physicist or chemist. Scientific students who are interested in these matters will find it worth while to consider the correspondence between these three types of energy, and that which is understood by the words, atoms, electrons, and ions.

All that manifests (from God to man)[84] is the result of these three types of energy or force, of their combination, their interplay, and their psychic action and reaction. During the great cycle of logoic appearance it is the second type of energy which dominates and which is of evolutionary importance, and this is why the etheric body which lies back of all that is visible is the most important. This is equally true of gods, of men and of atoms.

Much time is spent in speculating upon the sources of life, upon the springs of action, and upon the impulses which underlie the creative processes. Hitherto science has worked somewhat blindly and has spent much time investigating the lower three planes. It has dealt principally with the Mother, with the negative receptive matter, and is only now becoming aware of the Holy Spirit aspect, or of the energy which enables that Mother to fulfill her function, and to carry on her work.

Considering the same problem *microcosmically* it may be pointed out that men are only now beginning to be

[84] *The Secret Doctrine* says that:

God, Monad, and Atom are the correspondences of Spirit, Mind and Body.—S. D., I, 679.

The Logos is manifesting in this mahamanvantara as Manas (the Divine Manasaputras in their totality) utilising atomic sheaths for purposes of evolution and with the aim in view of developing the second aspect of buddhi or wisdom. Wisdom must have manas, or intelligent mind for its basis. He is the sumtotal of Intelligence, evolving in order to develop Love.

aware of the springs of spiritual action, and of the sources of spiritual life. The energy of the higher planes is only revealing itself as men begin to tread the Way, and to come under the influence of buddhi, which flows from the fourth cosmic etheric plane.

Finally, when scientists are willing to recognise and to co-operate with the intelligent forces that are to be found on etheric levels, and when they become convinced of the hylozoistic nature of all that exists, their findings and their work will be brought into a more accurate correspondence with things as they really are. This, as has been earlier pointed out, will be brought about as the race develops etheric vision, and the truth of the contentions of the occultist is proved past all controversy.

It will have been noted that in the enumeration of these two main groups, we did not touch upon that great group of Builders who are called esoterically "Those who transmit the Word." I have only dealt with the two groups who constitute the "Army of the Voice." This is due to the fact that in this section we are only dealing with that army, or with those builders, great and small, who are swept into activity as the Word of the physical plane sounds forth. The "Transmitters of the Word" upon the first subplane or atomic level are those who take up the vibratory sound as it reaches them from the astral plane and—passing it through their bodies—send it forth to the remaining subplanes. These transmitters may be, for purposes of clarity, considered as seven in number. In their totality they form the atomic physical bodies of the Raja Lord of the plane and in a peculiarly occult sense these seven form (in their lower differentiations on etheric levels) the sumtotal of the etheric centres of all human beings, just as on the cosmic etheric levels are found the centres of a Heavenly Man.

The connection between the centres and etheric substance, systemic and human, opens up a vast range for thought. The "Transmitters of the Word" on the atomic subplane of each plane are devas of vast power and prerogative who may be stated to be connected with the Father aspect, and embodiments of electric fire. They are all fully self-conscious, having passed through the human stage in earlier kalpas. They are also corporate parts of the seven primary head centres in the body of a solar Logos or planetary Logos.

Though connected with the Father aspect, they are nevertheless part of the body of the Son, and each of them, according to the plane which he energises, is a component part of one or other of the seven centres, either solar or planetary—planetary when only the particular centre is concerned, systemic when that centre is viewed as an integral part of the whole.

Each of these great lives (embodying deva energy of the first degree) is an emanation from the central spiritual sun in the first instance and from one of the three major constellations in the second instance. Systemically they fall into three groups: Group 1 includes those transmitters of the Word who are found on the three lower subplanes of the plane Adi, or the logoic plane. Group 2 comprises those great builders who transmit the Word on the three next systemic planes, the monadic, the atmic and the buddhic. Group 3 is formed of those who carry on a similar function in the three worlds of human endeavour. Fundamentally they are also emanations from one of the seven stars of the Great Bear in the third instance.

In these triple emanatory forces may be found the origin of all that is visible and objective, and through their agency our solar system takes its place within the greater cosmic scheme, and a certain basic cosmic fire is formed. They are the sumtotal of the head, the heart and the throat centres of the solar Logos, and their correspondences will be found within a Heavenly Man, a human being, and an atom. Hence the scientist, as he discovers the nature of the atom, is putting himself in touch with these three types of solar energy, and is unravelling the central mystery of the system. As the triple nature of the atom stands revealed, so likewise the triple nature of man and of God gradually becomes proven. The energy of these groups passes through the physical sun, and from thence they sound the Word for the particular plane of their specific endeavour.

The student must not make the mistake of thinking that these seven great transmitters are the seven Heavenly Men. They form one half of Their real nature. This is all that can be said of this great mystery, though it might be added that from another angle of vision, they form but one third of his threefold divine nature. Man is dual, being Spirit and matter; he is also, during evolution, a triplicity, so it is with a Heavenly Man, and hence the mystery.

The great Transmitter of the Word on the physical plane, which is the one under our consideration, is the energising factor of the throat centre of Brahma. An interesting tabulation of the threefold centres and the three divine aspects might here be given which may prove of use to the student, though he should carefully bear in mind that these centres are for the purpose of generating and transmitting energy.

1. The transmitter of energy on the physical plane forms the throat centre in the body of Brahma, the third aspect.
2. The transmitter of energy upon the astral plane forms the heart centre of Brahma.
3. The transmitter of the Word on the mental plane forms the head centre of this, the third aspect.

These three Raja Lords, devas, or transmitters, form the three centres of logoic force in the three worlds. They are the lowest energy aspect of Brahma.

4. The Transmitter of the Word upon the buddhic plane forms the throat centre of Vishnu, the second aspect. From thence the Word goes forth that builds the dense physical form of a Heavenly Man or of a solar Logos.

5. The Transmitter of energy upon the monadic plane forms the heart centre of Vishnu, the second aspect.

6. The Transmitter of force upon the atmic plane forms the head centre of Vishnu.

This tabulation will be confusing to students unless it is realised that we are here considering these aspects only as dualities, and are dealing with one of the dual parts. It will be apparent that in the Vishnu aspect, for instance, which manifests upon the second plane, the energy of that plane will act as the head centre to the succeeding planes, and this apprehension, rightly grasped, will clarify the others.

The Transmitter of the Word on the first plane of Adi is the embodiment of the throat centre of a cosmic entity. From this statement will come a just realisation of our place in the cosmic scheme, and the fundamentally physical nature of the seven planes of the solar system is also here demonstrated, the nature of **Brahma**, or the Holy Spirit, becoming apparent.

The old Commentary says:

"Brahma is One, yet includes His brother. Vishnu is One, yet existeth not apart from His brother, younger in point of time yet older far. Shiva is One, and antedates Them both, yet He appeareth not nor is He seen, until They both have cycled through Their courses."

The above sevenfold tabulation can be, under the law of correspondences, applied equally to every plane, for the transmitters and workers on each plane form similar groups. Equally well can man consider this tabulation in connection with his seven centres, and from a study of the two together he will gain knowledge as to the type of energy which flows through any particular centre. These transmitters likewise can be heard sounding forth the Word with particular force and power in that planetary scheme which corresponds to their note and is keyed to their vibration. The planetary schemes, therefore, will fall into a similar grouping, and this will open up for students a vast field of conjecture. The seven Prajapatis fall into two groups of three, with one dominating. Students will do well to remember in studying the solar system, the planes, the schemes, man and the atom, that the groupings of the lines or streams of energy during the evolutionary cycles fall naturally into four divisions:

1. 1—3—3
2. 4—3
3. 3—4
4. 3—1—3

Division 1 can be understood under the law of correspondences when the nature of the atomic plane of the solar system, the three cosmic etheric planes, and the three planes of human endeavour are investigated in connection with each other.

Division 2 becomes easier of comprehension when the close relation between the four cosmic etheric planes and the three lower planes is grasped. This can be illuminated by a study of the four physical ethers and the three lower subplanes of our physical plane.

Division 3 finds the clue to its mystery in the constitution of the mental plane, with its three formless levels, and its four levels of form.

Division 4 can be grasped as the student arrives at a comprehension of his own nature as a spiritual triad, an egoic body and a threefold lower man. He can likewise approach the first division in a similar manner, and view himself as a primary force or Monad, a triple secondary force or Ego, and a threefold lower energy, or personality, remembering that we are here dealing only with creative energy and with the Brahma aspect of manifestation as it co-ordinates itself with the Vishnu aspect.

The Transmitters of Prana. We have in an earlier section of this treatise considered somewhat the devas who are the transmitters of prana for the etheric body of man and of the planet. They are the reflection upon the lowest plane of the Vishnu aspect of divinity; the seven subplanes of our physical plane reflect in a dim and distorted fashion the three aspects, and are a shadow, dark and unrevealing, of the Godhead. This group of transmitters are responsible for three principal results, and are active along three main lines.

They are the devas who vitalise and produce the energy of all forms of sentient life. Theirs is the life which pulsates through the etheric body of every plant and animal and of all intermediate forms of life, and which constitutes the raging fire which is seen circulating through all etheric vehicles. Among many other functions they produce the warmth of the sun and of all bodies; they are the cause of solar, planetary, and human radiation, and they nourish and preserve all forms. They occultly mediate between the Father and the Mother on each plane, whether cosmic or systemic. They originate in the sun, and are closely related to the logoic and planetary solar plexus, for the evolutionary process, as in all manifestation, is the result of desire, acting upon the creative faculties and producing that which is objective.

They are the devas who energise the myriads of minute lives which build the etheric bodies of all that is seen and tangible, and who are the instigators of the creative processes on the three lowest subplanes of the physical plane. Systemically, the devas engaged in this line of activity can be subdivided into two groups:

a. Those who work on the four higher systemic planes and from thence influence in the three worlds, producing through reflex action the desired results.

b. Those who work in the three worlds of human endeavour, producing directly dense physical manifestation.

All the etheric devas who transmit energy on the physical plane belong to the second division above enumerated, and according to the subplane on which they work come under the guidance of a greater intelligence on a corresponding plane.

There are also the devas who form the attractive force of all subhuman forms, holding the forms of the three lower kingdoms of nature together in coherency, and thus producing the body of manifestation of the great Entity who is the sumtotal of the life of the kingdom, and of the lesser beings who ensoul different families and groups within any specific kingdom.

The Devas of the Etheric Double. The subject that we are to deal with now concerns those devas who are etheric doubles of all that is. It is full of profit therefore to the wise student, for it reveals the method whereby all forms materialise upon the physical plane.

It is not the purpose of this treatise to trace the materialisation of a form as it originates upon the archetypal planes, through the agency of divine thought, and from thence (through directed streams of intelligent energy) acquires substance as it is reproduced upon each plane, until eventually (upon the physical plane) the form stands revealed at its densest point of manifestation. No form is as yet perfect, and it is this fact which necessitates cyclic evolution, and the continual production of forms until they approximate reality in fact and in deed. The method of form production may be tabulated as follows:

FORM PRODUCTION

1. Divine thought ..... The cosmic mental plane.
2. Divine desire ....The cosmic astral plane.
3. Divine activity ..... The cosmic physical plane
(our seven systemic planes).

The logoic Breath...First plane...The Sound [85] *A.*

This is the first etheric appearance of a solar system upon the atomic subplane of the cosmic physical plane. The seeds of life are all latent. Faculty inheres from an earlier solar essence.

The logoic Sound...Second plane...The Sound A U
This is the body of the solar system in the second ether. This plane is the archetypal plane. The seeds of

---

[85] *Mantric Sounds.*

A mantram is a combination of sounds, of words and of phrases that, through virtue of certain rhythmic effects, achieve results that would not be possible apart from them. The most sacred of all the Eastern mantrams given out as yet to the public is the one embodied in the words: "Om mani padme hum." Every syllable of this phrase has a secret potency, and its totality has seven meanings and can bring about seven different results.

There are various mantric forms, based upon this formula and upon the Sacred Word, which, sounded rhythmically and in different keys, accomplish certain desired ends, such as the invoking of protective angels or devas, and definite work, either constructive or destructive upon the planes.

The potency of a mantram depends upon the point in evolution of the man who employs it. Uttered by an ordinary man it serves to stimulate the good within his bodies, to protect him, and it will also prove of beneficent influence upon his environment. Uttered by an adept or initiate its possibilities for good are infinite and far-reaching.

Mantrams are of many kinds, and generally speaking might be enumerated as follows:

1. Some very esoteric mantrams, existing in the original Sensa, in the custody of the Great White Lodge.
2. Some Sanskrit mantrams employed by initiates and adepts.
3. Mantrams connected with the different rays.
4. Mantrams used in healing.
5. Mantrams used in the departments of either the Manu, the Bodhisattva, or the Mahachohan.
6. Mantrams used in connection with the devas and the elemental kingdoms.
7. Special mantrams connected with fire.

All these mantrams depend for their potency upon the sound and rhythm and upon the syllabic emphasis imparted to them when enunciating and intoning. They depend too upon the capacity of the man who uses them to visualise and to *will* the desired effect.

life are vibrating or germinating. The seven centres of energy are apparent. The one deva Agni is seen as seven. The form is now potentially perfect.

> *The logoic triple Word..The third plane..The Sound*
> *A U M.*

The body of the solar system in substance of the third etheric plane is seen, and the three function as one. The triple energy of the Logos is co-ordinated, and nothing now can hinder the work of evolution. The three groups of devas are active, and the archetypal form is in process of materialization.

> *The logoic septenary word...The fourth...The seven*
> *The logoic etheric Centres   plane   syllabled*
> *   become active   Word.*

The etheric body of the solar system is now complete, though it will not be perfected till the end of another manvantara. The greater body of vitality is ready to energise the dense physical vehicle. The seven centres with their forty-nine major petals are vibrant, and con- sciousness thrills through every atom in the system.

An interlude or period of pause is to be found at this stage of development; in it the processes of co-ordination and of stabilisation are carried on; the energy or the vibration is increased until it becomes possible, by a simultaneous effort, emanating from all the three aspects, to bring into objectivity that which is as yet subjective. This is paralleled by man on the physical plane in the applied effort he has to make to bring through and ma- terialise, that which he has conceived and desired. The reason so many people fail in materialising their con- cepts, and hence come to be reckoned as failures, is owing to the fact of their inability to make a co-ordinated applied effort, and thus set in motion substance of the three lower subplanes of the physical plane. They succeed in bringing their concept through from the mental plane (as does the Logos on cosmic levels) as far as the fourth etheric level of the physical, and there their energy becomes exhausted owing to three things:

a. Lack of sustained will or concentration,

b. Lack of alignment with the Ego,

c. A weakness of co-ordination between the two parts of the physical vehicle.

The logoic Phrase...Fifth plane...The plane of the
The gaseous body.   *logoic mantram*
                                        of 35 stanzas.

The gaseous form of the solar system now appears, and the energy centres become veiled and hidden. Accretion and concretion rapidly proceeds. The three groups of builders co-ordinate their efforts afresh and a new influx of energy—bearing devas from the logoic head centre—pours in. The lesser builders respond to the logoic mantram chanted anew at each manvantara, and the seven streams of energy from the seven logoic centres are directed downwards.

The logoic Song of...The Sixth plane...A poem in
Love or Desire   *forty-two*
The logoic liquid body.   *verses.*

This song or vibration causes the bringing in of a body of devas from the logoic heart centre to swell the efforts of those already active. The liquid body of the solar Logos appears, and the form exists in its six differentiations. Concretion is very rapid, and activity is considerably more violent owing to the greater density of the accruing substance.

The logoic Book...Seventh plane...Exists in forty-
*   of Life*   *nine chapters.*

The entire form stands revealed. During evolution it must manifest its purpose and its nature. A third group of devas from the logoic throat centre appear, and co-operate with their brothers. All the fires are burning, all the centres are active, and every petal, forty-nine in number, on the fourth plane of Buddhi is producing a reflex activity upon the dense physical plane.

Men, when occupied in creation of any kind, and in the process of producing forms on earth which embody an idea, work along similar lines. The analogy is perfect.

In connection with those human beings who create nothing, but who are only swept into activity under the urge of circumstance—and they are the bulk of the human race—it should be pointed out that they are a part of the creative activity of some greater, and more advanced, entity. As self-conscious evolution proceeds, more and more of the human family will become creators and intelligent workers in connection with deva substance. In the initial stages, therefore, of their dissociation from a passive attitude, there will be found a revolt against law and order, a refusal to be governed, and an ability evidenced to follow out an individual concept at the expense of the group, great or small. This apparent defect, evolution itself and experience will remedy, and as the consciousness becomes alive to higher vibrations the man will become aware of the purpose and plan of the Intelligence of his group. He will awaken to the beauty of that plan and will begin to submerge his own interests in the greater, and to co-operate intelligently. The creative power which had before been of a separative nature will be offered as a willing sacrifice to the greater energy, and his small plans and ideas will be merged in the greater ones. He will no longer, however, be a passive unit, swept hither and thither by the energy of his group, but will become a positive, active potent force, self-immolated through intelligent recognition of the greater plan.

He will become alive to the fact that there are living

forces in nature. As the greater energy thrills through him, his own latent powers are awakened. He sees and knows the deva forces and can consequently work with them intelligently. Some he will control and manipulate, with others he will co-operate, and others still he will obey.

It is in the realisation of these facts anent deva substance, the power of sound, the law of vibration, and the ability to produce forms in conformity with law, that the true magician can be seen. Herein too lies one of the distinctions to be found between magicians of the Good Law, and those of the Left-hand Path. A white magician can control and manipulate deva substance, and he proceeds to do it through an intelligent co-operation with the greater builders. Owing to the purity and holiness of his life, and the height of his own vibration, he can contact them in some one or other of their grades. The magician of the shadows controls and manipulates deva substance on the astral and physical plane and on the lower levels of the mental plane through the force of his own vibration and knowledge, but not through co-operation with the directing builders. He cannot contact them, as his character is impure through selfishness, and his vibration is too low; his power therefore is limited and destructive, yet immense within certain restrictions.

The devas of the etheric doubles fall into two groups. They are those who are the lesser builders, and who, under direction from the greater builders, form the etheric doubles of all that can be seen and all that is tangible on the dense physical plane. They exist in vast hosts and are omnipresent; they gather and build the material needed to form the etheric double of everything, and they do this under certain laws and work under certain restrictions. They are called in occult phraseology *"the listening devas,"* for they are the ones who pick up that particular note and tone from the transmitters of the physical plane sound which is needed to gather the substance for any intended material form. Again, they are spoken of as "having ears but seeing not." They work in close co-operation with the elementals of the dense physical body. This second group are spoken of as the *"seeing elementals,"* for they exist in matter of the three lower subplanes and can therefore see on the objective plane in the occult sense which always implies an analogy between sight and knowledge. The *"listening builders"* gather the material; the "seeing elementals" take that gathered material, and build it into any specific form. They exist in many groups according to their point in evolution, and some of them might be tabulated as follows:

1. *The builders of the human vehicle.*

This is the highest group of lesser builders, who are highly specialised. These will be dealt with somewhat in detail later.

2. *The builders of the forms in the three kingdoms of nature in their two divisions.*

First. The builders of the mineral kingdom. These are the workers occultly called "the elemental alchemists." They are in many groups connected with the differing elements, metals, chemicals, and minerals, and with what are called active and radioactive substances. They are the custodians of two secrets, that of the immetalisation of the Monad, and the secret of the transmutation of metals.

Second. The builders of the vegetable kingdom. They exist in many groups and are termed "the surface alchemists" and "the bridging units." They build the doubles of every form of vegetable life, and just as the "alchemists" of the mineral kingdom are mostly concerned with the action of fire, these other alchemical workers are concerned with the liquid action of divine manifestation. They work, therefore, in co-operation with the devas of the waters, or liquid substance, whilst the earlier mentioned group work with the gaseous devas. A hint is here conveyed, but greater expansion of the statement is not possible, owing to the danger of the knowledge to be reached. With them is hidden three secrets: One is concerned with the earlier solar system, or the *green* solar system; another deals with the laws of bridging, or the interaction between the kingdoms of nature, and the third is connected with the history of the second round; this secret when revealed will make clear why man (under the law) should be a vegetarian and not carnivorous. Scientists are learning already certain things connected with the second secret, and they may hope, as the knowledge of the significance of colour is extended, to glean hints as to the first. The third secret will not be indicated more clearly till the sixth race is living upon earth.

Third. The builders of all animal etheric forms. These are a group closely allied with those who build the human form. They came in force from a reservoir of energy which was kept in a quiescent condition until the physical condition of any particular scheme warranted their activity. With them came in much that accounts for the present sad condition, for much of the fear, hatred, and destructive condition to be found among the animals is caused by their bodies being built, and the work of evolution carried on by the "imperfect gods" (as H. P. B. expresses it) working in imperfect matter as yet imperfectly manipulated. The secret of fear is hidden in the etheric body, and the particular type of substance out of which it may be built.

3. *The builders of the planetary etheric web.*

Their work is exceedingly obscure and exists in three divisions:

a. *The materialisation of the web.* This is only perfected by the fourth round, and was purposely hurried in connection with our planet owing to karmic conditions, and under the law of spiritual necessity. A correspondence to this can be seen in the case of man himself. The etheric web was very loosely co-ordinated in man at the beginning of the fourth rootrace. Spiritual necessity forced its rapid consolidation, and it is now so constituted that it forms a barrier between the physical and the astral plane.

b. *The preservation of the planetary web.* This will be continued until the sixth round. During this period spiritual evolution proceeds with a certain degree of planetary safety, for the web protects from certain solar influences, and acts largely as a sifter and a distributor of solar forces.

c. *The destruction of the web.* This takes place towards the end of planetary evolution, thus permitting the escape of the imprisoned planetary life and the absorption of the life essence into its synthesiser. The process of destruction can only be described in the words perforation and disintegration.

4. *The builders of the etheric body of the planetary Entity.*

This great involutionary life must remain for many aeons a mystery. His etheric body is now in process of building, and only in another solar system will he assume definite physical form. Sufficient energy has not yet been generated to permit of his manifestation objectively. He remains as yet subjective. He has his solar correspondence.

5. *The builders of the planetary body.*

This proceeds under the same law as that of the solar system and of man, but, as in the solar system, it proceeds upon the higher planes. Students are here recommended to trace the relation between the solar and cosmic planes in this specific connection.

6. *The etheric doubles of all that man creates.*

These are a special group of etheric builders who, under karma, are forced to act in conjunction with human beings.

These are but a few out of the many groups possible to touch upon; it is needless further to enlarge, as no substantial profit will eventuate from the impartation of further information. Only the briefest indications can be given and touched upon. It is neither safe nor advisable as yet to impart to men knowledge anent the workers in etheric matter, which would enable them to contact them, nor is it wise as yet to link up coherently the scattered facts already given in different occult books. Science is treading on the borderland of discovery, and trespassing already into the domain of the building devas. Caution is needed. Yet if the hints given above are studied, if the various secrets of the builders are pondered upon, and if the esoteric side of Masonry is carefully and persistently meditated upon, the work of the Great Architect and His many assistants will stand forth in a clearer and a fuller light. One hint may here be given, forgetting not that the work is twofold:

The construction of the tabernacle, or the building of the temporary forms is the work of the Divine Carpenter, whilst the building of the Temple of Solomon, or the construction of the more permanent structure is the work of the Supervising Architect. One concerns operative, and the other speculative Masonry in the true esoteric significance of the word.

The devas who form the etheric doubles of all objects out of their own substance must also be considered. These builders are the sumtotal of all physical plane substance, and constitute the matter of the etheric levels of the physical plane. They exist, therefore, in four groups, and each group has a curious karmic relation to one of the four kingdoms in nature:

Group.	Plane.	Kingdom.
First	One	Human
Second	Two	Animal
Third	Three	Vegetable
Fourth	Four	Mineral

The substance of the highest physical form of a human being is therefore atomic. The Master's physical body is made of atomic matter, and when He wishes to materialise it on the dense physical plane, He forms a sheath of gaseous substance upon that atomic matter, perfect in its delineation of all the known physical traits. The substance of the highest form of animal body is that of the second ether, and herein is to be found a clue as to the relation between all sea and watery forms to the animal. The highest form of body possible for the vegetable form of life is that of the third ether. These facts will be demonstrated in the seventh round when the present three kingdoms of nature—the human, the animal, and the vegetable will objectively exist in etheric matter; that will be for them their densest manifestation. The mineral kingdom will find its highest manifestation in matter of the fourth ether, and this transmutation is already taking place, for all the radioactive substances now being discovered are literally becoming matter of the fourth ether. The mineral kingdom is *relatively* nearing its possible manvantaric perfection, and by the time the seventh round is reached all mineral lives (not forms) will have been transferred to another planet. This will not be so with the other three kingdoms.

The etheric deva substance is acted upon in two ways:

It is awakened into a specific activity by the sounding of the physical plane word, and it is built into forms by the lesser builders.

It will, therefore, be apparent that it comes under the influence of two types of force or energy.

We will now briefly take up the subject of the work of the devas who build man's etheric and dense physical body. By dividing our thoughts into two sections, we may be able to cover the ground somewhat more easily, dealing first with the building devas and the microcosm and then with the lesser builders of the etheric levels.

d.   The Elementals and the Microcosm.

Man and the building devas. Man, in the process of evolution, as he pursues the method of reincarnation, works with four types of builders and three major grades of building essence or deva substance.

He connects with the transmitting devas who are found in connection with the microcosm on the fourth subplane of the mental plane, and on the atomic subplanes of the astral and physical plane. He connects next with the devas concerned with:

1.   The mental unit.
2.   The astral permanent atom.
3.   The physical permanent atom.

He co-operates with the work of the building devas who form the etheric body, and influences the building devas of the dense physical substances, so that the necessary physical vehicle for his objective manifestation becomes an actuality.

These are the four main groups of devas which come under the influence of any particular Ego. They unitedly produce the lower man, and bring into manifestation the Personality, that reflection of the Ego and shadow of the Monad. The three grades of building essence which are built into forms through the activity of the above four groups are here briefly recognised as the mental substance, built into the mental body, the astral substance, built into the astral vehicle and the matter of the physical body. These seven groups form, in their totality, what we might call the Brahma aspect of the microcosm.

From another point of view, we may be considered as studying the action of the solar Angel, or Lord, upon the lunar angels, and the process whereby the solar Lord imposes a certain rhythm and vibration upon different aspects of lower manifestation. Esoterically, this is all hidden in the words of a very ancient writing, which says:

"As the moon revolves, she reflects. As she reflects, she causes response in that which failed to radiate. These three, the Sun, the Moon, and the Mother, produce that which pursues a tiny cycle, and burns."

The first step of the Ego towards producing a "shadow" is expressed in the words "The Ego sounds his note." He utters his voice, and (as in the logoic process) the lesser "army of the voice" responds immediately to it. According to the tone and quality of the voice, so is the nature of the responsive agents. According to the depth or height of the note, and according to its volume, so is the status or grade of building deva which replies to the call. This egoic note produces, therefore, certain effects:

It sweeps into activity devas who proceed to transmit the sound. They utter a word.

It reaches the listening devas of the second grade who take up the word and proceed to elaborate it into what might be called a mantric phrase. The building process definitely begins in a sequential threefold manner. The

mental body begins to co-ordinate in three stages. All
the building stages overlap. When, for instance, the
co-ordination of the mental body is in its second stage,
the first stage of astral concretion begins. This is carried
on for seven stages (three major and four minor) which
overlap in an intricate fashion. Again, when the second
stage is reached, a vibration is produced which awakens
response in etheric matter on the physical plane, and the
builders of the etheric double commence their activity.
Again the process is repeated. When the second stage
of the work of these etheric devas is begun, *conception
takes place upon the physical plane.* This is a very important point to be remembered, for it brings the entire
process of human birth definitely into line with established karmic law. It shows the close connection between
that which is subjective and that which is tangible and
seen. The building of the physical body proceeds like
that of the three stages during the prenatal period:

- *a.* The work of the building devas during the three
  and a half months prior to the realisation of life.
  This period sees the third stage of the building of
  the etheric body entered upon.
- *b.* The building work of the next three and a half
  months of the gestation period.
- *c.* The final process of concretion carried on through
  the remaining two months.

Students will here find it interesting to trace out the
correspondence in this method of producing evolutionary
manifestation in a planetary scheme with its rounds and
races, and in a solar system with its manvantaras and
greater cycles.

In summing up this very cursory outline, the work of
the etheric devas does not cease at the birth of the man,
but is continued likewise in three stages, which find a
close analogy in the life period of a solar system.

First, their work is directed to the steady increase of the human physical vehicle, so that it may follow accurately the lines of growth of the two subtler bodies. This is carried on till maturity is reached. The next stage is that in which their work consists largely of repair work, and the preservation of the body during the years of full manhood so that it can measure up to the purpose of the subjective life. This purpose necessarily varies according to the stage of development of the man. Finally comes the stage when the work of building ceases. The vitality in the etheric body waxes dim, and the processes of destruction begin. The Ego begins to call in his forces. The "sound" becomes faint and dim; there is less and less volume for the transmitters to pass on, and the initial vibration gets fainter and fainter. The period of obscuration comes in. First the physical body waxes weak and useless; then the Ego withdraws from the centres, and functions for a few hours in the etheric double. This in turn is devitalised, and so the process is carried on till one by one the sheaths are discarded and the egoic "shadow" is dissipated.

The work of the building devas.

Let us now consider the work of the building devas on the three planes, dealing with them in two groups:

a. Those who are connected with the permanent atoms.

b. Those who are responsible for the building process.

The devas of the permanent atoms. This particular group of devas are the aggregate of the lives who form the mental unit and the two permanent atoms. They, as we know, have their place within the causal periphery, and are focal points of egoic energy. They are the very highest type of building devas, and form a group of lives which are closely allied to the solar Angels. *They exist in seven groups connected with three of the spirillae of*

*the logoic physical permanent atom. These three spiril-
lae are to these seven groups of lives what the three
major rays are to the seven groups of rays on the egoic
subplanes of the mental plane.* This phrase will bear
meditating upon, and may convey much information to
the intuitional thinker. There is a correspondence between the three permanent atomic triads, and the appearance of man in the third root race. A curiously
interesting sequence of the three lines of force can be
seen in:

    a. The triads of the involutionary group soul.
    b. The appearance of triple natured man in the third
        root race.
    c. The triads in the causal bodies of any self-conscious
        unit.

These building devas are the ones who take up the
sound as the Ego sends it forth through certain of the
transmitting deva agencies, and by the vibration which
this sets up they drive into activity the surrounding deva
essence in their two groups:

    a. Those who build the form.
    b. Those who are built into the form.

They only affect those of analogous vibration. The
stages of the building of any of the four forms through
which lower man (the Quaternary) functions, follow
exactly analogous stages to the building of the dense
physical body, for·instance, of a planet, or of a solar system. This can be traced all the way from the nebulous
and chaotic stages through the fiery to the solid, or to
the *relatively* solid where a subtle body is concerned.
There is no need for us further to enlarge. H. P. B. has
outlined these stages in the *Secret Doctrine,*[86] and they
have been dealt with in an earlier part of this Treatise.
    We have dealt at some length already with the work

[86] S. D., I, 279, 280.

of the transmitting devas upon the three planes in the three worlds, and with that of the devas connected with those relatively permanent focal points—the permanent atoms within the causal periphery. We can now consider the group of builders who, responding to the note of the transmitting agencies and to the initial vibration of the second group of builders concerned with the triple lower self, begin the work of aggregating and moulding the living substance necessary for egoic manifestation upon the lower planes.

We have seen that the first three stages of the egoic work are:

1. The sounding of the appropriate note, which note is indicative of man's place in evolution, and of the nature of his "psyche," or Ego.
2. The transmission of this note by the solar Angel, and the three groups of devas connected with the three permanent atoms.
3. The vibration set up within these atoms which is in line with the note sounded, and which becomes so strong as to make itself felt in the surrounding deva substance, thus awakening response.

These may be considered as the three primary stages, and we find demonstrated (in connection with the microcosm) the three factors of sound, colour and vibration, which, under the Law of Analogy, reflect the three aspects of the macrocosm. Here too is found a resemblance to the work of the first three Sephiroths of the Kabbalah,—the primary stage of manifestation finding its dim reflection in the work of the Ego in the three worlds.

The second stage now takes place, in which the work of building proceeds until the microcosm, man, makes his appearance upon the physical plane. This is succeeded by a third stage of evolution, in which the psychic nature of man is to demonstrate through the medium of the created forms. Then the next two groups of Sephiroth are seen reproduced in man. He is demonstrated to be nine from another angle but we are only concerned in this section with the builders of the form.

These groups of builders are four in number:

1. The builders of the mental body.
2. The builders of the astral body.
3. The builders of the etheric body.
4. The builders of the dense physical.

Each of these groups can be subdivided into four or seven or three, according to the plane concerned. Students must remember that matter from the two lowest subplanes of the physical and of the astral planes are never built into the human body as now constituted; it is of too low a vibration, and too coarse a grade for even the lowest type of men on earth at this time. It must be pointed out also that in the average man, the matter of some subplane will preponderate according to the depth of his nature and his place on the ladder of evolution. The "builders" of the human body work under the direction of one of the Lords of Karma from the lowest group. These Lords are to be found in three groups, and a Lord out of the third group has the work of superintending the builders of the human being on the three planes. Under Him are to be found certain karmic agents, who again are divided into the following groups:

1. Three karmic agents responsible to the karmic Lords for the work on the three planes.
2. Five karmic Lords who work in close connection with the Manus of the various races, and who are responsible for the correct building of the varying race types.
3. Karmic agents responsible for the subrace types of the present time.

4. Certain intermediary agents who represent (within these three groups) the seven Ray types.

5. Those agents of the good Law who are connected specifically with the work of the etheric centres, and their response to the different planetary centres.

6. The keepers of the records.

These various intelligences manipulate the building forces through the medium of streams of energy, which streams are set in motion when the Ego sounds his note. It must be remembered that in more or less degree upon his own plane the Ego is aware of his karma, and of what must be done to promote growth during the coming incarnation. He works, therefore, in connection with these Lords, but is only directly in touch with an agent of the sixth group and of the fourth. Through these two the work proceeds as far as the Ego is individually concerned, and they set in motion for him (*after he has sounded his note*) the machinery of the Law.

The builders of the human personality again are divided into seven main groups; all devas, just as is the case with the human Monads, come under one or other of the seven Rays, and are responsive to one or other of the seven logoic streams of fiery energy. According to a man's egoic Ray, so will be the type of deva substance influenced.

These builders work with certain elementals, but it is only upon the physical plane that any idea can be given as to their nature and work. These elementals are the little entities who, adhering to the plan as embodied by the builders, blindly construct the fabric of the body, and form the sheaths through which the Ego is to express himself. On the etheric planes they build the real "form" out of etheric substance, and produce the sheath of intricate lines of interlacing fiery strands, which is in reality an extension of the sutratma, or life thread. As it is woven and interlaced it becomes vitalised with the life energy sent down from the Ego, just as Shiva, the Father, gives to the Son the real "bios" or life, while the Mother warms, builds, and nourishes the body. The work of the etheric elementals reaches its primary consummation when the sutratma is connected with the three centres of the physical nature within the cranium—the pineal gland, the pituitary body, and the alta major centre. Occultly, the most important connection is the entrance of the sutratma into the centre at the top of the head, that through which the life of the etheric body withdraws at the moment of death. This is the vital point. The "thread" of life there, by the time the seventh year is reached, has divided itself into three branches, reaching out to the three centres. The realisation of this fact will eventually prove of much interest to scientists. A good deal of imbecility, or of arrested development will be found to have its origin in the etheric connection with these three centres. The etheric web is literally the fine network of fiery threads which spreads itself over the centre, and forms an area of fairly large dimensions. It separates the two bodies, astral and physical. A similar corresponding area will be found in the solar system. Through it the cosmic forces must pass to the different planetary schemes.

The elemental groups of the dense physical plane who are swept into activity by the builders, are three in number:

  a. The gaseous elementals.
  b. The liquid elementals.
  c. The strictly dense elementals.

One group concerns itself with the fiery channels, with the fires of the human body, and with the different gases to be found within the human periphery. Another group is to be seen working in connection with the circulatory system, and with all the liquids, juices, and waters of the body; whilst the third is largely involved in the construction of the frame, through the right apportioning of the minerals and .chemicals. A hint in connection with medicine is here to be found; it is occultly true that just as the liquid devas and elementals are closely related to the vegetable kingdom, and both to the plane of the emotions, the logoic liquid body, so the ills of men which affect the circulatory system, the kidneys, the bladder, and the lubrication of the joints, will find a CURE in vegetable constituents and above all in the right adjustment of the emotional nature.

Several influences other than those mentioned have to be considered when the subject of the work of these builders of man's body is under discussion. Not only are they affected by:

a. A man's note,
b. The colour poured forth by the transmitting agents,
c. The karmic agents,

but they come under:

d. Group karma and vibration which will sweep in another group of agencies and builders, and thus affect a man's bodies,
e. Racial karma, an extension of the above,
f. Forces playing upon the planet from another scheme, or through the formation of a systemic triangle,
g. A cosmic triangle of force of some specific kind which may bring in entities and energies of any particular scheme incident upon the karma of the planetary Logos.

It will, therefore, be apparent to the student how intricate this subject is and how truly each man is the outcome of force of some kind—egoic primarily, but also planetary, and even systemic. Yet withal, no man is ever put into circumstances which are insurmountable, once he has reached the point where he has *intelligently* put himself on the side of evolution, or of God. Prior to that he may, and will, be driven by the gales of circumstance; the press of group and racial karma will force him into situations necessary for the process of awakening him to his own innate possibilities. Once he becomes the conscious builder himself, seeking to control the forces and builders of his lower nature, and to construct the Temple of Solomon, then he is no longer *subject* to the earlier conditions. He becomes a ruler, a builder, and a transmitter, until the time comes when he is one with the solar Angels, and the work of human evolution is accomplished.

What has been said above is very superficial, and only that has been imparted which has a profound significance for man at this time. Much must be inferred, and more must be arrived at under the Law of Correspondences. It must ever be borne in mind likewise that our basic conception is one of *fiery energy,* of force centres set in motion, and kept in active vibration, by the pulsation of still greater centres. Every form is built of fiery atoms, or energetic lives, through the agency of greater lives, and is held in coherent form within the still greater sheaths,—that greater sheath being to the lesser what the macrocosm is to the microcosm. All these groups of building lives may be divided into three groups of energy units, and their nature deduced from the phrases:

1. Groups of lives animated by dynamic energy.
2. Groups of lives animated by radiant energy.
3. Groups of lives animated by atomic energy.

These again are the sumtotal of the three fires, electric fire, solar fire and fire by friction. In terms of the cosmic physical plane, the correspondence to the systemic plane can be seen in the following tabulation:

1. **Dynamic energy**..electric fire ......atomic subplane. First etheric substance. Plane adi.
2. **Radiant energy**...solar fire ....three cosmic etheric levels. Logoic etheric body.
3. **Atomic energy**...fire by friction...three planes of the three worlds. Logoic dense vehicle.

Each plane will be found to reflect this order in an interesting manner.

III. MAN AS A CREATOR IN MENTAL MATTER

1. *The Creation of Thought Forms.*

The subject we are now to deal with cannot be handled too explicitly on account of the attendant dangers. In the creative processes man is dealing with electrical phenomena of some kind, with that which is vitally affected by each thought emanating from him, and with those lesser lives who (aggregated together) form, from certain angles of vision, a source of very real danger to man. We might embody that which can be said in certain statements.

a. Much that is to be seen now of a distressing nature in the world can be directly traced to the wrong manipulation of mental matter by man; to erroneous conceptions as to the nature of matter itself, and to dangerous conditions brought about by the united creative attempts of human beings down the centuries.

Misunderstandings have arisen as to the the purpose of the vital fluids of the universe and this has added to the distress, as have certain distortions of the astral light, producing a subsidiary or secondary glamour, or reflected light which intensifies the maya already created. This secondary reflection has been produced by man himself in the evolutionary attempt to balance the pairs of opposites, and has produced a condition which must be surmounted before the true occult balancing begins. It might be regarded as the sumtotal of that great manifestation (created only by man) called "The Dweller on the Threshold."

One of the greatest impediments upon the Path of Return and one for which man is distinctly responsible within occult limits are those animated forms which he has produced ever since the middle of the Atlantean root race when the mind factor began slowly to assume increasing importance. The selfishness, the sordid motives, the prompt response to evil impulses for which the human race has been distinguished has brought about a condition of affairs unparalleled in the system. A gigantic thought form hovers over the entire human family, built by men everywhere during the ages, energised by the insane desires and evil inclinations of all that is worst in man's nature, and kept alive by the promptings of his lower desires. This thought form has to be broken up and dissipated by man himself during the latter part of this round before the conclusion of the cycle, and its dissipation will be one of the forces tending to the production of interplanetary pralaya. It is this piece of creative bungling, if so it might be called, which the Great Ones are occupied in destroying. Under the Law of Karma it has to be dissipated by those who have created it; the work of the Masters has to be carried on, therefore, indirectly, and must take the form of illuminating the sons of men in gradually increasing degree, so that they can see clearly this "Dweller on the Threshold" of the new life, and the antagonist who stands between the fourth kingdom of nature and the fifth. Every time a son of man stands upon the Probationary Path

Their work is facilitated, for it means that one small stream of life-energy is directed into new channels, and away from the old stream, which tends to vitalise and feed the evil form, and one more *conscious* assailant can be trained to co-operate in the work of destruction. Every time an initiate is admitted to the Lodge degrees, it means that a new and powerful agent is available for the bringing down of force from higher levels to aid in the work of disintegration. In the comprehension of these two methods of aggressive work (that of the aspirant and the initiate) will come much of vital interest to the careful student of analogy. Here lies the clue to the present problem of evil, and to the vitality of the hold which the matter aspect has on the spiritual. This gigantic thought form, the product of man's ignorance and selfishness, is kept alive and vitalised in three ways:

First, by the aggregate of the evil desires, wicked intentions, and selfish purposes of each individual man. Every wrong thought, when embodied in speech or manifested in action on the physical plane, goes to swell the proportions of this evil entity.

Second, by the fostering care of the brothers of the shadow, and those representatives of what may be called "cosmic evil" who (under the karma of the fourth or human family, in this fourth round), assume stupendous responsibilities, make possible the secondary vitalisation of the thought form and produce conditions of such a dire description that under law rapid crystallisation supervenes, and ultimate destruction becomes possible. Students would do well to broaden their concept as to the purpose of evil and the place the evil forces play in the general scheme.

Third, by the energy still extant and the vibration still to be felt which is the persistence of force from an earlier solar system, and an emanation from that which is no longer considered in this solar system to be a principle.

These three factors are the main ones to be considered by the Great Ones in Their work of enabling men to break loose from the influence of this self-imposed form, to destroy that which they have themselves constructed, and to shake themselves free from the illusion cast by the persistent vampire which they have nourished and strengthened for millennia of years.

This work of destruction the Great Ones are bringing about in four main ways:

(1) By the strength of Their united thoughts and meditations.

(2) By the work of the Hierarchy in training and teaching individuals, who thus break away from blind group activity, and become conscious centres of force and co-operators in the work of destruction. This work has to be carried on from mental levels. Hence the training of disciples to meditate and work in mental matter.

(3) By the use of certain mantrams and words which bring in interplanetary force of the fourth order. This force is then directed towards this distorted creation of the fourth Creative Hierarchy (the fourth or human kingdom) and tends to augment the work of destruction. Much of this work is carried on by the Nirmanakayas.

(4) By stimulating the egoic bodies of men so that the solar Angels may carry on with greater precision and force their conflict with the lunar gods. This is the true war in heaven. As the solar Gods [87] descend ever

---

[87] *The Solar Gods are the ''Fallen Angels.''*—S. D., II, 287.

   a. They *warm* the shadows . . . the human bodies.

   b. They in their turn are warmed by the Monad, or Atma.—S. D., II, 116, 117, 284.

   c. They are the Serpents of Wisdom.—S. D., II, 240.

   d. Their nature is Knowledge and Love.—S. D., II, 527.

   e. They come in from the cosmic mental plane.—S. D., III, 540.

nearer to the physical plane, and in their descent assume a steadily increasing control of the lunar natures, the thoughts and desires of men are consequently purified and refined. The solar fires put out the lunar light, and the lower nature is eventually purified and transmuted. In time the solar Angels blaze forth in all their glory through the medium of the lower nature on the physical plane, that lower nature providing fuel to the flames. The hated "Dweller on the Threshold" thus gradually dies for lack of sustenance, and disintegrates for lack of vitality, and man is set free.

b. At present much of the manipulation of mental matter and its direction into forms of some kind or another emanates from lower levels, and is the result of powerful desire based on physical attraction. The desire bodies, and not the mental bodies of the majority of men are the most powerful, and set up such a strong vibration (due to the force of two groups of lunar lords) that the third group of lunar entities who construct the mental body are swept into a willing response, and the whole threefold lower nature is immediately engaged in the dire process of feeding the dreaded "Dweller." This direction of energy follows the line of least resistance. One of the primary works of the Ego, as we well know, is to impose a new rhythm upon his shadow and reflection, the lower man, and it is this imposition which in time deflects energy away from man's distorted creation, and brings his vibration into tune with that of his solar Angel.

The devas who are the sumtotal of the energy of substance itself care not what form they build. They are

<hr>

The Ego, or Solar Angel is imprisoned.—S. D., I, 621.
    a. It has to liberate itself from the thraldom of sensuous perception.
    b. It has to see in the light of the one Reality.
    c. See S. D., II, 578.
    d. To redeem humanity.—S. D., II, 257.
    e. To endow him with human affections and aspirations.—S. D., II, 257.
    f. They give to men intelligence and consciousness.—S. D., I, 204.

irresponsibly responsive to energy currents, and theirs is not the problem of dealing with sources of energy. Therefore, the place of man in the cosmic plan becomes more vital and apparent when it is realised that one of his main responsibilities is the direction of energy currents from the mental plane, and the creation of that which is desired on *higher levels*. Men, as a whole, are undergoing evolutionary development in order that they may become conscious creators in matter. This involves

A realisation of the archetypal plan,

An understanding of the laws governing the building processes of nature,

A conscious process of willing creation, so that man co-operates with the ideal, works under law, and produces that which is in line with the planetary plan, and which tends to further the best interests of the race,

A comprehension as to the nature of energy, and an ability to direct energy currents, to disintegrate (or withdraw energy from) all forms in the three worlds,

An appreciation of the nature of the devas, their constitution and place as builders, and of the words and sounds whereby they are directed and controlled.

When the energy currents of the human family are directed from egoic levels only, when desire is transmuted, and the fifth principle awakened and finally illuminated by the sixth, then and only then will the strength of the impulse emanating from lower levels die out and the "Dweller on the Threshold" (who now haunts the human family) likewise die. In other words, when the dense physical body of the planetary Logos (composed of matter of the three worlds of human endeavour) is completely purified and vitalised by the force of the life flowing from etheric levels, and when all His centres (formed of human units) are fully awakened, then will those centres be channels for pure force, and such an entity as the "Dweller" be an impossibility.

All that I have here said anent this "Dweller on the Threshold" of the Path between the two great kingdoms, the fourth and the fifth, can be studied by the student with a personal application. Facing each earnest aspirant to the Mysteries is that vitalised form which he has himself constructed and nourished during the course of his previous incarnations, and which represents the sum-total of his evil desires, motives and thoughts. For ages it has vampirised him, and for ages it has represented that which he has failed to achieve. It affects not only himself but also all those units whom he contacts and meets. In its destruction he has to pursue methods similar to those followed by the Great Ones, and through the increasing power of his solar Angel, through the force of his Ego, and through a study of law, the knowledge of the power of sound, and the control of speech, he will eventually bring about its disintegration. The old Commentary says:

"The solar Angel must put out the light of the lunar angels and then for lack of warmth and light, that which has served to hinder no longer is."

c. As yet but few of the human family work deliberately and consciously in mental matter only. The energy exerted by men is mostly kama-manasic or desire coupled with lower mind, with a preponderance, as might be expected, of desire force. This is to be inferred from the second statement. The whole trend of evolution is to bring about ability to build in mental matter, and two things lie ahead of the race:

First. The gradual dissipation of the indefinite masses of kama-manasic matter which surround practically every unit of the human family, producing a condition of murkiness and fog within, and around, each aura. Grad·

ually this will clear away, and men will be seen surrounded by clear-cut thought forms, characterised by a distinctive vibration and distinguished by a particular quality incident to a man's ray and therefore to his type of mind.

Second. The aggregate of human thought forms which now are of a personal character, vibrating around each human being as the planets vibrate around the sun, will tend to approximate a *group* centre. Thought energy, which now emanates from each human being as a comparatively weak stream of an indefinite conglomeration of mental matter, of no particular character, forming no particularly distinct forms and persisting in animating those forms for but a brief period, will be directed towards the creation of that desired by *the group,* and not solely towards that desired by the unit. This is the basis, very largely, for the antagonism that all constructive thinkers and *group* workers encounter. The stream of energy which they emanate, and which constructs vital thought forms, runs counter to that of the masses of men, awakens opposition, and produces temporary chaos. The prominent workers and thinkers of the human family, under the direction of the Lodge, are engaged in three things:

a. The imposition of the newer and higher rhythm upon men.

b. The dissipation of the murky clouds of half-vitalised indefinite thought forms which surround our planet, thus permitting the entry of interplanetary force, and of force from the higher mental levels.

c. The awakening within men of the power to think clearly, to energise their thought forms accurately, and to hold in vital form those thought constructions whereby they may attain their objective, and bring about desired conditions upon the physical plane.

These three objectives necessitate a clear comprehension among such vital thinkers and workers, of the power of thought; of the direction of thought currents, of the science of thought building, of the manipulation under law and order of mental matter, and of the process of thought manifestation through the two factors of sound and vitalisation. It involves likewise the ability to negate or render futile all impulses arising from the lower self which are of a centralised and purely personal aspect, and the faculty of working in group form, each thought being sent upon the definite mission of adding its quota of energy and matter to some one stream which is specific and *known*. This last is of importance, for no worker for humanity becomes of real assistance until he (consciously and with full knowledge of his work) definitely directs his thought energy towards some particular channel of service to the race.

d. In all thought building, therefore, of a high order, men have several things to do, which might be enumerated as follows:

First, to purify their lower desires so that they are enabled to *see* clearly in the occult sense. No man has clear vision who is obsessed with his own needs, actions, and interests, and unconscious of that which is higher and of group activity. This clear vision brings about an ability to read, even if unconsciously at first, the akashic records, and thus ascertain the point of departure for the new and incoming thought impulses, an ability to lose sight of self interest in group interest, and thus co-operate with the plan, and a faculty that enables him to become aware of the keynote of the race, and aware of the "cry of humanity."

Next, to secure control over the mind. This involves

certain important things: A realisation of the nature of the mind and brain through concentration, an understanding of the relation which should exist between the physical brain and Man, the real Thinker on the physical plane, an ability, gradually developed once the mind is brought under control through concentration, to meditate in the occult sense, and thus bring through the plan from higher levels, ascertain his individual share in the plan, and then co-operate in the work of some particular group of Nirmanakayas. This is succeeded by a consideration of the laws of energy. A man discovers how to build a thought form of a particular quality and tone, to energise it with his own life, and thus have—on mental levels—a small creation, the child of his will, which he can use as a messenger, or as a means for the manifestation of an idea. Students will do well to consider these points with care, if they seek to become conscious operators.

Finally, having constructed a thought form, the next thing the servant of humanity has to learn is how to send it on its mission, whatever that may be, holding it through his own vital energy in its due form, keeping it vibrating to its own measure, and eventually bringing about its destruction when it has fulfilled its mission. The average man is often the victim of his own thought forms. He constructs them, but is neither strong enough to send them out to do their work, nor wise enough to dissipate them when required. This has brought about the thick swirling fog of half-formed, semi-vitalised forms in which eighty five percent of the human race is surrounded.

In his work as thought builder, man has to show forth the characteristics of the Logos, the great Architect or Builder of the universe. He has to parallel His work as:

The one who conceives the idea.

The one who clothes the idea in matter.

The one who energises the idea, and thus enables the form to preserve its outline and perform its mission.

The one who—in time and space—through desire and love, directs that thought form, vitalises it continuously, until the objective is attained.

The one who, when the desired end has been accomplished, destroys or disintegrates the thought form by withdrawing his energy (occultly, the "attention is withdrawn," or "the eye is no longer upon" it), so that the lesser lives (which had been built into the desired form) fall away and return to the general reservoir of deva substance.

Thus, in all creative work in mental matter, man is likewise to be seen as a Trinity at work; he is the creator, preserver, and destroyer.

e. *In all occult work in mental matter which has to manifest upon the physical plane, and thus achieve objectivity, man has to work as a unit.* This infers the ability, therefore, of the threefold lower man to be subordinated to the Ego, so that the dynamic will of the Ego may be imposed upon the physical brain.

The method of the man on the physical plane who is engaged in conscious work in mental matter is to be considered in two divisions: first, the initial process of alignment with the Ego, so that the plan, purpose and method of achievement may be impressed upon the physical brain, and then a secondary process in which the man, using the physical brain consciously, proceeds to carry out the plan, construct through will and purpose the necessitated form, and then, having built and energised the form, to "keep his eye upon it." This is stating occultly the great truth back of all processes of energising. "The eye of the Lord" is much referred to in the Christian Bible, and occultly understood, the eye is that which brings power to its servant, the thought form. Scientists are becoming interested in the power of the human eye, and that faculty of control and of recognition which is everywhere seen as existing will have its scientific and occult explanation when it is studied as *an instrument of initiatory energy.*

Therefore, it will be apparent that a thought form is the result of two types of energy:

That emanating in the first instance from the Ego on abstract levels.

That originating in a secondary sense from the man on the physical plane through the medium of the brain.

That men do not recognise the first factor as a general rule is that which is responsible for much that is evil. When the "Science of the Self" has assumed due proportions men will be careful to ascertain the egoic impulses in all thought process, and to utilise true egoic energy before they begin manipulating deva substance, and building forms of deva lives.

2. *Thought Form Building in the Three Worlds.*

I have a few more words to say anent this subject of man as a Creator in mental matter. The words are addressed to all those students who—through their ability to concentrate—have developed a certain measure of thought control, and who desire to understand the process of creation with greater scientific accuracy. We will, therefore, consider two factors in the process of thought-form building:

a. That of aligning with the Ego.[88]
b. The process of impressing the egoic will, on the physical brain, or (to word it otherwise) the initial utilisation of egoic energy.

[88] Alignment: See *Letters on Occult Meditation*, pp. 1-7.

Let us take them one by one:

a. Alignment with the Ego. This, as we know, is only possible to the man who has reached the Probationary Path, or a certain very definite point in evolution. Through knowledge and practice, the power has been acquired of automatically and scientifically utilising the sutratma (or channel) as a means of contact. When to this ability is added that of utilising with equal ease the antaskarana (or bridge between the Triad and the personality) then we have a powerful agent of the Hierarchy on the earth. We might generalise in the following manner as to the stages of growth and consequent ability to become the agent of ever increasing powers, tapping the resources of dynamic energy in the three worlds.

Lower types of humanity use the sutratma as it passes through the etheric body.

Average men utilise almost entirely that part of the sutratma which passes through the astral plane. Their reactions are largely based on desire, and are emotional.

Intellectual men utilise the sutratma as it passes through the lower levels of the mental plane, down through the astral to the physical in its two sections. Their activities are energised by mind and not by desire, as in the earlier cases.

Aspirants on the physical plane use the sutratma as it passes through the two lower subplanes of the abstract levels of the mental plane, and are beginning gradually to build the antaskarana, or the bridge between the Triad and the Personality. The power of the Ego can begin to make itself felt.

Applicants for initiation and initiates up to the third initiation use both the sutratma and the antaskarana, employing them as a unit. The power of the Triad begins to pour through, thus energising all human activities upon the physical plane, and vitalising in ever increasing degree the man's thought forms. The key to the formation of the Mayavirupa is found in the right comprehension of the process.

If students will study carefully the above differentiations, much light will be thrown upon the quality of the energy employed in thought-form building.

In the early stages of alignment, it has to be concisely and carefully brought about through concentration and meditation. Later, when the right rhythm has been set up in the bodies, and the purification of the sheaths has been rigidly pursued, the dual activity will become practically instantaneous, and the student can then turn his attention to the work of *conscious* building and vitalisation; his point of concentration will not then be given to the attainment of alignment.

Accurate alignment entails,

Mental quiescence, or stable vibration,

Emotional stability, resulting in limpid reflection,

Etheric poise, producing a condition in the head centre which would permit of the direct application of force to the physical brain via the centre.

b. Physical brain impression. The accurate realisation by the physical brain of what the Ego is seeking to convey concerning the work to be done only becomes possible when two things are realised:

Direct alignment.

The transmission of the egoic energy or will to one or other of the three physical centres in the head:

The pineal gland.

The pituitary body.

The alta major centre, or that nerve centre at the top of the spine, where the cranium and the spine make approximate contact. When this congery of nerves

Chart X

THE SCIENCE OF MEDITATION

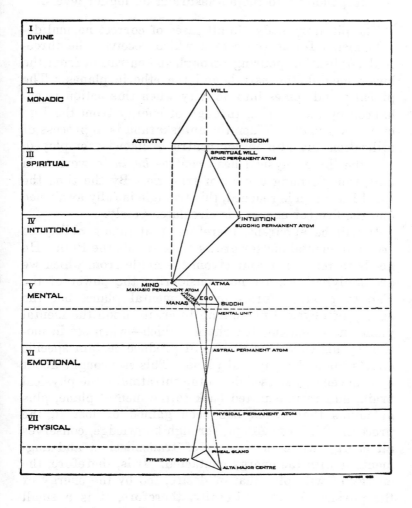

I
DIVINE

II
MONADIC

WILL

ACTIVITY   WISDOM

III
SPIRITUAL

SPIRITUAL WILL
ATMIC PERMANENT ATOM

IV
INTUITIONAL

INTUITION
BUDDHIC PERMANENT ATOM

V
MENTAL

MIND
MANASIC PERMANENT ATOM   ATMA

MANAS   EGO   BUDDHI

MENTAL UNIT

VI
EMOTIONAL

ASTRAL PERMANENT ATOM

VII
PHYSICAL

PHYSICAL PERMANENT ATOM

PINEAL GLAND

PITUITARY BODY

ALTA MAJOR CENTRE

is fully developed, it forms a centre of communication between the vital energy of the spinal column (the kundalini fire) and the energy of the two head centres above enumerated. It is the physical correspondence to the antaskarana on higher levels.

The pituitary body (in all cases of correct normal development) forms the centre which receives the threefold vitalisation pouring through the sutratma from the lower mental, the astral, and the etheric planes. The pineal gland comes into activity when this action is enhanced by the pouring through of energy from the Ego on its own plane. When the antaskarana is in process of utilisation the alta major centre is likewise employed, and the three physical head centres *begin* to work as a unit, thus forming a kind of triangle. By the time the third Initiation is reached, this triangle is fully awakened and the fire (or energy) is circulated freely.

It will be apparent, therefore, that man's ability to create in mental matter grows as he treads the Path. He needs to remember that (from the angle from which we are studying) we are not considering the power of the Ego to produce forms on the mental plane, but the ability of physical plane man to create upon the mental plane those vehicles for energy which—when set in motion by his conscious will—will produce certain specific effects upon the physical plane. This is brought about by egoic energy passed down the sutratma to the physical brain, and retransmitted back to the mental plane, plus or minus that which has been gained or lost in the process. The true Adept, through knowledge, conserves all energy while in process of transmission, and augments it with the energy contacted. It is, therefore, the energy of will, plus that of desire, fed by the energy of the physical brain. Literally, therefore, it is a small résumé of the creative process of the Godhead, being the energy of the three persons unified, and considered from the standpoint of the physical. It is the at-one-ment of the three fires in man, being in fact:

a. That much of the fire of spirit, or electric fire, which any particular Ego is embodying (relatively little prior to the third Initiation) or is able to transmit, coupled with,

b. That much of the fire of the solar Angel (solar fire) or the egoic aspect which the Ego is able to transmit. This is but little in average man, a good deal in the man on the probationary path, and a full downpour by the time the third Initiation is reached.

c. That much of the fire of substance in its purified state which can penetrate. This is dependent upon the purity of the three sheaths, and in the case of a highly advanced man is the kundalinic fire as it swells the blaze produced by the other two.

When, therefore, the alignment is corrected, and the physical head centres are awakening, it becomes possible for man to become a conscious creator in mental matter.

IV. MAN AND THE FIRE SPIRITS OR BUILDERS

This section we will consider in somewhat greater detail than the previous one, as it concerns much of present practical value to man. This will be seen particularly as we study the effects of speech, and the occult significance of the spoken word.

1. *The Will Aspect and Creation.*

In a previous division, we dealt somewhat with the transmission of the will of the Ego to the physical brain, and we saw how only in those persons who (through evolutionary development) had the sutratma and the antaskarana connected, and whose three physical head centres were more or less awakened, was the will of the Ego capable of transmission. In the other cases, such as the average man and little developed man, the purpose affecting the physical brain emanated from the astral or lower mental levels, and was, therefore, more likely to be the impulse of some lunar Lord, even if of a high order, than the divine will of the solar Angel, who is the true man.

a. The condition of the Magician. It is of value to remember that when the physical head centres are awakened (through alignment of the etheric centres) we have *the very lowest aspect of egoic influence.* From these three centres, man on the Probationary Path, and up to the third Initiation, directs and controls his sheath, and from them spreads that illumination which will irradiate the physical plane life. By the time the third Initiation is reached, the internal triangle is in full process of circulatory transmission, and the whole life of the Personality is subjected to the will of the Ego. "The Star absorbs the light of the moon, so that the rays of the Sun may be reflected back" is the occult way of expressing the truth anent this point in evolution. It might be of value here also to point out the condition of the etheric centres during this process of direct solar control.

Before the three physical head centres awaken, man is largely subjected to force flowing through the four minor etheric centres; later the three major centres—the head, the heart, and the throat—begin to vibrate, gradually assuming a greater sweep of activity, till their energy tends to negate that of the lower centres, to absorb their vitality and deflect the direction of their vitality, until the three higher wheels are in full fourth dimensional activity. As this proceeds, the three physical head centres begin to awake from dormancy into activity, the effect being felt as follows:

a. As the major head centre awakens, the pineal gland begins to function.

b. As the heart centre becomes fully alive, the pituitary body enters into activity.

c. As the throat centre assumes its right place in the process of evolution, the alta major centre vibrates adequately.

When the triangle of force that these three physical centres form is in circulatory effect, the greater triangle can be seen in circulation; it then becomes a "wheel turning upon itself." The major etheric centres are in full action, and the man is nearing the moment of liberation.

In the work of creation, as occultly carried on, all these three physical centres have to be utilised, and from a consideration of the subject it will become apparent why it has been necessary to deal with them in this order.

By means of *the pineal gland*,[89] the organ of spiritual perception, man ascertains the will and purpose of the Ego, and from thence he draws the necessary energy

---

[89] The Pineal Gland. The Third Eye.—S. D., III, 548.
  1. Goal of evolution to develop the inner vision.
  2. The occult significance of the eye.—S. D., III, 577.
  3. The "eye of Taurus the Bull."—(Compare bull's-eye.)
      The constellation of Taurus was called the Mother of Revelation and the interpreter of the divine Voice.—S. D., I, 721.
  4. The organs of inner vision:
      a. The exoteric organ.........Pineal gland........physical.
      b. The esoteric organ.........the third eye........etheric.
      Note: Students must be careful to distinguish between the third eye and the pineal gland.—See S. D., II, 308. "The third eye is dead and acts no longer." It has left behind a witness to its existence in the Pineal Gland.
  5. The Pineal gland is a small pea-like mass of grey nervous matter attached to the back of the third ventricle of the brain.
  6. The Pituitary Body stands to the Pineal gland as manas does to Buddhi, or mind to wisdom.—S. D., III, 504, 505.
  7. The Pineal gland reached its highest development proportionately with the Lowest Physical development.—S. D., II, 308, 313.
  8. The third eye exists in etheric matter.
      a. In front of the head.
      b. On a level with the eyes.
  9. It is an energy centre formed by a triangle of force:
      a. The Pituitary Body.
      b. The Pineal Gland.
      c. The alta major centre.
  10. The opened or third eye does not convey direct clairvoyance but is the organ through which direct and certain knowledge is obtained.—S. D., I, 77.

from the higher levels, via the head centre and the sutratma.

By means of *the pituitary body,* the second element of desire or of the form-building energy, becomes available, and under the law of attraction he can mould, and build in deva substance.

When *the alta major* centre, the synthesis of what might be called nervous energy, is awake, it becomes possible for him to materialise and activate the desired form which, through attractive energy, he is in process of constructing.

It will be apparent, therefore, why it is that so few people ever construct thought forms which are of constructive lasting benefit to humanity, and also why it is that the Great Ones, (as They work through Their disciples) are forced to work with groups, being seldom able to find a man or woman whose three physical head centres are simultaneously active. They frequently have to work with large groups before the quota of energy supplied to Them for the accomplishment of Their ends measures up to that necessitated.

It will be obvious, likewise, that the disciple's power for service for humanity is dependent largely upon three things:

> a. The initiate directs the eye towards the essence of things.
> b. The third eye must be acquired by the ascetic before he becomes an adept.—S. D., II, 651.
> 11. Students of occultism ought to know that the third eye is indissolubly connected with karma.—S. D., II, 312, note; S. D., II, 316, 320.
>> a. From its Atlantean past, the fifth root-race is working out fourth root-race causes.
>> b. Because it reveals that which is its past.—S. D., II, 297, 320, 813.
> 12. The third eye is the mirror of the soul.—S. D., II, 312.
> 13. To the inner spiritual eye the Gods are no more abstractions than our soul and body are to us.—S. D., I, 694.
>> a. The inner eye can see through the veil of matter.—S. D., I, 694.
>> b. The spiritual eye reveals the super-sensual states.—S. D., II, 561.
> 14. In the spiritual regenerated man the third eye is active.—S. D., II, 458.

a. The state of his bodies and their egoic alignment.
b. The condition of activity present in the physical head centres.
c. The circulatory action of the triangular transmission of force.

These factors are again dependent upon others, among which might be enumerated:

1. The ability of the disciple to meditate.
2. The capacity he displays for bringing through accurately from the subtler levels the plans and purposes of which his Ego is cognisant.
3. The purity of his motives.
4. His power to "hold a state of meditation," and while in that state begin to build the form for his idea, and thus materialise the plan of his Ego.
5. The amount of energy he can pour later into his thought form and thus procure for it a period of existence, or its tiny "day of Brahma."

These subsidiary factors are again dependent upon:

a. His place on the ladder of evolution.
b. The condition of his bodies.
c. His karmic condition.
d. The tenuosity of the etheric web.
e. The calibre of his physical body, and its relative refinement.

It is necessary here to warn the student against the error of making any hard or fast rule anent the sequential order of the development of the physical head centres, and the vitalisation of the force centres. This process is incident upon many things, such as the ray upon which the monad may be found, and the nature of the development in the past incarnations. Nature, in all departments of her corporate life, parallels her efforts, and overlaps her various processes, and it takes a seer of vast wisdom and experience to state exactly the stage at which any particular unit of the human family may be. He that is wise always refrains from assertion until he *knows*.

Let us now consider:

b. *The construction, vitalisation, and actuating of the thought form*. The Ego, having brought about a condition of receptivity, or of recognition in the physical brain of the man, and having drawn from him the necessary response, the process of building is thereupon begun.

This process of physical plane response is based—as is all else in nature—upon the relation of the polar opposites. The physical centres are receptive to the positive influence of the force centres. The physical brain is responsive to the positive influence of the lower nature in the earlier evolutionary stages, or to the reactions of the substance of the sheaths, the impress of the lunar Lords. It responds in the later stages to the positive influence of the Ego or the impress of the solar Lord.

As is apparent, this building process is divided into three parts, which overlap, and assume an appearance of simultaneity. When (as is the case with the majority of the human family) the process is an *unconscious* one, produced by reflex action and based largely on the accomplishment of desire, all is carried on with great rapidity, and leads to rapid results—these results being effective of accomplishment according to the ability of the man to vitalise and hold in coherent form his idea. Most of the thought forms created by average man are only relatively effective, and this within great limitations, and having but a restricted radius. When man is learning *consciously* to create, which he does through the organisation of thought, concentration and meditation, he proceeds more slowly, for he has two primary things to do before the creative process can be carried through:

a. To contact or communicate with the Ego, or solar Angel.

b. To study the process of creation and to make it conform step by step with natural evolutionary law.

The above is necessarily but another way of defining meditation and its objective.

Later on, when a man is an expert in meditation, the work of thought creation proceeds with ever increasing rapidity, until he surpasses (on a higher turn of the spiral) the activity of the earlier unconscious period.

Starting, therefore, with the recognition of the egoic intent in the physical brain, the man proceeds to build the form for his idea. He begins first to organise the material required upon the *mental plane*. It is on that plane that the impulse takes to itself its primary form. On the *desire or astral plane,* the process of vitalisation is largely pursued, for the length of the life of any thought form (even such an one as our solar system) is dependent upon the persistence of desire, and the strength of the desire.

On the *etheric levels* of the physical plane the process of physical concretion takes place; as the physical vehicle assumes the necessary proportions, the thought form becomes divorced from the one who is giving it form. Any idea of enough strength will inevitably materialise in dense physical matter, but the main work of its creator ceases when he has worked with it on mental, astral and etheric levels. The dense physical response is automatic and inevitable. Some ideas of a large and important nature, which have arisen in the consciousness of the Guides of the race, reach full manifestation only through the medium of many agents, and the dynamic impulses of many minds. A few work consciously, when this is the case, at the production of the necessitated form; many more are swept into activity and lend their aid through the very negativity of their natures; they are "forced" to be interested in spite of themselves, and are "swept into the movement," not through any mental apprehension or "vital desire," but because it is the thing to do. In this may be seen an instance of the ability of the Great Ones to utilise conditions of apparent inertia and negativity (due to little development), and thus produce good results.

We will here only deal with the man who is learning consciously to build, and will not consider the process as pursued by the adept, or the chaotic attempts of the little evolved. Having grasped the idea, and having with care discriminated the motive underlying the idea, thus ascertaining its utilitarian purposes, and its value to the group in the service of humanity, the man has certain things to do which, for the sake of clarity, we might sum up in certain statements:

He has, first of all, to hold the idea sufficiently long for it to be faithfully registered in the physical brain. Frequently the Ego will "get through" to the brain some concept, some portion of the plan, and yet will have to repeat the process continuously over quite a long period before the physical response is such that the solar Angel can rest assured that it is intelligently registered and recorded. It is perhaps unnecessary to say that the entire process is greatly facilitated if the "shadow," or the man, pursues regular meditation, cultivates the habit of a daily and hourly recollectedness of the higher Self, and before retiring at night endeavours to "hold the thought" of bringing through at the time of awakening as much as possible of any egoic impress. When the reaction between the two factors, the Ego and the receptive physical brain, is established, the interplay is reciprocal, and the two are keyed or tuned to each other, the second stage is entered upon. The idea is conceived.

A period of gestation is then pursued, itself divided into various stages. The man broods over the idea; he ponders upon it, thereby setting up activity in mental matter, and attracting to his germ thought the material necessary for its clothing. He pictures to himself the contour of the thought form, clothing it with colour, and painting in its details. Hence will be seen the great value of a true imagination, and its ordered scientific use. Imagination is kama-manasic in origin, being neither pure desire nor pure mind, and is a purely human product, being superseded by the intuition in perfected men, and in the higher Intelligences of Nature.

When his will, or the initial impulse is sufficiently strong, and when the imagination, or power of visualisation, is adequately vivid, the second part of the gestation period is entered upon, and the vitalisation by desire is begun. The interplay of mental impulse and desire produce what might be called a pulsation in the organising form of the idea, and it becomes *alive*. It is yet but nebulous and its tenuosity is great, but it shows signs of organisation and the outline of its form. Students must remember that this entire process is being carried on now during this stage which we are considering from within the brain. There is thus a definite correspondence to the work of the nine Sephiroth:

The initial three correspond to the egoic impulse with which we have earlier dealt.

The secondary group of Sephiroth find their analogy in the work pursued in the stage we are now dealing with, or the impulse of mind-desire, emanating consciously from man's brain.

The work of the final three is accomplished when the thought form, being clothed in mental and astral matter, passes into objectivity on the physical plane.

A later stage in the gestation period is pursued when the thought form, being clothed in mental matter, and having become vitalised by desire, takes to itself a layer of substance of astral matter, and is consequently enabled to function on the astral plane as well as the mental. Here its growth is rapid. It should be carefully borne in mind that the process of building in mental matter proceeds simultaneously, and that the development is now twofold. Here the conscious builder must be careful to hold the balance, and not to let imagination unduly assume too large proportions. The manasic element and the kamic element must be justly proportioned, or else will be seen that too common manifestation, an idea wrongly conceived and nurtured, and therefore impossible of playing its just part in the evolutionary plan, being but a grotesque distortion.

The idea now is reaching a critical stage, and should be ready for the assumption of physical matter and to take to itself an etheric form. When on etheric levels, it receives that final impulse which will lead to what may be called its "actuating," or its reception of that motivating impulse which will lead to its dissociation from its originator, and the sending out to assume

1. A dense form.
2. A separate existence.

It should be remembered that the thought form has now passed from the mental plane, taken to itself an astral sheath, and likewise is gathering to itself a body of etheric matter. When it has reached this stage its vitalisation is proceeding apace, and the hour of its separated existence is drawing near.

This vitalisation is consciously carried out by the man who—according to the original intent or initial impulse —directs to the thought form energy of some kind. This energy is directed from one or other of the three higher centres, according to the quality of the embodied idea,

and will be seen pouring towards the rapidly objectivising idea from the particular centre involved. We must
not forget that we are considering the thought form of
the *conscious* builder. The thought forms of the majority of human beings are energised from no such high
source, but find their active impulse emanating from
either the solar plexus, or the still lower organs of
generation.

It is this constant stream of emotional or sexual energy
which is responsible for the chaotic conditions of the
present; the balance is not preserved, the interaction between the two, and the myriads of thought forms consequently produced of a low order and vibration are producing a condition which is going to require all the efforts
of mental workers eventually to negate, offset, and
transmute. These forms, which scarce merit the pre-
fix "thought," being largely kamic with an admixture
of the lowest grade of mental matter, are responsible
for the heavy, slow vibrating or pulsating fog or cloak
which envelops the human family, and which produces
much of the present evil, crime and mental lethargy.
People are mainly polarised in the astral body, as we
know, and the lower centres are the most active; when
an atmosphere or environment of thought-forms of a low
key and vitalised by all the baser forms of astral energy
is coupled to this, it will become apparent how stupendous is the task of lifting humanity to a clearer, purer
and better atmosphere, and how easy it is for the lower
aspects and appetites to flourish and to grow.

As the vitalisation is pursued and the energy is poured
from one or other of the centres into the thought-form,
the *conscious* builder begins to extend this influence in
order to send it forth from him to perform its mission,
whatever that may be, to make it occultly "radiant" so
that its vibrations will emanate, and make themselves
felt, and finally to make it magnetic, so that something

in the thought form will call forth response from other thought forms or from the minds it may contact.

When these three objectives have been reached, the life of the form itself is now so strong that it can pursue its own little life cycle and fulfil its work, being only linked to its creator by a tiny thread of radiant substance, which is a correspondence to the sutratma. All forms have such a sutratma. It links a man's bodies to the inner Identity, or to that magnetic current which, emanating from the true Identity, the solar Logos, connects the Creator of the solar system with His great thought form by a stream of energy from the central Spiritual Sun to a point in the centre of the physical Sun.

As long as the attention of the creator of any thought form, great or small, is turned towards it, that magnetic link persists, the thought form is vitalised, and its work carried on. When the work has been accomplished, and the thought-form has served its purpose, every creator, consciously or unconsciously, turns his attention elsewhere, and his thought form disintegrates.

Hence the occult significance of all the processes occultly involved in sight, can be seen. As long as the eye of the Creator is upon that which is created, just so long does it persist; let the Creator withdraw "the light of his countenance" and the death of the thought form ensues, for vitality or energy follows the line of the eye. When, therefore, a man, in meditation, considers his work and builds his thought form for service, he is occultly looking, and consequently energising; he begins to use the third eye in its secondary aspect. The third or spiritual eye has several functions. Amongst others, it is the organ of illumination, the unveiled eye of the soul, through which light and illumination comes into the mind, and thus the entire lower life becomes irradiated. It is also the organ through which pours the directing energy which streams out from the conscious creating adept to the instruments of service, his thought-forms.

The little evolved do not, of course, employ the third eye for the stimulating of their thought forms. The energy used by them in the majority of cases originates in the solar plexus, and works in two directions, either via the organs of generation, or through the physical eyes. In many people these three points—the lower organs, the solar plexus, and the physical eyes—form a triangle of force, around which the stream of energy flows before going out to the objectivised thought form. In the aspirant, and the man who is intellectual, the triangle may be from the solar plexus, to the throat centre and thence to the eyes. Later, as the aspirant grows in knowledge and purity of motive, the triangle of energy will have the heart for its lowest point instead of the solar plexus, and the third eye will begin to do its work, though as yet very imperfectly.

Just as long as the "Eye" is directed to the created form, the current of force will be transmitted to it, and the more one-pointed the man may be the more this energy will be centralised and effective. Much of the ineffectiveness of people is due to the fact that their interests are not centralised but very diffuse, and no one thing engrosses their attention. They scatter their energy and are attempting to satisfy every wandering desire, and to dabble in everything which comes their way. Therefore, no thought they think ever assumes a proper form, or is ever duly energised. They are consequently surrounded by a dense cloud of half-formed disintegrating thought forms and clouds of partially energised matter in process of dissolution. This produces occultly a condition similar to the decay of a physical form, and is equally unpleasant and unwholesome. It accounts for much of the diseased condition of the human family at this time.

Failure in thought creation is due also to the fact that

the laws of thought are not taught, and men do not know how, through meditation, to create those children of their activity to carry on their work. Results on the physical plane are much more quickly achieved through scientific thought creation than through the directly physical plane means. This is becoming more realised, but until the race has reached a point of greater purity and unselfishness, the more detailed explanation of the process must necessarily be withheld.

Another reason for creative ineffectiveness is owing to the currents which emanate from the majority of people being of such a low order that the thought forms never reach the point of independent action, except through cumulative group work. Until matter of the three higher subplanes of the astral and physical planes finds its place in the thought form, it has to be energised principally by mob energy. When the higher substance begins to find its way into the form, then it can be seen acting independently, for the individual Ego of the man concerned can begin to work through the matter—a thing before impossible. The Ego cannot work freely in the personality until third subplane matter is found in his bodies; the correspondence consequently holds good.

Once the thought form has been vitalised and its etheric form is completed or "sealed" as it is called, it can attain the dense physical form if desired. This does not mean that the individual thought forms of every man take dense substance upon the etheric, but they will eventuate in activity upon the physical plane. A man, for instance, is thinking a kindly thought; he has built it up and vitalised it; it is objective to the clairvoyant and exists in etheric matter close to the man. It will, therefore, find physical expression in an act of kindness or a physical caress. When the act is over, the caress consummated, the interest of the man in that particular thought form fades out and it dies. Similarly with a crime—the thought form has been built up and inevitably it will find its physical expression in some deed of one kind or another. All activity of every kind is the result:

    a. Of thought forms built consciously or unconsciously.
    b. Of self-initiated thought forms or of the effect of the thought forms of others.
    c. Of responsiveness to one's own inner impulses, or of responsiveness to the impulses of others, and therefore to group thought forms.

It will be apparent, therefore, how vital is this matter, and how influenced men and women are by the thought forms they themselves create, or the mental children of other men.

    c. The occult significance of speech. The old Scripture saith: "In the multitude of words there wanteth not sin," [90] because in a tide of words at this stage of man's evolution, many are spoken purposelessly or from motives which (when analysed) will be found to be based purely in the personality. The greater the progress that is made along the path of approach to the Mysteries, the greater the care that must be taken by the aspirant. This is necessary for three reasons:

First, owing to his stage in evolution, he is able to enforce his words in a manner which would surprise him could he but see on the mental plane. He builds more accurately than the average men, his subsequent thought-form is more strongly vitalised, and it performs the function whereon it is sent by the "Sound" or speech with greater precision.

Second, any word spoken and consequent thought-form built (unless along the higher path and not based on personality impulses) is apt to cause a barrier of mental matter between a man and his goal. This matter or separating wall has to be dissipated before further

[90] Bible. Prov. 10:19.

advance can be made, and this process is karmic and unavoidable.

Third, speech is very largely a mode of communication on the physical levels; on the subtler levels whereon the worker stands, and in his communications with his fellow workers and chosen co-operators it will play an ever lessening part. Intuitive perception and telepathic interplay will distinguish the intercourse between aspirants and disciples, and when this is coupled with a full trust, sympathy and united effort for the plan we will have a formation wherewith the Master can work, and through which He can pour His force. The Master works through groups (large or small) and the work is facilitated for Them if the interplay between units of the group is steady and uninterrupted. One of the most frequent causes of difficulty in group work and consequent arrest of the inflow of force from the Master temporarily is based on misuse of speech. It brings about a clogging of the channel for the time being on the mental plane.

I mention these three factors for this question of group work is of vital importance and much is hoped from it in these days. If in any organisation on the physical plane the Masters can get a nucleus of even three people who mutually interact (I choose the word deliberately) and who disinterestedly follow the path of service, They can produce more definite results in a shorter space of time than is possible with a large and active body of people who may be sincere and earnest but do not know the meaning of trust in, and co-operation with each other and who guard not the gate of speech.

If a man succeeds in understanding the significance of speech, if he learns how to speak, when to speak, what is gained by speech, and what happens when he speaks, he is well on the way to achieving his goal. The person who regulates his speech rightly is the person who is going to make the most progress. This has ever been realised by all leaders of occult movements. That most occult order of Pythagoras at Crotona, and many other of the esoteric schools in Europe and Asia had a rule that all neophytes and probationers were not permitted to speak for two years after entering the school and when they had learned to keep silence for that period, they were given the right to speak, for they had learned a specific reticence.

It might be of value here if students realised that every good speaker is doing a most occult work. A good lecturer (for instance) is one who is doing work that is analogous on a small scale to that done by the solar Logos. What did He do? He thought, He built, He vitalised. A lecturer, therefore, segregates the material with which he is going to build his lecture and which he is going to vitalise. Out of all the thought matter of the world he gathers together the substance which he individually seeks to use. Next he copies the work of the second Logos in wisely building it into form. He constructs the form, and then when it is constructed, he finishes up by playing the part of the first Person of the Trinity putting his Spirit, vitality and force into it so that it is a vibrant, living manifestation. When a lecturer or speaker of any kind can accomplish that, he can always hold his audience and his audience will always learn from him; they will recognise that which the thought form is intended to convey.

In everyday life when the student speaks, he is doing just the same thing, only the trouble frequently arises that in his speech he constructs something that is usually not worth while and vitalises it with the wrong kind of energy, so that the form, instead of being a constructive, vital, helpful force, is a destructive one in the world. If we study the various cosmologies of the world, we shall see that the process of creation was carried on by the means of sound or speech or the Word. We have it in the Christian Bible, "In the beginning was the Word, and the Word was God. All things were made by Him and without Him was not anything made that was made." [91] Thus, according to the Christian teaching, the worlds were made by the Word of God.

In the Hindu Scriptures we will find that the Lord Vishnu, Who stands for the second Person of the Trinity, is called "The Voice." He is the great Singer Who has built the worlds and the universe by His song. He is the Revealer of the thought of God Who has constructed the universe of solar systems. Just as the Christian speaks about the great Word, the Word of God, the Christ, so the Hindu speaks of Vishnu, the great Singer, creating by means of His song.

In physical plane manifestation, we are known by our speech; we are known by our reticence, by the things we say, and by the things we leave unsaid and are judged by the quality of our conversation. We think of people in terms of what they say, because their words disclose the type of thought-matter in which they work and the quality of energy or life which they put behind their words. To the various solar Logoi of the vast constellations that are apparent when we scan the starry heavens, the quality of the Logos of our solar system is seen through the medium of that great thought form He has built by the power of His speech, and which is energised by His particular quality of love. When God speaks, the worlds are made and at this present time He is only in process of speaking. He has not yet concluded what He has to say, and hence the present apparent imperfection. When that great divine phrase or sentence which occupies His thought is brought to a close, we

[91] Bible. John I.

will have a perfect solar system inhabited by perfect existences.

Through speech a thought is evoked and becomes present; it is brought out of abstraction and out of a nebulous condition and materialised upon the physical plane, producing (could we but see it) something very definite on etheric levels. Objective manifestation is produced, for "Things are that which the Word makes them in naming them." Speech is literally a great magical force, and the adepts or white magicians, through knowledge of the forces and power of silence and of speech, can produce effects upon the physical plane. As we well know, there is a branch of magical work which consists in the utilisation of this knowledge in the form of Words of Power and of those mantrams and formulae which set in motion the hidden energies of nature and call the devas to their work.

Speech is one of the keys which opens the doors of communication between men and subtler beings. It gives the clue to the discovery of those entities who are contacted on the other side of the veil. But only he who has learned to keep silent, and has arrived at the knowledge of the times to speak can pass this veil and make certain esoteric contacts. Magic consists, we are told in the *Secret Doctrine,* in addressing the Gods in Their own language; therefore, the speech of average man cannot reach Them.

Therefore, those who seek to learn the occult language, those who yearn to become aware of the words which will penetrate to the ears of those who stand on the other side, and those who seek to utilise the formulae and phrases which will give them power over the Builders, have to unlearn their previous use of words and to refrain from ordinary methods of talking. Then the new language will be theirs and the new expressions, words, mantrams and formulas will be entrusted to their care.

The laws of speech are the laws of matter and students can apply the laws governing physical plane substance to their use of words, for it concerns the manipulation of matter on other levels. Speech is the great medium whereby we make apparent the nature of the little system we are constructing—that system of which each human unit is the central sun, for under the Law of Attraction he draws to himself that which he needs.

2. *The Nature of Magic.*[92]

We have considered somewhat at length the building of thought forms, and have seen that the process pursued by man is analogous to that pursued by the threefold Logos in the creation of the solar system. We are to deal now with that great department in occultism which is usually termed magic. The man who masters the esoteric significance of what is here said will take his place in the ranks of those entitled to call themselves the "Brothers of White Magic." The subject is too immense to be more than briefly touched upon, for it covers

[92] *Magic.*—S. D., I, 284.
1. Magic is a divine science which leads to a participation in the attributes of divinity itself.—Isis Unveiled, I, 25-27.
2. All magical operations consist in freeing oneself from the coils of the Ancient Serpent.—Isis Unveiled, I, 138.
3. The object of the art of magic is the perfection of man.—Isis Unveiled, I, 309.
4. Magic explores the essence and power of everything.—Isis Unveiled, I, 282; S. D., II, 538.
5. Magic and magnetism are synonymous terms.—Isis Unveiled, I, 279.
6. Magic is the sum-total of natural knowledge.—Isis Unveiled II, 99, 189.
7. Magic does not imply a transgression of the laws of nature.—Isis Unveiled, I, Preface.

The Basis of Magic.
1. Magic is based on the inner powers in man's soul.—Isis Unveiled, I, 459.
2. The trinity of nature is the lock of magic, the trinity of man the key that fits it.—Isis Unveiled, II, 635.
3. Magic is occult psychology.—Isis Unveiled, I, 612-616.
4. The astral light is the chief agent of magic.—Isis Unveiled, I, 128, 616; S. D., I, 275; II, 537.

the entire range of endeavour in the field of material construction.

We must deal first with the mental attitude of man as he faces the work of creation, and his ability to bring through, via the mental body, the purpose of the Ego, thereby impressing the building agents on the mental plane with a certain rate of rhythm, and a certain vibratory activity. This is the prime factor which results (on the physical plane) in direct egoic activity. We must also bear in mind, that in the consideration of this matter we are not dealing with the every day work of average man, but are speaking of the organised creative work, under law and rule, of the advanced man. We thereby set a standard and emphasise the ideal towards which occult students should strive.

We must also consider the work of the wise magical student upon the astral plane, whereon, through purified desire and sanctified emotion, he provides those equilibrised conditions and those stable vibrations, which will permit of the transmission without hindrance to the physical plane via the physical brain of the man, of the vibratory activity emanating from the Ego, and of the circulatory action of the higher force. Hence (if a remark of a practical nature may be interpolated for the average student) the cultivation of emotional tranquillity is one of the first steps towards the achievement of the needed equipment of the white magician. This tranquillity is not to be achieved by an effort of the will which succeeds in strangling all astral vibratory activity, but by the cultivation of response to the Ego, and a negation of all response to the inherent vibration of the astral sheath itself.

We will take up the work of force transmission on the physical plane via the etheric centres and the physical brain, studying somewhat the effect of sound as it is emitted unconsciously in everyday speech, and con-

sciously in the ordered regulated words of the true
worker in magic.[93]

In this connection, therefore, owing to the vital practical value of this section, and to the dangers attendant
upon a comprehension of these matters by those who
are as yet unready for the work of conscious manipulation of force, it is proposed to impart the necessary
teaching under the formula of "Rules of Magic," with
certain elucidating comments. In this way, the magical
work is fully safeguarded, and at the same time sufficient
is imparted to those who have the inner ear attentive,
and the eye of wisdom in process of opening.

   a. *Black Magicians and White.* Much is said among
occult students these days anent white and black magic,[94]
and much that is said is without force, or truth. It has

[93] Magic.—The very word Magic bears within itself proof of its high
origin. The Latin Magus, the Greek Magos, a magician, gives us all
those other words that are so indicative of authority, wisdom, superiority.
Then we have magnitude, magnificent, magniloquent, to express greatness
in position, in action and in speech. With the termination slightly changed
the same words become majesty, implying dominion, and again, we have
magistrate, anything that is magisterial which again has been simplified
into Master, and finally by the process of word evolution has become plain
Mister. But the Latin is only a transmitter of words. We can equally
follow up the historical development of this root until we reach the Zend
where we find it doing duty as the name for the whole priestly caste. The
magí were renowned all over the world for their wisdom and skill in
occultism and no doubt our word magic is mostly indebted to that source
for its present existence and meaning. That we need not pause even here
for back of the Zend "mag," "looms up the sanskrit, maha, signifying
great." It is thought by good scholars that maha was originally spelled
magha. To be sure, there is in the Sanskrit the word Maga meaning a
priest of the Sun, but this was evidently a later borrowing from the Zend
which had originally derived its root from its neighbour the Sanskrit.—
Lucifer, Vol. X, p. 157.

[94] Magic.—The art of divine Magic consists in the ability to perceive
the essence of things in the light of nature (astral light), and—by using
the soul-powers of the Spirit—to produce material things from the unseen
universe, and in such operations the Above and the Below must be brought
together and made to act harmoniously.—S. D., II, 538.

   Magic is the second of the four Vidyas, and is the great maha-Vidya
in the Tantric writings. It needs the light of the fourth vidya (atma-
vidya) thrown on it in order to be *White* magic.—S. D., I, 192.

   Black Magic is defined by H. P. B. as follows:

   a. Black magic employs the astral light for purposes of deception and
      seduction, whereas the white magician employs it for purposes
      of information, and the aiding of evolution.—S. D., I, 274.
   b. Black magic works with opposing poles. The white magician seeks

been truly said that between the two types of workers, the line of demarcation is so slight as to be difficult of recognition by those who, as yet, merit not the term "knower."

The distinction between the two exists in both motive and method, and might be summed up as follows:

The white magician has for motive that which will be of benefit to the group for whom he is expending his energy and time. The magician of the left hand path ever works *alone,* or if he at any time co-operates with others, it is with a hidden selfish purpose. The exponent of white magic interests himself in the work of constructive endeavour in order to co-operate in hierarchical plans, and to further the desires of the planetary Logos. The Brother of Darkness occupies himself with that which lies outside the plans of the Hierarchy and with that which is not included in the purpose of the Lord of the planetary Ray.

The white magician, as has been earlier said, works entirely through the greater Deva Builders, and through sound and numbers he blends their work, and thus influences the lesser Builders who form the substance of their bodies, and therefore of all that is. He works

the point of equilibrium or balance, and of synthesis.—S. D., I, 448.

c. Black magic has for its symbol the inverted 5-pointed star.
   White magic uses the same symbol with the point uppermost.

d. Black magic is maha-vidya without the light of atma-vidya.
   White magic is maha-vidya illumined by atma-vidya.—S. D., I, 592.

e. Black magic is ruled over by the moon.
   White magic is ruled over by the sun.

f. Black and white magic arose during the great schism which started during the fourth root-race.—S. D., II, 221, 445, 520.

g. Black magic is based on the degradation of sex and of the creative function.
   White magic is based on the transmutation of the creative faculty into the higher creative thought, the generative organs being neglected by the inner fire, which passes to the throat, the centre of creative sound.

h. Black magic deals with the forces of involution.
   White magic works with the powers of evolution.

i. Black magic is concerned with the form, with matter.
   White magic is concerned with the life within the form, with Spirit.

through group centres and vital points of energy, and from thence produces, in substance, the desired results. The dark brother works directly with substance itself, and with the lesser builders; He does not co-operate with the forces which emanate from egoic levels. The lesser cohorts of the "Army of the Voice" are his servants, and not the directing Intelligences in the three worlds, and he therefore works primarily on the astral and physical planes, only in rare cases working with the mental forces, and only in a few special cases, hidden in cosmic karma, is a black magician found working on the higher mental levels. Yet the cases which are there to be discovered are the main contributing causes of all manifesting black magic.

The Brother of Light works ever through the inherent force of the second aspect as long as he is functioning in connection with the three lower planes. After the third Initiation, he works increasingly with spiritual energy, or with the force of the first aspect. He impresses the lower substances, and manipulates the lesser building lives with the vibration of love, and the attractive coherency of the Son, and through wisdom the forms are built. He learns to work from the heart, and therefore to manipulate that energy which streams from the "Heart of the Sun" until (when he becomes a Buddha) he can dispense somewhat the force emanating from the "Spiritual Sun." Therefore, the heart centre in the Brother of the right hand path is the transmitting agency for the building force, and the triangle he uses in this work is

- a. The centre in the head which corresponds to the heart.
- b. The heart centre itself.
- c. The throat centre.

The Brothers of the left hand path work with the forces of the third aspect entirely, and this it is which gives them so much apparent power, for the second aspect is only in process of reaching its vibratory consummation, whereas the third aspect is at the height of its vibratory activity, being the product of the evolutionary processes of the preceding major solar system. He works from the throat centre almost entirely, and manipulates primarily the forces of the physical sun. This is the reason why he achieves many of his ends through the method of pranic stimulation or of pranic devitalisation, and why, also, most of his effects are carried out on the physical plane. He works, therefore, through

- a. The centre in the head corresponding to the throat centre.
- b. The throat centre.
- c. The centre at the base of the spine.

The white magician works always in co-operation with others, and is himself under the direction of certain group Heads. For instance, the Brothers of the White Lodge work under the three great Lords and conform to the plans laid down, subordinating Their individual purposes and ideas to the great general scheme. The black magician usually works in an intensely individualistic way, and can be seen carrying out his schemes alone, or with the aid of subordinates. He brooks usually no known superior, but is nevertheless frequently the victim of agents on higher levels of cosmic evil, who use him as he uses his inferior co-operators, that is, he works (as far as the bigger purpose is involved) blindly and unconsciously.

The white magician, as is well known, works on the side of evolution or in connection with the Path of Return. The black brother occupies himself with the forces of involution, or with the Path of Outgoing. They form the great balancing force in evolution, and though they are occupied with the material side of manifestation and the Brother of Light is concerned with the aspect of soul or consciousness, they and their work, under the great law of evolution, contribute to the general purpose of the solar Logos, though (and this is of tremendous occult significance to the illuminated student) *not to the individual purpose of the planetary* Logos.

Finally, it might be briefly said in connection with the distinctions between magicians that the magician of the Good Law works with the soul of things. His brothers of darkness work with the material aspect.

The white magician works through the force centres, on the first and fourth subplanes of each plane. The black magician works through the permanent atoms, and with the substance and forms concerned. The white magician utilises in this connection the higher three centres. The black magician uses the energy of the lower three centres (the organs of generation, the spleen, and the solar plexus) synthesising their energy by an act of the will and directing it to the centre at the base of the spine, so that the fourfold energy is thence transmitted to the throat centre.

The white magician uses the kundalini force as it is transmitted via the central spinal channel. The black magician uses the inferior channels, dividing the fourfold energy in two units, which mount via the two channels, leaving the central one dormant. Hence it will be apparent that one works with duality and the other with unity. On the planes of duality, therefore, it is apparent why the black magician has so much power. The plane of unity for humanity is the mental plane. The planes of diversity are the astral and the physical. Hence the black magician is of more apparent power than the white brother on the two lower planes in the three worlds.

The white brother works under the Hierarchy, or under the great King, carrying out His planetary pur-

poses. The dark brother works under certain separated
Entities, unknown to him, who are connected with the
forces of matter itself. Much more could be given in this
connection, but what is here imparted suffices for our
purpose.

b. The Source of Black Magic. In touching upon this
point, we are trespassing into the realms of the mystery
and the domain of the inexplicable. Certain statements
can, however, be made here which, if pondered upon, may
throw a little light upon this dark subject.

First. It should be remembered that the whole subject of planetary evil (and students must distinguish
carefully between planetary and cosmic evil) lies hid in
the individual life cycles and in the history of the Great
Being who is the planetary Logos of the Earth. Therefore, until a man has taken certain initiations and thus
achieved a measure of planetary consciousness, it is useless for him to speculate upon that record. H. P. B. has
touched, in the *Secret Doctrine*,[95] upon the subject of
"the imperfect Gods," and in these words lies the key to
planetary evil.

Second. It might briefly be said that, as far as our
humanity is concerned, the terms planetary evil and cosmic evil might be interpreted thus:

Planetary evil arises from certain relations existing
between our planetary Logos and another planetary
Logos. When this condition of polar opposition is adjusted, then planetary evil will cease. The adjustment
will be brought about through the mediation (occultly
understood) of a third planetary Logos. These three
will eventually form an equilateral triangle, and then
planetary evil will cease. Free circulation will ensue;
planetary obscuration will become possible, and the "imperfect Gods" will have achieved a relative perfection.
Thus will the karma of the manvantara, or secondary

[95] S. D., III, 62; Section 6, page 67.

cycle, be adjusted, and so much planetary karmic evil be "worked off." All the above must be interpreted in its esoteric sense and not its exoteric.

Cosmic evil from the standpoint of our planet consists in the relation between that spiritual intelligent Unit or "Rishi of the Superior Constellation" as He is called (who is the informing Life of one of the seven stars of the Great Bear, and our planetary prototype) and one of the forces of the Pleiades.[96] Students need here to remember that the "seven sisters" are occultly called the "seven wives" of the Rishis, and that the dual forces (resultant from that relationship) converge and play through that one of the planetary Logoi who is the Logos of any particular planet, and is the "reflection" of any specific Rishi. In this relation, at present lacking perfect adjustment, lies hid the mystery of cosmic evil as it makes itself felt in any particular planetary scheme. Again, when the heavenly triangle is duly equilibrated, and the force circulates freely through

a. One of the stars of the Great Bear,
b. The Pleiad involved,
c. The planetary scheme concerned,

then again cosmic evil will be negated, and a relative perfection achieved. This will mark the attainment of primary perfection, and the consummation of the greater cycle.

Cyclic evil, or tertiary evil, lies hid in the relation between the globes in any particular scheme, two of them ever being in opposition until equilibrised by force emanating from a third. Students will only apprehend the significance of this teaching as they study the pairs of opposites in their own cycles, and the equilibrising work of the Ego.

A fourth type of evil growing out of the above finds

[96] S. D., II, 579-581.

its main expression in the sorrows and troubles of the fourth or human kingdom, and will find its solution in two ways: by the balancing of the forces of the three kingdoms (the spiritual or fifth kingdom, the human, and the animal), and secondly, by the negation of the attractive power of the three lower kingdoms (the mineral, the vegetable, and the animal, who thus form one unit), by the spiritual kingdom, utilising the fourth or human kingdom.   In all these cases, triangles of force are formed which, when balanced, procure the desired end.

Black magic is spoken of as making its appearance upon our planet during the fourth root race.[97]   It should be borne in mind here that this means strictly in connection with the fourth kingdom and its conscious use by wrongly developed men.   The forces of evil of the planetary and cosmic kind have been present since manifestation set in, being latent in the karma of the planetary Logos, but human beings began consciously to work with these forces and to use them for specified selfish ends in this round during the fourth root race.

Black magicians work under certain great Entities, six in number, who are spoken of, for instance, in the Christian Bible as having the number 666.[98]   They came in (being cosmic, not systemic) on that stream of force emanating from cosmic mental levels which produced the three worlds of human endeavour.   Students should remember here the fact that the three lower planes of our solar system are not considered as embodying a cosmic principle, for they form the dense physical body of the Logos, and the dense physical body is not considered a principle.   There is an occult significance in the expression "unprincipled."   These entities are the sumtotal of the substance of the three lower subplanes of the cosmic physical plane (our three lower systemic

[97] S. D., I, 451, 452; II, 221, 234, 519.
[98] Bible.   Rev. 13:18.

planes), and it is under them that the black magicians are swept into activity, often unconsciously, but rising to power as they work consciously.[99]

In the early stages of human unfoldment all men are unconscious black magicians, but are not occultly "damned" thereby. As evolution proceeds they come under the force of the second aspect, and the majority respond to it, escaping from the meshes of the black magicians, and coming under the force of a different number. The few who do not do so in this manvantara are the "failures" who have to continue the struggle at a later date. A tiny percentage wilfully refuse to "pass on," and they become the true "black magicians." For them the end is ever the same, *first,* severance of the Ego from the Monad, entailing a wait for many aeons until another solar system has its being. In the case of the "failures" the Ego severed itself from the personality or lower self, entailing a setback for a lesser period, but still having opportunity within the system. *Second,* a cycle of existence, spent in unlimited evil, and dependent upon the vitality of the severed egoic body and its innate persistence. These are the ordinary "lost souls" spoken of in the *Secret Doctrine.*[1] If students will study these conditions, and will extend the same concept to an earlier and more matured solar system, they will get

[99] It might here be asked what, if any, relation there may be in this connection with the inner round? The inner round has many meanings, some impossible to give, but two things may here be said: That it concerns itself with the effect of the triangular balancing of forces towards the close of the cycle, when the force or energy involved is circulating unimpeded, even if slowly, through:

1. Two constellations of the solar system,
2. The planetary schemes,
3. Three globes in the scheme.

It should be remembered that all these three are interdependent. The force begins thus to flow when any cycle is two thirds run. It deals with the greater Initiations, and is the correspondence on the higher planes to the occult short cut to wisdom and knowledge which we call the Path of Initiation.

[1] No soul can be lost where:
  a. One good aspiration is present.
  b. One unselfish deed is done.

some light upon the problem of the origin of evil in this solar system.

c. Conditions for White Magic.   In considering the factors requiring adjustment prior to undertaking the work of magic, we are dealing with that which is of eminently practical value.   Unless students of magic enter upon this pursuit fortified by pure motive, clean bodies, and high aspiration, they are foredoomed to disappointment and even to disaster.   All those who seek to work consciously with the forces of manifestation, and who endeavour to control the Energies of all that is seen, need the strong protection of purity.   This is a point which cannot be too strongly emphasised and urged, and hence the constant injunctions to self control, comprehension of the nature of man, and devotion to the cause of humanity.   The pursuit of magical investigation is dangerous in three ways.

If a man's bodies are not sufficiently purified and their atomic vibration is not sufficiently high, he is in danger of over-stimulation when brought in contact with the forces of nature, and this inevitably entails the destruction and disintegration of one or other of his bodies. At times it may entail the destruction of two or more, and when this is the case, it involves a definite setback to egoic unfoldment, for it requires, in such cases, a much longer interval between incarnations, owing to the difficulty of assembling the needed materials in the sheaths.

Further, unless a man is strengthened in his endeavour by right motive, he is liable to be led astray by the acquisition of power.   Knowledge of the laws of magic puts into the hands of the student powers which enable him to create, to acquire, and to control.   Such powers

c. The life is strong in virtue.
d. The life is righteous.
e. The life is a naturally pure life.—Isis Unveiled, II, 368.
    Read S. D., III, 528, 529.

are fraught with menace to the unprepared and unready, for the student can, in this case, turn them to selfish ends, use them for his own temporal material advancement, and acquire in this way that which will feed the desires of the lower nature. He takes, therefore, the first step towards the left hand path, and each life may see him progressing towards it with greater readiness, until (almost unconsciously) he will find himself in the ranks of the black masters. Such a state of affairs can only be offset through the cultivation of altruism, sincere love of man, and a steady negation of all lower desire.

The third danger which menaces the unwary student of magic lies in the fact that when he tampers with these forces and energies he is dealing with that which is akin to his own lower nature. He, therefore, follows the line of least resistance; he augments these energies, thereby increasing their response to the lower and to the material aspects of his nature. This he does at the expense of his higher nature, retarding its unfoldment and delaying his progress. Incidentally also, he attracts the attention of those masters of the left hand path who are ever on the lookout for those who can be bent to their purposes, and he becomes (unwittingly at first), an agent on the side of evil.

It will be apparent, therefore, that the student has need of the following qualities before he undertakes the arduous task of becoming a conscious Master of Magic:

Physical Purity. This is a thing not easily to be acquired, but entailing many lives of strenuous effort. Through abstinence, right continence, clean living, vegetarian diet, and rigid self-control, the man gradually raises the vibration of his physical atoms, builds a body of ever greater resistance and strength, and succeeds in "manifesting" forth in a sheath of greater refinement.

Etheric Freedom. This term does not convey all that

I seek to impart, but it suffices for need of a better. The student of magic who can safely undertake the enterprise, will have constructed an etheric body of such a nature that vitality, or pranic force and energy, can circulate unimpeded; he will have formed an etheric web of such tenuosity that it forms no barrier to consciousness. This is all that can be said on this subject, owing to the danger involved, but it suffices for the conveyance of information to those who are beginning to know.

Astral Stability. The student of magic aims, above all, to purify his desires, and so to transmute his emotions that the lower physical purity and the higher mental responsiveness and transmutative power may equally be available. Every magician has to learn the fact that, in this solar system, during the cycle of humanity, the astral body is the pivotal point of endeavour, having a reflex effect on both the other sheaths, the physical and the mental. He, therefore, aims at transmuting (as has often been said) lower desire into aspiration; at changing the lower cruder colors which distinguish the astral body of average man, for the clearer, purer tones of the spiritual man, and of transforming its normal chaotic vibration, and the "stormy sea of life," for the steady rhythmic response to that which is highest and the centre of peace. These things he effects by constant watchfulness, unremitting control, and steady meditation.

Mental Poise. These words are used in the occult sense, wherein the mind (as it is commonly understood) becomes the keen steady instrument of the indwelling thinker, and the point from which he can travel onwards to higher realms of comprehension. It is the foundation stone whence the higher expansion can be initiated.

Let not the would-be student of magic proceed in his investigations and his experiments until he has attended to these injunctions, and until the whole bent of his thought is towards their manifestation and their demonstration in his every day life. When he has so worked, ceaselessly and untiringly, and his physical plane life and service bear witness to the inner transmutation, then he can proceed to parallel this life with magical studies and work. Only the solar Angel can do the work of the white magician, and he effects it through the control of the lunar angels and their complete subjugation. They are arrayed against him, until, through meditation, aspiration, and control, he bends them to his will and they become his servants.

This thought brings us to the vital and real distinction between the white brother and the brother of darkness, and in this summation we will conclude the present discussion and proceed with the rules.

The worker in white magic utilises ever the energy of the Solar Angel to effect his ends. The dark brother works through the inherent force of the lunar lords, which are allied in nature to all that is objective. In an old book of magic, hidden in the caves of learning, guarded by the Masters, are the following conclusive words, which find their place in this *Treatise on Fire* through their very appropriateness:

"The Brothers of the Sun, through the force of solar fire, fanned to a flame in the blazing vault of the second Heaven, put out the lower lunar fires, and render naught that lower 'fire by friction.'

"The Brother of the Moon ignores the sun and solar heat; borrows his fire from all that triply is, and pursues his cycle. The fires of hell await, and lunar fire dies out. Then neither sun nor moon avails him, only the highest heaven awaits the spark electric, seeking vibration synchronous from that which lies beneath. And yet it cometh not."

3. *Fifteen Rules for Magic.*

These rules will necessarily be of an esoteric nature, and the student will need to remember that the terminology is in the nature of a blind, which ever carries revelation to those who have the clue, but tends to perplex and to bewilder the student who as yet is unready for the truth. I would also remind the student to bear in mind that all that is here imparted concerns *"white magic,"* and is given from the standpoint of the solar Angel, and of solar Fire. Bearing these two points in mind the student will find much in these rules to produce eventual internal illumination. We will divide them into three groups of aphorisms or occult phrases; of these, the first will concern itself with the work of the magician on the mental plane, with his manipulation of solar energy, and his ability to sweep the Builders into co-operation with his purposes.

The second group will carry the work on down to the plane of desire, and of vitalisation, and will convey information as to the balancing of the pairs of opposites, and their equilibrising, so that eventual manifestation becomes possible.

The third group of rules will deal with the physical plane, with the transmission of force:

  a. Through the centres,
  b. Through the brain,
  c. Through the physical plane itself.

a. Six Rules for the Mental Plane. Certain of the laws of speech will be given, and the significance of colour and of sound will appear beneath the exoteric form of the phrasing to those whose perception suffices.

RULE I. *The Solar Angel collects himself, scatters not his force, but in meditation deep communicates with his reflection.*

The significance of this rule is easily to be seen. The white magician is ever one who, through conscious alignment with his Ego, with his "Angel," is receptive to his plans and purposes, and therefore capable of receiving the higher impression. We must remember that

white magic works from above downwards, and is the
result of solar vibration, and not of the heating impulses
emanating from one or other of the lunar Pitris; the
downflow of the impressing energy from the solar Pitri
is the result of his internal recollectedness, his indraw-
ing of his forces prior to sending them out concen-
tratedly to his shadow, man, and his steady meditation
upon the purpose and the plan. It may be of use to the
student if he here remembers that the Ego (as well as
the Logos) is in deep meditation during the whole cycle
of physical incarnation. This solar meditation is cyclic
in nature, the Pitri involved sending out to his "reflection" rhythmic streams of energy, which streams are
recognised by the man concerned as his "higher impulses," his dreams and aspirations. Therefore, it will
be apparent why workers in white magic are ever advanced, and spiritual men, for the "reflection" is seldom responsive to the Ego or the solar Angel until
many cycles or incarnation have transpired. The solar
Pitri communicates with his "shadow" or reflection by
means of the sutratma, which passes down through the
bodies to a point of entrance in the physical brain.

RULE II. *When the shadow hath responded, in meditation deep the work proceedeth. The
lower light is thrown upward; the greater
light illuminates the three, and the work
of the four proceedeth.*

Here the work of the two, the Ego on its own plane,
and its instrument in the three worlds, is shown as
linked and co-ordinated. As we well know, the main
function of meditation is to bring the lower instrument
into such a condition of receptivity and vibratory response that the Ego, or solar Angel, can use it, and produce specific results. This involves, therefore, a downflow of force from the upper levels of the mental plane

(the habitat of the real Man) and a reciprocal vibration, emanating from Man, the Reflection. When these two vibrations are attuned, and the interplay is rhythmic, then the two meditations proceed synchronously, and the work of magic and of creation can proceed unimpeded. It will, therefore, be apparent that the brain is the physical correspondence to the force centres upon the mental plane, and that the vibration has to be *consciously* set up by the man when meditating. When this is effected, the man can be a *conscious* creator, and the work proceeds therefore in a triple manner; the force circulates freely via three points of centralised activity:

First. From that circle of petals in the egoic lotus which the Ego chooses to use, or is in a position to use. This is conditioned by the objective in view, and the state of egoic unfoldment.

Secondly. The centre in the physical brain which is active in meditation. This is also conditioned by the man's point in evolution, and the particular goal in mind.

Thirdly. The centre of force generated by the man upon the lower mental plane, as he proceeds to form the necessitated thought form, and to sweep into activity those builders who can respond to the vibration sent forth. This is likewise conditioned by the strength of his meditation, the fullness of the note sent forth by him, and the strength of his initiated vibration.

Hence, the first thing the solar Angel does is to form a triangle, consisting of himself, the man on the physical plane, and the tiny point of force which is the result of their united endeavour. It will be of value to students of meditation to ponder upon this procedure, and to study the correspondence between it and the work of the solar Logos as He created ''the Heavens and the Earth.'' The

Highest and the lowest aspects met, spirit and matter were brought into contact with each other; the consequence of this interplay was the birth of the Son, or the great solar thought form. In the three worlds, man, the lesser Deity, within his limits, proceeds along analogous lines. The three who are illumined by the light of the One are the three persons of the lower Triad, the mental body, the astral body, and the physical body. They, with the Illuminator, make the "Four" referred to, and thus becomes apparent the microcosmic Tetraktys.

The two rules above form the esoteric basis of all meditation, and need to be carefully studied if results are to be achieved.

RULE III.   *The Energy circulates. The point of light, the product of the labours of the Four, waxeth and groweth. The myriads gather round its glowing warmth until its light recedes. Its fire grows dim. Then shall the second sound go forth.*

The white magician, having, through meditation and conscious purpose, formed a focal point of energy upon the mental plane, increases the vibration through strenuous concentration; he begins then to visualise in detail the form he is seeking to build; he pictures it with all its component parts, and sees "before his mind's eye" the consummated product of the egoic meditation as he has succeeded in bringing it through. This produces what is here called "the secondary note," the first being the note emanating from the Ego on its own plane, which awakened the "reflection" and called forth response. The vibration becomes stronger, and the note sounded by the man on the physical plane ascends and is heard upon the mental plane. Hence, in all meditation that is of occult value, the man has to do certain things in order to aid in bringing about the results.

He tranquilises his bodies in order that there be no impediment to the egoic intent, and listens for the "Voice of the Silence." He responds then to that Voice consciously, and broods over the imparted plans.

He then sounds the Sacred Word, taking up the note of the Ego as he believes he hears it, and sending it forth to swell the egoic sound, and to set in motion matter on the mental plane. He (synchronously with this sounding) visualises the proposed thought form which is to embody egoic purposes, and pictures it in detail.

We must not forget that we are here dealing with those conscious meditations, based on knowledge and long experience, which produce magical results on the physical plane. We are not dealing here with those meditations which have for their purpose the revelation of the inner God, and the bringing in of the illuminating fire of the Ego.

When this process is proceeding under rule and order, the focal point of energy on the lower mental plane gains in strength; its light or fire makes itself felt; it becomes, in the occult sense, visually objective, and attracts the attention of the lesser builders through

a. Its radiation or warmth,
b. Its active vibration,
c. Its sound or note,
d. Its light.

The elemental workers of responsive capacity are gathered and swept into the radius of the force, and begin to gather around. The intended form begins to be apparent, and tiny life after tiny life takes its place in its construction. The result of this "coherency" is that the inner light becomes veiled, its brilliancy dimmed, just as the inner light of the Ego in its shadow, or thought form, man, is similarly dimmed and hidden.

Rule IV.   *Sound, light, vibration, and the form blend*
and merge, and thus the work is one. It
proceedeth under the law, and naught
can hinder now the work from going for-
ward. The man breathes deeply. He
concentrates his forces, and drives the
thought-form from him.

Here we have a very important piece of work of magic
dealt with, and one that is little considered and known.
The force used by the Ego in the work of forcing the
man to carry out His purpose has been *dynamic* will,
and the petal, or energy centre, employed has been one
of the *will* petals. The man has, up till now, been
driven by egoic will, but has blended with this much of
the energy of the attraction aspect (desire or love)
thereby gathering to himself on the mental plane, the
material needed for his thought form. He has succeeded
so far that on the concrete levels of the mental plane is
to be seen a form in mental matter which is coherent,
alive, vibrant, and of a desired nature. Its internal
activity is such that its persistence for the length of time
necessary to ensure achievement of the egoic purpose
is assured; it stands ready to be sent forth upon its mission, to gather to itself material of a denser nature upon
the astral plane, and to achieve greater consolidation.
This is brought about by an act of will emanating from
the man, and he gives the living form power "to break
loose." It is exactly at this point, fortunately for the
human race, that the majority of magical investigators
fail in their work. They build a form in mental matter,
but do not know how to send it forth, so that inevitably
it will fulfill its mission. Thus many thought forms die
a natural death on the mental plane owing to the inability of the man to exert the will faculty constructively,
and his failure to understand the laws of thought-form
construction. Another factor is his lack of knowledge

of the formula which releases the elemental builders from their surroundings, and forces them to cohere within the periphery of the thought form for as long as the thinker desires.

Finally, they die owing to the incapacity of the man, which prevents him holding a meditation long enough, and formulating his ideas clearly enough to bring about ultimate materialisation.

Men are, as yet, too impure and too selfish to be trusted with this knowledge. Their thought forms would be constructed in order to be sent on selfish missions and for destructive ends, and until they are more spiritual, and have gained control over their lower nature, the magical words which galvanise into separated activity the form in mental substance will not be available for their use.

It might be asked how it is that men do achieve their ends, through concentration and visualisation, and do manage to send forth thought forms which reach their objective. In two ways this can be brought about:

First. By an unconscious recollection of methods and formulas known and used in Atlantean days, when the magical formulas were public property, and men produced results through the pronouncement of certain sounds. They did not achieve their ends through mental ability, but principally through a parrot-like capacity to repeat mantrams. These are, at times, hidden in the subconscious nature, and are used unwittingly by the man who is *feeling* strongly enough.

Second. Through the thoughts and ideas of the man fitting in with the plans and purposes of those who *do* know, either on the path of white or black magic. Then they utilise the form with its inherent force and galvanise it into activity, and a temporary separate identity, thus sending it forth to accomplish its purpose. This accounts for many of the apparently phenomenal results achieved by selfish or by incompetent (though good) thinkers.

The magical words are only communicated under the seal of secrecy, to men working under the Brotherhood of Light, to initiates, and to pledged chelas, owing to the great danger involved. Occasionally, too, they are ascertained by men and women who have brought about a condition of alignment with the Ego, and are, therefore, in touch with the inner centre of all knowledge within themselves. When this is so, the knowledge is safe, for the Ego ever works on the side of law and righteousness, and the words being emanated by the Ego are "lost in His sound" (as it is occultly termed) and will not be remembered by the physical brain when not under the influence of the solar Angel.

The six rules for the mental plane are necessarily brief, owing to the fact that the plane of mind is as yet an unknown land to the majority,—unknown in so far as its *conscious* control is concerned. These two remaining rules concern, in the first case, the brother engaged in white magic, and in the second the thought form he is constructing.

> RULE V. *Three things engage the solar Angel before the sheath created passes downward: the condition of the waters, the safety of the one who thus creates, and steady contemplation. Thus are the heart, the throat, and the eye, allied for triple service.*

The focal point of energy that the man, the magician, has now created upon the mental plane, has reached a vibratory activity which makes it certain that response will be called forth from the matter required for the providing of the next, and denser sheath. This vibration will result in an aggregation of a different type of divine life-substance around the central nucleus. The form, occultly, is made to be sent forth, to descend, to

fly as a bird forth upon its mission, and a critical moment is near for the magician.   One of the things the
magician has to see to is that this form which he has
constructed, and which he holds linked to him by a fine
thread of animated substance (a correspondence on a
minute scale of the sutratmic thread whereby the Monad
or the Ego holds in connection its "form of manifestation") shall neither die for lack of vital sustenance nor
return to him with its mission unfulfilled.   When this
latter catastrophe is the case, the thought form becomes
a menace to the magician, and he becomes the prey of
that which he has created.   The devas who form the
body of the idea which has failed in its purpose form
a drain upon his vital force.   He, therefore, sees to it
that the motive or desire lying back of the "idea," now
clothed with its first sheath, retains its pristine purity;
that no trace of selfish intent, no perversion of the initial
purpose of the solar Angel has been permitted to bring
in an unworthy vibration.   This is what is meant by at-
tending to the "condition of the waters."   As we well
know, water stands for matter, and the substances of the
astral plane which are now under consideration are of
prime importance in all form-building.   According to the
substance used and the nature of the Builders who respond to the note of the form in mental matter, will the
purpose be accomplished.   This is the most important
stage in many ways, for the astral body of any form
conditions:

a. The nature of the physical vehicle.
b. The transmission of force from the next highest
    plane.

Provided the man on the physical plane can hold the
purpose steady, and refuse to permit its distortion by
the influences and vibrations emanating from the lower
man, then the "devas of kama" can carry on their work.

I would remind students at this juncture that any thought form necessarily finds its way into greater streams of force or energy, emanating from advanced thinkers of every grade, from the planetary Logos downward, and according to its nature and motive so the work of evolution is assisted or retarded. It is in this connection that the Nirmanakayas work, manipulating streams of thought energy, vitalising the forms created by men, and thus carrying on the work of construction or destruction. They have to use that which exists; hence the necessity for clear thinking. Having "purified" the waters, or safeguarded his desires, the thinker next proceeds (through the use of certain words which are imparted to him by the solar Angel) to protect himself from the devas of elemental nature with which he is purposing to work. On the mental plane, the nature and vibration of the solar Angel proved sufficient protection, but he is now proposing to work with the most dangerous elementals and existences in the three worlds.[2]

These protective formulas are sounded forth by the thinker, in conjunction with the solar Angel, at the moment the thought form is ready to receive its astral sheath. The mantram deals with the forces which impel activity in the Agnisuryans, and starts a stream of protective energy from one of the heart petals of the Egoic lotus. This circulates through the throat centre of the man, and sets up a circulatory stream of energy around him which automatically repulses the devas who might (through their blind unintelligent work) menace his peace. These two matters attended to—desire adjusted and the identity guarded—both the solar Angel and the worker in magic maintain an attitude of contemplation,

---

[2] H. P. B. has said that the elementals of the air are the most wicked and dangerous. He refers there to the physical plane, and to dangers menacing the physical body. They are the most dangerous where the physical plane is concerned, but in the case we are considering, we are dealing with man, the unity in the three worlds.

or that profound condition which succeeds that called meditation.

In contemplation, the inner eye is fixed upon the object of contemplation, and this produces (unconsciously in most cases) a steady stream of energy which is focussed upon the objective, producing vitalisation and activity. It is the basis of the "work of transmutation," for instance, when the human substance is transmuted into solar substance. The Ego contemplates his lunar bodies, and gradually the work is accomplished. When his reflection, man, has reached a point in evolution where he can meditate and contemplate, the work is more rapidly accelerated, and transmutation proceeds with rapidity, particularly on the physical plane. In the work of thought-form building, the man, in contemplation, pursues the work of energising and vitalising. It might here be said that the eye is the great directing agency. When the third eye is used, which is the case in contemplation, it is the synthesiser and director of triple energy; hence the powerful work performed by those in whom it is functioning. The third eye only begins to function when the third circle of egoic petals is beginning slowly to unfold.

If students will study the effect of the human eye on the physical plane, and then extend the concept to the work of the interior Thinker, as he utilises the third eye, they will get an interesting light upon the subject of thought control. The old Commentary says:

"When the eye is blind, the forms created revolve in circles and fulfill not the law. When the eye is open, force streams forth, direction is assured, fulfillment is certain, and the plans proceed under law; the eye which is blue in color, and the eye which sees not red, when open, produce that which is intended with great facility."

The final rule is contained in the words:

RULE VI. *The devas of the lower four feel the force when the eye opens; they are driven forth and lose their master.*

The egoic energy, transmitted via the physical brain, is directed now to the work of sending forth the form, so that it may clothe itself in astral matter. The eye of the Thinker opens, and repulsing vitality streams forth. More need not be said here, for until the eye is functioning, it is not possible for men to comprehend the nature of the energy which they will then wield or direct.

b. Five Rules for the Astral Plane. Before we take up the consideration of the second set of "Rules for Magic," I would like to make a few remarks anent the "eye of the Magician," to which reference has been earlier made. One of the fundamental rules back of all magical processes is that no man is a magician or worker in white magic until the third eye is opened, or in process of opening, for it is by means of that eye that the thought form is energised, directed and controlled and the lesser builders or forces are swept into any particular line of activity. Among the coming discoveries, and among the next revelations of materialistic science will be one which will concern itself with the force-directing faculty of the human eye, alone or collectively, and this will indicate one of the first stages towards the rediscovery of the third eye, or the "Eye of Shiva." Shiva is, as we know, one of the names for the first great logoic aspect, and under that name is hidden much of esoteric moment. Shiva stands for:

a. The Will aspect,
b. The Spirit aspect,
c. The Father in Heaven,
d. The directing purpose,
e. Conscious energy,
f. Dynamic intent,

and in the consideration of these phrases the innate faculties of the third eye will become apparent.

The "Eye of Shiva" in the human being has its position, as is already known, in the centre of the forehead between the two physical eyes.[3]

It is not to be confounded with the pineal gland, which is distinctly a physical centre or gland. The third eye exists in etheric matter, and is an etheric centre of force, being made of the substance of the ethers, whereas the pineal gland is formed of matter of the three lower subplanes of the physical plane. The latter, nevertheless, has to be functioning more or less before the "Eye of Shiva" becomes in any degree active, and it is this fact that has led writers of occult books in the past purposely to confound the two, in order to protect the knowledge.

The third eye is formed through the activity of three factors:

First, through the direct impulse of the Ego on its own plane. During the greater part of evolution the Ego makes its contact with its reflection, physical plane man, through the centre at the top of the head. When man is more highly evolved, and is nearing or treading the Path, the indwelling Self takes a more complete grasp of its lower vehicle, and descends to a point in the head or brain which is found approximately in the centre of the forehead. This is its lowest contact. It is interesting here to note the correspondence with the evolution of the senses. The three major senses and the three first to demonstrate in order are, hearing, touch, sight. For the greater part of evolution, *hearing* is the guiding impulse of human life through egoic contact with the top of the head. Later, when the Ego descends a little lower, the etheric centre which is active in connection with the pituitary body, is added, and man becomes re-

[3] S. D., I, 77; II, 297, 309, 316.

sponsive to subtler and higher vibrations; the occult correspondence to the physical sense of *touch* awakens. Finally, the third *eye* opens and the pineal gland simultaneously begins to function. At first, the sight is dim, and the gland is only partially responsive to vibration, but gradually the eye opens fully, the gland is fully active, and we have the "fully awakened" man. When this is the case, the alta major centre vibrates and then the three physical head centres are functioning.

Second, through the co-ordinated activity of the major head centre, the many petalled lotus above the top of the head. This centre directly affects the pineal gland, and the interplay of force behind the two (the correspondence, on a tiny scale, of the pairs of opposites, spirit and matter), produces the great organ of consciousness, the "Eye of Shiva." It is the instrument of wisdom, and in these three centres of energy we have the correspondence of the three aspects within the head of man.

1. Major head centre	Will Aspect....	Spirit	Father in Heaven
2. Pineal gland	Love - Wisdom aspect	Conscious-ness	Son
3. Third eye.	Activity aspect	Matter ...	Mother

The third eye is the director of energy or force, and thus an instrument of the will or Spirit; it is responsive only to that will as controlled by the Son-aspect, the revealer of the love-wisdom nature of gods and man, and it is therefore the sign of the white magician.

Third, the reflex action of the pineal gland itself.

As these three types of energy, or the vibration of these three centres, begin to contact each other, a definite interplay is set up. This triple interplay forms *in time* a vortex or centre of force, which finds its place in the centre of the forehead, and takes eventually the semblance of an eye looking out between the other two.

It is the eye of the inner vision, and he who has opened it can direct and control the energy of matter, see all things in the Eternal Now, and therefore be in touch with causes more than with effects, read the akashic records, and see clairvoyantly. Therefore, its possessor can control the builders of low degree.

The "Eye of Shiva," when perfected, is blue in colour, and as our solar Logos is the "Blue Logos" so do His children occultly resemble Him; but this colour must be interpreted esoterically. It must be remembered also that prior to the final two Initiations (the sixth and seventh), the eye of the white magician, when developed, will be coloured according to the man's ray—again esoterically understood. More anent this question of colour may not be communicated. According to the colour, so will be the type of energy manipulated, but here it must be borne in mind that all magicians work with three types of energy:

a. That which is the same as their own Ray,
b. That which is complementary to their own type of force,
c. Their polar opposite,

and they work, therefore, either along the line of least resistance, or through attraction, and repulsion.

It is through the medium of this "all-seeing eye" that the Adept can at any moment put Himself in touch with His disciples anywhere; that He can communicate with His compeers on the planet, on the polar opposite of our planet, and on the third planet which, with ours, forms a triangle; that He can, through the energy directed from it, control and direct the builders, and hold any thought form He may have created within His sphere of influence, and upon its intended path of service; and that through his eye by means of directed energy currents He can help and stimulate His disciples or groups of men in any place at any time.

The pineal gland is subject to two lines of stimulation: *First,* that which emanates from the Ego itself via the etheric force centres. This downflow of egoic energy (the result of the awakening of the centres through meditation and spirituality of life), impinges upon the gland and in the course of years gradually increases its secretion, enlarges its form, and starts it into a new cycle of activity.

The second line of stimulation affecting the pineal gland is that which is the consequence of the discipline of the physical body, and its subjugation to the laws of spiritual unfoldment. As the disciple lives a regulated life, avoids meat, nicotine and alcohol, and practises continence, the pineal gland becomes no longer atrophied, but resumes its earlier activity.

More cannot here be given but enough has been indicated to give the student food for thought.

In meditation, by the sounding of the word, the student awakens response in the major head centre, causes reciprocal vibration between it and the physical head centre, and gradually co-ordinates the forces in the head. Through the practice of the power of visualisation, the third eye is developed. The forms visualised, and the ideas and abstractions which are, in the process, mentally clothed and vehicled, are pictured a few inches from the third eye. It is the knowledge of this which causes the Eastern yogi to speak of "concentration upon the tip of the nose." Behind this misleading phrase a great truth is veiled.

In proceeding with the "Rules for Magic," we will take up those concerned with the second set, which deal with the form-building impulses, and those attractive tendencies which are the basis of physical plane manifestation. We have considered certain rules which deal with the work of the solar Angel, who (in all true magical work of any kind), is the active agent. We have

considered the rules whereby He constructs a thought
form upon the mental plane, or that germ body which
will (through accretion and vibratory sound), take to
itself other forms.

RULE VII. *The dual forces on the plane whereon the
vital power must be sought, are seen; the two paths
face the Solar Angel; the poles vibrate. A choice
confronts the one who meditates.*

Upon the astral plane the thought form must now
function, and a body must be provided so as to make this
possible. The energy of desire enters it, and "he who
meditates" has to energise the form with one of two
types of force before it passes into objectivity. Upon
the action taken depends the construction of the etheric
body, and the consequent physical manifestation. This
point is but little realised by the average thinker, but
the parallel with his own life experience is exact, as is
the correspondence with the cosmic process. The
"nature of the deva" (as it is called), enters in, and
upon the quality of its love nature, and the specific type
of that which is the object of love will depend the nature
of the thought form. If the deva, or solar Angel,
is as yet in love with manifestation, and has a desire for
objective existence, thus identifying himself voluntarily
with substance, there ensues the phenomenon of reincarnated physical life. If the deva, or solar Angel, is no
longer attracted by matter, then there is no identification, and objective life is no longer the law of his existence. He identifies himself then with quality, or energy,
and becomes an expression of the divine attributes.
Objectivity may then ensue as a voluntary offering to
the good of the group or planetary existence, but identification with the separated form is no longer the case.
The human vehicle then created is as much a thought
form in this case as any other particularised idea, and

the greatest act of conscious magic is to be seen. All other magical creations are subsidiary to this. Through manipulation of negative and positive energy, thus bringing them to the point of equilibrium before informing them, the perfected body of the Adept is formed. All magical work on the astral plane has to be along the line of equilibrising activity, and the distinctive nature of this type of work on the three planes in the three worlds might be summed up as follows:

On the mental plane, the *positive* force of the solar Angel drives the substance needed into the correct form.

On the astral plane, the *equilibrising* force of the solar Angel gathers the needed material and energy from all directions and builds it into the necessary astral sheath.

On the physical plane the *negative* force of the solar Angel is all that is needed to gather the desired etheric substance. By this I mean the form has now achieved a vitality and distinction of its own, so that no aggressive action emanating from the egoic centre is required to continue the work. The note and vibration of the form itself suffices.

RULE VIII. *The Agnisuryans respond to the sound. The waters ebb and flow. Let the magician guard himself from drowning at the point where land and water meet. The midway spot which is neither dry nor wet must provide the standing place whereon his feet are set. When water, land and air meet there is the place for magic to be wrought.*

It will be noted that in this rule, no mention is made of the fourth element, fire. The reason for this is that the magician has to accomplish the stupendous task of generating the needed fire at this triple "meeting place." This is one of the most occult and most puzzling of the

rules.   Some light is thrown on it by the following three
sentences from the old Commentary:

"When the fire is drawn from the inmost point within the
heart the waters suffice not to subdue it.   Like a stream of flame
it issues forth, and traverses the waters, which disappear before
it.   Thus the goal is found."

"When the fire descends from the One Who watches above,
the wind suffices not to blow it out.   The very winds protect,
shield and aid the work, guiding the falling fire unto the point
of entrance."

"When the fire emanates from the mouth of the one who
thinks and sees, then the earth sufficeth not to hide or kill the
flame.   It feeds the flame, causing a growth and magnitude of
fire which reaches to the narrow door of entrance."

Under this symbology much is hidden anent the life-
giving energy, the centres symbolised to focalise it, and
to drive it forth, and the place the various types of receptive matter play in the magical work.   As is ever the
case in all white magic, the activity of the solar Angel
is the primary factor and the work of the man upon the
physical plane is regarded as secondary; his physical
body, and the work engendered therein, being frequently
referred to as "fuel and its warmth."   This needs careful remembering, and will give the clue to the necessity
of egoic alignment, and to the problem of the extinction
of certain workers in magic, who were "destroyed by
their own fire" or energy.   The discreet magician is one
who sees to the readiness of his lowest vehicle to carry
the fire wherewith he works, and this he accomplishes
through discipline and strict purity.

The magician guards himself from "drowning" or
from coming under the influence of the water or astral
elementals, through a knowledge of certain formulas,
and until these sounds and mantrams are imparted and
known, it is not safe for the man on the physical plane
to attempt magical creation.   These formulas are three
in number:

First, those which blend the two notes, add a third, and thus call into activity the builders of the astral plane, the Agnisuryans, in some one or other of their grades. These are based on the initiatory sound of the Ego, and distinguish between it and the sound of the note of the builders and lives of the tiny thought form already formed. The formula is chanted on a basis of these three notes, variation of tone and note, though not of formula, producing the types of forms.

Second, those which are of a purely protective nature, and which, through a knowledge of the laws of sound as they are known in connection with water (or the astral plane), place a vacuum between the magician and the waters, as well as between him and his creation. This formula is based on the sounds connected with air as well, for it is through placing around himself a protecting shell of air atoms, esoterically understood, that the magician guards himself from the approach of the water builders.

Third, those which, when sounded, produce two results: the sending forth of the perfected creation, so that it may take to itself a physical body, and next, the dispersal of the building forces, now that their work is completed.

This last set of formulas is of exceeding interest, and were they not so powerful the magician might find himself cumbered with the produce of his thought, and the prey of a vital form, and of certain "devas of the waters" who would never leave him until they had completely drained from him all the "waters of his nature," absorbing it into their own nature, and producing his astral death. The curious phenomenon would then be seen of the Ego or solar Angel being incarnated in the mental sheath, yet separated from the physical body, owing to the occult "drowning" of the magician. There is nothing left for the Ego to do then but to snap the sutratma or thread, and sever all connection with the lowest sheath. This lowest sheath then may persist for a short time, according to the strength of the animal life, but more probably death would immediately ensue.[4] Several magicians have perished thus.

RULE IX. *Condensation next ensues. The fire and waters meet, the form swells and grows. Let the magician set his form upon the proper path.*

This rule is very briefly summed up in the injunction: Let desire and mind be so pure and so equally apportioned and the created form so justly balanced that it cannot be attracted towards the destructive or "left-hand" path.

RULE X. *As the waters bathe the form created, they are absorbed and used. The form increases in its strength; let the magician thus continue until the work suffices. Let the outer builders cease their labors then, and let the inner workers enter on their cycle.*

One of the fundamental concepts which is grasped by all magical workers, is that both will and desire are *force emanations.* They differ in quality and vibration, but are essentially currents of energy, one forming an initial vortex or centre of activity, being centrifugal, and the other being centripetal, and the main factor in the accretion of matter into a form around the central vortex. This can be seen demonstrating in an interesting way in the case of the egoic lotus, where we have the will aspect forming the "jewel in the lotus," or the inner

---

[4] The courses open to the Divine Ego after separation are two.—S. D., III, 524.
    a. It can start a fresh series of incarnations.
    b. It can return to the 'bosom of the Father' and be gathered back to the Monad.
Two courses are open to the lower discarded self.—S. D., III, 525, 527.
    a. If with a physical body it becomes a soulless man.
      In this case there is hope.
    b. If without a physical body it becomes a spook, or one form of the Dweller on the Threshold.

centre of electrical energy, and the desire or love aspect forming the egoic lotus itself, or the form which hides the centre. The analogy in all form building holds good for gods, men and atoms. The solar system is (from the higher cosmic planes), seen as a vast blue lotus, and so on down the scale; even the tiny atom of substance can be so considered. The distinction between these various lotuses exists in the number and arrangement of the petals. The solar system is literally a twelve-petalled lotus, each petal being formed of forty-nine lesser petals. The planetary lotuses differ in each scheme, and one of the secrets of initiation is revealed when the number of the petals of

   a. Our earth planet,
   b. Our planetary polar opposite,
   c. Our complementary or equilibrising planet,

is committed to the initiate. Armed with this knowledge, he can then work out certain formulas of magic which enable him to create in the three spheres. It is the same basic concept which governs thought form building, and which enables a magician of white magic to produce objective phenomena on the physical plane. He works with the two types of energy, will and desire, and their equilibrising is what leads to the balancing of the pairs of opposites, and the subsequent release of energy-substance in the formation of the physical plane structure. The magician has to know the following facts:

The formulas for the two aspects of logoic energy, will and desire. This is literally apprehension of the note and formula of the Brahma or substance aspect, and the note and formula of the Vishnu, or building aspect. One he ascertains because he has mastered matter; the other is revealed to him when he has achieved group consciousness.

The formula for the particular type of energy substance which he is seeking to employ. This will have relation to that particular petal in the solar lotus from which the desired force emanates.

The formula for the particular type of energy which is transmitted to him via one or other of the three circles of petals in his own egoic lotus.

The formula for the particular petal in a circle of petals with which he may choose to work. All these concern primarily the will aspect, *as far as the thought form to be produced is concerned,* for the magician is the will, or purpose, or spirit behind the objective phenomenon which he is in process of producing.

The formula which sweeps into activity (and thus produces a form), those Agnisuryans who are energised by any particular aspect of solar force. Where the two forces are brought into contact, the form is produced, or the third energy centre appears or manifests:

a. The energy of the will aspect.

b. The energy of the desire or love aspect.

c. The energy of the consequent thought form.

There is no contradiction here to the occult teaching that Father and Mother, or Spirit and Matter, when brought into contact, produce the Son. The difficulty which students have to surmount consists in the true interpretation of the three terms: Mother—Matter—Moisture (or the waters).

In creation, the three vibratory spheres:

1. The dense physical...... Mother..... Matter,
2. The etheric..............Matter .....Holy Spirit,
3. The astral.............. Moisture... Water,

work as a unit, and in the occult teaching, during the earlier stages of creation, must not be separated or distinguished apart. On the path of involution, if the subject may be approached from a different angle, and thus somewhat clarify, distinctions are made, and on the path of evolution, or of return, they are, as we well know, surmounted; on the middle point of equilibrium, as on our globe, for instance, confusion ensues in the mind of the student owing to the occult fact that the various formulas are being employed simultaneously, the thought-forms are at all stages of construction, and the ensuing chaos is terrible.

The rule which we are commenting upon may be interpreted as stating that in the magical work, the energy of the waters becomes paramount, and desire for the form and the fulfilment of its objective increases. This takes place after the will energy has formed the central nucleus by being brought into contact with the desire force. The magician, through desire (or strong motive), increases the vitality of the form until it is so powerful and intense in its own separated life that it is ready to go forth on its mission upon the physical plane. The building devas who have been impelled to construct the form out of the myriads of elemental lives available, have completed their work, and now cease from constructing; this particular type of energy no longer drives the lesser lives in any specific direction, and the final cycle of work upon the astral plane is entered upon. This is summed up in the next rule.

> Rule XI. *Three things the worker with the law must now accomplish. First, ascertain the formula which will confine the lives within the ensphering wall; next, pronounce the words which will tell them what to do and where to carry that which has been made; and finally, to utter forth the mystic phrase which will save him from their work.*

The embodied idea has now form and shape upon the astral plane; but all is as yet in a state of flux, and the lives are only held in place through the fixed attention of the magician, working through the greater builders. He must, through knowledge of certain magical phrases, make the work more permanent and independent and fix the place of the vitalising elements within the form, and give them an impetus that will result in more settled concretion. Having accomplished that, he becomes, if it might so be expressed, an agent of Karma, and sends forth the dual thought form (clothed in mental and astral matter), to fulfil its mission, whatever that may be. Finally, he has to take steps to protect himself from the attractive forces of his own nature, which might eventuate in his holding the thought form so closely within the radius of his own influence that it would be rendered useless, its own inherent energy neutralised, and its purpose negated.

They might also produce such a powerful, attractive force that he would draw the form so closely to himself that he would be forced to absorb it. This can be harmlessly accomplished by the man who knows how, but results, nevertheless, in a waste of energy which is forbidden under the Law of Economy. With the majority of men, who are oft unconscious magicians, many thought forms are malicious or destructive, and react back upon their creators in a disastrous manner.

c. Four Rules for the Physical Plane. In the magical work of form creation, we have carried the thought form down from the mental plane where the solar Angel initiated the work, through the astral, where the equilibrising work was done, to the physical plane, or to the etheric levels. Here the work of producing objectivity is carried forward, and here the worker in magic is in critical danger of failure should he not be cognisant of the forms and mantrams by which the new group of builders can be reached, and the gap between the astral plane and the gaseous subplane of the physical be bridged. It might be useful here to remember that in the work of creation the white magician avails himself *of the current Ray influence.* When the third, fifth and seventh rays are in power, either coming in, at full meridian, or passing out, the work is much easier than when the second, sixth or fourth are dominant. At the present time, the seventh Ray, as we know, is rapidly dominating, and it is one of the easiest of the forces with which man has to work. Under this Ray it will be possible to build a new structure for the rapidly decaying civilisation, and to erect the new temple desired for the religious impulse. Under its influence the work of the numerous unconscious magicians will be much facilitated. This will eventuate in the rapid growth of unconscious psychic phenomena, in the spread of mental science, and the consequent ability of thinkers to acquire and to create those tangible benefits they desire. Nevertheless, this magic of the unconscious or selfish kind leads to karmic results of a deplorable nature, for only those who work with the law and who control the lesser lives through knowledge, love and will, evade the consequences entailed on those who manipulate living matter for selfish ends.

The white magician utilises solar forces. As the planet passes around the sun different types of solar energy are contacted, and expert knowledge is required to utilise the influences in due *time,* and to have the form so constituted that it can respond at the needed hour to the differentiated energy.

He manipulates planetary force of a triple nature:

a. That which is the product of his own planet, and the most easily available.
b. That which emanates from the polar opposite of our planet.
c. That which can be felt originating from that planet which forms, with our earth and its opposite, the esoteric triangle.

Students need here to remember that we are now dealing with etheric matter and vital energy, and are therefore concerning ourselves with the physical plane and all that is included in that term. They need likewise to remember that the magician (as he is working on the plane of objectivity) is in a position to use his own vital forces in the work of thought form creation, but this is only possible and permissible when he has reached the point in evolution where he is a channel for force and knows how to draw it within himself, transmute it, or combine it with the forces of his own body, and then transmit it to the thought form which he is in process of constructing. Much of interest will open up before the thinker who extends this idea to the planetary Logos and His work of form creating.

With these few preliminary remarks, we can now continue with the Rules of Magic for the physical plane.

RULE XII. *The web pulsates. It contracts and expands. Let the magician seize the midway point and thus release those "prisoners of the planet" whose note is right and justly tuned to that which must be made.*

It is necessary for the magician here to remember that all that takes place upon the earth is to be found within the planetary etheric web. The worker in white magic, being an occultist, deals in universals, and starts his magical work on the confines of the physical etheric sphere. His problem is to locate those lesser lives, within the web, who are of the right order to be built into the proposed thought vehicle. Such work can necessarily only be done by the man who, through the severance of the confining web of his own etheric web, can reach out to that which is consciously recognised by him as the planetary vital body. *Only he who is free can control and utilise those who are prisoners.* This is an occult axiom

of real moment, and much of the failure undergone by
would-be workers in magic is to be traced to the fact that
they themselves are not free. The "prisoners of the
planet" are those myriads of deva lives who form the
planetary pranic body, and are swept in on the floods of
vital force emanating from the physical sun.

> RULE XIII. *The magician must recognise the four; note
> in his work the shade of violet which they evidence,
> and thus construct the shadow. When this is so, the
> shadow clothes itself, and the four become the seven.*

This means literally that the magician must be in a
position to discriminate between the different ethers, and
to note the special hue of the different levels, thereby
ensuring a balanced building of the "shadow." He "recognises" them in the occult sense; that is, he knows their
note and key, and is aware of the particular type of
energy they embody. Enough emphasis has not been
laid upon the fact that the three higher levels of the
etheric planes are in vibratory communication with the
three higher planes of the cosmic physical plane, and
they (with their ensphering fourth level) have been called
in the occult books "the inverted Tetraktys." It is this
knowledge which puts the magician in possession of the
three types of planetary force and their combination, or
the fourth type, and thus releases for him that vital
energy which will drive this idea into objectivity. As the
different types of forces meet and coalesce, a dim shadowy
form clothes itself upon the vibrating astral and mental
sheath, and the idea of the solar Angel is attaining definite concretion.

> RULE XIV. *The sound swells out. The hour of danger
> to the soul courageous draweth near. The waters
> have not hurt the white creator and naught could
> drown nor drench him. Danger from fire and flame*

menaces now, and dimly yet the rising smoke is seen. Let him again, after the cycle of peace, call on the solar Angel.

The work of creation assumes now serious proportions, and for the final time the body of the magician is menaced by destruction. The "shadow" having been formed, it is now ready to take to itself a "fiery" or gaseous body, and it is these fire builders who menace the life of the magician, and this for the following reasons.

Firstly, because the fires of the human body are closely allied to the fires with which the magician seeks to work, and should these latent fires of the body and the latent fires of the planet be brought into too close juxtaposition, the creator is in danger of burning and destruction.

Secondly, the Agnichaitans, being *allied* to the "fire devas" of the mental plane, have much power, and can only be controlled properly by the solar Angel Himself.

Thirdly, on this planet the planetary fires are not as yet dominated by solar fire, and are very easily driven into the work of destruction.

The solar Angel must, therefore, now again be invoked. This means that the magician (when his "shadow" is completed, and prior to the final stages of concretion) must see to it that his alignment with the Ego is just and unimpeded, and the communicating currents in full play. He must literally "renew his meditation," and make direct contact afresh before proceeding with the work. Otherwise, the fires of his own body may get out of control, and his etheric body suffer in consequence. He, therefore, fights fire with fire, and draws down solar fire for his protection. This was not necessary on the astral plane. For the magician, the moments of the greatest danger in the work of creating are at certain junctures on the astral plane, where he is in danger of occult drowning, and at the transition from etheric levels

to the planes of tangible concretion, when he is menaced
by "occult burning." In the one case, he does not call
on the Ego, but stems the tide by love and the equilibrising powers of his own nature. In the latter case, he
must call in that which represents the will aspect in the
three worlds, the impulsive, dynamic thinker or solar
Angel. He accomplishes this by means of a mantram.
No clue can be given to this, owing to the powers it
confers.

> RULE XV. *The fires approach the shadow, yet burn it
> not. The fire sheath is completed. Let the magician
> chant the words that blend the fire and water.*

Little can here be said in interpretation of these words,
beyond a reference to the general sense. The gaseous
sheath is created, and the hour for the formation of the
sheath for the sixth subplane, the liquid, is near. The two
must blend. This is the moment of the greatest danger,
as far as the thought form itself is concerned. Earlier
dangers have menaced the magician. Now the form he is
creating must be protected. The nature of the danger is
hinted at in the words: "Where fire and water meet apart
from chanted sound, all dissipates in steam. The fire
ceases to be." This danger is hid in the karmic enmity
existing between the two great groups of devas. These
groups can only be united by the mediator, man.

It might be asked of what use the fifteen rules for magic
communicated above may be. Naught, as yet, as far as
practical work is concerned, but much where inner intellectual development is desired. He who meditates and
broods over these rules in the light of what has been earlier communicated anent the devas and building forces,
will arrive at an understanding of the Laws of Construction in the macrocosm, which will avail him much, and
save him much time when the magical work and formulas
are put in his hands.

SECTION TWO

DIVISION E

MOTION ON THE PLANE OF MIND

I. INTRODUCTORY REMARKS

We have now concluded our consideration of thought forms, having viewed the whole universe (including man) as an embodied thought, and having dealt with the ability

1027

of man himself to create forms for the clothing of his
ideas.

We now return once more to the realm of technicalities, and to the more scientific part of our thesis. I use
the word "scientific," for that which will be said concerns
that which is proven and known to occultists, and deals
with *facts*. The modern fact of the modern scientist is
his approximation of a part, and often an infinitesimal
part, of some greater whole, and even then it concerns
only the most objective part of manifestation, for that
which is the essence is not regarded as a reality at all by
them as it is by the real occult knower. That which we
see and can touch is but an *effect* of inner underlying
causes. The occultist does not concern himself with
effects, but only with their originating cause. The modern scientist, therefore, is not as yet occupying himself
with causes, and during the past only approached the
realm of these initiatory impulses when he began to comprehend the energy aspect of matter, and to consider
the nature of the atom. When he can pass more directly
in his thoughts to the discussion and consideration of the
etheric substratum which underlies the tangible, then and
only then will he be entering the domain of causes, and
even in this case, only those physical causes which underlie the grossly objective; he will not really have ascertained the vital impulses which produce Being. Yet a
great step will have been made for, under the Law of
Analogy, he will then be in a position to comprehend some
of the major secrets of solar manifestation; for the
planes of our solar system constitute, as we know, and
as this Treatise seeks to demonstrate, the seven subplanes of the cosmic physical plane.

It is apparent to all careful students of this *Treatise
on Fire* that in this section we are concerned with:

First, that mode of activity which distinguishes the
Vishnu aspect of Deity, or the motion of the Divine Man-

asaputras. This involves, therefore, a consideration of the effects of this motion:

   a. Within the planetary schemes, Their bodies.

   b. Upon the atoms or "Points" in those bodies, the human and deva Monads.

Second, that impulse which is the basis of the Law of Periodicity, and which results in the cyclic incarnation of all Beings. This impulse manifests in three cycles or in three turns of the wheel of Being.

   a. The activity which produces involution, or the submergence in matter of Life or Spirit.

   b. The activity which produces the equilibrium of these two forces, matter and Spirit, or manifestation, or the processes of evolution.

   c. The activity which withdraws the central energy from out of the responsive form and produces obscuration.

Third, that activity which causes the interplay—attraction and consequent repulsion—between all atoms, from the great cosmic atom, a solar system, to the tiny atom of the chemist or the physicist. This activity, therefore, may be viewed as:

   a. Inter-cosmic, or affecting constellations.

   b. Inter-planetary, or affecting the schemes.

   c. Inter-chain, or affecting the chains.

   d. Inter-globular, or producing an interchange of force between the globes of the chains.

   e. Inter-sectional, or affecting the transference of force between the five kingdoms of nature.

   f. Inter-human, or relating to the interplay between the various human units.

   g. Inter-atomic, or the passage of force from one atom to another atom.

Students need here to remember that we are concerned with the energy or activity which produces *forms*, and, therefore, with the forces which tend to coherence, to concretion, and to the stabilisation of the work of the builders. If they but realised it, the key to much that is connected with the production of forms, or of the Son, the second aspect, is contained in the above tabulation, for all nature holds together, and the life of any scheme, globe, kingdom, or atom, becomes in turn the animating principle of another scheme, globe, kingdom, or atom. Everything in the solar system is in a state of flux, as is everything in the universe, and the vital energy circulates, as the blood or the nervous energy of the body circulates, throughout the entire system. This is the basis of the occult fact that all in nature, for instance, will be, is, or has been, through the human kingdom.[5] Under this type of solar activity, the ultimate good is attained by the method of interplay, interchange, and in mutual attraction and repulsion.

It would be advisable here if students would study that which was communicated in the early part of this treatise upon motion upon the physical and astral planes. Under the Law of Analogy, much will be noted as necessarily translated on to the higher plane, and to be transmuted into the energy of the form-building impulse. We will consider what we have to say in this section under the following heads:

1. The nature of this motion...........spiral cycling
2. The results of its activity. These results can be viewed as four subsidiary laws or adjuncts to the major law of Attraction, and may be called:
    The Law of Expansion.
    The Law of Monadic Return.
    The Law of Solar Evolution.
    The Law of Radiation.

[5] S. D., I, 215, 242, 295.

It will, therefore, be apparent that, as we consider these laws, we are dealing with matters that concern:

The process of initiation.

The life of the divine pilgrims upon the upward arc.

The impulse which produces the Son, and which drives Him to gain experience through the medium of the solar system.

Magnetism, or Divine Alchemy.

3. The turning of the wheel,
    a. The solar wheel,
    b. The planetary wheel,
    c. The human wheel.

This will involve our taking up the consideration of the orbital paths of these various spheres, their centres, interplay and intercommunication, and of force transference, and will bring out the concept that all spiral-cyclic activity is not the result of the rotary action of matter itself, but of an impulse emanating from without any particular atom, and therefore extraneous to it.

4. Motion, or the form-building impulse latent in:
    a. The mental sheath itself, both cosmically and humanly considered.
    b. The causal body of the macrocosm and the microcosm.
    c. The centres, divine and human.

5. The effects of the united activity of the sheath, the centres, and the causal body as it produces:
    a. Periodic manifestation.
    b. The linking of the triangles.
    c. The relation between the throat centre, the alta major centre, and the mental centre, macrocosmically and microcosmically considered.

II. THE NATURE OF THIS MOTION

As we well know, the nature of the motion on the plane of matter is *rotary*. Each atom of matter rotates on its own axis, and each larger atom, from the purely physical standpoint, likewise does the same; a cosmic atom, a solar system, a planetary atom, and a human atom, man, can be seen equally rotating at differing degrees of velocity upon their own axis or around their own pole. When we arrive at the plane of mind, and have to consider the activity of the second aspect of divinity, that which builds and holds the forms in coherent form, and which is the basis of the phenomenon we call *time* (literally, the awareness of the form), a different type of force or motion becomes apparent. This type of energy in no way negates or renders useless the atomic rotary type, but involves it, and yet at the same time it brings the atoms of all degrees under the influence of its own activity, so that in every form which is in manifestation, the two types are manifested. I would here remind the student that we are primarily considering the force of the second aspect as it concerns the human and superhuman kingdoms, or as the Manasaputras and their various groups are concerned. On the involutionary arc, the Vishnu force is likewise felt, but until the nature of the group soul is more apprehended, and the quality of the Life who informs each of the subhuman kingdoms of nature is known with greater accuracy, it will profit us more to deal with force as it affects the human being, the planet on which he may be found, and the system in which that planet is playing its part.

The activity of the second aspect has been called *spiral-cyclic,* which in itself involves the concept of duality. This activity is the cause of all cyclic evolution, and has been called in the occult phraseology ''the activity of Brahma's year.'' It is that which brings about the periodical appearing and disappearing cf all existences, great or small. It is intimately linked with the will aspect of Divinity, and with the Lipika Lords of the highest degree and its origin is, therefore, difficult for us to comprehend. Perhaps all that can be said about it is that it is largely due to certain impulses which (as far as our solar system is concerned) can be traced to the sun Sirius. These impulses find their analogy in the impulses emanating in cyclic fashion from the causal body of man, which impulses bring about his appearance upon the plane of maya for a temporary period. A hint may here be given to the earnest student; in the threefold Ego (the lives who form the central bud, the lives of the petals, and the triple group of lives who form the three permanent atoms) is seen a correspondence to the three groups of Lipika Lords who are the karmic cause of solar manifestation, and who control its periodic manifestation. These three groups are related to Their guiding Intelligences on Sirius.

The Law of Periodicity is the effect produced by the amalgamation of these two types of force with a third. The two types of force or energy are the activity of the first Aspect, the logoic will or purpose, and the energy of the second aspect. This purpose is hidden in foreknowledge of the Logos and is completely hidden even from the Adept of the fifth Initiation. The Adept has achieved a comprehension of the purpose of the Son, and for Him there remains the problem to recognise the purpose of the Father. The one is the impulse behind the *forward* movement of all life, and the other the impulse behind its cyclic activity, and this is called spiral-cyclic. When this blended dual force is brought in touch with the rotary activity of matter itself, we have the triple activity of the Ego, for instance, which is rotary-spiral-cyclic, and that which results in the stimulation of the self-contained atom, in the periodical emergence of form, and in the steady, though slow, progress towards a goal. We might, for the sake of clarity, differentiate the effects thus:

1. Rotary activity .. The internal activity of every atom viewed as a unity, the activity of Brahma or the Holy Spirit, perfected in the first solar system. It is unified *individual* consciousness . . . "I am."

2. Cyclic activity ... The activity of all forms, viewing them from the aspect of consciousness, and of time. It is unified group consciousness . . . "I am That," the activity of Vishnu in process of being perfected in this the second solar system.

3. Spiral activity .. The influence which impresses all forms, which emanates from their greater centre, and which merges itself a little, a very little, with the two other modes of motion, being practically lost sight of in the stronger vibration. It is the activity which will be perfected in the third solar system, and is the Shiva form of motion, and the unified consciousness of all groups. It is the consciousness which proclaims "I am That I am."

One of the primary things the occult student should remember when considering the nature of spiral-cyclic activity, is that it has two effects.

First, it is an attractive force, gathering the rotating atoms of matter into definite types and forms, and holding them there as long as necessity demands.

Secondly, it is itself gradually dominated by another and higher vibration, and through its spiralling progress through matter it sweeps those forms systematically nearer and nearer to another and stronger point of energy.

These effects are to be seen clearly demonstrated in man's evolution in the approach he makes uniformly through the cycles to the centre of the spiral-cyclic energy, and subsequently to the still more impressive point, that of his "Father in Heaven." The Angel first attracts animal man; cyclically He actuates the material sheaths, thus giving them coherence, and ever swings them into closer relation to himself. Later, as the momentum is increased, the man is swung more definitely into relation with the monadic aspect, until that higher rhythm is imposed upon him. This is equally true of a planetary Logos, and of a solar Logos.

The spiral-cyclic force demonstrates, as might be expected, in seven ways; of these, the three major methods of demonstration are symbolised in the Rod of Initiation of Sanat Kumara. The Rod most frequently recognised by men is that of the Hierophant, the Bodhisattva, which consists of the straight central serpent with the two others entwined around it, thus picturing, among other things:

a. The three outpourings,
b. The three worlds,
c. The spinal column and its channels,

or those main factors with which the initiate concerns himself. He has to understand somewhat the nature of matter and what is occultly involved in that expression, his own triple constitution, the three worlds in which he has to play his part, and the instrument which he has to use. This rod of the Bodhisattva is surmounted by a diamond which is not as great a diamond as the "Flaming Diamond" of the first Kumara, but is of rare beauty. At the time of initiation when the electrical forces are tapped, this diamond revolves on its axis, picturing the rotary nature of atomic matter.

The Rod of Sanat Kumara is far more intricate, and instead of the central Rod, or Serpent, standing on the tip of its tail, all the three serpents are interwoven in a spiral fashion, and the Flaming Diamond which sur-

mounts it is of such radiance that the effect is produced
of a spheroidal aura, cast around the interlaced serpents,
typifying the form-building nature of the Vishnu
activity.

According to the initiation taken, a reflection will be
seen from a part of the interlaced serpents, and the
illusion will be created that the diamond is cycling up and
down between the summit, and the irradiated portion.

At the same time, each serpent revolves upon itself,
and likewise cycles around its neighbor, producing an
effect of extraordinary brilliance and beauty, and typifying rotary-spiral-cyclic force.

The seven types of spiral-cyclic energy are suggestive
of the nature of the planetary Logoi which they represent, and produce, therefore, the distinctions which exist
between men; they are accountable for the nature of
cycles, and this is a point oft overlooked. Students discuss the periods of the emergence of the Rays, setting
arbitrary dates, such as 2500 years, for the manifestation
of any particular ray. One ray does pass through its
cycle in that length of time, but only one, the others
being either longer or shorter. The difference has a
great effect upon the egoic cycles, and is responsible for
the length of time between incarnations. Some Egos
cycle through their incarnations and their pralayas very
rapidly; others spend untold aeons, and hence it is impossible to say that there are even "averages" connected with the appearance of Egos on the astral plane,
for instance. This fact has bearing upon the statement
of H. P. B. anent the Lodge effort each one hundred
years. Under the particular type of cyclic force emanating from the Lodge, the high water mark of its activity
is to be found once in every seven cycles. All that originates on that Ray is controlled by spiral-cyclic efforts
based upon the number 10 and its multiples, and finding
its highest cyclic vibration, as it happens, during the last

quarter of each century. What our more modern students are apt to forget in this connection is that this activity is but the demonstration of one type of force out of seven possible and that it concerns primarily that group of adepts who are on that particular line of energy, and will necessarily affect greatly all disciples and people on a similar line. At the same time, the work it initiates is endorsed by the Lodge as a whole, for it is part of the force emanation of the planetary Logos. It is naturally of great importance owing to the fact that this ray-energy is that of one of the three major Rays; but it will be, in the equilibrising process, balanced by analogous cyclic emanatory activity from the two other major Rays.

It might be added here that when this is recognised it will become apparent that the revolutionising scientific discoveries which can be traced down the centuries, such as the formulation of the Law of Gravitation, the circulation of the blood, the ascertainment of the nature of steam, the discovery by man of that form of electrical phenomena which he has harnessed, and the more recent discovery of radium, are in their own department (that of the Mahachohan), analogous to the effort made during the last quarter of each century to stimulate the evolution of men through a further revelation of some part of the *Secret Doctrine*. Newton, Copernicus, Galileo, Harvey, and the Curies are, on their own line of force, lightbringers of equal rank with H. P. B. All revolutionised the thought of their time; all gave a great impulse to the ability of man to interpret the laws of nature, and to understand the cosmic process, and only those of circumscribed vision will fail to recognise the unity of the many force impulses emanating from the one Lodge.

These cycles will not coincide, for they are not all similar to the one hundred year spiral. Some idea as to the Mahachohan's cycle of emanatory impulses may be gathered by considering the dates of the foremost scientific discoveries since Plato's time; the cycles of the second ray may also be averaged by a summary of the appearances of the great Teachers down the ages.

The force emanations from the Manu, or those of the first Ray, are easily traced when the races are considered, and this has been done in the recognition of the races and subraces. What is oft overlooked is that each of these rays of energy demonstrates *constructively,* through the form-building agencies, and *destructively* through the ability of the force to destroy prior to building. Thus the cycles can be viewed from two angles.

It is at this point that students in one branch of our theosophical movement must recognise the fact that just as H. P. B. came forth on a cyclic tide of energy to destroy the limiting forms to be found in the world of science and religion, so his work must fit in with other force emanations, such as the constructive work of the second ray in conjunction with the energy of the seventh at this time.

When students learn to blend the one hundred year cycles of the first type of energy with the equally powerful impulses from the second Ray and the third, we shall then have a cessation of many controversies. *No great impulse will come from the Lodge along the line of the first Ray of Will or Power till the close of a century.* One such impulse along another line of force came when the discovery of the nature of the atom was arrived at through the study of electricity, and of radioactive substances, and *an impulse from the second aspect is imminent.* It is not safe for students with limited vision to dogmatise anent this question of cycles. Apart from the cyclic impulses continuously going forth, overlapping and superseding, and intermingling with each other, there are many which we might call lesser impulses (and the cycle of one hundred years to which H. P. B. refers.

is but one of the lesser impulses. There is a one thousand year cycle of greater moment). There are vaster cycles, of 2500 years, of 7,000 years, of 9,000 years, of 15,000 years, and many others which only advanced initiates know of or can follow; these can break in upon any of the lesser impulses, and can be seen appearing, unexpectedly, as far as average man's knowledge is concerned, and yet they are but the returning impulses set in cyclic motion perhaps thousands of years ago.

H. P. B. is right in his affirmation as far as the impulse of the first ray is concerned; but his followers are not right, in so far as they overlook and negate the six other types of impulses, of equal or of more importance, which may emanate cyclically from the Lodge, and which will meet with response from those who vibrate to that particular type of energy.

III.   RESULTS OF ITS ACTIVITY.

These results can be studied in four ways, considering each as a subsidiary Law of the basic Law of Attraction and Repulsion. All motion is the result literally of the impact, or intercourse, between atoms, and there is no atom anywhere which escapes this force. In the case of *rotary* motion, which governs the activity of the atom of substance, the impulse emanates from within the ring-pass-not, and is produced by the impact of the positive charge upon the negative charges. This is true of all atoms, cosmic, solar, individual, chemical, and so forth.

When, however, the effect of the rotation of the atom is so strong that it begins to affect other atoms outside its individual ring-pass-not, another influence begins to make itself felt, which draws together, or dissipates, those contacting coalescing atoms. Thus forms are built under the impulse of aggregated forces of some one kind, and these forms in turn produce effects on other cohering atomic forms, until the rhythm is built up, and a vibra-

tion instigated which is a continuation of the rotary motion of the individual atoms, and the modification produced on them by their group activity. This causes progression and simultaneous rotation. The movement forward is modified considerably by the internal atomic
activity, and this it is which causes that motion we call
spiral cyclic. It demonstrates in all forms as a tendency
to repeat, owing to the backward pull of the rotating
atoms, and yet is offset by the strong progressive impulse of the form activity. Students can work this out
in connection with:

The planetary Logos, as He manifests through the
    rounds, each one of which, in its earlier stages, re-
    capitulates all that has previously occurred.
Man, in the ante-natal period, in which he runs through
    the various stages of development.
Spiritual man, as he creates that which will destroy
    the "Dweller on the Threshold."

This spiral-cyclic activity, which is distinctive of all
forms, can perhaps be comprehended more practically if
we study it as an expression of four laws, taking each
one briefly in turn:

1. *The Law of Expansion.*

This law of a gradual evolutionary expansion of the
consciousness indwelling every form is the cause of the
spheroidal form of every life in the entire solar system.
It is a fact in nature that all that is in existence dwells
within a sphere.[6] The chemical atom is spheroidal; man

---

[6] *The Atom.*—S. D., I, 113, 566. It is on the illusive nature of matter
and the infinite divisibility of the atom that the whole Science of Occultism
is built.
  1. Everything is atomic—God, Monads, atoms.
      a. The sphere of solar manifestation................... God
          The mundane egg. The logoic auric egg............ Macrocosm
      b. The sphere of monadic manifestation................ Monads
          The monadic auric egg............................ Microcosm
      c. The sphere of the ultimate physical atom............ Atoms

dwells within a sphere, as does the planetary Logos and the solar Logos, this sphere being the form matter takes when its own internal activity, and the activity of the form are working in unison. It requires the two types of force—rotary and spiral-cyclic—to produce this. Scientists are beginning to recognise this more or less, and to realise that it is the Law of Relativity, or the relation between all atoms, which produces that which is called Light, and which, in its aggregated phenomena, forms that composite sphere, a solar system. The motion of the constellations *external* to the solar sphere is responsible for its form in conjunction with its own rotary motion in space. As the wave lengths of the light from the constellations, and their relation to the sun are better understood, and as the effect of those wave lengths or light vibrations (which are either attractive to, or repulsive to, the sun) are understood, much will be revealed. Little has as yet been grasped as to the effect

2. The solar system is a cosmic atom.
3. Each plane is an atom or complete sphere.
4. Each planet is an atom.
5. Each Heavenly man is an atomic unit.
6. Each human Monad is an atom in the body of one of the Heavenly Men.
7. The causal body is an atom, or sphere.
8. The physical plane elemental is an atomic unit.
What is an atom?
1. A sheath formed of the matter of the solar system in one or other of its seven grades and indwelt by life of some kind.
    a. Absolute intelligence informs each atom.—S. D., I, 298.
    b. Absolute life informs each atom.—S. D., I, 278, 281; II, 742, note.
2. Atoms and souls are synonymous terms.—S. D., I, 620-622.
    a. In this solar system atoms and souls are synonymous terms. The Primordial Ray plus the Divine Ray of Wisdom.
    b. In the previous solar system atoms and mind were probably synonymous terms. It resulted in the Primordial Ray of active intelligent matter, the basis of the present evolution.
    c. In the next system atoms and the third factor, pure spirit may be synonymous terms. The Primordial Ray and The Divine Ray plus the third cosmic Ray of Will or Power.
3. Atoms are inseparable from Spirit.—S. D., I, 367.
    a. They are the sheaths through which the informing God manifests
    b. The form of the sheath is a sphere.
    c. The quality of the sheath is latent love.
    d. The matter of the sheath is active intelligent substance.

those constellations in the heavens (which are antagonistic to the solar system), have upon it, and whose wave
lengths it will not transmit, whose rays of light do not
pierce (if it might be expressed in so unscientific a manner) through the solar periphery.

We are told in the *Secret Doctrine* that "the seven
solar Rays dilate to seven suns and set fire to the whole
cosmos."[7] This it is which produces that final burning
which ushers in the great pralaya, and brings to an end
the logoic incarnation. It is produced under this Law
of Expansion, and causes that eventual merging and
blending of the seven sacred planetary schemes which
marks the achievement of the goal, and their eventual
perfection.

In occult literature this term "Law of Expansion" is
limited to the discussion of the seven Rays, and to the
subject of the *planetary* initiations. When dealing with
the expansions of consciousness of the human being, and
his initiations, we group them under the second "Law of
Monadic Return."

Students should here remember that we are dealing
with the expansions of consciousness of a planetary
Logos through the medium of:

a. The chains.
b. The rounds.
c. The kingdoms of nature.
d. The root races.

It should be remembered that the consciousness He is
in process of developing is that of the absolute will and
purpose of the solar Logos, as it is the expression of the
desire of the cosmic Logos.[8] Therefore, the expansions
might be grouped as follows:

[7] S. D., II, 72.
[8] The four sub-divisions of desire should be studied in the **Brahmana**
of the Sama-veda. (1) The desire to know; whence (2) **the desire to**
possess; thereafter (3) the desire to secure possession, *i.e.,* **to take the**

1. The solar Logos expands His consciousness to include the desire of the cosmic Logos.
2. The planetary Logos expands His consciousness to measure up to the will and purpose of the Solar Logos.
3. The Lords of the Chains are working at the *desire* consciousness (the love nature) of the planetary Logos.
4. The informing Lives of the globe in the chain are working at the intelligent consciousness of the planetary Logos.

This can be worked out in connection with a globe in a chain (such as our earth-chain) in the following manner.

The Lord of the world, the planetary Logos, in physical incarnation, works at His own peculiar problem, the bringing through (into physical manifestation upon the planet) of the *purpose* or will of the solar Logos in any particular scheme. This He does through meditation.

The totality of Dhyan Chohans of the fifth or spiritual kingdom are occupied with the working out into active manifestation of the will and purpose of the planetary Logos.

The human family, or the fourth kingdom, is seeking to make manifest the desire, or love nature, of the planetary Logos.

The three subhuman kingdoms have for objective the

---

necessary steps, the action, that will bring possession; and finally (4) the attainment—these respectively are the four sub-divisions, cognitive-desire, desire-proper, active-desire and summation-desire.

" 'The ruler of desire is Shiva and his instruction to his sub-hierarchs takes this shape: Behold, our work is the work of destruction. The order and the way thereof are these. This should be destroyed first, this afterwards; and such and such work of the nature of negation should be performed. First, make enquiry, entertain the 'desire to know,' and thoroughly and fully understand the nature of the I and the This. Then entertain the desire to possess, 'I shall obtain the This and the I.' Having obtained them, you will pass on to the Negation, to the declaration, 'no (I want them no more).' In the Negation is the summation, sam-a-hara, 'bringing all together,' and it is the sam-hara also, the 'taking all in,' re-absorption, destruction.' "—*Pranava-Vada*, p. 364.

manifesting of the intelligent nature of the planetary Logos.

All this done under the Law of Expansion, by the method of spiralling progression, cyclic growth, rotary repetition, and the summation of each greater spiral is the expansion of the consciousness into that of the sphere which enclosed the lesser ovoid, and the escape of the life imprisoned in the sphere. It is merged in its greater whole. As the fires of the sphere concerned blaze up, the "fire by friction" which produces rotary motion, and "solar fire," which is the basis of the spiral-cyclic activity, blend and merge. The ring-pass-not of the confining spheroidal wall is negated, and a blaze results.

The old Commentary expressed this as follows in connection with the planets, and it is equally, though relatively, true of the atom of substance, or the solar atom:

1. "The life pulsates, and the pole performs its function. The sphere revolves in many cycles. As it revolves it senses other spheres, and seeks to know their secret.

2. They meet each other. They seek a greater intimacy or reject with hatred any more approach. Some pass away; others return and marry. They know each other. They spiral through their courses hand in hand. Through union the fires blaze up, the two become the one, and live again in their Son, who is the Third."

Through the study of these significant words students may learn somewhat concerning "polar affinity," the "Marriage in the Heavens," the transference of the germs of life from the male attractive planet to the negative and receptive one, and finally, at a later period, the absorption of the life of the two planets by a third planet, who is called occultly "the Son." This refers to the synthesising planet which forms the apex of the solar triangle.

In summing up the effect of the union of individual atomic rotary motion and the spiral cyclic activity of all atomic groups, it is necessary to point out, therefore, that the following units are affected.

The essential individual atom. Its evolutionary progress towards self-determination is brought about by the effect of its group activity, or the motion of the form modifying its own inherent action.

The atomic form, likewise an atomic unit, rotating on its own axis and influenced and driven towards the centre of force of a higher macrocosm by the activity of its embracing kingdom.

The human atom, self-determined and individual, yet driven progressively forward by the influence of its group, or the potent activity of the Heavenly Man in Whose body it is the cell.

The planetary atom, equally self-determined, a composite of all planetary groups, rotating on its own axis, yet conforming to the cyclic-spiralling action, induced by the activity of the greater sphere in which it finds its place.

The solar Atom, also an individualised Life, the Son in incarnation, through the medium of the Sun, pursuing its own inherent cycle, yet spiralling in cyclic fashion through the heavens, and therefore, progressing through the effect of the extra-cosmic active Lives who either attract or repulse it.

These are the main sets of atomic groups, but there are many intermediate forms upon which it is not possible as yet to touch. All in nature affects that which it contacts, and these effects work either as

a.   Attractive or repulsive impulses.
b.   Retarding or accelerating impulses.
c.   Destructive or constructive impulses.
d.   Devitalising or stimulating impulses.
e.   Energising or disintegrating impulses.

Yet all can be expressed in terms of negative and positive force, manifesting as rotary or spiral activity. The lesser cycle can, from certain angles of vision, be regarded as appertaining to the rotary activity of certain atomic forms, and the greater cycles, which are so much more difficult for man to follow, as relating to the spiral action of the enclosing Life of the greater sphere. Every atom is part of a greater whole, even the solar atom is not a separated Life but a fragment of an immensity of Existence beyond the ken of man, and which is but dimly cognised by the most advanced Dhyan Chohan.

2. *The Law of Monadic Return.*

Here it is possible to study the Monad from the cyclic and energetic standpoint, and divorce our minds temporarily from that aspect of manifestation we call the human, or man.

In considering the "Divine Pilgrim" we can study him as demonstrating in the form of:

a. Three focal points of energy or force.
b. Three fires, each producing a definite effect, and each in turn producing effects upon each other.

In relation to a solar system, these three fires on the cosmic planes are called: [9]

[9] 1. The Names of the Sun mentioned in the *Secret Doctrine* are:
  a. Marttanda.—S. D., I, 61, 126-129, 483; II, 221.
  b. Agni.—S. D., II, 60, 400.
  c. Surya.—S. D., I, 127, 643.
  d. Helios.—S. D., II, 47.
  e. Apollo.—S. D., II, 6, 129.
2. The Sun in the S. D. is used in the three following connotations:
  a. The Central Spiritual Sun.—S. D., I, 519, 520, 700, 736; S. D., II, 120, 249, 251.
  b. The visible physical Sun.—S. D., I, 628.
  c. The three secondary Suns.—As above.
  Consider the Microcosm, manifesting through the causal body, which contains the three permanent atoms, the centres of force for the three bodies, the mental, astral and physical.
3. Consider the following three statements.—S. D. I., 574.
  a. In the Kosmos.......The Sun is the kama-rupa, or desire body of Akasha (the second aspect of Brahma). Compare 'Son of necessity.'—S. D., I, 74.

1. The central spiritual sun (essential).
2. The sun (subjective), called 'the heart of the sun.'
3. The physical sun (objective).

and the same thought can be carried through the monadic manifestation. The three monadic centres are distinguished by different types of energy:

1. Monadic—dynamic   energy . . . electric   impulse . . . pure fire.
2. Egoic—magnetic   energy . . . radiatory   impulse . . . solar fire.
3. Personal—individual energy . . . rotary impulse . . . fire by friction.

The first produces light, the second heat, and the third moisture or concretion.

By the interplay of the three types of force which constitute the three monadic aspects, a rhythm is set up which eventuates in the formation of:

A ring-pass-not, or ovoidal sphere, wherein the pilgrim is confined, and which contains within itself three major centres of force, corresponding to

    a. The three major logoic centres when the subjective or force side of existence is contemplated.

    b. The three permanent atoms if the purely objective side is in question.

A cyclic pulsation, which is the cause of every evolutionary impulse.

b. In the system........The Sun is the sixth principle, buddhi, and its vehicle. (The Dragons of Wisdom taking form on the fourth cosmic ether, our buddhic plane).

c. As an entity.........The Sun is the seventh principle of Brahma, or the aspect of active intelligent matter.

Hence 'rejection' as it is called ensues because *consciousness* or the development of the Ego (logoic or human) is the goal of evolution, and not the matter aspect. "The Primordial Ray is only the vehicle of the Divine Ray."—S. D., I, 108.

These evolutionary impulses may be regarded as three in number for a solar system, or for a Monad:

There is the impulse which drives every atom to self-determination, and is the secret of the phenomenon called individualisation. It is largely the force called Brahma.

There is the impulse which forces the individual atom towards group determination, and is the secret of the phenomenon termed "Initiation," or the process of passing out of the human or self-determined individualised Life into the higher kingdom. It is the sum total of the force of Vishnu, the second aspect, and produces the higher states of consciousness.

There is finally the impulse which forces the planetary groups, the sum total of all atoms and forms, to a conscious realisation of the nature of the all-enclosing group, the solar atom.

The Monad, acted upon by the Heavenly Man, intelligently forms his ring-pass-not. There his work ceases from the purely monadic standpoint; the inherent life of the atomic matter thus constituted produces the later phenomena. The rotary life of the atoms, and their interplay, modified by the Life of the planetary group, or Heavenly Man, pursued through long aeons, causes the phenomena of the various involutionary stages up to the point where certain of the atoms have evolved to the consciousness of animal-man. All through this inconceivable period (that is, in connection with our earth sphere) the milliards of atomic lives have pursued their courses, energised by the Life of the Monad, as it pulsates through the medium of the monadic heart on the spiritual plane; and equally they have responded to the larger rhythm of the Heavenly Man. This it is which has produced graded concretion, and brought animal-man to the stage where the upward pull of the Monad itself began to be felt. At the same time, the Monad on its own plane began to respond to the self-engendered energy of the lower form, the two rhythms contacted, individualisation occurred and the pilgrim manifested in his true nature.

Then—as far as concerns the Monad—progressive life forward begins. It is truly cyclic, repetitive and spiralling. At first the action, or the interplay between the rotary lower atomic form, and the influence of the Monad, is lethargic, slow and heavy, and the form retards the action of the Monad, and its heavy vibration tends to offset the higher. Gradually, as the sweeping spirals play their part, the higher vibration makes itself felt, and the activity, or motion, is more balanced, but lighter. Thus the cycles run until the higher rhythm or vibration is so dominant that the influence of the form is negated, and leads to its eventual discarding. Simultaneously with this, the highest rhythm of all makes itself felt, leading to increased activity upon the highest planes, and producing in time a negation of the sheath life of the Ego. As the old Commentary again says:

"The drops of moisture grow heavier. They break as rain upon the lowest plane. They sink into the clay and cause it to blossom. Thus do the waters cover the earth and all the cycles.

Two are the objectives of the fathering drops, and each attained in vastly separated cycles; one is to sink and lose itself in the dark soil of earth; the other to rise and merge itself in the clear air of heaven.

Between the two vast periods the heat doth play its part.

But when the heat grows fierce, and the fires within the earth and beneath the waters burn hot and flow, the nature of the many drops is seen to undergo a change. They dissipate in steam. Thus doth the heat perform its part.

Later again the fire electric flashes forth, and turns the steam to that which will permit its passage through the air."

We will now sum up briefly the various vibratory impulses which have a definite effect upon the Monad, and which must be borne in mind as we consider the evolution of the Divine Pilgrim. It is not the purpose of this *Treatise* to enlarge upon each distinctive impulse. It but seeks to indicate, leaving to later individual students the expansion of the imparted ideas.

1. Three impulses inherent in the three periodical vehicles, as H. P. B. terms the three main centres of energy through which the Monad manifests:

   a. The energy of the monadic ring-pass-not, viewing it as a unit.

   b. The energy of the causal body, within the monadic periphery.

   c. The energy of the physical body, the synthesis upon the physical plane of the force pouring through into manifestation through the three permanent atoms.

2. The activity set up in the seven etheric centres of force, the result of the activity of the seven principles:

   a. The head centre—an esoteric seven with an exoteric three.

   b. The throat centre.

   c. The heart centre—an esoteric three and exoteric seven.

   d. The solar plexus—an esoteric three and exoteric four.

   e. The organs of generation—an esoteric two.

   f. The base of the spine—an esoteric unity.

3. The inherent activity of every atom in every sheath, which produces the rhythm of the sheath.

4. The unified activity of every sheath or form which the divine Pilgrim uses.

5. The united active motion produced by the unification of the three vehicles, the seven sheaths, the force centres, and the atomic substance.

6. The effect produced by the action of the groups karmically allied with the Pilgrim. They are:

a. His Ray vibration, his monadic group.

b. His subray vibration, or the vibration of the egoic group.

c. His personality affiliations, such as his family, racial, and national energy. All of these play upon the sensitive atoms in the various bodies and produce specific effects.

7. The activity or motion initiated and stimulated by the life of any of the three lower kingdoms in nature,— all of which produce definite results.

8. The vibration of the particular planet upon which the monad may be seeking expression and experience.

9. The effect produced in the substance of the sheaths by the influences, or vibrations, of the various planets. This, esoterically understood, is the influence of some one or other of the solar centres, as the forces emanating from them play upon the planetary centres and thereby affect the involved monadic units. This is hidden in the karma of the Heavenly Man, and when true esoteric astrology comes into being then more anent this will be given out. Astrology as now studied and taught misleads more than it helps, and astrological students are as yet learning but the a-b-c of this stupendous subject, and are occupied with the exoteric fringes of that great veil which has been wisely thrown over all planetary lore.

10. Another form of energy which must ever be considered is that of the planetary Logos, as He pours His force through some one chain or some one globe upon the groups of evolving human units. This—from the human standpoint—cannot as yet be calculated, as it is dependent upon the occult "turning of the attention" by the planetary Logos in meditation upon any centre in His body corporate. It is, of course, all under cosmic law, but beyond the realisation of man. It involves cogni-

sance of the planetary individual purpose, which is not
revealed until the later initiations.

11. The inherent energy of the solar atom itself has
likewise a rhythmic effect upon the individual Monad,
and though it only reaches the monad via the greater
centres of Existence yet it has its effect upon one and
all. This is another factor not sufficiently recognised.

12. Finally, the energy of the greater life (in which
our solar system but forms a part) has to be reckoned
with, and the impulses emanating from the cosmic Logos,
the ONE ABOUT WHOM NAUGHT MAY BE SAID reach the
monadic lives and produce stimulation or retardation
according to the nature of the cosmic ideation. These
are necessarily entirely outside the ken of average man
and are only touched upon as no tabulation would be
complete without them.

13. There is also to be borne in mind the play of
energy which emanates from any one of those "Twelve
signs of the Zodiac" with which astrology concerns itself. This type of force is primarily concerned with
planetary stimulation, with the planetary Logoi, and is
hidden in Their cyclic karma,—a karma which of course
will incidentally involve those monads and devas which
form Their bodies and centres.

14. We must not ignore the three great waves of energy which sweep cyclically through the entire solar
system from:

a. The seven stars of the Great Bear. The strength
    of these vibrations depends upon the closeness of
    the connection and the accuracy of the alignment
    between any particular Heavenly Man and His
    Prototype. The mystery here is profound; it is
    connected with the stage in evolution of the "im-
    perfect gods" and the objective of the planetary
    deities.

b. The Seven Sisters, or the Pleiades, and from that one in particular who is occultly termed "the wife" of the planetary Logos whose scheme will eventually receive the seeds of life from our planet, which is not considered a sacred planet, as has before been stated.

c. The sun Sirius.

There are other streams of energetic force which have an effect upon the Pilgrim everywhere, but the above enumeration will serve to show the complexity of the subject and the vastness of the scheme of evolution. All these vibratory emanations pass through the sphere cyclically; they come and go, and according to their presence or their non presence and according to the stage of evolution of the emanating Existence will depend the phenomenal character of all life, will depend the nature of any specific period, and the quality of the manifesting Monads. It is the appearance or the disappearance of these waves of life-force (planetary, inter-planetary, systemic, cosmic and inter-cosmic) which sweeps into incarnation the divine pilgrims, and which brings about the cyclic manifestation of such great Lives as the "Silent Watcher" and the "Great Sacrifice"; it is this which causes also the dissolution of a scheme, and its reappearance, and is responsible for the transportation of the life seeds from one scheme to another, or from one solar system to another.

In this great tide of forces, the Monads are swept along; their aggregate is termed the "force of evolution," and the life and persistence of the initiatory Being sets the term for their duration. Man is but the plaything of the forces which gather him up and carry him on, just as the atom, in the human frame is but the obedient servant of the man's imposing direction; yet within limits man is the controller of his destiny; within limits he wields forces and energies, he manipulates lesser lives and controls lesser centres of energy, and as time slips away his radius of control becomes ever more extensive.

The atom controls its own central life; man can control the sets of lives who form his three bodies; the initiate and the adept are controlling energies of many kinds in the three worlds, as the Chohan does on the five planes of evolution. Thus the plan is carried forward until the Army of the Voice become themselves the Sounder of the Words, and the Sounders of the Words become the Word itself.

It will, therefore, be apparent, that the "Law of Monadic Return" which we have just been considering, is the sumtotal of those influences which have a direct bearing upon the monadic atoms, which affect its progress cyclically, and which stimulate it, or retard its activity according to the strength of the initiating life. It is only after initiation that the human atom reaches a stage in its development where forces and influences begin to be comprehended. When the methods are understood whereby adjustment is consciously made to extraneous force currents, resistance to retarding forces is initiated *consciously* and with scientific accuracy, and the man consciously puts himself into line with forces which will swing him along on the path of return. There is in this thought no undue complexity or cause for discouragement, for ever the potent force of electrical energy will offset the more lethargic vibration of solar fire, and solar fire itself in due time will negate the effects of "fire by friction."

3. *The Law of Solar Evolution.*

It is, of course, a truism to state that the Law of Solar Evolution is the sum-total of all the lesser activities.

We might consider this point in connection with the planetary atom, and the solar atom.

The planetary atom has, as all else in nature, three main activities:

First. It rotates upon its own axis, revolves cyclically within its own ring-pass-not, and thus displays its own inherent energy. What is meant by this phrase? Surely that the milliards of atoms which compose the planetary body (whether dense or subtle) pursue an orbital course around the central energetic positive unit. This dynamic force centre must be considered as subsisting naturally in two locations (if such an unsuitable term is permissible) according to the stage, usage, and particular type of the indwelling planetary entity.

    a. In what corresponds to the head centre in man, if the planetary Logos is of very advanced development.

    b. In the planetary correspondence to the heart centre.

The throat centre is, of course, ever vibrant in all the Logoi, as all are fully intelligent Creators, having perfected this capacity in an earlier solar system.

Students should here bear in mind that these centres of force are to be found depicted in the central Triangles upon the chart on page 373, though no indication is to be found through a study of such triangles as to the relative attainment of the planetary Logos. Within the chains likewise, will be found corresponding centres of energy, and also within the dense physical body of the Logos of any scheme, the physical planet.

One such centre is to be found at the North Pole, and two more are located within the planetary sphere, and frequently the inflow of force or energy to these internal centres (via the polar centre) results in those disasters we call earthquakes, and volcanic eruptions.

There is, as we know, a cyclic shifting of polar inclination, due to the gradually increasing responsiveness of the planetary Logos to His heavenly Prototype, whereby influences from the Great Bear draw, or occultly "attract," the attention of the Logos, and bring Him more into line with a greater impulsive Will. This shifting causes disruption in His lower manifestation, which is a condition on the cosmic Path of Initiation analogous to that undergone by a disciple.

The planetary atom revolves upon its axis and comes periodically under influences which produce definite effects. These influences are, among others, those of the moon, and of the two planets which lie nearest to it on either side—nearer and farther away from the Sun. The moon's influence is exceedingly strong, and has a curious resemblance (as far as the *physical* planet is concerned) to the "Dweller on the Threshold," which has such a familiar and potent effect upon the human atom. The resemblance must not be strained, for it should be borne in mind that the moon has no effect upon the Heavenly Man Himself, as His stage of evolution negates such a thing, but that the influence felt is by the planetary Entity—the sumtotal of the elemental essences of the planet. Scientific occult students will learn much anent the planetary scheme when they consider the influence of the moon's *karmic* pull upon the earth, coupled with the effect of the two neighboring planets, occultly understood.

Second, the planetary atom also revolves orbitally around its solar centre. This is its expression of rotary-spiral-cyclic action, and its recognition of the divine central magnet. This brings it under the constant impression of other schemes, each of which produces effects upon the planet. It likewise brings it under the inflowing streams of energy from what are termed the zodiacal constellations which reach the planetary scheme via the great centre, the Sun. It will be apparent to any student who has even slightly developed the power of visualisation, and has some realisation of the force currents of the solar system, that all can be regarded as the swirling tide of intermingling currents, with numerous focal points of energy demonstrating here and there, yet in no way static as to location.

The third activity of the planetary atom is that which carries it through space along with the entire solar system, and which embodies its "drift" or inclination towards the systemic orbit in the heavens.

The solar atom must be considered as pursuing analogous lines of activity and as paralleling on a vast scale the evolution of the planetary atom. The entire solar sphere, the logoic ring-pass-not, rotates upon its axis, and thus all that is included within the sphere is carried in a circular manner through the Heavens. The exact figures of the cycle which covers the vast rotation must remain as yet esoteric, but it may be stated that it approximates one hundred thousand years, being, as might be supposed, controlled by the energy of the first aspect, and therefore of the first Ray. This of itself is sufficient to account for varying and diverse influences which may be traced over vast periods by those with the "seeing eye," for it causes a turning of varying parts of the sphere to the differing zodiacal constellations. This influence (in connection with the planets) is increased or mitigated according to the place of the planets on their various orbital paths. Hence the immense complexity of the matter and the impossibility for the average astronomical and astrological student to make accurate computations or to draw accurate horoscopes. Within the Hall of Wisdom, there exists a department of which the modern varying astrological organisations are but the dim and uncertain reflections. The Adepts connected with it work not with humanity but concern Themselves specifically with "casting the horoscopes" (thus ascertaining the nature of the work immediately to be done) of the various great lives who inform the globes and kingdoms of nature, with ascertaining the nature of the karmic influences working out in the manifestation of three of the planetary Logoi:

1. Our own planetary Logos.
2. The planetary Logos of our polar opposite.
3. The planetary Logos of the scheme which makes with the two above mentioned a planetary triangle.

Beyond that, They may not go. They progress these various horoscopes for the next stated cycle, and Their records are of profound and significant interest. I would conjure students here to refrain from attempting (in years to come) to form cyclic computations of any kind, for as yet the many constellations which exist only in physical matter of an etheric nature are unknown and unseen. Yet they are potent in influence and until etheric vision is developed, all calculations will be full of error. It suffices for man as yet to master his own dharma, to fulfil group karma, and to dominate what is called "his stars."

Like the planetary atom, the solar atom not only rotates on its axis but likewise spirals in a cyclic fashion through the Heavens. This is a different activity to the *drift* or progressive dynamic motion through the Heavens. It deals with the revolution of our Sun around a central point and with its relation to the three constellations so oft referred to in this *Treatise:*

The Great Bear.
The Pleiades.
The Sun Sirius.

These three groups of solar bodies are of paramount influence where the spiral cyclic activity of our system is concerned. Just as in the human atom the spiral cyclic activity is egoic and controlled from the egoic body, so in connection with the solar system these three groups are related to the logoic Spiritual Triad, atma-buddhi-manas, and their influence is dominant in connection with solar incarnation, with solar evolution, and with solar progress.

Further, it must be added that the third type of motion to which our system is subjected, that of progress onward, is the result of the united activity of the seven constellations (our solar system forming one of the seven) which form the seven centres of the cosmic Logos. This united activity produces a uniform and steady *push* (if it might so be expressed) toward a point in the heavens unknown as yet to even the planetary Logoi.

The confines of the Heavens Themselves are illimitable and utterly unknown. Naught but the wildest speculation is possible to the tiny finite minds of men and it profits us not to consider the question. Go out on some clear starlit night and seek to realise that in the many thousands of suns and constellations visible to the unaided eye of man, and in the tens of millions which the modern telescope reveals there is seen the physical manifestation of as many millions of intelligent existences; this infers that what is visible is simply those existences who are in incarnation. But only one-seventh of the possible appearances are incarnating. Six-sevenths are out of incarnation, waiting their turn to manifest, and holding back from incarnation until, in the turning of the great wheel, suitable and better conditions may eventuate.

Realise further that the bodies of all these sentient intelligent cosmic, solar and planetary Logoi are constituted of living sentient beings, and the brain reels, and the mind draws back in dismay before such a staggering concept. Yet so it is, and so all moves forward to some unfathomable and magnificent consummation which will only in part begin to be visioned by us when our consciousness has expanded beyond the cosmic physical plane, and beyond the cosmic astral until it can "conceive and think" upon the cosmic mental plane. That supposes a realisation beyond that of the Buddhas who have the consciousness of the cosmic physical plane, and beyond that of the planetary Logoi. It is the consciousness and knowledge of a solar Logos.

To the occult student, who has developed the power of the inner vision, the vault of Heaven can therefore be seen as a blazing fire of light, and the stars as focal points of flame from which radiate streams of dynamic energy. Darkness is light to the illumined Seer, and the secret of the Heavens can be read and expressed in terms of force currents, energy centres, and dynamic fiery systemic peripheries.

4. *The Law of Radiation.*

It will be found that more time will be given to this expression of divine activity than to any other in this section, as it is the one of the most practical utility. This Law of Radiation is one that is beginning to be recognised by scientists since their acceptation of the radio-activity of certain substances, and when they are willing to approximate the occult conception of the radiatory, or emanatory condition, of all substances at a specific point in evolution, then they will very definitely approach Reality.

Radiation is the outer effect produced by all forms in all kingdoms when their internal activity has reached such a stage of vibratory activity that the confining walls of the form no longer form a prison, but permit of the escape of the subjective essence. It marks a specific point of attainment in the evolutionary process, and this is equally true of the atom of substance with which the chemist and physicist deal, when working with the elements, as it is of the forms in the vegetable kingdom, the

forms in the animal kingdom, in the human, and, likewise, in the divine.

From some angles of vision, it might be regarded as
the "true form" (which is to be understood occultly as
the etheric form of energy) making its presence felt in
such a way that it becomes apparent even to the scientist.
Students should here remember two things:

First, that in all occult conclusions, it is the body of
energy which is dealt with and the subjective life
back of the form which is recognised as being of
supreme importance.

Second, that the dense objective manifestation, as has
been reiterated frequently, is not regarded as a principle at all; the occultist deals with principles alone.

It might be of value here to remind the student also that
three things have to be recognised in all manifestation:

First, that the tangible objective exterior, negative, receptive, and occultly unorganised, is without form
and usefulness *apart from the inner energy.*

Second, that the "true form" or the force-vehicle energises and produces the cohesion of that which is
unorganised.

Third, that the "volatile essence," or the spiritual
essential Life, focuses itself in some one point within
the "true form." [10]

---

[10] *Form:* "The model according to which nature does its external work.
—S. D., II, 107; see S. D., I, 619.
1. Divine ideation passes from the abstract to the concrete or visible form.
    a. The objective is an emanation of the subjective.—S. D., I, 407.
    b. Impulse is Spirit energy causing objectivity.—S. D., I, 349, 683.
    c. The Logos renders objective a concealed thought.—S. D., II, 28.
2. Three things required before any form of energy can become objective:—S. D., I, 89.
    1. Privation.... Separation. Initial impulse. Energy. Will.
    2. Form....... Quality or shape. Nature. Love.
    3. Matter...... Objective sphere. Intelligent activity.
                 See S. D., III, 561.
3. Life precedes form.—S. D., I, 242.
    a. The Thinker ever remains.—S. D., II, 28.
    b. Force of life is the transformation into energy of the thought
of the Logos.—See S. D., III, 179.

In studying the subject of radiatory activity, we are dealing with the effect produced by the inner essence as it makes its presence felt through the form, when the form has been brought to a stage of such refinement that it becomes possible.

When this realisation is applied to all the forms in all the kingdoms, it will be found possible to bridge the gaps existing between the different forms of life, and the "elements" in every kingdom, and those unifying radiating centres will be found. The word "element" is yet confined to the basic substances in what is called essential matter, and the chemist and physicist are busy with such lives; but their correspondence (in the occult sense of the term) is to be found in every kingdom in nature, and there are forms of life in the vegetable kingdom which are occultly regarded as "radioactive," the eucalyptus tree being one such form. There are forms of animal life equally at an analogous stage and the human unit (as it approaches "liberation") demonstrates a similar phenomenon.

Again, as a planetary scheme nears its consummation, it becomes "radioactive," and through radiation transfers its essence to another "absorbent planet," or planets, as is the case with a solar system also. Its essence, or true Life, is absorbed by a receiving constellation, and the outer "case" returns to its original unorganised condition.

4. Spirit evolves through form and out of form.—S. D., I, 680.
    a. Spirit has to acquire full self-consciousness.—S. D., I, 215.
    b. Form imprisons Spirit.—S. D., II, 775.
    c. The principle of limitation is form.—S. D., III, 561.
    d. Spirit informs all sheaths.—S. D., I, 669, note.
    e. Spirit passes through the cycle of Being.—S. D., I, 160
5. The devas are the origin of form.—S. D., I, 488.
    They exist in two great groups:
    a. The Ahhi are the vehicle of divine thought.—S. D., I, 70.
    b. The Army of the Voice.—S. D., I, 124.
    They are the sum-total of the substance of the four higher planes and of the three lower.
6. There is a form which combines all forms.—S. D., I, 77, 118.

Under our consideration of the law of radiation, we will first of all take up the topic of the cause of radiation.

a.   *The Cause of Radiation.*   The student will only be able to get a true view of this matter if he views the subject in a large way.   Two aspects of the matter naturally come before his mental vision, both of which must be dealt with if any adequate concept of this subject is to be reached,—a subject which has engrossed philosophers, scientists and alchemists for hundreds of years consciously or unconsciously.   We must, therefore, consider:

a.   That which radiates.
b.   That which is the subjective cause of radiation.

It might be very briefly stated that when any form becomes radioactive, certain conditions have been fulfilled and certain results brought about, which conditions and results might be summed up as follows:

The radioactive form is one which has run through its appointed cycles, through its wheel of life, great or small, which has been turned with adequate frequency, so that the volatile life-essence is ready to escape from that form and merge itself in the greater form of which the lesser is but a part.   It must be remembered in this connection that radiation occurs when the etheric or true form becomes responsive to certain types of force.   Radiation, as it is occultly understood, does not concern itself with the escape from the physical or dense form, but with that period in the life of any living entity (atomic, human or divine) wherein the etheric or pranic body is in such a state that it can no longer limit or confine the indwelling life.

Radiation   comes   about   when   the   internal,   self-sufficient life of any atom is offset by a stronger urge, or pull, emanating from the enveloping greater existence of whose body it may form a part.   This is nevertheless only true when it is caused by the *pull upon the essential*

life by the essential life of the greater form; it is not due
to the attractive power of the form aspect of that greater
life. A very definite distinction must here be made. It
is the failure to recognise this that has led so many alchemical students and scientific investigators to lose their
way, and thus negate the conclusions of years of study.
They confuse the impulse of the atom to respond to the
vibratory magnetic pull of the more powerful and comprehensive form with the true esoteric attraction which
alone produces "occult radiation,"—that of the central
essential life of the form in which the element under consideration may have place. It is very necessary to make
this clear from the start. Perhaps the whole subject
may be clearer if we consider it in the following way.

The atom in a form revolves upon its own axis, follows
its own revolution, and lives its own internal life. This
concerns its primary awareness. As time progresses it
becomes magnetically aware of the attractive nature of
that which envelops it on all sides, and becomes conscious of the form which surrounds it. This is its *secondary* awareness but it still concerns what we might, for
lack of a better term, call matter. The atom, therefore,
has an interplay with other atoms.

Later, the atom in a form becomes aware that it not
only revolves upon its axis, but that it also follows an
orbit around a greater centre of force within a greater
form. This is *tertiary* awareness, and is caused by the
magnetic pull of the greater centre being felt, thus causing an urge within the atom which impels it to move
within certain specific cycles. This awareness, esoterically understood, concerns itself with substance or with
the true form within the objective form.

Finally, the attractive pull of the greater centre becomes so powerful that the positive life within the atom
(whatever type of atom it may be and in whatever kingdom) feels the force of the central energy which holds it,

along with other atoms, coherently fulfilling their function. This energy penetrates through the ring-pass-not, evokes no response from what might be called the electronic or negative lives within the atomic periphery, but does evoke a response from the essential, positive nucleus of the atom. This is due to the fact that the essential life of any atom, its highest positive aspect, is ever of the same nature as that of the greater life which is drawing it to itself. When this is felt sufficiently strongly, the atomic cycle is completed, the dense form is dispelled, the true form is dissipated, and the central life escapes to find its greater magnetic focal point.

Through this process (which is found throughout the solar system in all its departments) every atom in turn becomes an electron. The positive life of any atom in due course of evolution becomes negative to a greater life toward which it is impelled or drawn, and thus the process of evolution carries every life invariably through the four stages enumerated above. Within the three lower kingdoms of nature, the process is undergone unconsciously, according to the human connotation of that term; it is consciously passed through in the human kingdom, and in the higher spheres of existence, with an enveloping consciousness which can only be hinted at in the ambiguous term "self-conscious group realisation."

It was in connection with this transmutative process that the alchemists of old occupied themselves, but seldom did they reach the stage wherein it was possible for them to concern themselves with the response of the two types of positive energy to each other, and with the consequent escape of a lesser positive force to its greater attractive centre. When they did (with a few exceptions) they were brought up against a dead wall, for though they had succeeded in locating the radiating principle in substance, or in the true form, and had managed to pierce through (or to negate) both the dense physical body and the etheric form, yet they had no perception of the nature of the central force which was drawing the life they were concerned with out of its apparently legitimate sphere into a new realm of activity. Some few did possess this knowledge but (realising the danger of their conclusions) refused to put in writing the result of their investigations.

If students will study the laws of transmutation,[11] as already apprehended, and above all, as incorporated in the writings of Hermes Trismegistus, bearing this in mind, some interesting results might be brought about. Let them remember that that which "seeks liberty" is the central electric spark; that this liberty is achieved first of all through the results brought about by the activity of the "frictional fire" which speeds up its internal vibration; then by the work upon the atom, or the substance of solar fire, which causes:

    a. Orbital progression,

    b. Stimulative vibration,

    c. Awakened internal response,

until finally electric fire is contacted. This is true of all atoms:

[11] In connection with Transmutation the following ancient formula is of interest. It was the basis of the alchemical work of olden days.

"True, without error, certain and most true; that which is above is as that which is below and that which is below is as that which is above, for performing the miracles of the one Thing; and as all things were from one by the mediation of one so all things arose from this one thing by adaptation.

The Father of it is the sun, the mother of it is the moon; the wind carries it in its belly and the Mother of it is the earth. This is the Father of all perfection, and consummation of the whole world. The power of it is integral if it be turned into earth.

Thou shalt separate the earth from the fire and subtle from the gross, gently with much sagacity; it ascends from earth to Heaven, and again descends to earth; and receives the strength of the superiors and the inferiors—so thou hast the glory of the whole world; therefore let all obscurity fly before thee. This is the strong fortitude of all fortitudes, overcoming every subtle and penetrating every solid thing. So the world was created."—*Emerald Tablet of Hermes.*

a. The atom of substance,
b. The atom of a form whatsoever it be,
c. The atom of a kingdom in nature,
d. The atom of a planet,
e. The atom of a solar system.

In every case the three fires or types of energy play their part; in every case the four stages are passed through; in every case transmutation, transference, or radiation takes place, and the result of the escape of the central positive energy is achieved, and its absorption into a greater form, to be held in place for a specific cycle by the stronger energy.

This process of rendering radioactive all the elements has, as we have seen, occupied students down the ages. The alchemists of the middle ages beginning with the simpler elements and starting with the mineral kingdom sought to find out the secret of the liberating process, to know the method of release, and to understand the laws of transmutation. They did not succeed in the majority of cases because, having located the essence, they had no idea how to deal with it when released, nor (as we have seen) had they any conception as to the magnetic force which was drawing the released essence to itself.

To comprehend the law and therefore to be able to work perfectly with it, the experimenting student must have the ability to release the essence from its form. He must know the formulae and words which will direct it to that particular focal point in the mineral kingdom which stands in the same correspondential relation to the mineral monad as the Ego on its own plane stands to the man who casts off his physical and true forms through death. This involves knowledge only committed to the pledged disciple; if chance students stumble upon the law, and theoretically know the process, they would do well to proceed no further until they have learned how to protect themselves from the interplay of forces. As we well know, the workers with radium, and those who experiment in the world's laboratories, suffer frequently from loss of limb or life; this is due to their ignorance of the forces they are dealing with. The liberated essences become conductors of the greater force which is their magnetic centre, because they are responsive to it, and it is this force which produces the distressing conditions sometimes present in connection with radioactive substances. Every radioactive atom becomes, through this conductive faculty, a releasing agent; and they consequently cause what we call burns. These burns are the result of the process of releasing the essential life of the atom of physical substance being dealt with.

There might here be noted the curious phenomenon, in the human kingdom which is erroneously termed the prolongation of life; it might more truthfully be called the perpetuation of the form. Medical science today strains every effort to retain life in forms diseased and inadequate; these Nature, if left to herself, would long ago have discarded. They thereby imprison the life, and force back the life essence again and again into the sheath at the moment of liberation. In course of time and with more knowledge, true medical science will become purely preventative. It will concentrate its ability on preserving the atomic life of the human atom, and at furthering the preservative protective processes, and the functionary smoothness of the atomic rotary life, thus conducing to the correct following of the human orbital path. But further than that it will not go, and when the course of nature has been run, when the wheel of life has run down, when the hour for liberation has struck, when the time has come for the return of the essence to its centre, then the work will be recognised as completed, and the form discarded. But this will not, however, be possible until the human family has reached a stage when, through pure living and clean thinking, the present corruptions have been eliminated. Men will then function on into old age, or until the Ego, realising the particular work to be accomplished in any one life has been duly worked out, calls in the lower spark of life, and withdraws the central point of fire. This naturally presupposes knowledge and faculties at present lacking.

All these thoughts can be extended to include entire kingdoms of nature, the globes of a chain, the chains themselves, a planetary scheme or a solar system.

The moon is an interesting instance of the transmutative or liberating process practically completed in a globe: the essential life of the human kingdom has withdrawn and found a new field of expression. All animal life has equally been absorbed by a greater centre in another chain. Practically the same can be said of the vegetable kingdom on the moon though there are a few of the lower forms of the vegetable life (of a kind unrecognisable by us) still to be found there; whilst the mineral kingdom is radioactive and the essence of all mineral forms is fast escaping.

In connection with the kingdoms of nature, it must be remembered that their growth and eventual radiation is dependent upon the cyclic purpose of the planetary Logos, and upon the currents of force which play upon His planetary body, and which emanate from other planetary schemes.

All atoms become radioactive as the result of a response to a stronger magnetic centre which response is brought about through the gradual evolutionary development of consciousness of some kind or another. This is known to be true in a small degree in connection with the mineral kingdom though scientists have not yet admitted that radiation is thus caused. Later they will, but only when this general theory which is here laid down in connection with all atoms is admitted by them to be a plausible hypothesis. Then the goal of their endeavour will be somewhat changed; they will seek to ascertain through clear thinking and a study of the involved analogy what focal points of magnetic energy may be regarded as existing, and how they affect the atoms in their environment. One hint only can here be given. Light upon these dark problems will come along two lines.

First, it will come through the study of the place of the solar system in the universal whole, and the effect that certain constellations have upon it; secondly, it will come through a close study of the effect of one planetary scheme upon another, and the place of the moon in our own planetary life. This will lead to a close investigation of polar conditions in the earth, of the planetary magnetic currents, and of the electrical intercourse between our earth, and the Venusian and Martian planetary schemes. When this has been accomplished, astronomy and esoteric astrology will be revolutionised, and the nature of solar energy as an expression of an Entity of the fourth rank will be appreciated. This will come at the close of this century after a scientific discovery of even greater importance to the scientific world than that as to the nature of the atom. Until that time it will be as difficult to express the hylozoistic conception in terms of exact science as it would be for the sixteenth century ancestor of present humanity to conceive of the atom as being simply an aspect of force, and not objective and tangible. Hence further elucidation will but serve to confuse.

In considering this vast subject of radiation, which is the result of spiral-progressive movement, it might be of interest if I here pointed out that in every kingdom of nature there are certain focal points of energy which, as the æons gradually sweep along, bring the atomic substance of which all forms in all kingdoms are composed to the point where they become radioactive and achieve liberation. (The term "liberation" really means the ability of any conscious atom to pass out of one sphere of energised influence into another of a higher vibration, of larger and wider expanse of conscious realisation.)

Broadly speaking, it might be said that:

The *mineral kingdom* is responsive to that type of energy which is the lowest aspect of fire, of those internal furnaces which exert an influence upon the elements in the mineral world, and which resolve these atomic lives into a gradual series of ever-higher types of mineral energy. For instance, the type of energy which plays upon iron ore, or which produces tin, is emanated from a different centre in the body of the Entity informing the mineral kingdom to that which converts the elements into those wondrous jewels, the diamond, the sapphire, the emerald or the ruby. The energy of the particular centre involved is likewise responsive to force originating in the centre in the body of the planetary Logos—which centre depends upon the kingdom to be vivified. In dealing with these kingdoms, therefore, the relations might be briefly indicated—

KINGDOM	PLANETARY CENTRE
a. Human	Heart centre.
b. Animal	Throat centre.
c. Vegetable	Solar plexus.
d. Mineral	Spleen.

The planetary egoic centre is, of course, the transmitter to all the others, and it should be borne in mind in this connection that every centre transmits three types of force, with the exception of the spleen which hands on the solar fires, pranic force, pure and simple. Students will eventually ascertain how to group the various types in the different kingdoms according to the type of energy they display in fullest measure, remembering that only in the fourth kingdom, the human, is the highest of the three types (that which produces self-consciousness) manifesting; in the others it is latent. This will become apparent if the method of lunar individualisation is studied.

The *vegetable kingdom* is responsive to the particular type of energy which produces the phenomenon of water, or moisture. Through the effect of water every higher type of plant life is evolved, and through the combination of heat and water results are brought about which produce new types. The herbal scientist who is producing new species is really occupied with the effect of sex energy in the second kingdom of nature; he will do well to deal with all plant life as energy points responsive to other and greater energy centres. Much will be learned along this line when electricity and colored lights are more freely used in experimental stations. Sex, in the mineral kingdom, or chemical affinity, is the display in that kingdom of the second type of magnetic force; in the vegetable kingdom the same thing can be studied in the seed life, and in the fertilisation processes of all plants. Neptune, the God of the Waters, has a curious relationship to our planetary Logos, and also to the Entity Who is the informing life of the second kingdom.

The *animal kingdom* is responsive to a type of energy which is neither fire nor water but is a combination of the two. They are also the first of the kingdoms on the physical plane to be responsive to *sound,* or to the energy emanating from that which we call noise. This is an occult fact worthy of close attention. The energy emanating from the Entity Who is the informing Life of the third kingdom in nature has five channels of approach, that is five centres. That animating the fourth kingdom has seven, for the mind and the intuition are added. In the second kingdom there are three centres, but their manifestation is so obscure as to seem practically nonexistent to the human mind. In the first or mineral kingdom, the avenue of approach is limited to one centre.

It will be observed, therefore, that the stimulation of magnetic energy proceeds from what might be regarded as jumps, 1-3-5-7. Each kingdom starts with a specific equipment, and during the process of evolution within the kingdom adds to it so that the liberated life enters the next kingdom with its old equipment plus one.

The *human kingdom* is equally responsive to energy. This time it is the energy of fire at its highest manifestation in the three worlds. It must be borne in mind that we are referring to the positive energy of the greater Whole as it affects the lesser *positive* energetic points. We are not referring to form energy.

The atom becomes responsive to form energy or to that which surrounds it. It becomes conscious and then becomes responsive to the force of the *kingdom* in which it is a part. It gradually becomes responsive to stronger influences or to the force emanating from the Entity Who is the life of that kingdom.

Finally, the atom becomes conscious of planetary energy, or responsive to the Heavenly Man Himself. It then transcends the kingdom in which it has been, and is elevated into another kingdom in which the cycle is again repeated.

This can all be expressed in terms of consciousness but in this section we will limit the thought simply to that of energy. In summation it might be said that:

1. The planetary Logos has seven centres, as has man.
2. The informing Life of the animal kingdom has five centres, and the animal kingdom has five prototypes on the archetypal plane, whereas man has seven prototypes.
3. The informing Life of the vegetable kingdom has three centres of force on His Own plane, and there are, therefore, but three basic types of plant life.

All that we know are but differentiations of those three.

4. The informing Life of the mineral kingdom works through one centre.

b. *Radiation in the Five Kingdoms.* We have seen that the cause of radiation is the response of the positive life in any atom to the attractive power of the positive life in a greater atom. Expressed in other words, we might say that the deva life of any atomic form proceeds with its evolution, and by a series of "releases" transfers itself during the manvantaric cycles out of one kingdom into another until every atom has achieved self-determination, and thus the purpose of the Heavenly Man for any particular mahamanvantara is satisfactorily accomplished. As might be expected, therefore, when the subject is viewed as a whole and not from the standpoint of any one kingdom, there are in the evolutionary process five major at-one-ments.

1. At-one-ment with the mineral kingdom.
2. At-one-ment of the mineral monad with the vegetable kingdom.
3. At-one-ment of the vegetable monad with the animal kingdom.

   The progressive life has now made three at-one-ments or expanded its realisation three times.
4. At-one-ment with the human kingdom.
5. At-one-ment with the Heavenly Man or with the great planetary life.

Along these five stages, one of them is considered in this solar system to be the most important, and that is the at-one-ment with the human kingdom. For this particular greater cycle, the goal of evolution is man; when individualisation is achieved and self-determination is awakened, the Monad or Divine Pilgrim has attained that which expresses the logoic purpose most perfectly. The later stages but set the crown upon the victor, and the final at-one-ment with the divine Self is but the consummation of the fourth stage. Students will find it of interest to work out the correspondence between the five initiations and these five unifications. There is a close connection between the two. By understanding the laws of the different kingdoms, much can be learned anent the conditions governing the five Initiations. It will be found that the initiations mark stages in response to contact and to realisation which have their interesting germs in the five kingdoms.

It might here be pointed out with propriety that radiation is the result of transmutation; transmutation marks the completion of a cycle of rotary-spiralling activity. No atom becomes radioactive until its own internal rhythm has been stimulated to a point where the positive central life is ready for the imposition of a higher vibratory activity, and when the negative lives within the atomic periphery are repulsed by the intensity of its vibration, and are no longer attracted by its drawing qualities. This is due to the coming in and consequent response to the magnetic vibration of a still stronger positive life which releases the imprisoned central spark and causes what might from some aspects be called the dissipation of the atom. This process, nevertheless, in the majority of cases covers such a vast period of time that the human mind is unable to follow the process.

The radioactive period is much the longest in the mineral kingdom, and shortest of all in the human. We are not concerned with radiation in the spiritual kingdom at the close of the mahamanvantara, so no comment will here be made.

It is interesting to note that during this round, owing to planetary decision, the process of producing human radiation or "release" is being artificially stimulated through the method which we call initiation, and the short cut to intensive purification and stimulation is open to all who are willing to pass through the divine alchemical fire. Simultaneously, in the other kingdoms of nature a process somewhat similar in kind though not in degree is being attempted. The tremendous manipulation of ores, the scientific work of the chemist, and scientific investigation is analogous in the mineral kingdom to the world processes which are being utilised to liberate the human spark. Out of the chaos and turmoil of the World War, for instance, and the weight of metal undergoing violent disintegration the mineral monad emerged as from an initiatory test, incomprehensible as this may seem. It will be apparent that a great simultaneous movement is on foot to produce more rapid radiation in all the kingdoms of nature so that when the cycle is run the process of planetary radiation may be consummated. This intensive culture is not proceeding upon all the planets but only upon a very few. The others will run a longer cycle. The initiatory cultural process which has in view the stimulation of magnetic radiation or transmutation is but an experiment. It was tried first on Venus, and on the whole proved successful, resulting in the consummation of the planetary purpose in five rounds instead of seven. This was what made it possible to utilise Venusian energy upon the Venus chain and the Venus globe of our scheme and thus cause the phenomenon of forced individualisation in Lemurian days. It was the intensive stimulation of the third kingdom of nature during the third root race which artificially unified the three aspects. The process of stimulating through the medium of Venusian energy was really begun in the third round when the triangle of force was completed, and ready to function. It is this factor which occultly makes the third Initiation of such tremendous importance. In it the human triangle is linked, the Monad, the

Ego and the personality, or Venus, the Sun and the Earth are symbolically allied.

Enough has here been indicated to give the student room for thought, though one more word in this connection might be added. In the potentially radioactive qualities of the four kingdoms of nature with which we are most concerned will be found an interesting analogy to the functions of the four planetary schemes which (in their totality) form the logoic quaternary. This applies also in a lesser degree to the four chains which form the planetary quaternary. All have to become radioactive and all their principles have to be transmuted and the form for which they are responsible transcended.

When the subject of radiation is more completely comprehended, it will be found that it demonstrates one more instance of the unity of all life, and furnishes one more corroborative indication of the synthetic nature of the entire evolutionary process. In every instance that which radiates from each kingdom of nature is one and the same. The radioactive human being is the same in nature (differing only in degree and in conscious response) as the radioactive mineral; in every case it is the central positive life, the electric spark or that which is its correspondence, which radiates. There are, therefore, seven correspondences in this connection in the solar system, seven types which radiate, or seven classes of entities which demonstrate ability to transcend their normal motion and to transfer themselves into some greater sphere in due course of evolution. These are:

1. The mineral monad of the mineral kingdom, or the central positive nucleus in all atoms and elements.
2. The monad in the vegetable kingdom, or the central positive life of every plant and vegetable growth.
3. The monad in the animal kingdom or the positive life of each type.

4. The human Monads in their myriads of groups.
5. The Monad of any particular type, or form.
6. The planetary Monad, the sum total of all the lives within a planetary scheme.
7. The solar Monad or the sum total of all lives in the solar system.

Each of these is first rotary in its activity, or self-centred; later each simultaneously with its original motion demonstrates spiral-cyclic activity. Thereby it becomes "aware" of form, and finally becomes radioactive. During this final period it transcends the form, and escapes from out of it, becoming thus conscious of, and able to participate in, the activity of the still greater enveloping whole.

c. *Radiation and Cyclic Law.*   Scattered throughout this *Treatise,* are numerous indications of the cyclic nature of this phenomenon, and students should bear in mind that in all which concerns radiation, as in all else, there will be periods of quiescence, and periods of intensified activity. This will be seen quite clearly in connection with the fourth kingdom of nature. A period of radioactivity is being entered upon now in which men and women will achieve a larger realisation; they will begin to transcend their human limitations, and to enter the fifth kingdom one by one, and unit by unit. This period, as far as the larger cycle is concerned, began when the Door of Initiation was opened in Atlantean days, but many lesser cycles have occurred, for the influx into the fifth kingdom is equally governed by cyclic law, by periodic ebb and flow. At the close of the fourth root race there was a period of distinctive radioactivity, and many hundreds of men passed out of the fourth Creative Hierarchy into another and a higher one. Many posts held hitherto by Venusian Entities were vacated in order that our humanity might occupy them, and a vast interchain

radiation went on as many of the Kumaras and certain
lesser existences quitted our earth chain, and entered
upon subtler, and more advanced work. Then the activity gradually ebbed until a recurring cycle brought in
influences which produced a new radiation, though not of
such a strength as in the preceding period.

Another period of radioactivity occurred during the
time of the Buddha and many achieved Arhatship in those
days. That period was the highest point of what is occultly termed "a cycle of the third degree," and a similar
degree of radiatory activity has not been reached since
that time. Human radiation of a very slight nature was
felt about the time of Christ, but it only lasted for a couple
of hundred years, and though individuals here and there
have since achieved the goal, yet no large numbers have
passed successfully through the fires of transmutation,
and thus transcended the fourth kingdom. The cycle is
again on the upward turn; about the fourteenth century
the human kingdom began to be noticeably radioactive,
and we are on the way to the fulfilment of a "cycle of the
second order" or of a period of transcendence of a still
greater activity than in the time of the Buddha. It will
become demonstrably great when certain conditions have
been fulfilled.

First, when the present world chaos has subsided.
Next, when the present generation has consummated its
work of reconstruction. Third, when the coming great
Lord has entered upon His mission upon earth, thereby
increasing the vibration in every kingdom of nature, but
particularly in the second and fourth.

Fourth, when the movement, inaugurated at the close
of each century by the Trans-Himalayan Lodge is under
way, and the psycho-scientific Egos who are its agents
have made their presence felt.

Finally, when a movement is instituted by the Lodge,
working in connection with the fourth root race; it will

also be part of the stimulative process, and will result in the rendering radioactive of some of the foremost thinkers of that race. It will be their day of opportunity, and so great is the importance attached to this that a Member of the Lodge, Confucius as he has been called in the past, will incarnate in order to superintend the work. The preliminary steps are being taken now, and Egos are coming in who will endeavour to direct the energies of this race on to the right line though the peak of the cycle of stimulation will not be until the middle of the next century. It is needless for me to point out that all such movements are first felt as disturbing, and only when the dust of turmoil, and the noise of clashing forces have died away will *purpose* be seen emerging. This is very apparent in Russia at the present time.

A great factor and one that it is hard to explain so that the average thinker can understand it is the cyclic coming in of egos who are at a point in evolution where they are ready for their first radioactive life. In one great department of hierarchical endeavour all Egos are divided into two groups, according to their cycle and according to their type of energy. These grades are in turn subdivided according to the quality and the vibratory effect to be induced upon any one kingdom of nature by their united, or single, incarnation. This might be illustrated by pointing out that by the gradual coming in of human beings who are vegetarians by natural inclination and by the appearance of egos who are interested specifically in the welfare and nurture of the animals (as is the case so noticeably now) we have the cyclic appearance of a whole group of human units who have a definite karmic relation to the third kingdom. This relation is of a kind differing in specific detail from the meat-eating, and oft inhuman, groups of the past five hundred years.

It might be of profit and of interest if we here enumerated some of the occult terms applied to some of these differentiated groups, remembering that we are only touching upon a few out of a vast number, and only name those the terminology of which conveys information and educational benefit to the student:

1. The units of inertia,
2. Atoms of rhythmic centralisation,
3. Units of primary radiation,
4. The sons of heavy rhythm,
5. The points of fiery excellence (a name given oft to magnetic, highly-evolved types),
6. Tertiary points of secondary fire,
7. Magnetic flames (given to chelas and initiates of certain degrees),
8. Positive sons of electricity,
9. Rotating units of the seventh order,
10. Points of light of the fourth progression,
11. Electric sparks,
12. Units of negative resistance,
13. The equilibrised atoms.

Many more names might be given but these will suffice to indicate the general nature of these energy summations, under which all the members of the human family are gathered and placed according to:

a. Their rhythm,
b. Their quality,
c. Their heat,
d. Their light,
e. Their magnetic influence,
f. Their radiation,
g. Their activity.

This tabulation is but an extension of the major one which grouped all Egos under the divisions of colour, sound and vibration. A similar enumeration has also grouped the atoms in the other kingdoms of nature, and even the Dhyan Chohans of the highest rank find their place in the hierarchical archives of this fifth (or third) department.

A cyclic tabulation is of equal interest but is of a totally different nature, carrying to the initiated and intuitive investigator many hints of an evolutionary and historical value. Again we might append a brief epitome of some of the expressions used and of some of the names under which human beings are grouped in the archives of this the seventh department:

1. Units of the fire-mist stage,
2. Points of lunar origin,
3. Sons of the sun,
4. Devas of the fourth degree,
5. Flames from interplanetary spheres,
6. Atoms from the crimson sphere—a reference to certain Egos who have come to the earth from the planetary scheme whose note is red,
7. The successful Vyasians,
8. The points in the third planetary petal, and groups of others related to the twelve petalled planetary lotus,
9. The lovers of low vibration,
10. The rejectors of the eighth scheme,
11. The points of triple resistance,
12. The followers of the ARHAT,
13. The cyclic sons of peace,
14. The recurring sons of war,
15. The specks within the planetary eye,
16. The recognised points within the chakras. These naturally exist in ten groups.

Each name conveys to the mind of the initiate some knowledge as to the place in evolution of the Monad concerned, the nature of its incarnations, and its place in cyclic evolution.

The same method of grouping is used in connection with all the kingdoms though only in the case of the fourth and the fifth kingdoms are individual atoms dealt with; the tabulations and records for the other kingdoms are concerned with groups. When a group is known, the nature, vibration, and rhythm of the atom within that group is immediately apparent.

IV. THE TURNING OF THE WHEEL [12]

We come now to the consideration of another point, and one of very real moment; it emerges out of what we have been saying anent cycles and is the basis of all periodic phenomena. One of the most elementary of scientific truths is that the earth revolves upon its axis, and that it travels around the sun. One of the truths less recognised, yet withal of equal importance, is that the entire solar system equally revolves upon its axis but in a cycle so vast as to be beyond the powers of ordinary man to comprehend, and which necessitates mathematical for-

---

[12] Man must understand the nature of the wheel in which he is turned, called in Sanskrit the wheel of Samsara. This latter word derived from the root Sru, to move, indicates a motion wheel or the great wheel of changing life in which the human entities have been called upon to work and which must never be abandoned out of compassion for man and in obedience to the law of oneness which connects the many, in the opinion of all true yogees and Sri Krishna. The Teacher gives the nature of the samsaric wheel in a certain peculiar way which deserves to be thought over by you all. He says ''all bhootas spring up from food and food from Parjanya or rain. Rain comes out of yagna and yagna out of Karma. Karma is out of the Veda and Veda is of the Eternal.'' Here you see a Septenary gamut is given with the bhoota (or manifested form) at one end and the eternal substance unmanifested to us at the other end. If we divide this seven according to the theosophical plane of a lower four dominated over by a higher triad, we get form, food, rain and yagna as the lower four and karma, Veda and eternal substance as the higher triad. The eternal substance that pervades all space, worked on by the world song and giving rise to all the laws of karma that govern the development of the world, develops a lower four and this four is started by yagna—the spirit of evolution that connects the higher and lower or in Puranic fashion, the spirit that seeks to add to the harmony of the unmanifested by giving it a field of disharmony to work upon and establish its own greatness. This spirit of yagna in its way to produce the manifested form gives rise to the Parjanya or rain. The word Parjanya is applied to rain and often times to a spirit whose function is to produce rain.—*Some Thoughts on the Gita*, p. 127.

mulae of great intricacy. The orbital path of the solar system in the heavens around its cosmic centre is now being sensed, and the general drift also of our constellation is being taken into consideration as a welcome hypothesis. Scientists have not yet admitted into their calculations the fact that our solar system is revolving around a cosmic centre along with six other constellations of even greater magnitude in the majority of cases than ours, only one being approximately of the same magnitude as our solar system. This cosmic centre in turn forms part of a great wheel till—to the eye of the illumined seer—the entire vault of Heaven is seen to be in motion. All the constellations, viewing them as a whole, are impelled in one direction.

The old Commentary expresses this obscure truth as follows:

"The one wheel turns. One turn alone is made, and every sphere, and suns of all degrees, follow its course. The night of time is lost in it, and kalpas measure less than seconds in the little day of man.

Ten million million kalpas pass, and twice ten million million Brahmic cycles and yet one hour of cosmic time is not completed.

Within the wheel, forming that wheel, are all the lesser wheels from the first to the tenth dimension. These in their cyclic turn hold in their spheres of force other and lesser wheels. Yet many suns compose the cosmic One.

Wheels within wheels, spheres within spheres. Each pursues his course and attracts or rejects his brother, and yet cannot escape from the encircling arms of the mother.

When the wheels of the fourth dimension, of which our sun is one and all that is of lesser force and higher number, such as the eighth and ninth degrees, turn upon themselves, devour each other, and turn and rend their mother, then will the cosmic wheel be ready for a faster revolution."

It will, therefore, be apparent that the power of man to conceive of these whirling constellations, to measure their interaction, and to realise their essential unity is not as yet great enough. We are told that even to the liberated Dhyan Chohan the mystery of that which lies beyond his own solar Ring-Pass-Not is hid.

Certain influences indicate to Him and certain lines of force demonstrate to Him the fact that some constellations are knit with His system in a close and corporate union. We know that the Great Bear, the Pleiades, Draco or the Dragon are in some way associated with the solar system but as yet He knows not their function nor the nature of the other constellations. It must also be remembered that the turning of our tiny systemic wheel, and the revolution of a cosmic wheel can be hastened, or retarded, by influences emanating from unknown or unrealised constellations whose association with a systemic or a cosmic Logos is as mysterious relatively as the effect individuals have upon each other in the human family. This effect is hidden in logoic karma and is beyond the ken of man.

The wheels in order of their importance might be enumerated as follows:

The wheel of the universe, or the sumtotal of all stars and starry systems.

A cosmic wheel, or a group of seven constellations. These are grouped according to:

  a. Their magnitude,
  b. Their vibration,
  c. Their colour,
  d. Their influence upon each other.

These cosmic wheels, according to the esoteric books, are divided into forty-nine groups, each comprising millions of septenary constellations. For purposes of study by the Adepts, they are each known by a symbol, and these forty-nine symbols embody all that can be apprehended anent the size, magnitude, quality, vibratory activity, and objective of those great forms through which an Existence is experiencing. The Chohans of high degree know the forty-nine sounds which give the *quality* of the consciousness aspect of these great Beings Who are as far removed from the consciousness of our solar Logos as the consciousness of man is removed from that of a crystal. The knowledge thus appreciated by the Chohans is naturally but theoretical and conveys only to their relatively limited consciousness the general nature of the group of constellations, and the force occasionally emanating from them which has at times to be taken into calculation. For instance, the interest awakened in the public mind lately by the giant star Betelgeuse in the constellation of Orion is due to the fact that at this particular time there has been an interplay of force between our tiny system and this giant one, and communication between the two informing Existences.

Systemic wheels or the atomic life of individual constellations. These again are divided into 343 groups, known to the Adept again through a series of characters forming a word which—through its ideographic nature—conveys essential information to the Adept. The ideograph for our solar system may in part be disclosed—not the characters themselves but a digest of that for which the characters stand. Our solar system is disclosed as being:

a. A system of the fourth order, having its force centres upon the fourth cosmic plane, and making its objective manifestation from the fourth systemic plane, via the fourth subplane of the systemic physical plane.

b. Blue in colour, esoteric orange and green.

c. A system which is occultly known to the Adept as "in an airy sign in which the Bird can fly."

d. A system formed of "three fires which form a fourth."

e. A system in which the Bird has "four tail feathers"

and hence can occultly "mount to a higher plane and find its fifth."

f. A system which has four major cycles, and minor periods of manifestation which are multiples of that figure.

g. A system which in the alchemical phraseology of the Masters is viewed as being "a product of the fourth; the fourth itself in process of transmutation; and the living stone with four shells." All this can be seen at one glance by the Master who has the ideographic word before Him. Other ideograms are available for His use which give Him the immediate information as He studies the influences contacting our solar system.

Planetary wheels. For these there are ten modes of expression.

Chain wheels, called in some of the books rounds.

The revolution of any one globe.

The cycle of the three worlds.

The wheel of a plane.

The revolution or cyclic appearance of a kingdom in nature. This applies within a scheme but only to the four kingdoms in objective appearance.

The revolution of a planetary centre producing monadic appearance.

The monadic wheel, or the periodic appearance of units of the fourth Creative Hierarchy. Thus we pass down the scale through all the kingdoms and forms till we arrive at the tiny revolution of an atom of substance.

In concluding our remarks concerning the diverse wheels of the universe, we will touch with brevity upon the "wheels" which concern the human monad. This is a subject but little dealt with as yet, though a few words have been spoken anent the egoic wheel.

It must be borne in mind that the evolution of the

Monad is a much more intricate thing than appears in the books as yet given to the public. In those books the development of consciousness and its transition through the kingdoms of nature are the points dwelt upon. Yet there have been earlier cycles which it will be only possible to comprehend as the history and evolution of the planetary Logoi become gradually revealed. They are parts of His body of manifestation, cells within that greater vehicle, and thus vitalised by His life, qualified by His nature, and distinguished by His characteristics. This will take the history, therefore, of a Monad back to the earlier kalpas. Such history it is not possible to reveal, and no purpose would be served by such a revelation. The fact only can be touched upon as it must be considered along general lines if the true nature of the Self is to be accurately known.

We might consider that the Monad of the human being passes through cycles analogous to those through which the Heavenly Man travels. There is, first, the vast cycle of unfoldment through which a "spark" passes. This covers the period of three major solar systems—that preceding this one, the present, and the succeeding one. In these three, the totality of the cosmic Past, Present, and Future, embodying the three aspects of the divine Life of the solar Logos, are carried to the point of perfection in an individualised Monad. It must be remembered that in this solar system, for instance, certain developments are only recapitulations of evolutionary processes undergone in an earlier solar system; the clue to this lies in the consideration of the manasic or mind principle. The solar Angels, the intelligent individualising factor, were (from certain angles of vision) the product of an earlier system, and only waited for the time in the present system when the forms in the three kingdoms had reached the point of synthetic development which made it possible for them to be impressed and influenced from on high. We have in this concept an idea analogous to the entering in of those Monads, during Atlantean days, who, having individualised upon another chain, tarried in the interplanetary spaces until earth conditions were such that the occupation of adequate forms became possible. The correspondence is not exact but is indicative of the truth. The vast cycle of unfoldment (which rendered later evolution possible) preceded this solar system, and might be regarded as the monadic correspondence to a cosmic wheel. In the Old Commentary this point of development is hinted at in the words:

"The fifth did not appear as the product of the present. The five spokes of that wheel had each a cycle of development, and one in which they were welded at the centre."

The Monad has cycles analogous, though on a miniature scale, to those of the one Life Who permeates and animates all lesser lives. Certain of these cycles cover periods of time so vast, and so long past, that their history can only be conveyed to the investigating Adepts through the medium of sound and symbol. The details of that development are lost in the night of other kalpas, and all that can be seen are the *results*,—the cause must be accepted as existing, though for us remaining inexplicable until the higher initiations are taken.

In the fact of the turning of the monadic Wheel covering the period of three solar systems, lies hid the mystery of monadic self-will, and the secret as to why some of the Monads refused to incarnate, whilst others "fell," and thus proceeded along the present lines of evolution. They refused to incarnate because of internal group conditions brought about through the evolutionary processes of the past kalpas. It will, therefore, be apparent that the question of what constitutes sin and evil is far more intricate than even appears upon the surface. From our limited vision, it appears to be "sin" to fall into incarnation, and equally sin or self-will, self-satisfaction, to remain unevolved upon the higher planes. Yet both groups followed the law of their being, and the solution of the mystery lies in that which is to come.

If the student will with care meditate upon the fact that the three lower planes—the mental, the astral, and the physical—form the dense physical body of the planetary Logos and are, therefore, no principle, it will become apparent to him that through necessity certain units or cells in the body are more active in space and time than others. He must also bear in mind that groups of Monads come into incarnation according to which centre in a Heavenly Man of a particular planetary scheme, or which centre of the solar Logos, is in process of vivification or cyclic activity, and that certain of the centres of a solar Logos *and this particular solar system* are in a condition of partial pralaya through the process of the absorption of the lower solar life forces by the centres of higher vitality. Again, he must remember that the entire aspect of the Divine Life is not intended to reach its full unfoldment at any time in this solar system but must wait for the vitalising impulses of a later. This is due to the fact that there exist in this solar system effects of causes originating in earlier kalpas or—to word it otherwise— the karmic seeds of earlier logoic activities.

Our solar Logos has not yet attained true rhythm, but for millennia of cycles the equilibrising process must go on. Nor has our planetary Logos achieved equilibrium, and the even balancing of forces, therefore until His point in evolution and His objective vision is known and it is known also which centre in the solar body is vitalised by His life, it will be the part of wisdom to refrain from dogmatic assertion, and a too free utterance in connection with incarnating, and non-incarnating, Monads. All are turning upon the monadic cosmic wheel; each is being swept into some form of activity upon the lesser revolution of this particular systemic wheel, but not all in any particular cycle are to be found revolving upon a specific planetary wheel. Many wait for development and for more appropriate seasons in interplanetary spaces, and some must wait until the entering in of a new mahamanvantara. Students should bear carefully in mind the words of H. P. B. where he tells students of the *Secret Doctrine* that the stanzas and their Commentary deal primarily with our particular planetary Logos. This is oft forgotten.

It may interest students to know that there are certain colours, veiling these groups of non-incarnating Monads, at present totally unknown to humanity. These will sweep into the consciousness of the human being in another solar system, or after the taking of the sixth Initiation. All that we have on earth are reflections of the true colours, and likewise the reflection of the lowest aspect.

Every colour in the cosmos exists in three forms:

1. The true colour.
2. The illusory appearance of the colour.
3. Its reflection.

The reflection is that with which we are familiar; the appearance, or that which veils the reality, is contacted and known when we see with the eye of the soul, the Eye of Shiva, and the true colour [14] is contacted after the fifth kingdom has been passed through, and group consciousness is merging in that of the divine. Students will, therefore, note that the monadic cosmic wheel can be

---

[14] *Colour.*—Originally meant a "covering." From root "celare" to cover or hide. Also Occultare, to hide.

Symbology of colours. The language of the prism, of which "the seven mother colours have each seven sons," that is to say, forty-nine shades or "sons" between the seven, which graduated tints are so many letters or alphabetical characters. The language of colours has, therefore, fifty-six letters for the initiate. Of these letters each septenary is absorbed by the mother colour, as each of the seven mother colours is absorbed finally in the white ray, Divine Unity symbolised by these colours.

visioned in terms of "true colour," and is seen by the illumined seer as the combined blending of the primary colours of the three solar systems.

The monadic systemic wheel, which concerns this solar system alone, is distinguished by being the totality of the seven colours of the seven Heavenly Men, and from the vision of the adept of the fifth Initiation is the sumtotal of the primary colours of the egoic groups of the differing planetary schemes.

The monadic planetary wheel, which concerns the particular group of Monads incarnating in a particular scheme, is seen by the seer as the blending of egoic groups, but with the difference that the colour is a dual one, and the colouring of the personality ray of the incarnating Ego is also seen.

The egoic cycle, or the turning of the wheel of the incarnating Ego, is of the most practical interest to man, and has already been somewhat dealt with. For purposes of clarity and elucidation, this wheel may also be seen as turning in three cycles and as making three kinds of revolutions, covering varying periods of time.

There is first, *the Wheel of the chain,* or the cycling of the Monad around an entire chain, and its passage through all the globes and kingdoms. The consideration of this is complicated by the fact that in any particular chain, the Monads seldom begin and end their evolution; they seldom emerge, pass through their cycle and achieve their objective. It is not possible to dissociate a chain from its preceding or succeeding chain. Many Monads who achieved self-consciousness in the moon chain only entered into renewed activity in the middle of the fourth root race; others, who have individualised on this earth, will not succeed in reaching their goal upon this planet. There is here a correspondence to systemic evolution, and there is an analogy between the Monads who refused to incarnate and the Egos who were unable to take bodies in the Lemurian or third root race.

There is next, *the Wheel of a globe,* or the process of evolution upon any particular globe. The student must bear in mind that the Monad, after planetary dissolution, passes the time between incarnations on other and subtler globes, which are the correspondence to the interplanetary and intersystemic spheres.

There is also, *the Wheel of a race,* or the lesser cycle of incarnations—forming a definite series—wherein the incarnating Monad cycles through a number of lives in a particular race.

All these cycles of periodic manifestation are concerned primarily with the appearance, or the manifesting of the "sparks" upon one or other of the three planes in the three worlds, or in some part of the physical body of the planetary Logos. The lesser cycles deal with this; the greater turning of the wheel concerns also the appearance, or flashing forth, of the sparks in the planetary or systemic etheric body, or on the four higher planes of our solar system. We can picture to ourselves the glory of this concept; the downpouring of the streams of fiery sparks; their flashing forth into points of intensified fire as they meet conditions which produce occult "ignition"; and the constant circulation of the forty-nine fires constructed of the sixty thousand million human Monads and the countless streams of deva monads: fire on every side —a network of fiery rivers of living energy, focal points of intensified brilliancy and everywhere the sparks.

There are a few more remarks to be made anent the turning of the various wheels, and we can then take up the consideration of motion and the sheaths.

Within all those wheels which we have enumerated, are many lesser wheels all governed by the same laws, actuated by the same three forms of activity, and all (in their totality) forming one great whole. It will be apparent to all conscientious students that the founders of the symbolical method managed to convey in the symbol of the wheel an idea of the triplicity of all atomic activity:

a. The central point of active...the hub.
   positive force.
b. The negative stream of life...the radiating spokes.
c. The sphere of activity itself..the circumference of
   the effect of the interplay   the wheel.
   of these two.

If the student can picture those wheels in activity, if he can visualise all parts of the wheel as composed of lesser living wheels, and if he can work into his picture a hint of the interplay of all these fiery essences, coloured with certain predominant hues, he will become aware of conditions, and see before him a picture which is ever apparent to the illuminated seer. If, before doing this, he can vision the whole of the systemic wheel as in a constant state of circulation, in which the tiny lesser lives are impelled by the force of the central solar life to pass throughout the extent of the wheel so that they come in contact with all parts of the wheel, and are impressed by all the varying types of "power-substance," then the general nature of the method can be somewhat ascertained. We use the term "motion," but what do we really mean? Simply and literally, the manifestation of the energy generated through the bringing together of certain aspects of energy, and the triple result thereby produced; the activities resulting from this stream of dynamic electrical energy, emanating from some centre, which sweeps into response all that it contacts, and which holds the responsive units in some form or another.

From the occult standpoint, all that manifests is spheroidal in form, and is appropriately called a wheel, yet (in dense physical manifestation) the forms are diverse, and many, and unless etheric vision is present, the spheroidal forms of all lives are not apparent. How can this be explained? There are three major reasons for this illusion, and these we might here touch upon, finding in the word "illusion" [15] the key to the mystery.

We have been told in connection with the dense physical body that it is not considered a principle and is not (in this second solar system) expressing those qualities which are characteristic of the solar Logos and His present incarnation. We are told, further, that the grosser dense forms of substance, all that is objective and tangible upon the physical plane, are vibrating to a key which is characteristic of the preceding system, being a left-over (if so it might be expressed) of an earlier kalpa.

These two points must be carefully borne in mind and latitude allowed for them, when endeavouring to express the truth anent motion. Therefore, a number of the atoms of matter are as yet governed by an internal life which has for its main, distinctive feature, the faculty of a much closer adhesion, and a decisiveness of grouping that is inherently characteristic of the present body of manifestation of the solar system. We must remember when considering this, that all that is dense and gross in all forms, concerns only those forms on the three lower subplanes of the lowest systemic planes; the forms are constructed of matter of all the planes, but the percentage of gross matter is as we can plainly see but small. Interaction for the mineral monad exists, and completely negatives the vibration of the three lower subplanes of the physical plane; it passes eventually into forms which are more closely allied to the "true form."

The mineral monad has a problem slightly at variance with that of the other kingdoms, for it is specifically an

[15] Maya or Illusion. The word Maya is one which has to be properly understood by you in order that you may catch the spirit of the ancient philosophy. The derivation that is given for the word is Ma + Ya or not that. Maya is therefore a power that makes a thing appear as what it is not, or *a power of illusion* that arises out of limitation in the ancient concept of a true unity periodically appearing as multiplicity by the power of Maya that coexists with that unity.

expression of the lives which were classed as the failures of a previous solar system, and which were doomed to immerse themselves in the forms of the mineral kingdom. Liberation for man comes when he succeeds in freeing himself from the vibration of the three lower planes of our solar system, from that part of the logoic manifestation which constitutes His *dense* body, and which He does not therefore regard as a principle. It will, consequently, be apparent that there is a correspondence worthy of study to be found in the relation between the mineral monad, a human being, and a solar Logos. Viewing these three as an esoteric triplicity much light may be gained by meditation upon them as

a. The residual vibration of system 1,
b. The medial point of activity of system 2,
c. The subjective energy of the present system.

In the comprehension of this, and in the realisation that there are forces present in nature which are in the nature of left-overs, we have the clue to much of the puzzling side of manifestation, to the cruelty and death, the suffering, and the agony which are seen in the vegetable and animal kingdoms. In the term animal kingdom I include man's physical body. We have also the clue to some aspects of the left hand Path, and a clue to the problem of the basic cause of the appearance of such existences as black magicians. Just as no human being can escape the effects of energy generated by him in an early life, so the solar Logos Himself is working out and so held back by influences which are the result of His earlier activities in System 1.

The dense physical forms are an illusion because they are due to the reaction of the eye to those forces about which we have been speaking. Etheric vision, or the power to see energy-substance, is true vision for the human being, just as the etheric is the true form. But until the race is further evolved, the eye is aware of, and responds to the heavier vibration only. Gradually it will shake itself free from the lower and coarser reactions, and become an organ of true vision. It might be of interest here to remember the occult fact that as the atoms in the physical body of the human being pursue their evolution, they pass on and on to ever better forms, and eventually find their place within the eye, first of animals and then of man. This is the highest dense form into which they are built, and marks the consummation of the atom of *dense* matter. Occultly understood, the eye is formed through the interplay of certain streams of force, of which there are three in the animal, and five in the human being. By their conjunction and interaction, they form what is called "the triple opening" or the "fivefold door" out of which the animal soul or the human spirit can "look out upon the world illusion."

The final reason why the spheroidal true form of everything is apparently not seen on the planet can only at this stage be expressed through a quotation from an old esoteric manuscript in the Masters' archives:

"The vision of the higher sphere is hidden in the destiny of the fourth form of substance. The eye looks downwards and, behold, the atom disappears from view. The eye looks sideways and the dimensions merge, and again the atom disappears.

Outward it looks but sees the atom out of all proportion. When the eye negates the downward vision, and sees all from within outwards, the spheres again will be seen."

V. MOTION AND THE FORM-BUILDING IMPULSE

1. *Motion and the Mental Sheath.*

In the first section of this treatise we dealt somewhat with various phases of activity when considering "fire by friction," and the fiery motion of substance itself. We will only touch on some further aspects of the matter, for it is necessary that the student should bear in mind cer-

tain things. He should endeavour to ascertain the relationship between the universal mind (or the systemic
mind) and cosmic mind, and seek to comprehend the purpose of the mental sheath, which is one of the most interesting of the various bodies on account of its fiery
gaseous constitution. He should also seek to bring about
through meditation that mental control and alignment
which will result in stabilisation, and a responsiveness
to causal impression. This will lead to the transmission
of egoic instruction to the man on the physical plane.

Certain points in connection with the mental sheath
require emphasising, though it is not our purpose to do
more than call attention to their nature. Under the law
of correspondence, the student should be able to arrive at
certain conclusions and judge wisely the assignment of
purpose and place to the particular set of lunar pitris who
form the vehicle.

The mental body is composed of only four types of essence, whereas the astral body and the physical are
formed of seven types. The devas who compose this
body are grouped together as "the cohorts of the fourth
order" and have a close connection with that group of
cosmic Lives who (through the impress of their influence
upon solar matter) are responsible for the fact that our
solar system is a system of the fourth order. This group
of Lives is manipulated and controlled, in the macrocosmic sense, from cosmic mental levels via the central
spiritual sun, and through what is called in esoteric parlance "the fourth solar cavity." If students will meditate upon the nature of the human heart and its various
divisions, and particularly upon one of the valves, light
upon this complex problem may be forthcoming. There
is a constant inflow of energy from these great Entities
on cosmic mental levels; this inflow is the very life itself
of the solar units who are the sumtotal of the four lower
subplanes of the mental plane, and consequently the life

of the individual units who form the mental bodies of all human beings.

It will be apparent to all careful students that on all the planes, the fourth subplane has a peculiar and close relation to the fourth Creative Hierarchy, that of the human monads, and this is peculiarly the case in connection with the mental body. Through the medium of the plane number (five), and the subplane number (four), the possibility of initiation for the human being becomes a fact and that particular form of activity which distinguishes his progress is brought about. There are, therefore, two main streams of energy responsible for the form of the mental sheaths,

a. That emanating from the fourth subplane of the cosmic mental plane, including consequently the remaining three subplanes.

b. That emanating from the aggregate of those lives who form the fourth Creative Hierarchy. As we know, the esoteric number of this Hierarchy is nine, the exoteric number being four.

It is the blending of these two streams of force which (within the confines of the three worlds) results in the *progressive* activity of man. When this is coupled with the self-engendered action of the individual atoms of any sheath, we have spiral-progressive motion. This is true macrocosmically and microcosmically, for the activity of the cosmic physical plane (our seven systemic planes), is largely dependent upon the co-ordinated activity of certain force manifestations, which might be enumerated as follows:

a. That of the fourth Creative Hierarchy, who, in their aggregate, form the force centres.

b. The emanating influences of the fourth cosmic ether, the buddhic plane, upon which is dependent, throughout the system, the manifestation of that which is tangible and objective.

c. The opening up, both macrocosmically and microcosmically, of the fourth aspect of the solar and human egoic lotus; this is the revelation of the "Jewel in the Lotus," and macrocosmically is the perfect co-ordination of the three aspects through the medium of substance; this is the completion of logoic purpose, which is that of the fourth group. It might be expressed otherwise:

"When all is known of the significance of fourth dimensional existence, then the fourth order with the fifth will complete the sacred nine."

d. The specific alignment, interplay or free circulation of force simultaneously through the following manifestations of the one life:

1. The logoic Quaternary and equally the human.
2. The fourth systemic ether.
3. The fourth cosmic ether, the buddhic.
4. The fourth Creative Hierarchy.

When this has been completed, the goal universal will have been reached, and the Logos will have assumed the desired control of His physical body; the human units will be then functioning upon the buddhic plane, and the groups of lives who form the mental bodies of the human beings (who are numerically allied with the above progression) will have equally achieved.

Certain influences and forces play upon the mental sheath of any human being, and produce in it that activity which is termed "spiral progressive." These forces might be briefly considered as comprising the following:

1. The energies of the atoms of substance which compose the mental body.
2. The energies of the lunar father who is the coherent

life of the mental group body. These two groups
concern the Not-Self, the third aspect of monadic
manifestation.

3. The energies of the solar Angel, or Father, which
   is the co-ordinating principle behind manifestation in the three worlds.

4. The energies of the intelligent lives who form the
   body egoic. These lives find their emanating
   source on other levels than the systemic. These
   two groups concern the egoic principle, the middle
   principle which links the above and the below, and
   is the second aspect of monadic manifestation.

5. The energy emanating from the "Jewel in the Lotus" itself, the focal point of energy in the Upper
   Triad. This concerns the Self, the highest aspect
   of monadic manifestation.

The effects produced by the play of these five types
of energy upon each other produce (through the medium
of the mental unit) that which we term the mental sheath.
This sheath is after all only the aggregate of those atoms
within a specific area with which the Thinker has to do,
which he holds magnetically within his ring-pass-not, and
which serve as the medium for his mental expression, according to his point of evolution. This same definition
will be recognised as true of all atomic sheaths, and one
of the things which students of the occult sciences will
eventually do is to investigate the nature of the informing lives of the sheaths, the qualities of the energies influencing such lives, and the character and force of the
basic underlying principles. They will thus arrive at
facts concerning energies in the human kingdom which
will prove of inestimable value.

In order to keep the basic idea of this Treatise corresponding in its various divisions, I might call your attention to the four points we considered relative to motion

in the physical and astral sheaths. We found that the effects of such motion might be regarded as four altogether:

Separation.
Momentum.
Frictional Activity.
Absorption.

Separation. This separation is brought about through the initial activity of the Ego who produces the first of those forms which he intends to use during the cycle of incarnation, through the bringing together of these energies through self-engendered impulse. He, for purposes of development, identifies himself with that form, and thus *temporarily* separates himself off from his own real Self. Through the veil of mental matter he first knows separation, and undergoes his first experiences of the three worlds. This deals with separation from the highest aspect. Viewing it from the personality standpoint, separation is again to be seen, for the activity of the monadic sheath, its own internal volition produces the formation of a sphere of activity, distinct in its nature and governed by laws of its own, which—until a certain amount of alignment has been achieved during evolution—lives its own separate existence apart from the two lower sheaths, astral and physical. Thus it can be truly said that the "mind slays the Real"[16] and serves as the "great Deluder" of the Self in the one case, and as the "great Separator" in another; it comes between the centralised egoic life and the personality existences.

This life of separation becomes steadily stronger as the rotary-spiral action of the mental body becomes intensified during the cycles of manifestation, and the "individu-

[16] "Mind the Slayer of the Real."—*Voice of the Silence*, pp. 14-15.

alised" Idea becomes daily more dominant. The "Aham-kara" principle,[17] as it is called in the *Secret Doctrine,* does its work, and man becomes strongly self-centred, and self-conscious *in the lower connotation of the term.* Later, as higher energies come into play and the effort is made to balance the three types of force manifestations in the three worlds through the three vehicles, the Ego becomes aware of delusion and eventually frees himself. When this is in process of consummation during the final stages of evolution, the mental body becomes a transmitter for force currents from the egoic mind, the antaskarana between the higher mind and the mental sheath is built, and the "transmitting mind body" blends itself with the "reflecting astral body." Thus separation is negated.

Students will note, therefore, that the goal for the mental body is simply that it should become a transmitter of the thoughts and wishes of the solar Angel, and should act as the agent for the Triad. The goal for the astral body is that it should be the reflector in a similar way of the buddhic impulses, which reach the emotional body via certain petals in the egoic lotus, and the astral permanent atom. The process of equilibrising the forces in the personality (thus producing stability, and alignment) is brought about through the scientific manifestation of the electrical reactions of the three sheaths.

The *mental sheath* is regarded in its totality of force as positive. The *physical bodies* are regarded as negative to the mental. The *astral vehicle* is the point of the at-one-ment of the energies; it is the battleground whereon the dualities are adjusted to each other, and equilibrium is attained. This is the underlying thought when the words "kama-manasic" body are used, because for two-thirds of the pilgrim's journey this body serves a dual purpose. It is only during the later stage that a

[17] *Ahamkara.* The "I" making principle necessary in order that self-consciousness may be evolved, but transcended when its work is over.

man differentiates between will and desire, and between his mental body and his desire body.

Momentum: The activity of the mental sheath and its gradually increasing rate of vibration is brought about by the inflow of energies of different kinds. These various factors, as they are brought to bear upon the mental sheath produce an increased activity and speed in the rotary motion of the individual atoms, and also greater speed in the progress of the entire sheath. This means a more rapid transference of the atoms of low vibration out of the sheath and the substitution of atoms of high quality.

It involves also more rapid transition of the various energies, or increased spiral action. This is one of the factors resulting in more rapid incarnation, and more rapid assimilation of the experiences learnt. Curiously enough, from the standpoint of the average thinker, this factor causes longer devachanic periods, for these cycles of interior mental consideration are of ever increasing activity. They are cycles of intense mental adjustment, and of the generation of force until (towards the close of the cycle of incarnation) the activity which has been generated is so strong that continuity of consciousness becomes an accomplished fact. The man frequently then foregoes devachan as he needs it no more. Other results are the fourth dimensional activity of the various "wheels," which begin not only to rotate but to "turn upon themselves," and the vivification of the four spirillae of the mental unit. Some of the energies which produce increased momentum in the mental sheath might be enumerated, and as the students consider them it will again become apparent what a complicated thing human unfoldment really is. These energies are:

1. The direct increasing influence of the solar Angel. This influence is felt in four stages:

    As the three rows of petals unfold.

As the "interior jewel" rays forth more powerfully.

2. The reflex action from the physical personality, or
the thought currents sent through in course of
time from the physical brain.

3. The activities of the astral body.

4. The thought currents or energy units initiated by
identification with groups, national, family, racial
and egoic.

5. The currents which impinge upon the mental bodies
of all human beings as different Rays pass in and
out of incarnation.

6. The forces and energies which become active or
latent during different cycles.

7. The interplay between planets, or between systems
and constellations, of which an illustration can be
seen in the effect of Venusian energy upon our
Earth

and many more factors too numerous to mention. All
these energies have their effects, and serve either to
speed, or in some cases, to retard the evolutionary
process.

It should be borne in mind by students that all egoic
groups come under the Law of Karma, but only as it affects the Heavenly Man, and not the law as it demonstrates in the three worlds. This karmic law, which is the
governing impulse of His centres, will show itself in peculiar ways, and as the human monads compose those
centres, each group will have its own "activity" problems, will spiral through the round of Being in its own
peculiar manner, and will demonstrate qualities and motions different from its brothers. For instance, through
withdrawal of energy and not through basic inertia those
monads who are the sum total of the centre of creative
force of the Heavenly Man show qualities of violent

reaction on the physical plane against certain "laws of nature" and in the period of their transition from the lowest centre to the throat centre of the Heavenly Man, betray qualities of revolt which make them a puzzle to their brothers.

We have now to consider the "frictional activity" of the mental sheath, and the activity of the sheath as it manifests as absorption. These two concern, let us remember, the motion of the mental sheath as a whole. The result of this activity is rotary-spiral progressive action.

Frictional activity. This, as is apparent from the words, deals with the "Fire by friction" aspect of substance, and therefore with the lowest aspect of the energy of the mental sheath. The force of the Life within the sheath manifests in the attractive and repulsive action of the individual atoms, and this constant and ceaseless interplay results in the "occult heat" of the body, and its increased radiation. It is one of the factors also which produces the gradual building in of new atoms of substance (ever of a better and more adequate quality) and the expulsion of that which fails to suffice as a medium for intelligent expression.

The mental unit is the synthesis of the four types of force with which we are dealing, and of the four expressions of it which we are in process of considering.

Each of the groups of lives which are the living essence of four subplanes and which focalise through one of the spirillae of the unit and thus influence

a. The sheath itself
b. The man on the physical plane
c. Part of the head centre

express in greater or less degree these four qualities.

It might be noted here that the groups are called certain names by some occult teachers, which names convey the idea of the active enterprise which is their predominant function.

The "Lives" on the fourth subplane (that on which the mental unit has its place) are called "The absorbers of the above and the below" or the "Transmitting faces of the fourth order." They receive energy and absorb from the Ego on the one hand in the first stage of the incarnation process, and on the other absorb the energies of the personality at the close of the period of manifestation. They have, therefore, an activity which might be regarded as corresponding to the first aspect. When it is remembered that the cosmic process repeats itself on every plane, and that the Ego in the three worlds stands for the unmanifested, it will be seen that they are the primal separators, and the final "destroyers."

The lives of the next plane (which utilise the second spirilla of the mental unit) are called "The interacting points of cyclic momentum." These points which gather momentum through the process of attraction and repulsion represent, in the mental body, *dual force,* for it is only through the coming together and the separation of atoms, great and small, macrocosmic and microcosmic, that manifestation of any kind becomes possible.

On the subplane which is formed of lives functioning through the third spirilla, are found "the points of fric‚ tional activity" or the "heat producers" and these three —the absorbers, the points of momentum, and the heat producers, pour their united forces through the "separated lives" which form the real barrier between the next body and the mental sheath. This is only possible when their work is unified and synthesised. The student must here remember that the lives are the expression of one Life but that one or other of the spirillae will be the agency for lives which express specific qualities. We are dealing specifically with the fourth effect of motion in the mental sheath as it manifests throughout the entire vehicle.

Absorption: This is the faculty which produces the forms of the mental ring-pass-not, and which (at the close of the cycle) is the active principle behind *devachanic* manifestation. The student, through a consideration of the macrocosmic process, can arrive at a knowledge of the separation of the mental body and its individual functioning. It is anent the process of "heavenly withdrawal" that we are speaking; under the law of analogy it is not easily possible to follow the various steps and stages and this for the following reasons:

All our planes, being the cosmic physical subplanes, form the logoic physical body. At His final withdrawal from manifestation, He functions in His cosmic astral body, and the cosmic devachan is as yet far from Him, and impossible to conceive of. Certain points, therefore, anent man's "rest in Heaven" are all that is possible for us to deal with.

Absorption into devachan is absorption into a definite stage of consciousness within the logoic physical body; devachan, therefore, is occultly a state of consciousness, but of consciousness thinking in terms of time and space in the three worlds. It has therefore no location for the unit of consciousness, but has location from the standpoint of the Heavenly Man. Prakriti (matter) and consciousness are—in manifestation—inseparable.

The "devachan" of the occult books is connected with the consciousness of the logoic planetary body, and with the gaseous subplane of the cosmic physical plane. It is, consequently, transcended the moment a man begins to function in the cosmic ethers, such as the fourth cosmic ether, the buddhic plane. It is closely allied with certain karmic forces for, whilst in devachan, the man is occupied with the aggregate of the thought forms he has built, which are essentially of an occult, a mental, and a persistent nature.

It is in devachan that the man shapes and polishes the stones which are built into the Temple of Solomon. It is the workshop to which the individual stones (good deeds and thoughts) are taken for fashioning, after being extracted from the quarry of the personal life.

Being of mental matter, devachan might be regarded as a centre, or heart of peace, within the periphery of the sphere of influence of the mental unit. The four spirillae form four protecting streams of force. A correspondence to this stream of force can be seen in the four rivers which emanated from the Garden of Eden. Out of this garden man is driven into the world of physical incarnation and the Angel with the flaming sword protects the entrance, driving him back from entry until the time comes when evolution has progressed so far that he can come to the portal laden with stones which can withstand the action of fire. When he submits these stones to the fire and they stand the test, he can enter "Heaven" again, his time though being limited by the nature and the quality of what he brought.

When the consciousness within devachan has absorbed all the essences of life experience even that locality, or that aspect of matter, cannot enfold him, and he escapes from limitation into the causal vehicle.

2. *Motion in the Causal Body.*

We have studied somewhat this activity as it manifests in fourfold fashion in the mental sheath, and the reason that there has not been much to say anent this matter has been that the mental sheath comes under the laws of the matter aspect, and is subject to the same rules as are the material vehicles of all existences. It is only matter of a finer grade. The student, therefore, can apply what has been earlier said anent the astral and physical bodies

to the mental body, and thus negate the necessity of our
entering upon the subject in greater detail. The causal
body differs from the Brahma aspect in that it is a fuller
embodiment of the life of the second aspect, its predominant characteristics are those of the second aspect. To
study the nature of motion in the causal vehicle involves
much clarity of thought, and due appreciation of the nature of that body.

It should here be remembered that in considering the
causal body, we are dealing specifically with the vehicle
of manifestation of a solar Angel who is its informing life
and who is in process of constructing it, of perfecting it,
and of enlarging it, and thus reflecting on a tiny scale the
work of the Logos on His own plane.

Each part of the causal body is actuated by a type of
force emanating from some one or other great centre, and
it might be of interest, therefore, if we considered the
component parts of this "Temple of the Soul," if we
studied the type of animating activity and arrived at a
knowledge of the forces playing upon it and through it.
We will take them one by one, beginning with the outer
row of petals.

The Knowledge Petals. These are the petals which
represent the lowest aspect of the Triad and are responsive to the lowest forms of egoic force. These petals are
three in number and come under the influence of certain
streams of activity.

    a. One stream of energy emanates from the lower triad
        of permanent atoms, particularly the physical per-
        manent atom, via that one of the three petals called
        the knowledge petal. The stream of force engen-
        dered in the lower self circulates in a triple stream
        (the reflection in the lower self of the threefold
        Path to God) around the atomic triangle at the base
        of the egoic lotus. When of sufficient strength and

purity, it affects the outer row of petals. This begins to be felt during the third period of man's evolution when he is an average intelligent unit or atom. This energy, when it blends with the inherent life of the atomic lives which form the petals, produces eventually that intimate fusing of soul and body which makes man a living soul.

b. Another stream of energy emanates in time from the second tier of petals when in activity; this second tier is peculiarly instinctive with the life and quality of the Manasaputra in manifestation. The second tier of petals in any egoic lotus is the one that gives us the key to the nature of the solar Angel, just as the outer tier is—to the inner vision of the Adept—a clue to the point in evolution of the personality. By looking at the egoic lotus, the seer can tell the nature of the:

> *Personal self* through the condition of the atomic triangle, and the outer tier of petals.
>
> *Higher Self,* through the colour and arrangement of the central tier of petals. This tier gives the "family" of the solar Angel through the arrangement of atomic lives which form the petals, and the circulation of the streams of forces in those petals.
>
> *Monad,* through the inner circle of petals; its stage of lower awareness is revealed in a similar way.
>
> The *number of the Ray* concerned is known through the quality of the "light" of the concealed jewel.

In all these petals, groups of lives, solar and otherwise, are concerned, and streams of energy from them focus through the petals. This is apparent to the man who has the key. It is a curious fact that the streams of force which form the petals and which are in constant flux produce apparently "key symbols" within the periphery of the egoic wheel, and thus reveal themselves through their activity.

c. A third type of energy is that which—at the close of evolution—makes itself felt through the inner circle of petals, and which is the result of an inflow of monadic force, or atma.

d. Finally, therefore, when the petals are unfolded they are therefore transmitters of life or energy from three sources:

1. The lower self. . Lunar Pitri. . . Knowledge petals.
2. Ego. . . . . Solar Angel. . Love petals
3. Monad. . . . . .Father in
Heaven. . . . .Sacrifice petals.

It then becomes possible for a still higher form of energy to be felt, that which is the energy of the centre of the body of the Heavenly Man or planetary Logos, and which uses the "Jewel in the Lotus" as its focal point.

In this summation, we have dealt with the main types of energy manifesting in the egoic or causal body. Certain other influences must likewise be considered in connection with the outer tier of petals.

e. There is the energy reaching directly to the knowledge petals from the manasic permanent atom. The permanent atoms of the Spiritual Triad, as well as the bodies which are built around them, bring in certain groups of deva lives which have not as yet been much considered. They are not the lunar pitris, as that term is commonly understood, but have a direct connection with what is called "the cosmic moon" or to that dying solar system which has the same relation to our system as the moon has to the earth chain. This "cosmic moon'' transmits its energy to the manasic atomic subplane, via the planet Saturn. It is a triple energy and there is an esoteric connection between this triple energy, and Saturn's rings.

The old Commentary expresses this truth about an interesting group of sons of manas as follows:

"These Sons of mind clung to the old and dying form, and refused to leave their Mother. They chose to pass into dissolution with her, but a younger son (Saturn) sought to rescue his brothers, and to this end he built a triple bridge between the old and new. This bridge persists, and forms a path whereon escape is possible.

Some escaped and came to the help of the incarnating Sons of Mind who had left the Mother for the Father. The greater gulf was bridged. The lesser gulf persisted, and must be bridged by the living Sons of Mind themselves."

(This latter clause, refers to the building of the antaskarana.)

The energy transmitted from the manasic permanent atom of each incarnating jiva, its union with its reflection, the energy of the mental unit, and the triple stream of force thus created on the mental plane, has its planetary reflection in the relation of Saturn to another planetary scheme, and the three rings which are energy rings, and symbols of an inner verity.

f. Energy also pours in upon the knowledge petals from the egoic group, or from the aggregated knowledge petals of all the other lotuses in the group affiliated with any particular solar Angel. These groups have been earlier dealt with.

g. Energy is transmitted also to the petals via the groups and emanations from those planetary schemes and streams of force which form the outer petals of that great centre which is our solar system, and which we are told is seen from the higher planes as a twelve-petalled lotus. These streams do not emanate from the seven sacred planets but from other planetary bodies within the solar Ring-Pass-Not. Streams of force from *the Sacred Planets* play upon the central tier of petals. Herein lies a hint to the wise student, and a clue to the nature of the lower aspect of the solar Angel.

The Love Wisdom Petals. The streams of energy playing upon and through this second tier of petals closely resemble those already dealt with, but originate in differing groups of lives (lunar and solar).

a. The lowest form of energy, reaching this circle, emanates from the lower self, via the astral permanent atom, and the second petal of the outer tier. It is transmuted astral energy; it is more powerful than its correspondence in the first tier, owing to the inherent nature of the astral body, and the fact that it is augmented by the energy of the outer tier itself. This is one of the factors which brings about the more rapid progress made towards the close of the evolutionary period. There are certain streams of force in the evolution of the Monad which might be regarded as embodying for it the line of least resistance and they are specifically, beginning at the lowest:

    a. Emanations from the vegetable kingdom.
    b. Astral energy.
    c. The energy of the second circle of petals.
    d. Buddhic force.
    e. The activity of the second Logos, planetary or solar.

This is, of course, only true of this solar system, being the system of regenerative love.

b. Another form of influencing energy originates in the inner circle of petals, which is the focal point of force for the Monad, considered as atma. It must be pointed out that the streams of force which form the "petals of will" have a dynamic activity and (when in action) produce very rapid unfoldment. It is the inner of the two types of force; their mutual interplay provides the necessary stimulus, and results in the opening of the bud and the revelation of the Jewel.

The other types of energy find their correspondence with those already enumerated but I seek only to mention one of them,—that one which reaches the second tier of love petals, via the buddhic permanent atom. The energy thus originating is of a peculiarly interesting kind being the basic energy of all manifestation, and the sum total of the forces which form the sevenfold heart of the physical sun, and which are located within its sheltering luminosity. They in their turn are transmitters of the life-impulses from the heart of the central Spiritual Sun, so that we have a direct graded chain of transmitting energies.

a. The Heart of the central Spiritual Sun.
b. The sevenfold heart of the physical Sun.
c. The buddhic devas

to

d. The central circle of petals.
e. The astral permanent atom.
f. The heart centre within the Head.
g. The heart centre.

This buddhic energy is the sumtotal of the life force of Vishnu or the Son, Who is the transmitter and representative of a still greater cosmic Deity.

All the above serves to demonstrate the oneness of the tiniest unit with the one great informing Life, and shows the integral beauty of the scheme. The life of the greatest cosmic Lord of Love pulsates in infinitesimal degree in the heart of His tiniest reflection, and for this reason the atom man can likewise say "I too am God; His Life is mine."

The Sacrifice Petals. The energies or forces flowing through, and thus producing activity in the inner tier of petals, *the Sacrifice Petals,* are again similar in nature to those already enumerated, plus a definite stimulation of power in two directions.

One stimulating influence comes from the Will Aspect of the Monad, and thus (through transmission) from the first Aspect of the planetary Logos, and the other emanates from the "Sacred Bud which veils the Jewel." This is a particularly strong vibration because, when the inner circle is unfolded, the jewel is revealed, and the three "veils" or "sacred petals" open successively when the three tiers unfold.

It is thus apparent what numerous energising agencies are responsible for the "motion," occultly understood, of the egoic lotus. There is the inherent life of the atomic units forming each petal, and the circulatory life of the petal itself, regarding it as an individual unit. There is likewise the life of the circle of three petals and to this we must add the unified activity of the outer three circles, or the blending of *knowledge forces* absorbed from the personal self, of *love forces* which are the natural energies of the solar Angel, and of *sacrifice forces* pouring in from the Monad. Thus we have a marvellous aggregate of streams of energies, all representing interior and still greater (because cosmic) energies.

Finally, we have the dynamic force of the "Jewel" at the Heart, which is itself the focal point for the life of the planetary Logos, and through the planetary Logos of all the other Logoi.

Thus the potentialities latent in the incarnating jiva are stupendous, and he can become as God, provided he submits to the evolutionary process, and does not "refrain from being stretched upon the wheel.'' Thus the expansions of consciousness, which will admit an individual point of spiritual life into the councils, and the Wisdom of the Deity, are no idle promise but are guaranteed by the very constitution of the vehicle employed, and the place in the scheme of the ''developing Point,'' as the Ego is sometimes called. Naught in time and space can hinder, for every form being simply an expression of energised life, tends to serve every other form. Stimulation of some kind, the tendency to increase the vibration of contacting streams of energy, the accentuation of the activity of each centralised point as it contacts other points in the general heightening of the vibration through the interplay of those forces, all this sweeps the entire system on to its consummation, and to the revelation of the ''glory which shall some day be revealed.'' [18] All these forces form the aggregate of what is called ''fohatic life.'' As the system, or the body of the Logos, is carried forward through the energy in all its parts, so is each infinitesimal part speeded on to its similar individual glorification. The many which form the All, and the units which constitute the One, cannot be differentiated as the consummation is achieved. They are merged, and lost in the general ''beatific light,'' as it is sometimes called. We can then extend the concept somewhat further, and realise the cosmic interplay which is likewise being carried forward. We can picture the cosmic stimulation and intensification which proceeds as constellations form the units in the Whole instead of planets or human atoms. Whole suns with their allied systems in their immensity play the part of atoms. Thus some idea may be gained of the unified purpose underlying the turning of the great Wheel of the cosmic Heaven, and the working through of the life purposes of those stupendous Existences Who

[18] Bible. I. Peter, 5:1.

hold a position in the cosmic Hierarchy similar to that of the "ONE ABOUT WHOM NAUGHT MAY BE SAID."

It is not possible to give students an adequate idea of the beauty of the egoic lotus when it has reached the stage of complete unfoldment. The radiancy of its colour is not here referred to, but the brilliancy of the fires, and the rapid scintillation of the ceaselessly moving streams and points of energy. Each petal pulsates with quivering fire "points," and each tier of petals vibrates with life, whilst at the centre glows the Jewel, raying forth streams of energy from the centre to the periphery of the outermost circle.

The fires of living energy circulate around each individual petal and the method of interweaving and the circulation of the fires is (as may be well realised) sevenfold in nature according to the sevenfold nature of the Logos involved. Each circle of petals becomes, as evolution proceeds, likewise active, and revolves around the central Jewel, so that we have, not only the activity of the petals, not only the activity of the living points or the deva lives within the petal circumference, but likewise the unified activity of each tier of the threefold lotus. At a specific stage in evolution, prior to the opening of the central veiling bud, the three tiers of petals, considered as a unit, begin to revolve, so that the entire lotus appears to be in motion. At the final stages the central circle of petals opens, revealing that which is hid, and revolves around the Jewel, only in a contrary direction to the rapidly circulating outer lotus. The reason may not here be revealed for it is hid in the nature of the electric Fire of Spirit itself.

The Jewel itself remains occultly static, and does not circulate. It is a point of peace; it pulsates rhythmically as does the heart of man, and from it ray forth eight streams of living fire which extend to the tips of the four love petals and the four sacrifice petals. This eight-

fold energy is atma-buddhi. It is this final raying forth
which produces the eventual disintegration of the body
of the Ego. The knowledge petals, not being the subject
of the attention of this central fire in due time cease to be
active; knowledge is superseded by divine wisdom and
the love petals have their forces equally absorbed.
Naught is eventually left but the desire to "sacrifice,"
and as the vibratory impulse is akin to the nature of the
living Jewel, it is synthesised in the central living unit
and only the Jewel of fire remains. When all the petals
have merged their forces elsewhere, the process of revelation is completed. The lower fires die out; the central
fire is absorbed, and only the radiant point of electric
fire persists. Then a curious phenomenon is to be seen at
the final Initiation. The Jewel of fire blazes forth as
seven jewels within the one, or as the sevenfold electric
spark, and in the intensity of the blaze thus created is
reabsorbed into the Monad or the One. This process is
paralleled at the final consummation of solar evolution
when the seven Suns blaze forth before the great Pralaya.

All these modes of expression are but pictures which
serve to convey some small idea of the beauty, and the
intricacy of the divine process as it is carried on in the
microcosm, and in the macrocosm. They all serve to
limit and circumscribe the reality, but to the man who has
the divine eye in process of opening, and to him who has
the faculty of the higher intuition awakened, such pictures serve as a clue or key to the higher interpretation.
They reveal to the student certain ideas as to the nature
of fire.

In concluding what is to be said anent motion in the
causal body, I would like to point out that it too—on its
own plane—has the three characteristics of inertia, mobility and rhythm.

Inertia characterises the stage prior to the revolution of
the different tiers of petals, and this revolution only be-

gins to be felt when the petals are becoming active. It might be stated that the passing of the Pilgrim through the Hall of Ignorance corresponds to the period of "egoic inertia." During this period, the permanent atoms are the most noticeable points of light in the lotus; they constitute the "energy feeders" of the petal. Later, as the Pilgrim on the physical plane becomes more active and the egoic lotus is consequently unfolding with greater rapidity, the stage of *mobility* supervenes, and the circles commence their revolution. Finally, when the man treads the Path and his purpose is intensified, the central bud unfolds, the revolution is unified, and through the raying forth of the fires of the Jewel, a specific rhythm is imposed upon the lotus, and its energies are stabilised. This rhythm is diverse according to the type of Monad concerned, or the nature of the planetary Logos of a man's ray, his divine Prototype.

By the use of certain terms, information is conveyed to the Workers of the planet, the Brotherhood of Light, as to the *nature* of Ego concerned, the *quality* of his Ray, the number of his vibration, and the point of evolution attained. It will be apparent therefore, why it is not permitted here to make public the names of the seven rhythmic groups.

One of the effects produced in the lower man via the centres, through the unified activity of the causal body, is the co-ordination of the lower energies of the human being. These lower energies, as we know, demonstrate through the medium of:

   a. The three groups of centres in the three bodies.
   b. The etheric body itself.
   c. Certain centres in the physical body such as the pineal gland, the pituitary body and the spleen.

We are not here referring to the work of those centres as it is self-initiated because inherent in their very nature,

but to the effects to be seen in them as the three tiers of
petals function with increasing coherence, and the force
latent in the Jewel makes its presence felt. It might
specifically be said that these effects show themselves in
a threefold manner:

First, they cause the group of "wheels" or centres on
   each plane (or in each of the subtler vehicles) to become fourth dimensional, and to function as "wheels
   which turn upon themselves."

Secondly, they produce the orderly distribution of force
   by the forming of various triangles of energy within
   the bodies. This has been earlier dealt with, and
   it is only necessary here to point out that it is the
   energy, accumulating in the causal body and from
   thence making its presence felt, which produces
   among the centres the esoteric circulation of force
   which eventually links each centre up in a peculiar
   geometrical fashion, thus bringing every part of the
   nature of the lower man into subjection.

Thirdly, they bring about the stimulation of certain of
   the glands of the body which are deemed at present
   purely physical, and thus enable the solar Angel to
   grip and hold to His purpose the *dense* physical body.

It may be helpful if the student bears in mind the fact
that every centre may be considered as an evidence of
solar energy or fire, manifesting as a medium of lower
energy or fire by friction. Where these centres exist the
solar Angel is enabled gradually to impose his rhythm
and vibration upon that which vibrates to what is regarded as a lower rhythm. Thus He gradually swings the
entire lower form-substance into His control.

Before the final liberation but *after* the major part of
the purificatory and aligning processes are complete, the
vehicles of the initiate present a wonderful appearance,
due to the streams of energy from the egoic body which

can reach him. The egoic lotus is unfolded, and the central "fire" displayed. Each petal and each circle of petals is pulsating with life and colour, and is in active movement, revolving with great rapidity and with the stream of living energy circulating in every part of the lotus. The three permanent atoms glow and blaze and form, through their rapid revolution and interplay, what appears to be a blazing point of fire, so that it has been called at times "the reflection of the Jewel in the Mother's forehead." The eighteen centres on the three planes (four on the mental and seven on each of the two lower planes) are radiant wheels of fire, each group distinguished by a specific colour, and revolving with such rapidity that the eye can scarce follow them. The bodies are formed of the highest grades of substance, each individual atom, therefore, being capable of intensified vibration, and glowing with the light of its own central fire. The etheric body especially is to be noticed as it is a transmitter at this stage of the purest type of prana, and deserves the name sometimes given to it of "the body of the Sun." It is the envelope which holds the fires of the microcosmic system; in it are centred not only the pranic fires, but those seven centres which are the transmitters of all the higher energies from the Ego, and from the two higher material bodies. All is centralised, and the etheric vehicle waits for use on the physical plane in co-operation with the dense medium until the man can succeed in linking the consciousness of the two aspects of the dense body so that the continuity is preserved. This work accomplished, the three centres which are of a strictly physical nature—the pineal gland, the pituitary body and the spleen—themselves become luminous and radiant, and all the fires of the body are so stimulated that the atoms which form the physical sheath appear to radiate. This is the occult truth behind the belief that every messenger from the Lodge and every Saviour of man is naturally a healer. The forces which flow through a man whose atoms, centres, sheaths, and causal body form a coherent unit in full and radiant activity are of such strength and purity as to have a definite effect upon the nature of those they contact. They heal, stimulate and increase the vibration of their fellow men.

All this must be somewhat realised and visioned before a man on the physical plane will be willing to undergo the purifying discipline, and tread the Path whereby he finds his centre and works from that standpoint of power. He has to align these various factors, or energy centres, and thus bring on to the physical plane power to be used in the healing of the nations. When the glory of a man's inner God is seen, when his radiance shines forth then will it be said of him as of those who have preceded him along the Path: "Then shall the Sun of Righteousness arise with healing in his wings." [19]

There are, in connection with human evolution, certain factors which produce definite and important results, when connected with each other through linking streams of energy and therefore consciously functioning. These factors might be considered as follows, dividing them into two groups, each of them emphasising the duality of the microcosmic manifestation:

Group I.

1. The Knowledge Petals.
2. The knowledge petal in each of the two inner circles.
3. The centres on the mental plane.
4. The throat centre in etheric matter.
5. The alta major centre.
6. The physical brain.

Group II.

1. The Love Petals.
2. The love petal in each circle.

[19] Bible. Malachi, 4:2.

3. The centres on the astral plane.
4. The heart centre in etheric matter.
5. The pituitary body.
6. The sympathetic nervous system.

These various alignments (when functioning with due adjustment) result in the transmission of energy in the first case from the manasic permanent atom, and in the second case from the buddhic permanent atom. It will be apparent, therefore, how important it is that the student duly considers the process of bringing about a uniform alignment, and a conscious appreciation of the vibratory processes of these two groups. As he brings this adjustment about, the effect upon the physical plane will be the manifestation of the powers of the Soul, and of the healing capacity; the man will become a focal point for egoic energy and a server of his race. The black magician brings about similar results by means of the first group, only with the exception that he cannot align the knowledge petals in the two inner groups, as the love-wisdom aspect is atrophied in his case. He does, however, bring through the energy of the manasic permanent atom, for the force of Mahat (of which Manas is an expression) is closely connected with what is erroneously called "evil." Mahat and cosmic Evil have a close connection.

The great Existences Who are the principle of Mahat in its cosmic sense are connected with the lesser existences who express systemic evil. They are the sum total of the separative instrument, and where separation in any *form* exists, there is to be found ignorance, and therefore evil. Separation negates comprehension, or knowledge of that which is to be found outside the separated consciousness, for separative knowledge entails identification with that which is expressing itself through the medium of a form. Therefore, the Brothers of the Shadow can, and do, reach high levels along one aspect of consciousness, and touch certain specific heights of spiritual evil, going a great way along the line of Mahat, or knowledge, the principle of Universal Mind. They can reach, in their later stages, expansions of consciousness and of power that will take them far beyond the confines of our solar system, and give them attributes and capacities which prove a menace to the unfolding of the second Aspect.

The first group of alignments, when not balanced by the second group, is the line of the black magician; it will lead him eventually out of the stream of fivefold energy we call *manasic* on to the cosmic path of fohatic energy, the strictly mahatic. When on that Path two directions are possible to him; one will keep him in touch with the natural substance aspect concerned with the cosmic incarnations of *our* solar Logos; the other will sweep him on to that centre in the universe which is the emanating source of the mahatic principle; it is the focal point where is generated that type of energy which makes possible the *dense* physical manifestation of Gods and men.

In making this statement, it is necessary to bear in mind that the dense physical sheath is never considered a principle. It is ever deemed *occultly* evil. The matter might be more simply expressed by stating that the black adept is frankly concerned with what is termed "the residue of that which earlier was." He responds to the vibration of the solar system of an earlier greater cycle in which the knowledge, or the manasic principle, was the goal of achievement. He does not respond to the impulse of this solar system, but this lack of response is hid in the karma of the earlier manifestation. As we know, the Sons of Mind or the incarnating jivas are the returning nirvanis of a previous logoic incarnation. They have achieved mind, and need love. Some few, through a mysterious cycle of events inexplicable to man in this solar system, repudiated opportunity and linked themselves with that great deva existence which is the impulse of the dense physical, and they cannot loose themselves. Their destination, as well as his, is hidden in the plans of the ONE ABOUT WHOM NAUGHT MAY BE SAID, and in this solar system there is no hope for them. Fortunately, they are little likely to make themselves known to average man; it is the Adepts of the Good Law Who meet them the most often.

The subject is most intricate, but some light may come, if we remember that manas on the mental plane is found in two expressions:—the mental unit on the form levels and the manasic permanent atom on the formless planes. These two types of manas may be regarded as embodying the qualities of the two kinds, white and black. The mental unit or the mind aspect of a man, for instance, is after all but the sixth sense, and has to be transcended by the higher mind and the intuition. The black brother carries the evolution of the senses on to a stage inconceivable to man now and this sixth mahatic sense is of vaster extent and service to them than it ever is to the white Adept. Therefore, it will be apparent that for a long cycle of time, the black magician can persist and develop his powers because one-third of the force of the egoic lotus is his and he knows well how to utilise it to the best advantage. He builds also an antaskarana, but of quality and objective different to that of the student of the white magic. It is called "the path of manasic evil," and bridges a gap between the mental unit of the magician concerned, and certain correspondences on mental levels in the vehicles of the devas of that plane. Through this medium, and through *identification with the devas,* he can escape from the three worlds to spheres of evil incomprehensible to us. The point to be remembered here is that the black magician remains ever a prisoner; he cannot escape from substance and from form.

There is no need to enlarge further on this subject. I would like to enumerate the lines of alignment of the third group which eventually transcends the other two, and effects the final illumination and liberation of the man.

Group III.

1. The Sacrifice Petals.
2. The sacrifice petals in the two outer groups.
3. The three *major* centres in each of the three planes of the three worlds, producing thus absorption of the lower four centres on each plane.
4. The head centre, or the thousand-petalled lotus.
5. The pineal gland, producing the vivification and irradiation of the entire lower nature.

These three groups of forces in man, when synthesised, produce eventually that perfect co-ordination and adaptation to all conditions, forms and circumstances which eventuate in the escape of the liberated vital spark. This is technically accomplished when the ''bud'' opens, and it becomes possible for the Hierophant at initiation to liberate the energy of the Monad, and to direct that energy (through the agency of the Rod) so that eventually it circulates free and untrammelled through every part of the lower threefold manifestation. As it circulates, it destroys by burning, for it arouses the kundalini aspect perfectly by the time the fifth Initiation is taken. The destroyer aspect becomes dominated, and the form is ''burnt upon the altar.''

These ideas can also be studied in their larger aspect; a clue to the mystery of cosmic evil may be found in the difference existing between the sacred and non-sacred planets, and in the purpose and place, hitherto unrecognised, of the lives of the informing existences of the many planets and planetoids in the solar system. Some are purely mahatic or of the third Aspect, dominated by the devas. Others (of which the sacred planets are examples) are controlled by the second Aspect, and that second aspect will work through unconquerably into manifestation.

A few, like our Earth planet, are battlegrounds, and the two Aspects are in collision, with the indication of the eventual triumph of the "white" magic.

VI. EFFECTS OF SYNTHETIC MOTION

1. *Introductory remarks on alignment.*

The effects of the synthetic activity of the centres, sheaths and causal body produce:

Periodicity of manifestation.
The linking of the Triangles.
The relation between:
a. The alta major centre.
b. The throat centre.
c. The centres on the mental plane.

If we summarize the thoughts conveyed here, we will find that it deals with some aspects of that very necessary alignment which must take place prior to full ability to serve in final liberation. We have studied from many angles the component parts of man, the microcosm, and the mode whereby he manifests on earth in order to express that which lies hidden, and to make his energy felt in the group and place where he finds himself. The constitution of the causal body has been seen to consist of a triple form of energy, with a fourth and more dynamic type of force latent at the heart, ready to demonstrate when the other three forms are active, thus utilising them as a vehicle. We have noted also that there are also three forms of energy which we call the sheaths of the personal self, and which have also to be actively functioning before the triple egoic force can make itself felt through their medium. Added to these factors, must be mentioned the seven centres in etheric matter which find their place in the etheric body, and which awaken and become active as the sheaths swing into rhythmic activity. Of these centres the three major are of the main importance where egoic alignment is concerned, and their vital force only begins to make itself felt *after* the lower four are fully active.

A second factor which works into the general scheme here is the latent triple kundalini fire which is aroused and mounts through the triple spinal channel just as soon as the three major centres (the head, the heart and the throat) form an esoteric triangle, and can thus pass the fiery energy hidden in each centre in circulatory fashion. To summarise therefore: we have perfected alignment just as soon as the following factors have been put in touch with each other, or as soon as their motion or activity is synthesised; this is a most important subject for students of meditation, and for those who tread the Path of attainment to consider and practically realise.

1. The three tiers of petals.
2. The three sheaths.
3. The three major centres.
4. The threefold Kundalini fire.
5. The threefold spinal channel.
6. The three head centres, the pineal gland, the pituitary body, the alta major centre.[20]

Another factor which must be allowed for in advanced stages of development, is the third eye which is to the occultist and true white magician what the fourth energy centre (the jewel in the lotus) is to the lotus, or to the three tiers of petals. The correspondence is interesting:

The jewel in the lotus is the director of energy from the monad, whilst the third eye directs the energy of the Ego on the physical plane.

The jewel in the Lotus is the centre of force which links

---

[20] The alta major centre, which is formed at the point where the spinal channel contacts the skull and is therefore situated in the lowest part of the back of the head is formed of the lowest grade of etheric matter, matter of the fourth ether, whereas the etheric centres of the disciples are composed of matter of the higher ethers.

the buddhic and mental planes. When it is to be
seen and felt, the man can function consciously on
the buddhic plane. The third eye links the awakened
physical plane man with the astral or subjective
world, and enables him to function consciously there.
The jewel, or diamond concealed by the egoic lotus, is
the window of the Monad or Spirit whereby he looks
outward into the three worlds. The third eye is the
window of the Ego or soul functioning on the physical
plane whereby he looks inward into the three worlds.
The jewel in the lotus is situated between manas and
buddhi whilst the third eye is found between the right
and left eyes.

One of the main functions of the Master in this cycle
(though not in all cycles) is to teach His pupil how to
reconcile all these factors, how to synthesise their various
modes of motion or expression, and how to co-ordinate
them all so that the vibration is uniform. When energy
from the Ego controls, or imposes its rhythm upon the
various sheaths via their respective major centres, when
the triple fire is mounting in orderly fashion via the triple
channel, and when the three head centres are united in
triangular fashion, then we have illumination or the irra-
diance of the entire personality life, darkness gives place
to light, and the Sun of Knowledge arises and dispels the
darkness of ignorance. The minor centres are concerned
with the internal co-ordination of the sheath, the major
with the group co-ordination or the interrelation of one
sheath to another. The man becomes a burning and a
shining light, radiating forth a light which burns from
within.

When the next step is accomplished, and the energy of
the Monad, focussed through the jewel, makes itself felt
also on the physical plane, passing through the triple
egoic lotus via the channels already utilised by the Ego,

we have a man who is "inspired," who is a spiritual creator, and who is himself "a Sun of Healing Radiance."

These are the objectives before all those who tread the path and the goal ahead for those who follow the necessary discipline of life, and the stages of unfoldment through meditation. There are, needless to say, certain modes of work and mantric formulas known to the Masters which enable Them to hasten the process (when necessary) for Their disciples, but these are secrets scrupulously guarded and not frequently used. The usual method, a lengthy and laborious one, is to let the pupil find out each step of the way for himself, to teach him the constitution of his own body, the nature of the sheaths, and the function and apparatus of energy and so let him gradually become aware of the forces latent in himself. What is meant by the "three periodical vehicles" and the seven principles or qualities of force, is slowly revealed to him, and through experience, experiment, frequent failures, occasional success, mature reflection and introspection, and frequent incarnation, he is brought to the point where he has produced a certain measure of alignment through self-induced and continuous effort. He is then taught how to utilise that alignment, and how to manipulate energy consciously so that he can bring about on the physical plane results in service that for many lives have been probably a dream or an impossible vision. When he is proficient in these two things—stabilisation and manipulation—then, and only then, are committed to him the words and secrets which produce the demonstration on the physical plane of spiritual, or monadic, energy by means of the soul or egoic energy, utilising in its turn the energy of the material forms in the worlds, or what we might call bodily energy. This has been expressed in the following mystical and occult phrase:

"When the jewel sparkles as does the diamond under the influence of the rays of the blazing sun, then the setting likewise gleams and rays forth light. As the diamond shines with in-creasing brilliance, the fire is generated which sets on fire that which held and enclosed.''

2. *Motion produces periodic manifestation.*

We must here bear in mind, that we are considering *synthetic* alignment in connection with the second aspect, and are therefore dealing with the activity of those forms of divine manifestation which are nearing their objective. This objective might be defined as ability to vibrate syn-chronously with the greater unit of which it is a part. This must, therefore, be considered by the student in seven ways.

The first three ways concern the relation of the per-fected or nearly perfected units in the three kingdoms of nature with their immediate group soul, and their con-tinued manifestation in any particular kingdom.

Fourth, the relation of the disciple, or man on the path, to his immediate group, and the laws which govern his reappearance in physical incarnation.

Fifth, the relation of a planetary Spirit to His group of planets, and the processes of man's obscuration, or with-drawal, from physical plane manifestation.

Sixth, the relation of the major three planetary Spirits, or the three major aspects of the Logos and their mani-festation.

Seventh, the relation of the informing Life of a solar system to the group of constellations of which He forms part, and His periodic manifestation.

These subjects have been touched upon when we studied incarnation and, earlier still, when considering pralaya or obscuration, but we dealt then with them in general terms. We might now deal more specifically with the final activi-ties, or modes of motion, in these various congeries of lives, and see what occurs during the final stages of con-scious existence, and of limited manifestation. The subject is peculiarly abstruse, particularly where the elemental groups are concerned, but certain interesting points might here be brought out which will bear the closest study. Let us consider the three lower kingdoms first and pass later to the methods and activities of a human being, of a planetary Logos, and of a solar Logos.

The appearance, and the final disappearance, of any manifested Life is intimately concerned with the possession, the evolutionary development, and the final disintegration, of the permanent atom. Permanent atoms, as the term is usually understood, are the property of those lives only who have achieved self-consciousness, or individuality, and therefore relative permanence in time and space. The permanent atom may be viewed as the focal point of manifestation on any particular plane. It serves, if I may use so peculiar a term, as the anchor for any particular individual in any particular sphere, and this is true of the three great groups of self-conscious Lives:

a. The incarnating Jivas, or human beings,
b. The planetary Logoi,
c. The solar Logos.

We must remember here that all the atomic subplanes of the seven planes form the seven spirillae of the logoic permanent atom, for this has a close bearing upon the subject under consideration.

The units, therefore, in the three lower kingdoms possess no permanent atoms but contribute to the formation of those atoms in the higher kingdoms. Certain wide generalisations might here be made, though too literal or too identified an interpretation should not be put upon them.

First, it might be said that the lowest or *mineral kingdom* provides that vital something which is the essence of the physical permanent atom of the human being. It provides that energy which is the negative basis for the positive inflow which can be seen pouring in through the upper depression of the physical permanent atom.

Secondly, the *vegetable kingdom* similarly provides the negative energy for the astral permanent atom of a man, and thirdly, the *animal kingdom* provides the negative force which when energised by the positive is seen as the mental unit. This energy which is contributed by the three lower kingdoms is formed of the very highest vibration of which that kingdom is capable, and serves as a link between man and his various sheaths, all of which are allied to one or other of the lower kingdoms.

a. The mental body.. mental unit...animal kingdom.
b. The astral body...astral perma- vegetable king-
    nent atom... dom.
c. The physical body. physical per- mineral king-
    manent atom. dom.

In man these three types of energy are brought together, and synthesised, and when perfection of the personality is reached, and the vehicles aligned, we have:

a. The energy of the mental unit........positive.
b. The energy of the astral permanent
    atom..............................equilibrised.
c. The energy of the physical permanent
    atom ....negative.

Man is then closely linked with the three lower kingdoms by the best that they can provide, and they have literally given him his permanent atoms, and enabled him to manifest through their activity. The above three groups might be studied also from the standpoint of the three Gunas: [21]

[21] "Hence every manifested God is spoken of as a Trinity. The joining of these three Aspects, or phases of manifestation, at their outer points of contact with the circle, gives the basic Triangle of contact with Matter, which, with the three Triangles made with the lines traced by the Point, thus yields the divine Tetractys, sometimes called the Kosmic Quaternary, the three divine Aspects in contact with Matter, ready to create. These, in their totality, are the Oversoul, of the kosmos that is to be.

"Under Form we may first glance at the effects of these Aspects as

1. Tamas ...inertia .....mineral kingdom..physical   permanent atom.
2. Rajas .. activity ....vegetable   astral permanent kingdom ...... atom.
3. Sattva ...rhythm ....animal kingdom..mental unit.

All these must be regarded only from the point of view of the personality, the lower self, or not-self. In illustration of this idea, it might be pointed out that when the animal body of prehuman man was rhythmically adjusted, and had attained its highest or sattvic vibration, then individualisation became possible, and a true human being appeared in manifestation.

Each kingdom is *positive* to the one next below it, and between them is found that period of manifestation which bridges the two, and connects the positive and the negative. The types of most intense rajas or activity in the mineral kingdom are found in those forms of life which are neither mineral nor vegetable but which bridge the two. Similarly in the vegetable kingdom, the rajas period is seen in fullest expression just before the activity becomes rhythmic and the vegetable merges in the animal. In the animal kingdom the same is seen in the animals which individualise, passing out of the group soul into separated identity. These types of activity must be regarded as constituting for the mineral, physical activity, for the vegetable, sentient activity, and for the animal, rudimentary mental activity.

When this triple activity is achieved it might be noted that the dense physical body of the solar or planetary Logos is fully developed, and conscious contact can then

responded to from the side of Matter. These are not, of course, due to the Logos of a system, but are the correspondences in universal Matter with the Aspects of the universal Self. The Aspect of Bliss, or Will, imposes on Matter the quality of Inertia—Tamas, the power of resistance, stability, quietude. The Aspect of Activity gives to Matter its responsiveness to action—Rajas, mobility. The Aspect of Wisdom gives it Rhythm—Sattva, vibration, harmony. It is by the aid of Matter thus prepared that the Aspects of Logoic Consciousness can manifest themselves as Beings.''— *A Study in Consciousness,* by Annie Besant, p. 9.

be made with the etheric or vital body. *It is this contact which produces man,* for Spirit (as man understands the term) is after all but the energy, vitality, or essential life of the solar, or planetary Logos. Its correspondence in man is prana. A comprehension of this will be brought about if man realises that all the planes of our solar system are but the seven subplanes of the cosmic physical plane. It is the realisation of this which will eventually unite science and religion, for what the scientist calls energy, the religious man calls God, and yet the two are one, being but the manifested purpose, in physical matter, of a great extra-systemic Identity. Nature is the appearance of the physical body of the Logos, and the laws of nature are the laws governing the natural processes of that body. The Life of God, His energy, and vitality, are found in every manifested atom; His essence indwells all forms. This we call Spirit, yet He Himself is other than those forms, just as man knows himself to be other than his bodies. He knows himself to be a will, and a purpose, and as he progresses in evolution that purpose and will become to him ever more consciously defined. So with the planetary Logos and solar Logos. They dwell within, yet are found without, the planetary scheme or solar system.

It is useful to remember that in the three lower kingdoms, manifestation, or appearance on the physical plane, is ever *group* manifestation and not the appearance of separated units. Each group soul, as it is called, is divided into seven parts which appear in each of the seven races of a world period, and there is an interesting distinction between them and the units of the human kingdom. When portions of the group soul in one of its seven parts are out of incarnation they are to be found on the astral plane, even though the Mother group soul is found on the mental plane. Human units of the fourth kingdom when out of incarnation pass through the astral to the mental and descend again to incarnation from mental levels.

Each group soul, therefore, subjectively forms a triangle of force with one point (the highest) to be found on the mental plane, the lowest on the etheric levels of the physical plane, and another on the astral plane. The third point for the mineral group-soul is found on the second subplane of the astral, the vegetable on the third, and the animal on the fourth. It is owing to the fact that a centre of force for the animal group soul is found on the fourth subplane of the astral plane that it is possible for transference eventually to be made out of that kingdom into the fourth.

Certain laws govern the appearance periodically of the three kingdoms of nature, which are the laws of involution, the laws of the elemental kingdoms, and the laws of the three great groups which hold the germs and seeds of all manifested forms. We have in logoic manifestation the following seven groups for consideration:

1. 2. 3. Three groups of superhuman existence:
   - *a.* The group forming the Father aspect of which little can here be predicated.
   - *b.* The group of seven planetary Logoi.
   - *c.* The group of seven raja devas, or the life of each of the physical planes.
4. A group of solar lives who are the manasaputras or man.
5. 6. 7. Three groups of elemental lives, who form the three involutionary elemental kingdoms.

These three lower groups achieve concretion, and enter the upward arc, through the medium of the three lower kingdoms. The fourth group is the most important in some ways during the present cycle for it borrows from all the other six groups and is therefore the synthesis of energies taken from each and manifested. The higher three groups are closely allied, and until a man has passed out of the period of existence wherein he is controlled by that which he has borrowed from the three lower king-doms, he cannot comprehend the nature and purpose of the three higher. We might express the matter as follows:

The three higher groups are sattvic.

The three lower groups are tamasic.

The fourth group, or human, is rajasic.

Again, the three higher groups are energised by three streams of force which enter along the line of the three spirillae of the logoic permanent atom. The three lower groups are energised by energy entering by the three lowest spirillae (which we call the three lowest planes) and these spirillae energise the logoic dense body, were vitalised in the previous solar system, and are no longer in any way controlling factors in logoic existence. The fourth group, the human, is energised by the force of the fourth spirilla, to which we give the name of buddhic energy, and this fourth group has, therefore, the problem of bringing about conditions whereby the buddhic vibrations may dominate the other, and lower, three. It is this imposition which eventually releases the human units, and permits of their passing into the higher group. The elemental group souls find correspondences in the higher —first, in the human kingdom in the three main groups of Egos, in whom the three types of energy predominate; again in the three main or major planetary groups, and finally in the three aspects.

Elemental
   group....animal kingdom..Sattvic..Solar Logos....Uranus.
                          Father aspect.
Elemental
   group....vegetable kingdom..Rajasic..Planetary..Neptune.
                                       Logoi
                          Son aspect.
Elemental
   group....mineral kingdom..Tamasic..Plane devas..Saturn.
                          Mother, Brahma aspect

The fourth or human group, unites all three lives. The periodic manifestation of the three elemental groups (through the medium of the three lower kingdoms) is, therefore, governed by factors hidden in the nature of that great vibration which we call *tamasic,* or heavy rhythm. It is the vibration of Brahma, the third aspect, the mother or matter aspect. Their appearance, therefore, is one of a very slow manifestation, the seven subsidiary vibrations bringing in one or other of the seven groups of each group soul in a very slow alternation. The cycles cannot be given; two things only can be said: the appearance of these groups as units in manifestation is controlled by three factors:

1. The moon, for these are the many lunar fathers.
2. The ray in manifestation at any time.
3. The karma of the informing Life of any kingdom.

The second consideration is the karma and life-history of the planetary entity. He sleeps and awakes; he is the embodiment of tamas, and as he progresses and evolves so do the lower kingdoms.

The lunar pitris are to the planetary entity what the three major centres are to man or to the Logoi. The lunar Pitris who contribute the human form are (to the planetary entity) the correspondence to the *head centre.* Those who are the fathers of the vegetable forms correspond to his *heart centre,* whilst the Pitris of the mineral kingdom are analogous to the *throat centre.* This is all very obscure but hints of much value lie here.

It is not possible to give much further information relative to the periodical appearing of the subhuman forms of life. The subject is too obscure, and the detail too vast. Until the student has fitted himself to appreciate the symbolic, or hieroglyphic writings of the adepts,[22] it is impossible for him to grasp the matter. Much of the teaching on this matter is found in records in the department of the Manu, as it concerns primarily the initial stages of form building. It might be said that the appearance of any life in manifestation is due to primary activity on the part of some Entity, which activity is largely the expression of the first Ray. This concerns the periodical manifestation of the life or lives of any round just as it concerns also the ephemeral existence of a dragon fly; it deals with the form through which what we call a race is evolving and concerns itself with the tiny life of an individual in that race. The same laws govern all, though the response to the law may be relative and in degree. This law has the generic name of the "Law of Cycles," and is expressed in terms of time;

[22] *Symbols.*
  "In a symbol lies concealment or revelation."—Carlyle.
    1. Symbols are intended for:—
        a. The little evolved. They teach great truths in simple form.
        b. The bulk of humanity. They preserve truth intact and embody cosmic facts.
        c. The pupils of the Masters. They develop intuition.
    2. Symbolic books in the Master's archives used for instruction. These books are interpreted:—
        a. By their colour.
        b. By their position, i.e. above, on and beneath a line.
        c. By their connection with each other.
        d. By their key. One page may be read four ways:—
            1. From above downwards................involution.
            2. From beneath upwards................evolution.
            3. Right to left..........................greater cycles, etc.
            4. Left to right.......................... lesser cycles.
    3. *The three keys:—*
        1. Cosmic interpretation. The symbols standing for cosmic facts. i.e., Darkness. Light. The cross. The triangle.
        2. Systemic interpretation. Dealing with evolution of system and all therein.
        3. Human interpretation. Dealing with man himself. The cross of humanity. Seven-branched candlestick.
    4. *Four kinds of symbols:—*
        1. Symbols of extraneous objects....physical plane things.
        2. Symbols of emotional nature.....astral plane things; pictures.
        3. Numerical symbolism............Lower mental. Man used himself to count by.
        4. Geometrical symbolism.......... abstract   symbolism,   higher mental.

but the secret to the cycles may not as yet be given as it would convey to the intuitive too much dangerous information. It is the knowledge of this law as it concerns rounds, races, subraces, groups (involutionary and evolutionary) and individuals (human and superhuman) which enables the Lords of Karma, and the Adepts of the good Law, to manipulate force or energy, and so carry all that is, on to its triumphant conclusion. In connection with this, students may get much light on this difficult question of force if they bear in mind that every form in every kingdom on the downward, and the upward arc, is in itself a negative force impelled into activity by a positive force and demonstrating as a combination of the two. The distinctions are demonstrated in the fact that some forms are negative-positive, others positive-negative, whilst still others are at the point of equilibrium. This includes all the intermediate stages. The Builders of the cosmos work under cyclic law *consciously,* and utilise the aggregate of these forces in any kingdom, any group or any unit to bring about the consummation of the plan.

It would interest men much if they could see and interpret some of the records in the hierarchical records, for in them men and angels, minerals and elements, animals and vegetables, kingdoms and groups, Gods and ants are *specified in terms of energy formulas* and by a scrutiny of these records the approximate increase of vibration in any form of any kind can be found out at any time. This might be expressed in terms also of the Gunas; it will be found by disciples (when permitted access to the records) that they themselves, along with every other expression of the divine life, are described by a triple formula which conveys to the mind of the initiate the proportions of tamas or inertia, of rajas or activity, and of sattva or rhythm to be found in any form. This, therefore, through correspondences, imparts knowledge as to past achievement, present opportunity and the immediate future of any unit or embodied life, manifesting under any of the three aspects.

Another series of files in the records give—under a different formula—information as to what is esoterically called "the heat content" of any unit, "the radiating light" of any form, and the "magnetic force" of every life. It is through this knowledge that the Lipikas control the bringing in, and the passing out, of every Life, divine, superhuman, solar and human, and it is through a consideration of that formula which is the basic formula for a solar system that the physical plane appearance of a solar Logos is controlled, and the length of a cosmic pralaya settled. We must not forget that the Lipika Lords of the solar system have Their cosmic prototypes, and that These have Their feeble and groping human reflections in the great astronomical scientists who endeavour to ascertain facts anent the heavenly bodies, being subconsciously aware of the existence of these cosmic formulas conveying information as to the specific gravity, constitution, radiation, magnetic pull, heat and light of any sun, solar system, or constellation. Many of them in future and remote ages will pass to a full comprehension, and will have the formulas committed to their care, thus joining the ranks of the Lipikas. It is a peculiar line, requiring cycles of careful training in divine mathematics.

The Lipika Lords, controlling the periodical manifestation of life are, roughly speaking, divided into the following groups, which it might be of interest to note:

1. Three extra-systemic or cosmic Lords of Karma, Who work from a centre in Sirius through the medium of three representatives. These form a group around the solar Logos, and hold to Him a position analogous to the three Buddhas of Activity Who stand around Sanat Kumara.

2. Three Lipika Lords Who are the karmic agents working through the three aspects.
3. Nine Lipikas Who are the sumtotal of the agents for the Law working through what the *Qabbalah* calls the nine Sephiroth.
4. Seven presiding agents of karma for each one of the seven schemes.

These four groups correspond in manifestation to the Unmanifested, manifesting through the triple Aspects, and under Them work an infinity of lesser agents. These lesser agents might again be somewhat differentiated, each of the following groups being found in every scheme and on every ray-emanation.

1. The Lipika Lords of a scheme Who, through the manipulation of forces, make it possible for a planetary Logos to incarnate under the Law, and work out His cyclic problem.
2. Those who (under the first group) control the destiny of a chain.
3. Those who are the energy-directors of a globe.
4. Agents of every kind Who are concerned with the karmic adjustments, incident upon the periodical manifestation of such forms as:
   a. A round, seven in all.
   b. A kingdom in nature, seven in all.
   c. The human kingdom.
   d. A rootrace, subrace and branch race.
   e. A nation, a family, a group, and their correspondences in all the kingdoms.
   f. A plane.
   g. The reptile and insect world.
   h. The bird evolution.
   i. The devas.
   j. Human units, egoic groups, monadic lives,

and myriads of other forms, objective and subjective, planetary and interplanetary, in connection with the Sun, and in connection with the planetoids.

All work with energy emanations, and with force units under cyclic law, and all have the same objective,—the producing of perfected activity, intensification of heat, and of radiant magnetic light as an expression of the will or purpose of each embodied life.

Periodicity of manifestation is the cyclic appearance of certain forms of specified energy, and this is true whether a man is speaking of a solar system, of a Ray, of the appearance of a planet in space, or of the phenomenon of human birth. Certain factors extraneous to any energy unit under consideration, will inevitably affect its appearance, and act as deflecting or directing agents. The Law of Cycles has ever been regarded as one of the most difficult for a man to master, and it has been truly said that when a man has mastered its technicalities, and can understand its methods of time computation, he has attained initiation. Its intricacies are so numerous and so bound up with the still greater law, that of cause and effect, that practically the whole range of possible knowledge is thereby surmounted. To comprehend this law involves ability to:

a. Deal with the higher mathematical formulas of the solar system.

b. Compute the relationship between a unit of any degree and the greater whole upon whose vibration that unit is swept into periodic display.

c. Read the akashic records of a planetary system.

d. Judge of karmic effects in time and space.

e. Differentiate between the four streams of karmic effects as they concern the four kingdoms of nature.

f. Distinguish between the three main streams of en-

ergy—the units of inertia, mobility and rhythm—
and note the key of each unit, and its place in the
great group of transitional points.   These latter
units are those who are on the crest of one of the
three waves, and ready, therefore, to be transferred
into a wave of a higher vibratory capacity.

g. Enter the Hall of Records and there read a peculiar
group of documents dealing with planetary manifestation in a fourfold manner.   It concerns the
planetary Logos, and deals with the transference of
energy from the moon chain.   It concerns the transmission of energy to another planetary scheme,
and concerns the interaction between the human
Hierarchy (the fourth Kingdom) and the great informing Life of the animal kingdom.

When a man can do all these things and has earned the
right to know that which produces the phenomenon of
manifestation, he has earned the right to enter into the
councils of the planetary Hierarchy, and himself to direct
streams of energy upon, through and out of the planet.

Some idea of the complexity governing the periodical
manifestation of a human being may be gathered by a consideration of the forces which bring human units into
manifestation, which produce individualisation; this is,
after all, the appearing of a third stream of energy in conjunction with two others.   A man is the meeting ground
of three streams of force, one or other preponderating
according to his peculiar type.

Let us briefly enumerate these factors and thus get
some idea as to the complexity of the matter:

The first and paramount factor is the ray upon which
a particular human unit is found.   This means, that there
are seven specialised force streams, each with its peculiar
quality, type and rhythm.   The matter is further complicated by the fact that though the Ray of the Monad is its

main qualifying factor, yet two subsidiary Rays, those of the Ego and of the personality, have likewise to be considered.

Secondly, it must be borne in mind that the human units now upon this planet fall naturally into two great groups —those who reached individualisation, or became "units of self-directing energy," upon the moon, and those who attained self-consciousness upon the earth. There are important distinctions between these two groups, for the units of the moon chain are distinguished, not only by a more advanced development, owing to the longer period of their evolution, but also by the quality of great and intelligent activity, for (as might be expected) on the third or moon chain, the third Ray was a dominant factor. In this fourth chain, the quaternary dominates, or the synthesis of the three so as to produce a fourth, and this is one reason for the intensely material nature of those who entered the human kingdom on this planet. The distinctions between the two groups are very great, and one of the mysteries lying behind the main divisions of humanity—rulers and the ruled, capitalists and labourers, the governed and those who govern—is found right here. No system of sociological reform will be successfully worked out without a due consideration of this important fact. Other distinguishing features might be enumerated but would only serve at this stage to complicate the matter.

A third factor differentiating the groups of human units who reached self-consciousness on our planet is hidden in the methods employed by the Lords of the Flame at that time. They, we are told, employed three methods.

First, They themselves took bodies and thus energised certain of the higher forms of the animal kingdom, so that they appeared as man, and thus initiated a particular group. Their descendants can be seen in the highest specimens of the earth humanity now on earth. They are not even now, however, as far advanced as the groups of units from the moon chain who came in in Atlantean days. Their heredity is peculiar.

They implanted a germ of mind in the secondary group of animal-men who were ready for individualisation. This group, for a long time, was unable to express itself, and was most carefully nurtured by the Lords of Flame, nearly proving a failure. By the time, however, that the last subrace of the Lemurian root race was at its height it suddenly came into the forefront of the then civilisation, and justified hierarchical effort.

Thirdly, They fostered the germ of instinct in certain groups of animal-men until it flowered into mind. It must never be forgotten that men have within themselves (apart from any extraneous fostering) the ability to *arrive,* and to achieve full self-consciousness.

These three methods bring us to the fourth factor which must be remembered, that of the three modes of motion which powerfully affect the incarnating jivas.

The Sons of Mind are distinguished by the three qualities of matter as has been earlier brought out, and they have been generically called:

1. The Sons of sattvic rhythm,
2. The Sons of mobility,
3. The Sons of inertia.

These qualities are the characteristics of the three major Rays, and of the three Persons of the Godhead; they are the qualities of consciousness—material, intelligent, and divine. They are the predominating characteristics of the chains of which our earth is one.

Earth Planetary Scheme

First Chain............Archetypal.
Second Chain..........Sattvic Rhythm.

Third Chain...........Mobility.
Fourth Chain..........Inertia.
Fifth Chain...........Mobility.
Sixth Chain...........Sattvic Rhythm.
Seventh Chain.........Perfection.

The factors which we have considered as affecting the different incarnating units have a vital effect on their cyclic evolution, and the ray and the three main types produce varying periodic appearance. Certain statements have been made in occult books as to the length of time varying between incarnations. Such statements are in the main inaccurate, for they make no allowance for Ray difference, and permit of no calculations as to whether the human unit involved is a unit of inertia, a sattvic point, or a rajasic entity. No hard and fast rule can be laid down at this time for the general public, though such rules exist, and are governed by seven different formulas for the three main types. Within this sevenfold differentiation, exist many lesser, and the wise student refrains from dogmatic assertion on this most peculiar and difficult subject. The fringe of the matter has but been touched upon here. It should be remembered that in the earlier stages of incarnation, the unit is governed mainly by group appearance, and comes into incarnation with his group.

As time progresses and his own will or purpose becomes more distinctive, he will at times force himself into manifestation independently of his group, as will other group units, and this leads to an apparent confusion which is detrimental to the surface calculations of the superficial student. When this is the case, the particular unit concerned has his record transferred into another file in the hierarchical archives, and becomes what is occultly termed "a self directed point of fire." He is then strongly individualised, entirely self-engrossed, free of all group sense, except the earthly affiliations to which he adheres from the instinct of self-protection and personal well-being. In this stage he remains for a vast period of time, and has before him the mastering of a later stage in which he returns to the earlier group recognition on a higher turn of the spiral.

The rules governing the incarnations of average man have been considered elsewhere, and much information has been given in this treatise and in *Letters on Occult Meditation* which—if collated—will provide sufficient data for study for a long time. Not much has been given anent the incarnations of disciples and the methods involved in the later stages of evolution.

It should here be borne in mind that (for a disciple) direct alignment with the Ego via the centres and the physical brain is the goal of his life of meditation and of discipline. This is in order that the Inner God may function in full consciousness and wield full control on the physical plane. Thus will humanity be helped and group concerns furthered. Again it must be remembered that the basic Ray laws and the disciple's particular type will paramountly dictate his appearances, but certain other forces begin to hold sway which might here be touched upon.

The factors governing the appearance in incarnation of a disciple are as follows:

First, *his desire to work off karma rapidly* and so liberate himself for service. The Ego impresses this desire upon the disciple during incarnation, and thus obviates any counter desire on his part for the bliss of devachan, or even for work on the astral plane. The whole objective, therefore, of the disciple after death is to get rid of his subtler bodies, and acquire new ones. There is no desire for a period of rest, and as desire is the governing factor in this system of desire, and particularly in this planetary scheme, if it exists not, there is no incentive to fulfilment.

The man, therefore, absents himself from the physical plane for a very brief time, and is driven by his Ego into a physical body with great rapidity.

Second, *to work out some piece of service* under direction of his Master. This will involve some adjustments, and occasionally the temporary arresting of his karma. These adjustments are made by the Master with the concurrence of the disciple, and are only possible in the case of an accepted disciple of some standing. It does not mean that karma is set aside, but only that certain forces are kept in abeyance until a designated group work has been accomplished.

Third, *a disciple will return into incarnation occasionally so as to fit into the plan of a greater than himself*. When a messenger of the Great Lodge needs a vehicle through which to express Himself, and cannot use a physical body Himself, owing to the rarity of its substance, He will utilise the body of a disciple. We have an instance of this in the manner the Christ used the body of the initiate Jesus, taking possession of it at the time of the Baptism. Again when a message has to be given out to the world during some recurring cycle, a disciple of high position in a Master's group will appear in physical incarnation, and be "overshadowed" or "inspired" (in the technically occult sense) by some teacher greater than he.

Fourth, a disciple may, through lack of rounded development, be very far advanced along certain lines but lack what is called the full intensification of a particular principle. He may, therefore, decide (with the full concurrence of his Ego and of his Master) to *take a series of rapidly recurring incarnations* with the intention of working specifically at bringing a certain quality, or series of qualities, to a point of higher vibratory content, thus completing the rounding of his sphere of manifestation. This accounts for the peculiar, yet powerful, people who are met at times; they are so one-pointed and apparently so unbalanced that their sole attention is given to one line of development only, so much so that the other lines are hardly apparent. Yet their influence seems great, and out of all proportion to their *superficial* worth. A realisation of these factors will deter the wise student from hasty judgments, and from rapid conclusions concerning his fellow men.

Occasionally a variation of this reason for rapid and immediate incarnation is seen when an initiate (who has nearly completed his cycle) appears in incarnation to express almost entirely one perfected principle. This he does for the good of a particular group which—though engaged in work for humanity—is failing somewhat in its objective through the lack of a particular quality, or stream of force. When this becomes apparent on the inner side, some advanced disciple puts the energy of that particular quality at the disposal of the Hierarchy, and is sent forth to *balance* that group, and frequently to do so for a period of rapidly succeeding lives.

These are a few of the causes governing the periodic manifestation of those who are grouped in the Hierarchical records as "the aligned points of fire." They are distinguished by the energy flowing through them, by the magnetic quality of their work, by their powerful group effects, and by their physical plane realisation of the plan.

The coming into manifestation of the superhuman lives (such as greater liberated Existences, or the raja-devas of a plane), the appearing of the planetary Logoi and the solar Logoi in physical incarnation is governed by laws similar in nature to those governing the human unit, but of a cosmic scope. It will be apparent to the most superficial student that the gradual emergence of a plane out of the darkness which exists between systems is produced not only as the result of vibratory response to the enunciated Word, but as the working out of the karma of a cosmic Life and the relationship existing between that particular Life and the cosmic Existence Whom we call Brahma or the third Person of the Trinity. The deva Ruler of a plane is a superhuman Entity Who comes in under a great cosmic impulse to provide the vibratory form which will make possible the appearing of other and lesser forms. The Lords of the Rays, or the planetary Logoi, are similarly and karmically linked with the second aspect logoic, or with that manifesting Life we call Vishnu. It will thus be seen that three main impulses, each emanating from the will, plan, or conscious purpose of a cosmic Entity are responsible for all that is seen and known in our solar system. This, of course, has been oft emphasised in different occult books but the following tabulation may be of service:

Cosmic Entity	Systemic Entities	Number of Impulses	Quality
1. Brahma	The Raja Lords	7	Activity ... Inertia.
2. Vishnu	The Planetary Logoi	7	Wisdom ... Mobility.
3. Shiva	The Solar Logos	1	Will ... Rhythm.

It should be noted here that the above tabulation will apply to the microcosm as well as the macrocosm, and students will find it interesting to work it out.

3. *Triangular Linking.*

Enough has been indicated in this *Treatise* to show the general plan underlying and accounting for systemic emergence or incarnation, and it is not my purpose here to enlarge at great length. Just as it is not possible for a man in an early incarnation to conceive of the effects of evolution upon him and to realise the nature of the man upon the Path, so it is not possible for even great

systemic existences to conceive (except in the broadest
and most general terms) of the nature of the solar Logos,
and of the effect evolution will have on Him. Suffice it to
add, anent this matter, that when certain vast cosmic
alignments have been made and the energy from the
logoic causal ovoid on the cosmic mental planes is able
to flow unimpeded through to the physical plane atom
(our solar system) great eventualities and unconceived of
possibilities will then take place.

Certain phenomena likewise of a secondary nature to
this major happening will also take place as the cycles
slip away which may be generally summarised as follows:

First. Certain systemic triangles will be formed which
will permit of the interplay of energy between the different planetary schemes, and thus bring to more rapid maturity the plans and purposes of the Lives concerned.
It should be noted here that when we are considering the
transmission of energy through alignment and through
the forming of certain triangles, it is always in connection with the energy of the first aspect. It deals with the
transmission of electric fire. It is important to bear this
in mind, as it preserves the analogy between the macrocosm and the microcosm with accuracy.

Second. A final systemic triangle will be formed which
will be one of supreme force, for it will be utilised by the
abstracted essence and energies of the septenate of
schemes as the negative basis for the reception of positive electric energy. This electric energy is able to circulate through the schemes owing to the bringing about of
a cosmic alignment. It is the bringing in of this terrific
spiritual force during the final stages of manifestation
which results in the blazing forth of the seven suns.[23]
Though the seven have become the three, this is only in

[23] The rising and setting of the Sun symbolises manifestation and
obscuration.—S. D., II, 72.
Pralaya is of different kinds:—

connection with the dense physical planets. The blazing forth spoken of in the occult books and in the *Secret Doctrine* is in etheric matter; it is this etheric fiery energy which brings to a consummation (and so destroys) the remaining three major schemes. In this we have a *correspondence* to the burning of the causal body at the fourth Initiation through the merging of the three fires. It is only a correspondence, and the details must not be pushed too far. The Saturn scheme is esoterically regarded as having absorbed the "frictional fires of systemic space"; Neptune is looked upon as the repository of the "solar flames," and Uranus as the home of "fire electric." When, through extra-systemic activity based upon three causes:

1. Logoic alignment,
2. The taking of a logoic Initiation,
3. The action of the "ONE ABOUT WHOM NAUGHT MAY BE SAID,"

these three schemes are simultaneously stimulated and the fires pass from one to another in a triangular manner, they then too pass into obscuration. Naught is left save the blazing etheric suns and these—through very intensity of burning—dissipate with great rapidity.

1. Cosmic pralaya.........The obscuration of the three suns, or of three solar systems.
2. Solar pralaya..........The obscuration of a system at the end of one hundred years of Brahma. Period between solar systems.
3. Incidental pralaya......The obscuration of a scheme. Period between manvantaras.

Man repeats this at seventh, fifth initiations and at each rebirth in three worlds.

The Pleiades are the centre around which our solar system revolves.—S. D., II, 251, 581, 582.

The Sun is the kernel and matrix of all in the solar system.—S. D., I, 309, 310, 590, 591.

Kernel comes from the same word as corn.

Compare the words in Bible:—

"Except a corn of wheat fall into the ground and die it abideth alone, but if it die it bringeth forth much fruit."

The Sun is governed by the same laws as all other atoms.—S. D., I, 168, 667.

4. *Relation between the Throat, Alta Major and Mental Centres.*

The question of the centres has always had a great deal of interest for men, and much harm has been done through the directing of attention upon the physical centres. Unfortunately, names have been given to the centres which have their counterparts in the physical form, and with the usual aptitude of man to identify himself with that which is tangible and physical, a mass of data has accumulated which is based (not on spiritual knowledge) but on a study of the effects produced through meditation on the physical centres. Such meditation is only safely undertaken when a man is no longer polarised in the lower personal self but views all things from the standpoint of the Ego with whom he is completely identified. When this is the case, the centres in physical matter are recognised as being simply focal points of energy located in the etheric body, and having a definite use. This use is to act as transmitters of certain forms of energy *consciously* directed by the Ego or Self, with the intent of driving the physical body (which is *not* a principle) to fulfil egoic purpose. To do this the Ego has to follow certain rules, to conform to law, and to have attained not only conscious control of the physical body, but a knowledge of the laws of energy, and of the constitution of the etheric body, and its relation to the physical. The attention of students must be called to certain fundamental facts anent the centres and thus supplement, correlate, and summarise that already given in this *Treatise.* That a certain amount of repetition will be necessary is of value, and the information here given and the correspondences indicated, should provide all followers of raja yoga with a basis for sane consideration, wise meditation and a fuller comprehension of the truths involved. Owing to the rapid development of the race, and the future quick unfoldment of etheric vision, the gain will be very real if occult students have at least a theoretical concept of the nature of that which will be seen relatively so soon.

The centres, as we know, are seven in number and are formed in matter of the etheric subplanes of the physical plane. As we have been told, there are literally ten, but the lower three are not considered as subjects for the direction of egoic energy. They relate to the perpetuation of the physical form and have a close connection with:

a. The three lower kingdoms in nature.
b. The three lower subplanes of the physical plane.
c. The third solar system, from the logoic standpoint.

It must be borne in mind that though the three solar systems (the past, the present and that which is to come) are differentiated in time and space where the consciousness of man is concerned, from the point of view of the Logos they represent more accurately, highest, intermediate and lowest, and the three form but one expression. The past system, therefore, is deemed esoterically the third, being the lowest and being related to the dense and negative matter. It will be apparent that the past solar system has consequently a close relation to the third or animal kingdom, and this, man has presumably transcended.

The seven centres with which man is concerned are themselves found to exist in two groups: a lower four, which are related to the four Rays of Attributes, or the four minor rays, and are, therefore, closely connected with the quaternary, both microcosmic and macrocosmic, and a higher three which are transmitters for the three rays of aspect.

These energy centres are transmitters of energy from

many and varied sources which might be briefly enumerated as follows:

a. From the seven Rays, via the seven subrays of any specific monadic ray.

b. From the triple aspects of the planetary Logos as He manifests through a scheme.

c. From what are called "the sevenfold divisions of the logoic Heart," or the sun in its sevenfold essential nature, as it is seen lying esoterically behind the outer physical solar form.

d. From the seven Rishis of the Great Bear; this pours in via the Monad and is transmitted downward, merging on the higher levels of the mental plane with seven streams of energy from the Pleiades which come in as the psychical force demonstrating through the solar Angel.

All these various streams of energy are passed through certain groups or centres, becoming more active and demonstrating with a freer flow as the course of evolution is pursued. As far as man is concerned at present, this energy all converges, and seeks to energise his physical body, and direct his action via the seven etheric centres. These centres receive the force in a threefold manner:

a. Force from the Heavenly Man and, therefore, from the seven Rishis of the Great Bear via the Monad.

b. Force from the Pleiades, via the solar Angel or Ego.

c. Force from the planes, from the Raja Devas of a plane, or fohatic energy, via the spirillae of a permanent atom.

It is this fact which accounts for the gradual growth and development of a man. At first it is the force of the plane substance, which directs him, causing him to identify himself with the grosser substance and to consider himself a man, a member of the fourth Kingdom, and to be convinced, therefore, that he is the Not-Self. Later as force from the Ego pours in, his psychical evolution proceeds (I use the word "psychical" here in its higher connotation) and he begins to consider himself as the Ego, the Thinker, the One who uses the form. Finally, energy from the Monad begins to be responded to and he knows himself to be neither the man nor the angel, but a divine essence or Spirit. These three types of energy demonstrate during manifestation as Spirit, Soul, and Body, and through them the three aspects of the Godhead meet and converge in man, and lie latent in every atom.

The sevenfold energy of the planes, and therefore of substance, finds its consummation when the four lower centres are fully active. The sevenfold energy of the psyche, the consciousness aspect, demonstrates when the three higher in the three worlds are vibrating with accuracy. The sevenfold activity of spirit makes itself felt when each of these seven centres is not only fully active but is rotating as "wheels turning upon themselves," when they are fourth dimensional and are not only individually alive but are all linked up with the sevenfold head centre. A man is then seen as he is truly—a network of fire with flaming focal points, transmitting and circulating fiery energy. These centres not only receive the energy through the top of the head, or through a point slightly above the top of the head, to be more accurate, but pass it out through the head centre likewise, that which is being passed out being seen as differing in colour, being brighter and vibrating more rapidly than that which is being received. The etheric body is formed of a negative aspect of fire, and is the recipient of a positive fire. As the various types of fire blend, merge, and circulate, they gain thereby and produce definite effects in the fires of the microcosmic system.

The centre at the base of the spine (the lowest with which man has consciously to deal) is one of a peculiar interest, owing to its being the originating centre for three long streams of energy which pass up and down the spinal column. This triple stream of force has most interesting correspondences which can be worked out by the intuitive student. Some hints may here be given. This channel of threefold energy has itself three points of supreme interest, which (to word it so as to convey sense to the interested) may be regarded as:

1. The basic centre at the extreme lowest point of the spine.
2. The alta major centre at the top of the spine.
3. The supreme head centre.

It is, therefore, a miniature picture of the whole evolution of spirit and matter for,

1. The lowest centre corresponds to the personality,
2. The middle centre to the Ego, or the Thinker,
3. The supreme head centre to the Monad.

In the evolution of the fires of the spine, we have a correspondence to the sutratma with its three points of interest, the monadic auric egg, its emitting point, the egoic auric egg, the medial point, and the body or gross form, its lowest point.

Another hint of interest lies in the fact that there exist between these spinal centres, certain gaps (if I may so express it) which have (in the course of evolution) to be bridged by the energetic action of the rapidly growing vibration of the force unit. Between the triple energy of the spinal column and the alta major centre, there is a hiatus, just as there exists that which must be bridged between the triple lower man and the egoic body, or between the mental unit on the fourth subplane of the mental plane and the solar Angel on the third subplane. Though we are told that the permanent atomic triad is enclosed in the causal periphery, nevertheless, *from the standpoint of consciousness* there is that which must be bridged. Again, between the alta major centre and the supreme head centre, exists another gulf—a correspondence to the gulf found between the plane of the Ego and the lowest point of the Triad, the manasic permanent atom. When man has constructed the antaskarana (which he does during the final stages of his evolution in the three worlds) that gulf is bridged and the Monad and the Ego are closely linked. When man is polarised in his mental body, he begins to bridge the antaskarana. When the centre between the shoulder blades, referred to earlier in this *Treatise* as the manasic centre, is vibrating forcefully, then the alta major centre and the head centre, *via the throat centre* can be united.

Man, when he reaches this stage, is a creator in mental matter of a calibre different from the unconsciously working average man. He constructs in unison with the plan and the divine Manasaputra, the Son of Mind, will turn his attention from being a Son of Power in the three worlds and centre his attention in the Spiritual Triad, thus recapitulating on a higher turn of the spiral, the work he earlier did as man. This becomes possible when the growth of the triangle just above dealt with (base of spine, alta major centre and throat, as they unify in the head) is paralleled by another triplicity, the solar plexus, the heart and the third eye; the energy merging through them is similarly unified in the same head centre. The third eye is an energy centre constructed by man; it is a correspondence to the energy centre, the causal body, constructed by the Monad. The alta major centre is similarly constructed by other streams of force and corresponds interestingly to the triple form constructed by the ego in the three worlds.

When this dual work has proceeded to a certain evolutionary point, another triplicity becomes alive within the head itself as the result of these dual streams of triple energy. This triangle transmits fiery energy via the pineal gland, the pituitary body and the alta major centre and this reaches the head centre. In this way in these three triangles we have nine streams of energy converging and passing into the highest head lotus. The correspondence to certain macrocosmical forces will here be apparent to all discerning students.

We have seen the close connection between the different centres and the gradually demonstrating effects to be noted as they are linked up and eventually produce a synthetic circulatory system for egoic energy in conjunction with the energy of the lower man, which forms a kind of medium by which the egoic force makes itself felt. Macrocosmically, but little can be said which would prove intelligible to man at his present stage of evolution. Some brief statements might, nevertheless, be given which (if pondered on and correlated with each other) may throw some light on planetary evolution and on the relation of the planetary Logoi to the solar Logos.

A solar Logos uses for His energy centres the planetary schemes, each of which embodies a peculiar type of energy, and each of which, therefore, vibrates to the key of the logoic solar Angel, of which the human solar Angel is a dim reflection. It is interesting here to note that as the human solar Angel is a unity, manifesting through three tiers of petals, the logoic correspondence is even more interesting, for that great cosmic Entity demonstrates on the cosmic mental plane as a triple flame working through seven tiers of petals, and it is the energy from these seven circles of energy which pulsates through the medium of any scheme. All this is hidden in the mystery of the ONE ABOUT WHOM NAUGHT MAY BE SAID, and it is not possible for men to solve it,—the truth being obscure to even the highest Dhyan Chohan of our system.

The energy centres of the solar Logos are themselves

in the form of vast lotuses [24] or wheels, at the centre of
which lies hidden that central cosmic Life, we call a planetary Logos. He is the meeting place for two types of
force, spiritual or logoic, which reaches Him (via the
logoic Lotus on cosmic mental planes) from the seven
Rishis of the Great Bear on Their own plane, and, secondly, of buddhic force, which is transmitted via the
Seven Sisters or the Pleiades from a constellation called
the Dragon in some books, and from which has come the
appellation "The Dragon of Wisdom."

A third type of energy is added and, therefore, can be
detected in these centres, that of manasic type. This
reaches the logoic centres via the star Sirius, and is transmitted from that constellation which (as earlier I have

---

[24] See Section VIII, *Secret Doctrine*, Volume I.

The Lotus is symbolical of both the Macrocosm and of the Microcosm.
  a. The seeds of the Lotus contain in miniature the perfect plant.
  b. It is the product of fire and matter.
  c. It has its roots in the mud, it grows up through the water, it is
      fostered by the warmth of the sun, it blossoms in the air.

MACROCOSM

The mud	The objective physical solar system.
Water	The emotional or astral nature.
Flower on water	Fruition of the spiritual.
Method	Cosmic fire or intelligence.

MICROCOSM

The mud	The physical body.
Water	Emotional or astral nature.
Flower on water	Fruition of the buddhic or spiritual.
Method	Fire of mind.

"The significance of the tradition that Brahma is born from or in the
lotus, is the same. The lotus symbolises a world-system, and Brahma dwells
therein representing action; he is therefore called the Kamal-asana, the
Lotus-seated. The lotus, again, is said to arise from or in the navel of
Vishnu, because the navel of Vishnu or all-knowledge is *necessary desire*,
the primal form of which, as embodied in the Veda-text, is: May I be born
forth (as multitudinous progeny). From such central and essential desire,
the will to live, arises the whole of becoming, all the operations, all the
whirls and whorls, of change and manifestation which make up life. In
such becoming dwells Brahma, and from him and by him, i.e., by incessant
activity, arises and manifests the organised world, the trib huvanam, the
triple world. Because first *manifested*, therefore is Brahma *named* the first
of the gods; by action is manifestation, and he is the actor; and because
actor, therefore is he also sometimes called the preserver or protector of
the world; for he who makes a thing desires also the maintenance and
preservation of his handiwork, and, moreover, by the making of the thing
supplies the basis and opportunity for the operation of preservation, which,
in strictness, of course, belong to Vishnu."— *Pranava-Vada*, pp. 84, 311.

hinted) must remain obscure at present. These three great streams of energy form the total manifestation of a logoic centre. This is known to us as a planetary scheme.

Within the planetary scheme, these streams of energy work paramountly in the following manner:

a. Spiritual energy. .three higher
                              planes . . . . .the Monads.
b. Buddhic force. . . .fourth plane. . the solar Angels.
c. Manasic force. . . . two   lower. .the four kingdoms
                              planes   of nature.

Physical energy, the left-over of a previous solar system, demonstrates through the dense physical form and in the material which is energised during the involutionary cycle. It is not considered a principle; and is regarded as the basis of maya or illusion.

The various planetary schemes are not all alike and differ as to:

a. Type of energy,
b. Point in evolution,
c. Position in the general plan,
d. Karmic opportunity,
e. Rate of vibration.

The main distinction exists in the fact, as we have so oft repeated, that three of them form the three higher etheric energy centres of the Logos, and four constitute the lower centres.

Saturn is of interest to us here because the Logos of Saturn holds a position in the body logoic similar to that held by the throat centre in the microcosm. Three centres towards the close of manifestation will become aligned in the same way as the centre at the base of the spine, the throat centre and the alta major centre. Here it must be pointed out that there are three planetary schemes which hold a place analogous to that held by the pineal gland, the pituitary body, and the alta major centre, but they are not the schemes referred to as centres, or known to us as informed by planetary Logoi. Certain of the planetoids have their place here, and one scheme which has passed out of activity, and is in a condition of quiescence and non-activity. This latter scheme is the correspondence in the logoic body to the atrophied third eye in the fourth kingdom of nature. When man has developed etheric vision and thus has expanded his range of vision, he will become aware of these facts, for he will see. Many planetary schemes which are found only in etheric matter will be revealed to his astonished gaze, and he will find that (as in the body microcosmic) there are seven (or ten), paramount centres but numbers of other centres for the purpose of energising various organs. So likewise the body macrocosmic has myriads of energy focal points or feeders which have their place, their function, and their felt effects. These centres, with no dense physical globe, constitute what has sometimes been called "the inner round" and transmit their force through those greater centres which have been spoken of in occult books as having a connection with the inner round.

Each of these planetary schemes can be seen as a lotus having seven major petals, of which each chain forms one petal, but having also subsidiary petals of a secondary colour according to the nature and karma of the Entity concerned. It is in the enumeration of these solar lotuses that occult students go astray. It is, for instance, correct to say that the planetary scheme corresponding to the microcosmic base of the spine is a fourfold lotus and has, therefore, four petals. There are four outstanding petals of a peculiar hue, but there are three of a secondary colour, and nine of a tertiary nature. (To students with intuition the hint here conveyed may reveal the name of the planet, and the nature of its evolution).

Each of these solar lotuses, or planetary schemes, unfolds in three great stages of activity, in each one of which one of the three types of energy dominates. As the unfolding proceeds, the vibratory activity increases, and the *appearance* of the manifesting activity changes.

  a. The motion of the lotus or wheel for a long time is simply that of a slow revolution.

  b. Later, for a still vaster period, each petal revolves within the greater whole, and at an angle different to that of the whole revolution.

  c. Finally, these two activities are increased by the appearance of a form of energy which, originating from the centre, pulsates so powerfully that it produces what look to be streams of energy passing backwards and forwards from the centre to the periphery.

  d. When these three are working in unison, the effect is wonderful in the extreme, and impossible for the eye to follow, the mind of man to conceive, or the pen to express in words. It is this stage, macrocosmic and microcosmic, which constitutes the different grades of alignment, for it must never be forgotten by students that all that manifests is a sphere, and alignment really consists in unimpeded communication between the heart of the sphere and the periphery or the bound of the influence of the dynamic will and the centre.

Within each planetary scheme, are found the seven chains which are the seven planetary centres, and again within the chain are the seven globes which are the chain centres, but students would do well not to study the globes from the point of view of centres until their knowledge of the mystery underlying dense physical substance is greater, or they will be led into error. The lower down one seeks to carry the correspondence, the more the likelihood of error. The correspondence must lie in quality and in principle expressed, but not in form.

SECTION TWO

Division F.

THE LAW OF ATTRACTION

I. The Subsidiary Laws.
    1. Law of Chemical Affinity.
    2. Law of Progress.
    3. Law of Sex.
    4. Law of Magnetism.
    5. Law of Radiation.
    6. Law of the Lotus.
    7. Law of Colour.
    8. Law of Gravitation.
    9. Law of Planetary Affinity.
    10. Law of Solar Unity.
    11. Law of the Schools.

II. Its Effects.
    1. Association.
    2. Form Building.
    3. Adaptation of form to life.
    4. Group Unity.

III. Group Relations.
    1. Three atomic relations.
    2. Seven laws of group work.
    3. Twenty-two methods of interplay.

This law is, as we know, the basic law of all manifestation, and the paramount law for this solar system. It might strictly be called the Law of Adjustment or of Balance, for it conditions that aspect of electrical phenomena which we call *neutral*. The Law of Economy is the basic law of one pole, that of the negative aspect; the Law of Synthesis is the basic law of the positive pole, but the Law of Attraction is the law for the fire which is produced by the merging during evolution of the two poles. From the standpoint of the human being, it is that which brings about the realisation of self-consciousness; from the point of view of the subhuman beings it is that which draws all forms of life on to self-realisation; whilst in connection with the superhuman aspect it may be stated that this law of life expands into the processes conditioned by the higher law of Synthesis, of which the Law of Attraction is but a subsidiary branch.

Strictly speaking, the Law of Attraction is a generic term under which are grouped several other laws similar in nature but diverse in their manifestations. It might be useful if we enumerated a few of these laws, thereby enabling the student to get (as he studies them in their totality) a broad general idea as to the Law and its modifications, its spheres of influence and the scope of its activity. It should be noted here as a basic proposition in connection with all atoms that the Law of Attraction governs the Soul aspect. *The Law of Economy is the law of the negative electron; the Law of Synthesis is the Law of the positive central life; whilst the Law of Attraction governs that which is produced by the relation of these two,* and is itself controlled by a greater cosmic law which is the principle of the intelligence of substance. It is the law of Akasha.

It must be borne in mind that these three laws are the expression of the intent or purpose of the three Logoic Aspects. The Law of Economy is the governing principle of Brahma or the Holy Spirit; the Law of Synthesis is the law of the Father's life; whilst the Son's life is governed by, and manifests forth divine attraction. Yet these three are the three subsidiary laws of a greater impulse which governs the life of the Unmanifested Logos.[25]

[25] S. D., I, 56, 73, 74.

I. THE SUBSIDIARY LAWS

The subsidiary aspects, or laws, of the Law of Attraction might be enumerated as follows:

1. *The Law of Chemical Affinity.* This law governs the soul aspect in the mineral kingdom. It concerns the marriage of the atoms, and the romance of the elements. It serves to perpetuate the life of the mineral kingdom and to preserve its integrity.

It is the cause of the immetalisation of the Monad.

2. *The Law of Progress.* It is called this in the vegetable kingdom owing to the fact that it is in this kingdom that definite objective response to stimulation can be noted. It is the basis of the phenomenon of sensation, which is the key to this solar system of love, our system being a "Son of Necessity" or of desire. This law is the working out into manifestation of the informing consciousness of a part of the deva kingdom, and of certain pranic energies. The student will find much of esoteric interest in the following line of living forces:

a. The second chain, globe and round,
b. The vegetable kingdom,
c. The devas of desire in their second *reflected* groupings,
d. The heart of the Sun,
e. The second Ray force.

3. *The Law of Sex.* This is the term applied to the force which brings about the physical merging of the two poles in connection with the animal kingdom, and of man, viewing him as responsive to the call of his animal nature. It concerns itself with the due guarding of the form in this particular cycle and its perpetuation. It is only powerful during the period of the duality of the sexes and their separation and, in the case of man, will be offset by a higher expression of the law when man is again androgynous. It is

the law of marriage, and finds some aspects of its manifestation not only in marriage of men and animals in the physical sense, but in the "occult marriage" of

a. The Soul and the Spirit.
b. The Son with his Mother (or the Soul with the physical substance).
c. The negative planetary lives with the positive ones earlier pointed out.
d. The systemic marriage, or the merging of the two final planetary schemes after their absorption of the other forces.
e. The cosmic marriage, or the merging of our solar system with its opposite cosmic pole, another constellation. The cosmic marriage of stars and Systems is the cause of the occasional irregular flaring-up or intensification of suns and their increased luminosity which is sometimes seen, and which has frequently been the subject of discussion.

4. *The Law of Magnetism.* This is the law which produces the unifying of a personality, and though it is an expression of lunar force, is, nevertheless, of a much higher order than the law of physical sex. It is the expression of the law as it is demonstrated by the three major groups of lunar pitris. These three groups are not concerned with the building of the forms of the animal kingdom, for they are the builders of the body of man in the final three stages of the path of evolution:

a. The stage of high intellectuality, or of artistic attainment,
b. The stage of discipleship,
c. The stage of treading the Path.

The lower four groups concern themselves with the earlier stages, and with the animal aspects of attraction in both the kingdoms.

5. *The Law of Radiation*. This is one of the most interesting of the laws for it only comes into activity in connection with the highest specimens of the various kingdoms, and concerns itself with the attraction that a higher kingdom of nature will have for the highest lives of the next lower kingdom. It governs the radioactivity of minerals, the radiations of the vegetable kingdom and (curiously enough) the entire question of *perfumes*. Smell is the highest of the purely physical senses; so in the vegetable kingdom a certain series of perfumes are evidence of radiation in that kingdom.

There is, moreover, an interesting link between those who are members of the fifth kingdom (the spiritual) and the vegetable, for in esotericism the two and the five, the Son, and the Sons of Mind, are closely allied. It is not possible to indicate more, but it is not without significance that certain Rays are, through the initiates and Masters, represented by vegetable perfumes. It signifies radiation, and to those who have the key reveals the *quality* of the egoic lotus and the place it holds in any particular planetary lotus, as well as a connection with certain devas who are the sevenfold life of the vegetable kingdom. We must not forget that man is occultly a "seven-leaved plant, the saptaparna." [26]

This law in a mysterious manner, inexplicable to those ignorant of the karma of our planetary Logos, is not operative in the animal kingdom during this Cycle or chain. One of the problems of the next chain will be the bringing in of animal radiation; thus offsetting the method of initiation now pursued. It must never be forgotten that the chain process of individualisation, and the earlier three Initiations concern the animal kingdom and man is viewed therein as an animal. In the final Initiation. or the offering up of the entire bodily nature,

[26] S. D., I, 251; II, 625.

this part of the general karma of the planetary Logos and the Life of the informing Spirit of the animal kingdom become adjusted. If this is meditated upon, some light may be thrown upon the problem as to why the Adepts of the left hand path in Atlantean days were called "the Trees," [27] and were destroyed with the entire Atlantean vegetation. In the oldest of all the Commentaries the mystery is expressed thus:

"They (the Adepts of the Left Hand Path) became thus separated through their own fault. Their smell rose not up to Heaven; they refused to merge. No perfume was theirs. They hugged to their greedy bosoms all the gains of the flowering plant."

6. *The Law of the Lotus.* This is the name given to the mysterious influence from the cosmic Law of Attraction which brought in the divine Sons of Mind, and thus linked the two poles of Spirit and matter, producing upon the plane of mind that which we call the egoic lotus, or "the Flower of the Self." It is the law which enables the lotus to draw from the lower nature (the matter aspect and the water aspect) the moisture and heat necessary for its unfoldment, and to bring down from the levels of the Spirit that which is to it what the rays of the sun are to the vegetable kingdom. It governs the process of petal unfoldment, and therefore itself demonstrates as a triple law:

a. The Law of Solar Heat....Knowledge petals.
b. The Law of Solar Light....Love petals.
c. The Law of Solar Fire.....Sacrifice petals.

7. *The Law of Colour.*

To get any comprehension of this law students should remember that colour serves a twofold purpose. It acts as a veil for that which lies behind, and is therefore at-

[27] S. D., II, 519, 520, 521.

tracted to the central spark; it demonstrates the attractive quality of the central life.

All colours, therefore, are centres of attraction, are
complementary, or are antipathetic to each other, and
students who study along these lines can find out the law,
and comprehend its working through a realisation of the
purpose, the activity, and the relation of colours to or for
each other.

8. *The Law of Gravitation.* This law is for the non-
occult student the most puzzling and confusing of all the
laws. It shows itself in one aspect as the power, and the
stronger urge that a more vital life may have upon the
lesser, such as the power of the spirit of the Earth (the
planetary Entity, not the planetary Logos) to hold all
physical forms to itself and prevent their "scattering."
This is due to the heavier vibration, the greater accumulative force, and the aggregated tamasic lives of the body
of the planetary Entity. This force works upon the negative, or lowest, aspect of all physical forms. The Law of
Gravitation shows itself also in the response of the soul
of all things to the greater Soul in which the lesser finds
itself. This law, therefore, affects the two lowest forms
of divine life, but not the highest. It emanates in the
first instance from the physical sun and the heart of the
Sun. The final synthesising forces which might be regarded as forms of spiritual gravitational activity are,
nevertheless, not so, but are due to the working of another
law, emanating from the central spiritual Sun. The one
is purely systemic, the other a cosmic law.

9. *The Law of Planetary Affinity.* This term is used
in the occult teaching specifically in connection with the
interaction of the planets with each other and their
eventual marriage. As we know, the planetary schemes
(the seven sacred planets) will eventually synthesise, or
absorb the life of the planets which are not termed sacred
and the numerous planetoids, as far as the four kingdoms

of nature are concerned. The absorption of the Spirit aspect proceeds under the Law of Synthesis. The minor four planetary schemes become first the two, and then the one. This one, with the major three, forms a second and higher quaternary which again repeats the process, producing from the four, the two, and from the two, the one. This final one is eventually merged in the Sun, producing in this prolonged process, and over a vast period of time, the appearance of the "seven Suns who run together, and thus blaze forth, producing one flaming ball of fire."

On a lesser scale the same law governs the merging of the chains in a scheme.

10. *The Law of Solar Union.* When the interplay of the Suns is being dealt with from the material aspect and from the consciousness aspect, this term is occultly used. It is not possible to enlarge upon it, but only to point out the universality of this Law of Attraction.

11. *The Law of the Schools.* (The Law of Love and Light.) This is a mysterious term used to cover the law as it affects the expansions of consciousness which an initiate undergoes, and his ability to attract to himself through knowledge,

a. His own Higher Self, so as to produce alignment and illumination,
b. His Guru,
c. That which he seeks to know,
d. That which he can utilise in his work of service,
e. Other souls with whom he can work.

It will be evident, therefore, to the thoughtful student that this Law of the Schools is primarily applicable to all units of divine life who have arrived at, or transcended the stage of self-consciousness. It has consequently a vital connection with the human kingdom, and there is an occult significance in the fact that this is the eleventh

Law. It is the law which enables a man to unite two of
his aspects (the personal self and the Higher Self). It
is the law which governs the transition of the human
atom into another and a higher kingdom. It is the law
which (when comprehended and conformed to) enables a
man to enter into a new cycle. It is the law of the adept,
of the Master, and of the perfected man. For this reason
it might be of profit here if we dealt with it a little more
fully than with the other laws, for mankind is now at the
stage where a number of its units are ready to come under the specific influence of this law, and thus be transferred out of the Hall of Learning, via the Hall of Wisdom, into the fifth or spiritual kingdom.

This Law of the Schools does not specifically apply to
the deva evolution. They come under another law called
"The Law of Passive Resistance" which does not concern us here, nor would it profit us to consider it. Three
main groups of existences are controlled by it:

1. Human beings from the moment they tread the Probationary Path.
2. All the units of the fifth kingdom, therefore, all the
   members of the Hierarchy.
3. The planetary Logoi throughout the system.

It will be apparent, therefore, that this law concerns
the great experiment which has been inaugurated on earth
by our planetary Logos in connection with the process of
initiation, and it has only held sway since the Door of
Initiation was opened in Atlantean days. It does *not*,
therefore, apply to all the members of the human family;
some of whom will achieve slowly and under the sway of
the basic Law of Evolution. It does not affect, in any
way, for instance, those members of the human family
who have individualised on the earth chain through the
fanning of the spark of mind—one of the methods employed by the Lords of the Flame, as earlier seen.

It can be studied in two main divisions, first, in connection with the human units passing under hierarchical influence in the Hall of Wisdom, and also in connection with the various planetary schemes. Each scheme exists in order to teach a specific aspect of consciousness, and each planetary school or Hierarchy subjects its pupils to this law, only in manners diverse. These planetary schools are necessarily governed by certain factors of which the two most important are the peculiar karma of the planetary Logos concerned, and His particular Ray.

It is not possible at this stage to convey to students the information as to the nature of each planetary school. They exist in five great groups:

1. *The exoteric non-sacred planets,* called in occult parlance "the outer round" or outer circle of initiates. Of these our earth is one, but being aligned in a peculiar fashion with certain spheres on the inner round, a dual opportunity exists for mankind, which facilitates, whilst it complicates, the evolutionary process.

2. *The sacred planets,* called sometimes (when this Law of the Schools is under consideration) the "seven grades of psychic knowledge" or the "seven divisions of the field of knowledge."

3. *The inner round,* which carries with it vast opportunity for those who can surmount its problems and withstand its temptations. This inner round has a peculiar appeal to units on certain Rays, and has its own specific dangers. The inner round is the round that is followed by those who have passed through the human stage and have *consciously* developed the faculty of etheric living and can follow the etheric cycles, functioning consciously on the three higher etheric planes in all parts of the system. They have—for certain occult and specific purposes —broken the connection between the third etheric and the four lower subplanes of the physical plane. This

round is followed only by a prepared percentage of humanity, and is closely associated with a group who pass with facility and develop with equal facility on the three planets that make a triangle with the earth, namely Mars, Mercury, and Earth. These three planets—in connection with this inner round—are considered only as existing in etheric matter, and (in relation to one of the Heavenly Men) hold a place analogous to the etheric triangle found in the human etheric body. I have here conveyed more than has as yet been exoterically communicated anent this inner round and by the study of the human etheric triangle, its function, and the type of force which circulates around it, much may be deduced about the planetary inner round. We must bear in mind in this connection that just as the human etheric triangle is but the preparatory stage to a vast circulation within the sphere of the entire etheric body, so the etheric planetary triangle—passing from the Earth to Mars and Mercury—is but the preparatory circulatory system to a vaster round included within the sphere of influence of one planetary Lord.

4. *The circle of the planetoids*. Students of the Ageless Wisdom are apt to forget that the Life of the Logos manifests itself through those circling spheres which (though not large enough to be regarded as planets) pursue their orbital paths around the solar centre and have their own evolutionary problems and are functioning as part of the solar Body. They are informed—as are the planets—by a cosmic Entity and are under the influence of the Life impulses of the solar Logos as are the greater bodies. The evolutions upon them are analogous to, though not identical with, those of our planet, and they swing through their cycles in the Heavens under the same laws as do the greater planets.

5. *The absorbing Triangles*. This term is applied to the evolutionary schools found located in the three major

planets of our system—Uranus, Neptune and Saturn—
and to those found in the three major chains, and three
major globes in a planetary scheme. The Rulers of these
planets, chains and globes are called the "Divine Examin-
ers," and Their work concerns the human kingdom specifically and entirely. They are responsible

a. For the work of transferring men from one school to
another, and from one grade to another.

b. For the expanding of the human consciousness under the law,

c. For the transmutation of the forms of the human
unit in the three worlds and the consequent negation of the form,

d. For the radioactivity of the fourth kingdom in
nature.

We might regard the presiding lives in these departmental schools as the custodians of the Path, and responsible,
therefore, for the divine Pilgrim during the final stages
of the treading of the Path of Evolution. They begin to
work with men from the moment they first set foot upon
the Probationary Path and They continue Their work
until the seventh initiation is taken.

The Masters, therefore, Who take pupils for training,
are numbered amongst them, whilst the Masters Who do
not concern Themselves with individuals and their development are not.

It is not possible to give fully the types of schools
and teaching which is given on the different planets.
All that can be done is to give an occult phrase which will
convey to the intuitive student the necessary hint.

Planetary Schools

URANUS—The School of Magic of the tenth order. It is
sometimes called "the planet of the violet

force,'' and its graduates wield the power of cosmic etheric prana.

EARTH—The School of Magnetic Response. Another name given to its pupils is ''The graduates of painful endeavour'' or the ''adjudicators between the polar opposites.''

A further hint to be taken in connection with the two names above given, is that its graduates are said to undergo examination upon the third subplane of the astral plane.

VULCAN—The School for Fiery Stones. There is a curious connection between the human units who pass through its halls and the mineral kingdom. The human units on the earth scheme are called in mystical parlance ''the living stones''; on Vulcan they are called ''fiery stones.''

JUPITER—The School of Beneficent Magicians. This planet is sometimes called in the parlance of the schools, the ''College of Quadruple Force units,'' for its members wield four kinds of force in *constructive* magical work. Another name given to its halls is ''The Palace of Opulence'' for its graduates work with the Law of Supply, and are frequently called ''The Sowers.''

MERCURY—The pupils in this planetary school are called ''The Sons of Aspiration'' or ''The Points of Yellow Life.'' They have a close connection with our Earth scheme, and the Old Commentary refers to this in the words:

''The points of golden flame merge and blend with the four-leaved plant of tender green, and change its colour to a tinge of autumn yellow. The four-leaved plant through new and fresh inflow becomes the plant with seven leaves and three white flowers.''

VENUS—The School with five strict Grades. This again is a planetary scheme closely related to ours, but its planetary Logos is in a more advanced group of students in the cosmic sense than is our planetary Logos. Most of its hierarchical instructors come from the fifth cosmic plane, and are a peculiar group of Manasadevas of very exalted rank. They are each depicted in the archives of our Hierarchy as holding a trident of fire surmounted by five green emeralds.

MARS—The School for Warriors, or the open grades for soldiers. Four of these planetary schools are responsible for the energy flowing through the foremost exponents of the four castes and this not only in India but in all parts of the world. Its teachers are spoken of as the ''Graduates of the ruddy Fire,'' and are frequently portrayed as clothed in red robes, and carrying ebony wands. They work under the first Aspect logoic and train those whose work is along the lines of the destroyer.

NEPTUNE—This school concerns itself with the development and fostering of the desire element and its graduates are called ''the Sons of Vishnu.'' Their symbol is a robe with a full sailed boat portrayed over the heart, the significance of which will be apparent to those who have eyes to see.

It is not permissible to touch upon the other planetary schools, nor would it profit. Certain further facts can be ascertained by the student of meditation who is aligned with his Ego, and in touch with his egoic group.

The teaching given on our earth scheme in the Hall of Wisdom has been dealt with in many occult books, including *Initiation, Human and Solar,* and need not be enlarged upon here.

Some of the aspects of this law are here indicated. The ground is by no means covered but enough has been shown to indicate its magnitude and extent. In closing, it must be pointed out that the *Law of Karma* is from some angles of vision the sum total of this Law of Attraction for it governs the relation of all forms to that which uses the form, and of all lives to each other.

Students of the Law of Attraction must be careful to bear in mind certain things. These should be carefully considered and realised as the subject is studied.

They must remember first, that all these subsidiary laws are really only the manifestation of the One Law; that they are but differentiated terms, employed to express one great method of manifestation.

Secondly, that all energy, demonstrating in the solar system, is after all the energy of the logoic physical permanent atom, having its nucleus on the atomic subplane of the cosmic physical. This physical permanent atom (as is the case with fhe corresponding atom of the incarnating jiva), has its place within the causal body of the Logos on His own plane; it is, therefore, *impressed* by the totality of the force of the egoic cosmic lotus, or the attractive quality of cosmic love. This force is transmitted to the solar system in two ways: Through the medium of the Sun, which is in an occult sense the physical permanent atom; it, therefore, attracts, and holds attracted, all within its sphere of influence, thus producing the logoic physical body: through the medium of the planes which are the correspondences to the seven spirillae of the physical permanent atom of a human being. Thus a dual type of attractive force is found: one, basic and fundamental; the other more differentiated and sec-

Chart XI

ETHERIO—ATOMIC PHILOSOPHY OF FORCE.

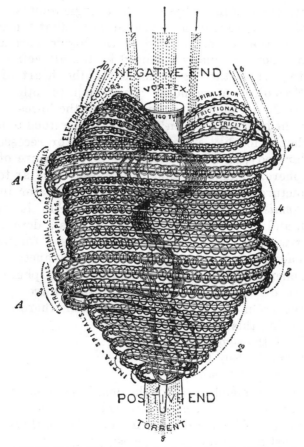

Fig. 135. The general Form of an Atom, including the spirals and 1st Spirillæ, together with influx and efflux ethers, represented by dots, which pass through these spirillæ. The 2d and 3d spirillæ with their still finer ethers are not shown.

From the Principles of Light and Color.
EDWIN D. BABBITT, NEW YORK, 1878.

ondary. These streams of energy, judged by their effects, are called in human terminology *laws,* because their results are ever immutable and irresistible, and their effects remain unchangeably the same, varying only according to the form which is the subject of the energic impulse.

Thirdly, the student must bear in mind that the seven planes, or the seven spirillae of the logoic permanent atom, are not all equally vitalised by the attractive pull emanating from the logoic lotus via the heart of the Sun. Five of them are more "alive" than the other two; these five do not include the highest and the lowest. The words "the heart of the Sun" must be understood to mean more than a locality situated in the interior recesses of the solar body, and have reference to the nature of the solar sphere. This solar sphere is closely similar to the atom pictured in the book by Babbitt and later in *Occult Chemistry* by Mrs. Besant. The Sun is heart-shaped, and (seen from cosmic angles) has a depression at what we might call its north pole. This is formed by the impact of logoic energy upon solar substance.

This energy which impinges upon the solar sphere, and is thence distributed to all parts of the entire system, emanates from three cosmic centres and, therefore, is triple during this particular cycle.

a. From the sevenfold great Bear.
b. From the Sun Sirius.
c. From the Pleiades.

It must be remembered that the possible cosmic streams of energy available for use in our solar system are seven in number, of which three are major. These three vary during vast and incalculable cycles.

Students may find it of use to remember that,

a. The Law of Economy demonstrates as an *urge,*
b. The Law of Attraction as a *pull,*
c. The Law of Synthesis as a tendency to concentrate at a centre, or to merge.

The streams of energy which pour forth through the medium of the Sun from the egoic lotus and which are in reality "logoic Soul energy" attract to them that which is akin to them in vibration. This may sound rather like the statement of a platitude, but is susceptible of really deep significance to the student, being accountable for all systemic phenomena. These streams pass in different directions, and in the knowledge of occult direction comes knowledge of the various hierarchies of being, and the secret of the esoteric symbols.

The main stream of energy enters at the top depression in the solar sphere and passes through the entire ring-pass-not, bisecting it into two halves.

With this stream enters that group of active lives whom we call the "Lords of Karma." They preside over the attractive forces, and distribute them justly. They enter, pass to the centre of the sphere and there (if I may so express it) locate, and set up the "Holy Temple of Divine Justice," sending out to the four quarters of the circle the four Maharajahs, their representatives. So is the equal armed Cross formed—and all the wheels of energy set in motion. This is conditioned by the karmic seeds of an earlier system, and only that substance is utilised by the Logos, and only those lives come into manifestation who have set up a mutual attraction.

These five streams of living energy (the one and the four) are the basis of the onward march of all things; these are sometimes esoterically called "the forward moving Lives." They embody the *Will* of the Logos. It is the note they sound and the attractive pull which they initiate which bring into contact with the solar sphere a group of existences whose mode of activity is spiral and not forward.

These groups are seven in number and pass into manifestation through what is for them a great door of Initiation. In some of the occult books, these seven groups are spoken of as the "seven cosmic Initiates Who have passed within the Heart, and there remain until the test is passed." These are the seven Hierarchies of Beings, the seven Dhyan Chohans. They spiral into manifestation, cutting across the fourfold cross, and touching the cruciform stream of energy in certain places. The places where the streams of love energy cross the streams of will and karmic energy are mystically called the "Caves of dual light" and when a reincarnating or liberated jiva enters one of these Caves in the course of his pilgrimage, he takes an initiation, and passes on to a higher turn of the spiral.

Another stream of energy follows a different route, which is a little difficult to make clear. This particular set of active lives enter the heart shaped depression, pass around the *edge* of the ring-pass-not to the lowest part of the solar sphere and then mount upwards, coming into opposition therefore with the stream of downpouring energy. This stream of force is called "lunar" force for lack of a better term. They form the body of the raja Lord of each of the planes, and are governed by the Law of Economy.

All these streams of energy form geometrical designs of great beauty to the eye of the initiated seer. We have the transverse and bisecting lines, the seven lines of force which form the planes, and the seven spiralling lines, thus forming lines of systemic latitude and longitude, and their interplay and interaction produce a whole of wondrous beauty and design. When these are visualised in colour, and seen in their true radiance, it will be realised that the point of attainment of our solar Logos is very high, for the beauty of the logoic Soul is expressed by that which is seen.

The Law of Attraction produces certain effects which it might profit us to touch upon here, provided we remember that only a few effects out of many possible are being considered.

1. *Association.*

The first effect might be called association.   Under this law the karmic Lords are enabled to bring together those lives (human, subhuman, and superhuman) which have earlier been associated, and have, therefore, somewhat to work out.   The seven Heavenly Men, for instance, are a few out of the great band of associated Lives Who have chosen to come into incarnation in this kalpa for purposes of mutual help and mutual correction.   They are really destined to work together, but nevertheless on other cosmic planes have points of contact unknown to us.

Under this attractive pull the informing existences of the various kingdoms of nature are engaged in mutual interaction, and thus swing into lesser but similar activity all the lives of these various bodies of manifestation. These lines of attraction are veiled in mystery, and all that it is possible to indicate is the karma of the Lord of the second or vegetable kingdom with the Lord of the fifth kingdom, and a close line of linking energy between the Lord of the mineral kingdom and the human. These points are only for reference to our own planetary scheme.   The Lord of the Moon chain and the Lord of our present animal kingdom are "blood brothers" and in their relationship and the esoteric interference of the "Man of Men" (the human family personified) is hidden the mystery of present animal karma and the slaughter of animal forms, the terror of wild beasts and the work of vivisectionists.

Under this Law, too, is found "the Path" upon which

men lift themselves out of the human state of consciousness into the divine, but on this there is no need to enlarge.

2. *Form Building.*

The second effect is form building. Upon this we will not enlarge at any length, as all that it is at present possible to impart anent this subject has already been given in this Treatise, and other works of a similar nature. It is the middle, or second aspect which is ever responsible for the construction of a form around a central nucleus. Students would find it useful to study and meditate upon the appended tabulation of energy streams and their objectivising through mutual interplay.

As time goes on, science will become aware of the basic nature and fundamental accuracy of the method whereby every form can be divided into its three aspects, and viewed as an Entity energised by three types of force, emanating from various points extraneous to the form under consideration. It can be considered also as expressing in some way or another, in its various parts, force or energy originating in the three forces of manifestation, Brahma, Vishnu and Shiva. Where this is the case and the premise admitted, the entire outlook on life, on nature, medicine and science and on methods of construction or destruction will be changed. Things will be viewed as essential triplicities, men will be regarded as a combination of energy units, and work with things and with men from the *form* aspect will be revolutionised.

In the tabulation much information is given anent the form building aspects of energy and the Law of Attraction as it shows itself in the working of the various groups of the Army of the Voice. It is this Army which is responsible for the attraction which is the medium of bringing together the material required by the free Spirits in order to construct their bodies of manifestation. The

TABULATION VII
ENERGIES

SOLAR LOGOS:

Source	Focal Point	Medium	Type of Energy	Nature of Fire
1. Causal Body.	Jewel	Central Spiritual Sun.	Cosmic Will .	Electric Fire. Positive.
2. Causal Body.	Lotus (two-petalled).	Heart of the Sun.	Cosmic Love (The Son).	Solar Fire. Harmony. Equilibrium.
3. Physical Plane Nucleus.	Permanent Atom.	The Physical Sun.	Cosmic Activ-ity (Universal Mind).	Fire by Friction. Negative.

PLANETARY LOGOS:

Source	Focal Point	Medium	Type of Energy	Nature of Fire
1. Planetary Causal Body.	Jewel	Heavenly Man (On his own plane.)	Systemic Will.	Electric Fire. Positive.
2. Planetary Causal Body.	Lotus	Egoic Groups.	Systemic Love	Solar Fire. Harmony. Balance.
3. Physical Plane Nucleus.	Permanent Atom.	Physical Planet.	Systemic Activity.	Fire by Friction. Negative.

MAN:

Source	Focal Point	Medium	Type of Energy	Nature of Fire
1. Human Causal Body.	Jewel	Monad Spirit.	Atma-Buddhi	Electric Fire. Positive Force.
2. Human Causal Body.	Lotus	Solar Angel	Manasic Ego	Solar Fire. Equilibrising Force.
3. Plane Nucleus.	Permanent Atom.	Lunar Angels.	Lower Threefold Man.	Fire by Friction. Negative.

PLANES:

Source	Focal Point	Medium	Type of Energy	Nature of Fire
1. Plane Raja Lord.	A Deva Hierarchy.	Atomic Sub-plane.	Fohatic	Central Fire. Initiatory.
2. Plane Devas.	Centres	Prana	Solar Energy	Form building Fire.
3. Elementals	Elemental Essence.	Molecular Substance.	Lunar Force	The Mother's Heat.

ATOMS:

Source	Focal Point	Medium	Type of Energy	Nature of Fire
1. Atom	Nucleus	Plane Deva	Positive	Electric.
2. Atomic Unit. of Form.	Sphere	Plane Devas	Balancing	Solar Fire.
3. Electrons	Nuclei	Elementals	Negative	Fire by Friction.

vibration initiated by the Sound, which is the expression of the Law of Synthesis, is succeeded by the Voice or Word, and that Word as it progresses outward from the centre to the periphery (for, occultly understood, the Word is "spoken from the Heart") becomes

    a. A phrase.
    b. Phrases.
    c. Sentences.
    d. Speech.
    e. The myriad sounds of nature.

Each of these terms can be explained in terms of attractive energy, and this attractive energy is likewise the demonstration of the life of an Existence of some grade or other.

"God speaks and the forms are made." This tabulation should form the basis of a complete phase of study along this line and is one of the most basic given in this *Treatise*.

3. *Adaptation of the form to the life.*

This is the process of gradually providing forms which are due expressions of the indwelling consciousness which is the great purpose of what we call "Mother Nature"; this she does, working under the Law of Attraction which we are considering. This law, therefore, governs two aspects of unfoldment, that which concerns the soul or consciousness aspect and that relating to the Spirit on its own plane. It is the cause of that continuous cycle of form taking, of form utilisation and of form rejection which characterises the incarnations of every kind and type of living being. The student should here remember that the Existences who are the attractive force in manifestation, the Dhyan Chohans, are seven in number, and that, therefore, the quality of the vehicles which form Their bodies will have the sevenfold variation according to the specific nature of the Lords of Life.

The only way to arrive at a realisation of the basic qualities of these planetary Logoi is through a consideration of the energy emanating from Them, and it is this which the true esoteric astrology will eventually reveal. The time is not yet; it will come when the scientific consideration of human magnetism, of the distinctions between the seven types of men, and the nature of the Ego is more truly followed. Then will be revealed the nature of planetary magnetism and the quality of any specific planetary *soul* as it is known through the aggregated nature of the men, responsive to and exponents of any particular planetary Ray. The mystery is increased by the fact that there are not only certain logoic qualities manifesting which are not included by the term "sacred," but that there are numerous other aspects of what we might term "secondary centres of fire," generated and making their presence felt. We have a correspondence to this in the fact that there are centres of energy in man which are not purely etheric centres but are the product of the interaction of the etheric centres and certain forms of negative energy of the lowest kind. Such, for instance, is the heart. There is the heart centre, one of the major centers on the etheric planes, but there is also the physical heart which is an energy generator also; there are the lower organs of generation which are equally a reflex product with an energy which is the resultant of the higher vibrations yet which has a quality all its own. This has its correspondence in the solar system. Many are the lesser planets and numerous are the planetoids which have an energy or attractive quality all their own and which, from the systemic standpoint, must be allowed for in the measuring of the attraction producing the forms of or upon any particular planet.

As we know from a study of the *Secret Doctrine,* certain of the planetary Logoi are pure and passionless whilst others are still under the domination of desire and of passion.[28] This quality of Theirs necessarily attracts to Them that which They need for the due expression of Their life in any scheme, and controls the nature of those egoic groups who are (for Them) generating force centres. Hence the nature of men upon earth. All human beings are paramountly governed by certain planetary attractions, impressions or influences which might be enumerated in the order of their importance.

There is, first of all, the attractive pull of the Life of the planetary Logos of this particular planet. This is necessarily the strongest and is one of the basic factors which have settled the lines the human form has taken upon this planet. There are human beings, or exponents of self-consciousness on other planets, but the forms they utilise are not the same as ours.

There is next, the attractive pull of the planetary Logos Who is the complementary Life to that of our Logos. This involves a planetary Logos responsive to a vibration which harmonises with that of our Logos but Who, when in union with Him, forms what might be called "the Third" or His dominant, as the case may be. It is not possible to reveal whether the blending of the note will mean that our scheme will absorb that which expresses the note of another scheme, or vice versa. It means that somewhere in the solar system is a planetary scheme of some kind (not necessarily one of the seven or of the ten) which has an interplay with ours and which, therefore, inevitably affects the egoic groups. We must note also the fact that—in connection with the expression of a Heavenly Man—the egoic groups are energy centres and make His dense physical body eventually an accomplished fact.

Finally, there is the attractive pull of that planetary scheme which is esoterically regarded as our polar oppo-

---

[28] S. D., I, 214, 449; II, 223.

site. (What is here said has reference to the other schemes, for the law persists throughout the solar system.)

It will be apparent, therefore, that the real and esoteric astrology will deal with four kinds of force, when it seeks to explain the nature of the Energies which influence any human being:

1. The quality of the solar system.
2. The quality of the Logos of the planet as it pours through the chains and globes and rounds in a sevenfold differentiation.
3. The quality of our earth's complementary planet.
4. The quality of the attraction of our earth's polar opposites.

This involves information as yet veiled in deepest mystery, but which will unfold as the true psychology is studied, and which will eventually embody itself in a fourth fundamental of the *Secret Doctrine* so that later students will have the three as they are now found in the Proem to that book, plus the fourth.[29] This might be expected in this fourth round. The true astrology will reveal the nature of this fourth proposition at some later date. More attention will eventually be paid to the planetary influences, and not so much to the signs of the zodiac where the nature of an Ego is concerned. The great signs of the zodiac concern the Heavenly Man, and necessarily, therefore, the Monads of every human being. The planetary influences must be studied to find out the quality of a man's Ray, and this in the above indicated threefold manner. Man is the Monad, therefore, he expresses a small part of his enfolding life. In this solar system he is essentially the Ego.

Astrologers should study the planetary schemes in the light of the Heavenly Man, viewing them as an incarna-

[29] S. D., I, 42-46.

tion of a planetary Logos, and thus strive to cast the horoscope of the planetary Logos. They cannot succeed in doing so, but in the attempt may learn much and achieve new light upon a most difficult subject.

In considering this question of the adaptation of the form to vibration, or the construction of a vehicle which will be a fitting instrument for spirit, the following factors must be borne in mind:

1. That it is the *quality* of the indwelling life which decides the type of form.
2. That these qualities are the sumtotal of the attributes of divinity which the indwelling life has succeeded in unfolding.
3. That these qualities—as may well be surmised—fall into the usual septennate.
4. That they fall also into two groups, those which concern the lower principles, and are, therefore, four in number, and those which concern the higher and middle and are, therefore, three.

This is true of all men, of the Heavenly Men and of the solar Logos likewise, and there is a mysterious analogy concerned in the manifestation of the three higher principles in man (which may be considered as demonstrating through the perfected Adept, the Bodhisattva) and the three higher principles of the solar Logos as they demonstrate through the major three aspects. They form but one principle showing forth in three ways. So it is with the unmanifested Monad (unmanifested from the standpoint of the lower man). That Monad can—at a certain very advanced stage in evolution, and one far beyond that of the Adept—have its triple simultaneous manifestation, and show forth as a Master in the three worlds, as a Bodhisattva on His own plane and as the emancipated Dhyani Buddha; yet these Three will be but One, will be the result of a great spiritual vibration and will perform the triple work which may (from the standpoint of the three worlds) appear as the work of three separate great Existences. They are forms of three monadic "vestures," worn by the one Monad as a man wears his three bodies simultaneously, and functions in them separately.[30]

One or other of these three can, if so He will, occupy a body on the physical plane which will not be simply a created mayavirupa. This is done in one of two ways: either through the occupancy of a willingly vacated body, as was the case when the Christ occupied the body of Jesus, or by a divine overshadowing of a disciple, as has been and will be the case. The quality of the form occupied or used, and the nature of its work depends upon which of the three higher aspects of the initiating impulse, is manifesting. Very rarely a more mysterious phenomenon occurs and the overshadowing Buddha, Bodhisattva, or Adept each makes His "appearance"

---

* The Three Vestures.—"*The stream is crossed. 'Tis true thou hast a right to Dharmakaya vesture; but Sambhogakaya is greater than a Nirvani, and greater still is a Nirmanakaya—the Buddha of Compassion.*"—*Voice of the Silence*, p. 97.

"The three Buddhic bodies or forms are styled: Nirmanakaya, Sambhogakaya, Dharmakaya.

The first is that ethereal form which one would assume when leaving his physical he would appear in his astral body—having in addition all the knowledge of an Adept. The Bodhisattva develops it in himself as he proceeds on the path. Having reached the goal and refused its fruition, he remains on earth, as an Adept; and when he dies, instead of going into Nirvana, he remains in that glorious body he has woven for himself, invisible to uninitiated mankind, to watch over and protect it.

Sambhogakaya is the same, but with the additional lustre of three perfections, one of which is entire obliteration of all earthly concerns.

The Dharmakaya body is that of complete Buddha, *i.e.*, no body at all, but an ideal breath; consciousness merged in the universal consciousness, or soul devoid of every attribute. Once a Dharmakaya, an Adept or Buddha leaves behind every possible relation with, or thought for, this earth. Thus to be enabled to help humanity, an Adept who has won the right to Nirvana, 'renounces the Dharmakaya body' in mystic parlance; keeps, of the Sambhogakaya, only the great and complete knowledge, and remains in his Nirmanakaya. The esoteric school teaches that Gautama Buddha, with several of his Arhats, is such a Nirmanakaya, higher than whom, on account of his great renunciation and sacrifice for mankind, there is none known."—*Voice of the Silence*, p. 98.

upon earth thus demonstrating the three aspects of knowledge, love and will and all taking form.

This may seem to be a great complexity, but it is not so much stranger after all than the phenomenon of the Monad (in time and space and during evolution) demonstrating forth as the Triad, the Ego and the Personality. This type of triple Avatar only makes its appearance under a peculiar series of cycles concerned with a group of Monads who were the most progressed and advanced at the opening of the mahamanvantara. As yet, there are not many progressed enough to do this triple work; the Buddha and nine others being the only Ones as yet remaining in touch with our particular planet in this particular manner. A few are as Christ is, and have the power to make a dual appearance. This type of monad is only found on Rays two, four, six.

If the student bears in mind that the nature of the form is dependent upon the *quality* of the incarnating Life, he will have also to bear in mind the distinctions between the various groups of Hierarchies, for the Lives in those groups are of a quality diverse to each other and the forms through which they manifest are equally distinct and diverse. Therefore, we must distinguish between:

1. The involutionary groups.
2. The evolutionary groups.
3. The seven groups of lives which we call the lunar Fathers:
    a. Three incorporeal who are the elemental kingdoms.
    b. Four material who are the forms of the four kingdoms on the upward arc.
4. The seven hierarchies of Lives.
5. The seven groups of solar Angels.

There must not be confusion as to the distinction between the hierarchies of Beings and the seven Rays, for though there is close connection, there is no resemblance. The "Rays" are but the primordial forms of certain Lives who "carry in their Hearts" all the Seeds of Form. The Hierarchies are the manifold groups of lives, at all stages of unfoldment and growth who will use the forms.[31] The Rays are vehicles and are, therefore, negative receivers. The Hierarchies are the users of the vehicles, and it is the nature of these lives and the quality of their vibration which under this great Law of Attraction brings to them the needed forms. These are the two primal distinctions, Life and Form, and these two are the "Son of God," the second Person of the Trinity in His form-building aspect. They are the Builders and equally exist in three groups with their lesser differentiations. It is not necessary here to place these groups on certain planes in the solar system.

These hierarchies of Beings Who come in on the Ray of Light from the centre are the seeds of all that later is and it is only as they pass out into manifestation and the forms which they are to occupy are gradually evolved, that consideration of the planes becomes necessary. The planes are to certain of these hierarchies what the sheaths of the Monad are to it; they are veils for the Life indwelling; they are media of expression, and exponents of force or energy of a specialised kind. The quality of a

[31] *The Twelve Creative Hierarchies.* Students are often puzzled in trying to account for the "twelves" in the cosmos. A correspondent sends the following suggestion: In a Study in Consciousness, the three, by an arrangement of internal groupings, show seven groups; these may be represented as ABC, ACB, BCA, BAC, CAB, CBA, and a seventh, a synthesis in which the three are equal. A second six would be represented by (AB) C, C (AB), A (BC), (BC) A, (CA) B, B (AC), the two bracketed being equal and the third stronger or weaker. The two groups of six, and the group in which the three are equal, would make thirteen. "This thirteen may be arranged as a circle of twelve, with one in the centre. The central one will be synthetic, and will be that class in which all three are equal. The physical correspondence of this will be the twelve signs of the Zodiac with the Sun at the centre, synthesising all of them. The spiritual correspondence will be the twelve Creative Orders with the Logos at the centre, synthesising all." The arrangement is quite legitimate.—*The Theosophist,* Vol. XXIX, p. 100.
Compare also the Twelve Signs of the Zodiac.

Ray is dependent upon the quality of the hierarchy of Beings who use it as a means of expression. These seven hierarchies are veiled by the Rays, but each is found behind the veil of every ray, for in their totality they are the informing lives of every planetary scheme within the system; they are the life of all interplanetary space, and the existences who are expressing themselves through the planetoids, and all forms of lesser independent life than a planet. Let me briefly give certain hints concerning these hierarchies which may serve to elucidate that contained in the *Secret Doctrine* concerning them.

What is here imparted is not in itself new, but is the synthesising of much already known and its gathering together in the form of brief enunciated facts.

Each of these seven hierarchies of Beings Who are the Builders or the *Attractive* Agents are (in their degree) intermediaries; all embody one of the types of force emanating from the seven constellations. Their intermediary work, therefore, is dual:

1. They are the mediators between Spirit and matter.
2. They are the transmitters of force from sources extraneous to the solar system to forms within the solar system.

Each of these groups of beings is likewise septenary in nature, and the forty-nine fires of Brahma are the lowest manifestation of their fiery nature. Each group also may be regarded as "fallen" in the cosmic sense, because involved in the building process, or the occupiers of forms of some degree of density or another.

Hierarchy I.   The first great Hierarchy is emanated from the Heart of the central Spiritual Sun.[32] It is the Son of God Himself, the First Born in a cosmic sense, even as the Christ was the "Eldest in a vast family of

[32] S. D., I, 233-250; III, 565-566.

brothers," and the "first flower on the human plant."
The symbol of this Hierarchy is the Golden Lotus with
its twelve petals folded.

It should be remembered that this Hierarchy is literally
the sixth, for five hierarchies have passed on, being the
product of the earlier system, that wherein Intelligence
or Manas was the goal. The five liberated hierarchies
are in their totality the sumtotal of manas. It is the
Hierarchy which is the fifth in order, and which we are
told is in process of achieving final liberation, or taking
its fourth Initiation, which is the cause of certain phenomena upon our planet which has merited our planet
being called the "Star of Suffering." There is a karmic
link between the animal kingdom and the fifth Creative
Hierarchy of the earlier system which makes itself felt
in man in the necessary crucifixion of the animal physical
nature, particularly along sex lines. We must remember
that the hierarchies work under the Law of Attraction;
it is the law of the Builders.

This first (sixth) Hierarchy has for its type of energy
the first aspect of the sixth type of cosmic electricity, and
wields special power, therefore, in conjunction with the
lowest fire, or "fire by friction," as it makes itself felt on
the sixth plane. These lives are called "the burning
Sons of Desire" and were the Sons of Necessity. It is
said of them in the old Commentary:

"They burned to know. They rushed into the spheres. They
are the longing of the Father for the Mother. Hence do they
suffer, burn, and long through the sixth sphere of sense."

Hierarchy II. The second Hierarchy is closely allied
with the Great Bear. We are told that They entered
through the second ventricle within the Sacred Heart,
and are (as we are told in the *Secret Doctrine*) the
prototypes of the Monads. They are the source of
monadic Life, but They are not the Monads; They are
far higher.

This Hierarchy, which is literally the seventh, is the influx into our system of those Lives who in the first solar system remained on their own plane, being too sinless and holy to find opportunity in that very material and intellectual evolution. Even in this, they will find it impossible to do more than influence the incarnating Jivas, imparting to them ability to realise the nature of group consciousness, the quality of the seven Heavenly Men, but not being able to express themselves fully. Some clue to this mystery will come if the student carefully bears in mind that in our solar system and our seven planes, we have only the physical body of the Logos, and that that physical body is a limitation of the expression of His threefold nature. The first (sixth) Hierarchy might be viewed as endeavouring to express the *mental* vibration of the solar Logos and the second, His emotional, or cosmic astral, nature.

This second (seventh) Hierarchy has for its type of force the second aspect of the seventh type of force from out of the many. Some idea of the relative point in evolution of the solar Logos may be gained by study of the varying aspects of force which He is demonstrating in this particular incarnation. It is this energy which drives the Monads through into physical incarnation for it makes itself felt on the seventh plane. The energies which are functioning are those which the Logos has unfolded, and are the *gain* of previous incarnations. Gaps necessarily occur, and certain types of force are lacking, because He has as yet much cosmically to gain.

It is the energy of this Hierarchy (whose numbers are two and seven) which results in the manifestation of the Divine Androgyne, and in the seven centres of force which are the seven Spiritual Energies.

Hierarchy III. The third Creative Hierarchy (or the eighth) is a peculiarly interesting one. They are called "the Triads" for they hold in themselves the potencies of triple evolution, mental, psychical, and spiritual. These Triads of Life are inherently the three Persons and the flower of the earlier system from a certain angle. From another angle, when studied as the "flower of the earlier Eight," They are the eightfold points awaiting opportunity to flame forth. They are the devas who are ready for service, which is to give to another hierarchy certain qualities which are lacking. This Hierarchy is regarded as the great donors of immortality whilst themselves "standing aloof from incarnation." Lords of Sacrifice and Love are They, but They cannot pass out of the logoic etheric body into the dense physical vehicle.

This third Hierarchy wields the third aspect of electric force of the first type of cosmic energy. They stand for a recurrent cycle of that first type symbolised by the number 8. The formulæ for these electrical energies are too complicated to be given here, but the student should bear in mind that these hierarchies express:

1. Septenary cosmic energy.
2. Cosmic prana.
3. Solar energy or electric fire, solar fire and fire by friction.

Each hierarchy manifests a triple energy or an aspect of each of the above, and that necessitates a ninefold differentiation, for the two first are triple as is the third. It is the rejection of the Triadal Lives by units in the fourth Hierarchy, that of the human Monads, which precipitates a man eventually into the eighth sphere. He refuses to become a Christ, a Saviour and remains self-centred.

We have dealt with the first three hierarchies which are regarded as ever "seeing the Face of the Ruler of the Deep," or as being so pure and holy that Their forces are in realised contact with Their emanating source.

We now take up for brief consideration two hierarchies which closely concern ourselves, the human self-conscious entities. These two groups are literally three, as the fifth Hierarchy is a dual one and it is this which has led to some confusion and is the occult significance behind the ill-omened number thirteen. They are the "Seekers of satisfaction" and the cause of the second fall into generation, the fact behind the taking of a lower nature by the Ego. The fourth and the fifth Hierarchies are the ninth and tenth, or the "Initiates" and the "Perfect Ones." All human beings, or "Imperishable Jivas," are those who evolve through a graded series of initiations either self-induced or brought about on our planet with extraneous aid. This they achieve through a "marriage" with the order next to them, the fifth. They are then completed or perfected, and it is owing to this occult fact that the fourth Hierarchy is regarded as masculine and the fifth as feminine.

Hierarchy IV. The fourth Creative Hierarchy is the group wherein the highest aspect of man, his "Father in Heaven" finds place. These lives are the points of fire who must become the flame; this they do through the agency of the fifth Hierarchy and the four wicks, or the two dual lower hierarchies. Thus it can be seen that where man is concerned, the fourth, fifth, sixth and seventh hierarchies are, during the cycle of incarnation, his very self. They are the "Lords of Sacrifice" and "Lords of Love," the flower of Atma-buddhi.

In studying these hierarchies, one of the most valuable lessons to be learned is the place and importance of man in the scheme. The hierarchy, for instance, which is the essence of the intangible Life of Spirit, and principle of Buddhi, is the esoteric cause of the cosmic marriage of spirit and matter, based on the love and desire of the Logos, but each hierarchy also expresses itself through one particular manifestation which comes to be regarded by the finite mind of man as the hierarchy itself. This is not so, and care must be taken to distinguish between these hierarchies.

They are latent germs of force centres and manifest subjectively; they warm and vitalise groups of forms; they flower forth and express themselves through the medium of a form, or another hierarchy. These hierarchies are all interrelated and are negative or positive to each other as the case may be.

As is stated in the *Secret Doctrine,* this hierarchy is the nursery for the incarnating Jivas; [33] and it carried in it the germs of the Lives which achieved the human stage in another solar system, but were not able to proceed beyond that owing to the coming in of pralaya, which projected them into a state of latency. The condition of the hierarchy is similar, only on a cosmic scale, to the condition of the seeds of human life held in a state of obscuration during an interchain period. The three other hierarchies dealt with (first, second, and third) were those who have (in previous kalpas of logoic manifestation) passed beyond the human stage altogether. They are, therefore, the formless groups, as the remaining are the rupa groups or those having forms.

The fourth Creative Hierarchy, or the ninth, must ever be regarded in this solar system as occupying what might be considered as the third place,

First, the Lives or the three Persons of the Trinity.

Second, the Prototypes of man, the seven Spirits.

Third, man or the lowest manifestation of the self-conscious Spirit aspect.

This needs to be carefully considered and has no reference to the form aspect but solely to the nature of the lives expressing themselves through other lives who are also *self-conscious,* or fully intelligent. This, certain of the hierarchies are not.

[33] S. D., I, 238.

The four lower hierarchies are all concerned with manifestation in the three worlds, or in the dense physical body of the solar Logos. They are those who can discard or pass through the etheric body of the solar Logos and take forms composed of either gaseous, liquid, or dense substance. The others cannot. They cannot fall into physical generation.

Students must bear in mind that from the standpoint of the Logos, the solar Angels on the mental plane (the fifth subplane of the cosmic physical plane) are in physical incarnation, and what is called the "second fall" applies to this. The first fall has reference to the taking of a form of cosmic etheric matter, such as is the case with the Heavenly Men, the prototypes of the human jivas. In this latter case the bodies used are called "formless" from our standpoint, and are "vital bodies" animated by cosmic prana. In the case of ourselves and the remaining groups, the forms are composed of substance of the three lower planes (that which the Logos does not regard as principle) and, therefore, matter responding still to the vibration of the earlier system. This means that the four lower hierarchies are *links* between the life of the past and of the future. They are the present. They had not finished their contacts with the active intelligent principle of the preceding kalpa, and so must continue such contacts in this. They will work out of it in this system, the four will become the three and they will then be the three higher arupa hierarchies of the next system.

Before continuing our consideration of the particular hierarchies, it is necessary to point out that in these hierarchies, certain of them are termed "dominant hierarchies" and others "subsidiary hierarchies." By this is meant that certain of them are in this solar system expressing themselves more fully than the others, and this necessarily entails the consequence that their vibration is more to be felt than that of the subsidiary groups.

The dominant groups are the second, fourth and fifth, and this because:

a. *The second* is the great expression of duality, of the Son as He vitalises the Sun.

b. *The fourth* is the hierarchy of human Monads who are the mediators or the synthesisers; they express the gain of System 1 and the goal of System 2.

c. *The fifth* or tenth is closely linked with the five liberated hierarchies, and is an expression of their synthesised life. It might, therefore, be said that the fifth Hierarchy serves as the representative of the five liberated groups and the fourth is the representative group in this system, whilst the second represents (for man, or these two groups united) that which is the Spirit aspect, the Father, the Unknown.

Hierarchy V. The fifth Creative Hierarchy is, as we know from study of the *Secret Doctrine,* a most mysterious one. This mystery is incident upon the relation of the fifth Hierarchy to the five liberated groups. This relation, *in connection with our particular planet, which is not a sacred planet,* can be somewhat understood if the history of the Buddha and his work is contemplated. This is hinted at in the third volume of the *Secret Doctrine.*[34]

The relation of the fifth Hierarchy to a certain constellation has also a bearing upon this mystery. This is hidden in the karma of the solar Logos, and concerns His relationship to another solar Logos, and the interplay of force between them in a greater mahakalpa. This is the true "secret of the Dragon," and it was the dragon-influence or the "serpent energy" which caused the influx of manasic or mind energy into the solar system. Entangled closely with the karma of these two cosmic

[34] S. D., I, 239; III, Sections 43, 44, 45.

Entities, was that of the lesser cosmic Entity Who is the Life of our planet, the planetary Logos. It was this triple karma which brought in the "serpent religion" and the "Serpents or Dragons of Wisdom" in Lemurian days. It had to do with solar and planetary Kundalini, or serpent fire. A hint lies in the fact that the constellation of the Dragon has the same relation to the ONE greater than our Logos as the centre at the base of the spine has to a human being. It concerns stimulation, and vitalisation with a consequent co-ordination of the manifesting fires.

A clue to the mystery lies also in the relation of this fifth group to the two contracting poles. They are the fivefold Links, the "Benign Uniters" and "the Producers of the Atonement." Esoterically, they are the "Saviours of the Race" and from Them emanates that principle which—in conjunction with the highest aspect— lifts the lower aspect up to Heaven.

When these mysteries are carefully studied, and due application made to the lives of the greatest exponents of the at-one-ing principle, it will become apparent how great and all-important is their place in the scheme.

It is for this reason that the units of the fifth Hierarchy are called "The Hearts of Fiery Love"; they save through love, and in their turn these lives are peculiarly close to the great Heart of Love of the solar Logos. These great redeeming Angels, who are the Sons of Men on their own true plane, the mental, are ever, therefore, pictured as taking the form of twelve-petalled lotuses— this symbology linking them up with "the Son of Divine Love," the manifested solar system, which is said to be a cosmic twelve-petalled lotus, and with the logoic causal lotus, equally of a twelve-petalled nature.

We have, therefore, a direct flow of energy flowing through:

a. The logoic twelve-petalled egoic Lotus.   Cosmic
    mental plane.
b. The solar twelve-petalled Lotus.
c. The planetary logoic Heart, also a twelve-petalled
    Lotus.
d. The twelve-petalled human egoic lotus on the mental
    plane.
e. The twelve-petalled heart centre in a human being.

Or, to word it otherwise, energy flows directly from:

a. The solar Logos via three great cosmic centres:
    1. The central spiritual Sun.
    2. The heart of the Sun.
    3. The physical Sun.
b. The heart centre of the planetary Logos, situated
    on the fourth cosmic etheric plane (our buddhic
    plane).
c. The egoic lotus of a human being on the mental
    plane, which is literally a correspondence to the
    "heart of the sun."   The monadic point is a re-
    flection in the human system of the "central spir-
    itual sun."
d. The heart centre of a man on the etheric plane of
    the physical plane, which is in its turn a correspon-
    dence to the physical sun.

Thus the tiny atom man is linked with the great central
Life of the solar system.

This Fifth Hierarchy is equally, under the law, a distributor of energy to the fifth subplane of each plane in
the system, only it must be borne in mind that in the three
worlds, it is the fifth subplane counting from above downward whilst in the worlds of superhuman evolution, it is
the fifth counting from below upwards.   This hierarchy
wields, as we know, the dual aspects of manas, one in the
three worlds and one which makes itself felt in higher
spheres.

It is necessary to bear in mind that all these groups are (even when termed "formless") the true forms of all that persists, for all are in the *etheric* body of the solar Logos or planetary Logos. This is a point requiring careful emphasis; students have for too long regarded the form as being the dense physical body, whereas to the occultist the physical body is not the form, but a gross maya, or illusion, and the true form is the body of vitality. Therefore, these hierarchies are the sumtotal of the vital lives and the substratum or the substance of all that is. We might regard the subject as follows:

a. The four superior groups are the hierarchies expressing themselves through the three cosmic ethers, the second, third and fourth.

b. The two lowest groups are the lives which are found functioning as the involutionary matter (organised and unorganised) of the logoic dense physical body, the liquid and gaseous, with the living substance of the four higher subplanes of the systemic dense physical body.

c. The fifth Hierarchy has an interesting position as the "mediating" body between the higher four and those which are found on the lower three subplanes. There is a vital and significant correspondence to be found between the seven head centres and the seven groups of Egos on the mental plane, and there is an occult analogy *between the three head centres (pineal gland, pituitary body, and the alta major centre) and the expression of these seven groups of Egos in the three worlds.* This is a most important esoteric fact, and all students of meditation upon the laws of at-one-ment must take this analogy into consideration.

It is useful to remember the place of these hierarchies in the scheme, and to realise that upon the sumtotal of these vital bodies is gradually gathered the dense manifestation which we regard as the evolutionary matter. The forms are built (from the form of all atoms to the body of the Ego, from the form of a flower to the vast planetary or solar lotus) because the hierarchies exist as the aggregate of germ lives, giving the impulse, providing the model, and procuring, through their very existence, the entire *raison d'être* of all that is seen on all planes.

Hierarchies VI and VII. These sixth and seventh Hierarchies which provide the substance forms of the three worlds have a vital use and a most interesting place. From the logoic standpoint, they are not regarded as providing principles, but from the standpoint of man they do provide him with *his* lowest principles. They hold the same relation to the Logos as the dense physical body does to man, and all that concerns the evolution of man must (in this particular place) be studied as going on within the physical, logoic vehicle. They deal with the display of physical energy; with the working out in the physical vehicle, of all divine purposes, and with the physical organisation of a certain great cosmic Life.

Particulaily is this so when we view the two hierarchies under consideration. They are the lowest residue of the previous system, and the energy of that matter (liquid, gaseous and dense) which the vibration of the logoic permanent atom (on the plane adi) attracts to itself in the building of the divine form. For purposes of clarification and of generalisation, it might be noted that the seventh Hierarchy is the life or energy found at the heart of every atom, its positive aspect, and the sixth Hierarchy is the life of the forms of all the etheric bodies of every tangible object. The function of this Hierarchy is well described in the words of the old Commentary:

"The devas hear the word go forth. They sacrifice themselves and out of their own substance they build the form desired. They draw life and the material from themselves, and yield themselves to the divine impulse."

It is not possible to say much more anent these two last Hierarchies. Much that concerns them has been covered in the section of this *Treatise* which deals with the fire of matter. I would only point out that just as we teach in the occult wisdom that there is a definite progression from one kingdom into the next higher above, so there is a similar activity in the realm of the hierarchies. The lives which compose a Hierarchy pass in ordered cycles into the next above, though the word "above" but serves to mislead. It is *consciousness* and realisation which must be considered as being transferred and the consciousness of one hierarchy expands into that of the next higher.

This can also be viewed in terms of energy. The negative lives of a hierarchy follow the following sequence:

1. Negative energy.
2. Equilibrised energy.
3. Positive energy.

The positive lives of one hierarchy become the negative lives of another when they pass into it, and this it is which leads to the general confusion of ideas under which the average student labours. If he is to comprehend the matter with accuracy, he must study each hierarchy in a threefold manner, and view it also in its transitional state, as the negative blends and merges into the positive, and the positive becomes the negative pole of a higher vibratory stage. There are, therefore, nine states of consciousness through which each hierarchy has to pass, and some idea of the significance of this and their relativity can be gained by a consideration of the nine Initiations of the fourth Creative Hierarchy. Within these nine distinct expansions through which each life in each hierarchy must pass, are to be found lesser expansions and it is here that the main difficulty for the student of divine psychology lies. The whole subject concerns the psyche, or second aspect, of every life—superhuman, human and subhuman—and only when the true psychology is better understood will the subject take on its true importance. Then the nine unfoldments of each hierarchy will be somewhat comprehended, and their relative importance assigned.

Study of the matter in each kingdom will not as yet bring full enlightenment regarding the constitution of the elements of the human kingdom and its principles, which are the manifestations of the different hierarchies. The true revelation will only come as the following points are recognised:

1. The triple nature of man.
2. The distinctions between the vehicle and that which utilises the vehicle.
3. The distinction between a Ray which is the expression of logoic energy and a *positive* emanation, and a hierarchy which is a negative emanation of the Logos, upon which His positive energy impresses itself, driving that hierarchy on to self expression and forcing the "marriage of the poles."

The whole subject is very involved and difficult but light will begin to dawn before long when science recognises the nature, place and responsibility of the etheric body in man, or of his vital body, and its position as the true form, and basic unit of the dense physical body. When this has been admitted, and the illuminating facts recorded and known, when the connection between the two is grasped, and the necessary deductions and correlations are made, the whole subject of logoic manifestation and the work of the Lives on the four higher planes, with their effect upon the Logoic dense physical plane (our three worlds of expression) will take on a new colouring. The thoughts of men will be revolutionised on the subject of creation;

the terms and expressions now used will be corrected, and
all will be expressed in terms of form-building energy,
and the three modes of electrical phenomena. This realisation is rapidly on its way but only the generation after
the one which the children of the present age are expressing, will see it demonstrated to such an extent as to place
etheric electrical phenomena beyond all dispute. This
will be done by the coming in of egos who are fully conscious on the etheric levels and who can *see* all that which
is now the subject of speculation. They—from their
great numbers and high stage of intellectuality—will rescue the whole matter from the realm of controversy and
demonstrate the facts.

The work of building forms will never be understood
till the true function of the etheric body is realised. It
is the attractive agent for those lives which are so low
an order as to be occultly *inert.* These lives, which are
not included in the list of hierarchies, are acted upon by
the sixth and seventh groups and by the energy emanating from them. They are stirred from the inertia in
which they have rested, and are driven to take their place,
and to form the concrete vehicles of all that is. They are
the lowest manifestation of that which is abstract; they
are the densest concretion of Spirit; they are the failures
of the system preceding this, and their failure is so complete (from the standpoint of consciousness) that all the
response they can make to the positive vibration of the
seventh Hierarchy is simply to be attracted. They can
be occultly drawn into place but only at the close of
this solar system will they be in a condition to pass into
and become the seventh Hierarchy of the next solar
system.

The goal for that which is not a principle is that it shall
become a vital principle through the play of energy upon
it. We are dealing here with that mysterious something
which has been called "the refuse of that which earlier

was seen,'' with that latent energy which hid the lowest vibration of the system before ours, and which was so heavy, and so inert, as to be regarded beyond the ken of the Logos. He was unaware of it, and the object before these peculiar lives which live (and yet are occultly dead) is that they must force themselves into the range of His *conscious* control by response to those lives which are consciously directed by Him, and who are, therefore, the Saviours of the lowest.

4. *Group Unity.*

Group unity must be viewed somewhat from the mystical standpoint. It is a truism in occultism to say that nothing stands alone, yet it is a fact that each infinitesimal part of the whole has three relations:

1. To those units which form its body of manifestation.
2. To its own unitary life.
3. To that greater unit of which it forms a part.

One of the main things which, it has been said, underlies logoic purpose, is the working out of ways which will result in true group unity. All that is to be seen might be regarded as a gigantic endeavour on the part of a great Intelligence to produce a group, and evolution is to be regarded, therefore, as a vast experiment with this objective in view.

This triple responsibility above referred to exists for the atom or for the solar Logos, and the trend of the evolutionary process is to make each unit, microcosm and macrocosm, an intelligent co-operator, responsive to forces impinging upon it externally, and aware of its own internal economy and of the latent forces and energies which it has to contribute to the good of the whole. Man, standing as he does at the middle point in evolution, and marking the stage in the evolution of consciousness where a triple awareness is possible,—awareness of individuality, awareness of the forces which are subhuman and which must be controlled, and awareness of a place within the plan and purpose of a greater Man—must, therefore, rightly be regarded as the most important of the evolutions, for through him can be worked out intelligently the laws of group unity for all the three groups, superhuman, human, and subhuman.

Above him stand those who are too pure or, as it is called, "too cold" to be immersed in the matter of the three worlds, below him are found those lives which are too impure (occultly understood) or "too full of burning matter and veiled in smoke" to be able to mount of themselves into regions where stand the unveiled sons of God. Man, therefore, acts as the mediator, and in him and through him can be worked out group methods and laws which—in a later solar system—can form a basic law for unified work. It is this fact which brings about so much of the peculiar trouble and nature of the human kingdom, and it might here be said that on our planet, which is, it must be remembered, one of the "profane" planets, certain experiments in connection with this problem have been undertaken by our planetary Logos. These (if successful) will result in a great expansion of the knowledge of the planetary Logos regarding the laws governing all bodies, and masses. Our planetary Logos has been given the name of the "experimenting divine Physicist." It is this condition which makes the humanity of this planet unique in some respects, for they may be regarded as working out two main problems:

1. The problem of establishing a *conscious* relation and response, to the animal kingdom.
2. The problem of simultaneously receiving and holding vibrations from superhuman lives and of transmitting them consciously to the subhuman states.

All this has to be accomplished by the units of the human kingdom in full individual consciousness, and the work of each human being might be regarded therefore as having in view the establishment of a sympathetic relation with other human units and with the pitris of the animal kingdom, and also the development of the power to act as the transmitter of energies from greater lives than his own, and to become a transmuting mediating agency.

It might be of interest here to note that it is the problem of establishing a relation between the animal and himself which was the original basis of what is called Hatha-Yoga and tantric magic. The link was sought in this yoga with that which was known to be similar in the two kingdoms (the physical body with its activities and purposes) and that which should be negative in the human kingdom was stimulated into a positive agency through the power of the will. That followers of Hatha-Yoga are not aware of this purpose may be true, but the originating exponents of the Hatha-Yoga mysteries were well aware of this objective, and in their zeal for unity between the two kingdoms, sought unity in the lower aspects, and neglected the real method.

III. GROUP RELATIONS

In establishing group relation with the superhuman kingdoms, man has not so erred, though relatively little progress has as yet been made, and few are the human units who have merged their consciousness with that of the greater directing Intelligences and yet remained in the human family. This is the true Raja Yoga.

It will be apparent, therefore, that in the fourth or human kingdom, wherein the fourth Hierarchy is seeking experience, there is an effort on foot to effect the merging or centralisation of the forces of three groups,

   a. Of the energy for which the animal kingdom stands,
   b. Of purely human energy,

c. Of the spiritual energy of the group which is the exponent of buddhic force, thus bringing in at the third great realisation, the force of atma itself, of which buddhi is but the vehicle.

These three streams of force should hold the following place:

Buddhic force ....Positive.
Human energy ....Equilibrised.
Animal energy ....Negative.

Or, to word it otherwise, the positive controlling factor in the human group should be spiritual energy, toward which the animal nature should be entirely receptive, these two holding towards each other the relative position of Father-Mother. The purely human energy serves as the balancing factor and brings about an adjustment between the Spirit aspect and the material. It is this triple group relation which makes the microcosm such a genuine reflection of the greater Man and the Fourth Kingdom a true exponent of cosmic processes.

The same laws govern the relationship of these three factors as govern the group inter-relation of the Brahma-Vishnu-Shiva aspects; time and space or "divine opportunity" play their parts in microcosmic group work as they do in the macrocosmic, and cyclic evolution proceeds in its work of group adjustment for both units, in order to produce eventual group harmony in both cases. It is the harmony of the individual with himself and with his environing units, and his realisation of the essential oneness of all life which brings about the great expansions of consciousness and leads to individual identification with some greater whole.

The work of a human atom, therefore, is but a replica of that which proceeds in the planetary, or solar atom, and serves as an incentive to those minute individual lives which find their place in the six subhuman kingdoms (the three elemental, and the three material). In one case we have a correspondence of so close a nature as to be almost a replica on a tiny scale; in the other we have analogies which produce what may be regarded as a reflection of the whole; in both cases we have basic group relations, fundamental group laws which produce group inter-relations, and bring about an essential union between all the forms of life. It is not my intention to say much anent group forms and work. It is for the student to study himself and that which surrounds him, and thus arrive at his own conclusions. We will, therefore, close this part of our *Treatise* by a brief enumeration of:

1. The three atomic relations.
2. The seven laws of group work.
3. The twenty-two methods of interplay.

These thirty-two phases and ideas must be applied in degree to all atoms, the tiny lives which are the sumtotal of all material worlds, the planetary atom, the macrocosm for all on the five planes, and the solar atom, the synthesis of all on the seven planes and of the seven evolutions.

1. *Three Atomic Relations.*

Individual. This concerns the central fire of all atoms and affects the relation of that positive centre to all within its sphere of influence.

Systemic. This concerns the relation of all atoms to other atoms which come within their range of influence, or their scale of contacts.

Universal. This deals with the identification of all atoms with these particular groups, and their consequent submergence in the interests of the greater whole.

It might be noted here that the immediate objective of the human kingdom is *consciously* to establish systemic relations, and be actively, and consciously, part of group work. The individual consciousness of relationship is somewhat established owing to there being self-consciousness. The work for the subhuman kingdoms is the establishment of conscious self-realisation, or the bringing about of a distinct individualism in every form of atomic life, whilst the object for the superhuman lives is the establishment of a universal consciousness which will enable every planet and solar life to be consciously and intelligently part of a cosmic whole.

2. *The Seven Laws of Group Work.*

These can only be expressed largely through the medium of mystical terms, and it is left to the intuition of the student to apply them to the more material forms of life.

Law 1. The.Law of Sacrifice. This involves the immolation and sacrifice of that which has been realised. This is crucifixion, the basic law of all group work, the governing principle which results in each human unit eventually becoming a Saviour.

Law 2. The Law of Magnetic Impulse. The law governing the primary realisations by any atom of its environing contacts, and the going out, or feeling after, by that atom so that eventually a relation between that which is realised as part of the group and the unit is established. This is not the same thing as making sense contacts, as the relation established is between the Self in all, and not between aspects of the Not-Self. This law is sometimes called "The first step towards marriage," for it results in an eventual union between the man or atom and the group which produces harmonious group relations.

Law 3. The Law of Service. This law, for want of a better name, concerns the identification of an atom with the group interest, and the steady negation of the atom's own material interests; it really deals with the process or method whereby an atom (positive in its own centralised life) gradually becomes responsive and receptive to the positive life of the group.

Law 4. The Law of Repulsion. This law concerns itself with the ability of an atom to throw off, or refuse to contact, any energy deemed inimical to group activity. It is literally a law of service, but only comes consciously into play when the atom has established certain basic discriminations, and guides its activities through a knowledge of the laws of its own being. This law is not the same as the Law of Repulsion which is used in connection with the Law of Attraction between forms which have relation to the material. The laws we are now considering have relation to the psyche, or to the Vishnu aspect. One group of laws concern energies emanating from the physical sun; the ones we are now considering emanate from the heart of the Sun. The "repulsion" here dealt with has the effect (when consciously applied through the developed heart energy of a human atom, for instance) of furthering the interests of the repulsed unit and of driving this unit closer to its own centre. Perhaps some idea of the great beauty of this law as it works out can be gathered from an occult phrase in a certain old book:

"This repulsive force drives in seven directions, and forces all that it contacts back to the bosom of the seven spiritual fathers."

Through repulsion, the units are driven home and the straying unconscious ones are forced towards their own centre. The Law of Repulsion, or the stream of energy for which it is but a name, can work from any centre, but as dealt with here, *it must emanate from the heart* if it is to bring about the necessary group work.

Law 5. The Law of Group Progress. This is sometimes called "the Law of Elevation" for it concerns the mysteries of group realisation, and expansions of con-

sciousness and the part each unit plays in the general
progress of a group. In relation to the human family,
for instance, the truth must ever be borne in mind that no
human atom arrives at "fullness of life" without adding
much to the general nature of his own group. The elevation of a unit results in the raising of the group; the
realisation of the unit brings about eventually group
recognition; the initiation of the unit leads finally to planetary initiation, and the attainment of the goal by the
human atom and his achievement of his objective brings
about steadily and ceaselessly group achievement. No
man liveth to himself, and the crucifixion of the units
throughout the aeons, and their realisation of their essential nature, only in order to offer up the best they have
and realise to the interests of the group, are but the
methods whereby the work of liberation is carried forward.

Sacrifice, Service, Magnetism (*"I, if I be lifted up,
will draw"*), Group Progress, Divine Repulsion, these are
but the inadequate terms whereby we seek to express the
divine truth that the whole life and expression of the
solar Logos will only be possible, and His purpose only
be revealed, when He has brought each atomic unit to the
stage of self-realisation. Then He will lead them on to
the point of sacrificing that realised self so that divine
purpose and will may be consummated, and the divine
life and glory shine forth in perfect radiance.

This might be expressed in more material terms by saying that through the dominance of these laws of the Soul,
the logoic physical body will become an active expression
of His self-realised purpose.

The final two laws concerning group activity can only
be very briefly treated as their true significance is only
apparent to pledged disciples. They concern primarily
the astral and the mental planes, and, therefore the corresponding vehicles of the group units. A group, it

should be remembered, which is functioning on the physical plane is also found in a still larger form on the astral and the mental. Just as the astral body of a man is larger than his physical body, and, therefore, has built into its structure a larger number of atomic units, so a group contains (astrally considered) more units than on the physical plane. The laws we are touching upon concern the relation of the physical plane units to those units who form a part of the group, and yet are functioning without the physical plane sheaths or vehicles. The same idea must be applied to the units devoid of a physical vehicle who form a component part of the mental body of the group.

These two laws are termed:

6. The Law of Expansive Response.
7. The Law of the Lower Four.

These laws only become operative in units on the physical plane which are becoming responsive consciously to those group workers who are discarnate.

All these laws, from the point of view of a disciple, need only be considered as operative in the three worlds, though it is needless to point out that parallels will be found on all planes. These seven laws are those which are ascertained and consciously studied in all groups working under the Masters.

For each of these Laws, there is a definite formula and symbol. At this stage of teaching or through this Treatise, it is not possible to reveal or impart the formulas. The symbol may be described, and if the student will carefully ponder upon the nomenclature of the Law, its occult name and its symbol, much may be gathered anent group inter-relations. It is these laws which the coming cycle of regeneration will enunciate, and which the Great Lord will demonstrate upon His appearing, and it is these laws which will gradually be applied to the working meth-

THE LAWS AND SYMBOLS

No. Exoteric Name	Esoteric Name	Symbol	Ray Energy
1. Law of Sacrifice.	The Law of Those Who Choose to Die.	A Rosy Cross with Golden Bird.	Out-pouring 4th Ray. At-one-ing factor.
2. Law of Magnetic Impulse.	The Law of the Polar Union.	Two fiery balls and triangle.	Radiatory energy 2nd Ray. Manifesting factor.
3. Law of Service.	The Law of Water and of Fishes.	A Pitcher on the head of a man.	Out-going energy 6th Ray. Vivifying factor.
4. Law of Repulse.	The Law of all Destroying Angels	An Angel with a flaming sword.	Rejecting energy 1st Ray. Dispersing factor.
5. Law of Group Progress.	The Law of Elevation.	The Mountain and the Goat.	Progressive energy 7th Ray. Evolving factor.
6. Law of Expansive Response.	(Name not given.)	Flaming Rosy Sun.	Expansive energy 3rd Ray. Adapting factor.
7. Law of the Lower Four.	The Law of Etheric Union.	A Male and Female Form, placed back to back.	Fiery energy 5th Ray. Vitalizing factor.

ods of all organisations, brotherhoods, fraternities and masonic circles. The symbols are as follows:

Law 1. A rosy cross, with a bird hovering above it.

Law 2. Two balls of fire united by a triangle of fire, thus picturing the triple interplay between all atomic structures.

Law 3. A pitcher of water, balanced on the head of a man, standing in the form of a cross. It is this law which brings in the energy, symbolised by the sign Aquarius, and this law is the governing factor of the Aquarian age. It might here be added that the symbol for Law 2 was the

origin of the balance or scales of the sign
Libra, but in the course of the ages its true
form was distorted. Not all the astrological
signs can be traced to the symbols, for only a
few can be traced back as far as the Master's
ashram.

Law 4. Here we have the angel with the flaming sword
turning in all directions. This symbolism is
held true in the Bible where the Angel guards
the treasure, and drives man forth in search
of another way of entrance, thus forcing him
through the cycle of rebirth until he finds the
portal of initiation. This portal is occultly
regarded as freed from the intervention of the
sword as man has developed the ability to soar
and mount as an eagle on wings.

Law 5. The symbol for this is the mountain with a goat
standing on the summit, and again an astrological sign, that of Capricorn, can be noted.
All hard places can be surmounted, and the
summit reached by the "Divine Goat," symbol of the group, viewed as a unit.

Law 6. The symbol contains a flaming rosy sun with a
sign in the centre—a sign symbolising the
union of fire and water; below this sign is
found a hieroglyphic which may not be given
as it gives the clue to the Earth sign, and the
keynote of the physical body of the planetary
Logos.

Law 7. This symbol takes the form of a male and female figure standing back to back, the male
figure holding above his head what looks like a
shield or tray of silver, a great reflector, whilst
the female figure holds aloft an urn full of oil.
Below this sign is another hieroglyphic which

contains the secret of the astral plane, which has to be dominated by the mental.

These seven laws can be worked out along the line of correspondences. It will be found that the energy of any particular centre and that of any one law can be brought into line with each other.

3. *The Twenty-two methods of Group Interplay.*

These methods of group interplay can only be grasped through a consideration of the fact that all groups are to be found on one or other of the seven Rays, and that their interaction will, therefore, be triple. This must again be regarded as having:

a. A triple internal interplay.
b. A triple external interaction.

We might, therefore, take the seven Rays and give the names for the three ways in which the groups on any particular ray interact with each other, remembering that as we consider them, we are really studying the twenty-one vibrations of the Law of Attraction or motion, with the basic vibration, which is the synthesis of the twenty-one added, thus making the twenty-two:

RAY METHODS OF ACTIVITY

I. *Ray of Power.*
  1. Destruction of forms through group interplay.
  2. Stimulation of the Self, or egoic principle.
  3. Spiritual impulse, or energy.

II. *Ray of Love Wisdom.*
  4. Construction of forms through group intercourse.
  5. Stimulation of desire, the love principle.
  6. Soul impulse, or energy.

III. *Ray of Activity or Adaptability.*
  7. Vitalising of forms through group work.
  8. Stimulation of forms, the etheric or pranic principle.
  9. Material impulse, or energy.

   IV.   Ray of Harmony, Union.
      10. Perfecting of forms through group interplay.
      11. Stimulation of the solar Angels, or the manasic principle.
      12. Buddhic energy.

   V.   Ray of Concrete Knowledge.
      13. Correspondence of forms to type, through group influence.
      14. Stimulation of logoic dense physical body, the three worlds.
      15. Manasic energy or impulse.

   VI.   Ray of Abstract Idealism or Devotion.
      16. Reflection of reality through group work.
      17. Stimulation of the Man through desire.
      18. Desire energy, instinct and aspiration.

   VII.   Ray of Ceremonial Order.
      19. Union of energy and substance through group activity.
      20. Stimulation of all etheric forms.
      21. Vital energy.

These twenty-one methods and their synthesis sum up very largely all that can be said anent the actions and motions of all deva substance and all forms. Under the Law of Attraction, the interplay between these ray forces and all atomic forms is brought about, and manifestation becomes a fact in nature, and the great Maya *is*. It might here be noted in conclusion that the following factors:

> 3 Atomic Relations
> 7 Laws
> 22 Methods of activity
> ――
> 32

make the thirty-two vibrations necessary to produce, as far as man is concerned, the five planes of evolution. There are, as we know, the thirty-five subplanes, or in reality the thirty-two minor vibrations and the three which dominate. Just as the three planes of the Ego on

THE SEVEN HIERARCHIES

Hierarchy	Nos.	Symbol	Force Aspect	Type
1. The Divine Lives.	1 or 6	Closed twelve-petalled Lotus Golden.	One of the	6th Cosmic Force or shakti.
2. The Burning Sons of Desire.	2 or 7	Seven coloured Spheres, each with a central fire.	Two of the	7th Shakti.
3. The Triads or the Triple Flowers.	3 or 8	A triple Flame hovering over a glowing altar.	Three of the	1st Shakti or type of force.
4. The Lords of Sacrifice or The Initiates.	4 or 9	The Son, standing with outstretched arms in space.	Second of the	4th Cosmic energy.
5. The Crocodiles or the Perfect Ones.	5 or 10	The five-pointed Star with the symbol of System 1 in the centre.	Fourth of the	5th Cosmic force (Mahat).
6. The Sacrificial Fires. The Aspirants.	6 or 11	A silver Moon surmounted by an equal armed Cross.	Third of the	6th Cosmic force.
7. The Baskets of Nourishment or The Blinded Lives.	7 or 12	A Man reversed with his eyes closed.	Fourth of the	7th Creative force.

the mental plane dominate the remaining planes in the three worlds, so in the five worlds of the Hierarchy the three higher subplanes of the atmic plane hold an analogous place.

In closing, we might give certain of the symbols for the twelve Creative Hierarchies. It is not possible to give the symbols whereby the Adepts know them, for in those symbols would be revealed much that it is deemed wiser to guard in secrecy, but the symbols, as they are found in records accessible to disciples, may be given, and from the close scrutiny of these some knowledge as to the essential character of the hierarchy may be revealed.

The symbols for the five hierarchies which have passed on may be stated as follows:

1. A ball of green fire with three rays of rose.
2. A sphere, divided by a Tau, in colours green and silver.
3. A bird, with plumage dark and with the eye of radiant fire.
4. Two stars of vivid rose linked by a band of violet.
5. An ovoid of colour indigo with five letters or symbolic words within its borders.

These hierarchies are also classed together and viewed as one and are called in esoteric parlance:

"The Lives of that which appeared, rotated and gathered to themselves the fifth aspect of Mahat."

This symbol, which signifies the liberation achieved and the gains attained in System One, takes the form of a blazing altar of pure fire out of which is escaping a bird of green and gold plumage with five wings outspread. Above this symbol appear certain hieroglyphics in the earliest Sensa script signifying, "Still I seek."

The symbols of the seven Creative Hierarchies now in manifestation are all enclosed in a circle denoting limitation and the circumscribing of the Life. All these hierarchies are Sons of Desire, and are paramountly an expression of the desire for manifested life of the solar Logos. They receive their primary impulse from the cosmic astral plane. They are also the expression of a vibration emanating from the second row of petals in the logoic Lotus on the cosmic mental plane.

They are, therefore, one and all an expression of His love nature, and it is for this reason that buddhi is found at the heart of the tiniest atom, or what we call in this system, electric fire. For the positive central life of every form is but an expression of cosmic buddhi, and the downpouring of a love which has its source in the Heart of the Solar Logos; this is itself an emanating principle from the ONE ABOVE OUR LOGOS, HE OF WHOM NAUGHT MAY BE SAID.

It is love limiting itself by desire, and for that which is desired. It is love pouring itself out into forms which are stimulated and aided thereby; it is the fulfillment of divine obligations incurred in the dim and distant kalpas which antedate the triplicity of solar systems which we can dimly vision, and it is the "Father of Light" (in a cosmic connotation) pouring Himself out for that which binds Him and which it is His dharma to lift up to His Throne. It is not possible to picture the revelation of the Love of the solar Logos as it reveals itself to the eye of the illuminated seer, nor to show the nature of the cosmic Lord of Sacrifice as He limits Himself in order to save. At each step along the Path, the extent of that love and sacrifice is opened up as the disciple knows himself to be in tiny measure also a Lord of Sacrifice and Love. It can only be appreciated as the two inner rows of egoic petals are unfolded; knowledge would not reveal it, and it is only as a man transcends knowledge, and knows himself to be something non-separative, and inclusive that this particular revelation comes to him.

This is the secret behind the seven symbols, each one of which hides an aspect of the sevenfold Love of God as it is revealed through the hierarchy of Beings, or as the Son reveals it, Who is the sumtotal of the Love of God.

We might at the same time consider the type of force wielded by a particular hierarchy.

SECTION THREE

(The Electric Fire of Spirit)

SECTION THREE

A. Certain Basic Statements.

In connection with this final section of the *Treatise on Cosmic Fire,* dealing with the Electric Fire of Spirit it should be remembered that it will be quite impossible to impart information of a definite character; this subject is considered (from the standpoint of the esoteric student) to be devoid of form and therefore incognisable by the lower concrete mind. The nature of Spirit can only be intelligibly revealed to the higher grades of the initiates, that is, to those who (through the medium of the work effected in the third Initiation) have been put in conscious contact with their "Father in Heaven," the Monad. Esoteric students, disciples and the initiates of lower degree are developing contact with the soul, or the second aspect, and only when this contact is firmly established can the higher concept be entertained. The nature of Spirit is dealt with in the New Testament in one of the esoteric statements addressed by the Great Lord to the initiate, Nicodemus. As he was an initiate of the second degree it may be supposed that he had some glimmering of understanding as to the meaning of the words, which were spoken to him as part of his training in preparation for the third Initiation.

"The wind (prana or Spirit) bloweth where it listeth, and thou hearest the sound thereof but canst not tell whence it cometh nor whither it goeth. So is everyone that is born of the Spirit."

Two ideas are conveyed in this thought-form,—those of an emanating sound and direction, and that which is

CHART XII

PARABRAHM.

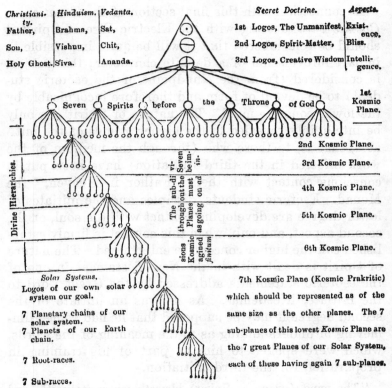

Christianity.	Hinduism.	Vedanta.		Secret Doctrine.	Aspects.
Father,	Brahma,	Sat,		1st Logos, The Unmanifest,	Existence.
Son,	Vishnu,	Chit,		2nd Logos, Spirit-Matter,	Bliss.
Holy Ghost.	S'iva.	Ananda.		3rd Logos, Creative Wisdom	Intelligence.

Seven   Spirits   before   the   Throne   of God

1st Kosmic Plane.

2nd Kosmic Plane.

3rd Kosmic Plane.

4th Kosmic Plane.

5th Kosmic Plane.

6th Kosmic Plane.

Divine Hierarchies.

The sub-divisions throughout the Seven Kosmic Planes must be imagined as going on ad infinitum

Solar Systems.

Logos of our own solar system our goal.

7 Planetary chains of our solar system.
7 Planets of our Earth chain.

7 Root-races.

7 Sub-races.

7th Kosmic Plane (Kosmic Prakritic) which should be represented as of the same size as the other planes. The 7 sub-planes of this lowest *Kosmic* Plane are the 7 great Planes of our Solar System, each of these having again 7 sub-planes.

FROM "THE THEOSOPHIST" FOR DECEMBER, 1899.

the result of the sound. This is evolution and the effect of the directing energy or activity of Spirit. From the point of view of consciousness these are the only things which the disciple can intelligently comprehend.

All that it will be possible for us to do in this section will be to impart the truth in three ways. Through the illumination of the student's mind as he studies the stanzas of Dzyan which will be found at the commencement of the treatise. Secondly, through the realisation that will come to the student as he correlates and ponders upon the various occult fragments found scattered through the pages, primarily centering his attention upon the following words:

"The secret of the Fire lies hid in the second letter of the Sacred Word. The mystery of life is concealed within the heart. When the lower point vibrates, when the Sacred Triangle glows, when the point, the middle centre and the apex, connect and circulate the Fire, when the threefold apex likewise burns, then the two triangles—the greater and the lesser—merge into one Flame, which burneth up the whole."

Thirdly, through the consideration of the various charts and word pictures which will be found also scattered through the *Treatise*. The student of the new era will approach much that he has to master through the medium of the eye, learning thereby to appreciate and solve that which is presented to him in the form of lines and diagrams. All is symbol and these symbols must be mastered.

It must also be borne in mind that students who approach the subject of SPIRIT need to grasp the following facts.

I. Whilst in manifestation and therefore during the period of an entire solar system, it is not possible for the highest Dhyan Chohan to think in terms of the negation of organised substance and of the non-existence of form. The goal of realisation for man is consciousness of the nature of the Soul, the medium through which the Spirit aspect, ever works. More it is not possible for him to do. Having learnt to function as the soul, detached from the three worlds, man then becomes a conscious corporate active part of that Soul which permeates and pervades all that is in manifestation. Then, and only then, the pure light of Spirit *per se* becomes visible to him through a just appreciation of the Jewel hidden at the heart of his own being; then only does he become aware of that greater Jewel which lies hidden at the heart of solar manifestation. Even then at that advanced stage all that he can be aware of, can contact and visualise, is the light which emanates from the Jewel and the radiance which veils the inner glory.

The seer (see-er) has then become pure vision. He perceives but as yet comprehends not the nature of that which is perceived, and it remains for another solar system and another kalpa to reveal to him the meaning of that revelation, the source of that illumination, and the essence of that Life whose quality is known to him already by its vibratory rate, its heat and its light. Needless it is, therefore, for us to study and consider that which the initiate of high degree can only dimly sense; useless it is for us to seek for terms to express that which lies safely hidden behind all ideas and all thought, when thought itself is not perfectly understood, and the machinery for comprehension is not perfected. Man himself—a great idea and a specific one—knows not the nature of that which he is seeking to express.

All that we can do is to apprehend the fact that there exists THAT which may not as yet be defined, to realise that a central life persists which permeates and animates the Soul and which seeks to utilise the form through which the soul expresses itself. This can be stated to be true of all forms, of all souls, human, subhuman, planetary and solar.

II. The wise student will likewise regard all forms of expression as in the nature of symbols. A symbol has three interpretations; it is itself an expression of an idea, and that idea has behind it, in its turn, a purpose inconceivable as yet. The three interpretations of a symbol might be considered in the following way:

1. *The exoteric interpretation* of a symbol is based largely upon its objective utility, and upon the nature of the form. That which is exoteric and substantial serves two purposes:

a. To give some faint indications as to the idea or the concept. This links the symbol in its exoteric nature with the mental plane, but does not release it from the three worlds of human appreciation.

b. To limit and confine and imprison the idea and so adapt it to the point in evolution which the solar Logos, the planetary Logos and man have reached. The true nature of the latent idea is ever more potent, complete and full than the form or symbol through which it is seeking expression. Matter is but a symbol of a central energy. Forms of all kinds in all the kingdoms of nature, and the manifested sheaths in their widest connotation and totality are only symbols of life—what that Life itself may be remains as yet a mystery.

These exoteric symbolic forms are of many kinds and serve many purposes, and this is largely responsible for the confusion in the minds of men on these matters. All symbols emanate from three groups of Creators:

The *solar Logos,* Who is constructing a "Temple in the Heavens not made with hands."

The *Planetary Logoi,* who—in Their seven groups—create through seven ways and methods, and thus produce a diversity of symbols and are responsible for concretion.

Man, who builds forms and creates symbols in his work of every day, but who as yet works blindly and largely unconsciously. Nevertheless, he merits the name of creator, because he utilises the faculty of mind and employs the rational quality.

The lesser devas and all the subhuman entities and all those builders who must in some distant future pass through the human state of consciousness are not regarded as creators. They work under impulses emanating from the other three groups. Each of the three groups is free within certain specified limits.

2. *The subjective interpretation* is the one which reveals the idea lying behind the objective manifestation. This idea, incorporeal in itself, becomes a concretion on the plane of objectivity, and as stated above, an idea lies behind every form without exception and no matter which group of creators is responsible for its construction. These ideas become apparent to the student after he has entered the Hall of Learning, just as the exoteric form of the symbol is all that is noted by the man who is as yet in the Hall of Ignorance. As soon as a man begins to use his mental apparatus and has made even a small contact with his ego three things occur:

a. He reaches out beyond the form and seeks to account for it.

b. He arrives in time at the soul which every form veils, and this he does through a knowledge of his own soul.

c. He begins then himself to formulate ideas in the occult sense of the term and to create and make manifest that soul-energy or substance which he finds he can manipulate.

To train people to work in mental matter is to train them to create; to teach people to know the nature of the soul is to put them in conscious touch with the subjective side of manifestation and to put into their hands the power to work with soul energy; to enable people to unfold the potencies of the soul aspect is to put them en rapport with the forces and energies hidden in the akasha and the anima mundi.

A man can then (as his soul contact and his subjective perception is strengthened and developed) become a conscious creator, co-operating with the plans of the Hierarchy of Adepts who work with ideas, and who seek to bring these ideas (planetary ideas) into manifestation upon the physical plane. As he passes through the different grades in the Hall of Learning his ability so to work and his capacity to get at the thought lying behind all symbols increases. He is no longer taken in by the appearance but knows it as the illusory form which veils and imprisons some thought.

3. *The spiritual meaning* is that which lies behind the subjective sense and which is veiled by the idea or thought just as the idea itself is veiled by the form it assumes when in exoteric manifestation. This can be regarded as the purpose which prompted the idea and led to its emanation into the world of forms. It is the central dynamic energy which is responsible for the subjective activity.

These three aspects of a symbol can be studied in connection with all atomic forms. There is, for instance, that unit of energy which we call the atom of the physicist or chemist. It has itself a form which is the symbol of the energy which produces it. This form of the atom is its exoteric manifestation. There are likewise those atomic aspects which we call—for lack of a better term—the electrons; these electrons are largely responsible for the quality of any particular atom, just as the soul of a man is responsible for his peculiar nature. They represent the subjective aspect or life. Then, finally, there is the positive aspect, the energy responsible for the coherence of the whole and for the uniformity of the dual manifestation, exoteric and subjective. This is analogous to the spiritual meaning, and who can read that meaning?

In man likewise, the human atom, these three aspects are found. Man on the physical plane is the exoteric symbol of an inner subjective idea which is possessed of quality and attributes and a form through which it seeks expression. That soul in its turn is the result of a spiritual impulse, but who shall say what that impulse is? Who as yet shall define the purpose behind the soul or idea, whether logoic or human? All these three factors are yet in process of evolution; all are as yet "imperfect Gods," each in their degree and therefore unable to express fully that which is the spiritual factor lying behind the conscious soul.

III. The wise student will also ponder well the words "the mystery of electricity," which is the mystery surrounding that process which is responsible for the production of light and therefore of vibration itself. We have concerned ourselves in the other two sections primarily with *effects,* with the results produced through the operation of the subjective side of nature (that alone which the occultist considers and works with) and the consequent production of objective manifestation. Now we arrive at the realisation that there is a cause lying behind that which has hitherto itself been regarded as a cause, for we discover that behind all subjective phenomena there lies an essentially spiritual incentive. This incentive, this latent spiritual cause, is the object of the attention of the spiritual man. The man of the world is occupied with objective phenomena, with that which can be seen, be touched, and handled; the occult student is engaged in studying the subjective side of life, and is occupied with the forces which produce all that is familiar upon the terrestrial plane. These forces fall into three main groups:

a. Forces emanating from the mental plane in its two divisions.

b. Forces of a kamic nature.

c. Forces of a purely physical description.

These the occult student studies, experiments with, manipulates and correlates; through the knowledge thus gained there comes an understanding of all that can be known in the three worlds, and likewise an understanding of his own nature.

The spiritual man is he who having been both a man of the world and an occult student has reached the conclusion that behind all those causes with which he has been hitherto engaged is a CAUSE; this causal unity then becomes the goal of his search. This is the mystery lying behind all mysteries; this is the secret of which all that has hitherto been known and conceived is but the veil; this is the heart of the Unknown which holds hid the purpose and the key to all that IS, and which is only put into the hands of those exalted Beings Who—having worked their way through the manifold web of life—know Themselves indeed and in truth to be Atma, or Spirit itself, and veritable sparks in the one great Flame.

Three times the cry goes out to all the Pilgrims upon the Path of Life: "Know thyself" is the first great injunction and long is the process of attaining that knowledge. "Know the Self" comes next and when that is achieved, man knows not only himself but all selves; the soul of the universe is to him no longer the sealed book of life but one with the seven seals broken. Then when the man stands adept, the cry goes forth "Know the One" and the words ring in the adepts' ears: "Search for that which is the responsible Cause, and having known the

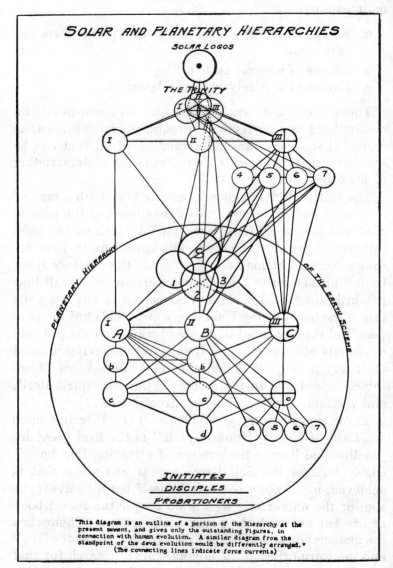

SOLAR AND PLANETARY HIERARCHIES

SOLAR LOGOS

THE TRINITY

PLANETARY HIERARCHY

OF THE EARTH SCHEME

INITIATES
DISCIPLES
PROBATIONERS

"This diagram is an outline of a portion of the Hierarchy at the present moment, and gives only the outstanding Figures, in connection with human evolution. A similar diagram from the standpoint of the deva evolution would be differently arranged."
(The connecting lines indicate force currents)

KEY TO DIAGRAM OF SOLAR AND PLANETARY HIERARCHIES

THE SOLAR HIERARCHY

The Solar Logos.

The Solar Trinity or Logoi

I   The Father ....Will.
II   The Son ....Love-Wisdom.
III   The Holy Spirit...Active Intelligence.

The Seven Rays
Three Rays of Aspect.
Four Rays of Attribute.

I.   Will or Power....II.   Love-Wisdom....III.   Active Intelligence.

4. Harmony or Beauty.
5. Concrete Knowledge.
6. Devotion or Idealism.
7. Ceremonial magic.

THE PLANETARY HIERARCHY

S. Sanat Kumara, the Lord of the World.
(The Ancient of Days.
The One Initiator.)

The Three Kumaras.
(The Buddhas of Activity.)
1   2   3

The reflections of the 3 major and 4 minor Rays.
The 3 Departmental Heads.

I.   *The Will Aspect*....II.   *The Love-Wisdom*   III.   *Intelligence Aspect.*
Aspect.

A.   The Manu.   B.   The Bodhisattva.   C.   The Mahachohan.
(The Christ.   (Lord of Civilisation)
The World Teacher.)

b.   Master Jupiter.   b.   A European Master.

c.   Master M—.   c.   Master K.H.   c.   The Venetian Master.

d.   Master D.K.   4.   The Master Serapis.
5.   Master Hilarion.
6.   Master Jesus.
7.   Master R—.

Four grades of initiates.

Various grades of disciples.

People on the Probationary Path.

Average humanity of all degrees.

soul, and its expression, form, search for THAT which the soul reveals.''

Here is to be found the clue to the search which the adept or perfected man undertakes when He puts His foot upon one of the seven possible paths. The only way in which any light can be thrown upon the mystery lies in the consideration of those seven cosmic Paths, of their names, and symbols. Very little can be said for the secrets of the higher initiations may not be revealed, nor the information given in a book for exoteric publication. All that can be done is to make certain suggestions, caution against certain conclusions, and indicate certain symbols which, if pondered upon, may bring a certain amount of illumination.

B. The Nature of the Seven Cosmic Paths.

It should be carefully borne in mind that when the term PATH is used, it is simply an energy term, and streams of energy are indicated,—seven streams which blend and merge to form one Path. It should also be noted that the Adept Who undergoes the discipline and who passes through initiatory rites which will enable him to tread those seven Paths, has transcended *colour,* has passed beyond the veil and has expanded His consciousness so that he is at-one with the conscious life of His planetary Logos. He has therefore arrived at a stage incomprehensible to man now; He is passing out of the realm of substantial forms altogether into the realm of energy. He knows the life of the two aspects, the soul and the body, and is passing away from the realm of *awareness* altogether. This will sound to the average reader as a foolish jingling of words and a splitting of hairs but he who reasons by the Law of Correspondences and who has grasped the basic essential relativity of the three aspects to each other has arrived at the knowledge that back of all form is a subjective Life which is known by its quality, its colour, and its attributes; he has expanded his consciousness until gradually he has ascertained and made a part of his own conscious ensemble those attributes and qualities. But the pulsating dynamic vibration which is the producing cause of both the subjective life and its qualitative form is as yet—to him—the mystery of mysteries and the ineffable secret. It becomes the goal of his endeavour as he sets foot upon one of the seven Paths which face him after the fifth Initiation. If a Master of the Wisdom and the one who has unified both the manas (intellect) and wisdom (buddhi) knows not what shall be revealed to him as he treads the cosmic Path which is his choice, surely it is needless for us to try and comprehend (at our relatively low stage of evolution) what is the true connotation of the word "Spirit." Pondering upon these matters is (for the average man) not only useless but also dangerous. He has not yet the apparatus of thought necessary for its safe undertaking. It is as if one tried to force a child in the first grade in school to comprehend the differential calculus and the laws of trigonometry.

These seven Paths, when trodden, prepare a man to pass certain cosmic initiations, including those upon the Sun Sirius. One hint may here be given. Each of these Paths eventually leads to one or other of the six constellations which (with ours) form the seven centres in the body of the ONE ABOUT WHOM NAUGHT MAY BE SAID. Those adepts therefore who stay for a prescribed length of time upon our planet are a correspondence to those greater initiates who remain for many kalpas within the solar system, taking certain mysterious initiations concerned entirely with solar evolution. Their work is concerned with the system as a centre in the body of that Existence Who vitalises the Logos of our own system.

It might be of value here to list the seven cosmic Paths as follows: [35]

Path   I .... The Path of Earth Service.
Path II .... The Path of Magnetic Work.
Path III .... The Path of the Planetary Logos.
Path IV .... The Path to Sirius.
Path   V .... The Ray Path.
Path VI .... The Path of the Solar Logos.
Path VII .... The Path of Absolute Sonship.

[35] Students must be careful to distinguish in their minds between these seven cosmic Paths and the seven ray Paths upon which all humanity are found and which have been earlier treated in this Treatise. As we have already seen the seven ray paths become three when units upon the four minor rays merge themselves into one of the three major rays. These three form the synthetic ray of Love-Wisdom by the time the sons of men have taken the final systemic Initiations. When this stage is reached and men realise the unity of the solar system not only theoretically but also as a practical reality with which they have identified themselves, then there is borne in upon their consciousness a something which transcends consciousness altogether and which can only be expressed by the limiting word *identification*. This identification is a cosmic and not a systemic process, and is itself sevenfold in nature. This sevenfold process for lack of a better term we call the sevenfold cosmic Path.

It must be borne in mind and no confusion of thought must be permitted that these terms are the generic names given in the mystic parlance of the Lodge of Masters to the seven methods of work, of endeavour and of aspiration whereby the perfected sons of Earth's humanity pass on to specific cosmic Paths or streams of energy, making in their totality one great cosmic WAY.

The seven paths at a certain stage which may not be defined become the four paths, owing to the fact that our solar system is one of the fourth order. This merging is effected in the following way:

The initiates upon Path I "fight their way" on to path VI.

The initiates upon Path II "alchemise themselves" on to Path VII.

The initiates upon Path III through "piercing the veil" find themselves upon Path V.

This leaves Path IV to be accounted for. Upon this Path pass all those who, through devotion and activity combined, achieve the goal but who lack as yet the full development of the manasic principle. This being the solar system of love-wisdom, or of astral buddhic development, the fourth Path includes the larger number of the sons of men. In the hierarchy of our planet the "Lords of Compassion" are numerically greater than the "Masters of the Wisdom." The former must therefore all pass to the sun Sirius there to undergo a tremendous manasic stimulation, for Sirius is the emanating source of manas. There the mystic must go and become what is called "a spark of mahatic electricity."

These seven Paths are not concerned with nature or the balancing of the pairs of opposites. They are concerned only with unity, with that which utilises the pairs of opposites as factors in the production of LIGHT. They deal with that unknown quantity which is responsible for the pairs of opposites; therefore they are primarily concerned with that which lies outside the manifested forms, with the true abstraction or the Absolute. Spirit and matter are never dissociated during manifestation; they are the duality lying back of all that is objective. Yet some factor is responsible for them—that which is neither Spirit nor matter, that which will be regarded as non-existent by anyone except the initiate. At the third Initiation some glimmering light upon this Abstraction is sensed by the initiate, and by the time the fifth Initiation is reached enough is apprehended by him to enable him to set forth with ardour on the search for its, secret.

Path I. *The Path of Earth Service.*

The nature of the spiritual force which animates the group of our peculiar planetary initiates will become apparent perhaps if the methods and purposes of their work are studied from the standpoint of subjective energy, and not so specifically of the material form. This point of view can be gleaned most easily from a consideration of the animating impulse lying behind all world groups which are particularly consecrated to the uplift of the race. This will necessarily include all political, religious, scientific and metaphysical organisations. It will be found that each and all are definitely related and have a point of at-one-ment with certain of the numerous occult bodies which are (usually unknown to the affiliated group) responsible for the vitalisation of the principal units in any of these organisations doing this pioneer work.

This first path is the one that keeps a man linked to the Hierarchy which is pledged to the service of our planetary scheme. It comprises those who work under the Lord of the World in the seven groups into which our Masters of the Wisdom are divided. Not so many Masters follow this Path as some of the others, and only enough are permitted to do so to carry on planetary evolution satisfactorily. More is known about this Path than about any of the others, and more will continuously be found out as members of our humanity fit themselves to contact the Brothers of the Hierarchy. Their field of employ, Their methods of work will eventually become exoteric, and as the seven groups are recognised and known, schools of development for the filling of posts in these groups will be the logical sequence.

The adepts who stay upon this Path are distinguished by a dual attribute, which is their guarantee of attainment along this line of spiritual endeavour. They are animated by *wise-compassion*. These words should be carefully studied for they hold the clue to the nature of this first Path. The adepts who choose this Path are called esoterically the "beneficent dragons," and the energy with which they work and the stream of living force upon which they are found emanates from the constellation of the Dragon, working through the zodiacal sign Libra. This special spiritual energy produces in all those groups which come under its direct influence a profound faculty for identification. This identification does not concern the form nor the soul but only the spiritual point of positive life which in the human unit we call the "Jewel in the Lotus." It should be remembered in this connection that there is a jewel at the heart of every atom. Every jewel has seven facets which are the seven doorways to the seven Paths.

The "beneficent dragons" are distinguished by their "luminosity," and it is this basic quality which lies behind the injunction given by all spiritual teachers to their pupils in the words "let your light shine forth."

When the adept enters through the "luminous door" he has before him four very peculiar and esoteric IDENTIFICATIONS. This entrance takes place after he has passed the fifth Initiation and has demonstrated his fitness so to do through a long period of service in connection with our planetary evolution. These identifications eventually bring about within the jewel, which is essentially the true spiritual unit, a momentous happening, and are undergone within the monadic consciousness after the transcendence of the atmic sheath. These four identifications are connected with the fourfold lotus of the solar Logos, or with His twelve-petalled heart centre. This lotus is sometimes called the "heart of the Sun," and concerns the subjective sun. It is not, however, possible to say more along this line.

These four Identifications are only undergone upon this particular Path and are each preceded by three lesser identifications which make a totality of twelve Identifications, corresponding to the twelve-petalled lotus. It will be noted by the accurate student that we are now discontinuing the use of the word "initiation" which has to do specifically with consciousness and therefore with duality and are utilising a word which connotes synthesis, though very inadequately.

The energy which is manipulated in the process of these identifications is largely that pouring through the sixth Hierarchy, which has an esoteric relation to the sixth Path on to which the initiates of Path I have eventually to fight their way. The form through which the adept must work in order to demonstrate his control of the energy concerned may not here be given. It may only be stated that luminosity is gained upon the battle ground through a fight with a dragon. The following summation may be found suggestive:

Path I. Earth Service

Attributes	Wise-compassion.
Source	Constellation of the Dragon, via Libra.
Method	Twelve cosmic Identifications.
Hierarchy	The sixth.
Symbol	A green dragon issuing from the centre of a blazing sun. Behind the sun and overtopping it can be seen two pillars on either side of a closed door.
Quality gained	Luminosity.

Path II. The Path of Magnetic Work.

In considering this Path students must bear in mind that they are dealing with that Path which of all the seven expresses most fully the effects of the Law of Attraction. It will be remembered by those who have carefully read this *Treatise* that this law is the expression of the spiritual will which produces the manifestation of the Son (Sun). Magnetism—physical, attractive and dynamic—is the expression of the law in the three worlds as far as the human unit is concerned. It will be apparent, therefore, that the adept who passes upon this Path is dealing with that reality which is the basis of all *coherency* in nature, and with that essence which through the force of its own innate quality produces the attractive energy which brings together the pairs of opposites; it is the force which is responsible for the interplay of electrical phenomena of every kind. The adept who chooses this cosmic stream of energy upon which to make certain cosmic approaches and upon which to make a series of cosmic unfoldments is one who has worked primarily upon the second ray path prior to the fifth Initiation, and who frequently has also been upon the fourth ray path. Adepts who have been upon the fourth ray path and who pass from thence upon the second ray do not as a rule choose this cosmic line of endeavour.

Those who do the work of wielding forces or electrical magnetism for the use of the Great Ones on all planes pass to this Path. They wield the elemental formative energy, manipulating matter of every density and vibration. Great waves of ideas and surging currents of public opinion on astral levels as well as on the higher levels where work the Great Ones, are manipulated by them. A large number of fifth Ray people, those who have the Ray of Concrete Knowledge for their monadic ray, pass to this line of endeavour. The inherent quality in the type of the Monad settles the line of activity. The karma of the fifth ray is one of the factors which produces this. These Monads work with fohat, and must, to the end of the greater manvantara. They have their eventual position on the cosmic mental plane, but as yet the capacity for abstract thought is so little developed that it is impossible for us to comprehend the significance of this expression.

Three types of magnetic work have been mastered by the adept who treads this second Path. He has mastered (in the three worlds) the magical work of form construction through the manipulation of magnetic energy and the utilisation of fohatic attractive energy in order to "bind the builders." This he does through the medium of a purified lower nature which can act as a perfect transmitter.

He has learnt also the secret of group coherence on the higher levels of the mental plane in connection with his own planetary Logos, and with those two other Logoi Who form with his own Logos a systemic triangle within the solar system. He has passed on also to a comprehension of the forces which unite the various streams of living energy emanating from Them in the furthering of the plans of solar evolution. This becomes possible to him when he can function in the monadic vehicle and is conscious in that unit of force.

This has been expressed in the old Commentary in the following words:

"The seven Brothers love each other, yet each seeketh for many æons the path of hatred. They hate and kill each other until they find that which dieth not and is not hurt. Together then they stand and serve and through their service the seven suns burn up."

The seven suns are destroyed because when synthesis and unity are reached and when the differentiated forces become one homogeneous force, the attractive or magnetic effect of this coherence is a manifested unit on the physical plane as well as on the subjective side of nature. This produces necessarily the destruction of all limiting forms, the merging of the fires, and the blazing forth into objectivity of the vital body of the Logos prior to the final abstraction and the subsequent dying out or obscuration of the solar system.

The will or purpose aspect which is the spiritual life behind all subjective and objective phenomena suddenly makes itself felt and also seen. It is the production of this which is the main work of the adept who passes on to Path II from off his particular ray path.

Those who tread this second Path work with magnetic or attractive energy because they have identified themselves with it. Eventually they will all pass on to Path VII, which is the Path of Absolute Sonship. All that can be said here in regard to their efforts is the statement that this Path carries them (through the medium of the logoic head centre) into the Heart of the ONE ABOUT WHOM NAUGHT MAY BE SAID. They are swept out of systemic evolution altogether upon a great tide of attractive energy which emanates from one of the major centres of that great Existence Who is the source of the life of the solar Logos. This centre is of course one of the seven constellations. As it is the most potent constellation as far as our system is concerned owing to the fact that this system predominantly expresses love or attractive energy and our Logos is as yet polarised in His cosmic astral body, it is not permitted to hint at the name of the constellation. The reason is that if the name were known and if enough people could do the work of occult meditation and visualisation, accompanying the work with a vivid imagination, it might be possible to attract into our system such a downpour of attractive energy from the constellation involved as to unduly speed up the processes of evolution upon our planet, and thus upset the systemic economy most dangerously. People do not yet realise the potency of meditation and especially of group meditation.

The zodiacal sign concerned is Gemini, and the reason will be apparent to all trained initiates.

A word here is necessary in explanation of the expression used earlier in connection with the passing of adepts from off this second Path on to the Seventh Path. It is stated that they "alchemise themselves" on to it. Some idea as to the meaning of this phrase may be gained through a consideration of the purposes of heat, when divorced from moisture, and of the method of employing such heat. The adepts use the "dry alchemical fires" to produce the results they desire in aiding the evolutionary process. As they use these "dry fires" the reaction upon themselves is such that they transmute the electrical spark (or the Monad within the flame of the planetary Life) and break it up in such a manner that it can pass through the systemic etheric web and on to that stream of cosmic energy emanating from the constellation mentioned above.

They are then known as "Absolute sparks of parental love," or (in the exoteric language of the initiates) they pass on to Path VII, that of "Absolute Sonship."

The attributes which the adept on this path has to possess prior to taking the needed training for the seventh cosmic method of approach is *responsiveness to heat and a knowledge of rhythm*. These words will, of course, mean nothing to the uninitiated but to some it will convey much and when it is noted that there will be found coupled with these two attributes an ability to ''see the dancing of the particles of heat and the waves of warm vibration'' (as it is called in an old manual which those in training for this path employ) it will be apparent that the effects of fire and the laws of fiery energy and vibration are here dealt with. Those sons of men who at this time search for the ''heat of the love nature'' of the human unit and who add to that search a cultivation of a vivid imagination and an intense power to visualise are laying a groundwork upon which this later knowledge may be superimposed. But this is not the easy thing it sounds, for it involves an identification at present impossible to the majority, and a power to realise the nature of that which is visualised which negates the idea of duality,—that which visualises and that which is visualised.

The *method* employed can only be expressed as the ''entering of the burning-ground.'' The power to do this is gained through passing through three preliminary burning-grounds, as is easily to be seen:

1. The burning-ground which lies between the Hall of Ignorance, and the Hall of Learning. This is the destructive fire which man creates under the working of the Law of Karma.

2. The burning-ground of the dead personality which lies between the Hall of Learning and the Hall of Wisdom. It is found upon the shores of the river of life and has to be passed prior to the third Initiation.

3. The burning-ground which is found when a man is ready to pass out of the Hall of Wisdom as a full adept. It is a triple burning-ground and is found "upon the mountain top, being kept alive and flaming by all the winds of heaven." It is responsible for the destruction of the egoic or causal body.

The third produces a spiritual alchemicalisation, whereas the other two produced results in the objective or form side and the subjective or consciousness aspect of his triple nature. When these three burning grounds are passed then the adept is prepared for another and fiercer experience.

The hierarchies connected with this Path are mainly the third and the fourth. Only the human units can pass on to these two paths. The deva hierarchies of the third order have already passed upon them, and it is their previous work which enables man to do so. This is a great mystery and more must not be revealed about it. The group of the Silent Watchers of all degrees are closely connected with this second cosmic path. All of Them are Lords of Sacrifice, and are animated solely by love, and all have therefore passed through the sacrificial burning grounds.

It is only possible to give the most elementary of the exoteric symbols. It takes the form of a funeral pyre in full conflagration, and with four flaming torches one at each corner. From the centre of the pyre a fivefold star mounts like a rocket towards a flaming sun of a predominantly rosy hue.

PATH II. PATH OF MAGNETIC WORK

Attributes ....Responsiveness to heat and knowledge of rhythm.
Source ....An unknown constellation via Gemini.
Method ....The entering of the burning-ground.
Hierarchy ....The third and fourth.

Symbol ....A funeral pyre, four torches, and a fivefold
                    star mounting towards the sun.
Quality gained .....Electrical velocity.

Path III. Path of training for Planetary Logoi.

This path is one that attracts to itself only a few comparatively of the sons of men. It involves a peculiar form
of development and the faculty of continued *awareness*
along with spiritual identification which is the distinguishing characteristic of the seven cosmic paths.

The adept who chooses this path preserves in a peculiar
way the faculty of sense-perception plus identification
with the spiritual aspect. They are constantly spoken of
in the occult archives as the "Lords Whose mayavirupa
continuously recurs." As they work with the psyche or
the soul of manifestation and are primarily concerned
with the subjective side of life they are connected with
that centre in the Body of the ONE ABOUT WHOM NAUGHT
MAY BE SAID which is the source of conscious sensation. Therefore, they are vitalised from the solar
plexus of that great Existence Whose all-embracing
vitality holds our Logos, along with other solar Logoi,
within the sphere of His consciousness. As is well known,
the solar plexus is the centre which synthesises the reactions and the essential virtues of the lower three centres.
This point must be borne in mind when studying this
cosmic path.

These adepts are also called the "Lords of cosmic
Maya" for they work with that faculty which is responsible for illusion and with the relation of the Knower to
that which is to be known. Remember here that we are
not considering the three worlds of human endeavour
except in so far as they form a part of a whole.

The attributes which predispose a man for the work of
training himself for the path of a planetary Logos are
three in number and may be expressed thus:

1. Cosmic vision. These adepts are connected with the logoic third eye.
2. Deva hearing.
3. Psychic correlation.

All the senses are, as we know, connected with some centre, and these centres are in turn connected with planetary centres which are themselves energised from an analogous cosmic source. The adept on this third Path has a specific connection with the energy which emanates from those cosmic centres which are related to spiritual vision and spiritual hearing. *The sense of touch* has primarily to do with the objectivity of the dense physical form, and with it this particular group of adepts has nothing to do. Sight, hearing and the power to correlate the relation between the Self and the Not-Self is theirs, but the Not-self comes specifically under the guidance and the stimulation of a totally different group of cosmic workers. It is difficult to convey a clear meaning in this connection and the student must remember that we are dealing with spirit and with the other two types of cosmic energy.

This path is trodden by those who will take up the work of the seven planetary Logoi of the next solar system, and of the forty-nine sub-planetary Logoi, Their assistants and of certain other entities working in that particular department. There will be seven systems, though we are only concerned with the major three, of which our present solar system is but the second.

Each Chohan of a Ray takes a certain number of initiates of the sixth Initiation and trains them specially for this work. Special aptitude in colour and sound predisposes the choice, and the ability to work with "psyche," or with the Spirits in evolution, marks a man out for this high post. We might say that the planetary Logoi are the divine psychologists, and therefore in the training for this post psychology is the basic subject, though it is a psychology inconceivable as yet to us.

Every planetary Logos has, in His own special planet, schools for the development of subordinate Logoi, and there trains them, giving them opportunity for wide experience. Even the Logoi Themselves progress onward, and Their places must be taken.

Students may be surprised to know that the source of the peculiar cosmic energy which is found streaming towards our system along this cosmic Path is that of the sun Betelgeuse. This name is, however, a blind. The reason that certain facts connected with this sun have lately come more prominently before the public is in reality a subjective one. The science of the soul in its various aspects (mental, psychical, and spiritual) is making much headway now in the world, and is absorbing more and more the attention of thinkers. This is the result of certain waves of energy impinging upon our solar system and thus eventually finding their way to our planet. Betelgeuse from the occult standpoint is a system of the second order, just as our solar system is one of the fourth order. There is consequently a relation between these two numbers both in the system and the cosmos. This influence reaches our system via *the sign Sagittarius.*

The work that adepts on this path have to accomplish primarily is to make possible the manifestation of the Monad of the solar Logos through the medium of the body of consciousness, or through the soul-form. They thus repeat on a higher level the work of those Builders who create and make manifest the body through which the soul seeks to express itself. They are not concerned with objectivity, and have a relation to that fifth Hierarchy which gives to man his egoic body.

The adepts on our Earth planet who seek this path do so through the department of the Mahachohan, which works with the intelligence or mental aspects of manifestation. From this third department they pass under the direct training of one of the Buddhas of Activity, and in the final stages are personally taught by Sanat Kumara, functioning as the embodied planetary Logos. This training concerns itself with three main subjects:

1. With colour, that which veils the Spirit aspect, as dense form veils the soul.

2. With sound, that which Spirit utters in order to make itself conscious, and to produce psychic awareness. The whole science of mantra yoga is mastered by them, but only in connection with the higher planes and where the cosmic planes are concerned.

3. With the nature of duality, that which is basically the science of the soul.

It is difficult to express in words *the method* employed by a Master of the Wisdom as he enters this cosmic Path. It has been called the *method of prismatic identification,* for it concerns the colour veils which shroud the spiritual energy. Another mode of expressing the same truth is to say that it is the method of understanding the song of life. As the "stars sing together," as the "chant of the Gods" peals forth in the great choir of the Heavens, it produces a corresponding colour symphony. This particular mode of identification enables the adept to act as a director in the chorus and to produce the needed colour effects and chords. When he can do this to perfection he is then in a position to take up office as a planetary Logos. More it is not permitted to say and the above is but a symbolic way of expressing a basic and difficult truth.

The *symbol* of this Path (and the only one it is possible to make exoteric) is a radiant Cross of coloured light; it has the long limb formed of the seven colours of the solar spectrum, and the transverse limb is composed of twelve gradations of colours as yet unknown to man. In the centre of the Cross is to be seen a five-pointed star in a deep indigo shade, and behind it is a blazing sun of a warm dark blue. Above the whole are certain Sensa characters, depicted in gold, and conveying to the initiated adept the name of one or other of the planetary Schools in which this particular line of study is undertaken. There are, as has been already said, seven such schools and candidates for this Path from our planetary scheme are transferred to the inner round and from thence to the Jupiter scheme.

The *quality* gained is cosmic etheric vision, the extent of the vision developed being within the seven systems which form (along with our solar system) the seven centres in the cosmic Life with whom our solar Logos is allied. This is sometimes called septenary cosmic clairvoyance.

One more fact of interest might here be added. This Path is sometimes called the "Lotus Path," as it concerns itself with the construction of the logoic Lotuses of solar Logoi. The schools which prepare for this work are called in the mystic parlance of the adepts the "lotus lands." The curriculum is termed at times the "Lotus sleep," as it involves a condition of complete negation where the form side of manifestation is concerned and an entire abstraction, thus producing a type of solar samadhi. Whilst this is being undergone the adept functions in a form or vehicle which is a correspondence upon the plane of atma to the mayavirupa on the plane of mind.

PATH III. THE PATH OF TRAINING FOR PLANETARY LOGOI

Attributes ....cosmic vision, deva hearing and psychic correlation.

Source ....Betelgeuse, via the sign Sagittarius.

Hierarchy ....the fifth.

Method ....prismatic identification.

Symbol ....a coloured Cross, with a star at the centre, and backed by a blazing sun, surmounted by a Sensa Word.

Quality ....cosmic etheric vision or septenary clairvoyance.

Path IV. The Path to Sirius.

This path is of all the Paths the most veiled in the clouds of mystery. The reason for this mystery will only be apparent to the pledged initiate, though a clue to the secret may be gained if it is realised that in a peculiar and esoteric sense the sun Sirius and the Pleiades hold a close relation to each other. It is a relation analogous to that which lower mind holds to higher mind. The lower is receptive to, or negatively polarised to the higher. Sirius is the seat of higher mind and mahat (as it is called, or universal mind) sweeps into manifestation in our solar system through the channel of the Pleiades. It is almost as if a great triangle of mahatic energy was thus formed. Sirius transmits energy to our solar system via that

". . . sevenfold brooding Mother, the silver constellation, whose voice is as a tinkling bell, and whose feet pass lightly o'er the radiant path between our worlds and hers."

Within the solar system there is an interesting correspondence to this cosmic interplay in the relation between the Venus scheme, our Earth scheme and the Venus chain in our scheme.

Curiously enough it will be through a comprehension of the human antaskarana, or the path which links higher and lower mind and which is constructed by the Thinker during the process of evolution, that light on this abstruse matter will come. There is (in connection with our planetary Logos) just such an antaskarana, and as He builds and constructs it, it forms part of the fourth Path, and permits the passage of the bulk of our humanity to this distant objective, and this without obstruction. A clue to the nature of this Path and as to the reason why so many of the human Monads seek this particular stream of energy lies in the right understanding of the above suggestion.

The initiates who tread this way are primarily those of the fourth and the sixth order. As earlier pointed out, this is the Path that the "lords of compassion" most frequently follow, and at this time the Egyptian Master and the Master Jesus are preparing Themselves to tread it. The mystics of the Occident who have come into incarnation during the past one thousand years are a peculiar group of Egos whose impulse is towards this type of cosmic energy. In this system they have developed certain basic recognitions and the "ecstasy" of the occidental mystic is the germ, latent within him, which will some day flower forth into that cosmic rapture for which we have as yet no name.

Cosmic rapture and rhythmic bliss are the attributes of the fourth path. It is a form of identification which is divorced from consciousness altogether. The reason also why the majority of the sons of men follow this Path lies in the fact of its numerical position. These units of the fourth kingdom, the bulk of the fourth Creative Hierarchy on this fourth globe of the fourth scheme in a solar system of the fourth order are innately compelled to seek this fourth WAY in order to perfect themselves. They are called the "blissful dancing points of fanatical devotion." This is as near as we can get to the true description. They have also been described as the "revolving wheels which turn upon themselves, and find the open door to perfect bliss."

The energy of Path IV reaches us from *Sirius via the Sun*. This must be understood as a blind behind which one of the signs of the zodiac veils itself.

The hierarchies concerned with this specific type of

cosmic force hide themselves under the numbers fourteen and seventeen. This will serve as a complete blind
to the average reader, but will carry to the pledged chela
the hint needed to produce illumination.

The *method* whereby the adept fits himself to pass
upon this path is termed that of duplex rotary motion
and "rhythmic dancing upon the square."

The *symbol,* which is first given to the pledged disciple
to study but which may, however, be described, is a duality of interlocked wheels revolving at a great pace in
opposite directions, and producing a unified whole. These
wheels are portrayed as manifesting electric blue flame,
rotating and revolving with great rapidity around an
equal-armed Cross. The Cross is pictured in orange fire
with a deep emerald green circle, flaming at the point in
the centre where the four arms of the Cross meet. The
symbolism of these colours links this fourth path to the
solar system preceding this one. In that system the
Sirian influence was more potent than in the present one.

It is not possible to add more to this beyond pointing
out that the *quality* gained by the adept who treads this
path may not be revealed. He comes under the concentrated influence of the energy which is identified with the
planetary antaskarana. It is not permitted, therefore,
to state what its specific quality may be, as it would convey too much information to the intelligent reader as to
the nature and the objective of our particular planetary
Logos.

Path IV. The Path to Sirius

Attributes ....cosmic rapture and rhythmic bliss.
Source ....Sirius via the Sun which veils a zodiacal
                    sign.
Hierarchy ....veiled by the numbers 14 and 17.
Method ....duplex rotary motion and rhythmic danc-
                    ing upon the square.

symbol ....two wheels of electric fire, revolving around an orange Cross, with an emerald at the centre.

quality ....unrevealed.

Path V. The Ray Path.

This Path is one of the great distributing paths of the system, and is trodden by the adept who has a clear understanding of the laws of vibration. It leads to the next cosmic plane with great facility and is therefore called "the outer door of entry." As we know, the seven Rays which manifest throughout our solar system, are but the seven subrays of one great ray, that of Love-Wisdom. This ray Path is the one upon which the majority of the "Masters of the Wisdom" pass. In the same way many of the "Lords of Compassion" pass on to Path IV. Five-eighths of the former pass on to this path just as four-fifths of the adepts of suffering pass on to Path IV. In considering these numbers it must be borne in mind that the figures are of very great magnitude. One-fifth of the Compassionate Lords is a vast number, whilst three-eighths is a stupendous number of monads. We must remember in this connection also that we are only dealing with the adepts of the fifth Initiation, and are not taking into consideration initiates of lower degrees nor disciples of many grades. It is useless for average man to ponder upon these figures. They are too difficult to compute and involve calculations most abstruse and intricate. This can be demonstrated by pointing out that from these figures must be subtracted that two-fifths which (in the next round) pass before the Judgment Throne and are rejected. Out of the remaining three-fifths only a percentage which may not be revealed reach final adeptship, though all pass upon the Path. The five-eighths above referred to and the four-fifths have reference only to the two great groups of asekha initiates.

Adepts who pass upon the Ray Path have to possess attributes which make them exceedingly responsive to vibration. In their group work (regarding all the units upon this Path as forming a unified Whole) the results achieved might be compared to that of a compass upon a ship. They respond primarily to a basic vibration, not through sensation but through that which is the outgrowth of sensation. It is a form of realisation which is the cosmic correspondence to the reaction which comes when the skin is touched. It is not consciousness but *knowledge through vibration*. They are themselves identified with a certain vibration and they respond to that vibration alone which is the higher correspondence upon the cosmic planes. Other vibrations they ignore.

They are taught how to insulate themselves so that no vibration save the one which reaches them from the cosmic source of the synthetic ray can touch them. Students can get some idea of the lower correspondence to this as they study the compass, its responsiveness to a certain magnetic current, and the tendency which it demonstrates to point ever towards the north. These adepts of the fifth Path are the constituent factor which occultly holds our solar system steadily equilibrised in one specific direction. Their main characteristic or attribute may be described as a *sense of cosmic direction.*

The source of energy to which they respond may be regarded as the Pole Star. It should nevertheless be pointed out that this star serves only as a blind for a constellation which lies behind,—a constellation which exists only in etheric matter. It is consequently ignored by astronomers, though its influence is exceedingly potent within our system. It should be borne in mind also that upon another planet within our solar ring-pass-not this fifth Path is the one that the majority of their adepts follow. Adepts who are on this Path, therefore, will pass to this other planetary scheme prior to finding their way to the Sun and from thence to cosmic spheres. Adepts from other schemes are not transferred to our Earth scheme as a school of training as it is not a sacred planet and therefore lacks such a specific school.

The influence which emanates from the Pole Star and which is such a potent factor in our solar system reaches our planet via the sign Aquarius. The reasons will be noted if the student bears in mind the significance of water as a symbol of the emotions, which are but a lower manifestation of love-desire. Aquarius is a force centre from which the adept draws the "water of life" and carries it to the multitude. This force from the Pole Star, via Aquarius, is of special power at this time and the day of opportunity is therefore great. It is one of the agencies which make the coming of the Great Lord a possibility. He is Himself upon the fifth Path just as the Manu is upon the third. Hence the close link between the two paths, for those on the fifth path can pass to the third and vice versa. The first and the seventh, the second and the fourth, and the third and the fifth are but the two sides of one whole, or the two aspects of the one Path. These three paths (with the fourth Path) constitute two Paths and the two Paths are but one. This great mystery may not further be enlarged upon.

The Hierarchies which play a great part in the introduction of polar influence are *the first and the second.* It was this occult truth which had such a bearing upon the nature of the first two races of mankind and upon their habitat.

The method whereby the adept develops the needed powers for this Path have been hinted at above. They might be expressed as *a process of electrical insulation and the imprisonment of polar magnetism.* It is not permitted to say more.

The symbol of this path is five balls of fire (blue fire) confined within a sphere. This sphere is formed by a serpent biting its tail, and the entire body of the serpent is closely covered with written Sensa characters; these characters embody the mantram whereby the adept insulates himself from the magnetic flow of all currents save that for which he is responsible.

The quality which the adept develops as he treads this Path can only be given in the words of the old Commentary:

"The depression at the northern point permits entrance of that which stabilises, and acts as the factor of resistance to that which seeketh to deter or to distract."

Perhaps *cosmic stability and magnetic equilibrium* serve best to convey the necessary idea.

PATH V. THE RAY PATH

Attributes ....A sense of cosmic direction.
Source ....The Pole Star via Aquarius.
Hierarchies ....The first and the second.
Method ....A process of electrical insulation and the imprisonment of polar magnetism.
Symbol ....Five balls of fire enclosed within a sphere. Sphere is formed of a serpent inscribed with the mantram of insulation.
Quality ....Cosmic stability and magnetic equilibrium.

There is no way in which we can express any teaching or give any information anent the sixth and seventh Paths. All that can be said is as follows:

Path VI. The Path the Logos Himself is on.

It will be apparent to all those students who have studied with care the world processes in the light of the law of correspondences that the Logos on the cosmic planes is evolving inner cosmic vision, just as man in his lesser degree is aiming at the same vision in the system. This might be called the development of the cosmic third

Eye. In the physical plane structure of the eye lies hid the secret and in its study may come some revelation of the mystery.

A certain portion of the eye is the nucleus of sight and the apparatus of vision itself. The remainder of the eye acts as a protecting shell; both parts are required, and neither can exist without the other. It is so in the cosmic sense also, but the analogy exists on such high levels that words only dim and blur the truth. Certain of the sons of men, a nucleus who reached a very high initiation in a previous solar system, formed an esoteric group around the Logos when He decided upon further progress. In consequence He formed this solar system, desire for cosmic manifestation urging Him on. This esoteric group remains with the Logos upon the atomic or the first plane of the system, on the subjective or inner side, and it corresponds in an occult sense to the pupil of the eye. The real home of these great Entities is upon the cosmic buddhic plane.

Gradually and by dint of hard effort, certain Masters have qualified themselves, or are qualifying themselves, to take the place of the original members of this group thus permitting of Their return to a cosmic centre around which our system, and the greater system of Sirius, revolves.

Only one adept here and there has the necessary qualities, for the development involves a certain type of response to cosmic vibration. It means a specialising of the inner sight, and the development of a certain amount of cosmic vision. More of the deva evolution pass to this Path than do the human. Human beings pass to it via the deva evolution, which can be entered by transference to the fifth, or Ray Path. On this latter Path the two evolutions merge and from the fifth, the sixth Path can be entered.

Path VII.   The Path of Absolute Sonship.

This sonship is a correspondence on the highest plane to that grade of discipleship which we call "Son of the Master." It is the Sonship to a Being higher than our Logos of Whom we may not speak. It is also the great controlling Path of Karma. The Lipika Lords are upon this Path, and all who are fitted for that line of work, and who are close to the Logos in a personal and intimate sense pass to this seventh Path. It is the Path of the special intimates of the Logos and into their hands He has put the working out of karma in the solar system. They know His wishes, His will and His aim, and to Them He entrusts the carrying out of His behests. This group, associated with the Logos, forms a special group linked to a still higher Logos.

These two paths enter into cosmic states of consciousness as inconceivable to man as the consciousness of the Ego of a human being is to an atom of substance. It is unnecessary and profitless therefore to enlarge further upon these exalted states.

C. Seven Esoteric Stanzas.

Stanza I

(From Archaic Formulas. No. 49)

Path 1. *The Path of Earth Service.*

The Dragon who hideth within the lowest of the Sacred Three ariseth in His might. In His mouth He holdeth the balances, and in the balances He weigheth the sons of men who—upon the field of battle—are impaled upon His spear.

In the great balance upon which His eyes are fixed, one scale is veiled in fire of vivid green; the other hides itself behind a screen of red.

Those sons of men whose note responds not to the note of red enter the scale upon the right hand side. From thence they pass upon a path which dimly can be seen behind the dragon's form.

This path is entered by a fourfold door. The sacred phrases of the Sons of Light define it thus: "The portal of the luminous light, which leadeth from the green into the heart of indigo, by that rare fire and

NOTE: These seven stanzas form only one true stanza out of the oldest book in the world, and one which the eye of the average man has never contacted. Only the sense is here given and not a literal translation, and certain phrases are eliminated in all of them for one or other of the three following reasons: Either the manuscript from which these extracts are taken lacks certain of the words or symbols which are missing on account of the extreme age of the material upon which the text is indited, or their insertion would convey too much knowledge to the man whose perception is sufficiently awakened. Thirdly, the insertion of the omitted words would only serve to awaken confusion and even ridicule on account of the impossibility of translating them correctly; they concern realisations far in advance of the comprehension of man at this time.

richly coloured blaze for which no name on earth hath yet been found.'' Its tone is hidden.

The sons of men (and few their number is) enter that door of luminous fire when they surmount the crest of gold which riseth on the dragon's head above the point where gleams "the eye of fire."

This eye of fire transmits a strong vibration from the triple Lhas unto a centre in the Adept's head. This, when aroused, reveals the Life that is, the form that shall be, and the work united of the two and four.

These two are drawn together. Their essence blends. The man who seeks this path is then impaled upon the spear and thrust within the fiery light which veils the balance. The mystic process then proceeds and . . . Thus is the work of SATURN seen, and thus the consummation is effected.

Through SATURN's fateful force the victor then is swiftly projected to the summit of the crest, and thence to that vibrating disk which guards the fourfold door of luminosity.

Three Words are then committed to the Liberated One. He stands triumphant on the speeding disk and when their utterance has . . . the door is seen ajar, and from its other side a voice is heard to say: "Son of Compassion, Master of Love and Life, the wheel turns all the time for those who battle on the fiery ground beneath the dragon's feet."

The first Word having entered on its mission, the victor lifts His head and seeks to utter forth the second Word. But, as He sounds it forth, He arrests its wide vibration, drawing again its power within His heart.

The motion of the disk slows down. The portal of the fiery light opens more widely yet. A form is seen. Unto the Master of the Fiery Heart, this form presents three precious jewels. Their names are hidden from those sons of men who have not yet attained the dragon's crest.

These jewels three give to the Master of the Fiery Heart a portion of the triple force which circulates within the planet's sphere.

With eye intent and heart alive with burning love the Master utters not the final Word. He steps from off the disk and turns His Lotus Feet back to that Path He earlier left behind, and from the other side remounts the Dragon's crest. Himself a dragon, He now identifies Himself with those who seek the beast. And thus He serves, turning His back upon the door of light. He is the offspring of the dragon and serves His time. . . .

Unknown and unseen by Him, a greater disk becomes apparent, turning unceasingly. He seeth not its movement for His eyes are on the world He has returned to serve. The disk revolves and brings around—before His yet unseeing eye—a greater wider Door. . . . His eye of vision opens. . . . He treads the first great path, yet knows it not.

The note that sounds forth from that first great WAY is yet unheard by Him. Its sound is lost in the uprising cry of the children of the lesser dragon.

Stanza XVII

(From Archaic Formulas. No. 49)

Path II. *The Path of Magnetic Work.*

The cosmic Burning-ground of living fire lieth in the nethermost part of the western heavens. Its smoke riseth unto that high place where dwell the Sacred Lhas to Whom the triple Unity within our solar space tender Their offerings and Their fealty. Its scent of spices sweet and faint aroma of incandescent . . . reach to the utmost confines of the starry vault.

The Two arise and pass the essential Flame through Their burning-ground, blending Their lesser smoke with the greater.

This smoke formeth a Path which reacheth forth unto those spheres within the radiant form of that Attractive Life, to Whom the sons of being and of men in all their many grades offer their prayers, their life and adoration.

The Master on this sphere, which is known as the fourth and is not holy, seeth the fiery Way; He respondeth to its heat and seeks to warm Himself within its waves of radiant fire electric.

A centre at the midway point within the great Kumaric Body formeth the pyre. It pulsates and it glows. It becomes a sea of living fire and draws within itself its own. The smoke which issues from this fiery wheel formeth a living Way, veiling the steps ahead.

The Master—with the midway wheel on fire—enters within the smoke, and enters blind. He sees no step ahead. He hears no voice. He feels no guiding hand. Only the fifth and latest known aids Him to forward grope, and pass straight onward through the veiling clouds; only the awakening of His wheel may indicate His progress through the new magnetic field.

Only the sons of . . . (GEMINI) know the way in; only the sons with blazing fire, issuing from the midway point, may enter in. They throw their beams ahead to illuminate the WAY. The Adept of the funeral pyre, the Master of the blazing sphere consumes Himself. Offering Himself the One that is, the new-made threefold Word, the sacred OM, the fire of God, He treads the burning-ground, and blazes forth to those who watch as a radiant flaming sun.

He . . . and draws the people onward to their goal, warming their hearts, producing dual fire, and leading all towards the portal of the sun and thence to . . . (GEMINI).

The mystic Word is veiled by letters four—E, M, and A and O—. In the significance of their numbers and the utilisation of their colours is the smoke dissipated.

(From Archaic Formulas. No. 49)

Path III. *Training for Planetary Logoi.*

The eye of Shiva opens wide and those within its range of vision awaken to another form of sleep. They sleep, but yet they see and hear; their eyes are closed, yet naught that passes in the greater cosmic Seven is missed by them. They see, and yet they vision not; they hear and yet their ears are deaf.

Three times the eye of Shiva closes and three times it opens wide. Thus three great groups of Lotus Lords are impelled upon Their way.

One group is called the "Lotus Lords of deep unseeing sleep." They dream, and as Their dreams take form, the worlds speed on. The great and cruel maya of the planes of sweet illusion comes into being, draws into its snare the points of unconnected light, and dims their lustre.

Thus is the work pursued. . . .

The eye through which these Lotus Lords contact the planes of cosmic vision is *inward* turned. They see not that which is upon the outer rim.

The second group has for its name "the Lords of the Inner Lotus." These are They who sleep, yet not so deep. They wake enough to guard Themselves from straying o'er the secret ring-pass-not which rims the great Illusion. They straitly stand, and, through Their very steadfastness, the forms are held together.

The eye through which these Lotus Lords look out

upon the great Illusion is *upward* turned. They see but that which lieth just above Them; they onward look to that vast mountain top which pierceth through the circumscribing wheel. This mountain top shineth with radiant light, reflected from the face of Him Whom the Lords of worlds within our solar sphere have never seen.

*   *   *   *   *   *   *

The third group is the strange mysterious triple group whose name must not be heard as yet within those planetary spheres whose colour blends not with the blue in just proportion.

The eye through which these Lotus Lords gaze out upon the cosmic Path is *outward* turned. Its hue is indigo. The eye through which the middle group of Lotus Lords look up is turquoise blue, whilst the Lords of deep unmoving slumber gaze in through sapphire blue. Thus is the WAY of triple blue formed into one.

This latter aspect of the eye of Shiva directs the other two, and gathers all its energy from a far distant cosmic sphere. The two respond, and in the treading of the cosmic WAY weave triple force into that path which meets the need of those who later seek to tread it.

They see; They hear; They dream, and dreaming build; Their eyes are blind; Their ears are deaf, and yet They are not dumb. They sound the several cosmic Words, and weave the seven with the twelve and multiply the five.

*   *   *   *   *   *   *

Thus are the planets built; thus guided, ruled and known.

Path IV. *The Path to Sirius.*

The mysterious Lhas of the sacred hidden fire withdraw Their thought, emerge from meditation, and all that is—between the first and third—is lost to sight. Naught is. Sound dies away. The Words are lost, for there is none to hear. The colours fade, and every point grows dim.

The ocean passes into quietude. The Mother slumbers and forgets her Son. The Father too retreats within the unknown place where fire lies hidden.

The serpent stretches forth inert. Its coils smother the lower fire and choke the sparks. . . . Silence reigns. The absent Lhas forget the worlds and play at other games. . . . All passes into nothingness. Yet still the Lhas themselves remain.

* * * * * * *

The mysterious Lhas of the fivefold force unite Their thought, sink into meditation deep and link the first and third. The worlds emerge, and—rushing into forms prepared—pursue their cycles.

* * * * * * *

The twelve-pointed play Their part and are the result of the communion of the One above the Sun with one of the seven wives.

* * * * * * *

The Master of the Sacred Heart is He who builds a Path between the sphere whereon His lot is cast and the great manasic orb. He builds it knowingly, calling in the aid of points of blue. These emerge from the heart of one of the seven. (The PLEIADES.)

These He bloweth upon and they find their place as stones in the one Way He constructeth for the treading of the many as they wend their way through mind to mind and thence to understanding. (Manas to mahat and thence to buddhi.)

PATH V. *The Ray Path.*

The Adjuster holds the balances, and the scales are duly set. The energies converge, and shake them out of equilibrium. They descend sometimes upon the right hand side and sometimes upon the left.

The Energies are five in number and their major hue is gold.

*   *   *   *   *   *   *

Three great Words are spoken by the Adjuster, and each Word is heard by those whose ears have been deaf for seven cycles and whose lips have been sealed for nigh upon fourteen rounded terms.

The first Word contains the value numerical of the synthetic indigo. It reverberates forth. The scales descend. He who hath ears to hear it, mounteth the scales and addeth to that Word another sound. None have heard it save he who hath stood before the Prince of Doom, and hath seen darkness descend upon the fivefold sons of flesh.

This dual Word buildeth a wall which surroundeth the Son of Man whose lips are dumb. It holdeth Him secure until the Word is spoken which will unseal the fount of speech.

This silence lasteth for seven times forty-nine years and each year for a day.

When the Silent One within the wall seeth the Ray

approach, when He changeth the key of the earlier spoken Word, the disruption of the wall is seen and a door openeth before Him.

*   *   *   *   *   *   *

The second Word holds hid the number of the sacred blue. As it reverberates, the scales ascend, and the man who seeketh to mount within them seeth the moment pass and knoweth not what to do.

He struggleth for speech and raiseth His right hand in supplication to the great Adjuster. From the sacred halls of the City of the White Island there issueth a messenger who speaketh to Him the following mystic words:

"As the power enters by that which is uppermost, and as it issues from the lotus within the head of Him who hath held His peace, utter this WORD . . . and look within."

He who hath held His speech breaks then the silence. He utters the four deep sounds which cause the scale again to drop within His reach. Another door is seen; it opens wide and thus the WAY is trodden.

*   *   *   *   *   *   *

The third Word holds securely sealed the key to the outer blue. It contains the order for inversion, and only those can hear that Word whose ears have been closed for eleven æons. It is never heard within the realms of pain. Few therefore hear it, and those few elude the scales, escape the fiery eye of the great Adjuster and in Their very blindness find the Path which lieth upon the further side of the scales.

*   *   *   *   *   *   *

These Words of high direction issue from that which lieth upon the . . . of the directing Life which holdeth our Lord of Life upon His Path.

Stanza VI

(From Archive 49)

Path VI. *The Path of the Solar Logos.*

The major Third carrieth within it the vibration of that which hath already been. The cosmic Lord from out the greater seven (Whose sacred Name is hid) seeketh the centre of His life from out the sacred seven. This is the mystery hid, the inner secret found in the heart of cosmic space within the groups divine.

The sacred seven with the greater seven approach their primary, the One Who standeth above, and in their cyclic outer sweep will some day touch. The two become the One and are lost in their primary.

Seek ye the same on lesser scale within the inner round and on the plane of density see the lesser primary manifest. The law holds good; the mystery dissolves in Time.

The major Third in both the lesser and the greater, the cosmic Lord—with His dim reflection solar—completes His cycle, meets His brother, becomes the Son, contacts the Mother, and is Himself the Father. All is One, and naught divides save in transition and through the agency of time.

*   *   *   *   *   *   *

The major fifth within the Eternal Now carrieth with it the vibration of that which is. It marks the point of cosmic knowledge that extendeth far ahead into the lengthening present. The cosmic Lord, Whose sacred Name holdeth for us the wisdom of the spheres, seeketh a form wherein to veil the Essence, and through the progress of the æons to perfect the great triplicity.

Hid is the mystery, and veiled by that which is. Deep is the essence, and sheathed by that which moves. Profound the darkness, lost in the heart of being; dense are the forms, which hide the inner light; gross is the sheath that acteth as a barrier, and crude the material veiling the latent life.

The major fifth includes the minor third; the double major marks the point attained. When the major third is synchronised to the greater fifth and the cosmic note—apportioned to the Lord of Cosmic Love Whose essence is the fire—the sacred Name is heard.

The cosmic Second approaches to the denser and the greater. He merges and He blends, and all is lost in dissonance adjusted. The spheres respond; the Now becomes the past and blends within the time to be. The essence and the life, the point within the circle, and the eternal ring-pass-not becomes as one, and all is peace for æons. Time ends; space disperses; naught is. Darkness reigns and silence on the waters. The central calm persists.

*　　*　　*　　*　　*　　*　　*

The completed chord, the third, the fifth and seventh within the Eternal Now, carrieth with it the vibration of that which is to be. Cometh the Day Be With Us on the greater cosmic plane. Then life and love and power shew forth as one.

The cosmic Lord, Whose sacred Name as yet is hid

e'en from the highest Chohan, holdeth within Himself the source of cosmic action, and the gain of cosmic love. The triple All enters—from out of time and space—into the centre of pralayic peace.

All is, yet all is not. The wheels turn not. The fires burn not. The veils of colour dissipate. The Three retire within the point of peace. The triple ring-pass-not acteth no longer as a barrier.

(From Archive 63)

PATH VII. *The Path of Absolute Sonship*

That which hath no beginning and no end; That
which is seen and yet remains unknown; That which
we touch and yet find unattained, That is the One
Who passeth on His WAY.

That which we call the Father and the Son; That
which we deem too high for words to grasp; That
which the Mother deems her Lord and God, That is
the One Who mounts the cosmic stair.

That which is seen when each point of heavenly
light sends out its beam upon the midnight blue; That
which we hear in every cosmic note and sense beneath
the sound of every form, That is the One Who chants
the heavenly lay and lends His light to swell the
cosmic fire.

That which is known by every Son of God, who
masters step by step the Path of Gold; That which
is heard by every deva lord who hears the Word go
forth as the æons pass away; That which sounds forth
the triple cyclic AUM, reserving yet another sound
for higher cosmic planes, That is the One unknown,
the Unrevealed, the One Who chants a note within a
cosmic chord.

That which in every æon cometh forth and passeth
through His cycle upon a cosmic Path; That which
in greater kalpas will play a god-like game; That

which in all the cosmic spheres is called "the One above the Son of violet hue," That is the One Who shineth in the galaxy of stars.

Such is the One to Whom the sons of glory give everlasting homage as He passes on His WAY. To Him be glory as the Mother, Father, Son, as the One Who hath existed in the past, the now and That which is to come.

FINALE

The morning stars sang in their courses.

The great pæan of creation echoeth yet, and arouseth the vibration.

There comes cessation of the song when perfection is achieved.

When all are blended into one full chord, the work is done.

Dissonance in space soundeth yet. Discord ariseth in many systems. When all is resolved into harmony, when all is blended into symphony, the grand chorale will reverberate to the uttermost bounds of the known universe.

Then will occur that which is beyond the comprehension of the highest Chohan—the marriage song of the Heavenly Man.

Training for new age
discipleship is provided
by the *Arcane School*.
The principles of the
Ageless Wisdom are
presented through esoteric
meditation, study and
service as a *way of life*.

*Write to the publishers
for information.*

THE GREAT INVOCATION

From the point of Light within the Mind of God
Let light stream forth into the minds of men.
Let Light descend on Earth.

From the point of Love within the Heart of God
Let love stream forth into the hearts of men.
May Christ return to Earth.

From the centre where the Will of God is known
Let purpose guide the little wills of men —
The purpose which the Masters know and serve.

From the centre which we call the race of men
Let the Plan of Love and Light work out
And may it seal the door where evil dwells.

Let Light and Love and Power restore the Plan on Earth.

"The above Invocation or Prayer does not belong to any person or group but to all Humanity. The beauty and the strength of this Invocation lies in its simplicity, and in its expression of certain central truths which all men, innately and normally, accept—the truth of the existence of a basic Intelligence to Whom we vaguely give the name of God; the truth that behind all outer seeming, the motivating power of the universe is Love; the truth that a great Individuality came to earth, called by Christians, the Christ, and embodied that love so that we could understand; the truth that both love and intelligence are effects of what is called the Will of God; and finally the self-evident truth that only through *humanity* itself can the Divine Plan work out."

ALICE A. BAILEY

INDEX

H

1332   INDEX

M

Macrocosm—
  and microcosm, 7, 47
  four planes of super-conscious
    life, 916
Macrocosmic—
  happening producing effects in
    microcosm, 702
  nature of Logos and man, 671
Magic—
  agents, deva, 645
  basis, 982
  beneficent, secret, 892
  black—
    definitions, 984-985
    responsibility for, 837
    source, 989-993
  concern, 638
  investigation, danger, 993-994
  nature of, 982-996
  of unconscious or selfish kind,
    karmic results, 1022
  rules, fifteen, 996-1026
  white—
    conditions for, 993-996
    definitions, 984-985
    distinction from black, 984-
      989
    requirement, 1008
Magical investigators, failure, 1002
Magician—
  becoming with safety, 625
  black, evolution of senses and
    powers, 1126
  black, work with involution, 987
  condition, 964-968
  knowledge of facts, 1018-1019
  life, menace to, 1025-1026
  occult drowning, 1016-1017
  protection from his creations,
    1016
  task of generating fire at triple
    "meeting place", 1014
  white—
    avails himself of current Ray
      influence, 1022
    beginning of work on etheric
      sphere, 1023
    body menaced by destruction,
      causes, 1025
    control and manipulation of
      deva substance, 930
    critical moment near, 1004-
      1005
    definition, 997
    equipment, 981, 983, 994-996
    formulas enabling him to
      create in three spheres,
      1018

  problems, 1023, 1024
  production of objective phe-
    nomena, 1018
  sign of, 1010
  use of own vital forces, condi-
    tions, 1023
  utilisation of solar forces, 1022
  work with soul aspect or soul
    of things, 988
Magicians—
  black, characteristics, 642
  black, use of seventh order of
    devas, 668
  control and manipulation of
    deva substance, 930
  of Good Law, distinction from
    those on left, 930
  old, coming into incarnation,
    455
  white—
    and black, comparison, 466,
      482, 488, 490-491, 930
    use of silence and speech, 981
    work, method, 668
    work, three types of energy,
      1011
Magnetic—
  attraction between seven sys-
    temic groups, 232
  force, 283-284
  interaction, 701
  repulsion and attraction, 91
  spots of earth, devas presiding,
    912
  stimulation, 247, 249, 254, 258
Magnetisation—
  lesser devas of, 915
  means of contacting green
    devas, 912
  path of service of green devas,
    913
Magnetism—
  and capacity to show love, 576
  definitions, 44, 53-54
  group, 465
  manifestation, electrical, 315
  radiatory, of man, 313
Mahachohan—
  cooperation, 869
  department, 484-485, 1037-1038
  influence, 871
  office, period, 871
  Ray, 236, 361, 588
  work, 120, 599, 906-910
Mahadeva—
  aspect, control, 147
  Vishnu, and Brahma in man,
    317